Apocrypha Complete:
Lost Books of the Bible. Including Psalms, Jasher and Book of Enoch

Table of Contents

Introduction

Welcome to *"Apocrypha Complete: Lost Books of the Bible"*, a comprehensive collection of ancient texts that have captivated scholars and theologians for centuries. This volume brings together a diverse array of writings, many of which have been historically excluded from the canonical Scriptures. These texts offer profound insights into the religious, cultural, and historical contexts of the Judeo-Christian tradition.

The term "Apocrypha" refers to a set of books and writings that were not included in the standard Biblical canon but have been revered and studied by various religious traditions. These texts provide additional narratives, teachings, and theological perspectives that complement and enrich the understanding of the canonical Bible. In this volume, we present a wide-ranging selection of these works, organized into four main sections:

Universal Deuterocanonical Books: These texts are recognized and valued across many Christian denominations. They include stories of faith, wisdom literature, and historical accounts that expand on the narratives found in the canonical Bible.

Orthodox-Specific Deuterocanonical Books: Unique to the Orthodox Christian tradition, these writings offer further insights and traditions that are not found in other branches of Christianity.

Judeo-Christian Pseudepigrapha and Other Non-Canonical Texts: This section includes a variety of texts that provide a deeper look into the beliefs and traditions of early Jewish and Christian communities. These writings, while not part of the standard canon, have influenced religious thought and practice throughout history.

Ethiopian Orthodox Canonical Texts: The Ethiopian Orthodox Church has preserved a distinctive set of canonical texts that reflect its unique theological and historical heritage. These writings offer a rich and diverse perspective on the Biblical narrative.

Each section of this book is introduced with context and commentary to help you navigate the rich and complex world of the Apocrypha. From the moral tales of Tobit and Judith to the profound wisdom of Solomon and Sirach, from the dramatic histories of the Maccabees to the mystical visions of Enoch, this collection invites you to explore the full breadth of ancient Judeo-Christian literature.

By bringing these lost books together in one volume, "Apocrypha Complete" aims to provide readers with a deeper appreciation of the spiritual and cultural legacy of these ancient texts. Whether you are a scholar, a student, or simply a curious reader, this book offers a unique opportunity to delve into the forgotten corners of Biblical history and uncover the hidden treasures of the Apocrypha.

Prepare to embark on a journey through the lost books of the Bible, where every page offers new insights and discoveries that have shaped the faith and understanding of countless generations.

Universal Deuterocanonical Books

Introduction

Welcome to the first section of "Apocrypha Complete" which introduces a collection of texts held in esteem across various Christian traditions—Catholic and Orthodox—yet absent from the Hebrew Bible and Protestant Old Testament. These books, often described as 'Deuterocanonical,' meaning 'second canon,' offer rich historical, theological, and literary insights that bridge the intertestamental period, shaping the theological contours of early Christianity and providing a fuller understanding of the Judaic world that predated it.

Historical Context - The Deuterocanonical books were primarily written between the third century BCE and the first century BCE, a period marked by significant upheaval and transformation within the Jewish community. The Greek conquests under Alexander the Great and the subsequent Hellenistic influence, followed by Roman domination, presented the Jewish religion with new challenges and syncretic pressures. These texts were initially included in the Septuagint, the Greek translation of the Hebrew Scriptures, which was widely used by Diaspora Jews whose primary language had become Greek. The inclusion of these books in the Septuagint but not in the later Hebrew Masoretic Text, compiled between the 7th and 10th centuries CE, highlights differing canonical processes influenced by varying linguistic, cultural, and religious contexts.

Theological Significance - Theologically, the Deuterocanonical books enrich the narrative continuity between the Old and New Testaments. They delve into themes such as the nature of God's wisdom (Wisdom of Solomon, Sirach), the interplay of faith and history (1 and 2 Maccabees), and the role of divine justice and mercy (Tobit, Judith). Moreover, texts like the Wisdom of Solomon and Sirach offer meditative reflections on wisdom as both a divine gift and a practical guide for ethical living, presaging themes found in New Testament writings.

Rationale for Inclusion - The inclusion of these texts in various Christian canons but their exclusion from the Jewish canon can be attributed to differences in usage and reverence across communities during the formative years of rabbinic Judaism and early Christianity. For the Christian communities, especially those conversant in Greek, these books formed an integral part of the scriptural tradition that informed their theological reflections, liturgical practices, and moral teachings.

- **Tobit and Judith** provide narratives of piety and divine intervention, emphasizing themes of justice, fidelity, and prayer.

- Wisdom of Solomon and Sirach engage with the pursuit of wisdom, articulating a blend of traditional Jewish thought and Hellenistic philosophy.

- **Baruch and the Additions to Esther and Daniel** underscore providential history and the importance of faithful Jewish identity under foreign rule.

- **1 and 2 Maccabees** document the historical struggle for religious freedom against Hellenistic rulers, celebrating the Maccabean heroes who became symbols of resistance and piety.

These texts not only complement the canonical scriptures but also serve as crucial links in understanding the religious and cultural ethos that shaped early Jewish and Christian thought. As such, they are indispensable for scholars, theologians, and lay readers interested in the depths of biblical heritage and its ongoing theological dialogue. The "Universal Deuterocanonical Books" are thus presented in this compilation not as historical footnotes but as vibrant, dynamic texts that contribute to the ongoing narrative of faith, culture, and theological reflection.

Tobit

Tob.1

[1] The book of the words of Tobit, son of Tobiel, the son of Ananiel, the son of Aduel, the son of Gabael, of the seed of Asael, of the tribe of Nephthali;[2] Who in the time of Enemessar king of the Assyrians was led captive out of Thisbe, which is at the right hand of that city, which is called properly Nephthali in Galilee above Aser.[3] I Tobit have walked all the days of my life in the ways of truth and justice, and I did many almsdeeds to my brethren, and my nation, who came with me to Nineve, into the land of the Assyrians.[4] And when I was in mine own country, in the land of

Israel being but young, all the tribe of Nephthali my father fell from the house of Jerusalem, which was chosen out of all the tribes of Israel, that all the tribes should sacrifice there, where the temple of the habitation of the most High was consecrated and built for all ages.[5] Now all the tribes which together revolted, and the house of my father Nephthali, sacrificed unto the heifer Baal.[6] But I alone went often to Jerusalem at the feasts, as it was ordained unto all the people of Israel by an everlasting decree, having the firstfruits and tenths of increase, with that which was first shorn; and them gave I at the altar to the priests the children of Aaron.[7] The first tenth part of all increase I gave to the sons of Aaron, who ministered at Jerusalem: another tenth part I sold away, and went, and spent it every year at Jerusalem:[8] And the third I gave unto them to whom it was meet, as Debora my father's mother had commanded me, because I was left an orphan by my father.[9] Furthermore, when I was come to the age of a man, I married Anna of mine own kindred, and of her I begat Tobias.[10] And when we were carried away captives to Nineve, all my brethren and those that were of my kindred did eat of the bread of the Gentiles.[11] But I kept myself from eating;[12] Because I remembered God with all my heart.[13] And the most High gave me grace and favour before Enemessar, so that I was his purveyor.[14] And I went into Media, and left in trust with Gabael, the brother of Gabrias, at Rages a city of Media ten talents of silver.[15] Now when Enemessar was dead, Sennacherib his son reigned in his stead; whose estate was troubled, that I could not go into Media.[16] And in the time of Enemessar I gave many alms to my brethren, and gave my bread to the hungry,[17] And my clothes to the naked: and if I saw any of my nation dead, or cast about the walls of Nineve, I buried him.[18] And if the king Sennacherib had slain any, when he was come, and fled from Judea, I buried them privily; for in his wrath he killed many; but the bodies were not found, when they were sought for of the king.[19] And when one of the Ninevites went and complained of me to the king, that I buried them, and hid myself; understanding that I was sought for to be put to death, I withdrew myself for fear.[20] Then all my goods were forcibly taken away, neither was there any thing left me, beside my wife Anna and my son Tobias.[21] And there passed not five and fifty days, before two of his sons killed him, and they fled into the mountains of Ararath; and Sarchedonus his son reigned in his stead; who appointed over his father's accounts, and over all his affairs, Achiacharus my brother Anael's son.[22] And Achiacharus intreating for me, I returned to Nineve. Now Achiacharus was cupbearer, and keeper of the signet, and steward, and overseer of the accounts: and Sarchedonus appointed him next unto him: and he was my brother's son.

Tob.2

[1] Now when I was come home again, and my wife Anna was restored unto me, with my son Tobias, in the feast of Pentecost, which is the holy feast of the seven weeks, there was a good dinner prepared me, in the which I sat down to eat.[2] And when I saw abundance of meat, I said to my son, Go and bring what poor man soever thou shalt find out of our brethren, who is mindful of the Lord; and, lo, I tarry for thee.[3] But he came again, and said, Father, one of our nation is strangled, and is cast out in the marketplace.[4] Then before I had tasted of any meat, I started up, and took him up into a room until the going down of the sun.[5] Then I returned, and washed myself, and ate my meat in heaviness,[6] Remembering that prophecy of Amos, as he said, Your feasts shall be turned into mourning, and all your mirth into lamentation.[7] Therefore I wept: and after the going down of the sun I went and made a grave, and buried him.[8] But my neighbours mocked me, and said, This man is not yet afraid to be put to death

for this matter: who fled away; and yet, lo, he burieth the dead again.[9] The same night also I returned from the burial, and slept by the wall of my courtyard, being polluted and my face was uncovered:[10] And I knew not that there were sparrows in the wall, and mine eyes being open, the sparrows muted warm dung into mine eyes, and a whiteness came in mine eyes: and I went to the physicians, but they helped me not: moreover Achiacharus did nourish me, until I went into Elymais.[11] And my wife Anna did take women's works to do.[12] And when she had sent them home to the owners, they paid her wages, and gave her also besides a kid.[13] And when it was in my house, and began to cry, I said unto her, From whence is this kid? is it not stolen? render it to the owners; for it is not lawful to eat any thing that is stolen.[14] But she replied upon me, It was given for a gift more than the wages. Howbeit I did not believe her, but bade her render it to the owners: and I was abashed at her. But she replied upon me, Where are thine alms and thy righteous deeds? behold, thou and all thy works are known.

Tob.3

[1] Then I being grieved did weep, and in my sorrow prayed, saying,[2] O Lord, thou art just, and all thy works and all thy ways are mercy and truth, and thou judgest truly and justly for ever.[3] Remember me, and look on me, punish me not for my sins and ignorances, and the sins of mg fathers, who have sinned before thee:[4] For they obeyed not thy commandments: wherefore thou hast delivered us for a spoil, and unto captivity, and unto death, and for a proverb of reproach to all the nations among whom we are dispersed.[5] And now thy judgments are many and true: deal with me according to my sins and my fathers': because we have not kept thy commandments, neither have walked in truth before thee.[6] Now therefore deal with me as seemeth best unto thee, and command my spirit to be taken from me, that I may be dissolved, and become earth: for it is profitable for me to die rather than to live, because I have heard false reproaches, and have much sorrow: command therefore that I may now be delivered out of this distress, and go into the everlasting place: turn not thy face away from me.[7] It came to pass the same day, that in Ecbatane a city of Media Sara the daughter of Raguel was also reproached by her father's maids;[8] Because that she had been married to seven husbands, whom Asmodeus the evil spirit had killed, before they had lain with her. Dost thou not know, said they, that thou hast strangled thine husbands? thou hast had already seven husbands, neither wast thou named after any of them.[9] Wherefore dost thou beat us for them? if they be dead, go thy ways after them, let us never see of thee either son or daughter.[10] Whe she heard these things, she was very sorrowful, so that she thought to have strangled herself; and she said, I am the only daughter of my father, and if I do this, it shall be a reproach unto him, and I shall bring his old age with sorrow unto the grave.[11] Then she prayed toward the window, and said, Blessed art thou, O Lord my God, and thine holy and glorious name is blessed and honourable for ever: let all thy works praise thee for ever.[12] And now, O Lord, I set I mine eyes and my face toward thee,[13] And say, Take me out of the earth, that I may hear no more the reproach.[14] Thou knowest, Lord, that I am pure from all sin with man,[15] And that I never polluted my name, nor the name of my father, in the land of my captivity: I am the only daughter of my father, neither hath he any child to be his heir, neither any near kinsman, nor any son of his alive, to whom I may keep myself for a wife: my seven husbands are already dead; and why should I live? but if it please not thee that I should die, command some regard to be had of me, and pity taken of me, that I hear no more reproach.[16] So the prayers of them both were heard before the majesty of the great God.[17] And Raphael was sent to heal them both,

that is, to scale away the whiteness of Tobit's eyes, and to give Sara the daughter of Raguel for a wife to Tobias the son of Tobit; and to bind Asmodeus the evil spirit; because she belonged to Tobias by right of inheritance. The selfsame time came Tobit home, and entered into his house, and Sara the daughter of Raguel came down from her upper chamber.

Tob.4

[1] In that day Tobit remembered the money which he had committed to Gabael in Rages of Media,[2] And said with himself, I have wished for death; wherefore do I not call for my son Tobias that I may signify to him of the money before I die?[3] And when he had called him, he said, My son, when I am dead, bury me; and despise not thy mother, but honour her all the days of thy life, and do that which shall please her, and grieve her not.[4] Remember, my son, that she saw many dangers for thee, when thou wast in her womb: and when she is dead, bury her by me in one grave.[5] My son, be mindful of the Lord our God all thy days, and let not thy will be set to sin, or to transgress his commandments: do uprightly all thy life long, and follow not the ways of unrighteousness.[6] For if thou deal truly, thy doings shall prosperously succeed to thee, and to all them that live justly.[7] Give alms of thy substance; and when thou givest alms, let not thine eye be envious, neither turn thy face from any poor, and the face of God shall not be turned away from thee.[8] If thou hast abundance give alms accordingly: if thou have but a little, be not afraid to give according to that little:[9] For thou layest up a good treasure for thyself against the day of necessity.[10] Because that alms do deliver from death, and suffereth not to come into darkness.[11] For alms is a good gift unto all that give it in the sight of the most High.[12] Beware of all whoredom, my son, and chiefly take a wife of the seed of thy fathers, and take not a strange woman to wife, which is not of thy father's tribe: for we are the children of the prophets, Noe, Abraham, Isaac, and Jacob: remember, my son, that our fathers from the beginning, even that they all married wives of their own kindred, and were blessed in their children, and their seed shall inherit the land.[13] Now therefore, my son, love thy brethren, and despise not in thy heart thy brethren, the sons and daughters of thy people, in not taking a wife of them: for in pride is destruction and much trouble, and in lewdness is decay and great want: for lewdness is the mother of famine.[14] Let not the wages of any man, which hath wrought for thee, tarry with thee, but give him it out of hand: for if thou serve God, he will also repay thee: be circumspect my son, in all things thou doest, and be wise in all thy conversation.[15] Do that to no man which thou hatest: drink not wine to make thee drunken: neither let drunkenness go with thee in thy journey.[16] Give of thy bread to the hungry, and of thy garments to them that are naked; and according to thine abundance give alms: and let not thine eye be envious, when thou givest alms.[17] Pour out thy bread on the burial of the just, but give nothing to the wicked.[18] Ask counsel of all that are wise, and despise not any counsel that is profitable.[19] Bless the Lord thy God alway, and desire of him that thy ways may be directed, and that all thy paths and counsels may prosper: for every nation hath not counsel; but the Lord himself giveth all good things, and he humbleth whom he will, as he will; now therefore, my son, remember my commandments, neither let them be put out of thy mind.[20] And now I signify this to they that I committed ten talents to Gabael the son of Gabrias at Rages in Media.[21] And fear not, my son, that we are made poor: for thou hast much wealth, if thou fear God, and depart from all sin, and do that which is pleasing in his sight.

Tob.5

[1] Tobias then answered and said, Father, I will do all things which thou hast commanded me:[2] But how can I receive the money, seeing I know him not?[3] Then he gave him the handwriting, and said unto him, Seek thee a man which may go with thee, whiles I yet live, and I will give him wages: and go and receive the money.[4] Therefore when he went to seek a man, he found Raphael that was an angel.[5] But he knew not; and he said unto him, Canst thou go with me to Rages? and knowest thou those places well?[6] To whom the angel said, I will go with thee, and I know the way well: for I have lodged with our brother Gabael.[7] Then Tobias said unto him, Tarry for me, till I tell my father.[8] Then he said unto him, Go and tarry not. So he went in and said to his father, Behold, I have found one which will go with me. Then he said, Call him unto me, that I may know of what tribe he is, and whether he be a trusty man to go with thee.[9] So he called him, and he came in, and they saluted one another.[10] Then Tobit said unto him, Brother, shew me of what tribe and family thou art.[11] To whom he said, Dost thou seek for a tribe or family, or an hired man to go with thy son? Then Tobit said unto him, I would know, brother, thy kindred and name.[12] Then he said, I am Azarias, the son of Ananias the great, and of thy brethren.[13] Then Tobit said, Thou art welcome, brother; be not now angry with me, because I have enquired to know thy tribe and thy family; for thou art my brother, of an honest and good stock: for I know Ananias and Jonathas, sons of that great Samaias, as we went together to Jerusalem to worship, and offered the firstborn, and the tenths of the fruits; and they were not seduced with the error of our brethren: my brother, thou art of a good stock.[14] But tell me, what wages shall I give thee? wilt thou a drachm a day, and things necessary, as to mine own son?[15] Yea, moreover, if ye return safe, I will add something to thy wages.[16] So they were well pleased. Then said he to Tobias, Prepare thyself for the journey, and God send you a good journey. And when his son had prepared all things far the journey, his father said, Go thou with this man, and God, which dwelleth in heaven, prosper your journey, and the angel of God keep you company. So they went forth both, and the young man's dog with them.[17] But Anna his mother wept, and said to Tobit, Why hast thou sent away our son? is he not the staff of our hand, in going in and out before us?[18] Be not greedy to add money to money: but let it be as refuse in respect of our child.[19] For that which the Lord hath given us to live with doth suffice us.[20] Then said Tobit to her, Take no care, my sister; he shall return in safety, and thine eyes shall see him.[21] For the good angel will keep him company, and his journey shall be prosperous, and he shall return safe.[22] Then she made an end of weeping.

Tob.6

[1] And as they went on their journey, they came in the evening to the river Tigris, and they lodged there.[2] And when the young man went down to wash himself, a fish leaped out of the river, and would have devoured him.[3] Then the angel said unto him, Take the fish. And the young man laid hold of the fish, and drew it to land.[4] To whom the angel said, Open the fish, and take the heart and the liver and the gall, and put them up safely.[5] So the young man did as the angel commanded him; and when they had roasted the fish, they did eat it: then they both went on their way, till they drew near to Ecbatane.[6] Then the young man said to the angel, Brother Azarias, to what use is the heart and the liver and the gal of the fish?[7] And he said unto him, Touching the heart and the liver, if a devil or an evil spirit trouble any, we must make a smoke thereof before the man or the woman, and the party shall be no more vexed.[8] As for the gall, it is good to anoint a man that hath whiteness in his eyes, and he shall be healed.[9] And when they were come near to Rages,[10] The angel said to the young man, Brother, to day we shall lodge with Raguel, who is thy cousin; he also hath one only daughter, named Sara; I will speak for her, that she may be given thee for a

wife.[11] For to thee doth the right of her appertain, seeing thou only art of her kindred.[12] And the maid is fair and wise: now therefore hear me, and I will speak to her father; and when we return from Rages we will celebrate the marriage: for I know that Raguel cannot marry her to another according to the law of Moses, but he shall be guilty of death, because the right of inheritance doth rather appertain to thee than to any other.[13] Then the young man answered the angel, I have heard, brother Azarias that this maid hath been given to seven men, who all died in the marriage chamber.[14] And now I am the only son of my father, and I am afraid, lest if I go in unto her, I die, as the other before: for a wicked spirit loveth her, which hurteth no body, but those which come unto her; wherefore I also fear lest I die, and bring my father's and my mother's life because of me to the grave with sorrow: for they have no other son to bury them.[15] Then the angel said unto him, Dost thou not remember the precepts which thy father gave thee, that thou shouldest marry a wife of thine own kindred? wherefore hear me, O my brother; for she shall be given thee to wife; and make thou no reckoning of the evil spirit; for this same night shall she be given thee in marriage.[16] And when thou shalt come into the marriage chamber, thou shalt take the ashes of perfume, and shalt lay upon them some of the heart and liver of the fish, and shalt make a smoke with it:[17] And the devil shall smell it, and flee away, and never come again any more: but when thou shalt come to her, rise up both of you, and pray to God which is merciful, who will have pity on you, and save you: fear not, for she is appointed unto thee from the beginning; and thou shalt preserve her, and she shall go with thee. Moreover I suppose that she shall bear thee children. Now when Tobias had heard these things, he loved her, and his heart was effectually joined to her.

Tob.7

[1] And when they were come to Ecbatane, they came to the house of Raguel, and Sara met them: and after they had saluted one another, she brought them into the house.[2] Then said Raguel to Edna his wife, How like is this young man to Tobit my cousin![3] And Raguel asked them, From whence are ye, brethren? To whom they said, We are of the sons of Nephthalim, which are captives in Nineve.[4] Then he said to them, Do ye know Tobit our kinsman? And they said, We know him. Then said he, Is he in good health?[5] And they said, He is both alive, and in good health: and Tobias said, He is my father.[6] Then Raguel leaped up, and kissed him, and wept,[7] And blessed him, and said unto him, Thou art the son of an honest and good man. But when he had heard that Tobit was blind, he was sorrowful, and wept.[8] And likewise Edna his wife and Sara his daughter wept. Moreover they entertained them cheerfully; and after that they had killed a ram of the flock, they set store of meat on the table. Then said Tobias to Raphael, Brother Azarias, speak of those things of which thou didst talk in the way, and let this business be dispatched.[9] So he communicated the matter with Raguel: and Raguel said to Tobias, Eat and drink, and make merry:[10] For it is meet that thou shouldest marry my daughter: nevertheless I will declare unto thee the truth.[11] I have given my daughter in marriage te seven men, who died that night they came in unto her: nevertheless for the present be merry. But Tobias said, I will eat nothing here, till we agree and swear one to another.[12] Raguel said, Then take her from henceforth according to the manner, for thou art her cousin, and she is thine, and the merciful God give you good success in all things.[13] Then he called his daughter Sara, and she came to her father, and he took her by the hand, and gave her to be wife to Tobias, saying, Behold, take her after the law of Moses, and lead her away to thy father. And he blessed them;[14] And called Edna his wife, and took paper, and did write an instrument of covenants, and sealed it.[15] Then they began to eat.[16] After Raguel called his wife

Edna, and said unto her, Sister, prepare another chamber, and bring her in thither.[17] Which when she had done as he had bidden her, she brought her thither: and she wept, and she received the tears of her daughter, and said unto her,[18] Be of good comfort, my daughter; the Lord of heaven and earth give thee joy for this thy sorrow: be of good comfort, my daughter.

Tob.8

[1] And when they had supped, they brought Tobias in unto her.[2] And as he went, he remembered the words of Raphael, and took the ashes of the perfumes, and put the heart and the liver of the fish thereupon, and made a smoke therewith.[3] The which smell when the evil spirit had smelled, he fled into the utmost parts of Egypt, and the angel bound him.[4] And after that they were both shut in together, Tobias rose out of the bed, and said, Sister, arise, and let us pray that God would have pity on us.[5] Then began Tobias to say, Blessed art thou, O God of our fathers, and blessed is thy holy and glorious name for ever; let the heavens bless thee, and all thy creatures.[6] Thou madest Adam, and gavest him Eve his wife for an helper and stay: of them came mankind: thou hast said, It is not good that man should be alone; let us make unto him an aid like unto himself.[7] And now, O Lord, I take not this my sister for lush but uprightly: therefore mercifully ordain that we may become aged together.[8] And she said with him, Amen.[9] So they slept both that night. And Raguel arose, and went and made a grave,[10] Saying, I fear lest he also be dead.[11] But when Raguel was come into his house,[12] He said unto his wife Edna. Send one of the maids, and let her see whether he be alive: if he be not, that we may bury him, and no man know it.[13] So the maid opened the door, and went in, and found them both asleep,[14] And came forth, and told them that he was alive.[15] Then Raguel praised God, and said, O God, thou art worthy to be praised with all pure and holy praise; therefore let thy saints praise thee with all thy creatures; and let all thine angels and thine elect praise thee for ever.[16] Thou art to be praised, for thou hast made me joyful; and that is not come to me which I suspected; but thou hast dealt with us according to thy great mercy.[17] Thou art to be praised because thou hast had mercy of two that were the only begotten children of their fathers: grant them mercy, O Lord, and finish their life in health with joy and mercy.[18] Then Raguel bade his servants to fill the grave.[19] And he kept the wedding feast fourteen days.[20] For before the days of the marriage were finished, Raguel had said unto him by an oath, that he should not depart till the fourteen days of the marriage were expired;[21] And then he should take the half of his goods, and go in safety to his father; and should have the rest when I and my wife be dead.

Tob.9

[1] Then Tobias called Raphael, and said unto him,[2] Brother Azarias, take with thee a servant, and two camels, and go to Rages of Media to Gabael, and bring me the money, and bring him to the wedding.[3] For Raguel hath sworn that I shall not depart.[4] But my father counteth the days; and if I tarry long, he will be very sorry.[5] So Raphael went out, and lodged with Gabael, and gave him the handwriting: who brought forth bags which were sealed up, and gave them to him.[6] And early in the morning they went forth both together, and came to the wedding: and Tobias blessed his wife.

Tob.10

[1] Now Tobit his father counted every day: and when the days of the journey were expired, and they came not,[2] Then Tobit said, Are they detained? or is Gabael dead, and there is no man to give him the money?[3] Therefore he was very sorry.[4] Then his wife said unto him, My son is dead, seeing he stayeth long; and she began to wail him, and said,[5] Now I care for nothing, my son, since I have let thee go, the light of mine eyes.[6] To whom Tobit said, Hold thy peace, take

no care, for he is safe.[7] But she said, Hold thy peace, and deceive me not; my son is dead. And she went out every day into the way which they went, and did eat no meat on the daytime, and ceased not whole nights to bewail her son Tobias, until the fourteen days of the wedding were expired, which Raguel had sworn that he should spend there. Then Tobias said to Raguel, Let me go, for my father and my mother look no more to see me.[8] But his father in law said unto him, Tarry with me, and I will send to thy father, and they shall declare unto him how things go with thee.[9] But Tobias said, No; but let me go to my father.[10] Then Raguel arose, and gave him Sara his wife, and half his goods, servants, and cattle, and money:[11] And he blessed them, and sent them away, saying, The God of heaven give you a prosperous journey, my children.[12] And he said to his daughter, Honour thy father and thy mother in law, which are now thy parents, that I may hear good report of thee. And he kissed her. Edna also said to Tobias, The Lord of heaven restore thee, my dear brother, and grant that I may see thy children of my daughter Sara before I die, that I may rejoice before the Lord: behold, I commit my daughter unto thee of special trust; where are do not entreat her evil.

Tob.11

[1] After these things Tobias went his way, praising God that he had given him a prosperous journey, and blessed Raguel and Edna his wife, and went on his way till they drew near unto Nineve.[2] Then Raphael said to Tobias, Thou knowest, brother, how thou didst leave thy father:[3] Let us haste before thy wife, and prepare the house.[4] And take in thine hand the gall of the fish. So they went their way, and the dog went after them.[5] Now Anna sat looking about toward the way for her son.[6] And when she espied him coming, she said to his father, Behold, thy son cometh, and the man that went with him.[7] Then said Raphael, I know, Tobias, that thy father will open his eyes.[8] Therefore anoint thou his eyes with the gall, and being pricked therewith, he shall rub, and the whiteness shall fall away, and he shall see thee.[9] Then Anna ran forth, and fell upon the neck of her son, and said unto him, Seeing I have seen thee, my son, from henceforth I am content to die. And they wept both.[10] Tobit also went forth toward the door, and stumbled: but his son ran unto him,[11] And took hold of his father: and he strake of the gall on his fathers' eyes, saying, Be of good hope, my father.[12] And when his eyes began to smart, he rubbed them;[13] And the whiteness pilled away from the corners of his eyes: and when he saw his son, he fell upon his neck.[14] And he wept, and said, Blessed art thou, O God, and blessed is thy name for ever; and blessed are all thine holy angels:[15] For thou hast scourged, and hast taken pity on me: for, behold, I see my son Tobias. And his son went in rejoicing, and told his father the great things that had happened to him in Media.[16] Then Tobit went out to meet his daughter in law at the gate of Nineve, rejoicing and praising God: and they which saw him go marvelled, because he had received his sight.[17] But Tobias gave thanks before them, because God had mercy on him. And when he came near to Sara his daughter in law, he blessed her, saying, Thou art welcome, daughter: God be blessed, which hath brought thee unto us, and blessed be thy father and thy mother. And there was joy among all his brethren which were at Nineve.[18] And Achiacharus, and Nasbas his brother's son, came:[19] And Tobias' wedding was kept seven days with great joy.

Tob.12

[1] Then Tobit called his son Tobias, and said unto him, My son, see that the man have his wages, which went with thee, and thou must give him more.[2] And Tobias said unto him, O father, it is no harm to me to give him half of those things which I have brought:[3] For he hath brought me again to thee in safety, and made whole my wife, and brought me the money, and likewise healed thee.[4] Then the old man said, It is due unto him.[5] So he called the angel, and he said unto him, Take half of all that ye have brought and go away in safety.[6] Then he took them both apart, and said unto them, Bless God, praise him, and magnify him, and praise him for the things which he hath done unto you in the sight of all that live. It is good to praise God, and exalt his name, and honourably to shew forth the works of God; therefore be not slack to praise him.[7] It is good to keep close the secret of a king, but it is honourable to reveal the works of God. Do that which is good, and no evil shall touch you.[8] Prayer is good with fasting and alms and righteousness. A little with righteousness is better than much with unrighteousness. It is better to give alms than to lay up gold:[9] For alms doth deliver from death, and shall purge away all sin. Those that exercise alms and righteousness shall be filled with life:[10] But they that sin are enemies to their own life.[11] Surely I will keep close nothing from you. For I said, It was good to keep close the secret of a king, but that it was honourable to reveal the works of God.[12] Now therefore, when thou didst pray, and Sara thy daughter in law, I did bring the remembrance of your prayers before the Holy One: and when thou didst bury the dead, I was with thee likewise.[13] And when thou didst not delay to rise up, and leave thy dinner, to go and cover the dead, thy good deed was not hid from me: but I was with thee.[14] And now God hath sent me to heal thee and Sara thy daughter in law.[15] I am Raphael, one of the seven holy angels, which present the prayers of the saints, and which go in and out before the glory of the Holy One.[16] Then they were both troubled, and fell upon their faces: for they feared.[17] But he said unto them, Fear not, for it shall go well with you; praise God therefore.[18] For not of any favour of mine, but by the will of our God I came; wherefore praise him for ever.[19] All these days I did appear unto you; but I did neither eat nor drink, but ye did see a vision.[20] Now therefore give God thanks: for I go up to him that sent me; but write all things which are done in a book.[21] And when they arose, they saw him no more.[22] Then they confessed the great and wonderful works of God, and how the angel of the Lord had appeared unto them.

Tob.13

[1] Then Tobit wrote a prayer of rejoicing, and said, Blessed be God that liveth for ever, and blessed be his kingdom.[2] For he doth scourge, and hath mercy: he leadeth down to hell, and bringeth up again: neither is there any that can avoid his hand.[3] Confess him before the Gentiles, ye children of Israel: for he hath scattered us among them.[4] There declare his greatness, and extol him before all the living: for he is our Lord, and he is the God our Father for ever.[5] And he will scourge us for our iniquities, and will have mercy again, and will gather us out of all nations, among whom he hath scattered us.[6] If ye turn to him with your whole heart, and with your whole mind, and deal uprightly before him, then will he turn unto you, and will not hide his face from you. Therefore see what he will do with you, and confess him with your whole mouth, and praise the Lord of might, and extol the everlasting King. In the land of my captivity do I praise him, and declare his might and majesty to a sinful nation. O ye sinners, turn and do justice before him: who can tell if he will accept you, and have mercy on you?[7] I will extol my God, and my soul shall praise the King of heaven, and shall rejoice in his greatness.[8] Let all men speak, and let all praise him for his righteousness.[9] O Jerusalem, the holy city, he will scourge thee for thy children's works, and will have mercy again on the sons of the righteous.[10] Give praise to the Lord, for he is good: and praise the everlasting King, that his tabernacle may be builded in thee again with joy, and let him make joyful there in thee those that are captives, and love in thee for ever those that are miserable.[11] Many nations

shall come from far to the name of the Lord God with gifts in their hands, even gifts to the King of heaven; all generations shall praise thee with great joy.[12] Cursed are all they which hate thee, and blessed shall all be which love thee for ever.[13] Rejoice and be glad for the children of the just: for they shall be gathered together, and shall bless the Lord of the just.[14] O blessed are they which love thee, for they shall rejoice in thy peace: blessed are they which have been sorrowful for all thy scourges; for they shall rejoice for thee, when they have seen all thy glory, and shall be glad for ever.[15] Let my soul bless God the great King.[16] For Jerusalem shall be built up with sapphires and emeralds, and precious stone: thy walls and towers and battlements with pure gold.[17] And the streets of Jerusalem shall be paved with beryl and carbuncle and stones of Ophir.[18] And all her streets shall say, Alleluia; and they shall praise him, saying, Blessed be God, which hath extolled it for ever.

Tob.14

[1] So Tobit made an end of praising God.[2] And he was eight and fifty years old when he lost his sight, which was restored to him after eight years: and he gave alms, and he increased in the fear of the Lord God, and praised him.[3] And when he was very aged he called his son, and the sons of his son, and said to him, My son, take thy children; for, behold, I am aged, and am ready to depart out of this life.[4] Go into Media my son, for I surely believe those things which Jonas the prophet spake of Nineve, that it shall be overthrown; and that for a time peace shall rather be in Media; and that our brethren shall lie scattered in the earth from that good land: and Jerusalem shall be desolate, and the house of God in it shall be burned, and shall be desolate for a time;[5] And that again God will have mercy on them, and bring them again into the land, where they shall build a temple, but not like to the first, until the time of that age be fulfilled; and afterward they shall return from all places of their captivity, and build up Jerusalem gloriously, and the house of God shall be built in it for ever with a glorious building, as the prophets have spoken thereof.[6] And all nations shall turn, and fear the Lord God truly, and shall bury their idols.[7] So shall all nations praise the Lord, and his people shall confess God, and the Lord shall exalt his people; and all those which love the Lord God in truth and justice shall rejoice, shewing mercy to our brethren.[8] And now, my son, depart out of Nineve, because that those things which the prophet Jonas spake shall surely come to pass.[9] But keep thou the law and the commandments, and shew thyself merciful and just, that it may go well with thee.[10] And bury me decently, and thy mother with me; but tarry no longer at Nineve. Remember, my son, how Aman handled Achiacharus that brought him up, how out of light he brought him into darkness, and how he rewarded him again: yet Achiacharus was saved, but the other had his reward: for he went down into darkness. Manasses gave alms, and escaped the snares of death which they had set for him: but Aman fell into the snare, and perished.[11] Wherefore now, my son, consider what alms doeth, and how righteousness doth deliver. When he had said these things, he gave up the ghost in the bed, being an hundred and eight and fifty years old; and he buried him honourably.[12] And when Anna his mother was dead, he buried her with his father. But Tobias departed with his wife and children to Ecbatane to Raguel his father in law,[13] Where he became old with honour, and he buried his father and mother in law honourably, and he inherited their substance, and his father Tobit's.[14] And he died at Ecbatane in Media, being an hundred and seven and twenty years old.[15] But before he died he heard of the destruction of Nineve, which was taken by Nabuchodonosor and Assuerus: and before his death he rejoiced over Nineve.

Judith

Jdt.1

[1] In the twelfth year of the reign of Nabuchodonosor, who reigned in Nineve, the great city; in the days of Arphaxad, which reigned over the Medes in Ecbatane,[2] And built in Ecbatane walls round about of stones hewn three cubits broad and six cubits long, and made the height of the wall seventy cubits, and the breadth thereof fifty cubits:[3] And set the towers thereof upon the gates of it an hundred cubits high, and the breadth thereof in the foundation threescore cubits:[4] And he made the gates thereof, even gates that were raised to the height of seventy cubits, and the breadth of them was forty cubits, for the going forth of his mighty armies, and for the setting in array of his footmen:[5] Even in those days king Nabuchodonosor made war with king Arphaxad in the great plain, which is the plain in the borders of Ragau.[6] And there came unto him all they that dwelt in the hill country, and all that dwelt by Euphrates, and Tigris and Hydaspes, and the plain of Arioch the king of the Elymeans, and very many nations of the sons of Chelod, assembled themselves to the battle.[7] Then Nabuchodonosor king of the Assyrians sent unto all that dwelt in Persia, and to all that dwelt westward, and to those that dwelt in Cilicia, and Damascus, and Libanus, and Antilibanus, and to all that dwelt upon the sea coast,[8] And to those among the nations that were of Carmel, and Galaad, and the higher Galilee, and the great plain of Esdrelom,[9] And to all that were in Samaria and the cities thereof, and beyond Jordan unto Jerusalem, and Betane, and Chelus, and Kades, and the river of Egypt, and Taphnes, and Ramesse, and all the land of Gesem,[10] Until ye come beyond Tanis and Memphis, and to all the inhabitants of Egypt, until ye come to the borders of Ethiopia.[11] But all the inhabitants of the land made light of the commandment of Nabuchodonosor king of the Assyrians, neither went they with him to the battle; for they were not afraid of him: yea, he was before them as one man, and they sent away his ambassadors from them without effect, and with disgrace.[12] Therefore Nabuchodonosor was very angry with all this country, and sware by his throne and kingdom, that he would surely be avenged upon all those coasts of Cilicia, and Damascus, and Syria, and that he would slay with the sword all the inhabitants of the land of Moab, and the children of Ammon, and all Judea, and all that were in Egypt, till ye come to the borders of the two seas.[13] Then he marched in battle array with his power against king Arphaxad in the seventeenth year, and he prevailed in his battle: for he overthrew all the power of Arphaxad, and all his horsemen, and all his chariots,[14] And became lord of his cities, and came unto Ecbatane, and took the towers, and spoiled the streets thereof, and turned the beauty thereof into shame.[15] He took also Arphaxad in the mountains of Ragau, and smote him through with his darts, and destroyed him utterly that day.[16] So he returned afterward to Nineve, both he and all his company of sundry nations being a very great multitude of men of war, and there he took his ease, and banqueted, both he and his army, an hundred and twenty days.

Jdt.2

[1] And in the eighteenth year, the two and twentieth day of the first month, there was talk in the house of Nabuchodonosor king of the Assyrians that he should, as he said, avenge himself on all the earth.[2] So he called unto him all his officers, and all his nobles, and communicated with them his secret counsel, and concluded the afflicting of the whole earth out of his own mouth.[3] Then they decreed to destroy all flesh, that did not obey the commandment of his mouth.[4] And when he had ended his counsel, Nabuchodonosor king of the Assyrians called Holofernes the chief captain of his army, which was next unto him, and said unto him.[5] Thus saith the great king, the lord of the whole earth, Behold, thou shalt go forth from

my presence, and take with thee men that trust in their own strength, of footmen an hundred and twenty thousand; and the number of horses with their riders twelve thousand.[6] And thou shalt go against all the west country, because they disobeyed my commandment.[7] And thou shalt declare unto that they prepare for me earth and water: for I will go forth in my wrath against them and will cover the whole face of the earth with the feet of mine army, and I will give them for a spoil unto them:[8] So that their slain shall fill their valleys and brooks and the river shall be filled with their dead, till it overflow:[9] And I will lead them captives to the utmost parts of all the earth.[10] Thou therefore shalt go forth. and take beforehand for me all their coasts: and if they will yield themselves unto thee, thou shalt reserve them for me till the day of their punishment.[11] But concerning them that rebel, let not thine eye spare them; but put them to the slaughter, and spoil them wheresoever thou goest.[12] For as I live, and by the power of my kingdom, whatsoever I have spoken, that will I do by mine hand.[13] And take thou heed that thou transgress none of the commandments of thy lord, but accomplish them fully, as I have commanded thee, and defer not to do them.[14] Then Holofernes went forth from the presence of his lord, and called all the governors and captains, and the officers of the army of Assur;[15] And he mustered the chosen men for the battle, as his lord had commanded him, unto an hundred and twenty thousand, and twelve thousand archers on horseback;[16] And he ranged them, as a great army is ordered for the war.[17] And he took camels and asses for their carriages, a very great number; and sheep and oxen and goats without number for their provision:[18] And plenty of victual for every man of the army, and very much gold and silver out of the king's house.[19] Then he went forth and all his power to go before king Nabuchodonosor in the voyage, and to cover all the face of the earth westward with their chariots, and horsemen, and their chosen footmen.[20] A great number also sundry countries came with them like locusts, and like the sand of the earth: for the multitude was without number.[21] And they went forth of Nineve three days' journey toward the plain of Bectileth, and pitched from Bectileth near the mountain which is at the left hand of the upper Cilicia.[22] Then he took all his army, his footmen, and horsemen and chariots, and went from thence into the hill country;[23] And destroyed Phud and Lud, and spoiled all the children of Rasses, and the children of Israel, which were toward the wilderness at the south of the land of the Chellians.[24] Then he went over Euphrates, and went through Mesopotamia, and destroyed all the high cities that were upon the river Arbonai, till ye come to the sea.[25] And he took the borders of Cilicia, and killed all that resisted him, and came to the borders of Japheth, which were toward the south, over against Arabia.[26] He compassed also all the children of Madian, and burned up their tabernacles, and spoiled their sheepcotes.[27] Then he went down into the plain of Damascus in the time of wheat harvest, and burnt up all their fields, and destroyed their flocks and herds, also he spoiled their cities, and utterly wasted their countries, and smote all their young men with the edge of the sword.[28] Therefore the fear and dread of him fell upon all the inhabitants of the sea coasts, which were in Sidon and Tyrus, and them that dwelt in Sur and Ocina, and all that dwelt in Jemnaan; and they that dwelt in Azotus and Ascalon feared him greatly.

Jdt.3

[1] So they sent ambassadors unto him to treat of peace, saying,[2] Behold, we the servants of Nabuchodonosor the great king lie before thee; use us as shall be good in thy sight.[3] Behold, our houses, and all our places, and all our fields of wheat, and flocks, and herds, and all the lodges of our tents lie before thy face; use them as it pleaseth thee.[4] Behold, even our cities and the inhabitants thereof are thy servants; come and deal with them as seemeth good unto thee.[5] So the men came to Holofernes, and declared unto him after this manner.[6] Then came he down toward the sea coast, both he and his army, and set garrisons in the high cities, and took out of them chosen men for aid.[7] So they and all the country round about received them with garlands, with dances, and with timbrels.[8] Yet he did cast down their frontiers, and cut down their groves: for he had decreed to destroy all the gods of the land, that all nations should worship Nabuchodonosor only, and that all tongues and tribes should call upon him as god.[9] Also he came over against Esdraelon near unto Judea, over against the great strait of Judea.[10] And he pitched between Geba and Scythopolis, and there he tarried a whole month, that he might gather together all the carriages of his army.

Jdt.4

[1] Now the children of Israel, that dwelt in Judea, heard all that Holofernes the chief captain of Nabuchodonosor king of the Assyrians had done to the nations, and after what manner he had spoiled all their temples, and brought them to nought.[2] Therefore they were exceedingly afraid of him, and were troubled for Jerusalem, and for the temple of the Lord their God:[3] For they were newly returned from the captivity, and all the people of Judea were lately gathered together: and the vessels, and the altar, and the house, were sanctified after the profanation.[4] Therefore they sent into all the coasts of Samaria, and the villages and to Bethoron, and Belmen, and Jericho, and to Choba, and Esora, and to the valley of Salem:[5] And possessed themselves beforehand of all the tops of the high mountains, and fortified the villages that were in them, and laid up victuals for the provision of war: for their fields were of late reaped.[6] Also Joacim the high priest, which was in those days in Jerusalem, wrote to them that dwelt in Bethulia, and Betomestham, which is over against Esdraelon toward the open country, near to Dothaim,[7] Charging them to keep the passages of the hill country: for by them there was an entrance into Judea, and it was easy to stop them that would come up, because the passage was straight, for two men at the most.[8] And the children of Israel did as Joacim the high priest had commanded them, with the ancients of all the people of Israel, which dwelt at Jerusalem.[9] Then every man of Israel cried to God with great fervency, and with great vehemency did they humble their souls:[10] Both they, and their wives and their children, and their cattle, and every stranger and hireling, and their servants bought with money, put sackcloth upon their loins.[11] Thus every man and women, and the little children, and the inhabitants of Jerusalem, fell before the temple, and cast ashes upon their heads, and spread out their sackcloth before the face of the Lord: also they put sackcloth about the altar,[12] And cried to the God of Israel all with one consent earnestly, that he would not give their children for a prey, and their wives for a spoil, and the cities of their inheritance to destruction, and the sanctuary to profanation and reproach, and for the nations to rejoice at.[13] So God heard their prayers, and looked upon their afflictions: for the people fasted many days in all Judea and Jerusalem before the sanctuary of the Lord Almighty.[14] And Joacim the high priest, and all the priests that stood before the Lord, and they which ministered unto the Lord, had their loins girt with sackcloth, and offered the daily burnt offerings, with the vows and free gifts of the people,[15] And had ashes on their mitres, and cried unto the Lord with all their power, that he would look upon all the house of Israel graciously.

Jdt.5

[1] Then was it declared to Holofernes, the chief captain of the army of Assur, that the children of Israel had prepared for war, and had shut up the passages of the hill country, and had fortified all the tops

of the high hills and had laid impediments in the champaign countries:[2] Wherewith he was very angry, and called all the princes of Moab, and the captains of Ammon, and all the governors of the sea coast,[3] And he said unto them, Tell me now, ye sons of Chanaan, who this people is, that dwelleth in the hill country, and what are the cities that they inhabit, and what is the multitude of their army, and wherein is their power and strength, and what king is set over them, or captain of their army;[4] And why have they determined not to come and meet me, more than all the inhabitants of the west.[5] Then said Achior, the captain of all the sons of Ammon, Let my lord now hear a word from the mouth of thy servant, and I will declare unto thee the truth concerning this people, which dwelleth near thee, and inhabiteth the hill countries: and there shall no lie come out of the mouth of thy servant.[6] This people are descended of the Chaldeans:[7] And they sojourned heretofore in Mesopotamia, because they would not follow the gods of their fathers, which were in the land of Chaldea.[8] For they left the way of their ancestors, and worshipped the God of heaven, the God whom they knew: so they cast them out from the face of their gods, and they fled into Mesopotamia, and sojourned there many days.[9] Then their God commanded them to depart from the place where they sojourned, and to go into the land of Chanaan: where they dwelt, and were increased with gold and silver, and with very much cattle.[10] But when a famine covered all the land of Chanaan, they went down into Egypt, and sojourned there, while they were nourished, and became there a great multitude, so that one could not number their nation.[11] Therefore the king of Egypt rose up against them, and dealt subtilly with them, and brought them low with labouring in brick, and made them slaves.[12] Then they cried unto their God, and he smote all the land of Egypt with incurable plagues: so the Egyptians cast them out of their sight.[13] And God dried the Red sea before them,[14] And brought them to mount Sina, and Cades-Barne, and cast forth all that dwelt in the wilderness.[15] So they dwelt in the land of the Amorites, and they destroyed by their strength all them of Esebon, and passing over Jordan they possessed all the hill country.[16] And they cast forth before them the Chanaanite, the Pherezite, the Jebusite, and the Sychemite, and all the Gergesites, and they dwelt in that country many days.[17] And whilst they sinned not before their God, they prospered, because the God that hateth iniquity was with them.[18] But when they departed from the way which he appointed them, they were destroyed in many battles very sore, and were led captives into a land that was not their's, and the temple of their God was cast to the ground, and their cities were taken by the enemies.[19] But now are they returned to their God, and are come up from the places where they were scattered, and have possessed Jerusalem, where their sanctuary is, and are seated in the hill country; for it was desolate.[20] Now therefore, my lord and governor, if there be any error against this people, and they sin against their God, let us consider that this shall be their ruin, and let us go up, and we shall overcome them.[21] But if there be no iniquity in their nation, let my lord now pass by, lest their Lord defend them, and their God be for them, and we become a reproach before all the world.[22] And when Achior had finished these sayings, all the people standing round about the tent murmured, and the chief men of Holofernes, and all that dwelt by the sea side, and in Moab, spake that he should kill him.[23] For, say they, we will not be afraid of the face of the children of Israel: for, lo, it is a people that have no strength nor power for a strong battle[24] Now therefore, lord Holofernes, we will go up, and they shall be a prey to be devoured of all thine army.

Jdt.6

[1] And when the tumult of men that were about the council was ceased, Holofernes the chief captain of the army of Assur said unto Achior and all the Moabites before all the company of other nations,[2] And who art thou, Achior, and the hirelings of Ephraim, that thou hast prophesied against us as to day, and hast said, that we should not make war with the people of Israel, because their God will defend them? and who is God but Nabuchodonosor?[3] He will send his power, and will destroy them from the face of the earth, and their God shall not deliver them: but we his servants will destroy them as one man; for they are not able to sustain the power of our horses.[4] For with them we will tread them under foot, and their mountains shall be drunken with their blood, and their fields shall be filled with their dead bodies, and their footsteps shall not be able to stand before us, for they shall utterly perish, saith king Nabuchodonosor, lord of all the earth: for he said, None of my words shall be in vain.[5] And thou, Achior, an hireling of Ammon, which hast spoken these words in the day of thine iniquity, shalt see my face no more from this day, until I take vengeance of this nation that came out of Egypt.[6] And then shall the sword of mine army, and the multitude of them that serve me, pass through thy sides, and thou shalt fall among their slain, when I return.[7] Now therefore my servants shall bring thee back into the hill country, and shall set thee in one of the cities of the passages:[8] And thou shalt not perish, till thou be destroyed with them.[9] And if thou persuade thyself in thy mind that they shall be taken, let not thy countenance fall: I have spoken it, and none of my words shall be in vain.[10] Then Holofernes commanded his servants, that waited in his tent, to take Achior, and bring him to Bethulia, and deliver him into the hands of the children of Israel.[11] So his servants took him, and brought him out of the camp into the plain, and they went from the midst of the plain into the hill country, and came unto the fountains that were under Bethulia.[12] And when the men of the city saw them, they took up their weapons, and went out of the city to the top of the hill: and every man that used a sling kept them from coming up by casting of stones against them.[13] Nevertheless having gotten privily under the hill, they bound Achior, and cast him down, and left him at the foot of the hill, and returned to their lord.[14] But the Israelites descended from their city, and came unto him, and loosed him, and brought him to Bethulia, and presented him to the governors of the city:[15] Which were in those days Ozias the son of Micha, of the tribe of Simeon, and Chabris the son of Gothoniel, and Charmis the son of Melchiel.[16] And they called together all the ancients of the city, and all their youth ran together, and their women, to the assembly, and they set Achior in the midst of all their people. Then Ozias asked him of that which was done.[17] And he answered and declared unto them the words of the council of Holofernes, and all the words that he had spoken in the midst of the princes of Assur, and whatsoever Holofernes had spoken proudly against the house of Israel.[18] Then the people fell down and worshipped God, and cried unto God. saying,[19] O Lord God of heaven, behold their pride, and pity the low estate of our nation, and look upon the face of those that are sanctified unto thee this day.[20] Then they comforted Achior, and praised him greatly.[21] And Ozias took him out of the assembly unto his house, and made a feast to the elders; and they called on the God of Israel all that night for help.

Jdt.7

[1] The next day Holofernes commanded all his army, and all his people which were come to take his part, that they should remove their camp against Bethulia, to take aforehand the ascents of the hill country, and to make war against the children of Israel.[2] Then their strong men removed their camps in that day, and the army of the men of war was an hundred and seventy thousand footmen, and

twelve thousand horsemen, beside the baggage, and other men that were afoot among them, a very great multitude.³ And they camped in the valley near unto Bethulia, by the fountain, and they spread themselves in breadth over Dothaim even to Belmaim, and in length from Bethulia unto Cynamon, which is over against Esdraelon.⁴ Now the children of Israel, when they saw the multitude of them, were greatly troubled, and said every one to his neighbour, Now will these men lick up the face of the earth; for neither the high mountains, nor the valleys, nor the hills, are able to bear their weight.⁵ Then every man took up his weapons of war, and when they had kindled fires upon their towers, they remained and watched all that night.⁶ But in the second day Holofernes brought forth all his horsemen in the sight of the children of Israel which were in Bethulia,⁷ And viewed the passages up to the city, and came to the fountains of their waters, and took them, and set garrisons of men of war over them, and he himself removed toward his people.⁸ Then came unto him all the chief of the children of Esau, and all the governors of the people of Moab, and the captains of the sea coast, and said,⁹ Let our lord now hear a word, that there be not an overthrow in thine army.¹⁰ For this people of the children of Israel do not trust in their spears, but in the height of the mountains wherein they dwell, because it is not easy to come up to the tops of their mountains.¹¹ Now therefore, my lord, fight not against them in battle array, and there shall not so much as one man of thy people perish.¹² Remain in thy camp, and keep all the men of thine army, and let thy servants get into their hands the fountain of water, which issueth forth of the foot of the mountain:¹³ For all the inhabitants of Bethulia have their water thence; so shall thirst kill them, and they shall give up their city, and we and our people shall go up to the tops of the mountains that are near, and will camp upon them, to watch that none go out of the city.¹⁴ So they and their wives and their children shall be consumed with fire, and before the sword come against them, they shall be overthrown in the streets where they dwell.¹⁵ Thus shalt thou render them an evil reward; because they rebelled, and met not thy person peaceably.¹⁶ And these words pleased Holofernes and all his servants, and he appointed to do as they had spoken.¹⁷ So the camp of the children of Ammon departed, and with them five thousand of the Assyrians, and they pitched in the valley, and took the waters, and the fountains of the waters of the children of Israel.¹⁸ Then the children of Esau went up with the children of Ammon, and camped in the hill country over against Dothaim: and they sent some of them toward the south, and toward the east over against Ekrebel, which is near unto Chusi, that is upon the brook Mochmur; and the rest of the army of the Assyrians camped in the plain, and covered the face of the whole land; and their tents and carriages were pitched to a very great multitude.¹⁹ Then the children of Israel cried unto the Lord their God, because their heart failed, for all their enemies had compassed them round about, and there was no way to escape out from among them.²⁰ Thus all the company of Assur remained about them, both their footmen, chariots, and horsemen, four and thirty days, so that all their vessels of water failed all the inhabitants of Bethulia.²¹ And the cisterns were emptied, and they had not water to drink their fill for one day; for they gave them drink by measure.²² Therefore their young children were out of heart, and their women and young men fainted for thirst, and fell down in the streets of the city, and by the passages of the gates, and there was no longer any strength in them.²³ Then all the people assembled to Ozias, and to the chief of the city, both young men, and women, and children, and cried with a loud voice, and said before all the elders,²⁴ God be judge between us and you: for ye have done us great injury, in that ye have not required peace of the children of Assur.²⁵ For now we have no

helper: but God hath sold us into their hands, that we should be thrown down before them with thirst and great destruction.²⁶ Now therefore call them unto you, and deliver the whole city for a spoil to the people of Holofernes, and to all his army.²⁷ For it is better for us to be made a spoil unto them, than to die for thirst: for we will be his servants, that our souls may live, and not see the death of our infants before our eyes, nor our wives nor our children to die.²⁸ We take to witness against you the heaven and the earth, and our God and Lord of our fathers, which punisheth us according to our sins and the sins of our fathers, that he do not according as we have said this day.²⁹ Then there was great weeping with one consent in the midst of the assembly; and they cried unto the Lord God with a loud voice.³⁰ Then said Ozias to them, Brethren, be of good courage, let us yet endure five days, in the which space the Lord our God may turn his mercy toward us; for he will not forsake us utterly.³¹ And if these days pass, and there come no help unto us, I will do according to your word.³² And he dispersed the people, every one to their own charge; and they went unto the walls and towers of their city, and sent the women and children into their houses: and they were very low brought in the city.

Jdt.8

¹ Now at that time Judith heard thereof, which was the daughter of Merari, the son of Ox, the son of Joseph, the son of Ozel, the son of Elcia, the son of Ananias, the son of Gedeon, the son of Raphaim, the son of Acitho, the son of Eliu, the son of Eliab, the son of Nathanael, the son of Samael, the son of Salasadal, the son of Israel.² And Manasses was her husband, of her tribe and kindred, who died in the barley harvest.³ For as he stood overseeing them that bound sheaves in the field, the heat came upon his head, and he fell on his bed, and died in the city of Bethulia: and they buried him with his fathers in the field between Dothaim and Balamo.⁴ So Judith was a widow in her house three years and four months.⁵ And she made her a tent upon the top of her house, and put on sackcloth upon her loins and ware her widow's apparel.⁶ And she fasted all the days of her widowhood, save the eves of the sabbaths, and the sabbaths, and the eves of the new moons, and the new moons and the feasts and solemn days of the house of Israel.⁷ She was also of a goodly countenance, and very beautiful to behold: and her husband Manasses had left her gold, and silver, and menservants and maidservants, and cattle, and lands; and she remained upon them.⁸ And there was none that gave her an ill word; ar she feared God greatly.⁹ Now when she heard the evil words of the people against the governor, that they fainted for lack of water; for Judith had heard all the words that Ozias had spoken unto them, and that he had sworn to deliver the city unto the Assyrians after five days;¹⁰ Then she sent her waitingwoman, that had the government of all things that she had, to call Ozias and Chabris and Charmis, the ancients of the city.¹¹ And they came unto her, and she said unto them, Hear me now, O ye governors of the inhabitants of Bethulia: for your words that ye have spoken before the people this day are not right, touching this oath which ye made and pronounced between God and you, and have promised to deliver the city to our enemies, unless within these days the Lord turn to help you.¹² And now who are ye that have tempted God this day, and stand instead of God among the children of men?¹³ And now try the Lord Almighty, but ye shall never know any thing.¹⁴ For ye cannot find the depth of the heart of man, neither can ye perceive the things that he thinketh: then how can ye search out God, that hath made all these things, and know his mind, or comprehend his purpose? Nay, my brethren, provoke not the Lord our God to anger.¹⁵ For if he will not help us within these five days, he hath power to defend us when he will, even every day, or to destroy us before our

enemies.[16] Do not bind the counsels of the Lord our God: for God is not as man, that he may be threatened; neither is he as the son of man, that he should be wavering.[17] Therefore let us wait for salvation of him, and call upon him to help us, and he will hear our voice, if it please him.[18] For there arose none in our age, neither is there any now in these days neither tribe, nor family, nor people, nor city among us, which worship gods made with hands, as hath been aforetime.[19] For the which cause our fathers were given to the sword, and for a spoil, and had a great fall before our enemies.[20] But we know none other god, therefore we trust that he will not dispise us, nor any of our nation.[21] For if we be taken so, all Judea shall lie waste, and our sanctuary shall be spoiled; and he will require the profanation thereof at our mouth.[22] And the slaughter of our brethren, and the captivity of the country, and the desolation of our inheritance, will he turn upon our heads among the Gentiles, wheresoever we shall be in bondage; and we shall be an offence and a reproach to all them that possess us.[23] For our servitude shall not be directed to favour: but the Lord our God shall turn it to dishonour.[24] Now therefore, O brethren, let us shew an example to our brethren, because their hearts depend upon us, and the sanctuary, and the house, and the altar, rest upon us.[25] Moreover let us give thanks to the Lord our God, which trieth us, even as he did our fathers.[26] Remember what things he did to Abraham, and how he tried Isaac, and what happened to Jacob in Mesopotamia of Syria, when he kept the sheep of Laban his mother's brother.[27] For he hath not tried us in the fire, as he did them, for the examination of their hearts, neither hath he taken vengeance on us: but the Lord doth scourge them that come near unto him, to admonish them.[28] Then said Ozias to her, All that thou hast spoken hast thou spoken with a good heart, and there is none that may gainsay thy words.[29] For this is not the first day wherein thy wisdom is manifested; but from the beginning of thy days all the people have known thy understanding, because the disposition of thine heart is good.[30] But the people were very thirsty, and compelled us to do unto them as we have spoken, and to bring an oath upon ourselves, which we will not break.[31] Therefore now pray thou for us, because thou art a godly woman, and the Lord will send us rain to fill our cisterns, and we shall faint no more.[32] Then said Judith unto them, Hear me, and I will do a thing, which shall go throughout all generations to the children of our nation.[33] Ye shall stand this night in the gate, and I will go forth with my waitingwoman: and within the days that ye have promised to deliver the city to our enemies the Lord will visit Israel by mine hand.[34] But enquire not ye of mine act: for I will not declare it unto you, till the things be finished that I do.[35] Then said Ozias and the princes unto her, Go in peace, and the Lord God be before thee, to take vengeance on our enemies.[36] So they returned from the tent, and went to their wards.

Jdt.9

[1] Judith fell upon her face, and put ashes upon her head, and uncovered the sackcloth wherewith she was clothed; and about the time that the incense of that evening was offered in Jerusalem in the house of the Lord Judith cried with a loud voice, and said,[2] O Lord God of my father Simeon, to whom thou gavest a sword to take vengeance of the strangers, who loosened the girdle of a maid to defile her, and discovered the thigh to her shame, and polluted her virginity to her reproach; for thou saidst, It shall not be so; and yet they did so:[3] Wherefore thou gavest their rulers to be slain, so that they dyed their bed in blood, being deceived, and smotest the servants with their lords, and the lords upon their thrones;[4] And hast given their wives for a prey, and their daughters to be captives, and all their spoils to be divided among thy dear children; which were moved with thy zeal, and abhorred the pollution of their blood, and called upon thee for aid: O God, O my God, hear me also a widow.[5] For thou hast wrought not only those things, but also the things which fell out before, and which ensued after; thou hast thought upon the things which are now, and which are to come.[6] Yea, what things thou didst determine were ready at hand, and said, Lo, we are here: for all thy ways are prepared, and thy judgments are in thy foreknowledge.[7] For, behold, the Assyrians are multiplied in their power; they are exalted with horse and man; they glory in the strength of their footmen; they trust in shield, and spear, and bow, and sling; and know not that thou art the Lord that breakest the battles: the Lord is thy name.[8] Throw down their strength in thy power, and bring down their force in thy wrath: for they have purposed to defile thy sanctuary, and to pollute the tabernacle where thy glorious name resteth and to cast down with sword the horn of thy altar.[9] Behold their pride, and send thy wrath upon their heads: give into mine hand, which am a widow, the power that I have conceived.[10] Smite by the deceit of my lips the servant with the prince, and the prince with the servant: break down their stateliness by the hand of a woman.[11] For thy power standeth not in multitude nor thy might in strong men: for thou art a God of the afflicted, an helper of the oppressed, an upholder of the weak, a protector of the forlorn, a saviour of them that are without hope.[12] I pray thee, I pray thee, O God of my father, and God of the inheritance of Israel, Lord of the heavens and earth, Creator of the waters, king of every creature, hear thou my prayer:[13] And make my speech and deceit to be their wound and stripe, who have purposed cruel things against thy covenant, and thy hallowed house, and against the top of Sion, and against the house of the possession of thy children.[14] And make every nation and tribe to acknowledge that thou art the God of all power and might, and that there is none other that protecteth the people of Israel but thou.

Jdt.10

[1] Now after that she had ceased to cry unto the God of Israel, and bad made an end of all these words.[2] She rose where she had fallen down, and called her maid, and went down into the house in the which she abode in the sabbath days, and in her feast days,[3] And pulled off the sackcloth which she had on, and put off the garments of her widowhood, and washed her body all over with water, and anointed herself with precious ointment, and braided the hair of her head, and put on a tire upon it, and put on her garments of gladness, wherewith she was clad during the life of Manasses her husband.[4] And she took sandals upon her feet, and put about her her bracelets, and her chains, and her rings, and her earrings, and all her ornaments, and decked herself bravely, to allure the eyes of all men that should see her.[5] Then she gave her maid a bottle of wine, and a cruse of oil, and filled a bag with parched corn, and lumps of figs, and with fine bread; so she folded all these things together, and laid them upon her.[6] Thus they went forth to the gate of the city of Bethulia, and found standing there Ozias and the ancients of the city, Chabris and Charmis.[7] And when they saw her, that her countenance was altered, and her apparel was changed, they wondered at her beauty very greatly, and said unto her.[8] The God, the God of our fathers give thee favour, and accomplish thine enterprizes to the glory of the children of Israel, and to the exaltation of Jerusalem. Then they worshipped God.[9] And she said unto them, Command the gates of the city to be opened unto me, that I may go forth to accomplish the things whereof ye have spoken with me. So they commanded the young men to open unto her, as she had spoken.[10] And when they had done so, Judith went out, she, and her maid with her; and the men of the city looked after her, until she was gone down the mountain, and till she had passed the valley, and could see her no more.[11] Thus they went straight forth in the valley:

and the first watch of the Assyrians met her,[12] And took her, and asked her, Of what people art thou? and whence comest thou? and whither goest thou? And she said, I am a woman of the Hebrews, and am fled from them: for they shall be given you to be consumed:[13] And I am coming before Holofernes the chief captain of your army, to declare words of truth; and I will shew him a way, whereby he shall go, and win all the hill country, without losing the body or life of any one of his men.[14] Now when the men heard her words, and beheld her countenance, they wondered greatly at her beauty, and said unto her,[15] Thou hast saved thy life, in that thou hast hasted to come down to the presence of our lord: now therefore come to his tent, and some of us shall conduct thee, until they have delivered thee to his hands.[16] And when thou standest before him, be not afraid in thine heart, but shew unto him according to thy word; and he will entreat thee well.[17] Then they chose out of them an hundred men to accompany her and her maid; and they brought her to the tent of Holofernes.[18] Then was there a concourse throughout all the camp: for her coming was noised among the tents, and they came about her, as she stood without the tent of Holofernes, till they told him of her.[19] And they wondered at her beauty, and admired the children of Israel because of her, and every one said to his neighbour, Who would despise this people, that have among them such women? surely it is not good that one man of them be left who being let go might deceive the whole earth.[20] And they that lay near Holofernes went out, and all his servants and they brought her into the tent.[21] Now Holofernes rested upon his bed under a canopy, which was woven with purple, and gold, and emeralds, and precious stones.[22] So they shewed him of her; and he came out before his tent with silver lamps going before him.[23] And when Judith was come before him and his servants they all marvelled at the beauty of her countenance; and she fell down upon her face, and did reverence unto him: and his servants took her up.

Jdt.11

[1] Then said Holofernes unto her, Woman, be of good comfort, fear not in thine heart: for I never hurt any that was willing to serve Nabuchodonosor, the king of all the earth.[2] Now therefore, if thy people that dwelleth in the mountains had not set light by me, I would not have lifted up my spear against them: but they have done these things to themselves.[3] But now tell me wherefore thou art fled from them, and art come unto us: for thou art come for safeguard; be of good comfort, thou shalt live this night, and hereafter:[4] For none shall hurt thee, but entreat thee well, as they do the servants of king Nabuchodonosor my lord.[5] Then Judith said unto him, Receive the words of thy servant, and suffer thine handmaid to speak in thy presence, and I will declare no lie to my lord this night.[6] And if thou wilt follow the words of thine handmaid, God will bring the thing perfectly to pass by thee; and my lord shall not fail of his purposes.[7] As Nabuchodonosor king of all the earth liveth, and as his power liveth, who hath sent thee for the upholding of every living thing: for not only men shall serve him by thee, but also the beasts of the field, and the cattle, and the fowls of the air, shall live by thy power under Nabuchodonosor and all his house.[8] For we have heard of thy wisdom and thy policies, and it is reported in all the earth, that thou only art excellent in all the kingdom, and mighty in knowledge, and wonderful in feats of war.[9] Now as concerning the matter, which Achior did speak in thy council, we have heard his words; for the men of Bethulia saved him, and he declared unto them all that he had spoken unto thee.[10] Therefore, O lord and governor, respect not his word; but lay it up in thine heart, for it is true: for our nation shall not be punished, neither can sword prevail against them, except they sin against their God.[11] And now, that my lord be not defeated and frustrate of his purpose, even death is now

fallen upon them, and their sin hath overtaken them, wherewith they will provoke their God to anger whensoever they shall do that which is not fit to be done:[12] For their victuals fail them, and all their water is scant, and they have determined to lay hands upon their cattle, and purposed to consume all those things, that God hath forbidden them to eat by his laws:[13] And are resolved to spend the firstfruits of the the tenths of wine and oil, which they had sanctified, and reserved for the priests that serve in Jerusalem before the face of our God; the which things it is not lawful for any of the people so much as to touch with their hands.[14] For they have sent some to Jerusalem, because they also that dwell there have done the like, to bring them a licence from the senate.[15] Now when they shall bring them word, they will forthwith do it, and they shall be given to thee to be destroyed the same day.[16] Wherefore I thine handmaid, knowing all this, am fled from their presence; and God hath sent me to work things with thee, whereat all the earth shall be astonished, and whosoever shall hear it.[17] For thy servant is religious, and serveth the God of heaven day and night: now therefore, my lord, I will remain with thee, and thy servant will go out by night into the valley, and I will pray unto God, and he will tell me when they have committed their sins:[18] And I will come and shew it unto thee: then thou shalt go forth with all thine army, and there shall be none of them that shall resist thee.[19] And I will lead thee through the midst of Judea, until thou come before Jerusalem; and I will set thy throne in the midst thereof; and thou shalt drive them as sheep that have no shepherd, and a dog shall not so much as open his mouth at thee: for these things were told me according to my foreknowledge, and they were declared unto me, and I am sent to tell thee.[20] Then her words pleased Holofernes and all his servants; and they marvelled at her wisdom, and said,[21] There is not such a woman from one end of the earth to the other, both for beauty of face, and wisdom of words.[22] Likewise Holofernes said unto her. God hath done well to send thee before the people, that strength might be in our hands and destruction upon them that lightly regard my lord.[23] And now thou art both beautiful in thy countenance, and witty in thy words: surely if thou do as thou hast spoken thy God shall be my God, and thou shalt dwell in the house of king Nabuchodonosor, and shalt be renowned through the whole earth.

Jdt.12

[1] Then he commanded to bring her in where his plate was set; and bade that they should prepare for her of his own meats, and that she should drink of his own wine.[2] And Judith said, I will not eat thereof, lest there be an offence: but provision shall be made for me of the things that I have brought.[3] Then Holofernes said unto her, If thy provision should fail, how should we give thee the like? for there be none with us of thy nation.[4] Then said Judith unto him As thy soul liveth, my lord, thine handmaid shall not spend those things that I have, before the Lord work by mine hand the things that he hath determined.[5] Then the servants of Holofernes brought her into the tent, and she slept till midnight, and she arose when it was toward the morning watch,[6] And sent to Holofernes, saving, Let my lord now command that thine handmaid may go forth unto prayer.[7] Then Holofernes commanded his guard that they should not stay her: thus she abode in the camp three days, and went out in the night into the valley of Bethulia, and washed herself in a fountain of water by the camp.[8] And when she came out, she besought the Lord God of Israel to direct her way to the raising up of the children of her people.[9] So she came in clean, and remained in the tent, until she did eat her meat at evening.[10] And in the fourth day Holofernes made a feast to his own servants only, and called none of the officers to the banquet.[11] Then said he to Bagoas the eunuch, who had charge over all that he had, Go now, and persuade this Hebrew

woman which is with thee, that she come unto us, and eat and drink with us.[12] For, lo, it will be a shame for our person, if we shall let such a woman go, not having had her company; for if we draw her not unto us, she will laugh us to scorn.[13] Then went Bagoas from the presence of Holofernes, and came to her, and he said, Let not this fair damsel fear to come to my lord, and to be honoured in his presence, and drink wine, and be merry with us and be made this day as one of the daughters of the Assyrians, which serve in the house of Nabuchodonosor.[14] Then said Judith unto him, Who am I now, that I should gainsay my lord? surely whatsoever pleaseth him I will do speedily, and it shall be my joy unto the day of my death.[15] So she arose, and decked herself with her apparel and all her woman's attire, and her maid went and laid soft skins on the ground for her over against Holofernes, which she had received of Bagoas far her daily use, that she might sit and eat upon them.[16] Now when Judith came in and sat down, Holofernes his heart was ravished with her, and his mind was moved, and he desired greatly her company; for he waited a time to deceive her, from the day that he had seen her.[17] Then said Holofernes unto her, Drink now, and be merry with us.[18] So Judith said, I will drink now, my lord, because my life is magnified in me this day more than all the days since I was born.[19] Then she took and ate and drank before him what her maid had prepared.[20] And Holofernes took great delight in her, and drank more wine than he had drunk at any time in one day since he was born.

Jdt.13

[1] Now when the evening was come, his servants made haste to depart, and Bagoas shut his tent without, and dismissed the waiters from the presence of his lord; and they went to their beds: for they were all weary, because the feast had been long.[2] And Judith was left along in the tent, and Holofernes lying along upon his bed: for he was filled with wine.[3] Now Judith had commanded her maid to stand without her bedchamber, and to wait for her. coming forth, as she did daily: for she said she would go forth to her prayers, and she spake to Bagoas according to the same purpose.[4] So all went forth and none was left in the bedchamber, neither little nor great. Then Judith, standing by his bed, said in her heart, O Lord God of all power, look at this present upon the works of mine hands for the exaltation of Jerusalem.[5] For now is the time to help thine inheritance, and to execute thine enterprizes to the destruction of the enemies which are risen against us.[6] Then she came to the pillar of the bed, which was at Holofernes' head, and took down his fauchion from thence,[7] And approached to his bed, and took hold of the hair of his head, and said, Strengthen me, O Lord God of Israel, this day.[8] And she smote twice upon his neck with all her might, and she took away his head from him.[9] And tumbled his body down from the bed, and pulled down the canopy from the pillars; and anon after she went forth, and gave Holofernes his head to her maid;[10] And she put it in her bag of meat: so they twain went together according to their custom unto prayer: and when they passed the camp, they compassed the valley, and went up the mountain of Bethulia, and came to the gates thereof.[11] Then said Judith afar off, to the watchmen at the gate, Open, open now the gate: God, even our God, is with us, to shew his power yet in Jerusalem, and his forces against the enemy, as he hath even done this day.[12] Now when the men of her city heard her voice, they made haste to go down to the gate of their city, and they called the elders of the city.[13] And then they ran all together, both small and great, for it was strange unto them that she was come: so they opened the gate, and received them, and made a fire for a light, and stood round about them.[14] Then she said to them with a loud voice, Praise, praise God, praise God, I say, for he hath not taken away his mercy from

15

the house of Israel, but hath destroyed our enemies by mine hands this night.[15] So she took the head out of the bag, and shewed it, and said unto them, behold the head of Holofernes, the chief captain of the army of Assur, and behold the canopy, wherein he did lie in his drunkenness; and the Lord hath smitten him by the hand of a woman.[16] As the Lord liveth, who hath kept me in my way that I went, my countenance hath deceived him to his destruction, and yet hath he not committed sin with me, to defile and shame me.[17] Then all the people were wonderfully astonished, and bowed themselves and worshipped God, and said with one accord, Blessed be thou, O our God, which hast this day brought to nought the enemies of thy people.[18] Then said Ozias unto her, O daughter, blessed art thou of the most high God above all the women upon the earth; and blessed be the Lord God, which hath created the heavens and the earth, which hath directed thee to the cutting off of the head of the chief of our enemies.[19] For this thy confidence shall not depart from the heart of men, which remember the power of God for ever.[20] And God turn these things to thee for a perpetual praise, to visit thee in good things because thou hast not spared thy life for the affliction of our nation, but hast revenged our ruin, walking a straight way before our God. And all the people said; So be it, so be it.

Jdt.14

[1] Then said Judith unto them, Hear me now, my brethren, and take this head, and hang it upon the highest place of your walls.[2] And so soon as the morning shall appear, and the sun shall come forth upon the earth, take ye every one his weapons, and go forth every valiant man out of the city, and set ye a captain over them, as though ye would go down into the field toward the watch of the Assyrians; but go not down.[3] Then they shall take their armour, and shall go into their camp, and raise up the captains of the army of Assur, and shall run to the tent of Holofernes, but shall not find him: then fear shall fall upon them, and they shall flee before your face.[4] So ye, and all that inhabit the coast of Israel, shall pursue them, and overthrow them as they go.[5] But before ye do these things, call me Achior the Ammonite, that he may see and know him that despised the house of Israel, and that sent him to us as it were to his death.[6] Then they called Achior out of the house of Ozias; and when he was come, and saw the head of Holofernes in a man's hand in the assembly of the people, he fell down on his face, and his spirit failed.[7] But when they had recovered him, he fell at Judith's feet, and reverenced her, and said, Blessed art thou in all the tabernacles of Juda, and in all nations, which hearing thy name shall be astonished.[8] Now therefore tell me all the things that thou hast done in these days. Then Judith declared unto him in the midst of the people all that she had done, from the day that she went forth until that hour she spake unto them.[9] And when she had left off speaking, the people shouted with a loud voice, and made a joyful noise in their city.[10] And when Achior had seen all that the God of Israel had done, he believed in God greatly, and circumcised the flesh of his foreskin, and was joined unto the house of Israel unto this day.[11] And as soon as the morning arose, they hanged the head of Holofernes upon the wall, and every man took his weapons, and they went forth by bands unto the straits of the mountain.[12] But when the Assyrians saw them, they sent to their leaders, which came to their captains and tribunes, and to every one of their rulers.[13] So they came to Holofernes' tent, and said to him that had the charge of all his things, Waken now our lord: for the slaves have been bold to come down against us to battle, that they may be utterly destroyed.[14] Then went in Bagoas, and knocked at the door of the tent; for he thought that he had slept with Judith.[15] But because none answered, he opened it, and went into the bedchamber, and found him cast upon the floor dead, and his head was taken from him.[16] Therefore he cried with a loud voice,

with weeping, and sighing, and a mighty cry, and rent his garments.[17] After he went into the tent where Judith lodged: and when he found her not, he leaped out to the people, and cried,[18] These slaves have dealt treacherously; one woman of the Hebrews hath brought shame upon the house of king Nabuchodonosor: for, behold, Holofernes lieth upon the ground without a head.[19] When the captains of the Assyrians' army heard these words, they rent their coats and their minds were wonderfully troubled, and there was a cry and a very great noise throughout the camp.

Jdt.15

[1] And when they that were in the tents heard, they were astonished at the thing that was done.[2] And fear and trembling fell upon them, so that there was no man that durst abide in the sight of his neighbour, but rushing out all together, they fled into every way of the plain, and of the hill country.[3] They also that had camped in the mountains round about Bethulia fled away. Then the children of Israel, every one that was a warrior among them, rushed out upon them.[4] Then sent Ozias to Betomasthem, and to Bebai, and Chobai, and Cola and to all the coasts of Israel, such as should tell the things that were done, and that all should rush forth upon their enemies to destroy them.[5] Now when the children of Israel heard it, they all fell upon them with one consent, and slew them unto Chobai: likewise also they that came from Jerusalem, and from all the hill country, (for men had told them what things were done in the camp of their enemies) and they that were in Galaad, and in Galilee, chased them with a great slaughter, until they were past Damascus and the borders thereof.[6] And the residue that dwelt at Bethulia, fell upon the camp of Assur, and spoiled them, and were greatly enriched.[7] And the children of Israel that returned from the slaughter had that which remained; and the villages and the cities, that were in the mountains and in the plain, gat many spoils: for the multitude was very great.[8] Then Joacim the high priest, and the ancients of the children of Israel that dwelt in Jerusalem, came to behold the good things that God had shewed to Israel, and to see Judith, and to salute her.[9] And when they came unto her, they blessed her with one accord, and said unto her, Thou art the exaltation of Jerusalem, thou art the great glory of Israel, thou art the great rejoicing of our nation:[10] Thou hast done all these things by thine hand: thou hast done much good to Israel, and God is pleased therewith: blessed be thou of the Almighty Lord for evermore. And all the people said, So be it.[11] And the people spoiled the camp the space of thirty days: and they gave unto Judith Holofernes his tent, and all his plate, and beds, and vessels, and all his stuff: and she took it and laid it on her mule; and made ready her carts, and laid them thereon.[12] Then all the women of Israel ran together to see her, and blessed her, and made a dance among them for her: and she took branches in her hand, and gave also to the women that were with her.[13] And they put a garland of olive upon her and her maid that was with her, and she went before all the people in the dance, leading all the women: and all the men of Israel followed in their armour with garlands, and with songs in their mouths.

Jdt.16

[1] Then Judith began to sing this thanksgiving in all Israel, and all the people sang after her this song of praise.[2] And Judith said, Begin unto my God with timbrels, sing unto my Lord with cymbals: tune unto him a new psalm: exalt him, and call upon his name.[3] For God breaketh the battles: for among the camps in the midst of the people he hath delivered me out of the hands of them that persecuted me.[4] Assur came out of the mountains from the north, he came with ten thousands of his army, the multitude whereof stopped the torrents, and their horsemen have covered the hills.[5] He bragged that he would burn up my borders, and kill my young men with the sword, and dash the sucking children against the ground, and make mine infants as a prey, and my virgins as a spoil.[6] But the Almighty Lord hath disappointed them by the hand of a woman.[7] For the mighty one did not fall by the young men, neither did the sons of the Titans smite him, nor high giants set upon him: but Judith the daughter of Merari weakened him with the beauty of her countenance.[8] For she put off the garment of her widowhood for the exaltation of those that were oppressed in Israel, and anointed her face with ointment, and bound her hair in a tire, and took a linen garment to deceive him.[9] Her sandals ravished his eyes, her beauty took his mind prisoner, and the fauchion passed through his neck.[10] The Persians quaked at her boldness, and the Medes were daunted at her hardiness.[11] Then my afflicted shouted for joy, and my weak ones cried aloud; but they were astonished: these lifted up their voices, but they were overthrown.[12] The sons of the damsels have pierced them through, and wounded them as fugatives' children: they perished by the battle of the Lord.[13] I will sing unto the Lord a new song: O Lord, thou art great and glorious, wonderful in strength, and invincible.[14] Let all creatures serve thee: for thou spakest, and they were made, thou didst send forth thy spirit, and it created them, and there is none that can resist thy voice.[15] For the mountains shall be moved from their foundations with the waters, the rocks shall melt as wax at thy presence: yet thou art merciful to them that fear thee.[16] For all sacrifice is too little for a sweet savour unto thee, and all the fat is not sufficient for thy burnt offering: but he that feareth the Lord is great at all times.[17] Woe to the nations that rise up against my kindred! the Lord Almighty will take vengeance of them in the day of judgment, in putting fire and worms in their flesh; and they shall feel them, and weep for ever.[18] Now as soon as they entered into Jerusalem, they worshipped the Lord; and as soon as the people were purified, they offered their burnt offerings, and their free offerings, and their gifts.[19] Judith also dedicated all the stuff of Holofernes, which the people had given her, and gave the canopy, which she had taken out of his bedchamber, for a gift unto the Lord.[20] So the people continued feasting in Jerusalem before the sanctuary for the space of three months and Judith remained with them.[21] After this time every one returned to his own inheritance, and Judith went to Bethulia, and remained in her own possession, and was in her time honourable in all the country.[22] And many desired her, but none knew her all the days of her life, after that Manasses her husband was dead, and was gathered to his people.[23] But she increased more and more in honour, and waxed old in her husband's house, being an hundred and five years old, and made her maid free; so she died in Bethulia: and they buried her in the cave of her husband Manasses.[24] And the house of Israel lamented her seven days: and before she died, she did distribute her goods to all them that were nearest of kindred to Manasses her husband, and to them that were the nearest of her kindred.[25] And there was none that made the children of Israel any more afraid in the days of Judith, nor a long time after her death.

Wisdom of Solomon

Wis.1

[1] Love righteousness, ye that be judges of the earth: think of the Lord with a good (heart,) and in simplicity of heart seek him.[2] For he will be found of them that tempt him not; and sheweth himself unto such as do not distrust him.[3] For froward thoughts separate from God: and his power, when it is tried, reproveth the unwise.[4] For into a malicious soul wisdom shall not enter; nor dwell in the body that is subject unto sin.[5] For the holy spirit of discipline

will flee deceit, and remove from thoughts that are without understanding, and will not abide when unrighteousness cometh in.[6] For wisdom is a loving spirit; and will not acquit a blasphemer of his words: for God is witness of his reins, and a true beholder of his heart, and a hearer of his tongue.[7] For the Spirit of the Lord filleth the world: and that which containeth all things hath knowledge of the voice.[8] Therefore he that speaketh unrighteous things cannot be hid: neither shall vengeance, when it punisheth, pass by him.[9] For inquisition shall be made into the counsels of the ungodly: and the sound of his words shall come unto the Lord for the manifestation of his wicked deeds.[10] For the ear of jealousy heareth all things: and the noise of murmurings is not hid.[11] Therefore beware of murmuring, which is unprofitable; and refrain your tongue from backbiting: for there is no word so secret, that shall go for nought: and the mouth that belieth slayeth the soul.[12] Seek not death in the error of your life: and pull not upon yourselves destruction with the works of your hands.[13] For God made not death: neither hath he pleasure in the destruction of the living.[14] For he created all things, that they might have their being: and the generations of the world were healthful; and there is no poison of destruction in them, nor the kingdom of death upon the earth:[15] (For righteousness is immortal:)[16] But ungodly men with their works and words called it to them: for when they thought to have it their friend, they consumed to nought, and made a covenant with it, because they are worthy to take part with it.

Wis.2

[1] For the ungodly said, reasoning with themselves, but not aright, Our life is short and tedious, and in the death of a man there is no remedy: neither was there any man known to have returned from the grave.[2] For we are born at all adventure: and we shall be hereafter as though we had never been: for the breath in our nostrils is as smoke, and a little spark in the moving of our heart:[3] Which being extinguished, our body shall be turned into ashes, and our spirit shall vanish as the soft air,[4] And our name shall be forgotten in time, and no man shall have our works in remembrance, and our life shall pass away as the trace of a cloud, and shall be dispersed as a mist, that is driven away with the beams of the sun, and overcome with the heat thereof.[5] For our time is a very shadow that passeth away; and after our end there is no returning: for it is fast sealed, so that no man cometh again.[6] Come on therefore, let us enjoy the good things that are present: and let us speedily use the creatures like as in youth.[7] Let us fill ourselves with costly wine and ointments: and let no flower of the spring pass by us:[8] Let us crown ourselves with rosebuds, before they be withered:[9] Let none of us go without his part of our voluptuousness: let us leave tokens of our joyfulness in every place: for this is our portion, and our lot is this.[10] Let us oppress the poor righteous man, let us not spare the widow, nor reverence the ancient gray hairs of the aged.[11] Let our strength be the law of justice: for that which is feeble is found to be nothing worth.[12] Therefore let us lie in wait for the righteous; because he is not for our turn, and he is clean contrary to our doings: he upbraideth us with our offending the law, and objecteth to our infamy the transgressings of our education.[13] He professeth to have the knowledge of God: and he calleth himself the child of the Lord.[14] He was made to reprove our thoughts.[15] He is grievous unto us even to behold: for his life is not like other men's, his ways are of another fashion.[16] We are esteemed of him as counterfeits: he abstaineth from our ways as from filthiness: he pronounceth the end of the just to be blessed, and maketh his boast that God is his father.[17] Let us see if his words be true: and let us prove what shall happen in the end of him.[18] For if the just man be the son of God, he will help him, and deliver him from the hand of his enemies.[19] Let us examine him with despitefulness and torture, that we may know his meekness, and prove his patience.[20] Let us condemn him with a shameful death: for by his own saying he shall be respected.[21] Such things they did imagine, and were deceived: for their own wickedness hath blinded them.[22] As for the mysteries of God, they kn ew them not: neither hoped they for the wages of righteousness, nor discerned a reward for blameless souls.[23] For God created man to be immortal, and made him to be an image of his own eternity.[24] Nevertheless through envy of the devil came death into the world: and they that do hold of his side do find it.

Wis.3

[1] But the souls of the righteous are in the hand of God, and there shall no torment touch them.[2] In the sight of the unwise they seemed to die: and their departure is taken for misery,[3] And their going from us to be utter destruction: but they are in peace.[4] For though they be punished in the sight of men, yet is their hope full of immortality.[5] And having been a little chastised, they shall be greatly rewarded: for God proved them, and found them worthy for himself.[6] As gold in the furnace hath he tried them, and received them as a burnt offering.[7] And in the time of their visitation they shall shine, and run to and fro like sparks among the stubble.[8] They shall judge the nations, and have dominion over the people, and their Lord shall reign for ever.[9] They that put their trust in him shall understand the truth: and such as be faithful in love shall abide with him: for grace and mercy is to his saints, and he hath care for his elect.[10] But the ungodly shall be punished according to their own imaginations, which have neglected the righteous, and forsaken the Lord.[11] For whoso despiseth wisdom and nurture, he is miserable, and their hope is vain, their labours unfruitful, and their works unprofitable:[12] Their wives are foolish, and their children wicked:[13] Their offspring is cursed. Wherefore blessed is the barren that is undefiled, which hath not known the sinful bed: she shall have fruit in the visitation of souls.[14] And blessed is the eunuch, which with his hands hath wrought no iniquity, nor imagined wicked things against God: for unto him shall be given the special gift of faith, and an inheritance in the temple of the Lord more acceptable to his mind.[15] For glorious is the fruit of good labours: and the root of wisdom shall never fall away.[16] As for the children of adulterers, they shall not come to their perfection, and the seed of an unrighteous bed shall be rooted out.[17] For though they live long, yet shall they be nothing regarded: and their last age shall be without honour.[18] Or, if they die quickly, they have no hope, neither comfort in the day of trial.[19] For horrible is the end of the unrighteous generation.

Wis.4

[1] Better it is to have no children, and to have virtue: for the memorial thereof is immortal: because it is known with God, and with men.[2] When it is present, men take example at it; and when it is gone, they desire it: it weareth a crown, and triumpheth for ever, having gotten the victory, striving for undefiled rewards.[3] But the multiplying brood of the ungodly shall not thrive, nor take deep rooting from bastard slips, nor lay any fast foundation.[4] For though they flourish in branches for a time; yet standing not last, they shall be shaken with the wind, and through the force of winds they shall be rooted out.[5] The imperfect branches shall be broken off, their fruit unprofitable, not ripe to eat, yea, meet for nothing.[6] For children begotten of unlawful beds are witnesses of wickedness against their parents in their trial.[7] But though the righteous be prevented with death, yet shall he be in rest.[8] For honourable age is not that which standeth in length of time, nor that is measured by number of years.[9] But wisdom is the gray hair unto men, and an unspotted life is old age.[10] He pleased God, and was beloved of him:

so that living among sinners he was translated.[11] Yea speedily was he taken away, lest that wickedness should alter his understanding, or deceit beguile his soul.[12] For the bewitching of naughtiness doth obscure things that are honest; and the wandering of concupiscence doth undermine the simple mind.[13] He, being made perfect in a short time, fulfilled a long time:[14] For his soul pleased the Lord: therefore hasted he to take him away from among the wicked.[15] This the people saw, and understood it not, neither laid they up this in their minds, That his grace and mercy is with his saints, and that he hath respect unto his chosen.[16] Thus the righteous that is dead shall condemn the ungodly which are living; and youth that is soon perfected the many years and old age of the unrighteous.[17] For they shall see the end of the wise, and shall not understand what God in his counsel hath decreed of him, and to what end the Lord hath set him in safety.[18] They shall see him, and despise him; but God shall laugh them to scorn: and they shall hereafter be a vile carcase, and a reproach among the dead for evermore.[19] For he shall rend them, and cast them down headlong, that they shall be speechless; and he shall shake them from the foundation; and they shall be utterly laid waste, and be in sorrow; and their memorial shall perish.[20] And when they cast up the accounts of their sins, they shall come with fear: and their own iniquities shall convince them to their face.

Wis.5

[1] Then shall the righteous man stand in great boldness before the face of such as have afflicted him, and made no account of his labours.[2] When they see it, they shall be troubled with terrible fear, and shall be amazed at the strangeness of his salvation, so far beyond all that they looked for.[3] And they repenting and groaning for anguish of spirit shall say within themselves, This was he, whom we had sometimes in derision, and a proverb of reproach:[4] We fools accounted his life madness, and his end to be without honour:[5] How is he numbered among the children of God, and his lot is among the saints![6] Therefore have we erred from the way of truth, and the light of righteousness hath not shined unto us, and the sun of righteousness rose not upon us.[7] We wearied ourselves in the way of wickedness and destruction: yea, we have gone through deserts, where there lay no way: but as for the way of the Lord, we have not known it.[8] What hath pride profited us? or what good hath riches with our vaunting brought us?[9] All those things are passed away like a shadow, and as a post that hasted by;[10] And as a ship that passeth over the waves of the water, which when it is gone by, the trace thereof cannot be found, neither the pathway of the keel in the waves;[11] Or as when a bird hath flown through the air, there is no token of her way to be found, but the light air being beaten with the stroke of her wings and parted with the violent noise and motion of them, is passed through, and therein afterwards no sign where she went is to be found;[12] Or like as when an arrow is shot at a mark, it parteth the air, which immediately cometh together again, so that a man cannot know where it went through:[13] Even so we in like manner, as soon as we were born, began to draw to our end, and had no sign of virtue to shew; but were consumed in our own wickedness.[14] For the hope of the Godly is like dust that is blown away with the wind; like a thin froth that is driven away with the storm; like as the smoke which is dispersed here and there with a tempest, and passeth away as the remembrance of a guest that tarrieth but a day.[15] But the righteous live for evermore; their reward also is with the Lord, and the care of them is with the most High.[16] Therefore shall they receive a glorious kingdom, and a beautiful crown from the Lord's hand: for with his right hand shall he cover them, and with his arm shall he protect them.[17] He shall take to him his jealousy for complete armour, and make the creature his weapon for the revenge of his enemies.[18] He shall put on

righteousness as a breastplate, and true judgment instead of an helmet.[19] He shall take holiness for an invincible shield.[20] His severe wrath shall he sharpen for a sword, and the world shall fight with him against the unwise.[21] Then shall the right aiming thunderbolts go abroad; and from the clouds, as from a well drawn bow, shall they fly to the mark.[22] And hailstones full of wrath shall be cast as out of a stone bow, and the water of the sea shall rage against them, and the floods shall cruelly drown them.[23] Yea, a mighty wind shall stand up against them, and like a storm shall blow them away: thus iniquity shall lay waste the whole earth, and ill dealing shall overthrow the thrones of the mighty.

Wis.6

[1] Hear therefore, O ye kings, and understand; learn, ye that be judges of the ends of the earth.[2] Give ear, ye that rule the people, and glory in the multitude of nations.[3] For power is given you of the Lord, and sovereignty from the Highest, who shall try your works, and search out your counsels.[4] Because, being ministers of his kingdom, ye have not judged aright, nor kept the law, nor walked after the counsel of God;[5] Horribly and speedily shall he come upon you: for a sharp judgment shall be to them that be in high places.[6] For mercy will soon pardon the meanest: but mighty men shall be mightily tormented.[7] For he which is Lord over all shall fear no man's person, neither shall he stand in awe of any man's greatness: for he hath made the small and great, and careth for all alike.[8] But a sore trial shall come upon the mighty.[9] Unto you therefore, O kings, do I speak, that ye may learn wisdom, and not fall away.[10] For they that keep holiness holily shall be judged holy: and they that have learned such things shall find what to answer.[11] Wherefore set your affection upon my words; desire them, and ye shall be instructed.[12] Wisdom is glorious, and never fadeth away: yea, she is easily seen of them that love her, and found of such as seek her.[13] She preventeth them that desire her, in making herself first known unto them.[14] Whoso seeketh her early shall have no great travail: for he shall find her sitting at his doors.[15] To think therefore upon her is perfection of wisdom: and whoso watcheth for her shall quickly be without care.[16] For she goeth about seeking such as are worthy of her, sheweth herself favourably unto them in the ways, and meeteth them in every thought.[17] For the very true beginning of her is the desire of discipline; and the care of discipline is love;[18] And love is the keeping of her laws; and the giving heed unto her laws is the assurance of incorruption;[19] And incorruption maketh us near unto God:[20] Therefore the desire of wisdom bringeth to a kingdom.[21] If your delight be then in thrones and sceptres, O ye kings of the people, honour wisdom, that ye may reign for evermore.[22] As for wisdom, what she is, and how she came up, I will tell you, and will not hide mysteries from you: but will seek her out from the beginning of her nativity, and bring the knowledge of her into light, and will not pass over the truth.[23] Neither will I go with consuming envy; for such a man shall have no fellowship with wisdom.[24] But the multitude of the wise is the welfare of the world: and a wise king is the upholding of the people.[25] Receive therefore instruction through my words, and it shall do you good.

Wis.7

[1] I myself also am a mortal man, like to all, and the offspring of him that was first made of the earth,[2] And in my mother's womb was fashioned to be flesh in the time of ten months, being compacted in blood, of the seed of man, and the pleasure that came with sleep.[3] And when I was born, I drew in the common air, and fell upon the earth, which is of like nature, and the first voice which I uttered was crying, as all others do.[4] I was nursed in swaddling clothes, and that with cares.[5] For there is no king that had any other beginning of birth.[6] For all men have one entrance into life, and the

like going out.[7] Wherefore I prayed, and understanding was given me: I called upon God, and the spirit of wisdom came to me.[8] I preferred her before sceptres and thrones, and esteemed riches nothing in comparison of her.[9] Neither compared I unto her any precious stone, because all gold in respect of her is as a little sand, and silver shall be counted as clay before her.[10] I loved her above health and beauty, and chose to have her instead of light: for the light that cometh from her never goeth out.[11] All good things together came to me with her, and innumerable riches in her hands.[12] And I rejoiced in them all, because wisdom goeth before them: and I knew not that she was the mother of them.[13] I learned diligently, and do communicate her liberally: I do not hide her riches.[14] For she is a treasure unto men that never faileth: which they that use become the friends of God, being commended for the gifts that come from learning.[15] God hath granted me to speak as I would, and to conceive as is meet for the things that are given me: because it is he that leadeth unto wisdom, and directeth the wise.[16] For in his hand are both we and our words; all wisdom also, and knowledge of workmanship.[17] For he hath given me certain knowledge of the things that are, namely, to know how the world was made, and the operation of the elements:[18] The beginning, ending, and midst of the times: the alterations of the turning of the sun, and the change of seasons:[19] The circuits of years, and the positions of stars:[20] The natures of living creatures, and the furies of wild beasts: the violence of winds, and the reasonings of men: the diversities of plants and the virtues of roots:[21] And all such things as are either secret or manifest, them I know.[22] For wisdom, which is the worker of all things, taught me: for in her is an understanding spirit holy, one only, manifold, subtil, lively, clear, undefiled, plain, not subject to hurt, loving the thing that is good quick, which cannot be letted, ready to do good,[23] Kind to man, steadfast, sure, free from care, having all power, overseeing all things, and going through all understanding, pure, and most subtil, spirits.[24] For wisdom is more moving than any motion: she passeth and goeth through all things by reason of her pureness.[25] For she is the breath of the power of God, and a pure influence flowing from the glory of the Almighty: therefore can no defiled thing fall into her.[26] For she is the brightness of the everlasting light, the unspotted mirror of the power of God, and the image of his goodness.[27] And being but one, she can do all things: and remaining in herself, she maketh all things new: and in all ages entering into holy souls, she maketh them friends of God, and prophets.[28] For God loveth none but him that dwelleth with wisdom.[29] For she is more beautiful than the sun, and above all the order of stars: being compared with the light, she is found before it.[30] For after this cometh night: but vice shall not prevail against wisdom.

Wis.8

[1] Wisdom reacheth from one end to another mightily: and sweetly doth she order all things.[2] I loved her, and sought her out from my youth, I desired to make her my spouse, and I was a lover of her beauty.[3] In that she is conversant with God, she magnifieth her nobility: yea, the Lord of all things himself loved her.[4] For she is privy to the mysteries of the knowledge of God, and a lover of his works.[5] If riches be a possession to be desired in this life; what is richer than wisdom, that worketh all things?[6] And if prudence work; who of all that are is a more cunning workman than she?[7] And if a man love righteousness her labours are virtues: for she teacheth temperance and prudence, justice and fortitude: which are such things, as en can have nothing more profitable in their life.[8] If a man desire much experience, she knoweth things of old, and conjectureth aright what is to come: she knoweth the subtilties of speeches, and can expound dark sentences: she foreseeth signs and wonders, and

the events of seasons and times.[9] Therefore I purposed to take her to me to live with me, knowing that she would be a counsellor of good things, and a comfort in cares and grief.[10] For her sake I shall have estimation among the multitude, and honour with the elders, though I be young.[11] I shall be found of a quick conceit in judgment, and shall be admired in the sight of great men.[12] When I hold my tongue, they shall bide my leisure, and when I speak, they shall give good ear unto me: if I talk much, they shall lay their hands upon their mouth.[13] Moreover by the means of her I shall obtain immortality, and leave behind me an everlasting memorial to them that come after me.[14] I shall set the people in order, and the nations shall be subject unto me.[15] Horrible tyrants shall be afraid, when they do but hear of me; I shall be found good among the multitude, and valiant in war.[16] After I am come into mine house, I will repose myself with her: for her conversation hath no bitterness; and to live with her hath no sorrow, but mirth and joy.[17] Now when I considered these things in myself, and pondered them in my heart, how that to be allied unto wisdom is immortality;[18] And great pleasure it is to have her friendship; and in the works of her hands are infinite riches; and in the exercise of conference with her, prudence; and in talking with her, a good report; I went about seeking how to take her to me.[19] For I was a witty child, and had a good spirit.[20] Yea rather, being good, I came into a body undefiled.[21] Nevertheless, when I perceived that I could not otherwise obtain her, except God gave her me; and that was a point of wisdom also to know whose gift she was; I prayed unto the Lord, and besought him, and with my whole heart I said,

Wis.9

[1] O God of my fathers, and Lord of mercy, who hast made all things with thy word,[2] And ordained man through thy wisdom, that he should have dominion over the creatures which thou hast made,[3] And order the world according to equity and righteousness, and execute judgment with an upright heart:[4] Give me wisdom, that sitteth by thy throne; and reject me not from among thy children:[5] For I thy servant and son of thine handmaid am a feeble person, and of a short time, and too young for the understanding of judgment and laws.[6] For though a man be never so perfect among the children of men, yet if thy wisdom be not with him, he shall be nothing regarded.[7] Thou hast chosen me to be a king of thy people, and a judge of thy sons and daughters:[8] Thou hast commanded me to build a temple upon thy holy mount, and an altar in the city wherein thou dwellest, a resemblance of the holy tabernacle, which thou hast prepared from the beginning.[9] And wisdom was with thee: which knoweth thy works, and was present when thou madest the world, and knew what was acceptable in thy sight, and right in thy commandments.[10] O send her out of thy holy heavens, and from the throne of thy glory, that being present she may labour with me, that I may know what is pleasing unto thee.[11] For she knoweth and understandeth all things, and she shall lead me soberly in my doings, and preserve me in her power.[12] So shall my works be acceptable, and then shall I judge thy people righteously, and be worthy to sit in my father's seat.[13] For what man is he that can know the counsel of God? or who can think what the will of the Lord is?[14] For the thoughts of mortal men are miserable, and our devices are but uncertain.[15] For the corruptible body presseth down the soul, and the earthy tabernacle weigheth down the mind that museth upon many things.[16] And hardly do we guess aright at things that are upon earth, and with labour do we find the things that are before us: but the things that are in heaven who hath searched out?[17] And thy counsel who hath known, except thou give wisdom, and send thy Holy Spirit from above?[18] For so the ways of them which lived on

the earth were reformed, and men were taught the things that are pleasing unto thee, and were saved through wisdom.

Wis.10

¹ She preserved the first formed father of the world, that was created alone, and brought him out of his fall,² And gave him power to rule all things.³ But when the unrighteous went away from her in his anger, he perished also in the fury wherewith he murdered his brother.⁴ For whose cause the earth being drowned with the flood, wisdom again preserved it, and directed the course of the righteous in a piece of wood of small value.⁵ Moreover, the nations in their wicked conspiracy being confounded, she found out the righteous, and preserved him blameless unto God, and kept him strong against his tender compassion toward his son.⁶ When the ungodly perished, she delivered the righteous man, who fled from the fire which fell down upon the five cities.⁷ Of whose wickedness even to this day the waste land that smoketh is a testimony, and plants bearing fruit that never come to ripeness: and a standing pillar of salt is a monument of an unbelieving soul.⁸ For regarding not wisdom, they gat not only this hurt, that they knew not the things which were good; but also left behind them to the world a memorial of their foolishness: so that in the things wherein they offended they could not so much as be hid.⁹ Rut wisdom delivered from pain those that attended upon her.¹⁰ When the righteous fled from his brother's wrath she guided him in right paths, shewed him the kingdom of God, and gave him knowledge of holy things, made him rich in his travels, and multiplied the fruit of his labours.¹¹ In the covetousness of such as oppressed him she stood by him, and made him rich.¹² She defended him from his enemies, and kept him safe from those that lay in wait, and in a sore conflict she gave him the victory; that he might know that goodness is stronger than all.¹³ When the righteous was sold, she forsook him not, but delivered him from sin: she went down with him into the pit,¹⁴ And left him not in bonds, till she brought him the sceptre of the kingdom, and power against those that oppressed him: as for them that had accused him, she shewed them to be liars, and gave him perpetual glory.¹⁵ She delivered the righteous people and blameless seed from the nation that oppressed them.¹⁶ She entered into the soul of the servant of the Lord, and withstood dreadful kings in wonders and signs;¹⁷ Rendered to the righteous a reward of their labours, guided them in a marvellous way, and was unto them for a cover by day, and a light of stars in the night season;¹⁸ Brought them through the Red sea, and led them through much water:¹⁹ But she drowned their enemies, and cast them up out of the bottom of the deep.²⁰ Therefore the righteous spoiled the ungodly, and praised thy holy name, O Lord, and magnified with one accord thine hand, that fought for them.²¹ For wisdom opened the mouth of the dumb, and made the tongues of them that cannot speak eloquent.

Wis.11

¹ She prospered their works in the hand of the holy prophet.² They went through the wilderness that was not inhabited, and pitched tents in places where there lay no way.³ They stood against their enemies, and were avenged of their adversaries.⁴ When they were thirsty, they called upon thee, and water was given them out of the flinty rock, and their thirst was quenched out of the hard stone.⁵ For by what things their enemies were punished, by the same they in their need were benefited.⁶ For instead of of a perpetual running river troubled with foul blood,⁷ For a manifest reproof of that commandment, whereby the infants were slain, thou gavest unto them abundance of water by a means which they hoped not for:⁸ Declaring by that thirst then how thou hadst punished their adversaries.⁹ For when they were tried albeit but in mercy chastised, they knew how the ungodly were judged in wrath and tormented,

thirsting in another manner than the just.¹⁰ For these thou didst admonish and try, as a father: but the other, as a severe king, thou didst condemn and punish.¹¹ Whether they were absent or present, they were vexed alike.¹² For a double grief came upon them, and a groaning for the remembrance of things past.¹³ For when they heard by their own punishments the other to be benefited, they had some feeling of the Lord.¹⁴ For whom they respected with scorn, when he was long before thrown out at the casting forth of the infants, him in the end, when they saw what came to pass, they admired.¹⁵ But for the foolish devices of their wickedness, wherewith being deceived they worshipped serpents void of reason, and vile beasts, thou didst send a multitude of unreasonable beasts upon them for vengeance;¹⁶ That they might know, that wherewithal a man sinneth, by the same also shall he be punished.¹⁷ For thy Almighty hand, that made the world of matter without form, wanted not means to send among them a multitude of bears or fierce lions,¹⁸ Or unknown wild beasts, full of rage, newly created, breathing out either a fiery vapour, or filthy scents of scattered smoke, or shooting horrible sparkles out of their eyes:¹⁹ Whereof not only the harm might dispatch them at once, but also the terrible sight utterly destroy them.²⁰ Yea, and without these might they have fallen down with one blast, being persecuted of vengeance, and scattered abroad through the breath of thy power: but thou hast ordered all things in measure and number and weight.²¹ For thou canst shew thy great strength at all times when thou wilt; and who may withstand the power of thine arm?²² For the whole world before thee is as a little grain of the balance, yea, as a drop of the morning dew that falleth down upon the earth.²³ But thou hast mercy upon all; for thou canst do all things, and winkest at the sins of men, because they should amend.²⁴ For thou lovest all the things that are, and abhorrest nothing which thou hast made: for never wouldest thou have made any thing, if thou hadst hated it.²⁵ And how could any thing have endured, if it had not been thy will? or been preserved, if not called by thee?²⁶ But thou sparest all: for they are thine, O Lord, thou lover of souls.

Wis.12

¹ For thine incorruptible Spirit is in all things.² Therefore chastenest thou them by little and little that offend, and warnest them by putting them in remembrance wherein they have offended, that leaving their wickedness they may believe on thee, O Lord.³ For it was thy will to destroy by the hands of our fathers both those old inhabitants of thy holy land,⁴ Whom thou hatedst for doing most odious works of witchcrafts, and wicked sacrifices;⁵ And also those merciless murderers of children, and devourers of man's flesh, and the feasts of blood,⁶ With their priests out of the midst of their idolatrous crew, and the parents, that killed with their own hands souls destitute of help:⁷ That the land, which thou esteemedst above all other, might receive a worthy colony of God's children.⁸ Nevertheless even those thou sparedst as men, and didst send wasps, forerunners of thine host, to destroy them by little and little.⁹ Not that thou wast unable to bring the ungodly under the hand of the righteous in battle, or to destroy them at once with cruel beasts, or with one rough word:¹⁰ But executing thy judgments upon them by little and little, thou gavest them place of repentance, not being ignorant that they were a naughty generation, and that their malice was bred in them, and that their cogitation would never be changed.¹¹ For it was a cursed seed from the beginning; neither didst thou for fear of any man give them pardon for those things wherein they sinned.¹² For who shall say, What hast thou done? or who shall withstand thy judgment? or who shall accuse thee for the nations that perish, whom thou made? or who shall come to stand against thee, to be revenged for the unrighteous men?¹³ For neither is there

any God but thou that careth for all, to whom thou mightest shew that thy judgment is not unright.[14] Neither shall king or tyrant be able to set his face against thee for any whom thou hast punished.[15] Forsomuch then as thou art righteous thyself, thou orderest all things righteously: thinking it not agreeable with thy power to condemn him that hath not deserved to be punished.[16] For thy power is the beginning of righteousness, and because thou art the Lord of all, it maketh thee to be gracious unto all.[17] For when men will not believe that thou art of a full power, thou shewest thy strength, and among them that know it thou makest their boldness manifest.[18] But thou, mastering thy power, judgest with equity, and orderest us with great favour: for thou mayest use power when thou wilt.[19] But by such works hast thou taught thy people that the just man should be merciful, and hast made thy children to be of a good hope that thou givest repentance for sins.[20] For if thou didst punish the enemies of thy children, and the condemned to death, with such deliberation, giving them time and place, whereby they might be delivered from their malice:[21] With how great circumspection didst thou judge thine own sons, unto whose fathers thou hast sworn, and made covenants of good promises?[22] Therefore, whereas thou dost chasten us, thou scourgest our enemies a thousand times more, to the intent that, when we judge, we should carefully think of thy goodness, and when we ourselves are judged, we should look for mercy.[23] Wherefore, whereas men have lived dissolutely and unrighteously, thou hast tormented them with their own abominations.[24] For they went astray very far in the ways of error, and held them for gods, which even among the beasts of their enemies were despised, being deceived, as children of no understanding.[25] Therefore unto them, as to children without the use of reason, thou didst send a judgment to mock them.[26] But they that would not be reformed by that correction, wherein he dallied with them, shall feel a judgment worthy of God.[27] For, look, for what things they grudged, when they were punished, that is, for them whom they thought to be gods; [now] being punished in them, when they saw it, they acknowledged him to be the true God, whom before they denied to know: and therefore came extreme damnation upon them.

Wis.13

[1] Surely vain are all men by nature, who are ignorant of God, and could not out of the good things that are seen know him that is: neither by considering the works did they acknowledge the workmaster;[2] But deemed either fire, or wind, or the swift air, or the circle of the stars, or the violent water, or the lights of heaven, to be the gods which govern the world.[3] With whose beauty if they being delighted took them to be gods; let them know how much better the Lord of them is: for the first author of beauty hath created them.[4] But if they were astonished at their power and virtue, let them understand by them, how much mightier he is that made them.[5] For by the greatness and beauty of the creatures proportionably the maker of them is seen.[6] But yet for this they are the less to be blamed: for they peradventure err, seeking God, and desirous to find him.[7] For being conversant in his works they search him diligently, and believe their sight: because the things are beautiful that are seen.[8] Howbeit neither are they to be pardoned.[9] For if they were able to know so much, that they could aim at the world; how did they not sooner find out the Lord thereof?[10] But miserable are they, and in dead things is their hope, who call them gods, which are the works of men's hands, gold and silver, to shew art in, and resemblances of beasts, or a stone good for nothing, the work of an ancient hand.[11] Now a carpenter that felleth timber, after he hath sawn down a tree meet for the purpose, and taken off all the bark skilfully round about, and hath wrought it handsomely, and made a

vessel thereof fit for the service of man's life;[12] And after spending the refuse of his work to dress his meat, hath filled himself;[13] And taking the very refuse among those which served to no use, being a crooked piece of wood, and full of knots, hath carved it diligently, when he had nothing else to do, and formed it by the skill of his understanding, and fashioned it to the image of a man;[14] Or made it like some vile beast, laying it over with vermilion, and with paint colouring it red, and covering every spot therein;[15] And when he had made a convenient room for it, set it in a wall, and made it fast with iron:[16] For he provided for it that it might not fall, knowing that it was unable to help itself; for it is an image, and hath need of help:[17] Then maketh he prayer for his goods, for his wife and children, and is not ashamed to speak to that which hath no life.[18] For health he calleth upon that which is weak: for life prayeth to that which is dead; for aid humbly beseecheth that which hath least means to help: and for a good journey he asketh of that which cannot set a foot forward:[19] And for gaining and getting, and for good success of his hands, asketh ability to do of him, that is most unable to do any thing.

Wis.14

[1] Again, one preparing himself to sail, and about to pass through the raging waves, calleth upon a piece of wood more rotten than the vessel that carrieth him.[2] For verily desire of gain devised that, and the workman built it by his skill.[3] But thy providence, O Father, governeth it: for thou hast made a way in the sea, and a safe path in the waves;[4] Shewing that thou canst save from all danger: yea, though a man went to sea without art.[5] Nevertheless thou wouldest not that the works of thy wisdom should be idle, and therefore do men commit their lives to a small piece of wood, and passing the rough sea in a weak vessel are saved.[6] For in the old time also, when the proud giants perished, the hope of the world governed by thy hand escaped in a weak vessel, and left to all ages a seed of generation.[7] For blessed is the wood whereby righteousness cometh.[8] But that which is made with hands is cursed, as well it, as he that made it: he, because he made it; and it, because, being corruptible, it was called god.[9] For the ungodly and his ungodliness are both alike hateful unto God.[10] For that which is made shall be punished together with him that made it.[11] Therefore even upon the idols of the Gentiles shall there be a visitation: because in the creature of God they are become an abomination, and stumblingblocks to the souls of men, and a snare to the feet of the unwise.[12] For the devising of idols was the beginning of spiritual fornication, and the invention of them the corruption of life.[13] For neither were they from the beginning, neither shall they be for ever.[14] For by the vain glory of men they entered into the world, and therefore shall they come shortly to an end.[15] For a father afflicted with untimely mourning, when he hath made an image of his child soon taken away, now honoured him as a god, which was then a dead man, and delivered to those that were under him ceremonies and sacrifices.[16] Thus in process of time an ungodly custom grown strong was kept as a law, and graven images were worshipped by the commandments of kings.[17] Whom men could not honour in presence, because they dwelt far off, they took the counterfeit of his visage from far, and made an express image of a king whom they honoured, to the end that by this their forwardness they might flatter him that was absent, as if he were present.[18] Also the singular diligence of the artificer did help to set forward the ignorant to more superstition.[19] For he, peradventure willing to please one in authority, forced all his skill to make the resemblance of the best fashion.[20] And so the multitude, allured by the grace of the work, took him now for a god, which a little before was but honoured.[21] And this was an occasion to deceive the world: for men,

serving either calamity or tyranny, did ascribe unto stones and stocks the incommunicable name.²² Moreover this was not enough for them, that they erred in the knowledge of God; but whereas they lived in the great war of ignorance, those so great plagues called they peace.²³ For whilst they slew their children in sacrifices, or used secret ceremonies, or made revellings of strange rites;²⁴ They kept neither lives nor marriages any longer undefiled: but either one slew another traiterously, or grieved him by adultery.²⁵ So that there reigned in all men without exception blood, manslaughter, theft, and dissimulation, corruption, unfaithfulness, tumults, perjury,²⁶ Disquieting of good men, forgetfulness of good turns, defiling of souls, changing of kind, disorder in marriages, adultery, and shameless uncleanness.²⁷ For the worshipping of idols not to be named is the beginning, the cause, and the end, of all evil.²⁸ For either they are mad when they be merry, or prophesy lies, or live unjustly, or else lightly forswear themselves.²⁹ For insomuch as their trust is in idols, which have no life; though they swear falsely, yet they look not to be hurt.³⁰ Howbeit for both causes shall they be justly punished: both because they thought not well of God, giving heed unto idols, and also unjustly swore in deceit, despising holiness.³¹ For it is not the power of them by whom they swear: but it is the just vengeance of sinners, that punisheth always the offence of the ungodly.

Wis.15

¹ But thou, O God, art gracious and true, longsuffering, and in mercy ordering all things,² For if we sin, we are thine, knowing thy power: but we will not sin, knowing that we are counted thine.³ For to know thee is perfect righteousness: yea, to know thy power is the root of immortality.⁴ For neither did the mischievous invention of men deceive us, nor an image spotted with divers colours, the painter's fruitless labour;⁵ The sight whereof enticeth fools to lust after it, and so they desire the form of a dead image, that hath no breath.⁶ Both they that make them, they that desire them, and they that worship them, are lovers of evil things, and are worthy to have such things to trust upon.⁷ For the potter, tempering soft earth, fashioneth every vessel with much labour for our service: yea, of the same clay he maketh both the vessels that serve for clean uses, and likewise also all such as serve to the contrary: but what is the use of either sort, the potter himself is the judge.⁸ And employing his labours lewdly, he maketh a vain god of the same clay, even he which a little before was made of earth himself, and within a little while after returneth to the same, out when his life which was lent him shall be demanded.⁹ Notwithstanding his care is, not that he shall have much labour, nor that his life is short: but striveth to excel goldsmiths and silversmiths, and endeavoureth to do like the workers in brass, and counteth it his glory to make counterfeit things.¹⁰ His heart is ashes, his hope is more vile than earth, and his life of less value than clay:¹¹ Forasmuch as he knew not his Maker, and him that inspired into him an active soul, and breathed in a living spirit.¹² But they counted our life a pastime, and our time here a market for gain: for, say they, we must be getting every way, though it be by evil means.¹³ For this man, that of earthly matter maketh brittle vessels and graven images, knoweth himself to offend above all others.¹⁴ And all the enemies of thy people, that hold them in subjection, are most foolish, and are more miserable than very babes.¹⁵ For they counted all the idols of the heathen to be gods: which neither have the use of eyes to see, nor noses to draw breath, nor ears to hear, nor fingers of hands to handle; and as for their feet, they are slow to go.¹⁶ For man made them, and he that borrowed his own spirit fashioned them: but no man can make a god like unto himself.¹⁷ For being mortal, he worketh a dead thing with wicked hands: for he himself is better than the things which he worshippeth:

whereas he lived once, but they never.¹⁸ Yea, they worshipped those beasts also that are most hateful: for being compared together, some are worse than others.¹⁹ Neither are they beautiful, so much as to be desired in respect of beasts: but they went without the praise of God and his blessing.

Wis.16

¹ Therefore by the like were they punished worthily, and by the multitude of beasts tormented.² Instead of which punishment, dealing graciously with thine own people, thou preparedst for them meat of a strange taste, even quails to stir up their appetite:³ To the end that they, desiring food, might for the ugly sight of the beasts sent among them lothe even that, which they must needs desire; but these, suffering penury for a short space, might be made partakers of a strange taste.⁴ For it was requisite, that upon them exercising tyranny should come penury, which they could not avoid: but to these it should only be shewed how their enemies were tormented.⁵ For when the horrible fierceness of beasts came upon these, and they perished with the stings of crooked serpents, thy wrath endured not for ever:⁶ But they were troubled for a small season, that they might be admonished, having a sign of salvation, to put them in remembrance of the commandment of thy law.⁷ For he that turned himself toward it was not saved by the thing that he saw, but by thee, that art the Saviour of all.⁸ And in this thou madest thine enemies confess, that it is thou who deliverest from all evil:⁹ For them the bitings of grasshoppers and flies killed, neither was there found any remedy for their life: for they were worthy to be punished by such.¹⁰ But thy sons not the very teeth of venomous dragons overcame: for thy mercy was ever by them, and healed them.¹¹ For they were pricked, that they should remember thy words; and were quickly saved, that not falling into deep forgetfulness, they might be continually mindful of thy goodness.¹² For it was neither herb, nor mollifying plaister, that restored them to health: but thy word, O Lord, which healeth all things.¹³ For thou hast power of life and death: thou leadest to the gates of hell, and bringest up again.¹⁴ A man indeed killeth through his malice: and the spirit, when it is gone forth, returneth not; neither the soul received up cometh again.¹⁵ But it is not possible to escape thine hand.¹⁶ For the ungodly, that denied to know thee, were scourged by the strength of thine arm: with strange rains, hails, and showers, were they persecuted, that they could not avoid, and through fire were they consumed.¹⁷ For, which is most to be wondered at, the fire had more force in the water, that quencheth all things: for the world fighteth for the righteous.¹⁸ For sometime the flame was mitigated, that it might not burn up the beasts that were sent against the ungodly; but themselves might see and perceive that they were persecuted with the judgment of God.¹⁹ And at another time it burneth even in the midst of water above the power of fire, that it might destroy the fruits of an unjust land.²⁰ Instead whereof thou feddest thine own people with angels' food, and didst send them from heaven bread prepared without their labour, able to content every man's delight, and agreeing to every taste.²¹ For thy sustenance declared thy sweetness unto thy children, and serving to the appetite of the eater, tempered itself to every man's liking.²² But snow and ice endured the fire, and melted not, that they might know that fire burning in the hail, and sparkling in the rain, did destroy the fruits of the enemies.²³ But this again did even forget his own strength, that the righteous might be nourished.²⁴ For the creature that serveth thee, who art the Maker increaseth his strength against the unrighteous for their punishment, and abateth his strength for the benefit of such as put their trust in thee.²⁵ Therefore even then was it altered into all fashions, and was obedient to thy grace, that nourisheth all things, according to the desire of them that had

need:[26] That thy children, O Lord, whom thou lovest, might know, that it is not the growing of fruits that nourisheth man: but that it is thy word, which preserveth them that put their trust in thee.[27] For that which was not destroyed of the fire, being warmed with a little sunbeam, soon melted away:[28] That it might be known, that we must prevent the sun to give thee thanks, and at the dayspring pray unto thee.[29] For the hope of the unthankful shall melt away as the winter's hoar frost, and shall run away as unprofitable water.

Wis.17

[1] For great are thy judgments, and cannot be expressed: therefore unnurtured souls have erred.[2] For when unrighteous men thought to oppress the holy nation; they being shut up in their houses, the prisoners of darkness, and fettered with the bonds of a long night, lay [there] exiled from the eternal providence.[3] For while they supposed to lie hid in their secret sins, they were scattered under a dark veil of forgetfulness, being horribly astonished, and troubled with [strange] apparitions.[4] For neither might the corner that held them keep them from fear: but noises [as of waters] falling down sounded about them, and sad visions appeared unto them with heavy countenances.[5] No power of the fire might give them light: neither could the bright flames of the stars endure to lighten that horrible night.[6] Only there appeared unto them a fire kindled of itself, very dreadful: for being much terrified, they thought the things which they saw to be worse than the sight they saw not.[7] As for the illusions of art magick, they were put down, and their vaunting in wisdom was reproved with disgrace.[8] For they, that promised to drive away terrors and troubles from a sick soul, were sick themselves of fear, worthy to be laughed at.[9] For though no terrible thing did fear them; yet being scared with beasts that passed by, and hissing of serpents,[10] They died for fear, denying that they saw the air, which could of no side be avoided.[11] For wickedness, condemned by her own witness, is very timorous, and being pressed with conscience, always forecasteth grievous things.[12] For fear is nothing else but a betraying of the succours which reason offereth.[13] And the expectation from within, being less, counteth the ignorance more than the cause which bringeth the torment.[14] But they sleeping the same sleep that night, which was indeed intolerable, and which came upon them out of the bottoms of inevitable hell,[15] Were partly vexed with monstrous apparitions, and partly fainted, their heart failing them: for a sudden fear, and not looked for, came upon them.[16] So then whosoever there fell down was straitly kept, shut up in a prison without iron bars,[17] For whether he were husbandman, or shepherd, or a labourer in the field, he was overtaken, and endured that necessity, which could not be avoided: for they were all bound with one chain of darkness.[18] Whether it were a whistling wind, or a melodious noise of birds among the spreading branches, or a pleasing fall of water running violently,[19] Or a terrible sound of stones cast down, or a running that could not be seen of skipping beasts, or a roaring voice of most savage wild beasts, or a rebounding echo from the hollow mountains; these things made them to swoon for fear.[20] For the whole world shined with clear light, and none were hindered in their labour:[21] Over them only was spread an heavy night, an image of that darkness which should afterward receive them: but yet were they unto themselves more grievous than the darkness.

Wis.18

[1] Nevertheless thy saints had a very great light, whose voice they hearing, and not seeing their shape, because they also had not suffered the same things, they counted them happy.[2] But for that they did not hurt them now, of whom they had been wronged before, they thanked them, and besought them pardon for that they had been enemies.[3] Instead whereof thou gavest them a burning pillar of fire, both to be a guide of the unknown journey, and an harmless sun to entertain them honourably.[4] For they were worthy to be deprived of light and imprisoned in darkness, who had kept thy sons shut up, by whom the uncorrupt light of the law was to be given unto the world.[5] And when they had determined to slay the babes of the saints, one child being cast forth, and saved, to reprove them, thou tookest away the multitude of their children, and destroyedst them altogether in a mighty water.[6] Of that night were our fathers certified afore, that assuredly knowing unto what oaths they had given credence, they might afterwards be of good cheer.[7] So of thy people was accepted both the salvation of the righteous, and destruction of the enemies.[8] For wherewith thou didst punish our adversaries, by the same thou didst glorify us, whom thou hadst called.[9] For the righteous children of good men did sacrifice secretly, and with one consent made a holy law, that the saints should be like partakers of the same good and evil, the fathers now singing out the songs of praise.[10] But on the other side there sounded an ill according cry of the enemies, and a lamentable noise was carried abroad for children that were bewailed.[11] The master and the servant were punished after one manner; and like as the king, so suffered the common person.[12] So they all together had innumerable dead with one kind of death; neither were the living sufficient to bury them: for in one moment the noblest offspring of them was destroyed.[13] For whereas they would not believe any thing by reason of the enchantments; upon the destruction of the firstborn, they acknowledged this people to be the sons of God.[14] For while all things were in quiet silence, and that night was in the midst of her swift course,[15] Thine Almighty word leaped down from heaven out of thy royal throne, as a fierce man of war into the midst of a land of destruction,[16] And brought thine unfeigned commandment as a sharp sword, and standing up filled all things with death; and it touched the heaven, but it stood upon the earth.[17] Then suddenly visions of horrible dreams troubled them sore, and terrors came upon them unlooked for.[18] And one thrown here, and another there, half dead, shewed the cause of his death.[19] For the dreams that troubled them did foreshew this, lest they should perish, and not know why they were afflicted.[20] Yea, the tasting of death touched the righteous also, and there was a destruction of the multitude in the wilderness: but the wrath endured not long.[21] For then the blameless man made haste, and stood forth to defend them; and bringing the shield of his proper ministry, even prayer, and the propitiation of incense, set himself against the wrath, and so brought the calamity to an end, declaring that he was thy servant.[22] So he overcame the destroyer, not with strength of body, nor force of arms, but with a word subdued him that punished, alleging the oaths and covenants made with the fathers.[23] For when the dead were now fallen down by heaps one upon another, standing between, he stayed the wrath, and parted the way to the living.[24] For in the long garment was the whole world, and in the four rows of the stones was the glory of the fathers graven, and thy Majesty upon the daidem of his head.[25] Unto these the destroyer gave place, and was afraid of them: for it was enough that they only tasted of the wrath.

Wis.19

[1] As for the ungodly, wrath came upon them without mercy unto the end: for he knew before what they would do;[2] How that having given them leave to depart, and sent them hastily away, they would repent and pursue them.[3] For whilst they were yet mourning and making lamentation at the graves of the dead, they added another foolish device, and pursued them as fugitives, whom they had intreated to be gone.[4] For the destiny, whereof they were worthy, drew them unto this end, and made them forget the things that had already happened, that they might fulfil the punishment which was

23

wanting to their torments:[5] And that thy people might pass a wonderful way: but they might find a strange death.[6] For the whole creature in his proper kind was fashioned again anew, serving the peculiar commandments that were given unto them, that thy children might be kept without hurt:[7] As namely, a cloud shadowing the camp; and where water stood before, dry land appeared; and out of the Red sea a way without impediment; and out of the violent stream a green field:[8] Wherethrough all the people went that were defended with thy hand, seeing thy marvellous strange wonders.[9] For they went at large like horses, and leaped like lambs, praising thee, O Lord, who hadst delivered them.[10] For they were yet mindful of the things that were done while they sojourned in the strange land, how the ground brought forth flies instead of cattle, and how the river cast up a multitude of frogs instead of fishes.[11] But afterwards they saw a new generation of fowls, when, being led with their appetite, they asked delicate meats.[12] For quails came up unto them from the sea for their contentment.[13] And punishments came upon the sinners not without former signs by the force of thunders: for they suffered justly according to their own wickedness, insomuch as they used a more hard and hateful behaviour toward strangers.[14] For the Sodomites did not receive those, whom they knew not when they came: but these brought friends into bondage, that had well deserved of them.[15] And not only so, but peradventure some respect shall be had of those, because they used strangers not friendly:[16] But these very grievously afflicted them, whom they had received with feastings, and were already made partakers of the same laws with them.[17] Therefore even with blindness were these stricken, as those were at the doors of the righteous man: when, being compassed about with horrible great darkness, every one sought the passage of his own doors.[18] For the elements were changed in themselves by a kind of harmony, like as in a psaltery notes change the name of the tune, and yet are always sounds; which may well be perceived by the sight of the things that have been done.[19] For earthly things were turned into watery, and the things, that before swam in the water, now went upon the ground.[20] The fire had power in the water, forgetting his own virtue: and the water forgat his own quenching nature.[21] On the other side, the flames wasted not the flesh of the corruptible living things, though they walked therein; neither melted they the icy kind of heavenly meat that was of nature apt to melt.[22] For in all things, O Lord, thou didst magnify thy people, and glorify them, neither didst thou lightly regard them: but didst assist them in every time and place.

Prologue to Wisdom of Jesus Son of Sirach

"A Prologue made by an uncertain Author" This Jesus was the son of Sirach, and grandchild to Jesus of the same name with him: this man therefore lived in the latter times, after the people had been led away captive, and called home a again, and almost after all the prophets. Now his grandfather Jesus, as he himself witnesseth, was a man of great diligence and wisdom among the Hebrews, who did not only gather the grave and short sentences of wise men, that had been before him, but himself also uttered some of his own, full of much understanding and wisdom. When as therefore the first Jesus died, leaving this book almost perfected, Sirach his son receiving it after him left it to his own son Jesus, who, having gotten it into his hands, compiled it all orderly into one volume, and called it Wisdom, intituling it both by his own name, his father's name, and his grandfather's; alluring the hearer by the very name of Wisdom to have a greater love to the study of this book. It containeth therefore wise sayings, dark sentences, and parables, and certain particular ancient godly stories of men that pleased God; also his prayer and song; moreover, what benefits God had vouchsafed his people, and what plagues he had heaped upon their enemies. This Jesus did imitate Solomon, and was no less famous for wisdom and learning, both being indeed a man of great learning, and so reputed also. [The Prologue of the Wisdom of Jesus the Son of Sirach.] Whereas many and great things have been delivered unto us by the law and the prophets, and by others that have followed their steps, for the which things Israel ought to be commended for learning and wisdom; and whereof not only the readers must needs become skilful themselves, but also they that desire to learn be able to profit them which are without, both by speaking and writing: my grandfather Jesus, when he had much given himself to the reading of the law, and the prophets, and other books of our fathers, and had gotten therein good judgment, was drawn on also himself to write something pertaining to learning and wisdom; to the intent that those which are desirous to learn, and are addicted to these things, might profit much more in living according to the law. Wherefore let me intreat you to read it with favour and attention, and to pardon us, wherein we may seem to come short of some words, which we have laboured to interpret. For the same things uttered in Hebrew, and translated into another tongue, have not the same force in them: and not only these things, but the law itself, and the prophets, and the rest of the books, have no small difference, when they are spoken in their own language. For in the eight and thirtieth year coming into Egypt, when Euergetes was king, and continuing there some time, I found a book of no small learning: therefore I thought it most necessary for me to bestow some diligence and travail to interpret it; using great watchfulness and skill in that space to bring the book to an end, and set it forth for them also, which in a strange country are willing to learn, being prepared before in manners to live after the law.

Wisdom of Jesus Son of Sirach
Sir.1

[1] All wisdom cometh from the Lord, and is with him for ever.[2] Who can number the sand of the sea, and the drops of rain, and the days of eternity?[3] Who can find out the height of heaven, and the breadth of the earth, and the deep, and wisdom?[4] Wisdom hath been created before all things, and the understanding of prudence from everlasting.[5] The word of God most high is the fountain of wisdom; and her ways are everlasting commandments.[6] To whom hath the root of wisdom been revealed? or who hath known her wise counsels?[7] [Unto whom hath the knowledge of wisdom been made manifest? and who hath understood her great experience?][8] There is one wise and greatly to be feared, the Lord sitting upon his throne.[9] He created her, and saw her, and numbered her, and poured her out upon all his works.[10] She is with all flesh according to his gift, and he hath given her to them that love him.[11] The fear of the Lord is honour, and glory, and gladness, and a crown of rejoicing.[12] The fear of the Lord maketh a merry heart, and giveth joy, and gladness, and a long life.[13] Whoso feareth the Lord, it shall go well with him at the last, and he shall find favour in the day of his death.[14] To fear the Lord is the beginning of wisdom: and it was created with the faithful in the womb.[15] She hath built an everlasting foundation with men, and she shall continue with their seed.[16] To fear the Lord is fulness of wisdom, and filleth men with her fruits.[17] She filleth all their house with things desirable, and the garners with her increase.[18] The fear of the Lord is a crown of wisdom, making peace and perfect health to flourish; both which are the gifts of God: and it enlargeth their rejoicing that love him.[19] Wisdom raineth down skill and knowledge of understanding standing, and exalteth them to honour that hold her fast.[20] The root of wisdom is to fear the Lord, and the branches thereof are long life.[21] The fear of the Lord driveth away sins: and where it is present,

it turneth away wrath.²² A furious man cannot be justified; for the sway of his fury shall be his destruction.²³ A patient man will tear for a time, and afterward joy shall spring up unto him.²⁴ He will hide his words for a time, and the lips of many shall declare his wisdom.²⁵ The parables of knowledge are in the treasures of wisdom: but godliness is an abomination to a sinner.²⁶ If thou desire wisdom, keep the commandments, and the Lord shall give her unto thee.²⁷ For the fear of the Lord is wisdom and instruction: and faith and meekness are his delight.²⁸ Distrust not the fear of the Lord when thou art poor: and come not unto him with a double heart.²⁹ Be not an hypocrite in the sight of men, and take good heed what thou speakest.³⁰ Exalt not thyself, lest thou fall, and bring dishonour upon thy soul, and so God discover thy secrets, and cast thee down in the midst of the congregation, because thou camest not in truth to the fear of the Lord, but thy heart is full of deceit.

Sir.2

¹ My son, if thou come to serve the Lord, prepare thy soul for temptation.² Set thy heart aright, and constantly endure, and make not haste in time of trouble.³ Cleave unto him, and depart not away, that thou mayest be increased at thy last end.⁴ Whatsoever is brought upon thee take cheerfully, and be patient when thou art changed to a low estate.⁵ For gold is tried in the fire, and acceptable men in the furnace of adversity.⁶ Believe in him, and he will help thee; order thy way aright, and trust in him.⁷ Ye that fear the Lord, wait for his mercy; and go not aside, lest ye fall.⁸ Ye that fear the Lord, believe him; and your reward shall not fail.⁹ Ye that fear the Lord, hope for good, and for everlasting joy and mercy.¹⁰ Look at the generations of old, and see; did ever any trust in the Lord, and was confounded? or did any abide in his fear, and was forsaken? or whom did he ever despise, that called upon him?¹¹ For the Lord is full of compassion and mercy, longsuffering, and very pitiful, and forgiveth sins, and saveth in time of affliction.¹² Woe be to fearful hearts, and faint hands, and the sinner that goeth two ways!¹³ Woe unto him that is fainthearted! for he believeth not; therefore shall he not be defended.¹⁴ Woe unto you that have lost patience! and what will ye do when the Lord shall visit you?¹⁵ They that fear the Lord will not disobey his Word; and they that love him will keep his ways.¹⁶ They that fear the Lord will seek that which is well, pleasing unto him; and they that love him shall be filled with the law.¹⁷ They that fear the Lord will prepare their hearts, and humble their souls in his sight,¹⁸ Saying, We will fall into the hands of the Lord, and not into the hands of men: for as his majesty is, so is his mercy.

Sir.3

¹ Hear me your father, O children, and do thereafter, that ye may be safe.² For the Lord hath given the father honour over the children, and hath confirmed the authority of the mother over the sons.³ Whoso honoureth his father maketh an atonement for his sins:⁴ And he that honoureth his mother is as one that layeth up treasure.⁵ Whoso honoureth his father shall have joy of his own children; and when he maketh his prayer, he shall be heard.⁶ He that honoureth his father shall have a long life; and he that is obedient unto the Lord shall be a comfort to his mother.⁷ He that feareth the Lord will honour his father, and will do service unto his parents, as to his masters.⁸ Honour thy father and mother both in word and deed, that a blessing may come upon thee from them.⁹ For the blessing of the father establisheth the houses of children; but the curse of the mother rooteth out foundations.¹⁰ Glory not in the dishonour of thy father; for thy father's dishonour is no glory unto thee.¹¹ For the glory of a man is from the honour of his father; and a mother in dishonour is a reproach to the children.¹² My son, help thy father in his age, and grieve him not as long as he liveth.¹³ And if his understanding fail, have patience with him; and despise him

not when thou art in thy full strength.¹⁴ For the relieving of thy father shall not be forgotten: and instead of sins it shall be added to build thee up.¹⁵ In the day of thine affliction it shall be remembered; thy sins also shall melt away, as the ice in the fair warm weather.¹⁶ He that forsaketh his father is as a blasphemer; and he that angereth his mother is cursed: of God.¹⁷ My son, go on with thy business in meekness; so shalt thou be beloved of him that is approved.¹⁸ The greater thou art, the more humble thyself, and thou shalt find favour before the Lord.¹⁹ Many are in high place, and of renown: but mysteries are revealed unto the meek.²⁰ For the power of the Lord is great, and he is honoured of the lowly.²¹ Seek not out things that are too hard for thee, neither search the things that are above thy strength.²² But what is commanded thee, think thereupon with reverence, for it is not needful for thee to see with thine eyes the things that are in secret.²³ Be not curious in unnecessary matters: for more things are shewed unto thee than men understand.²⁴ For many are deceived by their own vain opinion; and an evil suspicion hath overthrown their judgment.²⁵ Without eyes thou shalt want light: profess not the knowledge therefore that thou hast not.²⁶ A stubborn heart shall fare evil at the last; and he that loveth danger shall perish therein.²⁷ An obstinate heart shall be laden with sorrows; and the wicked man shall heap sin upon sin.²⁸ In the punishment of the proud there is no remedy; for the plant of wickedness hath taken root in him.²⁹ The heart of the prudent will understand a parable; and an attentive ear is the desire of a wise man.³⁰ Water will quench a flaming fire; and alms maketh an atonement for sins.³¹ And he that requiteth good turns is mindful of that which may come hereafter; and when he falleth, he shall find a stay.

Sir.4

¹ My son, defraud not the poor of his living, and make not the needy eyes to wait long.² Make not an hungry soul sorrowful; neither provoke a man in his distress.³ Add not more trouble to an heart that is vexed; and defer not to give to him that is in need.⁴ Reject not the supplication of the afflicted; neither turn away thy face from a poor man.⁵ Turn not away thine eye from the needy, and give him none occasion to curse thee:⁶ For if he curse thee in the bitterness of his soul, his prayer shall be heard of him that made him.⁷ Get thyself the love of the congregation, and bow thy head to a great man.⁸ Let it not grieve thee to bow down thine ear to the poor, and give him a friendly answer with meekness.⁹ Deliver him that suffereth wrong from the hand of the oppressor; and be not fainthearted when thou sittest in judgment.¹⁰ Be as a father unto the fatherless, and instead of an husband unto their mother: so shalt thou be as the son of the most High, and he shall love thee more than thy mother doth.¹¹ Wisdom exalteth her children, and layeth hold of them that seek her.¹² He that loveth her loveth life; and they that seek to her early shall be filled with joy.¹³ He that holdeth her fast shall inherit glory; and wheresoever she entereth, the Lord will bless.¹⁴ They that serve her shall minister to the Holy One: and them that love her the Lord doth love.¹⁵ Whoso giveth ear unto her shall judge the nations: and he that attendeth unto her shall dwell securely.¹⁶ If a man commit himself unto her, he shall inherit her; and his generation shall hold her in possession.¹⁷ For at the first she will walk with him by crooked ways, and bring fear and dread upon him, and torment him with her discipline, until she may trust his soul, and try him by her laws.¹⁸ Then will she return the straight way unto him, and comfort him, and shew him her secrets.¹⁹ But if he go wrong, she will forsake him, and give him over to his own ruin.²⁰ Observe the opportunity, and beware of evil; and be not ashamed when it concerneth thy soul.²¹ For there is a shame that bringeth sin; and there is a shame which is glory and grace.²² Accept no person against thy soul, and let not the reverence of any man

cause thee to fall.²³ And refrain not to speak, when there is occasion to do good, and hide not thy wisdom in her beauty.²⁴ For by speech wisdom shall be known: and learning by the word of the tongue.²⁵ In no wise speak against the truth; but be abashed of the error of thine ignorance.²⁶ Be not ashamed to confess thy sins; and force not the course of the river.²⁷ Make not thyself an underling to a foolish man; neither accept the person of the mighty.²⁸ Strive for the truth unto death, and the Lord shall fight for thee.²⁹ Be not hasty in thy tongue, and in thy deeds slack and remiss.³⁰ Be not as a lion in thy house, nor frantick among thy servants.³¹ Let not thine hand be stretched out to receive, and shut when thou shouldest repay.

Sir.5

¹ Set thy heart upon thy goods; and say not, I have enough for my life.² Follow not thine own mind and thy strength, to walk in the ways of thy heart:³ And say not, Who shall controul me for my works? for the Lord will surely revenge thy pride.⁴ Say not, I have sinned, and what harm hath happened unto me? for the Lord is longsuffering, he will in no wise let thee go.⁵ Concerning propitiation, be not without fear to add sin unto sin:⁶ And say not His mercy is great; he will be pacified for the multitude of my sins: for mercy and wrath come from him, and his indignation resteth upon sinners.⁷ Make no tarrying to turn to the Lord, and put not off from day to day: for suddenly shall the wrath of the Lord come forth, and in thy security thou shalt be destroyed, and perish in the day of vengeance.⁸ Set not thine heart upon goods unjustly gotten, for they shall not profit thee in the day of calamity.⁹ Winnow not with every wind, and go not into every way: for so doth the sinner that hath a double tongue.¹⁰ Be stedfast in thy understanding; and let thy word be the same.¹¹ Be swift to hear; and let thy life be sincere; and with patience give answer.¹² If thou hast understanding, answer thy neighbour; if not, lay thy hand upon thy mouth.¹³ Honour and shame is in talk: and the tongue of man is his fall.¹⁴ Be not called a whisperer, and lie not in wait with thy tongue: for a foul shame is upon the thief, and an evil condemnation upon the double tongue.¹⁵ Be not ignorant of any thing in a great matter or a small.

Sir.6

¹ Instead of a friend become not an enemy; for [thereby] thou shalt inherit an ill name, shame, and reproach: even so shall a sinner that hath a double tongue.² Extol not thyself in the counsel of thine own heart; that thy soul be not torn in pieces as a bull [straying alone.]³ Thou shalt eat up thy leaves, and lose thy fruit, and leave thyself as a dry tree.⁴ A wicked soul shall destroy him that hath it, and shall make him to be laughed to scorn of his enemies.⁵ Sweet language will multiply friends: and a fairspeaking tongue will increase kind greetings.⁶ Be in peace with many: nevertheless have but one counsellor of a thousand.⁷ If thou wouldest get a friend, prove him first and be not hasty to credit him.⁸ For some man is a friend for his own occasion, and will not abide in the day of thy trouble.⁹ And there is a friend, who being turned to enmity, and strife will discover thy reproach.¹⁰ Again, some friend is a companion at the table, and will not continue in the day of thy affliction.¹¹ But in thy prosperity he will be as thyself, and will be bold over thy servants.¹² If thou be brought low, he will be against thee, and will hide himself from thy face.¹³ Separate thyself from thine enemies, and take heed of thy friends.¹⁴ A faithfull friend is a strong defence: and he that hath found such an one hath found a treasure.¹⁵ Nothing doth countervail a faithful friend, and his excellency is invaluable.¹⁶ A faithful friend is the medicine of life; and they that fear the Lord shall find him.¹⁷ Whoso feareth the Lord shall direct his friendship aright: for as he is, so shall his neighbour be also.¹⁸ My son, gather instruction from thy youth up: so shalt thou find wisdom till thine

old age.¹⁹ Come unto her as one that ploweth and soweth, and wait for her good fruits: for thou shalt not toil much in labouring about her, but thou shalt eat of her fruits right soon.²⁰ She is very unpleasant to the unlearned: he that is without understanding will not remain with her.²¹ She will lie upon him as a mighty stone of trial; and he will cast her from him ere it be long.²² For wisdom is according to her name, and she is not manifest unto many.²³ Give ear, my son, receive my advice, and refuse not my counsel,²⁴ And put thy feet into her fetters, and thy neck into her chain.²⁵ Bow down thy shoulder, and bear her, and be not grieved with her bonds.²⁶ Come unto her with thy whole heart, and keep her ways with all thy power.²⁷ Search, and seek, and she shall be made known unto thee: and when thou hast got hold of her, let her not go.²⁸ For at the last thou shalt find her rest, and that shall be turned to thy joy.²⁹ Then shall her fetters be a strong defence for thee, and her chains a robe of glory.³⁰ For there is a golden ornament upon her, and her bands are purple lace.³¹ Thou shalt put her on as a robe of honour, and shalt put her about thee as a crown of joy.³² My son, if thou wilt, thou shalt be taught: and if thou wilt apply thy mind, thou shalt be prudent.³³ If thou love to hear, thou shalt receive understanding: and if thou bow thine ear, thou shalt be wise,³⁴ Stand in the multitude of the elders; and cleave unto him that is wise.³⁵ Be willing to hear every godly discourse; and let not the parables of understanding escape thee.³⁶ And if thou seest a man of understanding, get thee betimes unto him, and let thy foot wear the steps of his door.³⁷ Let thy mind be upon the ordinances of the Lord and meditate continually in his commandments: he shall establish thine heart, and give thee wisdom at thine owns desire.

Sir.7

¹ Do no evil, so shall no harm come unto thee.² Depart from the unjust, and iniquity shall turn away from thee.³ My son, sow not upon the furrows of unrighteousness, and thou shalt not reap them sevenfold.⁴ Seek not of the Lord preeminence, neither of the king the seat of honour.⁵ justify not thyself before the Lord; and boast not of thy wisdom before the king.⁶ Seek not to be judge, being not able to take away iniquity; lest at any time thou fear the person of the mighty, an stumblingblock in the way of thy uprightness.⁷ Offend not against the multitude of a city, and then thou shalt not cast thyself down among the people.⁸ Bind not one sin upon another; for in one thou shalt not be unpunished.⁹ Say not, God will look upon the multitude of my oblations, and when I offer to the most high God, he will accept it.¹⁰ Be not fainthearted when thou makest thy prayer, and neglect not to give alms.¹¹ Laugh no man to scorn in the bitterness of his soul: for there is one which humbleth and exalteth.¹² Devise not a lie against thy brother; neither do the like to thy friend.¹³ Use not to make any manner of lie: for the custom thereof is not good.¹⁴ Use not many words in a multitude of elders, and make not much babbling when thou prayest.¹⁵ Hate not laborious work, neither husbandry, which the most High hath ordained.¹⁶ Number not thyself among the multitude of sinners, but remember that wrath will not tarry long.¹⁷ Humble thyself greatly: for the vengeance of the ungodly is fire and worms.¹⁸ Change not a friend for any good by no means; neither a faithful brother for the gold of Ophir.¹⁹ Forego not a wise and good woman: for her grace is above gold.²⁰ Whereas thy servant worketh truly, entreat him not evil. nor the hireling that bestoweth himself wholly for thee.²¹ Let thy soul love a good servant, and defraud him not of liberty.²² Hast thou cattle? have an eye to them: and if they be for thy profit, keep them with thee.²³ Hast thou children? instruct them, and bow down their neck from their youth.²⁴ Hast thou daughters? have a care of their body, and shew not thyself cheerful toward them.²⁵ Marry thy daughter, and so shalt thou have performed a weighty matter: but

give her to a man of understanding.[26] Hast thou a wife after thy mind? forsake her not: but give not thyself over to a light woman.[27] Honour thy father with thy whole heart, and forget not the sorrows of thy mother.[28] Remember that thou wast begotten of them; and how canst thou recompense them the things that they have done for thee?[29] Fear the Lord with all thy soul, and reverence his priests.[30] Love him that made thee with all thy strength, and forsake not his ministers.[31] Fear the Lord, and honor the priest; and give him his portion, as it is commanded thee; the firstfruits, and the trespass offering, and the gift of the shoulders, and the sacrifice of sanctification, and the firstfruits of the holy things.[32] And stretch thine hand unto the poor, that thy blessing may be perfected.[33] A gift hath grace in the sight of every man living; and for the dead detain it not.[34] Fail not to be with them that weep, and mourn with them that mourn.[35] Be not slow to visit the sick: fir that shall make thee to be beloved.[36] Whatsoever thou takest in hand, remember the end, and thou shalt never do amiss.

Sir.8

[1] Strive not with a mighty man' lest thou fall into his hands.[2] Be not at variance with a rich man, lest he overweigh thee: for gold hath destroyed many, and perverted the hearts of kings.[3] Strive not with a man that is full of tongue, and heap not wood upon his fire.[4] Jest not with a rude man, lest thy ancestors be disgraced.[5] Reproach not a man that turneth from sin, but remember that we are all worthy of punishment.[6] Dishonour not a man in his old age: for even some of us wax old.[7] Rejoice not over thy greatest enemy being dead, but remember that we die all.[8] Despise not the discourse of the wise, but acquaint thyself with their proverbs: for of them thou shalt learn instruction, and how to serve great men with ease.[9] Miss not the discourse of the elders: for they also learned of their fathers, and of them thou shalt learn understanding, and to give answer as need requireth.[10] Kindle not the coals of a sinner, lest thou be burnt with the flame of his fire.[11] Rise not up [in anger] at the presence of an injurious person, lest he lie in wait to entrap thee in thy words[12] Lend not unto him that is mightier than thyself; for if thou lendest him, count it but lost.[13] Be not surety above thy power: for if thou be surety, take care to pay it.[14] Go not to law with a judge; for they will judge for him according to his honour.[15] Travel not by the way with a bold fellow, lest he become grievous unto thee: for he will do according to his own will, and thou shalt perish with him through his folly.[16] Strive not with an angry man, and go not with him into a solitary place: for blood is as nothing in his sight, and where there is no help, he will overthrow thee.[17] Consult not with a fool; for he cannot keep counsel.[18] Do no secret thing before a stranger; for thou knowest not what he will bring forth.[19] Open not thine heart to every man, lest he requite thee with a shrewd turn.

Sir.9

[1] Be not jealous over the wife of thy bosom, and teach her not an evil lesson against thyself.[2] Give not thy soul unto a woman to set her foot upon thy substance.[3] Meet not with an harlot, lest thou fall into her snares.[4] Use not much the company of a woman that is a singer, lest thou be taken with her attempts.[5] Gaze not on a maid, that thou fall not by those things that are precious in her.[6] Give not thy soul unto harlots, that thou lose not thine inheritance.[7] Look not round about thee in the streets of the city, neither wander thou in the solitary place thereof.[8] Turn away thine eye from a beautiful woman, and look not upon another's beauty; for many have been deceived by the beauty of a woman; for herewith love is kindled as a fire.[9] Sit not at all with another man's wife, nor sit down with her in thine arms, and spend not thy money with her at the wine; lest thine heart incline unto her, and so through thy desire thou fall into destruction.[10] Forsake not an old friend; for the new is not comparable to him: a new friend is as new wine; when it is old, thou shalt drink it with pleasure.[11] Envy not the glory of a sinner: for thou knowest not what shall be his end.[12] Delight not in the thing that the ungodly have pleasure in; but remember they shall not go unpunished unto their grave.[13] Keep thee far from the man that hath power to kill; so shalt thou not doubt the fear of death: and if thou come unto him, make no fault, lest he take away thy life presently: remember that thou goest in the midst of snares, and that thou walkest upon the battlements of the city.[14] As near as thou canst, guess at thy neighbour, and consult with the wise.[15] Let thy talk be with the wise, and all thy communication in the law of the most High.[16] And let just men eat and drink with thee; and let thy glorying be in the fear of the Lord.[17] For the hand of the artificer the work shall be commended: and the wise ruler of the people for his speech.[18] A man of an ill tongue is dangerous in his city; and he that is rash in his talk shall be hated.

Sir.10

[1] A wise judge will instruct his people; and the government of a prudent man is well ordered.[2] As the judge of the people is himself, so are his officers; and what manner of man the ruler of the city is, such are all they that dwell therein.[3] An unwise king destroyeth his people; but through the prudence of them which are in authority the city shall be inhabited.[4] The power of the earth is in the hand of the Lord, and in due time he will set over it one that is profitable.[5] In the hand of God is the prosperity of man: and upon the person of the scribe shall he lay his honour.[6] Bear not hatred to thy neighbour for every wrong; and do nothing at all by injurious practices.[7] Pride is hateful before God and man: and by both doth one commit iniquity.[8] Because of unrighteous dealings, injuries, and riches got by deceit, the kingdom is translated from one people to another.[9] Why is earth and ashes proud? There is not a more wicked thing than a covetous man: for such an one setteth his own soul to sale; because while he liveth he casteth away his bowels.[10] The physician cutteth off a long disease; and he that is to day a king to morrow shall die.[11] For when a man is dead, he shall inherit creeping things, beasts, and worms.[12] The beginning of pride is when one departeth from God, and his heart is turned away from his Maker.[13] For pride is the beginning of sin, and he that hath it shall pour out abomination: and therefore the Lord brought upon them strange calamities, and overthrew them utterly.[14] The Lord hath cast down the thrones of proud princes, and set up the meek in their stead.[15] The Lord hath plucked up the roots of the proud nations, and planted the lowly in their place.[16] The Lord overthrew countries of the heathen, and destroyed them to the foundations of the earth.[17] He took some of them away, and destroyed them, and hath made their memorial to cease from the earth.[18] Pride was not made for men, nor furious anger for them that are born of a woman.[19] They that fear the Lord are a sure seed, and they that love him an honourable plant: they that regard not the law are a dishonourable seed; they that transgress the commandments are a deceivable seed.[20] Among brethren he that is chief is honorable; so are they that fear the Lord in his eyes.[21] The fear of the Lord goeth before the obtaining of authority: but roughness and pride is the losing thereof.[22] Whether he be rich, noble, or poor, their glory is the fear of the Lord.[23] It is not meet to despise the poor man that hath understanding; neither is it convenient to magnify a sinful man.[24] Great men, and judges, and potentates, shall be honoured; yet is there none of them greater than he that feareth the Lord.[25] Unto the servant that is wise shall they that are free do service: and he that hath knowledge will not grudge when he is reformed.[26] Be not overwise in doing thy business; and boast not thyself in the time of thy distress.[27] Better is he that laboureth, and

aboundeth in all things, than he that boasteth himself, and wanteth bread.[28] My son, glorify thy soul in meekness, and give it honour according to the dignity thereof.[29] Who will justify him that sinneth against his own soul? and who will honour him that dishonoureth his own life?[30] The poor man is honoured for his skill, and the rich man is honoured for his riches.[31] He that is honoured in poverty, how much more in riches? and he that is dishonourable in riches, how much more in poverty?

Sir.11

[1] Wisdom lifteth up the head of him that is of low degree, and maketh him to sit among great men.[2] Commend not a man for his beauty; neither abhor a man for his outward appearance.[3] The bee is little among such as fly; but her fruit is the chief of sweet things.[4] Boast not of thy clothing and raiment, and exalt not thyself in the day of honour: for the works of the Lord are wonderful, and his works among men are hidden.[5] Many kings have sat down upon the ground; and one that was never thought of hath worn the crown.[6] Many mighty men have been greatly disgraced; and the honourable delivered into other men's hands.[7] Blame not before thou hast examined the truth: understand first, and then rebuke.[8] Answer not before thou hast heard the cause: neither interrupt men in the midst of their talk.[9] Strive not in a matter that concerneth thee not; and sit not in judgment with sinners.[10] My son, meddle not with many matters: for if thou meddle much, thou shalt not be innocent; and if thou follow after, thou shalt not obtain, neither shalt thou escape by fleeing.[11] There is one that laboureth, and taketh pains, and maketh haste, and is so much the more behind.[12] Again, there is another that is slow, and hath need of help, wanting ability, and full of poverty; yet the eye of the Lord looked upon him for good, and set him up from his low estate,[13] And lifted up his head from misery; so that many that saw from him is peace over all the[14] Prosperity and adversity, life and death, poverty and riches, come of the Lord.[15] Wisdom, knowledge, and understanding of the law, are of the Lord: love, and the way of good works, are from him.[16] Error and darkness had their beginning together with sinners: and evil shall wax old with them that glory therein.[17] The gift of the Lord remaineth with the ungodly, and his favour bringeth prosperity for ever.[18] There is that waxeth rich by his wariness and pinching, and this his the portion of his reward:[19] Whereas he saith, I have found rest, and now will eat continually of my goods; and yet he knoweth not what time shall come upon him, and that he must leave those things to others, and die.[20] Be stedfast in thy covenant, and be conversant therein, and wax old in thy work.[21] Marvel not at the works of sinners; but trust in the Lord, and abide in thy labour: for it is an easy thing in the sight of the Lord on the sudden to make a poor man rich.[22] The blessing of the Lord is in the reward of the godly, and suddenly he maketh his blessing flourish.[23] Say not, What profit is there of my service? and what good things shall I have hereafter?[24] Again, say not, I have enough, and possess many things, and what evil shall I have hereafter?[25] In the day of prosperity there is a forgetfulness of affliction: and in the day of affliction there is no more remembrance of prosperity.[26] For it is an easy thing unto the Lord in the day of death to reward a man according to his ways.[27] The affliction of an hour maketh a man forget pleasure: and in his end his deeds shall be discovered.[28] Judge none blessed before his death: for a man shall be known in his children.[29] Bring not every man into thine house: for the deceitful man hath many trains.[30] Like as a partridge taken [and kept] in a cage, so is the heart of the proud; and like as a spy, watcheth he for thy fall:[31] For he lieth in wait, and turneth good into evil, and in things worthy praise will lay blame upon thee.[32] Of a spark of fire a heap of coals is kindled: and a sinful man layeth wait for blood.[33] Take heed of a mischievous man, for he worketh wickedness; lest he bring upon thee a perpetual blot.[34] Receive a stranger into thine house, and he will disturb thee, and turn thee out of thine own.

Sir.12

[1] When thou wilt do good know to whom thou doest it; so shalt thou be thanked for thy benefits.[2] Do good to the godly man, and thou shalt find a recompence; and if not from him, yet from the most High.[3] There can no good come to him that is always occupied in evil, nor to him that giveth no alms.[4] Give to the godly man, and help not a sinner.[5] Do well unto him that is lowly, but give not to the ungodly: hold back thy bread, and give it not unto him, lest he overmaster thee thereby: for [else] thou shalt receive twice as much evil for all the good thou shalt have done unto him.[6] For the most High hateth sinners, and will repay vengeance unto the ungodly, and keepeth them against the mighty day of their punishment.[7] Give unto the good, and help not the sinner.[8] A friend cannot be known in prosperity: and an enemy cannot be hidden in adversity.[9] In the prosperity of a man enemies will be grieved: but in his adversity even a friend will depart.[10] Never trust thine enemy: for like as iron rusteth, so is his wickedness.[11] Though he humble himself, and go crouching, yet take good heed and beware of him, and thou shalt be unto him as if thou hadst wiped a lookingglass, and thou shalt know that his rust hath not been altogether wiped away.[12] Set him not by thee, lest, when he hath overthrown thee, he stand up in thy place; neither let him sit at thy right hand, lest he seek to take thy seat, and thou at the last remember my words, and be pricked therewith.[13] Who will pity a charmer that is bitten with a serpent, or any such as come nigh wild beasts?[14] So one that goeth to a sinner, and is defiled with him in his sins, who will pity?[15] For a while he will abide with thee, but if thou begin to fall, he will not tarry.[16] An enemy speaketh sweetly with his lips, but in his heart he imagineth how to throw thee into a pit: he will weep with his eyes, but if he find opportunity, he will not be satisfied with blood.[17] If adversity come upon thee, thou shalt find him there first; and though he pretend to help thee, yet shall he undermine thee.[18] He will shake his head, and clap his hands, and whisper much, and change his countenance.

Sir.13

[1] He that toucheth pitch shall be defiled therewith; and he that hath fellowship with a proud man shall be like unto him.[2] Burden not thyself above thy power while thou livest; and have no fellowship with one that is mightier and richer than thyself: for how agree the kettle and the earthen pot together? for if the one be smitten against the other, it shall be broken.[3] The rich man hath done wrong, and yet he threateneth withal: the poor is wronged, and he must intreat also.[4] If thou be for his profit, he will use thee: but if thou have nothing, he will forsake thee.[5] If thou have any thing, he will live with thee: yea, he will make thee bare, and will not be sorry for it.[6] If he have need of thee, he will deceive thee, and smile upon thee, and put thee in hope; he will speak thee fair, and say, What wantest thou?[7] And he will shame thee by his meats, until he have drawn thee dry twice or thrice, and at the last he will laugh thee to scorn afterward, when he seeth thee, he will forsake thee, and shake his head at thee.[8] Beware that thou be not deceived and brought down in thy jollity.[9] If thou be invited of a mighty man, withdraw thyself, and so much the more will he invite thee.[10] Press thou not upon him, lest thou be put back; stand not far off, lest thou be forgotten.[11] Affect not to be made equal unto him in talk, and believe not his many words: for with much communication will he tempt thee, and smiling upon thee will get out thy secrets:[12] But cruelly he will lay up thy words, and will not spare to do thee hurt, and to put thee in prison.[13] Observe, and take good heed, for thou

walkest in peril of thy overthrowing: when thou hearest these things, awake in thy sleep.[14] Love the Lord all thy life, and call upon him for thy salvation.[15] Every beast loveth his like, and every man loveth his neighbor.[16] All flesh consorteth according to kind, and a man will cleave to his like.[17] What fellowship hath the wolf with the lamb? so the sinner with the godly.[18] What agreement is there between the hyena and a dog? and what peace between the rich and the poor?[19] As the wild ass is the lion's prey in the wilderness: so the rich eat up the poor.[20] As the proud hate humility: so doth the rich abhor the poor.[21] A rich man beginning to fall is held up of his friends: but a poor man being down is thrust away by his friends.[22] When a rich man is fallen, he hath many helpers: he speaketh things not to be spoken, and yet men justify him: the poor man slipped, and yet they rebuked him too; he spake wisely, and could have no place.[23] When a rich man speaketh, every man holdeth his tongue, and, look, what he saith, they extol it to the clouds: but if the poor man speak, they say, What fellow is this? and if he stumble, they will help to overthrow him.[24] Riches are good unto him that hath no sin, and poverty is evil in the mouth of the ungodly.[25] The heart of a man changeth his countenance, whether it be for good or evil: and a merry heart maketh a cheerful countenance.[26] A cheerful countenance is a token of a heart that is in prosperity; and the finding out of parables is a wearisome labour of the mind.

Sir.14

[1] Blessed is the man that hath not slipped with his mouth, and is not pricked with the multitude of sins.[2] Blessed is he whose conscience hath not condemned him, and who is not fallen from his hope in the Lord.[3] Riches are not comely for a niggard: and what should an envious man do with money?[4] He that gathereth by defrauding his own soul gathereth for others, that shall spend his goods riotously.[5] He that is evil to himself, to whom will he be good? he shall not take pleasure in his goods.[6] There is none worse than he that envieth himself; and this is a recompence of his wickedness.[7] And if he doeth good, he doeth it unwillingly; and at the last he will declare his wickedness.[8] The envious man hath a wicked eye; he turneth away his face, and despiseth men.[9] A covetous man's eye is not satisfied with his portion; and the iniquity of the wicked drieth up his soul.[10] A wicked eye envieth [his] bread, and he is a niggard at his table.[11] My son, according to thy ability do good to thyself, and give the Lord his due offering.[12] Remember that death will not be long in coming, and that the covenant of the grave is not shewed unto thee.[13] Do good unto thy friend before thou die, and according to thy ability stretch out thy hand and give to him.[14] Defraud not thyself of the good day, and let not the part of a good desire overpass thee.[15] Shalt thou not leave thy travails unto another? and thy labours to be divided by lot?[16] Give, and take, and sanctify thy soul; for there is no seeking of dainties in the grave.[17] All flesh waxeth old as a garment: for the covenant from the beginning is, Thou shalt die the death.[18] As of the green leaves on a thick tree, some fall, and some grow; so is the generation of flesh and blood, one cometh to an end, and another is born.[19] Every work rotteth and consumeth away, and the worker thereof shall go withal.[20] Blessed is the man that doth meditate good things in wisdom, and that reasoneth of holy things by his understanding. ing.[21] He that considereth her ways in his heart shall also have understanding in her secrets.[22] Go after her as one that traceth, and lie in wait in her ways.[23] He that prieth in at her windows shall also hearken at her doors.[24] He that doth lodge near her house shall also fasten a pin in her walls.[25] He shall pitch his tent nigh unto her, and shall lodge in a lodging where good things are.[26] He shall set his children under her shelter, and shall lodge under her branches.[27] By her he shall be covered from heat, and in her glory shall he dwell.

Sir.15

[1] He that feareth the Lord will do good, and he that hath the knowledge of the law shall obtain her.[2] And as a mother shall she meet him, and receive him as a wife married of a virgin.[3] With the bread of understanding shall she feed him, and give him the water of wisdom to drink.[4] He shall be stayed upon her, and shall not be moved; and shall rely upon her, and shall not be confounded.[5] She shall exalt him above his neighbours, and in the midst of the congregation shall she open his mouth.[6] He shall find joy and a crown of gladness, and she shall cause him to inherit an everlasting name.[7] But foolish men shall not attain unto her, and sinners shall not see her.[8] For she is far from pride, and men that are liars cannot remember her.[9] Praise is not seemly in the mouth of a sinner, for it was not sent him of the Lord.[10] For praise shall be uttered in wisdom, and the Lord will prosper it.[11] Say not thou, It is through the Lord that I fell away: for thou oughtest not to do the things that he hateth.[12] Say not thou, He hath caused me to err: for he hath no need of the sinful man.[13] The Lord hateth all abomination; and they that fear God love it not.[14] He himself made man from the beginning, and left him in the hand of his counsel;[15] If thou wilt, to keep the commandments, and to perform acceptable faithfulness.[16] He hath set fire and water before thee: stretch forth thy hand unto whether thou wilt.[17] Before man is life and death; and whether him liketh shall be given him.[18] For the wisdom of the Lord is great, and he is mighty in power, and beholdeth all things:[19] And his eyes are upon them that fear him, and he knoweth every work of man.[20] He hath commanded no man to do wickedly, neither hath he given any man licence to sin.

Sir.16

[1] Desire not a multitude of unprofitable children, neither delight in ungodly sons.[2] Though they multiply, rejoice not in them, except the fear of the Lord be with them.[3] Trust not thou in their life, neither respect their multitude: for one that is just is better than a thousand; and better it is to die without children, than to have them that are ungodly.[4] For by one that hath understanding shall the city be replenished: but the kindred of the wicked shall speedily become desolate.[5] Many such things have I seen with mine eyes, and mine ear hath heard greater things than these.[6] In the congregation of the ungodly shall a fire be kindled; and in a rebellious nation wrath is set on fire.[7] He was not pacified toward the old giants, who fell away in the strength of their foolishness.[8] Neither spared he the place where Lot sojourned, but abhorred them for their pride.[9] He pitied not the people of perdition, who were taken away in their sins:[10] Nor the six hundred thousand footmen, who were gathered together in the hardness of their hearts.[11] And if there be one stiffnecked among the people, it is marvel if he escape unpunished: for mercy and wrath are with him; he is mighty to forgive, and to pour out displeasure.[12] As his mercy is great, so is his correction also: he judgeth a man according to his works[13] The sinner shall not escape with his spoils: and the patience of the godly shall not be frustrate.[14] Make way for every work of mercy: for every man shall find according to his works.[15] The Lord hardened Pharaoh, that he should not know him, that his powerful works might be known to the world.[16] His mercy is manifest to every creature; and he hath separated his light from the darkness with an adamant.[17] Say not thou, I will hide myself from the Lord: shall any remember me from above? I shall not be remembered among so many people: for what is my soul among such an infinite number of creatures?[18] Behold, the heaven, and the heaven of heavens, the deep, and the earth, and all that therein is, shall be moved when he shall visit.[19] The mountains also and foundations of the earth be shaken with trembling, when the Lord looketh upon them.[20] No heart can think

upon these things worthily: and who is able to conceive his ways?²¹ It is a tempest which no man can see: for the most part of his works are hid.²² Who can declare the works of his justice? or who can endure them? for his covenant is afar off, and the trial of all things is in the end.²³ He that wanteth understanding will think upon vain things: and a foolish man erring imagineth follies.²⁴ by son, hearken unto me, and learn knowledge, and mark my words with thy heart.²⁵ I will shew forth doctrine in weight, and declare his knowledge exactly.²⁶ The works of the Lord are done in judgment from the beginning: and from the time he made them he disposed the parts thereof.²⁷ He garnished his works for ever, and in his hand are the chief of them unto all generations: they neither labour, nor are weary, nor cease from their works.²⁸ None of them hindereth another, and they shall never disobey his word.²⁹ After this the Lord looked upon the earth, and filled it with his blessings.³⁰ With all manner of living things hath he covered the face thereof; and they shall return into it again.

Sir.17

¹ The Lord created man of the earth, and turned him into it again.² He gave them few days, and a short time, and power also over the things therein.³ He endued them with strength by themselves, and made them according to his image,⁴ And put the fear of man upon all flesh, and gave him dominion over beasts and fowls.⁵ They received the use of the five operations of the Lord, and in the sixth place he imparted them understanding, and in the seventh speech, an interpreter of the cogitations thereof.]⁶ Counsel, and a tongue, and eyes, ears, and a heart, gave he them to understand.⁷ Withal he filled them with the knowledge of understanding, and shewed them good and evil.⁸ He set his eye upon their hearts, that he might shew them the greatness of his works.⁹ He gave them to glory in his marvellous acts for ever, that they might declare his works with understanding.¹⁰ And the elect shall praise his holy name.¹¹ Beside this he gave them knowledge, and the law of life for an heritage.¹² He made an everlasting covenant with them, and shewed them his judgments.¹³ Their eyes saw the majesty of his glory, and their ears heard his glorious voice.¹⁴ And he said unto them, Beware of all unrighteousness; and he gave every man commandment concerning his neighbour.¹⁵ Their ways are ever before him, and shall not be hid from his eyes.¹⁶ Every man from his youth is given to evil; neither could they make to themselves fleshy hearts for stony.¹⁷ For in the division of the nations of the whole earth he set a ruler over every people; but Israel is the Lord's portion:¹⁸ Whom, being his firstborn, he nourisheth with discipline, and giving him the light of his love doth not forsake him.¹⁹ Therefore all their works are as the sun before him, and his eyes are continually upon their ways.²⁰ None of their unrighteous deeds are hid from him, but all their sins are before the Lord²¹ But the Lord being gracious and knowing his workmanship, neither left nor forsook them, but spared them.²² The alms of a man is as a signet with him, and he will keep the good deeds of man as the apple of the eye, and give repentance to his sons and daughters.²³ Afterwards he will rise up and reward them, and render their recompence upon their heads.²⁴ But unto them that repent, he granted them return, and comforted those that failed in patience.²⁵ Return unto the Lord, and forsake thy sins, make thy prayer before his face, and offend less.²⁶ Turn again to the most High, and turn away from iniquity: for he will lead thee out of darkness into the light of health, and hate thou abomination vehemently.²⁷ Who shall praise the most High in the grave, instead of them which live and give thanks?²⁸ Thanksgiving perisheth from the dead, as from one that is not: the living and sound in heart shall praise the Lord.²⁹ How great is the lovingkindness of the Lord our God, and his compassion unto such as turn unto him in holiness!³⁰ For all things cannot be in men, because the son of man is not immortal.³¹ What is brighter than the sun? yet the light thereof faileth; and flesh and blood will imagine evil.³² He vieweth the power of the height of heaven; and all men are but earth and ashes.

Sir.18

¹ He that liveth for ever Hath created all things in general.² The Lord only is righteous, and there is none other but he,³ Who governeth the world with the palm of his hand, and all things obey his will: for he is the King of all, by his power dividing holy things among them from profane.⁴ To whom hath he given power to declare his works? and who shall find out his noble acts?⁵ Who shall number the strength of his majesty? and who shall also tell out his mercies?⁶ As for the wondrous works of the Lord, there may nothing be taken from them, neither may any thing be put unto them, neither can the ground of them be found out.⁷ When a man hath done, then he beginneth; and when he leaveth off, then he shall be doubtful.⁸ What is man, and whereto serveth he? what is his good, and what is his evil?⁹ The number of a man's days at the most are an hundred years.¹⁰ As a drop of water unto the sea, and a gravelstone in comparison of the sand; so are a thousand years to the days of eternity.¹¹ Therefore is God patient with them, and poureth forth his mercy upon them.¹² He saw and perceived their end to be evil; therefore he multiplied his compassion.¹³ The mercy of man is toward his neighbour; but the mercy of the Lord is upon all flesh: he reproveth, and nurtureth, and teacheth and bringeth again, as a shepherd his flock.¹⁴ He hath mercy on them that receive discipline, and that diligently seek after his judgments.¹⁵ My son, blemish not thy good deeds, neither use uncomfortable words when thou givest any thing.¹⁶ Shall not the dew asswage the heat? so is a word better than a gift?¹⁷ Lo, is not a word better than a gift? but both are with a gracious man.¹⁸ A fool will upbraid churlishly, and a gift of the envious consumeth the eyes.¹⁹ Learn before thou speak, and use physick or ever thou be sick.²⁰ Before judgment examine thyself, and in the day of visitation thou shalt find mercy.²¹ Humble thyself before thou be sick, and in the time of sins shew repentance.²² Let nothing hinder thee to pay thy vow in due time, and defer not until death to be justified.²³ Before thou prayest, prepare thyself; and be not as one that tempteth the Lord.²⁴ Think upon the wrath that shall be at the end, and the time of vengeance, when he shall turn away his face.²⁵ When thou hast enough, remember the time of hunger: and when thou art rich, think upon poverty and need.²⁶ From the morning until the evening the time is changed, and all things are soon done before the Lord.²⁷ A wise man will fear in every thing, and in the day of sinning he will beware of offence: but a fool will not observe time.²⁸ Every man of understanding knoweth wisdom, and will give praise unto him that found her.²⁹ They that were of understanding in sayings became also wise themselves, and poured forth exquisite parables.³⁰ Go not after thy lusts, but refrain thyself from thine appetites.³¹ If thou givest thy soul the desires that please her, she will make thee a laughingstock to thine enemies that malign thee.³² Take not pleasure in much good cheer, neither be tied to the expence thereof.³³ Be not made a beggar by banqueting upon borrowing, when thou hast nothing in thy purse: for thou shalt lie in wait for thine own life, and be talked on.

Sir.19

¹ A labouring man that A is given to drunkenness shall not be rich: and he that contemneth small things shall fall by little and little.² Wine and women will make men of understanding to fall away: and he that cleaveth to harlots will become impudent.³ Moths and worms shall have him to heritage, and a bold man shall be taken away.⁴ He that is hasty to give credit is lightminded; and he that

sinneth shall offend against his own soul.[5] Whoso taketh pleasure in wickedness shall be condemned: but he that resisteth pleasures crowneth his life.[6] He that can rule his tongue shall live without strife; and he that hateth babbling shall have less evil.[7] Rehearse not unto another that which is told unto thee, and thou shalt fare never the worse.[8] Whether it be to friend or foe, talk not of other men's lives; and if thou canst without offence, reveal them not.[9] For he heard and observed thee, and when time cometh he will hate thee.[10] If thou hast heard a word, let it die with thee; and be bold, it will not burst thee.[11] A fool travaileth with a word, as a woman in labour of a child.[12] As an arrow that sticketh in a man's thigh, so is a word within a fool's belly.[13] Admonish a friend, it may be he hath not done it: and if he have done it, that he do it no more.[14] Admonish thy friend, it may be he hath not said it: and if he have, that he speak it not again.[15] Admonish a friend: for many times it is a slander, and believe not every tale.[16] There is one that slippeth in his speech, but not from his heart; and who is he that hath not offended with his tongue?[17] Admonish thy neighbour before thou threaten him; and not being angry, give place to the law of the most High.[18] The fear of the Lord is the first step to be accepted [of him,] and wisdom obtaineth his love.[19] The knowledge of the commandments of the Lord is the doctrine of life: and they that do things that please him shall receive the fruit of the tree of immortality.[20] The fear of the Lord is all wisdom; and in all wisdom is the performance of the law, and the knowledge of his omnipotency.[21] If a servant say to his master, I will not do as it pleaseth thee; though afterward he do it, he angereth him that nourisheth him.[22] The knowledge of wickedness is not wisdom, neither at any time the counsel of sinners prudence.[23] There is a wickedness, and the same an abomination; and there is a fool wanting in wisdom.[24] He that hath small understanding, and feareth God, is better than one that hath much wisdom, and transgresseth the law of the most High.[25] There is an exquisite subtilty, and the same is unjust; and there is one that turneth aside to make judgment appear; and there is a wise man that justifieth in judgment.[26] There is a wicked man that hangeth down his head sadly; but inwardly he is full of deceit,[27] Casting down his countenance, and making as if he heard not: where he is not known, he will do thee a mischief before thou be aware.[28] And if for want of power he be hindered from sinning, yet when he findeth opportunity he will do evil.[29] A man may be known by his look, and one that hath understanding by his countenance, when thou meetest him.[30] A man's attire, and excessive laughter, and gait, shew what he is.

Sir.20

[1] There is a reproof that is not comely: again, some man holdeth his tongue, and he is wise.[2] It is much better to reprove, than to be angry secretly: and he that confesseth his fault shall be preserved from hurt.[3] How good is it, when thou art reproved, to shew repentance! for so shalt thou escape wilful sin.[4] As is the lust of an eunuch to deflower a virgin; so is he that executeth judgment with violence.[5] There is one that keepeth silence, and is found wise: and another by much babbling becometh hateful.[6] Some man holdeth his tongue, because he hath not to answer: and some keepeth silence, knowing his time.[7] A wise man will hold his tongue till he see opportunity: but a babbler and a fool will regard no time.[8] He that useth many words shall be abhorred; and he that taketh to himself authority therein shall be hated.[9] There is a sinner that hath good success in evil things; and there is a gain that turneth to loss.[10] There is a gift that shall not profit thee; and there is a gift whose recompence is double.[11] There is an abasement because of glory; and there is that lifteth up his head from a low estate.[12] There is that buyeth much for a little, and repayeth it sevenfold.[13] A wise man by

his words maketh him beloved: but the graces of fools shall be poured out.[14] The gift of a fool shall do thee no good when thou hast it; neither yet of the envious for his necessity: for he looketh to receive many things for one.[15] He giveth little, and upbraideth much; he openeth his mouth like a crier; to day he lendeth, and to morrow will he ask it again: such an one is to be hated of God and man.[16] The fool saith, I have no friends, I have no thank for all my good deeds, and they that eat my bread speak evil of me.[17] How oft, and of how many shall he be laughed to scorn! for he knoweth not aright what it is to have; and it is all one unto him as if he had it not.[18] To slip upon a pavement is better than to slip with the tongue: so the fall of the wicked shall come speedily.[19] An unseasonable tale will always be in the mouth of the unwise.[20] A wise sentence shall be rejected when it cometh out of a fool's mouth; for he will not speak it in due season.[21] There is that is hindered from sinning through want: and when he taketh rest, he shall not be troubled.[22] There is that destroyeth his own soul through bashfulness, and by accepting of persons overthroweth himself.[23] There is that for bashfulness promiseth to his friend, and maketh him his enemy for nothing.[24] A lie is a foul blot in a man, yet it is continually in the mouth of the untaught.[25] A thief is better than a man that is accustomed to lie: but they both shall have destruction to heritage.[26] The disposition of a liar is dishonourable, and his shame is ever with him.[27] A wise man shall promote himself to honour with his words: and he that hath understanding will please great men.[28] He that tilleth his land shall increase his heap: and he that pleaseth great men shall get pardon for iniquity.[29] Presents and gifts blind the eyes of the wise, and stop up his mouth that he cannot reprove.[30] Wisdom that is hid, and treasure that is hoarded up, what profit is in them both?[31] Better is he that hideth his folly than a man that hideth his wisdom.[32] Necessary patience in seeking ing the Lord is better than he that leadeth his life without a guide.

Sir.21

[1] My son, hast thou sinned? do so no more, but ask pardon for thy former sins.[2] Flee from sin as from the face of a serpent: for if thou comest too near it, it will bite thee: the teeth thereof are as the teeth of a lion, slaying the souls of men.[3] All iniquity is as a two edged sword, the wounds whereof cannot be healed.[4] To terrify and do wrong will waste riches: thus the house of proud men shall be made desolate.[5] A prayer out of a poor man's mouth reacheth to the ears of God, and his judgment cometh speedily.[6] He that hateth to be reproved is in the way of sinners: but he that feareth the Lord will repent from his heart.[7] An eloquent man is known far and near; but a man of understanding knoweth when he slippeth.[8] He that buildeth his house with other men's money is like one that gathereth himself stones for the tomb of his burial.[9] The congregation of the wicked is like tow wrapped together: and the end of them is a flame of fire to destroy them.[10] The way of sinners is made plain with stones, but at the end thereof is the pit of hell.[11] He that keepeth the law of the Lord getteth the understanding thereof: and the perfection of the fear of the Lord is wisdom.[12] He that is not wise will not be taught: but there is a wisdom which multiplieth bitterness.[13] The knowledge of a wise man shall abound like a flood: and his counsel is like a pure fountain of life.[14] The inner parts of a fool are like a broken vessel, and he will hold no knowledge as long as he liveth.[15] If a skilful man hear a wise word, he will commend it, and add unto it: but as soon as one of no understanding heareth it, it displeaseth him, and he casteth it behind his back.[16] The talking of a fool is like a burden in the way: but grace shall be found in the lips of the wise.[17] They enquire at the mouth of the wise man in the congregation, and they shall ponder his words in their heart.[18] As is a house that is destroyed, so is wisdom to a fool: and the knowledge

of the unwise is as talk without sense.[19] Doctrine unto fools is as fetters on the feet, and like manacles on the right hand.[20] A fool lifteth up his voice with laughter; but a wise man doth scarce smile a little.[21] Learning is unto a wise man as an ornament of gold, and like a bracelet upon his right arm.[22] A foolish man's foot is soon in his [neighbour's] house: but a man of experience is ashamed of him.[23] A fool will peep in at the door into the house: but he that is well nurtured will stand without.[24] It is the rudeness of a man to hearken at the door: but a wise man will be grieved with the disgrace.[25] The lips of talkers will be telling such things as pertain not unto them: but the words of such as have understanding are weighed in the balance.[26] The heart of fools is in their mouth: but the mouth of the wise is in their heart.[27] When the ungodly curseth Satan, he curseth his own soul.[28] A whisperer defileth his own soul, and is hated wheresoever he dwelleth.

Sir.22

[1] A slothful man is compared to a filthy stone, and every one will hiss him out to his disgrace.[2] A slothful man is compared to the filth of a dunghill: every man that takes it up will shake his hand.[3] An evilnurtured man is the dishonour of his father that begat him: and a [foolish] daughter is born to his loss.[4] A wise daughter shall bring an inheritance to her husband: but she that liveth dishonestly is her father's heaviness.[5] She that is bold dishonoureth both her father and her husband, but they both shall despise her.[6] A tale out of season [is as] musick in mourning: but stripes and correction of wisdom are never out of time.[7] Whoso teacheth a fool is as one that glueth a potsherd together, and as he that waketh one from a sound sleep.[8] He that telleth a tale to a fool speaketh to one in a slumber: when he hath told his tale, he will say, What is the matter?[9] If children live honestly, and have wherewithal, they shall cover the baseness of their parents.[10] But children, being haughty, through disdain and want of nurture do stain the nobility of their kindred.[11] Weep for the dead, for he hath lost the light: and weep for the fool, for he wanteth understanding: make little weeping for the dead, for he is at rest: but the life of the fool is worse than death.[12] Seven days do men mourn for him that is dead; but for a fool and an ungodly man all the days of his life.[13] Talk not much with a fool, and go not to him that hath no understanding: beware of him, lest thou have trouble, and thou shalt never be defiled with his fooleries: depart from him, and thou shalt find rest, and never be disquieted with madness.[14] What is heavier than lead? and what is the name thereof, but a fool?[15] Sand, and salt, and a mass of iron, is easier to bear, than a man without understanding.[16] As timber girt and bound together in a building cannot be loosed with shaking: so the heart that is stablished by advised counsel shall fear at no time.[17] A heart settled upon a thought of understanding is as a fair plaistering on the wall of a gallery.[18] Pales set on an high place will never stand against the wind: so a fearful heart in the imagination of a fool cannot stand against any fear.[19] He that pricketh the eye will make tears to fall: and he that pricketh the heart maketh it to shew her knowledge.[20] Whoso casteth a stone at the birds frayeth them away: and he that upbraideth his friend breaketh friendship.[21] Though thou drewest a sword at thy friend, yet despair not: for there may be a returning [to favour.][22] If thou hast opened thy mouth against thy friend, fear not; for there may be a reconciliation: except for upbraiding, or pride, or disclosing of secrets, or a treacherous wound: for for these things every friend will depart.[23] Be faithful to thy neighbour in his poverty, that thou mayest rejoice in his prosperity: abide stedfast unto him in the time of his trouble, that thou mayest be heir with him in his heritage: for a mean estate is not always to be contemned: nor the rich that is foolish to be had in admiration.[24] As the vapour and smoke of a

furnace goeth before the fire; so reviling before blood.[25] I will not be ashamed to defend a friend; neither will I hide myself from him.[26] And if any evil happen unto me by him, every one that heareth it will beware of him.[27] Who shall set a watch before my mouth, and a seal of wisdom upon my lips, that I fall not suddenly by them, and that my tongue destroy me not?

Sir.23

[1] O Lord, Father and Governor of all my whole life, leave me not to their counsels, and let me not fall by them.[2] Who will set scourges over my thoughts, and the discipline of wisdom over mine heart? that they spare me not for mine ignorances, and it pass not by my sins:[3] Lest mine ignorances increase, and my sins abound to my destruction, and I fall before mine adversaries, and mine enemy rejoice over me, whose hope is far from thy mercy.[4] O Lord, Father and God of my life, give me not a proud look, but turn away from thy servants always a haughty mind.[5] Turn away from me vain hopes and concupiscence, and thou shalt hold him up that is desirous always to serve thee.[6] Let not the greediness of the belly nor lust of the flesh take hold of me; and give not over me thy servant into an impudent mind.[7] Hear, O ye children, the discipline of the mouth: he that keepeth it shall never be taken in his lips.[8] The sinner shall be left in his foolishness: both the evil speaker and the proud shall fall thereby.[9] Accustom not thy mouth to swearing; neither use thyself to the naming of the Holy One.[10] For as a servant that is continually beaten shall not be without a blue mark: so he that sweareth and nameth God continually shall not be faultless.[11] A man that useth much swearing shall be filled with iniquity, and the plague shall never depart from his house: if he shall offend, his sin shall be upon him: and if he acknowledge not his sin, he maketh a double offence: and if he swear in vain, he shall not be innocent, but his house shall be full of calamities.[12] There is a word that is clothed about with death: God grant that it be not found in the heritage of Jacob; for all such things shall be far from the godly, and they shall not wallow in their sins.[13] Use not thy mouth to intemperate swearing, for therein is the word of sin.[14] Remember thy father and thy mother, when thou sittest among great men. Be not forgetful before them, and so thou by thy custom become a fool, and wish that thou hadst not been born, and curse they day of thy nativity.[15] The man that is accustomed to opprobrious words will never be reformed all the days of his life.[16] Two sorts of men multiply sin, and the third will bring wrath: a hot mind is as a burning fire, it will never be quenched till it be consumed: a fornicator in the body of his flesh will never cease till he hath kindled a fire.[17] All bread is sweet to a whoremonger, he will not leave off till he die.[18] A man that breaketh wedlock, saying thus in his heart, Who seeth me? I am compassed about with darkness, the walls cover me, and no body seeth me; what need I to fear? the most High will not remember my sins:[19] Such a man only feareth the eyes of men, and knoweth not that the eyes of the Lord are ten thousand times brighter than the sun, beholding all the ways of men, and considering the most secret parts.[20] He knew all things ere ever they were created; so also after they were perfected he looked upon them all.[21] This man shall be punished in the streets of the city, and where he suspecteth not he shall be taken.[22] Thus shall it go also with the wife that leaveth her husband, and bringeth in an heir by another.[23] For first, she hath disobeyed the law of the most High; and secondly, she hath trespassed against her own husband; and thirdly, she hath played the whore in adultery, and brought children by another man.[24] She shall be brought out into the congregation, and inquisition shall be made of her children.[25] Her children shall not take root, and her branches shall bring forth no fruit.[26] She shall leave her memory to be cursed, and her reproach shall not be blotted

out.²⁷ And they that remain shall know that there is nothing better than the fear of the Lord, and that there is nothing sweeter than to take heed unto the commandments of the Lord.²⁸ It is great glory to follow the Lord, and to be received of him is long life.

Sir.24

¹ Wisdom shall praise herself, and shall glory in the midst of her people.² In the congregation of the most High shall she open her mouth, and triumph before his power.³ I came out of the mouth of the most High, and covered the earth as a cloud.⁴ I dwelt in high places, and my throne is in a cloudy pillar.⁵ I alone compassed the circuit of heaven, and walked in the bottom of the deep.⁶ In the waves of the sea and in all the earth, and in every people and nation, I got a possession.⁷ With all these I sought rest: and in whose inheritance shall I abide?⁸ So the Creator of all things gave me a commandment, and he that made me caused my tabernacle to rest, and said, Let thy dwelling be in Jacob, and thine inheritance in Israel.⁹ He created me from the beginning before the world, and I shall never fail.¹⁰ In the holy tabernacle I served before him; and so was I established in Sion.¹¹ Likewise in the beloved city he gave me rest, and in Jerusalem was my power.¹² And I took root in an honourable people, even in the portion of the Lord's inheritance.¹³ I was exalted like a cedar in Libanus, and as a cypress tree upon the mountains of Hermon.¹⁴ I was exalted like a palm tree in En-gaddi, and as a rose plant in Jericho, as a fair olive tree in a pleasant field, and grew up as a plane tree by the water.¹⁵ I gave a sweet smell like cinnamon and aspalathus, and I yielded a pleasant odour like the best myrrh, as galbanum, and onyx, and sweet storax, and as the fume of frankincense in the tabernacle.¹⁶ As the turpentine tree I stretched out my branches, and my branches are the branches of honour and grace.¹⁷ As the vine brought I forth pleasant savour, and my flowers are the fruit of honour and riches.¹⁸ I am the mother of fair love, and fear, and knowledge, and holy hope: I therefore, being eternal, am given to all my children which are named of him.¹⁹ Come unto me, all ye that be desirous of me, and fill yourselves with my fruits.²⁰ For my memorial is sweeter than honey, and mine inheritance than the honeycomb.²¹ They that eat me shall yet be hungry, and they that drink me shall yet be thirsty.²² He that obeyeth me shall never be confounded, and they that work by me shall not do amiss.²³ All these things are the book of the covenant of the most high God, even the law which Moses commanded for an heritage unto the congregations of Jacob.²⁴ Faint not to be strong in the Lord; that he may confirm you, cleave unto him: for the Lord Almighty is God alone, and beside him there is no other Saviour.²⁵ He filleth all things with his wisdom, as Phison and as Tigris in the time of the new fruits.²⁶ He maketh the understanding to abound like Euphrates, and as Jordan in the time of the harvest.²⁷ He maketh the doctrine of knowledge appear as the light, and as Geon in the time of vintage.²⁸ The first man knew her not perfectly: no more shall the last find her out.²⁹ For her thoughts are more than the sea, and her counsels profounder than the great deep.³⁰ I also came out as a brook from a river, and as a conduit into a garden.³¹ I said, I will water my best garden, and will water abundantly my garden bed: and, lo, my brook became a river, and my river became a sea.³² I will yet make doctrine to shine as the morning, and will send forth her light afar off.³³ I will yet pour out doctrine as prophecy, and leave it to all ages for ever.³⁴ Behold that I have not laboured for myself only, but for all them that seek wisdom.

Sir.25

¹ In three things I was beautified, and stood up beautiful both before God and men: the unity of brethren, the love of neighbours, a man and a wife that agree together.² Three sorts of men my soul hateth,

and I am greatly offended at their life: a poor man that is proud, a rich man that is a liar, and an old adulterer that doateth.³ If thou hast gathered nothing in thy youth, how canst thou find any thing in thine age?⁴ O how comely a thing is judgment for gray hairs, and for ancient men to know counsel!⁵ O how comely is the wisdom of old men, and understanding and counsel to men of honour.⁶ Much experience is the crown of old men, and the fear of God is their glory.⁷ There be nine things which I have judged in mine heart to be happy, and the tenth I will utter with my tongue: A man that hath joy of his children; and he that liveth to see the fall of his enemy:⁸ Well is him that dwelleth with a wife of understanding, and that hath not slipped with his tongue, and that hath not served a man more unworthy than himself:⁹ Well is him that hath found prudence, and he that speaketh in the ears of them that will hear:¹⁰ O how great is he that findeth wisdom! yet is there none above him that feareth the Lord.¹¹ But the love of the Lord passeth all things for illumination: he that holdeth it, whereto shall he be likened?¹² The fear of the Lord is the beginning of his love: and faith is the beginning of cleaving unto him.¹³ [Give me] any plague, but the plague of the heart: and any wickedness, but the wickedness of a woman:¹⁴ And any affliction, but the affliction from them that hate me: and any revenge, but the revenge of enemies.¹⁵ There is no head above the head of a serpent; and there is no wrath above the wrath of an enemy.¹⁶ I had rather dwell with a lion and a dragon, than to keep house with a wicked woman.¹⁷ The wickedness of a woman changeth her face, and darkeneth her countenance like sackcloth.¹⁸ Her husband shall sit among his neighbours; and when he heareth it shall sigh bitterly.¹⁹ All wickedness is but little to the wickedness of a woman: let the portion of a sinner fall upon her.²⁰ As the climbing up a sandy way is to the feet of the aged, so is a wife full of words to a quiet man.²¹ Stumble not at the beauty of a woman, and desire her not for pleasure.²² A woman, if she maintain her husband, is full of anger, impudence, and much reproach.²³ A wicked woman abateth the courage, maketh an heavy countenance and a wounded heart: a woman that will not comfort her husband in distress maketh weak hands and feeble knees.²⁴ Of the woman came the beginning of sin, and through her we all die.²⁵ Give the water no passage; neither a wicked woman liberty to gad abroad.²⁶ If she go not as thou wouldest have her, cut her off from thy flesh, and give her a bill of divorce, and let her go.

Sir.26

¹ Blessed is the man that hath a virtuous wife, for the number of his days shall be double.² A virtuous woman rejoiceth her husband, and he shall fulfil the years of his life in peace.³ A good wife is a good portion, which shall be given in the portion of them that fear the Lord.⁴ Whether a man be rich or poor, if he have a good heart toward the Lord, he shall at all times rejoice with a cheerful countenance.⁵ There be three things that mine heart feareth; and for the fourth I was sore afraid: the slander of a city, the gathering together of an unruly multitude, and a false accusation: all these are worse than death.⁶ But a grief of heart and sorrow is a woman that is jealous over another woman, and a scourge of the tongue which communicateth with all.⁷ An evil wife is a yoke shaken to and fro: he that hath hold of her is as though he held a scorpion.⁸ A drunken woman and a gadder abroad causeth great anger, and she will not cover her own shame.⁹ The whoredom of a woman may be known in her haughty looks and eyelids.¹⁰ If thy daughter be shameless, keep her in straitly, lest she abuse herself through overmuch liberty.¹¹ Watch over an impudent eye: and marvel not if she trespass against thee.¹² She will open her mouth, as a thirsty traveller when he hath found a fountain, and drink of every water near her: by every hedge will she sit down, and open her quiver against every

arrow. [13] The grace of a wife delighteth her husband, and her discretion will fatten her bones. [14] A silent and loving woman is a gift of the Lord; and there is nothing so much worth as a mind well instructed. [15] A shamefaced and faithful woman is a double grace, and her continent mind cannot be valued. [16] As the sun when it ariseth in the high heaven; so is the beauty of a good wife in the ordering of her house. [17] As the clear light is upon the holy candlestick; so is the beauty of the face in ripe age. [18] As the golden pillars are upon the sockets of silver; so are the fair feet with a constant heart. [19] My son, keep the flower of thine age sound; and give not thy strength to strangers. [20] When thou hast gotten a fruitful possession through all the field, sow it with thine own seed, trusting in the goodness of thy stock. [21] So thy race which thou leavest shall be magnified, having the confidence of their good descent. [22] An harlot shall be accounted as spittle; but a married woman is a tower against death to her husband. [23] A wicked woman is given as a portion to a wicked man: but a godly woman is given to him that feareth the Lord. [24] A dishonest woman contemneth shame: but an honest woman will reverence her husband. [25] A shameless woman shall be counted as a dog; but she that is shamefaced will fear the Lord. [26] A woman that honoureth her husband shall be judged wise of all; but she that dishonoureth him in her pride shall be counted ungodly of all. [27] A loud crying woman and a scold shall be sought out to drive away the enemies. [28] There be two things that grieve my heart; and the third maketh me angry: a man of war that suffereth poverty; and men of understanding that are not set by; and one that returneth from righteousness to sin; the Lord prepareth such an one for the sword. [29] A merchant shall hardly keep himself from doing wrong; and an huckster shall not be freed from sin.

Sir.27

[1] Many have sinned for a small matter; and he that seeketh for abundance will turn his eyes away. [2] As a nail sticketh fast between the joinings of the stones; so doth sin stick close between buying and selling. [3] Unless a man hold himself diligently in the fear of the Lord, his house shall soon be overthrown. [4] As when one sifteth with a sieve, the refuse remaineth; so the filth of man in his talk. [5] The furnace proveth the potter's vessels; so the trial of man is in his reasoning. [6] The fruit declareth if the tree have been dressed; so is the utterance of a conceit in the heart of man. [7] Praise no man before thou hearest him speak; for this is the trial of men. [8] If thou followest righteousness, thou shalt obtain her, and put her on, as a glorious long robe. [9] The birds will resort unto their like; so will truth return unto them that practise in her. [10] As the lion lieth in wait for the prey; so sin for them that work iniquity. [11] The discourse of a godly man is always with wisdom; but a fool changeth as the moon. [12] If thou be among the indiscreet, observe the time; but be continually among men of understanding. [13] The discourse of fools is irksome, and their sport is the wantonness of sin. [14] The talk of him that sweareth much maketh the hair stand upright; and their brawls make one stop his ears. [15] The strife of the proud is bloodshedding, and their revilings are grievous to the ear. [16] Whoso discovereth secrets loseth his credit; and shall never find friend to his mind. [17] Love thy friend, and be faithful unto him: but if thou betrayest his secrets, follow no more after him. [18] For as a man hath destroyed his enemy; so hast thou lost the love of thy neighbor. [19] As one that letteth a bird go out of his hand, so hast thou let thy neighbour go, and shalt not get him again [20] Follow after him no more, for he is too far off; he is as a roe escaped out of the snare. [21] As for a wound, it may be bound up; and after reviling there may be reconcilement: but he that betrayeth secrets is without hope. [22] He that winketh with the eyes worketh evil: and he that knoweth him will depart from him. [23] When thou art present, he will speak sweetly, and will admire thy words: but at the last he will writhe his mouth, and slander thy sayings. [24] I have hated many things, but nothing like him; for the Lord will hate him. [25] Whoso casteth a stone on high casteth it on his own head; and a deceitful stroke shall make wounds. [26] Whoso diggeth a pit shall fall therein: and he that setteth a trap shall be taken therein. [27] He that worketh mischief, it shall fall upon him, and he shall not know whence it cometh. [28] Mockery and reproach are from the proud; but vengeance, as a lion, shall lie in wait for them. [29] They that rejoice at the fall of the righteous shall be taken in the snare; and anguish shall consume them before they die. [30] Malice and wrath, even these are abominations; and the sinful man shall have them both.

Sir.28

[1] He that revengeth shall find vengeance from the Lord, and he will surely keep his sins [in remembrance.] [2] Forgive thy neighbour the hurt that he hath done unto thee, so shall thy sins also be forgiven when thou prayest. [3] One man beareth hatred against another, and doth he seek pardon from the Lord? [4] He sheweth no mercy to a man, which is like himself: and doth he ask forgiveness of his own sins? [5] If he that is but flesh nourish hatred, who will intreat for pardon of his sins? [6] Remember thy end, and let enmity cease; [remember] corruption and death, and abide in the commandments. [7] Remember the commandments, and bear no malice to thy neighbour: [remember] the covenant of the Highest, and wink at ignorance. [8] Abstain from strife, and thou shalt diminish thy sins: for a furious man will kindle strife, [9] A sinful man disquieteth friends, and maketh debate among them that be at peace. [10] As the matter of the fire is, so it burneth: and as a man's strength is, so is his wrath; and according to his riches his anger riseth; and the stronger they are which contend, the more they will be inflamed. [11] An hasty contention kindleth a fire: and an hasty fighting sheddeth blood. [12] If thou blow the spark, it shall burn: if thou spit upon it, it shall be quenched: and both these come out of thy mouth. [13] Curse the whisperer and doubletongued: for such have destroyed many that were at peace. [14] A backbiting tongue hath disquieted many, and driven them from nation to nation: strong cities hath it pulled down, and overthrown the houses of great men. [15] A backbiting tongue hath cast out virtuous women, and deprived them of their labours. [16] Whoso hearkeneth unto it shall never find rest, and never dwell quietly. [17] The stroke of the whip maketh marks in the flesh: but the stroke of the tongue breaketh the bones. [18] Many have fallen by the edge of the sword: but not so many as have fallen by the tongue. [19] Well is he that is defended through the venom thereof; who hath not drawn the yoke thereof, nor hath been bound in her bands. [20] For the yoke thereof is a yoke of iron, and the bands thereof are bands of brass. [21] The death thereof is an evil death, the grave were better than it. [22] It shall not have rule over them that fear God, neither shall they be burned with the flame thereof. [23] Such as forsake the Lord shall fall into it; and it shall burn in them, and not be quenched; it shall be sent upon them as a lion, and devour them as a leopard. [24] Look that thou hedge thy possession about with thorns, and bind up thy silver and gold, [25] And weigh thy words in a balance, and make a door and bar for thy mouth. [26] Beware thou slide not by it, lest thou fall before him that lieth in wait.

Sir.29

[1] He that is merciful will lend unto his neighbour; and he that strengtheneth his hand keepeth the commandments. [2] Lend to thy neighbour in time of his need, and pay thou thy neighbour again in due season. [3] Keep thy word, and deal faithfully with him, and thou shalt always find the thing that is necessary for thee. [4] Many, when a thing was lent them, reckoned it to be found, and put them to

trouble that helped them.[5] Till he hath received, he will kiss a man's hand; and for his neighbour's money he will speak submissly: but when he should repay, he will prolong the time, and return words of grief, and complain of the time.[6] If he prevail, he shall hardly receive the half, and he will count as if he had found it: if not, he hath deprived him of his money, and he hath gotten him an enemy without cause: he payeth him with cursings and railings; and for honour he will pay him disgrace.[7] Many therefore have refused to lend for other men's ill dealing, fearing to be defrauded.[8] Yet have thou patience with a man in poor estate, and delay not to shew him mercy.[9] Help the poor for the commandment's sake, and turn him not away because of his poverty.[10] Lose thy money for thy brother and thy friend, and let it not rust under a stone to be lost.[11] Lay up thy treasure according to the commandments of the most High, and it shall bring thee more profit than gold.[12] Shut up alms in thy storehouses: and it shall deliver thee from all affliction.[13] It shall fight for thee against thine enemies better than a mighty shield and strong spear.[14] An honest man is surety for his neighbour: but he that is impudent will forsake him.[15] Forget not the friendship of thy surety, for he hath given his life for thee.[16] A sinner will overthrow the good estate of his surety:[17] And he that is of an unthankful mind will leave him [in danger] that delivered him.[18] Suretiship hath undone many of good estate, and shaken them as a wave of the sea: mighty men hath it driven from their houses, so that they wandered among strange nations.[19] A wicked man transgressing the commandments of the Lord shall fall into suretiship: and he that undertaketh and followeth other men's business for gain shall fall into suits.[20] Help thy neighbour according to thy power, and beware that thou thyself fall not into the same.[21] The chief thing for life is water, and bread, and clothing, and an house to cover shame.[22] Better is the life of a poor man in a mean cottage, than delicate fare in another man's house.[23] Be it little or much, hold thee contented, that thou hear not the reproach of thy house.[24] For it is a miserable life to go from house to house: for where thou art a stranger, thou darest not open thy mouth.[25] Thou shalt entertain, and feast, and have no thanks: moreover thou shalt hear bitter words:[26] Come, thou stranger, and furnish a table, and feed me of that thou hast ready.[27] Give place, thou stranger, to an honourable man; my brother cometh to be lodged, and I have need of mine house.[28] These things are grievous to a man of understanding; the upbraiding of houseroom, and reproaching of the lender.

Sir.30

[1] He that loveth his son causeth him oft to feel the rod, that he may have joy of him in the end.[2] He that chastiseth his son shall have joy in him, and shall rejoice of him among his acquaintance.[3] He that teacheth his son grieveth the enemy: and before his friends he shall rejoice of him.[4] Though his father die, yet he is as though he were not dead: for he hath left one behind him that is like himself.[5] While he lived, he saw and rejoiced in him: and when he died, he was not sorrowful.[6] He left behind him an avenger against his enemies, and one that shall requite kindness to his friends.[7] He that maketh too much of his son shall bind up his wounds; and his bowels will be troubled at every cry.[8] An horse not broken becometh headstrong: and a child left to himself will be wilful.[9] Cocker thy child, and he shall make thee afraid: play with him, and he will bring thee to heaviness.[10] Laugh not with him, lest thou have sorrow with him, and lest thou gnash thy teeth in the end.[11] Give him no liberty in his youth, and wink not at his follies.[12] Bow down his neck while he is young, and beat him on the sides while he is a child, lest he wax stubborn, and be disobedient unto thee, and so bring sorrow to thine heart.[13] Chastise thy son, and hold him to labour, lest his lewd behaviour be an offence unto thee.[14] Better is the poor, being sound and strong of constitution, than a rich man that is afflicted in his body.[15] Health and good estate of body are above all gold, and a strong body above infinite wealth.[16] There is no riches above a sound body, and no joy above the joy of the heart.[17] Death is better than a bitter life or continual sickness.[18] Delicates poured upon a mouth shut up are as messes of meat set upon a grave.[19] What good doeth the offering unto an idol? for neither can it eat nor smell: so is he that is persecuted of the Lord.[20] He seeth with his eyes and groaneth, as an eunuch that embraceth a virgin and sigheth.[21] Give not over thy mind to heaviness, and afflict not thyself in thine own counsel.[22] The gladness of the heart is the life of man, and the joyfulness of a man prolongeth his days.[23] Love thine own soul, and comfort thy heart, remove sorrow far from thee: for sorrow hath killed many, and there is no profit therein.[24] Envy and wrath shorten the life, and carefulness bringeth age before the time.[25] A cheerful and good heart will have a care of his meat and diet.

Sir.31

[1] Watching for riches consumeth the flesh, and the care thereof driveth away sleep.[2] Watching care will not let a man slumber, as a sore disease breaketh sleep,[3] The rich hath great labour in gathering riches together; and when he resteth, he is filled with his delicates.[4] The poor laboureth in his poor estate; and when he leaveth off, he is still needy.[5] He that loveth gold shall not be justified, and he that followeth corruption shall have enough thereof.[6] Gold hath been the ruin of many, and their destruction was present.[7] It is a stumblingblock unto them that sacrifice unto it, and every fool shall be taken therewith.[8] Blessed is the rich that is found without blemish, and hath not gone after gold.[9] Who is he? and we will call him blessed: for wonderful things hath he done among his people.[10] Who hath been tried thereby, and found perfect? then let him glory. Who might offend, and hath not offended? or done evil, and hath not done it?[11] His goods shall be established, and the congregation shall declare his alms.[12] If thou sit at a bountiful table, be not greedy upon it, and say not, There is much meat on it.[13] Remember that a wicked eye is an evil thing: and what is created more wicked than an eye? therefore it weepeth upon every occasion.[14] Stretch not thine hand whithersoever it looketh, and thrust it not with him into the dish.[15] Judge not thy neighbour by thyself: and be discreet in every point.[16] Eat as it becometh a man, those things which are set before thee; and devour note, lest thou be hated.[17] Leave off first for manners' sake; and be not unsatiable, lest thou offend.[18] When thou sittest among many, reach not thine hand out first of all.[19] A very little is sufficient for a man well nurtured, and he fetcheth not his wind short upon his bed.[20] Sound sleep cometh of moderate eating: he riseth early, and his wits are with him: but the pain of watching, and choler, and pangs of the belly, are with an unsatiable man.[21] And if thou hast been forced to eat, arise, go forth, vomit, and thou shalt have rest.[22] My son, hear me, and despise me not, and at the last thou shalt find as I told thee: in all thy works be quick, so shall there no sickness come unto thee.[23] Whoso is liberal of his meat, men shall speak well of him; and the report of his good housekeeping will be believed.[24] But against him that is a niggard of his meat the whole city shall murmur; and the testimonies of his niggardness shall not be doubted of.[25] Shew not thy valiantness in wine; for wine hath destroyed many.[26] The furnace proveth the edge by dipping: so doth wine the hearts of the proud by drunkeness.[27] Wine is as good as life to a man, if it be drunk moderately: what life is then to a man that is without wine? for it was made to make men glad.[28] Wine measurably drunk and in season bringeth gladness of the heart, and cheerfulness of the mind:[29] But wine drunken with excess maketh bitterness of the mind, with brawling and quarrelling.[30] Drunkenness increaseth the

rage of a fool till he offend: it diminisheth strength, and maketh wounds.[31] Rebuke not thy neighbour at the wine, and despise him not in his mirth: give him no despiteful words, and press not upon him with urging him [to drink.]

Sir.32

[1] If thou be made the master [of a feast,] lift not thyself up, but be among them as one of the rest; take diligent care for them, and so sit down.[2] And when thou hast done all thy office, take thy place, that thou mayest be merry with them, and receive a crown for thy well ordering of the feast.[3] Speak, thou that art the elder, for it becometh thee, but with sound judgment; and hinder not musick.[4] Pour not out words where there is a musician, and shew not forth wisdom out of time.[5] A concert of musick in a banquet of wine is as a signet of carbuncle set in gold.[6] As a signet of an emerald set in a work of gold, so is the melody of musick with pleasant wine.[7] Speak, young man, if there be need of thee: and yet scarcely when thou art twice asked.[8] Let thy speech be short, comprehending much in few words; be as one that knoweth and yet holdeth his tongue.[9] If thou be among great men, make not thyself equal with them; and when ancient men are in place, use not many words.[10] Before the thunder goeth lightning; and before a shamefaced man shall go favour.[11] Rise up betimes, and be not the last; but get thee home without delay.[12] There take thy pastime, and do what thou wilt: but sin not by proud speech.[13] And for these things bless him that made thee, and hath replenished thee with his good things.[14] Whoso feareth the Lord will receive his discipline; and they that seek him early shall find favour.[15] He that seeketh the law shall be filled therewith: but the hypocrite will be offended thereat.[16] They that fear the Lord shall find judgment, and shall kindle justice as a light.[17] A sinful man will not be reproved, but findeth an excuse according to his will.[18] A man of counsel will be considerate; but a strange and proud man is not daunted with fear, even when of himself he hath done without counsel.[19] Do nothing without advice; and when thou hast once done, repent not.[20] Go not in a way wherein thou mayest fall, and stumble not among the stones.[21] Be not confident in a plain way.[22] And beware of thine own children.[23] In every good work trust thy own soul; for this is the keeping of the commandments.[24] He that believeth in the Lord taketh heed to the commandment; and he that trusteth in him shall fare never the worse.

Sir.33

[1] There shall no evil happen unto him that feareth the Lord; but in temptation even again he will deliver him.[2] A wise man hateth not the law; but he that is an hypocrite therein is as a ship in a storm.[3] A man of understanding trusteth in the law; and the law is faithful unto him, as an oracle.[4] Prepare what to say, and so thou shalt be heard: and bind up instruction, and then make answer.[5] The heart of the foolish is like a cartwheel; and his thoughts are like a rolling axletree.[6] A stallion horse is as a mocking friend, he neigheth under every one that sitteth upon him.[7] Why doth one day excel another, when as all the light of every day in the year is of the sun?[8] By the knowledge of the Lord they were distinguished: and he altered seasons and feasts.[9] Some of them hath he made high days, and hallowed them, and some of them hath he made ordinary days.[10] And all men are from the ground, and Adam was created of earth:[11] In much knowledge the Lord hath divided them, and made their ways diverse.[12] Some of them hath he blessed and exalted and some of them he sanctified, and set near himself: but some of them hath he cursed and brought low, and turned out of their places.[13] As the clay is in the potter's hand, to fashion it at his pleasure: so man is in the hand of him that made him, to render to them as liketh him best.[14] Good is set against evil, and life against death: so is the godly against the sinner, and the sinner against the godly.[15] So look upon all the works of the most High; and there are two and two, one against another.[16] I awaked up last of all, as one that gathereth after the grapegatherers: by the blessing of the Lord I profited, and tred my winepress like a gatherer of grapes.[17] Consider that I laboured not for myself only, but for all them that seek learning.[18] Hear me, O ye great men of the people, and hearken with your ears, ye rulers of the congregation.[19] Give not thy son and wife, thy brother and friend, power over thee while thou livest, and give not thy goods to another: lest it repent thee, and thou intreat for the same again.[20] As long as thou livest and hast breath in thee, give not thyself over to any.[21] For better it is that thy children should seek to thee, than that thou shouldest stand to their courtesy.[22] In all thy works keep to thyself the preeminence; leave not a stain in thine honour.[23] At the time when thou shalt end thy days, and finish thy life, distribute thine inheritance.[24] Fodder, a wand, and burdens, are for the ass; and bread, correction, and work, for a servant. .[25] If thou set thy servant to labour, thou shalt find rest: but if thou let him go idle, he shall seek liberty.[26] A yoke and a collar do bow the neck: so are tortures and torments for an evil servant.[27] Send him to labour, that he be not idle; for idleness teacheth much evil.[28] Set him to work, as is fit for him: if he be not obedient, put on more heavy fetters.[29] But be not excessive toward any; and without discretion do nothing.[30] If thou have a servant, let him be unto thee as thyself, because thou hast bought him with a price.[31] If thou have a servant, entreat him as a brother: for thou hast need of him, as of thine own soul: if thou entreat him evil, and he run from thee, which way wilt thou go to seek him?

Sir.34

[1] The hopes of a man void of understanding are vain and false: and dreams lift up fools.[2] Whoso regardeth dreams is like him that catcheth at a shadow, and followeth after the wind.[3] The vision of dreams is the resemblance of one thing to another, even as the likeness of a face to a face.[4] Of an unclean thing what can be cleansed? and from that thing which is false what truth can come?[5] Divinations, and soothsayings, and dreams, are vain: and the heart fancieth, as a woman's heart in travail.[6] If they be not sent from the most High in thy visitation, set not thy heart upon them.[7] For dreams have deceived many, and they have failed that put their trust in them.[8] The law shall be found perfect without lies: and wisdom is perfection to a faithful mouth.[9] A man that hath travelled knoweth many things; and he that hath much experience will declare wisdom.[10] He that hath no experience knoweth little: but he that hath travelled is full of prudence.[11] When I travelled, I saw many things; and I understand more than I can express.[12] I was ofttimes in danger of death: yet I was delivered because of these things.[13] The spirit of those that fear the Lord shall live; for their hope is in him that saveth them.[14] Whoso feareth the Lord shall not fear nor be afraid; for he is his hope.[15] Blessed is the soul of him that feareth the Lord: to whom doth he look? and who is his strength?[16] For the eyes of the Lord are upon them that love him, he is their mighty protection and strong stay, a defence from heat, and a cover from the sun at noon, a preservation from stumbling, and an help from falling.[17] He raiseth up the soul, and lighteneth the eyes: he giveth health, life, and blessing.[18] He that sacrificeth of a thing wrongfully gotten, his offering is ridiculous; and the gifts of unjust men are not accepted.[19] The most High is not pleased with the offerings of the wicked; neither is he pacified for sin by the multitude of sacrifices.[20] Whoso bringeth an offering of the goods of the poor doeth as one that killeth the son before his father's eyes.[21] The bread of the needy is their life: he that defraudeth him thereof is a man of blood.[22] He that taketh away his neighbour's living slayeth him; and

he that defraudeth the labourer of his hire is a bloodshedder.[23] When one buildeth, and another pulleth down, what profit have they then but labour?[24] When one prayeth, and another curseth, whose voice will the Lord hear?[25] He that washeth himself after the touching of a dead body, if he touch it again, what availeth his washing?[26] So is it with a man that fasteth for his sins, and goeth again, and doeth the same: who will hear his prayer? or what doth his humbling profit him?

Sir.35

[1] He that keepeth the law bringeth offerings enough: he that taketh heed to the commandment offereth a peace offering.[2] He that requiteth a goodturn offereth fine flour; and he that giveth alms sacrificeth praise.[3] To depart from wickedness is a thing pleasing to the Lord; and to forsake unrighteousness is a propitiation.[4] Thou shalt not appear empty before the Lord.[5] For all these things [are to be done] because of the commandment.[6] The offering of the righteous maketh the altar fat, and the sweet savour thereof is before the most High.[7] The sacrifice of a just man is acceptable. and the memorial thereof shall never be forgotten.[8] Give the Lord his honour with a good eye, and diminish not the firstfruits of thine hands.[9] In all thy gifts shew a cheerful countenance, and dedicate thy tithes with gladness.[10] Give unto the most High according as he hath enriched thee; and as thou hast gotten, give with a cheerful eye.[11] For the Lord recompenseth, and will give thee seven times as much.[12] Do not think to corrupt with gifts; for such he will not receive: and trust not to unrighteous sacrifices; for the Lord is judge, and with him is no respect of persons.[13] He will not accept any person against a poor man, but will hear the prayer of the oppressed.[14] He will not despise the supplication of the fatherless; nor the widow, when she poureth out her complaint.[15] Do not the tears run down the widow's cheeks? and is not her cry against him that causeth them to fall?[16] He that serveth the Lord shall be accepted with favour, and his prayer shall reach unto the clouds.[17] The prayer of the humble pierceth the clouds: and till it come nigh, he will not be comforted; and will not depart, till the most High shall behold to judge righteously, and execute judgment.[18] For the Lord will not be slack, neither will the Mighty be patient toward them, till he have smitten in sunder the loins of the unmerciful, and repayed vengeance to the heathen; till he have taken away the multitude of the proud, and broken the sceptre of the unrighteous;[19] Till he have rendered to every man according to his deeds, and to the works of men according to their devices; till he have judged the cause of his people, and made them to rejoice in his mercy.[20] Mercy is seasonable in the time of affliction, as clouds of rain in the time of drought.

Sir.36

[1] Have mercy upon us, O Lord God of all, and behold us:[2] And send thy fear upon all the nations that seek not after thee.[3] Lift up thy hand against the strange nations, and let them see thy power.[4] As thou wast sanctified in us before them: so be thou magnified among them before us.[5] And let them know thee, as we have known thee, that there is no God but only thou, O God.[6] Shew new signs, and make other strange wonders: glorify thy hand and thy right arm, that they may set forth thy wondrous works.[7] Raise up indignation, and pour out wrath: take away the adversary, and destroy the enemy.[8] Sake the time short, remember the covenant, and let them declare thy wonderful works.[9] Let him that escapeth be consumed by the rage of the fire; and let them perish that oppress the people.[10] Smite in sunder the heads of the rulers of the heathen, that say, There is none other but we.[11] Gather all the tribes of Jacob together, and inherit thou them, as from the beginning.[12] O Lord, have mercy upon the people that is called by thy name, and upon

Israel, whom thou hast named thy firstborn.[13] O be merciful unto Jerusalem, thy holy city, the place of thy rest.[14] Fill Sion with thine unspeakable oracles, and thy people with thy glory:[15] Give testimony unto those that thou hast possessed from the beginning, and raise up prophets that have been in thy name.[16] Reward them that wait for thee, and let thy prophets be found faithful.[17] O Lord, hear the prayer of thy servants, according to the blessing of Aaron over thy people, that all they which dwell upon the earth may know that thou art the Lord, the eternal God.[18] The belly devoureth all meats, yet is one meat better than another.[19] As the palate tasteth divers kinds of venison: so doth an heart of understanding false speeches.[20] A froward heart causeth heaviness: but a man of experience will recompense him.[21] A woman will receive every man, yet is one daughter better than another.[22] The beauty of a woman cheereth the countenance, and a man loveth nothing better.[23] If there be kindness, meekness, and comfort, in her tongue, then is not her husband like other men.[24] He that getteth a wife beginneth a possession, a help like unto himself, and a pillar of rest.[25] Where no hedge is, there the possession is spoiled: and he that hath no wife will wander up and down mourning.[26] Who will trust a thief well appointed, that skippeth from city to city? so [who will believe] a man that hath no house, and lodgeth wheresoever the night taketh him?

Sir.37

[1] Every friend saith, I am his friend also: but there is a friend, which is only a friend in name.[2] Is it not a grief unto death, when a companion and friend is turned to an enemy?[3] O wicked imagination, whence camest thou in to cover the earth with deceit?[4] There is a companion, which rejoiceth in the prosperity of a friend, but in the time of trouble will be against him.[5] There is a companion, which helpeth his friend for the belly, and taketh up the buckler against the enemy.[6] Forget not thy friend in thy mind, and be not unmindful of him in thy riches.[7] Every counsellor extolleth counsel; but there is some that counselleth for himself.[8] Beware of a counsellor, and know before what need he hath; for he will counsel for himself; lest he cast the lot upon thee,[9] And say unto thee, Thy way is good: and afterward he stand on the other side, to see what shall befall thee.[10] Consult not with one that suspecteth thee: and hide thy counsel from such as envy thee.[11] Neither consult with a woman touching her of whom she is jealous; neither with a coward in matters of war; nor with a merchant concerning exchange; nor with a buyer of selling; nor with an envious man of thankfulness; nor with an unmerciful man touching kindness; nor with the slothful for any work; nor with an hireling for a year of finishing work; nor with an idle servant of much business: hearken not unto these in any matter of counsel.[12] But be continually with a godly man, whom thou knowest to keep the commandments of the Lord, whose, mind is according to thy mind, and will sorrow with thee, if thou shalt miscarry.[13] And let the counsel of thine own heart stand: for there is no man more faithful unto thee than it.[14] For a man's mind is sometime wont to tell him more than seven watchmen, that sit above in an high tower.[15] And above all this pray to the most High, that he will direct thy way in truth.[16] Let reason go before every enterprize, and counsel before every action.[17] The countenance is a sign of changing of the heart.[18] Four manner of things appear: good and evil, life and death: but the tongue ruleth over them continually.[19] There is one that is wise and teacheth many, and yet is unprofitable to himself.[20] There is one that sheweth wisdom in words, and is hated: he shall be destitute of all food.[21] For grace is not given, him from the Lord, because he is deprived of all wisdom.[22] Another is wise to himself; and the fruits of understanding are commendable in his mouth.[23] A wise man

instructeth his people; and the fruits of his understanding fail not.²⁴ A wise man shall be filled with blessing; and all they that see him shall count him happy.²⁵ The days of the life of man may be numbered: but the days of Israel are innumerable.²⁶ A wise man shall inherit glory among his people, and his name shall be perpetual.²⁷ My son, prove thy soul in thy life, and see what is evil for it, and give not that unto it.²⁸ For all things are not profitable for all men, neither hath every soul pleasure in every thing.²⁹ Be not unsatiable in any dainty thing, nor too greedy upon meats:³⁰ For excess of meats bringeth sickness, and surfeiting will turn into choler.³¹ By surfeiting have many perished; but he that taketh heed prolongeth his life.

Sir.38

¹ Honour a physician with the honour due unto him for the uses which ye may have of him: for the Lord hath created him.² For of the most High cometh healing, and he shall receive honour of the king.³ The skill of the physician shall lift up his head: and in the sight of great men he shall be in admiration.⁴ The Lord hath created medicines out of the earth; and he that is wise will not abhor them.⁵ Was not the water made sweet with wood, that the virtue thereof might be known?⁶ And he hath given men skill, that he might be honoured in his marvellous works.⁷ With such doth he heal [men,] and taketh away their pains.⁸ Of such doth the apothecary make a confection; and of his works there is no end; and from him is peace over all the earth,⁹ My son, in thy sickness be not negligent: but pray unto the Lord, and he will make thee whole.¹⁰ Leave off from sin, and order thine hands aright, and cleanse thy heart from all wickedness.¹¹ Give a sweet savour, and a memorial of fine flour; and make a fat offering, as not being.¹² Then give place to the physician, for the Lord hath created him: let him not go from thee, for thou hast need of him.¹³ There is a time when in their hands there is good success.¹⁴ For they shall also pray unto the Lord, that he would prosper that, which they give for ease and remedy to prolong life.¹⁵ He that sinneth before his Maker, let him fall into the hand of the physician.¹⁶ My son, let tears fall down over the dead, and begin to lament, as if thou hadst suffered great harm thyself; and then cover his body according to the custom, and neglect not his burial.¹⁷ Weep bitterly, and make great moan, and use lamentation, as he is worthy, and that a day or two, lest thou be evil spoken of: and then comfort thyself for thy heaviness.¹⁸ For of heaviness cometh death, and the heaviness of the heart breaketh strength.¹⁹ In affliction also sorrow remaineth: and the life of the poor is the curse of the heart.²⁰ Take no heaviness to heart: drive it away, and member the last end.²¹ Forget it not, for there is no turning again: thou shalt not do him good, but hurt thyself.²² Remember my judgment: for thine also shall be so; yesterday for me, and to day for thee.²³ When the dead is at rest, let his remembrance rest; and be comforted for him, when his Spirit is departed from him.²⁴ The wisdom of a learned man cometh by opportunity of leisure: and he that hath little business shall become wise.²⁵ How can he get wisdom that holdeth the plough, and that glorieth in the goad, that driveth oxen, and is occupied in their labours, and whose talk is of bullocks?²⁶ He giveth his mind to make furrows; and is diligent to give the kine fodder.²⁷ So every carpenter and workmaster, that laboureth night and day: and they that cut and grave seals, and are diligent to make great variety, and give themselves to counterfeit imagery, and watch to finish a work:²⁸ The smith also sitting by the anvil, and considering the iron work, the vapour of the fire wasteth his flesh, and he fighteth with the heat of the furnace: the noise of the hammer and the anvil is ever in his ears, and his eyes look still upon the pattern of the thing that he maketh; he setteth his mind to finish his work, and watcheth to polish it perfectly:²⁹ So doth the potter sitting

at his work, and turning the wheel about with his feet, who is alway carefully set at his work, and maketh all his work by number;³⁰ He fashioneth the clay with his arm, and boweth down his strength before his feet; he applieth himself to lead it over; and he is diligent to make clean the furnace:³¹ All these trust to their hands: and every one is wise in his work.³² Without these cannot a city be inhabited: and they shall not dwell where they will, nor go up and down:³³ They shall not be sought for in publick counsel, nor sit high in the congregation: they shall not sit on the judges' seat, nor understand the sentence of judgment: they cannot declare justice and judgment; and they shall not be found where parables are spoken.³⁴ But they will maintain the state of the world, and [all] their desire is in the work of their craft.

Sir.39

¹ But he that giveth his mind to the law of the most High, and is occupied in the meditation thereof, will seek out the wisdom of all the ancient, and be occupied in prophecies.² He will keep the sayings of the renowned men: and where subtil parables are, he will be there also.³ He will seek out the secrets of grave sentences, and be conversant in dark parables.⁴ He shall serve among great men, and appear before princes: he will travel through strange countries; for he hath tried the good and the evil among men.⁵ He will give his heart to resort early to the Lord that made him, and will pray before the most High, and will open his mouth in prayer, and make supplication for his sins.⁶ When the great Lord will, he shall be filled with the spirit of understanding: he shall pour out wise sentences, and give thanks unto the Lord in his prayer.⁷ He shall direct his counsel and knowledge, and in his secrets shall he meditate.⁸ He shall shew forth that which he hath learned, and shall glory in the law of the covenant of the Lord.⁹ Many shall commend his understanding; and so long as the world endureth, it shall not be blotted out; his memorial shall not depart away, and his name shall live from generation to generation.¹⁰ Nations shall shew forth his wisdom, and the congregation shall declare his praise.¹¹ If he die, he shall leave a greater name than a thousand: and if he live, he shall increase it.¹² Yet have I more to say, which I have thought upon; for I am filled as the moon at the full.¹³ Hearken unto me, ye holy children, and bud forth as a rose growing by the brook of the field:¹⁴ And give ye a sweet savour as frankincense, and flourish as a lily, send forth a smell, and sing a song of praise, bless the Lord in all his works.¹⁵ Magnify his name, and shew forth his praise with the songs of your lips, and with harps, and in praising him ye shall say after this manner:¹⁶ All the works of the Lord are exceeding good, and whatsoever he commandeth shall be accomplished in due season.¹⁷ And none may say, What is this? wherefore is that? for at time convenient they shall all be sought out: at his commandment the waters stood as an heap, and at the words of his mouth the receptacles of waters.¹⁸ At his commandment is done whatsoever pleaseth him; and none can hinder, when he will save.¹⁹ The works of all flesh are before him, and nothing can be hid from his eyes.²⁰ He seeth from everlasting to everlasting; and there is nothing wonderful before him.²¹ A man need not to say, What is this? wherefore is that? for he hath made all things for their uses.²² His blessing covered the dry land as a river, and watered it as a flood.²³ As he hath turned the waters into saltness: so shall the heathen inherit his wrath.²⁴ As his ways are plain unto the holy; so are they stumblingblocks unto the wicked.²⁵ For the good are good things created from the beginning: so evil things for sinners.²⁶ The principal things for the whole use of man's life are water, fire, iron, and salt, flour of wheat, honey, milk, and the blood of the grape, and oil, and clothing.²⁷ All these things are for good to the godly: so to the sinners they are turned into evil.²⁸ There be spirits that are

created for vengeance, which in their fury lay on sore strokes; in the time of destruction they pour out their force, and appease the wrath of him that made them.[29] Fire, and hail, and famine, and death, all these were created for vengeance;[30] Teeth of wild beasts, and scorpions, serpents, and the sword punishing the wicked to destruction.[31] They shall rejoice in his commandment, and they shall be ready upon earth, when need is; and when their time is come, they shall not transgress his word.[32] Therefore from the beginning I was resolved, and thought upon these things, and have left them in writing.[33] All the works of the Lord are good: and he will give every needful thing in due season.[34] So that a man cannot say, This is worse than that: for in time they shall all be well approved.[35] And therefore praise ye the Lord with the whole heart and mouth, and bless the name of the Lord.

Sir.40

[1] Great travail is created for every man, and an heavy yoke is upon the sons of Adam, from the day that they go out of their mother's womb, till the day that they return to the mother of all things.[2] Their imagination of things to come, and the day of death, [trouble] their thoughts, and [cause] fear of heart;[3] From him that sitteth on a throne of glory, unto him that is humbled in earth and ashes;[4] From him that weareth purple and a crown, unto him that is clothed with a linen frock.[5] Wrath, and envy, trouble, and unquietness, fear of death, and anger, and strife, and in the time of rest upon his bed his night sleep, do change his knowledge.[6] A little or nothing is his rest, and afterward he is in his sleep, as in a day of keeping watch, troubled in the vision of his heart, as if he were escaped out of a battle.[7] When all is safe, he awaketh, and marvelleth that the fear was nothing.[8] [Such things happen] unto all flesh, both man and beast, and that is sevenfold more upon sinners.[9] Death, and bloodshed, strife, and sword, calamities, famine, tribulation, and the scourge;[10] These things are created for the wicked, and for their sakes came the flood.[11] All things that are of the earth shall turn to the earth again: and that which is of the waters doth return into the sea.[12] All bribery and injustice shall be blotted out: but true dealing shall endure for ever.[13] The goods of the unjust shall be dried up like a river, and shall vanish with noise, like a great thunder in rain.[14] While he openeth his hand he shall rejoice: so shall transgressors come to nought.[15] The children of the ungodly shall not bring forth many branches: but are as unclean roots upon a hard rock.[16] The weed growing upon every water and bank of a river shall be pulled up before all grass.[17] Bountifulness is as a most fruitful garden, and mercifulness endureth for ever.[18] To labour, and to be content with that a man hath, is a sweet life: but he that findeth a treasure is above them both.[19] Children and the building of a city continue a man's name: but a blameless wife is counted above them both.[20] Wine and musick rejoice the heart: but the love of wisdom is above them both.[21] The pipe and the psaltery make sweet melody: but a pleasant tongue is above them both.[22] Thine eye desireth favour and beauty: but more than both corn while it is green.[23] A friend and companion never meet amiss: but above both is a wife with her husband.[24] Brethren and help are against time of trouble: but alms shall deliver more than them both.[25] Gold and silver make the foot stand sure: but counsel is esteemed above them both.[26] Riches and strength lift up the heart: but the fear of the Lord is above them both: there is no want in the fear of the Lord, and it needeth not to seek help.[27] The fear of the Lord is a fruitful garden, and covereth him above all glory.[28] My son, lead not a beggar's life; for better it is to die than to beg.[29] The life of him that dependeth on another man's table is not to be counted for a life; for he polluteth himself with other men's meat: but a wise man well nurtured will beware thereof.[30] Begging is sweet in the mouth of the shameless: but in his belly there shall burn a fire.

Sir.41

[1] O death, how bitter is the remembrance of thee to a man that liveth at rest in his possessions, unto the man that hath nothing to vex him, and that hath prosperity in all things: yea, unto him that is yet able to receive meat![2] O death, acceptable is thy sentence unto the needy, and unto him whose strength faileth, that is now in the last age, and is vexed with all things, and to him that despaireth, and hath lost patience![3] Fear not the sentence of death, remember them that have been before thee, and that come after; for this is the sentence of the Lord over all flesh.[4] And why art thou against the pleasure of the most High? there is no inquisition in the grave, whether thou have lived ten, or an hundred, or a thousand years.[5] The children of sinners are abominable children, and they that are conversant in the dwelling of the ungodly.[6] The inheritance of sinners' children shall perish, and their posterity shall have a perpetual reproach.[7] The children will complain of an ungodly father, because they shall be reproached for his sake.[8] Woe be unto you, ungodly men, which have forsaken the law of the most high God! for if ye increase, it shall be to your destruction:[9] And if ye be born, ye shall be born to a curse: and if ye die, a curse shall be your portion.[10] All that are of the earth shall turn to earth again: so the ungodly shall go from a curse to destruction.[11] The mourning of men is about their bodies: but an ill name of sinners shall be blotted out.[12] Have regard to thy name; for that shall continue with thee above a thousand great treasures of gold.[13] A good life hath but few days: but a good name endureth for ever.[14] My children, keep discipline in peace: for wisdom that is hid, and a treasure that is not seen, what profit is in them both?[15] A man that hideth his foolishness is better than a man that hideth his wisdom.[16] Therefore be shamefaced according to my word: for it is not good to retain all shamefacedness; neither is it altogether approved in every thing.[17] Be ashamed of whoredom before father and mother: and of a lie before a prince and a mighty man;[18] Of an offence before a judge and ruler; of iniquity before a congregation and people; of unjust dealing before thy partner and friend;[19] And of theft in regard of the place where thou sojournest, and in regard of the truth of God and his covenant; and to lean with thine elbow upon the meat; and of scorning to give and take;[20] And of silence before them that salute thee; and to look upon an harlot;[21] And to turn away thy face from thy kinsman; or to take away a portion or a gift; or to gaze upon another man's wife.[22] Or to be overbusy with his maid, and come not near her bed; or of upbraiding speeches before friends; and after thou hast given, upbraid not;[23] Or of iterating and speaking again that which thou hast heard; and of revealing of secrets.[24] So shalt thou be truly shamefaced and find favour before all men.

Sir.42

[1] Of these things be not thou ashamed, and accept no person to sin thereby:[2] Of the law of the most High, and his covenant; and of judgment to justify the ungodly;[3] Of reckoning with thy partners and travellers; or of the gift of the heritage of friends;[4] Of exactness of balance and weights; or of getting much or little;[5] And of merchants' indifferent selling; of much correction of children; and to make the side of an evil servant to bleed.[6] Sure keeping is good, where an evil wife is; and shut up, where many hands are.[7] Deliver all things in number and weight; and put all in writing that thou givest out, or receivest in.[8] Be not ashamed to inform the unwise and foolish, and the extreme aged that contendeth with those that are young: thus shalt thou be truly learned, and approved of all men living.[9] The father waketh for the daughter, when no man knoweth; and the care for her taketh away sleep: when she is young, lest she pass away the

flower of her age; and being married, lest she should be hated:[10] In her virginity, lest she should be defiled and gotten with child in her father's house; and having an husband, lest she should misbehave herself; and when she is married, lest she should be barren.[11] Keep a sure watch over a shameless daughter, lest she make thee a laughingstock to thine enemies, and a byword in the city, and a reproach among the people, and make thee ashamed before the multitude.[12] Behold not every body's beauty, and sit not in the midst of women.[13] For from garments cometh a moth, and from women wickedness.[14] Better is the churlishness of a man than a courteous woman, a woman, I say, which bringeth shame and reproach.[15] I will now remember the works of the Lord, and declare the things that I have seen: In the words of the Lord are his works.[16] The sun that giveth light looketh upon all things, and the work thereof is full of the glory of the Lord.[17] The Lord hath not given power to the saints to declare all his marvellous works, which the Almighty Lord firmly settled, that whatsoever is might be established for his glory.[18] He seeketh out the deep, and the heart, and considereth their crafty devices: for the Lord knoweth all that may be known, and he beholdeth the signs of the world.[19] He declareth the things that are past, and for to come, and revealeth the steps of hidden things.[20] No thought escapeth him, neither any word is hidden from him.[21] He hath garnished the excellent works of his wisdom, and he is from everlasting to everlasting: unto him may nothing be added, neither can he be diminished, and he hath no need of any counsellor.[22] Oh how desirable are all his works! and that a man may see even to a spark.[23] All these things live and remain for ever for all uses, and they are all obedient.[24] All things are double one against another: and he hath made nothing imperfect.[25] One thing establisheth the good or another: and who shall be filled with beholding his glory?

Sir.43

[1] The pride of the height, the clear firmament, the beauty of heaven, with his glorious shew;[2] The sun when it appeareth, declaring at his rising a marvellous instrument, the work of the most High:[3] At noon it parcheth the country, and who can abide the burning heat thereof?[4] A man blowing a furnace is in works of heat, but the sun burneth the mountains three times more; breathing out fiery vapours, and sending forth bright beams, it dimmeth the eyes.[5] Great is the Lord that made it; and at his commandment runneth hastily.[6] He made the moon also to serve in her season for a declaration of times, and a sign of the world.[7] From the moon is the sign of feasts, a light that decreaseth in her perfection.[8] The month is called after her name, increasing wonderfully in her changing, being an instrument of the armies above, shining in the firmament of heaven;[9] The beauty of heaven, the glory of the stars, an ornament giving light in the highest places of the Lord.[10] At the commandment of the Holy One they will stand in their order, and never faint in their watches.[11] Look upon the rainbow, and praise him that made it; very beautiful it is in the brightness thereof.[12] It compasseth the heaven about with a glorious circle, and the hands of the most High have bended it.[13] By his commandment he maketh the snow to fall aplace, and sendeth swiftly the lightnings of his judgment.[14] Through this the treasures are opened: and clouds fly forth as fowls.[15] By his great power he maketh the clouds firm, and the hailstones are broken small.[16] At his sight the mountains are shaken, and at his will the south wind bloweth.[17] The noise of the thunder maketh the earth to tremble: so doth the northern storm and the whirlwind: as birds flying he scattereth the snow, and the falling down thereof is as the lighting of grasshoppers:[18] The eye marvelleth at the beauty of the whiteness thereof, and the heart is astonished at the raining of it.[19] The hoarfrost also as salt he poureth on the earth, and being congealed, it lieth on the top of sharp

stakes.[20] When the cold north wind bloweth, and the water is congealed into ice, it abideth upon every gathering together of water, and clotheth the water as with a breastplate.[21] It devoureth the mountains, and burneth the wilderness, and consumeth the grass as fire.[22] A present remedy of all is a mist coming speedily, a dew coming after heat refresheth.[23] By his counsel he appeaseth the deep, and planteth islands therein.[24] They that sail on the sea tell of the danger thereof; and when we hear it with our ears, we marvel threat.[25] For therein be strange and wondrous works, variety of all kinds of beasts and whales created.[26] By him the end of them hath prosperous success, and by his word all things consist.[27] We may speak much, and yet come short: wherefore in sum, he is all.[28] How shall we be able to magnify him? for he is great above all his works.[29] The Lord is terrible and very great, and marvellous is his power.[30] When ye glorify the Lord, exalt him as much as ye can; for even yet will he far exceed: and when ye exalt him, put forth all your strength, and be not weary; for ye can never go far enough.[31] Who hath seen him, that he might tell us? and who can magnify him as he is?[32] There are yet hid greater things than these be, for we have seen but a few of his works.[33] For the Lord hath made all things; and to the godly hath he given wisdom.

Sir.44

[1] Let us now praise famous men, and our fathers that begat us.[2] The Lord hath wrought great glory by them through his great power from the beginning.[3] Such as did bear rule in their kingdoms, men renowned for their power, giving counsel by their understanding, and declaring prophecies:[4] Leaders of the people by their counsels, and by their knowledge of learning meet for the people, wise and eloquent are their instructions:[5] Such as found out musical tunes, and recited verses in writing:[6] Rich men furnished with ability, living peaceably in their habitations:[7] All these were honoured in their generations, and were the glory of their times.[8] There be of them, that have left a name behind them, that their praises might be reported.[9] And some there be, which have no memorial; who are perished, as though they had never been; and are become as though they had never been born; and their children after them.[10] But these were merciful men, whose righteousness hath not been forgotten.[11] With their seed shall continually remain a good inheritance, and their children are within the covenant.[12] Their seed standeth fast, and their children for their sakes.[13] Their seed shall remain for ever, and their glory shall not be blotted out.[14] Their bodies are buried in peace; but their name liveth for evermore.[15] The people will tell of their wisdom, and the congregation will shew forth their praise.[16] Enoch pleased the Lord, and was translated, being an example of repentance to all generations.[17] Noah was found perfect and righteous; in the time of wrath he was taken in exchange [for the world;] therefore was he left as a remnant unto the earth, when the flood came.[18] An everlasting covenant was made with him, that all flesh should perish no more by the flood.[19] Abraham was a great father of many people: in glory was there none like unto him;[20] Who kept the law of the most High, and was in covenant with him: he established the covenant in his flesh; and when he was proved, he was found faithful.[21] Therefore he assured him by an oath, that he would bless the nations in his seed, and that he would multiply him as the dust of the earth, and exalt his seed as the stars, and cause them to inherit from sea to sea, and from the river unto the utmost part of the land.[22] With Isaac did he establish likewise [for Abraham his father's sake] the blessing of all men, and the covenant, And made it rest upon the head of Jacob. He acknowledged him in his blessing, and gave him an heritage, and divided his portions; among the twelve tribes did he part them.

Sir.45

[1] And he brought out of him a merciful man, which found favour in the sight of all flesh, even Moses, beloved of God and men, whose memorial is blessed.[2] He made him like to the glorious saints, and magnified him, so that his enemies stood in fear of him.[3] By his words he caused the wonders to cease, and he made him glorious in the sight of kings, and gave him a commandment for his people, and shewed him part of his glory.[4] He sanctified him in his faithfuless and meekness, and chose him out of all men.[5] He made him to hear his voice, and brought him into the dark cloud, and gave him commandments before his face, even the law of life and knowledge, that he might teach Jacob his covenants, and Israel his judgments.[6] He exalted Aaron, an holy man like unto him, even his brother, of the tribe of Levi.[7] An everlasting covenant he made with him and gave him the priesthood among the people; he beautified him with comely ornaments, and clothed him with a robe of glory.[8] He put upon him perfect glory; and strengthened him with rich garments, with breeches, with a long robe, and the ephod.[9] And he compassed him with pomegranates, and with many golden bells round about, that as he went there might be a sound, and a noise made that might be heard in the temple, for a memorial to the children of his people;[10] With an holy garment, with gold, and blue silk, and purple, the work of the embroidere, with a breastplate of judgment, and with Urim and Thummim;[11] With twisted scarlet, the work of the cunning workman, with precious stones graven like seals, and set in gold, the work of the jeweller, with a writing engraved for a memorial, after the number of the tribes of Israel.[12] He set a crown of gold upon the mitre, wherein was engraved Holiness, an ornament of honour, a costly work, the desires of the eyes, goodly and beautiful.[13] Before him there were none such, neither did ever any stranger put them on, but only his children and his children's children perpetually.[14] Their sacrifices shall be wholly consumed every day twice continually.[15] Moses consecrated him, and anointed him with holy oil: this was appointed unto him by an everlasting covenant, and to his seed, so long as the heavens should remain, that they should minister unto him, and execute the office of the priesthood, and bless the people in his name.[16] He chose him out of all men living to offer sacrifices to the Lord, incense, and a sweet savour, for a memorial, to make reconciliation for his people.[17] He gave unto him his commandments, and authority in the statutes of judgments, that he should teach Jacob the testimonies, and inform Israel in his laws.[18] Strangers conspired together against him, and maligned him in the wilderness, even the men that were of Dathan's and Abiron's side, and the congregation of Core, with fury and wrath.[19] This the Lord saw, and it displeased him, and in his wrathful indignation were they consumed: he did wonders upon them, to consume them with the fiery flame.[20] But he made Aaron more honourable, and gave him an heritage, and divided unto him the firstfruits of the increase; especially he prepared bread in abundance:[21] For they eat of the sacrifices of the Lord, which he gave unto him and his seed.[22] Howbeit in the land of the people he had no inheritance, neither had he any portion among the people: for the Lord himself is his portion and inheritance.[23] The third in glory is Phinees the son of Eleazar, because he had zeal in the fear of the Lord, and stood up with good courage of heart: when the people were turned back, and made reconciliation for Israel.[24] Therefore was there a covenant of peace made with him, that he should be the chief of the sanctuary and of his people, and that he and his posterity should have the dignity of the priesthood for ever:[25] According to the covenant made with David son of Jesse, of the tribe of Juda, that the inheritance of the king should be to his posterity alone: so the inheritance of Aaron should also be unto his seed.[26] God give you wisdom in your heart to judge his people in righteousness, that their good things be not abolished, and that their glory may endure for ever.

Sir.46

[1] Jesus the son a Nave was valiant in the wars, and was the successor of Moses in prophecies, who according to his name was made great for the saving of the elect of God, and taking vengeance of the enemies that rose up against them, that he might set Israel in their inheritance.[2] How great glory gat he, when he did lift up his hands, and stretched out his sword against the cities![3] Who before him so stood to it? for the Lord himself brought his enemies unto him.[4] Did not the sun go back by his means? and was not one day as long as two?[5] He called upon the most high Lord, when the enemies pressed upon him on every side; and the great Lord heard him.[6] And with hailstones of mighty power he made the battle to fall violently upon the nations, and in the descent [of Beth-horon] he destroyed them that resisted, that the nations might know all their strength, because he fought in the sight of the Lord, and he followed the Mighty One.[7] In the time of Moses also he did a work of mercy, he and Caleb the son of Jephunne, in that they withstood the congregation, and withheld the people from sin, and appeased the wicked murmuring.[8] And of six hundred thousand people on foot, they two were preserved to bring them in to the heritage, even unto the land that floweth with milk and honey.[9] The Lord gave strength also unto Caleb, which remained with him unto his old age: so that he entered upon the high places of the land, and his seed obtained it for an heritage:[10] That all the children of Israel might see that it is good to follow the Lord.[11] And concerning the judges, every one by name, whose heart went not a whoring, nor departed from the Lord, let their memory be blessed.[12] Let their bones flourish out of their place, and let the name of them that were honoured be continued upon their children.[13] Samuel, the prophet of the Lord, beloved of his Lord, established a kingdom, and anointed princes over his people.[14] By the law of the Lord he judged the congregation, and the Lord had respect unto Jacob.[15] By his faithfulness he was found a true prophet, and by his word he was known to be faithful in vision.[16] He called upon the mighty Lord, when his enemies pressed upon him on every side, when he offered the sucking lamb.[17] And the Lord thundered from heaven, and with a great noise made his voice to be heard.[18] And he destroyed the rulers of the Tyrians, and all the princes cf the Philistines.[19] And before his long sleep he made protestations in the sight of the Lord and his anointed, I have not taken any man's goods, so much as a shoe: and no man did accuse him.[20] And after his death he prophesied, and shewed the king his end, and lifted up his voice from the earth in prophecy, to blot out the wickedness of the people.

Sir.47

[1] And after him rose up Nathan to prophesy in the time of David.[2] As is the fat taken away from the peace offering, so was David chosen out of the children of Israel.[3] He played with lions as with kids, and with bears as with lambs.[4] Slew he not a giant, when he was yet but young? and did he not take away reproach from the people, when he lifted up his hand with the stone in the sling, and beat down the boasting of Goliath?[5] For he called upon the most high Lord; and he gave him strength in his right hand to slay that mighty warrior, and set up the horn of his people.[6] So the people honoured him with ten thousands, and praised him in the blessings of the Lord, in that he gave him a crown of glory.[7] For he destroyed the enemies on every side, and brought to nought the Philistines his adversaries, and brake their horn in sunder unto this day.[8] In all his works he praised the Holy One most high with words of glory; with his whole heart he sung songs, and loved him that made him.[9] He

set singers also before the altar, that by their voices they might make sweet melody, and daily sing praises in their songs.[10] He beautified their feasts, and set in order the solemn times until the end, that they might praise his holy name, and that the temple might sound from morning.[11] The Lord took away his sins, and exalted his horn for ever: he gave him a covenant of kings, and a throne of glory in Israel.[12] After him rose up a wise son, and for his sake he dwelt at large.[13] Solomon reigned in a peaceable time, and was honoured; for God made all quiet round about him, that he might build an house in his name, and prepare his sanctuary for ever.[14] How wise wast thou in thy youth and, as a flood, filled with understanding![15] Thy soul covered the whole earth, and thou filledst it with dark parables.[16] Thy name went far unto the islands; and for thy peace thou wast beloved.[17] The countries marvelled at thee for thy songs, and proverbs, and parables, and interpretations.[18] By the name of the Lord God, which is called the Lord God of Israel, thou didst gather gold as tin and didst multiply silver as lead.[19] Thou didst bow thy loins unto women, and by thy body thou wast brought into subjection.[20] Thou didst stain thy honour, and pollute thy seed: so that thou broughtest wrath upon thy children, and wast grieved for thy folly.[21] So the kingdom was divided, and out of Ephraim ruled a rebellious kingdom.[22] But the Lord will never leave off his mercy, neither shall any of his works perish, neither will he abolish the posterity of his elect, and the seed of him that loveth him he will not take away: wherefore he gave a remnant unto Jacob, and out of him a root unto David.[23] Thus rested Solomon with his fathers, and of his seed he left behind him Roboam, even the foolishness of the people, and one that had no understanding, who turned away the people through his counsel. There was also Jeroboam the son of Nebat, who caused Israel to sin, and shewed Ephraim the way of sin:[24] And their sins were multiplied exceedingly, that they were driven out of the land.[25] For they sought out all wickedness, till the vengeance came upon them.

Sir.48

[1] Then stood up Elias the prophet as fire, and his word burned like a lamp.[2] He brought a sore famine upon them, and by his zeal he diminished their number.[3] By the word of the Lord he shut up the heaven, and also three times brought down fire.[4] O Elias, how wast thou honoured in thy wondrous deeds! and who may glory like unto thee![5] Who didst raise up a dead man from death, and his soul from the place of the dead, by the word of the most High:[6] Who broughtest kings to destruction, and honorable men from their bed:[7] Who heardest the rebuke of the Lord in Sinai, and in Horeb the judgment of vengeance:[8] Who annointedst kings to take revenge, and prophets to succeed after him:[9] Who was taken up in a whirlwind of fire, and in a chariot of fiery horses:[10] Who wast ordained for reproofs in their times, to pacify the wrath of the Lord's judgment, before it brake forth into fury, and to turn the heart of the father unto the son, and to restore the tribes of Jacob.[11] Blessed are they that saw thee, and slept in love; for we shall surely live.[12] Elias it was, who was covered with a whirlwind: and Eliseus was filled with his spirit: whilst he lived, he was not moved with the presence of any prince, neither could any bring him into subjection.[13] No word could overcome him; and after his death his body prophesied.[14] He did wonders in his life, and at his death were his works marvellous.[15] For all this the people repented not, neither departed they from their sins, till they were spoiled and carried out of their land, and were scattered through all the earth: yet there remained a small people, and a ruler in the house of David:[16] Of whom some did that which was pleasing to God, and some multiplied sins.[17] Ezekias fortified his city, and brought in water into the midst thereof: he digged the hard rock with iron, and made wells

42

for waters.[18] In his time Sennacherib came up, and sent Rabsaces, and lifted up his hand against Sion, and boasted proudly.[19] Then trembled their hearts and hands, and they were in pain, as women in travail.[20] But they called upon the Lord which is merciful, and stretched out their hands toward him: and immediately the Holy One heard them out of heaven, and delivered them by the ministry of Esay.[21] He smote the host of the Assyrians, and his angel destroyed them.[22] For Ezekias had done the thing that pleased the Lord, and was strong in the ways of David his father, as Esay the prophet, who was great and faithful in his vision, had commanded him.[23] In his time the sun went backward, and he lengthened the king's life.[24] He saw by an excellent spirit what should come to pass at the last, and he comforted them that mourned in Sion.[25] He shewed what should come to pass for ever, and secret things or ever they came.

Sir.49

[1] The remembrance of Josias is like the composition of the perfume that is made by the art of the apothecary: it is sweet as honey in all mouths, and as musick at a banquet of wine.[2] He behaved himself uprightly in the conversion of the people, and took away the abominations of iniquity.[3] He directed his heart unto the Lord, and in the time of the ungodly he established the worship of God.[4] All, except David and Ezekias and Josias, were defective: for they forsook the law of the most High, even the kings of Juda failed.[5] Therefore he gave their power unto others, and their glory to a strange nation.[6] They burnt the chosen city of the sanctuary, and made the streets desolate, according to the prophecy of Jeremias.[7] For they entreated him evil, who nevertheless was a prophet, sanctified in his mother's womb, that he might root out, and afflict, and destroy; and that he might build up also, and plant.[8] It was Ezekiel who saw the glorious vision, which was shewed him upon the chariot of the cherubims.[9] For he made mention of the enemies under the figure of the rain, and directed them that went right.[10] And of the twelve prophets let the memorial be blessed, and let their bones flourish again out of their place: for they comforted Jacob, and delivered them by assured hope.[11] How shall we magnify Zorobabel? even he was as a signet on the right hand:[12] So was Jesus the son of Josedec: who in their time builded the house, and set up an holy temple to the Lord, which was prepared for everlasting glory.[13] And among the elect was Neemias, whose renown is great, who raised up for us the walls that were fallen, and set up the gates and the bars, and raised up our ruins again.[14] But upon the earth was no man created like Enoch; for he was taken from the earth.[15] Neither was there a young man born like Joseph, a governor of his brethren, a stay of the people, whose bones were regarded of the Lord.[16] Sem and Seth were in great honour among men, and so was Adam above every living thing in creation.

Sir.50

[1] Simon the high priest, the son of Onias, who in his life repaired the house again, and in his days fortified the temple:[2] And by him was built from the foundation the double height, the high fortress of the wall about the temple:[3] In his days the cistern to receive water, being in compass as the sea, was covered with plates of brass:[4] He took care of the temple that it should not fall, and fortified the city against besieging:[5] How was he honoured in the midst of the people in his coming out of the sanctuary![6] He was as the morning star in the midst of a cloud, and as the moon at the full:[7] As the sun shining upon the temple of the most High, and as the rainbow giving light in the bright clouds:[8] And as the flower of roses in the spring of the year, as lilies by the rivers of waters, and as the branches of the frankincense tree in the time of summer:[9] As fire and incense in the censer, and as a vessel of beaten gold set with all manner of precious

stones:[10] And as a fair olive tree budding forth fruit, and as a cypress tree which groweth up to the clouds.[11] When he put on the robe of honour, and was clothed with the perfection of glory, when he went up to the holy altar, he made the garment of holiness honourable.[12] When he took the portions out of the priests' hands, he himself stood by the hearth of the altar, compassed about, as a young cedar in Libanus; and as palm trees compassed they him round about.[13] So were all the sons of Aaron in their glory, and the oblations of the Lord in their hands, before all the congregation of Israel.[14] And finishing the service at the altar, that he might adorn the offering of the most high Almighty,[15] He stretched out his hand to the cup, and poured of the blood of the grape, he poured out at the foot of the altar a sweetsmelling savour unto the most high King of all.[16] Then shouted the sons of Aaron, and sounded the silver trumpets, and made a great noise to be heard, for a remembrance before the most High.[17] Then all the people together hasted, and fell down to the earth upon their faces to worship their Lord God Almighty, the most High.[18] The singers also sang praises with their voices, with great variety of sounds was there made sweet melody.[19] And the people besought the Lord, the most High, by prayer before him that is merciful, till the solemnity of the Lord was ended, and they had finished his service.[20] Then he went down, and lifted up his hands over the whole congregation of the children of Israel, to give the blessing of the Lord with his lips, and to rejoice in his name.[21] And they bowed themselves down to worship the second time, that they might receive a blessing from the most High.[22] Now therefore bless ye the God of all, which only doeth wondrous things every where, which exalteth our days from the womb, and dealeth with us according to his mercy.[23] He grant us joyfulness of heart, and that peace may be in our days in Israel for ever:[24] That he would confirm his mercy with us, and deliver us at his time![25] There be two manner of nations which my heart abhorreth, and the third is no nation:[26] They that sit upon the mountain of Samaria, and they that dwell among the Philistines, and that foolish people that dwell in Sichem.[27] Jesus the son of Sirach of Jerusalem hath written in this book the instruction of understanding and knowledge, who out of his heart poured forth wisdom.[28] Blessed is he that shall be exercised in these things; and he that layeth them up in his heart shall become wise.[29] For if he do them, he shall be strong to all things: for the light of the Lord leadeth him, who giveth wisdom to the godly. Blessed be the name of the Lord for ever. Amen, Amen.

Sir.51

[A Prayer of Jesus the son of Sirach.][1] I will thank thee, O Lord and King, and praise thee, O God my Saviour: I do give praise unto thy name:[2] For thou art my defender and helper, and has preserved my body from destruction, and from the snare of the slanderous tongue, and from the lips that forge lies, and has been mine helper against mine adversaries:[3] And hast delivered me, according to the multitude of they mercies and greatness of thy name, from the teeth of them that were ready to devour me, and out of the hands of such as sought after my life, and from the manifold afflictions which I had;[4] From the choking of fire on every side, and from the midst of the fire which I kindled not;[5] From the depth of the belly of hell, from an unclean tongue, and from lying words.[6] By an accusation to the king from an unrighteous tongue my soul drew near even unto death, my life was near to the hell beneath.[7] They compassed me on every side, and there was no man to help me: I looked for the succour of men, but there was none.[8] Then thought I upon thy mercy, O Lord, and upon thy acts of old, how thou deliverest such as wait for thee, and savest them out of the hands of the enemies.[9] Then lifted I up my supplications from the earth, and

prayed for deliverance from death.[10] I called upon the Lord, the Father of my Lord, that he would not leave me in the days of my trouble, and in the time of the proud, when there was no help.[11] I will praise thy name continually, and will sing praises with thanksgiving; and so my prayer was heard:[12] For thou savedst me from destruction, and deliveredst me from the evil time: therefore will I give thanks, and praise thee, and bless they name, O Lord.[13] When I was yet young, or ever I went abroad, I desired wisdom openly in my prayer.[14] I prayed for her before the temple, and will seek her out even to the end.[15] Even from the flower till the grape was ripe hath my heart delighted in her: my foot went the right way, from my youth up sought I after her.[16] I bowed down mine ear a little, and received her, and gat much learning.[17] I profited therein, therefore will I ascribe glory unto him that giveth me wisdom.[18] For I purposed to do after her, and earnestly I followed that which is good; so shall I not be confounded.[19] My soul hath wrestled with her, and in my doings I was exact: I stretched forth my hands to the heaven above, and bewailed my ignorances of her.[20] I directed my soul unto her, and I found her in pureness: I have had my heart joined with her from the beginning, therefore shall I not be foresaken.[21] My heart was troubled in seeking her: therefore have I gotten a good possession.[22] The Lord hath given me a tongue for my reward, and I will praise him therewith.[23] Draw near unto me, ye unlearned, and dwell in the house of learning.[24] Wherefore are ye slow, and what say ye to these things, seeing your souls are very thirsty?[25] I opened my mouth, and said, Buy her for yourselves without money.[26] Put your neck under the yoke, and let your soul receive instruction: she is hard at hand to find.[27] Behold with your eyes, how that I have but little labour, and have gotten unto me much rest.[28] Get learning with a great sum of money, and get much gold by her.[29] Let your soul rejoice in his mercy, and be not ashamed of his praise.[30] Work your work betimes, and in his time he will give you your reward.

Baruch

Bar.1

[1] And these are the words of the book, which Baruch the son of Nerias, the son of Maasias, the son of Sedecias, the son of Asadias, the son of Chelcias, wrote in Babylon,[2] In the fifth year, and in the seventh day of the month, what time as the Chaldeans took Jerusalem, and burnt it with fire.[3] And Baruch did read the words of this book in the hearing of Jechonias the son of Joachim king of Juda, and in the ears of all the people that came to hear the book,[4] And in the hearing of the nobles, and of the king's sons, and in the hearing of the elders, and of all the people, from the lowest unto the highest, even of all them that dwelt at Babylon by the river Sud.[5] Whereupon they wept, fasted, and prayed before the Lord.[6] They made also a collection of money according to every man's power:[7] And they sent it to Jerusalem unto Joachim the high priest, the son of Chelcias, son of Salom, and to the priests, and to all the people which were found with him at Jerusalem,[8] At the same time when he received the vessels of the house of the Lord, that were carried out of the temple, to return them into the land of Juda, the tenth day of the month Sivan, namely, silver vessels, which Sedecias the son of Josias king of Jada had made,[9] After that Nabuchodonosor king of Babylon had carried away Jechonias, and the princes, and the captives, and the mighty men, and the people of the land, from Jerusalem, and brought them unto Babylon.[10] And they said, Behold, we have sent you money to buy you burnt offerings, and sin offerings, and incense, and prepare ye manna, and offer upon the altar of the Lord our God;[11] And pray for the life of Nabuchodonosor king of Babylon, and for the life of Balthasar his

son, that their days may be upon earth as the days of heaven:[12] And the Lord will give us strength, and lighten our eyes, and we shall live under the shadow of Nabuchodonosor king of Babylon, and under the shadow of Balthasar his son, and we shall serve them many days, and find favour in their sight.[13] Pray for us also unto the Lord our God, for we have sinned against the Lord our God; and unto this day the fury of the Lord and his wrath is not turned from us.[14] And ye shall read this book which we have sent unto you, to make confession in the house of the Lord, upon the feasts and solemn days.[15] And ye shall say, To the Lord our God belongeth righteousness, but unto us the confusion of faces, as it is come to pass this day, unto them of Juda, and to the inhabitants of Jerusalem,[16] And to our kings, and to our princes, and to our priests, and to our prophets, and to our fathers:[17] For we have sinned before the Lord,[18] And disobeyed him, and have not hearkened unto the voice of the Lord our God, to walk in the commandments that he gave us openly:[19] Since the day that the Lord brought our forefathers out of the land of Egypt, unto this present day, we have been disobedient unto the Lord our God, and we have been negligent in not hearing his voice.[20] Wherefore the evils cleaved unto us, and the curse, which the Lord appointed by Moses his servant at the time that he brought our fathers out of the land of Egypt, to give us a land that floweth with milk and honey, like as it is to see this day.[21] Nevertheless we have not hearkened unto the voice of the Lord our God, according unto all the words of the prophets, whom he sent unto us:[22] But every man followed the imagination of his own wicked heart, to serve strange gods, and to do evil in the sight of the Lord our God.

Bar.2

[1] Therefore the Lord hath made good his word, which he pronounced against us, and against our judges that judged Israel, and against our kings, and against our princes, and against the men of Israel and Juda,[2] To bring upon us great plagues, such as never happened under the whole heaven, as it came to pass in Jerusalem, according to the things that were written in the law of Moses;[3] That a man should eat the flesh of his own son, and the flesh of his own daughter.[4] Moreover he hath delivered them to be in subjection to all the kingdoms that are round about us, to be as a reproach and desolation among all the people round about, where the Lord hath scattered them.[5] Thus we were cast down, and not exalted, because we have sinned against the Lord our God, and have not been obedient unto his voice.[6] To the Lord our God appertaineth righteousness: but unto us and to our fathers open shame, as appeareth this day.[7] For all these plagues are come upon us, which the Lord hath pronounced against us[8] Yet have we not prayed before the Lord, that we might turn every one from the imaginations of his wicked heart.[9] Wherefore the Lord watched over us for evil, and the Lord hath brought it upon us: for the Lord is righteous in all his works which he hath commanded us.[10] Yet we have not hearkened unto his voice, to walk in the commandments of the Lord, that he hath set before us.[11] And now, O Lord God of Israel, that hast brought thy people out of the land of Egypt with a mighty hand, and high arm, and with signs, and with wonders, and with great power, and hast gotten thyself a name, as appeareth this day:[12] O Lord our God, we have sinned, we have done ungodly, we have dealt unrighteously in all thine ordinances.[13] Let thy wrath turn from us: for we are but a few left among the heathen, where thou hast scattered us.[14] Hear our prayers, O Lord, and our petitions, and deliver us for thine own sake, and give us favour in the sight of them which have led us away:[15] That all the earth may know that thou art the Lord our God, because Israel and his posterity is called by thy name.[16] O Lord, look down from thine holy house, and consider us:

bow down thine ear, O Lord, to hear us.[17] Open thine eyes, and behold; for the dead that are in the graves, whose souls are taken from their bodies, will give unto the Lord neither praise nor righteousness:[18] But the soul that is greatly vexed, which goeth stooping and feeble, and the eyes that fail, and the hungry soul, will give thee praise and righteousness, O Lord.[19] Therefore we do not make our humble supplication before thee, O Lord our God, for the righteousness of our fathers, and of our kings.[20] For thou hast sent out thy wrath and indignation upon us, as thou hast spoken by thy servants the prophets, saying,[21] Thus saith the Lord, Bow down your shoulders to serve the king of Babylon: so shall ye remain in the land that I gave unto your fathers.[22] But if ye will not hear the voice of the Lord, to serve the king of Babylon,[23] I will cause to cease out of the cites of Judah, and from without Jerusalem, the voice of mirth, and the voice of joy, the voice of the bridegroom, and the voice of the bride: and the whole land shall be desolate of inhabitants.[24] But we would not hearken unto thy voice, to serve the king of Babylon: therefore hast thou made good the words that thou spakest by thy servants the prophets, namely, that the bones of our kings, and the bones of our fathers, should be taken out of their place.[25] And, lo, they are cast out to the heat of the day, and to the frost of the night, and they died in great miseries by famine, by sword, and by pestilence.[26] And the house which is called by thy name hast thou laid waste, as it is to be seen this day, for the wickedness of the house of Israel and the house of Juda.[27] O Lord our God, thou hast dealt with us after all thy goodness, and according to all that great mercy of thine,[28] As thou spakest by thy servant Moses in the day when thou didst command him to write the law before the children of Israel, saying,[29] If ye will not hear my voice, surely this very great multitude shall be turned into a small number among the nations, where I will scatter them.[30] For I knew that they would not hear me, because it is a stiffnecked people: but in the land of their captivities they shall remember themselves.[31] And shall know that I am the Lord their God: for I will give them an heart, and ears to hear:[32] And they shall praise me in the land of their captivity, and think upon my name,[33] And return from their stiff neck, and from their wicked deeds: for they shall remember the way of their fathers, which sinned before the Lord.[34] And I will bring them again into the land which I promised with an oath unto their fathers, Abraham, Isaac, and Jacob, and they shall be lords of it: and I will increase them, and they shall not be diminished.[35] And I will make an everlasting covenant with them to be their God, and they shall be my people: and I will no more drive my people of Israel out of the land that I have given them.

Bar.3

[1] O Lord Almighty, God of Israel, the soul in anguish the troubled spirit, crieth unto thee.[2] Hear, O Lord, and have mercy; ar thou art merciful: and have pity upon us, because we have sinned before thee.[3] For thou endurest for ever, and we perish utterly.[4] O Lord Almighty, thou God of Israel, hear now the prayers of the dead Israelites, and of their children, which have sinned before thee, and not hearkened unto the voice of thee their God: for the which cause these plagues cleave unto us.[5] Remember not the iniquities of our forefathers: but think upon thy power and thy name now at this time.[6] For thou art the Lord our God, and thee, O Lord, will we praise.[7] And for this cause thou hast put thy fear in our hearts, to the intent that we should call upon thy name, and praise thee in our captivity: for we have called to mind all the iniquity of our forefathers, that sinned before thee.[8] Behold, we are yet this day in our captivity, where thou hast scattered us, for a reproach and a curse, and to be subject to payments, according to all the iniquities of our fathers, which departed from the Lord our God.[9] Hear, Israel,

the commandments of life: give ear to understand wisdom.[10] How happeneth it Israel, that thou art in thine enemies' land, that thou art waxen old in a strange country, that thou art defiled with the dead,[11] That thou art counted with them that go down into the grave?[12] Thou hast forsaken the fountain of wisdom.[13] For if thou hadst walked in the way of God, thou shouldest have dwelled in peace for ever.[14] Learn where is wisdom, where is strength, where is understanding; that thou mayest know also where is length of days, and life, where is the light of the eyes, and peace.[15] Who hath found out her place? or who hath come into her treasures ?[16] Where are the princes of the heathen become, and such as ruled the beasts upon the earth;[17] They that had their pastime with the fowls of the air, and they that hoarded up silver and gold, wherein men trust, and made no end of their getting?[18] For they that wrought in silver, and were so careful, and whose works are unsearchable,[19] They are vanished and gone down to the grave, and others are come up in their steads.[20] Young men have seen light, and dwelt upon the earth: but the way of knowledge have they not known,[21] Nor understood the paths thereof, nor laid hold of it: their children were far off from that way.[22] It hath not been heard of in Chanaan, neither hath it been seen in Theman.[23] The Agarenes that seek wisdom upon earth, the merchants of Meran and of Theman, the authors of fables, and searchers out of understanding; none of these have known the way of wisdom, or remember her paths.[24] O Israel, how great is the house of God! and how large is the place of his possession![25] Great, and hath none end; high, and unmeasurable.[26] There were the giants famous from the beginning, that were of so great stature, and so expert in war.[27] Those did not the Lord choose, neither gave he the way of knowledge unto them:[28] But they were destroyed, because they had no wisdom, and perished through their own foolishness.[29] Who hath gone up into heaven, and taken her, and brought her down from the clouds?[30] Who hath gone over the sea, and found her, and will bring her for pure gold?[31] No man knoweth her way, nor thinketh of her path.[32] But he that knoweth all things knoweth her, and hath found her out with his understanding: he that prepared the earth for evermore hath filled it with fourfooted beasts:[33] He that sendeth forth light, and it goeth, calleth it again, and it obeyeth him with fear.[34] The stars shined in their watches, and rejoiced: when he calleth them, they say, Here we be; and so with cheerfulness they shewed light unto him that made them.[35] This is our God, and there shall none other be accounted of in comparison of him[36] He hath found out all the way of knowledge, and hath given it unto Jacob his servant, and to Israel his beloved.[37] Afterward did he shew himself upon earth, and conversed with men.

Bar.4

[1] This is the book of the commandments of God, and the law that endureth for ever: all they that keep it shall come to life; but such as leave it shall die.[2] Turn thee, O Jacob, and take hold of it: walk in the presence of the light thereof, that thou mayest be illuminated.[3] Give not thine honour to another, nor the things that are profitable unto thee to a strange nation.[4] O Israel, happy are we: for things that are pleasing to God are made known unto us.[5] Be of good cheer, my people, the memorial of Israel.[6] Ye were sold to the nations, not for [your] destruction: but because ye moved God to wrath, ye were delivered unto the enemies.[7] For ye provoked him that made you by sacrificing unto devils, and not to God.[8] Ye have forgotten the everlasting God, that brought you up; and ye have grieved Jerusalem, that nursed you.[9] For when she saw the wrath of God coming upon you, she said, Hearken, O ye that dwell about Sion: God hath brought upon me great mourning;[10] For I saw the captivity of my sons and daughters, which the Everlasting brought upon them.[11] With joy did I nourish them; but sent them away with weeping and mourning.[12] Let no man rejoice over me, a widow, and forsaken of many, who for the sins of my children am left desolate; because they departed from the law of God.[13] They knew not his statutes, nor walked in the ways of his commandments, nor trod in the paths of discipline in his righteousness.[14] Let them that dwell about Sion come, and remember ye the captivity of my sons and daughters, which the Everlasting hath brought upon them.[15] For he hath brought a nation upon them from far, a shameless nation, and of a strange language, who neither reverenced old man, nor pitied child.[16] These have carried away the dear beloved children of the widow, and left her that was alone desolate without daughters.[17] But what can I help you?[18] For he that brought these plagues upon you will deliver you from the hands of your enemies.[19] Go your way, O my children, go your way: for I am left desolate.[20] I have put off the clothing of peace, and put upon me the sackcloth of my prayer: I will cry unto the Everlasting in my days.[21] Be of good cheer, O my children, cry unto the Lord, and he will deliver you from the power and hand of the enemies.[22] For my hope is in the Everlasting, that he will save you; and joy is come unto me from the Holy One, because of the mercy which shall soon come unto you from the Everlasting our Saviour.[23] For I sent you out with mourning and weeping: but God will give you to me again with joy and gladness for ever.[24] Like as now the neighbours of Sion have seen your captivity: so shall they see shortly your salvation from our God which shall come upon you with great glory, and brightness of the Everlasting.[25] My children, suffer patiently the wrath that is come upon you from God: for thine enemy hath persecuted thee; but shortly thou shalt see his destruction, and shalt tread upon his neck.[26] My delicate ones have gone rough ways, and were taken away as a flock caught of the enemies.[27] Be of good comfort, O my children, and cry unto God: for ye shall be remembered of him that brought these things upon you.[28] For as it was your mind to go astray from God: so, being returned, seek him ten times more.[29] For he that hath brought these plagues upon you shall bring you everlasting joy with your salvation.[30] Take a good heart, O Jerusalem: for he that gave thee that name will comfort thee.[31] Miserable are they that afflicted thee, and rejoiced at thy fall.[32] Miserable are the cities which thy children served: miserable is she that received thy sons.[33] For as she rejoiced at thy ruin, and was glad of thy fall: so shall she be grieved for her own desolation.[34] For I will take away the rejoicing of her great multitude, and her pride shall be turned into mourning.[35] For fire shall come upon her from the Everlasting, long to endure; and she shall be inhabited of devils for a great time.[36] O Jerusalem, look about thee toward the east, and behold the joy that cometh unto thee from God.[37] Lo, thy sons come, whom thou sentest away, they come gathered together from the east to the west by the word of the Holy One, rejoicing in the glory of God.

Bar.5

[1] Put off, O Jerusalem, the garment of mourning and affliction, and put on the comeliness of the glory that cometh from God for ever.[2] Cast about thee a double garment of the righteousness which cometh from God; and set a diadem on thine head of the glory of the Everlasting.[3] For God will shew thy brightness unto every country under heaven.[4] For thy name shall be called of God for ever The peace of righteousness, and The glory of God's worship.[5] Arise, O Jerusalem, and stand on high, and look about toward the east, and behold thy children gathered from the west unto the east by the word of the Holy One, rejoicing in the remembrance of God.[6] For they departed from thee on foot, and were led away of their enemies: but God bringeth them unto thee exalted with glory, as children of the kingdom.[7] For God hath appointed that every high hill, and

banks of long continuance, should be cast down, and valleys filled up, to make even the ground, that Israel may go safely in the glory of God,[8] Moreover even the woods and every sweetsmelling tree shall overshadow Israel by the commandment of God.[9] For God shall lead Israel with joy in the light of his glory with the mercy and righteousness that cometh from him.

Additions to the Book of Esther

AddEsth.1

[1] Then Mardocheus said, God hath done these things.[2] For I remember a dream which I saw concerning these matters, and nothing thereof hath failed.[3] A little fountain became a river, and there was light, and the sun, and much water: this river is Esther, whom the king married, and made queen:[4] And the two dragons are I and Aman.[5] And the nations were those that were assembled to destroy the name of the Jews:[6] And my nation is this Israel, which cried to God, and were saved: for the Lord hath saved his people, and the Lord hath delivered us from all those evils, and God hath wrought signs and great wonders, which have not been done among the Gentiles.[7] Therefore hath he made two lots, one for the people of God, and another for all the Gentiles.[8] And these two lots came at the hour, and time, and day of judgment, before God among all nations.[9] So God remembered his people, and justified his inheritance.[10] Therefore those days shall be unto them in the month Adar, the fourteenth and fifteenth day of the same month, with an assembly, and joy, and with gladness before God, according to the generations for ever among his people.

AddEsth.2

[1] In the fourth year of the reign of Ptolemeus and Cleopatra, Dositheus, who said he was a priest and Levite, and Ptolemeus his son, brought this epistle of Phurim, which they said was the same, and that Lysimachus the son of Ptolemeus, that was in Jerusalem, had interpreted it.[2] In the second year of the reign of Artexerxes the great, in the first day of the month Nisan, Mardocheus the son of Jairus, the son of Semei, the son of Cisai, of the tribe of Benjamin, had a dream;[3] Who was a Jew, and dwelt in the city of Susa, a great man, being a servitor in the king's court.[4] He was also one of the captives, which Nabuchodonosor the king of Babylon carried from Jerusalem with Jechonias king of Judea; and this was his dream:[5] Behold a noise of a tumult, with thunder, and earthquakes, and uproar in the land:[6] And, behold, two great dragons came forth ready to fight, and their cry was great.[7] And at their cry all nations were prepared to battle, that they might fight against the righteous people.[8] And lo a day of darkness and obscurity, tribulation and anguish, affliction and great uproar, upon earth.[9] And the whole righteous nation was troubled, fearing their own evils, and were ready to perish.[10] Then they cried unto God, and upon their cry, as it were from a little fountain, was made a great flood, even much water.[11] The light and the sun rose up, and the lowly were exalted, and devoured the glorious.[12] Now when Mardocheus, who had seen this dream, and what God had determined to do, was awake, he bare this dream in mind, and until night by all means was desirous to know it.

AddEsth.3

[1] And Mardocheus took his rest in the court with Gabatha and Tharra, the two eunuchs of the king, and keepers of the palace.[2] And he heard their devices, and searched out their purposes, and learned that they were about to lay hands upon Artexerxes the king; and so he certified the king of them.[3] Then the king examined the two eunuchs, and after that they had confessed it, they were strangled.[4] And the king made a record of these things, and Mardocheus also wrote thereof.[5] So the king commanded,

Mardocheus to serve in the court, and for this he rewarded him.[6] Howbeit Aman the son of Amadathus the Agagite, who was in great honour with the king, sought to molest Mardocheus and his people because of the two eunuchs of the king.

AddEsth.4

[1] The copy of the letters was this: The great king Artexerxes writeth these things to the princes and governours that are under him from India unto Ethiopia in an hundred and seven and twenty provinces.[2] After that I became lord over many nations and had dominion over the whole world, not lifted up with presumption of my authority, but carrying myself always with equity and mildness, I purposed to settle my subjects continually in a quiet life, and making my kingdom peaceable, and open for passage to the utmost coasts, to renew peace, which is desired of all men.[3] Now when I asked my counsellors how this might be brought to pass, Aman, that excelled in wisdom among us, and was approved for his constant good will and steadfast fidelity, and had the honour of the second place in the kingdom,[4] Declared unto us, that in all nations throughout the world there was scattered a certain malicious people, that had laws contrary to ail nations, and continually despised the commandments of kings, so as the uniting of our kingdoms, honourably intended by us cannot go forward.[5] Seeing then we understand that this people alone is continually in opposition unto all men, differing in the strange manner of their laws, and evil affected to our state, working all the mischief they can that our kingdom may not be firmly established:[6] Therefore have we commanded, that all they that are signified in writing unto you by Aman, who is ordained over the affairs, and is next unto us, shall all, with their wives and children, be utterly destroyed by the sword of their enemies, without all mercy and pity, the fourteenth day of the twelfth month Adar of this present year:[7] That they, who of old and now also are malicious, may in one day with violence go into the grave, and so ever hereafter cause our affairs to be well settled, and without trouble.[8] Then Mardocheus thought upon all the works of the Lord, and made his prayer unto him,[9] Saying, O Lord, Lord, the King Almighty: for the whole world is in thy power, and if thou hast appointed to save Israel, there is no man that can gainsay thee:[10] For thou hast made heaven and earth, and all the wondrous things under the heaven.[11] Thou art Lord of all things, and and there is no man that can resist thee, which art the Lord.[12] Thou knowest all things, and thou knowest, Lord, that it was neither in contempt nor pride, nor for any desire of glory, that I did not bow down to proud Aman.[13] For I could have been content with good will for the salvation of Israel to kiss the soles of his feet.[14] But I did this, that I might not prefer the glory of man above the glory of God: neither will I worship any but thee, O God, neither will I do it in pride.[15] And now, O Lord God and King, spare thy people: for their eyes are upon us to bring us to nought; yea, they desire to destroy the inheritance, that hath been thine from the beginning.[16] Despise not the portion, which thou hast delivered out of Egypt for thine own self.[17] Hear my prayer, and be merciful unto thine inheritance: turn our sorrow into joy, that we may live, O Lord, and praise thy name: and destroy not the mouths of them that praise thee, O Lord.[18] All Israel in like manner cried most earnestly unto the Lord, because their death was before their eyes.

AddEsth.5

[1] Queen Esther also, being in fear of death, resorted unto the Lord:[2] And laid away her glorious apparel, and put on the garments of anguish and mourning: and instead of precious ointments, she covered her head with ashes and dung, and she humbled her body greatly, and all the places of her joy she filled with her torn hair.[3] And she prayed unto the Lord God of Israel, saying, O my Lord, thou

only art our King: help me, desolate woman, which have no helper but thee:[4] For my danger is in mine hand.[5] From my youth up I have heard in the tribe of my family that thou, O Lord, tookest Israel from among all people, and our fathers from all their predecessors, for a perpetual inheritance, and thou hast performed whatsoever thou didst promise them.[6] And now we have sinned before thee: therefore hast thou given us into the hands of our enemies,[7] Because we worshipped their gods: O Lord, thou art righteous.[8] Nevertheless it satisfieth them not, that we are in bitter captivity: but they have stricken hands with their idols,[9] That they will abolish the thing that thou with thy mouth hast ordained, and destroy thine inheritance, and stop the mouth of them that praise thee, and quench the glory of thy house, and of thine altar,[10] And open the mouths of the heathen to set forth the praises of the idols, and to magnify a fleshly king for ever.[11] O Lord, give not thy sceptre unto them that be nothing, and let them not laugh at our fall; but turn their device upon themselves, and make him an example, that hath begun this against us.[12] Remember, O Lord, make thyself known in time of our affliction, and give me boldness, O King of the nations, and Lord of all power.[13] Give me eloquent speech in my mouth before the lion: turn his heart to hate him that fighteth against us, that there may be an end of him, and of all that are likeminded to him:[14] But deliver us with thine hand, and help me that am desolate, and which have no other help but thee.[15] Thou knowest all things, O Lord; thou knowest that I hate the glory of the unrighteous, and abhor the bed of the uncircumcised, and of all the heathen.[16] Thou knowest my necessity: for I abhor the sign of my high estate, which is upon mine head in the days wherein I shew myself, and that I abhor it as a menstruous rag, and that I wear it not when I am private by myself.[17] And that thine handmaid hath not eaten at Aman's table, and that I have not greatly esteemed the king's feast, nor drunk the wine of the drink offerings.[18] Neither had thine handmaid any joy since the day that I was brought hither to this present, but in thee, O Lord God of Abraham.[19] O thou mighty God above all, hear the voice of the forlorn and deliver us out of the hands of the mischievous, and deliver me out of my fear.

AddEsth.6

[1] And upon the third day, when she had ended her prayers, she laid away her mourning garments, and put on her glorious apparel.[2] And being gloriously adorned, after she had called upon God, who is the beholder and saviour of all things, she took two maids with her:[3] And upon the one she leaned, as carrying herself daintily;[4] And the other followed, bearing up her train.[5] And she was ruddy through the perfection of her beauty, and her countenance was cheerful and very amiable: but her heart was in anguish for fear.[6] Then having passed through all the doors, she stood before the king, who sat upon his royal throne, and was clothed with all his robes of majesty, all glittering with gold and precious stones; and he was very dreadful.[7] Then lifting up his countenance that shone with majesty, he looked very fiercely upon her: and the queen fell down, and was pale, and fainted, and bowed herself upon the head of the maid that went before her.[8] Then God changed the spirit of the king into mildness, who in a fear leaped from his throne, and took her in his arms, till she came to herself again, and comforted her with loving words and said unto her,[9] Esther, what is the matter? I am thy brother, be of good cheer:[10] Thou shalt not die, though our our commandment be general: come near.[11] And so he held up his golden sceptre, and laid it upon her neck,[12] And embraced her, and said, Speak unto me.[13] Then said she unto him, I saw thee, my lord, as an angel of God, and my heart was troubled for fear of thy majesty.[14] For wonderful art thou, lord, and thy countenance is full of grace.[15] And as she was speaking, she fell down for

47

faintness.[16] Then the king was troubled, and all his servants comforted her.

AddEsth.7

[1] The great king Artexerxes unto the princes and governors of an hundred and seven and twenty provinces from India unto Ethiopia, and unto all our faithful subjects, greeting.[2] Many, the more often they are honoured with the great bounty of their gracious princes, the more proud they are waxen,[3] And endeavour to hurt not our subjects only, but not being able to bear abundance, do take in hand to practise also against those that do them good:[4] And take not only thankfulness away from among men, but also lifted up with the glorious words of lewd persons, that were never good, they think to escape the justice of God, that seeth all things and hateth evil.[5] Oftentimes also fair speech of those, that are put in trust to manage their friends' affairs, hath caused many that are in authority to be partakers of innocent blood, and hath enwrapped them in remediless calamities:[6] Beguiling with the falsehood and deceit of their lewd disposition the innocency and goodness of princes.[7] Now ye may see this, as we have declared, not so much by ancient histories, as ye may, if ye search what hath been wickedly done of late through the pestilent behaviour of them that are unworthily placed in authority.[8] And we must take care for the time to come, that our kingdom may be quiet and peaceable for all men,[9] Both by changing our purposes, and always judging things that are evident with more equal proceeding.[10] For Aman, a Macedonian, the son of Amadatha, being indeed a stranger from the Persian blood, and far distant from our goodness, and as a stranger received of us,[11] Had so far forth obtained the favour that we shew toward every nation, as that he was called our father, and was continually honoured of all the next person unto the king.[12] But he, not bearing his great dignity, went about to deprive us of our kingdom and life:[13] Having by manifold and cunning deceits sought of us the destruction, as well of Mardocheus, who saved our life, and continually procured our good, as also of blameless Esther, partaker of our kingdom, with their whole nation.[14] For by these means he thought, finding us destitute of friends to have translated the kingdom of the Persians to the Macedonians.[15] But we find that the Jews, whom this wicked wretch hath delivered to utter destruction, are no evildoers, but live by most just laws:[16] And that they be children of the most high and most mighty, living God, who hath ordered the kingdom both unto us and to our progenitors in the most excellent manner.[17] Wherefore ye shall do well not to put in execution the letters sent unto you by Aman the son of Amadatha.[18] For he that was the worker of these things, is hanged at the gates of Susa with all his family: God, who ruleth all things, speedily rendering vengeance to him according to his deserts.[19] Therefore ye shall publish the copy of this letter in all places, that the Jews may freely live after their own laws.[20] And ye shall aid them, that even the same day, being the thirteenth day of the twelfth month Adar, they may be avenged on them, who in the time of their affliction shall set upon them.[21] For Almighty God hath turned to joy unto them the day, wherein the chosen people should have perished.[22] Ye shall therefore among your solemn feasts keep it an high day with all feasting:[23] That both now and hereafter there may be safety to us and the well affected Persians; but to those which do conspire against us a memorial of destruction.[24] Therefore every city and country whatsoever, which shall not do according to these things, shall be destroyed without mercy with fire and sword, and shall be made not only unpassable for men, but also most hateful to wild beasts and fowls for ever.

Prayer of Azariah and Song of the Three Holy Children

¹ And they walked in the midst of the fire, praising God, and blessing the Lord.² Then Azarias stood up, and prayed on this manner; and opening his mouth in the midst of the fire said,³ Blessed art thou, O Lord God of our fathers: thy name is worthy to be praised and glorified for evermore:⁴ For thou art righteous in all the things that thou hast done to us: yea, true are all thy works, thy ways are right, and all thy judgments truth.⁵ In all the things that thou hast brought upon us, and upon the holy city of our fathers, even Jerusalem, thou hast executed true judgment: for according to truth and judgment didst thou bring all these things upon us because of our sins.⁶ For we have sinned and committed iniquity, departing from thee.⁷ In all things have we trespassed, and not obeyed thy commandments, nor kept them, neither done as thou hast commanded us, that it might go well with us.⁸ Wherefore all that thou hast brought upon us, and every thing that thou hast done to us, thou hast done in true judgment.⁹ And thou didst deliver us into the hands of lawless enemies, most hateful forsakers of God, and to an unjust king, and the most wicked in all the world.¹⁰ And now we cannot open our mouths, we are become a shame and reproach to thy servants; and to them that worship thee.¹¹ Yet deliver us not up wholly, for thy name's sake, neither disannul thou thy covenant:¹² And cause not thy mercy to depart from us, for thy beloved Abraham's sake, for thy servant Issac's sake, and for thy holy Israel's sake;¹³ To whom thou hast spoken and promised, that thou wouldest multiply their seed as the stars of heaven, and as the sand that lieth upon the seashore.¹⁴ For we, O Lord, are become less than any nation, and be kept under this day in all the world because of our sins.¹⁵ Neither is there at this time prince, or prophet, or leader, or burnt offering, or sacrifice, or oblation, or incense, or place to sacrifice before thee, and to find mercy.¹⁶ Nevertheless in a contrite heart and an humble spirit let us be accepted.¹⁷ Like as in the burnt offerings of rams and bullocks, and like as in ten thousands of fat lambs: so let our sacrifice be in thy sight this day, and grant that we may wholly go after thee: for they shall not be confounded that put their trust in thee.¹⁸ And now we follow thee with all our heart, we fear thee, and seek thy face.¹⁹ Put us not to shame: but deal with us after thy lovingkindness, and according to the multitude of thy mercies.²⁰ Deliver us also according to thy marvellous works, and give glory to thy name, O Lord: and let all them that do thy servants hurt be ashamed;²¹ And let them be confounded in all their power and might, and let their strength be broken;²² And let them know that thou art God, the only God, and glorious over the whole world.²³ And the king's servants, that put them in, ceased not to make the oven hot with rosin, pitch, tow, and small wood;²⁴ So that the flame streamed forth above the furnace forty and nine cubits.²⁵ And it passed through, and burned those Chaldeans it found about the furnace.²⁶ But the angel of the Lord came down into the oven together with Azarias and his fellows, and smote the flame of the fire out of the oven;²⁷ And made the midst of the furnace as it had been a moist whistling wind, so that the fire touched them not at all, neither hurt nor troubled them.²⁸ Then the three, as out of one mouth, praised, glorified, and blessed, God in the furnace, saying,²⁹ Blessed art thou, O Lord God of our fathers: and to be praised and exalted above all for ever.³⁰ And blessed is thy glorious and holy name: and to be praised and exalted above all for ever.³¹ Blessed art thou in the temple of thine holy glory: and to be praised and glorified above all for ever.³² Blessed art thou that beholdest the depths, and sittest upon the cherubims: and to be praised and exalted above all for ever.³³ Blessed art thou on the glorious throne of thy kingdom: and to be praised and glorified above all for ever.³⁴ Blessed art thou in the firmament of heaven: and above ail to be praised and glorified for ever.³⁵ O all ye works of the Lord, bless ye the Lord : praise and exalt him above all for ever,³⁶ O ye heavens, bless ye the Lord : praise and exalt him above all for ever.³⁷ O ye angels of the Lord, bless ye the Lord: praise and exalt him above all for ever.³⁸ O all ye waters that be above the heaven, bless ye the Lord: praise and exalt him above all for ever.³⁹ O all ye powers of the Lord, bless ye the Lord: praise and exalt him above all for ever.⁴⁰ O ye sun and moon, bless ye the Lord: praise and exalt him above all for ever.⁴¹ O ye stars of heaven, bless ye the Lord: praise and exalt him above all for ever.⁴² O every shower and dew, bless ye the Lord: praise and exalt him above all for ever.⁴³ O all ye winds, bless ye the Lord: praise and exalt him above all for ever,⁴⁴ O ye fire and heat, bless ye the Lord: praise and exalt him above all for ever.⁴⁵ O ye winter and summer, bless ye the Lord: praise and exalt him above all for ever.⁴⁶ 0 ye dews and storms of snow, bless ye the Lord: praise and exalt him above all for ever.⁴⁷ O ye nights and days, bless ye the Lord: bless and exalt him above all for ever.⁴⁸ O ye light and darkness, bless ye the Lord: praise and exalt him above all for ever.⁴⁹ O ye ice and cold, bless ye the Lord: praise and exalt him above all for ever.⁵⁰ O ye frost and snow, bless ye the Lord: praise and exalt him above all for ever.⁵¹ O ye lightnings and clouds, bless ye the Lord: praise and exalt him above all for ever.⁵² O let the earth bless the Lord: praise and exalt him above all for ever.⁵³ O ye mountains and little hills, bless ye the Lord: praise and exalt him above all for ever.⁵⁴ O all ye things that grow in the earth, bless ye the Lord: praise and exalt him above all for ever.⁵⁵ O ye mountains, bless ye the Lord: Praise and exalt him above all for ever.⁵⁶ O ye seas and rivers, bless ye the Lord: praise and exalt him above all for ever.⁵⁷ O ye whales, and all that move in the waters, bless ye the Lord: praise and exalt him above all for ever.⁵⁸ O all ye fowls of the air, bless ye the Lord: praise and exalt him above all for ever.⁵⁹ O all ye beasts and cattle, bless ye the Lord: praise and exalt him above all for ever.⁶⁰ O ye children of men, bless ye the Lord: praise and exalt him above all for ever.⁶¹ O Israel, bless ye the Lord: praise and exalt him above all for ever.⁶² O ye priests of the Lord, bless ye the Lord: praise and exalt him above all for ever.⁶³ O ye servants of the Lord, bless ye the Lord: praise and exalt him above all for ever.⁶⁴ O ye spirits and souls of the righteous, bless ye the Lord: praise and exalt him above all for ever.⁶⁵ O ye holy and humble men of heart, bless ye the Lord: praise and exalt him above all for ever.⁶⁶ O Ananias, Azarias, and Misael, bless ye the Lord: praise and exalt him above all for ever: far he hath delivered us from hell, and saved us from the hand of death, and delivered us out of the midst of the furnace and burning flame: even out of the midst of the fire hath he delivered us.⁶⁷ O give thanks unto the Lord, because he is gracious: for his mercy endureth for ever.⁶⁸ O all ye that worship the Lord, bless the God of gods, praise him, and give him thanks: for his mercy endureth for ever.

Susanna

¹ There dwelt a man in Babylon, called Joacim:² And he took a wife, whose name was Susanna, the daughter of Chelcias, a very fair woman, and one that feared the Lord.³ Her parents also were righteous, and taught their daughter according to the law of Moses.⁴ Now Joacim was a great rich man, and had a fair garden joining unto his house: and to him resorted the Jews; because he was more honourable than all others.⁵ The same year were appointed two of the ancients of the people to be judges, such as the Lord spake of, that wickedness came from Babylon from ancient judges, who seemed to govern the people.⁶ These kept much at Joacim's house: and all that had any suits in law came unto them.⁷ Now when the people departed away at noon, Susanna went into her husband's garden to walk.⁸ And the two elders saw her going in every day, and walking; so that their lust was inflamed toward her.⁹ And they

perverted their own mind, and turned away their eyes, that they might not look unto heaven, nor remember just judgments.[10] And albeit they both were wounded with her love, yet durst not one shew another his grief.[11] For they were ashamed to declare their lust, that they desired to have to do with her.[12] Yet they watched diligently from day to day to see her.[13] And the one said to the other, Let us now go home: for it is dinner time.[14] So when they were gone out, they parted the one from the other, and turning back again they came to the same place; and after that they had asked one another the cause, they acknowledged their lust: then appointed they a time both together, when they might find her alone.[15] And it fell out, as they watched a fit time, she went in as before with two maids only, and she was desirous to wash herself in the garden: for it was hot.[16] And there was no body there save the two elders, that had hid themselves, and watched her.[17] Then she said to her maids, Bring me oil and washing balls, and shut the garden doors, that I may wash me.[18] And they did as she bade them, and shut the garden doors, and went out themselves at privy doors to fetch the things that she had commanded them: but they saw not the elders, because they were hid.[19] Now when the maids were gone forth, the two elders rose up, and ran unto her, saying,[20] Behold, the garden doors are shut, that no man can see us, and we are in love with thee; therefore consent unto us, and lie with us.[21] If thou wilt not, we will bear witness against thee, that a young man was with thee: and therefore thou didst send away thy maids from thee.[22] Then Susanna sighed, and said, I am straitened on every side: for if I do this thing, it is death unto me: and if I do it not I cannot escape your hands.[23] It is better for me to fall into your hands, and not do it, than to sin in the sight of the Lord.[24] With that Susanna cried with a loud voice: and the two elders cried out against her.[25] Then ran the one, and opened the garden door.[26] So when the servants of the house heard the cry in the garden, they rushed in at the privy door, to see what was done unto her.[27] But when the elders had declared their matter, the servants were greatly ashamed: for there was never such a report made of Susanna.[28] And it came to pass the next day, when the people were assembled to her husband Joacim, the two elders came also full of mischievous imagination against Susanna to put her to death;[29] And said before the people, Send for Susanna, the daughter of Chelcias, Joacim's wife. And so they sent.[30] So she came with her father and mother, her children, and all her kindred.[31] Now Susanna was a very delicate woman, and beauteous to behold.[32] And these wicked men commanded to uncover her face, (for she was covered) that they might be filled with her beauty.[33] Therefore her friends and all that saw her wept.[34] Then the two elders stood up in the midst of the people, and laid their hands upon her head.[35] And she weeping looked up toward heaven: for her heart trusted in the Lord.[36] And the elders said, As we walked in the garden alone, this woman came in with two maids, and shut the garden doors, and sent the maids away.[37] Then a young man, who there was hid, came unto her, and lay with her.[38] Then we that stood in a corner of the garden, seeing this wickedness, ran unto them.[39] And when we saw them together, the man we could not hold: for he was stronger than we, and opened the door, and leaped out.[40] But having taken this woman, we asked who the young man was, but she would not tell us: these things do we testify.[41] Then the assembly believed them as those that were the elders and judges of the people: so they condemned her to death.[42] Then Susanna cried out with a loud voice, and said, O everlasting God, that knowest the secrets, and knowest all things before they be:[43] Thou knowest that they have borne false witness against me, and, behold, I must die; whereas I never did such things as these men have maliciously invented against me.[44] And the Lord heard her voice.[45] Therefore when she was led to be put to death,

49

the Lord raised up the holy spirit of a young youth whose name was Daniel:[46] Who cried with a loud voice, I am clear from the blood of this woman.[47] Then all the people turned them toward him, and said, What mean these words that thou hast spoken?[48] So he standing in the midst of them said, Are ye such fools, ye sons of Israel, that without examination or knowledge of the truth ye have condemned a daughter of Israel?[49] Return again to the place of judgment: for they have borne false witness against her.[50] Wherefore all the people turned again in haste, and the elders said unto him, Come, sit down among us, and shew it us, seeing God hath given thee the honour of an elder.[51] Then said Daniel unto them, Put these two aside one far from another, and I will examine them.[52] So when they were put asunder one from another, he called one of them, and said unto him, O thou that art waxen old in wickedness, now thy sins which thou hast committed aforetime are come to light.[53] For thou hast pronounced false judgment and hast condemned the innocent and hast let the guilty go free; albeit the Lord saith, The innocent and righteous shalt thou not slay.[54] Now then, if thou hast seen her, tell me, Under what tree sawest thou them companying together? Who answered, Under a mastick tree.[55] And Daniel said, Very well; thou hast lied against thine own head; for even now the angel of God hath received the sentence of God to cut thee in two.[56] So he put him aside, and commanded to bring the other, and said unto him, O thou seed of Chanaan, and not of Juda, beauty hath deceived thee, and lust hath perverted thine heart.[57] Thus have ye dealt with the daughters of Israel, and they for fear companied with you: but the daughter of Juda would not abide your wickedness.[58] Now therefore tell me, Under what tree didst thou take them companying together? Who answered, Under an holm tree.[59] Then said Daniel unto him, Well; thou hast also lied against thine own head: for the angel of God waiteth with the sword to cut thee in two, that he may destroy you.[60] With that all the assembly cried out with a loud voice, and praised God, who saveth them that trust in him.[61] And they arose against the two elders, for Daniel had convicted them of false witness by their own mouth:[62] And according to the law of Moses they did unto them in such sort as they maliciously intended to do to their neighbour: and they put them to death. Thus the innocent blood was saved the same day.[63] Therefore Chelcias and his wife praised God for their daughter Susanna, with Joacim her husband, and all the kindred, because there was no dishonesty found in her.[64] From that day forth was Daniel had in great reputation in the sight of the people.

Bel and the Dragon

[1] And king Astyages was gathered to his fathers, and Cyrus of Persia received his kingdom.[2] And Daniel conversed with the king, and was honoured above all his friends.[3] Now the Babylons had an idol, called Bel, and there were spent upon him every day twelve great measures of fine flour, and forty sheep, and six vessels of wine.[4] And the king worshipped it and went daily to adore it: but Daniel worshipped his own God. And the king said unto him, Why dost not thou worship Bel?[5] Who answered and said, Because I may not worship idols made with hands, but the living God, who hath created the heaven and the earth, and hath sovereignty over all flesh.[6] Then said the king unto him, Thinkest thou not that Bel is a living God? seest thou not how much he eateth and drinketh every day?[7] Then Daniel smiled, and said, O king, be not deceived: for this is but clay within, and brass without, and did never eat or drink any thing.[8] So the king was wroth, and called for his priests, and said unto them, If ye tell me not who this is that devoureth these expences, ye shall die.[9] But if ye can certify me that Bel devoureth them, then Daniel shall die: for he hath spoken blasphemy against

Bel. And Daniel said unto the king, Let it be according to thy word.¹⁰ Now the priests of Bel were threescore and ten, beside their wives and children. And the king went with Daniel into the temple of Bel.¹¹ So Bel's priests said, Lo, we go out: but thou, O king, set on the meat, and make ready the wine, and shut the door fast and seal it with thine own signet;¹² And to morrow when thou comest in, if thou findest not that Bel hath eaten up all, we will suffer death: or else Daniel, that speaketh falsely against us.¹³ And they little regarded it: for under the table they had made a privy entrance, whereby they entered in continually, and consumed those things.¹⁴ So when they were gone forth, the king set meats before Bel. Now Daniel had commanded his servants to bring ashes, and those they strewed throughout all the temple in the presence of the king alone: then went they out, and shut the door, and sealed it with the king's signet, and so departed.¹⁵ Now in the night came the priests with their wives and children, as they were wont to do, and did eat and drinck up all.¹⁶ In the morning betime the king arose, and Daniel with him.¹⁷ And the king said, Daniel, are the seals whole? And he said, Yea, O king, they be whole.¹⁸ And as soon as he had opened the dour, the king looked upon the table, and cried with a loud voice, Great art thou, O Bel, and with thee is no deceit at all.¹⁹ Then laughed Daniel, and held the king that he should not go in, and said, Behold now the pavement, and mark well whose footsteps are these.²⁰ And the king said, I see the footsteps of men, women, and children. And then the king was angry,²¹ And took the priests with their wives and children, who shewed him the privy doors, where they came in, and consumed such things as were upon the table.²² Therefore the king slew them, and delivered Bel into Daniel's power, who destroyed him and his temple.²³ And in that same place there was a great dragon, which they of Babylon worshipped.²⁴ And the king said unto Daniel, Wilt thou also say that this is of brass? lo, he liveth, he eateth and drinketh; thou canst not say that he is no living god: therefore worship him.²⁵ Then said Daniel unto the king, I will worship the Lord my God: for he is the living God.²⁶ But give me leave, O king, and I shall slay this dragon without sword or staff. The king said, I give thee leave.²⁷ Then Daniel took pitch, and fat, and hair, and did seethe them together, and made lumps thereof: this he put in the dragon's mouth, and so the dragon burst in sunder : and Daniel said, Lo, these are the gods ye worship.²⁸ When they of Babylon heard that, they took great indignation, and conspired against the king, saying, The king is become a Jew, and he hath destroyed Bel, he hath slain the dragon, and put the priests to death.²⁹ So they came to the king, and said, Deliver us Daniel, or else we will destroy thee and thine house.³⁰ Now when the king saw that they pressed him sore, being constrained, he delivered Daniel unto them:³¹ Who cast him into the lions' den: where he was six days.³² And in the den there were seven lions, and they had given them every day two carcases, and two sheep: which then were not given to them, to the intent they might devour Daniel.³³ Now there was in Jewry a prophet, called Habbacuc, who had made pottage, and had broken bread in a bowl, and was going into the field, for to bring it to the reapers.³⁴ But the angel of the Lord said unto Habbacuc, Go, carry the dinner that thou hast into Babylon unto Daniel, who is in the lions' den.³⁵ And Habbacuc said, Lord, I never saw Babylon; neither do I know where the den is.³⁶ Then the angel of the Lord took him by the crown, and bare him by the hair of his head, and through the vehemency of his spirit set him in Babylon over the den.³⁷ And Habbacuc cried, saying, O Daniel, Daniel, take the dinner which God hath sent thee.³⁸ And Daniel said, Thou hast remembered me, O God: neither hast thou forsaken them that seek thee and love thee.³⁹ So Daniel arose, and did eat: and the angel of the Lord set Habbacuc in his

own place again immediately.⁴⁰ Upon the seventh day the king went to bewail Daniel: and when he came to the den, he looked in, and behold, Daniel was sitting.⁴¹ Then cried the king with a loud voice, saying, Great art Lord God of Daniel, and there is none other beside thee.⁴² And he drew him out, and cast those that were the cause of his destruction into the den: and they were devoured in a moment before his face.

1 Maccabees

1Mac.1

¹ And it happened, after that Alexander son of Philip, the Macedonian, who came out of the land of Chettiim, had smitten Darius king of the Persians and Medes, that he reigned in his stead, the first over Greece,² And made many wars, and won many strong holds, and slew the kings of the earth,³ And went through to the ends of the earth, and took spoils of many nations, insomuch that the earth was quiet before him; whereupon he was exalted and his heart was lifted up.⁴ And he gathered a mighty strong host and ruled over countries, and nations, and kings, who became tributaries unto him.⁵ And after these things he fell sick, and perceived that he should die.⁶ Wherefore he called his servants, such as were honourable, and had been brought up with him from his youth, and parted his kingdom among them, while he was yet alive.⁷ So Alexander reigned twelves years, and then died.⁸ And his servants bare rule every one in his place.⁹ And after his death they all put crowns upon themselves; so did their sons after them many years: and evils were multiplied in the earth.¹⁰ And there came out of them a wicked root Antiochus surnamed Epiphanes, son of Antiochus the king, who had been an hostage at Rome, and he reigned in the hundred and thirty and seventh year of the kingdom of the Greeks.¹¹ In those days went there out of Israel wicked men, who persuaded many, saying, Let us go and make a covenant with the heathen that are round about us: for since we departed from them we have had much sorrow.¹² So this device pleased them well.¹³ Then certain of the people were so forward herein, that they went to the king, who gave them licence to do after the ordinances of the heathen:¹⁴ Whereupon they built a place of exercise at Jerusalem according to the customs of the heathen:¹⁵ And made themselves uncircumcised, and forsook the holy covenant, and joined themselves to the heathen, and were sold to do mischief.¹⁶ Now when the kingdom was established before Antiochus, he thought to reign over Egypt that he might have the dominion of two realms.¹⁷ Wherefore he entered into Egypt with a great multitude, with chariots, and elephants, and horsemen, and a great navy,¹⁸ And made war against Ptolemee king of Egypt: but Ptolemee was afraid of him, and fled; and many were wounded to death.¹⁹ Thus they got the strong cities in the land of Egypt and he took the spoils thereof.²⁰ And after that Antiochus had smitten Egypt, he returned again in the hundred forty and third year, and went up against Israel and Jerusalem with a great multitude,²¹ And entered proudly into the sanctuary, and took away the golden altar, and the candlestick of light, and all the vessels thereof,²² And the table of the shewbread, and the pouring vessels, and the vials. and the censers of gold, and the veil, and the crown, and the golden ornaments that were before the temple, all which he pulled off.²³ He took also the silver and the gold, and the precious vessels: also he took the hidden treasures which he found.²⁴ And when he had taken all away, he went into his own land, having made a great massacre, and spoken very proudly.²⁵ Therefore there was a great mourning in Israel, in every place where they were;²⁶ So that the princes and elders mourned, the virgins and young men were made feeble, and the beauty of women was changed.²⁷ Every bridegroom took up

lamentation, and she that sat in the marriage chamber was in heaviness,²⁸ The land also was moved for the inhabitants thereof, and all the house of Jacob was covered with confusion.²⁹ And after two years fully expired the king sent his chief collector of tribute unto the cities of Juda, who came unto Jerusalem with a great multitude,³⁰ And spake peaceable words unto them, but all was deceit: for when they had given him credence, he fell suddenly upon the city, and smote it very sore, and destroyed much people of Israel.³¹ And when he had taken the spoils of the city, he set it on fire, and pulled down the houses and walls thereof on every side.³² But the women and children took they captive, and possessed the cattle.³³ Then builded they the city of David with a great and strong wall, and with mighty towers, and made it a strong hold for them.³⁴ And they put therein a sinful nation, wicked men, and fortified themselves therein.³⁵ They stored it also with armour and victuals, and when they had gathered together the spoils of Jerusalem, they laid them up there, and so they became a sore snare:³⁶ For it was a place to lie in wait against the sanctuary, and an evil adversary to Israel.³⁷ Thus they shed innocent blood on every side of the sanctuary, and defiled it:³⁸ Insomuch that the inhabitants of Jerusalem fled because of them: whereupon the city was made an habitation of strangers, and became strange to those that were born in her; and her own children left her.³⁹ Her sanctuary was laid waste like a wilderness, her feasts were turned into mourning, her sabbaths into reproach her honour into contempt.⁴⁰ As had been her glory, so was her dishonour increased, and her excellency was turned into mourning.⁴¹ Moreover king Antiochus wrote to his whole kingdom, that all should be one people,⁴² And every one should leave his laws: so all the heathen agreed according to the commandment of the king.⁴³ Yea, many also of the Israelites consented to his religion, and sacrificed unto idols, and profaned the sabbath.⁴⁴ For the king had sent letters by messengers unto Jerusalem and the cities of Juda that they should follow the strange laws of the land,⁴⁵ And forbid burnt offerings, and sacrifice, and drink offerings, in the temple; and that they should profane the sabbaths and festival days:⁴⁶ And pollute the sanctuary and holy people:⁴⁷ Set up altars, and groves, and chapels of idols, and sacrifice swine's flesh, and unclean beasts:⁴⁸ That they should also leave their children uncircumcised, and make their souls abominable with all manner of uncleanness and profanation:⁴⁹ To the end they might forget the law, and change all the ordinances.⁵⁰ And whosoever would not do according to the commandment of the king, he said, he should die.⁵¹ In the selfsame manner wrote he to his whole kingdom, and appointed overseers over all the people, commanding the cities of Juda to sacrifice, city by city.⁵² Then many of the people were gathered unto them, to wit every one that forsook the law; and so they committed evils in the land;⁵³ And drove the Israelites into secret places, even wheresoever they could flee for succour.⁵⁴ Now the fifteenth day of the month Casleu, in the hundred forty and fifth year, they set up the abomination of desolation upon the altar, and builded idol altars throughout the cities of Juda on every side;⁵⁵ And burnt incense at the doors of their houses, and in the streets.⁵⁶ And when they had rent in pieces the books of the law which they found, they burnt them with fire.⁵⁷ And whosoever was found with any the book of the testament, or if any committed to the law, the king's commandment was, that they should put him to death.⁵⁸ Thus did they by their authority unto the Israelites every month, to as many as were found in the cities.⁵⁹ Now the five and twentieth day of the month they did sacrifice upon the idol altar, which was upon the altar of God.⁶⁰ At which time according to the commandment they put to death certain women, that had caused their children to be circumcised.⁶¹ And they hanged the infants about their necks, and

rifled their houses, and slew them that had circumcised them.⁶² Howbeit many in Israel were fully resolved and confirmed in themselves not to eat any unclean thing.⁶³ Wherefore the rather to die, that they might not be defiled with meats, and that they might not profane the holy covenant: so then they died.⁶⁴ And there was very great wrath upon Israel.

1Mac.2

¹ In those days arose Mattathias the son of John, the son of Simeon, a priest of the sons of Joarib, from Jerusalem, and dwelt in Modin.² And he had five sons, Joannan, called Caddis:³ Simon; called Thassi:⁴ Judas, who was called Maccabeus:⁵ Eleazar, called Avaran: and Jonathan, whose surname was Apphus.⁶ And when he saw the blasphemies that were committed in Juda and Jerusalem,⁷ He said, Woe is me! wherefore was I born to see this misery of my people, and of the holy city, and to dwell there, when it was delivered into the hand of the enemy, and the sanctuary into the hand of strangers?⁸ Her temple is become as a man without glory.⁹ Her glorious vessels are carried away into captivity, her infants are slain in the streets, her young men with the sword of the enemy.¹⁰ What nation hath not had a part in her kingdom and gotten of her spoils?¹¹ All her ornaments are taken away; of a free woman she is become a bondslave.¹² And, behold, our sanctuary, even our beauty and our glory, is laid waste, and the Gentiles have profaned it.¹³ To what end therefore shall we live any longer?¹⁴ Then Mattathias and his sons rent their clothes, and put on sackcloth, and mourned very sore.¹⁵ In the mean while the king's officers, such as compelled the people to revolt, came into the city Modin, to make them sacrifice.¹⁶ And when many of Israel came unto them, Mattathias also and his sons came together.¹⁷ Then answered the king's officers, and said to Mattathias on this wise, Thou art a ruler, and an honourable and great man in this city, and strengthened with sons and brethren:¹⁸ Now therefore come thou first, and fulfil the king's commandment, like as all the heathen have done, yea, and the men of Juda also, and such as remain at Jerusalem: so shalt thou and thy house be in the number of the king's friends, and thou and thy children shall be honoured with silver and gold, and many rewards.¹⁹ Then Mattathias answered and spake with a loud voice, Though all the nations that are under the king's dominion obey him, and fall away every one from the religion of their fathers, and give consent to his commandments:²⁰ Yet will I and my sons and my brethren walk in the covenant of our fathers.²¹ God forbid that we should forsake the law and the ordinances.²² We will not hearken to the king's words, to go from our religion, either on the right hand, or the left.²³ Now when he had left speaking these words, there came one of the Jews in the sight of all to sacrifice on the altar which was at Modin, according to the king's commandment.²⁴ Which thing when Mattathias saw, he was inflamed with zeal, and his reins trembled, neither could he forbear to shew his anger according to judgment: wherefore he ran, and slew him upon the altar.²⁵ Also the king's commissioner, who compelled men to sacrifice, he killed at that time, and the altar he pulled down.²⁶ Thus dealt he zealously for the law of God like as Phinees did unto Zambri the son of Salom.²⁷ And Mattathias cried throughout the city with a loud voice, saying, Whosoever is zealous of the law, and maintaineth the covenant, let him follow me.²⁸ So he and his sons fled into the mountains, and left all that ever they had in the city.²⁹ Then many that sought after justice and judgment went down into the wilderness, to dwell there:³⁰ Both they, and their children, and their wives; and their cattle; because afflictions increased sore upon them.³¹ Now when it was told the king's servants, and the host that was at Jerusalem, in the city of David, that certain men, who had broken the king's commandment, were gone down into the secret

places in the wilderness, [32] They pursued after them a great number, and having overtaken them, they camped against them, and made war against them on the sabbath day. [33] And they said unto them, Let that which ye have done hitherto suffice; come forth, and do according to the commandment of the king, and ye shall live. [34] But they said, We will not come forth, neither will we do the king's commandment, to profane the sabbath day. [35] So then they gave them the battle with all speed. [36] Howbeit they answered them not, neither cast they a stone at them, nor stopped the places where they lay hid; [37] But said, Let us die all in our innocency: heaven and earth will testify for us, that ye put us to death wrongfully. [38] So they rose up against them in battle on the sabbath, and they slew them, with their wives and children and their cattle, to the number of a thousand people. [39] Now when Mattathias and his friends understood hereof, they mourned for them right sore. [40] And one of them said to another, If we all do as our brethren have done, and fight not for our lives and laws against the heathen, they will now quickly root us out of the earth. [41] At that time therefore they decreed, saying, Whosoever shall come to make battle with us on the sabbath day, we will fight against him; neither will we die all, as our brethren that were murdered im the secret places. [42] Then came there unto him a company of Assideans who were mighty men of Israel, even all such as were voluntarily devoted unto the law. [43] Also all they that fled for persecution joined themselves unto them, and were a stay unto them. [44] So they joined their forces, and smote sinful men in their anger, and wicked men in their wrath: but the rest fled to the heathen for succour. [45] Then Mattathias and his friends went round about, and pulled down the altars: [46] And what children soever they found within the coast of Israel uncircumcised, those they circumcised valiantly. [47] They pursued also after the proud men, and the work prospered in their hand. [48] So they recovered the law out of the hand of the Gentiles, and out of the hand of kings, neither suffered they the sinner to triumph. [49] Now when the time drew near that Mattathias should die, he said unto his sons, Now hath pride and rebuke gotten strength, and the time of destruction, and the wrath of indignation: [50] Now therefore, my sons, be ye zealous for the law, and give your lives for the covenant of your fathers. [51] Call to remembrance what acts our fathers did in their time; so shall ye receive great honour and an everlasting name. [52] Was not Abraham found faithful in temptation, and it was imputed unto him for righteousness? [53] Joseph in the time of his distress kept the commandment and was made lord of Egypt. [54] Phinees our father in being zealous and fervent obtained the covenant of an everlasting priesthood. [55] Jesus for fulfilling the word was made a judge in Israel. [56] Caleb for bearing witness before the congregation received the heritage of the land. [57] David for being merciful possessed the throne of an everlasting kingdom. [58] Elias for being zealous and fervent for the law was taken up into heaven. [59] Ananias, Azarias, and Misael, by believing were saved out of the flame. [60] Daniel for his innocency was delivered from the mouth of lions. [61] And thus consider ye throughout all ages, that none that put their trust in him shall be overcome. [62] Fear not then the words of a sinful man: for his glory shall be dung and worms. [63] To day he shall be lifted up and to morrow he shall not be found, because he is returned into his dust, and his thought is come to nothing. [64] Wherefore, ye my sons, be valiant and shew yourselves men in the behalf of the law; for by it shall ye obtain glory. [65] And behold, I know that your brother Simon is a man of counsel, give ear unto him alway: he shall be a father unto you. [66] As for Judas Maccabeus, he hath been mighty and strong, even from his youth up: let him be your captain, and fight the battle of the people. [67] Take also unto you all those that observe the law, and avenge ye the wrong of your people. [68] Recompense

fully the heathen, and take heed to the commandments of the law. [69] So he blessed them, and was gathered to his fathers. [70] And he died in the hundred forty and sixth year, and his sons buried him in the sepulchres of his fathers at Modin, and all Israel made great lamentation for him.

1Mac.3

[1] Then his son Judas, called Maccabeus, rose up in his stead. [2] And all his brethren helped him, and so did all they that held with his father, and they fought with cheerfulness the battle of Israel. [3] So he gat his people great honour, and put on a breastplate as a giant, and girt his warlike harness about him, and he made battles, protecting the host with his sword. [4] In his acts he was like a lion, and like a lion's whelp roaring for his prey. [5] For He pursued the wicked, and sought them out, and burnt up those that vexed his people. [6] Wherefore the wicked shrunk for fear of him, and all the workers of iniquity were troubled, because salvation prospered in his hand. [7] He grieved also many kings, and made Jacob glad with his acts, and his memorial is blessed for ever. [8] Moreover he went through the cities of Juda, destroying the ungodly out of them, and turning away wrath from Israel: [9] So that he was renowned unto the utmost part of the earth, and he received unto him such as were ready to perish. [10] Then Apollonius gathered the Gentiles together, and a great host out of Samaria, to fight against Israel. [11] Which thing when Judas perceived, he went forth to meet him, and so he smote him, and slew him: many also fell down slain, but the rest fled. [12] Wherefore Judas took their spoils, and Apollonius' sword also, and therewith he fought all his life long. [13] Now when Seron, a prince of the army of Syria, heard say that Judas had gathered unto him a multitude and company of the faithful to go out with him to war; [14] He said, I will get me a name and honour in the kingdom; for I will go fight with Judas and them that are with him, who despise the king's commandment. [15] So he made him ready to go up, and there went with him a mighty host of the ungodly to help him, and to be avenged of the children of Israel. [16] And when he came near to the going up of Bethhoron, Judas went forth to meet him with a small company: [17] Who, when they saw the host coming to meet them, said unto Judas, How shall we be able, being so few, to fight against so great a multitude and so strong, seeing we are ready to faint with fasting all this day? [18] Unto whom Judas answered, It is no hard matter for many to be shut up in the hands of a few; and with the God of heaven it is all one, to deliver with a great multitude, or a small company: [19] For the victory of battle standeth not in the multitude of an host; but strength cometh from heaven. [20] They come against us in much pride and iniquity to destroy us, and our wives and children, and to spoil us: [21] But we fight for our lives and our laws. [22] Wherefore the Lord himself will overthrow them before our face: and as for you, be ye not afraid of them. [23] Now as soon as he had left off speaking, he leapt suddenly upon them, and so Seron and his host was overthrown before him. [24] And they pursued them from the going down of Bethhoron unto the plain, where were slain about eight hundred men of them; and the residue fled into the land of the Philistines. [25] Then began the fear of Judas and his brethren, and an exceeding great dread, to fall upon the nations round about them: [26] Insomuch as his fame came unto the king, and all nations talked of the battles of Judas. [27] Now when king Antiochus heard these things, he was full of indignation: wherefore he sent and gathered together all the forces of his realm, even a very strong army. [28] He opened also his treasure, and gave his soldiers pay for a year, commanding them to be ready whensoever he should need them. [29] Nevertheless, when he saw that the money of his treasures failed and that the tributes in the country were small, because of the dissension and plague, which he had brought upon the land in taking

away the laws which had been of old time;[30] He feared that he should not be able to bear the charges any longer, nor to have such gifts to give so liberally as he did before: for he had abounded above the kings that were before him.[31] Wherefore, being greatly perplexed in his mind, he determined to go into Persia, there to take the tributes of the countries, and to gather much money.[32] So he left Lysias, a nobleman, and one of the blood royal, to oversee the affairs of the king from the river Euphrates unto the borders of Egypt:[33] And to bring up his son Antiochus, until he came again.[34] Moreover he delivered unto him the half of his forces, and the elephants, and gave him charge of all things that he would have done, as also concerning them that dwelt in Juda and Jerusalem:[35] To wit, that he should send an army against them, to destroy and root out the strength of Israel, and the remnant of Jerusalem, and to take away their memorial from that place;[36] And that he should place strangers in all their quarters, and divide their land by lot.[37] So the king took the half of the forces that remained, and departed from Antioch, his royal city, the hundred forty and seventh year; and having passed the river Euphrates, he went through the high countries.[38] Then Lysias chose Ptolemee the son of Dorymenes, Nicanor, and Gorgias, mighty men of the king's friends:[39] And with them he sent forty thousand footmen, and seven thousand horsemen, to go into the land of Juda, and to destroy it, as the king commanded.[40] So they went forth with all their power, and came and pitched by Emmaus in the plain country.[41] And the merchants of the country, hearing the fame of them, took silver and gold very much, with servants, and came into the camp to buy the children of Israel for slaves: a power also of Syria and of the land of the Philistines joined themselves unto them.[42] Now when Judas and his brethren saw that miseries were multiplied, and that the forces did encamp themselves in their borders: for they knew how the king had given commandment to destroy the people, and utterly abolish them;[43] They said one to another, Let us restore the decayed fortune of our people, and let us fight for our people and the sanctuary.[44] Then was the congregation gathered together, that they might be ready for battle, and that they might pray, and ask mercy and compassion.[45] Now Jerusalem lay void as a wilderness, there was none of her children that went in or out: the sanctuary also was trodden down, and aliens kept the strong hold; the heathen had their habitation in that place; and joy was taken from Jacob, and the pipe with the harp ceased.[46] Wherefore the Israelites assembled themselves together, and came to Maspha, over against Jerusalem; for in Maspha was the place where they prayed aforetime in Israel.[47] Then they fasted that day, and put on sackcloth, and cast ashes upon their heads, and rent their clothes,[48] And laid open the book of the law, wherein the heathen had sought to paint the likeness of their images.[49] They brought also the priests' garments, and the firstfruits, and the tithes: and the Nazarites they stirred up, who had accomplished their days.[50] Then cried they with a loud voice toward heaven, saying, What shall we do with these, and whither shall we carry them away?[51] For thy sanctuary is trodden down and profaned, and thy priests are in heaviness, and brought low.[52] And lo, the heathen are assembled together against us to destroy us: what things they imagine against us, thou knowest.[53] How shall we be able to stand against them, except thou, O God, be our help?[54] Then sounded they with trumpets, and cried with a loud voice.[55] And after this Judas ordained captains over the people, even captains over thousands, and over hundreds, and over fifties, and over tens.[56] But as for such as were building houses, or had betrothed wives, or were planting vineyards, or were fearful, those he commanded that they should return, every man to his own house, according to the law.[57] So the camp removed, and pitched upon the south side of Emmaus.[58] And Judas said, arm yourselves, and be valiant men, and see that ye be in readiness against the morning, that ye may fight with these nations, that are assembled together against us to destroy us and our sanctuary:[59] For it is better for us to die in battle, than to behold the calamities of our people and our sanctuary.[60] Nevertheless, as the will of God is in heaven, so let him do.

1Mac.4

[1] Then took Gorgias five thousand footmen, and a thousand of the best horsemen, and removed out of the camp by night;[2] To the end he might rush in upon the camp of the Jews, and smite them suddenly. And the men of the fortress were his guides.[3] Now when Judas heard thereof he himself removed, and the valiant men with him, that he might smite the king's army which was at Emmaus,[4] While as yet the forces were dispersed from the camp.[5] In the mean season came Gorgias by night into the camp of Judas: and when he found no man there, he sought them in the mountains: for said he, These fellows flee from us[6] But as soon as it was day, Judas shewed himself in the plain with three thousand men, who nevertheless had neither armour nor swords to their minds.[7] And they saw the camp of the heathen, that it was strong and well harnessed, and compassed round about with horsemen; and these were expert of war.[8] Then said Judas to the men that were with him, Fear ye not their multitude, neither be ye afraid of their assault.[9] Remember how our fathers were delivered in the Red sea, when Pharaoh pursued them with an army.[10] Now therefore let us cry unto heaven, if peradventure the Lord will have mercy upon us, and remember the covenant of our fathers, and destroy this host before our face this day:[11] That so all the heathen may know that there is one who delivereth and saveth Israel.[12] Then the strangers lifted up their eyes, and saw them coming over against them.[13] Wherefore they went out of the camp to battle; but they that were with Judas sounded their trumpets.[14] So they joined battle, and the heathen being discomfited fled into the plain.[15] Howbeit all the hindmost of them were slain with the sword: for they pursued them unto Gazera, and unto the plains of Idumea, and Azotus, and Jamnia, so that there were slain of them upon a three thousand men.[16] This done, Judas returned again with his host from pursuing them,[17] And said to the people, Be not greedy of the spoil inasmuch as there is a battle before us,[18] And Gorgias and his host are here by us in the mountain: but stand ye now against our enemies, and overcome them, and after this ye may boldly take the spoils.[19] As Judas was yet speaking these words, there appeared a part of them looking out of the mountain:[20] Who when they perceived that the Jews had put their host to flight and were burning the tents; for the smoke that was seen declared what was done:[21] When therefore they perceived these things, they were sore afraid, and seeing also the host of Judas in the plain ready to fight,[22] They fled every one into the land of strangers.[23] Then Judas returned to spoil the tents, where they got much gold, and silver, and blue silk, and purple of the sea, and great riches.[24] After this they went home, and sung a song of thanksgiving, and praised the Lord in heaven: because it is good, because his mercy endureth forever.[25] Thus Israel had a great deliverance that day.[26] Now all the strangers that had escaped came and told Lysias what had happened:[27] Who, when he heard thereof, was confounded and discouraged, because neither such things as he would were done unto Israel, nor such things as the king commanded him were come to pass.[28] The next year therefore following Lysias gathered together threescore thousand choice men of foot, and five thousand horsemen, that he might subdue them.[29] So they came into Idumea, and pitched their tents at Bethsura, and Judas met them with ten thousand men.[30] And when

he saw that mighty army, he prayed and said, Blessed art thou, O Saviour of Israel, who didst quell the violence of the mighty man by the hand of thy servant David, and gavest the host of strangers into the hands of Jonathan the son of Saul, and his armourbearer;[31] Shut up this army in the hand of thy people Israel, and let them be confounded in their power and horsemen:[32] Make them to be of no courage, and cause the boldness of their strength to fall away, and let them quake at their destruction:[33] Cast them down with the sword of them that love thee, and let all those that know thy name praise thee with thanksgiving.[34] So they joined battle; and there were slain of the host of Lysias about five thousand men, even before them were they slain.[35] Now when Lysias saw his army put to flight, and the manliness of Judas' soldiers, and how they were ready either to live or die valiantly, he went into Antiochia, and gathered together a company of strangers, and having made his army greater than it was, he purposed to come again into Judea.[36] Then said Judas and his brethren, Behold, our enemies are discomfited: let us go up to cleanse and dedicate the sanctuary.[37] Upon this all the host assembled themselves together, and went up into mount Sion.[38] And when they saw the sanctuary desolate, and the altar profaned, and the gates burned up, and shrubs growing in the courts as in a forest, or in one of the mountains, yea, and the priests' chambers pulled down;[39] They rent their clothes, and made great lamentation, and cast ashes upon their heads,[40] And fell down flat to the ground upon their faces, and blew an alarm with the trumpets, and cried toward heaven.[41] Then Judas appointed certain men to fight against those that were in the fortress, until he had cleansed the sanctuary.[42] So he chose priests of blameless conversation, such as had pleasure in the law:[43] Who cleansed the sanctuary, and bare out the defiled stones into an unclean place.[44] And when as they consulted what to do with the altar of burnt offerings, which was profaned;[45] They thought it best to pull it down, lest it should be a reproach to them, because the heathen had defiled it: wherefore they pulled it down,[46] And laid up the stones in the mountain of the temple in a convenient place, until there should come a prophet to shew what should be done with them.[47] Then they took whole stones according to the law, and built a new altar according to the former;[48] And made up the sanctuary, and the things that were within the temple, and hallowed the courts.[49] They made also new holy vessels, and into the temple they brought the candlestick, and the altar of burnt offerings, and of incense, and the table.[50] And upon the altar they burned incense, and the lamps that were upon the candlestick they lighted, that they might give light in the temple.[51] Furthermore they set the loaves upon the table, and spread out the veils, and finished all the works which they had begun to make.[52] Now on the five and twentieth day of the ninth month, which is called the month Casleu, in the hundred forty and eighth year, they rose up betimes in the morning,[53] And offered sacrifice according to the law upon the new altar of burnt offerings, which they had made.[54] Look, at what time and what day the heathen had profaned it, even in that was it dedicated with songs, and citherns, and harps, and cymbals.[55] Then all the people fell upon their faces, worshipping and praising the God of heaven, who had given them good success.[56] And so they kept the dedication of the altar eight days and offered burnt offerings with gladness, and sacrificed the sacrifice of deliverance and praise.[57] They decked also the forefront of the temple with crowns of gold, and with shields; and the gates and the chambers they renewed, and hanged doors upon them.[58] Thus was there very great gladness among the people, for that the reproach of the heathen was put away.[59] Moreover Judas and his brethren with the whole congregation of Israel ordained, that the days of the dedication of the altar should be kept in their season

from year to year by the space of eight days, from the five and twentieth day of the month Casleu, with mirth and gladness.[60] At that time also they builded up the mount Sion with high walls and strong towers round about, lest the Gentiles should come and tread it down as they had done before.[61] And they set there a garrison to keep it, and fortified Bethsura to preserve it; that the people might have a defence against Idumea.

1Mac.5

[1] Now when the nations round about heard that the altar was built and the sanctuary renewed as before, it displeased them very much.[2] Wherefore they thought to destroy the generation of Jacob that was among them, and thereupon they began to slay and destroy the people.[3] Then Judas fought against the children of Esau in Idumea at Arabattine, because they besieged Gael: and he gave them a great overthrow, and abated their courage, and took their spoils.[4] Also he remembered the injury of the children of Bean, who had been a snare and an offence unto the people, in that they lay in wait for them in the ways.[5] He shut them up therefore in the towers, and encamped against them, and destroyed them utterly, and burned the towers of that place with fire, and all that were therein.[6] Afterward he passed over to the children of Ammon, where he found a mighty power, and much people, with Timotheus their captain.[7] So he fought many battles with them, till at length they were discomfited before him; and he smote them.[8] And when he had taken Jazar, with the towns belonging thereto, he returned into Judea.[9] Then the heathen that were at Galaad assembled themselves together against the Israelites that were in their quarters, to destroy them; but they fled to the fortress of Dathema.[10] And sent letters unto Judas and his brethren, The heathen that are round about us are assembled together against us to destroy us:[11] And they are preparing to come and take the fortress whereunto we are fled, Timotheus being captain of their host.[12] Come now therefore, and deliver us from their hands, for many of us are slain:[13] Yea, all our brethren that are in the places of Tobie are put to death: their wives and their children also they have carried away captives, and borne away their stuff; and they have destroyed there about a thousand men.[14] While these letters were yet reading, behold, there came other messengers from Galilee with their clothes rent, who reported on this wise,[15] And said, They of Ptolemais, and of Tyrus, and Sidon, and all Galilee of the Gentiles, are assembled together against us to consume us.[16] Now when Judas and the people heard these words, there assembled a great congregation together, to consult what they should do for their brethren, that were in trouble, and assaulted of them.[17] Then said Judas unto Simon his brother, Choose thee out men, and go and deliver thy brethren that are in Galilee, for I and Jonathan my brother will go into the country of Galaad.[18] So he left Joseph the son of Zacharias, and Azarias, captains of the people, with the remnant of the host in Judea to keep it.[19] Unto whom he gave commandment, saying, Take ye the charge of this people, and see that ye make not war against the heathen until the time that we come again.[20] Now unto Simon were given three thousand men to go into Galilee, and unto Judas eight thousand men for the country of Galaad.[21] Then went Simon into Galilee, where he fought many battles with the heathen, so that the heathen were discomfited by him.[22] And he pursued them unto the gate of Ptolemais; and there were slain of the heathen about three thousand men, whose spoils he took.[23] And those that were in Galilee, and in Arbattis, with their wives and their children, and all that they had, took he away with him, and brought them into Judea with great joy.[24] Judas Maccabeus also and his brother Jonathan went over Jordan, and travelled three days' journey in the wilderness,[25] Where they met with the Nabathites, who came unto them in a peaceable manner, and told

them every thing that had happened to their brethren in the land of Galaad:²⁶ And how that many of them were shut up in Bosora, and Bosor, and Alema, Casphor, Maked, and Carnaim; all these cities are strong and great:²⁷ And that they were shut up in the rest of the cities of the country of Galaad, and that against to morrow they had appointed to bring their host against the forts, and to take them, and to destroy them all in one day.²⁸ Hereupon Judas and his host turned suddenly by the way of the wilderness unto Bosora; and when he had won the city, he slew all the males with the edge of the sword, and took all their spoils, and burned the city with fire,²⁹ From whence he removed by night, and went till he came to the fortress.³⁰ And betimes in the morning they looked up, and, behold, there was an innumerable people bearing ladders and other engines of war, to take the fortress: for they assaulted them.³¹ When Judas therefore saw that the battle was begun, and that the cry of the city went up to heaven, with trumpets, and a great sound,³² He said unto his host, Fight this day for your brethren.³³ So he went forth behind them in three companies, who sounded their trumpets, and cried with prayer.³⁴ Then the host of Timotheus, knowing that it was Maccabeus, fled from him: wherefore he smote them with a great slaughter; so that there were killed of them that day about eight thousand men.³⁵ This done, Judas turned aside to Maspha; and after he had assaulted it he took and slew all the males therein, and received the spoils thereof and and burnt it with fire.³⁶ From thence went he, and took Casphon, Maged, Bosor, and the other cities of the country of Galaad.³⁷ After these things gathered Timotheus another host and encamped against Raphon beyond the brook.³⁸ So Judas sent men to espy the host, who brought him word, saying, All the heathen that be round about us are assembled unto them, even a very great host.³⁹ He hath also hired the Arabians to help them and they have pitched their tents beyond the brook, ready to come and fight against thee. Upon this Judas went to meet them.⁴⁰ Then Timotheus said unto the captains of his host, When Judas and his host come near the brook, if he pass over first unto us, we shall not be able to withstand him; for he will mightily prevail against us:⁴¹ But if he be afraid, and camp beyond the river, we shall go over unto him, and prevail against him.⁴² Now when Judas came near the brook, he caused the scribes of the people to remain by the brook: unto whom he gave commandment, saying, Suffer no man to remain in the camp, but let all come to the battle.⁴³ So he went first over unto them, and all the people after him: then all the heathen, being discomfited before him, cast away their weapons, and fled unto the temple that was at Carnaim.⁴⁴ But they took the city, and burned the temple with all that were therein. Thus was Carnaim subdued, neither could they stand any longer before Judas.⁴⁵ Then Judas gathered together all the Israelites that were in the country of Galaad, from the least unto the greatest, even their wives, and their children, and their stuff, a very great host, to the end they might come into the land of Judea.⁴⁶ Now when they came unto Ephron, (this was a great city in the way as they should go, very well fortified) they could not turn from it, either on the right hand or the left, but must needs pass through the midst of it.⁴⁷ Then they of the city shut them out, and stopped up the gates with stones.⁴⁸ Whereupon Judas sent unto them in peaceable manner, saying, Let us pass through your land to go into our own country, and none shall do you any hurt; we will only pass through on foot: howbeit they would not open unto him.⁴⁹ Wherefore Judas commanded a proclamation to be made throughout the host, that every man should pitch his tent in the place where he was.⁵⁰ So the soldiers pitched, and assaulted the city all that day and all that night, till at the length the city was delivered into his hands:⁵¹ Who then slew all the males with the edge of the sword, and rased the city, and took the spoils thereof, and

passed through the city over them that were slain.⁵² After this went they over Jordan into the great plain before Bethsan.⁵³ And Judas gathered together those that came behind, and exhorted the people all the way through, till they came into the land of Judea.⁵⁴ So they went up to mount Sion with joy and gladness, where they offered burnt offerings, because not one of them were slain until they had returned in peace.⁵⁵ Now what time as Judas and Jonathan were in the land of Galaad, and Simon his brother in Galilee before Ptolemais,⁵⁶ Joseph the son of Zacharias, and Azarias, captains of the garrisons, heard of the valiant acts and warlike deeds which they had done.⁵⁷ Wherefore they said, Let us also get us a name, and go fight against the heathen that are round about us.⁵⁸ So when they had given charge unto the garrison that was with them, they went toward Jamnia.⁵⁹ Then came Gorgias and his men out of the city to fight against them.⁶⁰ And so it was, that Joseph and Azaras were put to flight, and pursued unto the borders of Judea: and there were slain that day of the people of Israel about two thousand men.⁶¹ Thus was there a great overthrow among the children of Israel, because they were not obedient unto Judas and his brethren, but thought to do some valiant act.⁶² Moreover these men came not of the seed of those, by whose hand deliverance was given unto Israel.⁶³ Howbeit the man Judas and his brethren were greatly renowned in the sight of all Israel, and of all the heathen, wheresoever their name was heard of;⁶⁴ Insomuch as the the people assembled unto them with joyful acclamations.⁶⁵ Afterward went Judas forth with his brethren, and fought against the children of Esau in the land toward the south, where he smote Hebron, and the towns thereof, and pulled down the fortress of it, and burned the towers thereof round about.⁶⁶ From thence he removed to go into the land of the Philistines, and passed through Samaria.⁶⁷ At that time certain priests, desirous to shew their valour, were slain in battle, for that they went out to fight unadvisedly.⁶⁸ So Judas turned to Azotus in the land of the Philistines, and when he had pulled down their altars, and burned their carved images with fire, and spoiled their cities, he returned into the land of Judea.

1Mac.6

¹ About that time king Antiochus travelling through the high countries heard say, that Elymais in the country of Persia was a city greatly renowned for riches, silver, and gold;² And that there was in it a very rich temple, wherein were coverings of gold, and breastplates, and shields, which Alexander, son of Philip, the Macedonian king, who reigned first among the Grecians, had left there.³ Wherefore he came and sought to take the city, and to spoil it; but he was not able, because they of the city, having had warning thereof,⁴ Rose up against him in battle: so he fled, and departed thence with great heaviness, and returned to Babylon.⁵ Moreover there came one who brought him tidings into Persia, that the armies, which went against the land of Judea, were put to flight:⁶ And that Lysias, who went forth first with a great power was driven away of the Jews; and that they were made strong by the armour, and power, and store of spoils, which they had gotten of the armies, whom they had destroyed:⁷ Also that they had pulled down the abomination, which he had set up upon the altar in Jerusalem, and that they had compassed about the sanctuary with high walls, as before, and his city Bethsura.⁸ Now when the king heard these words, he was astonished and sore moved: whereupon he laid him down upon his bed, and fell sick for grief, because it had not befallen him as he looked for.⁹ And there he continued many days: for his grief was ever more and more, and he made account that he should die.¹⁰ Wherefore he called for all his friends, and said unto them, The sleep is gone from mine eyes, and my heart faileth for very care.¹¹ And I thought with myself, Into what tribulation am I come,

and how great a flood of misery is it, wherein now I am! for I was bountiful and beloved in my power. [12] But now I remember the evils that I did at Jerusalem, and that I took all the vessels of gold and silver that were therein, and sent to destroy the inhabitants of Judea without a cause. [13] I perceive therefore that for this cause these troubles are come upon me, and, behold, I perish through great grief in a strange land. [14] Then called he for Philip, one of his friends, who he made ruler over all his realm, [15] And gave him the crown, and his robe, and his signet, to the end he should bring up his son Antiochus, and nourish him up for the kingdom. [16] So king Antiochus died there in the hundred forty and ninth year. [17] Now when Lysias knew that the king was dead, he set up Antiochus his son, whom he had brought up being young, to reign in his stead, and his name he called Eupator. [18] About this time they that were in the tower shut up the Israelites round about the sanctuary, and sought always their hurt, and the strengthening of the heathen. [19] Wherefore Judas, purposing to destroy them, called all the people together to besiege them. [20] So they came together, and besieged them in the hundred and fiftieth year, and he made mounts for shot against them, and other engines. [21] Howbeit certain of them that were besieged got forth, unto whom some ungodly men of Israel joined themselves: [22] And they went unto the king, and said, How long will it be ere thou execute judgment, and avenge our brethren? [23] We have been willing to serve thy father, and to do as he would have us, and to obey his commandments; [24] For which cause they of our nation besiege the tower, and are alienated from us: moreover as many of us as they could light on they slew, and spoiled our inheritance. [25] Neither have they stretched out their hand against us only, but also against their borders. [26] And, behold, this day are they besieging the tower at Jerusalem, to take it: the sanctuary also and Bethsura have they fortified. [27] Wherefore if thou dost not prevent them quickly, they will do the greater things than these, neither shalt thou be able to rule them. [28] Now when the king heard this, he was angry, and gathered together all his friends, and the captains of his army, and those that had charge of the horse. [29] There came also unto him from other kingdoms, and from isles of the sea, bands of hired soldiers. [30] So that the number of his army was an hundred thousand footmen, and twenty thousand horsemen, and two and thirty elephants exercised in battle. [31] These went through Idumea, and pitched against Bethsura, which they assaulted many days, making engines of war; but they of Bethsura came out, and burned them with fire, and fought valiantly. [32] Upon this Judas removed from the tower, and pitched in Bathzacharias, over against the king's camp. [33] Then the king rising very early marched fiercely with his host toward Bathzacharias, where his armies made them ready to battle, and sounded the trumpets. [34] And to the end they might provoke the elephants to fight, they shewed them the blood of grapes and mulberries. [35] Moreover they divided the beasts among the armies, and for every elephant they appointed a thousand men, armed with coats of mail, and with helmets of brass on their heads; and beside this, for every beast were ordained five hundred horsemen of the best. [36] These were ready at every occasion: wheresoever the beast was, and whithersoever the beast went, they went also, neither departed they from him. [37] And upon the beasts were there strong towers of wood, which covered every one of them, and were girt fast unto them with devices: there were also upon every one two and thirty strong men, that fought upon them, beside the Indian that ruled him. [38] As for the remnant of the horsemen, they set them on this side and that side at the two parts of the host giving them signs what to do, and being harnessed all over amidst the ranks. [39] Now when the sun shone upon the shields of gold and brass, the mountains glistered therewith, and shined like

lamps of fire. [40] So part of the king's army being spread upon the high mountains, and part on the valleys below, they marched on safely and in order. [41] Wherefore all that heard the noise of their multitude, and the marching of the company, and the rattling of the harness, were moved: for the army was very great and mighty. [42] Then Judas and his host drew near, and entered into battle, and there were slain of the king's army six hundred men. [43] Eleazar also, surnamed Savaran, perceiving that one of the beasts, armed with royal harness, was higher than all the rest, and supposing that the king was upon him, [44] Put himself in jeopardy, to the end he might deliver his people, and get him a perpetual name: [45] Wherefore he ran upon him courageously through the midst of the battle, slaying on the right hand and on the left, so that they were divided from him on both sides. [46] Which done, he crept under the elephant, and thrust him under, and slew him: whereupon the elephant fell down upon him, and there he died. [47] Howbeit the rest of the Jews seeing the strength of the king, and the violence of his forces, turned away from them. [48] Then the king's army went up to Jerusalem to meet them, and the king pitched his tents against Judea, and against mount Sion. [49] But with them that were in Bethsura he made peace: for they came out of the city, because they had no victuals there to endure the siege, it being a year of rest to the land. [50] So the king took Bethsura, and set a garrison there to keep it. [51] As for the sanctuary, he besieged it many days: and set there artillery with engines and instruments to cast fire and stones, and pieces to cast darts and slings. [52] Whereupon they also made engines against their engines, and held them battle a long season. [53] Yet at the last, their vessels being without victuals, (for that it was the seventh year, and they in Judea that were delivered from the Gentiles, had eaten up the residue of the store;) [54] There were but a few left in the sanctuary, because the famine did so prevail against them, that they were fain to disperse themselves, every man to his own place. [55] At that time Lysias heard say, that Philip, whom Antiochus the king, whiles he lived, had appointed to bring up his son Antiochus, that he might be king, [56] Was returned out of Persia and Media, and the king's host also that went with him, and that he sought to take unto him the ruling of the affairs. [57] Wherefore he went in all haste, and said to the king and the captains of the host and the company, We decay daily, and our victuals are but small, and the place we lay siege unto is strong, and the affairs of the kingdom lie upon us: [58] Now therefore let us be friends with these men, and make peace with them, and with all their nation; [59] And covenant with them, that they shall live after their laws, as they did before: for they are therefore displeased, and have done all these things, because we abolished their laws. [60] So the king and the princes were content: wherefore he sent unto them to make peace; and they accepted thereof. [61] Also the king and the princes made an oath unto them: whereupon they went out of the strong hold. [62] Then the king entered into mount Sion; but when he saw the strength of the place, he broke his oath that he had made, and gave commandment to pull down the wall round about. [63] Afterward departed he in all haste, and returned unto Antiochia, where he found Philip to be master of the city: so he fought against him, and took the city by force.

1Mac.7

[1] In the hundred and one and fiftieth year Demetrius the son of Seleucus departed from Rome, and came up with a few men unto a city of the sea coast, and reigned there. [2] And as he entered into the palace of his ancestors, so it was, that his forces had taken Antiochus and Lysias, to bring them unto him. [3] Wherefore, when he knew it, he said, Let me not see their faces. [4] So his host slew them. Now when Demetrius was set upon the throne of his kingdom, [5] There came unto him all the wicked and ungodly men of Israel, having

Alcimus, who was desirous to be high priest, for their captain:[6] And they accused the people to the king, saying, Judas and his brethren have slain all thy friends, and driven us out of our own land.[7] Now therefore send some man whom thou trustest, and let him go and see what havock he hath made among us, and in the king's land, and let him punish them with all them that aid them.[8] Then the king chose Bacchides, a friend of the king, who ruled beyond the flood, and was a great man in the kingdom, and faithful to the king,[9] And him he sent with that wicked Alcimus, whom he made high priest, and commanded that he should take vengeance of the children of Israel.[10] So they departed, and came with a great power into the land of Judea, where they sent messengers to Judas and his brethren with peaceable words deceitfully.[11] But they gave no heed to their words; for they saw that they were come with a great power.[12] Then did there assemble unto Alcimus and Bacchides a company of scribes, to require justice.[13] Now the Assideans were the first among the children of Israel that sought peace of them:[14] For said they, One that is a priest of the seed of Aaron is come with this army, and he will do us no wrong.[15] So he spake unto them, peaceably, and sware unto them, saying, we will procure the harm neither of you nor your friends.[16] Whereupon they believed him: howbeit he took of them threescore men, and slew them in one day, according to the words which he wrote,[17] The flesh of thy saints have they cast out, and their blood have they shed round about Jerusalem, and there was none to bury them.[18] Wherefore the fear and dread of them fell upon all the people, who said, There is neither truth nor righteousness in them; for they have broken the covenant and oath that they made.[19] After this, removed Bacchides from Jerusalem, and pitched his tents in Bezeth, where he sent and took many of the men that had forsaken him, and certain of the people also, and when he had slain them, he cast them into the great pit.[20] Then committed he the country to Alcimus, and left with him a power to aid him: so Bacchides went to the king.[21] But Alcimus contended for the high priesthood.[22] And unto him resorted all such as troubled the people, who, after they had gotten the land of Juda into their power, did much hurt in Israel.[23] Now when Judas saw all the mischief that Alcimus and his company had done among the Israelites, even above the heathen,[24] He went out into all the coasts of Judea round about, and took vengeance of them that had revolted from him, so that they durst no more go forth into the country.[25] On the other side, when Alcimus saw that Judas and his company had gotten the upper hand, and knew that he was not able to abide their force, he went again to the king, and said all the worst of them that he could.[26] Then the king sent Nicanor, one of his honourable princes, a man that bare deadly hate unto Israel, with commandment to destroy the people.[27] So Nicanor came to Jerusalem with a great force; and sent unto Judas and his brethren deceitfully with friendly words, saying,[28] Let there be no battle between me and you; I will come with a few men, that I may see you in peace.[29] He came therefore to Judas, and they saluted one another peaceably. Howbeit the enemies were prepared to take away Judas by violence.[30] Which thing after it was known to Judas, to wit, that he came unto him with deceit, he was sore afraid of him, and would see his face no more.[31] Nicanor also, when he saw that his counsel was discovered, went out to fight against Judas beside Capharsalama:[32] Where there were slain of Nicanor's side about five thousand men, and the rest fled into the city of David.[33] After this went Nicanor up to mount Sion, and there came out of the sanctuary certain of the priests and certain of the elders of the people, to salute him peaceably, and to shew him the burnt sacrifice that was offered for the king.[34] But he mocked them, and laughed at them, and abused them shamefully, and spake proudly,[35] And sware in his wrath, saying, Unless Judas and his host

be now delivered into my hands, if ever I come again in safety, I will burn up this house: and with that he went out in a great rage.[36] Then the priests entered in, and stood before the altar and the temple, weeping, and saying,[37] Thou, O Lord, didst choose this house to be called by thy name, and to be a house of prayer and petition for thy people:[38] Be avenged of this man and his host, and let them fall by the sword: remember their blasphemies, and suffer them not to continue any longer.[39] So Nicanor went out of Jerusalem, and pitched his tents in Bethhoron, where an host out of Syria met him.[40] But Judas pitched in Adasa with three thousand men, and there he prayed, saying,[41] O Lord, when they that were sent from the king of the Assyrians blasphemed, thine angel went out, and smote an hundred fourscore and five thousand of them.[42] Even so destroy thou this host before us this day, that the rest may know that he hath spoken blasphemously against thy sanctuary, and judge thou him according to his wickedness.[43] So the thirteenth day of the month Adar the hosts joined battle: but Nicanor's host was discomfited, and he himself was first slain in the battle.[44] Now when Nicanor's host saw that he was slain, they cast away their weapons, and fled.[45] Then they pursued after them a day's journey, from Adasa unto Gazera, sounding an alarm after them with their trumpets.[46] Whereupon they came forth out of all the towns of Judea round about, and closed them in; so that they, turning back upon them that pursued them, were all slain with the sword, and not one of them was left.[47] Afterwards they took the spoils, and the prey, and smote off Nicanors head, and his right hand, which he stretched out so proudly, and brought them away, and hanged them up toward Jerusalem.[48] For this cause the people rejoiced greatly, and they kept that day a day of great gladness.[49] Moreover they ordained to keep yearly this day, being the thirteenth of Adar.[50] Thus the land of Juda was in rest a little while.

1Mac.8

[1] Now Judas had heard of the the Romans, that they were mighty and valiant men, and such as would lovingly accept all that joined themselves unto them, and make a league of amity with all that came unto them;[2] And that they were men of great valour. It was told him also of their wars and noble acts which they had done among the Galatians, and how they had conquered them, and brought them under tribute;[3] And what they had done in the country of Spain, for the winning of the mines of the silver and gold which is there;[4] And that by their policy and patience they had conquered all the place, though it were very far from them; and the kings also that came against them from the uttermost part of the earth, till they had discomfited them, and given them a great overthrow, so that the rest did give them tribute every year:[5] Beside this, how they had discomfited in battle Philip, and Perseus, king of the Citims, with others that lifted up themselves against them, and had overcome them:[6] How also Antiochus the great king of Asia, that came against them in battle, having an hundred and twenty elephants, with horsemen, and chariots, and a very great army, was discomfited by them;[7] And how they took him alive, and covenanted that he and such as reigned after him should pay a great tribute, and give hostages, and that which was agreed upon,[8] And the country of India, and Media and Lydia and of the goodliest countries, which they took of him, and gave to king Eumenes:[9] Moreover how the Grecians had determined to come and destroy them;[10] And that they, having knowledge thereof sent against them a certain captain, and fighting with them slew many of them, and carried away captives their wives and their children, and spoiled them, and took possession of their lands, and pulled down their strong holds, and brought them to be their servants unto this day:[11] It was told him besides, how they destroyed and brought under their dominion all

other kingdoms and isles that at any time resisted them;[12] But with their friends and such as relied upon them they kept amity: and that they had conquered kingdoms both far and nigh, insomuch as all that heard of their name were afraid of them:[13] Also that, whom they would help to a kingdom, those reign; and whom again they would, they displace: finally, that they were greatly exalted:[14] Yet for all this none of them wore a crown or was clothed in purple, to be magnified thereby:[15] Moreover how they had made for themselves a senate house, wherein three hundred and twenty men sat in council daily, consulting alway for the people, to the end they might be well ordered:[16] And that they committed their government to one man every year, who ruled over all their country, and that all were obedient to that one, and that there was neither envy nor emmulation among them.[17] In consideration of these things, Judas chose Eupolemus the son of John, the son of Accos, and Jason the son of Eleazar, and sent them to Rome, to make a league of amity and confederacy with them,[18] And to intreat them that they would take the yoke from them; for they saw that the kingdom of the Grecians did oppress Israel with servitude.[19] They went therefore to Rome, which was a very great journey, and came into the senate, where they spake and said.[20] Judas Maccabeus with his brethren, and the people of the Jews, have sent us unto you, to make a confederacy and peace with you, and that we might be registered your confederates and friends.[21] So that matter pleased the Romans well.[22] And this is the copy of the epistle which the senate wrote back again in tables of brass, and sent to Jerusalem, that there they might have by them a memorial of peace and confederacy:[23] Good success be to the Romans, and to the people of the Jews, by sea and by land for ever: the sword also and enemy be far from them,[24] If there come first any war upon the Romans or any of their confederates throughout all their dominion,[25] The people of the Jews shall help them, as the time shall be appointed, with all their heart:[26] Neither shall they give any thing unto them that make war upon them, or aid them with victuals, weapons, money, or ships, as it hath seemed good unto the Romans; but they shall keep their covenants without taking any thing therefore.[27] In the same manner also, if war come first upon the nation of the Jews, the Romans shall help them with all their heart, according as the time shall be appointed them:[28] Neither shall victuals be given to them that take part against them, or weapons, or money, or ships, as it hath seemed good to the Romans; but they shall keep their covenants, and that without deceit.[29] According to these articles did the Romans make a covenant with the people of the Jews.[30] Howbeit if hereafter the one party or the other shall think to meet to add or diminish any thing, they may do it at their pleasures, and whatsoever they shall add or take away shall be ratified.[31] And as touching the evils that Demetrius doeth to the Jews, we have written unto him, saying, Wherefore thou made thy yoke heavy upon our friends and confederates the Jews?[32] If therefore they complain any more against thee, we will do them justice, and fight with thee by sea and by land.

1Mac.9

[1] Furthermore, when Demetrius heard the Nicanor and his host were slain in battle, he sent Bacchides and Alcimus into the land of Judea the second time, and with them the chief strength of his host:[2] Who went forth by the way that leadeth to Galgala, and pitched their tents before Masaloth, which is in Arbela, and after they had won it, they slew much people.[3] Also the first month of the hundred fifty and second year they encamped before Jerusalem:[4] From whence they removed, and went to Berea, with twenty thousand footmen and two thousand horsemen.[5] Now Judas had pitched his tents at Eleasa, and three thousand chosen men with

him:[6] Who seeing the multitude of the other army to he so great were sore afraid; whereupon many conveyed themselves out of the host, insomuch as abode of them no more but eight hundred men.[7] When Judas therefore saw that his host slipt away, and that the battle pressed upon him, he was sore troubled in mind, and much distressed, for that he had no time to gather them together.[8] Nevertheless unto them that remained he said, Let us arise and go up against our enemies, if peradventure we may be able to fight with them.[9] But they dehorted him, saying, We shall never be able: let us now rather save our lives, and hereafter we will return with our brethren, and fight against them: for we are but few.[10] Then Judas said, God forbid that I should do this thing, and flee away from them: if our time be come, let us die manfully for our brethren, and let us not stain our honour.[11] With that the host of Bacchides removed out of their tents, and stood over against them, their horsemen being divided into two troops, and their slingers and archers going before the host and they that marched in the foreward were all mighty men.[12] As for Bacchides, he was in the right wing: so the host drew near on the two parts, and sounded their trumpets.[13] They also of Judas' side, even they sounded their trumpets also, so that the earth shook at the noise of the armies, and the battle continued from morning till night.[14] Now when Judas perceived that Bacchides and the strength of his army were on the right side, he took with him all the hardy men,[15] Who discomfited the right wing, and pursued them unto the mount Azotus.[16] But when they of the left wing saw that they of the right wing were discomfited, they followed upon Judas and those that were with him hard at the heels from behind:[17] Whereupon there was a sore battle, insomuch as many were slain on both parts.[18] Judas also was killed, and the remnant fled.[19] THen Jonathan and Simon took Judas their brother, and buried him in the sepulchre of his fathers in Modin.[20] Moreover they bewailed him, and all Israel made great lamentation for him, and mourned many days, saying,[21] How is the valiant man fallen, that delivered Israel![22] As for the other things concerning Judas and his wars, and the noble acts which he did, and his greatness, they are not written: for they were very many.[23] Now after the death of Judas the wicked began to put forth their heads in all the coasts of Israel, and there arose up all such as wrought iniquity.[24] In those days also was there a very great famine, by reason whereof the country revolted, and went with them.[25] Then Bacchides chose the wicked men, and made them lords of the country.[26] And they made enquiry and search for Judas' friends, and brought them unto Bacchides, who took vengeance of them, and used them despitefully.[27] So was there a great affliction in Israel, the like whereof was not since the time that a prophet was not seen among them.[28] For this cause all Judas' friends came together, and said unto Jonathan,[29] Since thy brother Judas died, we have no man like him to go forth against our enemies, and Bacchides, and against them of our nation that are adversaries to us.[30] Now therefore we have chosen thee this day to be our prince and captain in his stead, that thou mayest fight our battles.[31] Upon this Jonathan took the governance upon him at that time, and rose up instead of his brother Judas.[32] But when Bacchides gat knowledge thereof, he sought for to slay him[33] Then Jonathan, and Simon his brother, and all that were with him, perceiving that, fled into the wilderness of Thecoe, and pitched their tents by the water of the pool Asphar.[34] Which when Bacchides understood, he came near to Jordan with all his host upon the sabbath day.[35] Now Jonathan had sent his brother John, a captain of the people, to pray his friends the Nabathites, that they might leave with them their carriage, which was much.[36] But the children of Jambri came out of Medaba, and took John, and all that he had, and went their way with it.[37] After this came word to

Jonathan and Simon his brother, that the children of Jambri made a great marriage, and were bringing the bride from Nadabatha with a great train, as being the daughter of one of the great princes of Chanaan.[38] Therefore they remembered John their brother, and went up, and hid themselves under the covert of the mountain:[39] Where they lifted up their eyes, and looked, and, behold, there was much ado and great carriage: and the bridegroom came forth, and his friends and brethren, to meet them with drums, and instruments of musick, and many weapons.[40] Then Jonathan and they that were with him rose up against them from the place where they lay in ambush, and made a slaughter of them in such sort, as many fell down dead, and the remnant fled into the mountain, and they took all their spoils.[41] Thus was the marriage turned into mourning, and the noise of their melody into lamentation.[42] So when they had avenged fully the blood of their brother, they turned again to the marsh of Jordan.[43] Now when Bacchides heard hereof, he came on the sabbath day unto the banks of Jordan with a great power.[44] Then Jonathan said to his company, Let us go up now and fight for our lives, for it standeth not with us to day, as in time past:[45] For, behold, the battle is before us and behind us, and the water of Jordan on this side and that side, the marsh likewise and wood, neither is there place for us to turn aside.[46] Wherefore cry ye now unto heaven, that ye may be delivered from the hand of your enemies.[47] With that they joined battle, and Jonathan stretched forth his hand to smite Bacchides, but he turned back from him.[48] Then Jonathan and they that were with him leapt into Jordan, and swam over unto the other bank: howbeit the other passed not over Jordan unto them.[49] So there were slain of Bacchides' side that day about a thousand men.[50] Afterward returned Bacchides to Jerusalem and repaired the strong cites in Judea; the fort in Jericho, and Emmaus, and Bethhoron, and Bethel, and Thamnatha, Pharathoni, and Taphon, these did he strengthen with high walls, with gates and with bars.[51] And in them he set a garrison, that they might work malice upon Israel.[52] He fortified also the city Bethsura, and Gazera, and the tower, and put forces in them, and provision of victuals.[53] Besides, he took the chief men's sons in the country for hostages, and put them into the tower at Jerusalem to be kept.[54] Moreover in the hundred fifty and third year, in the second month, Alcimus commanded that the wall of the inner court of the sanctuary should be pulled down; he pulled down also the works of the prophets[55] And as he began to pull down, even at that time was Alcimus plagued, and his enterprizes hindered: for his mouth was stopped, and he was taken with a palsy, so that he could no more speak any thing, nor give order concerning his house.[56] So Alcimus died at that time with great torment.[57] Now when Bacchides saw that Alcimus was dead, he returned to the king: whereupon the land of Judea was in rest two years.[58] Then all the ungodly men held a council, saying, Behold, Jonathan and his company are at ease, and dwell without care: now therefore we will bring Bacchides hither, who shall take them all in one night.[59] So they went and consulted with him.[60] Then removed he, and came with a great host, and sent letters privily to his adherents in Judea, that they should take Jonathan and those that were with him: howbeit they could not, because their counsel was known unto them.[61] Wherefore they took of the men of the country, that were authors of that mischief, about fifty persons, and slew them.[62] Afterward Jonathan, and Simon, and they that were with him, got them away to Bethbasi, which is in the wilderness, and they repaired the decays thereof, and made it strong.[63] Which thing when Bacchides knew, he gathered together all his host, and sent word to them that were of Judea.[64] Then went he and laid siege against Bethbasi; and they fought against it a long season and made engines

59

of war.[65] But Jonathan left his brother Simon in the city, and went forth himself into the country, and with a certain number went he forth.[66] And he smote Odonarkes and his brethren, and the children of Phasiron in their tent.[67] And when he began to smite them, and came up with his forces, Simon and his company went out of the city, and burned up the engines of war,[68] And fought against Bacchides, who was discomfited by them, and they afflicted him sore: for his counsel and travail was in vain.[69] Wherefore he was very wroth at the wicked men that gave him counsel to come into the country, inasmuch as he slew many of them, and purposed to return into his own country.[70] Whereof when Jonathan had knowledge, he sent ambassadors unto him, to the end he should make peace with him, and deliver them the prisoners.[71] Which thing he accepted, and did according to his demands, and sware unto him that he would never do him harm all the days of his life.[72] When therefore he had restored unto him the prisoners that he had taken aforetime out of the land of Judea, he returned and went his way into his own land, neither came he any more into their borders.[73] Thus the sword ceased from Israel: but Jonathan dwelt at Machmas, and began to govern the people; and he destroyed the ungodly men out of Israel.

1Mac.10

[1] In the hundred and sixtieth year Alexander, the son of Antiochus surnamed Epiphanes, went up and took Ptolemais: for the people had received him, by means whereof he reigned there,[2] Now when king Demetrius heard thereof, he gathered together an exceeding great host, and went forth against him to fight.[3] Moreover Demetrius sent letters unto Jonathan with loving words, so as he magnified him.[4] For said he, Let us first make peace with him, before he join with Alexander against us:[5] Else he will remember all the evils that we have done against him, and against his brethren and his people.[6] Wherefore he gave him authority to gather together an host, and to provide weapons, that he might aid him in battle: he commanded also that the hostages that were in the tower should be delivered him.[7] Then came Jonathan to Jerusalem, and read the letters in the audience of all the people, and of them that were in the tower:[8] Who were sore afraid, when they heard that the king had given him authority to gather together an host.[9] Whereupon they of the tower delivered their hostages unto Jonathan, and he delivered them unto their parents.[10] This done, Jonathan settled himself in Jerusalem, and began to build and repair the city.[11] And he commanded the workmen to build the walls and the mount Sion and about with square stones for fortification; and they did so.[12] Then the strangers, that were in the fortresses which Bacchides had built, fled away;[13] Insomuch as every man left his place, and went into his own country.[14] Only at Bethsura certain of those that had forsaken the law and the commandments remained still: for it was their place of refuge.[15] Now when king Alexander had heard what promises Demetrius had sent unto Jonathan: when also it was told him of the battles and noble acts which he and his brethren had done, and of the pains that they had endured,[16] He said, Shall we find such another man? now therefore we will make him our friend and confederate.[17] Upon this he wrote a letter, and sent it unto him, according to these words, saying,[18] King Alexander to his brother Jonathan sendeth greeting:[19] We have heard of thee, that thou art a man of great power, and meet to be our friend.[20] Wherefore now this day we ordain thee to be the high priest of thy nation, and to be called the king's friend; (and therewithal he sent him a purple robe and a crown of gold:) and require thee to take our part, and keep friendship with us.[21] So in the seventh month of the hundred and sixtieth year, at the feast of the tabernacles, Jonathan put on the holy robe, and gathered together forces, and provided much armour.[22] Whereof when Demetrius heard, he was very sorry, and

said,[23] What have we done, that Alexander hath prevented us in making amity with the Jews to strengthen himself?[24] I also will write unto them words of encouragement, and promise them dignities and gifts, that I may have their aid.[25] He sent unto them therefore to this effect: King Demetrius unto the people of the Jews sendeth greeting:[26] Whereas ye have kept covenants with us, and continued in our friendship, not joining yourselves with our enemies, we have heard hereof, and are glad.[27] Wherefore now continue ye still to be faithful unto us, and we will well recompense you for the things ye do in our behalf,[28] And will grant you many immunities, and give you rewards.[29] And now do I free you, and for your sake I release all the Jews, from tributes, and from the customs of salt, and from crown taxes,[30] And from that which appertaineth unto me to receive for the third part or the seed, and the half of the fruit of the trees, I release it from this day forth, so that they shall not be taken of the land of Judea, nor of the three governments which are added thereunto out of the country of Samaria and Galilee, from this day forth for evermore.[31] Let Jerusalem also be holy and free, with the borders thereof, both from tenths and tributes.[32] And as for the tower which is at Jerusalem, I yield up authority over it, and give the high priest, that he may set in it such men as he shall choose to keep it.[33] Moreover I freely set at liberty every one of the Jews, that were carried captives out of the land of Judea into any part of my kingdom, and I will that all my officers remit the tributes even of their cattle.[34] Furthermore I will that all the feasts, and sabbaths, and new moons, and solemn days, and the three days before the feast, and the three days after the feast shall be all of immunity and freedom for all the Jews in my realm.[35] Also no man shall have authority to meddle with or to molest any of them in any matter.[36] I will further, that there be enrolled among the king's forces about thirty thousand men of the Jews, unto whom pay shall be given, as belongeth to all king's forces.[37] And of them some shall be placed in the king's strong holds, of whom also some shall be set over the affairs of the kingdom, which are of trust: and I will that their overseers and governors be of themselves, and that they live after their own laws, even as the king hath commanded in the land of Judea.[38] And concerning the three governments that are added to Judea from the country of Samaria, let them be joined with Judea, that they may be reckoned to be under one, nor bound to obey other authority than the high priest's.[39] As for Ptolemais, and the land pertaining thereto, I give it as a free gift to the sanctuary at Jerusalem for the necessary expences of the sanctuary.[40] Moreover I give every year fifteen thousand shekels of silver out of the king's accounts from the places appertaining.[41] And all the overplus, which the officers payed not in as in former time, from henceforth shall be given toward the works of the temple.[42] And beside this, the five thousand shekels of silver, which they took from the uses of the temple out of the accounts year by year, even those things shall be released, because they appertain to the priests that minister.[43] And whosoever they be that flee unto the temple at Jerusalem, or be within the liberties hereof, being indebted unto the king, or for any other matter, let them be at liberty, and all that they have in my realm.[44] For the building also and repairing of the works of the sanctuary expences shall be given of the king's accounts.[45] Yea, and for the building of the walls of Jerusalem, and the fortifying thereof round about, expences shall be given out of the king's accounts, as also for the building of the walls in Judea.[46] Now when Jonathan and the people heard these words, they gave no credit unto them, nor received them, because they remembered the great evil that he had done in Israel; for he had afflicted them very sore.[47] But with Alexander they were well pleased, because he was the first that entreated of true peace with them, and they were confederate with

60

him always.[48] Then gathered king Alexander great forces, and camped over against Demetrius.[49] And after the two kings had joined battle, Demetrius' host fled: but Alexander followed after him, and prevailed against them.[50] And he continued the battle very sore until the sun went down: and that day was Demetrius slain.[51] Afterward Alexander sent ambassadors to Ptolemee king of Egypt with a message to this effect:[52] Forasmuch as I am come again to my realm, and am set in the throne of my progenitors, and have gotten the dominion, and overthrown Demetrius, and recovered our country;[53] For after I had joined battle with him, both he and his host was discomfited by us, so that we sit in the throne of his kingdom:[54] Now therefore let us make a league of amity together, and give me now thy daughter to wife: and I will be thy son in law, and will give both thee and her as according to thy dignity.[55] Then Ptolemee the king gave answer, saying, Happy be the day wherein thou didst return into the land of thy fathers, and satest in the throne of their kingdom.[56] And now will I do to thee, as thou hast written: meet me therefore at Ptolemais, that we may see one another; for I will marry my daughter to thee according to thy desire.[57] So Ptolemee went out of Egypt with his daughter Cleopatra, and they came unto Ptolemais in the hundred threescore and second year:[58] Where king Alexander meeting him, he gave unto him his daughter Cleopatra, and celebrated her marriage at Ptolemais with great glory, as the manner of kings is.[59] Now king Alexander had written unto Jonathan, that he should come and meet him.[60] Who thereupon went honourably to Ptolemais, where he met the two kings, and gave them and their friends silver and gold, and many presents, and found favour in their sight.[61] At that time certain pestilent fellows of Israel, men of a wicked life, assembled themselves against him, to accuse him: but the king would not hear them.[62] Yea more than that, the king commanded to take off his garments, and clothe him in purple: and they did so.[63] And he made him sit by himself, and said unto his princes, Go with him into the midst of the city, and make proclamation, that no man complain against him of any matter, and that no man trouble him for any manner of cause.[64] Now when his accusers saw that he was honored according to the proclamation, and clothed in purple, they fled all away.[65] So the king honoured him, and wrote him among his chief friends, and made him a duke, and partaker of his dominion.[66] Afterward Jonathan returned to Jerusalem with peace and gladness.[67] Furthermore in the; hundred threescore and fifth year came Demetrius son of Demetrius out of Crete into the land of his fathers:[68] Whereof when king Alexander heard tell, he was right sorry, and returned into Antioch.[69] Then Demetrius made Apollonius the governor of Celosyria his general, who gathered together a great host, and camped in Jamnia, and sent unto Jonathan the high priest, saying,[70] Thou alone liftest up thyself against us, and I am laughed to scorn for thy sake, and reproached: and why dost thou vaunt thy power against us in the mountains?[71] Now therefore, if thou trustest in thine own strength, come down to us into the plain field, and there let us try the matter together: for with me is the power of the cities.[72] Ask and learn who I am, and the rest that take our part, and they shall tell thee that thy foot is not able to to flight in their own land.[73] Wherefore now thou shalt not be able to abide the horsemen and so great a power in the plain, where is neither stone nor flint, nor place to flee unto.[74] So when Jonathan heard these words of Apollonius, he was moved in his mind, and choosing ten thousand men he went out of Jerusalem, where Simon his brother met him for to help him.[75] And he pitched his tents against Joppa: but; they of Joppa shut him out of the city, because Apollonius had a garrison there.[76] Then Jonathan laid siege unto it: whereupon they of the city let him in for fear: and so Jonathan won

Joppa.[77] Whereof when Apollonius heard, he took three thousand horsemen, with a great host of footmen, and went to Azotus as one that journeyed, and therewithal drew him forth into the plain. because he had a great number of horsemen, in whom he put his trust.[78] Then Jonathan followed after him to Azotus, where the armies joined battle.[79] Now Apollonius had left a thousand horsemen in ambush.[80] And Jonathan knew that there was an ambushment behind him; for they had compassed in his host, and cast darts at the people, from morning till evening.[81] But the people stood still, as Jonathan had commanded them: and so the enemies' horses were tired.[82] Then brought Simon forth his host, and set them against the footmen, (for the horsemen were spent) who were discomfited by him, and fled.[83] The horsemen also, being scattered in the field, fled to Azotus, and went into Bethdagon, their idol's temple, for safety.[84] But Jonathan set fire on Azotus, and the cities round about it, and took their spoils; and the temple of Dagon, with them that were fled into it, he burned with fire.[85] Thus there were burned and slain with the sword well nigh eight thousand men.[86] And from thence Jonathan removed his host, and camped against Ascalon, where the men of the city came forth, and met him with great pomp.[87] After this returned Jonathan and his host unto Jerusalem, having any spoils.[88] Now when king ALexander heard these things, he honoured Jonathan yet more.[89] And sent him a buckle of gold, as the use is to be given to such as are of the king's blood: he gave him also Accaron with the borders thereof in possession.

1Mac.11

[1] And the king of Egypt gathered together a great host, like the sand that lieth upon the sea shore, and many ships, and went about through deceit to get Alexander's kingdom, and join it to his own.[2] Whereupon he took his journey into Spain in peaceable manner, so as they of the cities opened unto him, and met him: for king Alexander had commanded them so to do, because he was his brother in law.[3] Now as Ptolemee entered into the cities, he set in every one of them a garrison of soldiers to keep it.[4] And when he came near to Azotus, they shewed him the temple of Dagon that was burnt, and Azotus and the suburbs thereof that were destroyed, and the bodies that were cast abroad and them that he had burnt in the battle; for they had made heaps of them by the way where he should pass.[5] Also they told the king whatsoever Jonathan had done, to the intent he might blame him: but the king held his peace.[6] Then Jonathan met the king with great pomp at Joppa, where they saluted one another, and lodged.[7] Afterward Jonathan, when he had gone with the king to the river called Eleutherus, returned again to Jerusalem.[8] King Ptolemee therefore, having gotten the dominion of the cities by the sea unto Seleucia upon the sea coast, imagined wicked counsels against Alexander.[9] Whereupon he sent ambasadors unto king Demetrius, saying, Come, let us make a league betwixt us, and I will give thee my daughter whom Alexander hath, and thou shalt reign in thy father's kingdom:[10] For I repent that I gave my daughter unto him, for he sought to slay me.[11] Thus did he slander him, because he was desirous of his kingdom.[12] Wherefore he took his daughter from him, and gave her to Demetrius, and forsook Alexander, so that their hatred was openly known.[13] Then Ptolemee entered into Antioch, where he set two crowns upon his head, the crown of Asia, and of Egypt.[14] In the mean season was king Alexander in Cilicia, because those that dwelt in those parts had revolted from him.[15] But when Alexander heard of this, he came to war against him: whereupon king Ptolemee brought forth his host, and met him with a mighty power, and put him to flight.[16] So Alexander fled into Arabia there to be defended; but king Ptolemee was exalted:[17] For Zabdiel the Arabian took off Alexander's head, and sent it unto Ptolemee.[18] King Ptolemee also died the third day after, and they that were in the strong holds were slain one of another.[19] By this means Demetrius reigned in the hundred threescore and seventh year.[20] At the same time Jonathan gathered together them that were in Judea to take the tower that was in Jerusalem: and he made many engines of war against it.[21] Then came ungodly persons, who hated their own people, went unto the king, and told him that Jonathan besieged the tower,[22] Whereof when he heard, he was angry, and immediately removing, he came to Ptolemais, and wrote unto Jonathan, that he should not lay siege to the tower, but come and speak with him at Ptolemais in great haste.[23] Nevertheless Jonathan, when he heard this, commanded to besiege it still: and he chose certain of the elders of Israel and the priests, and put himself in peril;[24] And took silver and gold, and raiment, and divers presents besides, and went to Ptolemais unto the king, where he found favour in his sight.[25] And though certain ungodly men of the people had made complaints against him,[26] Yet the king entreated him as his predecessors had done before, and promoted him in the sight of all his friends,[27] And confirmed him in the high priesthood, and in all the honours that he had before, and gave him preeminence among his chief friends.[28] Then Jonathan desired the king, that he would make Judea free from tribute, as also the three governments, with the country of Samaria; and he promised him three hundred talents.[29] So the king consented, and wrote letters unto Jonathan of all these things after this manner:[30] King Demetrius unto his brother Jonathan, and unto the nation of the Jews, sendeth greeting:[31] We send you here a copy of the letter which we did write unto our cousin Lasthenes concerning you, that ye might see it.[32] King Demetrius unto his father Lasthenes sendeth greeting:[33] We are determined to do good to the people of the Jews, who are our friends, and keep covenants with us, because of their good will toward us.[34] Wherefore we have ratified unto them the borders of Judea, with the three governments of Apherema and Lydda and Ramathem, that are added unto Judea from the country of Samaria, and all things appertaining unto them, for all such as do sacrifice in Jerusalem, instead of the payments which the king received of them yearly aforetime out of the fruits of the earth and of trees.[35] And as for other things that belong unto us, of the tithes and customs pertaining unto us, as also the saltpits, and the crown taxes, which are due unto us, we discharge them of them all for their relief.[36] And nothing hereof shall be revoked from this time forth for ever.[37] Now therefore see that thou make a copy of these things, and let it be delivered unto Jonathan, and set upon the holy mount in a conspicuous place.[38] After this, when king Demetrius saw that the land was quiet before him, and that no resistance was made against him, he sent away all his forces, every one to his own place, except certain bands of strangers, whom he had gathered from the isles of the heathen: wherefore all the forces of his fathers hated him.[39] Moreover there was one Tryphon, that had been of Alexander's part afore, who, seeing that all the host murmured against Demetrius, went to Simalcue the Arabian that brought up Antiochus the young son of Alexander,[40] And lay sore upon him to deliver him this young Antiochus, that he might reign in his father's stead: he told him therefore all that Demetrius had done, and how his men of war were at enmity with him, and there he remained a long season.[41] In the mean time Jonathan sent unto king Demetrius, that he would cast those of the tower out of Jerusalem, and those also in the fortresses: for they fought against Israel.[42] So Demetrius sent unto Jonathan, saying, I will not only do this for thee and thy people, but I will greatly honour thee and thy nation, if opportunity serve.[43] Now therefore thou shalt do well, if thou send me men to help me; for all my forces are gone from me.[44] Upon this Jonathan

sent him three thousand strong men unto Antioch: and when they came to the king, the king was very glad of their coming.[45] Howbeit they that were of the city gathered themselves together into the midst of the city, to the number of an hundred and twenty thousand men, and would have slain the king.[46] Wherefore the king fled into the court, but they of the city kept the passages of the city, and began to fight.[47] Then the king called to the Jews for help, who came unto him all at once, and dispersing themselves through the city slew that day in the city to the number of an hundred thousand.[48] Also they set fire on the city, and gat many spoils that day, and delivered the king.[49] So when they of the city saw that the Jews had got the city as they would, their courage was abated: wherefore they made supplication to the king, and cried, saying,[50] Grant us peace, and let the Jews cease from assaulting us and the city.[51] With that they cast away their weapons, and made peace; and the Jews were honoured in the sight of the king, and in the sight of all that were in his realm; and they returned to Jerusalem, having great spoils.[52] So king Demetrius sat on the throne of his kingdom, and the land was quiet before him.[53] Nevertheless he dissembled in all that ever he spake, and estranged himself from Jonathan, neither rewarded he him according to the benefits which he had received of him, but troubled him very sore.[54] After this returned Tryphon, and with him the young child Antiochus, who reigned, and was crowned.[55] Then there gathered unto him all the men of war, whom Demetrius had put away, and they fought against Demetrius, who turned his back and fled.[56] Moreover Tryphon took the elephants, and won Antioch.[57] At that time young Antiochus wrote unto Jonathan, saying, I confirm thee in the high priesthood, and appoint thee ruler over the four governments, and to be one of the king's friends.[58] Upon this he sent him golden vessels to be served in, and gave him leave to drink in gold, and to be clothed in purple, and to wear a golden buckle.[59] His brother Simon also he made captain from the place called The ladder of Tyrus unto the borders of Egypt.[60] Then Jonathan went forth, and passed through the cities beyond the water, and all the forces of Syria gathered themselves unto him for to help him: and when he came to Ascalon, they of the city met him honourably.[61] From whence he went to Gaza, but they of Gaza shut him out; wherefore he laid siege unto it, and burned the suburbs thereof with fire, and spoiled them.[62] Afterward, when they of Gaza made supplication unto Jonathan, he made peace with them, and took the sons of their chief men for hostages, and sent them to Jerusalem, and passed through the country unto Damascus.[63] Now when Jonathan heard that Demetrius' princes were come to Cades, which is in Galilee, with a great power, purposing to remove him out of the country,[64] He went to meet them, and left Simon his brother in the country.[65] Then Simon encamped against Bethsura and fought against it a long season, and shut it up:[66] But they desired to have peace with him, which he granted them, and then put them out from thence, and took the city, and set a garrison in it.[67] As for Jonathan and his host, they pitched at the water of Gennesar, from whence betimes in the morning they gat them to the plain of Nasor.[68] And, behold, the host of strangers met them in the plain, who, having laid men in ambush for him in the mountains, came themselves over against him.[69] So when they that lay in ambush rose out of their places and joined battle, all that were of Jonathan's side fled;[70] Insomuch as there was not one of them left, except Mattathias the son of Absalom, and Judas the son of Calphi, the captains of the host.[71] Then Jonathan rent his clothes, and cast earth upon his head, and prayed.[72] Afterwards turning again to battle, he put them to flight, and so they ran away.[73] Now when his own men that were fled saw this, they turned again unto him, and with him pursued them to Cades, even unto their own tents, and

there they camped.[74] So there were slain of the heathen that day about three thousand men: but Jonathan returned to Jerusalem.

1Mac.12

[1] Now when Jonathan saw that time served him, he chose certain men, and sent them to Rome, for to confirm and renew the friendship that they had with them.[2] He sent letters also to the Lacedemonians, and to other places, for the same purpose.[3] So they went unto Rome, and entered into the senate, and said, Jonathan the high priest, and the people of the Jews, sent us unto you, to the end ye should renew the friendship, which ye had with them, and league, as in former time.[4] Upon this the Romans gave them letters unto the governors of every place that they should bring them into the land of Judea peaceably.[5] And this is the copy of the letters which Jonathan wrote to the Lacedemonians:[6] Jonathan the high priest, and the elders of the nation, and the priests, and the other of the Jews, unto the Lacedemonians their brethren send greeting:[7] There were letters sent in times past unto Onias the high priest from Darius, who reigned then among you, to signify that ye are our brethren, as the copy here underwritten doth specify.[8] At which time Onias entreated the ambassador that was sent honourably, and received the letters, wherein declaration was made of the league and friendship.[9] Therefore we also, albeit we need none of these things, that we have the holy books of scripture in our hands to comfort us,[10] Have nevertheless attempted to send unto you for the renewing of brotherhood and friendship, lest we should become strangers unto you altogether: for there is a long time passed since ye sent unto us.[11] We therefore at all times without ceasing, both in our feasts, and other convenient days, do remember you in the sacrifices which we offer, and in our prayers, as reason is, and as it becometh us to think upon our brethren:[12] And we are right glad of your honour.[13] As for ourselves, we have had great troubles and wars on every side, forsomuch as the kings that are round about us have fought against us.[14] Howbeit we would not be troublesome unto you, nor to others of our confederates and friends, in these wars:[15] For we have help from heaven that succoureth us, so as we are delivered from our enemies, and our enemies are brought under foot.[16] For this cause we chose Numenius the son of Antiochus, and Antipater he son of Jason, and sent them unto the Romans, to renew the amity that we had with them, and the former league.[17] We commanded them also to go unto you, and to salute and to deliver you our letters concerning the renewing of our brotherhood.[18] Wherefore now ye shall do well to give us an answer thereto.[19] And this is the copy of the letters which Oniares sent.[20] Areus king of the Lacedemonians to Onias the high priest, greeting:[21] It is found in writing, that the Lacedemonians and Jews are brethren, and that they are of the stock of Abraham:[22] Now therefore, since this is come to our knowledge, ye shall do well to write unto us of your prosperity.[23] We do write back again to you, that your cattle and goods are our's, and our's are your's We do command therefore our ambassadors to make report unto you on this wise.[24] Now when Jonathan heard that Demebius' princes were come to fight against him with a greater host than afore,[25] He removed from Jerusalem, and met them in the land of Amathis: for he gave them no respite to enter his country.[26] He sent spies also unto their tents, who came again, and told him that they were appointed to come upon them in the night season.[27] Wherefore so soon as the sun was down, Jonathan commanded his men to watch, and to be in arms, that all the night long they might be ready to fight: also he sent forth centinels round about the host.[28] But when the adversaries heard that Jonathan and his men were ready for battle, they feared, and trembled in their hearts, and they kindled fires in their camp.[29] Howbeit Jonathan and his company knew it not till the

morning: for they saw the lights burning.[30] Then Jonathan pursued after them, but overtook them not: for they were gone over the river Eleutherus.[31] Wherefore Jonathan turned to the Arabians, who were called Zabadeans, and smote them, and took their spoils.[32] And removing thence, he came to Damascus, and so passed through all the country,[33] Simon also went forth, and passed through the country unto Ascalon, and the holds there adjoining, from whence he turned aside to Joppa, and won it.[34] For he had heard that they would deliver the hold unto them that took Demetrius' part; wherefore he set a garrison there to keep it.[35] After this came Jonathan home again, and calling the elders of the people together, he consulted with them about building strong holds in Judea,[36] And making the walls of Jerusalem higher, and raising a great mount between the tower and the city, for to separate it from the city, that so it might be alone, that men might neither sell nor buy in it.[37] Upon this they came together to build up the city, forasmuch as part of the wall toward the brook on the east side was fallen down, and they repaired that which was called Caphenatha.[38] Simon also set up Adida in Sephela, and made it strong with gates and bars.[39] Now Tryphon went about to get the kingdom of Asia, and to kill Antiochus the king, that he might set the crown upon his own head.[40] Howbeit he was afraid that Jonathan would not suffer him, and that he would fight against him; wherefore he sought a way how to take Jonathan, that he might kill him. So he removed, and came to Bethsan.[41] Then Jonathan went out to meet him with forty thousand men chosen for the battle, and came to Bethsan.[42] Now when Tryphon saw Jonathan came with so great a force, he durst not stretch his hand against him;[43] But received him honourably, and commended him unto all his friends, and gave him gifts, and commanded his men of war to be as obedient unto him, as to himself.[44] Unto Jonathan also he said, Why hast thou brought all this people to so great trouble, seeing there is no war betwixt us?[45] Therefore send them now home again, and choose a few men to wait on thee, and come thou with me to Ptolemais, for I will give it thee, and the rest of the strong holds and forces, and all that have any charge: as for me, I will return and depart: for this is the cause of my coming.[46] So Jonathan believing him did as he bade him, and sent away his host, who went into the land of Judea.[47] And with himself he retained but three thousand men, of whom he sent two thousand into Galilee, and one thousand went with him.[48] Now as soon as Jonathan entered into Ptolemais, they of Ptolemais shut the gates and took him, and all them that came with him they slew with the sword.[49] Then sent Tryphon an host of footmen and horsemen into Galilee, and into the great plain, to destroy all Jonathan's company.[50] But when they knew that Jonathan and they that were with him were taken and slain, they encouraged one another; and went close together, prepared to fight.[51] They therefore that followed upon them, perceiving that they were ready to fight for their lives, turned back again.[52] Whereupon they all came into the land of Judea peaceably, and there they bewailed Jonathan, and them that were with him, and they were sore afraid; wherefore all Israel made great lamentation.[53] Then all the heathen that were round about then sought to destroy them: for said they, They have no captain, nor any to help them: now therefore let us make war upon them, and take away their memorial from among men.

1Mac.13

[1] Now when Simon heard that Tryphon had gathered together a great host to invade the land of Judea, and destroy it,[2] And saw that the people was in great trembling and fear, he went up to Jerusalem, and gathered the people together,[3] And gave them exhortation, saying, Ye yourselves know what great things I, and my brethren, and my father's house, have done for the laws and the sanctuary, the battles also and troubles which we have seen.[4] By reason whereof all my brethren are slain for Israel's sake, and I am left alone.[5] Now therefore be it far from me, that I should spare mine own life in any time of trouble: for I am no better than my brethren.[6] Doubtless I will avenge my nation, and the sanctuary, and our wives, and our children: for all the heathen are gathered to destroy us of very malice.[7] Now as soon as the people heard these words, their spirit revived.[8] And they answered with a loud voice, saying, Thou shalt be our leader instead of Judas and Jonathan thy brother.[9] Fight thou our battles, and whatsoever, thou commandest us, that will we do.[10] So then he gathered together all the men of war, and made haste to finish the walls of Jerusalem, and he fortified it round about.[11] Also he sent Jonathan the son of Absolom, and with him a great power, to Joppa: who casting out them that were therein remained there in it.[12] So Tryphon removed from Ptolemaus with a great power to invade the land of Judea, and Jonathan was with him in ward.[13] But Simon pitched his tents at Adida, over against the plain.[14] Now when Tryphon knew that Simon was risen up instead of his brother Jonathan, and meant to join battle with him, he sent messengers unto him, saying,[15] Whereas we have Jonathan thy brother in hold, it is for money that he is owing unto the king's treasure, concerning the business that was committed unto him.[16] Wherefore now send an hundred talents of silver, and two of his sons for hostages, that when he is at liberty he may not revolt from us, and we will let him go.[17] Hereupon Simon, albeit he perceived that they spake deceitfully unto him yet sent he the money and the children, lest peradventure he should procure to himself great hatred of the people:[18] Who might have said, Because I sent him not the money and the children, therefore is Jonathan dead.[19] So he sent them the children and the hundred talents: howbeit Tryphon dissembled neither would he let Jonathan go.[20] And after this came Tryphon to invade the land, and destroy it, going round about by the way that leadeth unto Adora: but Simon and his host marched against him in every place, wheresoever he went.[21] Now they that were in the tower sent messengers unto Tryphon, to the end that he should hasten his coming unto them by the wilderness, and send them victuals.[22] Wherefore Tryphon made ready all his horsemen to come that night: but there fell a very great snow, by reason whereof he came not. So he departed, and came into the country of Galaad.[23] And when he came near to Bascama he slew Jonathan, who was buried there.[24] Afterward Tryphon returned and went into his own land.[25] Then sent Simon, and took the bones of Jonathan his brother, and buried them in Modin, the city of his fathers.[26] And all Israel made great lamentation for him, and bewailed him many days.[27] Simon also built a monument upon the sepulchre of his father and his brethren, and raised it aloft to the sight, with hewn stone behind and before.[28] Moreover he set up seven pyramids, one against another, for his father, and his mother, and his four brethren.[29] And in these he made cunning devices, about the which he set great pillars, and upon the pillars he made all their armour for a perpetual memory, and by the armour ships carved, that they might be seen of all that sail on the sea.[30] This is the sepulchre which he made at Modin, and it standeth yet unto this day.[31] Now Tryphon dealt deceitfully with the young king Antiochus, and slew him.[32] And he reigned in his stead, and crowned himself king of Asia, and brought a great calamity upon the land.[33] Then Simon built up the strong holds in Judea, and fenced them about with high towers, and great walls, and gates, and bars, and laid up victuals therein.[34] Moreover Simon chose men, and sent to king Demetrius, to the end he should give the land an immunity, because all that Tryphon did was to spoil.[35] Unto whom king Demetrius answered and wrote after this manner:[36] King Demetrius unto Simon the high

priest, and friend of kings, as also unto the elders and nation of the Jews, sendeth greeting:[37] The golden crown, and the scarlet robe, which ye sent unto us, we have received: and we are ready to make a stedfast peace with you, yea, and to write unto our officers, to confirm the immunities which we have granted.[38] And whatsoever covenants we have made with you shall stand; and the strong holds, which ye have builded, shall be your own.[39] As for any oversight or fault committed unto this day, we forgive it, and the crown tax also, which ye owe us: and if there were any other tribute paid in Jerusalem, it shall no more be paid.[40] And look who are meet among you to be in our court, let then be enrolled, and let there be peace betwixt us.[41] Thus the yoke of the heathen was taken away from Israel in the hundred and seventieth year.[42] Then the people of Israel began to write in their instruments and contracts, In the first year of Simon the high priest, the governor and leader of the Jews.[43] In those days Simon camped against Gaza and besieged it round about; he made also an engine of war, and set it by the city, and battered a certain tower, and took it.[44] And they that were in the engine leaped into the city; whereupon there was a great uproar in the city:[45] Insomuch as the people of the city rent their clothes, and climbed upon the walls with their wives and children, and cried with a loud voice, beseeching Simon to grant them peace.[46] And they said, Deal not with us according to our wickedness, but according to thy mercy.[47] So Simon was appeased toward them, and fought no more against them, but put them out of the city, and cleansed the houses wherein the idols were, and so entered into it with songs and thanksgiving.[48] Yea, he put all uncleanness out of it, and placed such men there as would keep the law, and made it stronger than it was before, and built therein a dwellingplace for himself.[49] They also of the tower in Jerusalem were kept so strait, that they could neither come forth, nor go into the country, nor buy, nor sell: wherefore they were in great distress for want of victuals, and a great number of them perished through famine.[50] Then cried they to Simon, beseeching him to be at one with them: which thing he granted them; and when he had put them out from thence, he cleansed the tower from pollutions:[51] And entered into it the three and twentieth day of the second month in the hundred seventy and first year, with thanksgiving, and branches of palm trees, and with harps, and cymbals, and with viols, and hymns, and songs: because there was destroyed a great enemy out of Israel.[52] He ordained also that that day should be kept every year with gladness. Moreover the hill of the temple that was by the tower he made stronger than it was, and there he dwelt himself with his company.[53] And when Simon saw that John his son was a valiant man, he made him captain of all the hosts; and he dwelt in Gazera.

1Mac.14

[1] Now in the hundred threescore and twelfth year king Demetrius gathered his forces together, and went into Media to get him help to fight against Tryphone.[2] But when Arsaces, the king of Persia and Media, heard that Demetrius was entered within his borders, he sent one of his princes to take him alive:[3] Who went and smote the host of Demetrius, and took him, and brought him to Arsaces, by whom he was put in ward.[4] As for the land of Judea, that was quiet all the days of Simon; for he sought the good of his nation in such wise, as that evermore his authority and honour pleased them well.[5] And as he was honourable in all his acts, so in this, that he took Joppa for an haven, and made an entrance to the isles of the sea,[6] And enlarged the bounds of his nation, and recovered the country,[7] And gathered together a great number of captives, and had the dominion of Gazera, and Bethsura, and the tower, out of the which he took all uncleaness, neither was there any that resisted him.[8] Then did they till their ground in peace, and the earth gave her increase, and the

trees of the field their fruit.[9] The ancient men sat all in the streets, communing together of good things, and the young men put on glorious and warlike apparel.[10] He provided victuals for the cities, and set in them all manner of munition, so that his honourable name was renowned unto the end of the world.[11] He made peace in the land, and Israel rejoiced with great joy:[12] For every man sat under his vine and his fig tree, and there was none to fray them:[13] Neither was there any left in the land to fight against them: yea, the kings themselves were overthrown in those days.[14] Moreover he strengthened all those of his people that were brought low: the law he searched out; and every contemner of the law and wicked person he took away.[15] He beautified the sanctuary, and multiplied vessels of the temple.[16] Now when it was heard at Rome, and as far as Sparta, that Jonathan was dead, they were very sorry.[17] But as soon as they heard that his brother Simon was made high priest in his stead, and ruled the country, and the cities therein:[18] They wrote unto him in tables of brass, to renew the friendship and league which they had made with Judas and Jonathan his brethren:[19] Which writings were read before the congregation at Jerusalem.[20] And this is the copy of the letters that the Lacedemonians sent; The rulers of the Lacedemonians, with the city, unto Simon the high priest, and the elders, and priests, and residue of the people of the Jews, our brethren, send greeting:[21] The ambassadors that were sent unto our people certified us of your glory and honour: wherefore we were glad of their coming,[22] And did register the things that they spake in the council of the people in this manner; Numenius son of Antiochus, and Antipater son of Jason, the Jews' ambassadors, came unto us to renew the friendship they had with us.[23] And it pleased the people to entertain the men honourably, and to put the copy of their ambassage in publick records, to the end the people of the Lacedemonians might have a memorial thereof: furthermore we have written a copy thereof unto Simon the high priest.[24] After this Simon sent Numenius to Rome with a great shield of gold of a thousand pound weight to confirm the league with them.[25] Whereof when the people heard, they said, What thanks shall we give to Simon and his sons?[26] For he and his brethren and the house of his father have established Israel, and chased away in fight their enemies from them, and confirmed their liberty.[27] So then they wrote it in tables of brass, which they set upon pillars in mount Sion: and this is the copy of the writing; The eighteenth day of the month Elul, in the hundred threescore and twelfth year, being the third year of Simon the high priest,[28] At Saramel in the great congregation of the priests, and people, and rulers of the nation, and elders of the country, were these things notified unto us.[29] Forasmuch as oftentimes there have been wars in the country, wherein for the maintenance of their sanctuary, and the law, Simon the son of Mattathias, of the posterity of Jarib, together with his brethren, put themselves in jeopardy, and resisting the enemies of their nation did their nation great honour:[30] (For after that Jonathan, having gathered his nation together, and been their high priest, was added to his people,[31] Their enemies prepared to invade their country, that they might destroy it, and lay hands on the sanctuary:[32] At which time Simon rose up, and fought for his nation, and spent much of his own substance, and armed the valiant men of his nation and gave them wages,[33] And fortified the cities of Judea, together with Bethsura, that lieth upon the borders of Judea, where the armour of the enemies had been before; but he set a garrison of Jews there:[34] Moreover he fortified Joppa, which lieth upon the sea, and Gazera, that bordereth upon Azotus, where the enemies had dwelt before: but he placed Jews there, and furnished them with all things convenient for the reparation thereof.)[35] The people therefore sang the acts of Simon, and unto what glory he thought to bring his nation, made him their governor and chief priest, because he had done all these things, and for the justice and faith which he kept to his nation, and for that he sought by all means to exalt his people.[36] For in his time things prospered in his hands, so that the heathen were taken out of their country, and they also that were in the city of David in Jerusalem, who had made themselves a tower, out of which they issued, and polluted all about the sanctuary, and did much hurt in the holy place:[37] But he placed Jews therein. and fortified it for the safety of the country and the city, and raised up the walls of Jerusalem.[38] King Demetrius also confirmed him in the high priesthood according to those things,[39] And made him one of his friends, and honoured him with great honour.[40] For he had heard say, that the Romans had called the Jews their friends and confederates and brethren; and that they had entertained the ambassadors of Simon honourably;[41] Also that the Jews and priests were well pleased that Simon should be their governor and high priest for ever, until there should arise a faithful prophet;[42] Moreover that he should be their captain, and should take charge of the sanctuary, to set them over their works, and over the country, and over the armour, and over the fortresses, that, I say, he should take charge of the sanctuary;[43] Beside this, that he should be obeyed of every man, and that all the writings in the country should be made in his name, and that he should be clothed in purple, and wear gold:[44] Also that it should be lawful for none of the people or priests to break any of these things, or to gainsay his words, or to gather an assembly in the country without him, or to be clothed in purple, or wear a buckle of gold;[45] And whosoever should do otherwise, or break any of these things, he should be punished.[46] Thus it liked all the people to deal with Simon, and to do as hath been said.[47] Then Simon accepted hereof, and was well pleased to be high priest, and captain and governor of the Jews and priests, and to defend them all.[48] So they commanded that this writing should be put in tables of brass, and that they should be set up within the compass of the sanctuary in a conspicuous place;[49] Also that the copies thereof should be laid up in the treasury, to the end that Simon and his sons might have them.

1Mac.15

[1] Moreover Antiochus son of Demetrius the king sent letters from the isles of the sea unto Simon the priest and prince of the Jews, and to all the people;[2] The contents whereof were these: King Antiochus to Simon the high priest and prince of his nation, and to the people of the Jews, greeting:[3] Forasmuch as certain pestilent men have usurped the kingdom of our fathers, and my purpose is to challenge it again, that I may restore it to the old estate, and to that end have gathered a multitude of foreign soldiers together, and prepared ships of war;[4] My meaning also being to go through the country, that I may be avenged of them that have destroyed it, and made many cities in the kingdom desolate:[5] Now therefore I confirm unto thee all the oblations which the kings before me granted thee, and whatsoever gifts besides they granted.[6] I give thee leave also to coin money for thy country with thine own stamp.[7] And as concerning Jerusalem and the sanctuary, let them be free; and all the armour that thou hast made, and fortresses that thou hast built, and keepest in thine hands, let them remain unto thee.[8] And if anything be, or shall be, owing to the king, let it be forgiven thee from this time forth for evermore.[9] Furthermore, when we have obtained our kingdom, we will honour thee, and thy nation, and thy temple, with great honour, so that your honour shall be known throughout the world.[10] In the hundred threescore and fourteenth year went Antiochus into the land of his fathers: at which time all the forces came together unto him, so that few were left with Tryphon.[11] Wherefore being pursued by king Antiochus, he fled unto Dora, which lieth by the sea side:[12] For he saw that troubles came upon him all at once, and that his forces had forsaken him.[13] Then camped Antiochus against Dora, having with him an hundred and twenty thousand men of war, and eight thousand horsemen.[14] And when he had compassed the city round about, and joined ships close to the town on the sea side, he vexed the city by land and by sea, neither suffered he any to go out or in.[15] In the mean season came Numenius and his company from Rome, having letters to the kings and countries; wherein were written these things:[16] Lucius, consul of the Romans unto king Ptolemee, greeting:[17] The Jews' ambassadors, our friends and confederates, came unto us to renew the old friendship and league, being sent from Simon the high priest, and from the people of the Jews:[18] And they brought a shield of gold of a thousand pound.[19] We thought it good therefore to write unto the kings and countries, that they should do them no harm, nor fight against them, their cities, or countries, nor yet aid their enemies against them.[20] It seemed also good to us to receive the shield of them.[21] If therefore there be any pestilent fellows, that have fled from their country unto you, deliver them unto Simon the high priest, that he may punish them according to their own law.[22] The same things wrote he likewise unto Demetrius the king, and Attalus, to Ariarathes, and Arsaces,[23] And to all the countries and to Sampsames, and the Lacedemonians, and to Delus, and Myndus, and Sicyon, and Caria, and Samos, and Pamphylia, and Lycia, and Halicarnassus, and Rhodus, and Aradus, and Cos, and Side, and Aradus, and Gortyna, and Cnidus, and Cyprus, and Cyrene.[24] And the copy hereof they wrote to Simon the high priest.[25] So Antiochus the king camped against Dora the second day, assaulting it continually, and making engines, by which means he shut up Tryphon, that he could neither go out nor in.[26] At that time Simon sent him two thousand chosen men to aid him; silver also, and gold, and much armour.[27] Nevertheless he would not receive them, but brake all the covenants which he had made with him afore, and became strange unto him.[28] Furthermore he sent unto him Athenobius, one of his friends, to commune with him, and say, Ye withhold Joppa and Gazera; with the tower that is in Jerusalem, which are cities of my realm.[29] The borders thereof ye have wasted, and done great hurt in the land, and got the dominion of many places within my kingdom.[30] Now therefore deliver the cities which ye have taken, and the tributes of the places, whereof ye have gotten dominion without the borders of Judea:[31] Or else give me for them five hundred talents of silver; and for the harm that ye have done, and the tributes of the cities, other five hundred talents: if not, we will come and fight against you.[32] So Athenobius the king's friend came to Jerusalem: and when he saw the glory of Simon, and the cupboard of gold and silver plate, and his great attendance, he was astonished, and told him the king's message.[33] Then answered Simon, and said unto him, We have neither taken other men's land, nor holden that which appertaineth to others, but the inheritance of our fathers, which our enemies had wrongfully in possession a certain time.[34] Wherefore we, having opportunity, hold the inheritance of our fathers.[35] And whereas thou demandest Joppa and Gazera, albeit they did great harm unto the people in our country, yet will we give thee an hundred talents for them. Hereunto Athenobius answered him not a word;[36] But returned in a rage to the king, and made report unto him of these speeches, and of the glory of Simon, and of all that he had seen: whereupon the king was exceeding wroth.[37] In the mean time fled Tryphon by ship unto Orthosias.[38] Then the king made Cendebeus captain of the sea coast, and gave him an host of footmen and horsemen,[39] And commanded him to remove his host toward Judea; also he commanded him to build up Cedron, and to fortify the gates, and to war against the people; but as for the king himself, he pursued Tryphon.[40] So

Cendebeus came to Jamnia and began to provoke the people and to invade Judea, and to take the people prisoners, and slay them.[41] And when he had built up Cedrou, he set horsemen there, and an host of footmen, to the end that issuing out they might make outroads upon the ways of Judea, as the king had commanded him.

1Mac.16

[1] Then came up John from Gazera, and told Simon his father what Cendebeus had done.[2] Wherefore Simon called his two eldest sons, Judas and John, and said unto them, I, and my brethren, and my father's house, have ever from my youth unto this day fought against the enemies of Israel; and things have prospered so well in our hands, that we have delivered Israel oftentimes.[3] But now I am old, and ye, by God's mercy, are of a sufficient age: be ye instead of me and my brother, and go and fight for our nation, and the help from heaven be with you.[4] So he chose out of the country twenty thousand men of war with horsemen, who went out against Cendebeus, and rested that night at Modin.[5] And when as they rose in the morning, and went into the plain, behold, a mighty great host both of footmen and horsemen came against them: howbeit there was a water brook betwixt them.[6] So he and his people pitched over against them: and when he saw that the people were afraid to go over the water brook, he went first over himself, and then the men seeing him passed through after him.[7] That done, he divided his men, and set the horsemen in the midst of the footmen: for the enemies' horsemen were very many.[8] Then sounded they with the holy trumpets: whereupon Cendebeus and his host were put to flight, so that many of them were slain, and the remnant gat them to the strong hold.[9] At that time was Judas John's brother wounded; but John still followed after them, until he came to Cedron, which Cendebeus had built.[10] So they fled even unto the towers in the fields of Azotus; wherefore he burned it with fire: so that there were slain of them about two thousand men. Afterward he returned into the land of Judea in peace.[11] Moreover in the plain of Jericho was Ptolemeus the son of Abubus made captain, and he had abundance of silver and gold:[12] For he was the high priest's son in law.[13] Wherefore his heart being lifted up, he thought to get the country to himself, and thereupon consulted deceitfully against Simon and his sons to destroy them.[14] Now Simon was visiting the cities that were in the country, and taking care for the good ordering of them; at which time he came down himself to Jericho with his sons, Mattathias and Judas, in the hundred threescore and seventeenth year, in the eleventh month, called Sabat:[15] Where the son of Abubus receiving them deceitfully into a little hold, called Docus, which he had built, made them a great banquet: howbeit he had hid men there.[16] So when Simon and his sons had drunk largely, Ptolemee and his men rose up, and took their weapons, and came upon Simon into the banqueting place, and slew him, and his two sons, and certain of his servants.[17] In which doing he committed a great treachery, and recompensed evil for good.[18] Then Ptolemee wrote these things, and sent to the king, that he should send him an host to aid him, and he would deliver him the country and cities.[19] He sent others also to Gazera to kill John: and unto the tribunes he sent letters to come unto him, that he might give them silver, and gold, and rewards.[20] And others he sent to take Jerusalem, and the mountain of the temple.[21] Now one had run afore to Gazera and told John that his father and brethren were slain, and, quoth he, Ptolemee hath sent to slay thee also.[22] Hereof when he heard, he was sore astonished: so he laid hands on them that were come to destroy him, and slew them; for he knew that they sought to make him away.[23] As concerning the rest of the acts of John, and his wars, and worthy deeds which he did, and the building of the walls which he made, and his doings,[24] Behold, these are written in the chronicles

66

of his priesthood, from the time he was made high priest after his father.

2 Maccabees

2Mac.1

[1] The brethren, the Jews that be at Jerusalem and in the land of Judea, wish unto the brethren, the Jews that are throughout Egypt health and peace:[2] God be gracious unto you, and remember his covenant that he made with Abraham, Isaac, and Jacob, his faithful servants;[3] And give you all an heart to serve him, and to do his will, with a good courage and a willing mind;[4] And open your hearts in his law and commandments, and send you peace,[5] And hear your prayers, and be at one with you, and never forsake you in time of trouble.[6] And now we be here praying for you.[7] What time as Demetrius reigned, in the hundred threescore and ninth year, we the Jews wrote unto you in the extremity of trouble that came upon us in those years, from the time that Jason and his company revolted from the holy land and kingdom,[8] And burned the porch, and shed innocent blood: then we prayed unto the Lord, and were heard; we offered also sacrifices and fine flour, and lighted the lamps, and set forth the loaves.[9] And now see that ye keep the feast of tabernacles in the month Casleu.[10] In the hundred fourscore and eighth year, the people that were at Jerusalem and in Judea, and the council, and Judas, sent greeting and health unto Aristobulus, king Ptolemeus' master, who was of the stock of the anointed priests, and to the Jews that were in Egypt:[11] Insomuch as God hath delivered us from great perils, we thank him highly, as having been in battle against a king.[12] For he cast them out that fought within the holy city.[13] For when the leader was come into Persia, and the army with him that seemed invincible, they were slain in the temple of Nanea by the deceit of Nanea's priests.[14] For Antiochus, as though he would marry her, came into the place, and his friends that were with him, to receive money in name of a dowry.[15] Which when the priests of Nanea had set forth, and he was entered with a small company into the compass of the temple, they shut the temple as soon as Antiochus was come in:[16] And opening a privy door of the roof, they threw stones like thunderbolts, and struck down the captain, hewed them in pieces, smote off their heads and cast them to those that were without.[17] Blessed be our God in all things, who hath delivered up the ungodly.[18] Therefore whereas we are now purposed to keep the purification of the temple upon the five and twentieth day of the month Casleu, we thought it necessary to certify you thereof, that ye also might keep it, as the feast of the tabernacles, and of the fire, which was given us when Neemias offered sacrifice, after that he had builded the temple and the altar.[19] For when our fathers were led into Persia, the priests that were then devout took the fire of the altar privily, and hid it in an hollow place of a pit without water, where they kept it sure, so that the place was unknown to all men.[20] Now after many years, when it pleased God, Neemias, being sent from the king of Persia, did send of the posterity of those priests that had hid it to the fire: but when they told us they found no fire, but thick water;[21] Then commanded he them to draw it up, and to bring it; and when the sacrifices were laid on, Neemias commanded the priests to sprinkle the wood and the things laid thereupon with the water.[22] When this was done, and the time came that the sun shone, which afore was hid in the cloud, there was a great fire kindled, so that every man marvelled.[23] And the priests made a prayer whilst the sacrifice was consuming, I say, both the priests, and all the rest, Jonathan beginning, and the rest answering thereunto, as Neemias did.[24] And the prayer was after this manner; O Lord, Lord God, Creator of all things, who art fearful and strong, and righteous, and merciful, and the only and gracious

King,²⁵ The only giver of all things, the only just, almighty, and everlasting, thou that deliverest Israel from all trouble, and didst choose the fathers, and sanctify them:²⁶ Receive the sacrifice for thy whole people Israel, and preserve thine own portion, and sanctify it.²⁷ Gather those together that are scattered from us, deliver them that serve among the heathen, look upon them that are despised and abhorred, and let the heathen know that thou art our God.²⁸ Punish them that oppress us, and with pride do us wrong.²⁹ Plant thy people again in thy holy place, as Moses hath spoken.³⁰ And the priests sung psalms of thanksgiving.³¹ Now when the sacrifice was consumed, Neemias commanded the water that was left to be poured on the great stones.³² When this was done, there was kindled a flame: but it was consumed by the light that shined from the altar.³³ So when this matter was known, it was told the king of Persia, that in the place, where the priests that were led away had hid the fire, there appeared water, and that Neemias had purified the sacrifices therewith.³⁴ Then the king, inclosing the place, made it holy, after he had tried the matter.³⁵ And the king took many gifts, and bestowed thereof on those whom he would gratify.³⁶ And Neemias called this thing Naphthar, which is as much as to say, a cleansing: but many men call it Nephi.

2Mac.2

¹ It is also found in the records, that Jeremy the prophet commanded them that were carried away to take of the fire, as it hath been signified:² And how that the prophet, having given them the law, charged them not to forget the commandments of the Lord, and that they should not err in their minds, when they see images of silver and gold, with their ornaments.³ And with other such speeches exhorted he them, that the law should not depart from their hearts.⁴ It was also contained in the same writing, that the prophet, being warned of God, commanded the tabernacle and the ark to go with him, as he went forth into the mountain, where Moses climbed up, and saw the heritage of God.⁵ And when Jeremy came thither, he found an hollow cave, wherein he laid the tabernacle, and the ark, and the altar of incense, and so stopped the door.⁶ And some of those that followed him came to mark the way, but they could not find it.⁷ Which when Jeremy perceived, he blamed them, saying, As for that place, it shall be unknown until the time that God gather his people again together, and receive them unto mercy.⁸ Then shall the Lord shew them these things, and the glory of the Lord shall appear, and the cloud also, as it was shewed under Moses, and as when Solomon desired that the place might be honourably sanctified.⁹ It was also declared, that he being wise offered the sacrifice of dedication, and of the finishing of the temple.¹⁰ And as when Moses prayed unto the Lord, the fire came down from heaven, and consumed the sacrifices: even so prayed Solomon also, and the fire came down from heaven, and consumed the burnt offerings.¹¹ And Moses said, Because the sin offering was not to be eaten, it was consumed.¹² So Solomon kept those eight days.¹³ The same things also were reported in the writings and commentaries of Neemias; and how he founding a library gathered together the acts of the kings, and the prophets, and of David, and the epistles of the kings concerning the holy gifts.¹⁴ In like manner also Judas gathered together all those things that were lost by reason of the war we had, and they remain with us,¹⁵ Wherefore if ye have need thereof, send some to fetch them unto you.¹⁶ Whereas we then are about to celebrate the purification, we have written unto you, and ye shall do well, if ye keep the same days.¹⁷ We hope also, that the God, that delivered all his people, and gave them all an heritage, and the kingdom, and the priesthood, and the sanctuary,¹⁸ As he promised in the law, will shortly have mercy upon us, and gather us together out of every land under heaven into the holy place: for he hath

delivered us out of great troubles, and hath purified the place.¹⁹ Now as concerning Judas Maccabeus, and his brethren, and the purification of the great temple, and the dedication of the altar,²⁰ And the wars against Antiochus Epiphanes, and Eupator his son,²¹ And the manifest signs that came from heaven unto those that behaved themselves manfully to their honour for Judaism: so that, being but a few, they overcame the whole country, and chased barbarous multitudes,²² And recovered again the temple renowned all the world over, and freed the city, and upheld the laws which were going down, the Lord being gracious unto them with all favour:²³ All these things, I say, being declared by Jason of Cyrene in five books, we will assay to abridge in one volume.²⁴ For considering the infinite number, and the difficulty which they find that desire to look into the narrations of the story, for the variety of the matter,²⁵ We have been careful, that they that will read may have delight, and that they that are desirous to commit to memory might have ease, and that all into whose hands it comes might have profit.²⁶ Therefore to us, that have taken upon us this painful labour of abridging, it was not easy, but a matter of sweat and watching;²⁷ Even as it is no ease unto him that prepareth a banquet, and seeketh the benefit of others: yet for the pleasuring of many we will undertake gladly this great pains;²⁸ Leaving to the author the exact handling of every particular, and labouring to follow the rules of an abridgement.²⁹ For as the master builder of a new house must care for the whole building; but he that undertaketh to set it out, and paint it, must seek out fit things for the adorning thereof: even so I think it is with us.³⁰ To stand upon every point, and go over things at large, and to be curious in particulars, belongeth to the first author of the story:³¹ But to use brevity, and avoid much labouring of the work, is to be granted to him that will make an abridgment.³² Here then will we begin the story: only adding thus much to that which hath been said, that it is a foolish thing to make a long prologue, and to be short in the story itself.

2Mac.3

¹ Now when the holy city was inhabited with all peace, and the laws were kept very well, because of the godliness of Onias the high priest, and his hatred of wickedness,² It came to pass that even the kings themselves did honour the place, and magnify the temple with their best gifts;³ Insomuch that Seleucus of Asia of his own revenues bare all the costs belonging to the service of the sacrifices.⁴ But one Simon of the tribe of Benjamin, who was made governor of the temple, fell out with the high priest about disorder in the city.⁵ And when he could not overcome Onias, he gat him to Apollonius the son of Thraseas, who then was governor of Celosyria and Phenice,⁶ And told him that the treasury in Jerusalem was full of infinite sums of money, so that the multitude of their riches, which did not pertain to the account of the sacrifices, was innumerable, and that it was possible to bring all into the king's hand.⁷ Now when Apollonius came to the king, and had shewed him of the money whereof he was told, the king chose out Heliodorus his treasurer, and sent him with a commandment to bring him the foresaid money.⁸ So forthwith Heliodorus took his journey; under a colour of visiting the cities of Celosyria and Phenice, but indeed to fulfil the king's purpose.⁹ And when he was come to Jerusalem, and had been courteously received of the high priest of the city, he told him what intelligence was given of the money, and declared wherefore he came, and asked if these things were so indeed.¹⁰ Then the high priest told him that there was such money laid up for the relief of widows and fatherless children:¹¹ And that some of it belonged to Hircanus son of Tobias, a man of great dignity, and not as that wicked Simon had misinformed: the sum whereof in all was four hundred talents of silver, and two hundred of gold:¹² And that it was

altogether impossible that such wrongs should be done unto them, that had committed it to the holiness of the place, and to the majesty and inviolable sanctity of the temple, honoured over all the world.[13] But Heliodorus, because of the king's commandment given him, said, That in any wise it must be brought into the king's treasury.[14] So at the day which he appointed he entered in to order this matter: wherefore there was no small agony throughout the whole city.[15] But the priests, prostrating themselves before the altar in their priests' vestments, called unto heaven upon him that made a law concerning things given to he kept, that they should safely be preserved for such as had committed them to be kept.[16] Then whoso had looked the high priest in the face, it would have wounded his heart: for his countenance and the changing of his colour declared the inward agony of his mind.[17] For the man was so compassed with fear and horror of the body, that it was manifest to them that looked upon him, what sorrow he had now in his heart.[18] Others ran flocking out of their houses to the general supplication, because the place was like to come into contempt.[19] And the women, girt with sackcloth under their breasts, abounded in the streets, and the virgins that were kept in ran, some to the gates, and some to the walls, and others looked out of the windows.[20] And all, holding their hands toward heaven, made supplication.[21] Then it would have pitied a man to see the falling down of the multitude of all sorts, and the fear of the high priest being in such an agony.[22] They then called upon the Almighty Lord to keep the things committed of trust safe and sure for those that had committed them.[23] Nevertheless Heliodorus executed that which was decreed.[24] Now as he was there present himself with his guard about the treasury, the Lord of spirits, and the Prince of all power, caused a great apparition, so that all that presumed to come in with him were astonished at the power of God, and fainted, and were sore afraid.[25] For there appeared unto them an horse with a terrible rider upon him, and adorned with a very fair covering, and he ran fiercely, and smote at Heliodorus with his forefeet, and it seemed that he that sat upon the horse had complete harness of gold.[26] Moreover two other young men appeared before him, notable in strength, excellent in beauty, and comely in apparel, who stood by him on either side; and scourged him continually, and gave him many sore stripes.[27] And Heliodorus fell suddenly unto the ground, and was compassed with great darkness: but they that were with him took him up, and put him into a litter.[28] Thus him, that lately came with a great train and with all his guard into the said treasury, they carried out, being unable to help himself with his weapons: and manifestly they acknowledged the power of God.[29] For he by the hand of God was cast down, and lay speechless without all hope of life.[30] But they praised the Lord, that had miraculously honoured his own place: for the temple; which a little afore was full of fear and trouble, when the Almighty Lord appeared, was filled with joy and gladness.[31] Then straightways certain of Heliodorus' friends prayed Onias, that he would call upon the most High to grant him his life, who lay ready to give up the ghost.[32] So the high priest, suspecting lest the king should misconceive that some treachery had been done to Heliodorus by the Jews, offered a sacrifice for the health of the man.[33] Now as the high priest was making an atonement, the same young men in the same clothing appeared and stood beside Heliodorus, saying, Give Onias the high priest great thanks, insomuch as for his sake the Lord hath granted thee life:[34] And seeing that thou hast been scourged from heaven, declare unto all men the mighty power of God. And when they had spoken these words, they appeared no more.[35] So Heliodorus, after he had offered sacrifice unto the Lord, and made great vows unto him that had saved his life, and saluted Onias, returned with his host to the king.[36] Then testified he to all men the works of the great God, which he had seen with his eyes.[37] And when the king Heliodorus, who might be a fit man to be sent yet once again to Jerusalem, he said,[38] If thou hast any enemy or traitor, send him thither, and thou shalt receive him well scourged, if he escape with his life: for in that place, no doubt; there is an especial power of God.[39] For he that dwelleth in heaven hath his eye on that place, and defendeth it; and he beateth and destroyeth them that come to hurt it.[40] And the things concerning Heliodorus, and the keeping of the treasury, fell out on this sort.

2Mac.4

[1] This Simon now, of whom we spake afore, having been a betrayer of the money, and of his country, slandered Onias, as if he ha terrified Heliodorus, and been the worker of these evils.[2] Thus was he bold to call him a traitor, that had deserved well of the city, and tendered his own nation, and was so zealous of the laws.[3] But when their hatred went so far, that by one of Simon's faction murders were committed,[4] Onias seeing the danger of this contention, and that Apollonius, as being the governor of Celosyria and Phenice, did rage, and increase Simon's malice,[5] He went to the king, not to be an accuser of his countrymen, but seeking the good of all, both publick and private:[6] For he saw that it was impossible that the state should continue quiet, and Simon leave his folly, unless the king did look thereunto.[7] But after the death of Seleucus, when Antiochus, called Epiphanes, took the kingdom, Jason the brother of Onias laboured underhand to be high priest,[8] Promising unto the king by intercession three hundred and threescore talents of silver, and of another revenue eighty talents:[9] Beside this, he promised to assign an hundred and fifty more, if he might have licence to set him up a place for exercise, and for the training up of youth in the fashions of the heathen, and to write them of Jerusalem by the name of Antiochians.[10] Which when the king had granted, and he had gotten into his hand the rule he forthwith brought his own nation to Greekish fashion.[11] And the royal privileges granted of special favour to the Jews by the means of John the father of Eupolemus, who went ambassador to Rome for amity and aid, he took away; and putting down the governments which were according to the law, he brought up new customs against the law:[12] For he built gladly a place of exercise under the tower itself, and brought the chief young men under his subjection, and made them wear a hat.[13] Now such was the height of Greek fashions, and increase of heathenish manners, through the exceeding profaneness of Jason, that ungodly wretch, and no high priest;[14] That the priests had no courage to serve any more at the altar, but despising the temple, and neglecting the sacrifices, hastened to be partakers of the unlawful allowance in the place of exercise, after the game of Discus called them forth;[15] Not setting by the honours of their fathers, but liking the glory of the Grecians best of all.[16] By reason whereof sore calamity came upon them: for they had them to be their enemies and avengers, whose custom they followed so earnestly, and unto whom they desired to be like in all things.[17] For it is not a light thing to do wickedly against the laws of God: but the time following shall declare these things.[18] Now when the game that was used every faith year was kept at Tyrus, the king being present,[19] This ungracious Jason sent special messengers from Jerusalem, who were Antiochians, to carry three hundred drachms of silver to the sacrifice of Hercules, which even the bearers thereof thought fit not to bestow upon the sacrifice, because it was not convenient, but to be reserved for other charges.[20] This money then, in regard of the sender, was appointed to Hercules' sacrifice; but because of the bearers thereof, it was employed to the making of gallies.[21] Now when Apollonius the son of Menestheus was sent into Egypt for the coronation of king Ptolemeus Philometor, Antiochus, understanding him not to be well

affected to his affairs, provided for his own safety: whereupon he came to Joppa, and from thence to Jerusalem:[22] Where he was honourably received of Jason, and of the city, and was brought in with torch alight, and with great shoutings: and so afterward went with his host unto Phenice.[23] Three years afterward Jason sent Menelaus, the aforesaid Simon's brother, to bear the money unto the king, and to put him in mind of certain necessary matters.[24] But he being brought to the presence of the king, when he had magnified him for the glorious appearance of his power, got the priesthood to himself, offering more than Jason by three hundred talents of silver.[25] So he came with the king's mandate, bringing nothing worthy the high priesthood, but having the fury of a cruel tyrant, and the rage of a savage beast.[26] Then Jason, who had undermined his own brother, being undermined by another, was compelled to flee into the country of the Ammonites.[27] So Menelaus got the principality: but as for the money that he had promised unto the king, he took no good order for it, albeit Sostratis the ruler of the castle required it:[28] For unto him appertained the gathering of the customs. Wherefore they were both called before the king.[29] Now Menelaus left his brother Lysimachus in his stead in the priesthood; and Sostratus left Crates, who was governor of the Cyprians.[30] While those things were in doing, they of Tarsus and Mallos made insurrection, because they were given to the king's concubine, called Antiochus.[31] Then came the king in all haste to appease matters, leaving Andronicus, a man in authority, for his deputy.[32] Now Menelaus, supposing that he had gotten a convenient time, stole certain vessels of gold out of the temple, and gave some of them to Andronicus, and some he sold into Tyrus and the cities round about.[33] Which when Onias knew of a surety, he reproved him, and withdrew himself into a sanctuary at Daphne, that lieth by Antiochia.[34] Wherefore Menelaus, taking Andronicus apart, prayed, him to get Onias into his hands; who being persuaded thereunto, and coming to Onias in deceit, gave him his right hand with oaths; and though he were suspected by him, yet persuaded he him to come forth of the sanctuary: whom forthwith he shut up without regard of justice.[35] For the which cause not only the Jews, but many also of other nations, took great indignation, and were much grieved for the unjust murder of the man.[36] And when the king was come again from the places about Cilicia, the Jews that were in the city, and certain of the Greeks that abhorred the fact also, complained because Onias was slain without cause.[37] Therefore Antiochus was heartily sorry, and moved to pity, and wept, because of the sober and modest behaviour of him that was dead.[38] And being kindled with anger, forthwith he took away Andronicus his purple, and rent off his clothes, and leading him through the whole city unto that very place, where he had committed impiety against Onias, there slew he the cursed murderer. Thus the Lord rewarded him his punishment, as he had deserved.[39] Now when many sacrileges had been committed in the city by Lysimachus with the consent of Menelaus, and the fruit thereof was spread abroad, the multitude gathered themselves together against Lysimachus, many vessels of gold being already carried away.[40] Whereupon the common people rising, and being filled with rage, Lysimachus armed about three thousand men, and began first to offer violence; one Auranus being the leader, a man far gone in years, and no less in folly.[41] They then seeing the attempt of Lysimachus, some of them caught stones, some clubs, others taking handfuls of dust, that was next at hand, cast them all together upon Lysimachus, and those that set upon them.[42] Thus many of them they wounded, and some they struck to the ground, and all of them they forced to flee: but as for the churchrobber himself, him they killed beside the treasury.[43] Of these matters therefore there was an accusation laid against

Menelaus.[44] Now when the king came to Tyrus, three men that were sent from the senate pleaded the cause before him:[45] But Menelaus, being now convicted, promised Ptolemee the son of Dorymenes to give him much money, if he would pacify the king toward him.[46] Whereupon Ptolemee taking the king aside into a certain gallery, as it were to take the air, brought him to be of another mind:[47] Insomuch that he discharged Menelaus from the accusations, who notwithstanding was cause of all the mischief: and those poor men, who, if they had told their cause, yea, before the Scythians, should have been judged innocent, them he condemned to death.[48] Thus they that followed the matter for the city, and for the people, and for the holy vessels, did soon suffer unjust punishment.[49] Wherefore even they of Tyrus, moved with hatred of that wicked deed, caused them to be honourably buried.[50] And so through the covetousness of them that were of power Menelaus remained still in authority, increasing in malice, and being a great traitor to the citizens.

2Mac.5

[1] About the same time Antiochus prepared his second voyage into Egypt:[2] And then it happened, that through all the city, for the space almost of forty days, there were seen horsemen running in the air, in cloth of gold, and armed with lances, like a band of soldiers,[3] And troops of horsemen in array, encountering and running one against another, with shaking of shields, and multitude of pikes, and drawing of swords, and casting of darts, and glittering of golden ornaments, and harness of all sorts.[4] Wherefore every man prayed that that apparition might turn to good.[5] Now when there was gone forth a false rumour, as though Antiochus had been dead, Jason took at the least a thousand men, and suddenly made an assault upon the city; and they that were upon the walls being put back, and the city at length taken, Menelaus fled into the castle:[6] But Jason slew his own citizens without mercy, not considering that to get the day of them of his own nation would be a most unhappy day for him; but thinking they had been his enemies, and not his countrymen, whom he conquered.[7] Howbeit for all this he obtained not the principality, but at the last received shame for the reward of his treason, and fled again into the country of the Ammonites.[8] In the end therefore he had an unhappy return, being accused before Aretas the king of the Arabians, fleeing from city to city, pursued of all men, hated as a forsaker of the laws, and being had in abomination as an open enemy of his country and countrymen, he was cast out into Egypt.[9] Thus he that had driven many out of their country perished in a strange land, retiring to the Lacedemonians, and thinking there to find succour by reason of his kindred:[10] And he that had cast out many unburied had none to mourn for him, nor any solemn funerals at all, nor sepulchre with his fathers.[11] Now when this that was done came to the king's car, he thought that Judea had revolted: whereupon removing out of Egypt in a furious mind, he took the city by force of arms,[12] And commanded his men of war not to spare such as they met, and to slay such as went up upon the houses.[13] Thus there was killing of young and old, making away of men, women, and children, slaying of virgins and infants.[14] And there were destroyed within the space of three whole days fourscore thousand, whereof forty thousand were slain in the conflict; and no fewer sold than slain.[15] Yet was he not content with this, but presumed to go intothe most holy temple of all the world; Menelaus, that traitor to the laws, and to his own country, being his guide:[16] And taking the holy vessels with polluted hands, and with profane hands pulling down the things that were dedicated by other kings to the augmentation and glory and honour of the place, he gave them away.[17] And so haughty was Antiochus in mind, that he considered not that the Lord was angry for a while for the sins of

them that dwelt in the city, and therefore his eye was not upon the place.[18] For had they not been formerly wrapped in many sins, this man, as soon as he had come, had forthwith been scourged, and put back from his presumption, as Heliodorus was, whom Seleucus the king sent to view the treasury.[19] Nevertheless God did not choose the people for the place's sake, but the place far the people's sake.[20] And therefore the place itself, that was partaker with them of the adversity that happened to the nation, did afterward communicate in the benefits sent from the Lord: and as it was forsaken in the wrath of the Almighty, so again, the great Lord being reconciled, it was set up with all glory.[21] So when Antiochus had carried out of the temple a thousand and eight hundred talents, he departed in all haste unto Antiochia, weening in his pride to make the land navigable, and the sea passable by foot: such was the haughtiness of his mind.[22] And he left governors to vex the nation: at Jerusalem, Philip, for his country a Phrygian, and for manners more barbarous than he that set him there;[23] And at Garizim, Andronicus; and besides, Menelans, who worse than all the rest bare an heavy hand over the citizens, having a malicious mind against his countrymen the Jews.[24] He sent also that detestable ringleader Apollonius with an army of two and twenty thousand, commanding him to slay all those that were in their best age, and to sell the women and the younger sort:[25] Who coming to Jerusalem, and pretending peace, did forbear till the holy day of the sabbath, when taking the Jews keeping holy day, he commanded his men to arm themselves.[26] And so he slew all them that were gone to the celebrating of the sabbath, and running through the city with weapons slew great multitudes.[27] But Judas Maccabeus with nine others, or thereabout, withdrew himself into the wilderness, and lived in the mountains after the manner of beasts, with his company, who fed on herbs continually, lest they should be partakers of the pollution.

2Mac.6

[1] Not long after this the king sent an old man of Athens to compel the Jews to depart from the laws of their fathers, and not to live after the laws of God:[2] And to pollute also the temple in Jerusalem, and to call it the temple of Jupiter Olympius; and that in Garizim, of Jupiter the Defender of strangers, as they did desire that dwelt in the place.[3] The coming in of this mischief was sore and grievous to the people:[4] For the temple was filled with riot and revelling by the Gentiles, who dallied with harlots, and had to do with women within the circuit of the holy places, and besides that brought in things that were not lawful.[5] The altar also was filled with profane things, which the law forbiddeth.[6] Neither was it lawful for a man to keep sabbath days or ancient fasts, or to profess himself at all to be a Jew.[7] And in the day of the king's birth every month they were brought by bitter constraint to eat of the sacrifices; and when the fast of Bacchus was kept, the Jews were compelled to go in procession to Bacchus, carrying ivy.[8] Moreover there went out a decree to the neighbour cities of the heathen, by the suggestion of Ptolemee, against the Jews, that they should observe the same fashions, and be partakers of their sacrifices:[9] And whoso would not conform themselves to the manners of the Gentiles should be put to death. Then might a man have seen the present misery.[10] For there were two women brought, who had circumcised their children; whom when they had openly led round about the city, the babes handing at their breasts, they cast them down headlong from the wall.[11] And others, that had run together into caves near by, to keep the sabbath day secretly, being discovered by Philip, were all burnt together, because they made a conscience to help themselves for the honour of the most sacred day.[12] Now I beseech those that read this book, that they be not discouraged for these calamities, but that they judge those

punishments not to be for destruction, but for a chastening of our nation.[13] For it is a token of his great goodness, when wicked doers are not suffered any long time, but forthwith punished.[14] For not as with other nations, whom the Lord patiently forbeareth to punish, till they be come to the fulness of their sins, so dealeth he with us,[15] Lest that, being come to the height of sin, afterwards he should take vengeance of us.[16] And therefore he never withdraweth his mercy from us: and though he punish with adversity, yet doth he never forsake his people.[17] But let this that we at spoken be for a warning unto us. And now will we come to the declaring of the matter in a few words.[18] Eleazar, one of the principal scribes, an aged man, and of a well favoured countenance, was constrained to open his mouth, and to eat swine's flesh.[19] But he, choosing rather to die gloriously, than to live stained with such an abomination, spit it forth, and came of his own accord to the torment,[20] As it behoved them to come, that are resolute to stand out against such things, as are not lawful for love of life to be tasted.[21] But they that had the charge of that wicked feast, for the old acquaintance they had with the man, taking him aside, besought him to bring flesh of his own provision, such as was lawful for him to use, and make as if he did eat of the flesh taken from the sacrifice commanded by the king;[22] That in so doing he might be delivered from death, and for the old friendship with them find favour.[23] But he began to consider discreetly, and as became his age, and the excellency of his ancient years, and the honour of his gray head, whereon was come, and his most honest education from a child, or rather the holy law made and given by God: therefore he answered accordingly, and willed them straightways to send him to the grave.[24] For it becometh not our age, said he, in any wise to dissemble, whereby many young persons might think that Eleazar, being fourscore years old and ten, were now gone to a strange religion;[25] And so they through mine hypocrisy, and desire to live a little time and a moment longer, should be deceived by me, and I get a stain to mine old age, and make it abominable.[26] For though for the present time I should be delivered from the punishment of men: yet should I not escape the hand of the Almighty, neither alive, nor dead.[27] Wherefore now, manfully changing this life, I will shew myself such an one as mine age requireth,[28] And leave a notable example to such as be young to die willingly and courageously for the honourable and holy laws. And when he had said these words, immediately he went to the torment:[29] They that led him changing the good will they bare him a little before into hatred, because the foresaid speeches proceeded, as they thought, from a desperate mind.[30] But when he was ready to die with stripes, he groaned, and said, It is manifest unto the Lord, that hath the holy knowledge, that whereas I might have been delivered from death, I now endure sore pains in body by being beaten: but in soul am well content to suffer these things, because I fear him.[31] And thus this man died, leaving his death for an example of a noble courage, and a memorial of virtue, not only unto young men, but unto all his nation.

2Mac.7

[1] It came to pass also, that seven brethren with their mother were taken, and compelled by the king against the law to taste swine's flesh, and were tormented with scourges and whips.[2] But one of them that spake first said thus, What wouldest thou ask or learn of us? we are ready to die, rather than to transgress the laws of our fathers.[3] Then the king, being in a rage, commanded pans and caldrons to be made hot:[4] Which forthwith being heated, he commanded to cut out the tongue of him that spake first, and to cut off the utmost parts of his body, the rest of his brethren and his mother looking on.[5] Now when he was thus maimed in all his members, he commanded him being yet alive to be brought to the

fire, and to be fried in the pan: and as the vapour of the pan was for a good space dispersed, they exhorted one another with the mother to die manfully, saying thus,[6] The Lord God looketh upon us, and in truth hath comfort in us, as Moses in his song, which witnessed to their faces, declared, saying, And he shall be comforted in his servants.[7] So when the first was dead after this number, they brought the second to make him a mocking stock: and when they had pulled off the skin of his head with the hair, they asked him, Wilt thou eat, before thou be punished throughout every member of thy body?[8] But he answered in his own language, and said, No. Wherefore he also received the next torment in order, as the former did.[9] And when he was at the last gasp, he said, Thou like a fury takest us out of this present life, but the King of the world shall raise us up, who have died for his laws, unto everlasting life.[10] After him was the third made a mocking stock: and when he was required, he put out his tongue, and that right soon, holding forth his hands manfully.[11] And said courageously, These I had from heaven; and for his laws I despise them; and from him I hope to receive them again.[12] Insomuch that the king, and they that were with him, marvelled at the young man's courage, for that he nothing regarded the pains.[13] Now when this man was dead also, they tormented and mangled the fourth in like manner.[14] So when he was ready to die he said thus, It is good, being put to death by men, to look for hope from God to be raised up again by him: as for thee, thou shalt have no resurrection to life.[15] Afterward they brought the fifth also, and mangled him.[16] Then looked he unto the king, and said, Thou hast power over men, thou art corruptible, thou doest what thou wilt; yet think not that our nation is forsaken of God;[17] But abide a while, and behold his great power, how he will torment thee and thy seed.[18] After him also they brought the sixth, who being ready to die said, Be not deceived without cause: for we suffer these things for ourselves, having sinned against our God: therefore marvellous things are done unto us.[19] But think not thou, that takest in hand to strive against God, that thou shalt escape unpunished.[20] But the mother was marvellous above all, and worthy of honourable memory: for when she saw her seven sons slain within the space of one day, she bare it with a good courage, because of the hope that she had in the Lord.[21] Yea, she exhorted every one of them in her own language, filled with courageous spirits; and stirring up her womanish thoughts with a manly stomach, she said unto them,[22] I cannot tell how ye came into my womb: for I neither gave you breath nor life, neither was it I that formed the members of every one of you;[23] But doubtless the Creator of the world, who formed the generation of man, and found out the beginning of all things, will also of his own mercy give you breath and life again, as ye now regard not your own selves for his laws' sake.[24] Now Antiochus, thinking himself despised, and suspecting it to be a reproachful speech, whilst the youngest was yet alive, did not only exhort him by words, but also assured him with oaths, that he would make him both a rich and a happy man, if he would turn from the laws of his fathers; and that also he would take him for his friend, and trust him with affairs.[25] But when the young man would in no case hearken unto him, the king called his mother, and exhorted her that she would counsel the young man to save his life.[26] And when he had exhorted her with many words, she promised him that she would counsel her son.[27] But she bowing herself toward him, laughing the cruel tyrant to scorn, spake in her country language on this manner; O my son, have pity upon me that bare thee nine months in my womb, and gave thee such three years, and nourished thee, and brought thee up unto this age, and endured the troubles of education.[28] I beseech thee, my son, look upon the heaven and the earth, and all that is therein, and consider that God made them of things that were not; and so was mankind made likewise.[29] Fear not this tormentor, but, being worthy of thy brethren, take thy death that I may receive thee again in mercy with thy brethren.[30] Whiles she was yet speaking these words, the young man said, Whom wait ye for? I will not obey the king's commandment: but I will obey the commandment of the law that was given unto our fathers by Moses.[31] And thou, that hast been the author of all mischief against the Hebrews, shalt not escape the hands of God.[32] For we suffer because of our sins.[33] And though the living Lord be angry with us a little while for our chastening and correction, yet shall he be at one again with his servants.[34] But thou, O godless man, and of all other most wicked, be not lifted up without a cause, nor puffed up with uncertain hopes, lifting up thy hand against the servants of God:[35] For thou hast not yet escaped the judgment of Almighty God, who seeth all things.[36] For our brethren, who now have suffered a short pain, are dead under God's covenant of everlasting life: but thou, through the judgment of God, shalt receive just punishment for thy pride.[37] But I, as my brethren, offer up my body and life for the laws of our fathers, beseeching God that he would speedily be merciful unto our nation; and that thou by torments and plagues mayest confess, that he alone is God;[38] And that in me and my brethren the wrath of the Almighty, which is justly brought upon our nation, may cease.[39] Than the king' being in a rage, handed him worse than all the rest, and took it grievously that he was mocked.[40] So this man died undefiled, and put his whole trust in the Lord.[41] Last of all after the sons the mother died.[42] Let this be enough now to have spoken concerning the idolatrous feasts, and the extreme tortures.

2Mac.8

[1] Then Judas Maccabeus, and they that were with him, went privily into the towns, and called their kinsfolks together, and took unto them all such as continued in the Jews' religion, and assembled about six thousand men.[2] And they called upon the Lord, that he would look upon the people that was trodden down of all; and also pity the temple profaned of ungodly men;[3] And that he would have compassion upon the city, sore defaced, and ready to be made even with the ground; and hear the blood that cried unto him,[4] And remember the wicked slaughter of harmless infants, and the blasphemies committed against his name; and that he would shew his hatred against the wicked.[5] Now when Maccabeis had his company about him, he could not be withstood by the heathen: for the wrath of the Lord was turned into mercy.[6] Therefore he came at unawares, and burnt up towns and cities, and got into his hands the most commodious places, and overcame and put to flight no small number of his enemies.[7] But specially took he advantage of the night for such privy attempts, insomuch that the fruit of his holiness was spread every where.[8] So when Philip saw that this man increased by little and little, and that things prospered with him still more and more, he wrote unto Ptolemeus, the governor of Celosyria and Phenice, to yield more aid to the king's affairs.[9] Then forthwith choosing Nicanor the son of Patroclus, one of his special friends, he sent him with no fewer than twenty thousand of all nations under him, to root out the whole generation of the Jews; and with him he joined also Gorgias a captain, who in matters of war had great experience.[10] So Nicanor undertook to make so much money of the captive Jews, as should defray the tribute of two thousand talents, which the king was to pay to the Romans.[11] Wherefore immediately he sent to the cities upon the sea coast, proclaiming a sale of the captive Jews, and promising that they should have fourscore and ten bodies for one talent, not expecting the vengeance that was to follow upon him from the Almighty God.[12] Now when word was brought unto Judas of Nicanor's coming, and he had imparted unto those

that were with him that the army was at hand,[13] They that were fearful, and distrusted the justice of God, fled, and conveyed themselves away.[14] Others sold all that they had left, and withal besought the Lord to deliver them, sold by the wicked Nicanor before they met together:[15] And if not for their own sakes, yet for the covenants he had made with their fathers, and for his holy and glorious name's sake, by which they were called.[16] So Maccabeus called his men together unto the number of six thousand, and exhorted them not to be stricken with terror of the enemy, nor to fear the great multitude of the heathen, who came wrongly against them; but to fight manfully,[17] And to set before their eyes the injury that they had unjustly done to the holy place, and the cruel handling of the city, whereof they made a mockery, and also the taking away of the government of their forefathers:[18] For they, said he, trust in their weapons and boldness; but our confidence is in the Almighty who at a beck can cast down both them that come against us, and also all the world.[19] Moreover, he recounted unto them what helps their forefathers had found, and how they were delivered, when under Sennacherib an hundred fourscore and five thousand perished.[20] And he told them of the battle that they had in Babylon with the Galatians, how they came but eight thousand in all to the business, with four thousand Macedonians, and that the Macedonians being perplexed, the eight thousand destroyed an hundred and twenty thousand because of the help that they had from heaven, and so received a great booty.[21] Thus when he had made them bold with these words, and ready to die for the law and the country, he divided his army into four parts;[22] And joined with himself his own brethren, leaders of each band, to wit Simon, and Joseph, and Jonathan, giving each one fifteen hundred men.[23] Also he appointed Eleazar to read the holy book: and when he had given them this watchword, The help of God; himself leading the first band,[24] And by the help of the Almighty they slew above nine thousand of their enemies, and wounded and maimed the most part of Nicanor's host, and so put all to flight;[25] And took their money that came to buy them, and pursued them far: but lacking time they returned:[26] For it was the day before the sabbath, and therefore they would no longer pursue them.[27] So when they had gathered their armour together, and spoiled their enemies, they occupied themselves about the sabbath, yielding exceeding praise and thanks to the Lord, who had preserved them unto that day, which was the beginning of mercy distilling upon them.[28] And after the sabbath, when they had given part of the spoils to the maimed, and the widows, and orphans, the residue they divided among themselves and their servants.[29] When this was done, and they had made a common supplication, they besought the merciful Lord to be reconciled with his servants for ever.[30] Moreover of those that were with Timotheus and Bacchides, who fought against them, they slew above twenty thousand, and very easily got high and strong holds, and divided among themselves many spoils more, and made the maimed, orphans, widows, yea, and the aged also, equal in spoils with themselves.[31] And when they had gathered their armour together, they laid them up all carefully in convenient places, and the remnant of the spoils they brought to Jerusalem.[32] They slew also Philarches, that wicked person, who was with Timotheus, and had annoyed the Jews many ways.[33] Furthermore at such time as they kept the feast for the victory in their country they burnt Callisthenes, that had set fire upon the holy gates, who had fled into a little house; and so he received a reward meet for his wickedness.[34] As for that most ungracious Nicanor, who had brought a thousand merchants to buy the Jews,[35] He was through the help of the Lord brought down by them, of whom he made least account; and putting off his glorious apparel, and discharging his company, he came like a

fugitive servant through the midland unto Antioch having very great dishonour, for that his host was destroyed.[36] Thus he, that took upon him to make good to the Romans their tribute by means of captives in Jerusalem, told abroad, that the Jews had God to fight for them, and therefore they could not be hurt, because they followed the laws that he gave them.

2Mac.9

[1] About that time came Antiochus with dishonour out of the country of Persia[2] For he had entered the city called Persepolis, and went about to rob the temple, and to hold the city; whereupon the multitude running to defend themselves with their weapons put them to flight; and so it happened, that Antiochus being put to flight of the inhabitants returned with shame.[3] Now when he came to Ecbatane, news was brought him what had happened unto Nicanor and Timotheus.[4] Then swelling with anger. he thought to avenge upon the Jews the disgrace done unto him by those that made him flee. Therefore commanded he his chariotman to drive without ceasing, and to dispatch the journey, the judgment of GOd now following him. For he had spoken proudly in this sort, That he would come to Jerusalem and make it a common burying place of the Jews.[5] But the Lord Almighty, the God of Isreal, smote him with an incurable and invisible plague: or as soon as he had spoken these words, a pain of the bowels that was remediless came upon him, and sore torments of the inner parts;[6] And that most justly: for he had tormented other men's bowels with many and strange torments.[7] Howbeit he nothing at all ceased from his bragging, but still was filled with pride, breathing out fire in his rage against the Jews, and commanding to haste the journey: but it came to pass that he fell down from his chariot, carried violently; so that having a sore fall, all the members of his body were much pained.[8] And thus he that a little afore thought he might command the waves of the sea, (so proud was he beyond the condition of man) and weigh the high mountains in a balance, was now cast on the ground, and carried in an horselitter, shewing forth unto all the manifest power of God.[9] So that the worms rose up out of the body of this wicked man, and whiles he lived in sorrow and pain, his flesh fell away, and the filthiness of his smell was noisome to all his army.[10] And the man, that thought a little afore he could reach to the stars of heaven, no man could endure to carry for his intolerable stink.[11] Here therefore, being plagued, he began to leave off his great pride, and to come to the knowledge of himself by the scourge of God, his pain increasing every moment.[12] And when he himself could not abide his own smell, he said these words, It is meet to be subject unto God, and that a man that is mortal should not proudly think of himself if he were God.[13] This wicked person vowed also unto the Lord, who now no more would have mercy upon him, saying thus,[14] That the holy city (to the which he was going in haste to lay it even with the ground, and to make it a common buryingplace,) he would set at liberty:[15] And as touching the Jews, whom he had judged not worthy so much as to be buried, but to be cast out with their children to be devoured of the fowls and wild beasts, he would make them all equals to the citizens of Athens:[16] And the holy temple, which before he had spoiled, he would garnish with goodly gifts, and restore all the holy vessels with many more, and out of his own revenue defray the charges belonging to the sacrifices:[17] Yea, and that also he would become a Jew himself, and go through all the world that was inhabited, and declare the power of God.[18] But for all this his pains would not cease: for the just judgment of God was come upon him: therefore despairing of his health, he wrote unto the Jews the letter underwritten, containing the form of a supplication, after this manner:[19] Antiochus, king and governor, to the good Jews his citizens wisheth much joy, health, and

prosperity:[20] If ye and your children fare well, and your affairs be to your contentment, I give very great thanks to God, having my hope in heaven.[21] As for me, I was weak, or else I would have remembered kindly your honour and good will returning out of Persia, and being taken with a grievous disease, I thought it necessary to care for the common safety of all:[22] Not distrusting mine health, but having great hope to escape this sickness.[23] But considering that even my father, at what time he led an army into the high countries. appointed a successor,[24] To the end that, if any thing fell out contrary to expectation, or if any tidings were brought that were grievous, they of the land, knowing to whom the state was left, might not be troubled:[25] Again, considering how that the princes that are borderers and neighbours unto my kingdom wait for opportunities, and expect what shall be the event. I have appointed my son Antiochus king, whom I often committed and commended unto many of you, when I went up into the high provinces; to whom I have written as followeth:[26] Therefore I pray and request you to remember the benefits that I have done unto you generally, and in special, and that every man will be still faithful to me and my son.[27] For I am persuaded that he understanding my mind will favourably and graciously yield to your desires.[28] Thus the murderer and blasphemer having suffered most grievously, as he entreated other men, so died he a miserable death in a strange country in the mountains.[29] And Philip, that was brought up with him, carried away his body, who also fearing the son of Antiochus went into Egypt to Ptolemeus Philometor.

2Mac.10

[1] Now Maccabeus and his company, the Lord guiding them, recovered the temple and the city:[2] But the altars which the heathen had built in the open street, and also the chapels, they pulled down.[3] And having cleansed the temple they made another altar, and striking stones they took fire out of them, and offered a sacrifice after two years, and set forth incense, and lights, and shewbread.[4] When that was done, they fell flat down, and besought the Lord that they might come no more into such troubles; but if they sinned any more against him, that he himself would chasten them with mercy, and that they might not be delivered unto the blasphemous and barbarous nations.[5] Now upon the same day that the strangers profaned the temple, on the very same day it was cleansed again, even the five and twentieth day of the same month, which is Casleu.[6] And they kept the eight days with gladness, as in the feast of the tabernacles, remembering that not long afore they had held the feast of the tabernacles, when as they wandered in the mountains and dens like beasts.[7] Therefore they bare branches, and fair boughs, and palms also, and sang psalms unto him that had given them good success in cleansing his place.[8] They ordained also by a common statute and decree, That every year those days should be kept of the whole nation of the Jews.[9] And this was the end of Antiochus, called Epiphanes.[10] Now will we declare the acts of Antiochus Eupator, who was the son of this wicked man, gathering briefly the calamities of the wars.[11] So when he was come to the crown, he set one Lysias over the affairs of his realm, and appointed him his chief governor of Celosyria and Phenice.[12] For Ptolemeus, that was called Macron, choosing rather to do justice unto the Jews for the wrong that had been done unto them, endeavoured to continue peace with them.[13] Whereupon being accused of the king's friends before Eupator, and called traitor at every word because he had left Cyprus, that Philometor had committed unto him, and departed to Antiochus Epiphanes, and seeing that he was in no honourable place, he was so discouraged, that he poisoned himself and died.[14] But when Gorgias was governor of the holds, he hired soldiers, and nourished war continually with the Jews:[15] And

therewithall the Idumeans, having gotten into their hands the most commodious holds, kept the Jews occupied, and receiving those that were banished from Jerusalem, they went about to nourish war.[16] Then they that were with Maccabeus made supplication, and besought God that he would be their helper; and so they ran with violence upon the strong holds of the Idumeans,[17] And assaulting them strongly, they won the holds, and kept off all that fought upon the wall, and slew all that fell into their hands, and killed no fewer than twenty thousand.[18] And because certain, who were no less than nine thousand, were fled together into two very strong castles, having all manner of things convenient to sustain the siege,[19] Maccabeus left Simon and Joseph, and Zaccheus also, and them that were with him, who were enough to besiege them, and departed himself unto those places which more needed his help.[20] Now they that were with Simon, being led with covetousness, were persuaded for money through certain of those that were in the castle, and took seventy thousand drachms, and let some of them escape.[21] But when it was told Maccabeus what was done, he called the governors of the people together, and accused those men, that they had sold their brethren for money, and set their enemies free to fight against them.[22] So he slew those that were found traitors, and immediately took the two castles.[23] And having good success with his weapons in all things he took in hand, he slew in the two holds more than twenty thousand.[24] Now Timotheus, whom the Jews had overcome before, when he had gathered a great multitude of foreign forces, and horses out of Asia not a few, came as though he would take Jewry by force of arms.[25] But when he drew near, they that were with Maccabeus turned themselves to pray unto God, and sprinkled earth upon their heads, and girded their loins with sackcloth,[26] And fell down at the foot of the altar, and besought him to be merciful to them, and to be an enemy to their enemies, and an adversary to their adversaries, as the law declareth.[27] So after the prayer they took their weapons, and went on further from the city: and when they drew near to their enemies, they kept by themselves.[28] Now the sun being newly risen, they joined both together; the one part having together with their virtue their refuge also unto the Lord for a pledge of their success and victory: the other side making their rage leader of their battle[29] But when the battle waxed strong, there appeared unto the enemies from heaven five comely men upon horses, with bridles of gold, and two of them led the Jews,[30] And took Maccabeus betwixt them, and covered him on every side weapons, and kept him safe, but shot arrows and lightnings against the enemies: so that being confounded with blindness, and full of trouble, they were killed.[31] And there were slain of footmen twenty thousand and five hundred, and six hundred horsemen.[32] As for Timotheus himself, he fled into a very strong hold, called Gawra, where Chereas was governor.[33] But they that were with Maccabeus laid siege against the fortress courageously four days.[34] And they that were within, trusting to the strength of the place, blasphemed exceedingly, and uttered wicked words.[35] Nevertheless upon the fifth day early twenty young men of Maccabeus' company, inflamed with anger because of the blasphemies, assaulted the wall manly, and with a fierce courage killed all that they met withal.[36] Others likewise ascending after them, whiles they were busied with them that were within, burnt the towers, and kindling fires burnt the blasphemers alive; and others broke open the gates, and, having received in the rest of the army, took the city,[37] And killed Timotheus, that was hid in a certain pit, and Chereas his brother, with Apollophanes.[38] When this was done, they praised the Lord with psalms and thanksgiving, who had done so great things for Israel, and given them the victory.

2Mac.11

[1] Not long after the, Lysias the king's protector and cousin, who also managed the affairs, took sore displeasure for the things that were done.[2] And when he had gathered about fourscore thousand with all the horsemen, he came against the Jews, thinking to make the city an habitation of the Gentiles,[3] And to make a gain of the temple, as of the other chapels of the heathen, and to set the high priesthood to sale every year:[4] Not at all considering the power of God but puffed up with his ten thousands of footmen, and his thousands of horsemen, and his fourscore elephants.[5] So he came to Judea, and drew near to Bethsura, which was a strong town, but distant from Jerusalem about five furlongs, and he laid sore siege unto it.[6] Now when they that were with Maccabeus heard that he besieged the holds, they and all the people with lamentation and tears besought the Lord that he would send a good angel to deliver Israel.[7] Then Maccabeus himself first of all took weapons, exhorting the other that they would jeopard themselves together with him to help their brethren: so they went forth together with a willing mind.[8] And as they were at Jerusalem, there appeared before them on horseback one in white clothing, shaking his armour of gold.[9] Then they praised the merciful God all together, and took heart, insomuch that they were ready not only to fight with men, but with most cruel beasts, and to pierce through walls of iron.[10] Thus they marched forward in their armour, having an helper from heaven: for the Lord was merciful unto them[11] And giving a charge upon their enemies like lions, they slew eleven thousand footmen, and sixteen hundred horsemen, and put all the other to flight.[12] Many of them also being wounded escaped naked; and Lysias himself fled away shamefully, and so escaped.[13] Who, as he was a man of understanding, casting with himself what loss he had had, and considering that the Hebrews could not be overcome, because the Almighty God helped them, he sent unto them,[14] And persuaded them to agree to all reasonable conditions, and promised that he would persuade the king that he must needs be a friend unto them.[15] Then Maccabeus consented to all that Lysias desired, being careful of the common good; and whatsoever Maccabeus wrote unto Lysias concerning the Jews, the king granted it.[16] For there were letters written unto the Jews from Lysias to this effect: Lysias unto the people of the Jews sendeth greeting:[17] John and Absolom, who were sent from you, delivered me the petition subscribed, and made request for the performance of the contents thereof.[18] Therefore what things soever were meet to be reported to the king, I have declared them, and he hath granted as much as might be.[19] And if then ye will keep yourselves loyal to the state, hereafter also will I endeavour to be a means of your good.[20] But of the particulars I have given order both to these and the other that came from me, to commune with you.[21] Fare ye well. The hundred and eight and fortieth year, the four and twentieth day of the month Dioscorinthius.[22] Now the king's letter contained these words: King Antiochus unto his brother Lysias sendeth greeting:[23] Since our father is translated unto the gods, our will is, that they that are in our realm live quietly, that every one may attend upon his own affairs.[24] We understand also that the Jews would not consent to our father, for to be brought unto the custom of the Gentiles, but had rather keep their own manner of living: for the which cause they require of us, that we should suffer them to live after their own laws.[25] Wherefore our mind is, that this nation shall be in rest, and we have determined to restore them their temple, that they may live according to the customs of their forefathers.[26] Thou shalt do well therefore to send unto them, and grant them peace, that when they are certified of our mind, they may be of good comfort, and ever go cheerfully about their own affairs.[27] And the letter of the king unto the nation of the Jews was after this manner: King Antiochus sendeth greeting unto the council, and the rest of the Jews:[28] If ye fare well, we have our desire; we are also in good health.[29] Menelaus declared unto us, that your desire was to return home, and to follow your own business:[30] Wherefore they that will depart shall have safe conduct till the thirtieth day of Xanthicus with security.[31] And the Jews shall use their own kind of meats and laws, as before; and none of them any manner of ways shall be molested for things ignorantly done.[32] I have sent also Menelaus, that he may comfort you.[33] Fare ye well. In the hundred forty and eighth year, and the fifteenth day of the month Xanthicus.[34] The Romans also sent unto them a letter containing these words: Quintus Memmius and Titus Manlius, ambassadors of the Romans, send greeting unto the people of the Jews.[35] Whatsoever Lysias the king's cousin hath granted, therewith we also are well pleased.[36] But touching such things as he judged to be referred to the king, after ye have advised thereof, send one forthwith, that we may declare as it is convenient for you: for we are now going to Antioch.[37] Therefore send some with speed, that we may know what is your mind.[38] Farewell. This hundred and eight and fortieth year, the fifteenth day of the month Xanthicus.

2Mac.12

[1] When these covenants were made, Lysias went unto the king, and the Jews were about their husbandry.[2] But of the governours of several places, Timotheus, and Apollonius the son of Genneus, also Hieronymus, and Demophon, and beside them Nicanor the governor of Cyprus, would not suffer them to be quiet and live in peace.[3] The men of Joppa also did such an ungodly deed: they prayed the Jews that dwelt among them to go with their wives and children into the boats which they had prepared, as though they had meant them no hurt.[4] Who accepted of it according to the common decree of the city, as being desirous to live in peace, and suspecting nothing: but when they were gone forth into the deep, they drowned no less than two hundred of them.[5] When Judas heard of this cruelty done unto his countrymen, he commanded those that were with him to make them ready.[6] And calling upon God the righteous Judge, he came against those murderers of his brethren, and burnt the haven by night, and set the boats on fire, and those that fled thither he slew.[7] And when the town was shut up, he went backward, as if he would return to root out all them of the city of Joppa.[8] But when he heard that the Jamnites were minded to do in like manner unto the Jews that dwelt among them,[9] He came upon the Jamnites also by night, and set fire on the haven and the navy, so that the light of the fire was seen at Jerusalem two hundred and forty furlongs off.[10] Now when they were gone from thence nine furlongs in their journey toward Timotheus, no fewer than five thousand men on foot and five hundred horsemen of the Arabians set upon him.[11] Whereupon there was a very sore battle; but Judas' side by the help of God got the victory; so that the Nomades of Arabia, being overcome, besought Judas for peace, promising both to give him cattle, and to pleasure him otherwise.[12] Then Judas, thinking indeed that they would be profitable in many things, granted them peace: whereupon they shook hands, and so they departed to their tents.[13] He went also about to make a bridge to a certain strong city, which was fenced about with walls, and inhabited by people of divers countries; and the name of it was Caspis.[14] But they that were within it put such trust in the strength of the walls and provision of victuals, that they behaved themselves rudely toward them that were with Judas, railing and blaspheming, and uttering such words as were not to be spoken.[15] Wherefore Judas with his company, calling upon the great Lord of the world, who without rams or engines of war did cast down Jericho in the time of Joshua, gave a fierce assault against the walls,[16] And took the city by the will of God, and made unspeakable slaughters, insomuch that a lake two furlongs broad

near adjoining thereunto, being filled full, was seen running with blood.[17] Then departed they from thence seven hundred and fifty furlongs, and came to Characa unto the Jews that are called Tubieni.[18] But as for Timotheus, they found him not in the places: for before he had dispatched any thing, he departed from thence, having left a very strong garrison in a certain hold.[19] Howbeit Dositheus and Sosipater, who were of Maccabeus' captains, went forth, and slew those that Timotheus had left in the fortress, above ten thousand men.[20] And Maccabeus ranged his army by bands, and set them over the bands, and went against Timotheus, who had about him an hundred and twenty thousand men of foot, and two thousand and five hundred horsemen.[21] Now when Timotheus had knowledge of Judas' coming, he sent the women and children and the other baggage unto a fortress called Carnion: for the town was hard to besiege, and uneasy to come unto, by reason of the straitness of all the places.[22] But when Judas his first band came in sight, the enemies, being smitten with fear and terror through the appearing of him who seeth all things, fled amain, one running into this way, another that way, so as that they were often hurt of their own men, and wounded with the points of their own swords.[23] Judas also was very earnest in pursuing them, killing those wicked wretches, of whom he slew about thirty thousand men.[24] Moreover Timotheus himself fell into the hands of Dositheus and Sosipater, whom he besought with much craft to let him go with his life, because he had many of the Jews' parents, and the brethren of some of them, who, if they put him to death, should not be regarded.[25] So when he had assured them with many words that he would restore them without hurt, according to the agreement, they let him go for the saving of their brethren.[26] Then Maccabeus marched forth to Carnion, and to the temple of Atargatis, and there he slew five and twenty thousand persons.[27] And after he had put to flight and destroyed them, Judas removed the host toward Ephron, a strong city, wherein Lysias abode, and a great multitude of divers nations, and the strong young men kept the walls, and defended them mightily: wherein also was great provision of engines and darts.[28] But when Judas and his company had called upon Almighty God, who with his power breaketh the strength of his enemies, they won the city, and slew twenty and five thousand of them that were within,[29] From thence they departed to Scythopolis, which lieth six hundred furlongs from Jerusalem,[30] But when the Jews that dwelt there had testified that the Scythopolitans dealt lovingly with them, and entreated them kindly in the time of their adversity;[31] They gave them thanks, desiring them to be friendly still unto them: and so they came to Jerusalem, the feast of the weeks approaching.[32] And after the feast, called Pentecost, they went forth against Gorgias the governor of Idumea,[33] Who came out with three thousand men of foot and four hundred horsemen.[34] And it happened that in their fighting together a few of the Jews were slain.[35] At which time Dositheus, one of Bacenor's company, who was on horseback, and a strong man, was still upon Gorgias, and taking hold of his coat drew him by force; and when he would have taken that cursed man alive, a horseman of Thracia coming upon him smote off his shoulder, so that Gorgias fled unto Marisa.[36] Now when they that were with Gorgias had fought long, and were weary, Judas called upon the Lord, that he would shew himself to be their helper and leader of the battle.[37] And with that he began in his own language, and sung psalms with a loud voice, and rushing unawares upon Gorgias' men, he put them to flight.[38] So Judas gathered his host, and came into the city of Odollam, And when the seventh day came, they purified themselves, as the custom was, and kept the sabbath in the same place.[39] And upon the day following, as the use had been, Judas and his company came to take up the bodies of them that were slain, and to bury them

with their kinsmen in their fathers' graves.[40] Now under the coats of every one that was slain they found things consecrated to the idols of the Jamnites, which is forbidden the Jews by the law. Then every man saw that this was the cause wherefore they were slain.[41] All men therefore praising the Lord, the righteous Judge, who had opened the things that were hid,[42] Betook themselves unto prayer, and besought him that the sin committed might wholly be put out of remembrance. Besides, that noble Judas exhorted the people to keep themselves from sin, forsomuch as they saw before their eyes the things that came to pass for the sins of those that were slain.[43] And when he had made a gathering throughout the company to the sum of two thousand drachms of silver, he sent it to Jerusalem to offer a sin offering, doing therein very well and honestly, in that he was mindful of the resurrection:[44] For if he had not hoped that they that were slain should have risen again, it had been superfluous and vain to pray for the dead.[45] And also in that he perceived that there was great favour laid up for those that died godly, it was an holy and good thought. Whereupon he made a reconciliation for the dead, that they might be delivered from sin.

2Mac.13

[1] In the hundred forty and ninth year it was told Judas, that Antiochus Eupator was coming with a great power into Judea,[2] And with him Lysias his protector, and ruler of his affairs, having either of them a Grecian power of footmen, an hundred and ten thousand, and horsemen five thousand and three hundred, and elephants two and twenty, and three hundred chariots armed with hooks.[3] Menelaus also joined himself with them, and with great dissimulation encouraged Antiochus, not for the safeguard of the country, but because he thought to have been made governor.[4] But the King of kings moved Antiochus' mind against this wicked wretch, and Lysias informed the king that this man was the cause of all mischief, so that the king commanded to bring him unto Berea, and to put him to death, as the manner is in that place.[5] Now there was in that place a tower of fifty cubits high, full of ashes, and it had a round instrument which on every side hanged down into the ashes.[6] And whosoever was condemned of sacrilege, or had committed any other grievous crime, there did all men thrust him unto death.[7] Such a death it happened that wicked man to die, not having so much as burial in the earth; and that most justly:[8] For inasmuch as he had committed many sins about the altar, whose fire and ashes were holy, he received his death in ashes.[9] Now the king came with a barbarous and haughty mind to do far worse to the Jews, than had been done in his father's time.[10] Which things when Judas perceived, he commanded the multitude to call upon the Lord night and day, that if ever at any other time, he would now also help them, being at the point to be put from their law, from their country, and from the holy temple:[11] And that he would not suffer the people, that had even now been but a little refreshed, to be in subjection to the blasphemous nations.[12] So when they had all done this together, and besought the merciful Lord with weeping and fasting, and lying flat upon the ground three days long, Judas, having exhorted them, commanded they should be in a readiness.[13] And Judas, being apart with the elders, determined, before the king's host should enter into Judea, and get the city, to go forth and try the matter in fight by the help of the Lord.[14] So when he had committed all to the Creator of the world, and exhorted his soldiers to fight manfully, even unto death, for the laws, the temple, the city, the country, and the commonwealth, he camped by Modin:[15] And having given the watchword to them that were about him, Victory is of God; with the most valiant and choice young men he went in into the king's tent by night, and slew in the camp about four thousand men, and the chiefest of the elephants, with all that were

upon him.[16] And at last they filled the camp with fear and tumult, and departed with good success.[17] This was done in the break of the day, because the protection of the Lord did help him.[18] Now when the king had taken a taste of the manliness of the Jews, he went about to take the holds by policy,[19] And marched toward Bethsura, which was a strong hold of the Jews: but he was put to flight, failed, and lost of his men:[20] For Judas had conveyed unto them that were in it such things as were necessary.[21] But Rhodocus, who was in the Jews' host, disclosed the secrets to the enemies; therefore he was sought out, and when they had gotten him, they put him in prison.[22] The king treated with them in Bethsum the second time, gave his hand, took their's, departed, fought with Judas, was overcome;[23] Heard that Philip, who was left over the affairs in Antioch, was desperately bent, confounded, intreated the Jews, submitted himself, and sware to all equal conditions, agreed with them, and offered sacrifice, honoured the temple, and dealt kindly with the place,[24] And accepted well of Maccabeus, made him principal governor from Ptolemais unto the Gerrhenians;[25] Came to Ptolemais: the people there were grieved for the covenants; for they stormed, because they would make their covenants void:[26] Lysias went up to the judgment seat, said as much as could be in defence of the cause, persuaded, pacified, made them well affected, returned to Antioch. Thus it went touching the king's coming and departing.

2Mac.14

[1] After three years was Judas informed, that Demetrius the son of Seleucus, having entered by the haven of Tripolis with a great power and navy,[2] Had taken the country, and killed Antiochus, and Lysias his protector.[3] Now one Alcimus, who had been high priest, and had defiled himself wilfully in the times of their mingling with the Gentiles, seeing that by no means he could save himself, nor have any more access to the holy altar,[4] Came to king Demetrius in the hundred and one and fiftieth year, presenting unto him a crown of gold, and a palm, and also of the boughs which were used solemnly in the temple: and so that day he held his peace.[5] Howbeit having gotten opportunity to further his foolish enterprize, and being called into counsel by Demetrius, and asked how the Jews stood affected, and what they intended, he answered thereunto:[6] Those of the Jews that he called Assideans, whose captain is Judas Maccabeus, nourish war and are seditious, and will not let the rest be in peace.[7] Therefore I, being deprived of mine ancestors' honour, I mean the high priesthood, am now come hither:[8] First, verily for the unfeigned care I have of things pertaining to the king; and secondly, even for that I intend the good of mine own countrymen: for all our nation is in no small misery through the unadvised dealing of them aforersaid.[9] Wherefore, O king, seeing knowest all these things, be careful for the country, and our nation, which is pressed on every side, according to the clemency that thou readily shewest unto all.[10] For as long as Judas liveth, it is not possible that the state should be quiet.[11] This was no sooner spoken of him, but others of the king's friends, being maliciously set against Judas, did more incense Demetrius.[12] And forthwith calling Nicanor, who had been master of the elephants, and making him governor over Judea, he sent him forth,[13] Commanding him to slay Judas, and to scatter them that were with him, and to make Alcimus high priest of the great temple.[14] Then the heathen, that had fled out of Judea from Judas, came to Nicanor by flocks, thinking the harm and calamities ot the Jews to be their welfare.[15] Now when the Jews heard of Nicanor's coming, and that the heathen were up against them, they cast earth upon their heads, and made supplication to him that had established his people for ever, and who always helpeth his portion with manifestation of his presence.[16] So at the commandment of the captain they removed straightways from thence, and came near unto them at the town of Dessau.[17] Now Simon, Judas' brother, had joined battle with Nicanor, but was somewhat discomfited through the sudden silence of his enemies.[18] Nevertheless Nicanor, hearing of the manliness of them that were with Judas, and the courageousness that they had to fight for their country, durst not try the matter by the sword.[19] Wherefore he sent Posidonius, and Theodotus, and Mattathias, to make peace.[20] So when they had taken long advisement thereupon, and the captain had made the multitude acquainted therewith, and it appeared that they were all of one mind, they consented to the covenants,[21] And appointed a day to meet in together by themselves: and when the day came, and stools were set for either of them,[22] Ludas placed armed men ready in convenient places, lest some treachery should be suddenly practised by the enemies: so they made a peaceable conference.[23] Now Nicanor abode in Jerusalem, and did no hurt, but sent away the people that came flocking unto him.[24] And he would not willingly have Judas out of his sight: for he love the man from his heart[25] He prayed him also to take a wife, and to beget children: so he married, was quiet, and took part of this life.[26] But Alcimus, perceiving the love that was betwixt them, and considering the covenants that were made, came to Demetrius, and told him that Nicanor was not well affected toward the state; for that he had ordained Judas, a traitor to his realm, to be the king's successor.[27] Then the king being in a rage, and provoked with the accusations of the most wicked man, wrote to Nicanor, signifying that he was much displeased with the covenants, and commanding him that he should send Maccabeus prisoner in all haste unto Antioch.[28] When this came to Nicanor's hearing, he was much confounded in himself, and took it grievously that he should make void the articles which were agreed upon, the man being in no fault.[29] But because there was no dealing against the king, he watched his time to accomplish this thing by policy.[30] Notwithstanding, when Maccabeus saw that Nicanor began to be churlish unto him, and that he entreated him more roughly than he was wont, perceiving that such sour behaviour came not of good, he gathered together not a few of his men, and withdrew himself from Nicanor.[31] But the other, knowing that he was notably prevented by Judas' policy, came into the great and holy temple, and commanded the priests, that were offering their usual sacrifices, to deliver him the man.[32] And when they sware that they could not tell where the man was whom he sought,[33] He stretched out his right hand toward the temple, and made an oath in this manner: If ye will not deliver me Judas as a prisoner, I will lay this temple of God even with the ground, and I will break down the altar, and erect a notable temple unto Bacchus.[34] After these words he departed. Then the priests lifted up their hands toward heaven, and besought him that was ever a defender of their nation, saying in this manner;[35] Thou, O Lord of all things, who hast need of nothing, wast pleased that the temple of thine habitation should be among us:[36] Therefore now, O holy Lord of all holiness, keep this house ever undefiled, which lately was cleansed, and stop every unrighteous mouth.[37] Now was there accused unto Nicanor one Razis, one of the elders of Jerusalem, a lover of his countrymen, and a man of very good report, who for his kindness was called a father of the Jews.[38] For in the former times, when they mingled not themselves with the Gentiles, he had been accused of Judaism, and did boldly jeopard his body and life with all vehemency for the religion of the Jews.[39] So Nicanor, willing to declare the hate that he bare unto the Jews, sent above five hundred men of war to take him:[40] For he thought by taking him to do the Jews much hurt.[41] Now when the multitude would have taken the tower, and violently broken into the outer door, and bade that fire should be brought to burn it, he being

ready to be taken on every side fell upon his sword;[42] Choosing rather to die manfully, than to come into the hands of the wicked, to be abused otherwise than beseemed his noble birth:[43] But missing his stroke through haste, the multitude also rushing within the doors, he ran boldly up to the wall, and cast himself down manfully among the thickest of them.[44] But they quickly giving back, and a space being made, he fell down into the midst of the void place.[45] Nevertheless, while there was yet breath within him, being inflamed with anger, he rose up; and though his blood gushed out like spouts of water, and his wounds were grievous, yet he ran through the midst of the throng; and standing upon a steep rock,[46] When as his blood was now quite gone, he plucked out his bowels, and taking them in both his hands, he cast them upon the throng, and calling upon the Lord of life and spirit to restore him those again, he thus died.

2Mac.15

[1] But Nicanor, hearing that Judas and his company were in the strong places about Samaria, resolved without any danger to set upon them on the sabbath day.[2] Nevertheless the Jews that were compelled to go with him said, O destroy not so cruelly and barbarously, but give honour to that day, which he, that seeth all things, hath honoured with holiness above all other days.[3] Then the most ungracious wretch demanded, if there were a Mighty one in heaven, that had commanded the sabbath day to be kept.[4] And when they said, There is in heaven a living Lord, and mighty, who commanded the seventh day to be kept:[5] Then said the other, And I also am mighty upon earth, and I command to take arms, and to do the king's business. Yet he obtained not to have his wicked will done.[6] So Nicanor in exceeding pride and haughtiness determined to set up a publick monument of his victory over Judas and them that were with him.[7] But Maccabeus had ever sure confidence that the Lord would help him:[8] Wherefore he exhorted his people not to fear the coming of the heathen against them, but to remember the help which in former times they had received from heaven, and now to expect the victory and aid, which should come unto them from the Almighty.[9] And so comforting them out of the law and the prophets, and withal putting them in mind of the battles that they won afore, he made them more cheerful.[10] And when he had stirred up their minds, he gave them their charge, shewing them therewithall the falsehood of the heathen, and the breach of oaths.[11] Thus he armed every one of them, not so much with defence of shields and spears, as with comfortable and good words: and beside that, he told them a dream worthy to be believed, as if it had been so indeed, which did not a little rejoice them.[12] And this was his vision: That Onias, who had been high priest, a virtuous and a good man, reverend in conversation, gentle in condition, well spoken also, and exercised from a child in all points of virtue, holding up his hands prayed for the whole body of the Jews.[13] This done, in like manner there appeared a man with gray hairs, and exceeding glorious, who was of a wonderful and excellent majesty.[14] Then Onias answered, saying, This is a lover of the brethren, who prayeth much for the people, and for the holy city, to wit, Jeremias the prophet of God.[15] Whereupon Jeremias holding forth his right hand gave to Judas a sword of gold, and in giving it spake thus,[16] Take this holy sword, a gift from God, with the which thou shalt wound the adversaries.[17] Thus being well comforted by the words of Judas, which were very good, and able to stir them up to valour, and to encourage the hearts of the young men, they determined not to pitch camp, but courageously to set upon them, and manfully to try the matter by conflict, because the city and the sanctuary and the temple were in danger.[18] For the care that they took for their wives, and their children, their brethren, and folks,

was in least account with them: but the greatest and principal fear was for the holy temple.[19] Also they that were in the city took not the least care, being troubled for the conflict abroad.[20] And now, when as all looked what should be the trial, and the enemies were already come near, and the army was set in array, and the beasts conveniently placed, and the horsemen set in wings,[21] Maccabeus seeing the coming of the multitude, and the divers preparations of armour, and the fierceness of the beasts, stretched out his hands toward heaven, and called upon the Lord that worketh wonders, knowing that victory cometh not by arms, but even as it seemeth good to him, he giveth it to such as are worthy:[22] Therefore in his prayer he said after this manner; O Lord, thou didst send thine angel in the time of Ezekias king of Judea, and didst slay in the host of Sennacherib an hundred fourscore and five thousand:[23] Wherefore now also, O Lord of heaven, send a good angel before us for a fear and dread unto them;[24] And through the might of thine arm let those be stricken with terror, that come against thy holy people to blaspheme. And he ended thus.[25] Then Nicanor and they that were with him came forward with trumpets and songs.[26] But Judas and his company encountered the enemies with invocation and prayer.[27] So that fighting with their hands, and praying unto God with their hearts, they slew no less than thirty and five thousand men: for through the appearance of God they were greatly cheered.[28] Now when the battle was done, returning again with joy, they knew that Nicanor lay dead in his harness.[29] Then they made a great shout and a noise, praising the Almighty in their own language.[30] And Judas, who was ever the chief defender of the citizens both in body and mind, and who continued his love toward his countrymen all his life, commanded to strike off Nicanor's head, and his hand with his shoulder, and bring them to Jerusalem.[31] So when he was there, and called them of his nation together, and set the priests before the altar, he sent for them that were of the tower,[32] And shewed them vile Nicanor's head, and the hand of that blasphemer, which with proud brags he had stretched out against the holy temple of the Almighty.[33] And when he had cut out the tongue of that ungodly Nicanor, he commanded that they should give it by pieces unto the fowls, and hang up the reward of his madness before the temple.[34] So every man praised toward the heaven the glorious Lord, saying, Blessed be he that hath kept his own place undefiled.[35] He hanged also Nicanor's head upon the tower, an evident and manifest sign unto all of the help of the Lord.[36] And they ordained all with a common decree in no case to let that day pass without solemnity, but to celebrate the thirtieth day of the twelfth month, which in the Syrian tongue is called Adar, the day before Mardocheus' day.[37] Thus went it with Nicanor: and from that time forth the Hebrews had the city in their power. And here will I make an end.[38] And if I have done well, and as is fitting the story, it is that which I desired: but if slenderly and meanly, it is that which I could attain unto.[39] For as it is hurtful to drink wine or water alone; and as wine mingled with water is pleasant, and delighteth the taste: even so speech finely framed delighteth the ears of them that read the story. And here shall be an end.

Orthodox-Specific Deuterocanonical Books

Introduction

This second section delves into a collection of texts that hold a unique place within the Eastern Orthodox Christian tradition. These books, while not universally acknowledged in the broader Christian canons such as those of the Roman Catholic Church, embody significant theological and liturgical value in the Orthodox community. Their recognition underscores the diversity and richness of Christian scriptural traditions and highlights the distinct historical paths of scriptural canonization and liturgical usage across Christianity.

Historical Context - The Eastern Orthodox Church has historically maintained a broader biblical canon than that of the Roman Catholic or Protestant traditions, partly due to different historical developments and theological emphases. The texts included in this section—1 Esdras, 3 Maccabees, Prayer of Manasseh, and Psalm 151—are part of the Septuagint, the ancient Greek version of the Hebrew Scriptures, which was widely used in the Eastern Mediterranean, particularly within Hellenistic Jewish and early Christian communities. The inclusion of these texts reflects the Orthodox Church's continuity with the early, culturally diverse Christian practices that were more aligned with the Septuagint's broader corpus.

Theological Significance - These texts enrich the Orthodox tradition with narratives and prayers that emphasize repentance, divine mercy, and the complexity of human governance under divine providence. Each text offers unique insights:

- **1 Esdras** revisits the story of the return from Babylonian exile, echoing themes from Ezra and Nehemiah but with unique additions that emphasize themes of piety and community restoration.
- **3 Maccabees**, despite its name, does not directly relate to the Maccabean revolt but describes a different persecution and miraculous salvation, enhancing themes of divine protection against oppression.
- **Prayer of Manasseh,** encapsulates the theme of repentance, traditionally attributed to the wicked King Manasseh of Judah, whose contrite prayer for forgiveness exemplifies the possibility of redemption.
- **Psalm 151**, considered canonical in the Orthodox tradition, provides a personal reflection attributed to David, offering a glimpse into his anointing as a shepherd boy, highlighting God's choice of the humble and pious.

Rationale for Inclusion - The inclusion of these texts in the Orthodox canon but not in the Catholic deuterocanon underscores the varying criteria and theological motifs valued by different traditions. For the Orthodox Church, these writings are not merely historical artifacts but are living texts that continue to inform liturgical life, doctrinal teaching, and personal piety. Their usage in liturgy and catechesis underscores the Orthodox emphasis on the transformative power of Scripture in personal and communal religious life.

The theological narratives and prayers contained within these books resonate deeply with the Orthodox understanding of history as a manifestation of God's ongoing conversation with humanity. Their scriptural status in the East as opposed to their apocryphal status in the West reflects broader ecclesiastical and theological trajectories that have historically differentiated the Christian East from the West.

In sum, this section offers readers a profound insight into the diversity of Christian scriptural tradition, highlighting how different communities have discerned and valued the texts that shape their faith and practice. Through these Orthodox-specific deuterocanonical books, we gain a richer understanding of the spiritual and theological heritage that has sustained Orthodox Christianity through the centuries.

1 Esdras (Ezra Sutuel)

1Esdr.1

[1] And Josias held the feast of the passover in Jerusalem unto his Lord, and offered the passover the fourteenth day of the first month;[2] Having set the priests according to their daily courses, being arrayed in long garments, in the temple of the Lord.[3] And he spake unto the Levites, the holy ministers of Israel, that they should hallow themselves unto the Lord, to set the holy ark of the Lord in the house that king Solomon the son of David had built:[4] And said, Ye shall no more bear the ark upon your shoulders: now therefore serve the Lord your God, and minister unto his people Israel, and prepare you after your families and kindreds,[5] According as David the king of Israel prescribed, and according to the magnificence of Solomon his son: and standing in the temple according to the several dignity of the families of you the Levites, who minister in the presence of your brethren the children of Israel,[6] Offer the passover in order, and make ready the sacrifices for your brethren, and keep the passover according to the commandment of the Lord, which was given unto Moses.[7] And unto the people that was found there Josias gave thirty thousand lambs and kids, and three thousand calves: these things were given of the king's allowance, according as he promised, to the people, to the priests, and to the Levites.[8] And Helkias, Zacharias, and Syelus, the governors of the temple, gave to the priests for the passover two thousand and six hundred sheep, and three hundred calves.[9] And Jeconias, and Samaias, and Nathanael his brother, and Assabias, and Ochiel, and Joram, captains over thousands, gave to the Levites for the passover five thousand sheep, and seven hundred calves.[10] And when these things were done, the priests and Levites, having the unleavened bread, stood in very comely order according to the kindreds,[11] And according to the several dignities of the fathers, before the people, to offer to the Lord, as it is written in the book of Moses: and thus did they in the morning.[12] And they roasted the passover with fire, as appertaineth: as for the sacrifices, they sod them in brass pots and pans with a good savour,[13] And set them before all the people: and afterward they prepared for themselves, and for the priests their brethren, the sons of Aaron.[14] For the priests offered the fat until night: and the Levites prepared for themselves, and the priests their brethren, the sons of Aaron.[15] The holy singers also, the sons of Asaph, were in their order, according to the appointment of David, to wit, Asaph, Zacharias, and Jeduthun, who was of the king's retinue.[16] Moreover the porters were at every gate; it was not lawful for any to go from his ordinary service: for their brethren the Levites prepared for them.[17] Thus were the things that belonged to the sacrifices of the Lord accomplished in that day, that they might hold the passover,[18] And offer sacrifices upon the altar of the Lord, according to the commandment of king Josias.[19] So the children of Israel which were present held the passover at that time, and the feast of sweet bread seven days.[20] And such a passover was not kept in Israel since the time of the prophet Samuel.[21] Yea, all the kings of Israel held not such a passover as Josias, and the priests, and the Levites, and the Jews, held with all Israel that were found dwelling at Jerusalem.[22] In the eighteenth year of the reign of Josias was this passover kept.[23] And the works or Josias were upright before his Lord with an heart full of godliness.[24] As for the things that came to pass in his time, they were written in former times, concerning those that sinned, and did wickedly against the Lord above all people and kingdoms, and how they grieved him exceedingly, so that the words of the Lord rose up against Israel.[25] Now after all these acts of Josias it came to pass, that Pharaoh the king of Egypt came to raise war at Carchamis upon Euphrates: and Josias went out against him.[26] But the king of Egypt sent to him, saying, What have I to do with thee, O king of Judea?[27] I am not sent out from the Lord God against thee; for my war is upon Euphrates: and now the Lord is with me, yea, the Lord is with me hasting me forward: depart from me, and be not against the Lord.[28] Howbeit Josias did not turn back his chariot from him, but undertook to fight with him, not regarding

the words of the prophet Jeremy spoken by the mouth of the Lord:[29] But joined battle with him in the plain of Magiddo, and the princes came against king Josias.[30] Then said the king unto his servants, Carry me away out of the battle; for I am very weak. And immediately his servants took him away out of the battle.[31] Then gat he up upon his second chariot; and being brought back to Jerusalem died, and was buried in his father's sepulchre.[32] And in all Jewry they mourned for Josias, yea, Jeremy the prophet lamented for Josias, and the chief men with the women made lamentation for him unto this day: and this was given out for an ordinance to be done continually in all the nation of Israel.[33] These things are written in the book of the stories of the kings of Judah, and every one of the acts that Josias did, and his glory, and his understanding in the law of the Lord, and the things that he had done before, and the things now recited, are reported in the book of the kings of Israel and Judea.[34] And the people took Joachaz the son of Josias, and made him king instead of Josias his father, when he was twenty and three years old.[35] And he reigned in Judea and in Jerusalem three months: and then the king of Egypt deposed him from reigning in Jerusalem.[36] And he set a tax upon the land of an hundred talents of silver and one talent of gold.[37] The king of Egypt also made king Joacim his brother king of Judea and Jerusalem.[38] And he bound Joacim and the nobles: but Zaraces his brother he apprehended, and brought him out of Egypt.[39] Five and twenty years old was Joacim when he was made king in the land of Judea and Jerusalem; and he did evil before the Lord.[40] Wherefore against him Nabuchodonosor the king of Babylon came up, and bound him with a chain of brass, and carried him into Babylon.[41] Nabuchodonosor also took of the holy vessels of the Lord, and carried them away, and set them in his own temple at Babylon.[42] But those things that are recorded of him, and of his uncleaness and impiety, are written in the chronicles of the kings.[43] And Joacim his son reigned in his stead: he was made king being eighteen years old;[44] And reigned but three months and ten days in Jerusalem; and did evil before the Lord.[45] So after a year Nabuchodonosor sent and caused him to be brought into Babylon with the holy vessels of the Lord;[46] And made Zedechias king of Judea and Jerusalem, when he was one and twenty years old; and he reigned eleven years:[47] And he did evil also in the sight of the Lord, and cared not for the words that were spoken unto him by the prophet Jeremy from the mouth of the Lord.[48] And after that king Nabuchodonosor had made him to swear by the name of the Lord, he forswore himself, and rebelled; and hardening his neck, his heart, he transgressed the laws of the Lord God of Israel.[49] The governors also of the people and of the priests did many things against the laws, and passed all the pollutions of all nations, and defiled the temple of the Lord, which was sanctified in Jerusalem.[50] Nevertheless the God of their fathers sent by his messenger to call them back, because he spared them and his tabernacle also.[51] But they had his messengers in derision; and, look, when the Lord spake unto them, they made a sport of his prophets:[52] So far forth, that he, being wroth with his people for their great ungodliness, commanded the kings of the Chaldees to come up against them;[53] Who slew their young men with the sword, yea, even within the compass of their holy temple, and spared neither young man nor maid, old man nor child, among them; for he delivered all into their hands.[54] And they took all the holy vessels of the Lord, both great and small, with the vessels of the ark of God, and the king's treasures, and carried them away into Babylon.[55] As for the house of the Lord, they burnt it, and brake down the walls of Jerusalem, and set fire upon her towers:[56] And as for her glorious things, they never ceased till they had consumed and brought them all to nought: and the people that were not slain with the sword he

carried unto Babylon:[57] Who became servants to him and his children, till the Persians reigned, to fulfil the word of the Lord spoken by the mouth of Jeremy:[58] Until the land had enjoyed her sabbaths, the whole time of her desolation shall she rest, until the full term of seventy years.

1Esdr.2

[1] In the first year of Cyrus king of the Persians, that the word of the Lord might be accomplished, that he had promised by the mouth of Jeremy;[2] The Lord raised up the spirit of Cyrus the king of the Persians, and he made proclamation through all his kingdom, and also by writing,[3] Saying, Thus saith Cyrus king of the Persians; The Lord of Israel, the most high Lord, hath made me king of the whole world,[4] And commanded me to build him an house at Jerusalem in Jewry.[5] If therefore there be any of you that are of his people, let the Lord, even his Lord, be with him, and let him go up to Jerusalem that is in Judea, and build the house of the Lord of Israel: for he is the Lord that dwelleth in Jerusalem.[6] Whosoever then dwell in the places about, let them help him, those, I say, that are his neighbours, with gold, and with silver,[7] With gifts, with horses, and with cattle, and other things, which have been set forth by vow, for the temple of the Lord at Jerusalem.[8] Then the chief of the families of Judea and of the tribe of Benjamin stood up; the priests also, and the Levites, and all they whose mind the Lord had moved to go up, and to build an house for the Lord at Jerusalem,[9] And they that dwelt round about them, and helped them in all things with silver and gold, with horses and cattle, and with very many free gifts of a great number whose minds were stirred up thereto.[10] King Cyrus also brought forth the holy vessels, which Nabuchodonosor had carried away from Jerusalem, and had set up in his temple of idols.[11] Now when Cyrus king of the Persians had brought them forth, he delivered them to Mithridates his treasurer:[12] And by him they were delivered to Sanabassar the governor of Judea.[13] And this was the number of them; A thousand golden cups, and a thousand of silver, censers of silver twenty nine, vials of gold thirty, and of silver two thousand four hundred and ten, and a thousand other vessels.[14] So all the vessels of gold and of silver, which were carried away, were five thousand four hundred threescore and nine.[15] These were brought back by Sanabassar, together with them of the captivity, from Babylon to Jerusalem.[16] But in the time of Artexerxes king of the Persians Belemus, and Mithridates, and Tabellius, and Rathumus, and Beeltethmus, and Semellius the secretary, with others that were in commission with them, dwelling in Samaria and other places, wrote unto him against them that dwelt in Judea and Jerusalem these letters following;[17] To king Artexerxes our lord, Thy servants, Rathumus the storywriter, and Semellius the scribe, and the rest of their council, and the judges that are in Celosyria and Phenice.[18] Be it now known to the lord king, that the Jews that are up from you to us, being come into Jerusalem, that rebellious and wicked city, do build the marketplaces, and repair the walls of it and do lay the foundation of the temple.[19] Now if this city and the walls thereof be made up again, they will not only refuse to give tribute, but also rebel against kings.[20] And forasmuch as the things pertaining to the temple are now in hand, we think it not meet to neglect such a matter,[21] But to speak unto our lord the king, to the intent that, if it be thy pleasure it may be sought out in the books of thy fathers:[22] And thou shalt find in the chronicles what is written concerning these things, and shalt understand that that city was rebellious, troubling both kings and cities:[23] And that the Jews were rebellious, and raised always wars therein; for the which cause even this city was made desolate.[24] Wherefore now we do declare unto thee, O lord the king, that if this city be built again, and the walls thereof set up anew, thou shalt from henceforth have no passage

into Celosyria and Phenice.²⁵ Then the king wrote back again to Rathumus the storywriter, to Beeltethmus, to Semellius the scribe, and to the rest that were in commission, and dwellers in Samaria and Syria and Phenice, after this manner;²⁶ I have read the epistle which ye have sent unto me: therefore I commanded to make diligent search, and it hath been found that that city was from the beginning practising against kings;²⁷ And the men therein were given to rebellion and war: and that mighty kings and fierce were in Jerusalem, who reigned and exacted tributes in Celosyria and Phenice.²⁸ Now therefore I have commanded to hinder those men from building the city, and heed to be taken that there be no more done in it;²⁹ And that those wicked workers proceed no further to the annoyance of kings,³⁰ Then king Artexerxes his letters being read, Rathumus, and Semellius the scribe, and the rest that were in commission with them, removing in haste toward Jerusalem with a troop of horsemen and a multitude of people in battle array, began to hinder the builders; and the building of the temple in Jerusalem ceased until the second year of the reign of Darius king of the Persians.

1Esdr.3

¹ Now when Darius reigned, he made a great feast unto all his subjects, and unto all his household, and unto all the princes of Media and Persia,² And to all the governors and captains and lieutenants that were under him, from India unto Ethiopia, of an hundred twenty and seven provinces.³ And when they had eaten and drunken, and being satisfied were gone home, then Darius the king went into his bedchamber, and slept, and soon after awaked.⁴ Then three young men, that were of the guard that kept the king's body, spake one to another;⁵ Let every one of us speak a sentence: he that shall overcome, and whose sentence shall seem wiser than the others, unto him shall the king Darius give great gifts, and great things in token of victory:⁶ As, to be clothed in purple, to drink in gold, and to sleep upon gold, and a chariot with bridles of gold, and an headtire of fine linen, and a chain about his neck:⁷ And he shall sit next to Darius because of his wisdom, and shall be called Darius his cousin.⁸ And then every one wrote his sentence, sealed it, and laid it under king Darius his pillow;⁹ And said that, when the king is risen, some will give him the writings; and of whose side the king and the three princes of Persia shall judge that his sentence is the wisest, to him shall the victory be given, as was appointed.¹⁰ The first wrote, Wine is the strongest.¹¹ The second wrote, The king is strongest.¹² The third wrote, Women are strongest: but above all things Truth beareth away the victory.¹³ Now when the king was risen up, they took their writings, and delivered them unto him, and so he read them:¹⁴ And sending forth he called all the princes of Persia and Media, and the governors, and the captains, and the lieutenants, and the chief officers;¹⁵ And sat him down in the royal seat of judgment; and the writings were read before them.¹⁶ And he said, Call the young men, and they shall declare their own sentences. So they were called, and came in.¹⁷ And he said unto them, Declare unto us your mind concerning the writings. Then began the first, who had spoken of the strength of wine;¹⁸ And he said thus, O ye men, how exceeding strong is wine! it causeth all men to err that drink it:¹⁹ It maketh the mind of the king and of the fatherless child to be all one; of the bondman and of the freeman, of the poor man and of the rich:²⁰ It turneth also every thought into jollity and mirth, so that a man remembereth neither sorrow nor debt:²¹ And it maketh every heart rich, so that a man remembereth neither king nor governor; and it maketh to speak all things by talents:²² And when they are in their cups, they forget their love both to friends and brethren, and a little after draw out swords:²³ But when they are from the wine, they remember not what they have done.²⁴ O ye men,

is not wine the strongest, that enforceth to do thus? And when he had so spoken, he held his peace.

1Esdr.4

¹ Then the second, that had spoken of the strength of the king, began to say,² O ye men, do not men excel in strength that bear rule over sea and land and all things in them?³ But yet the king is more mighty: for he is lord of all these things, and hath dominion over them; and whatsoever he commandeth them they do.⁴ If he bid them make war the one against the other, they do it: if he send them out against the enemies, they go, and break down mountains walls and towers.⁵ They slay and are slain, and transgress not the king's commandment: if they get the victory, they bring all to the king, as well the spoil, as all things else.⁶ Likewise for those that are no soldiers, and have not to do with wars, but use husbundry, when they have reaped again that which they had sown, they bring it to the king, and compel one another to pay tribute unto the king.⁷ And yet he is but one man: if he command to kill, they kill; if he command to spare, they spare;⁸ If he command to smite, they smite; if he command to make desolate, they make desolate; if he command to build, they build;⁹ If he command to cut down, they cut down; if he command to plant, they plant.¹⁰ So all his people and his armies obey him: furthermore he lieth down, he eateth and drinketh, and taketh his rest:¹¹ And these keep watch round about him, neither may any one depart, and do his own business, neither disobey they him in any thing.¹² O ye men, how should not the king be mightiest, when in such sort he is obeyed? And he held his tongue.¹³ Then the third, who had spoken of women, and of the truth, (this was Zorobabel) began to speak.¹⁴ O ye men, it is not the great king, nor the multitude of men, neither is it wine, that excelleth; who is it then that ruleth them, or hath the lordship over them? are they not women?¹⁵ Women have borne the king and all the people that bear rule by sea and land.¹⁶ Even of them came they: and they nourished them up that planted the vineyards, from whence the wine cometh.¹⁷ These also make garments for men; these bring glory unto men; and without women cannot men be.¹⁸ Yea, and if men have gathered together gold and silver, or any other goodly thing, do they not love a woman which is comely in favour and beauty?¹⁹ And letting all those things go, do they not gape, and even with open mouth fix their eyes fast on her; and have not all men more desire unto her than unto silver or gold, or any goodly thing whatsoever?²⁰ A man leaveth his own father that brought him up, and his own country, and cleaveth unto his wife.²¹ He sticketh not to spend his life with his wife. and remembereth neither father, nor mother, nor country.²² By this also ye must know that women have dominion over you: do ye not labour and toil, and give and bring all to the woman?²³ Yea, a man taketh his sword, and goeth his way to rob and to steal, to sail upon the sea and upon rivers;²⁴ And looketh upon a lion, and goeth in the darkness; and when he hath stolen, spoiled, and robbed, he bringeth it to his love.²⁵ Wherefore a man loveth his wife better than father or mother.²⁶ Yea, many there be that have run out of their wits for women, and become servants for their sakes.²⁷ Many also have perished, have erred, and sinned, for women.²⁸ And now do ye not believe me? is not the king great in his power? do not all regions fear to touch him?²⁹ Yet did I see him and Apame the king's concubine, the daughter of the admirable Bartacus, sitting at the right hand of the king,³⁰ And taking the crown from the king's head, and setting it upon her own head; she also struck the king with her left hand.³¹ And yet for all this the king gaped and gazed upon her with open mouth: if she laughed upon him, he laughed also: but if she took any displeasure at him, the king was fain to flatter, that she might be reconciled to him again.³² O ye men, how can it be but women should be strong, seeing they do

thus?³³ Then the king and the princes looked one upon another: so he began to speak of the truth.³⁴ O ye men, are not women strong? great is the earth, high is the heaven, swift is the sun in his course, for he compasseth the heavens round about, and fetcheth his course again to his own place in one day.³⁵ Is he not great that maketh these things? therefore great is the truth, and stronger than all things.³⁶ All the earth crieth upon the truth, and the heaven blesseth it: all works shake and tremble at it, and with it is no unrighteous thing.³⁷ Wine is wicked, the king is wicked, women are wicked, all the children of men are wicked, and such are all their wicked works; and there is no truth in them; in their unrighteousness also they shall perish.³⁸ As for the truth, it endureth, and is alwaYs strong; it liveth and conquereth for evermore.³⁹ With her there is no accepting of persons or rewards; but she doeth the things that are just, and refraineth from all unjust and wicked things; and all men do well like of her works.⁴⁰ Neither in her judgment is any unrighteousness; and she is the strength, kingdom, power, and majesty, of all ages. Blessed be the God of truth.⁴¹ And with that he held his peace. And all the people then shouted, and said, Great is Truth, and mighty above all things.⁴² Then said the king unto him, Ask what thou wilt more than is appointed in the writing, and we will give it thee, because thou art found wisest; and thou shalt sit next me, and shalt be called my cousin.⁴³ Then said he unto the king, Remember thy vow, which thou hast vowed to build Jerusalem, in the day when thou camest to thy kingdom,⁴⁴ And to send away all the vessels that were taken away out of Jerusalem, which Cyrus set apart, when he vowed to destroy Babylon, and to send them again thither.⁴⁵ Thou also hast vowed to build up the temple, which the Edomites burned when Judea was made desolate by the Chaldees.⁴⁶ And now, O lord the king, this is that which I require, and which I desire of thee, and this is the princely liberality proceeding from thyself: I desire therefore that thou make good the vow, the performance whereof with thine own mouth thou hast vowed to the King of heaven.⁴⁷ Then Darius the king stood up, and kissed him, and wrote letters for him unto all the treasurers and lieutenants and captains and governors, that they should safely convey on their way both him, and all those that go up with him to build Jerusalem.⁴⁸ He wrote letters also unto the lieutenants that were in Celosyria and Phenice, and unto them in Libanus, that they should bring cedar wood from Libanus unto Jerusalem, and that they should build the city with him.⁴⁹ Moreover he wrote for all the Jews that went out of his realm up into Jewry, concerning their freedom, that no officer, no ruler, no lieutenant, nor treasurer, should forcibly enter into their doors;⁵⁰ And that all the country which they hold should be free without tribute; and that the Edomites should give over the villages of the Jews which then they held:⁵¹ Yea, that there should be yearly given twenty talents to the building of the temple, until the time that it were built;⁵² And other ten talents yearly, to maintain the burnt offerings upon the altar every day, as they had a commandment to offer seventeen:⁵³ And that all they that went from Babylon to build the city should have free liberty, as well they as their posterity, and all the priests that went away.⁵⁴ He wrote also concerning. the charges, and the priests' vestments wherein they minister;⁵⁵ And likewise for the charges of the Levites, to be given them until the day that the house were finished, and Jerusalem builded up.⁵⁶ And he commanded to give to all that kept the city pensions and wages.⁵⁷ He sent away also all the vessels from Babylon, that Cyrus had set apart; and all that Cyrus had given in commandment, the same charged he also to be done, and sent unto Jerusalem.⁵⁸ Now when this young man was gone forth, he lifted up his face to heaven toward Jerusalem, and praised the King of heaven,⁵⁹ And said, From thee cometh victory, from thee cometh wisdom, and thine is the glory,

and I am thy servant.⁶⁰ Blessed art thou, who hast given me wisdom: for to thee I give thanks, O Lord of our fathers.⁶¹ And so he took the letters, and went out, and came unto Babylon, and told it all his brethren.⁶² And they praised the God of their fathers, because he had given them freedom and liberty⁶³ To go up, and to build Jerusalem, and the temple which is called by his name: and they feasted with instruments of musick and gladness seven days.

1Esdr.5

¹ After this were the principal men of the families chosen according to their tribes, to go up with their wives and sons and daughters, with their menservants and maidservants, and their cattle.² And Darius sent with them a thousand horsemen, till they had brought them back to Jerusalem safely, and with musical [instruments] tabrets and flutes.³ And all their brethren played, and he made them go up together with them.⁴ And these are the names of the men which went up, according to their families among their tribes, after their several heads.⁵ The priests, the sons of Phinees the son of Aaron: Jesus the son of Josedec, the son of Saraias, and Joacim the son of Zorobabel, the son of Salathiel, of the house of David, out of the kindred of Phares, of the tribe of Judah;⁶ Who spake wise sentences before Darius the king of Persia in the second year of his reign, in the month Nisan, which is the first month.⁷ And these are they of Jewry that came up from the captivity, where they dwelt as strangers, whom Nabuchodonosor the king of Babylon had carried away unto Babylon.⁸ And they returned unto Jerusalem, and to the other parts of Jewry, every man to his own city, who came with Zorobabel, with Jesus, Nehemias, and Zacharias, and Reesaias, Enenius, Mardocheus. Beelsarus, Aspharasus, Reelius, Roimus, and Baana, their guides.⁹ The number of them of the nation, and their governors, sons of Phoros, two thousand an hundred seventy and two; the sons of Saphat, four hundred seventy and two:¹⁰ The sons of Ares, seven hundred fifty and six:¹¹ The sons of Phaath Moab, two thousand eight hundred and twelve:¹² The sons of Elam, a thousand two hundred fifty and four: the sons of Zathul, nine hundred forty and five: the sons of Corbe, seven hundred and five: the sons of Bani, six hundred forty and eight:¹³ The sons of Bebai, six hundred twenty and three: the sons of Sadas, three thousand two hundred twenty and two:¹⁴ The sons of Adonikam, six hundred sixty and seven: the sons of Bagoi, two thousand sixty and six: the sons of Adin, four hundred fifty and four:¹⁵ The sons of Aterezias, ninety and two: the sons of Ceilan and Azetas threescore and seven: the sons of Azuran, four hundred thirty and two:¹⁶ The sons of Ananias, an hundred and one: the sons of Arom, thirty two: and the sons of Bassa, three hundred twenty and three: the sons of Azephurith, an hundred and two:¹⁷ The sons of Meterus, three thousand and five: the sons of Bethlomon, an hundred twenty and three:¹⁸ They of Netophah, fifty and five: they of Anathoth, an hundred fifty and eight: they of Bethsamos, forty and two:¹⁹ They of Kiriathiarius, twenty and five: they of Caphira and Beroth, seven hundred forty and three: they of Pira, seven hundred:²⁰ They of Chadias and Ammidoi, four hundred twenty and two: they of Cirama and Gabdes, six hundred twenty and one:²¹ They of Macalon, an hundred twenty and two: they of Betolius, fifty and two: the sons of Nephis, an hundred fifty and six:²² The sons of Calamolalus and Onus, seven hundred twenty and five: the sons of Jerechus, two hundred forty and five:²³ The sons of Annas, three thousand three hundred and thirty.²⁴ The priests: the sons of Jeddu, the son of Jesus among the sons of Sanasib, nine hundred seventy and two: the sons of Meruth, a thousand fifty and two:²⁵ The sons of Phassaron, a thousand forty and seven: the sons of Carme, a thousand and seventeen.²⁶ The Levites: the sons of Jessue, and Cadmiel, and Banuas, and Sudias, seventy and four.²⁷ The holy singers: the sons

of Asaph, an hundred twenty and eight.[28] The porters: the sons of Salum, the sons of Jatal, the sons of Talmon, the sons of Dacobi, the sons of Teta, the sons of Sami, in all an hundred thirty and nine.[29] The servants of the temple: the sons of Esau, the sons of Asipha, the sons of Tabaoth, the sons of Ceras, the sons of Sud, the sons of Phaleas, the sons of Labana, the sons of Graba,[30] The sons of Acua, the sons of Uta, the sons of Cetab, the sons of Agaba, the sons of Subai, the sons of Anan, the sons of Cathua, the sons of Geddur,[31] The sons of Airus, the sons of Daisan, the sons of Noeba, the sons of Chaseba, the sons of Gazera, the sons of Azia, the sons of Phinees, the sons of Azare, the sons of Bastai, the sons of Asana, the sons of Meani, the sons of Naphisi, the sons of Acub, the sons of Acipha, the sons of Assur, the sons of Pharacim, the sons of Basaloth,[32] The sons of Meeda, the sons of Coutha, the sons of Charea, the sons of Charcus, the sons of Aserer, the sons of Thomoi, the sons of Nasith, the sons of Atipha.[33] The sons of the servants of Solomon: the sons of Azaphion, the sons of Pharira, the sons of Jeeli, the sons of Lozon, the sons of Israel, the sons of Sapheth,[34] The sons of Hagia, the sons of Pharacareth, the sons of Sabi, the sons of Sarothie, the sons of Masias, the sons of Gar, the sons of Addus, the sons of Suba, the sons of Apherra, the sons of Barodis, the sons of Sabat, the sons of Allom.[35] All the ministers of the temple, and the sons of the servants of Solomon, were three hundred seventy and two.[36] These came up from Thermeleth and Thelersas, Charaathalar leading them, and Aalar;[37] Neither could they shew their families, nor their stock, how they were of Israel: the sons of Ladan, the son of Ban, the sons of Necodan, six hundred fifty and two.[38] And of the priests that usurped the office of the priesthood, and were not found: the sons of Obdia, the sons of Accoz, the sons of Addus, who married Augia one of the daughters of Barzelus, and was named after his name.[39] And when the description of the kindred of these men was sought in the register, and was not found, they were removed from executing the office of the priesthood:[40] For unto them said Nehemias and Atharias, that they should not be partakers of the holy things, till there arose up an high priest clothed with doctrine and truth.[41] So of Israel, from them of twelve years old and upward, they were all in number forty thousand, beside menservants and womenservants two thousand three hundred and sixty.[42] Their menservants and handmaids were seven thousand three hundred forty and seven: the singing men and singing women, two hundred forty and five:[43] Four hundred thirty and five camels, seven thousand thirty and six horses, two hundred forty and five mules, five thousand five hundred twenty and five beasts used to the yoke.[44] And certain of the chief of their families, when they came to the temple of God that is in Jerusalem, vowed to set up the house again in his own place according to their ability,[45] And to give into the holy treasury of the works a thousand pounds of gold, five thousand of silver, and an hundred priestly vestments.[46] And so dwelt the priests and the Levites and the people in Jerusalem, and in the country, the singers also and the porters; and all Israel in their villages.[47] But when the seventh month was at hand, and when the children of Israel were every man in his own place, they came all together with one consent into the open place of the first gate which is toward the east.[48] Then stood up Jesus the son of Josedec, and his brethren the priests and Zorobabel the son of Salathiel, and his brethren, and made ready the altar of the God of Israel,[49] To offer burnt sacrifices upon it, according as it is expressly commanded in the book of Moses the man of God.[50] And there were gathered unto them out of the other nations of the land, and they erected the altar upon his own place, because all the nations of the land were at enmity with them, and oppressed them; and they offered sacrifices according to the time, and burnt offerings to the Lord both morning and evening.[51] Also they held the feast of tabernacles, as it is commanded in the law, and offered sacrifices daily, as was meet:[52] And after that, the continual oblations, and the sacrifice of the sabbaths, and of the new moons, and of all holy feasts.[53] And all they that had made any vow to God began to offer sacrifices to God from the first day of the seventh month, although the temple of the Lord was not yet built.[54] And they gave unto the masons and carpenters money, meat, and drink, with cheerfulness.[55] Unto them of Zidon also and Tyre they gave carrs, that they should bring cedar trees from Libanus, which should be brought by floats to the haven of Joppa, according as it was commanded them by Cyrus king of the Persians.[56] And in the second year and second month after his coming to the temple of God at Jerusalem began Zorobabel the son of Salathiel, and Jesus the son of Josedec, and their brethren, and the priests, and the Levites, and all they that were come unto Jerusalem out of the captivity:[57] And they laid the foundation of the house of God in the first day of the second month, in the second year after they were come to Jewry and Jerusalem.[58] And they appointed the Levites from twenty years old over the works of the Lord. Then stood up Jesus, and his sons and brethren, and Cadmiel his brother, and the sons of Madiabun, with the sons of Joda the son of Eliadun, with their sons and brethren, all Levites, with one accord setters forward of the business, labouring to advance the works in the house of God. So the workmen built the temple of the Lord.[59] And the priests stood arrayed in their vestments with musical instruments and trumpets; and the Levites the sons of Asaph had cymbals,[60] Singing songs of thanksgiving, and praising the Lord, according as David the king of Israel had ordained.[61] And they sung with loud voices songs to the praise of the Lord, because his mercy and glory is for ever in all Israel.[62] And all the people sounded trumpets, and shouted with a loud voice, singing songs of thanksgiving unto the Lord for the rearing up of the house of the Lord.[63] Also of the priests and Levites, and of the chief of their families, the ancients who had seen the former house came to the building of this with weeping and great crying.[64] But many with trumpets and joy shouted with loud voice,[65] Insomuch that the trumpets might not be heard for the weeping of the people: yet the multitude sounded marvellously, so that it was heard afar off.[66] Wherefore when the enemies of the tribe of Judah and Benjamin heard it, they came to know what that noise of trumpets should mean.[67] And they perceived that they that were of the captivity did build the temple unto the Lord God of Israel.[68] So they went to Zorobabel and Jesus, and to the chief of the families, and said unto them, We will build together with you.[69] For we likewise, as ye, do obey your Lord, and do sacrifice unto him from the days of Azbazareth the king of the Assyrians, who brought us hither.[70] Then Zorobabel and Jesus and the chief of the families of Israel said unto them, It is not for us and you to build together an house unto the Lord our God.[71] We ourselves alone will build unto the Lord of Israel, according as Cyrus the king of the Persians hath commanded us.[72] But the heathen of the land lying heavy upon the inhabitants of Judea, and holding them strait, hindered their building;[73] And by their secret plots, and popular persuasions and commotions, they hindered the finishing of the building all the time that king Cyrus lived: so they were hindered from building for the space of two years, until the reign of Darius.

1Esdr.6

[1] Now in the second year of the reign of Darius Aggeus and Zacharias the son of Addo, the prophets, prophesied unto the Jews in Jewry and Jerusalem in the name of the Lord God of Israel, which was upon them.[2] Then stood up Zorobabel the son of Salatiel, and Jesus the son of Josedec, and began to build the house of the Lord

at Jerusalem, the prophets of the Lord being with them, and helping them.³ At the same time came unto them Sisinnes the governor of Syria and Phenice, with Sathrabuzanes and his companions, and said unto them,⁴ By whose appointment do ye build this house and this roof, and perform all the other things? and who are the workmen that perform these things?⁵ Nevertheless the elders of the Jews obtained favour, because the Lord had visited the captivity;⁶ And they were not hindered from building, until such time as signification was given unto Darius concerning them, and an answer received.⁷ The copy of the letters which Sisinnes, governor of Syria and Phenice, and Sathrabuzanes, with their companions, rulers in Syria and Phenice, wrote and sent unto Darius; To king Darius, greeting:⁸ Let all things be known unto our lord the king, that being come into the country of Judea, and entered into the city of Jerusalem we found in the city of Jerusalem the ancients of the Jews that were of the captivity⁹ Building an house unto the Lord, great and new, of hewn and costly stones, and the timber already laid upon the walls.¹⁰ And those works are done with great speed, and the work goeth on prosperously in their hands, and with all glory and diligence is it made.¹¹ Then asked we these elders, saying, By whose commandment build ye this house, and lay the foundations of these works?¹² Therefore to the intent that we might give knowledge unto thee by writing, we demanded of them who were the chief doers, and we required of them the names in writing of their principal men.¹³ So they gave us this answer, We are the servants of the Lord which made heaven and earth.¹⁴ And as for this house, it was builded many years ago by a king of Israel great and strong, and was finished.¹⁵ But when our fathers provoked God unto wrath, and sinned against the Lord of Israel which is in heaven, he gave them over into the power of Nabuchodonosor king of Babylon, of the Chaldees;¹⁶ Who pulled down the house, and burned it, and carried away the people captives unto Babylon.¹⁷ But in the first year that king Cyrus reigned over the country of Babylon Cyrus the king wrote to build up this house.¹⁸ And the holy vessels of gold and of silver, that Nabuchodonosor had carried away out of the house at Jerusalem, and had set them in his own temple those Cyrus the king brought forth again out of the temple at Babylon, and they were delivered to Zorobabel and to Sanabassarus the ruler,¹⁹ With commandment that he should carry away the same vessels, and put them in the temple at Jerusalem; and that the temple of the Lord should be built in his place.²⁰ Then the same Sanabassarus, being come hither, laid the foundations of the house of the Lord at Jerusalem; and from that time to this being still a building, it is not yet fully ended.²¹ Now therefore, if it seem good unto the king, let search be made among the records of king Cyrus:²² And if it be found that the building of the house of the Lord at Jerusalem hath been done with the consent of king Cyrus, and if our lord the king be so minded, let him signify unto us thereof.²³ Then commanded king Darius to seek among the records at Babylon: and so at Ecbatane the palace, which is in the country of Media, there was found a roll wherein these things were recorded.²⁴ In the first year of the reign of Cyrus king Cyrus commanded that the house of the Lord at Jerusalem should be built again, where they do sacrifice with continual fire:²⁵ Whose height shall be sixty cubits and the breadth sixty cubits, with three rows of hewn stones, and one row of new wood of that country; and the expences thereof to be given out of the house of king Cyrus:²⁶ And that the holy vessels of the house of the Lord, both of gold and silver, that Nabuchodonosor took out of the house at Jerusalem, and brought to Babylon, should be restored to the house at Jerusalem, and be set in the place where they were before.²⁷ And also he commanded that Sisinnes the governor of Syria and Phenice, and Sathrabuzanes, and their companions, and

those which were appointed rulers in Syria and Phenice, should be careful not to meddle with the place, but suffer Zorobabel, the servant of the Lord, and governor of Judea, and the elders of the Jews, to build the house of the Lord in that place.²⁸ I have commanded also to have it built up whole again; and that they look diligently to help those that be of the captivity of the Jews, till the house of the Lord be finished:²⁹ And out of the tribute of Celosyria and Phenice a portion carefully to be given these men for the sacrifices of the Lord, that is, to Zorobabel the governor, for bullocks, and rams, and lambs;³⁰ And also corn, salt, wine, and oil, and that continually every year without further question, according as the priests that be in Jerusalem shall signify to be daily spent:³¹ That offerings may be made to the most high God for the king and for his children, and that they may pray for their lives.³² And he commanded that whosoever should transgress, yea, or make light of any thing afore spoken or written, out of his own house should a tree be taken, and he thereon be hanged, and all his goods seized for the king.³³ The Lord therefore, whose name is there called upon, utterly destroy every king and nation, that stretcheth out his hand to hinder or endamage that house of the Lord in Jerusalem.³⁴ I Darius the king have ordained that according unto these things it be done with diligence.

1Esdr.7

¹ Then Sisinnes the governor of Celosyria and Phenice, and Sathrabuzanes, with their companions following the commandments of king Darius,² Did very carefully oversee the holy works, assisting the ancients of the Jews and governors of the temple.³ And so the holy works prospered, when Aggeus and Zacharias the prophets prophesied.⁴ And they finished these things by the commandment of the Lord God of Israel, and with the consent of Cyrus, Darius, and Artexerxes, kings of Persia.⁵ And thus was the holy house finished in the three and twentieth day of the month Adar, in the sixth year of Darius king of the Persians⁶ And the children of Israel, the priests, and the Levites, and others that were of the captivity, that were added unto them, did according to the things written in the book of Moses.⁷ And to the dedication of the temple of the Lord they offered an hundred bullocks two hundred rams, four hundred lambs;⁸ And twelve goats for the sin of all Israel, according to the number of the chief of the tribes of Israel.⁹ The priests also and the Levites stood arrayed in their vestments, according to their kindreds, in the service of the Lord God of Israel, according to the book of Moses: and the porters at every gate.¹⁰ And the children of Israel that were of the captivity held the passover the fourteenth day of the first month, after that the priests and the Levites were sanctified.¹¹ They that were of the captivity were not all sanctified together: but the Levites were all sanctified together.¹² And so they offered the passover for all them of the captivity, and for their brethren the priests, and for themselves.¹³ And the children of Israel that came out of the captivity did eat, even all they that had separated themselves from the abominations of the people of the land, and sought the Lord.¹⁴ And they kept the feast of unleavened bread seven days, making merry before the Lord,¹⁵ For that he had turned the counsel of the king of Assyria toward them, to strengthen their hands in the works of the Lord God of Israel.

1Esdr.8

¹ And after these things, when Artexerxes the king of the Persians reigned came Esdras the son of Saraias, the son of Ezerias, the son of Helchiah, the son of Salum,² The son of Sadduc, the son of Achitob, the son of Amarias, the son of Ezias, the son of Meremoth, the son of Zaraias, the son of Savias, the son of Boccas, the son of Abisum, the son of Phinees, the son of Eleazar, the son of Aaron

the chief priest.[3] This Esdras went up from Babylon, as a scribe, being very ready in the law of Moses, that was given by the God of Israel.[4] And the king did him honour: for he found grace in his sight in all his requests.[5] There went up with him also certain of the children of Israel, of the priest of the Levites, of the holy singers, porters, and ministers of the temple, unto Jerusalem,[6] In the seventh year of the reign of Artexerxes, in the fifth month, this was the king's seventh year; for they went from Babylon in the first day of the first month, and came to Jerusalem, according to the prosperous journey which the Lord gave them.[7] For Esdras had very great skill, so that he omitted nothing of the law and commandments of the Lord, but taught all Israel the ordinances and judgments.[8] Now the copy of the commission, which was written from Artexerxes the king, and came to Esdras the priest and reader of the law of the Lord, is this that followeth;[9] King Artexerxes unto Esdras the priest and reader of the law of the Lord sendeth greeting:[10] Having determined to deal graciously, I have given order, that such of the nation of the Jews, and of the priests and Levites being within our realm, as are willing and desirous should go with thee unto Jerusalem.[11] As many therefore as have a mind thereunto, let them depart with thee, as it hath seemed good both to me and my seven friends the counsellors;[12] That they may look unto the affairs of Judea and Jerusalem, agreeably to that which is in the law of the Lord;[13] And carry the gifts unto the Lord of Israel to Jerusalem, which I and my friends have vowed, and all the gold and silver that in the country of Babylon can be found, to the Lord in Jerusalem,[14] With that also which is given of the people for the temple of the Lord their God at Jerusalem: and that silver and gold may be collected for bullocks, rams, and lambs, and things thereunto appertaining;[15] To the end that they may offer sacrifices unto the Lord upon the altar of the Lord their God, which is in Jerusalem.[16] And whatsoever thou and thy brethren will do with the silver and gold, that do, according to the will of thy God.[17] And the holy vessels of the Lord, which are given thee for the use of the temple of thy God, which is in Jerusalem, thou shalt set before thy God in Jerusalem.[18] And whatsoever thing else thou shalt remember for the use of the temple of thy God, thou shalt give it out of the king's treasury.[19] And I king Artexerxes have also commanded the keepers of the treasures in Syria and Phenice, that whatsoever Esdras the priest and the reader of the law of the most high God shall send for, they should give it him with speed,[20] To the sum of an hundred talents of silver, likewise also of wheat even to an hundred cors, and an hundred pieces of wine, and other things in abundance.[21] Let all things be performed after the law of God diligently unto the most high God, that wrath come not upon the kingdom of the king and his sons.[22] I command you also, that ye require no tax, nor any other imposition, of any of the priests, or Levites, or holy singers, or porters, or ministers of the temple, or of any that have doings in this temple, and that no man have authority to impose any thing upon them.[23] And thou, Esdras, according to the wisdom of God ordain judges and justices, that they may judge in all Syria and Phenice all those that know the law of thy God; and those that know it not thou shalt teach.[24] And whosoever shall transgress the law of thy God, and of the king, shall be punished diligently, whether it be by death, or other punishment, by penalty of money, or by imprisonment.[25] Then said Esdras the scribe, Blessed be the only Lord God of my fathers, who hath put these things into the heart of the king, to glorify his house that is in Jerusalem:[26] And hath honoured me in the sight of the king, and his counsellors, and all his friends and nobles.[27] Therefore was I encouraged by the help of the Lord my God, and gathered together men of Israel to go up with me.[28] And these are the chief according to their families and several

dignities, that went up with me from Babylon in the reign of king Artexerxes:[29] Of the sons of Phinees, Gerson: of the sons of Ithamar, Gamael: of the sons of David, Lettus the son of Sechenias:[30] Of the sons of Pharez, Zacharias; and with him were counted an hundred and fifty men:[31] Of the sons of Pahath Moab, Eliaonias, the son of Zaraias, and with him two hundred men:[32] Of the sons of Zathoe, Sechenias the son of Jezelus, and with him three hundred men: of the sons of Adin, Obeth the son of Jonathan, and with him two hundred and fifty men:[33] Of the sons of Elam, Josias son of Gotholias, and with him seventy men:[34] Of the sons of Saphatias, Zaraias son of Michael, and with him threescore and ten men:[35] Of the sons of Joab, Abadias son of Jezelus, and with him two hundred and twelve men:[36] Of the sons of Banid, Assalimoth son of Josaphias, and with him an hundred and threescore men:[37] Of the sons of Babi, Zacharias son of Bebai, and with him twenty and eight men:[38] Of the sons of Astath, Johannes son of Acatan, and with him an hundred and ten men:[39] Of the sons of Adonikam the last, and these are the names of them, Eliphalet, Jewel, and Samaias, and with them seventy men:[40] Of the sons of Bago, Uthi the son of Istalcurus, and with him seventy men.[41] And these I gathered together to the river called Theras, where we pitched our tents three days: and then I surveyed them.[42] But when I had found there none of the priests and Levites,[43] Then sent I unto Eleazar, and Iduel, and Masman,[44] And Alnathan, and Mamaias, and Joribas, and Nathan, Eunatan, Zacharias, and Mosollamon, principal men and learned.[45] And I bade them that they should go unto Saddeus the captain, who was in the place of the treasury:[46] And commanded them that they should speak unto Daddeus, and to his brethren, and to the treasurers in that place, to send us such men as might execute the priests' office in the house of the Lord.[47] And by the mighty hand of our Lord they brought unto us skilful men of the sons of Moli the son of Levi, the son of Israel, Asebebia, and his sons, and his brethren, who were eighteen.[48] And Asebia, and Annus, and Osaias his brother, of the sons of Channuneus, and their sons, were twenty men.[49] And of the servants of the temple whom David had ordained, and the principal men for the service of the Levites to wit, the servants of the temple two hundred and twenty, the catalogue of whose names were shewed.[50] And there I vowed a fast unto the young men before our Lord, to desire of him a prosperous journey both for us and them that were with us, for our children, and for the cattle:[51] For I was ashamed to ask the king footmen, and horsemen, and conduct for safeguard against our adversaries.[52] For we had said unto the king, that the power of the Lord our God should be with them that seek him, to support them in all ways.[53] And again we besought our Lord as touching these things, and found him favourable unto us.[54] Then I separated twelve of the chief of the priests, Esebrias, and Assanias, and ten men of their brethren with them:[55] And I weighed them the gold, and the silver, and the holy vessels of the house of our Lord, which the king, and his council, and the princes, and all Israel, had given.[56] And when I had weighed it, I delivered unto them six hundred and fifty talents of silver, and silver vessels of an hundred talents, and an hundred talents of gold,[57] And twenty golden vessels, and twelve vessels of brass, even of fine brass, glittering like gold.[58] And I said unto them, Both ye are holy unto the Lord, and the vessels are holy, and the gold and the silver is a vow unto the Lord, the Lord of our fathers.[59] Watch ye, and keep them till ye deliver them to the chief of the priests and Levites, and to the principal men of the families of Israel, in Jerusalem, into the chambers of the house of our God.[60] So the priests and the Levites, who had received the silver and the gold and the vessels, brought them unto Jerusalem, into the temple of the Lord.[61] And from the river Theras we departed the twelfth day of the first month, and came to Jerusalem by the mighty hand of our Lord, which was with us: and from the beginning of our journey the Lord delivered us from every enemy, and so we came to Jerusalem.[62] And when we had been there three days, the gold and silver that was weighed was delivered in the house of our Lord on the fourth day unto Marmoth the priest the son of Iri.[63] And with him was Eleazar the son of Phinees, and with them were Josabad the son of Jesu and Moeth the son of Sabban, Levites: all was delivered them by number and weight.[64] And all the weight of them was written up the same hour.[65] Moreover they that were come out of the captivity offered sacrifice unto the Lord God of Israel, even twelve bullocks for all Israel, fourscore and sixteen rams,[66] Threescore and twelve lambs, goats for a peace offering, twelve; all of them a sacrifice to the Lord.[67] And they delivered the king's commandments unto the king's stewards' and to the governors of Celosyria and Phenice; and they honoured the people and the temple of God.[68] Now when these things were done, the rulers came unto me, and said,[69] The nation of Israel, the princes, the priests and Levites, have not put away from them the strange people of the land, nor the pollutions of the Gentiles to wit, of the Canaanites, Hittites, Pheresites, Jebusites, and the Moabites, Egyptians, and Edomites.[70] For both they and their sons have married with their daughters, and the holy seed is mixed with the strange people of the land; and from the beginning of this matter the rulers and the great men have been partakers of this iniquity.[71] And as soon as I had heard these things, I rent my clothes, and the holy garment, and pulled off the hair from off my head and beard, and sat me down sad and very heavy.[72] So all they that were then moved at the word of the Lord God of Israel assembled unto me, whilst I mourned for the iniquity: but I sat still full of heaviness until the evening sacrifice.[73] Then rising up from the fast with my clothes and the holy garment rent, and bowing my knees, and stretching forth my hands unto the Lord,[74] I said, O Lord, I am confounded and ashamed before thy face;[75] For our sins are multiplied above our heads, and our ignorances have reached up unto heaven.[76] For ever since the time of our fathers we have been and are in great sin, even unto this day.[77] And for our sins and our fathers' we with our brethren and our kings and our priests were given up unto the kings of the earth, to the sword, and to captivity, and for a prey with shame, unto this day.[78] And now in some measure hath mercy been shewed unto us from thee, O Lord, that there should be left us a root and a name in the place of thy sanctuary;[79] And to discover unto us a light in the house of the Lord our God, and to give us food in the time of our servitude.[80] Yea, when we were in bondage, we were not forsaken of our Lord; but he made us gracious before the kings of Persia, so that they gave us food;[81] Yea, and honoured the temple of our Lord, and raised up the desolate Sion, that they have given us a sure abiding in Jewry and Jerusalem.[82] And now, O Lord, what shall we say, having these things? for we have transgressed thy commandments, which thou gavest by the hand of thy servants the prophets, saying,[83] That the land, which ye enter into to possess as an heritage, is a land polluted with the pollutions of the strangers of the land, and they have filled it with their uncleanness.[84] Therefore now shall ye not join your daughters unto their sons, neither shall ye take their daughters unto your sons.[85] Moreover ye shall never seek to have peace with them, that ye may be strong, and eat the good things of the land, and that ye may leave the inheritance of the land unto your children for evermore.[86] And all that is befallen is done unto us for our wicked works and great sins; for thou, O Lord, didst make our sins light,[87] And didst give unto us such a root: but we have turned back again to transgress thy law, and to mingle ourselves with the

uncleanness of the nations of the land.[88] Mightest not thou be angry with us to destroy us, till thou hadst left us neither root, seed, nor name?[89] O Lord of Israel, thou art true: for we are left a root this day.[90] Behold, now are we before thee in our iniquities, for we cannot stand any longer by reason of these things before thee.[91] And as Esdras in his prayer made his confession, weeping, and lying flat upon the ground before the temple, there gathered unto him from Jerusalem a very great multitude of men and women and children: for there was great weeping among the multitude.[92] Then Jechonias the son of Jeelus, one of the sons of Israel, called out, and said, O Esdras, we have sinned against the Lord God, we have married strange women of the nations of the land, and now is all Israel aloft.[93] Let us make an oath to the Lord, that we will put away all our wives, which we have taken of the heathen, with their children,[94] Like as thou hast decreed, and as many as do obey the law of the Lord.[95] Arise and put in execution: for to thee doth this matter appertain, and we will be with thee: do valiantly.[96] So Esdras arose, and took an oath of the chief of the priests and Levites of all Israel to do after these things; and so they sware.

1Esdr.9

[1] Then Esdras rising from the court of the temple went to the chamber of Joanan the son of Eliasib,[2] And remained there, and did eat no meat nor drink water, mourning for the great iniquities of the multitude.[3] And there was a proclamation in all Jewry and Jerusalem to all them that were of the captivity, that they should be gathered together at Jerusalem:[4] And that whosoever met not there within two or three days according as the elders that bare rule appointed, their cattle should be seized to the use of the temple, and himself cast out from them that were of the captivity.[5] And in three days were all they of the tribe of Judah and Benjamin gathered together at Jerusalem the twentieth day of the ninth month.[6] And all the multitude sat trembling in the broad court of the temple because of the present foul weather.[7] So Esdras arose up, and said unto them, Ye have transgressed the law in marrying strange wives, thereby to increase the sins of Israel.[8] And now by confessing give glory unto the Lord God of our fathers,[9] And do his will, and separate yourselves from the heathen of the land, and from the strange women.[10] Then cried the whole multitude, and said with a loud voice, Like as thou hast spoken, so will we do.[11] But forasmuch as the people are many, and it is foul weather, so that we cannot stand without, and this is not a work of a day or two, seeing our sin in these things is spread far:[12] Therefore let the rulers of the multitude stay, and let all them of our habitations that have strange wives come at the time appointed,[13] And with them the rulers and judges of every place, till we turn away the wrath of the Lord from us for this matter.[14] Then Jonathan the son of Azael and Ezechias the son of Theocanus accordingly took this matter upon them: and Mosollam and Levis and Sabbatheus helped them.[15] And they that were of the captivity did according to all these things.[16] And Esdras the priest chose unto him the principal men of their families, all by name: and in the first day of the tenth month they sat together to examine the matter.[17] So their cause that held strange wives was brought to an end in the first day of the first month.[18] And of the priests that were come together, and had strange wives, there were found:[19] Of the sons of Jesus the son of Josedec, and his brethren; Matthelas and Eleazar, and Joribus and Joadanus.[20] And they gave their hands to put away their wives and to offer rams to make reconcilement for their errors.[21] And of the sons of Emmer; Ananias, and Zabdeus, and Eanes, and Sameius, and Hiereel, and Azarias.[22] And of the sons of Phaisur; Elionas, Massias Israel, and Nathanael, and Ocidelus and Talsas.[23] And of the Levites; Jozabad, and Semis, and Colius, who was called Calitas, and Patheus, and Judas, and Jonas.[24] Of the holy

singers; Eleazurus, Bacchurus.[25] Of the porters; Sallumus, and Tolbanes.[26] Of them of Israel, of the sons of Phoros; Hiermas, and Eddias, and Melchias, and Maelus, and Eleazar, and Asibias, and Baanias.[27] Of the sons of Ela; Matthanias, Zacharias, and Hierielus, and Hieremoth, and Aedias.[28] And of the sons of Zamoth; Eliadas, Elisimus, Othonias, Jarimoth, and Sabatus, and Sardeus.[29] Of the sons of Babai; Johannes, and Ananias and Josabad, and Amatheis.[30] Of the sons of Mani; Olamus, Mamuchus, Jedeus, Jasubus, Jasael, and Hieremoth.[31] And of the sons of Addi; Naathus, and Moosias, Lacunus, and Naidus, and Mathanias, and Sesthel, Balnuus, and Manasseas.[32] And of the sons of Annas; Elionas and Aseas, and Melchias, and Sabbeus, and Simon Chosameus.[33] And of the sons of Asom; Altaneus, and Matthias, and Baanaia, Eliphalet, and Manasses, and Semei.[34] And of the sons of Maani; Jeremias, Momdis, Omaerus, Juel, Mabdai, and Pelias, and Anos, Carabasion, and Enasibus, and Mamnitanaimus, Eliasis, Bannus, Eliali, Samis, Selemias, Nathanias: and of the sons of Ozora; Sesis, Esril, Azaelus, Samatus, Zambis, Josephus.[35] And of the sons of Ethma; Mazitias, Zabadaias, Edes, Juel, Banaias.[36] All these had taken strange wives, and they put them away with their children.[37] And the priests and Levites, and they that were of Israel, dwelt in Jerusalem, and in the country, in the first day of the seventh month: so the children of Israel were in their habitations.[38] And the whole multitude came together with one accord into the broad place of the holy porch toward the east:[39] And they spake unto Esdras the priest and reader, that he would bring the law of Moses, that was given of the Lord God of Israel.[40] So Esdras the chief priest brought the law unto the whole multitude from man to woman, and to all the priests, to hear law in the first day of the seventh month.[41] And he read in the broad court before the holy porch from morning unto midday, before both men and women; and the multitude gave heed unto the law.[42] And Esdras the priest and reader of the law stood up upon a pulpit of wood, which was made for that purpose.[43] And there stood up by him Mattathias, Sammus, Ananias, Azarias, Urias, Ezecias, Balasamus, upon the right hand:[44] And upon his left hand stood Phaldaius, Misael, Melchias, Lothasubus, and Nabarias.[45] Then took Esdras the book of the law before the multitude: for he sat honourably in the first place in the sight of them all.[46] And when he opened the law, they stood all straight up. So Esdras blessed the Lord God most High, the God of hosts, Almighty.[47] And all the people answered, Amen; and lifting up their hands they fell to the ground, and worshipped the Lord.[48] Also Jesus, Anus, Sarabias, Adinus, Jacubus, Sabateas, Auteas, Maianeas, and Calitas, Asrias, and Joazabdus, and Ananias, Biatas, the Levites, taught the law of the Lord, making them withal to understand it.[49] Then spake Attharates unto Esdras the chief priest. and reader, and to the Levites that taught the multitude, even to all, saying,[50] This day is holy unto the Lord; (for they all wept when they heard the law:)[51] Go then, and eat the fat, and drink the sweet, and send part to them that have nothing;[52] For this day is holy unto the Lord: and be not sorrowful; for the Lord will bring you to honour.[53] So the Levites published all things to the people, saying, This day is holy to the Lord; be not sorrowful.[54] Then went they their way, every one to eat and drink, and make merry, and to give part to them that have nothing, and to make great cheer;[55] Because they understood the words wherein they were instructed, and for the which they had been assembled.

3 Maccabees

3Mac.1

[1] When Philopator learned from those who returned that the regions which he had controlled had been seized by Antiochus, he gave orders to all his forces, both infantry and cavalry, took with him his sister Arsinoe, and marched out to the region near Raphia, where Antiochus's supporters were encamped. [2] But a certain Theodotus, determined to carry out the plot he had devised, took with him the best of the Ptolemaic arms that had been previously issued to him, and crossed over by night to the tent of Ptolemy, intending single-handed to kill him and thereby end the war. [3] But Dositheus, known as the son of Drimylus, a Jew by birth who later changed his religion and apostatized from the ancestral traditions, had led the king away and arranged that a certain insignificant man should sleep in the tent; and so it turned out that this man incurred the vengeance meant for the king. [4] When a bitter fight resulted, and matters were turning out rather in favor of Antiochus, Arsinoe went to the troops with wailing and tears, her locks all disheveled, and exhorted them to defend themselves and their children and wives bravely, promising to give them each two minas of gold if they won the battle. [5] And so it came about that the enemy was routed in the action, and many captives also were taken. [6] Now that he had foiled the plot, Ptolemy decided to visit the neighboring cities and encourage them. [7] By doing this, and by endowing their sacred enclosures with gifts, he strengthened the morale of his subjects. [8] Since the Jews had sent some of their council and elders to greet him, to bring him gifts of welcome, and to congratulate him on what had happened, he was all the more eager to visit them as soon as possible. [9] After he had arrived in Jerusalem, he offered sacrifice to the supreme God and made thank-offerings and did what was fitting for the holy place. Then, upon entering the place and being impressed by its excellence and its beauty, [10] he marveled at the good order of the temple, and conceived a desire to enter the holy of holies. [11] When they said that this was not permitted, because not even members of their own nation were allowed to enter, nor even all of the priests, but only the high priest who was pre-eminent over all, and he only once a year, the king was by no means persuaded. [12] Even after the law had been read to him, he did not cease to maintain that he ought to enter, saying, "Even if those men are deprived of this honor, I ought not to be." [13] And he inquired why, when he entered every other temple, no one there had stopped him. [14] And someone heedlessly said that it was wrong to take this as a sign in itself. [15] "But since this has happened," the king said, "why should not I at least enter, whether they wish it or not?" [16] Then the priests in all their vestments prostrated themselves and entreated the supreme God to aid in the present situation and to avert the violence of this evil design, and they filled the temple with cries and tears; [17] and those who remained behind in the city were agitated and hurried out, supposing that something mysterious was occurring. [18] The virgins who had been enclosed in their chambers rushed out with their mothers, sprinkled their hair with dust, and filled the streets with groans and lamentations. [19] Those women who had recently been arrayed for marriage abandoned the bridal chambers prepared for wedded union, and, neglecting proper modesty, in a disorderly rush flocked together in the city. [20] Mothers and nurses abandoned even newborn children here and there, some in houses and some in the streets, and without a backward look they crowded together at the most high temple. [21] Various were the supplications of those gathered there because of what the king was profanely plotting. [22] In addition, the bolder of the citizens would not tolerate the completion of his plans or the fulfillment of his intended purpose. [23] They shouted to their fellows to take arms and die courageously for the ancestral law, and created a considerable disturbance in the holy place; and being barely restrained by the old men and the elders, they resorted to the same posture of supplication as the others. [24] Meanwhile the crowd, as before, was engaged in prayer, [25] while the elders near the king tried

in various ways to change his arrogant mind from the plan that he had conceived.[26] But he, in his arrogance, took heed of nothing, and began now to approach, determined to bring the aforesaid plan to a conclusion.[27] When those who were around him observed this, they turned, together with our people, to call upon him who has all power to defend them in the present trouble and not to overlook this unlawful and haughty deed.[28] The continuous, vehement, and concerted cry of the crowds resulted in an immense uproar;[29] for it seemed that not only the men but also the walls and the whole earth around echoed, because indeed all at that time preferred death to the profanation of the place.

3Mac.2

[1]Then the high priest Simon, facing the sanctuary, bending his knees and extending his hands with calm dignity, prayed as follows:[2] "Lord, Lord, king of the heavens, and sovereign of all creation, holy among the holy ones, the only ruler, almighty, give attention to us who are suffering grievously from an impious and profane man, puffed up in his audacity and power.[3] For you, the creator of all things and the governor of all, are a just Ruler, and you judge those who have done anything in insolence and arrogance.[4] You destroyed those who in the past committed injustice, among whom were even giants who trusted in their strength and boldness, whom you destroyed by bringing upon them a boundless flood.[5] You consumed with fire and sulphur the men of Sodom who acted arrogantly, who were notorious for their vices; and you made them an example to those who should come afterward.[6] You made known your mighty power by inflicting many and varied punishments on the audacious Pharaoh who had enslaved your holy people Israel.[7] And when he pursued them with chariots and a mass of troops, you overwhelmed him in the depths of the sea, but carried through safely those who had put their confidence in you, the Ruler over the whole creation.[8] And when they had seen works of your hands, they praised you, the Almighty.[9] You, O King, when you had created the boundless and immeasurable earth, chose this city and sanctified this place for your name, though you have no need of anything; and when you had glorified it by your magnificent manifestation, you made it a firm foundation for the glory of your great and honored name.[10] And because you love the house of Israel, you promised that if we should have reverses, and tribulation should overtake us, you would listen to our petition when we come to this place and pray.[11] And indeed you are faithful and true.[12] And because oftentimes when our fathers were oppressed you helped them in their humiliation, and rescued them from great evils,[13] see now, O holy King, that because of our many and great sins we are crushed with suffering, subjected to our enemies, and overtaken by helplessness.[14] In our downfall this audacious and profane man undertakes to violate the holy place on earth dedicated to your glorious name.[15] For your dwelling, the heaven of heavens, is unapproachable by man.[16] But because you graciously bestowed your glory upon your people Israel, you sanctified this place.[17] Do not punish us for the defilement committed by these men, or call us to account for this profanation, lest the transgressors boast in their wrath or exult in the arrogance of their tongue, saying,[18] `We have trampled down the house of the sanctuary as offensive houses are trampled down.'[19] Wipe away our sins and disperse our errors, and reveal your mercy at this hour.[20] Speedily let your mercies overtake us, and put praises in the mouth of those who are downcast and broken in spirit, and give us peace."[21]Thereupon God, who oversees all things, the first Father of all, holy among the holy ones, having heard the lawful supplication, scourged him who had exalted himself in insolence and audacity.[22] He shook him on this side and that as a reed is shaken by

the wind, so that he lay helpless on the ground and, besides being paralyzed in his limbs, was unable even to speak, since he was smitten by a righteous judgment.[23] Then both friends and bodyguards, seeing the severe punishment that had overtaken him, and fearing lest he should lose his life, quickly dragged him out, panic-stricken in their exceedingly great fear.[24] After a while he recovered, and though he had been punished, he by no means repented, but went away uttering bitter threats.[25]When he arrived in Egypt, he increased in his deeds of malice, abetted by the previously mentioned drinking companions and comrades, who were strangers to everything just.[26] He was not content with his uncounted licentious deeds, but he also continued with such audacity that he framed evil reports in the various localities; and many of his friends, intently observing the king's purpose, themselves also followed his will.[27] He proposed to inflict public disgrace upon the Jewish community, and he set up a stone on the tower in the courtyard with this inscription:[28] "None of those who do not sacrifice shall enter their sanctuaries, and all Jews shall be subjected to a registration involving poll tax and to the status of slaves. Those who object to this are to be taken by force and put to death;[29] those who are registered are also to be branded on their bodies by fire with the ivy-leaf symbol of Dionysus, and they shall also be reduced to their former limited status."[30] In order that he might not appear to be an enemy to all, he inscribed below: "But if any of them prefer to join those who have been initiated into the mysteries, they shall have equal citizenship with the Alexandrians."[31]Now some, however, with an obvious abhorrence of the price to be exacted for maintaining the religion of their city, readily gave themselves up, since they expected to enhance their reputation by their future association with the king.[32] But the majority acted firmly with a courageous spirit and did not depart from their religion; and by paying money in exchange for life they confidently attempted to save themselves from the registration.[33] They remained resolutely hopeful of obtaining help, and they abhorred those who separated themselves from them, considering them to be enemies of the Jewish nation, and depriving them of common fellowship and mutual help.

3Mac.3

[1]When the impious king comprehended this situation, he became so infuriated that not only was he enraged against those Jews who lived in Alexandria, but was still more bitterly hostile toward those in the countryside; and he ordered that all should promptly be gathered into one place, and put to death by the most cruel means.[2] While these matters were being arranged, a hostile rumor was circulated against the Jewish nation by men who conspired to do them ill, a pretext being given by a report that they hindered others from the observance of their customs.[3] The Jews, however, continued to maintain good will and unswerving loyalty toward the dynasty;[4] but because they worshiped God and conducted themselves by his law, they kept their separateness with respect to foods. For this reason they appeared hateful to some;[5] but since they adorned their style of life with the good deeds of upright people, they were established in good repute among all men.[6] Nevertheless those of other races paid no heed to their good service to their nation, which was common talk among all;[7] instead they gossiped about the differences in worship and foods, alleging that these people were loyal neither to the king nor to his authorities, but were hostile and greatly opposed to his government. So they attached no ordinary reproach to them.[8]The Greeks in the city, though wronged in no way, when they saw an unexpected tumult around these people and the crowds that suddenly were forming, were not strong enough to help them, for they lived under tyranny. They did try to console them, being grieved

at the situation, and expected that matters would change;[9] for such a great community ought not to be left to its fate when it had committed no offense.[10] And already some of their neighbors and friends and business associates had taken some of them aside privately and were pledging to protect them and to exert more earnest efforts for their assistance.[11]Then the king, boastful of his present good fortune, and not considering the might of the supreme God, but assuming that he would persevere constantly in his same purpose, wrote this letter against them:[12] "King Ptolemy Philopator to his generals and soldiers in Egypt and all its districts, greetings and good health.[13] I myself and our government are faring well.[14] When our expedition took place in Asia, as you yourselves know, it was brought to conclusion, according to plan, by the gods' deliberate alliance with us in battle,[15] and we considered that we should not rule the nations inhabiting Coele-Syria and Phoenicia by the power of the spear but should cherish them with clemency and great benevolence, gladly treating them well.[16] And when we had granted very great revenues to the temples in the cities, we came on to Jerusalem also, and went up to honor the temple of those wicked people, who never cease from their folly.[17] They accepted our presence by word, but insincerely by deed, because when we proposed to enter their inner temple and honor it with magnificent and most beautiful offerings,[18] they were carried away by their traditional conceit, and excluded us from entering; but they were spared the exercise of our power because of the benevolence which we have toward all.[19] By maintaining their manifest ill-will toward us, they become the only people among all nations who hold their heads high in defiance of kings and their own benefactors, and are unwilling to regard any action as sincere.[20]"But we, when we arrived in Egypt victorious, accommodated ourselves to their folly and did as was proper, since we treat all nations with benevolence.[21] Among other things, we made known to all our amnesty toward their compatriots here, both because of their alliance with us and the myriad affairs liberally entrusted to them from the beginning; and we ventured to make a change, by deciding both to deem them worthy of Alexandrian citizenship and to make them participants in our regular religious rites.[22] But in their innate malice they took this in a contrary spirit, and disdained what is good. Since they incline constantly to evil,[23] they not only spurn the priceless citizenship, but also both by speech and by silence they abominate those few among them who are sincerely disposed toward us; in every situation, in accordance with their infamous way of life, they secretly suspect that we may soon alter our policy.[24] Therefore, fully convinced by these indications that they are ill-disposed toward us in every way, we have taken precautions lest, if a sudden disorder should later arise against us, we should have these impious people behind our backs as traitors and barbarous enemies.[25] Therefore we have given orders that, as soon as this letter shall arrive, you are to send to us those who live among you, together with their wives and children, with insulting and harsh treatment, and bound securely with iron fetters, to suffer the sure and shameful death that befits enemies.[26] For when these all have been punished, we are sure that for the remaining time the government will be established for ourselves in good order and in the best state.[27] But whoever shelters any of the Jews, old people or children or even infants, will be tortured to death with the most hateful torments, together with his family.[28] Any one willing to give information will receive the property of the one who incurs the punishment, and also two thousand drachmas from the royal treasury, and will be awarded his freedom.[29] Every place detected sheltering a Jew is to be made unapproachable and burned with fire, and shall become useless for all time to any mortal creature."[30] The letter was written in the above form.

3Mac.4

[1]In every place, then, where this decree arrived, a feast at public expense was arranged for the Gentiles with shouts and gladness, for the inveterate enmity which had long ago been in their minds was now made evident and outspoken.[2] But among the Jews there was incessant mourning, lamentation, and tearful cries; everywhere their hearts were burning, and they groaned because of the unexpected destruction that had suddenly been decreed for them.[3] What district or city, or what habitable place at all, or what streets were not filled with mourning and wailing for them?[4] For with such a harsh and ruthless spirit were they being sent off, all together, by the generals in the several cities, that at the sight of their unusual punishments, even some of their enemies, perceiving the common object of pity before their eyes, reflected upon the uncertainty of life and shed tears at the most miserable expulsion of these people.[5] For a multitude of gray-headed old men, sluggish and bent with age, was being led away, forced to march at a swift pace by the violence with which they were driven in such a shameful manner.[6] And young women who had just entered the bridal chamber to share married life exchanged joy for wailing, their myrrh-perfumed hair sprinkled with ashes, and were carried away unveiled, all together raising a lament instead of a wedding song, as they were torn by the harsh treatment of the heathen.[7] In bonds and in public view they were violently dragged along as far as the place of embarkation.[8] Their husbands, in the prime of youth, their necks encircled with ropes instead of garlands, spent the remaining days of their marriage festival in lamentations instead of good cheer and youthful revelry, seeing death immediately before them.[9] They were brought on board like wild animals, driven under the constraint of iron bonds; some were fastened by the neck to the benches of the boats, others had their feet secured by unbreakable fetters,[10] and in addition they were confined under a solid deck, so that with their eyes in total darkness, they should undergo treatment befitting traitors during the whole voyage.[11]When these men had been brought to the place called Schedia, and the voyage was concluded as the king had decreed, he commanded that they should be enclosed in the hippodrome which had been built with a monstrous perimeter wall in front of the city, and which was well suited to make them an obvious spectacle to all coming back into the city and to those from the city going out into the country, so that they could neither communicate with the king's forces nor in any way claim to be inside the circuit of the city.[12] And when this had happened, the king, hearing that the Jews' compatriots from the city frequently went out in secret to lament bitterly the ignoble misfortune of their brothers,[13] ordered in his rage that these men be dealt with in precisely the same fashion as the others, not omitting any detail of their punishment.[14] The entire race was to be registered individually, not for the hard labor that has been briefly mentioned before, but to be tortured with the outrages that he had ordered, and at the end to be destroyed in the space of a single day.[15] The registration of these people was therefore conducted with bitter haste and zealous intentness from the rising of the sun till its setting, and though uncompleted it stopped after forty days.[16]The king was greatly and continually filled with joy, organizing feasts in honor of all his idols, with a mind alienated from truth and with a profane mouth, praising speechless things that are not able even to communicate or to come to one's help, and uttering improper words against the supreme God.[17] But after the previously mentioned interval of time the scribes declared to the king that they were no longer able to take the census of the Jews because of their innumerable multitude,[18] although most of them were still in the country, some still residing in their homes, and some at the place; the task was

impossible for all the generals in Egypt.[19] After he had threatened them severely, charging that they had been bribed to contrive a means of escape, he was clearly convinced about the matter[20] when they said and proved that both the paper and the pens they used for writing had already given out.[21] But this was an act of the invincible providence of him who was aiding the Jews from heaven.

3Mac.5

[1]Then the king, completely inflexible, was filled with overpowering anger and wrath; so he summoned Hermon, keeper of the elephants,[2] and ordered him on the following day to drug all the elephants -- five hundred in number -- with large handfuls of frankincense and plenty of unmixed wine, and to drive them in, maddened by the lavish abundance of liquor, so that the Jews might meet their doom.[3] When he had given these orders he returned to his feasting, together with those of his friends and of the army who were especially hostile toward the Jews.[4] And Hermon, keeper of the elephants, proceeded faithfully to carry out the orders.[5] The servants in charge of the Jews went out in the evening and bound the hands of the wretched people and arranged for their continued custody through the night, convinced that the whole nation would experience its final destruction.[6] For to the Gentiles it appeared that the Jews were left without any aid,[7] because in their bonds they were forcibly confined on every side. But with tears and a voice hard to silence they all called upon the Almighty Lord and Ruler of all power, their merciful God and Father, praying[8] that he avert with vengeance the evil plot against them and in a glorious manifestation rescue them from the fate now prepared for them.[9] So their entreaty ascended fervently to heaven.[10]Hermon, however, when he had drugged the pitiless elephants until they had been filled with a great abundance of wine and satiated with frankincense, presented himself at the courtyard early in the morning to report to the king about these preparations.[11] But the Lord sent upon the king a portion of sleep, that beneficence which from the beginning, night and day, is bestowed by him who grants it to whomever he wishes.[12] And by the action of the Lord he was overcome by so pleasant and deep a sleep that he quite failed in his lawless purpose and was completely frustrated in his inflexible plan.[13] Then the Jews, since they had escaped the appointed hour, praised their holy God and again begged him who is easily reconciled to show the might of his all-powerful hand to the arrogant Gentiles.[14]But now, since it was nearly the middle of the tenth hour, the person who was in charge of the invitations, seeing that the guests were assembled, approached the king and nudged him.[15] And when he had with difficulty roused him, he pointed out that the hour of the banquet was already slipping by, and he gave him an account of the situation.[16] The king, after considering this, returned to his drinking, and ordered those present for the banquet to recline opposite him.[17] When this was done he urged them to give themselves over to revelry and to make the present portion of the banquet joyful by celebrating all the more.[18] After the party had been going on for some time, the king summoned Hermon and with sharp threats demanded to know why the Jews had been allowed to remain alive through the present day.[19] But when he, with the corroboration of his friends, pointed out that while it was still night he had carried out completely the order given him,[20] the king, possessed by a savagery worse than that of Phalaris, said that the Jews were benefited by today's sleep, "but," he added, "tomorrow without delay prepare the elephants in the same way for the destruction of the lawless Jews!"[21] When the king had spoken, all those present readily and joyfully with one accord gave their approval, and each departed to his own home.[22] But they did not so much employ the duration of the night in sleep as in devising all sorts of insults for those they thought to be doomed.[23]Then, as soon as the cock had crowed in the early morning, Hermon, having equipped the beasts, began to move them along in the great colonnade.[24] The crowds of the city had been assembled for this most pitiful spectacle and they were eagerly waiting for daybreak.[25] But the Jews, at their last gasp, since the time had run out, stretched their hands toward heaven and with most tearful supplication and mournful dirges implored the supreme God to help them again at once.[26] The rays of the sun were not yet shed abroad, and while the king was receiving his friends, Hermon arrived and invited him to come out, indicating that what the king desired was ready for action.[27] But he, upon receiving the report and being struck by the unusual invitation to come out -- since he had been completely overcome by incomprehension -- inquired what the matter was for which this had been so zealously completed for him.[28] This was the act of God who rules over all things, for he had implanted in the king's mind a forgetfulness of the things he had previously devised.[29] Then Hermon and all the king's friends pointed out that the beasts and the armed forces were ready, "O king, according to your eager purpose."[30] But at these words he was filled with an overpowering wrath, because by the providence of God his whole mind had been deranged in regard to these matters; and with a threatening look he said,[31] "Were your parents or children present, I would have prepared them to be a rich feast for the savage beasts instead of the Jews, who give me no ground for complaint and have exhibited to an extraordinary degree a full and firm loyalty to my ancestors.[32] In fact you would have been deprived of life instead of these, were it not for an affection arising from our nurture in common and your usefulness."[33] So Hermon suffered an unexpected and dangerous threat, and his eyes wavered and his face fell.[34] The king's friends one by one sullenly slipped away and dismissed the assembled people, each to his own occupation.[35] Then the Jews, upon hearing what the king had said, praised the manifest Lord God, King of kings, since this also was his aid which they had received.[36]The king, however, reconvened the party in the same manner and urged the guests to return to their celebrating.[37] After summoning Hermon he said in a threatening tone, "How many times, you poor wretch, must I give you orders about these things?[38] Equip the elephants now once more for the destruction of the Jews tomorrow!"[39] But the officials who were at table with him, wondering at his instability of mind, remonstrated as follows:[40] "O king, how long will you try us, as though we are idiots, ordering now for a third time that they be destroyed, and again revoking your decree in the matter?[41] As a result the city is in a tumult because of its expectation; it is crowded with masses of people, and also in constant danger of being plundered."[42] Upon this the king, a Phalaris in everything and filled with madness, took no account of the changes of mind which had come about within him for the protection of the Jews, and he firmly swore an irrevocable oath that he would send them to death without delay, mangled by the knees and feet of the beasts,[43] and would also march against Judea and rapidly level it to the ground with fire and spear, and by burning to the ground the temple inaccessible to him would quickly render it forever empty of those who offered sacrifices there.[44] Then the friends and officers departed with great joy, and they confidently posted the armed forces at the places in the city most favorable for keeping guard.[45] Now when the beasts had been brought virtually to a state of madness, so to speak, by the very fragrant draughts of wine mixed with frankincense and had been equipped with frightful devices, the elephant keeper[46] entered at about dawn into the courtyard -- the city now being filled with countless masses of people crowding their way into the hippodrome -- and urged the king on to the matter at hand.[47] So he, when he had filled his impious

mind with a deep rage, rushed out in full force along with the beasts, wishing to witness, with invulnerable heart and with his own eyes, the grievous and pitiful destruction of the aforementioned people.[48] And when the Jews saw the dust raised by the elephants going out at the gate and by the following armed forces, as well as by the trampling of the crowd, and heard the loud and tumultuous noise,[49] they thought that this was their last moment of life, the end of their most miserable suspense, and giving way to lamentation and groans they kissed each other, embracing relatives and falling into one another's arms -- parents and children, mothers and daughters, and others with babies at their breasts who were drawing their last milk.[50] Not only this, but when they considered the help which they had received before from heaven they prostrated themselves with one accord on the ground, removing the babies from their breasts,[51] and cried out in a very loud voice, imploring the Ruler over every power to manifest himself and be merciful to them, as they stood now at the gates of death.

3Mac.6

[1]Then a certain Eleazar, famous among the priests of the country, who had attained a ripe old age and throughout his life had been adorned with every virtue, directed the elders around him to cease calling upon the holy God and prayed as follows:[2] "King of great power, Almighty God Most High, governing all creation with mercy,[3] look upon the descendants of Abraham, O Father, upon the children of the sainted Jacob, a people of your consecrated portion who are perishing as foreigners in a foreign land.[4] Pharaoh with his abundance of chariots, the former ruler of this Egypt, exalted with lawless insolence and boastful tongue, you destroyed together with his arrogant army by drowning them in the sea, manifesting the light of your mercy upon the nation of Israel.[5] Sennacherib exulting in his countless forces, oppressive king of the Assyrians, who had already gained control of the whole world by the spear and was lifted up against your holy city, speaking grievous words with boasting and insolence, you, O Lord, broke in pieces, showing your power to many nations.[6] The three companions in Babylon who had voluntarily surrendered their lives to the flames so as not to serve vain things, you rescued unharmed, even to a hair, moistening the fiery furnace with dew and turning the flame against all their enemies.[7] Daniel, who through envious slanders was cast down into the ground to lions as food for wild beasts, you brought up to the light unharmed.[8] And Jonah, wasting away in the belly of a huge, sea-born monster, you, Father, watched over and restored unharmed to all his family.[9] And now, you who hate insolence, all-merciful and protector of all, reveal yourself quickly to those of the nation of Israel -- who are being outrageously treated by the abominable and lawless Gentiles.[10] Even if our lives have become entangled in impieties in our exile, rescue us from the hand of the enemy, and destroy us, Lord, by whatever fate you choose.[11] Let not the vain-minded praise their vanities at the destruction of your beloved people, saying, `Not even their god has rescued them.'[12] But you, O Eternal One, who have all might and all power, watch over us now and have mercy upon us who by the senseless insolence of the lawless are being deprived of life in the manner of traitors.[13] And let the Gentiles cower today in fear of your invincible might, O honored One, who have power to save the nation of Jacob.[14] The whole throng of infants and their parents entreat you with tears.[15] Let it be shown to all the Gentiles that you are with us, O Lord, and have not turned your face from us; but just as you have said, `Not even when they were in the land of their enemies did I neglect them,' so accomplish it, O Lord."[16]Just as Eleazar was ending his prayer, the king arrived at the hippodrome with the beasts and all the arrogance of his forces.[17] And when the Jews observed

this they raised great cries to heaven so that even the nearby valleys resounded with them and brought an uncontrollable terror upon the army.[18] Then the most glorious, almighty, and true God revealed his holy face and opened the heavenly gates, from which two glorious angels of fearful aspect descended, visible to all but the Jews.[19] They opposed the forces of the enemy and filled them with confusion and terror, binding them with immovable shackles.[20] Even the king began to shudder bodily, and he forgot his sullen insolence.[21] The beasts turned back upon the armed forces following them and began trampling and destroying them.[22] Then the king's anger was turned to pity and tears because of the things that he had devised beforehand.[23] For when he heard the shouting and saw them all fallen headlong to destruction, he wept and angrily threatened his friends, saying,[24] "You are committing treason and surpassing tyrants in cruelty; and even me, your benefactor, you are now attempting to deprive of dominion and life by secretly devising acts of no advantage to the kingdom.[25] Who is it that has taken each man from his home and senselessly gathered here those who faithfully have held the fortresses of our country?[26] Who is it that has so lawlessly encompassed with outrageous treatment those who from the beginning differed from all nations in their goodwill toward us and often have accepted willingly the worst of human dangers?[27] Loose and untie their unjust bonds! Send them back to their homes in peace, begging pardon for your former actions![28] Release the sons of the almighty and living God of heaven, who from the time of our ancestors until now has granted an unimpeded and notable stability to our government."[29] These then were the things he said; and the Jews, immediately released, praised their holy God and Savior, since they now had escaped death.[30]Then the king, when he had returned to the city, summoned the official in charge of the revenues and ordered him to provide to the Jews both wines and everything else needed for a festival of seven days, deciding that they should celebrate their rescue with all joyfulness in that same place in which they had expected to meet their destruction.[31] Accordingly those disgracefully treated and near to death, or rather, who stood at its gates, arranged for a banquet of deliverance instead of a bitter and lamentable death, and full of joy they apportioned to celebrants the place which had been prepared for their destruction and burial.[32] They ceased their chanting of dirges and took up the song of their fathers, praising God, their Savior and worker of wonders. Putting an end to all mourning and wailing, they formed choruses as a sign of peaceful joy.[33] Likewise also the king, after convening a great banquet to celebrate these events, gave thanks to heaven unceasingly and lavishly for the unexpected rescue which he had experienced.[34] And those who had previously believed that the Jews would be destroyed and become food for birds, and had joyfully registered them, groaned as they themselves were overcome by disgrace, and their fire-breathing boldness was ignominiously quenched.[35] But the Jews, when they had arranged the aforementioned choral group, as we have said before, passed the time in feasting to the accompaniment of joyous thanksgiving and psalms.[36] And when they had ordained a public rite for these things in their whole community and for their descendants, they instituted the observance of the aforesaid days as a festival, not for drinking and gluttony, but because of the deliverance that had come to them through God.[37] Then they petitioned the king, asking for dismissal to their homes.[38] So their registration was carried out from the twenty-fifth of Pachon to the fourth of Epeiph, for forty days; and their destruction was set for the fifth to the seventh of Epeiph, the three days[39] on which the Lord of all most gloriously revealed his mercy and rescued them all together and unharmed.[40] Then they feasted, provided with everything by the king, until the fourteenth day, on which also they made the petition for their dismissal.[41] The king granted their request at once and wrote the following letter for them to the generals in the cities, magnanimously expressing his concern:

3Mac.7

[1]"King Ptolemy Philopator to the generals in Egypt and all in authority in his government, greetings and good health.[2] We ourselves and our children are faring well, the great God guiding our affairs according to our desire.[3] Certain of our friends, frequently urging us with malicious intent, persuaded us to gather together the Jews of the kingdom in a body and to punish them with barbarous penalties as traitors;[4] for they declared that our government would never be firmly established until this was accomplished, because of the ill-will which these people had toward all nations.[5] They also led them out with harsh treatment as slaves, or rather as traitors, and, girding themselves with a cruelty more savage than that of Scythian custom, they tried without any inquiry or examination to put them to death.[6] But we very severely threatened them for these acts, and in accordance with the clemency which we have toward all men we barely spared their lives. Since we have come to realize that the God of heaven surely defends the Jews, always taking their part as a father does for his children,[7] and since we have taken into account the friendly and firm goodwill which they had toward us and our ancestors, we justly have acquitted them of every charge of whatever kind.[8] We also have ordered each and every one to return to his own home, with no one in any place doing them harm at all or reproaching them for the irrational things that have happened.[9] For you should know that if we devise any evil against them or cause them any grief at all, we always shall have not man but the Ruler over every power, the Most High God, in everything and inescapably as an antagonist to avenge such acts. Farewell."[10]Upon receiving this letter the Jews did not immediately hurry to make their departure, but they requested of the king that at their own hands those of the Jewish nation who had willfully transgressed against the holy God and the law of God should receive the punishment they deserved.[11] For they declared that those who for the belly's sake had transgressed the divine commandments would never be favorably disposed toward the king's government.[12] The king then, admitting and approving the truth of what they said, granted them a general license so that freely and without royal authority or supervision they might destroy those everywhere in his kingdom who had transgressed the law of God.[13] When they had applauded him in fitting manner, their priests and the whole multitude shouted the Hallelujah and joyfully departed.[14] And so on their way they punished and put to a public and shameful death any whom they met of their fellow-countrymen who had become defiled.[15] In that day they put to death more than three hundred men; and they kept the day as a joyful festival, since they had destroyed the profaners.[16] But those who had held fast to God even to death and had received the full enjoyment of deliverance began their departure from the city, crowned with all sorts of very fragrant flowers, joyfully and loudly giving thanks to the one God of their fathers, the eternal Savior of Israel, in words of praise and all kinds of melodious songs.[17]When they had arrived at Ptolemais, called "rose-bearing" because of a characteristic of the place, the fleet waited for them, in accord with the common desire, for seven days.[18] There they celebrated their deliverance, for the king had generously provided all things to them for their journey, to each as far as his own house.[19] And when they had landed in peace with appropriate thanksgiving, there too in like manner they decided to observe these days as a joyous festival during the time of their stay.[20] Then, after inscribing them as holy on a pillar and dedicating a place of prayer

at the site of the festival, they departed unharmed, free, and overjoyed, since at the king's command they had been brought safely by land and sea and river each to his own place.[21] They also possessed greater prestige among their enemies, being held in honor and awe; and they were not subject at all to confiscation of their belongings by any one.[22] Besides they all recovered all of their property, in accordance with the registration, so that those who held any restored it to them with extreme fear. So the supreme God perfectly performed great deeds for their deliverance.[23] Blessed be the Deliverer of Israel through all times! Amen.

Prayer of Manasseh

O Lord, Almighty God of our fathers, Abraham, Isaac, and Jacob, and of their righteous seed; who hast made heaven and earth, with all the ornament thereof; who hast bound the sea by the word of thy commandment; who hast shut up the deep, and sealed it by thy terrible and glorious name; whom all men fear, and tremble before thy power; for the majesty of thy glory cannot be borne, and thine angry threatening toward sinners is importable: but thy merciful promise is unmeasurable and unsearchable; for thou art the most high Lord, of great compassion, longsuffering, very merciful, and repentest of the evils of men. Thou, O Lord, according to thy great goodness hast promised repentance and forgiveness to them that have sinned against thee: and of thine infinite mercies hast appointed repentance unto sinners, that they may be saved. Thou therefore, O Lord, that art the God of the just, hast not appointed repentance to the just, as to Abraham, and Isaac, and Jacob, which have not sinned against thee; but thou hast appointed repentance unto me that am a sinner: for I have sinned above the number of the sands of the sea. My transgressions, O Lord, are multiplied: my transgressions are multiplied, and I am not worthy to behold and see the height of heaven for the multitude of mine iniquities. I am bowed down with many iron bands, that I cannot life up mine head, neither have any release: for I have provoked thy wrath, and done evil before thee: I did not thy will, neither kept I thy commandments: I have set up abominations, and have multiplied offences. Now therefore I bow the knee of mine heart, beseeching thee of grace. I have sinned, O Lord, I have sinned, and I acknowledge mine iniquities: wherefore, I humbly beseech thee, forgive me, O Lord, forgive me, and destroy me not with mine iniquites. Be not angry with me for ever, by reserving evil for me; neither condemn me to the lower parts of the earth. For thou art the God, even the God of them that repent; and in me thou wilt shew all thy goodness: for thou wilt save me, that am unworthy, according to thy great mercy. Therefore I will praise thee for ever all the days of my life: for all the powers of the heavens do praise thee, and thine is the glory for ever and ever. Amen.

Psalm 151

[1] I was small among my brothers, and the youngest in my father's house; I tended my father's sheep. [2] My hands made a harp; my fingers fashioned a lyre. [3] And who will tell my Lord? The Lord himself; it is he who hears. [4] It was he who sent his messenger and took me from my father's sheep, and anointed me with his anointing oil. [5] My brothers were handsome and tall, but the Lord was not pleased with them. [6] I went out to meet the Philistine, and he cursed me by his idols. [7] But I drew his own sword; I beheaded him, and took away disgrace from the people of Israel.

Additional Orthodox Canonical Texts (not universally recognized)

Introduction

This section focuses on texts that have found canonical acceptance in specific Orthodox communities, yet remain outside the broader Christian canonical frameworks. This section includes 2 Esdras and 4 Maccabees—texts that, while not universally recognized, play significant roles in the liturgical and theological traditions of certain Eastern Orthodox churches.

Historical Context - The texts in this section represent the diversity within the Christian scriptural traditions, especially in how different communities have historically interacted with and valued these writings. 2 Esdras, known in some traditions as the Apocalypse of Ezra, is an apocalyptic text likely composed in the late first century CE, reflecting Jewish apocalyptic responses to the destruction of Jerusalem. In Orthodox Christianity, it is recognized particularly in Slavic traditions, which often include it in their biblical canon. 4 Maccabees, a philosophical treatise that uses the martyrdom of the Maccabean brothers to expound on the supremacy of pious reason over passion, is included in the Greek Bible's appendix and recognized by the Georgian Orthodox Church.

Theological Significance

2 Esdras and 4 Maccabees offer deep theological insights:

- **2 Esdras**, grapples with theodicy and divine justice in the aftermath of catastrophic loss, presenting visions and dialogues that explore themes of redemption, resurrection, and messianic hope. Its inclusion in some Slavic Orthodox Bibles underscores the text's role in offering theological explanations for suffering and divine providence.

- **4 Maccabees,** elaborates on the philosophical discourse of Hellenistic Judaism, emphasizing the Stoic idea that reason governed by virtue can control passions. Its canonical status in the Georgian Church highlights the integration of Hellenistic philosophical concepts with early Christian thought on martyrdom and virtue.

Rationale for Inclusion - The inclusion of these texts in specific Orthodox canons but not in others illustrates the regional and cultural variations that have influenced the formation of biblical canons. These texts have been preserved and revered where they resonated with local theological concerns and liturgical practices. For Orthodox communities that embrace these books, they provide not only historical insights into Jewish and early Christian thought but also serve as ongoing sources for theological reflection and spiritual formation.

This section not only enriches our understanding of the diversity within Orthodox scriptural tradition but also invites broader Christian audiences to explore how different communities have engaged with these complex and profound texts. The inclusion of these books highlights the dynamic and living tradition of Scripture interpretation within the Orthodox Church, reflecting a unique blend of cultural, philosophical, and theological currents that have shaped these communities' faith practices.

2 Esdras (4 Ezra)

4Ezra.1

[1] The second book of the prophet Esdras, the son of Saraias, the son of Azarias, the son of Helchias, the son of Sadamias, the sou of Sadoc, the son of Achitob,[2] The son of Achias, the son of Phinees, the son of Heli, the son of Amarias, the son of Aziei, the son of Marimoth, the son of And he spake unto the of Borith, the son of Abisei, the son of Phinees, the son of Eleazar,[3] The son of Aaron, of the tribe of Levi; which was captive in the land of the Medes, in the reign of Artexerxes king of the Persians.[4] And the word of the Lord came unto me, saying,[5] Go thy way, and shew my people their sinful deeds, and their children their wickedness which they have done against me; that they may tell their children's children:[6] Because the sins of their fathers are increased in them: for they have forgotten me, and have offered unto strange gods.[7] Am not I even he that brought them out of the land of Egypt, from the house of bondage? but they have provoked me unto wrath, and despised my counsels.[8] Pull thou off then the hair of thy head, and cast all evil upon them, for they have not been obedient unto my law, but it is a rebellious people.[9] How long shall I forbear them, into whom I have done so much good?[10] Many kings have I destroyed for their sakes; Pharaoh with his servants and all his power have I smitten down.[11] All the nations have I destroyed before them, and in the east I have scattered the people of two provinces, even of Tyrus and Sidon, and have slain all their enemies.[12] Speak thou therefore unto them, saying, Thus saith the Lord,[13] I led you through the sea and in the beginning gave you a large and safe passage; I gave you Moses for a leader, and Aaron for a priest.[14] I gave you light in a pillar of fire, and great wonders have I done among you; yet have ye forgotten me, saith the Lord.[15] Thus saith the Almighty Lord, The quails were as a token to you; I gave you tents for your safeguard: nevertheless ye murmured there,[16] And triumphed not in my name for the destruction of your enemies, but ever to this day do ye yet murmur.[17] Where are the benefits that I have done for you? when ye were hungry and thirsty in the wilderness, did ye not cry unto me,[18] Saying, Why hast thou brought us into this wilderness to kill us? it had been better for us to have served the Egyptians, than to die in this wilderness.[19] Then had I pity upon your mournings, and gave you manna to eat; so ye did eat angels' bread.[20] When ye were thirsty, did I not cleave the rock, and waters flowed out to your fill? for the heat I covered you with the leaves of the trees.[21] I divided among you a fruitful land, I cast out the Canaanites, the Pherezites, and the Philistines, before you: what shall I yet do more for you? saith the Lord.[22] Thus saith the Almighty Lord, When ye were in the wilderness, in the river of the Amorites, being athirst, and blaspheming my name,[23] I gave you not fire for your blasphemies, but cast a tree in the water, and made the river sweet.[24] What shall I do unto thee, O Jacob? thou, Juda, wouldest not obey me: I will turn me to other nations, and unto those will I give my name, that they may keep my statutes.[25] Seeing ye have forsaken me, I will forsake you also; when ye desire me to be gracious unto you, I shall have no mercy upon you.[26] Whensoever ye shall call upon me, I will not hear you: for ye have defiled your hands with blood, and your feet are swift to commit manslaughter.[27] Ye have not as it were forsaken me, but your own selves, saith the Lord.[28] Thus saith the Almighty Lord, Have I not prayed you as a father his sons, as a mother her daughters, and a nurse her young babes,[29] That ye would be my people, and I should be your God; that ye would be my children, and I should be your father?[30] I gathered you together, as a hen gathereth her chickens under her wings: but now, what shall I do unto you? I will cast you out from my face.[31] When ye offer unto me, I will turn my face from you: for your solemn feastdays, your new moons, and your circumcisions, have I forsaken.[32] I sent unto you my servants the prophets, whom ye have taken and slain, and torn their bodies in pieces, whose blood I will require of your hands, saith the Lord.[33] Thus saith the Almighty Lord, Your house is desolate, I will cast you out as the wind doth stubble.[34] And your children shall not be fruitful; for they have despised my commandment, and done the thing that is an evil before me.[35] Your houses will I give to a people that shall come; which not having heard of me yet shall believe me; to whom I have shewed no signs, yet they shall do that I have commanded them.[36] They have seen no prophets, yet they shall call their sins to remembrance, and

acknowledge them.[37] I take to witness the grace of the people to come, whose little ones rejoice in gladness: and though they have not seen me with bodily eyes, yet in spirit they believe the thing that I say.[38] And now, brother, behold what glory; and see the people that come from the east:[39] Unto whom I will give for leaders, Abraham, Isaac, and Jacob, Oseas, Amos, and Micheas, Joel, Abdias, and Jonas,[40] Nahum, and Abacuc, Sophonias, Aggeus, Zachary, and Malachy, which is called also an angel of the Lord.

4Ezra.2

[1] Thus saith the Lord, I brought this people out of bondage, and I gave them my commandments by menservants the prophets; whom they would not hear, but despised my counsels.[2] The mother that bare them saith unto them, Go your way, ye children; for I am a widow and forsaken.[3] I brought you up with gladness; but with sorrow and heaviness have I lost you: for ye have sinned before the Lord your God, and done that thing that is evil before him.[4] But what shall I now do unto you? I am a widow and forsaken: go your way, O my children, and ask mercy of the Lord.[5] As for me, O father, I call upon thee for a witness over the mother of these children, which would not keep my covenant,[6] That thou bring them to confusion, and their mother to a spoil, that there may be no offspring of them.[7] Let them be scattered abroad among the heathen, let their names be put out of the earth: for they have despised my covenant.[8] Woe be unto thee, Assur, thou that hidest the unrighteous in thee! O thou wicked people, remember what I did unto Sodom and Gomorrha;[9] Whose land lieth in clods of pitch and heaps of ashes: even so also will I do unto them that hear me not, saith the Almighty Lord.[10] Thus saith the Lord unto Esdras, Tell my people that I will give them the kingdom of Jerusalem, which I would have given unto Israel.[11] Their glory also will I take unto me, and give these the everlasting tabernacles, which I had prepared for them.[12] They shall have the tree of life for an ointment of sweet savour; they shall neither labour, nor be weary.[13] Go, and ye shall receive: pray for few days unto you, that they may be shortened: the kingdom is already prepared for you: watch.[14] Take heaven and earth to witness; for I have broken the evil in pieces, and created the good: for I live, saith the Lord.[15] Mother, embrace thy children, and bring them up with gladness, make their feet as fast as a pillar: for I have chosen thee, saith the Lord.[16] And those that be dead will I raise up again from their places, and bring them out of the graves: for I have known my name in Israel.[17] Fear not, thou mother of the children: for I have chosen thee, saith the Lord.[18] For thy help will I send my servants Esau and Jeremy, after whose counsel I have sanctified and prepared for thee twelve trees laden with divers fruits,[19] And as many fountains flowing with milk and honey, and seven mighty mountains, whereupon there grow roses and lilies, whereby I will fill thy children with joy.[20] Do right to the widow, judge for the fatherless, give to the poor, defend the orphan, clothe the naked,[21] Heal the broken and the weak, laugh not a lame man to scorn, defend the maimed, and let the blind man come into the sight of my clearness.[22] Keep the old and young within thy walls.[23] Wheresoever thou findest the dead, take them and bury them, and I will give thee the first place in my resurrection.[24] Abide still, O my people, and take thy rest, for thy quietness still come.[25] Nourish thy children, O thou good nurse; stablish their feet.[26] As for the servants whom I have given thee, there shall not one of them perish; for I will require them from among thy number.[27] Be not weary: for when the day of trouble and heaviness cometh, others shall weep and be sorrowful, but thou shalt be merry and have abundance.[28] The heathen shall envy thee, but they shall be able to do nothing against thee, saith the Lord.[29] My hands shall cover thee, so that thy children shall not see hell.[30] Be joyful, O thou mother, with thy children; for I will deliver thee, saith the Lord.[31] Remember thy children that sleep, for I shall bring them out of the sides of the earth, and shew mercy unto them: for I am merciful, saith the Lord Almighty.[32] Embrace thy children until I come and shew mercy unto them: for my wells run over, and my grace shall not fail.[33] I Esdras received a charge of the Lord upon the mount Oreb, that I should go unto Israel; but when I came unto them, they set me at nought, and despised the commandment of the Lord.[34] And therefore I say unto you, O ye heathen, that hear and understand, look for your Shepherd, he shall give you everlasting rest; for he is nigh at hand, that shall come in the end of the world.[35] Be ready to the reward of the kingdom, for the everlasting light shall shine upon you for evermore.[36] Flee the shadow of this world, receive the joyfulness of your glory: I testify my Saviour openly.[37] O receive the gift that is given you, and be glad, giving thanks unto him that hath led you to the heavenly kingdom.[38] Arise up and stand, behold the number of those that be sealed in the feast of the Lord;[39] Which are departed from the shadow of the world, and have received glorious garments of the Lord.[40] Take thy number, O Sion, and shut up those of thine that are clothed in white, which have fulfilled the law of the Lord.[41] The number of thy children, whom thou longedst for, is fulfilled: beseech the power of the Lord, that thy people, which have been called from the beginning, may be hallowed.[42] I Esdras saw upon the mount Sion a great people, whom I could not number, and they all praised the Lord with songs.[43] And in the midst of them there was a young man of a high stature, taller than all the rest, and upon every one of their heads he set crowns, and was more exalted; which I marvelled at greatly.[44] So I asked the angel, and said, Sir, what are these?[45] He answered and said unto me, These be they that have put off the mortal clothing, and put on the immortal, and have confessed the name of God: now are they crowned, and receive palms.[46] Then said I unto the angel, What young person is it that crowneth them, and giveth them palms in their hands?[47] So he answered and said unto me, It is the Son of God, whom they have confessed in the world. Then began I greatly to commend them that stood so stiffly for the name of the Lord.[48] Then the angel said unto me, Go thy way, and tell my people what manner of things, and how great wonders of the Lord thy God, thou hast seen.

4Ezra.3

[1] In the thirtieth year after the ruin of the city I was in Babylon, and lay troubled upon my bed, and my thoughts came up over my heart:[2] For I saw the desolation of Sion, and the wealth of them that dwelt at Babylon.[3] And my spirit was sore moved, so that I began to speak words full of fear to the most High, and said,[4] O Lord, who bearest rule, thou spakest at the beginning, when thou didst plant the earth, and that thyself alone, and commandedst the people,[5] And gavest a body unto Adam without soul, which was the workmanship of thine hands, and didst breathe into him the breath of life, and he was made living before thee.[6] And thou leadest him into paradise, which thy right hand had planted, before ever the earth came forward.[7] And unto him thou gavest commandment to love thy way: which he transgressed, and immediately thou appointedst death in him and in his generations, of whom came nations, tribes, people, and kindreds, out of number.[8] And every people walked after their own will, and did wonderful things before thee, and despised thy commandments.[9] And again in process of time thou broughtest the flood upon those that dwelt in the world, and destroyedst them.[10] And it came to pass in every of them, that as death was to Adam, so was the flood to these.[11] Nevertheless one of them thou leftest, namely, Noah with his household, of whom came all righteous men.[12] And it happened, that when they that dwelt upon

the earth began to multiply, and had gotten them many children, and were a great people, they began again to be more ungodly than the first.¹³ Now when they lived so wickedly before thee, thou didst choose thee a man from among them, whose name was Abraham.¹⁴ Him thou lovedst, and unto him only thou shewedst thy will:¹⁵ And madest an everlasting covenant with him, promising him that thou wouldest never forsake his seed.¹⁶ And unto him thou gavest Isaac, and unto Isaac also thou gavest Jacob and Esau. As for Jacob, thou didst choose him to thee, and put by Esau: and so Jacob became a great multitude.¹⁷ And it came to pass, that when thou leadest his seed out of Egypt, thou broughtest them up to the mount Sinai.¹⁸ And bowing the heavens, thou didst set fast the earth, movedst the whole world, and madest the depths to tremble, and troubledst the men of that age.¹⁹ And thy glory went through four gates, of fire, and of earthquake, and of wind, and of cold; that thou mightest give the law unto the seed of Jacob, and diligence unto the generation of Israel.²⁰ And yet tookest thou not away from them a wicked heart, that thy law might bring forth fruit in them.²¹ For the first Adam bearing a wicked heart transgressed, and was overcome; and so be all they that are born of him.²² Thus infirmity was made permanent; and the law (also) in the heart of the people with the malignity of the root; so that the good departed away, and the evil abode still.²³ So the times passed away, and the years were brought to an end: then didst thou raise thee up a servant, called David:²⁴ Whom thou commandedst to build a city unto thy name, and to offer incense and oblations unto thee therein.²⁵ When this was done many years, then they that inhabited the city forsook thee,²⁶ And in all things did even as Adam and all his generations had done: for they also had a wicked heart:²⁷ And so thou gavest thy city over into the hands of thine enemies.²⁸ Are their deeds then any better that inhabit Babylon, that they should therefore have the dominion over Sion?²⁹ For when I came thither, and had seen impieties without number, then my soul saw many evildoers in this thirtieth year, so that my heart failed me.³⁰ For I have seen how thou sufferest them sinning, and hast spared wicked doers: and hast destroyed thy people, and hast preserved thine enemies, and hast not signified it.³¹ I do not remember how this way may be left: Are they then of Babylon better than they of Sion?³² Or is there any other people that knoweth thee beside Israel? or what generation hath so believed thy covenants as Jacob?³³ And yet their reward appeareth not, and their labour hath no fruit: for I have gone here and there through the heathen, and I see that they flow in wealth, and think not upon thy commandments.³⁴ Weigh thou therefore our wickedness now in the balance, and their's also that dwell the world; and so shall thy name no where be found but in Israel.³⁵ Or when was it that they which dwell upon the earth have not sinned in thy sight? or what people have so kept thy commandments?³⁶ Thou shalt find that Israel by name hath kept thy precepts; but not the heathen.

4Ezra.4

¹ And the angel that was sent unto me, whose name was Uriel, gave me an answer,² And said, Thy heart hath gone to far in this world, and thinkest thou to comprehend the way of the most High?³ Then said I, Yea, my lord. And he answered me, and said, I am sent to shew thee three ways, and to set forth three similitudes before thee:⁴ Whereof if thou canst declare me one, I will shew thee also the way that thou desirest to see, and I shall shew thee from whence the wicked heart cometh.⁵ And I said, Tell on, my lord. Then said he unto me, Go thy way, weigh me the weight of the fire, or measure me the blast of the wind, or call me again the day that is past.⁶ Then answered I and said, What man is able to do that, that thou shouldest ask such things of me?⁷ And he said unto me, If I should ask thee

how great dwellings are in the midst of the sea, or how many springs are in the beginning of the deep, or how many springs are above the firmament, or which are the outgoings of paradise:⁸ Peradventure thou wouldest say unto me, I never went down into the deep, nor as yet into hell, neither did I ever climb up into heaven.⁹ Nevertheless now have I asked thee but only of the fire and wind, and of the day wherethrough thou hast passed, and of things from which thou canst not be separated, and yet canst thou give me no answer of them.¹⁰ He said moreover unto me, Thine own things, and such as are grown up with thee, canst thou not know;¹¹ How should thy vessel then be able to comprehend the way of the Highest, and, the world being now outwardly corrupted to understand the corruption that is evident in my sight?¹² Then said I unto him, It were better that we were not at all, than that we should live still in wickedness, and to suffer, and not to know wherefore.¹³ He answered me, and said, I went into a forest into a plain, and the trees took counsel,¹⁴ And said, Come, let us go and make war against the sea that it may depart away before us, and that we may make us more woods.¹⁵ The floods of the sea also in like manner took counsel, and said, Come, let us go up and subdue the woods of the plain, that there also we may make us another country.¹⁶ The thought of the wood was in vain, for the fire came and consumed it.¹⁷ The thought of the floods of the sea came likewise to nought, for the sand stood up and stopped them.¹⁸ If thou wert judge now betwixt these two, whom wouldest thou begin to justify? or whom wouldest thou condemn?¹⁹ I answered and said, Verily it is a foolish thought that they both have devised, for the ground is given unto the wood, and the sea also hath his place to bear his floods.²⁰ Then answered he me, and said, Thou hast given a right judgment, but why judgest thou not thyself also?²¹ For like as the ground is given unto the wood, and the sea to his floods: even so they that dwell upon the earth may understand nothing but that which is upon the earth: and he that dwelleth above the heavens may only understand the things that are above the height of the heavens.²² Then answered I and said, I beseech thee, O Lord, let me have understanding:²³ For it was not my mind to be curious of the high things, but of such as pass by us daily, namely, wherefore Israel is given up as a reproach to the heathen, and for what cause the people whom thou hast loved is given over unto ungodly nations, and why the law of our forefathers is brought to nought, and the written covenants come to none effect,²⁴ And we pass away out of the world as grasshoppers, and our life is astonishment and fear, and we are not worthy to obtain mercy.²⁵ What will he then do unto his name whereby we are called? of these things have I asked.²⁶ Then answered he me, and said, The more thou searchest, the more thou shalt marvel; for the world hasteth fast to pass away,²⁷ And cannot comprehend the things that are promised to the righteous in time to come: for this world is full of unrighteousness and infirmities.²⁸ But as concerning the things whereof thou askest me, I will tell thee; for the evil is sown, but the destruction thereof is not yet come.²⁹ If therefore that which is sown be not turned upside down, and if the place where the evil is sown pass not away, then cannot it come that is sown with good.³⁰ For the grain of evil seed hath been sown in the heart of Adam from the beginning, and how much ungodliness hath it brought up unto this time? and how much shall it yet bring forth until the time of threshing come?³¹ Ponder now by thyself, how great fruit of wickedness the grain of evil seed hath brought forth.³² And when the ears shall be cut down, which are without number, how great a floor shall they fill?³³ Then I answered and said, How, and when shall these things come to pass? wherefore are our years few and evil?³⁴ And he answered me, saying, Do not thou hasten above the most Highest: for thy haste is in vain to be above him, for thou hast much exceeded.³⁵ Did not the souls also of the righteous ask question of these things in their chambers, saying, How long shall I hope on this fashion? when cometh the fruit of the floor of our reward?³⁶ And unto these things Uriel the archangel gave them answer, and said, Even when the number of seeds is filled in you: for he hath weighed the world in the balance.³⁷ By measure hath he measured the times; and by number hath he numbered the times; and he doth not move nor stir them, until the said measure be fulfilled.³⁸ Then answered I and said, O Lord that bearest rule, even we all are full of impiety.³⁹ And for our sakes peradventure it is that the floors of the righteous are not filled, because of the sins of them that dwell upon the earth.⁴⁰ So he answered me, and said, Go thy way to a woman with child, and ask of her when she hath fulfilled her nine months, if her womb may keep the birth any longer within her.⁴¹ Then said I, No, Lord, that can she not. And he said unto me, In the grave the chambers of souls are like the womb of a woman:⁴² For like as a woman that travaileth maketh haste to escape the necessity of the travail: even so do these places haste to deliver those things that are committed unto them.⁴³ From the beginning, look, what thou desirest to see, it shall be shewed thee.⁴⁴ Then answered I and said, If I have found favour in thy sight, and if it be possible, and if I be meet therefore,⁴⁵ Shew me then whether there be more to come than is past, or more past than is to come.⁴⁶ What is past I know, but what is for to come I know not.⁴⁷ And he said unto me, Stand up upon the right side, and I shall expound the similitude unto thee.⁴⁸ So I stood, and saw, and, behold, an hot burning oven passed by before me: and it happened that when the flame was gone by I looked, and, behold, the smoke remained still.⁴⁹ After this there passed by before me a watery cloud, and sent down much rain with a storm; and when the stormy rain was past, the drops remained still.⁵⁰ Then said he unto me, Consider with thyself; as the rain is more than the drops, and as the fire is greater than the smoke; but the drops and the smoke remain behind: so the quantity which is past did more exceed.⁵¹ Then I prayed, and said, May I live, thinkest thou, until that time? or what shall happen in those days?⁵² He answered me, and said, As for the tokens whereof thou askest me, I may tell thee of them in part: but as touching thy life, I am not sent to shew thee; for I do not know it.

4Ezra.5

¹ Nevertheless as coming the tokens, behold, the days shall come, that they which dwell upon earth shall be taken in a great number, and the way of truth shall be hidden, and the land shall be barren of faith.² But iniquity shall be increased above that which now thou seest, or that thou hast heard long ago.³ And the land, that thou seest now to have root, shalt thou see wasted suddenly.⁴ But if the most High grant thee to live, thou shalt see after the third trumpet that the sun shall suddenly shine again in the night, and the moon thrice in the day:⁵ And blood shall drop out of wood, and the stone shall give his voice, and the people shall be troubled:⁶ And even he shall rule, whom they look not for that dwell upon the earth, and the fowls shall take their flight away together:⁷ And the Sodomitish sea shall cast out fish, and make a noise in the night, which many have not known: but they shall all hear the voice thereof.⁸ There shall be a confusion also in many places, and the fire shall be oft sent out again, and the wild beasts shall change their places, and menstruous women shall bring forth monsters:⁹ And salt waters shall be found in the sweet, and all friends shall destroy one another; then shall wit hide itself, and understanding withdraw itself into his secret chamber,¹⁰ And shall be sought of many, and yet not be found: then shall unrighteousness and incontinency be multiplied upon earth.¹¹ One land also shall ask another, and say, Is righteousness that maketh a man righteous gone through thee? And it shall say,

No.¹² At the same time shall men hope, but nothing obtain: they shall labour, but their ways shall not prosper.¹³ To shew thee such tokens I have leave; and if thou wilt pray again, and weep as now, and fast even days, thou shalt hear yet greater things.¹⁴ Then I awaked, and an extreme fearfulness went through all my body, and my mind was troubled, so that it fainted.¹⁵ So the angel that was come to talk with me held me, comforted me, and set me up upon my feet.¹⁶ And in the second night it came to pass, that Salathiel the captain of the people came unto me, saying, Where hast thou been? and why is thy countenance so heavy?¹⁷ Knowest thou not that Israel is committed unto thee in the land of their captivity?¹⁸ Up then, and eat bread, and forsake us not, as the shepherd that leaveth his flock in the hands of cruel wolves.¹⁹ Then said I unto him, Go thy ways from me, and come not nigh me. And he heard what I said, and went from me.²⁰ And so I fasted seven days, mourning and weeping, like as Uriel the angel commanded me.²¹ And after seven days so it was, that the thoughts of my heart were very grievous unto me again,²² And my soul recovered the spirit of understanding, and I began to talk with the most High again,²³ And said, O Lord that bearest rule, of every wood of the earth, and of all the trees thereof, thou hast chosen thee one only vine:²⁴ And of all lands of the whole world thou hast chosen thee one pit: and of all the flowers thereof one lily:²⁵ And of all the depths of the sea thou hast filled thee one river: and of all builded cities thou hast hallowed Sion unto thyself:²⁶ And of all the fowls that are created thou hast named thee one dove: and of all the cattle that are made thou hast provided thee one sheep:²⁷ And among all the multitudes of people thou hast gotten thee one people: and unto this people, whom thou lovedst, thou gavest a law that is approved of all.²⁸ And now, O Lord, why hast thou given this one people over unto many? and upon the one root hast thou prepared others, and why hast thou scattered thy only one people among many?²⁹ And they which did gainsay thy promises, and believed not thy covenants, have trodden them down.³⁰ If thou didst so much hate thy people, yet shouldest thou punish them with thine own hands.³¹ Now when I had spoken these words, the angel that came to me the night afore was sent unto me,³² And said unto me, Hear me, and I will instruct thee; hearken to the thing that I say, and I shall tell thee more.³³ And I said, Speak on, my Lord. Then said he unto me, Thou art sore troubled in mind for Israel's sake: lovest thou that people better than he that made them?³⁴ And I said, No, Lord: but of very grief have I spoken: for my reins pain me every hour, while I labour to comprehend the way of the most High, and to seek out part of his judgment.³⁵ And he said unto me, Thou canst not. And I said, Wherefore, Lord? whereunto was I born then? or why was not my mother's womb then my grave, that I might not have seen the travail of Jacob, and the wearisome toil of the stock of Israel?³⁶ And he said unto me, Number me the things that are not yet come, gather me together the dross that are scattered abroad, make me the flowers green again that are withered,³⁷ Open me the places that are closed, and bring me forth the winds that in them are shut up, shew me the image of a voice: and then I will declare to thee the thing that thou labourest to know.³⁸ And I said, O Lord that bearest rule, who may know these things, but he that hath not his dwelling with men?³⁹ As for me, I am unwise: how may I then speak of these things whereof thou askest me?⁴⁰ Then said he unto me, Like as thou canst do none of these things that I have spoken of, even so canst thou not find out my judgment, or in the end the love that I have promised unto my people.⁴¹ And I said, Behold, O Lord, yet art thou nigh unto them that be reserved till the end: and what shall they do that have been before me, or we that be now, or they that shall come after us?⁴² And he said unto me, I will liken my judgment unto a ring: like as there is no slackness of the last, even so there is no swiftness of the first.[43] So I answered and said, Couldest thou not make those that have been made, and be now, and that are for to come, at once; that thou mightest shew thy judgment the sooner?[44] Then answered he me, and said, The creature may not haste above the maker; neither may the world hold them at once that shall be created therein.[45] And I said, As thou hast said unto thy servant, that thou, which givest life to all, hast given life at once to the creature that thou hast created, and the creature bare it: even so it might now also bear them that now be present at once.[46] And he said unto me, Ask the womb of a woman, and say unto her, If thou bringest forth children, why dost thou it not together, but one after another? pray her therefore to bring forth ten children at once.[47] And I said, She cannot: but must do it by distance of time.[48] Then said he unto me, Even so have I given the womb of the earth to those that be sown in it in their times.[49] For like as a young child may not bring forth the things that belong to the aged, even so have I disposed the world which I created.[50] And I asked, and said, Seeing thou hast now given me the way, I will proceed to speak before thee: for our mother, of whom thou hast told me that she is young, draweth now nigh unto age.[51] He answered me, and said, Ask a woman that beareth children, and she shall tell thee.[52] Say unto her, Wherefore are unto they whom thou hast now brought forth like those that were before, but less of stature?[53] And she shall answer thee, They that be born in the the strength of youth are of one fashion, and they that are born in the time of age, when the womb faileth, are otherwise.[54] Consider thou therefore also, how that ye are less of stature than those that were before you.[55] And so are they that come after you less than ye, as the creatures which now begin to be old, and have passed over the strength of youth.[56] Then said I, Lord, I beseech thee, if I have found favour in thy sight, shew thy servant by whom thou visitest thy creature.

4Ezra.6

[1] And he said unto me, In the beginning, when the earth was made, before the borders of the world stood, or ever the winds blew,[2] Before it thundered and lightened, or ever the foundations of paradise were laid,[3] Before the fair flowers were seen, or ever the moveable powers were established, before the innumerable multitude of angels were gathered together,[4] Or ever the heights of the air were lifted up, before the measures of the firmament were named, or ever the chimneys in Sion were hot,[5] And ere the present years were sought out, and or ever the inventions of them that now sin were turned, before they were sealed that have gathered faith for a treasure:[6] Then did I consider these things, and they all were made through me alone, and through none other: by me also they shall be ended, and by none other.[7] Then answered I and said, What shall be the parting asunder of the times? or when shall be the end of the first, and the beginning of it that followeth?[8] And he said unto me, From Abraham unto Isaac, when Jacob and Esau were born of him, Jacob's hand held first the heel of Esau.[9] For Esau is the end of the world, and Jacob is the beginning of it that followeth.[10] The hand of man is betwixt the heel and the hand: other question, Esdras, ask thou not.[11] I answered then and said, O Lord that bearest rule, if I have found favour in thy sight,[12] I beseech thee, shew thy servant the end of thy tokens, whereof thou shewedst me part the last night.[13] So he answered and said unto me, Stand up upon thy feet, and hear a mighty sounding voice.[14] And it shall be as it were a great motion; but the place where thou standest shall not be moved.[15] And therefore when it speaketh be not afraid: for the word is of the end, and the foundation of the earth is understood.[16] And why? because the speech of these things trembleth and is moved: for it knoweth that the end of these things must be changed.[17] And

it happened, that when I had heard it I stood up upon my feet, and hearkened, and, behold, there was a voice that spake, and the sound of it was like the sound of many waters.[18] And it said, Behold, the days come, that I will begin to draw nigh, and to visit them that dwell upon the earth,[19] And will begin to make inquisition of them, what they be that have hurt unjustly with their unrighteousness, and when the affliction of Sion shall be fulfilled;[20] And when the world, that shall begin to vanish away, shall be finished, then will I shew these tokens: the books shall be opened before the firmament, and they shall see all together:[21] And the children of a year old shall speak with their voices, the women with child shall bring forth untimely children of three or four months old, and they shall live, and be raised up.[22] And suddenly shall the sown places appear unsown, the full storehouses shall suddenly be found empty:[23] And tha trumpet shall give a sound, which when every man heareth, they shall be suddenly afraid.[24] At that time shall friends fight one against another like enemies, and the earth shall stand in fear with those that dwell therein, the springs of the fountains shall stand still, and in three hours they shall not run.[25] Whosoever remaineth from all these that I have told thee shall escape, and see my salvation, and the end of your world.[26] And the men that are received shall see it, who have not tasted death from their birth: and the heart of the inhabitants shall be changed, and turned into another meaning.[27] For evil shall be put out, and deceit shall be quenched.[28] As for faith, it shall flourish, corruption shall be overcome, and the truth, which hath been so long without fruit, shall be declared.[29] And when he talked with me, behold, I looked by little and little upon him before whom I stood.[30] And these words said he unto me; I am come to shew thee the time of the night to come.[31] If thou wilt pray yet more, and fast seven days again, I shall tell thee greater things by day than I have heard.[32] For thy voice is heard before the most High: for the Mighty hath seen thy righteous dealing, he hath seen also thy chastity, which thou hast had ever since thy youth.[33] And therefore hath he sent me to shew thee all these things, and to say unto thee, Be of good comfort and fear not[34] And hasten not with the times that are past, to think vain things, that thou mayest not hasten from the latter times.[35] And it came to pass after this, that I wept again, and fasted seven days in like manner, that I might fulfil the three weeks which he told me.[36] And in the eighth night was my heart vexed within me again, and I began to speak before the most High.[37] For my spirit was greatly set on fire, and my soul was in distress.[38] And I said, O Lord, thou spakest from the beginning of the creation, even the first day, and saidst thus; Let heaven and earth be made; and thy word was a perfect work.[39] And then was the spirit, and darkness and silence were on every side; the sound of man's voice was not yet formed.[40] Then commandedst thou a fair light to come forth of thy treasures, that thy work might appear.[41] Upon the second day thou madest the spirit of the firmament, and commandedst it to part asunder, and to make a division betwixt the waters, that the one part might go up, and the other remain beneath.[42] Upon the third day thou didst command that the waters should be gathered in the seventh part of the earth: six pats hast thou dried up, and kept them, to the intent that of these some being planted of God and tilled might serve thee.[43] For as soon as thy word went forth the work was made.[44] For immediately there was great and innumerable fruit, and many and divers pleasures for the taste, and flowers of unchangeable colour, and odours of wonderful smell: and this was done the third day.[45] Upon the fourth day thou commandedst that the sun should shine, and the moon give her light, and the stars should be in order:[46] And gavest them a charge to do service unto man, that was to be made.[47] Upon the fifth day thou saidst unto the seventh part, where the waters were gathered that it should bring forth living creatures, fowls and fishes: and so it came to pass.[48] For the dumb water and without life brought forth living things at the commandment of God, that all people might praise thy wondrous works.[49] Then didst thou ordain two living creatures, the one thou calledst Enoch, and the other Leviathan;[50] And didst separate the one from the other: for the seventh part, namely, where the water was gathered together, might not hold them both.[51] Unto Enoch thou gavest one part, which was dried up the third day, that he should dwell in the same part, wherein are a thousand hills:[52] But unto Leviathan thou gavest the seventh part, namely, the moist; and hast kept him to be devoured of whom thou wilt, and when.[53] Upon the sixth day thou gavest commandment unto the earth, that before thee it should bring forth beasts, cattle, and creeping things:[54] And after these, Adam also, whom thou madest lord of all thy creatures: of him come we all, and the people also whom thou hast chosen.[55] All this have I spoken before thee, O Lord, because thou madest the world for our sakes[56] As for the other people, which also come of Adam, thou hast said that they are nothing, but be like unto spittle: and hast likened the abundance of them unto a drop that falleth from a vessel.[57] And now, O Lord, behold, these heathen, which have ever been reputed as nothing, have begun to be lords over us, and to devour us.[58] But we thy people, whom thou hast called thy firstborn, thy only begotten, and thy fervent lover, are given into their hands.[59] If the world now be made for our sakes, why do we not possess an inheritance with the world? how long shall this endure?

4Ezra.7

[1] And when I had made an end of speaking these words, there was sent unto me the angel which had been sent unto me the nights afore:[2] And he said unto me, Up, Esdras, and hear the words that I am come to tell thee.[3] And I said, Speak on, my God. Then said he unto me, The sea is set in a wide place, that it might be deep and great.[4] But put the case the entrance were narrow, and like a river;[5] Who then could go into the sea to look upon it, and to rule it? if he went not through the narrow, how could he come into the broad?[6] There is also another thing; A city is builded, and set upon a broad field, and is full of all good things:[7] The entrance thereof is narrow, and is set in a dangerous place to fall, like as if there were a fire on the right hand, and on the left a deep water:[8] And one only path between them both, even between the fire and the water, so small that there could but one man go there at once.[9] If this city now were given unto a man for an inheritance, if he never shall pass the danger set before it, how shall he receive this inheritance?[10] And I said, It is so, Lord. Then said he unto me, Even so also is Israel's portion.[11] Because for their sakes I made the world: and when Adam transgressed my statutes, then was decreed that now is done.[12] Then were the entrances of this world made narrow, full of sorrow and travail: they are but few and evil, full of perils,: and very painful.[13] For the entrances of the elder world were wide and sure, and brought immortal fruit.[14] If then they that live labour not to enter these strait and vain things, they can never receive those that are laid up for them.[15] Now therefore why disquietest thou thyself, seeing thou art but a corruptible man? and why art thou moved, whereas thou art but mortal?[16] Why hast thou not considered in thy mind this thing that is to come, rather than that which is present?[17] Then answered I and said, O Lord that bearest rule, thou hast ordained in thy law, that the righteous should inherit these things, but that the ungodly should perish.[18] Nevertheless the righteous shall suffer strait things, and hope for wide: for they that have done wickedly have suffered the strait things, and yet shall not see the wide.[19] And he said unto me. There is no judge above God, and none that hath understanding above the Highest.[20] For there be

many that perish in this life, because they despise the law of God that is set before them.[21] For God hath given strait commandment to such as came, what they should do to live, even as they came, and what they should observe to avoid punishment.[22] Nevertheless they were not obedient unto him; but spake against him, and imagined vain things;[23] And deceived themselves by their wicked deeds; and said of the most High, that he is not; and knew not his ways:[24] But his law have they despised, and denied his covenants; in his statutes have they not been faithful, and have not performed his works.[25] And therefore, Esdras, for the empty are empty things, and for the full are the full things.[26] Behold, the time shall come, that these tokens which I have told thee shall come to pass, and the bride shall appear, and she coming forth shall be seen, that now is withdrawn from the earth.[27] And whosoever is delivered from the foresaid evils shall see my wonders.[28] For my son Jesus shall be revealed with those that be with him, and they that remain shall rejoice within four hundred years.[29] After these years shall my son Christ die, and all men that have life.[30] And the world shall be turned into the old silence seven days, like as in the former judgments: so that no man shall remain.[31] And after seven days the world, that yet awaketh not, shall be raised up, and that shall die that is corrupt[32] And the earth shall restore those that are asleep in her, and so shall the dust those that dwell in silence, and the secret places shall deliver those souls that were committed unto them.[33] And the most High shall appear upon the seat of judgment, and misery shall pass away, and the long suffering shall have an end:[34] But judgment only shall remain, truth shall stand, and faith shall wax strong:[35] And the work shall follow, and the reward shall be shewed, and the good deeds shall be of force, and wicked deeds shall bear no rule.[36] Then said I, Abraham prayed first for the Sodomites, and Moses for the fathers that sinned in the wilderness:[37] And Jesus after him for Israel in the time of Achan:[38] And Samuel and David for the destruction: and Solomon for them that should come to the sanctuary:[39] And Helias for those that received rain; and for the dead, that he might live:[40] And Ezechias for the people in the time of Sennacherib: and many for many.[41] Even so now, seeing corruption is grown up, and wickedness increased, and the righteous have prayed for the ungodly: wherefore shall it not be so now also?[42] He answered me, and said, This present life is not the end where much glory doth abide; therefore have they prayed for the weak.[43] But the day of doom shall be the end of this time, and the beginning of the immortality for to come, wherein corruption is past,[44] Intemperance is at an end, infidelity is cut off, righteousness is grown, and truth is sprung up.[45] Then shall no man be able to save him that is destroyed, nor to oppress him that hath gotten the victory.[46] I answered then and said, This is my first and last saying, that it had been better not to have given the earth unto Adam: or else, when it was given him, to have restrained him from sinning.[47] For what profit is it for men now in this present time to live in heaviness, and after death to look for punishment?[48] O thou Adam, what hast thou done? for though it was thou that sinned, thou art not fallen alone, but we all that come of thee.[49] For what profit is it unto us, if there be promised us an immortal time, whereas we have done the works that bring death?[50] And that there is promised us an everlasting hope, whereas ourselves being most wicked are made vain?[51] And that there are laid up for us dwellings of health and safety, whereas we have lived wickedly?[52] And that the glory of the most High is kept to defend them which have led a wary life, whereas we have walked in the most wicked ways of all?[53] And that there should be shewed a paradise, whose fruit endureth for ever, wherein is security and medicine, since we shall not enter into it?[54] (For we have walked in unpleasant places.)[55] And that the faces of them which have used abstinence shall shine above the stars, whereas our faces shall be blacker than darkness?[56] For while we lived and committed iniquity, we considered not that we should begin to suffer for it after death.[57] Then answered he me, and said, This is the condition of the battle, which man that is born upon the earth shall fight;[58] That, if he be overcome, he shall suffer as thou hast said: but if he get the victory, he shall receive the thing that I say.[59] For this is the life whereof Moses spake unto the people while he lived, saying, Choose thee life, that thou mayest live.[60] Nevertheless they believed not him, nor yet the prophets after him, no nor me which have spoken unto them,[61] That there should not be such heaviness in their destruction, as shall be joy over them that are persuaded to salvation.[62] I answered then, and said, I know, Lord, that the most High is called merciful, in that he hath mercy upon them which are not yet come into the world,[63] And upon those also that turn to his law;[64] And that he is patient, and long suffereth those that have sinned, as his creatures;[65] And that he is bountiful, for he is ready to give where it needeth;[66] And that he is of great mercy, for he multiplieth more and more mercies to them that are present, and that are past, and also to them which are to come.[67] For if he shall not multiply his mercies, the world would not continue with them that inherit therein.[68] And he pardoneth; for if he did not so of his goodness, that they which have committed iniquities might be eased of them, the ten thousandth part of men should not remain living.[69] And being judge, if he should not forgive them that are cured with his word, and put out the multitude of contentions,[70] There should be very few left peradventure in an innumerable multitude.

4Ezra.8

[1] And he answered me, saying, The most High hath made this world for many, but the world to come for few.[2] I will tell thee a similitude, Esdras; As when thou askest the earth, it shall say unto thee, that it giveth much mould whereof earthen vessels are made, but little dust that gold cometh of: even so is the course of this present world.[3] There be many created, but few shall be saved.[4] So answered I and said, Swallow then down, O my soul, understanding, and devour wisdom.[5] For thou hast agreed to give ear, and art willing to prophesy: for thou hast no longer space than only to live.[6] O Lord, if thou suffer not thy servant, that we may pray before thee, and thou give us seed unto our heart, and culture to our understanding, that there may come fruit of it; how shall each man live that is corrupt, who beareth the place of a man?[7] For thou art alone, and we all one workmanship of thine hands, like as thou hast said.[8] For when the body is fashioned now in the mother's womb, and thou givest it members, thy creature is preserved in fire and water, and nine months doth thy workmanship endure thy creature which is created in her.[9] But that which keepeth and is kept shall both be preserved: and when the time cometh, the womb preserved delivereth up the things that grew in it.[10] For thou hast commanded out of the parts of the body, that is to say, out of the breasts, milk to be given, which is the fruit of the breasts,[11] That the thing which is fashioned may be nourished for a time, till thou disposest it to thy mercy.[12] Thou broughtest it up with thy righteousness, and nurturedst it in thy law, and reformedst it with thy judgment.[13] And thou shalt mortify it as thy creature, and quicken it as thy work.[14] If therefore thou shalt destroy him which with so great labour was fashioned, it is an easy thing to be ordained by thy commandment, that the thing which was made might be preserved.[15] Now therefore, Lord, I will speak; touching man in general, thou knowest best; but touching thy people, for whose sake I am sorry;[16] And for thine inheritance, for whose cause I mourn; and for Israel, for whom I am heavy; and for Jacob, for whose sake I am troubled;[17] Therefore will I begin to pray before thee for myself and for them: for I see the

falls of us that dwell in the land.[18] But I have heard the swiftness of the judge which is to come.[19] Therefore hear my voice, and understand my words, and I shall speak before thee. This is the beginning of the words of Esdras, before he was taken up: and I said,[20] O Lord, thou that dwellest in everlastingness which beholdest from above things in the heaven and in the air;[21] Whose throne is inestimable; whose glory may not be comprehended; before whom the hosts of angels stand with trembling,[22] Whose service is conversant in wind and fire; whose word is true, and sayings constant; whose commandment is strong, and ordinance fearful;[23] Whose look drieth up the depths, and indignation maketh the mountains to melt away; which the truth witnesseth:[24] O hear the prayer of thy servant, and give ear to the petition of thy creature.[25] For while I live I will speak, and so long as I have understanding I will answer.[26] O look not upon the sins of thy people; but on them which serve thee in truth.[27] Regard not the wicked inventions of the heathen, but the desire of those that keep thy testimonies in afflictions.[28] Think not upon those that have walked feignedly before thee: but remember them, which according to thy will have known thy fear.[29] Let it not be thy will to destroy them which have lived like beasts; but to look upon them that have clearly taught thy law.[30] Take thou no indignation at them which are deemed worse than beasts; but love them that always put their trust in thy righteousness and glory.[31] For we and our fathers do languish of such diseases: but because of us sinners thou shalt be called merciful.[32] For if thou hast a desire to have mercy upon us, thou shalt be called merciful, to us namely, that have no works of righteousness.[33] For the just, which have many good works laid up with thee, shall out of their own deeds receive reward.[34] For what is man, that thou shouldest take displeasure at him? or what is a corruptible generation, that thou shouldest be so bitter toward it?[35] For in truth them is no man among them that be born, but he hath dealt wickedly; and among the faithful there is none which hath not done amiss.[36] For in this, O Lord, thy righteousness and thy goodness shall be declared, if thou be merciful unto them which have not the confidence of good works.[37] Then answered he me, and said, Some things hast thou spoken aright, and according unto thy words it shall be.[38] For indeed I will not think on the disposition of them which have sinned before death, before judgment, before destruction:[39] But I will rejoice over the disposition of the righteous, and I will remember also their pilgrimage, and the salvation, and the reward, that they shall have.[40] Like as I have spoken now, so shall it come to pass.[41] For as the husbandman soweth much seed upon the ground, and planteth many trees, and yet the thing that is sown good in his season cometh not up, neither doth all that is planted take root: even so is it of them that are sown in the world; they shall not all be saved.[42] I answered then and said, If I have found grace, let me speak.[43] Like as the husbandman's seed perisheth, if it come not up, and receive not thy rain in due season; or if there come too much rain, and corrupt it:[44] Even so perisheth man also, which is formed with thy hands, and is called thine own image, because thou art like unto him, for whose sake thou hast made all things, and likened him unto the husbandman's seed.[45] Be not wroth with us but spare thy people, and have mercy upon thine own inheritance: for thou art merciful unto thy creature.[46] Then answered he me, and said, Things present are for the present, and things to cometh for such as be to come.[47] For thou comest far short that thou shouldest be able to love my creature more than I: but I have ofttimes drawn nigh unto thee, and unto it, but never to the unrighteous.[48] In this also thou art marvellous before the most High:[49] In that thou hast humbled thyself, as it becometh thee, and hast not judged thyself worthy to be much glorified among the righteous.[50] For many great miseries shall be done to them that in the latter time shall dwell in the world, because they have walked in great pride.[51] But understand thou for thyself, and seek out the glory for such as be like thee.[52] For unto you is paradise opened, the tree of life is planted, the time to come is prepared, plenteousness is made ready, a city is builded, and rest is allowed, yea, perfect goodness and wisdom.[53] The root of evil is sealed up from you, weakness and the moth is hid from you, and corruption is fled into hell to be forgotten:[54] Sorrows are passed, and in the end is shewed the treasure of immortality.[55] And therefore ask thou no more questions concerning the multitude of them that perish.[56] For when they had taken liberty, they despised the most High, thought scorn of his law, and forsook his ways.[57] Moreover they have trodden down his righteous,[58] And said in their heart, that there is no God; yea, and that knowing they must die.[59] For as the things aforesaid shalt receive you, so thirst and pain are prepared for them: for it was not his will that men should come to nought:[60] But they which be created have defiled the name of him that made them, and were unthankful unto him which prepared life for them.[61] And therefore is my judgment now at hand.[62] These things have I not shewed unto all men, but unto thee, and a few like thee. Then answered I and said,[63] Behold, O Lord, now hast thou shewed me the multitude of the wonders, which thou wilt begin to do in the last times: but at what time, thou hast not shewed me.

4Ezra.9

[1] He answered me then, and said, Measure thou the time diligently in itself: and when thou seest part of the signs past, which I have told thee before,[2] Then shalt thou understand, that it is the very same time, wherein the Highest will begin to visit the world which he made.[3] Therefore when there shall be seen earthquakes and uproars of the people in the world:[4] Then shalt thou well understand, that the most High spake of those things from the days that were before thee, even from the beginning.[5] For like as all that is made in the world hath a beginning and an end, and the end is manifest:[6] Even so the times also of the Highest have plain beginnings in wonder and powerful works, and endings in effects and signs.[7] And every one that shall be saved, and shall be able to escape by his works, and by faith, whereby ye have believed,[8] Shall be preserved from the said perils, and shall see my salvation in my land, and within my borders: for I have sanctified them for me from the beginning.[9] Then shall they be in pitiful case, which now have abused my ways: and they that have cast them away despitefully shall dwell in torments.[10] For such as in their life have received benefits, and have not known me;[11] And they that have loathed my law, while they had yet liberty, and, when as yet place of repentance was open unto them, understood not, but despised it;[12] The same must know it after death by pain.[13] And therefore be thou not curious how the ungodly shall be punished, and when: but enquire how the righteous shall be saved, whose the world is, and for whom the world is created.[14] Then answered I and said,[15] I have said before, and now do speak, and will speak it also hereafter, that there be many more of them which perish, than of them which shall be saved:[16] Like as a wave is greater than a drop.[17] And he answered me, saying, Like as the field is, so is also the seed; as the flowers be, such are the colours also; such as the workman is, such also is the work; and as the husbandman is himself, so is his husbandry also: for it was the time of the world.[18] And now when I prepared the world, which was not yet made, even for them to dwell in that now live, no man spake against me.[19] For then every one obeyed: but now the manners of them which are created in this world that is made are corrupted by a perpetual seed, and by a law which is unsearchable rid themselves.[20] So I considered the world, and, behold, there was peril because of the devices that were come into it.[21] And I saw, and

99

spared it greatly, and have kept me a grape of the cluster, and a plant of a great people.[22] Let the multitude perish then, which was born in vain; and let my grape be kept, and my plant; for with great labour have I made it perfect.[23] Nevertheless, if thou wilt cease yet seven days more, (but thou shalt not fast in them,[24] But go into a field of flowers, where no house is builded, and eat only the flowers of the field; taste no flesh, drink no wine, but eat flowers only;)[25] And pray unto the Highest continually, then will I come and talk with thee.[26] So I went my way into the field which is called Ardath, like as he commanded me; and there I sat among the flowers, and did eat of the herbs of the field, and the meat of the same satisfied me.[27] After seven days I sat upon the grass, and my heart was vexed within me, like as before:[28] And I opened my mouth, and began to talk before the most High, and said,[29] O Lord, thou that shewest thyself unto us, thou wast shewed unto our fathers in the wilderness, in a place where no man treadeth, in a barren place, when they came out of Egypt.[30] And thou spakest saying, Hear me, O Israel; and mark my words, thou seed of Jacob.[31] For, behold, I sow my law in you, and it shall bring fruit in you, and ye shall be honoured in it for ever.[32] But our fathers, which received the law, kept it not, and observed not thy ordinances: and though the fruit of thy law did not perish, neither could it, for it was thine;[33] Yet they that received it perished, because they kept not the thing that was sown in them.[34] And, lo, it is a custom, when the ground hath received seed, or the sea a ship, or any vessel meat or drink, that, that being perished wherein it was sown or cast into,[35] That thing also which was sown, or cast therein, or received, doth perish, and remaineth not with us: but with us it hath not happened so.[36] For we that have received the law perish by sin, and our heart also which received it[37] Notwithstanding the law perisheth not, but remaineth in his force.[38] And when I spake these things in my heart, I looked back with mine eyes, and upon the right side I saw a woman, and, behold, she mourned and wept with a loud voice, and was much grieved in heart, and her clothes were rent, and she had ashes upon her head.[39] Then let I my thoughts go that I was in, and turned me unto her,[40] And said unto her, Wherefore weepest thou? why art thou so grieved in thy mind?[41] And she said unto me, Sir, let me alone, that I may bewail myself, and add unto my sorrow, for I am sore vexed in my mind, and brought very low.[42] And I said unto her, What aileth thee? tell me.[43] She said unto me, I thy servant have been barren, and had no child, though I had an husband thirty years,[44] And those thirty years I did nothing else day and night, and every hour, but make my, prayer to the Highest.[45] After thirty years God heard me thine handmaid, looked upon my misery, considered my trouble, and gave me a son: and I was very glad of him, so was my husband also, and all my neighbours: and we gave great honour unto the Almighty.[46] And I nourished him with great travail.[47] So when he grew up, and came to the time that he should have a wife, I made a feast.

4Ezra.10

[1] And it so came to pass, that when my son was entered into his wedding chamber, he fell down, and died.[2] Then we all overthrew the lights, and all my neighbours rose up to comfort me: so I took my rest unto the second day at night.[3] And it came to pass, when they had all left off to comfort me, to the end I might be quiet; then rose I up by night and fled, and came hither into this field, as thou seest.[4] And I do now purpose not to return into the city, but here to stay, and neither to eat nor drink, but continually to mourn and to fast until I die.[5] Then left I the meditations wherein I was, and spake to her in anger, saying,[6] Thou foolish woman above all other, seest thou not our mourning, and what happeneth unto us?[7] How that Sion our mother is full of all heaviness, and much humbled,

mourning very sore? [8] And now, seeing we all mourn and are sad, for we are all in heaviness, art thou grieved for one son? [9] For ask the earth, and she shall tell thee, that it is she which ought to mourn for the fall of so many that grow upon her. [10] For out of her came all at the first, and out of her shall all others come, and, behold, they walk almost all into destruction, and a multitude of them is utterly rooted out. [11] Who then should make more mourning than she, that hath lost so great a multitude; and not thou, which art sorry but for one? [12] But if thou sayest unto me, My lamentation is not like the earth's, because I have lost the fruit of my womb, which I brought forth with pains, and bare with sorrows; [13] But the earth not so: for the multitude present in it according to the course of the earth is gone, as it came: [14] Then say I unto thee, Like as thou hast brought forth with labour; even so the earth also hath given her fruit, namely, man, ever since the beginning unto him that made her. [15] Now therefore keep thy sorrow to thyself, and bear with a good courage that which hath befallen thee. [16] For if thou shalt acknowledge the determination of God to be just, thou shalt both receive thy son in time, and shalt be commended among women. [17] Go thy way then into the city to thine husband. [18] And she said unto me, That will I not do: I will not go into the city, but here will I die. [19] So I proceeded to speak further unto her, and said, [20] Do not so, but be counselled. by me: for how many are the adversities of Sion? be comforted in regard of the sorrow of Jerusalem. [21] For thou seest that our sanctuary is laid waste, our altar broken down, our temple destroyed; [22] Our psaltery is laid on the ground, our song is put to silence, our rejoicing is at an end, the light of our candlestick is put out, the ark of our covenant is spoiled, our holy things are defiled, and the name that is called upon us is almost profaned: our children are put to shame, our priests are burnt, our Levites are gone into captivity, our virgins are defiled, and our wives ravished; our righteous men carried away, our little ones destroyed, our young men are brought in bondage, and our strong men are become weak; [23] And, which is the greatest of all, the seal of Sion hath now lost her honour; for she is delivered into the hands of them that hate us. [24] And therefore shake off thy great heaviness, and put away the multitude of sorrows, that the Mighty may be merciful unto thee again, and the Highest shall give thee rest and ease from thy labour. [25] And it came to pass while I was talking with her, behold, her face upon a sudden shined exceedingly, and her countenance glistered, so that I was afraid of her, and mused what it might be. [26] And, behold, suddenly she made a great cry very fearful: so that the earth shook at the noise of the woman. [27] And I looked, and, behold, the woman appeared unto me no more, but there was a city builded, and a large place shewed itself from the foundations: then was I afraid, and cried with a loud voice, and said, [28] Where is Uriel the angel, who came unto me at the first? for he hath caused me to fall into many trances, and mine end is turned into corruption, and my prayer to rebuke. [29] And as I was speaking these words behold, he came unto me, and looked upon me. [30] And, lo, I lay as one that had been dead, and mine understanding was taken from me: and he took me by the right hand, and comforted me, and set me upon my feet, and said unto me, [31] What aileth thee? and why art thou so disquieted? and why is thine understanding troubled, and the thoughts of thine heart? [32] And I said, Because thou hast forsaken me, and yet I did according to thy words, and I went into the field, and, lo, I have seen, and yet see, that I am not able to express. [33] And he said unto me, Stand up manfully, and I will advise thee. [34] Then said I, Speak on, my lord, in me; only forsake me not, lest I die frustrate of my hope. [35] For I have seen that I knew not, and hear that I do not know. [36] Or is my sense deceived, or my soul in a dream? [37] Now therefore I beseech thee that thou wilt shew thy

servant of this vision. [38] He answered me then, and said, Hear me, and I shall inform thee, and tell thee wherefore thou art afraid: for the Highest will reveal many secret things unto thee. [39] He hath seen that thy way is right: for that thou sorrowest continually for thy people, and makest great lamentation for Sion. [40] This therefore is the meaning of the vision which thou lately sawest: [41] Thou sawest a woman mourning, and thou begannest to comfort her: [42] But now seest thou the likeness of the woman no more, but there appeared unto thee a city builded. [43] And whereas she told thee of the death of her son, this is the solution: [44] This woman, whom thou sawest is Sion: and whereas she said unto thee, even she whom thou seest as a city builded, [45] Whereas, I say, she said unto thee, that she hath been thirty years barren: those are the thirty years wherein there was no offering made in her. [46] But after thirty years Solomon builded the city and offered offerings: and then bare the barren a son. [47] And whereas she told thee that she nourished him with labour: that was the dwelling in Jerusalem. [48] But whereas she said unto thee, That my son coming into his marriage chamber happened to have a fail, and died: this was the destruction that came to Jerusalem. [49] And, behold, thou sawest her likeness, and because she mourned for her son, thou begannest to comfort her: and of these things which have chanced, these are to be opened unto thee. [50] For now the most High seeth that thou art grieved unfeignedly, and sufferest from thy whole heart for her, so hath he shewed thee the brightness of her glory, and the comeliness of her beauty: [51] And therefore I bade thee remain in the field where no house was builded: [52] For I knew that the Highest would shew this unto thee. [53] Therefore I commanded thee to go into the field, where no foundation of any building was. [54] For in the place wherein the Highest beginneth to shew his city, there can no man's building be able to stand. [55] And therefore fear not, let not thine heart be affrighted, but go thy way in, and see the beauty and greatness of the building, as much as thine eyes be able to see: [56] And then shalt thou hear as much as thine ears may comprehend. [57] For thou art blessed above many other, and art called with the Highest; and so are but few. [58] But to morrow at night thou shalt remain here; [59] And so shall the Highest shew thee visions of the high things, which the most High will do unto them that dwell upon the earth in the last days. So I slept that night and another, like as he commanded me.

4Ezra.11

[1] Then saw I a dream, and, behold, there came up from the sea an eagle, which had twelve feathered wings, and three heads. [2] And I saw, and, behold, she spread her wings over all the earth, and all the winds of the air blew on her, and were gathered together. [3] And I beheld, and out of her feathers there grew other contrary feathers; and they became little feathers and small. [4] But her heads were at rest: the head in the midst was greater than the other, yet rested it with the residue. [5] Moreover I beheld, and, lo, the eagle flew with her feathers, and reigned upon earth, and over them that dwelt therein. [6] And I saw that all things under heaven were subject unto her, and no man spake against her, no, not one creature upon earth. [7] And I beheld, and, lo, the eagle rose upon her talons, and spake to her feathers, saying, [8] Watch not all at once: sleep every one in his own place, and watch by course: [9] But let the heads be preserved for the last. [10] And I beheld, and, lo, the voice went not out of her heads, but from the midst of her body. [11] And I numbered her contrary feathers, and, behold, there were eight of them. [12] And I looked, and, behold, on the right side there arose one feather, and reigned over all the earth; [13] And so it was, that when it reigned, the end of it came, and the place thereof appeared no more: so the next following stood up. and reigned, and had a great time; [14] And it happened, that when it reigned, the end of it came also, like as the

first, so that it appeared no more.[15] Then came there a voice unto it, and said,[16] Hear thou that hast borne rule over the earth so long: this I say unto thee, before thou beginnest to appear no more,[17] There shall none after thee attain unto thy time, neither unto the half thereof.[18] Then arose the third, and reigned as the other before, and appeared no more also.[19] So went it with all the residue one after another, as that every one reigned, and then appeared no more.[20] Then I beheld, and, lo, in process of time the feathers that followed stood up upon the right side, that they might rule also; and some of them ruled, but within a while they appeared no more:[21] For some of them were set up, but ruled not.[22] After this I looked, and, behold, the twelve feathers appeared no more, nor the two little feathers:[23] And there was no more upon the eagle's body, but three heads that rested, and six little wings.[24] Then saw I also that two little feathers divided themselves from the six, and remained under the head that was upon the right side: for the four continued in their place.[25] And I beheld, and, lo, the feathers that were under the wing thought to set up themselves and to have the rule.[26] And I beheld, and, lo, there was one set up, but shortly it appeared no more.[27] And the second was sooner away than the first.[28] And I beheld, and, lo, the two that remained thought also in themselves to reign:[29] And when they so thought, behold, there awaked one of the heads that were at rest, namely, it that was in the midst; for that was greater than the two other heads.[30] And then I saw that the two other heads were joined with it.[31] And, behold, the head was turned with them that were with it, and did eat up the two feathers under the wing that would have reigned.[32] But this head put the whole earth in fear, and bare rule in it over all those that dwelt upon the earth with much oppression; and it had the governance of the world more than all the wings that had been.[33] And after this I beheld, and, lo, the head that was in the midst suddenly appeared no more, like as the wings.[34] But there remained the two heads, which also in like sort ruled upon the earth, and over those that dwelt therein.[35] And I beheld, and, lo, the head upon the right side devoured it that was upon the left side.[36] Then I head a voice, which said unto me, Look before thee, and consider the thing that thou seest.[37] And I beheld, and lo, as it were a roaring lion chased out of the wood: and I saw that he sent out a man's voice unto the eagle, and said,[38] Hear thou, I will talk with thee, and the Highest shall say unto thee,[39] Art not thou it that remainest of the four beasts, whom I made to reign in my world, that the end of their times might come through them?[40] And the fourth came, and overcame all the beasts that were past, and had power over the world with great fearfulness, and over the whole compass of the earth with much wicked oppression; and so long time dwelt he upon the earth with deceit.[41] For the earth hast thou not judged with truth.[42] For thou hast afflicted the meek, thou hast hurt the peaceable, thou hast loved liars, and destroyed the dwellings of them that brought forth fruit, and hast cast down the walls of such as did thee no harm.[43] Therefore is thy wrongful dealing come up unto the Highest, and thy pride unto the Mighty.[44] The Highest also hath looked upon the proud times, and, behold, they are ended, and his abominations are fulfilled.[45] And therefore appear no more, thou eagle, nor thy horrible wings, nor thy wicked feathers nor thy malicious heads, nor thy hurtful claws, nor all thy vain body:[46] That all the earth may be refreshed, and may return, being delivered from thy violence, and that she may hope for the judgment and mercy of him that made her.

4Ezra.12

[1] And it came to pass, whiles the lion spake these words unto the eagle, I saw,[2] And, behold, the head that remained and the four wings appeared no more, and the two went unto it and set themselves up to reign, and their kingdom was small, and fill of uproar.[3] And I saw, and, behold, they appeared no more, and the whole body of the eagle was burnt so that the earth was in great fear: then awaked I out of the trouble and trance of my mind, and from great fear, and said unto my spirit,[4] Lo, this hast thou done unto me, in that thou searchest out the ways of the Highest.[5] Lo, yet am I weary in my mind, and very weak in my spirit; and little strength is there in me, for the great fear wherewith I was afflicted this night.[6] Therefore will I now beseech the Highest, that he will comfort me unto the end.[7] And I said, Lord that bearest rule, if I have found grace before thy sight, and if I am justified with thee before many others, and if my prayer indeed be come up before thy face;[8] Comfort me then, and shew me thy servant the interpretation and plain difference of this fearful vision, that thou mayest perfectly comfort my soul.[9] For thou hast judged me worthy to shew me the last times.[10] And he said unto me, This is the interpretation of the vision:[11] The eagle, whom thou sawest come up from the sea, is the kingdom which was seen in the vision of thy brother Daniel.[12] But it was not expounded unto him, therefore now I declare it unto thee.[13] Behold, the days will come, that there shall rise up a kingdom upon earth, and it shall be feared above all the kingdoms that were before it.[14] In the same shall twelve kings reign, one after another:[15] Whereof the second shall begin to reign, and shall have more time than any of the twelve.[16] And this do the twelve wings signify, which thou sawest.[17] As for the voice which thou heardest speak, and that thou sawest not to go out from the heads but from the midst of the body thereof, this is the interpretation:[18] That after the time of that kingdom there shall arise great strivings, and it shall stand in peril of failing: nevertheless it shall not then fall, but shall be restored again to his beginning.[19] And whereas thou sawest the eight small under feathers sticking to her wings, this is the interpretation:[20] That in him there shall arise eight kings, whose times shall be but small, and their years swift.[21] And two of them shall perish, the middle time approaching: four shall be kept until their end begin to approach: but two shall be kept unto the end.[22] And whereas thou sawest three heads resting, this is the interpretation:[23] In his last days shall the most High raise up three kingdoms, and renew many things therein, and they shall have the dominion of the earth,[24] And of those that dwell therein, with much oppression, above all those that were before them: therefore are they called the heads of the eagle.[25] For these are they that shall accomplish his wickedness, and that shall finish his last end.[26] And whereas thou sawest that the great head appeared no more, it signifieth that one of them shall die upon his bed, and yet with pain.[27] For the two that remain shall be slain with the sword.[28] For the sword of the one shall devour the other: but at the last shall he fall through the sword himself.[29] And whereas thou sawest two feathers under the wings passing over the head that is on the right side;[30] It signifieth that these are they, whom the Highest hath kept unto their end: this is the small kingdom and full of trouble, as thou sawest.[31] And the lion, whom thou sawest rising up out of the wood, and roaring, and speaking to the eagle, and rebuking her for her unrighteousness with all the words which thou hast heard;[32] This is the anointed, which the Highest hath kept for them and for their wickedness unto the end: he shall reprove them, and shall upbraid them with their cruelty.[33] For he shall set them before him alive in judgment, and shall rebuke them, and correct them.[34] For the rest of my people shall he deliver with mercy, those that have been pressed upon my borders, and he shall make them joyful until the coming of the day of judgment, whereof I have spoken unto thee from the the beginning.[35] This is the dream that thou sawest, and these are the interpretations.[36] Thou only hast been meet to know this secret of the Highest.[37] Therefore write all these things that thou hast seen in

a book, and hide them:[38] And teach them to the wise of the people, whose hearts thou knowest may comprehend and keep these secrets.[39] But wait thou here thyself yet seven days more, that it may be shewed thee, whatsoever it pleaseth the Highest to declare unto thee. And with that he went his way.[40] And it came to pass, when all the people saw that the seven days were past, and I not come again into the city, they gathered them all together, from the least unto the greatest, and came unto me, and said,[41] What have we offended thee? and what evil have we done against thee, that thou forsakest us, and sittest here in this place?[42] For of all the prophets thou only art left us, as a cluster of the vintage, and as a candle in a dark place, and as a haven or ship preserved from the tempest.[43] Are not the evils which are come to us sufficient?[44] If thou shalt forsake us, how much better had it been for us, if we also had been burned in the midst of Sion?[45] For we are not better than they that died there. And they wept with a loud voice. Then answered I them, and said,[46] Be of good comfort, O Israel; and be not heavy, thou house of Jacob:[47] For the Highest hath you in remembrance, and the Mighty hath not forgotten you in temptation.[48] As for me, I have not forsaken you, neither am I departed from you: but am come into this place, to pray for the desolation of Sion, and that I might seek mercy for the low estate of your sanctuary.[49] And now go your way home every man, and after these days will I come unto you.[50] So the people went their way into the city, like as I commanded them:[51] But I remained still in the field seven days, as the angel commanded me; and did eat only in those days of the flowers of the field, and had my meat of the herbs

4Ezra.13

[1] And it came to pass after seven days, I dreamed a dream by night:[2] And, lo, there arose a wind from the sea, that it moved all the waves thereof.[3] And I beheld, and, lo, that man waxed strong with the thousands of heaven: and when he turned his countenance to look, all the things trembled that were seen under him.[4] And whensoever the voice went out of his mouth, all they burned that heard his voice, like as the earth faileth when it feeleth the fire.[5] And after this I beheld, and, lo, there was gathered together a multitude of men, out of number, from the four winds of the heaven, to subdue the man that came out of the sea[6] But I beheld, and, lo, he had graved himself a great mountain, and flew up upon it.[7] But I would have seen the region or place whereout the hill was graven, and I could not.[8] And after this I beheld, and, lo, all they which were gathered together to subdue him were sore afraid, and yet durst fight.[9] And, lo, as he saw the violence of the multitude that came, he neither lifted up his hand, nor held sword, nor any instrument of war:[10] But only I saw that he sent out of his mouth as it had been a blast of fire, and out of his lips a flaming breath, and out of his tongue he cast out sparks and tempests.[11] And they were all mixed together; the blast of fire, the flaming breath, and the great tempest; and fell with violence upon the multitude which was prepared to fight, and burned them up every one, so that upon a sudden of an innumerable multitude nothing was to be perceived, but only dust and smell of smoke: when I saw this I was afraid.[12] Afterward saw I the same man come down from the mountain, and call unto him another peaceable Multitude.[13] And there came much people unto him, whereof some were glad, some were sorry, and some of them were bound, and other some brought of them that were offered: then was I sick through great fear, and I awaked, and said,[14] Thou hast shewed thy servant these wonders from the beginning, and hast counted me worthy that thou shouldest receive my prayer:[15] Shew me now yet the interpretation of this dream.[16] For as I conceive in mine understanding, woe unto them that shall be left in those days and much more woe unto them that are not left behind![17] For they

that were not left were in heaviness.[18] Now understand I the things that are laid up in the latter days, which shall happen unto them, and to those that are left behind.[19] Therefore are they come into great perils and many necessities, like as these dreams declare.[20] Yet is it easier for him that is in danger to come into these things, than to pass away as a cloud out of the world, and not to see the things that happen in the last days. And he answered unto me, and said,[21] The interpretation of the vision shall I shew thee, and I will open unto thee the thing that thou hast required.[22] Whereas thou hast spoken of them that are left behind, this is the interpretation:[23] He that shall endure the peril in that time hath kept himself: they that be fallen into danger are such as have works, and faith toward the Almighty.[24] Know this therefore, that they which be left behind are more blessed than they that be dead.[25] This is the meaning of the vision: Whereas thou sawest a man coming up from the midst of the sea:[26] The same is he whom God the Highest hath kept a great season, which by his own self shall deliver his creature: and he shall order them that are left behind.[27] And whereas thou sawest, that out of his mouth there came as a blast of wind, and fire, and storm;[28] And that he held neither sword, nor any instrument of war, but that the rushing in of him destroyed the whole multitude that came to subdue him; this is the interpretation:[29] Behold, the days come, when the most High will begin to deliver them that are upon the earth.[30] And he shall come to the astonishment of them that dwell on the earth.[31] And one shall undertake to fight against another, one city against another, one place against another, one people against another, and one realm against another.[32] And the time shall be when these things shall come to pass, and the signs shall happen which I shewed thee before, and then shall my Son be declared, whom thou sawest as a man ascending.[33] And when all the people hear his voice, every man shall in their own land leave the battle they have one against another.[34] And an innumerable multitude shall be gathered together, as thou sawest them, willing to come, and to overcome him by fighting.[35] But he shall stand upon the top of the mount Sion.[36] And Sion shall come, and shall be shewed to all men, being prepared and builded, like as thou sawest the hill graven without hands.[37] And this my Son shall rebuke the wicked inventions of those nations, which for their wicked life are fallen into the tempest;[38] And shall lay before them their evil thoughts, and the torments wherewith they shall begin to be tormented, which are like unto a flame: and he shall destroy them without labour by the law which is like unto me.[39] And whereas thou sawest that he gathered another peaceable multitude unto him;[40] Those are the ten tribes, which were carried away prisoners out of their own land in the time of Osea the king, whom Salmanasar the king of Assyria led away captive, and he carried them over the waters, and so came they into another land.[41] But they took this counsel among themselves, that they would leave the multitude of the heathen, and go forth into a further country, where never mankind dwelt,[42] That they might there keep their statutes, which they never kept in their own land.[43] And they entered into Euphrates by the narrow places of the river.[44] For the most High then shewed signs for them, and held still the flood, till they were passed over.[45] For through that country there was a great way to go, namely, of a year and a half: and the same region is called Arsareth.[46] Then dwelt they there until the latter time; and now when they shall begin to come,[47] The Highest shall stay the springs of the stream again, that they may go through: therefore sawest thou the multitude with peace.[48] But those that be left behind of thy people are they that are found within my borders.[49] Now when he destroyeth the multitude of the nations that are gathered together, he shall defend his people that remain.[50] And then shall he shew them great wonders.[51] Then said I, O Lord that bearest rule, shew me this: Wherefore have I seen the man coming up from the midst of the sea?[52] And he said unto me, Like as thou canst neither seek out nor know the things that are in the deep of the sea: even so can no man upon earth see my Son, or those that be with him, but in the day time.[53] This is the interpretation of the dream which thou sawest, and whereby thou only art here lightened.[54] For thou hast forsaken thine own way, and applied thy diligence unto my law, and sought it.[55] Thy life hast thou ordered in wisdom, and hast called understanding thy mother.[56] And therefore have I shewed thee the treasures of the Highest: after other three days I will speak other things unto thee, and declare unto thee mighty and wondrous things.[57] Then went I forth into the field, giving praise and thanks greatly unto the most High because of his wonders which he did in time;[58] And because he governeth the same, and such things as fall in their seasons: and there I sat three days.

4Ezra.14

[1] And it came to pass upon the third day, I sat under an oak, and, behold, there came a voice out of a bush over against me, and said, Esdras, Esdras.[2] And I said, Here am I, Lord And I stood up upon my feet.[3] Then said he unto me, In the bush I did manifestly reveal myself unto Moses, and talked with him, when my people served in Egypt:[4] And I sent him and led my people out of Egypt, and brought him up to the mount of where I held him by me a long season,[5] And told him many wondrous things, and shewed him the secrets of the times, and the end; and commanded him, saying,[6] These words shalt thou declare, and these shalt thou hide.[7] And now I say unto thee,[8] That thou lay up in thy heart the signs that I have shewed, and the dreams that thou hast seen, and the interpretations which thou hast heard:[9] For thou shalt be taken away from all, and from henceforth thou shalt remain with my Son, and with such as be like thee, until the times be ended.[10] For the world hath lost his youth, and the times begin to wax old.[11] For the world is divided into twelve parts, and the ten parts of it are gone already, and half of a tenth part:[12] And there remaineth that which is after the half of the tenth part.[13] Now therefore set thine house in order, and reprove thy people, comfort such of them as be in trouble, and now renounce corruption,[14] Let go from thee mortal thoughts, cast away the burdens of man, put off now the weak nature,[15] And set aside the thoughts that are most heavy unto thee, and haste thee to flee from these times.[16] For yet greater evils than those which thou hast seen happen shall be done hereafter.[17] For look how much the world shall be weaker through age, so much the more shall evils increase upon them that dwell therein.[18] For the time is fled far away, and leasing is hard at hand: for now hasteth the vision to come, which thou hast seen.[19] Then answered I before thee, and said,[20] Behold, Lord, I will go, as thou hast commanded me, and reprove the people which are present: but they that shall be born afterward, who shall admonish them? thus the world is set in darkness, and they that dwell therein are without light.[21] For thy law is burnt, therefore no man knoweth the things that are done of thee, or the work that shall begin.[22] But if I have found grace before thee, send the Holy Ghost into me, and I shall write all that hath been done in the world since the beginning, which were written in thy law, that men may find thy path, and that they which will live in the latter days may live.[23] And he answered me, saying, Go thy way, gather the people together, and say unto them, that they seek thee not for forty days.[24] But look thou prepare thee many box trees, and take with thee Sarea, Dabria, Selemia, Ecanus, and Asiel, these five which are ready to write swiftly;[25] And come hither, and I shall light a candle of understanding in thine heart, which shall not be put out, till the things be performed which thou shalt begin to write.[26] And when thou hast done, some things shalt thou publish, and some things shalt thou shew secretly to the wise: to morrow this hour shalt thou begin to write.[27] Then went I forth, as he commanded, and gathered all the people together, and said,[28] Hear these words, O Israel.[29] Our fathers at the beginning were strangers in Egypt, from whence they were delivered:[30] And received the law of life, which they kept not, which ye also have transgressed after them.[31] Then was the land, even the land of Sion, parted among you by lot: but your fathers, and ye yourselves, have done unrighteousness, and have not kept the ways which the Highest commanded you.[32] And forasmuch as he is a righteous judge, he took from you in time the thing that he had given you.[33] And now are ye here, and your brethren among you.[34] Therefore if so be that ye will subdue your own understanding, and reform your hearts, ye shall be kept alive and after death ye shall obtain mercy.[35] For after death shall the judgment come, when we shall live again: and then shall the names of the righteous be manifest, and the works of the ungodly shall be declared.[36] Let no man therefore come unto me now, nor seek after me these forty days.[37] So I took the five men, as he commanded me, and we went into the field, and remained there.[38] And the next day, behold, a voice called me, saying, Esdras, open thy mouth, and drink that I give thee to drink.[39] Then opened I my mouth, and, behold, he reached me a full cup, which was full as it were with water, but the colour of it was like fire.[40] And I took it, and drank: and when I had drunk of it, my heart uttered understanding, and wisdom grew in my breast, for my spirit strengthened my memory:[41] And my mouth was opened, and shut no more.[42] The Highest gave understanding unto the five men, and they wrote the wonderful visions of the night that were told, which they knew not: and they sat forty days, and they wrote in the day, and at night they ate bread.[43] As for me. I spake in the day, and I held not my tongue by night.[44] In forty days they wrote two hundred and four books.[45] And it came to pass, when the forty days were filled, that the Highest spake, saying, The first that thou hast written publish openly, that the worthy and unworthy may read it:[46] But keep the seventy last, that thou mayest deliver them only to such as be wise among the people:[47] For in them is the spring of understanding, the fountain of wisdom, and the stream of knowledge.[48] And I did so.

4Ezra.15

[1] Behold, speak thou in the ears of my people the words of prophecy, which I will put in thy mouth, saith the Lord:[2] And cause them to be written in paper: for they are faithful and true.[3] Fear not the imaginations against thee, let not the incredulity of them trouble thee, that speak against thee.[4] For all the unfaithful shall die in their unfaithfulness.[5] Behold, saith the Lord, I will bring plagues upon the world; the sword, famine, death, and destruction.[6] For wickedness hath exceedingly polluted the whole earth, and their hurtful works are fulfilled.[7] Therefore saith the Lord,[8] I will hold my tongue no more as touching their wickedness, which they profanely commit, neither will I suffer them in those things, in which they wickedly exercise themselves: behold, the innocent and righteous blood crieth unto me, and the souls of the just complain continually.[9] And therefore, saith the Lord, I will surely avenge them, and receive unto me all the innocent blood from among them.[10] Behold, my people is led as a flock to the slaughter: I will not suffer them now to dwell in the land of Egypt:[11] But I will bring them with a mighty hand and a stretched out arm, and smite Egypt with plagues, as before, and will destroy all the land thereof.[12] Egypt shall mourn, and the foundation of it shall be smitten with the plague and punishment that God shall bring upon it.[13] They that till the ground shall mourn: for their seeds shall fail through the blasting and hail, and with a fearful constellation.[14] Woe to the world and them that dwell

therein!15 For the sword and their destruction draweth nigh, and one people shall stand up and fight against another, and swords in their hands.16 For there shall be sedition among men, and invading one another; they shall not regard their kings nor princes, and the course of their actions shall stand in their power.17 A man shall desire to go into a city, and shall not be able.18 For because of their pride the cities shall be troubled, the houses shall be destroyed, and men shall be afraid.19 A man shall have no pity upon his neighbour, but shall destroy their houses with the sword, and spoil their goods, because of the lack of bread, and for great tribulation.20 Behold, saith God, I will call together all the kings of the earth to reverence me, which are from the rising of the sun, from the south, from the east, and Libanus; to turn themselves one against another, and repay the things that they have done to them.21 Like as they do yet this day unto my chosen, so will I do also, and recompense in their bosom. Thus saith the Lord God;22 My right hand shall not spare the sinners, and my sword shall not cease over them that shed innocent blood upon the earth.23 The fire is gone forth from his wrath, and hath consumed the foundations of the earth, and the sinners, like the straw that is kindled.24 Woe to them that sin, and keep not my commandments! saith the Lord.25 I will not spare them: go your way, ye children, from the power, defile not my sanctuary.26 For the Lord knoweth all them that sin against him, and therefore delivereth he them unto death and destruction.27 For now are the plagues come upon the whole earth and ye shall remain in them: for God shall not deliver you, because ye have sinned against him.28 Behold an horrible vision, and the appearance thereof from the east:29 Where the nations of the dragons of Arabia shall come out with many chariots, and the multitude of them shall be carried as the wind upon earth, that all they which hear them may fear and tremble.30 Also the Carmanians raging in wrath shall go forth as the wild boars of the wood, and with great power shall they come, and join battle with them, and shall waste a portion of the land of the Assyrians.31 And then shall the dragons have the upper hand, remembering their nature; and if they shall turn themselves, conspiring together in great power to persecute them,32 Then these shall be troubled bled, and keep silence through their power, and shall flee.33 And from the land of the Assyrians shall the enemy besiege them, and consume some of them, and in their host shall be fear and dread, and strife among their kings.34 Behold clouds from the east and from the north unto the south, and they are very horrible to look upon, full of wrath and storm.35 They shall smite one upon another, and they shall smite down a great multitude of stars upon the earth, even their own star; and blood shall be from the sword unto the belly,36 And dung of men unto the camel's hough.37 And there shall be great fearfulness and trembling upon earth: and they that see the wrath shall be afraid, and trembling shall come upon them.38 And then shall there come great storms from the south, and from the north, and another part from the west.39 And strong winds shall arise from the east, and shall open it; and the cloud which he raised up in wrath, and the star stirred to cause fear toward the east and west wind, shall be destroyed.40 The great and mighty clouds shall be puffed up full of wrath, and the star, that they may make all the earth afraid, and them that dwell therein; and they shall pour out over every high and eminent place an horrible star,41 Fire, and hail, and flying swords, and many waters, that all fields may be full, and all rivers, with the abundance of great waters.42 And they shall break down the cities and walls, mountains and hills, trees of the wood, and grass of the meadows, and their corn.43 And they shall go stedfastly unto Babylon, and make her afraid.44 They shall come to her, and besiege her, the star and all wrath shall they pour out upon her: then shall the dust and smoke go up unto the heaven, and all they that be about

104

her shall bewail her.45 And they that remain under her shall do service unto them that have put her in fear.46 And thou, Asia, that art partaker of the hope of Babylon, and art the glory of her person:47 Woe be unto thee, thou wretch, because thou hast made thyself like unto her; and hast decked thy daughters in whoredom, that they might please and glory in thy lovers, which have always desired to commit whoredom with thee.48 Thou hast followed her that is hated in all her works and inventions: therefore saith God,49 I will send plagues upon thee; widowhood, poverty, famine, sword, and pestilence, to waste thy houses with destruction and death.50 And the glory of thy Power shall be dried up as a flower, the heat shall arise that is sent over thee.51 Thou shalt be weakened as a poor woman with stripes, and as one chastised with wounds, so that the mighty and lovers shall not be able to receive thee.52 Would I with jealousy have so proceeded against thee, saith the Lord,53 If thou hadst not always slain my chosen, exalting the stroke of thine hands, and saying over their dead, when thou wast drunken,54 Set forth the beauty of thy countenance?55 The reward of thy whoredom shall be in thy bosom, therefore shalt thou receive recompence.56 Like as thou hast done unto my chosen, saith the Lord, even so shall God do unto thee, and shall deliver thee into mischief57 Thy children shall die of hunger, and thou shalt fall through the sword: thy cities shall be broken down, and all thine shall perish with the sword in the field.58 They that be in the mountains shall die of hunger, and eat their own flesh, and drink their own blood, for very hunger of bread, and thirst of water.59 Thou as unhappy shalt come through the sea, and receive plagues again.60 And in the passage they shall rush on the idle city, and shall destroy some portion of thy land, and consume part of thy glory, and shall return to Babylon that was destroyed.61 And thou shalt be cast down by them as stubble, and they shall be unto thee as fire;62 And shall consume thee, and thy cities, thy land, and thy mountains; all thy woods and thy fruitful trees shall they burn up with fire.63 Thy children shall they carry away captive, and, look, what thou hast, they shall spoil it, and mar the beauty of thy face.

4Ezra.16

1 Woe be unto thee, Babylon, and Asia! woe be unto thee, Egypt and Syria!2 Gird up yourselves with cloths of sack and hair, bewail your children, and be sorry; for your destruction is at hand.3 A sword is sent upon you, and who may turn it back?4 A fire is sent among you, and who may quench it?5 Plagues are sent unto you, and what is he that may drive them away?6 May any man drive away an hungry lion in the wood? or may any one quench the fire in stubble, when it hath begun to burn?7 May one turn again the arrow that is shot of a strong archer?8 The mighty Lord sendeth the plagues and who is he that can drive them away?9 A fire shall go forth from his wrath, and who is he that may quench it?10 He shall cast lightnings, and who shall not fear? he shall thunder, and who shall not be afraid?11 The Lord shall threaten, and who shall not be utterly beaten to powder at his presence?12 The earth quaketh, and the foundations thereof; the sea ariseth up with waves from the deep, and the waves of it are troubled, and the fishes thereof also, before the Lord, and before the glory of his power:13 For strong is his right hand that bendeth the bow, his arrows that he shooteth are sharp, and shall not miss, when they begin to be shot into the ends of the world.14 Behold, the plagues are sent, and shall not return again, until they come upon the earth.15 The fire is kindled, and shall not be put out, till it consume the foundation of the earth.16 Like as an arrow which is shot of a mighty archer returneth not backward: even so the plagues that shall be sent upon earth shall not return again.17 Woe is me! woe is me! who will deliver me in those days?18 The beginning of sorrows and great mournings; the beginning of famine and great death; the

beginning of wars, and the powers shall stand in fear; the beginning of evils! what shall I do when these evils shall come?[19] Behold, famine and plague, tribulation and anguish, are sent as scourges for amendment.[20] But for all these things they shall not turn from their wickedness, nor be always mindful of the scourges.[21] Behold, victuals shall be so good cheap upon earth, that they shall think themselves to be in good case, and even then shall evils grow upon earth, sword, famine, and great confusion.[22] For many of them that dwell upon earth shall perish of famine; and the other, that escape the hunger, shall the sword destroy.[23] And the dead shall be cast out as dung, and there shall be no man to comfort them: for the earth shall be wasted, and the cities shall be cast down.[24] There shall be no man left to till the earth, and to sow it[25] The trees shall give fruit, and who shall gather them?[26] The grapes shall ripen, and who shall tread them? for all places shall be desolate of men:[27] So that one man shall desire to see another, and to hear his voice.[28] For of a city there shall be ten left, and two of the field, which shall hide themselves in the thick groves, and in the clefts of the rocks.[29] As in an orchard of Olives upon every tree there are left three or four olives;[30] Or as when a vineyard is gathered, there are left some clusters of them that diligently seek through the vineyard:[31] Even so in those days there shall be three or four left by them that search their houses with the sword.[32] And the earth shall be laid waste, and the fields thereof shall wax old, and her ways and all her paths shall grow full of thorns, because no man shall travel therethrough.[33] The virgins shall mourn, having no bridegrooms; the women shall mourn, having no husbands; their daughters shall mourn, having no helpers.[34] In the wars shall their bridegrooms be destroyed, and their husbands shall perish of famine.[35] Hear now these things and understand them, ye servants of the Lord.[36] Behold, the word of the Lord, receive it: believe not the gods of whom the Lord spake.[37] Behold, the plagues draw nigh, and are not slack.[38] As when a woman with child in the ninth month bringeth forth her son, with two or three hours of her birth great pains compass her womb, which pains, when the child cometh forth, they slack not a moment:[39] Even so shall not the plagues be slack to come upon the earth, and the world shall mourn, and sorrows shall come upon it on every side.[40] O my people, hear my word: make you ready to thy battle, and in those evils be even as pilgrims upon the earth.[41] He that selleth, let him be as he that fleeth away: and he that buyeth, as one that will lose:[42] He that occupieth merchandise, as he that hath no profit by it: and he that buildeth, as he that shall not dwell therein:[43] He that soweth, as if he should not reap: so also he that planteth the vineyard, as he that shall not gather the grapes:[44] They that marry, as they that shall get no children; and they that marry not, as the widowers.[45] And therefore they that labour labour in vain:[46] For strangers shall reap their fruits, and spoil their goods, overthrow their houses, and take their children captives, for in captivity and famine shall they get children.[47] And they that occupy their merchandise with robbery, the more they deck their cities, their houses, their possessions, and their own persons:[48] The more will I be angry with them for their sin, saith the Lord.[49] Like as a whore envieth a right honest and virtuous woman:[50] So shall righteousness hate iniquity, when she decketh herself, and shall accuse her to her face, when he cometh that shall defend him that diligently searcheth out every sin upon earth.[51] And therefore be ye not like thereunto, nor to the works thereof.[52] For yet a little, and iniquity shall be taken away out of the earth, and righteousness shall reign among you.[53] Let not the sinner say that he hath not sinned: for God shall burn coals of fire upon his head, which saith before the Lord God and his glory, I have not sinned.[54] Behold, the Lord knoweth all the works of men, their imaginations, their thoughts, and their hearts:[55] Which spake but the word, Let the earth be made; and it was made: Let the heaven be made; and it was created.[56] In his word were the stars made, and he knoweth the number of them.[57] He searcheth the deep, and the treasures thereof; he hath measured the sea, and what it containeth.[58] He hath shut the sea in the midst of the waters, and with his word hath he hanged the earth upon the waters.[59] He spreadeth out the heavens like a vault; upon the waters hath he founded it.[60] In the desert hath he made springs of water, and pools upon the tops of the mountains, that the floods might pour down from the high rocks to water the earth.[61] He made man, and put his heart in the midst of the body, and gave him breath, life, and understanding.[62] Yea and the Spirit of Almighty God, which made all things, and searcheth out all hidden things in the secrets of the earth,[63] Surely he knoweth your inventions, and what ye think in your hearts, even them that sin, and would hide their sin.[64] Therefore hath the Lord exactly searched out all your works, and he will put you all to shame.[65] And when your sins are brought forth, ye shall be ashamed before men, and your own sins shall be your accusers in that day.[66] What will ye do? or how will ye hide your sins before God and his angels?[67] Behold, God himself is the judge, fear him: leave off from your sins, and forget your iniquities, to meddle no more with them for ever: so shall God lead you forth, and deliver you from all trouble.[68] For, behold, the burning wrath of a great multitude is kindled over you, and they shall take away certain of you, and feed you, being idle, with things offered unto idols.[69] And they that consent unto them shall be had in derision and in reproach, and trodden under foot.[70] For there shall be in every place, and in the next cities, a great insurrection upon those that fear the Lord.[71] They shall be like mad men, sparing none, but still spoiling and destroying those that fear the Lord.[72] For they shall waste and take away their goods, and cast them out of their houses.[73] Then shall they be known, who are my chosen; and they shall be tried as the gold in the fire.[74] Hear, O ye my beloved, saith the Lord: behold, the days of trouble are at hand, but I will deliver you from the same.[75] Be ye not afraid neither doubt; for God is your guide,[76] And the guide of them who keep my commandments and precepts, saith the Lord God: let not your sins weigh you down, and let not your iniquities lift up themselves.[77] Woe be unto them that are bound with their sins, and covered with their iniquities like as a field is covered over with bushes, and the path thereof covered with thorns, that no man may travel through![78] It is left undressed, and is cast into the fire to be consumed therewith.

4 Maccabees

4Mac.1

[1] The subject that I am about to discuss is most philosophical, that is, whether devout reason is sovereign over the emotions. So it is right for me to advise you to pay earnest attention to philosophy.[2] For the subject is essential to everyone who is seeking knowledge, and in addition it includes the praise of the highest virtue -- I mean, of course, rational judgment.[3] If, then, it is evident that reason rules over those emotions that hinder self-control, namely, gluttony and lust,[4] it is also clear that it masters the emotions that hinder one from justice, such as malice, and those that stand in the way of courage, namely anger, fear, and pain.[5] Some might perhaps ask, "If reason rules the emotions, why is it not sovereign over forgetfulness and ignorance?" Their attempt at argument is ridiculous![6] For reason does not rule its own emotions, but those that are opposed to justice, courage, and self-control; and it is not for the purpose of destroying them, but so that one may not give way to them.[7] I could prove to you from many and various examples that reason is dominant over the emotions,[8] but I can demonstrate it best from the noble bravery of those who died for the sake of

virtue, Eleazar and the seven brothers and their mother.[9] All of these, by despising sufferings that bring death, demonstrated that reason controls the emotions.[10] On this anniversary it is fitting for me to praise for their virtues those who, with their mother, died for the sake of nobility and goodness, but I would also call them blessed for the honor in which they are held.[11] For all people, even their torturers, marveled at their courage and endurance, and they became the cause of the downfall of tyranny over their nation. By their endurance they conquered the tyrant, and thus their native land was purified through them.[12] I shall shortly have an opportunity to speak of this; but, as my custom is, I shall begin by stating my main principle, and then I shall turn to their story, giving glory to the all-wise God.[13] Our inquiry, accordingly, is whether reason is sovereign over the emotions.[14] We shall decide just what reason is and what emotion is, how many kinds of emotions there are, and whether reason rules over all these.[15] Now reason is the mind that with sound logic prefers the life of wisdom.[16] Wisdom, next, is the knowledge of divine and human matters and the causes of these.[17] This, in turn, is education in the law, by which we learn divine matters reverently and human affairs to our advantage.[18] Now the kinds of wisdom are rational judgment, justice, courage, and self-control.[19] Rational judgment is supreme over all of these, since by means of it reason rules over the emotions.[20] The two most comprehensive types of the emotions are pleasure and pain; and each of these is by nature concerned with both body and soul.[21] The emotions of both pleasure and pain have many consequences.[22] Thus desire precedes pleasure and delight follows it.[23] Fear precedes pain and sorrow comes after.[24] Anger, as a man will see if he reflects on this experience, is an emotion embracing pleasure and pain.[25] In pleasure there exists even a malevolent tendency, which is the most complex of all the emotions.[26] In the soul it is boastfulness, covetousness, thirst for honor, rivalry, and malice;[27] in the body, indiscriminate eating, gluttony, and solitary gormandizing.[28] Just as pleasure and pain are two plants growing from the body and the soul, so there are many offshoots of these plants,[29] each of which the master cultivator, reason, weeds and prunes and ties up and waters and thoroughly irrigates, and so tames the jungle of habits and emotions.[30] For reason is the guide of the virtues, but over the emotions it is sovereign. Observe now first of all that rational judgment is sovereign over the emotions by virtue of the restraining power of self-control.[31] Self-control, then, is dominance over the desires.[32] Some desires are mental, others are physical, and reason obviously rules over both.[33] Otherwise how is it that when we are attracted to forbidden foods we abstain from the pleasure to be had from them? Is it not because reason is able to rule over appetites? I for one think so.[34] Therefore when we crave seafood and fowl and animals and all sorts of foods that are forbidden to us by the law, we abstain because of domination by reason.[35] For the emotions of the appetites are restrained, checked by the temperate mind, and all the impulses of the body are bridled by reason.

4Mac.2

[1] And why is it amazing that the desires of the mind for the enjoyment of beauty are rendered powerless?[2] It is for this reason, certainly, that the temperate Joseph is praised, because by mental effort he overcame sexual desire.[3] For when he was young and in his prime for intercourse, by his reason he nullified the frenzy of the passions.[4] Not only is reason proved to rule over the frenzied urge of sexual desire, but also over every desire.[5] Thus the law says, "You shall not covet your neighbor's wife...or anything that is your neighbor's."[6] In fact, since the law has told us not to covet, I could prove to you all the more that reason is able to control desires. Just so it is with the emotions that hinder one from justice.[7] Otherwise

how could it be that someone who is habitually a solitary gormandizer, a glutton, or even a drunkard can learn a better way, unless reason is clearly lord of the emotions?[8] Thus, as soon as a man adopts a way of life in accordance with the law, even though he is a lover of money, he is forced to act contrary to his natural ways and to lend without interest to the needy and to cancel the debt when the seventh year arrives.[9] If one is greedy, he is ruled by the law through his reason so that he neither gleans his harvest nor gathers the last grapes from the vineyard. In all other matters we can recognize that reason rules the emotions.[10] For the law prevails even over affection for parents, so that virtue is not abandoned for their sakes.[11] It is superior to love for one's wife, so that one rebukes her when she breaks the law.[12] It takes precedence over love for children, so that one punishes them for misdeeds.[13] It is sovereign over the relationship of friends, so that one rebukes friends when they act wickedly.[14] Do not consider it paradoxical when reason, through the law, can prevail even over enmity. The fruit trees of the enemy are not cut down, but one preserves the property of enemies from the destroyers and helps raise up what has fallen.[15] It is evident that reason rules even the more violent emotions: lust for power, vainglory, boasting, arrogance, and malice.[16] For the temperate mind repels all these malicious emotions, just as it repels anger -- for it is sovereign over even this.[17] When Moses was angry with Dathan and Abiram he did nothing against them in anger, but controlled his anger by reason.[18] For, as I have said, the temperate mind is able to get the better of the emotions, to correct some, and to render others powerless.[19] Why else did Jacob, our most wise father, censure the households of Simeon and Levi for their irrational slaughter of the entire tribe of the Shechemites, saying, "Cursed be their anger"?[20] For if reason could not control anger, he would not have spoken thus.[21] Now when God fashioned man, he planted in him emotions and inclinations,[22] but at the same time he enthroned the mind among the senses as a sacred governor over them all.[23] To the mind he gave the law; and one who lives subject to this will rule a kingdom that is temperate, just, good, and courageous.[24] How is it then, one might say, that if reason is master of the emotions, it does not control forgetfulness and ignorance?

4Mac.3

[1] This notion is entirely ridiculous; for it is evident that reason rules not over its own emotions, but over those of the body.[2] No one of us can eradicate that kind of desire, but reason can provide a way for us not to be enslaved by desire.[3] No one of us can eradicate anger from the mind, but reason can help to deal with anger.[4] No one of us can eradicate malice, but reason can fight at our side so that we are not overcome by malice.[5] For reason does not uproot the emotions but is their antagonist.[6] Now this can be explained more clearly by the story of King David's thirst.[7] David had been attacking the Philistines all day long, and together with the soldiers of his nation had slain many of them.[8] Then when evening fell, he came, sweating and quite exhausted, to the royal tent, around which the whole army of our ancestors had encamped.[9] Now all the rest were at supper,[10] but the king was extremely thirsty, and although springs were plentiful there, he could not satisfy his thirst from them.[11] But a certain irrational desire for the water in the enemy's territory tormented and inflamed him, undid and consumed him.[12] When his guards complained bitterly because of the king's craving, two staunch young soldiers, respecting the king's desire, armed themselves fully, and taking a pitcher climbed over the enemy's ramparts.[13] Eluding the sentinels at the gates, they went searching throughout the enemy camp[14] and found the spring, and from it boldly brought the king a drink.[15] But David, although he was burning with thirst, considered it an altogether fearful danger to his

soul to drink what was regarded as equivalent to blood.[16] Therefore, opposing reason to desire, he poured out the drink as an offering to God.[17] For the temperate mind can conquer the drives of the emotions and quench the flames of frenzied desires;[18] it can overthrow bodily agonies even when they are extreme, and by nobility of reason spurn all domination by the emotions.[19] The present occasion now invites us to a narrative demonstration of temperate reason.[20] At a time when our fathers were enjoying profound peace because of their observance of the law and were prospering, so that even Seleucus Nicanor, king of Asia, had both appropriated money to them for the temple service and recognized their commonwealth --[21] just at that time certain men attempted a revolution against the public harmony and caused many and various disasters.

4Mac.4

[1] Now there was a certain Simon, a political opponent of the noble and good man, Onias, who then held the high priesthood for life. When despite all manner of slander he was unable to injure Onias in the eyes of the nation, he fled the country with the purpose of betraying it.[2] So he came to Apollonius, governor of Syria, Phoenicia, and Cilicia, and said,[3] "I have come here because I am loyal to the king's government, to report that in the Jerusalem treasuries there are deposited tens of thousands in private funds, which are not the property of the temple but belong to King Seleucus."[4] When Apollonius learned the details of these things, he praised Simon for his service to the king and went up to Seleucus to inform him of the rich treasure.[5] On receiving authority to deal with this matter, he proceeded quickly to our country accompanied by the accursed Simon and a very strong military force.[6] He said that he had come with the king's authority to seize the private funds in the treasury.[7] The people indignantly protested his words, considering it outrageous that those who had committed deposits to the sacred treasury should be deprived of them, and did all that they could to prevent it.[8] But, uttering threats, Apollonius went on to the temple.[9] While the priests together with women and children were imploring God in the temple to shield the holy place that was being treated so contemptuously,[10] and while Apollonius was going up with his armed forces to seize the money, angels on horseback with lightning flashing from their weapons appeared from heaven, instilling in them great fear and trembling.[11] Then Apollonius fell down half dead in the temple area that was open to all, stretched out his hands toward heaven, and with tears besought the Hebrews to pray for him and propitiate the wrath of the heavenly army.[12] For he said that he had committed a sin deserving of death, and that if he were delivered he would praise the blessedness of the holy place before all people.[13] Moved by these words, Onias the high priest, although otherwise he had scruples about doing so, prayed for him lest King Seleucus suppose that Apollonius had been overcome by human treachery and not by divine justice.[14] So Apollonius, having been preserved beyond all expectations, went away to report to the king what had happened to him.[15] When King Seleucus died, his son Antiochus Epiphanes succeeded to the throne, an arrogant and terrible man,[16] who removed Onias from the priesthood and appointed Onias's brother Jason as high priest.[17] Jason agreed that if the office were conferred upon him he would pay the king three thousand six hundred and sixty talents annually.[18] So the king appointed him high priest and ruler of the nation.[19] Jason changed the nation's way of life and altered its form of government in complete violation of the law,[20] so that not only was a gymnasium constructed at the very citadel of our native land, but also the temple service was abolished.[21] The divine justice was angered by these acts and caused Antiochus himself to make war on them.[22] For when he was warring against Ptolemy in Egypt, he heard that a rumor of his death had spread and that the people of Jerusalem had rejoiced greatly. He speedily marched against them,[23] and after he had plundered them he issued a decree that if any of them should be found observing the ancestral law they should die.[24] When, by means of his decrees, he had not been able in any way to put an end to the people's observance of the law, but saw that all his threats and punishments were being disregarded,[25] even to the point that women, because they had circumcised their sons, were thrown headlong from heights along with their infants, though they had known beforehand that they would suffer this --[26] when, then, his decrees were despised by the people, he himself, through torture, tried to compel everyone in the nation to eat defiling foods and to renounce Judaism.

4Mac.5

[1] The tyrant Antiochus, sitting in state with his counselors on a certain high place, and with his armed soldiers standing about him,[2] ordered the guards to seize each and every Hebrew and to compel them to eat pork and food sacrificed to idols.[3] If any were not willing to eat defiling food, they were to be broken on the wheel and killed.[4] And when many persons had been rounded up, one man, Eleazar by name, leader of the flock, was brought before the king. He was a man of priestly family, learned in the law, advanced in age, and known to many in the tyrant's court because of his philosophy.[5] When Antiochus saw him he said,[6] "Before I begin to torture you, old man, I would advise you to save yourself by eating pork,[7] for I respect your age and your gray hairs. Although you have had them for so long a time, it does not seem to me that you are a philosopher when you observe the religion of the Jews.[8] Why, when nature has granted it to us, should you abhor eating the very excellent meat of this animal?[9] It is senseless not to enjoy delicious things that are not shameful, and wrong to spurn the gifts of nature.[10] It seems to me that you will do something even more senseless if, by holding a vain opinion concerning the truth, you continue to despise me to your own hurt.[11] Will you not awaken from your foolish philosophy, dispel your futile reasonings, adopt a mind appropriate to your years, philosophize according to the truth of what is beneficial,[12] and have compassion on your old age by honoring my humane advice?[13] For consider this, that if there is some power watching over this religion of yours, it will excuse you from any transgression that arises out of compulsion."[14] When the tyrant urged him in this fashion to eat meat unlawfully, Eleazar asked to have a word.[15] When he had received permission to speak, he began to address the people as follows:[16] "We, O Antiochus, who have been persuaded to govern our lives by the divine law, think that there is no compulsion more powerful than our obedience to the law.[17] Therefore we consider that we should not transgress it in any respect.[18] Even if, as you suppose, our law were not truly divine and we had wrongly held it to be divine, not even so would it be right for us to invalidate our reputation for piety.[19] Therefore do not suppose that it would be a petty sin if we were to eat defiling food;[20] to transgress the law in matters either small or great is of equal seriousness,[21] for in either case the law is equally despised.[22] You scoff at our philosophy as though living by it were irrational,[23] but it teaches us self-control, so that we master all pleasures and desires, and it also trains us in courage, so that we endure any suffering willingly;[24] it instructs us in justice, so that in all our dealings we act impartially, and it teaches us piety, so that with proper reverence we worship the only real God.[25] "Therefore we do not eat defiling food; for since we believe that the law was established by God, we know that in the nature of things the Creator of the world in giving us the law has shown sympathy toward

us.²⁶ He has permitted us to eat what will be most suitable for our lives, but he has forbidden us to eat meats that would be contrary to this.²⁷ It would be tyrannical for you to compel us not only to transgress the law, but also to eat in such a way that you may deride us for eating defiling foods, which are most hateful to us.²⁸ But you shall have no such occasion to laugh at me,²⁹ nor will I transgress the sacred oaths of my ancestors concerning the keeping of the law,³⁰ not even if you gouge out my eyes and burn my entrails.³¹ I am not so old and cowardly as not to be young in reason on behalf of piety.³² Therefore get your torture wheels ready and fan the fire more vehemently!³³ I do not so pity my old age as to break the ancestral law by my own act.³⁴ I will not play false to you, O law that trained me, nor will I renounce you, beloved self-control.³⁵ I will not put you to shame, philosophical reason, nor will I reject you, honored priesthood and knowledge of the law.³⁶ You, O king, shall not stain the honorable mouth of my old age, nor my long life lived lawfully.³⁷ The fathers will receive me as pure, as one who does not fear your violence even to death.³⁸ You may tyrannize the ungodly, but you shall not dominate my religious principles either by word or by deed."

4Mac.6

¹When Eleazar in this manner had made eloquent response to the exhortations of the tyrant, the guards who were standing by dragged him violently to the instruments of torture.² First they stripped the old man, who remained adorned with the gracefulness of his piety.³ And after they had tied his arms on each side they scourged him,⁴ while a herald opposite him cried out, "Obey the king's commands!"⁵ But the courageous and noble man, as a true Eleazar, was unmoved, as though being tortured in a dream;⁶ yet while the old man's eyes were raised to heaven, his flesh was being torn by scourges, his blood flowing, and his sides were being cut to pieces.⁷ And though he fell to the ground because his body could not endure the agonies, he kept his reason upright and unswerving.⁸ One of the cruel guards rushed at him and began to kick him in the side to make him get up again after he fell.⁹ But he bore the pains and scorned the punishment and endured the tortures.¹⁰ And like a noble athlete the old man, while being beaten, was victorious over his torturers;¹¹ in fact, with his face bathed in sweat, and gasping heavily for breath, he amazed even his torturers by his courageous spirit.¹²At that point, partly out of pity for his old age,¹³ partly out of sympathy from their acquaintance with him, partly out of admiration for his endurance, some of the king's retinue came to him and said,¹⁴ "Eleazar, why are you so irrationally destroying yourself through these evil things?¹⁵ We will set before you some cooked meat; save yourself by pretending to eat pork."¹⁶But Eleazar, as though more bitterly tormented by this counsel, cried out:¹⁷ "May we, the children of Abraham, never think so basely that out of cowardice we feign a role unbecoming to us!¹⁸ For it would be irrational if we, who have lived in accordance with truth to old age and have maintained in accordance with law the reputation of such a life, should now change our course¹⁹ become a pattern of impiety to the young, in becoming an example of the eating of defiling food.²⁰ It would be shameful if we should survive for a little while and during that time be a laughing stock to all for our cowardice,²¹ and if we should be despised by the tyrant as unmanly, and not protect our divine law even to death.²² Therefore, O children of Abraham, die nobly for your religion!²³ And you, guards of the tyrant, why do you delay?"²⁴When they saw that he was so courageous in the face of the afflictions, and that he had not been changed by their compassion, the guards brought him to the fire.²⁵ There they burned him with maliciously contrived instruments, threw him down, and poured stinking liquids

into his nostrils.²⁶ When he was now burned to his very bones and about to expire, he lifted up his eyes to God and said,²⁷ "You know, O God, that though I might have saved myself, I am dying in burning torments for the sake of the law.²⁸ Be merciful to your people, and let our punishment suffice for them.²⁹ Make my blood their purification, and take my life in exchange for theirs."³⁰ And after he said this, the holy man died nobly in his tortures, and by reason he resisted even to the very tortures of death for the sake of the law.³¹Admittedly, then, devout reason is sovereign over the emotions.³² For if the emotions had prevailed over reason, we would have testified to their domination.³³ But now that reason has conquered the emotions, we properly attribute to it the power to govern.³⁴ And it is right for us to acknowledge the dominance of reason when it masters even external agonies. It would be ridiculous to deny it.³⁵ And I have proved not only that reason has mastered agonies, but also that it masters pleasures and in no respect yields to them.

4Mac.7

¹For like a most skilful pilot, the reason of our father Eleazar steered the ship of religion over the sea of the emotions,² and though buffeted by the stormings of the tyrant and overwhelmed by the mighty waves of tortures,³ in no way did he turn the rudder of religion until he sailed into the haven of immortal victory.⁴ No city besieged with many ingenious war machines has ever held out as did that most holy man. Although his sacred life was consumed by tortures and racks, he conquered the besiegers with the shield of his devout reason.⁵ For in setting his mind firm like a jutting cliff, our father Eleazar broke the maddening waves of the emotions.⁶ O priest, worthy of the priesthood, you neither defiled your sacred teeth nor profaned your stomach, which had room only for reverence and purity, by eating defiling foods.⁷ O man in harmony with the law and philosopher of divine life!⁸ Such should be those who are administrators of the law, shielding it with their own blood and noble sweat in sufferings even to death.⁹ You, father, strengthened our loyalty to the law through your glorious endurance, and you did not abandon the holiness which you praised, but by your deeds you made your words of divine philosophy credible.¹⁰ O aged man, more powerful than tortures; O elder, fiercer than fire; O supreme king over the passions, Eleazar!¹¹ For just as our father Aaron, armed with the censer, ran through the multitude of the people and conquered the fiery angel,¹² so the descendant of Aaron, Eleazar, though being consumed by the fire, remained unmoved in his reason.¹³ Most amazing, indeed, though he was an old man, his body no longer tense and firm, his muscles flabby, his sinews feeble, he became young again¹⁴ in spirit through reason; and by reason like that of Isaac he rendered the many-headed rack ineffective.¹⁵ O man of blessed age and of venerable gray hair and of law-abiding life, whom the faithful seal of death has perfected!¹⁶If, therefore, because of piety an aged man despised tortures even to death, most certainly devout reason is governor of the emotions.¹⁷ Some perhaps might say, "Not every one has full command of his emotions, because not every one has prudent reason."¹⁸ But as many as attend to religion with a whole heart, these alone are able to control the passions of the flesh,¹⁹ since they believe that they, like our patriarchs Abraham and Isaac and Jacob, do not die to God, but live in God.²⁰ No contradiction therefore arises when some persons appear to be dominated by their emotions because of the weakness of their reason.²¹ What person who lives as a philosopher by the whole rule of philosophy, and trusts in God,²² and knows that it is blessed to endure any suffering for the sake of virtue, would not be able to overcome the emotions through godliness?²³ For only the wise and courageous man is lord of his emotions.

4Mac.8

[1]For this is why even the very young, by following a philosophy in accordance with devout reason, have prevailed over the most painful instruments of torture. [2]For when the tyrant was conspicuously defeated in his first attempt, being unable to compel an aged man to eat defiling foods, then in violent rage he commanded that others of the Hebrew captives be brought, and that any who ate defiling food should be freed after eating, but if any were to refuse, these should be tortured even more cruelly. [3]When the tyrant had given these orders, seven brothers -- handsome, modest, noble, and accomplished in every way -- were brought before him along with their aged mother. [4]When the tyrant saw them, grouped about their mother as if in a chorus, he was pleased with them. And struck by their appearance and nobility, he smiled at them, and summoned them nearer and said, [5]"Young men, I admire each and every one of you in a kindly manner, and greatly respect the beauty and the number of such brothers. Not only do I advise you not to display the same madness as that of the old man who has just been tortured, but I also exhort you to yield to me and enjoy my friendship. [6]Just as I am able to punish those who disobey my orders, so I can be a benefactor to those who obey me. [7]Trust me, then, and you will have positions of authority in my government if you will renounce the ancestral tradition of your national life. [8]And enjoy your youth by adopting the Greek way of life and by changing your manner of living. [9]But if by disobedience you rouse my anger, you will compel me to destroy each and every one of you with dreadful punishments through tortures. [10]Therefore take pity on yourselves. Even I, your enemy, have compassion for your youth and handsome appearance. [11]Will you not consider this, that if you disobey, nothing remains for you but to die on the rack?" [12]When he had said these things, he ordered the instruments of torture to be brought forward so as to persuade them out of fear to eat the defiling food. [13]And when the guards had placed before them wheels and joint-dislocators, rack and hooks and catapults and caldrons, braziers and thumbscrews and iron claws and wedges and bellows, the tyrant resumed speaking: [14]"Be afraid, young fellows, and whatever justice you revere will be merciful to you when you transgress under compulsion." [15]But when they had heard the inducements and saw the dreadful devices, not only were they not afraid, but they also opposed the tyrant with their own philosophy, and by their right reasoning nullified his tyranny. [16]Let us consider, on the other hand, what arguments might have been used if some of them had been cowardly and unmanly. Would they not have been these? [17]"O wretches that we are and so senseless! Since the king has summoned and exhorted us to accept kind treatment if we obey him, [18]why do we take pleasure in vain resolves and venture upon a disobedience that brings death? [19]O men and brothers, should we not fear the instruments of torture and consider the threats of torments, and give up this vain opinion and this arrogance that threatens to destroy us? [20]Let us take pity on our youth and have compassion on our mother's age; [21]and let us seriously consider that if we disobey we are dead! [22]Also, divine justice will excuse us for fearing the king when we are under compulsion. [23]Why do we banish ourselves from this most pleasant life and deprive ourselves of this delightful world? [24]Let us not struggle against compulsion nor take hollow pride in being put to the rack. [25]Not even the law itself would arbitrarily slay us for fearing the instruments of torture. [26]Why does such contentiousness excite us and such a fatal stubbornness please us, when we can live in peace if we obey the king?" [27]But the youths, though about to be tortured, neither said any of these things nor even seriously considered them. [28]For they were contemptuous of the emotions and sovereign over agonies, [29]so that as soon as the tyrant had ceased counseling them to eat defiling food, all with one voice together, as from one mind, said:

4Mac.9

[1]"Why do you delay, O tyrant? For we are ready to die rather than transgress our ancestral commandments; [2]we are obviously putting our forefathers to shame unless we should practice ready obedience to the law and to Moses our counselor. [3]Tyrant and counselor of lawlessness, in your hatred for us do not pity us more than we pity ourselves. [4]For we consider this pity of yours which insures our safety through transgression of the law to be more grievous than death itself. [5]You are trying to terrify us by threatening us with death by torture, as though a short time ago you learned nothing from Eleazar. [6]And if the aged men of the Hebrews because of their religion lived piously while enduring torture, it would be even more fitting that we young men should die despising your coercive tortures, which our aged instructor also overcame. [7]Therefore, tyrant, put us to the test; and if you take our lives because of our religion, do not suppose that you can injure us by torturing us. [8]For we, through this severe suffering and endurance, shall have the prize of virtue and shall be with God, for whom we suffer; [9]but you, because of your bloodthirstiness toward us, will deservedly undergo from the divine justice eternal torment by fire." [10]When they had said these things the tyrant not only was angry, as at those who are disobedient, but also was enraged, as at those who are ungrateful. [11]Then at his command the guards brought forward the eldest, and having torn off his tunic, they bound his hands and arms with thongs on each side. [12]When they had worn themselves out beating him with scourges, without accomplishing anything, they placed him upon the wheel. [13]When the noble youth was stretched out around this, his limbs were dislocated, [14]and though broken in every member he denounced the tyrant, saying, [15]"Most abominable tyrant, enemy of heavenly justice, savage of mind, you are mangling me in this manner, not because I am a murderer, or as one who acts impiously, but because I protect the divine law." [16]And when the guards said, "Agree to eat so that you may be released from the tortures," [17]he replied, "You abominable lackeys, your wheel is not so powerful as to strangle my reason. Cut my limbs, burn my flesh, and twist my joints. [18]Through all these tortures I will convince you that sons of the Hebrews alone are invincible where virtue is concerned." [19]While he was saying these things, they spread fire under him, and while fanning the flames they tightened the wheel further. [20]The wheel was completely smeared with blood, and the heap of coals was being quenched by the drippings of gore, and pieces of flesh were falling off the axles of the machine. [21]Although the ligaments joining his bones were already severed, the courageous youth, worthy of Abraham, did not groan, [22]but as though transformed by fire into immortality he nobly endured the rackings. [23]"Imitate me, brothers," he said. "Do not leave your post in my struggle or renounce our courageous brotherhood. [24]Fight the sacred and noble battle for religion. Thereby the just Providence of our ancestors may become merciful to our nation and take vengeance on the accursed tyrant." [25]When he had said this, the saintly youth broke the thread of life. [26]While all were marveling at his courageous spirit, the guards brought in the next eldest, and after fitting themselves with iron gauntlets having sharp hooks, they bound him to the torture machine and catapult. [27]Before torturing him, they inquired if he were willing to eat, and they heard this noble decision. [28]These leopard-like beasts tore out his sinews with the iron hands, flayed all his flesh up to his chin, and tore away his scalp. But he steadfastly endured this agony and said, [29]"How sweet is any kind of death for the religion of our fathers!" [30]To the tyrant he said, "Do you not think, you most savage tyrant, that you are being

tortured more than I, as you see the arrogant design of your tyranny being defeated by our endurance for the sake of religion?[31] I lighten my pain by the joys that come from virtue,[32] but you suffer torture by the threats that come from impiety. You will not escape, most abominable tyrant, the judgments of the divine wrath."

4Mac.10

[1]When he too had endured a glorious death, the third was led in, and many repeatedly urged him to save himself by tasting the meat.[2] But he shouted, "Do you not know that the same father begot me and those who died, and the same mother bore me, and that I was brought up on the same teachings?[3] I do not renounce the noble kinship that binds me to my brothers."[45] Enraged by the man's boldness, they disjointed his hands and feet with their instruments, dismembering him by prying his limbs from their sockets,[6] and breaking his fingers and arms and legs and elbows.[7] Since they were not able in any way to break his spirit, they abandoned the instruments and scalped him with their fingernails in a Scythian fashion.[8] They immediately brought him to the wheel, and while his vertebrae were being dislocated upon it he saw his own flesh torn all around and drops of blood flowing from his entrails.[9] When he was about to die, he said,[10] "We, most abominable tyrant, are suffering because of our godly training and virtue,[11] but you, because of your impiety and bloodthirstiness, will undergo unceasing torments."[12]When he also had died in a manner worthy of his brothers, they dragged in the fourth, saying,[13] "As for you, do not give way to the same insanity as your brothers, but obey the king and save yourself.[14] But he said to them, "You do not have a fire hot enough to make me play the coward.[15] No, by the blessed death of my brothers, by the eternal destruction of the tyrant, and by the everlasting life of the pious, I will not renounce our noble brotherhood.[16] Contrive tortures, tyrant, so that you may learn from them that I am a brother to those who have just been tortured."[17] When he heard this, the bloodthirsty, murderous, and utterly abominable Antiochus gave orders to cut out his tongue.[18] But he said, "Even if you remove my organ of speech, God hears also those who are mute.[19] See, here is my tongue; cut it off, for in spite of this you will not make our reason speechless.[20] Gladly, for the sake of God, we let our bodily members be mutilated.[21] God will visit you swiftly, for you are cutting out a tongue that has been melodious with divine hymns."

4Mac.11

[1]When this one died also, after being cruelly tortured, the fifth leaped up, saying,[2] "I will not refuse, tyrant, to be tortured for the sake of virtue.[3] I have come of my own accord, so that by murdering me you will incur punishment from the heavenly justice for even more crimes.[4] Hater of virtue, hater of mankind, for what act of ours are you destroying us in this way?[5] Is it because we revere the Creator of all things and live according to his virtuous law?[6] But these deeds deserve honors, not tortures."[79] While he was saying these things, the guards bound him and dragged him to the catapult;[10] they tied him to it on his knees, and fitting iron clamps on them, they twisted his back around the wedge on the wheel, so that he was completely curled back like a scorpion, and all his members were disjointed.[11] In this condition, gasping for breath and in anguish of body,[12] he said, "Tyrant, they are splendid favors that you grant us against your will, because through these noble sufferings you give us an opportunity to show our endurance for the law."[13]After he too had died, the sixth, a mere boy, was led in. When the tyrant inquired whether he was willing to eat and be released, he said,[14] "I am younger in age than my brothers, but I am their equal in mind.[15] Since to this end we were born and bred, we ought likewise to die for the same principles.[16] So if you intend to torture

me for not eating defiling foods, go on torturing!"[17] When he had said this, they led him to the wheel.[18] He was carefully stretched tight upon it, his back was broken, and he was roasted from underneath.[19] To his back they applied sharp spits that had been heated in the fire, and pierced his ribs so that his entrails were burned through.[20] While being tortured he said, "O contest befitting holiness, in which so many of us brothers have been summoned to an arena of sufferings for religion, and in which we have not been defeated![21] For religious knowledge, O tyrant, is invincible.[22] I also, equipped with nobility, will die with my brothers,[23] and I myself will bring a great avenger upon you, you inventor of tortures and enemy of those who are truly devout.[24] We six boys have paralyzed your tyranny![25] Since you have not been able to persuade us to change our mind or to force us to eat defiling foods, is not this your downfall?[26] Your fire is cold to us, and the catapults painless, and your violence powerless.[27] For it is not the guards of the tyrant but those of the divine law that are set over us; therefore, unconquered, we hold fast to reason."

4Mac.12

[1]When he also, thrown into the caldron, had died a blessed death, the seventh and youngest of all came forward.[2] Even though the tyrant had been fearfully reproached by the brothers, he felt strong compassion for this child when he saw that he was already in fetters. He summoned him to come nearer and tried to console him, saying,[3] "You see the result of your brothers' stupidity, for they died in torments because of their disobedience.[4] You too, if you do not obey, will be miserably tortured and die before your time,[5] but if you yield to persuasion you will be my friend and a leader in the government of the kingdom."[6] When he had so pleaded, he sent for the boy's mother to show compassion on her who had been bereaved of so many sons and to influence her to persuade the surviving son to obey and save himself.[7] But when his mother had exhorted him in the Hebrew language, as we shall tell a little later,[8] he said, "Let me loose, let me speak to the king and to all his friends that are with him.[9] Extremely pleased by the boy's declaration, they freed him at once.[10] Running to the nearest of the braziers,[11] he said, "You profane tyrant, most impious of all the wicked, since you have received good things and also your kingdom from God, were you not ashamed to murder his servants and torture on the wheel those who practice religion?[12] Because of this, justice has laid up for you intense and eternal fire and tortures, and these throughout all time will never let you go.[13] As a man, were you not ashamed, you most savage beast, to cut out the tongues of men who have feelings like yours and are made of the same elements as you, and to maltreat and torture them in this way?[14] Surely they by dying nobly fulfilled their service to God, but you will wail bitterly for having slain without cause the contestants for virtue."[15] Then because he too was about to die, he said,[16] "I do not desert the excellent example of my brothers,[17] and I call on the God of our fathers to be merciful to our nation;[18] but on you he will take vengeance both in this present life and when you are dead."[19] After he had uttered these imprecations, he flung himself into the braziers and so ended his life.

4Mac.13

[1]Since, then, the seven brothers despised sufferings even unto death, everyone must concede that devout reason is sovereign over the emotions.[2] For if they had been slaves to their emotions and had eaten defiling food, we would say that they had been conquered by these emotions.[3] But in fact it was not so. Instead, by reason, which is praised before God, they prevailed over their emotions.[4] The supremacy of the mind over these cannot be overlooked, for the brothers mastered both emotions and pains.[5] How then can one fail to confess the sovereignty of right reason over emotion in those

who were not turned back by fiery agonies?[6] For just as towers jutting out over harbors hold back the threatening waves and make it calm for those who sail into the inner basin,[7] so the seven-towered right reason of the youths, by fortifying the harbor of religion, conquered the tempest of the emotions.[8] For they constituted a holy chorus of religion and encouraged one another, saying,[9] "Brothers, let us die like brothers for the sake of the law; let us imitate the three youths in Assyria who despised the same ordeal of the furnace.[10] Let us not be cowardly in the demonstration of our piety."[11] While one said, "Courage, brother," another said, "Bear up nobly,"[12] and another reminded them, "Remember whence you came, and the father by whose hand Isaac would have submitted to being slain for the sake of religion."[13] Each of them and all of them together looking at one another, cheerful and undaunted, said, "Let us with all our hearts consecrate ourselves to God, who gave us our lives, and let us use our bodies as a bulwark for the law.[14] Let us not fear him who thinks he is killing us,[15] for great is the struggle of the soul and the danger of eternal torment lying before those who transgress the commandment of God.[16] Therefore let us put on the full armor of self-control, which is divine reason.[17] For if we so die, Abraham and Isaac and Jacob will welcome us, and all the fathers will praise us."[18] Those who were left behind said to each of the brothers who were being dragged away, "Do not put us to shame, brother, or betray the brothers who have died before us."[19] You are not ignorant of the affection of brotherhood, which the divine and all-wise Providence has bequeathed through the fathers to their descendants and which was implanted in the mother's womb.[20] There each of the brothers dwelt the same length of time and was shaped during the same period of time; and growing from the same blood and through the same life, they were brought to the light of day.[21] When they were born after an equal time of gestation, they drank milk from the same fountains. For such embraces brotherly-loving souls are nourished;[22] and they grow stronger from this common nurture and daily companionship, and from both general education and our discipline in the law of God.[23] Therefore, when sympathy and brotherly affection had been so established, the brothers were the more sympathetic to one another.[24] Since they had been educated by the same law and trained in the same virtues and brought up in right living, they loved one another all the more.[25] A common zeal for nobility expanded their goodwill and harmony toward one another,[26] because, with the aid of their religion, they rendered their brotherly love more fervent.[27] But although nature and companionship and virtuous habits had augmented the affection of brotherhood, those who were left endured for the sake of religion, while watching their brothers being maltreated and tortured to death.

4Mac.14

[1] Furthermore, they encouraged them to face the torture, so that they not only despised their agonies, but also mastered the emotions of brotherly love.[2] O reason, more royal than kings and freer than the free![3] O sacred and harmonious concord of the seven brothers on behalf of religion![4] None of the seven youths proved coward or shrank from death,[5] but all of them, as though running the course toward immortality, hastened to death by torture.[6] Just as the hands and feet are moved in harmony with the guidance of the mind, so those holy youths, as though moved by an immortal spirit of devotion, agreed to go to death for its sake.[7] O most holy seven, brothers in harmony! For just as the seven days of creation move in choral dance around religion,[8] so these youths, forming a chorus, encircled the sevenfold fear of tortures and dissolved it.[9] Even now, we ourselves shudder as we hear of the tribulations of these young men; they not only saw what was happening, yes, not only heard the direct word of threat, but also bore the sufferings patiently, and in agonies of fire at that.[10] What could be more excruciatingly painful than this? For the power of fire is intense and swift, and it consumed their bodies quickly.[11] Do not consider it amazing that reason had full command over these men in their tortures, since the mind of woman despised even more diverse agonies,[12] for the mother of the seven young men bore up under the rackings of each one of her children.[13] Observe how complex is a mother's love for her children, which draws everything toward an emotion felt in her inmost parts.[14] Even unreasoning animals, like mankind, have a sympathy and parental love for their offspring.[15] For example, among birds, the ones that are tame protect their young by building on the housetops,[16] and the others, by building in precipitous chasms and in holes and tops of trees, hatch the nestlings and ward off the intruder.[17] If they are not able to keep him away, they do what they can to help their young by flying in circles around them in the anguish of love, warning them with their own calls.[18] And why is it necessary to demonstrate sympathy for children by the example of unreasoning animals,[19] since even bees at the time for making honeycombs defend themselves against intruders as though with an iron dart sting those who approach their hive and defend it even to the death?[20] But sympathy for her children did not sway the mother of the young men; she was of the same mind as Abraham.

4Mac.15

[1] O reason of the children, tyrant over the emotions! O religion, more desirable to the mother than her children![2] Two courses were open to this mother, that of religion, and that of preserving her seven sons for a time, as the tyrant had promised.[3] She loved religion more, religion that preserves them for eternal life according to God's promise.[4] In what manner might I express the emotions of parents who love their children? We impress upon the character of a small child a wondrous likeness both of mind and of form. Especially is this true of mothers, who because of their birthpangs have a deeper sympathy toward their offspring than do the fathers.[5] Considering that mothers are the weaker sex and give birth to many, they are more devoted to their children.[6] The mother of the seven boys, more than any other mother, loved her children. In seven pregnancies she had implanted in herself tender love toward them,[7] and because of the many pains she suffered with each of them she had sympathy for them;[8] yet because of the fear of God she disdained the temporary safety of her children.[9] Not only so, but also because of the nobility of her sons and their ready obedience to the law she felt a greater tenderness toward them.[10] For they were righteous and self-controlled and brave and magnanimous, and loved their brothers and their mother, so that they obeyed her even to death in keeping the ordinances.[11] Nevertheless, though so many factors influenced the mother to suffer with them out of love for her children, in the case of none of them were the various tortures strong enough to pervert her reason.[12] Instead, the mother urged them on, each child singly and all together, to death for the sake of religion.[13] O sacred nature and affection of parental love, yearning of parents toward offspring, nurture and indomitable suffering by mothers![14] This mother, who saw them tortured and burned one by one, because of religion did not change her attitude.[15] She watched the flesh of her children consumed by fire, their toes and fingers scattered on the ground, and the flesh of the head to the chin exposed like masks.[16] O mother, tried now by more bitter pains than even the birth-pangs you suffered for them![17] O woman, who alone gave birth to such complete devotion![18] When the first-born breathed his last it did not turn you aside, nor when the second in torments looked at you piteously nor when the third expired;[19] nor did you weep when you looked at the eyes of each one in his tortures

gazing boldly at the same agonies, and saw in their nostrils the signs of the approach of death.[20] When you saw the flesh of children burned upon the flesh of other children, severed hands upon hands, scalped heads upon heads, and corpses fallen on other corpses and when you saw the place filled with many spectators of the torturings, you did not shed tears. [21] Neither the melodies of sirens nor the songs of swans attract the attention of their hearers as did the voices of the children in torture calling to their mother.[22] How great and how many torments the mother then suffered as her sons were tortured on the wheel and with the hot irons![23] But devout reason, giving her heart a man's courage in the very midst of her emotions, strengthened her to disregard her temporal love for her children.[24] Although she witnessed the destruction of seven children and the ingenious and various rackings, this noble mother disregarded all these because of faith in God.[25] For as in the council chamber of her own soul she saw mighty advocates -- nature, family, parental love, and the rackings of her children --[26] this mother held two ballots, one bearing death and the other deliverance for her children.[27] She did not approve the deliverance which would preserve the seven sons for a short time,[28] but as the daughter of God-fearing Abraham she remembered his fortitude.[29] O mother of the nation, vindicator of the law and champion of religion, who carried away the prize of the contest in your heart![30] O more noble than males in steadfastness, and more manly than men in endurance![31] Just as Noah's ark, carrying the world in the universal flood, stoutly endured the waves,[32] so you, O guardian of the law, overwhelmed from every side by the flood of your emotions and the violent winds, the torture of your sons, endured nobly and withstood the wintry storms that assail religion.

4Mac.16

[1] If, then, a woman, advanced in years and mother of seven sons, endured seeing her children tortured to death, it must be admitted that devout reason is sovereign over the emotions.[2] Thus I have demonstrated not only that men have ruled over the emotions, but also that a woman has despised the fiercest tortures.[3] The lions surrounding Daniel were not so savage, nor was the raging fiery furnace of Mishael so intensely hot, as was her innate parental love, inflamed as she saw her seven sons tortured in such varied ways.[4] But the mother quenched so many and such great emotions by devout reason.[5] Consider this also. If this woman, though a mother, had been fainthearted, she would have mourned over them and perhaps spoken as follows:[6] "O how wretched am I and many times unhappy! After bearing seven children, I am now the mother of none![7] O seven childbirths all in vain, seven profitless pregnancies, fruitless nurturings and wretched nursings![8] In vain, my sons, I endured many birth-pangs for you, and the more grievous anxieties of your upbringing.[9] Alas for my children, some unmarried, others married and without offspring. I shall not see your children or have the happiness of being called grandmother.[10] Alas, I who had so many and beautiful children am a widow and alone, with many sorrows.[11] Nor when I die, shall I have any of my sons to bury me."[12] Yet the sacred and God-fearing mother did not wail with such a lament for any of them, nor did she dissuade any of them from dying, nor did she grieve as they were dying,[13] but, as though having a mind like adamant and giving rebirth for immortality to the whole number of her sons, she implored them and urged them on to death for the sake of religion.[14] O mother, soldier of God in the cause of religion, elder and woman! By steadfastness you have conquered even a tyrant, and in word and deed you have proved more powerful than a man.[15] For when you and your sons were arrested together, you stood and watched Eleazar being tortured, and said to your sons in the Hebrew language,[16] "My sons, noble is the contest to which you are called to bear witness for the nation. Fight zealously for our ancestral law.[17] For it would be shameful if, while an aged man endures such agonies for the sake of religion, you young men were to be terrified by tortures.[18] Remember that it is through God that you have had a share in the world and have enjoyed life,[19] and therefore you ought to endure any suffering for the sake of God.[20] For his sake also our father Abraham was zealous to sacrifice his son Isaac, the ancestor of our nation; and when Isaac saw his father's hand wielding a sword and descending upon him, he did not cower.[21] And Daniel the righteous was thrown to the lions, and Hananiah, Azariah, and Mishael were hurled into the fiery furnace and endured it for the sake of God. [22] You too must have the same faith in God and not be grieved.[23] It is unreasonable for people who have religious knowledge not to withstand pain."[24] By these words the mother of the seven encouraged and persuaded each of her sons to die rather than violate God's commandment.[25] They knew also that those who die for the sake of God live in God, as do Abraham and Isaac and Jacob and all the patriarchs.

4Mac.17

[1] Some of the guards said that when she also was about to be seized and put to death she threw herself into the flames so that no one might touch her body.[2] O mother, who with your seven sons nullified the violence of the tyrant, frustrated his evil designs, and showed the courage of your faith![3] Nobly set like a roof on the pillars of your sons, you held firm and unswerving against the earthquake of the tortures. [4] Take courage, therefore, O holy-minded mother, maintaining firm an enduring hope in God.[5] The moon in heaven, with the stars, does not stand so august as you, who, after lighting the way of your star-like seven sons to piety, stand in honor before God and are firmly set in heaven with them.[6] For your children were true descendants of father Abraham.[7] If it were possible for us to paint the history of your piety as an artist might, would not those who first beheld it have shuddered as they saw the mother of the seven children enduring their varied tortures to death for the sake of religion?[8] Indeed it would be proper to inscribe upon their tomb these words as a reminder to the people of our nation:[9] "Here lie buried an aged priest and an aged woman and seven sons, because of the violence of the tyrant who wished to destroy the way of life of the Hebrews.[10] They vindicated their nation, looking to God and enduring torture even to death."[11] Truly the contest in which they were engaged was divine,[12] for on that day virtue gave the awards and tested them for their endurance. The prize was immortality in endless life.[13] Eleazar was the first contestant, the mother of the seven sons entered the competition, and the brothers contended.[14] The tyrant was the antagonist, and the world and the human race were the spectators.[15] Reverence for God was victor and gave the crown to its own athletes.[16] Who did not admire the athletes of the divine legislation? Who were not amazed?[17] The tyrant himself and all his council marveled at their endurance,[18] because of which they now stand before the divine throne and live through blessed eternity.[19] For Moses says, "All who are consecrated are under your hands."[20] These, then, who have been consecrated for the sake of God, are honored, not only with this honor, but also by the fact that because of them our enemies did not rule over our nation,[21] the tyrant was punished, and the homeland purified -- they having become, as it were, a ransom for the sin of our nation.[22] And through the blood of those devout ones and their death as an expiation, divine Providence preserved Israel that previously had been afflicted.[23] For the tyrant Antiochus, when he saw the courage of their virtue and their endurance under the tortures, proclaimed them to his soldiers as an example for their own endurance,[24] and

this made them brave and courageous for infantry battle and siege, and he ravaged and conquered all his enemies.

4Mac.18

[1] O Israelite children, offspring of the seed of Abraham, obey this law and exercise piety in every way,[2] knowing that devout reason is master of all emotions, not only of sufferings from within, but also of those from without.[3] Therefore those who gave over their bodies in suffering for the sake of religion were not only admired by men, but also were deemed worthy to share in a divine inheritance.[4] Because of them the nation gained peace, and by reviving observance of the law in the homeland they ravaged the enemy.[5] The tyrant Antiochus was both punished on earth and is being chastised after his death. Since in no way whatever was he able to compel the Israelites to become pagans and to abandon their ancestral customs, he left Jerusalem and marched against the Persians.[6] The mother of seven sons expressed also these principles to her children:[7] "I was a pure virgin and did not go outside my father's house; but I guarded the rib from which woman was made.[8] No seducer corrupted me on a desert plain, nor did the destroyer, the deceitful serpent, defile the purity of my virginity.[9] In the time of my maturity I remained with my husband, and when these sons had grown up their father died. A happy man was he, who lived out his life with good children, and did not have the grief of bereavement.[10] While he was still with you, he taught you the law and the prophets.[11] He read to you about Abel slain by Cain, and Isaac who was offered as a burnt offering, and of Joseph in prison.[12] He told you of the zeal of Phineas, and he taught you about Hananiah, Azariah, and Mishael in the fire.[13] He praised Daniel in the den of the lions and blessed him.[14] He reminded you of the scripture of Isaiah, which says, `Even though you go through the fire, the flame shall not consume you.'[15] He sang to you songs of the psalmist David, who said, `Many are the afflictions of the righteous.'[16] He recounted to you Solomon's proverb, `There is a tree of life for those who do his will.'[17] He confirmed the saying of Ezekiel, `Shall these dry bones live?'[18] For he did not forget to teach you the song that Moses taught, which says,[19] `I kill and I make alive: this is your life and the length of your days.'"[20] O bitter was that day -- and yet not bitter -- when that bitter tyrant of the Greeks quenched fire with fire in his cruel caldrons, and in his burning rage brought those seven sons of the daughter of Abraham to the catapult and back again to more tortures,[21] pierced the pupils of their eyes and cut out their tongues, and put them to death with various tortures.[22] For these crimes divine justice pursued and will pursue the accursed tyrant.[23] But the sons of Abraham with their victorious mother are gathered together into the chorus of the fathers, and have received pure and immortal souls from God,[24] to whom be glory for ever and ever. Amen.

Judeo-Christian Pseudepigrapha and Other Non-Canonical Texts

Introduction

This section is a fascinating compilation of writings that, while not included in the canonical scriptures of mainstream Judaism or Christianity, hold immense historical, religious, and cultural significance. These texts offer a window into the diverse theological ideas and practices that flourished in the intertestamental period and the early centuries of Christianity. This section presents an opportunity to explore the rich tapestry of religious thought that influenced and was peripheral to the dominant streams of Judeo-Christian tradition.

Historical Context - The Pseudepigrapha, a term meaning "falsely attributed," comprises a broad range of texts purportedly written by biblical figures but actually composed much later. These works reflect the religious and theological diversity of an era characterized by significant cultural and political changes. Written from about the third century BCE to the second century CE, these texts often arose from communities grappling with oppression, identity, and theological innovation.

Theological Significance - Theologically, these texts explore themes such as angelology, eschatology, theodicy, and divine justice, often presenting views divergent from those found in the canonical texts. This section focuses on five particularly influential texts:

- **1 Enoch** (The Book of Enoch): Offers extensive and detailed visions of heaven and the workings of the cosmos, significantly influencing early Christian eschatology and angelology. It elaborates on the Watchers, angels who sinned by taking human wives, and their progeny, the Nephilim, contributing significantly to Jewish and early Christian cosmology.

- **Jubilees**: Known as the "Lesser Genesis," it reinterprets the Genesis narrative, emphasizing strict legal observance and the role of angels in the transmission of divine laws, presenting a more deterministic universe closely guided by divine justice.

- **Testament of the Twelve Patriarchs:** Provides ethical teachings and apocalyptic visions attributed to the twelve sons of Jacob. Each testament offers moral instructions, prophecies concerning the descendants of its author, and reflections on virtue and sin.

- **Ascension of Isaiah**: Combines Christian theology with Jewish apocalyptic literature, describing the heavenly journey of the prophet Isaiah. It reflects early Christian beliefs about the nature of Christ and the spiritual world.

- **2 Baruch** (Syriac Apocalypse of Baruch): Written after the destruction of Jerusalem, this text addresses the problem of evil and the end of times, offering consolation to the oppressed through visions of the coming redemption and judgment.

Rationale for Inclusion- These texts were introduced into various Jewish and Christian circles to address specific communal needs, such as reinforcing communal identity, offering eschatological hope, or providing ethical instruction. Their exclusion from the canon often stemmed from their late authorship, geographical marginality, or theological content that diverged from emerging orthodoxies.

The inclusion of these texts in "Apocrypha Complete" not only enriches our understanding of the religious landscape from which mainstream Judaism and Christianity emerged but also highlights the ongoing relevance of these themes in contemporary religious and philosophical discourse. Through their study, scholars and lay readers alike can gain deeper insights into the complexity of early religious thought and the enduring human quest to understand the divine.

Testament of the Twelve Patriarchs

Test. 12 Pat. 1. The Testament of Reuben Concerning Thoughts

[1] The copy of the Testament of Reuben, what things he charged his sons before he died in the hundred and twenty-fifth year of his life. When he was sick two years after the death of Joseph, his sons and his sons' sons were gathered together to visit him. And he said to them, My children, I am dying, and go the way of my fathers. And when he saw there Judah and Gad and Asher, his brethren, he said to them, Raise me up, my brethren, that I may tell to my brethren and to my children what things I have hidden in my heart, for from henceforth my strength fails me. And he arose and kissed them, and said, weeping: Hear, my brethren, give ear to Reuben your father,

what things I command you. And, behold, I call to witness against you this day the God of heaven, that you walk not in the ignorance of youth and fornication wherein I ran greedily, and I defiled the bed of Jacob my father. For I tell you that He smote me with a sore plague in my loins for seven months; and had not Jacob our father prayed for me to the Lord, surely the Lord would have destroyed me. For I was thirty years old when I did this evil in the sight of the Lord, and for seven months I was sick even unto death; and I repented for seven years in the set purpose of my soul before the Lord. Wine and strong drink I drank not, and flesh entered not into my mouth, and I tasted not pleasant food, mourning over my sin, for it was great. And it shall not so be done in Israel. 2 And now hear me, my children, what things I saw in my repentance concerning the seven spirits of error. Seven spirits are given against man from Beliar, and they are chief of the works of youth; and seven spirits are given to him at his creation, that in them should be done every work of man. The first (1 spirit is of life, with which man's whole being is created. The second (2 spirit is of sight, with which arises desire. The third (3 spirit is of hearing, with which comes teaching. The fourth (4 spirit is of smelling, with which taste is given to draw air and breath. The fifth (5 spirit is of speech, with which comes knowledge. The sixth (6 spirit is of taste, with which comes the eating of meats and drinks; and by them strength is produced, for in food is the foundation of strength. The seventh (7 spirit is of begetting and sexual intercourse, with which through love of pleasure sin also enters in: wherefore it is the last in order of creation, and the first of youth, because it is filled with ignorance, which leads the young as a blind man to a pit, and as cattle to a precipice. 3 Besides all these, there is an eighth (8 spirit of sleep, with which is created entrancement of man's nature, and the image of death. With these spirits are mingled the spirits of error. The first (1, the spirit of fornication, dwells in the nature and in the senses; the second (2 spirit of insatiateness in the belly; the third (3 spirit of fighting in the liver and the gall. The fourth (4 is the spirit of fawning and trickery, that through over-officiousness a man may be fair in seeming. The fifth (5 is the spirit of arrogance, that a man may be stirred up and become high-minded. The sixth (6 is the spirit of lying, in perdition and in jealousy to feign words, and to conceal words from kindred and friends. The seventh (7 is the spirit of injustice, with which are theft and pilferings, that a man may work the desire of his heart; for injustice works together with the other spirits by means of craft. Besides all these, the spirit of sleep, the eighth (8 spirit, is conjoined with error and fantasy. And so perishes every young man, darkening his mind from the truth, and not understanding the law of God, nor obeying the admonitions of his fathers, as befell me also in my youth. And now, children, love the truth, and it shall preserve you. I counsel you, hear ye Reuben your father. Pay no heed to the sight of a woman, nor yet associate privately with a female under the authority of a husband, nor meddle with affairs of womankind. For had I not seen Bilhah bathing in a covered place, I had not fallen into this great iniquity. For my mind, dwelling on the woman's nakedness, suffered me not to sleep until I had done the abominable deed. For while Jacob our father was absent with Isaac his father, when we were in Gader, near to Ephratha in Bethlehem, Bilhah was drunk, and lay asleep uncovered in her chamber; and when I went in and beheld her nakedness, I wrought that impiety, and leaving her sleeping I departed. And immediately an angel of God revealed to my father Jacob concerning my impiety, and he came and mourned over me, and touched her no more. 4 Pay no heed, therefore, to the beauty of women, and muse not upon their doings; but walk in singleness of heart in the fear of the Lord, and be labouring in works, and roaming in study

and among your flocks, until the Lord give to you a wife whom He will, that you suffer not as I did. Until my father's death I had not boldness to look steadfastly into the face of Jacob, or to speak to any of my brethren, because of my reproach; and even until now my conscience afflicts me by reason of my sin. And my father comforted me; for he prayed for me unto the Lord, that the anger of the Lord might pass away from me, even as the Lord showed me. From henceforth, then, I was protected, and I sinned not. Therefore, my children, observe all things whatsoever I command you, and you shall not sin. For fornication is the destruction of the soul, separating it from God, and bringing it near to idols, because it deceives the mind and understanding, and brings down young men into hell before their time. For many has fornication destroyed; because, though a man be old or noble, it makes him a reproach and a laughing-stock with Beliar and the sons of men. For in that Joseph kept himself from every woman, and purged his thoughts from all fornication, he found favour before the Lord and men. For the Egyptian woman did many things unto him, and called for magicians, and offered him love potions, and the purpose of his soul admitted no evil desire. Therefore the God of my fathers delivered him from every visible and hidden death. For if fornication overcome not the mind, neither shall Beliar overcome you. 5 Hurtful are women, my children; because, since they have no power or strength over the man, they act subtly through outward guise how they may draw him to themselves; and whom they cannot overcome by strength, him they overcome by craft. For moreover the angel of God told me concerning them, and taught me that women are overcome by the spirit of fornication more than men, and they devise in their heart against men; and by means of their adornment they deceive first their minds, and instil the poison by the glance of their eye, and then they take them captive by their doings, for a woman cannot overcome a man by force. Therefore flee fornication, my children, and command your wives and your daughters that they adorn not their heads and their faces; because every woman who acts deceitfully in these things has been reserved to everlasting punishment. For thus they allured the Watchers before the flood; and as these continually beheld them, they fell into desire each of the other, and they conceived the act in their mind, and changed themselves into the shape of men, and appeared to them in their congress with their husbands; and the women, having in their minds desire toward their apparitions, gave birth to giants, for the Watchers appeared to them as reaching even unto heaven. 6 Beware, therefore, of fornication; and if you wish to be pure in your mind, guard your senses against every woman. And command them likewise not to company with men, that they also be pure in their mind. For constant meetings, even though the ungodly deed be not wrought, are to them an irremediable disease, and to us an everlasting reproach of Beliar; for fornication has neither understanding nor godliness in itself, and all jealousy dwells in the desire thereof. Therefore you will be jealous against the sons of Levi, and will seek to be exalted over them; but you shall not be able, for God will work their avenging, and you shall die by an evil death. For to Levi the Lord gave the sovereignty, and to Judah, and to me also with them, and to Dan and Joseph, that we should be for rulers. Therefore I command you to hearken to Levi, because he shall know the law of the Lord, and shall give ordinances for judgment and sacrifice for all Israel until the completion of the times of Christ, the High Priest whom the Lord has declared. I adjure you by the God of heaven to work truth each one with his neighbour; and draw near to Levi in humbleness of heart, that you may receive a blessing from his mouth. For he shall bless Israel; and specially Judah, because him has the Lord chosen to rule over all the peoples. And worship we his Seed, because He shall die for us in wars visible and invisible, and shall be among you an everlasting king. 7 And Reuben died after that he had given command to his sons; and they placed him in a coffin until they bore him up from Egypt, and buried him in Hebron in the double cave where his fathers were.

Test. 12 Pat. 2. The Testament of Simeon Concerning Envy

1 The copy of the words of Simeon, what things he spoke to his sons before he died, in the hundred and twentieth year of his life, in the year in which Joseph died. For they came to visit him when he was sick, and he strengthened himself and sat up and kissed them, and said to them: 2 Hear, O my children, hear Simeon your father, what things I have in my heart. I was born of Jacob my father, his second son; and my mother Leah called me Simeon, because the Lord heard her prayer. [Gen. 29³³] I became strong exceedingly; I shrank from no deed, nor was I afraid of anything. For my heart was hard, and my mind was unmoveable, and my bowels unfeeling: because valour also has been given from the Most High to men in soul and in body. And at that time I was jealous of Joseph because our father loved him; and I set my mind against him to destroy him, because the prince of deceit sent forth the spirit of jealousy and blinded my mind, that I regarded him not as a brother, and spared not Jacob my father. But his God and the God of his fathers sent forth His angel, and delivered him out of my hands. For when I went into Shechem to bring ointment for the flocks, and Reuben to Dotham, where were our necessaries and all our stores, Judah our brother sold him to the Ishmaelites. And when Reuben came he was grieved, for he wished to have restored him safe to his father. But I was angry against Judah in that he let him go away alive, and for five months I continued wrathful against him; but God restrained me, and withheld from me all working of my hands, for my right hand was half withered for seven days. And I knew, my children, that because of Joseph this happened to me, and I repented and wept; and I besought the Lord that He would restore my hand unto me, and that I might be kept from all pollution and envy, and from all folly. For I knew that I had devised an evil deed before the Lord and Jacob my father, on account of Joseph my brother, in that I envied him. 3 And now, children, take heed of the spirit of deceit and of envy. For envy rules over the whole mind of a man, and suffers him neither to eat, nor to drink, nor to do any good thing: it ever suggests to him to destroy him that he envies; and he that is envied ever flourishes, but he that envies fades away. Two years of days I afflicted my soul with fasting in the fear of the Lord, and I learned that deliverance from envy comes by the fear of God. If a man flee to the Lord, the evil spirit runs away from him, and his mind becomes easy. And henceforward he sympathizes with him whom he envied, and condemns not those who love him, and so ceases from his envy. 4 And my father asked concerning me, because he saw that I was sad; and I said, I am pained in my liver. For I mourned more than they all, because I was guilty of the selling of Joseph. And when we went down into Egypt, and he bound me as a spy, I knew that I was suffering justly, and I grieved not. Now Joseph was a good man, and had the Spirit of God within him: compassionate and pitiful, he bore not malice against me; nay, he loved me even as the rest of his brothers. Take heed, therefore, my children, of all jealousy and envy, and walk in singleness of soul and with good heart, keeping in mind the brother of your father, that God may give to you also grace and glory, and blessing upon your heads, even as you saw in him. All his days he reproached us not concerning this thing, but loved us as his own soul, and beyond his own sons; and he glorified us, and gave riches, and cattle, and fruits freely to us all. Then also, my beloved children, love each one his brother with a good heart, and remove from you the spirit of envy, for this makes

115

savage the soul and destroys the body; it turns his purposes into anger and war, and stirs up unto blood, and leads the mind into frenzy, and suffers not prudence to act in men: moreover, it takes away sleep, and causes tumult to the soul and trembling to the body. For even in sleep some malicious jealousy, deluding him, gnaws at his soul, and with wicked spirits disturbs it, and causes the body to be troubled, and the mind to awake from sleep in confusion; and as though having a wicked and poisonous spirit, so appears it to men. 5 Therefore was Joseph fair in appearance, and goodly to look upon, because there dwelt not in him any wickedness; for in trouble of the spirit the face declares it. And now, my children, make your hearts good before the Lord, and your ways straight before men, and you shall find grace before God and men. And take heed not to commit fornication, for fornication is mother of all evils, separating from God, and bringing near to Beliar. For I have seen it inscribed in the writing of Enoch that your sons shall with you be corrupted in fornication, and shall do wrong against Levi with the sword. But they shall not prevail against Levi, for he shall wage the war of the Lord, and shall conquer all your hosts; and there shall be a few divided in Levi and Judah, and there shall be none of you for sovereignty, even as also my father Jacob prophesied in his blessings. 6 Behold, I have foretold you all things, that I may be clear from the sin of your souls. Now, if you remove from you your envy, and all your stiffneckedness, as a rose shall my bones flourish in Israel, and as a lily my flesh in Jacob, and my odour shall be as the odour of Libanus; and as cedars shall holy ones be multiplied from me for ever, and their branches shall stretch afar off. Then shall perish the seed of Canaan, and a remnant shall not be to Amalek, and all the Cappadocians shall perish, and all the Hittites shall be utterly destroyed. Then shall fail the land of Ham, and every people shall perish. Then shall all the earth rest from trouble, and all the world under heaven from war. Then shall Shem be glorified, because the Lord God, the Mighty One of Israel, shall appear upon earth as man, and saved by Him Adam. Then shall all the spirits of deceit be given to be trampled under foot, and men shall rule over the wicked spirits. Then will I arise in joy, and will bless the Most High because of His marvellous works, because God has taken a body and eaten with men and saved men. 7 And now, my children, obey Levi, and in Judah shall you be redeemed: and be not lifted up against these two tribes, for from them shall arise to you the salvation of God. For the Lord shall raise up from Levi as it were a Priest, and from Judah as it were a King, God and man. So shall He save all the Gentiles and the race of Israel. Therefore I command you all things, in order that you also may command your children, that they may observe them throughout their generations. 8 And Simeon made an end of commanding his sons, and slept with his fathers, being an hundred and twenty years old. And they laid him in a coffin of incorruptible wood, to take up his bones to Hebron. And they carried them up in a war of the Egyptians secretly: for the bones of Joseph the Egyptians guarded in the treasure-house of the palace; for the sorcerers told them that at the departure of the bones of Joseph there should be throughout the whole of Egypt darkness and gloom, and an exceeding great plague to the Egyptians, so that even with a lamp a man should not recognise his brother. 9 And the sons of Simeon bewailed their father according to the law of mourning, and they were in Egypt until the day of their departure from Egypt by the hand of Moses.

Test. 12 Pat. 3. The Testament of Levi Concerning the Priesthood and Arrogance

1 The copy of the words of Levi, what things he appointed to his sons, according to all that they should do, and what things should befall them until the day of judgment. He was in sound health when

he called them to him, for it had been shown to him that he should die. And when they were gathered together he said to them: 2 I Levi was conceived in Haran and born there, and after that I came with my father to Shechem. And I was young, about twenty years of age, when with Simeon I wrought the vengeance on Hamor for our sister Dinah. And when we were feeding our flocks in Abel-Maul, a spirit of understanding of the Lord came upon me, and I saw all men corrupting their way, and that unrighteousness had built to itself walls, and iniquity sat upon towers; and I grieved for the race of men, and I prayed to the Lord that I might be saved. Then there fell upon me a sleep, and I beheld a high mountain: this is the mountain of Aspis in Abel-Maul. And behold, the heavens were opened, and an angel of God said to me, Levi, enter. And I entered from the first heaven into the second, and I saw there water hanging between the one and the other. And I saw a third heaven far brighter than those two, for there was in it a height without bounds. And I said to the angel, Wherefore is this? And the angel said to me, Marvel not at these, for you shall see four other heavens brighter than these, and without comparison, when you shall have ascended there: because you shall stand near the Lord, and shall be His minister, and shall declare His mysteries to men, and shall proclaim concerning Him who shall redeem Israel; [Luke 24²¹ and by you and Judah shall the Lord appear among men, saving in them every race of men; and of the portion of the Lord shall be your life, and He shall be your field and vineyard, fruits, gold, silver. ³ Hear, then, concerning the seven heavens. The lowest is for this cause more gloomy, in that it is near all the iniquities of men. The second has fire, snow, ice, ready for the day of the ordinance of the Lord, in the righteous judgment of God: in it are all the spirits of the retributions for vengeance on the wicked. In the third are the hosts of the armies which are ordained for the day of judgment, to work vengeance on the spirits of deceit and of Beliar. And the heavens up to the fourth above these are holy, for in the highest of all dwells the Great Glory, in the holy of holies, far above all holiness. In the heaven next to it are the angels of the presence of the Lord, who minister and make propitiation to the Lord for all the ignorances of the righteous; and they offer to the Lord a reasonable sweet-smelling savour, and a bloodless offering. And in the heaven below this are the angels who bear the answers to the angels of the presence of the Lord. And in the heaven next to this are thrones, dominions, in which hymns are ever offered to God. Therefore, whenever the Lord looks upon us, all of us are shaken; yea, the heavens, and the earth, and the abysses, are shaken at the presence of His majesty; but the sons of men, regarding not these things, sin, and provoke the Most High. ⁴ Now, therefore, know that the Lord will execute judgment upon the sons of men; because when the rocks are rent, and the sun quenched, and the waters dried up, and the fire trembling, and all creation troubled, and the invisible spirits melting away, and the grave spoiled in the suffering of the Most High, men unbelieving will abide in their iniquity, therefore with punishment shall they be judged. Therefore the Most High has heard your prayer, to separate you from iniquity, and that you should become to Him a son, and a servant, and a minister of His presence. A shining light of knowledge shall you shine in Jacob, and as the sun shall you be to all the seed of Israel. And a blessing shall be given to you, and to all your seed, until the Lord shall visit all the heathen in the tender mercies of His Son, even for ever. Nevertheless your sons shall lay hands upon Him to crucify Him; and therefore have counsel and understanding been given you, that you might instruct your sons concerning Him, because he that blesses Him shall be blessed, but they that curse Him shall perish. ⁵ And the angel opened to me the gates of heaven, and I saw the holy temple, and the Most High upon a throne of glory. And He

said to me, Levi, I have given you the blessings of the priesthood until that I shall come and sojourn in the midst of Israel. Then the angel brought me to the earth, and gave me a shield and a sword, and said, Work vengeance on Shechem because of Dinah, and I will be with you, because the Lord has sent me. And I destroyed at that time the sons of Hamor, as it is written in the heavenly tablets. And I said to Him, I pray You, O Lord, tell me Your name, that I may call upon You in a day of tribulation. And He said, I am the angel who intercedes for the race of Israel, that He smite them not utterly, because every evil spirit attacks it. And after these things I was as it were awaked, and blessed the Most High, and the angel that intercedes for the race of Israel, and for all the righteous. ⁶ And when I came to my father I found a brazen shield; wherefore also the name of the mountain is Aspis, which is near Gebal, on the right side of Abila; and I kept these words in my heart. I took counsel with my father, and with Reuben my brother, that he should bid the sons of Hamor that they should be circumcised; for I was jealous because of the abomination which they had wrought in Israel. And I slew Shechem at the first, and Simeon slew Hamor. And after this our brethren came and smote the city with the edge of the sword; and our father heard it and was angry, and he was grieved in that they had received the circumcision, and after that had been put to death, and in his blessings he dealt otherwise with us. For we sinned because we had done this thing against his will, and he was sick upon that day. But I knew that the sentence of God was for evil upon Shechem; for they sought to do to Sarah as they did to Dinah our sister, and the Lord hindered them. And so they persecuted Abraham our father when he was a stranger, and they harried his flocks when they were multiplied upon him; and Jeblae his servant, born in his house, they shamefully handled. And thus they did to all strangers, taking away their wives by force, and the men themselves driving into exile. But the wrath of the Lord came suddenly upon them to the uttermost. ⁷ And I said to my father, Be not angry, sir, because by you will the Lord bring to nought the Canaanites, and will give their land to you, and to your seed after you. For from this day forward shall Shechem be called a city of them that are without understanding; for as a man mocks at a fool, so did we mock them, because they wrought folly in Israel to defile our sister. And we took our sister from thence, and departed, and came to Bethel. ⁸ And there I saw a thing again even as the former, after we had passed seventy days. And I saw seven men in white raiment saying to me, Arise, put on the robe of the priesthood, and the crown of righteousness, and the breastplate of understanding, and the garment of truth, and the diadem of faith, and the tiara of miracle, and the ephod of prophecy. And each one of them bearing each of these things put them on me, and said, From henceforth become a priest of the Lord, you and your seed for ever. And the first anointed me with holy oil, and gave to me the rod of judgment. The second washed me with pure water, and fed me with bread and wine, the most holy things, and clad me with a holy and glorious robe. The third clothed me with a linen vestment like to an ephod. The fourth put round me a girdle like purple. The fifth gave to me a branch of rich olive. The sixth placed a crown on my head. The seventh placed on my head a diadem of priesthood, and filled my hands with incense, so that I served as a priest to the Lord. And they said to me, Levi, your seed shall be divided into three branches, for a sign of the glory of the Lord who is to come; and first shall he be that has been faithful; no portion shall be greater than his. The second shall be in the priesthood. The third — a new name shall be called over Him, because He shall arise as King from Judah, and shall establish a new priesthood, after the fashion of the Gentiles, to all the Gentiles. And His appearing shall be unutterable, as of an exalted prophet of the seed of Abraham our father. Every desirable thing in Israel shall be for you and for your seed, and everything fair to look upon shall you eat, and the table of the Lord shall your seed apportion, and some of them shall be high priests, and judges, and scribes; for by their mouth shall the holy place be guarded. And when I awoke, I understood that this thing was like the former. And I hid this also in my heart, and told it not to any man upon the earth. ⁹ And after two days I and Judah went up to Isaac after our father; and the father of my father blessed me according to all the words of the visions which I had seen: and he would not come with us to Bethel. And when we came to Bethel, my father Jacob saw in a vision concerning me, that I should be to them for a priest unto the Lord; and he rose up early in the morning, and paid tithes of all to the Lord through me. And we came to Hebron to dwell there, and Isaac called me continually to put me in remembrance of the law of the Lord, even as the angel of God showed to me. And he taught me the law of the priesthood, of sacrifices, whole burnt-offerings, first-fruits, free-will offerings, thank-offerings. And each day he was instructing me, and was busied for me before the Lord. And he said to me, Take heed, my child, of the spirit of fornication; for this shall continue, and shall by your seed pollute the holy things. Take therefore to yourself, while yet you are young, a wife, not having blemish, nor yet polluted, nor of the race of the Philistines or Gentiles. And before entering into the holy place, bathe; and when you offer the sacrifice, wash; and again when you finish the sacrifice, wash. Of twelve trees ever having leaves, offer up the fruits to the Lord, as also Abraham taught me; and of every clean beast and clean bird offer a sacrifice to the Lord, and of every firstling and of wine offer first-fruits; and every sacrifice you shall salt with salt. ¹⁰ Now, therefore, observe whatsoever I command you, children; for whatsoever things I have heard from my fathers I have made known to you. I am clear from all your ungodliness and transgression which you will do in the end of the ages against the Saviour of the world, acting ungodly, deceiving Israel, and raising up against it great evils from the Lord. And you will deal lawlessly with Israel, so that Jerusalem shall not endure your wickedness; but the veil of the temple shall be rent, so as not to cover your shame. And you shall be scattered as captives among the heathen, and shall be for a reproach and for a curse, and for a trampling under foot. For the house which the Lord shall choose shall be called Jerusalem, as is contained in the boo of Enoch the righteous. ¹¹ Therefore, when I took a wife I was twenty-eight years old, and her name was Melcha. And she conceived and bare a son, and she called his name Gersham, for we were sojourners in our land: for Gersham is interpreted sojourning. And I saw concerning him that he would not be in the first rank. And Kohath was born in my thirty-fifth year, towards the east. And I saw in a vision that he was standing on high in the midst of all the congregation. Therefore I called his name Kohath, which means, beginning of majesty and instruction. And thirdly, she bare to me Merari, in the fortieth year of my life; and since his mother bare him with difficulty, she called him Merari, which means my bitterness, because he also died. And Jochebed was born in my sixty-fourth year, in Egypt, for I was renowned then in the midst of my brethren. ¹² And Gersham took a wife, and she bare to him Lomni and Semei. And the sons of Kohath, Ambram, Isaar, Chebro, and Ozel. And the sons of Merari, Mooli and Homusi. And in my ninety-fourth year Ambram took Jochebed my daughter to him to wife, for they were born in one day, he and my daughter. Eight years old was I when I went into the land of Canaan, and eighteen years when I slew Shechem, and at nineteen years I became priest, and at twenty-eight years I took a wife, and at forty years I went into Egypt. And behold, you are my children, my children even of a third generation. In my hundred and eighteenth

117

year Joseph died. ¹³ And now, my children, I command you that you fear our Lord with your whole heart, and walk in simplicity according to all His law. And do ye also teach your children learning, that they may have understanding in all their life, reading unceasingly the law of God; for every one who shall know the law of God shall be honoured, and shall not be a stranger wheresoever he goes. Yea, many friends shall he gain more than his forefathers; and many men shall desire to serve him, and to hear the law from his mouth. Work righteousness, my children, upon the earth, that you may find treasure in the heavens, and sow good things in your souls, that you may find them in your life. For if you sow evil things, you shall reap all trouble and affliction. Get wisdom in the fear of God with diligence; for though there shall be a leading into captivity, and cities be destroyed, and lands and gold and silver and every possession shall perish, the wisdom of the wise none can take away, save the blindness of ungodliness and the palsy of sin: for even among his enemies shall it be to him glorious, and in a strange country a home, and in the midst of foes shall it be found a friend. If a man teach these things and do them, he shall be enthroned with kings, as was also Joseph our brother. ¹⁴ And now, my children, I have learned from the writing of Enoch that at the last you will deal ungodly, laying your hands upon the Lord in all malice; and your brethren shall be ashamed because of you, and to all the Gentiles shall it become a mocking. For our father Israel shall be pure from the ungodliness of the chief priests who shall lay their hands upon the Saviour of the world. Pure is the heaven above the earth, and you are the lights of the heaven as the sun and the moon. What shall all the Gentiles do if you be darkened in ungodliness? So shall you bring a curse upon our race for whom came the light of the world, which was given among you for the lighting up of every man. Him will you desire to slay, teaching commandments contrary to the ordinances of God. The offerings of the Lord will you rob, and from His portion will you steal; and before ye sacrifice to the Lord, you will take the choicest parts, in despitefulness eating them with harlots. Amid excesses will you teach the commandments of the Lord, the women that have husbands will you pollute, and the virgins of Jerusalem will you defile; and with harlots and adulteresses will you be joined. The daughters of the Gentiles will you take for wives, purifying them with an unlawful purification; and your union shall be like Sodom and Gomorrha in ungodliness. And ye will be puffed up because of the priesthood lifting yourselves up against men. And not only so, but being puffed up also against the commands of God, you will scoff at the holy things, mocking in despitefulness. ¹⁵ Therefore the temple which the Lord shall choose shall be desolate in uncleanness, and you shall be captives throughout all nations, and you shall be an abomination among them, and you shall receive reproach and everlasting shame from the righteous judgment of God; and all who see you shall flee from you. And were it not for Abraham, Isaac, and Jacob our fathers, not one from my seed should be left upon the earth. ¹⁶ And now I have learned in the boo of Enoch that for seventy weeks will you go astray, and will profane the priesthood, and pollute the sacrifices, and corrupt the law, and set at nought the words of the prophets. In perverseness you will persecute righteous men, and hate the godly; the words of the faithful will you abhor, and the man who renews the law in the power of the Most High will you call a deceiver; and at last, as you suppose, you will slay Him, not understanding His resurrection, wickedly taking upon your own heads the innocent blood. Because of Him shall your holy places be desolate, polluted even to the ground, and you shall have no place that is clean; but you shall be among the Gentiles a curse and a dispersion, until He shall again look upon you, and in pity shall take you to Himself through faith and water. [17] And because you have heard concerning the seventy weeks, hear also concerning the priesthood; for in each jubilee there shall be a priesthood. In the first jubilee, the first who is anointed into the priesthood shall be great, and shall speak to God as to a Father; and his priesthood shall be filled with the fear of the Lord, and in the day of his gladness shall he arise for the salvation of the world. In the second jubilee, he that is anointed shall be conceived in the sorrow of beloved ones; and his priesthood shall be honoured, and shall be glorified among all. And the third priest shall be held fast in sorrow; and the fourth shall be in grief, because unrighteousness shall be laid upon him exceedingly, and all Israel shall hate each one his neighbour. The fifth shall be held fast in darkness, likewise also the sixth and the seventh. And in the seventh there shall be such pollution as I am not able to express, before the Lord and men, for they shall know it who do these things. Therefore shall they be in captivity and for a prey, and their land and their substance shall be destroyed. And in the fifth week they shall return into their desolate country, and shall renew the house of the Lord. And in the seventh week shall come the priests, worshippers of idols, contentious, lovers of money, proud, lawless, lascivious, abusers of children and beasts. [18] And after their punishment shall have come from the Lord, then will the Lord raise up to the priesthood a new Priest, to whom all the words of the Lord shall be revealed; and He shall execute a judgment of truth upon the earth, in the fullness of days. And His star shall arise in heaven, as a king shedding forth the light of knowledge in the sunshine of day, and He shall be magnified in the world until His ascension. He shall shine forth as the sun in the earth, and shall drive away all darkness from the world under heaven, and there shall be peace in all the earth. The heavens shall rejoice in His days, and the earth shall be glad, and the clouds shall be joyful, and the knowledge of the Lord shall be poured forth upon the earth, as the water of seas; and the angels of the glory of the presence of the Lord shall be glad in Him. The heavens shall be opened, and from the temple of glory shall the sanctification come upon Him with the Father's voice, as from Abraham the father of Isaac. And the glory of the Most High shall be uttered over Him, and the spirit of understanding and of sanctification shall rest upon Him in the water. He shall give the majesty of the Lord to His sons in truth for evermore; and there shall none succeed Him for all generations, even for ever. And in His priesthood shall all sin come to an end, and the lawless shall rest from evil, and the just shall rest in Him. And He shall open the gates of paradise, and shall remove the threatening sword against Adam; and He shall give to His saints to eat from the tree of life, and the spirit of holiness shall be on them. And Beliar shall be bound by Him, and He shall give power to His children to tread upon the evil spirits. And the Lord shall rejoice in His children, and the Lord shall be well pleased in His beloved for ever. Then shall Abraham and Isaac and Jacob be joyful, and I will be glad, and all the saints shall put on gladness. [19] And now, my children, you have heard all; choose therefore for yourselves either the darkness or the light, either the law of the Lord or the works of Beliar. And we answered our father, saying, Before the Lord will we walk according to His law. And our father said, The Lord is witness, and His angels are witnesses, and I am witness, and you are witnesses, concerning the word of your mouth. And we said, We are witnesses. And thus Levi ceased giving charge to his sons; and he stretched out his feet, and was gathered to his fathers, after he had lived a hundred and thirty-seven years. And they laid him in a coffin, and afterwards they buried him in Hebron, by the side of Abraham, and Isaac, and Jacob.

Test. 12 Pat. 4. The Testament of Judah Concerning Fortitude, and Love of Money, and Fornication

[1] The copy of the words of Judah, what things he spoke to his sons before he died. They gathered themselves together, and came to him, and he said to them: I was the fourth son born to my father, and my mother called me Judah, saying, I give thanks to the Lord, because He has given to me even a fourth son. I was swift and active in my youth, and obedient to my father in everything. And I honoured my mother and my mother's sister. And it came to pass, when I became a man, that my father Jacob prayed over me, saying, You shall be a king, and prosperous in all things. [2] And the Lord showed me favour in all my works both in the field and at home. When I saw that I could run with the hind, then I caught it, and prepared meat for my father. I seized upon the roes in the chase, and all that was in the plains I outran. A wild mare I outran, and I caught it and tamed it; and I slew a lion, and plucked a kid out of its mouth. I took a bear by its paw, and rolled it over a cliff; and if any beast turned upon me, I rent it like a dog. I encountered the wild boar, and overtaking it in the chase, I tore it. A leopard in Hebron leaped upon the dog, and I caught it by the tail, and flung it from me, and it was dashed to pieces in the coasts of Gaza. A wild ox feeding in the field I seized by the horns; and whirling it round and stunning it, I cast it from me, and slew it. [3] And when the two kings of the Canaanites came in warlike array against our flocks, and much people with them, I by myself rushed upon King Sur and seized him; and I beat him upon the legs, and dragged him down, and so I slew him. And the other king, Taphue, I slew as he sat upon his horse, and so I scattered all the people. Achor the king, a man of giant stature, hurling darts before and behind as he sat on horseback, I slew; for I hurled a stone of sixty pounds weight, and cast it upon his horse, and killed him. And I fought with Achor for two hours, and I killed him; and I clave his shield into two parts, and I chopped off his feet. And as I stripped off his breastplate, behold, eight men his companions began to fight with me. I wound round therefore my garment in my hand; and I slang stones at them, and killed four of them, and the rest fled. And Jacob my father slew Beelisa, king of all the kings, a giant in strength, twelve cubits high; and fear fell upon them, and they ceased from making war with us. Therefore my father had no care in the wars when I was among my brethren. For he saw in a vision concerning me, that an angel of might followed me everywhere, that I should not be overcome. [4] And in the south there befell us a greater war than that in Shechem; and I joined in battle array with my brethren, and pursued a thousand men, and slew of them two hundred men and four kings. And I went up against them upon the wall, and two other kings I slew; and so we freed Hebron, and took all the captives of the kings. [5] On the next day we departed to Areta, a city strong and walled and inaccessible, threatening us with death. Therefore I and Gad approached on the east side of the city, and Reuben and Levi on the west and south. And they that were upon the wall, thinking that we were alone, charged down upon us; and so our brethren secretly climbed up the wall on both sides by ladders, and entered into the city, while the men knew it not. And we took it with the edge of the sword; and those who had taken refuge in the tower, we set fire to the tower, and took both it and them. And as we were departing the men of Thaffu set upon our captives, and we took it with our sons, and fought with them even to Thaffu; and we slew them, and burnt their city, and spoiled all the things that were therein. [6] And when I was at the waters of Chuzeba, the men of Jobel came against us to battle, and we fought with them; and their allies from Selom we slew, and we allowed them no means of escaping, and of coming against us. And the men of Machir came upon us on the fifth day, to carry away our captives; and we attacked them, and overcame them in fierce battle: for they were a host and mighty in themselves, and we slew

them before they had gone up the ascent of the hill. And when we came to their city, their women rolled upon us stones from the brow of the hill on which the city stood. And I and Simeon hid ourselves behind the town, and seized upon the heights, and utterly destroyed the whole city. 7 And the next day it was told us that the cities of the two kings with a great host were coming against us. I therefore and Dan feigned ourselves to be Amorites, and went as allies into their city. And in the depth of night our brethren came, and we opened to them the gates; and we destroyed all the men and their substance, and we took for a prey all that was theirs, and their three walls we cast down. And we drew near to Thamna, where was all the refuge of the hostile kings. Then having received hurt I was angry, and charged upon them to the brow of the hill; and they slang at me with stones and darts; and had not Dan my brother aided me, they would have been able to slay me. We came upon them therefore with wrath, and they all fled; and passing by another way, they besought my father, and he made peace with them, and we did to them no hurt, but made a truce with them, and restored to them all the captives. And I built Thamna, and my father built Rhambael. I was twenty years old when this war befell, and the Canaanites feared me and my brethren. 8 Moreover, I had much cattle, and I had for the chief of my herdsmen Iran [Gen. 38] the Adullamite. And when I went to him I saw Barsan, king of Adullam, and he made us a feast; and he entreated me, and gave me his daughter Bathshua to wife. She bare me Er, and Onan, and Shelah; and the two of them the Lord smote that they died childless: for Shelah lived, and his children are you. 9 Eighteen years we abode at peace, our father and we, with his brother Esau, and his sons with us, after that we came from Mesopotamia, from Laban. And when eighteen years were fulfilled, in the fortieth year of my life, Esau, the brother of my father, came upon us with much people and strong; and he fell by the bow of Jacob, and was taken up dead in Mount Seir: even as he went above Iramna was he slain. And we pursued after the sons of Esau. Now they had a city with walls of iron and gates of brass; and we could not enter into it, and we encamped around, and besieged them. And when they opened not to us after twenty days, I set up a ladder in the sight of all, and with my shield upon my head I climbed up, assailed with stones of three talents' weight; and I climbed up, and slew four who were mighty among them. And the next day Reuben and Gad entered in and slew sixty others. Then they asked from us terms of peace; and being aware of our father's purpose, we received them as tributaries. And they gave us two hundred cors of wheat, five hundred baths of oil, fifteen hundred measures of wine, until we went down into Egypt. 10 After these things, my son Er took to wife Tamar, from Mesopotamia, a daughter of Aram. Now Er was wicked, and he doubted concerning Tamar, because she was not of the land of Canaan. And on the third day an angel of the Lord smote him in the night, and he had not known her, according to the evil craftiness of his mother, for he did not wish to have children from her. In the days of the wedding-feast I espoused Onan to her; and he also in wickedness knew her not, though he lived with her a year. And when I threatened him, he lay with her, ...according to the command of his mother, and he also died in his wickedness. And I wished to give Shelah also to her, but my wife Bathshua suffered it not; for she bore a spite against Tamar, because she was not of the daughters of Canaan, as she herself was. 11 And I knew that the race of Canaan was wicked, but the thoughts of youth blinded my heart. And when I saw her pouring out wine, in the drunkenness of wine was I deceived, and I fell before her. And while I was away, she went and took for Shelah a wife from the land of Caanan. And when I knew what she had done, I cursed her in the anguish of my soul, and she also died in the wickedness of her sons. 12 And after these things,

while Tamar was a widow, she heard after two years that I was going up to shear my sheep; then she decked herself in bridal array, and sat over against the city by the gate. For it is a law of the Amorites, that she who is about to marry sit in fornication seven days by the gate. I therefore, being drunk at the waters of Chozeb, recognised her not by reason of wine; and her beauty deceived me, through the fashion of her adorning. And I turned aside to her, and said, I would enter in to you. And she said to me, What will you give me? And I gave her my staff, and my girdle, and my royal crown; and I lay with her, and she conceived. I then, not knowing what she had done, wished to slay her; but she privily sent my pledges, and put me to shame. And when I called her, I heard also the secret words which I spoke when lying with her in my drunkenness; and I could not slay her, because it was from the Lord. For I said, Lest haply she did it in subtlety, and received the pledge from another woman: but I came near her no more till my death, because I had done this abomination in all Israel. Moreover, they who were in the city said that there was no bride in the city, because she came from another place, and sat for awhile in the gate, and she thought that no one knew that I had gone in to her. And after this we came into Egypt to Joseph, because of the famine. Forty and six years old was I, and seventy and three years lived I there. 13 And now, my children, in what things so ever I command you hearken to your father, and keep all my sayings to perform the ordinances of the Lord, and to obey the command of the Lord God. And walk not after your lusts, nor in the thoughts of your imaginations in the haughtiness of your heart; and glory not in the works of the strength of youth, for this also is evil in the eyes of the Lord. For since I also gloried that in wars the face of no woman of goodly form ever deceived me, and upbraided Reuben my brother concerning Bilhah, the wife of my father, the spirits of jealousy and of fornication arrayed themselves within me, until I fell before Bathshua the Canaanite, and Tamar who was espoused to my sons. And I said to my father-in-law, I will counsel with my father, and so will I take your daughter. And he showed me a boundless store of gold in his daughter's behalf, for he was a king. And he decked her with gold and pearls, and caused her to pour out wine for us at the feast in womanly beauty. And the wine led my eyes astray, and pleasure blinded my heart; and I loved her, and I fell, and transgressed the commandment of the Lord and the commandment of my fathers, and I took her to wife. And the Lord rewarded me according to the thought of my heart, insomuch that I had no joy in her children. 14 And now, my children, be not drunk with wine; for wine turns the mind away from the truth, and kindles in it the passion of lust, and leads the eyes into error. For the spirit of fornication has wine as a minister to give pleasures to the mind; for these two take away the power from a man. For if a man drink wine to drunkenness, he disturbs his mind with filthy thoughts to fornication, and excites his body to carnal union; and if the cause of the desire be present, he works the sin, and is not ashamed. Such is wine, my children; for he who is drunken reverences no man. For, lo, it made me also to err, so that I was not ashamed of the multitude in the city, because before the eyes of all I turned aside unto Tamar, and I worked a great sin, and I uncovered the covering of the shame of my sons. After that I drank wine I reverenced not the commandment of God, and I took a woman of Canaan to wife. Wherefore, my children, he who drinks wine needs discretion; and herein is discretion in drinking wine, that a man should drink as long as he keeps decency; but if he go beyond this bound, the spirit of deceit attacks his mind and works his will; and it makes the drunkard to talk filthily, and to transgress and not to be ashamed, but even to exult in his dishonour, accounting himself to do well. 15 He that commits fornication, and uncovers his nakedness, has become the servant of fornication, and escapes not from the power thereof, even as I also was uncovered. For I gave my staff, that is, the stay of my tribe; and my girdle, that is, my power; and my diadem, that is, the glory of my kingdom. Then I repented for these things, and took no wine or flesh until my old age, nor did I behold any joy. And the angel of God showed me that for ever do women bear rule over king and beggar alike; and from the king they take away his glory, and from the valiant man his strength, and from the beggar even that little which is the stay of his poverty. 16 Observe therefore, my children, moderation in wine; for there are in it four evil spirits of (1 lust, of (2 wrath, of (3 riot, of (4 filthy lucre. If you drink wine in gladness, with shamefacedness, with the fear of God, you shall live. For if you drink not with shamefacedness, and the fear of God departs from you, then comes drunkenness, and shamelessness steals in. But even if you drink not at all, take heed lest ye sin in words of outrage, and fighting, and slander, and transgression of the commandments of God; so shall you perish before your time. Moreover, wine reveals the mysteries of God and men to aliens, even as I also revealed the commandments of God and the mysteries of Jacob my father to the Canaanitish Bathshua, to whom God forbade to declare them. And wine also is a cause of war and confusion. 17 I charge you, therefore, my children, not to love money, nor to gaze upon the beauty of women; because for the sake of money and beauty I was led astray to Bathshua the Canaanite. For I know that because of these two things shall you who are my race fall into wickedness; for even wise men among my sons shall they mar, and shall cause the kingdom of Judah to be diminished, which the Lord gave me because of my obedience to my father. For I never disobeyed a word of Jacob my father, for all things whatsoever he commanded I did. And Abraham, the father of my father, blessed me that I should be king in Israel, and Isaac further blessed me in like manner. And I know that from me shall the kingdom be established. 18 For I have read also in the books of Enoch the righteous what evils you shall do in the last days. Take heed, therefore, my children, of fornication and the love of money; hearken to Judah your father, for these things do withdraw you from the law of God, and blind the understanding of the soul, and teach arrogance, and suffer not a man to have compassion upon his neighbour: they rob his soul of all goodness, and bind him in toils and troubles, and take away his sleep and devour his flesh, and hinder the sacrifices of God; and he remembers not blessing, and he hearkens not to a prophet when he speaks, and is vexed at the word of godliness. For one who serves two passions contrary to the commandments of God cannot obey God, because they have blinded his soul, and he walks in the day-time as in the night. 19 My children, the love of money leads to idols; because, when led astray through money, men make mention of those who are no gods, and it causes him who has it to fall into madness. For the sake of money I lost my children, and but for the repentance of my flesh, and the humbling of my soul, and the prayers of Jacob my father, I should have died childless. But the God of my fathers, who is pitiful and merciful, pardoned me, because I did it in ignorance. For the prince of deceit blinded me, and I was ignorant as a man and as flesh, being corrupted in sins; and I learned my own weakness while thinking myself unconquerable. 20 Learn therefore, my children, that two spirits wait upon man: the spirit of truth and the spirit of error; and in the midst is the spirit of the understanding of the mind, to which it belongs to turn wherever it will. And the works of truth and the works of error are written upon the breast of men, and each one of them the Lord knows. And there is no time at which the works of men can be hid from Him; for on the bones of his breast has he been written down before the Lord. And the spirit of truth testifies

all things, and accuses all; and he who sins is burnt up by his own heart, and cannot raise his face unto the Judge. 21 And now, my children, love Levi, that you may abide, and exalt not yourselves against him, lest ye be utterly destroyed. For to me the Lord gave the kingdom, and to him the priesthood, and He set the kingdom beneath the priesthood. To me He gave the things upon the earth; to him the things in the heavens. As the heaven is higher than the earth, so is the priesthood of God higher than the kingdom upon the earth. For the Lord chose him above you, to draw near to Him, and to eat of His table and first-fruits, even the choice things of the sons of Israel, and you shall be to them as a sea. For as, on the sea, just and unjust are tossed about, some taken into captivity while others are enriched, so also shall every race of men be in you, some are in jeopardy and taken captive, and others shall grow rich by means of plunder. For they who rule will be as great sea-monsters, swallowing up men like fishes: free sons and daughters do they enslave; houses, lands, flocks, money, will they plunder; and with the flesh of many will they wrongfully feed the ravens and the cranes; and they will go on further in evil, advancing on still in covetousness. And there shall be false prophets like tempests, and they shall persecute all righteous men. 22 And the Lord shall bring upon them divisions one against another, and there shall be continual wars in Israel; and among men of other race shall my kingdom be brought to an end, until the salvation of Israel shall come, until the appearing of the God of righteousness, that Jacob and all the Gentiles may rest in peace. And he shall guard the might of my kingdom for ever: for the Lord swore to me with an oath that the kingdom should never fail from me, and from my seed for all days, even for ever. 23 Now I have much grief, my children, because of your lewdness, and witchcrafts, and idolatries, which you will work against the kingdom, following them that have familiar spirits; you will make your daughters singing girls and harlots for divinations and demons of error, and you will be mingled in the pollutions of the Gentiles: for which things' sake the Lord shall bring upon you famine and pestilence, death and the sword, avenging siege, and dogs for the rending in pieces of enemies, and revilings of friends, destruction and blighting of eyes, children slaughtered, wives carried off, possessions plundered, temple of God in flames, your land desolated, your own selves enslaved among the Gentiles, and they shall make some of you eunuchs for their wives; and whenever you will return to the Lord with humility of heart, repenting and walking in all the commandments of God, then will the Lord visit you in mercy and in love, bringing you from out of the bondage of your enemies. 24 And after these things shall a Star arise to you from Jacob in peace, and a Man shall rise from my seed, like the Sun of righteousness, walking with the sons of men in meekness and righteousness, and no sin shall be found in Him. And the heavens shall be opened above Him, to shed forth the blessing of the Spirit from the Holy Father; and He shall shed forth a spirit of grace upon you, and you shall be unto Him sons in truth, and you shall walk in His commandments, the first and the last. This is the Branch of God Most High, and this the Well-spring unto life for all flesh. Then shall the sceptre of my kingdom shine forth, and from your root shall arise a stem; and in it shall arise a rod of righteousness to the Gentiles, to judge and to save all that call upon the Lord. 25 And after these things shall Abraham and Isaac and Jacob arise unto life, and I and my brethren will be chiefs, even your sceptre in Israel: Levi first, I the second, Joseph third, Benjamin fourth, Simeon fifth, Issachar sixth, and so all in order. And the Lord blessed Levi; the Angel of the Presence, me; the powers of glory, Simeon; the heaven, Reuben; the earth, Issachar; the sea, Zebulun; the mountains, Joseph; the tabernacle, Benjamin; the lights of heaven, Dan; the fatness of earth, Naphtali; the sun, Gad; the olive, Asher: and there shall be one people of the Lord, and one tongue; and there shall no more be a spirit of deceit of Beliar, for he shall be cast into the fire for ever. And they who have died in grief shall arise in joy, and they who have lived in poverty for the Lord's sake shall be made rich, and they who have been in want shall be filled, and they who have been weak shall be made strong, and they who have been put to death for the Lord's sake shall awake in life. And the harts of Jacob shall run in joyfulness, and the eagles of Israel shall fly in gladness; but the ungodly shall lament, and sinners all weep, and all the people shall glorify the Lord for ever. 26 Observe, therefore, my children, all the law of the Lord, for there is hope for all them who follow His way aright. And he said to them: I die before your eyes this day, a hundred and nineteen years old. Let no one bury me in costly apparel, nor tear open my bowels, for this shall they who are kings do: and carry me up to Hebron with you. And Judah, when he had said these things, fell asleep; and his sons did according to all whatsoever he commanded them, and they buried him in Hebron with his fathers.

Test. 12 Pat. 5. The Testament of Issachar Concerning Simplicity

1 The record of the words of Issachar. He called his sons, and said to them: Hearken, my children, to Issachar your father; give ear to my words, you who are beloved of the Lord. I was the fifth son born to Jacob, even the hire of the mandrakes. For Reuben brought in mandrakes from the field, and Rachel met him and took them. And Reuben wept, and at his voice Leah my mother came forth. Now these mandrakes were sweet-smelling apples which the land of Aram produced on high ground below a ravine of water. And Rachel said, I will not give them to you, for they shall be to me instead of children. Now there were two apples; and Leah said, Let it suffice you that you have taken the husband of my virginity: will you also take these? And she said, Behold, let Jacob be to you this night instead of the mandrakes of your son. And Leah said to her, Boast not, and vaunt not yourself; for Jacob is mine, and I am the wife of his youth. But Rachel said, How so? For to me was he first espoused, and for my sake he served our father fourteen years. What shall I do to you, because the craft and the subtlety of men are increased, and craft prospers upon the earth? And were it not so, you would not now see the face of Jacob. For you are not his wife, but in craft were taken to him in my stead. And my father deceived me, and removed me on that night, and suffered me not to see him; for had I been there, it had not happened thus. And Rachel said, Take one mandrake, and for the other you shall hire him from me for one night. And Jacob knew Leah, and she conceived and bare me, and on account of the hire I was called Issachar. 2 Then appeared to Jacob an angel of the Lord, saying, Two children shall Rachel bear; for she has refused company with her husband, and has chosen continency. And had not Leah my mother given up the two apples for the sake of his company, she would have borne eight sons; and for this thing she bare six, and Rachel two: because on account of the mandrakes the Lord visited her. For He knew that for the sake of children she wished to company with Jacob, and not for lust of pleasure. For she went further, and on the morrow too gave up Jacob that she might receive also the other mandrake. Therefore the Lord hearkened to Rachel because of the mandrakes: for though she desired them, she ate them not, but brought them to the priest of the Most High who was at that time, and offered them up in the house of the Lord. 3 When, therefore, I grew up, my children, I walked in uprightness of heart, and I became a husbandman for my parents and my brethren, and I brought in fruits from the field according to their season; and my father blessed me, for he saw that

I walked in simplicity. And I was not a busybody in my doings, nor malicious and slanderous against my neighbour. I never spoke against any one, nor did I censure the life of any man, but walked in the simplicity of my eyes. Therefore when I was thirty years old I took to myself a wife, for my labour wore away my strength, and I never thought upon pleasure with women; but through my labour my sleep sufficed me, and my father always rejoiced in my simplicity. For on whatever I laboured I offered first to the Lord, by the hands of the priests, of all my produce and all first-fruits; then to my father, and then took for myself. And the Lord increased twofold His benefits in my hands; and Jacob also knew that God aided my simplicity, for on every poor man and every one in distress I bestowed the good things of the earth in simplicity of heart. 4 And now hearken to me, my children, and walk in simplicity of heart, for I have seen in it all that is well-pleasing to the Lord. The simple covets not gold, defrauds not his neighbour, longs not after manifold dainties, delights not in varied apparel, does not picture to himself to live a long life, but only waits for the will of God, and the spirits of error have no power against him. For he cannot allow within his mind a thought of female beauty, that he should not pollute his mind in corruption. No envy can enter into his thoughts, no jealousy melts away his soul, nor does he brood over gain with insatiate desire; for he walks in uprightness of life, and beholds all things in simplicity, not admitting in his eyes malice from the error of the world, lest he should see the perversion of any of the commandments of the Lord. 5 Keep therefore the law of God, my children, and get simplicity, and walk in guilelessness, not prying over-curiously into the commands of God and the business of your neighbour; but love the Lord and your neighbour, have compassion on the poor and weak. Bow down your back unto husbandry, and labour in tillage of the ground in all manner of husbandry, offering gifts unto the Lord with thanksgiving; for with the first-fruits of the earth did the Lord bless me, even as He blessed all the saints from Abel even until now. For no other portion is given to you than of the fatness of the earth, whose fruits are raised by toil; for our father Jacob blessed me with blessings of the earth and of first-fruits. And Levi and Judah were glorified by the Lord among the sons of Jacob; for the Lord made choice of them, and to the one He gave the priesthood, to the other the kingdom. Them therefore obey, and walk in the simplicity of your father; for unto Gad has it been given to destroy the temptations that are coming upon Israel. 6 I know, my children, that in the last times your sons will forsake simplicity, and will cleave unto avarice, and leaving guilelessness will draw near to malice, and forsaking the commandments of the Lord will cleave unto Beliar, and leaving husbandry will follow after their wicked devices, and shall be dispersed among the Gentiles, and shall serve their enemies. And do you therefore command these things to your children, that if they sin they may the more quickly return to the Lord; for He is merciful, and will deliver them even to bring them back into their land. 7 I am a hundred and twenty-two years old, and I know not against myself a sin unto death. Except my wife, I have not known any woman. I never committed fornication in the haughtiness of my eyes; I drank not wine, to be led astray thereby; I coveted not any desirable thing that was my neighbour's; guile never entered in my heart; a lie never passed through my lips; if any man grieved, I wept with him, and I shared my bread with the poor. I never ate alone; I moved no landmark; in all my days I wrought godliness and truth. I loved the Lord with all my strength; likewise also did I love every man even as my own children. So ye also do these things, my children, and every spirit of Beliar shall flee from you, and no deed of malicious men shall rule over you; and every wild beast shall you subdue, having with yourselves the God of heaven walking with men in simplicity of heart. And he commanded them that they should carry him up to Hebron, and bury him there in the cave with his fathers. And he stretched out his feet and died, the fifth son of Jacob, in a good old age; and with every limb sound, and with strength unabated, he slept the eternal sleep.

Test. 12 Pat. 6. The Testament of Zebulun Concerning Compassion and Mercy

[1] The record of Zebulun, which he enjoined his children in the hundred and fourteenth year of his life, thirty-two years after the death of Joseph. And he said to them: Hearken to me sons of Zebulun, attend to the words of your father. I am Zebulun, a good gift to my parents. For when I was born our father was increased very exceedingly, both in flocks and herds, when with the streaked rods he had his portion. I know not, my children, that in all my days I have sinned, save only in thought. Nor do I remember that I have done any iniquity, except the sin of ignorance which I committed against Joseph; for I screened my brethren, not telling to my father what had been done. And I wept sore in secret, for I feared my brethren, because they had all agreed together, that if any one should declare the secret, he should be slain with the sword. But when they wished to kill him, I adjured them much with tears not to be guilty of this iniquity. [2] For Simeon and Gad came against Joseph to kill him. And Joseph fell upon his face, and said unto them, Pity me, my brethren, have compassion upon the bowels of Jacob our father: lay not upon me your hands to shed innocent blood, for I have not sinned against you; yea, if I have sinned, with chastening chastise me, but lay not upon me your hand, for the sake of Jacob our father. And as he spoke these words, I pitied him and began to weep, and my heart melted within me, and all the substance of my bowels was loosened within my soul. And Joseph also wept, and I too wept with him; and my heart throbbed fast, and the joints of my body trembled, and I was not able to stand. And when he saw me weeping with him, and them coming against him to slay him, he fled behind me, beseeching them. And Reuben rose and said, My brethren, let us not slay him, but let us cast him into one of these dry pits which our fathers dug and found no water. For for this cause the Lord forbade that water should rise up in them, in order that Joseph might be preserved; and the Lord appointed it so, until they sold him to the Ishmaelites. [3] For in the price of Joseph, my children, I had no share; but Simeon and Gad and six other of our brethren took the price of Joseph, and bought sandals for themselves, their wives, and their children, saying, We will not eat of it, for it is the price of our brother's blood, but will tread it down under foot, because he said that he was king over us, and so let us see what his dreams mean. Therefore is it written in the writing of the law of Enoch, that whosoever will not raise up seed to his brother, his sandal shall be unloosed, and they shall spit into his face. And the brethren of Joseph wished not that their brother should live, and the Lord loosed unto them the sandal of Joseph. For when they came into Egypt they were unloosed by the servants of Joseph before the gate, and so made obeisance to Joseph after the fashion of Pharaoh. And not only did they make obeisance to Joseph, but were spit upon also, falling down before him immediately, and so they were put to shame before the Egyptians; for after this the Egyptians heard all the evils which we had done to Joseph. [4] After these things they brought forth food; for I through two days and two nights tasted nothing, through pity for Joseph. And Judah ate not with them, but watched the pit; for he feared lest Simeon and Gad should run back and slay him. And when they saw that I also ate not, they set me to watch him until he was sold. And he remained in the pit three days and three nights, and so was sold famishing. And when Reuben heard that while he was away Joseph had been sold, he rent his clothes about him, and mourned, saying, How shall I look in the face of Jacob my father? And he took the money, and ran after the merchants, and found no one; for they had left the main road, and journeyed hastily through rugged byways. And Reuben ate no food on that day. Dan therefore came to him, and said, Weep not, neither grieve; for I have found what we can say to our father Jacob. Let us slay a kid of the goats, and dip in it the coat of Joseph; and we will say, Look, if this is the coat of your son: for they stripped off from Joseph the coat of our father when they were about to sell him, and put upon him an old garment of a slave. Now Simeon had the coat, and would not give it up, wishing to rend it with his sword; for he was angry that Joseph lived, and that he had not slain him. Then we all rose up together against him, and said, If you give it not up, we will say that you alone did this wickedness in Israel; and so he gave it up, and they did even as Dan had said. [5] And now, my children, I bid you to keep the commands of the Lord, and to show mercy upon your neighbour, and to have compassion towards all, not towards men only, but also towards beasts. For for this thing's sake the Lord blessed me; and when all my brethren were sick I escaped without sickness, for the Lord knows the purposes of each. Have therefore compassion in your hearts, my children, because even as a man does to his neighbour, even so also will the Lord do to him. For the sons of my brethren were sickening, were dying on account of Joseph, because they showed not mercy in their hearts; but my sons were preserved without sickness, as you know. And when I was in Canaan, by the sea-coast, I caught spoil of fish for Jacob my father; and when many were choked in the sea, I abode unhurt. [6] I was the first who made a boat to sail upon the sea, for the Lord gave me understanding and wisdom therein; and I let down a rudder behind it, and I stretched a sail on an upright mast in the midst; and sailing therein along the shores, I caught fish for the house of my father until we went into Egypt; and through compassion, I gave of my fish to every stranger. And if any man were a stranger, or sick, or aged, I boiled the fish and dressed them well, and offered them to all men as every man had need, bringing them together and having compassion upon them. Wherefore also the Lord granted me to take much fish: for he that imparts unto his neighbour, receives manifold more from the Lord. For five years I caught fish, and gave thereof to every man whom I saw, and brought sufficient for all the house of my father. In the summer I caught fish, and in the winter I kept sheep with my brethren. [7] Now I will declare unto you what I did, I saw a man in distress and nakedness in wintertime, and had compassion upon him, and stole away a garment secretly from my house, and gave it to him who was in distress. Do you therefore, my children, from that which God bestows upon you, show compassion and mercy impartially to all men, and give to every man with a good heart. And if you have not at the time wherewith to give to him that asks you, have compassion for him in bowels of mercy. I know that my hand found not at the time wherewith to give to him that asked me, and I walked with him weeping for more than seven furlongs, and my bowels yearned towards him unto compassion. [8] Have therefore yourselves also, my children, compassion towards every man with mercy, that the Lord also may have compassion upon you, and have mercy upon you; because also in the last days God sends His compassion on the earth, and wheresoever He finds bowels of mercy, He dwells in him. For how much compassion a man has upon his neighbours, so much also has the Lord upon him. For when we went down into Egypt, Joseph bore no malice against us, and when he saw me he was filled with compassion. And looking towards him, do ye also, my children, approve yourselves without malice, and love one another; and reckon not each one the evil of his brother, for this breaks unity, and divides all kindred, and

122

troubles the soul: for he who bears malice has not bowels of mercy. ⁹ Mark the waters, that they flow together, and sweep along stones, trees, sand; but if they are divided into many streams, the earth sucks them up, and they become of no account. So also shall you be if you be divided. Divide not yourselves into two heads, for everything which the Lord made has but one head; He gave two shoulders, hands, feet, but all the members are subject unto the one head. I have learned by the writing of my fathers, that in the last days you will depart from the Lord, and be divided in Israel, and you will follow two kings, and will work every abomination, and every idol will you worship, and your enemies shall lead you captive, and you shall dwell among the nations with all infirmities and tribulations and anguish of soul. And after these things you will remember the Lord, and will repent, and He will lead you back; for He is merciful and full of compassion, not imputing evil to the sons of men, because they are flesh, and the spirits of error deceive them in all their doings. And after these things shall the Lord Himself arise to you, [Malachi ⁴²] the Light of righteousness, and healing and compassion shall be upon His wings. He shall redeem all captivity of the sons of men from Beliar, and every spirit of error shall be trodden down. And He shall bring back all the nations to zeal for Him, and you shall see God in the fashion of a man whom the Lord shall choose, Jerusalem is His name. And again with the wickedness of your words will you provoke Him to anger, and you shall be cast away, even unto the time of consummation. ¹⁰ And now, my children, grieve not that I am dying, nor be troubled in that I am passing away from you. For I shall arise once more in the midst of you, as a ruler in the midst of his sons; and I will rejoice in the midst of my tribe, as many as have kept the law of the Lord, and the commandments of Zebulun their father. But upon the ungodly shall the Lord bring everlasting fire, and will destroy them throughout all generations. I am hastening away unto my rest, as did my fathers; but do ye fear the Lord your God with all your strength all the days of your life. And when he had said these things he fell calmly asleep, and his sons laid him in a coffin; and afterwards they carried him up to Hebron, and buried him with his fathers.

Test. 12 Pat. 7. The Testament of Dan Concerning Anger and Lying

¹ The record of the words of Dan, which he spoke to his sons in his last days. In the hundred and twenty-fifth year of his life he called together his family, and said: Hearken to my words, you sons of Dan; give heed to the words of the mouth of your father. I have proved in my heart, and in my whole life, that truth with just dealing is good and well-pleasing to God, and that lying and anger are evil, because they teach man all wickedness. I confess this day to you, my children, that in my heart I rejoiced concerning the death of Joseph, a true and good man; and I rejoiced at the selling of Joseph, because his father loved him more than us. For the spirit of jealousy and of vainglory said to me, You also are his son. And one of the spirits of Beliar wrought with me, saying, Take this sword, and with it slay Joseph; so shall your father love you when he is slain. This is the spirit of anger that counselled me, that even as a leopard devours a kid, so should I devour Joseph. But the God of Jacob our father gave him not over into my hands that I should find him alone, nor suffered me to work this iniquity, that two tribes should be destroyed in Israel. ² And now, my children, I am dying, and I tell you of a truth, that unless ye keep yourselves from the spirit of lying and of anger, and love truth and long-suffering, you shall perish. There is blindness in anger, my children, and no wrathful man regards any person with truth: for though it be a father or a mother, he behaves towards them as enemies; though it be a brother, he knows him not; though it be a prophet of the Lord, he disobeys him;

123

though a righteous man, he regards him not; a friend he does not acknowledge. For the spirit of anger encompasses him with the nets of deceit, and blinds his natural eyes, and through lying darkens his mind, and gives him a sight of his own making. And wherewith encompasses he his eyes? In hatred of heart; and he gives him a heart of his own against his brother unto envy. ³ My children, mischievous is anger, for it becomes as a soul to the soul itself; and the body of the angry man it makes its own, and over his soul it gets the mastery, and it bestows upon the body its own power, that it may work all iniquity; and whenever the soul does anything, it justifies what has been done, since it sees not. Therefore he who is wrathful, if he be a mighty man, has a treble might in his anger; one by the might and aid of his servants, and a second by his wrath, whereby he persuades and overcomes in injustice: and having a third of the nature of his own body, and of his own self working the evil. And though the wrathful man be weak, yet has he a might twofold of that which is by nature; for wrath ever aids such in mischief. This spirit goes always with lying at the right hand of Satan, that his works may be wrought with cruelty and lying. ⁴ Understand ye therefore the might of wrath, that it is vain. For it first of all stings him in word: then by deeds it strengthens him who is angry, and with bitter punishments disturbs his mind, and so stirs up with great wrath his soul. Therefore, when any one speaks against you, be not ye moved unto anger. And if any man praises you as good, be not lifted up nor elated, either to the feeling or showing of pleasure. For first it pleases the hearing, and so stirs up the understanding to understand the grounds for anger; and then, being wrathful, he thinks that he is justly angry. If you fall into any loss or ruin, my children, be not troubled; for this very spirit makes men desire that which has perished, in order that they may be inflamed by the desire. If you suffer loss willingly, be not vexed, for from vexation he raises up wrath with lying. And wrath with lying is a twofold mischief; and they speak one with another that they may disturb the mind; and when the soul is continually disturbed, the Lord departs from it, and Beliar rules over it. ⁵ Observe, therefore, my children, the commandments of the Lord, and keep His law; and depart from wrath, and hate lying, that the Lord may dwell among you, and Beliar may flee from you. Speak truth each one with his neighbour, so shall you not fall into lust and confusion; but you shall be in peace, having the God of peace, so shall no war prevail over you. Love the Lord through all your life, and one another with a true heart. For I know that in the last days you will depart from the Lord, and will provoke Levi unto anger, and will fight against Judah; but you shall not prevail against them. For an angel of the Lord shall guide them both; for by them shall Israel stand. And whenever ye depart from the Lord, you will walk in all evil, working the abominations of the Gentiles, going astray with women of them that are ungodly; and the spirits of error shall work in you with all malice. For I have read in the boo of Enoch the righteous, that your prince is Satan, and that all the spirits of fornication and pride shall be subject unto Levi, to lay a snare for the sons of Levi, to cause them to sin before the Lord. And my sons will draw near unto Levi, and sin with them in all things; and the sons of Judah will be covetous, plundering other men's goods like lions. Therefore shall you be led away with them in captivity, and there shall you receive all the plagues of Egypt, and all the malice of the Gentiles: and so, when you return to the Lord, you shall obtain mercy, and He shall bring you into His sanctuary, calling peace upon you; and there shall arise unto you from the tribe of Judah and of Levi the salvation of the Lord; and He shall make war against Beliar, and He shall give the vengeance of victory to our coasts. And the captivity shall He take from Beliar, even the souls of the saints, and shall turn disobedient hearts unto the Lord, and shall give to them who call upon Him everlasting peace; and the saints shall rest in Eden, and the righteous shall rejoice in the new Jerusalem, which shall be unto the glory of God for ever and ever. And no longer shall Jerusalem endure desolation, nor Israel be led captive; for the Lord shall be in the midst of her, dwelling among men, even the Holy One of Israel reigning over them in humility and in poverty; and he who believes in Him shall reign in truth in the heavens. 6 And now, my children, fear the Lord, and take heed unto yourselves of Satan and his spirits; and draw near unto God, and to the Angel that intercedes for you, for He is a Mediator between God and man for the peace of Israel. He shall stand up against the kingdom of the enemy; therefore is the enemy eager to destroy all that call upon the Lord. For he knows that in the day on which Israel shall believe, the kingdom of the enemy shall be brought to an end; and the very angel of peace shall strengthen Israel, that it fall not into the extremity of evil. And it shall be in the time of the iniquity of Israel, that the Lord will depart from them, and will go after him that does His will, for unto none of His angels shall it be as unto him. And His name shall be in every place of Israel, and among the Gentiles, Saviour. Keep therefore yourselves, my children, from every evil work, and cast away wrath and all lying, and love truth and long-suffering; and the things which you have heard from your father, do ye also impart to your children, that the Father of the Gentiles may receive you: for He is true and long-suffering, meek and lowly, and teaches by His works the law of God. Depart, therefore, from all unrighteousness, and cleave unto the righteousness of the law of the Lord: and bury me near my fathers. 7 And when he had said these things he kissed them, and slept the long sleep. And his sons buried him, and after that they carried up his bones to the side of Abraham, and Isaac, and Jacob. Nevertheless, as Dan had prophesied unto them that they should forget the law of their God, and should be alienated from the land of their inheritance, and from the race of Israel, and from their kindred, so also it came to pass.

Test. 12 Pat. 8. The Testament of Naphtali Concerning Natural Goodness

1 The record of the testament of Naphtali, what things he ordained at the time of his death in the hundred and thirty-second year of his life. When his sons were gathered together in the seventh month, the fourth day of the month, he, being yet in good health, made them a feast and good cheer. And after he was awake in the morning, he said to them, I am dying; and they believed him not. And he blessed the Lord; and affirmed that after yesterday's feast he should die. He began then to say to his sons: Hear, my children; ye sons of Naphtali, hear the words of your father. I was born from Bilhah; and because Rachel dealt craftily, and gave Bilhah in place of herself to Jacob, and she bore me upon Rachel's lap, therefore was I called Naphtali. And Rachel loved me because I was born upon her lap; and when I was of young and tender form, she was wont to kiss me, and say, Would that I might see a brother of yours from my own womb, like you: whence also Joseph was like me in all things, according to the prayers of Rachel. Now my mother was Bilhah, daughter of Rotheus the brother of Deborah, Rebecca's nurse, and she was born on one and the self-same day with Rachel. And Rotheus was of the family of Abraham, a Chaldean, fearing God, free-born and noble; and he was taken captive, and was bought by Laban; and he gave him Aena his handmaid to wife, and she bore a daughter, and called her Zilpah, after the name of the village in which he had been taken captive. And next she bore Bilhah, saying, My daughter is eager after what is new, for immediately that she was born she was eager for the breast. 2 And since I was swift on my feet like a deer, my father Jacob appointed me for all errands and messages, and as a deer [Gen.s 49²¹ did he give me his blessing. For as the potter knows the vessel, what it contains, and brings clay thereto, so also does the Lord make the body in accordance with the spirit, and according to the capacity of the body does He implant the spirit, and the one is not deficient from the other by a third part of a hair; for by weight, and measure, and rule is every creature of the Most High. And as the potter knows the use of each vessel, whereto it suffices, so also does the Lord know the body, how far it is capable for goodness, and when it begins in evil; for there is no created thing and no thought which the Lord knows not, for He created every man after His own image. As man's strength, so also is his work; and as his mind, so also is his work; and as his purpose, so also is his doing; as his heart, so also is his mouth; as his eye, so also is his sleep; as his soul, so also is his word, either in the law of the Lord or in the law of Beliar. And as there is a division between light and darkness, between seeing and hearing, so also is there a division between man and man, and between woman and woman; neither is it to be said that there is any superiority in anything, either of the face or of other like things. For God made all things good in their order, the five senses in the head, and He joins on the neck to the head, the hair also for comeliness, the heart moreover for understanding, the belly for the dividing of the stomach, the calamus for health, the liver for wrath, the gall for bitterness. the spleen for laughter, the reins for craftiness, the loins for power, the ribs for containing, the back for strength, and so forth. So then, my children, be orderly unto good things in the fear of God, and do nothing disorderly in scorn or out of its due season. For if you bid the eye to hear, it cannot; so neither in darkness can you do the works of light. 3 Be not therefore eager to corrupt your doings through excess, or with empty words to deceive your souls; because if you keep silence in purity of heart, you shall be able to hold fast the will of God, and to cast away the will of the devil. Sun and moon and stars change not their order; so also you shall not change the law of God in the disorderliness of your doings. Nations went astray, and forsook the Lord, and changed their order, and followed stones and stocks, following after spirits of error. But you shall not be so, my children, recognising in the firmament, in the earth, and in the sea, and in all created things, the Lord who made them all, that you become not as Sodom, which changed the order of its nature, in like manner also the Watchers changed the order of their nature, whom also the Lord cursed at the flood, and for their sakes made desolate the earth, that it should be uninhabited and fruitless. 4 These things I say, my children, for I have read in the holy writing of Enoch that you yourselves also will depart from the Lord, walking according to all wickedness of the Gentiles, and ye will do according to all the iniquity of Sodom. And the Lord will bring captivity upon you, and there shall you serve your enemies, and you shall be covered with all affliction and tribulation, until the Lord shall have consumed you all. And after that you shall have been diminished and made few, you will return and acknowledge the Lord your God; and He will bring you back into your own land, according to His abundant mercy. And it shall be, after that they shall come into the land of their fathers, they will again forget the Lord and deal wickedly; and the Lord shall scatter them upon the face of all the earth, until the compassion of the Lord shall come, a Man working righteousness and showing mercy unto all them that are afar off, and them that are near. 5 For in the fortieth year of my life, I saw in a vision that the sun and the moon were standing still on the Mount of Olives, at the east of Jerusalem. And behold Isaac, the father of my father, says to us, Run and lay hold of them, each one according to his strength; and he that seizes them, his shall be the sun and the moon. And we all of us ran together, and Levi laid hold of the 49²¹ sun, and Judah outstripped the

others and seized the moon, and they were both of them lifted up with them. And when Levi became as a sun, a certain young man gave to him twelve branches of palm; and Judah was bright as the moon, and under his feet were twelve rays. And Levi and Judah ran, and laid hold each of the other. And, lo, a bull upon the earth, having two great horns, and an eagle's wings upon his back; and we wished to seize him, but could not. For Joseph outstripped us, and took him, and ascended up with him on high. And I saw, for I was there, and behold a holy writing appeared to us saying: Assyrians, Medes, Persians, Elamites, Gelachæans, Chaldeans, Syrians, shall possess in captivity the twelve tribes of Israel. 6 And again, after seven months, I saw our father Jacob standing by the sea of Jamnia, and we his sons were with him. And, behold, there came a ship sailing by, full of dried flesh, without sailors or pilot: and there was written upon the ship, Jacob. And our father says to us, Let us embark on our ship. And when we had gone on board, there arose a vehement storm, and a tempest of mighty wind; and our father, who was holding the helm, flew away from us. And we, being tost with the tempest, were borne along over the sea; and the ship was filled with water and beaten about with a mighty wave, so that it was nearly broken in pieces. And Joseph fled away upon a little boat, and we all were divided upon twelve boards, and Levi and Judah were together. We therefore all were scattered even unto afar off. Then Levi, girt about with sackcloth, prayed for us all unto the Lord. And when the storm ceased, immediately the ship reached the land, as though in peace. And, lo, Jacob our father came, and we rejoiced with one accord. 7 These two dreams I told to my father; and he said to me, These things must be fulfilled in their season, after that Israel has endured many things. Then my father says unto me, I believe that Joseph lives, for I see always that the Lord numbers him with you. And he said, weeping, You live, Joseph, my child, and I behold you not, and you see not Jacob that begot you. And he caused us also to weep at these words of his, and I burned in my heart to declare that he had been sold, but I feared my brethren. 8 Behold, my children, I have shown unto you the last times, that all shall come to pass in Israel. Do ye also therefore charge your children that they be united to Levi and to Judah. For through Judah shall salvation arise unto Israel, and in Him shall Jacob be blessed. For through his tribe shall God be seen dwelling among men on the earth, to save the race of Israel, and He shall gather together the righteous from the Gentiles. If you work that which is good, my children, both men and angels will bless you; and God will be glorified through you among the Gentiles, and the devil will flee from you, and the wild beasts will fear you, and the angels will cleave to you. For as if a man rear up a child well, he has a kindly remembrance thereof; so also for a good work there is a good remembrance with God. But him who does not that which is good, men and angels shall curse and God will be dishonoured among the heathen through him, and the devil makes him his own as his peculiar instrument, and every wild beast shall master him, and the Lord will hate him. For the commandments of the law are twofold, and through prudence must they be fulfilled. For there is a season for a man to embrace his wife, and a season to abstain therefrom for his prayer So then there are two commandments; and unless they be done in due order, they bring about sin. So also is it with the other commandments. Be therefore wise in God, and prudent, understanding the order of the commandments, and the laws of every work, that the Lord may love you. 9 And when he had charged them with many such words, he exhorted them that they should remove his bones to Hebron, and should bury him with his fathers. And when he had eaten and drunken with a merry heart, he covered his face and died. And his

sons did according to all things whatsoever Naphtali their father had charged them.

Test. 12 Pat. 9. The Testament of Gad Concerning Hatred

1 The record of the testament of Gad, what things he spoke unto his sons, in the hundred and twenty-seventh year of his life, saying: I was the seventh son born to Jacob, and I was valiant in keeping the flocks. I guarded at night the flock; and whenever the lion came, or wolf, or leopard, or bear, or any wild beast against the fold, I pursued it, and with my hand seizing its foot, and whirling it round, I stunned it, and hurled it over two furlongs, and so killed it. Now Joseph was feeding the flock with us for about thirty days, and being tender, he fell sick by reason of the heat. And he returned to Hebron to his father, who made him lie down near him, because he loved him. And Joseph told our father that the sons of Zilpah and Bilhah were slaying the best of the beasts, and devouring them without the knowledge of Judah and Reuben. For he saw that I delivered a lamb out of the mouth of the bear, and I put the bear to death; and the lamb I slew, being grieved concerning it that it could not live, and we ate it, and he told our father. And I was angry with Joseph for that thing until the day that he was sold into Egypt. And the spirit of hatred was in me, and I wished not either to see Joseph or to hear him. And he rebuked us to our faces for having eaten of the flock without Judah. And whatsoever things he told our father, he believed him. 2 I confess now my sin, my children, that oftentimes I wished to kill him, because I hated him to the death, and there were in no wise in me bowels of mercy towards him. Moreover, I hated him yet more because of his dreams; and I would have devoured him out of the land of the living, even as a calf devours the grass from the earth. Therefore I and Judah sold him to the Ishmaelites for thirty pieces of gold, and ten of them we hid, and showed the twenty to our brethren: and so through my covetousness I was fully bent on his destruction. And the God of my fathers delivered him from my hands, that I should not work iniquity in Israel. 3 And now, my children, hearken to the words of truth to work righteousness, and all the law of the Most High, and not go astray through the spirit of hatred, for it is evil in all the doings of men. Whatsoever a man does, that does the hater abhor: though he works the law of the Lord, he praises him not; though he fears the Lord, and takes pleasure in that which is righteous, he loves him not: he dispraises the truth, he envies him that orders his way aright, he delights in evil-speaking, he loves arrogance, for hatred has blinded his soul; even as I also looked on Joseph. 4 Take heed therefore, my children, of hatred; for it works iniquity against the Lord Himself: for it will not hear the words of His commandments concerning the loving of one's neighbour, and it sins against God. For if a brother stumble, immediately it wishes to proclaim it to all men, and is urgent that he should be judged for it, and be punished and slain. And if it be a servant, it accuses him to his master, and with all affliction it devises against him, if it be possible to slay him. For hatred works in envy, and it ever sickens with envy against them that prosper in well-doing, when it sees or hears thereof. For as love would even restore to life the dead, and would call back them that are condemned to die, so hatred would slay the living, and those that have offended in a small matter it would not suffer to live. For the spirit of hatred works together with Satan through hastiness of spirit in all things unto men's death; but the spirit of love works together with the law of God in long-suffering unto the salvation of men. 5 Hatred is evil, because it continually abides with lying, speaking against the truth; and it makes small things to be great, and gives heed to darkness as to light, and calls the sweet bitter, and teaches slander, and war, and violence, and every excess of evil; and it fills the heart with devilish poison. And these things I say to you from experience, my children,

that you may flee hatred, and cleave to the love of the Lord. Righteousness casts out hatred, humility destroys hatred. For he that is just and humble is ashamed to do wrong, being reproved not of another, but of his own heart, because the Lord views his intent: he speaks not against any man, because the fear of the Most High overcomes hatred. For, fearing lest he should offend the Lord, he will not do any wrong to any man, no, not even in thought. These things I learned at last, after that I had repented concerning Joseph. For true repentance after a godly sort destroys unbelief, and drives away the darkness, and enlightens the eyes, and gives knowledge to the soul, and guides the mind to salvation; and those things which it has not learned from man, it knows through repentance. For God brought upon me a disease of the heart; and had not the prayers of Jacob my father intervened, it had hardly failed that my spirit had departed. For by what things a man transgresses, by the same also is he punished. For in that my heart was set mercilessly against Joseph, in my heart too I suffered mercilessly, and was judged for eleven months, for so long a time as I had been envious against Joseph until he was sold. 6 And now, my children, love ye each one his brother, and put away hatred from your hearts, loving one another in deed, and in word, and in thought of the soul. For in the presence of our father I spoke peaceably with Joseph; and when I had gone out, the spirit of hatred darkened my mind, and moved my soul to slay him. Love ye therefore one another from your hearts; and if a man sin against you, tell him of it gently, and drive out the poison of hatred, and foster not guile in your soul. And if he confess and repent, forgive him; and if he deny it, strive not with him, lest he swear, and you sin doubly. Let not a stranger hear your secrets amid your striving, lest he hate and become your enemy, and work great sin against you; for ofttimes he will talk guilefully with you, or evilly overreach you, taking his poison from himself. Therefore, if he deny it, and is convicted and put to shame, and is silenced, do not tempt him on. For he who denies repents, so that he no more does wrong against you; yea also, he will honour you, and fear you, and be at peace with you. But if he be shameless, and abides in his wrongdoing, even then forgive him from the heart, and give the vengeance to God. 7 If a man prospers more than you, be not grieved, but pray also for him, that he may have perfect prosperity. For perchance it is expedient for you thus; and if he be further exalted, be not envious, remembering that all flesh shall die: and offer praise to God, who gives things good and profitable to all men. Seek out the judgments of the Lord, and so shall your mind rest and be at peace. And though a man become rich by evil means, even as Esau the brother of my father, be not jealous; but wait for the end of the Lord. For either He takes His benefits away from the wicked, or leaves them still to the repentant, or to the unrepentant reserves punishment for ever. For the poor man who is free from envy, giving thanks to the Lord in all things, is rich among all men, because he has not evil jealousy of men. Put away, therefore, hatred from your souls, and love one another with uprightness of heart. 8 And do ye also tell these things to your children, that they honour Judah and Levi, for from them shall the Lord raise up a Saviour to Israel. For I know that at the last your children shall depart from them, and shall walk in all wickedness, and mischief, and corruption before the Lord. And when he had rested for a little while, he said again to them, My children, obey your father, and bury me near to my fathers. And he drew up his feet, and fell asleep in peace. And after five years they carried him up, and laid him in Hebron with his fathers.

Test. 12 Pat. 10. The Testament of Asher Concerning Two Faces of Vice and Virtue

1 The record of the testament of Asher, what things he spoke to his sons in the hundred and twentieth year of his life. While he was still in health, he said to them: Hearken, you children of Asher, to your father, and I will declare to you all that is right in the sight of God. Two ways has God given to the sons of men, and two minds, and two doings, and two places, and two ends. Therefore all things are by twos, one corresponding to the other. There are two ways of good and evil, with which are the two minds in our breasts distinguishing them. Therefore if the soul take pleasure in good, all its actions are in righteousness; and though it sin, it straightway repents. For, having his mind set upon righteousness, and casting away maliciousness, he straightway overthrows the evil, and uproots the sin. But if his mind turn aside in evil, all his doings are in maliciousness, and he drives away the good, and takes unto him the evil, and is ruled by Beliar; and even though he work what is good, he perverts it in evil. For whenever he begins as though to do good, he brings the end of his doing to work evil, seeing that the treasure of the devil is filled with the poison of an evil spirit. 2 There is then, he says, a soul which speaks the good for the sake of the evil, and the end of the doing leads to mischief. There is a man who shows no compassion upon him who serves his turn in evil; and this thing has two aspects, but the whole is evil. And there is a man that loves him that works evil; he likewise dwells in evil, because he chooses even to die in an evil cause for his sake: and concerning this it is clear that it has two aspects, but the whole is an evil work. And though there is love, it is but wickedness concealing the evil, even as it bears a name that seems good, but the end of the doing tends unto evil. Another steals, works unjustly, plunders, defrauds, and withal pities the poor: this, too, has a twofold aspect, but the whole is evil. Defrauding his neighbour he provokes God, and swears falsely against the Most High, and yet pities the poor: the Lord who commands the law he sets at nought and provokes, and refreshes the poor; he defiles the soul, and makes gay the body; he kills many, and he pities a few: and this, too, has a twofold aspect. Another commits adultery and fornication, and abstains from meats; yet in his fasting he works evil, and by his power and his wealth perverts many, and out of his excessive wickedness works the commandments: this, too, has a twofold aspect, but the whole is evil. Such men are as swine or hares; for they are half clean, but in very deed are unclean. For God in the Heavenly Tablets has thus declared. 3 Do not ye therefore, my children, wear two faces like them, of goodness and of wickedness; but cleave unto goodness only, for in goodness does God rest, and men desire it. From wickedness flee away, destroying the devil by your good works; for they that are double-faced serve not God, but their own lusts, so that they may please Beliar and men like themselves. 4 For good men, even they that are single of face, though they be thought by them that are double-faced to err, are just before God. For many in killing the wicked do two works, an evil by a good; but the whole is good, because he has uprooted and destroyed that which is evil. One man hates him that shows mercy, and does wrong to the adulterer and the thief: this, too, is double-faced, but the whole work is good, because he follows the Lord's example, in that he receives not that which seems good with that which is really bad. Another desires not to see good days with them that riot, lest he defile his mouth and pollute his soul: this, too, is double-faced, but the whole is good, for such men are like to stags and to hinds, because in a wild condition they seem to be unclean, but they are altogether clean; because they walk in a zeal for God, and abstain from what God also hates and forbids by His commandments, and they ward off the evil from the good. 5 You see therefore, my children, how that there are two in all things, one against the other, and the one is hidden by the other. Death succeeds to life, dishonour to glory, night to day, and darkness to light; and all things are under the day, and just things

under life: wherefore also everlasting life awaits death. Nor may it be said that truth is a lie, nor right wrong; for all truth is under the light, even as all things are under God. All these things I proved in my life, and I wandered not from the truth of the Lord, and I searched out the commandments of the Most High, walking with singleness of face according to all my strength unto that which is good. ⁶ Take heed therefore ye also, my children, to the commandments of the Lord, following the truth with singleness of face, for they that are double-faced receive twofold punishment. Hate the spirits of error, which strive against men. Keep the law of the Lord, and give not heed to evil as unto good; but look unto the thing that is good indeed, and keep it in all commandments of the Lord, having your conversation unto Him, and resting in Him: for the ends at which men aim do show their righteousness, and know the angels of the Lord from the angels of Satan. For if the soul depart troubled, it is tormented by the evil spirit which also it served in lusts and evil works; but if quietly and with joy it has known the angel of peace, it shall comfort him in life. ⁷ Become not, my children, as Sodom, which knew not the angels of the Lord, and perished for ever. For I know that you will sin, and you shall be delivered into the hands of your enemies, and your land shall be made desolate, and you shall be scattered unto the four corners of the earth. And you shall be set at nought in the Dispersion as useless water, until the Most High shall visit the earth; and He shall come as man, with men eating and drinking, and in peace breaking the head of the dragon through water. He shall save Israel and all nations, God speaking in the person of man. Therefore tell ye these things to your children, that they disobey Him not. For I have read in the Heavenly Tablets that in very deed you will disobey Him, and act ungodly against Him, not giving heed to the law of God, but to the commandments of men. Therefore shall you be scattered as Gad and as Dan my brethren, who shall know not their own lands, tribe, and tongue. But the Lord will gather you together in faith through the hope of His tender mercy, for the sake of Abraham, and Isaac, and Jacob. ⁸ And when he had said these things unto them, he charged them, saying: Bury me in Hebron. And he fell into a peaceful sleep, and died; and after this his sons did as he had charged them, and they carried him up and buried him with his fathers.

Test. 12 Pat. 11. The Testament of Joseph Concerning Sobriety
¹ The record of the testament of Joseph. When he was about to die he called his sons and his brethren together, and said to them: My children and brethren, hearken to Joseph the beloved of Israel; give ear, my sons, unto your father. I have seen in my life envy and death, and I wandered not in the truth of the Lord. These my brethren hated me, and the Lord loved me: they wished to slay me, and the God of my fathers guarded me: they let me down into a pit, and the Most High brought me up again: I was sold for a slave, and the Lord made me free: I was taken into captivity, and His strong hand succoured me: I was kept in hunger, and the Lord Himself nourished me: I was alone, and God comforted me: I was sick, and the Most High visited me: I was in prison, and the Saviour showed favour unto me; in bonds, and He released me; amid slanders, and He pleaded my cause; amid bitter words of the Egyptians, and He rescued me; amid envy and guile, and He exalted me. ² And thus Potiphar the chief cook of Pharaoh entrusted to me his house, and I struggled against a shameless woman, urging me to transgress with her; but the God of Israel my father guarded me from the burning flame. I was cast into prison, I was beaten, I was mocked; and the Lord granted me to find pity in the sight of the keeper of the prison. For He will in no wise forsake them that fear Him, neither in darkness, nor in bonds, nor in tribulations, nor in necessities. For not as man is God ashamed, nor as the son of man is He afraid, nor

as one that is earth-born is He weak, or can He be thrust aside; but in all places is He at hand, and in various ways does He comfort, departing for a little to try the purpose of the soul. In ten temptations He showed me approved, and in all of them I endured; for endurance is a mighty charm, and patience gives many good things. ³ How often did the Egyptian threaten me with death! How often did she give me over to punishment, and then call me back, and threaten me when I would not company with her! And she said to me, You shall be lord of me, and all that is mine, if you will give yourself unto me, and you shall be as our master. Therefore I remembered the words of the fathers of my father Jacob, and I entered into my chamber and prayed unto the Lord; and I fasted in those seven years, and I appeared to my master as one living delicately, for they that fast for God's sake receive beauty of face. And if one gave me wine, I drank it not; and I fasted for three days, and took my food and gave it to the poor and sick. And I sought the Lord early, and wept for the Egyptian woman of Memphis, for very unceasingly did she trouble me, and at night she came to me under the pretence of visiting me; and at first, because she had no male child, she feigned to count me as a son. And I prayed unto the Lord, and she bare a male child; therefore for a time she embraced me as a son, and I knew it not. Last of all, she sought to draw me into fornication. And when I perceived it, I sorrowed even unto death; and when she had gone out I came to myself, and I lamented for her many days, because I saw her guile and her deceit. And I declared unto her the words of the Most High, if haply she would turn from her evil lust. ⁴ How often has she fawned upon me with words as a holy man, with guile in her talk, praising my chastity before her husband, while desiring to destroy me when we were alone. She lauded me openly as chaste, and in secret she said unto me, Fear not my husband; for he is persuaded concerning your chastity, so that even should one tell him concerning us he would in no wise believe. For all these things I lay upon the ground in sackcloth, and I besought God that the Lord would deliver me from the Egyptian. And when she prevailed nothing, she came again to me under the plea of instruction, that she might know the word of the Lord. And she said unto me, If you will that I should leave my idols, be persuaded by me, and I will persuade my husband to depart from his idols, and we will walk in the law of your Lord. And I said unto her, The Lord wills not that those who reverence Him should be in uncleanness, nor does He take pleasure in them that commit adultery. And she held her peace, longing to accomplish her evil desire. And I gave myself yet more to fasting and prayer, that the Lord should deliver me from her. ⁵ And again at another time she said unto me, If you will not commit adultery, I will kill my husband, and so will I lawfully take you to be my husband. I therefore, when I heard this, rent my garment, and said, Woman, reverence the Lord, and do not this evil deed, lest you be utterly destroyed; for I will declare your ungodly thought unto all men. She therefore, being afraid, besought that I would declare to no one her wickedness. And she departed, soothing me with gifts, and sending to me every delight of the sons of men. ⁶ And she sends to me food sprinkled with enchantments. And when the eunuch who brought it came, I looked up and beheld a terrible man giving me with the dish a sword, and I perceived that her scheme was for the deception of my soul. And when he had gone out I wept, nor did I taste that or any other of her food. So then after one day she came to me and observed the food, and said unto me, What is this, that you have not eaten of the food? And I said unto her, It is because you filled it with death; and how did you say, I come not near to idols but to the Lord alone? Now therefore know that the God of my father has revealed unto me by an angel your wickedness, and I have kept it to convict you, if haply you may see it and repent. But that you may learn that the wickedness of the ungodly has no power over them that reverence God in chastity, I took it and ate it before her, saying, The God of my fathers and the Angel of Abraham shall be with me. And she fell upon her face at my feet, and wept; and I raised her up and admonished her, and she promised to do this iniquity no more. 7 But because her heart was set upon me to commit lewdness, she sighed, and her countenance fell. And when her husband saw her, he said unto her, Why is your countenance fallen? And she said, I have a pain at my heart, and the groanings of my spirit do oppress me; and so he comforted her who was not sick. Then she rushed in to me while her husband was yet without, and said unto me, I will hang myself, or cast myself into a well or over a cliff, if you will not consent unto me. And when I saw the spirit of Beliar was troubling her, I prayed unto the Lord, and said unto her, Why are you troubled and disturbed, blinded in sins? Remember that if you kill yourself, Sethon, the concubine of your husband, your rival, will beat your children, and will destroy your memorial from off the earth. And she said unto me, Lo then you love me; this alone is sufficient for me, that you care for my life and my children: I have expectation that I shall enjoy my desire. And she knew not that because of my God I spoke thus, and not because of her. For if a man has fallen before the passion of a wicked desire, then by that has he become enslaved, even as also was she. And if he hear any good thing with regard to the passion whereby he is vanquished, he receives it unto his wicked desire. 8 I declare unto you, my children, that it was about the sixth hour when she departed from me; and I knelt before the Lord all that day, and continued all the night; and about dawn I rose up weeping, and praying for a release from the Egyptian. At last, then, she laid hold of my garments, forcibly dragging me to have connection with her. When, therefore, I saw that in her madness she was forcibly holding my garments, I fled away naked. And she falsely accused me to her husband, and the Egyptian cast me into the prison in his house; and on the morrow, having scourged me, the Egyptian sent me into the prison in his house. When, therefore, I was in fetters, the Egyptian woman fell sick from her vexation, and listened to me how I sang praises unto the Lord while I was in the abode of darkness, and with glad voice rejoiced and glorified my God only because by a pretext I had been rid of the Egyptian woman. 9 How often has she sent unto me, saying, Consent to fulfil my desire, and I will release you from your bonds, and I will free time from the darkness! And not even in thoughts did I incline unto her. For God loves him who in a den of darkness fasts with chastity, rather than him who in secret chambers lives delicately without restraint. And whosoever lives in chastity, and desires also glory, and if the Most High knows that it is expedient for him, He bestows this also upon him, even as upon me. How often, though she were sick, did she come down to me at unlooked-for times, and listened to my voice as I prayed! And when I heard her groanings I held my peace. For when I was in her house she was wont to bare her arms, and breasts, and legs, that I might fall before her; for she was very beautiful, splendidly adorned for my deception. And the Lord guarded me from her devices. 10 You see therefore, my children, how great things patience works, and prayer with fasting. And if you therefore follow after sobriety and purity in patience and humility of heart, the Lord will dwell among you, because He loves sobriety. And wheresoever the Most High dwells, even though a man fall into envy, or slavery, or slander, the Lord who dwells in him, for his sobriety's sake not only delivers him from evil, but also exalts and glorifies him, even as me. For in every way the man is guarded, whether in deed, or in word, or in thought. My brethren know how my father loved me, and I was not exalted in my heart; although I

was a child, I had the fear of God in my thoughts. For I knew that all things should pass away, and I kept myself within bounds, and I honoured my brethren; and through fear of them I held my peace when I was sold, and revealed not my family to the Ishmaelites, that I was the son of Jacob, a great man and a mighty. 11 Do ye also, therefore, have the fear of God in your works, and honour your brethren. For every one who works the law of the Lord shall be loved by Him. And when I came to the Indocolpitæ with the Ishmaelites, they asked me, and I said that I was a slave from their house, that I might not put my brethren to shame. And the eldest of them said unto me, You are not a slave, for even your appearance does make it manifest concerning you. And he threatened me even unto death. But I said that I was their slave. Now when we came into Egypt, they strove concerning me, which of them should buy me and take me. Therefore it seemed good to all that I should remain in Egypt with a merchant of their trade, until they should return bringing merchandise. And the Lord gave me favour in the eyes of the merchant, and he entrusted unto me his house. And the Lord blessed him by my means, and increased him in silver and gold, and I was with him three months and five days. 12 About that time the Memphian wife of Potiphar passed by with great pomp, and cast her eyes upon me, because her eunuchs told her concerning me. And she told her husband concerning the merchant, that he had become rich by means of a young Hebrew, saying, And they say that men have indeed stolen him out of the land of Canaan. Now therefore execute judgment with him, and take away the youth to be your steward; so shall the God of the Hebrews bless you, for grace from heaven is upon him. 13 And Potiphar was persuaded by her words, and commanded the merchant to be brought, and said unto him, What is this that I hear, that you steal souls out of the land of the Hebrews, and sellest them for slaves? The merchant therefore fell upon his face, and besought him, saying, I beseech you, my lord, I know not what you say. And he said, Whence then is your Hebrew servant? And he said, The Ishmaelites entrusted him to me until they should return. And he believed him not, but commanded him to be stripped and beaten. And when he persisted, Potiphar said, Let the youth be brought. And when I was brought in, I did obeisance to the chief of the eunuchs — for he was third in rank with Pharaoh, being chief of all the eunuchs, and having wives and children and concubines. And he took me apart from him, and said unto me, Are you a slave or free? And I said, A slave. And he said unto me, Whose slave are you? And I said unto him, The Ishmaelites'. And again he said unto me, How did you become their slave? And I said, They bought me out of the land of Canaan. And he believed me not, and said, You are lying: and he commanded me to be stripped and beaten. 14 Now the Memphian woman was looking through a window while I was being beaten, and she sent unto her husband, saying, Your judgment is unjust; for you even punish a free man who has been stolen, as though he were a transgressor. And when I gave no other answer though I was beaten, he commanded that we should be kept in guard, until, said he, the owners of the boy shall come. And his wife said unto him, Wherefore do you detain in captivity this noble child, who ought rather to be set at liberty, and wait upon you? For she wished to see me in desire of sin, and I was ignorant concerning all these things. Then said he to his wife, It is not the custom of the Egyptians to take away that which belongs to others before proof is given. This he said concerning the merchant, and concerning me, that I must be imprisoned. 15 Now, after four and twenty days came the Ishmaelites; and having heard that Jacob my father was mourning because of me, they said unto me, How is it that you said that you were a slave? And lo, we have learned that you are the son of a mighty man in the land of Canaan, and your father grieves for you in sackcloth. And again I would have wept, but I restrained myself, that I should not put my brethren to shame. And I said, I know not, I am a slave. Then they take counsel to sell me, that I should not be found in their hands. For they feared Jacob, lest he should work upon them a deadly vengeance. For it had been heard that he was mighty with the Lord and with men. Then said the merchant unto them, Release me from the judgment of Potiphar. They therefore came and asked for me, saying, He was bought by us with money. And he sent us away. ¹⁶ Now the Memphian woman pointed me out to her husband, that he should buy me; for I hear, said she, that they are selling him. And she sent a eunuch to the Ishmaelites, and asked them to sell me; and since he was not willing to traffic with them, he returned. So when the eunuch had made trial of them, he made known to his mistress that they asked a large price for their slave. And she sent another eunuch, saying, Even though they demand two minæ of gold, take heed not to spare the gold; only buy the boy, and bring him hither. And he gave them eighty pieces of gold for me, and told his mistress that a hundred had been given for me. And when I saw it I held my peace, that the eunuch should not be punished. ¹⁷ You see, my children, what great things I endured that I should not put my brethren to shame. Do ye also love one another, and with long-suffering hide ye one another's faults. For God delights in the unity of brethren, and in the purpose of a heart approved unto love. And when my brethren came into Egypt, and learned that I returned their money unto them, and upbraided them not, yea, that I even comforted them, and after the death of Jacob I loved them more abundantly, and all things whatsoever he commanded I did very abundantly, then they marvelled. For I suffered them not to be afflicted even unto the smallest matter; and all that was in my hand I gave unto them. Their children were my children, and my children were as their servants; their life was my life, and all their suffering was my suffering, and all their sickness was my infirmity. My land was their land, my counsel their counsel, and I exalted not myself among them in arrogance because of my worldly glory, but I was among them as one of the least. ¹⁸ If you also therefore walk in the commandments of the Lord, my children, He will exalt you there, and will bless you with good things for ever and ever. And if any one seeks to do evil unto you, by well-doing pray for him, and you shall be redeemed of the Lord from all evil. For, behold, you see that through long-suffering I took unto wife even the daughter of my master. And a hundred talents of gold were given me with her; for the Lord made them to serve me. And He gave me also beauty as a flower above the beautiful ones of Israel; and He preserved me unto old age in strength and in beauty, because I was like in all things to Jacob. ¹⁹ Hear ye also, my children, the visions which I saw. There were twelve deer feeding, and the nine were divided and scattered in the land, likewise also the three. And I saw that from Judah was born a virgin wearing a linen garment, and from her went forth a Lamb, without spot, and on His left hand there was as it were a lion; and all the beasts rushed against Him, and the lamb overcame them, and destroyed them, and trod them under foot. And because of Him the angels rejoiced, and men, and all the earth. And these things shall take place in their season, in the last days. Do ye therefore, my children, observe the commandments of the Lord, and honour Judah and Levi; for from them shall arise unto you the Lamb of God, by grace saving all the Gentiles and Israel. For His kingdom is an everlasting kingdom, which shall not be shaken; but my kingdom among you shall come to an end as a watcher's hammock, which after the summer will not appear. ²⁰ I know that after my death the Egyptians will afflict you, but God will undertake your cause, and will bring you into that which He promised to your fathers. But carry

ye up my bones with you; for when my bones are taken up, the Lord will be with you in light, and Beliar shall be in darkness with the Egyptians. And carry ye up Zilpah your mother, and lay her near Bilhah, by the hippodrome, by the side of Rachel. And when he had said these things, he stretched out his feet, and slept the long sleep. And all Israel bewailed him, and all Egypt, with a great lamentation. For he felt even for the Egyptians even as his own members, and showed them kindness, aiding them in every work, and counsel, and matter.

Test. 12 Pat. 12. The Testament of Benjamin Concerning a Pure Mind

¹ The record of the words of Benjamin, which he set forth to his sons, after he had lived a hundred and twenty years. And he kissed them, and said: As Isaac was born to Abraham in his hundredth year, so also was I to Jacob. Now since Rachel died in giving me birth, I had no milk; therefore I was suckled by Bilhah her handmaid. For Rachel remained barren for twelve years after that she had borne Joseph: and she prayed the Lord with fasting twelve days, and she conceived and bare me. For our father loved Rachel dearly, and prayed that he might see two sons born from her: therefore was I called the son of days, which is Benjamin. ² When therefore I went into Egypt, and Joseph my brother recognised me, he said unto me, What did they tell my father in that they sold me? And I said unto him, They dabbled your coat with blood and sent it, and said, Look if this is the coat of your son. And he said to me, Even so, brother; for when the Ishmaelites took me, one of them stripped off my coat, and gave me a girdle, and scourged me, and bade me run. And as he went away to hide my garment, a lion met him, and slew him; and so his fellows were afraid, and sold me to their companions. ³ Do ye also therefore, my children, love the Lord God of heaven, and keep His commandments, and be followers of the good and holy man Joseph; and let your mind be unto good, even as you know me. He that has his mind good sees all things rightly. Fear ye the Lord, and love your neighbour; and even though the spirits of Beliar allure you into all troublous wickedness, yet shall no troublous wickedness have dominion over you, even as it had not over Joseph my brother. How many men wished to slay him, and God shielded him! For he that fears God and loves his neighbour cannot be smitten by Beliar's spirit of the air, being shielded by the fear of God; nor can he be ruled over by the device of men or of beasts, for he is aided by the love of the Lord which he has towards his neighbour. For he even besought our father Jacob that he would pray for our brethren, that the Lord would not impute to them the evil that they devised concerning Joseph. And thus Jacob cried out, My child Joseph, you have prevailed over the bowels of your father Jacob. And he embraced him, and kissed him for two hours, saying, In you shall be fulfilled the prophecy of heaven concerning the Lamb of God, even the Saviour of the world, that spotless shall He be delivered up for transgressors, and sinless shall He be put to death for ungodly men in the blood of the covenant, for the salvation of the Gentiles and of Israel, and shall destroy Beliar, and them that serve him. ⁴ Know ye, my children, the end of the good man? Be followers of his compassion in a good mind, that you also may wear crowns of glory. The good man has not a dark eye; for he shows mercy to all men, even though they be sinners, even though they devise evil concerning him. So he that does good overcomes the evil, being shielded by Him that is good; and he loves the righteous as his own soul. If any one is glorified, he envies him not; if any one is enriched, he is not jealous; if any one is valiant, he praises him; he trusts and lauds him that is sober-minded; he shows mercy to the poor; he is kindly disposed toward the weak; he sings the praises of God; as for him who has the fear of God, he protects him as with a shield; him

that loves God he aids; him that rejects the Most High he admonishes and turns back; and him that has the grace of a good spirit, he loves even as his own soul. 5 If you have a good mind, my children, then will both wicked men be at peace with you, and the profligate will reverence you and turn unto good; and the covetous shall not only cease from their inordinate desire, but shall even give the fruits of their covetousness to them that are afflicted. If you do well, even the unclean spirits shall flee from you; yea, the very beasts shall flee from you in dread. For where the reverence for good works is present unto the mind, darkness flees away from him. For if any one is injurious to a holy man, he repents; for the holy man shows pity on his reviler, and holds his peace. And if any one betray a righteous soul, and the righteous man, though praying, be humbled for a little while, yet not long after he appears far more glorious, even as was Joseph my brother. 6 The mind of the good man is not in the power of the deceit of the spirit of Beliar, for the angel of peace guides his soul. He gazes not passionately on corruptible things, nor gathers together riches unto desire of pleasure; he delights not in pleasure, he hurts not his neighbour, he pampers not himself with food, he errs not in the pride of his eyes, for the Lord is his portion. The good mind admits not the glory and dishonour of men, neither knows it any guile or lie, fighting or reviling; for the Lord dwells in him and lights up his soul, and he rejoices towards all men at every time. The good mind has not two tongues, of blessing and of cursing, of insult and of honour, of sorrow and of joy, of quietness and of trouble, of hypocrisy and of truth, of poverty and of wealth; but it has one disposition, pure and uncorrupt, concerning all men. It has no double sight, nor double hearing; for in everything which he does, or speaks, or sees, he knows that the Lord watches his soul, and he cleanses his mind that he be not condemned by God and men. But of Beliar every work is twofold, and has no singleness. 7 Flee ye therefore, my children, the evil-doing of Beliar; for it gives a sword to them that obeys, and the sword is the mother of seven evils. First the mind conceives through Beliar, and first there is envy; secondly, desperation; thirdly, tribulation; fourthly, captivity; fifthly, neediness; sixthly, trouble; seventhly, desolation. Therefore also Cain is delivered over to seven vengeances by God, for in every hundred years the Lord brought one plague upon him. Two hundred years he suffered, and in the nine hundredth year he was brought to desolation at the flood, for Abel his righteous brother's sake. In seven hundred years was Cain judged, and Lamech in seventy times seven; because for ever those who are likened unto Cain in envy unto hatred of brethren shall be judged with the same punishment. 8 Do ye also therefore, my children, flee ill-doing, envy, and hatred of brethren, and cleave to goodness and love. He that has a pure mind in love, looks not after a woman unto fornication; for he has no defilement in his heart, because the Spirit of God rests in him. For as the sun is not defiled by shining over dung and mire, but rather dries up both and drives away the ill smell: so also the pure mind, constrained among the defilements of the earth, rather edifies, and itself suffers no defilement. 9 Now I suppose, from the words of the righteous Enoch, that there will be also evil-doings among you: for you will commit fornication with the fornication of Sodom, and shall perish all save a few, and will multiply inordinate lusts with women; and the kingdom of the Lord shall not be among you, for immediately He will take it away. Nevertheless the temple of God shall be built in your portion, and shall be glorious among you. For He shall take it, and the twelve tribes shall be gathered together there, and all the Gentiles, until the Most High shall send forth His salvation in the visitation of His only-begotten one. And He shall enter into the front of the temple, and there shall the Lord be treated with outrage, and He shall be lifted up upon a tree. And

130

the veil of the temple shall be rent, and the Spirit of God shall descend upon the Gentiles as fire poured forth. And He shall arise from the grave, and shall ascend from earth into heaven: and I know how lowly He shall be upon the earth, and how glorious in the heaven. 10 Now when Joseph was in Egypt, I longed to see his visage and the form of his countenance; and through the prayers of Jacob my father I saw him, while awake in the daytime, in his full and perfect shape. Know ye therefore, my children, that I am dying. Work therefore truth and righteousness each one with his neighbour, and judgment unto faithful doing, and keep the law of the Lord and His commandments; for these things do I teach you instead of all inheritance. Do ye also therefore give them to your children for an everlasting possession; for so did both Abraham, and Isaac, and Jacob. All these things they gave us for an inheritance, saying, Keep the commandments of God until the Lord shall reveal His salvation to all nations. Then shall you see Enoch, Noah, and Shem, and Abraham, and Isaac, and Jacob, arising on the right hand in gladness. Then shall we also arise, each one over our tribe, worshipping the King of heaven, who appeared upon the earth in the form of a man of humility. And as many as believed on Him on the earth shall rejoice with Him; and then shall all men arise, some unto glory and some unto shame. And the Lord shall judge Israel first, even for the wrong they did unto Him; for when He appeared as a deliverer, God in the flesh, they believed Him not. And then shall He judge all the Gentiles, as many as believed Him not when He appeared upon earth. And He shall reprove Israel among the chosen ones of the Gentiles, even as He reproved Esau among the Midianites, who deceived their brethren, so that they fell into fornication and idolatry; and they were alienated from God, and became as they that were no children in the portion of them that fear the Lord. But if you walk in holiness in the presence of the Lord, you shall dwell in hope again in me, and all Israel shall be gathered unto the Lord. 11 And I shall no longer be called a ravening wolf on account of your ravages, but a worker of the Lord, distributing food to them that work what is good. And one shall rise up from my seed in the latter times, beloved of the Lord, hearing upon the earth His voice, enlightening with new knowledge all the Gentiles, bursting in upon Israel for salvation with the light of knowledge, and tearing it away from it like a wolf, and giving it to the synagogue of the Gentiles. And until the consummation of the ages shall he be in the synagogues of the Gentiles, and among their rulers, as a strain of music in the mouth of all; and he shall be inscribed in the holy books, both his work and his word, and he shall be a chosen one of God for ever; and because of him my father Jacob instructed me, saying, He shall fill up that which lacks of your tribe. 12 And when he finished his words, he said: I charge you, my children, carry up my bones out of Egypt, and bury me at Hebron, near my fathers. So Benjamin died a hundred and twenty-five years old, in a good old age, and they placed him in a coffin. And in the ninety-first year of the departure of the children of Israel from Egypt, they and their brethren brought up the bones of their fathers secretly in a place which is called Canaan; and they buried them in Hebron, by the feet of their fathers. And they returned from the land of Canaan, and dwelt in Egypt until the day of their departing from the land of Egypt.

Jubilees

Moses receives the tables of the law and instruction on past and future history which he is to inscribe in a book, 1-4. Apostasy of Israel, 5-9. Captivity of Israel and Judah, 10-13. Return of Judah and rebuilding of the temple, 15-18. Moses' prayer for Israel, 19-21. God's promise to redeem and dwell with them, 22-5, 28. Moses bidden to write down the future history of the world (the Book of

THIS is the history of the division of the days of the law and of the testimony, of the events of the years, of their (year) weeks, of their Jubilees throughout all the years of the world, as the Lord spake to Moses on Mount Sinai when he went up to receive the tables of the law and of the commandment, according to the voice of God as he said unto him, 'Go up to the top of the Mount.'

Jub. 1

[1]And it came to pass in the first year of the exodus of the children of Israel out of Egypt, in the third month, on the sixteenth day of the month, [2450 Anno Mundi] that God spake to Moses, saying: 'Come up to Me on the Mount, and I will give thee two tables of stone of the law and of the commandment, which I have written, that thou mayst teach them.' [2]And Moses went up into the mount of God, and the glory of the Lord abode on Mount Sinai, and a cloud overshadowed it six days. [3]And He called to Moses on the seventh day out of the midst of the cloud, and the appearance of the glory of the Lord was like a flaming fire on the top of the mount. [4]And Moses was on the Mount forty days and forty nights, and God taught him the earlier and the later history of the division of all the days of the law and of the testimony. [5]And He said: 'Incline thine heart to every word which I shall speak to thee on this mount, and write them in a book in order that their generations may see how I have not forsaken them for all the evil which they have wrought in transgressing the covenant which I establish between Me and thee for their generations this day on Mount Sinai. [6]And thus it will come to pass when all these things come upon them, that they will recognise that I am more righteous than they in all their judgments and in all their actions, and they will recognise that I have been truly with them. [7]And do thou write for thyself all these words which I declare unto, thee this day, for I know their rebellion and their stiff neck, before I bring them into the land of which I sware to their fathers, to Abraham and to Isaac and to Jacob, saying: ' Unto your seed will I give a land flowing with milk and honey. [8]And they will eat and be satisfied, and they will turn to strange gods, to (gods) which cannot deliver them from aught of their tribulation: and this witness shall be heard for a witness against them. For they will forget all My commandments, (even) all that I command them, and they will walk after the Gentiles, and after their uncleanness, and after their shame, and will serve their gods, and these will prove unto them an offence and a tribulation and an affliction and a snare. [9]And many will perish and they will be taken captive, and will fall into the hands of the enemy, because they have forsaken My ordinances and My commandments, and the festivals of My covenant, and My sabbaths, and My holy place which I have hallowed for Myself in their midst, and My tabernacle, and My sanctuary, which I have hallowed for Myself in the midst of the land, that I should set my name upon it, and that it should dwell (there). [10]And they will make to themselves high places and groves and graven images, and they will worship, each his own (graven image), so as to go astray, and they will sacrifice their children to demons, and to all the works of the error of their hearts. [11]And I will send witnesses unto them, that I may witness against them, but they will not hear, and will slay the witnesses also, and they will persecute those who seek the law, and they will abrogate and change everything so as to work evil before My eyes. [12]And I will hide My face from them, and I will deliver them into the hand of the Gentiles for captivity, and for a prey, and for devouring, and I will remove them from the midst of the land, and I will scatter them amongst the Gentiles. [13]And they will forget all My law and all My commandments and all My judgments, and will go astray as to new moons, and sabbaths, and festivals, and jubilees, and ordinances. [14]And after this they will turn to Me from amongst the Gentiles with all their heart and with all their soul and with all their strength, and I will gather them from amongst all the Gentiles, and they will seek me, so that I shall be found of them, when they seek me with all their heart and with all their soul. [15]And I will disclose to them abounding peace with righteousness, and I will remove them the plant of uprightness, with all My heart and with all My soul, and they shall be for a blessing and not for a curse, and they shall be the head and not the tail. [16]And I will build My sanctuary in their midst, and I will dwell with them, and I will be their God and they shall be My people in truth and righteousness. [17]And I will not forsake them nor fail them; for I am the Lord their God.' [18]And Moses fell on his face and prayed and said, 'O Lord my God, do not forsake Thy people and Thy inheritance, so that they should wander in the error of their hearts, and do not deliver them into the hands of their enemies, the Gentiles, lest they should rule over them and cause them to sin against Thee. [19]Let thy mercy, O Lord, be lifted up upon Thy people, and create in them an upright spirit, and let not the spirit of Beliar rule over them to accuse them before Thee, and to ensnare them from all the paths of righteousness, so that they may perish from before Thy face. [20]But they are Thy people and Thy inheritance, which thou hast delivered with thy great power from the hands of the Egyptians: create in them a clean heart and a holy spirit, and let them not be ensnared in their sins from henceforth until eternity.' [21]And the Lord said unto Moses: 'I know their contrariness and their thoughts and their stiffneckedness, and they will not be obedient till they confess their own sin and the sin of their fathers. [22]And after this they will turn to Me in all uprightness and with all (their) heart and with all (their) soul, and I will circumcise the foreskin of their heart and the foreskin of the heart of their seed, and I will create in them a holy spirit, and I will cleanse them so that they shall not turn away from Me from that day unto eternity. [23]And their souls will cleave to Me and to all My commandments, and they will fulfil My commandments, and I will be their Father and they shall be My children. [24]And they all shall be called children of the living God, and every angel and every spirit shall know, yea, they shall know that these are My children, and that I am their Father in uprightness and righteousness, and that I love them. [25]And do thou write down for thyself all these words which I declare unto thee on this mountain, the first and the last, which shall come to pass in all the divisions of the days in the law and in the testimony and in the weeks and the jubilees unto eternity, until I descend and dwell with them throughout eternity.' [26]And He said to the angel of the presence: Write for Moses from the beginning of creation till My sanctuary has been built among them for all eternity. [27]And the Lord will appear to the eyes of all, and all shall know that I am the God of Israel and the Father of all the children of Jacob, and King on Mount Zion for all eternity. And Zion and Jerusalem shall be holy.' [28]And the angel of the presence who went before the camp of Israel took the tables of the divisions of the years -from the time of the creation- of the law and of the testimony of the weeks of the jubilees, according to the individual years, according to all the number of the jubilees [according, to the individual years], from the day of the [new] creation when the heavens and the earth shall be renewed and all their creation according to the powers of the heaven, and according to all the creation of the earth, until the sanctuary of the Lord shall be made in Jerusalem on Mount Zion, and all the luminaries be renewed for healing and for peace and for blessing for all the elect of Israel, and that thus it may be from that day and unto all the days of the earth.

Jub. 2

¹And the angel of the presence spake to Moses according to the word of the Lord, saying: Write the complete history of the creation, how in six days the Lord God finished all His works and all that He created, and kept Sabbath on the seventh day and hallowed it for all ages, and appointed it as a sign for all His works. ²For on the first day He created the heavens which are above and the earth and the waters and all the spirits which serve before him -the angels of the presence, and the angels of sanctification, and the angels [of the spirit of fire and the angels] of the spirit of the winds, and the angels of the spirit of the clouds, and of darkness, and of snow and of hail and of hoar frost, and the angels of the voices and of the thunder and of the lightning, and the angels of the spirits of cold and of heat, and of winter and of spring and of autumn and of summer and of all the spirits of his creatures which are in the heavens and on the earth, (He created) the abysses and the darkness, eventide <and night>, and the light, dawn and day, which He hath prepared in the knowledge of his heart.

³And thereupon we saw His works, and praised Him, and lauded before Him on account of all His works; for seven great works did He create on the first day. ⁴And on the second day He created the firmament in the midst of the waters, and the waters were divided on that day -half of them went up above and half of them went down below the firmament (that was) in the midst over the face of the whole earth. And this was the only work (God) created on the second day. ⁵And on the third day He commanded the waters to pass from off the face of the whole earth into one place, and the dry land to appear. ⁶And the waters did so as He commanded them, and they retired from off the face of the earth into one place outside of this firmament, and the dry land appeared. ⁷And on that day He created for them all the seas according to their separate gathering-places, and all the rivers, and the gatherings of the waters in the mountains and on all the earth, and all the lakes, and all the dew of the earth, and the seed which is sown, and all sprouting things, and fruit-bearing trees, and trees of the wood, and the garden of Eden, in Eden and all *plants after their kind*. ⁸These four great works God created on the third day. And on the fourth day He created the sun and the moon and the stars, and set them in the firmament of the heaven, to give light upon all the earth, and to rule over the day and the night, and divide the light from the darkness. ⁹And God appointed the sun to be a great sign on the earth for days and for sabbaths and for months and for feasts and for years and for sabbaths of years and for jubilees and for all seasons of the years. ¹⁰And it divideth the light from the darkness [and] for prosperity, that all things may prosper which shoot and grow on the earth. ¹¹These three kinds He made on the fourth day. And on the fifth day He created great sea monsters in the depths of the waters, for these were the first things of flesh that were created by his hands, the fish and everything that moves in the waters, and everything that flies, the birds and all their kind. ¹²And the sun rose above them to prosper (them), and above everything that was on the earth, everything that shoots out of the earth, and all fruit-bearing trees, and all flesh. ¹³These three kinds He created on the fifth day. And on the sixth day He created all the animals of the earth, and all cattle, and everything that moves on the earth. ¹⁴And after all this He created man, a man and a woman created He them, and gave him dominion over all that is upon the earth, and in the seas, and over everything that flies, and over beasts and over cattle, and over everything that moves on the earth, and over the whole earth, and over all this He gave him dominion. ¹⁵And these four kinds He

created on the sixth day. And there were altogether two and twenty kinds. ¹⁶And He finished all his work on the sixth day -all that is in the heavens and on the earth, and in the seas and in the abysses, and in the light and in the darkness, and in everything. ¹⁷And He gave us a great sign, the Sabbath day, that we should work six days, but keep Sabbath on the seventh day from all work. ¹⁸And all the angels of the presence, and all the angels of sanctification, these two great classes -He hath bidden us to keep the Sabbath with Him in heaven and on earth. ¹⁹And He said unto us: 'Behold, I will separate unto Myself a people from among all the peoples, and these shall keep the Sabbath day, and I will sanctify them unto Myself as My people, and will bless them; as I have sanctified the Sabbath day and do sanctify (it) unto Myself, even so will I bless them, and they shall be My people and I will be their God. ²⁰And I have chosen the seed of Jacob from amongst all that I have seen, and have written him down as My first-born son, and have sanctified him unto Myself for ever and ever; and I will teach them the Sabbath day, that they may keep Sabbath thereon from all work.' ²¹And thus He created therein a sign in accordance with which they should keep Sabbath with us on the seventh day, to eat and to drink, and to bless Him who has created all things as He has blessed and sanctified unto Himself a peculiar people above all peoples, and that they should keep Sabbath together with us. ²²And He caused His commands to ascend as a sweet savour acceptable before Him all the days . . . ²³There (were) two and twenty heads of mankind from Adam to Jacob, and two and twenty kinds of work were made until the seventh day; this is blessed and holy; and the former also is blessed and holy; and this one serves with that one for sanctification and blessing. ²⁴And to this (Jacob and his seed) it was granted that they should always be the blessed and holy ones of the first testimony and law, even as He had sanctified and blessed the Sabbath day on the seventh day. ²⁵He created heaven and earth and everything that He created in six days, and God made the seventh day holy, for all His works; therefore He commanded on its behalf that, whoever does any work thereon shall die, and that he who defiles it shall surely die. ²⁶Wherefore do thou command the children of Israel to observe this day that they may keep it holy and not do thereon any work, and not to defile it, as it is holier than all other days. ²⁷And whoever profanes it shall surely die, and whoever does thereon any work shall surely die eternally, that the children of Israel may observe this day throughout their generations, and not be rooted out of the land; for it is a holy day and a blessed day. ²⁸And every one who observes it and keeps Sabbath thereon from all his work, will be holy and blessed throughout all days like unto us. ²⁹Declare and say to the children of Israel the law of this day both that they should keep Sabbath thereon, and that they should not forsake it in the error of their hearts; (and) that it is not lawful to do any work thereon which is unseemly, to do thereon their own pleasure, and that they should not prepare thereon anything to be eaten or drunk, and (that it is not lawful) to draw water, or bring in or take out thereon through their gates any burden, which they had not prepared for themselves on the sixth day in their dwellings. ³⁰And they shall not bring in nor take out from house to house on that day; for that day is more holy and blessed than any jubilee day of the jubilees; on this we kept Sabbath in the heavens before it was made known to any flesh to keep Sabbath thereon on the earth. ³¹And the Creator of all things blessed it, but he did not sanctify all peoples and nations to keep Sabbath thereon, but Israel alone: them alone he permitted to eat and drink and to keep Sabbath thereon on the earth. ³²And the Creator of all things blessed this day which He had created for blessing and holiness and glory above all days. ³³This law and testimony was given to the children of Israel as a law for ever unto their generations.

Jub. 3

Adam names all creatures, 1-3. Creaton of Eve and enactment of Levitical laws of purification, 4-14. Adam and Eve in Paradise: their sin and expulsion, 15-29. Law of covering one's shame enacted, 30-2. Adam and Eve live in Êldâ, 32-5. (Cf.Gen. ii.18-25, iii.) [1]And on the six days of the second week we brought, according to the word of God, unto Adam all the beasts, and all the cattle, and all the birds, and everything that moves on the earth, and everything that moves in the water, according to their kinds, and according to their types: the beasts on the first day; the cattle on the second day; the birds on the third day; and all that which moves on the earth on the fourth day; and that which moves in the water on the fifth day. [2] And Adam named them all by their respective names, and as he called them, so was their name. [3] And on these five days Adam saw all these, male and female, according to every kind that was on the earth, but he was alone and found no helpmeet for him. [4] And the Lord said unto us: 'It is not good that the man should be alone: let us make a helpmeet for him.' [5] And the Lord our God caused a deep sleep to fall upon him, and he slept, and He took for the woman one rib from amongst his ribs, and this rib was the origin of the woman from amongst his ribs, and He built up the flesh in its stead, and built the woman. [6] And He awaked Adam out of his sleep and on awaking he rose on the sixth day, and He brought her to him, and he knew her, and said unto her: "This is now bone of my bones and flesh of my flesh; she shall be called [my] wife; because she was taken from her husband.' [7] Therefore shall man and wife be one and therefore shall a man leave his father and his mother, and cleave unto his wife, and they shall be one flesh. [8] In the first week was Adam created, and the rib -his wife: in the second week He showed her unto him: and for this reason the commandment was given to keep in their defilement, for a male seven days, and for a female twice seven days. [9] And after Adam had completed forty days in the land where he had been created, we brought him into the garden of Eden to till and keep it, but his wife they brought in on the eightieth day, and after this she entered into the garden of Eden. [10] And for this reason the commandment is written on the heavenly tablets in regard to her that gives birth: 'if she bears a male, she shall remain in her uncleanness seven days according to the first week of days, and thirty and three days shall she remain in the blood of her purifying, and she shall not touch any hallowed thing, nor enter into the sanctuary, until she accomplishes these days which (are enjoined) in the case of a male child. [11] But in the case of a female child she shall remain in her uncleanness two weeks of days, according to the first two weeks, and sixty-six days in the blood of her purification, and they will be in all eighty days.' [12] And when she had completed these eighty days we brought her into the garden of Eden, for it is holier than all the earth besides and every tree that is planted in it is holy. [13] Therefore, there was ordained regarding her who bears a male or a female child the statute of those days that she should touch no hallowed thing, nor enter into the sanctuary until these days for the male or female child are accomplished. [14] This is the law and testimony which was written down for Israel, in order that they should observe (it) all the days. [15] And in the first week of the first jubilee, [1-7 A.M.] Adam and his wife were in the garden of Eden for seven years tilling and keeping it, and we gave him work and we instructed him to do everything that is suitable for tillage. [16] And he tilled (the garden), and was naked and knew it not, and was not ashamed, and he protected the garden from the birds and beasts and cattle, and gathered its fruit, and eat, and put aside the residue for himself and for his wife [and put aside that which was being kept]. [17] And after the completion of the seven years, which he had completed there, seven years exactly, [8 A.M.] and in the second month, on the

seventeenth day (of the month), the serpent came and approached the woman, and the serpent said to the woman, 'Hath God commanded you, saying, Ye shall not eat of every tree of the garden?' [18] And she said to it, 'Of all the fruit of the trees of the garden God hath said unto us, Eat; but of the fruit of the tree which is in the midst of the garden God hath said unto us, Ye shall not eat thereof, neither shall ye touch it, lest ye die.' [19] And the serpent said unto the woman, 'Ye shall not surely die: for God doth know that on the day ye shall eat thereof, your eyes will be opened, and ye will be as gods, and ye will know good and evil. [20] And the woman saw the tree that it was agreeable and pleasant to the eye, and that its fruit was good for food, and she took thereof and eat. [21] And when she had first covered her shame with figleaves, she gave thereof to Adam and he eat, and his eyes were opened, and he saw that he was naked. [22] And he took figleaves and sewed (them) together, and made an apron for himself, and ,covered his shame. [23] And God cursed the serpent, and was wroth with it for ever . . . [24] And He was wroth with the woman, because she harkened to the voice of the serpent, and did eat; and He said unto her: 'I will greatly multiply thy sorrow and thy pains: in sorrow thou shalt bring forth children, and thy return shall be unto thy husband, and he will rule over thee.' [25] And to Adam also he said, ' Because thou hast harkened unto the voice of thy wife, and hast eaten of the tree of which I commanded thee that thou shouldst not eat thereof, cursed be the ground for thy sake: thorns and thistles shall it bring forth to thee, and thou shalt eat thy bread in the sweat of thy face, till thou returnest to the earth from whence thou wast taken; for earth thou art, and unto earth shalt thou return.' [26] And He made for them coats of skin, and clothed them, and sent them forth from the Garden of Eden. [27] And on that day on which Adam went forth from the Garden, he offered as a sweet savour an offering, frankincense, galbanum, and stacte, and spices in the morning with the rising of the sun from the day when he covered his shame. [28] And on that day was closed the mouth of all beasts, and of cattle, and of birds, and of whatever walks, and of whatever moves, so that they could no longer speak: for they had all spoken one with another with one lip and with one tongue. [29] And He sent out of the Garden of Eden all flesh that was in the Garden of Eden, and all flesh was scattered according to its kinds, and according to its types unto the places which had been created for them. [30] And to Adam alone did He give (the wherewithal) to cover his shame, of all the beasts and cattle. [31] On this account, it is prescribed on the heavenly tablets as touching all those who know the judgment of the law, that they should cover their shame, and should not uncover themselves as the Gentiles uncover themselves. [32] And on the new moon of the fourth month, Adam and his wife went forth from the Garden of Eden, and they dwelt in the land of Elda in the land of their creation. [33] And Adam called the name of his wife Eve. [34] And they had no son till the first jubilee, [8 A.M.] and after this he knew her. [35] Now he tilled the land as he had been instructed in the Garden of Eden.

Jub. 4

Cain and Abel and other children of Adam, 1-12. Enos, Kenan, Mahalalel, Jared, 13-15. Enoch and his history, 16-25. Four sacred places, 26. Methuselah, Lamech, Noah, 27, 28. Death of Adam and Cain, 29-32. Shem,Ham, and Japhet,32. (Cf. Gen. iv-v.) [1] And in the third week in the second jubilee [64-70 A.M.] she gave birth to Cain, and in the fourth [71-77 A.M.] she gave birth to Abel, and in the fifth [78-84 A.M.] she gave birth to her daughter Âwân. [2] And in the first (year) of the third jubilee [99-105 A.M.], Cain slew Abel because (God) accepted the sacrifice of Abel, and did not accept the offering of Cain. [3] And he slew him in the field: and his blood cried from the ground to heaven, complaining because he had slain him. 4 And the Lord reproved Cain because of Abel, because he had slain him, and he made him a fugitive on the earth because of the blood of his brother, and he cursed him upon the earth. 5 And on this account it is written on the heavenly tables, 'Cursed is ,he who smites his neighbour treacherously, and let all who have seen and heard say, So be it; and the man who has seen and not declared (it), let him be accursed as the other.' 6 And for this reason we announce when we come before the Lord our God all the sin which is committed in heaven and on earth, and in light and in darkness, and everywhere. 7 And Adam and his wife mourned for Abel four weeks of years, [99-127 A.M] and in the fourth year of the fifth week [130 A.M.] they became joyful, and Adam knew his wife again, and she bare him a son, and he called his name Seth; for he said 'GOD has raised up a second seed unto us on the earth instead of Abel; for Cain slew him.' 8 And in the sixth week [134-40 A.M.] he begat his daughter Azûrâ. 9 And Cain took Âwân his sister to be his wife and she bare him Enoch at the close of the fourth jubilee. [190-196 A.M.] And in the first year of the first week of the fifth jubilee, [197 A.M.] houses were built on the earth, and Cain built a city, and called its name after the name of his son Enoch. 10 And Adam knew Eve his wife and she bare yet nine sons. 11 And in the fifth week of the fifth jubilee [225-31 A.M.] Seth took Azûrâ his sister to be his wife, and in the fourth (year of the sixth week) [235 A.M.] she bare him Enos. 12 He began to call on the name of the Lord on the earth. 13 And in the seventh jubilee in the third week [309-15 A.M.] Enos took Nôâm his sister to be his wife, and she bare him a son in the third year of the fifth week, and he called his name Kenan. 14 And at the close of the eighth jubilee [325, 386-3992 A.M.] Kenan took Mûalêlêth his sister to be his wife, and she bare him a son in the ninth jubilee, in the first week in the third year of this week, [395 A.M] and he called his name Mahalalel. 15 And in the second week of the tenth jubilee [449-55 A.M.] Mahalalel took unto him to wife DinaH, the daughter of Barakiel the daughter of his father's brother, and she bare him a son in the third week in the sixth year, [461 A.M.] and he called his name Jared, for in his days the angels of the Lord descended on the earth, those who are named the Watchers, that they should instruct the children of men, and that they should do judgment and uprightness on the earth. 16 And in the eleventh jubilee [512-18 A.M.] Jared took to himself a wife, and her name was Baraka, the daughter of Râsûjâl, a daughter of his father's brother, in the fourth week of this jubilee, [522 A.M.] and she bare him a son in the fifth week, in the fourth year of the jubilee, and he called his name Enoch. 17 And he was the first among men that are born on earth who learnt writing and knowledge and wisdom and who wrote down the signs of heaven according to the order of their months in a book, that men might know the seasons of the years according to the order of their separate months. 18 And he was the first to write a testimony and he testified to the sons of men among the generations of the earth, and recounted the weeks of the jubilees, and made known to them the days of the years, and set in order the months and recounted the Sabbaths of the years as we made (them), known to him. 19 And what was and what will be he saw in a vision of his sleep, as it will happen to the children of men throughout their generations until the day of judgment; he saw and understood everything, and wrote his testimony, and placed the testimony on earth for all the children of men and for their generations. 20 And in the twelfth jubilee, [582-88] in the seventh week thereof, he took to himself a wife, and her name was Edna, the daughter of Danel, the daughter of his father's brother, and in the sixth year in this week [587 A.M.] she bare him a son and he called his name Methuselah. 21 And he was moreover with the angels of God these six jubilees of years, and they showed

134

him everything which is on earth and in the heavens, the rule of the sun, and he wrote down everything. 22 And he testified to the Watchers, who had sinned with the daughters of men; for these had begun to unite themselves, so as to be defiled, with the daughters of men, and Enoch testified against (them) all. 23 And he was taken from amongst the children of men, and we conducted him into the Garden of Eden in majesty and honour, and behold there he writes down the condemnation and judgment of the world, and all the wickedness of the children of men. 24 And on account of it (God) brought the waters of the flood upon all the land of Eden; for there he was set as a sign and that he should testify against all the children of men, that he should recount all the deeds of the generations until the day of condemnation. 25 And he burnt the incense of the sanctuary, (even) sweet spices acceptable before the Lord on the Mount. 26 For the Lord has four places on the earth, the Garden of Eden, and the Mount of the East, and this mountain on which thou art this day, Mount Sinai, and Mount Zion (which) will be sanctified in the new creation for a sanctification of the earth; through it will the earth be sanctified from all (its) guilt and its uncleanness through- out the generations of the world. 27 And in the fourteenth jubilee [652 A.M.] Methuselah took unto himself a wife, Edna the daughter of Azrial, the daughter of his father's brother, in the third week, in the first year of this week, [701-7 A.M.] and he begat a son and called his name Lamech. 28 And in the fifteenth jubilee in the third week Lamech took to himself a wife, and her name was Betenos the daughter of Baraki'il, the daughter of his father's brother, and in this week she bare him a son and he called his name Noah, saying, 'This one will comfort me for my trouble and all my work, and for the ground which the Lord hath cursed.' 29 And at the close of the nineteenth jubilee, in the seventh week in the sixth year [930 A.M.] thereof, Adam died, and all his sons buried him in the land of his creation, and he was the first to be buried in the earth. 30 And he lacked seventy years of one thousand years; for one thousand years are as one day in the testimony of the heavens and therefore was it written concerning the tree of knowledge: 'On the day that ye eat thereof ye shall die.' For this reason he did not complete the years of this day; for he died during it. 31 At the close of this jubilee Cain was killed after him in the same year; for his house fell upon him and he died in the midst of his house, and he was killed by its stones; for with a stone he had killed Abel, and by a stone was he killed in righteous judgment. 32 For this reason it was ordained on the heavenly tablets: With the instrument with which a man kills his neighbour with the same shall he be killed; after the manner that he wounded him, in like manner shall they deal with him.' 33 And in the twenty-fifth [1205 A.M.] jubilee Noah took to himself a wife, and her name was `Emzârâ, the daughter of Râkê'êl, the daughter of his father's brother, in the first year in the fifth week [1207 A.M.]: and in the third year thereof she bare him Shem, in the fifth year thereof [1209 A.M.] she bare him Ham, and in the first year in the sixth week [1212 A.M.] she bare him Japheth.

Jub. 5

The Angels of God marry the daughters of men, 1. Corruption of all creation, 2-3. Punishment of the fallen angels and their children, 4-9a. Final judgment announced, 9b-16. Day of Atonement, 17-18. The deluge foretold, Noah builds the ark, the deluge, 19-32. (Cf. Gen.vi-viii.19.) 1 And it came to pass when the children of men began to multiply on the face of the earth and daughters were born unto them, that the angels of God saw them on a certain year of this jubilee, that they were beautiful to look upon; and they took themselves wives of all whom they chose, and they bare unto them sons and they were giants. 2 And lawlessness increased on the earth and all flesh corrupted its way, alike men and cattle and beasts and birds and everything that walks on the earth -

all of them corrupted their ways and their orders, and they began to devour each other, and lawlessness increased on the earth and every imagination of the thoughts of all men (was) thus evil continually. 3 And God looked upon the earth, and behold it was corrupt, and all flesh had corrupted its orders, and all that were upon the earth had wrought all manner of evil before His eyes. 4 And He said that He would destroy man and all flesh upon the face of the earth which He had created. 5 But Noah found grace before the eyes of the Lord. 6 And against the angels whom He had sent upon the earth, He was exceedingly wroth, and He gave commandment to root them out of all their dominion, and He bade us to bind them in the depths of the earth, and behold they are bound in the midst of them, and are (kept) separate. 7 And against their sons went forth a command from before His face that they should be smitten with the sword, and be removed from under heaven. 8 And He said 'My spirit shall not always abide on man; for they also are flesh and their days shall be one hundred and twenty years'. 9 And He sent His sword into their midst that each should slay his neighbour, and they began to slay each other till they all fell by the sword and were destroyed from the earth. 10 And their fathers were witnesses (of their destruction), and after this they were bound in the depths of the earth for ever, until the day of the great condemnation, when judgment is executed on all those who have corrupted their ways and their works before the Lord. 11 And He destroyed all from their places, and there was not left one of them whom He judged not according to all their wickedness. 12 And he made for all his works a new and righteous nature, so that they should not sin in their whole nature for ever, but should be all righteous each in his kind alway. 13 And the judgment of all is ordained and written on the heavenly tablets in righteousness -even (the judgment of) all who depart from the path which is ordained for them to walk in; and if they walk not therein, judgment is written down for every creature and for every kind. 14 And there is nothing in heaven or on earth, or in light or in darkness, or in Sheol or in the depth, or in the place of darkness (which is not judged); and all their judgments are ordained and written and engraved. 15 In regard to all He will judge,the great according to his greatness, and the small according to his smallness, and each according to his way. 16 And He is not one who will regard the person (of any), nor is He one who will receive gifts, if He says that He will execute judgment on each: if one gave everything that is on the earth, He will not regard the gifts or the person (of any), nor accept anything at his hands, for He is a righteous judge. 17 [And of the children of Israel it has been written and ordained: If they turn to him in righteousness He will forgive all their transgressions and pardon all their sins. 18 It is written and ordained that He will show mercy to all who turn from all their guilt once each year.] 19 And as for all those who corrupted their ways and their thoughts before the flood, no man's person was accepted save that of Noah alone; for his person was accepted in behalf of his sons, whom (God) saved from the waters of the flood on his account; for his heart was righteous in all his ways, according as it was commanded regarding him, and he had not departed from aught that was ordained for him. 20 And the Lord said that he would destroy everything which was upon the earth, both men and cattle, and 21 beasts, and fowls of the air, and that which moveth on the earth. And He commanded Noah to make him an ark, that he might save himself from the waters of the flood. 22 And Noah made the ark in all respects as He commanded him, in the twenty-seventh jubilee of years, in the fifth week in the fifth year (on the new moon of the first month). [1307 A.M.] 23 And he entered in the sixth (year) thereof, [1308 A.M.] in the second month, on the new moon of the second month, till the sixteenth; and he entered, and all that we

brought to him, into the ark, and the Lord closed it from without on the seventeenth evening. 24 And the Lord opened seven flood-gates of heaven, And the mouths of the fountains of the great deep, seven mouths in number. 25 And the flood-gates began to pour down water from the heaven forty days and forty nights, And the fountains of the deep also sent up waters, until the whole world was full of water. 26 And the waters increased upon the earth: Fifteen cubits did the waters rise above all the high mountains, And the ark was lift up above the earth, And it moved upon the face of the waters. 27 And the water prevailed on the face of the earth five months -one hundred and fifty days. 28 And the ark went and rested on the top of Lubar, one of the mountains of Ararat. 29 And (on the new moon) in the fourth month the fountains of the great deep were closed and the flood-gates of heaven were restrained; and on the new moon of the seventh month all the mouths of the abysses of the earth were opened, and the water began to descend into the deep below. 30 And on the new moon of the tenth month the tops of the mountains were seen, and on the new moon of the first month the earth became visible. 31 And the waters disappeared from above the earth in the fifth week in the seventh year [1309 A.M.] thereof, and on the seventeenth day in the second month the earth was dry. 32 And on the twenty-seventh thereof he opened the ark, and sent forth from it beasts, and cattle, and birds, and every moving thing.

Jub. 6

Sacrifice of Noah, 1-3 (cf. Gen. vii.20-2). God's convenant with Noah, eating of blood forbidden, 4-10 (cf. Gen. ix. 1-17). Moses bidden to renew this law against the eating of blood, 11-14. Bow set in the clouds for a sign, 15-16. Feast of weeks instituted, history of its observances, 17-22. Feast of the new moons, 23-8. Division of the year into 364 days, 29-38. 1And on the new moon of the third month he went forth from the ark, and built an altar on that mountain. 2 And he made atonement for the earth, and took a kid and made atonement by its blood for all the guilt of the earth; for everything that had been on it had been destroyed, save those that were in the ark with Noah. 3 And he placed the fat thereof on the altar, and he took an ox, and a goat, and a sheep and kids, and salt, and a turtle-dove, and the young of a dove, and placed a burnt sacrifice on the altar, and poured thereon an offering mingled with oil, and sprinkled wine and strewed frankincense over everything, and caused a goodly savour to arise, acceptable before the Lord. 4 And the Lord smelt the goodly savour, and He made a covenant with him that there should not be any more a flood to destroy the earth; that all the days of the earth seed-time and harvest should never cease; cold and heat, and summer and winter, and day and night should not change their order, nor cease for ever. 5 'And you, increase ye and multiply upon the earth, and become many upon it, and be a blessing upon it. The fear of you and the dread of you I will inspire in everything that is on earth and in the sea. 6 And behold I have given unto you all beasts, and all winged things, and everything that moves on the earth, and the fish in the waters, and all things for food; as the green herbs, I have given you all things to eat. 7 But flesh, with the life thereof, with the blood, ye shall not eat; for the life of all flesh is in the blood, lest your blood of your lives be required. At the hand of every man, at the hand of every (beast) will I require the blood of man. 8 Whoso sheddeth man's blood by man shall his blood be shed, for in the image of God made He man. 9 And you, increase ye, and multiply on the earth.' 10 And Noah and his sons swore that they would not eat any blood that was in any flesh, and he made a covenant before the Lord God for ever throughout all the generations of the earth in this month. 11 On this account He spake to thee that thou shouldst make a covenant with the children of Israel in this month upon the mountain with an oath, and that thou shouldst sprinkle blood upon them because of all the words of the covenant, which the Lord made with them for ever. 12 And this testimony is written concerning you that you should observe it continually, so that you should not eat on any day any blood of beasts or birds or cattle during all the days of the earth, and the man who eats the blood of beast or of cattle or of birds during all the days of the earth, he and his seed shall be rooted out of the land. 13 And do thou command the children of Israel to eat no blood, so that their names and their seed may be before the Lord our God continually. 14 And for this law there is no limit of days, for it is for ever. They shall observe it throughout their generations, so that they may continue supplicating on your behalf with blood before the altar; every day and at the time of morning and evening they shall seek forgiveness on your behalf perpetually before the Lord that they may keep it and not be rooted out. 15 And He gave to Noah and his sons a sign that there should not again be a flood on the earth. 16 He set His bow in the cloud for a sign of the eternal covenant that there should not again be a flood on the earth to destroy it all the days of the earth. 17 For this reason it is ordained and written on the heavenly tablets, that they should celebrate the feast of weeks in this month once a year, to renew the covenant every year. 18 And this whole festival was celebrated in heaven from the day of creation till the days of Noah -twenty-six jubilees and five weeks of years [1309-1659 A.M.]: and Noah and his sons observed it for seven jubilees and one week of years, till the day of Noah's death, and from the day of Noah's death his sons did away with (it) until the days of Abraham, and they eat blood. 19 But Abraham observed it, and Isaac and Jacob and his children observed it up to thy days, and in thy days the children of Israel forgot it until ye celebrated it anew on this mountain. 20 And do thou command the children of Israel to observe this festival in all their generations for a commandment unto them: one day in the year in this month they shall celebrate the festival. 21 For it is the feast of weeks and the feast of first fruits: this feast is twofold and of a double nature: according to what is written and engraven concerning it, celebrate it. 22 For I have written in the book of the first law, in that which I have written for thee, that thou shouldst celebrate it in its season, one day in the year, and I explained to thee its sacrifices that the children of Israel should remember and should celebrate it throughout their generations in this month, one day in every year. 23 And on the new moon of the first month, and on the new moon of the fourth month, and on the new moon of the seventh month, and on the new moon of the tenth month are the days of remembrance, and the days of the seasons in the four divisions of the year. These are written and ordained as a testimony for ever. 24 And Noah ordained them for himself as feasts for the generations for ever, so that they have become thereby a memorial unto him. 25 And on the new moon of the first month he was bidden to make for himself an ark, and on that (day) the earth became dry and he opened (the ark) and saw the earth. 26 And on the new moon of the fourth month the mouths of the depths of the abyss beneath were closed. And on the new moon of the seventh month all the mouths of the abysses of the earth were opened, and the waters began to descend into them. 27 And on the new moon of the tenth month the tops of the mountains were seen, and Noah was glad. 28 And on this account he ordained them for himself as feasts for a memorial for ever, and thus are they ordained. 29 And they placed them on the heavenly tablets, each had thirteen weeks; from one to another (passed) their memorial, from the first to the second, and from the second to the third, and from the third to the fourth. 30 And all the days of the commandment will be two and fifty weeks of days, and (these will make) the entire year complete. Thus it is engraven and ordained on the heavenly tablets. 31 And there is no neglecting (this commandment) for a single year or from year to year. 32 And command thou the children of Israel that they observe the years according to this reckoning-three hundred and sixty-four days, and (these) will constitute a complete year, and they will not disturb its time from its days and from its feasts; for everything will fall out in them according to their testimony, and they will not leave out any day nor disturb any feasts. 33 But if they do neglect and do not observe them according to His commandment, then they will disturb all their seasons and the years will be dislodged from this (order), [and they will disturb the seasons and the years will be dislodged] and they will neglect their ordinances. 34 And all the children of Israel will forget and will not find the path of the years, and will forget the new moons, and seasons, and sabbaths and they will go wrong as to all the order of the years. 35 For I know and from henceforth will I declare it unto thee, and it is not of my own devising; for the book (lies) written before me, and on the heavenly tablets the division of days is ordained, lest they forget the feasts of the covenant and walk according to the feasts of the Gentiles after their error and after their ignorance. 36 For there will be those who will assuredly make observations of the moon -how (it) disturbs the seasons and comes in from year to year ten days too soon. 37 For this reason the years will come upon them when they will disturb (the order), and make an abominable (day) the day of testimony, and an unclean day a feast day, and they will confound all the days, the holy with the unclean, and the unclean day with the holy; for they will go wrong as to the months and sabbaths and feasts and jubilees. 38 For this reason I command and testify to thee that thou mayst testify to them; for after thy death thy children will disturb (them), so that they will not make the year three hundred and sixty-four days only, and for this reason they will go wrong as to the new moons and seasons and sabbaths and festivals, and they will eat all kinds of blood with all kinds of flesh.

Jub. 7

Noah plants a vineyard and offers a sacrifice, 1-5. Becomes drunk and exposes his person, 6-9. The cursing of Canaan and blessing of Shem and Japeth, 10-12 (cf. Gen. ix.20-8). Noah's sons and grandsons and their cities, 13-19. Noah teaches his sons regarding the causes of the deluge and admonishes them to avoid the eating of blood and murder, to keep the law regarding fruit trees and let the land lie fallow every seventh year, as Enoch had directed, 20-39. 1 And in the seventh week in the first year [1317 A.M.] thereof, in this jubilee, Noah planted vines on the mountain on which the ark had rested, named Lubar, one of the Ararat Mountains, and they produced fruit in the fourth year, [1320 A.M.] and he guarded their fruit, and gathered it in this year in the seventh month. 2 And he made wine therefrom and put it into a vessel, and kept it until the fifth year, [1321 A.M.] until the first day, on the new moon of the first month. 3 And he celebrated with joy the day of this feast, and he made a burnt sacrifice unto the Lord, one young ox and one ram, and seven sheep, each a year old, and a kid of the goats, that he might make atonement thereby for himself and his sons. 4 And he prepared the kid first, and placed some of its blood on the flesh that was on the altar which he had made, and all the fat he laid on the altar where he made the burnt sacrifice, and the ox and the ram and the sheep, and he laid all their flesh upon the altar. 5 And he placed all their offerings mingled with oil upon it, and afterwards he sprinkled wine on the fire which he had previously made on the altar, and he placed incense on the altar and caused a sweet savour to ascend acceptable before the Lord his God. 6 And he rejoiced and drank of this wine, he and his children with joy. 7 And it was evening, and he went into his tent, and being drunken he lay down and slept, and was uncovered in his tent as he slept. 8 And Ham saw

Noah his father naked, and went forth and told his two brethren without. 9 And Shem took his garment and arose, he and Japheth, and they placed the garment on their shoulders and went backward and covered the shame of their father, and their faces were backward. 10 And Noah awoke from his sleep and knew all that his younger son had done unto him, and he cursed his son and said: 'Cursed be Canaan; an enslaved servant shall he be unto his brethren.' 11 And he blessed Shem, and said: 'Blessed be the Lord God of Shem, and Canaan shall be his servant. 12 God shall enlarge Japheth, and God shall dwell in the dwelling of Shem, and Canaan shall be his servant.' 13 And Ham knew that his father had cursed his younger son, and he was displeased that he had cursed his son. and he parted from his father, he and his sons with him, Cush and Mizraim and Put and Canaan. 14 And he built for himself a city and called its name after the name of his wife Ne'elatama'uk. 15 And Japheth saw it, and became envious of his brother, and he too built for himself a city, and he called its name after the name of his wife 'Adataneses. 16 And Shem dwelt with his father Noah, and he built a city close to his father on the mountain, and he too called its name after the name of his wife Sedeqetelebab. 17 And behold these three cities are near Mount Lubar; Sedeqetelebab fronting the mountain on its east; and Na'eltama'uk on the south; 'Adatan'eses towards the west. 18 And these are the sons of Shem: Elam, and Asshur, and Arpachshad -this (son) was born two years after the flood- and Lud, and Aram. 19 The sons of Japheth: Gomer and Magog and Madai and Javan, Tubal and Meshech and Tiras: these are the sons of Noah. 20 And in the twenty-eighth jubilee [1324-1372 A.M.] Noah began to enjoin upon his sons' sons the ordinances and commandments, and all the judgments that he knew, and he exhorted his sons to observe righteousness, and to cover the shame of their flesh, and to bless their Creator, and honour father and mother, and love their neighbour, and guard their souls from fornication and uncleanness and all iniquity. 21 For owing to these three things came the flood upon the earth, namely, owing to the fornication wherein the Watchers against the law of their ordinances went a whoring after the daughters of men, and took themselves wives of all which they chose: and they made the beginning of uncleanness. 22 And they begat sons the Naphidim, and they were all unlike, and they devoured one another: and the Giants slew the Naphil, and the Naphil slew the Eljo, and the Eljo mankind, and one man another. 23 And every one sold himself to work iniquity and to shed much blood, and the earth was filled with iniquity. 24 And after this they sinned against the beasts and birds, and all that moves and walks on the earth: and much blood was shed on the earth, and every imagination and desire of men imagined vanity and evil continually. 25 And the Lord destroyed everything from off the face of the earth; because of the wickedness of their deeds, and because of the blood which they had shed in the midst of the earth He destroyed everything. 26 'And we were left, I and you, my sons, and everything that entered with us into the ark, and behold I see your works before me that ye do not walk in righteousness: for in the path of destruction ye have begun to walk, and ye are parting one from another, and are envious one of another, and (so it comes) that ye are not in harmony, my sons, each with his brother. 27 For I see, and behold the demons have begun (their) seductions against you and against your children and now I fear on your behalf, that after my death ye will shed the blood of men upon the earth, and that ye, too, will be destroyed from the face of the earth. 28 For whoso sheddeth man's blood, and whoso eateth the blood of any flesh, shall all be destroyed from the earth. 29 And there shall not be left any man that eateth blood, or that sheddeth the blood of man on the earth, Nor shall there be left to him any seed or descendants living

under heaven; For into Sheol shall they go, And into the place of condemnation shall they descend, And into the darkness of the deep shall they all be removed by a violent death. 30 There shall be no blood seen upon you of all the blood there shall be all the days in which ye have killed any beasts or cattle or whatever flies upon the earth, and work ye a good work to your souls by covering that which has been shed on the face of the earth. 31 And ye shall not be like him who eats with blood, but guard yourselves that none may eat blood before you: cover the blood, for thus have I been commanded to testify to you and your children, together with all flesh. 32 And suffer not the soul to be eaten with the flesh, that your blood, which is your life, may not be required at the hand of any flesh that sheds (it) on the earth. 33 For the earth will not be clean from the blood which has been shed upon it; for (only) through the blood of him that shed it will the earth be purified throughout all its generations. 34 And now, my children, harken: work judgment and righteousness that ye maybe planted in righteousness over the face of the whole earth, and your glory lifted up before my God, who saved me from the waters of the flood. 35 And behold, ye will go and build for yourselves cities, and plant in them all the plants that are upon the earth, and moreover all fruit-bearing trees. 36 For three years the fruit of everything that is eaten will not be gathered: and in the fourth year its fruit will be accounted holy [and they will offer the first-fruits], acceptable before the Most High God, who created heaven and earth and all things. Let them offer in abundance the first of the wine and oil (as) first-fruits on the altar of the Lord, who receives it, and what is left let the servants of the house of the Lord eat before the altar which receives (it). 37 And in the fifth year make ye the release so that ye release it in righteousness and uprightness, and ye shall be righteous, and all that you plant shall prosper. 38 For thus did Enoch, the father of your father command Methuselah, his son, and Methuselah his son Lamech, and Lamech commanded me all the things which his fathers commanded him. 39 And I also will give you commandment, my sons, as Enoch commanded his son in the first jubilees: whilst still living, the seventh in his generation, he commanded and testified to his son and to his son's sons until the day of his death.'

Jub. 8

Kâinâm discovers an inscription relating to the sun and stars, 1-4. His sons, 5-8. Noah's sons and Noah divide the earth, 10-11. Shem's inheritance, 12-21: Ham's, 22-4: Japheth's, 25-30. (Cf. Gen. x.) 1 In the twenty-ninth jubilee, in the first week, [1373 A.M.] in the beginning thereof Arpachshad took to himself a wife and her name was Rasu'eja, the daughter of Susan, the daughter of Elam, and she bare him a son in the third year in this week, [1375 A.M.] and he called his name Kainam. 2 And the son grew, and his father taught him writing, and he went to seek for himself a place where he might seize for himself a city. 3 And he found a writing which former (generations) had carved on the rock, and he read what was thereon, and he transcribed it and sinned owing to it; for it contained the teaching of the Watchers in accordance with which they used to observe the omens of the sun and moon and stars in all the signs of heaven. 4 And he wrote it down and said nothing regarding it; for he was afraid to speak to Noah about it lest he should be angry with him on account of it. 5 And in the thirtieth jubilee, [1429 A.M.] in the second week, in the first year thereof, he took to himself a wife, and her name was Melka, the daughter of Madai, the son of Japheth, and in the fourth year [1432 A.M.] he begat a son, and called his name Shelah; for he said: 'Truly I have been sent.' 6 [And in the fourth year he was born], and Shelah grew up and took to himself a wife, and her name was Mu'ak, the daughter of Kesed, his father's brother, in the one and thirtieth jubilee, in the fifth week, in the first year [1499 A.M.] thereof. 7 And she bare him a son in the fifth year [1503 A.M.] thereof, and he called his name Eber: and he took unto himself a wife, and her name was 'Azûrâd, the daughter of Nebrod, in the thirty-second jubilee, in the seventh week, in the third year thereof. [1564 A.M.] 8 And in the sixth year [1567 A.M.] thereof, she bare him son, and he called his name Peleg; for in the days when he was born the children of Noah began to divide the earth amongst themselves: for this reason he called his name Peleg. 9 And they divided (it) secretly amongst themselves, and told it to Noah. 10 And it came to pass in the beginning of the thirty-third jubilee [1569 A.M.] that they divided the earth into three parts, for Shem and Ham and Japheth, according to the inheritance of each, in the first year in the first week, when one of us who had been sent, was with them. 11 And he called his sons, and they drew nigh to him, they and their children, and he divided the earth into the lots, which his three sons were to take in possession, and they reached forth their hands, and took the writing out of the bosom of Noah, their father. 12 And there came forth on the writing as Shem's lot the middle of the earth which he should take as an inheritance for himself and for his sons for the generations of eternity, from the middle of the mountain range of Rafa, from the mouth of the water from the river Tina, and his portion goes towards the west through the midst of this river, and it extends till it reaches the water of the abysses, out of which this river goes forth and pours its waters into the sea Me'at, and this river flows into the great sea. And all that is towards the north is Japheth's, and all that is towards the south belongs to Shem. 13 And it extends till it reaches Karaso: this is in the bosom of the tongue which looks towards the south. 14 And his portion extends along the great sea, and it extends in a straight line till it reaches the west of the tongue which looks towards the south: for this sea is named the tongue of the Egyptian Sea. 15 And it turns from here towards the south towards the mouth of the great sea on the shore of (its) waters, and it extends to the west to 'Afra, and it extends till it reaches the waters of the river Gihon, and to the south of the waters of Gihon, to the banks of this river. 16 And it extends towards the east, till it reaches the Garden of Eden, to the south thereof, [to the south] and from the east of the whole land of Eden and of the whole east, it turns to the east and proceeds till it reaches the east of the mountain named Rafa, and it descends to the bank of the mouth of the river Tina. 17 This portion came forth by lot for Shem and his sons, that they should possess it for ever unto his generations for evermore. 18 And Noah rejoiced that this portion came forth for Shem and for his sons, and he remembered all that he had spoken with his mouth in prophecy; for he had said: 'Blessed be the Lord God of Shem And may the Lord dwell in the dwelling of Shem.' 19 And he knew that the Garden of Eden is the holy of holies, and the dwelling of the Lord, and Mount Sinai the centre of the desert, and Mount Zion -the centre of the navel of the earth: these three were created as holy places facing each other. 20 And he blessed the God of gods, who had put the word of the Lord into his mouth, and the Lord for evermore. 21 And he knew that a blessed portion and a blessing had come to Shem and his sons unto the generations for ever -the whole land of Eden and the whole land of the Red Sea, and the whole land of the east and India, and on the Red Sea and the mountains thereof, and all the land of Bashan, and all the land of Lebanon and the islands of Kaftur, and all the mountains of Sanir and 'Amana, and the mountains of Asshur in the north, and all the land of Elam, Asshur, and Babel, and Susan and Ma'edai, and all the mountains of Ararat, and all the region beyond the sea, which is beyond the mountains of Asshur towards the north, a blessed and spacious land, and all that is in it is very good. 22 And for Ham came forth the second portion, beyond the Gihon towards

the south to the right of the Garden, and it extends towards the south and it extends to all the mountains of fire, and it extends towards the west to the sea of 'Atel and it extends towards the west till it reaches the sea of Ma'uk -that (sea) into which everything which is not destroyed descends. 23 And it goes forth towards the north to the limits of Gadir, and it goes forth to the coast of the waters of the sea to the waters of the great sea till it draws near to the river Gihon, and goes along the river Gihon till it reaches the right of the Garden of Eden. 24 And this is the land which came forth for Ham as the portion which he was to occupy for ever for himself and his sons unto their generations for ever. 25 And for Japheth came forth the third portion beyond the river Tina to the north of the outflow of its waters, and it extends north- easterly to the whole region of Gog, and to all the country east thereof. 26 And it extends northerly to the north, and it extends to the mountains of Qelt towards the north, and towards the sea of Ma'uk, and it goes forth to the east of Gadir as far as the region of the waters of the sea. 27 And it extends until it approaches the west of Fara and it returns towards 'Aferag, and it extends easterly to the waters of the sea of Me'at. 28 And it extends to the region of the river Tina in a north-easterly direction until it approaches the boundary of its waters towards the mountain Rafa, and it turns round towards the north. 29 This is the land which came forth for Japheth and his sons as the portion of his inheritance which he should possess for himself and his sons, for their generations for ever; five great islands, and a great land in the north. 30 But it is cold, and the land of Ham is hot, and the land of Shem is neither hot nor cold, but it is of blended cold and heat.

Jub. 9

Subdivision of the three portions amongst the grandchildren of Noah. Amongst Ham's children, 1: Shem's, 2-6: Japheth's, 7-13. Oath taken by Noah's sons, 14-15. 1 And Ham divided amongst his sons, and the first portion came forth for Cush towards the east, and to the west of him for Mizraim, and to the west of him for Put, and to the west of him [and to the west thereof] on the sea for Canaan. 2 And Shem also divided amongst his sons, and the first portion came forth for Ham and his sons, to the east of the river Tigris till it approaches the east, the whole land of India, and on the Red Sea on its coast, and the waters of Dedan, and all the mountains of Mebri and Ela, and all the land of Susan and all that is on the side of Pharnak to the Red Sea and the river Tina. 3 And for Asshur came forth the second Portion, all the land of Asshur and Nineveh and Shinar and to the border of India, and it ascends and skirts the river. 4 And for Arpachshad came forth the third portion, all the land of the region of the Chaldees to the east of the Euphrates, bordering on the Red Sea, and all the waters of the desert close to the tongue of the sea which looks towards Egypt, all the land of Lebanon and Sanir and 'Amana to the border of the Euphrates. 5 And for Aram there came forth the fourth portion, all the land of Mesopotamia between the Tigris and the Euphrates to the north of the Chaldees to the border of the mountains of Asshur and the land of 'Arara. 6 And there came forth for Lud the fifth portion, the mountains of Asshur and all appertaining to them till it reaches the Great Sea, and till it reaches the east of Asshur his brother. 7 And Japheth also divided the land of his inheritance amongst his sons. 8 And the first portion came forth for Gomer to the east from the north side to the river Tina; and in the north there came forth for Magog all the inner portions of the north until it reaches to the sea of Me'at. 9 And for Madai came forth as his portion that he should posses from the west of his two brothers to the islands, and to the coasts of the islands. 10 And for Javan came forth the fourth portion every island and the islands which are towards the border of Lud. 11 And for Tubal there came forth the fifth portion in the midst of the tongue which approaches towards the border of the portion of Lud to the second tongue, to the region beyond the second tongue unto the third tongue. [12] And for Meshech came forth the sixth portion, all the region beyond the third tongue till it approaches the east of Gadir. [13] And for Tiras there came forth the seventh portion, four great islands in the midst of the sea, which reach to the portion of Ham [and the islands of Kamaturi came out by lot for the sons of Arpachshad as his inheritance]. [14] And thus the sons of Noah divided unto their sons in the presence of Noah their father, and he bound them all by an oath, imprecating a curse on every one that sought to seize the portion which had not fallen (to him) by his lot. [15] And they all said, 'So be it; so be it ' for themselves and their sons for ever throughout their generations till the day of judgment, on which the Lord God shall judge them with a sword and with fire for all the unclean wickedness of their errors, wherewith they have filled the earth with transgression and uncleanness and fornication and sin.

Jub. 10

Evil spirits leads astray the sons of Noah, 1-2. Noah's prayer, 3-6. Mastêmâ allowed to retain one-tenth of his subject spirits, 7-11. Noah taught the use of herbs by the angels for resisting the demons, 12-14. Noah dies, 15-17. Building of Babel and the confusion of tongues, 18-27. Canaan seizes on Palestine, 29-34. Madai receives Media, 33-6. [1] And in the third week of this jubilee the unclean demons began to lead astray the children of the sons of Noah, and to make to err and destroy them. [2] And the sons of Noah came to Noah their father, and they told him concerning the demons which were leading astray and blinding and slaying his sons' sons. [3] And he prayed before the Lord his God, and said: 'God of the spirits of all flesh, who hast shown mercy unto me And hast saved me and my sons from the waters of the flood, And hast not caused me to perish as Thou didst the sons of perdition; For Thy grace has been great towards me, And great has been Thy mercy to my soul; Let Thy grace be lift up upon my sons, And let not wicked spirits rule over them Lest they should destroy them from the earth. [4] But do Thou bless me and my sons, that we may increase and Multiply and replenish the earth. [5] And Thou knowest how Thy Watchers, the fathers of these spirits, acted in my day: and as for these spirits which are living, imprison them and hold them fast in the place of condemnation, and let them not bring destruction on the sons of thy servant, my God; for these are malignant, and created in order to destroy. [6] And let them not rule over the spirits of the living; for Thou alone canst exercise dominion over them. And let them not have power over the sons of the righteous from henceforth and for evermore.' [7] And the Lord our God bade us to bind all. [8] And the chief of the spirits, Mastêmâ, came and said: 'Lord, Creator, let some of them remain before me, and let them harken to my voice, and do all that I shall say unto them; for if some of them are not left to me, I shall not be able to execute the power of my will on the sons of men; for these are for corruption and leading astray before my judgment, for great is the wickedness of the sons of men.' [9] And He said: Let the tenth part of them remain before him, and let nine parts descend into the place of condemnation.' [10] And one of us He commanded that we should teach Noah all their medicines; for He knew that they would not walk in uprightness, nor strive in righteousness. [11] And we did according to all His words: all the malignant evil ones we bound in the place of condemnation and a tenth part of them we left that they might be subject before Satan on the earth. [12] And we explained to Noah all the medicines of their diseases, together with their seductions, how he might heal them with herbs of the earth. [13] And Noah wrote down all things in a book as we instructed him concerning every kind of medicine. Thus the evil spirits were precluded from (hurting) the sons of Noah. [14] And he gave all that

he had written to Shem, his eldest son; for he loved him exceedingly above all his sons. [15] And Noah slept with his fathers, and was buried on Mount Lubar in the land of Ararat. [16] Nine hundred and fifty years he completed in his life, nineteen jubilees and two weeks and five years. [1659 A.M.] [17] And in his life on earth he excelled the children of men save Enoch because of the righteousness, wherein he was perfect. For Enoch's office was ordained for a testimony to the generations of the world, so that he should recount all the deeds of generation unto generation, till the day of judgment. [18] And in the three and thirtieth jubilee, in the first year in the second week, Peleg took to himself a wife, whose name was Lomna the daughter of Sina'ar, and she bare him a son in the fourth year of this week, and he called his name Reu; for he said: 'Behold the children of men have become evil through the wicked purpose of building for themselves a city and a tower in the land of Shinar.' [19] For they departed from the land of Ararat eastward to Shinar; for in his days they built the city and the tower, saying, 'Go to, let us ascend thereby into heaven.' [20] And they began to build, and in the fourth week they made brick with fire, and the bricks served them for stone, and the clay with which they cemented them together was asphalt which comes out of the sea, and out of the fountains of water in the land of Shinar. [21] And they built it: forty and three years [1645-1688 A.M.] were they building it; its breadth was 203 bricks, and the height (of a brick) was the third of one; its height amounted to 5433 cubits and 2 palms, and (the extent of one wall was) thirteen stades (and of the other thirty stades). [22] And the Lord our God said unto us: Behold, they are one people, and (this) they begin to do, and now nothing will be withholden from them. Go to, let us go down and confound their language, that they may not understand one another's speech, and they may be dispersed into cities and nations, and one purpose will no longer abide with them till the day of judgment.' [23] And the Lord descended, and we descended with him to see the city and the tower which the children of men had built. [24] And he confounded their language, and they no longer understood one another's speech, and they ceased then to build the city and the tower. [25] For this reason the whole land of Shinar is called Babel, because the Lord did there confound all the language of the children of men, and from thence they were dispersed into their cities, each according to his language and his nation. [26] And the Lord sent a mighty wind against the tower and overthrew it upon the earth, and behold it was between Asshur and Babylon in the land of Shinar, and they called its name 'Overthrow'. [27] In the fourth week in the first year [1688 A.M.] in the beginning thereof in the four and thirtieth jubilee, were they dispersed from the land of Shinar. [28] And Ham and his sons went into the land which he was to occupy, which he acquired as his portion in the land of the south. [29] And Canaan saw the land of Lebanon to the river of Egypt, that it was very good, and he went not into the land of his inheritance to the west (that is to) the sea, and he dwelt in the land of Lebanon, eastward and westward from the border of Jordan and from the border of the sea. [30] And Ham, his father, and Cush and Mizraim his brothers said unto him: 'Thou hast settled in a land which is not thine, and which did not fall to us by lot: do not do so; for if thou dost do so, thou and thy sons will fall in the land and (be) accursed through sedition; for by sedition ye have settled, and by sedition will thy children fall, and thou shalt be rooted out for ever. [31] Dwell not in the dwelling of Shem; for to Shem and to his sons did it come by their lot. [32] Cursed art thou, and cursed shalt thou be beyond all the sons of Noah, by the curse by which we bound ourselves by an oath in the presence of the holy judge, and in the presence of Noah our father.' [33] But he did not harken unto them, and dwelt in the land of Lebanon from Hamath to the entering of Egypt, he and his sons until this day. [34] And for this reason that land is named Canaan. [35] And Japheth and his sons went towards the sea and dwelt in the land of their portion, and Madai saw the land of the sea and it did not please him, and he begged a (portion) from Ham and Asshur and Arpachshad, his wife's brother, and he dwelt in the land of Media, near to his wife's brother until this day. [36] And he called his dwelling-place, and the dwelling-place of his sons, Media, after the name of their father Madai.

Jub. 11

Reu and Serug, 1 (cf. Gen. xi.20, 21). Rise of war and bloodshed and eating of blood and idolatry, 2-7. Nachor and Terah, 8-14 (cf. Gen. xi.22-30). Abram's knowledge of God and wonderful deeds, 15-24. [1] And in the thirty-fifth jubilee, in the third week, in the first year [1681 A.M.] thereof, Reu took to himself a wife, and her name was 'Ôrâ, the daughter of 'Ûr, the son of Kesed, and she bare him a son, and he called his name Sêrôh, in the seventh year of this week in this jubilee. [1687 A.M.] [2] And the sons of Noah began to war on each other, to take captive and to slay each other, and to shed the blood of men on the earth, and to eat blood, and to build strong cities, and walls, and towers, and individuals (began) to exalt themselves above the nation, and to found the beginnings of kingdoms, and to go to war people against people, and nation against nation, and city against city, and all (began) to do evil, and to acquire arms, and to teach their sons war, and they began to capture cities, and to sell male and female slaves. [3] And 'Ûr, the son of Kesed, built the city of 'Ara of the Chaldees, and called its name after his own name and the name of his father. And they made for themselves molten images, and they worshipped each the idol, the molten image which they had made for themselves, and they began to make graven images and unclean simulacra, and malignant spirits assisted and seduced (them) into committing transgression and uncleanness. [4] And the prince Mastêmâ exerted himself to do all this, and he sent forth other spirits, those which were put under his hand, to do all manner of wrong and sin, and all manner of transgression, to corrupt and destroy, and to shed blood upon the earth. [5] For this reason he called the name of Sêrôh, Serug, for every one turned to do all manner of sin and transgression. [6] And he grew up, and dwelt in Ur of the Chaldees, near to the father of his wife's mother, and he worshipped idols, and he took to himself a wife in the thirty-sixth jubilee, in the fifth week, in the first year thereof, [1744 A.M.] and her name was Melka, the daughter of Kaber, the daughter of his father's brother. [7] And she bare him Nahor, in the first year of this week, and he grew and dwelt in Ur of the Chaldees, and his father taught him the researches of the Chaldees to divine and augur, according to the signs of heaven. [8] And in the thirty-seventh jubilee in the sixth week, in the first year thereof, [1800 A.M.] he took to himself a wife, and her name was 'Ijaska, the daughter of Nestag of the Chaldees. [9] And she bare him Terah in the seventh year of this week. [1806 A.M.] [10] And the prince Mastêmâ sent ravens and birds to devour the seed which was sown in the land, in order to destroy the land, and rob the children of men of their labours. Before they could plough in the seed, the ravens picked (it) from the surface of the ground. [11] And for this reason he called his name Terah because the ravens and the birds reduced them to destitution and devoured their seed. [12] And the years began to be barren, owing to the birds, and they devoured all the fruit of the trees from the trees: it was only with great effort that they could save a little of all the fruit of the earth in their days. [13] And in this thirty-ninth jubilee, in the second week in the first year, [1870 A.M.] Terah took to himself a wife, and her name was 'Edna, the daughter of 'Abram, the daughter of his father's sister. And in the seventh year of this week [1876 A.M.] she bare him a son, and he called his name Abram, by the name of the

140

father of his mother; [14] for he had died before his daughter had conceived a son. [15] And the child began to understand the errors of the earth that all went astray after graven images and after uncleanness, and his father taught him writing, and he was two weeks of years old, [1890 A.M.] and he separated himself from his father, that he might not worship idols with him. [16] And he began to pray to the Creator of all things that He might save him from the errors of the children of men, and that his portion should not fall into error after uncleanness and vileness. [17] And the seed time came for the sowing of seed upon the land, and they all went forth together to protect their seed against the ravens, and Abram went forth with those that went, and the child was a lad of fourteen years. [18] And a cloud of ravens came to devour the seed, and Abram ran to meet them before they settled on the ground, and cried to them before they settled on the ground to devour the seed, and said, ' Descend not: return to the place whence ye came,' and they proceeded to turn back. [19] And he caused the clouds of ravens to turn back that day seventy times, and of all the ravens throughout all the land where Abram was there settled there not so much as one. [20] And all who were with him throughout all the land saw him cry out, and all the ravens turn back, and his name became great in all the land of the Chaldees. [21] And there came to him this year all those that wished to sow, and he went with them until the time of sowing ceased: and they sowed their land, and that year they brought enough grain home and eat and were satisfied. [22] And in the first year of the fifth week [1891 A.M.] Abram taught those who made implements for oxen, the artificers in wood, and they made a vessel above the ground, facing the frame of the plough, in order to put the seed thereon, and the seed fell down therefrom upon the share of the plough, and was hidden in the earth, and they no longer feared the ravens. [23] And after this manner they made (vessels) above the ground on all the frames of the ploughs, and they sowed and tilled all the land, according as Abram commanded them, and they no longer feared the birds.

Jub. 12

Abram seeks to run Terah from idolatry, 1-8. Marries Sarai, 9. Haran and Nachor, 9-11. Abram burns the idols: death of Haran, 12-14 (cf. Gen. xi.28). Terah and his family go to Haran, 15. Abram observes the stars and prays, 16-21. Is bidden to go to Canaan and blessed, 22-4. Power of speaking Hebrew given to him, 25-7. Leaves Haran for Canaan, 28-31. (Cf. Gen. xi.31-xii.3.) [1] And it came to pass in the sixth week, in the seventh year thereof, [1904 A.M.] that Abram said to Terah his father, saying, 'Father!' [2] And he said, 'Behold, here am I, my son.' And he said, 'What help and profit have we from those idols which thou dost worship, And before which thou dost bow thyself? [3] For there is no spirit in them, For they are dumb forms, and a misleading of the heart. Worship them not: [4] Worship the God of heaven, Who causes the rain and the dew to descend on the earth And does everything upon the earth, And has created everything by His word, And all life is from before His face. [5] Why do ye worship things that have no spirit in them? For they are the work of (men's) hands, And on your shoulders do ye bear them, And ye have no help from them, But they are a great cause of shame to those who make them, And a misleading of the heart to those who worship them: Worship them not.' [6] And his father said unto him, I also know it, my son, but what shall I do with a people who have made me to serve before them? [7] And if I tell them the truth, they will slay me; for their soul cleaves to them to worship them and honour them. [8] Keep silent, my son, lest they slay thee.' And these words he spake to his two brothers, and they were angry with him and he kept silent. [9] And in the fortieth jubilee, in the second week, in the seventh year thereof, [1925 A.M.] Abram took to himself a wife, and her name was Sarai, the daughter of his father, and she became his wife. 10 And Haran, his brother, took to himself a wife in the third year of the third week, [1928 A.M.] and she bare him a son in the seventh year of this week, [1932 A.M.] and he called his name Lot. 11 And Nahor, his brother, took to himself a wife. 12 And in the sixtieth year of the life of Abram, that is, in the fourth week, in the fourth year thereof, [1936 A.M.] Abram arose by night, and burned the house of the idols, and he burned all that was in the house and no man knew it. 13 And they arose in the night and sought to save their gods from the midst of the fire. 14 And Haran hasted to save them, but the fire flamed over him, and he was burnt in the fire, and he died in Ur of the Chaldees before Terah his father, and they buried him in Ur of the Chaldees. 15 And Terah went forth from Ur of the Chaldees, he and his sons, to go into the land of Lebanon and into the land of Canaan, and he dwelt in the land of Haran, and Abram dwelt with Terah his father in Haran two weeks of years. 16 And in the sixth week, in the fifth year thereof, [1951 A.M.] Abram sat up throughout the night on the new moon of the seventh month to observe the stars from the evening to the morning, in order to see what would be the character of the year with regard to the rains, and he was alone as he sat and observed. 17 And a word came into his heart and he said: All the signs of the stars, and the signs of the moon and of the sun are all in the hand of the Lord. Why do I search (them) out? 18 If He desires, He causes it to rain, morning and evening; And if He desires, He withholds it, And all things are in his hand.' 19 And he prayed that night and said, 'My God, God Most High, Thou alone art my God, And Thee and Thy dominion have I chosen. And Thou hast created all things, And all things that are the work of thy hands. 20 Deliver me from the hands of evil spirits who have dominion over the thoughts of men's hearts, And let them not lead me astray from Thee, my God. And stablish Thou me and my seed for ever That we go not astray from henceforth and for evermore.' 21 And he said, 'Shall I return unto Ur of the Chaldees who seek my face that I may return to them, am I to remain here in this place? The right path before Thee prosper it in the hands of Thy servant that he may fulfil (it) and that I may not walk in the deceitfulness of my heart, O my God.' 22 And he made an end of speaking and praying, and behold the word of the Lord was sent to him through me, saying: 'Get thee up from thy country, and from thy kindred and from the house of thy father unto a land which I will show thee, and I shall make thee a great and numerous nation. 23 And I will bless thee And I will make thy name great, And thou shalt be blessed in the earth, And in Thee shall all families of the earth be blessed, And I will bless them that bless thee, And curse them that curse thee. 24 And I will be a God to thee and thy son, and to thy son's son, and to all thy seed: fear not, from henceforth and unto all generations of the earth I am thy God.' 25 And the Lord God said: 'Open his mouth and his ears, that he may hear and speak with his mouth, with the language which has been revealed'; for it had ceased from the mouths of all the children of men from the day of the overthrow (of Babel). 26 And I opened his mouth, and his ears and his lips, and I began to speak with him in Hebrew in the tongue of the creation. 27 And he took the books of his fathers, and these were written in Hebrew, and he transcribed them, and he began from henceforth to study them, and I made known to him that which he could not (understand), and he studied them during the six rainy months. 28 And it came to pass in the seventh year of the sixth week [1953 A.M.] that he spoke to his father and informed him, that he would leave Haran to go into the land of Canaan to see it and return to him. 29 And Terah his father said unto him; Go in peace: May the eternal God make thy path straight. And the Lord [(be) with thee, and] protect thee from all evil, And grant unto thee grace,

141

mercy and favour before those who see thee, And may none of the children of men have power over thee to harm thee; Go in peace. 30 And if thou seest a land pleasant to thy eyes to dwell in, then arise and take me to thee and take Lot with thee, the son of Haran thy brother as thine own son: the Lord be with thee. 31 And Nahor thy brother leave with me till thou returnest in peace, and we go with thee all together.'

Jub. 13

Abram journeys from Haran to Shechem in Canaan, thence to Hebron and thence to Egypt, 1-14a. Returns to Canaan where Lot separates from him, and receives the promise of Canaan and journeys to Hebron, 14b-21. Chedorlaomer's attack on Sodom and Gomorrah: Lot taken captive, 22-4. Law of tithes enacted, 25-9. (Cf. Gen. xii.4-10, 15-17, 19-20; xiii.11-18; xiv.8-14; 21-4.) 1 And Abram journeyed from Haran, and he took Sarai, his wife, and Lot, his brother Haran's son, to the land of Canaan, and he came into Asshur, and proceeded to Shechem, and dwelt near a lofty oak. 2 And he saw, and, behold, the land was very pleasant from the entering of Hamath to the lofty oak. 3 And the Lord said to him: "To thee and to thy seed will I give this land.' 4 And he built an altar there, and he offered thereon a burnt sacrifice to the Lord, who had appeared to him. 5 And he removed from thence unto the mountain . . . Bethel on the west and Ai on the east, and pitched his tent there. 6 And he saw and behold, the land was very wide and good, and everything grew thereon -vines and figs and pomegranates, oaks and ilexes, and terebinths and oil trees, and cedars and cypresses and date trees, and all trees of the field, and there was water on the mountains. 7 And he blessed the Lord who had led him out of Ur of the Chaldees, and had brought him to this land. 8 And it came to pass in the first year, in the seventh week, on the new moon of the first month, 1954 A.M.] that he built an altar on this mountain, and called on the name of the Lord: "Thou, the eternal God, art my God.' 9 And he offered on the altar a burnt sacrifice unto the Lord that He should be with him and not forsake him all the days of his life. 10 And he removed from thence and went towards the south, and he came to Hebron and Hebron was built at that time, and he dwelt there two years, and he went (thence) into the land of the south, to Bealoth, and there was a famine in the land. 11 And Abram went into Egypt in the third year of the week, and he dwelt in Egypt five years before his wife was torn away from him. 12 Now Tanais in Egypt was at that time built- seven years after Hebron. 13 And it came to pass when Pharaoh seized Sarai, the wife of Abram that the Lord plagued Pharaoh and his house with great plagues because of Sarai, Abram's wife. 14 And Abram was very glorious by reason of possessions in sheep, and cattle, and asses, and horses, and camels, and menservants, and maidservants, and in silver and gold exceedingly. And Lot also his brother's son, was wealthy. 15 And Pharaoh gave back Sarai, the wife of Abram, and he sent him out of the land of Egypt, and he journeyed to the place where he had pitched his tent at the beginning, to the place of the altar, with Ai on the east, and Bethel on the west, and he blessed the Lord his God who had brought him back in peace. 16 And it came to pass in the forty-first jubilee in the third year of the first week, [1963 A.M.] that he returned to this place and offered thereon a burnt sacrifice, and called on the name of the Lord, and said: "Thou, the most high God, art my God for ever and ever.' 17 And in the fourth year of this week [1964 A.M.] Lot parted from him, and Lot dwelt in Sodom, and the men of Sodom were sinners exceedingly. 18 And it grieved him in his heart that his brother's son had parted from him; for he had no children. 19 In that year when Lot was taken captive, the Lord said unto Abram, after that Lot had parted from him, in the fourth year of this week: 'Lift up thine eyes from the place where thou art dwelling, northward and southward, and westward and eastward. 20 For all the land which thou seest I will give to thee and to thy seed for ever, and I will make thy seed as the sand of the sea: though a man may number the dust of the earth, yet thy seed shall not be numbered. 21 Arise, walk (through the land) in the length of it and the breadth of it, and see it all; for to thy seed will I give it.' And Abram went to Hebron, and dwelt there. 22 And in this year came Chedorlaomer, king of Elam, and Amraphel, king of Shinar, and Arioch king of Sellasar, and Tergal, king of nations, and slew the king of Gomorrah, and the king of Sodom fled, and many fell through wounds in the vale of Siddim, by the Salt Sea. 23 And they took captive Sodom and Adam and Zeboim, and they took captive Lot also, the son of Abram's brother, and all his possessions, and they went to Dan. 24 And one who had escaped came and told Abram that his brother's son had been taken captive and (Abram) armed his household servants . . . 25 . . . . for Abram, and for his seed, a tenth of the first fruits to the Lord, and the Lord ordained it as an ordinance for ever that they should give it to the priests who served before Him, that they should possess it for ever. 26 And to this law there is no limit of days; for He hath ordained it for the generations for ever that they should give to the Lord the tenth of everything, of the seed and of the wine and of the oil and of the cattle and of the sheep. 27 And He gave (it) unto His priests to eat and to drink with joy before Him. 28 And the king of Sodom came to him and bowed himself before him, and said: 'Our Lord Abram, give unto us the souls which thou hast rescued, but let the booty be thine.' 29 And Abram said unto him: 'I lift up my hands to the Most High God, that from a thread to a shoe-latchet I shall not take aught that is thine lest thou shouldst say, I have made Abram rich; save only what the young men have eaten, and the portion of the men who went with me -Aner, Eschol, and Mamre. These shall take their portion.'

Jub. 14

Abram receives the promise of a son and of innumerable descendants, 1-7. Offers a sacrifice and is told of his seed being in Egypt, 8-17. God's convenant with Abram, 18-20. Hagar bears Ishmael, 21-4. (Cf. Gen. xv.; xvi.1-4, 11.)

1 After these things, in the fourth year of this week, on the new moon of the third month, the word of the Lord came to Abram in a dream, saying: 'Fear not, Abram; I am thy defender, and thy reward will be exceeding great.' 2 And he said: 'Lord, Lord, what wilt thou give me, seeing I go hence childless, and the son of Maseq, the son of my handmaid, is the Dammasek Eliezer: he will be my heir, and to me thou hast given no seed.' 3 And he said unto him: "This (man) will not be thy heir, but one that will come out of thine own bowels; he will be thine heir.' 4 And He brought him forth abroad, and said unto him: 'Look toward heaven and number the stars if thou art able to number them.' 5 And he looked toward heaven, and beheld the stars. And He said unto him: 'So shall thy seed be.' 6 And he believed in the Lord, and it was counted to him for righteousness. 7 And He said unto him: 'I am the Lord that brought thee out of Ur of the Chaldees, to give thee the land of the Canaanites to possess it for ever; and I will be God unto thee and to thy seed after thee.' 8 And he said: 'Lord, Lord, whereby shall I know that I shall inherit (it)?' 9 And He said unto him: 'Take Me an heifer of three years, and a goat of three years, and a sheep of three years, and a turtle-dove, and a pigeon.' 10 And he took all these in the middle of the month and he dwelt at the oak of Mamre, which is near Hebron. 11 And he built there an altar, and sacrificed all these; and he poured their blood upon the altar, and divided them in the midst, and laid them over against each other; but the birds divided he not. 12 And birds came down upon the pieces, and Abram drove them away, and did not suffer the birds to touch them. 13 And it came to pass, when the sun had set, that an ecstasy fell upon Abram, and lo ! an horror of great darkness fell upon him, and it was said unto Abram: 'Know of a

142

surety that thy seed shall be a stranger in a land (that is) not theirs, and they shall bring them into bondage, and afflict them four hundred years. 14 And the nation also to whom they will be in bondage will I judge, and after that they shall come forth thence with much substance. 15 And thou shalt go to thy fathers in peace, and be buried in a good old age. 16 But in the fourth generation they shall return hither; for the iniquity of the Amorites is not yet full.' 17 And he awoke from his sleep, and he arose, and the sun had set; and there was a flame, and behold ! a furnace was smoking, and a flame of fire passed between the pieces. 18 And on that day the Lord made a covenant with Abram, saying: "To thy seed will I give this land, from the river of Egypt unto the great river, the river Euphrates, the Kenites, the Kenizzites, the Kadmonites, the Perizzites, and the Rephaim, the Phakorites, and the Hivites, and the Amorites, and the Canaanites, and the Girgashites, and the Jebusites. 19 And the day passed, and Abram offered the pieces, and the birds, and their fruit offerings, and their drink offerings, and the fire devoured them. 20 And on that day we made a covenant with Abram, according as we had covenanted with Noah in this month; and Abram renewed the festival and ordinance for himself for ever. 21 And Abram rejoiced, and made all these things known to Sarai his wife; and he believed that he would have seed, but she did not bear. 22 And Sarai advised her husband Abram, and said unto him: 'Go in unto Hagar, my Egyptian maid: it may be that I shall build up seed unto thee by her.' 23 And Abram harkened unto the voice of Sarai his wife, and said unto her, 'Do (so).' And Sarai took Hagar, her maid, the Egyptian, and gave her to Abram, her husband, to be his wife. 24 And he went in unto her, and she conceived and bare him a son, and he called his name Ishmael, in the fifth year of this week [1965 A.M.]; and this was the eighty-sixth year in the life of Abram.

Jub. 15

Abram celebrates the feast of first fruits, 1-2: his name changed and circumcision instituted, 3-14. Sarai's name changed and Isaak promised, 15-21. Abraham, Ishmael, and all his household circumcised, 22-4. Circumcision an eternal ordination, 25, 26. Israel shares this honour with the highest angels who were created circumcised, 27-9. Israel subject to God alone: other nations to angels, 30-2. Future faithlessness of Israel, 33-4. (Cf. Gen. xvii.) 1 And in the fifth year of the fourth week of this jubilee, [1979 A.M.] in the third month, in the middle of the month, Abram celebrated the feast of the first-fruits of the grain harvest. 2 And he offered new offerings on the altar, the first-fruits of the produce, unto the Lord, an heifer and a goat and a sheep on the altar as a burnt sacrifice unto the Lord; their fruit offerings and their drink offerings he offered upon the altar with frankincense. 3 And the Lord appeared to Abram, and said unto him: 'I am God Almighty; approve thyself before me and be thou perfect. 4 And I will make My covenant between Me and thee, and I will multiply thee exceedingly.' 5 And Abram fell on his face, and God talked with him, and said: 6 'Behold my ordinance is with thee, And thou shalt be the father of many nations. 7 Neither shall thy name any more be called Abram, But thy name from henceforth, even for ever, shall be Abraham. For the father of many nations have I made thee. 8 And I will make thee very great, And I will make thee into nations, And kings shall come forth from thee. 9 And I shall establish My covenant between Me and thee, and thy seed after thee, throughout their generations, for an eternal covenant, so that I may be a God unto thee, and to thy seed after thee. 10 the land where thou hast been a sojourner, the land of Canaan, that thou mayst possess it for ever, and I will be their God.' 11 And the Lord said unto Abraham: 'And as for thee, do thou keep my covenant, thou and thy seed after thee: and circumcise ye every male among you, and circumcise your foreskins, and it shall be a token of an eternal covenant between Me and you. 12 And the child on the eighth day ye shall circumcise, every male throughout your generations, him that is born in the house, or whom ye have bought with money from any stranger, whom ye have acquired who is not of thy seed. 13 He that is born in thy house shall surely be circumcised, and those whom thou hast bought with money shall be circumcised, and My covenant shall be in your flesh for an eternal ordinance. 14 And the uncircumcised male who is not circumcised in the flesh of his foreskin on the eighth day, that soul shall be cut off from his people, for he has broken My covenant.' 15 And God said unto Abraham: 'As for Sarai thy wife, her name shall no more be called Sarai, but Sarah shall be her name. 16 And I will bless her, and give thee a son by her, and I will bless him, and he shall become a nation, and kings of nations shall proceed from him.' 17 And Abraham fell on his face, and rejoiced, and said in his heart: 'Shall a son be born to him that is a hundred years old, and shall Sarah, who is ninety years old, bring forth?' 18 And Abraham said unto God: 'O that Ishmael might live before thee!' 19 And God said: 'Yea, and Sarah also shall bear thee a son, and thou shalt call his name Isaac, and I will establish My covenant with him, an everlasting covenant, and for his seed after him. 20 And as for Ishmael also have I heard thee, and behold I will bless him, and make him great, and multiply him exceedingly, and he shall beget twelve princes, and I will make him a great nation. 21 But My covenant will I establish with Isaac, whom Sarah shall bear to thee, in these days, in the next year.' 22 And He left off speaking with him, and God went up from Abraham. 23 And Abraham did according as God had said unto him, and he took Ishmael his son, and all that were born in his house, and whom he had bought with his money, every male in his house, and circumcised the flesh of their foreskin. 24 And on the selfsame day was Abraham circumcised, and all the men of his house, , and all those, whom he had bought with money from the children of the stranger, were circumcised with him. 25 This law is for all the generations for ever, and there is no circumcision of the days, and no omission of one day out of the eight days; for it is an eternal ordinance, ordained and written on the heavenly tablets. 26 And every one that is born, the flesh of whose foreskin is not circumcised on the eighth day, belongs not to the children of the covenant which the Lord made with Abraham, but to the children of destruction; nor is there, moreover, any sign on him that he is the Lord's, but (he is destined) to be destroyed and slain from the earth, and to be rooted out of the earth, for he has broken the covenant of the Lord our God. 27 For all the angels of the presence and all the angels of sanctification have been so created from the day of their creation, and before the angels of the presence and the angels of sanctification He hath sanctified Israel, that they should be with Him and with His holy angels. 28 And do thou command the children of Israel and let them observe the sign of this covenant for their generations as an eternal ordinance, and they will not be rooted out of the land. 29 For the command is ordained for a covenant, that they should observe it for ever among all the children of Israel. 30 For Ishmael and his sons and his brothers and Esau, the Lord did not cause to approach Him, and he chose them not because they are the children of Abraham, because He knew them, but He chose Israel to be His people. 31 And He sanctified it, and gathered it from amongst all the children of men; for there are many nations and many peoples, and all are His, and over all hath He placed spirits in authority to lead them astray from Him. 32 But over Israel He did not appoint any angel or spirit, for He alone is their ruler, and He will preserve them and require them at the hand of His angels and His spirits, and at the hand of all His powers in order that He may preserve them and bless them, and that they may be His and He may be theirs from

henceforth for ever. 33 And now I announce unto thee that the children of Israel will not keep true to this ordinance, and they will not circumcise their sons according to all this law; for in the flesh of their circumcision they will omit this circumcision of their sons, and all of them, sons of Beliar, will leave their sons uncircumcised as they were born. 34 And there will be great wrath from the Lord against the children of Israel. because they have forsaken His covenant and turned aside from His word, and provoked and blasphemed, inasmuch as they do not observe the ordinance of this law; for they have treated their members like the Gentiles, so that they may be removed and rooted out of the land. And there will no more be pardon or forgiveness unto them [so that there should be forgiveness and pardon] for all the sin of this eternal error.

Jub. 16

Angels appear to Abraham in Hebron and Isaac again promised, 1-4. Destruction of Sodom and Lot's deliverance, 5-9. Abraham at Beersheba: birth of and circumcision of Isaac, whose seed was to be the portion of God, 10-19. Institution of the feast of Tabernacles, 20-31. (Cf. Gen. xviii.1, 10, 12; xix.24, 29, 33-7; xx.1, 4, 8; xxi. 1-4.) 1 And on the new moon of the fourth month we appeared unto Abraham, at the oak of Mamre, and we talked with him, and we announced to him that a son would be given to him by Sarah his wife. 2 And Sarah laughed, for she heard that we had spoken these words with Abraham, and we admonished her, and she became afraid, and denied that she had laughed on account of the words. 3 And we told her the name of her son, as his name is ordained and written in the heavenly tablets (i.e.) Isaac, 4 And (that) when we returned to her at a set time, she would have conceived a son. 5 And in this month the Lord executed his judgments on Sodom, and Gomorrah, and Zeboim, and all the region of the Jordan, and He burned them with fire and brimstone, and destroyed them until this day, even as [lo] I have declared unto thee all their works, that they are wicked and sinners exceedingly, and that they defile themselves and commit fornication in their flesh, and work uncleanness on the earth. 6 And, in like manner, God will execute judgment on the places where they have done according to the uncleanness of the Sodomites, like unto the judgment of Sodom. 7 But Lot we saved; for God remembered Abraham, and sent him out from the midst of the overthrow. 8 And he and his daughters committed sin upon the earth, such as had not been on the earth since the days of Adam till his time; for the man lay with his daughters. 9 And, behold, it was commanded and engraven concerning all his seed, on the heavenly tablets, to remove them and root them out, and to execute judgment upon them like the judgment of Sodom, and to leave no seed of the man on earth on the day of condemnation. 10 And in this month Abraham moved from Hebron, and departed and dwelt between Kadesh and Shur in the mountains of Gerar. 11 And in the middle of the fifth month he moved from thence, and dwelt at the Well of the Oath. 12 And in the middle of the sixth month the Lord visited Sarah and did unto her as He had spoken and she conceived. 13 And she bare a son in the third month, and in the middle of the month, at the time of which the Lord had spoken to Abraham, on the festival of the first fruits of the harvest, Isaac was born. 14 And Abraham circumcised his son on the eighth day: he was the first that was circumcised according to the covenant which is ordained for ever. 15 And in the sixth year of the fourth week we came to Abraham, to the Well of the Oath, and we appeared unto him [as we had told Sarah that we should return to her, and she would have conceived a son. 16 And we returned in the seventh month, and found Sarah with child before us] and we blessed him, and we announced to him all the things which had been decreed concerning him, that he should not die till he should beget six sons more, and should see (them) before he died; but (that) in Isaac should his name and seed be called: 17 And (that) all the seed of his sons should be Gentiles, and be reckoned with the Gentiles; but from the sons of Isaac one should become a holy seed, and should not be reckoned among the Gentiles. 18 For he should become the portion of the Most High, and all his seed had fallen into the possession of God, that it should be unto the Lord a people for (His) possession above all nations and that it should become a kingdom and priests and a holy nation. 19 And we went our way, and we announced to Sarah all that we had told him, and they both rejoiced with exceeding great joy. 20 And he built there an altar to the Lord who had delivered him, and who was making him rejoice in the land of his sojourning, and he celebrated a festival of joy in this month seven days, near the altar which he had built at the Well of the Oath. 21 And he built booths for himself and for his servants on this festival, and he was the first to celebrate the feast of tabernacles on the earth. 22 And during these seven days he brought each day to the altar a burnt offering to the Lord, two oxen, two rams, seven sheep, one he-goat, for a sin offering, that he might atone thereby for himself and for his seed. 23 And, as a thank-offering, seven rams, seven kids, seven sheep, and seven he-goats, and their fruit offerings and their drink offerings; and he burnt all the fat thereof on the altar, a chosen offering unto the Lord for a sweet smelling savour. 24 And morning and evening he burnt fragrant substances, frankincense and galbanum, and stackte, and nard, and myrrh, and spice, and costum; all these seven he offered, crushed, mixed together in equal parts (and) pure. 25 And he celebrated this feast during seven days, rejoicing with all his heart and with all his soul, he and all those who were in his house, and there was no stranger with him, nor any that was uncircumcised. 26 And he blessed his Creator who had created him in his generation, for He had created him according to His good pleasure; for He knew and perceived that from him would arise the plant of righteousness for the eternal generations, and from him a holy seed, so that it should become like Him who had made all things. 27 And he blessed and rejoiced, and he called the name of this festival the festival of the Lord, a joy acceptable to the Most High God. 28 And we blessed him for ever, and all his seed after him throughout all the generations of the earth, because he celebrated this festival in its season, according to the testimony of the heavenly tablets. 29 For this reason it is ordained on the heavenly tablets concerning Israel, that they shall celebrate the feast of tabernacles seven days with joy, in the seventh month, acceptable before the Lord -a statute for ever throughout their generations every year. 30 And to this there is no limit of days; for it is ordained for ever regarding Israel that they should celebrate it and dwell in booths, and set wreaths upon their heads, and take leafy boughs, and willows from the brook. 31 And Abraham took branches of palm trees, and the fruit of goodly trees, and every day going round the altar with the branches seven times [a day] in the morning, he praised and gave thanks to his God for all things in joy.

Jub. 17

Expulsion of Hagar and Ishmael, 1-14. Mastêmâ proposes that God should require Abraham to sacrifice Isaac in order to test his love and obedience: Abraham's ten trials, 15-18. (Cf. Gen.xxi.8-21.) 1 And in the first year of the fifth week Isaac was weaned in this jubilee, [1982 A.M.] and Abraham made a great banquet in the third month, on the day his son Isaac was weaned. 2 And Ishmael, the son of Hagar, the Egyptian, was before the face of Abraham, his father, in his place, and Abraham rejoiced and blessed God because he had seen his sons and had not died childless. 3 And he remembered the words which He had spoken to him on the day on which Lot had parted from him, and he rejoiced because the Lord had given him seed

144

upon the earth to inherit the earth, and he blessed with all his mouth the Creator of all things. 4 And Sarah saw Ishmael playing and dancing, and Abraham rejoicing with great joy, and she became jealous of Ishmael and said to Abraham, 'Cast out this bondwoman and her son; for the son of this bondwoman will not be heir with my son, Isaac.' 5 And the thing was grievous in Abraham's sight, because of his maidservant and because of his son, that he should drive them from him. 6 And God said to Abraham 'Let it not be grievous in thy sight, because of the child and because of the bondwoman; in all that Sarah hath said unto thee, harken to her words and do (them); for in Isaac shall thy name and seed be called. 7 But as for the son of this bondwoman I will make him a great nation, because he is of thy seed.' 8 And Abraham rose up early in the morning, and took bread and a bottle of water, and placed them on the shoulders of Hagar and the child, and sent her away. 9 And she departed and wandered in the wilderness of Beersheba, and the water in the bottle was spent, and the child thirsted, and was not able to go on, and fell down. 10 And his mother took him and cast him under an olive tree, and went and sat her down over against him, at the distance of a bow-shot; for she said, 'Let me not see the death of my child,' and as she sat she wept. 11 And an angel of God, one of the holy ones, said unto her, 'Why weepest thou, Hagar? Arise take the child, and hold him in thine hand; for God hath heard thy voice, and hath seen the child.' 12 And she opened her eyes, and she saw a well of water, and she went and filled her bottle with water, and she gave her child to drink, and she arose and went towards the wilderness of Paran. 13 And the child grew and became an archer, and God was with him, and his mother took him a wife from among the daughters of Egypt. 14 And she bare him a son, and he called his name Nebaioth; for she said, 'The Lord was nigh to me when I called upon him.' 15 And it came to pass in the seventh week, in the first year thereof, [2003 A.M.] in the first month in this jubilee, on the twelfth of this month, there were voices in heaven regarding Abraham, that he was faithful in all that He told him, and that he loved the Lord, and that in every affliction he was faithful. 16 And the prince Mastêmâ came and said before God, 'Behold, Abraham loves Isaac his son, and he delights in him above all things else; bid him offer him as a burnt-offering on the altar, and Thou wilt see if he will do this command, and Thou wilt know if he is faithful in everything wherein Thou dost try him. 17 And the Lord knew that Abraham was faithful in all his afflictions; for He had tried him through his country and with famine, and had tried him with the wealth of kings, and had tried him again through his wife, when she was torn (from him), and with circumcision; and had tried him through Ishmael and Hagar, his maid-servant, when he sent them away. 18 And in everything wherein He had tried him, he was found faithful, and his soul was not impatient, and he was not slow to act; for he was faithful and a lover of the Lord.

Jub. 18

Sacrifice of Isaac: Mastêmâ put to shame, 1-13. Abraham again blessed: returns to Beersheba 14-19. (Cf. Gen. xxii. 1-19.) 1 And God said to him, 'Abraham, Abraham'; and he said, Behold, (here) am I.' 2 And he said, Take thy beloved son whom thou lovest, (even) Isaac, and go unto the high country, and offer him on one of the mountains which I will point out unto thee.' 3 And he rose early in the morning and saddled his ass, and took his two young men with him, and Isaac his son, and clave the wood of the burnt offering, and he went to the place on the third day, and he saw the place afar off. 4 And he came to a well of water, and he said to his young men, 'Abide ye here with the ass, and I and the lad shall go (yonder), and when we have worshipped we shall come again to you.' 5 And he took the wood of the burnt-offering and laid it on Isaac his son, and he took in his hand the fire and the knife, and they went both of them together to that place. 6 And Isaac said to his father, 'Father;' and he said, 'Here am I, my son.' And he said unto him, 'Behold the fire, and the knife, and the wood; but where is the sheep for the burnt-offering, father?' 7 And he said, 'God will provide for himself a sheep for a burnt-offering, my son.' And he drew near to the place of the mount of God. 8 And he built an altar, and he placed the wood on the altar, and bound Isaac his son, and placed him on the wood which was upon the altar, and stretched forth his hand to take the knife to slay Isaac his son. 9 And I stood before him, and before the prince Mastêmâ, and the Lord said, 'Bid him not to lay his hand on the lad, nor to do anything to him, for I have shown that he fears the Lord.' 10 And I called to him from heaven, and said unto him: 'Abraham, Abraham;' and he was terrified and said: 'Behold, (here) am I.' 11 And I said unto him: 'Lay not thy hand upon the lad, neither do thou anything to him; for now I have shown that thou fearest the Lord, and hast not withheld thy son, thy first-born son, from me.' 12 And the prince Mastêmâ was put to shame; and Abraham lifted up his eyes and looked, and, behold a ram caught . . . by his horns, and Abraham went and took the ram and offered it for a burnt-offering in the stead of his son. 13 And Abraham called that place "The Lord hath seen', so that it is said in the mount the Lord hath seen: that is Mount Sion. 14 And the Lord called Abraham by his name a second time from heaven, as he caused us to appear to speak to him in the name of the Lord. 15 And he said: 'By Myself have I sworn, saith the Lord, Because thou hast done this thing, And hast not withheld thy son, thy beloved son, from Me, That in blessing I will bless thee, And in multiplying I will multiply thy seed As the stars of heaven, And as the sand which is on the seashore. And thy seed shall inherit the cities of its enemies, 16 And in thy seed shall all nations of the earth be blessed; Because thou hast obeyed My voice, And I have shown to all that thou art faithful unto Me in all that I have said unto thee: Go in peace.' 17 And Abraham went to his young men, and they arose and went together to Beersheba, and Abraham [2010 A.M.] dwelt by the Well of the Oath. 18 And he celebrated this festival every year, seven days with joy, and he called it the festival of the Lord according to the seven days during which he went and returned in peace. 19 And accordingly has it been ordained and written on the heavenly tablets regarding Israel and its seed that they should observe this festival seven days with the joy of festival.

Jub. 19

Return of Abraham to Hebron. Death and burial of Sarah, 1-9. Marriage of Isaac and second marriage of Abraham. Birth of Esau and Jacob, 10-14. Abraham commends Jacob to Rebecca and blesses him, 15-31. (Cf. Gen. xxiii.1-4, 11-16; xxiv.15; xxv.1-2, 25-7; xiii. 16.) 1 And in the first year of the first week in the forty-second jubilee, Abraham returned and dwelt opposite Hebron, that is Kirjath Arba, two weeks of years. 2 And in the first year of the third week of this jubilee the days of the life of Sarah were accomplished, and she died in Hebron. 3 And Abraham went to mourn over her and bury her, and we tried him [to see] if his spirit were patient and he were not indignant in the words of his mouth; and he was found patient in this, and was not disturbed. 4 For in patience of spirit he conversed with the children of Heth, to the intent that they should give him a place in which to bury his dead. 5 And the Lord gave him grace before all who saw him, and he besought in gentleness the sons of Heth, and they gave him the land of the double cave over against Mamre, that is Hebron, for four hundred pieces of silver. 6 And they besought him saying, We shall give it to thee for nothing; but he would not take it from their hands for nothing, for he gave the price

of the place, the money in full, and he bowed down before them twice, and after this he buried his dead in the double cave. 7 And all the days of the life of Sarah were one hundred and twenty-seven years, that is, two jubilees and four weeks and one year: these are the days of the years of the life of Sarah. 8 This is the tenth trial wherewith Abraham was tried, and he was found faithful, patient in spirit. 9 And he said not a single word regarding the rumour in the land how that God had said that He would give it to him and to his seed after him, and he begged a place there to bury his dead; for he was found faithful, and was recorded on the heavenly tablets as the friend of God. 10 And in the fourth year thereof he took a wife for his son Isaac and her name was Rebecca [2020 A.M.] [the daughter of Bethuel, the son of Nahor, the brother of Abraham] the sister of Laban and daughter of Bethuel; and Bethuel was the son of Melca, who was the wife of Nahor, the brother of Abraham. 11 And Abraham took to himself a third wife, and her name was Keturah, from among the daughters of his household servants, for Hagar had died before Sarah. And she bare him six sons, Zimram, and Jokshan, and Medan, and Midian, and Ishbak, and Shuah, in the two weeks of years. 12 And in the sixth week, in the second year thereof, Rebecca bare to Isaac two sons, Jacob and Esau, 13 and [2046 A.M.] Jacob was a smooth and upright man, and Esau was fierce, a man of the field, and hairy, and Jacob dwelt in tents. 14 And the youths grew, and Jacob learned to write; but Esau did not learn, for he was a man of the field and a hunter, and he learnt war, and all his deeds were fierce. 15 And Abraham loved Jacob, but Isaac loved Esau. 16 And Abraham saw the deeds of Esau, and he knew that in Jacob should his name and seed be called; and he called Rebecca and gave commandment regarding Jacob, for he knew that she (too) loved Jacob much more than Esau. 17 And he said unto her: My daughter, watch over my son Jacob, For he shall be in my stead on the earth, And for a blessing in the midst of the children of men, And for the glory of the whole seed of Shem. 18 For I know that the Lord will choose him to be a people for possession unto Himself, above all peoples that are upon the face of the earth. 19 And behold, Isaac my son loves Esau more than Jacob, but I see that thou truly lovest Jacob. 20 Add still further to thy kindness to him, And let thine eyes be upon him in love; For he shall be a blessing unto us on the earth from henceforth unto all generations of the earth. 21 Let thy hands be strong And let thy heart rejoice in thy son Jacob; For I have loved him far beyond all my sons. He shall be blessed for ever, And his seed shall fill the whole earth. 22 If a man can number the sand of the earth, His seed also shall be numbered. 23 And all the blessings wherewith the Lord hath blessed me and my seed shall belong to Jacob and his seed alway. 24 And in his seed shall my name be blessed, and the name of my fathers, Shem, and Noah, and Enoch, and Mahalalel, and Enos, and Seth, and Adam. 25 And these shall serve To lay the foundations of the heaven, And to strengthen the earth, And to renew all the luminaries which are in the firmament. 26 And he called Jacob before the eyes of Rebecca his mother, and kissed him, and blessed him, and said: 27 'Jacob, my beloved son, whom my soul loveth, may God bless thee from above the firmament, and may He give thee all the blessings wherewith He blessed Adam, and Enoch, and Noah, and Shem; and all the things of which He told me, and all the things which He promised to give me, may he cause to cleave to thee and to thy seed for ever, according to the days of heaven above the earth. 28 And the Spirits of Mastêmâ shall not rule over thee or over thy seed to turn thee from the Lord, who is thy God from henceforth for ever. 29 And may the Lord God be a father to thee and thou the first-born son, and to the people alway. 30 Go in peace, my son.' And they both went forth together from Abraham. 31 And Rebecca loved Jacob, with all her heart and with all her soul, very much more than Esau; but Isaac loved Esau much more than Jacob.

Jub. 20

Abraham admonishes his sons and his sons' sons to work righteousness, observe circumcision, and refrain from impurity and idolatry, 1-10. Dismisses them with gifts, 11. Dwelling-places of the Ishmaelites and of the sons of Keturah, 12-13. (Cf. Gen. xxv. 5-6.) [1] And in the forty-second jubilee, in the first year of the seventh week, Abraham called Ishmael, [2052 (2045?) A.M.] and his twelve sons, and Isaac and his two sons, and the six sons of Keturah, and their sons. [2] And he commanded them that they should observe the way of the Lord; that they should work righteousness, and love each his neighbour, and act on this manner amongst all men; that they should each so walk with regard to them as to do judgment and righteousness on the earth. [3] That they should circumcise their sons, according to the covenant which He had made with them, and not deviate to the right hand or the left of all the paths which the Lord had commanded us; and that we should keep ourselves from all fornication and uncleanness, [and renounce from amongst us all fornication and uncleanness]. [4] And if any woman or maid commit fornication amongst you, burn her with fire and let them not commit fornication with her after their eyes and their heart; and let them not take to themselves wives from the daughters of Canaan; for the seed of Canaan will be rooted out of the land. [5] And he told them of the judgment of the giants, and the judgment of the Sodomites, how they had been judged on account of their wickedness, and had died on account of their fornication, and uncleanness, and mutual corruption through fornication. [6] 'And guard yourselves from all fornication and uncleanness, And from all pollution of sin, Lest ye make our name a curse, And your whole life a hissing, And all your sons to be destroyed by the sword, And ye become accursed like Sodom, And all your remnant as the sons of Gomorrah. [7] I implore you, my sons, love the God of heaven And cleave ye to all His commandments. And walk not after their idols, and after their uncleannesses, [8] And make not for yourselves molten or graven gods; For they are vanity, And there is no spirit in them; For they are work of (men's) hands, And all who trust in them, trust in nothing. [9] Serve them not, nor worship them, But serve ye the most high God, and worship Him continually: And hope for His countenance always, And work uprightness and righteousness before Him, That He may have pleasure in you and grant you His mercy, And send rain upon you morning and evening, And bless all your works which ye have wrought upon the earth, And bless thy bread and thy water, And bless the fruit of thy womb and the fruit of thy land, And the herds of thy cattle, and the flocks of thy sheep. [10] And ye will be for a blessing on the earth, And all nations of the earth will desire you, And bless your sons in my name, That they may be blessed as I am. [11] And he gave to Ishmael and to his sons, and to the sons of Keturah, gifts, and sent them away from Isaac his son, and he gave everything to Isaac his son. [12] And Ishmael and his sons, and the sons of Keturah and their sons, went together and dwelt from Paran to the entering in of Babylon in all the land which is towards the East facing the desert. [13] And these mingled with each other, and their name was called Arabs, and Ishmaelites.

Jub. 21

Abraham's last words to Isaac regarding idolatry, the eating of blood, the offering of various sacrifices and the use of salt, 1-11. Also regarding the woods to be used in sacrifice and the duty of washing before sacrifice and of covering blood etc., 12-25. [1] And in the sixth year of the seventh week of this jubilee Abraham called Isaac his son, and [2057 (2050?) A.M.] commanded him: saying, 'I am become old, and know not the day of my death, and am full of my days. [2] And behold, I am one hundred and seventy-five years old, and throughout all the days of my life I have remembered the Lord, and sought with all my heart to do His will, and to walk uprightly in all His ways. [3] My soul has hated idols, that I might observe to do the will of Him who created me. [4] For He is the living God, and He is holy and faithful, and He is righteous beyond all, and there is with Him no accepting of (men's) persons and no accepting of gifts; for God is righteous, and executeth judgment on all those who transgress His commandments and despise His covenant. [5] And do thou, my son, observe His commandments and His ordinances and His judgments, and walk not after the abominations and after the graven images and after the molten images. [6] And eat no blood at all of animals or cattle, or of any bird which flies in the heaven. [7] And if thou dost slay a victim as an acceptable peace offering, slay ye it, and pour out its blood upon the altar, and all the fat of the offering offer on the altar with fine flour and the meat offering mingled with oil, with its drink offering -offer them all together on the altar of burnt offering; it is a sweet savour before the Lord. [8] And thou wilt offer the fat of the sacrifice of thank offerings on the fire which is upon the altar, and the fat which is on the belly, and all the fat on the inwards and the two kidneys, and all the fat that is upon them, and upon the loins and liver thou shalt remove, together with the kidneys. [9] And offer all these for a sweet savour acceptable before the Lord, with its meat-offering and with its drink- offering, for a sweet savour, the bread of the offering unto the Lord. [10] And eat its meat on that day and on the second day, and let not the sun on the second day go down upon it till it is eaten, and let nothing be left over for the third day; for it is not acceptable [for it is not approved] and let it no longer be eaten, and all who eat thereof will bring sin upon themselves; for thus I have found it written in the books of my forefathers, and in the words of Enoch, and in the words of Noah. [11] And on all thy oblations thou shalt strew salt, and let not the salt of the covenant be lacking in all thy oblations before the Lord. [12] And as regards the wood of the sacrifices, beware lest thou bring (other) wood for the altar in addition to these: cypress, bay, almond, fir, pine, cedar, savin, fig, olive, myrrh, laurel, aspalathus. [13] And of these kinds of wood lay upon the altar under the sacrifice, such as have been tested as to their appearance, and do not lay (thereon) any split or dark wood, (but) hard and clean, without fault, a sound and new growth; and do not lay (thereon) old wood, [for its fragrance is gone] for there is no longer fragrance in it as before. [14] Besides these kinds of wood there is none other that thou shalt place (on the altar), for the fragrance is dispersed, and the smell of its fragrance goes not up to heaven. [15] Observe this commandment and do it, my son, that thou mayst be upright in all thy deeds. [16] And at all times be clean in thy body, and wash thyself with water before thou approachest to offer on the altar, and wash thy hands and thy feet before thou drawest near to the altar; and when thou art done sacrificing, wash again thy hands and thy feet. [17] And let no blood appear upon you nor upon your clothes; be on thy guard, my son, against blood, be on thy guard exceedingly; cover it with dust. [18] And do not eat any blood for it is the soul; eat no blood whatever. [19] And take no gifts for the blood of man, lest it be shed with impunity, without judgment; for it is the blood that is shed that causes the earth to sin, and the earth cannot be cleansed from the blood of man save by the blood of him who shed it. [20] And take no present or gift for the blood of man: blood for blood, that thou mayest be accepted before the Lord, the Most High God; for He is the defence of the good: and that thou mayest be preserved from all evil, and that He may save thee from every kind of death. [21] I see, my son, That all the works of the children of men are sin and wickedness, And all their deeds are uncleanness and an

146

abomination and a pollution, And there is no righteousness with them. 22 Beware, lest thou shouldest walk in their ways And tread in their paths, And sin a sin unto death before the Most High God. Else He will [hide His face from thee And] give thee back into the hands of thy transgression, And root thee out of the land, and thy seed likewise from under heaven, And thy name and thy seed shall perish from the whole earth. 23 Turn away from all their deeds and all their uncleanness, And observe the ordinance of the Most High God, And do His will and be upright in all things. 24 And He will bless thee in all thy deeds, And will raise up from thee a plant of righteousness through all the earth, throughout all generations of the earth, And my name and thy name shall not be forgotten under heaven for ever. 25 Go, my son in peace. May the Most High God, my God and thy God, strengthen thee to do His will, And may He bless all thy seed and the residue of thy seed for the generations for ever, with all righteous blessings, That thou mayest be a blessing on all the earth.' 26 And he went out from him rejoicing.

Jub. 22

Isaac, Ishmael, and Jacob celebrate the feast of first fruits at Beersheba with Abraham, 1-5. Prayer of Abraham, 6-9. Abraham's last words to and blessings of Jacob, 10-30. 1 And it came to pass in the first week in the forty-fourth jubilee, in the second year, that is, the year in which Abraham died, that Isaac and Ishmael came from the Well of the Oath to celebrate the feast of weeks -that is, the feast of the first fruits of the harvest-to Abraham, their father, and Abraham rejoiced because his two sons had come. 2 For Isaac had many possessions in Beersheba, and Isaac was wont to go and see his possessions and to return to his father. 3 And in those days Ishmael came to see his father, and they both came together, and Isaac offered a sacrifice for a burnt offering, and presented it on the altar of his father which he had made in Hebron. 4 And he offered a thank offering and made a feast of joy before Ishmael, his brother: and Rebecca made new cakes from the new grain, and gave them to Jacob, her son, to take them to Abraham, his father, from the first fruits of the land, that he might eat and bless the Creator of all things before he died. 5 And Isaac, too, sent by the hand of Jacob to Abraham a best thank offering, that he might eat and drink. 6 And he eat and drank, and blessed the Most High God, Who hath created heaven and earth, Who hath made all the fat things of the earth, And given them to the children of men That they might eat and drink and bless their Creator. 7 'And now I give thanks unto Thee, my God, because thou hast caused me to see this day: behold, I am one hundred three score and fifteen years, an old man and full of days, and all my days have been unto me peace. 8 The sword of the adversary has not overcome me in all that Thou hast given me and my children all the days of my life until this day. 9 My God, may Thy mercy and Thy peace be upon Thy servant, and upon the seed of his sons, that they may be to Thee a chosen nation and an inheritance from amongst all the nations of the earth from henceforth unto all the days of the generations of the earth, unto all the ages.' 10 And he called Jacob and said: 'My son Jacob, may the God of all bless thee and strengthen thee to do righteousness, and His will before Him, and may He choose thee and thy seed that ye may become a people for His inheritance according to His will alway. 11 And do thou, my son, Jacob, draw near and kiss me.' And he drew near and kissed him, and he said: 'Blessed be my son Jacob And all the sons of God Most High, unto all the ages: May God give unto thee a seed of righteousness; And some of thy sons may He sanctify in the midst of the whole earth; May nations serve thee, And all the nations bow themselves before thy seed. 12 Be strong in the presence of men, And exercise authority over all the seed of Seth. Then thy ways and the ways of thy sons will be justified, So that they shall become a holy nation. 13 May the

147

Most High God give thee all the blessings Wherewith He has blessed me And wherewith He blessed Noah and Adam; May they rest on the sacred head of thy seed from generation to generation for ever. 14 And may He cleanse thee from all unrighteousness and impurity, That thou mayest be forgiven all the transgressions; which thou hast committed ignorantly. And may He strengthen thee, And bless thee. And mayest thou inherit the whole earth, 15 And may He renew His covenant with thee. That thou mayest be to Him a nation for His inheritance for all the ages, And that He may be to thee and to thy seed a God in truth and righteousness throughout all the days of the earth. 16 And do thou, my son Jacob, remember my words, And observe the commandments of Abraham, thy father: Separate thyself from the nations, And eat not with them: And do not according to their works, And become not their associate; For their works are unclean, And all their ways are a Pollution and an abomination and uncleanness. 17 They offer their sacrifices to the dead And they worship evil spirits, And they eat over the graves, And all their works are vanity and nothingness. 18 They have no heart to understand And their eyes do not see what their works are, And how they err in saying to a piece of wood: 'Thou art my God,' And to a stone: 'Thou art my Lord and thou art my deliverer.' [And they have no heart.] 19 And as for thee, my son Jacob, May the Most High God help thee And the God of heaven bless thee And remove thee from their uncleanness and from all their error. 20 Be thou ware, my son Jacob, of taking a wife from any seed of the daughters of Canaan; For all his seed is to be rooted out of the earth. 21 For, owing to the transgression of Ham, Canaan erred, And all his seed shall be destroyed from off the earth and all the residue thereof, And none springing from him shall be saved on the day of judgment. 22 And as for all the worshippers of idols and the profane (b) There shall be no hope for them in the land of the living; (c) And there shall be no remembrance of them on the earth; (c) For they shall descend into Sheol, (d) And into the place of condemnation shall they go, As the children of Sodom were taken away from the earth So will all those who worship idols be taken away. 23 Fear not, my son Jacob, And be not dismayed, O son of Abraham: May the Most High God preserve thee from destruction, And from all the paths of error may he deliver thee. 24 This house have I built for myself that I might put my name upon it in the earth: [it is given to thee and to thy seed for ever], and it will be named the house of Abraham; it is given to thee and to thy seed for ever; for thou wilt build my house and establish my name before God for ever: thy seed and thy name will stand throughout all generations of the earth.' 25 And he ceased commanding him and blessing him. 26 And the two lay together on one bed, and Jacob slept in the bosom of Abraham, his father's father and he kissed him seven times, and his affection and his heart rejoiced over him. 27 And he blessed him with all his heart and said: "The Most High God, the God of all, and Creator of all, who brought me forth from Ur of the Chaldees that he might give me this land to inherit it for ever, and that I might establish a holy seed-blessed be the Most High for ever.' 28 And he blessed Jacob and said: 'My son, over whom with all my heart and my affection I rejoice, may Thy grace and Thy mercy be lift up upon him and upon his seed alway. 29 And do not forsake him, nor set him at nought from henceforth unto the days of eternity, and may Thine eyes be opened upon him and upon his seed, that Thou mayst preserve him, and bless him, and mayest sanctify him as a nation for Thine inheritance; 30 And bless him with all Thy blessings from henceforth unto all the days of eternity, and renew Thy covenant and Thy grace with him and with his seed according to all Thy good pleasure unto all the generations of the earth.'

Jub. 23

¹ And he placed two fingers of Jacob on his eyes, and he blessed the God of gods, and he covered his face and stretched out his feet and slept the sleep of eternity, and was gathered to his fathers. ² And notwithstanding all this Jacob was lying in his bosom, and knew not that Abraham, his father's father, was dead. ³ And Jacob awoke from his sleep, and behold Abraham was cold as ice, and he said 'Father, father'; but there was none that spake, and he knew that he was dead. ⁴ And he arose from his bosom and ran and told Rebecca, his mother; and Rebecca went to Isaac in the night, and told him; and they went together, and Jacob with them, and a lamp was in his hand, and when they had gone in they found Abraham lying dead. ⁵ And Isaac fell on the face of his father and wept and kissed him. ⁶ And the voices were heard in the house of Abraham, and Ishmael his son arose, and went to Abraham his father, and wept over Abraham his father, he and all the house of Abraham, and they wept with a great weeping. ⁷ And his sons Isaac and Ishmael buried him in the double cave, near Sarah his wife, and they wept for him forty days, all the men of his house, and Isaac and Ishmael, and all their sons, and all the sons of Keturah in their places; and the days of weeping for Abraham were ended. ⁸ And he lived three jubilees and four weeks of years, one hundred and seventy-five years, and completed the days of his life, being old and full of days. ⁹ For the days of the forefathers, of their life, were nineteen jubilees; and after the Flood they began to grow less than nineteen jubilees, and to decrease in jubilees, and to grow old quickly, and to be full of their days by reason of manifold tribulation and the wickedness of their ways, with the exception of Abraham. ¹⁰ For Abraham was perfect in all his deeds with the Lord, and well-pleasing in righteousness all the days of his life; and behold, he did not complete four jubilees in his life, when he had grown old by reason of the wickedness, and was full of his days. ¹¹ And all the generations which shall arise from this time until the day of the great judgment shall grow old quickly, before they complete two jubilees, and their knowledge shall forsake them by reason of their old age Land all their know- ledge shall vanish away]. ¹² And in those days, if a man live a jubilee and a-half of years, they shall say regarding him: 'He has lived long, and the greater part of his days are pain and sorrow and tribulation, and there is no peace: ¹³ For calamity follows on calamity, and wound on wound, and tribulation on tribulation, and evil tidings on evil tidings, and illness on illness, and all evil judgments such as these, one with another, illness and overthrow, and snow and frost and ice, and fever, and chills, and torpor, and famine, and death, and sword, and captivity, and all kinds of calamities and pains.' ¹⁴ And all these shall come on an evil generation, which transgresses on the earth: their works are uncleanness and fornication, and pollution and abominations. ¹⁵ Then they shall say: "The days of the forefathers were many (even), unto a thousand years, and were good; but behold, the days of our life, if a man has lived many, are three score years and ten, and, if he is strong, four score years, and those evil, and there is no peace in the days of this evil generation.' ¹⁶ And in that generation the sons shall convict their fathers and their elders of sin and unrighteousness, and of the words of their mouth and the great wickednesses which they perpetrate, and concerning their forsaking the covenant which the Lord made between them and Him, that they should observe and do all His commandments and His ordinances and all His laws, without departing either to the right hand or the left. ¹⁷ For all have done evil, and every mouth speaks

148

iniquity and all their works are an uncleanness and an abomination, and all their ways are pollution, uncleanness and destruction. ¹⁸ Behold the earth shall be destroyed on account of all their works, and there shall be no seed of the vine, and no oil; for their works are altogether faithless, and they shall all perish together, beasts and cattle and birds, and all the fish of the sea, on account of the children of men. ¹⁹ And they shall strive one with another, the young with the old, and the old with the young, the poor with the rich, the lowly with the great, and the beggar with the prince, on account of the law and the covenant; for they have forgotten commandment, and covenant, and feasts, and months, and Sabbaths, and jubilees, and all judgments. ²⁰ And they shall stand swords and war to turn them back into the way; but they shall not return until much blood has been shed on the earth, one by another. ²¹ And those who have escaped shall not return from their wickedness to the way of righteousness, but they shall all exalt themselves to deceit and wealth, that they may each take all that is his neighbour's, and they shall name the great name, but not in truth and not in righteousness, and they shall defile the holy of holies with their uncleanness and the corruption of their pollution. ²² And a great punishment shall befall the deeds of this generation from the Lord, and He will give them over to the sword and to judgment and to captivity, and to be plundered and devoured. ²³ And He will wake up against them the sinners of the Gentiles, who have neither mercy nor compassion, and who shall respect the person of none, neither old nor young, nor any one, for they are more wicked and strong to do evil than all the children of men. And they shall use violence against Israel and transgression against Jacob, And much blood shall be shed upon the earth, And there shall be none to gather and none to bury. ²⁴ In those days they shall cry aloud, And call and pray that they may be saved from the hand of the sinners, the Gentiles; But none shall be saved. ²⁵ And the heads of the children shall be white with grey hair, And a child of three weeks shall appear old like a man of one hundred years, And their stature shall be destroyed by tribulation and oppression. ²⁶ And in those days the children shall begin to study the laws, And to seek the commandments, And to return to the path of righteousness. ²⁷ And the days shall begin to grow many and increase amongst those children of men Till their days draw nigh to one thousand years. And to a greater number of years than (before) was the number of the days. ²⁸ And there shall be no old man Nor one who is satisfied with his days, For all shall be (as) children and youths. ²⁹ And all their days they shall complete and live in peace and in joy, And there shall be no Satan nor any evil destroyer; For all their days shall be days of blessing and healing. ³⁰ And at that time the Lord will heal His servants, And they shall rise up and see great peace, And drive out their adversaries. And the righteous shall see and be thankful, And rejoice with joy for ever and ever, And shall see all their judgments and all their curses on their enemies. ³¹ And their bones shall rest in the earth, And their spirits shall have much joy, And they shall know that it is the Lord who executes judgment, And shows mercy to hundreds and thousands and to all that love Him ³² And do thou, Moses, write down these words; for thus are they written, and they record (them) on the heavenly tablets for a testimony for the generations for ever.

Jub. 24

¹ And it came to pass after the death of Abraham, that the Lord blessed Isaac his son, and he arose from Hebron and went and dwelt at the Well of the Vision in the first year of the third week [2073 A.M.] of this jubilee, seven years. ² And in the first year of the fourth week a famine began in the land, [2080 A.M.] besides the first famine, which had been in the days of

Abraham. ³ And Jacob sod lentil pottage, and Esau came from the field hungry. And he said to Jacob his brother: 'Give me of this red pottage.' And Jacob said to him: 'Sell to me thy [primogeniture, this] birthright and I will give thee bread, and also some of this lentil pottage.' ⁴ And Esau said in his heart: 'I shall die; of what profit to me is this birthright? ⁵ 'And he said to Jacob: 'I give it to thee.' And Jacob said: 'Swear to me, this day,' and he sware unto him. ⁶ And Jacob gave his brother Esau bread and pottage, and he eat till he was satisfied, and Esau despised his birthright; for this reason was Esau's name called Edom, on account of the red pottage which Jacob gave him for his birthright. ⁷ And Jacob became the elder, and Esau was brought down from his dignity. ⁸ And the famine was over the land, and Isaac departed to go down into Egypt in the second year of this week, and went to the king of the Philistines to Gerar, unto Abimelech. ⁹ And the Lord appeared unto him and said unto him: 'Go not down into Egypt; dwell in the land that I shall tell thee of, and sojourn in this land, and I will be with thee and bless thee. ¹⁰ For to thee and to thy seed will I give all this land, and I will establish My oath which I sware unto Abraham thy father, and I will multiply thy seed as the stars of heaven, and will give unto thy seed all this land. ¹¹ And in thy seed shall all the nations of the earth be blessed, because thy father obeyed My voice, and kept My charge and My commandments, and My laws, and My ordinances, and My covenant; and now obey My voice and dwell in this land.' ¹² And he dwelt in Gelar three weeks of years. ¹³ And Abimelech charged concerning him, [2080-2101 A.M.] and concerning all that was his, saying: 'Any man that shall touch him or aught that is his shall surely die.' ¹⁴ And Isaac waxed strong among the Philistines, and he got many possessions, oxen and sheep and camels and asses and a great household. ¹⁵ And he sowed in the land of the Philistines and brought in a hundred-fold, and Isaac became exceedingly great, and the Philistines envied him. ¹⁶ Now all the wells which the servants of Abraham had dug during the life of Abraham, the Philistines had stopped them after the death of Abraham, and filled them with earth. ¹⁷ And Abimelech said unto Isaac: 'Go from us, for thou art much mightier than we', and Isaac departed thence in the first year of the seventh week, and sojourned in the valleys of Gerar. ¹⁸ And they digged again the wells of water which the servants of Abraham, his father, had digged, and which the Philistines had closed after the death of Abraham his father, and he called their names as Abraham his father had named them. ¹⁹ And the servants of Isaac dug a well in the valley, and found living water, and the shepherds of Gerar strove with the shepherds of Isaac, saying: 'The water is ours'; and Isaac called the name of the well 'Perversity', because they had been perverse with us. ²⁰ And they dug a second well, and they strove for that also, and he called its name 'Enmity'. And he arose from thence and they digged another well, and for that they strove not, and he called the name of it 'Room', and Isaac said: 'Now the Lord hath made room for us, and we have increased in the land.' ²¹ And he went up from thence to the Well of the Oath in the first year of the first week in the [2108 A.M.] forty-fourth jubilee. ²² And the Lord appeared to him that night, on the new moon of the first month, and said unto him: 'I am the God of Abraham thy father; fear not, for I am with thee, and shall bless thee and shall surely multiply thy seed as the sand of the earth, for the sake of Abraham my servant.' ²³ And he built an altar there, which Abraham his father had first built, and he called upon the name of the Lord, and he offered sacrifice to the God of Abraham his father. ²⁴ And they digged a well and they found living water. ²⁵ And the servants of Isaac digged another well and did not find water, and they went and told Isaac that they had not found water, and Isaac said: 'I have sworn this day to the Philistines and this thing has been announced

to us.' ²⁶ And he called the name of that place the Well of the Oath; for there he had sworn to Abimelech and Ahuzzath his friend and Phicol the prefect Or his host. ²⁷ And Isaac knew that day that under constraint he had sworn to them to make peace with them. ²⁸ And Isaac on that day cursed the Philistines and said: 'Cursed be the Philistines unto the day of wrath and indignation from the midst of all nations; may God make them a derision and a curse and an object of wrath and indignation in the hands of the sinners the Gentiles and in the hands of the Kittim. ²⁹ And whoever escapes the sword of the enemy and the Kittim, may the righteous nation root out in judgment from under heaven; for they shall be the enemies and foes of my children throughout their generations upon the earth. ³⁰ And no remnant shall be left to them, Nor one that shall be saved on the day of the wrath of judgment; For destruction and rooting out and expulsion from the earth is the whole seed of the Philistines (reserved), And there shall no longer be left for these Caphtorim a name or a seed on the earth. ³¹ For though he ascend unto heaven, Thence shall he be brought down, And though he make himself strong on earth, Thence shall he be dragged forth, And though he hide himself amongst the nations, Even from thence shall he be rooted out; And though he descend into Sheol, There also shall his condemnation be great, And there also he shall have no peace. ³² And if he go into captivity, By the hands of those that seek his life shall they slay him on the way, And neither name nor seed shall be left to him on all the earth; For into eternal malediction shall he depart.' ³³ And thus is it written and engraved concerning him on the heavenly tablets, to do unto him on the day of judgment, so that he may be rooted out of the earth.

Jub. 25

Rebecca admonished Jacob not to marry a Canaanitish woman, 1-3. Jacob promises to marry a daughter of Laban despite the urgent requests of Esau that he should marry a Canaanitish woman, 4-10. Rebecca blessees Jacob, 11-23. (Cf. Gen. xxviii.1-4.) ¹ And in the second year of this week in this jubilee, Rebecca called Jacob her son, and spake unto [2109 A.M.] him, saying: 'My son, do not take thee a wife of the daughters of Canaan, as Esau, thy brother, who took him two wives of the daughters of Canaan, and they have embittered my soul with all their unclean deeds: for all their deeds are fornication and lust, and there is no righteousness with them, for (their deeds) are evil. ² And I, my son, love thee exceedingly, and my heart and my affection bless thee every hour of the day and watch of the night. ³ And now, my son, hearken to my voice, and do the will of thy mother, and do not take thee a wife of the daughters of this land, but only of the house of my father, and of my father's kindred. Thou shalt take thee a wife of the house of my father, and the Most High God will bless thee, and thy children shall be a righteous generation and a holy seed.' ⁴ And then spake Jacob to Rebecca, his mother, and said unto her: 'Behold, mother, I am nine weeks of years old, and I neither know nor have I touched any woman, nor have I betrothed myself to any, nor even think of taking me a wife of the daughters of Canaan. ⁵ For I remember, mother, the words of Abraham, our father, for he commanded me not to take a wife of the daughters of Canaan, but to take me a wife from the seed of my father's house and from my kindred. ⁶ I have heard before that daughters have been born to Laban, thy brother, and I have set my heart on them to take a wife from amongst them. ⁷ And for this reason I have guarded myself in my spirit against sinning or being corrupted in all my ways throughout all the days of my life; for with regard to lust and fornication, Abraham, my father, gave me many commands. ⁸ And, despite all that he has commanded me, these two and twenty years my brother has striven with me, and spoken frequently to me and said: 'My brother, take to wife a sister of my two wives'; but I refuse

149

to do as he has done. 9 I swear before thee, mother, that all the days of my life I will not take me a wife from the daughters of the seed of Canaan, and I will not act wickedly as my brother has done. 10 Fear not, mother; be assured that I shall do thy will and walk in uprightness, and not corrupt my ways for ever.' 11 And thereupon she lifted up her face to heaven and extended the fingers of her hands, and opened her mouth and blessed the Most High God, who had created the heaven and the earth, and she gave Him thanks and praise. 12 And she said: 'Blessed be the Lord God, and may His holy name be blessed for ever and ever, who has given me Jacob as a pure son and a holy seed; for he is Thine, and Thine shall his seed be continually and throughout all the generations for evermore. 13 Bless him, O Lord, and place in my mouth the blessing of righteousness, that I may bless him.' 14 And at that hour, when the spirit of righteousness descended into her mouth, she placed both her hands on the head of Jacob, and said: 15 Blessed art thou, Lord of righteousness and God of the ages And may He bless thee beyond all the generations of men. May He give thee, my Son, the path of righteousness, And reveal righteousness to thy seed. 16 And may He make thy sons many during thy life, And may they arise according to the number of the months of the year. And may their sons become many and great beyond the stars of heaven, And their numbers be more than the sand of the sea. 17 And may He give them this goodly land -as He said He would give it to Abraham and to his seed after him alway- And may they hold it as a possession for ever. 18 And may I see (born) unto thee, my son, blessed children during my life, And a blessed and holy seed may all thy seed be. 19 And as thou hast refreshed thy mother's spirit during her life, The womb of her that bare thee blesses thee thus, [My affection] and my breasts bless thee And my mouth and my tongue praise thee greatly. 20 Increase and spread over the earth, And may thy seed be perfect in the joy of heaven and earth for ever; And may thy seed rejoice, And on the great day of peace may it have peace. 21 And may thy name and thy seed endure to all the ages, And may the Most High God be their God, And may the God of righteousness dwell with them, And by them may His sanctuary be built unto all the ages. 22 Blessed be he that blesseth thee, And all flesh that curseth thee falsely, may it be cursed.' 23 And she kissed him, and said to him; 'May the Lord of the world love thee As the heart of thy mother and her affection rejoice in thee and bless thee.' And she ceased from blessing.

Jub. 26

Isaac scuds Esau for venison, 1-4. Rebecca instructs Jacob to obtain the blessing, 5-9. Jacob under the person of Esau obtains it, 10-24. Esau brings in his venison and by his importunity obtains a blessing, 25-34. Threatens Jacob, 35. (Cf. Gen.xxvii.) 1 And in the seventh year of this week Isaac called Esau, his elder Son, and said unto him: ' I am [2114 A.M.] old, my son, and behold my eyes are dim in seeing, and I know not the day of my death. 2 And now take thy hunting weapons thy quiver and thy bow, and go out to the field, and hunt and catch me (venison), my son, and make me savoury meat, such as my soul loveth, and bring it to me that I may eat, and that my soul may bless thee before I die.' 3 But Rebecca heard Isaac speaking to Esau. 4 And Esau went forth early to the field to hunt and catch and bring home to his father. 5 And Rebecca called Jacob, her son, and said unto him: 'Behold, I heard Isaac, thy father, speak unto Esau, thy brother, saying: "Hunt for me, and make me savoury meat, and bring (it) to me that 6 I may eat and bless thee before the Lord before I die." And now, my son, obey my voice in that which I command thee: Go to thy flock and fetch me two good kids of the goats, and I will make them savoury meat for thy father, such as he loves, and thou shalt bring (it) to thy father that he may eat and bless thee before the Lord

before he die, and that thou mayst be blessed.' 7 And Jacob said to Rebecca his mother: 'Mother, I shall not withhold anything which my father would eat, and which would please him: only I fear, my mother, that he will recognise my voice and wish to touch me. 8 And thou knowest that I am smooth, and Esau, my brother, is hairy, and I shall appear before his eyes as an evildoer, and shall do a deed which he had not commanded me, and he will be wroth with me, and I shall bring upon myself a curse, and not a blessing.' 9 And Rebecca, his mother, said unto him: 'Upon me be thy curse, my son, only obey my voice.' 10 And Jacob obeyed the voice of Rebecca, his mother, and went and fetched two good and fat kids of the goats, and brought them to his mother, and his mother made them ~savoury meat~ such as he loved. 11 And Rebecca took the goodly rainment of Esau, her elder son, which was with her in the house, and she clothed Jacob, her younger son, (with them), and she put the skins of the kids upon his hands and on the exposed parts of his neck. 12 And she gave the meat and the bread which she had prepared into the hand of her son Jacob. 13 And Jacob went in to his father and said: 'I am thy son: I have done according as thou badest me: arise and sit and eat of that which I have caught, father, that thy soul may bless me.' 14 And Isaac said to his son: 'How hast thou found so quickly, my son? 15 'And Jacob said: 'Because thy God caused me to find.' 16 And Isaac said unto him: Come near, that I may feel thee, my son, if thou art my son Esau or not.' 17 And Jacob went near to Isaac, his father, and he felt him and said: 'The voice is Jacob's voice, but the hands are the hands of Esau,' 18 and he discerned him not, because it was a dispensation from heaven to remove his power of perception and Isaac discerned not, for his hands were hairy as his brother Esau's, so that he blessed him. 19 And he said: 'Art thou my son Esau? ' and he said: 'I am thy son': and he said, 'Bring near to me that I may eat of that which thou hast caught, my son, that my soul may bless thee.' 20 And he brought near to him, and he did eat, and he brought him wine and he drank. 21 And Isaac, his father, said unto him: 'Come near and kiss me, my son. 22 And he came near and kissed him. And he smelled the smell of his raiment, and he blessed him and said: 'Behold, the smell of my son is as the smell of a field which the Lord hath blessed. 23 And may the Lord give thee of the dew of heaven And of the dew of the earth, and plenty of corn and oil: Let nations serve thee, And peoples bow down to thee. 24 Be lord over thy brethren, And let thy mother's sons bow down to thee; And may all the blessings wherewith the Lord hath blessed me and blessed Abraham, my father; Be imparted to thee and to thy seed for ever: Cursed be he that curseth thee, And blessed be he that blesseth thee.' 25 And it came to pass as soon as Isaac had made an end of blessing his son Jacob, and Jacob had gone forth from Isaac his father he hid himself and Esau, his brother, came in from his hunting. 26 And he also made savoury meat, and brought (it) to his father, and said unto his father: 'Let my father arise, and eat of my venison that thy soul may bless me.' 27 And Isaac, his father, said unto him: 'Who art thou? 'And he said unto him: 'I am thy first born, thy son Esau: I have done as thou hast commanded me.' 28 And Isaac was very greatly astonished, and said: 'Who is he that hath hunted and caught and brought (it) to me, and I have eaten of all before thou camest, and have blessed him: (and) he shall be blessed, and all his seed for ever.' 29 And it came to pass when Esau heard the words of his father Isaac that he cried with an exceeding great and bitter cry, and said unto his father: 'Bless me, (even) me also, father.' 30 And he said unto him: 'Thy brother came with guile, and hath taken away thy blessing.' And he said: 'Now I know why his name is named Jacob: behold, he hath supplanted me these two times: he took away my birth-right, and now he hath taken away my blessing.' 31 And he said: 'Hast thou

150

not reserved a blessing for me, father?' and Isaac answered and said unto Esau: 'Behold, I have made him thy lord, And all his brethren have I given to him for servants, And with plenty of corn and wine and oil have I strengthened him: And what now shall I do for thee, my son?' [32] And Esau said to Isaac, his father: 'Hast thou but one blessing, O father? Bless me, (even) me also, father: ' [33] And Esau lifted up his voice and wept. And Isaac answered and said unto him: 'Behold, far from the dew of the earth shall be thy dwelling, And far from the dew of heaven from above. [34] And by thy sword wilt thou live, And thou wilt serve thy brother. And it shall come to pass when thou becomest great, And dost shake his yoke from off thy neck, Thou shalt sin a complete sin unto death, And thy seed shall be rooted out from under heaven.' [35] And Esau kept threatening Jacob because of the blessing wherewith his father blessed him, and he: said in his heart: 'May the days of mourning for my father now come, so that I may slay my brother Jacob.'

Jub. 27

Rebecca alarmed at Esau's threats prevails on Isaac to send Jacob to Mesopotamia, 1-12. Isaac comforts Rebecca on the departure of Jacob, 13-18. Jacob's dream and vow at Bethel, 19-27. (Cf. Gen. xxviii.) [1] And the words of Esau, her elder son, were told to Rebecca in a dream, and Rebecca sent and called Jacob her younger son, [2] and said unto him: 'Behold Esau thy brother will take vengeance on thee so as to kill thee. [3] Now, therefore, my son, obey my voice, and arise and flee thou to Laban, my brother, to Haran, and tarry with him a few days until thy brother's anger turns away, and he remove his anger from thee, and forget all that thou hast done; then I will send and fetch thee from thence.' [4] And Jacob said: 'I am not afraid; if he wishes to kill me, I will kill him.' [5] But she said unto him: 'Let me not be bereft of both my sons on one day.' [6] And Jacob said to Rebecca his mother: 'Behold, thou knowest that my father has become old, and does not see because his eyes are dull, and if I leave him it will be evil in his eyes, because I leave him and go away from you, and my father will be angry, and will curse me. I will not go; when he sends me, then only will I go.' [7] And Rebecca said to Jacob: 'I will go in and speak to him, and he will send thee away.' [8] And Rebecca went in and said to Isaac: 'I loathe my life because of the two daughters of Heth, whom Esau has taken him as wives; and if Jacob take a wife from among the daughters of the land such as these, for what purpose do I further live, for the daughters of Canaan are evil.' [9] And Isaac called Jacob and blessed him, and admonished him and said unto him: 'Do not take thee a wife of any of the daughters of Canaan; [10] arise and go to Mesopotamia, to the house of Bethuel, thy mother's father, and take thee a wife from thence of the daughters of Laban, thy mother's brother. [11] And God Almighty bless thee and increase and multiply thee that thou mayest become a company of nations, and give thee the blessings of my father Abraham, to thee and to thy seed after thee, that thou mayest inherit the land of thy sojournings and all the land which God gave to Abraham: go, my son, in peace.' [12] And Isaac sent Jacob away, and he went to Mesopotamia, to Laban the son of Bethuel the Syrian, the brother of Rebecca, Jacob's mother. [13] And it came to pass after Jacob had arisen to go to Mesopotamia that the spirit of Rebecca was grieved after her son, and she wept. [14] And Isaac said to Rebecca: 'My sister, weep not on account of Jacob, my son; for he goeth in peace, and in peace will he return. [15] The Most High God will preserve him from all evil, and will be with him; for He will not forsake him all his days; [16] For I know that his ways will be prospered in all things wherever he goes, until he return in peace to us, and we see him in peace. [17] Fear not on his account, my sister, for he is on the upright path and he is a perfect man: and he is faithful and will not perish. Weep not.' [18] And Isaac comforted

Rebecca on account of her son Jacob, and blessed him. [19] And Jacob went from the Well of the Oath to go to Haran on the first year of the second week in the forty-fourth jubilee, and he came to Luz on the mountains, that is, Bethel, on the new moon of the first month of this week, [2115 A.M.] and he came to the place at even and turned from the way to the west of the road that night: and he slept there; for the sun had set. [20] And he took one of the stones of that place and laid under the tree, and he was journeying alone, and he slept. [21] And he dreamt that night, and behold a ladder set up on the earth, and the top of it reached to heaven, and behold, the angels of the Lord ascended and descended on it: and behold, the Lord stood upon it. [22] And he spake to Jacob and said: 'I am the Lord God of Abraham, thy father, and the God of Isaac; the land whereon thou art sleeping, to thee will I give it, and to thy seed after thee. [23] And thy seed shall be as the dust of the earth, and thou shalt increase to the west and to the east, to the north and the south, and in thee and in thy seed shall all the families of the nations be blessed. [24] And behold, I will be with thee, and will keep thee whithersoever thou goest, and I will bring thee again into this land in peace; for I will not leave thee until I do everything that I told thee of.' [25] And Jacob awoke from his sleep, and said, "Truly this place is the house of the Lord, and I knew it not.' And he was afraid and said: 'Dreadful is this place which is none other than the house of God, and this is the gate of heaven.' [26] And Jacob arose early in the morning, and took the stone which he had put under his head and set it up as a pillar for a sign, and he poured oil upon the top of it. And he called the name of that place Bethel; but the name of the place was Luz at the first. [27] And Jacob vowed a vow unto the Lord, saying: 'If the Lord will be with me, and will keep me in this way that I go, and give me bread to eat and raiment to put on, so that I come again to my father's house in peace, then shall the Lord be my God, and this stone which I have set up as a pillar for a sign in this place, shall be the Lord's house, and of all that thou givest me, I shall give the tenth to thee, my God.'

Jub. 28

Jacob marries leah and Rachel, 1-10. His children by Leah and Rachel and by their handmaids, 11-24. Jacob seeks to leave Laban, 25: but stays on at a certain wage, 26-8. Jacob becomes rich, 29-30. (Cf. Gen. xxix.1, 17, 18, 21-35; xxx.1-13,17-22, 24, 25, 28, 32, 39, 43; xxxi.1, 2.) [1] And he went on his journey, and came to the land of the east, to Laban, the brother of Rebecca, and he was with him, and served him for Rachel his daughter one week. [2] And in the first year of the third week [2122 A.M.] he said unto him: 'Give me my wife, for whom I have served thee seven years '; and Laban said unto Jacob: 'I will give thee thy wife.' [3] And Laban made a feast, and took Leah his elder daughter, and gave (her) to Jacob as a wife, and gave her Zilpah his handmaid for an hand- maid; and Jacob did not know, for he thought that she was Rachel. [4] And he went in unto her, and behold, she was Leah; and Jacob was angry with Laban, and said unto him: 'Why hast thou dealt thus with me? Did not I serve thee for Rachel and not for Leah? Why hast thou wronged me? [5] Take thy daughter, and I will go; for thou hast done evil to me.' For Jacob loved Rachel more than Leah; for Leah's eyes were weak, but her form was very handsome; but Rachel had beautiful eyes and a beautiful and very handsome form. [6] And Laban said to Jacob: 'It is not so done in our country, to give the younger before the elder.' And it is not right to do this; for thus it is ordained and written in the heavenly tablets, that no one should give his younger daughter before the elder; but the elder, one gives first and after her the younger -and the man who does so, they set down guilt against him in heaven, and none is righteous that does this thing, for this deed is evil before the Lord. [7] And command thou the children of Israel that they do not this thing; let them neither take nor give the younger before they have given the elder, for it is very wicked. 8 And Laban said to Jacob: 'Let the seven days of the feast of this one pass by, and I shall give thee Rachel, that thou mayst serve me another seven years, that thou mayst pasture my sheep as thou didst in the former week.' 9 And on the day when the seven days of the feast of Leah had passed, Laban gave Rachel to Jacob, that he might serve him another seven years, and he gave to Rachel Bilhah, the sister of Zilpah, as a handmaid. 10 And he served yet other seven years for Rachel, for Leah had been given to him for nothing. 11 And the Lord opened the womb of Leah, and she conceived and bare Jacob a son, and he called his name Reuben, on the fourteenth day of the ninth month, in the first year of the third week. [2122 A.M.] 12 But the womb of Rachel was closed, for the Lord saw that Leah was hated and Rachel loved. 13 And again Jacob went in unto Leah, and she conceived, and bare Jacob a second son, and he called his name Simeon, on the twenty-first of the tenth month, and in the third year of this week. [2124 A.M.] 14 And again Jacob went in unto Leah, and she conceived, and bare him a third son, and he called his name Levi, in the new moon of the first month in the sixth year of this week. [2127 A.M.] 15 And again Jacob went in unto her, and she conceived, and bare him a fourth son, and he called his name Judah, on the fifteenth of the third month, in the first year of the fourth week. [2129 A.M.] 16 And on account of all this Rachel envied Leah, for she did not bear, and she said to Jacob: 'Give me children'; and Jacob said: 'Have I withheld from thee the fruits of thy womb? Have I forsaken thee?' 17 And when Rachel saw that Leah had borne four sons to Jacob, Reuben and Simeon and Levi and Judah, she said unto him: 'Go in unto Bilhah my handmaid, and she will conceive, and bear a son unto me.' (And she gave (him) Bilhah her handmaid to wife). 18 And he went in unto her, and she conceived, and bare him a son, and he called his name Dan, on the ninth of the sixth month, in the sixth year of the third week. [2127 A.M.] 19 And Jacob went in again unto Bilhah a second time, and she conceived, and bare Jacob another son, and Rachel called his name Napthali, on the fifth of the seventh month, in the second year of the fourth week. [2130 A.M.] 20 And when Leah saw that she had become sterile and did not bear, she envied Rachel, and she also gave her handmaid Zilpah to Jacob to wife, and she conceived, and bare a son, and Leah called his name Gad, on the twelfth of the eighth month, in the third year of the fourth week. [2131 A.M.] 21 And he went in again unto her, and she conceived, and bare him a second son, and Leah called his name Asher, on the second of the eleventh month, in the fifth year of the fourth week. [2133 A.M.] 22 And Jacob went in unto Leah, and she conceived, and bare a son, and she called his name Issachar, on the fourth of the fifth month, in the fourth year of the fourth week,[2132 A.M.] and she gave him to a nurse. 23 And Jacob went in again unto her, and she conceived, and bare two (children), a son and a daughter, and she called the name of the son Zabulon, and the name of the daughter Dinah, in the seventh of the seventh month, in the sixth year of the fourth week. [2134 A.M.] 24 And the Lord was gracious to Rachel, and opened her womb, and she conceived, and bare a son, and she called his name Joseph, on the new moon of the fourth month, in the sixth year in this fourth week. [2134 A.M.] 25 And in the days when Joseph was born, Jacob said to Laban: 'Give me my wives and sons, and let me go to my father Isaac, and let me make me an house; for I have completed the years in which I have served thee for thy two daughters, and I will go to the house of my father.' 26 And Laban said to Jacob: "Tarry with me for thy wages, and pasture my flock for me again, and take thy wages.' 27 And they agreed with one another that he should give him as his wages those of the lambs and kids which were born black and

152

spotted and white, (these) were to be his wages. 28 And all the sheep brought forth spotted and speckled and black, variously marked, and they brought forth again lambs like themselves, and all that were spotted were Jacob's and those which were not were Laban's. 29 And Jacob's possessions multiplied exceedingly, and he possessed oxen and sheep and asses and camels, and menservants and maidservants. 30 And Laban and his sons envied Jacob, and Laban took back his sheep from him, and he observed him with evil intent.

Jub. 29

Jacob, departs secretly, 1-4. Laban pursues after him, 5-6. Covenant of Jacob and Laban, 7-8. Abodes of the Amorites (anciently of the Rephaim) destroyed in the time of the writer, 9-11. Laban departs, 12. Jacob is reconciled to Esau, 13. Jacob sends supplies of food to his parents four times a year to Hebron, 14-17, 19-20. Esau marries again, 18. (Cf. Gen. xxxi.3, 4, 10, 13, 19, 21, 23, 24, 46, 47; xxxii.22; xxxiii.10, 16.) 1 And it came to pass when Rachel had borne Joseph, that Laban went to shear his sheep; for they were distant from him a three days' journey. 2 And Jacob saw that Laban was going to shear his sheep, and Jacob called Leah and Rachel, and spake kindly unto them that they should come with him to the land of Canaan. 3 For he told them how he had seen everything in a dream, even all that He had spoken unto him that he should return to his father's house, and they said: "To every place whither thou goest we will go with thee.' 4 And Jacob blessed the God of Isaac his father, and the God of Abraham his father's father, and he arose and mounted his wives and his children, and took all his possessions and crossed the river, and came to the land of Gilead, and Jacob hid his intention from Laban and told him not. 5 And in the seventh year of the fourth week Jacob turned (his face) toward Gilead in the first month, on the twenty-first thereof. [2135 A.M.] And Laban pursued after him and overtook Jacob in the mountain of Gilead in the third month, on the thirteenth thereof. 6 And the Lord did not suffer him to injure Jacob; for he appeared to him in a dream by night. And Laban spake to Jacob. 7 And on the fifteenth of those days Jacob made a feast for Laban, and for all who came with him, and Jacob sware to Laban that day, and Laban also to Jacob, that neither should cross the mountain of Gilead to the other with evil purpose. 8 And he made there a heap for a witness; wherefore the name of that place is called: 'The Heap of Witness,' after this heap. 9 But before they used to call the land of Gilead the land of the Rephaim; for it was the land of the Rephaim, and the Rephaim were born (there), giants whose height was ten, nine, eight down to seven cubits. 10 And their habitation was from the land of the children of Ammon to Mount Hermon, and the seats of their kingdom were Karnaim and Ashtaroth, and Edrei, and Misur, and Beon. 11 And the Lord destroyed them because of the evil of their deeds; for they were very malignant, and the Amorites dwelt in their stead, wicked and sinful, and there is no people to-day which has wrought to the full all their sins, and they have no longer length of life on the earth. 12 And Jacob sent away Laban, and he departed into Mesopotamia, the land of the East, and Jacob returned to the land of Gilead. 13 And he passed over the Jabbok in the ninth month, on the eleventh thereof. And on that day Esau, his brother, came to him, and he was reconciled to him, and departed from him unto the land of Seir, but Jacob dwelt in tents. 14 And in the first year of the fifth week in this jubilee [2136 A.M.] he crossed the Jordan, and dwelt beyond the Jordan, and he pastured his sheep from the sea of the heap unto Bethshan, and unto Dothan and unto the forest of Akrabbim. 15 And he sent to his father Isaac of all his substance, clothing, and food, and meat, and drink, and milk, and butter, and cheese, and some dates of the valley. 16 And to his mother Rebecca also four times a year, between the times of the months, between ploughing and reaping, and between autumn and the rain (season) and between winter and spring, to the tower of Abraham. [17] For Isaac had returned from the Well of the Oath and gone up to the tower of his father Abraham, and he dwelt there apart from his son Esau. [18] For in the days when Jacob went to Mesopotamia, Esau took to himself a wife Mahalath, the daughter of Ishmael, and he gathered together all the flocks of his father and his wives, and went Up and dwelt on Mount Seir, and left Isaac his father at the Well of the Oath alone. [19] And Isaac went up from the Well of the Oath and dwelt in the tower of Abraham his father on the mountains of Hebron, [20] And thither Jacob sent all that he did send to his father and his mother from time to time, all they needed, and they blessed Jacob with all their heart and with all their soul.

Jub. 30

Dinah ravished, 1-3. Slaughter of the Shechemites, 4-6. Laws against intermarriage between Israel and the heathen, 7-17. Levi chosen for the priesthood on account of his slaughter of the Shechemites, 18-23. Dinah recovered, 24. Jacob's reproof, 25-6. (Cf. Gen. xxxiii.18, xxxiv.2, 4, 7, 13-14, 25-30, xxxv.5.) [1] And in the first year of the sixth week [2143 A.M.] he went up to Salem, to the east of Shechem, in peace, in the fourth month. [2] And there they carried off Dinah, the daughter of Jacob, into the house of Shechem, the son of Hamor, the Hivite, the prince of the land, and he lay with her and defiled her, and she was a little girl, a child of twelve years. [3] And he besought his father and her brothers that she might be given to him to wife. And Jacob and his sons were wroth because of the men of Shechem; for they had defiled Dinah, their sister, and they spake to them with evil intent and dealt deceitfully with them and beguiled them. [4] And Simeon and Levi came unexpectedly to Shechem and executed judgment on all the men of Shechem, and slew all the men whom they found in it, and left not a single one remaining in it: they slew all in torments because they had dishonoured their sister Dinah. [5] And thus let it not again be done from henceforth that a daughter of Israel be defiled; for judgment is ordained in heaven against them that they should destroy with the sword all the men of the Shechemites because they had wrought shame in Israel. [6] And the Lord delivered them into the hands of the sons of Jacob that they might exterminate them with the sword and execute judgment upon them, and that it might not thus again be done in Israel that a virgin of Israel should be defiled. [7] And if there is any man who wishes in Israel to give his daughter or his sister to any man who is of the seed of the Gentiles he shall surely die, and they shall stone him with stones; for he hath wrought shame in Israel; and they shall burn the woman with fire, because she has dishonoured the name of the house of her father, and she shall be rooted out of Israel. [8] And let not an adulteress and no uncleanness be found in Israel throughout all the days of the generations of the earth; for Israel is holy unto the Lord, and every man who has defiled (it) shall surely die: they shall stone him with stones. [9] For thus has it been ordained and written in the heavenly tablets regarding all the seed of Israel: he who defileth (it) shall surely die, and he shall be stoned with stones. [10] And to this law there is no limit of days, and no remission, nor any atonement: but the man who has defiled his daughter shall be rooted out in the midst of all Israel, because he has given of his seed to Moloch, and wrought impiously so as to defile it. [11] And do thou, Moses, command the children of Israel and exhort them not to give their daughters to the Gentiles, and not to take for their sons any of the daughters of the Gentiles, for this is abominable before the Lord. [12] For this reason I have written for thee in the words of the Law all the deeds of the Shechemites, which they wrought against Dinah, and how the sons of Jacob spake, saying: 'We will not give our daughter to a man who is uncircumcised; for that were a reproach unto us.' [13] And it is a reproach to Israel, to those who live, and to those that take the daughters of the Gentiles; for this is unclean and abominable to Israel. [14] And Israel will not be free from this uncleanness if it has a wife of the daughters of the Gentiles, or has given any of its daughters to a man who is of any of the Gentiles. [15] For there will be plague upon plague, and curse upon curse, and every judgment and plague and curse will come upon him: if he do this thing, or hide his eyes from those who commit uncleanness, or those who defile the sanctuary of the Lord, or those who profane His holy name, (then) will the whole nation together be judged for all the uncleanness and profanation of this man. [16] And there will be no respect of persons [and no consideration of persons] and no receiving at his hands of fruits and offerings and burnt-offerings and fat, nor the fragrance of sweet savour, so as to accept it: and so fare every man or woman in Israel who defiles the sanctuary. [17] For this reason I have commanded thee, saying: 'Testify this testimony to Israel: see how the Shechemites fared and their sons: how they were delivered into the hands of two sons of Jacob, and they slew them under tortures, and it was (reckoned) unto them for righteousness, and it is written down to them for righteousness. [18] And the seed of Levi was chosen for the priesthood, and to be Levites, that they might minister before the Lord, as we, continually, and that Levi and his sons may be blessed for ever; for he was zealous to execute righteousness and judgment and vengeance on all those who arose against Israel. [19] And so they inscribe as a testimony in his favour on the heavenly tablets blessing and righteousness before the God of all: [20] And we remember the righteousness which the man fulfilled during his life, at all periods of the year; until a thousand generations they will record it, and it will come to him and to his descendants after him, and he has been recorded on the heavenly tablets as a friend and a righteous man. [21] All this account I have written for thee, and have commanded thee to say to the children of Israel, that they should not commit sin nor transgress the ordinances nor break the covenant which has been ordained for them, (but) that they should fulfil it and be recorded as friends. [22] But if they transgress and work uncleanness in every way, they will be recorded on the heavenly tablets as adversaries, and they will be destroyed out of the book of life, and they will be recorded in the book of those who will be destroyed and with those who will be rooted out of the earth. [23] And on the day when the sons of Jacob slew Shechem a writing was recorded in their favour in heaven that they had executed righteousness and uprightness and vengeance on the sinners, and it was written for a blessing. [24] And they brought Dinah, their sister, out of the house of Shechem, and they took captive everything that was in Shechem, their sheep and their oxen and their asses, and all their wealth, and all their flocks, and brought them all to Jacob their father. [25] And he reproached them because they had put the city to the sword for he feared those who dwelt in the land, the Canaanites and the Perizzites. [26] And the dread of the Lord was upon all the cities which are around about Shechem, and they did not rise to pursue after the sons of Jacob; for terror had fallen upon them.

Jub. 31

Jacob goes to Bethel to offer sacrifice, 1-3 (cf. Gen. xxxv.2-4, 7, 14). Isaac blesses Levi, 4-17, and Judah, 18-22. Jacob recounts to Isaac how God prospered him, 24. Jacob goes to Bethel with Rebecca and Deborah, 26-30. Jacob blesses the God of his fathers, 31-2. [1] And on the new moon of the month Jacob spake to all the people of his house. saying: 'Purify yourselves and change your garments, and let us arise and go up to Bethel, where I vowed a vow to Him on the day when I fled from the face of Esau my brother, because he has been with me and brought me into this land in peace, and put ye away the strange gods that arc among you.' [2] And they gave up the strange gods and that

153

which was in their ears and which was on their necks and the idols which Rachel stole from Laban her father she gave wholly to Jacob. And he burnt and brake them to pieces and destroyed them, and hid them under an oak which is in the land of Shechem. ³ And he went up on the new moon of the seventh month to Bethel. And he built an altar at the place where he had slept, and he set up a pillar there, and he sent word to his father Isaac to come to him to his sacrifice, and to his mother Rebecca. ⁴ And Isaac said: 'Let my son Jacob come, and let me see him before I die.' ⁵ And Jacob went to his father Isaac and to his mother Rebecca, to the house of his father Abraham, and he took two of his sons with him, Levi and Judah, and he came to his father Isaac and to his mother Rebecca. ⁶ And Rebecca came forth from the tower to the front of it to kiss Jacob and embrace him; for her spirit had revived when she heard: 'Behold Jacob thy son has come'; and she kissed him. ⁷ And she saw his two sons, and she recognised them, and said unto him: 'Are these thy sons, my son?' and she embraced them and kissed them, and blessed them, saying: 'In you shall the seed of Abraham become illustrious, and ye shall prove a blessing on the earth.' ⁸ And Jacob went in to Isaac his father, to the chamber where he lay, and his two sons were with him, and he took the hand of his father, and stooping down he kissed him, and Isaac clung to the neck of Jacob his son, and wept upon his neck. ⁹ And the darkness left the eyes of Isaac, and he saw the two sons of Jacob, Levi, and Judah, and he said: 'Are these thy sons, my son? for they are like thee.' ¹⁰ And he said unto him that they were truly his sons: 'And thou hast truly seen that they are truly my sons'. ¹¹ And they came near to him, and he turned and kissed them and embraced them both together. ¹² And the spirit of prophecy came down into his mouth, and he took Levi by his right hand and Judah by his left. ¹³ And he turned to Levi first, and began to bless him first, and said unto him: May the God of all, the very Lord of all the ages, bless thee and thy children throughout all the ages. ¹⁴ And may the Lord give to thee and to thy seed greatness and great glory, and cause thee and thy seed, from among all flesh, to approach Him to serve in His sanctuary as the angels of the presence and as the holy ones. (Even) as they, shall the seed of thy sons be for glory and greatness and holiness, and may He make them great unto all the ages. ¹⁵ And they shall be judges and princes, and chiefs of all the seed of the sons of Jacob; They shall speak the word of the Lord in righteousness, And they shall judge all His judgments in righteousness. And they shall declare My ways to Jacob And My paths to Israel. The blessing of the Lord shall be given in their mouths To bless all the seed of the beloved. ¹⁶ Thy mother has called thy name Levi, And justly has she called thy name; Thou shalt be joined to the Lord And be the companion of all the sons of Jacob; Let His table be thine, And do thou and thy sons eat thereof; And may thy table be full unto all generations, And thy food fail not unto all the ages. ¹⁷ And let all who hate thee fall down before thee, And let all thy adversaries be rooted out and perish; And blessed be he that blesses thee, And cursed be every nation that curses thee.' ¹⁸ And to Judah he said: 'May the Lord give thee strength and power To tread down all that hate thee; A prince shalt thou be, thou and one of thy sons, over the sons of Jacob; May thy name and the name of thy sons go forth and traverse every land and region. Then shall the Gentiles fear before thy face, And all the nations shall quake [And all the peoples shall quake]. ¹⁹ In thee shall be the help of Jacob, And in thee be found the salvation of Israel. ²⁰ And when thou sittest on the throne of honour of thy righteousness There shall be great peace for all the seed of the sons of the beloved; Blessed be he that blesseth thee, And all that hate thee and afflict thee and curse thee Shall be rooted out and destroyed from the earth and be accursed.' ²¹ And turning he kissed him again and embraced him,

154

and rejoiced greatly; for he had seen the sons of Jacob his son in very truth. ²² And he went forth from between his feet and fell down and bowed down to him, and he blessed them and rested there with Isaac his father that night, and they eat and drank with joy. ²³ And he made the two sons of Jacob sleep, the one on his right hand and the other on his left, and it was counted to him for righteousness. ²⁴ And Jacob told his father everything during the night, how the Lord had shown him great mercy, and how he had prospered (him in) all his ways, and protected him from all evil. ²⁵ And Isaac blessed the God of his father Abraham, who had not withdrawn his mercy and his righteousness from the sons of his servant Isaac. ²⁶ And in the morning Jacob told his father Isaac the vow which he had vowed to the Lord, and the vision which he had seen, and that he had built an altar, and that everything was ready for the sacrifice to be made before the Lord as he had vowed, and that he had come to set him on an ass. ²⁷ And Isaac said unto Jacob his son: 'I am not able to go with thee; for I am old and not able to bear the way: go, my son, in peace; for I am one hundred and sixty-five years this day; I am no longer able to journey; set thy mother (on an ass) and let her go with thee. ²⁸ And I know, my son, that thou hast come on my account, and may this day be blessed on which thou hast seen me alive, and I also have seen thee, my son. ²⁹ Mayest thou prosper and fulfil the vow which thou hast vowed; and put not off thy vow; for thou shalt be called to account as touching the vow; now therefore make haste to perform it, and may He be pleased who has made all things, to whom thou hast vowed the vow.' ³⁰ And he said to Rebecca: 'Go with Jacob thy son'; and Rebecca went with Jacob her son, and Deborah with her, and they came to Bethel. ³¹ And Jacob remembered the prayer with which his father had blessed him and his two sons, Levi and Judah, and he rejoiced and blessed the God of his fathers, Abraham and Isaac. ³² And he said: 'Now I know that I have an eternal hope, and my sons also, before the God of all'; and thus is it ordained concerning the two; and they record it as an eternal testimony unto them on the heavenly tablets how Isaac blessed them.

Jub. 32

Levi's dream at Bethel, 1. Levi chosen to the priesthood, as the tenth son, 2-3. Jacob celebrates the feast of tabernacles and offers tithes through Levi: also the second tithe, 4-9. Law of tithes ordained, 10-15. Jacob's visions in which Jacob reads on the heavenly tablets his own future and that of his descendants, 16-26. Celebrates the eighty day of feast of tabernacles, 27-9. Death of Deborah, 30. Birth of Benjamin and death of Rachel, 33-4. (Cf. Gen. xxxv.8,10, 11, 13, 16-20.) ¹ And he abode that night at Bethel, and Levi dreamed that they had ordained and made him the priest of the Most High God, him and his sons for ever; and he awoke from his sleep and blessed the Lord. ² And Jacob rose early in the morning, on the fourteenth of this month, and he gave a tithe of all that came with him, both of men and cattle, both of gold and every vessel and garment, yea, he gave tithes of all. ³ And in those days Rachel became pregnant with her son Benjamin. And Jacob counted his sons from him upwards and Levi fell to the portion of the Lord, and his father clothed him in the garments of the priesthood and filled his hands. ⁴ And on the fifteenth of this month, he brought to the altar fourteen oxen from amongst the cattle, and twenty-eight rams, and forty-nine sheep, and seven lambs, and twenty-one kids of the goats as a burnt-offering on the altar of sacrifice, well pleasing for a sweet savour before God. ⁵ This was his offering, in consequence of the vow which he had vowed that he would give a tenth, with their fruit-offerings and their drink- offerings. ⁶ And when the fire had consumed it, he burnt incense on the fire over the fire, and for a thank-offering two oxen and four rams and four sheep, four he-goats, and two sheep of a year old, and two kids of the goats; and thus he did daily for seven days. 7 And he and all his sons and his men were eating (this) with joy there during seven days and blessing and thanking the Lord, who had delivered him out of all his tribulation and had given him his vow. 8 And he tithed all the clean animals, and made a burnt sacrifice, but the unclean animals he gave (not) to Levi his son, and he gave him all the souls of the men. 9 And Levi discharged the priestly office at Bethel before Jacob his father in preference to his ten brothers, and he was a priest there, and Jacob gave his vow: thus he tithed again the tithe to the Lord and sanctified it, and it became holy unto Him. 10 And for this reason it is ordained on the heavenly tablets as a law for the tithing again the tithe to eat before the Lord from year to year, in the place where it is chosen that His name should dwell, and to this law there is no limit of days for ever. 11 This ordinance is written that it may be fulfilled from year to year in eating the second tithe before the Lord in the place where it has been chosen, and nothing shall remain over from it from this year to the year following. 12 For in its year shall the seed be eaten till the days of the gathering of the seed of the year, and the wine till the days of the wine, and the oil till the days of its season. 13 And all that is left thereof and becomes old, let it be regarded as polluted: let it be burnt with fire, for it is unclean. 14 And thus let them eat it together in the sanctuary, and let them not suffer it to become old. 15 And all the tithes of the oxen and sheep shall be holy unto the Lord, and shall belong to his priests, which they will eat before Him from year to year; for thus is it ordained and engraven regarding the tithe on the heavenly tablets. 16 And on the following night, on the twenty-second day of this month, Jacob resolved to build that place, and to surround the court with a wall, and to sanctify it and make it holy for ever, for himself and his children after him. 17 And the Lord appeared to him by night and blessed him and said unto him: 'Thy name shall not be called Jacob, but Israel shall they name thy name.' 18 And He said unto him again: 'I am the Lord who created the heaven and the earth, and I will increase thee and multiply thee exceedingly, and kings shall come forth from thee, and they shall judge everywhere wherever the foot of the sons of men has trodden. 19 And I will give to thy seed all the earth which is under heaven, and they shall judge all the nations according to their desires, and after that they shall get possession of the whole earth and inherit it for ever.' 20 And He finished speaking with him, and He went up from him. and Jacob looked till He had ascended into heaven. 21 And he saw in a vision of the night, and behold an angel descended from heaven with seven tablets in his hands, and he gave them to Jacob, and he read them and knew all that was written therein which would befall him and his sons throughout all the ages. 22 And he showed him all that was written on the tablets, and said unto him: 'Do not build this place, and do not make it an eternal sanctuary, and do not dwell here; for this is not the place. Go to the house of Abraham thy father and dwell with Isaac thy father until the day of the death of thy father. 23 For in Egypt thou shalt die in peace, and in this land thou shalt be buried with honour in the sepulchre of thy fathers, with Abraham and Isaac. 24 Fear not, for as thou hast seen and read it, thus shall it all be; and do thou write down everything as thou hast seen and read.' 25 And Jacob said: 'Lord, how can I remember all that I have read and seen? 'And he said unto him: 'I will bring all things to thy remembrance.' 26 And he went up from him, and he awoke from his sleep, and he remembered everything which he had read and seen, and he wrote down all the words which he had read and seen. 27 And he celebrated there yet another day, and he sacrificed thereon according to all that he sacrificed on the former days, and called its name 'Addition,' for this day was added and the former days he called 'The Feast '. 28 And thus it was manifested that it should be, and it is written on the

155

heavenly tablets: wherefore it was revealed to him that he should celebrate it, and add it to the seven days of the feast. 29 And its name was called 'Addition,' because that it was recorded amongst the days of the feast days, according to the number of the days of the year. 30 And in the night, on the twenty-third of this month, Deborah Rebecca's nurse died, and they buried her beneath the city under the oak of the river, and he called the name of this place, 'The river of Deborah,' and the oak, 'The oak of the mourning of Deborah.' 31 And Rebecca went and returned to her house to his father Isaac, and Jacob sent by her hand rams and sheep and he-goats that she should prepare a meal for his father such as he desired. 32 And he went after his mother till he came to the land of Kabratan, and he dwelt there. 33 And Rachel bare a son in the night, and called his name 'Son of my sorrow '; for she suffered in giving him birth: but his father called his name Benjamin, on the eleventh of the eighth month in the first of the sixth week of this jubilee. [2143 A.M.] 34 And Rachel died there and she was buried in the land of Ephrath, the same is Bethlehem, and Jacob built a pillar on the grave of Rachel, on the road above her grave.

Jub. 33

Reuben sins with Bilhah, 1-9 (cf. Gen. xxxv.21, 22). Laws regarding incest, 10-20. Jacob's children, 22. (Cf. Gen. xxxv.23-7.) 1 And Jacob went and dwelt to the south of Magdalaadra'ef. And he went to his father Isaac, he and Leah his wife, on the new moon of the tenth month. 2 And Reuben saw Bilhah, Rachel's maid, the concubine of his father, bathing in water in a secret place, and he loved her. 3 And he hid himself at night, and he entered the house of Bilhah [at night], and he found her sleeping alone on a bed in her house. 4 And he lay with her, and she awoke and saw, and behold Reuben was lying with her in the bed, and she uncovered the border of her covering and seized him, and cried out, and discovered that it was Reuben. 5 And she was ashamed because of him, and released her hand from him, and he fled. 6 And she lamented because of this thing exceedingly, and did not tell it to any one. 7 And when Jacob returned and sought her, she said unto him: 'I am not clean for thee, for I have been defiled as regards thee; for Reuben has defiled me, and has lain with me in the night, and I was asleep, and did not discover until he uncovered my skirt and slept with me.' 8 And Jacob was exceedingly wroth with Reuben because he had lain with Bilhah, because he had uncovered his father's skirt. 9 And Jacob did not approach her again because Reuben had defiled her. And as for any man who uncovers his father's skirt his deed is wicked exceedingly, for he is abominable before the Lord. 10 For this reason it is written and ordained on the heavenly tablets that a man should not lie with his father's wife, and should not uncover his father's skirt, for this is unclean: they shall surely die together, the man who lies with his father's wife and the woman also, for they have wrought uncleanness on the earth. 11 And there shall be nothing unclean before our God in the nation which He has chosen for Himself as a possession. 12 And again, it is written a second time: 'Cursed be he who lieth with the wife of his father, for he hath uncovered his father's shame'; and all the holy ones of the Lord said 'So be it; so be it.' 13 And do thou, Moses, command the children of Israel that they observe this word; for it (entails) a punishment of death; and it is unclean, and there is no atonement for ever to atone for the man who has committed this, but he is to be put to death and slain, and stoned with stones, and rooted out from the midst of the people of our God. 14 For to no man who does so in Israel is it permitted to remain alive a single day on the earth, for he is abominable and unclean. 15 And let them not say: to Reuben was granted life and forgiveness after he had lain with his father's concubine, and to her also though she had a husband, and her husband Jacob, his father, was still alive. 16 For until that time there had not been revealed the ordinance and judgment and law in its completeness for all, but in thy days (it has been revealed) as a law of seasons and of days, and an everlasting law for the everlasting generations. 17 And for this law there is no consummation of days, and no atonement for it, but they must both be rooted out in the midst of the nation: on the day whereon they committed it they shall slay them. 18 And do thou, Moses, write (it) down for Israel that they may observe it, and do according to these words, and not commit a sin unto death; for the Lord our God is judge, who respects not persons and accepts not gifts. 19 And tell them these words of the covenant, that they may hear and observe, and be on their guard with respect to them, and not be destroyed and rooted out of the land; for an uncleanness, and an abomination, and a contamination, and a pollution are all they who commit it on the earth before our God. 20 And there is no greater sin than the fornication which they commit on earth; for Israel is a holy nation unto the Lord its God, and a nation of inheritance, and a priestly and royal nation and for (His own) possession; and there shall no such uncleanness appear in the midst of the holy nation. 21 And in the third year of this sixth week [2145 A.M.] Jacob and all his sons went and dwelt in the house of Abraham, near Isaac his father and Rebecca his mother. 22 And these were the names of the sons of Jacob: the first-born Reuben, Simeon, Levi, Judah, Issachar, Zebulon, the sons of Leah; and the sons of Rachel, Joseph and Benjamin; and the sons of Bilhah, Dan and Naphtali; and the sons of Zilpah, Gad and Asher; and Dinah, the daughter of Leah, the only daughter of Jacob. 23 And they came and bowed themselves to Isaac and Rebecca, and when they saw them they blessed Jacob and all his sons, and Isaac rejoiced exceedingly, for he saw the sons of Jacob, his younger son and he blessed them.

Jub. 34

Warfare of the Amorite kings against Jacob and his sons, 1-9. Jacob sends Joseph to visit his brethren, 10. Joseph sold and carried down into Egypt, 11-12 (cf. Gen. xxxvii.14, 17, 18, 25, 32-6). Deaths of Bilhah and Dinah, 15. Jacob mourns for Joseph, 13, 14, 17. Institution of Day of Atonement on day when news of Joseph's death arrived, 18-19. Wives of Jacob's son's, 20-1. 1 And in the sixth year of this week of this forty-fourth jubilee [2148 A.M.] Jacob sent his sons to pasture their sheep, and his servants with them to the pastures of Shechem. 2 And the seven kings of the Amorites assembled themselves together against them, to slay them, hiding themselves under the trees, and to take their cattle as a prey. 3 And Jacob and Levi and Judah and Joseph were in the house with Isaac their father; for his spirit was sorrowful, and they could not leave him: and Benjamin was the youngest, and for this reason remained with his father. 4 And there came the king[s] of Taphu and the king[s] of 'Aresa, and the king[s] of Seragan, and the king[s] of Selo, and the king[s] of Ga'as, and the king of Bethoron, and the king of Ma'anisakir, and all those who dwell in these mountains (and) who dwell in the woods in the land of Canaan. 5 And they announced this to Jacob saying: 'Behold, the kings of the Amorites have surrounded thy sons, and plundered their herds.' 6 And he arose from his house, he and his three sons and all the servants of his father, and his own servants, and he went against them with six thousand men, who carried swords. 7 And he slew them in the pastures of Shechem, and pursued those who fled, and he slew them with the edge of the sword, and he slew 'Aresa and Taphu and Saregan and Selo and 'Amani- sakir and Ga[ga]'as, and he recovered his herds. 8 And he prevailed over them, and imposed tribute on them that they should pay him tribute, five fruit products of their land, and he built Robel and Tamnatares. 9 And he returned in peace, and made peace with them, and they became his servants, until the day that he and his sons went down into Egypt. 10 And in the seventh year of this week

156

[2149 A.M.] he sent Joseph to learn about the welfare of his brothers from his house to the land of Shechem, and he found them in the land of Dothan. 11 And they dealt treacherously with him, and formed a plot against him to slay him, but changing their minds, they sold him to Ishmaelite merchants, and they brought him down into Egypt, and they sold him to Potiphar, the eunuch of Pharaoh, the chief of the cooks, priest of the city of 'Elew. 12 And the sons of Jacob slaughtered a kid, and dipped the coat of Joseph in the blood, and sent (it) to Jacob their father on the tenth of the seventh month. 13 And he mourned all that night, for they had brought it to him in the evening, and he became feverish with mourning for his death, and he said: 'An evil beast hath devoured Joseph'; and all the members of his house [mourned with him that day, and they] were grieving and mourning with him all that day. 14 And his sons and his daughter rose up to comfort him, but he refused to be comforted for his son. 15 And on that day Bilhah heard that Joseph had perished, and she died mourning him, and she was living in Qafratef, and Dinah also, his daughter, died after Joseph had perished. 16 And there came these three mournings upon Israel in one month. And they buried Bilhah over against the tomb of Rachel, and Dinah also. his daughter, they buried there. 17 And he mourned for Joseph one year, and did not cease, for he said 'Let me go down to the grave mourning for my son'. 18 For this reason it is ordained for the children of Israel that they should afflict themselves on the tenth of the seventh month -on the day that the news which made him weep for Joseph came to Jacob his father- that they should make atonement for themselves thereon with a young goat on the tenth of the seventh month, once a year, for their sins; for they had grieved the affection of their father regarding Joseph his son. 19 And this day has been ordained that they should grieve thereon for their sins, and for all their transgressions and for all their errors, so that they might cleanse themselves on that day once a year. 20 And after Joseph perished, the sons of Jacob took unto themselves wives. The name of Reuben's wife is 'Ada; and the name of Simeon's wife is 'Adlba'a, a Canaanite; and the name of Levi's wife is Melka, of the daughters of Aram, of the seed of the sons of Terah; and the name of Judah's wife, Betasu'el, a Canaanite; and the name of Issachar's wife, Hezaqa: and the name of Zabulon's wife, Ni'iman; and the name of Dan's wife, 'Egla; and the name of Naphtali's wife, Rasu'u, of Mesopotamia; and the name of Gad's wife, Maka; and the name of Asher's wife, 'Ijona; and the name of Joseph's wife, Asenath, the Egyptian; and the name of Benjamin's wife, 'Ijasaka. 21 And Simeon repented, and took a second wife from Mesopotamia as his brothers.

Jub. 35

Rebecca's admonition to Jacob and his reply, 1-8. Rebecca asks Isaac to make Esau swear that he will not injure Jacob, 9-12. Isaac consents, 13-17. Esau takes the oath and likewise Jacob, 18-26. Death of Rebecca, 27. 1 And in the first year of the first week of the forty-fifth jubilee [2157 A.M.] Rebecca called Jacob, her son, and commanded him regarding his father and regarding his brother, that he should honour them all the days of his life. 2 And Jacob said: 'I will do everything as thou hast commanded me; for this thing will be honour and greatness to me, and righteousness before the Lord, that I should honour them. 3 And thou too, mother, knowest from the time I was born until this day, all my deeds and all that is in my heart, that I always think good concerning all. 4 And how should I not do this thing which thou hast commanded me, that I should honour my father and my brother! 5 Tell me, mother, what perversity hast thou seen in me and I shall turn away from it, and mercy will be upon me.' 6 And she said unto him: 'My son, I have not seen in thee all my days any perverse but (only) upright deeds. And yet I will tell thee the truth, my son: I shall die this year, and I shall not survive this year in my life; for I have seen in a dream the day of my death, that I should not live beyond a hundred and fifty-five years: and behold I have completed all the days of my life which I am to live.' 7 And Jacob laughed at the words of his mother. because his mother had said unto him that she should die; and she was sitting opposite to him in possession of her strength, and she was not infirm in her strength; for she went in and out and saw, and her teeth were strong, and no ailment had touched her all the days of her life. 8 And Jacob said unto her: 'Blessed am I, mother, if my days approach the days of thy life, and my strength remain with me thus as thy strength: and thou wilt not die, for thou art jesting idly with me regarding thy death.' 9 And she went in to Isaac and said unto him: 'One petition I make unto thee: make Esau swear that he will not injure Jacob, nor pursue him with enmity; for thou knowest Esau's thoughts that they are perverse from his youth, and there is no goodness in him; for he desires after thy death to kill him. 10 And thou knowest all that he has done since the day Jacob his brother went to Haran until this day: how he has forsaken us with his whole heart, and has done evil to us; thy flocks he has taken to himself, and carried off all thy possessions from before thy face. 11 And when we implored and besought him for what was our own, he did as a man who was taking pity on us. 12 And he is bitter against thee because thou didst bless Jacob thy perfect and upright son; for there is no evil but only goodness in him, and since he came from Haran unto this day he has not robbed us of aught, for he brings us everything in its season always, and rejoices with all his heart when we take at his hands and he blesses us, and has not parted from us since he came from Haran until this day, and he remains with us continually at home honouring us.' 13 And Isaac said unto her: 'I, too, know and see the deeds of Jacob who is with us, how that with all his heart he honours us; but I loved Esau formerly more than Jacob, because he was the firstborn; but now I love Jacob more than Esau, for he has done manifold evil deeds, and there is no righteousness in him, for all his ways are unrighteousness and violence, [and there is no righteousness around him.] 14 And now my heart is troubled because of all his deeds, and neither he nor his seed is to be saved, for they are those who will be destroyed from the earth and who will be rooted out from under heaven, for he has forsaken the God of Abraham and gone after his wives and after their uncleanness and after their error, he and his children. 15 And thou dost bid me make him swear that he will not slay Jacob his brother; even if he swear he will not abide by his oath, and he will not do good but evil only. 16 But if he desires to slay Jacob, his brother, into Jacob's hands will he be given, and he will not escape from his hands, [for he will descend into his hands.] 17 And fear thou not on account of Jacob; for the guardian of Jacob is great and powerful and honoured, and praised more than the guardian of Esau.' 18 And Rebecca sent and called Esau and he came to her, and she said unto him: 'I have a petition, my son, to make unto thee, and do thou promise to do it, my son.' 19 And he said: 'I will do everything that thou sayest unto me, and I will not refuse thy petition.' 20 And she said unto him: 'I ask you that the day I die, thou wilt take me in and bury me near Sarah, thy father's mother, and that thou and Jacob will love each other and that neither will desire evil against the other, but mutual love only, and (so) ye will prosper, my sons, and be honoured in the midst of the land, and no enemy will rejoice over you, and ye will be a blessing and a mercy in the eyes of all those that love you.' 21 And he said: 'I will do all that thou hast told me, and I shall bury thee on the day thou diest near Sarah, my father's mother, as thou hast desired that her bones may be near thy bones. 22 And Jacob, my brother, also, I shall love above all flesh; for I have not a brother in all the earth but him only: and this is no great merit for me if I love

him; for he is my brother, and we were sown together in thy body, and together came we forth from thy womb, and if I do not love my brother, whom shall I love? 23 And I, myself, beg thee to exhort Jacob concerning me and concerning my sons, for I know that he will assuredly be king over me and my sons, for on the day my father blessed him he made him the higher and me the lower. 24 And I swear unto thee that I shall love him, and not desire evil against him all the days of my life but good only.' 25 And he sware unto her regarding all this matter. And she called Jacob before the eyes of Esau, and gave him commandment according to the words which she had spoken to Esau. 26 And he said: 'I shall do thy pleasure; believe me that no evil will proceed from me or from my sons against Esau, and I shall be first in naught save in love only.' 27 And they eat and drank, she and her sons that night, and she died, three jubilees and one week and one year old, on that night, and her two sons, Esau and Jacob, buried her in the double cave near Sarah, their father's mother.

Jub. 36

Isaac gives directions to his sons as to his burial: exhorts them to love one another and makes them imprecate destruction on him who injures his brother, 1-11. Divides his possessions, giving the larger portion to Jacob, and dies, 12-18. Leah dies: Jacob's sons come to comfort him, 21-4. 1 And in the sixth year of this week [2162 A.M.] Isaac called his two sons Esau and Jacob, and they came to him, and he said unto them: 'My sons, I am going the way of my fathers, to the eternal house where my fathers are. 2 Wherefore bury me near Abraham my father, in the double cave in the field of Ephron the Hittite, where Abraham purchased a sepulchre to bury in; in the sepulchre which I digged for myself, there bury me. 3 And this I command you, my sons, that ye practise righteousness and uprightness on the earth, so that the Lord may bring upon you all that the Lord said that he would do to Abraham and to his seed. 4 And love one another, my sons, your brothers as a man who loves his own soul, and let each seek in what he may benefit his brother, and act together on the earth; and let them love each other as their own souls. 5 And concerning the question of idols, I command and admonish you to reject them and hate them, and love them not, for they are full of deception for those that worship them and for those that bow down to them. 6 Remember ye, my sons, the Lord God of Abraham your father, and how I too worshipped Him and served Him in righteousness and in joy, that He might multiply you and increase your seed as the stars of heaven in multitude, and establish you on the earth as the plant of righteousness which will not be rooted out unto all the generations for ever. 7 And now I shall make you swear a great oath -for there is no oath which is greater than it by the name glorious and honoured and great and splendid and wonderful and mighty, which created the heavens and the earth and all things together- that ye will fear Him and worship Him. 8 And that each will love his brother with affection and righteousness, and that neither will desire evil against his brother from henceforth for ever all the days of your life so that ye may prosper in all your deeds and not be destroyed. 9 And if either of you devises evil against his brother, know that from henceforth everyone that devises evil against his brother shall fall into his hand, and shall be rooted out of the land of the living, and his seed shall be destroyed from under heaven. 10 But on the day of turbulence and execration and indignation and anger, with flaming devouring fire as He burnt Sodom, so likewise will He burn his land and his city and all that is his, and he shall be blotted out of the book of the discipline of the children of men, and not be recorded in the book of life, but in that which is appointed to destruction, and he shall depart into eternal execration; so that their condemnation may be always renewed in hate and in execration and in wrath and in torment and in indignation and in plagues and in disease for ever. [11] I say and testify to you, my sons, according to the judgment which shall come upon the man who wishes to injure his brother. [12] And he divided all his possessions between the two on that day and he gave the larger portion to him that was the first-born, and the tower and all that was about it, and all that Abraham possessed at the Well of the Oath. [13] And he said: 'This larger portion I will give to the firstborn.' [14] And Esau said, 'I have sold to Jacob and given my birthright to Jacob; to him let it be given, and I have not a single word to say regarding it, for it is his.' [15] And Isaac said, May a blessing rest upon you, my sons, and upon your seed this day, for ye have given me rest, and my heart is not pained concerning the birthright, lest thou shouldest work wickedness on account of it. [16] May the Most High God bless the man that worketh righteousness, him and his seed for ever.' [17] And he ended commanding them and blessing them, and they eat and drank together before him, and he rejoiced because there was one mind between them, and they went forth from him and rested that day and slept. [18] And Isaac slept on his bed that day rejoicing; and he slept the eternal sleep, and died one hundred and eighty years old. He completed twenty-five weeks and five years; and his two sons Esau and Jacob buried him. [19] And Esau went to the land of Edom, to the mountains of Seir, and dwelt there. [20] And Jacob dwelt in the mountains of Hebron, in the tower of the land of the sojournings of his father Abraham, and he worshipped the Lord with all his heart and according to the visible commands according as He had divided the days of his generations. [21] And Leah his wife died in the fourth year of the second week of the forty-fifth jubilee, [2167 A.M.] and he buried her in the double cave near Rebecca his mother to the left of the grave of Sarah, his father's mother [22] and all her sons and his sons came to mourn over Leah his wife with him and to comfort him regarding her, for he was lamenting her for he loved her exceedingly after Rachel her sister died; [23] for she was perfect and upright in all her ways and honoured Jacob, and all the days that she lived with him he did not hear from her mouth a harsh word, for she was gentle and peaceable and upright and honourable. [24] And he remembered all her deeds which she had done during her life and he lamented her exceedingly; for he loved her with all his heart and with all his soul.

Jub. 37

Esau's sons reproach him for his subordination to Jacob, and constrain him to war with the assistance of 4,000 mercenaries against Jacob, 1-15. Jacob reproves Esau, 16-17. Esau's reply, 18-25. [1] And on the day that Isaac the father of Jacob and Esau died, [2162 A.M.] the sons of Esau heard that Isaac had given the portion of the elder to his younger son Jacob and they were very angry. [2] And they strove with their father, saying 'Why has thy father given Jacob the portion of the elder and passed over thee, although thou art the elder and Jacob the younger?' [3] And he said unto them 'Because I sold my birthright to Jacob for a small mess of lentils, and on the day my father sent me to hunt and catch and bring him something that he should eat and bless me, he came with guile and brought my father food and drink, and my father blessed him and put me under his hand. [4] And now our father has caused us to swear, me and him, that we shall not mutually devise evil, either against his brother, and that we shall continue in love and in peace each with his brother and not make our ways corrupt.' [5] And they said unto him, 'We shall not hearken unto thee to make peace with him; for our strength is greater than his strength, and we are more powerful than he; we shall go against him and slay him, and destroy him and his sons. And if thou wilt not go with us, we shall do hurt to thee also. [6] And now hearken unto us: Let us send to Aram and Philistia and Moab and Ammon, and let us choose

for ourselves chosen men who are ardent for battle, and let us go against him and do battle with him, and let us exterminate him from the earth before he grows strong.' [7] And their father said unto them, 'Do not go and do not make war with him lest ye fall before him.' [8] And they said unto him, 'This too, is exactly thy mode of action from thy youth until this day, and thou art putting thy neck under his yoke. [9] We shall not hearken to these words.' And they sent to Aram, and to 'Aduram to the friend of their father, and they hired along with them one thousand fighting men, chosen men of war. [10] And there came to them from Moab and from the children of Ammon, those who were hired, one thousand chosen men, and from Philistia, one thousand chosen men of war, and from Edom and from the Horites one thousand chosen fighting men, and from the Kittim mighty men of war. [11] And they said unto their father: Go forth with them and lead them, else we shall slay thee.' [12] And he was filled with wrath and indignation on seeing that his sons were forcing him to go before (them) to lead them against Jacob his brother. [13] But afterward he remembered all the evil which lay hidden in his heart against Jacob his brother; and he remembered not the oath which he had sworn to his father and to his mother that he would devise no evil all his days against Jacob his brother. [14] And notwithstanding all this, Jacob knew not that they were coming against him to battle, and he was mourning for Leah, his wife, until they approached very near to the tower with four thousand warriors and chosen men of war. [15] And the men of Hebron sent to him saying, 'Behold thy brother has come against thee, to fight thee, with four thousand girt with the sword, and they carry shields and weapons'; for they loved Jacob more than Esau. So they told him; for Jacob was a more liberal and merciful man than Esau. [16] But Jacob would not believe until they came very near to the tower. [17] And he closed the gates of the tower; and he stood on the battlements and spake to his brother Esau and said, 'Noble is the comfort wherewith thou hast come to comfort me for my wife who has died. Is this the oath that thou didst swear to thy father and again to thy mother before they died? Thou hast broken the oath, and on the moment that thou didst swear to thy father wast thou condemned.' [18] And then Esau answered and said unto him, 'Neither the children of men nor the beasts of the earth have any oath of righteousness which in swearing they have sworn (an oath valid) for ever; but every day they devise evil one against another, and how each may slay his adversary and foe. [19] And thou dost hate me and my children for ever. And there is no observing the tie of brotherhood with thee. [20] Hear these words which I declare unto thee, If the boar can change its skin and make its bristles as soft as wool, Or if it can cause horns to sprout forth on its head like the horns of a stag or of a sheep, Then will I observe the tie of brotherhood with thee And if the breasts separated themselves from their mother, for thou hast not been a brother to me. [21] And if the wolves make peace with the lambs so as not to devour or do them violence, And if their hearts are towards them for good, Then there shall be peace in my heart towards thee [22] And if the lion becomes the friend of the ox and makes peace with him And if he is bound under one yoke with him and ploughs with him, Then will I make peace with thee. [23] And when the raven becomes white as the raza, Then know that I have loved thee And shall make peace with thee Thou shalt be rooted out, And thy sons shall be rooted out, And there shall be no peace for thee' [24] And when Jacob saw that he was (so) evilly disposed towards him with his heart, and with all his soul as to slay him, and that he had come springing like the wild boar which comes upon the spear that pierces and kills it, and recoils not from it; [25] then he spake to his own and to his servants that they should attack him and all his companions.

Jub. 38

War between Jacob and Esau. Death of Esau and overthrow of his forces, 1-10. Edom reduced to servitude 'till this day', 11-14. Kings of Edom, 15-24. (Cf. Gen. xxxvi.31-9.) [1] And after that Judah spake to Jacob, his father, and said unto him: 'Bend thy bow, father, and send forth thy arrows and cast down the adversary and slay the enemy; and mayst thou have the power, for we shall not slay thy brother, for he is such as thou, and he is like thee let us give him (this) honour.' [2] Then Jacob bent his bow and sent forth the arrow and struck Esau, his brother (on his right breast) and slew him. [3] And again he sent forth an arrow and struck 'Adoran the Aramaean, on the left breast, and drove him backward and slew him. [4] And then went forth the sons of Jacob, they and their servants, dividing themselves into companies on the four sides of the tower. [5] And Judah went forth in front, and Naphtali and Gad with him and fifty servants with him on the south side of the tower, and they slew all they found before them, and not one individual of them escaped. [6] And Levi and Dan and Asher went forth on the east side of the tower, and fifty (men) with them, and they slew the fighting men of Moab and Ammon. [7] And Reuben and Issachar and Zebulon went forth on the north side of the tower, and fifty men with them, and they slew the fighting men of the Philistines. [8] And Simeon and Benjamin and Enoch, Reuben's son, went forth on the west side of the tower, and fifty (men) with them, and they slew of Edom and of the Horites four hundred men, stout warriors; and six hundred fled, and four of the sons of Esau fled with them, and left their father lying slain, as he had fallen on the hill which is in 'Aduram. [9] And the sons of Jacob pursued after them to the mountains of Seir. And Jacob buried his brother on the hill which is in 'Aduram, and he returned to his house. [10] And the sons of Jacob pressed hard upon the sons of Esau in the mountains of Seir, and bowed their necks so that they became servants of the sons of Jacob. [11] And they sent to their father (to inquire) whether they should make peace with them or slay them. [12] And Jacob sent word to his sons that they should make peace, and they made peace with them, and placed the yoke of servitude upon them, so that they paid tribute to Jacob and to his sons always. [13] And they continued to pay tribute to Jacob until the day that he went down into Egypt. [14] And the sons of Edom have not got quit of the yoke of servitude which the twelve sons of Jacob had imposed on them until this day. [15] And these are the kings that reigned in Edom before there reigned any king over the children of Israel [until this day] in the land of Edom. [16] And Balaq, the son of Beor, reigned in Edom, and the name of his city was Danaba. [17] And Balaq died, and Jobab, the son of Zara of Boser, reigned in his stead. [18] And Jobab died, and 'Asam, of the land of Teman, reigned in his stead. [19] And 'Asam died, and 'Adath, the son of Barad, who slew Midian in the field of Moab, reigned in his stead, and the name of his city was Avith. [20] And 'Adath died, and Salman, from 'Amaseqa, reigned in his stead. [21] And Salman died, and Saul of Ra'aboth (by the) river, reigned in his stead. [22] And Saul died, and Ba'elunan, the son of Achbor, reigned in his stead. [23] And Ba'elunan, the son of Achbor died, and 'Adath reigned in his stead, and the name of his wife was Maitabith, the daughter of Matarat, the daughter of Metabedza'ab. [24] These are the kings who reigned in the land of Edom.

Jub. 39

Joseph set over Potiphar's house, 1-4. His purity and imprisonment, 5-13. Imprisonment of Pharaoh's chief butler and chief baker whose dreams Joseph interprets, 14-18. (Cf. Gen.xxxvii.2; xxxix.3-8, 12-15, 17-23; xl.1-5, 21-3; xli.1.) [1] And Jacob dwelt in the land of his father's sojournings in the land of Canaan. These are the generations of Jacob. [2] And Joseph was seventeen years old when they took him down into the land of Egypt, and Potiphar, an eunuch of Pharaoh, the chief cook bought him. [3] And he set Joseph over all his house and the blessing of the Lord came upon the house of the Egyptian on account of Joseph, and the Lord prospered him in all that he did. [4] And the Egyptian committed everything into the hands of Joseph; for he saw that the Lord was with him, and that the Lord prospered him in all that he did. [5] And Joseph's appearance was comely [and very beautiful was his appearance], and his master's wife lifted up her eyes and saw Joseph, and she loved him and besought him to lie with her. [6] But he did not surrender his soul, and he remembered the Lord and the words which Jacob, his father, used to read from amongst the words of Abraham, that no man should commit fornication with a woman who has a husband; that for him the punishment of death has been ordained in the heavens before the Most High God, and the sin will be recorded against him in the eternal books continually before the Lord. [7] And Joseph remembered these words and refused to lie with her. [8] And she besought him for a year, but he refused and would not listen. [9] But she embraced him and held him fast in the house in order to force him to lie with her, and closed the doors of the house and held him fast; but he left his garment in her hands and broke through the door and fled without from her presence. [10] And the woman saw that he would not lie with her, and she calumniated him in the presence of his lord, saying 'Thy Hebrew servant, whom thou lovest, sought to force me so that he might lie with me; and it came to pass when I lifted up my voice that he fled and left his garment in my hands when I held him, and he brake through the door.' [11] And the Egyptian saw the garment of Joseph and the broken door, and heard the words of his wife, and cast Joseph into prison into the place where the prisoners were kept whom the king imprisoned. [12] And he was there in the prison; and the Lord gave Joseph favour in the sight of the chief of the prison guards and compassion before him, for he saw that the Lord was with him, and that the Lord made all that he did to prosper. [13] And he committed all things into his hands, and the chief of the prison guards knew of nothing that was with him, for Joseph did every thing, and the Lord perfected it. [14] And he remained there two years. And in those days Pharaoh, king of Egypt was wroth against his two eunuchs, against the chief butler, and against the chief baker, and he put them in ward in the house of the chief cook, in the prison where Joseph was kept. [15] And the chief of the prison guards appointed Joseph to serve them; and he served before them. [16] And they both dreamed a dream, the chief butler and the chief baker, and they told it to Joseph. [17] And as he interpreted to them so it befell them, and Pharaoh restored the chief butler to his office and the (chief) baker he slew, as Joseph had interpreted to them. [18] But the chief butler forgot Joseph in the prison, although he had informed him what would befall him, and did not remember to inform Pharaoh how Joseph had told him, for he forgot.

Jub. 40

Pharoah's dreams and their interpretation, 1-4. Elevation and marriage of Joseph, 5-13. (Cf. Gen. xli.1-5, 7-9, 14 seqq., 25, 29-30, 34, 36, 38-43, 45-6, 49.) [1] And in those days Pharaoh dreamed two dreams in one night concerning a famine which was to be in all the land, and he awoke from his sleep and called all the interpreters of dreams that were in Egypt, and magicians, and told them his two dreams, and they were not able to declare (them). [2] And then the chief butler remembered Joseph and spake of him to the king, and he brought him forth from the prison, and he to|d his two dreams before him. [3] And he said before Pharaoh that his two dreams were one, and he said unto him: 'Seven years shall come (in which there shall be) plenty over all the land of Egypt, and after that seven years of famine, such a famine as has not been in all the land. 4 And now let Pharaoh appoint overseers in all the land of Egypt, and let them store up food in every city throughout the days of the years of plenty, and there will be food for the seven years of famine, and the land will not perish through the famine, for it will be very severe.' 5 And the Lord gave Joseph favour and mercy in the eyes of Pharaoh, and Pharaoh said unto his servants. We shall not find such a wise and discreet man as this man, for the spirit of the Lord is with him.' 6 And he appointed him the second in all his kingdom and gave him authority over all Egypt, and caused him to ride in the second chariot of Pharaoh. 7 And he clothed him with byssus garments, and he put a gold chain upon his neck, and (a herald) proclaimed before him ' 'El 'El wa 'Abirer,' and placed a ring on his hand and made him ruler over all his house, and magnified him, and said unto him. 'Only on the throne shall I be greater than thou.' 8 And Joseph ruled over all the land of Egypt, and all the princes of Pharaoh, and all his servants, and all who did the king's business loved him, for he walked in uprightness, for he was without pride and arrogance, and he had no respect of persons, and did not accept gifts, but he judged in uprightness all the people of the land. 9 And the land of Egypt was at peace before Pharaoh because of Joseph, for the Lord was with him, and gave him favour and mercy for all his generations before all those who knew him and those who heard concerning him, and Pharaoh's kingdom was well ordered, and there was no Satan and no evil person (therein). 10 And the king called Joseph's name Sephantiphans, and gave Joseph to wife the daughter of Potiphar, the daughter of the priest of Heliopolis, the chief cook. 11 And on the day that Joseph stood before Pharaoh he was thirty years old [when he stood before Pharaoh]. 12 And in that year Isaac died. And it came to pass as Joseph had said in the interpretation of his two dreams, according as he had said it, there were seven years of plenty over all the land of Egypt, and the land of Egypt abundantly produced, one measure (producing) eighteen hundred measures. 13 And Joseph gathered food into every city until they were full of corn until they could no longer count and measure it for its multitude.

Jub. 41

Judah's sons and Tamar, 1-7. Judah's incest with Tamar, 8-18. Tamar bears twins, 21-2. Judah forgiven, because he sinned ignorantly and repented when convicted, and because Tamar's marriage with his sons had not been consummated, 23-8. (Cf. Gen. xxxviii.6-18, 20-6, 29-30; xli.13.) 1 And in the forty-fifth jubilee, in the second week, (and) in the second year, [2165 A.M.] Judah took for his first-born Er, a wife from the daughters of Aram, named Tamar. 2 But he hated, and did not lie with her, because his mother was of the daughters of Canaan, and he wished to take him a wife of the kinsfolk of his mother, but Judah, his father, would not permit him. 3 And this Er, the first-born of Judah, was wicked, and the Lord slew him. 4 And Judah said unto Onan, his brother 'Go in unto thy brother's wife and perform the duty of a husband's brother unto her, and raise up seed unto thy brother.' 5 And Onan knew that the seed would not be his, (but) his brother's only, and he went into the house of his brother's wife, and spilt the seed on the ground, and he was wicked in the eyes of the Lord, and He slew him. 6 And Judah said unto Tamar, his daughter-in-law: 'Remain in thy father's house as a widow till Shelah my son be grown up, and I shall give thee to him to wife.' 7 And he grew up; but Bedsu'el, the wife of Judah, did not permit her son Shelah to marry. And Bedsu'el, the wife of Judah, died [2168 A.M.] in the fifth year of this week. 8 And in the sixth year Judah went up to shear his sheep at Timnah. [2169 A.M.] And they told Tamar: 'Behold thy father-in-law goeth up to Timnah to shear his sheep.' 9 And she put off her widow's clothes, and put on a veil, and adorned herself, and

sat in the gate adjoining the way to Timnah. 10 And as Judah was going along he found her, and thought her to be an harlot, and he said unto her: 'Let me come in unto thee'; and she said unto him Come in,' and he went in. 11 And she said unto him: 'Give me my hire'; and he said unto her: 'I have nothing in my hand save my ring that is on my finger, and my necklace, and my staff which is in my hand.' 12 And she said unto him 'Give them to me until thou dost send me my hire', and he said unto her: 'I will send unto thee a kid of the goats'; and he gave them to her, and he went in unto her, and she conceived by him. 13 And Judah went unto his sheep, and she went to her father's house. 14 And Judah sent a kid of the goats by the hand of his shepherd, an Adullamite, and he found her not; and he asked the people of the place, saying: 'Where is the harlot who was here?' And they said unto him; 'There is no harlot here with us.' 15 And he returned and informed him, and said unto him that he had not found her: 'I asked the people of the place, and they said unto me: "There is no harlot here." ' 16 And he said: 'Let her keep (them) lest we become a cause of derision.' And when she had completed three months, it was manifest that she was with child, and they told Judah, saying: 'Behold Tamar, thy daughter-in-law, is with child by whoredom.' 17 And Judah went to the house of her father, and said unto her father and her brothers: 'Bring her forth, and let them burn her, for she hath wrought uncleanness in Israel.' 18 And it came to pass when they brought her forth to burn her that she sent to her father-in-law the ring and the necklace, and the staff, saying: 'Discern whose are these, for by him am I with child.' 19 And Judah acknowledged, and said: "Tamar is more righteous than I am. 20 And therefore let them burn her not' And for that reason she was not given to Shelah, and he did not again approach her. 21 And after that she bare two sons, Perez [2170 A.M.] and Zerah, in the seventh year of this second week. 22 And thereupon the seven years of fruitfulness were accomplished, of which Joseph spake to Pharaoh. 23 And Judah acknowledged that the deed which he had done was evil, for he had lain with his daughter-in-law, and he esteemed it hateful in his eyes, and he acknowledged that he had transgressed and gone astray, for he had uncovered the skirt of his son, and he began to lament and to supplicate before the Lord because of his transgression. 24 And we told him in a dream that it was forgiven him because he supplicated earnestly, and lamented, and did not again commit it. 25 And he received forgiveness because he turned from his sin and from his ignorance, for he transgressed greatly before our God; and every one that acts thus, every one who lies with his mother-in-law, let them burn him with fire that he may burn therein, for there is uncleanness and pollution upon them, with fire let them burn them. 26 And do thou command the children of Israel that there be no uncleanness amongst them, for every one who lies with his daughter-in-law or with his mother-in-law hath wrought uncleanness; with fire let them burn the man who has lain with her, and likewise the woman, and He will turn away wrath and punishment from Israel. 27 And unto Judah we said that his two sons had not lain with her, and for this reason his seed was stablished for a second generation, and would not be rooted out. 28 For in singleness of eye he had gone and sought for punishment, namely, according to the judgment of Abraham, which he had commanded his sons, Judah had sought to burn her with fire.

Jub. 42

Owing to the famine Jacob sends his sons to Egypt for corn, 1-4. Joseph recognizes them and retains Simeon, and requires them to bring Benjamin when they returned, 5-12. Notwithstanding Jacob's reluctance his sons take Benjamin with them on their second journey and are entertained by Joseph, 13-25. (Cf. Gen. xli.54, 56; xlii.7-9, 13, 17, 20, 24-5, 29-30, 34-8; xliii.1-2, 4-5, 8-

160

9, 11, 15, 23, 26, 29, 34; xliv. 1-2.) ¹ And in the first year of the third week of the forty-fifth jubilee the famine began to come into the [2171 A.M.] land, and the rain refused to be given to the earth, for none whatever fell. ² And the earth grew barren, but in the land of Egypt there was food, for Joseph had gathered the seed of the land in the seven years of plenty and had preserved it. ³ And the Egyptians came to Joseph that he might give them food, and he opened the store-houses where was the grain of the first year, and he sold it to the people of the land for gold. ⁴ , and Jacob heard that there was food in Egypt, and he sent his ten sons that they should procure food for him in Egypt; but Benjamin he did not send, and arrived among those that went (there). ⁵ And Joseph recognised them, but they did not recognise him, and he spake unto them and questioned them, and he said unto them; 'Are ye not spies and have ye not come to explore the approaches of the land? 'And he put them in ward. ⁶ And after that he set them free again, and detained Simeon alone and sent off his nine brothers. ⁷ And he filled their sacks with corn, and he put their gold in their sacks, and they did not know. ⁸ And he commanded them to bring their younger brother, for they had told him their father was living and their younger brother. ⁹ And they went up from the land of Egypt and they came to the land of Canaan; and they told their father all that had befallen them, and how the lord of the country had spoken roughly to them, and had seized Simeon till they should bring Benjamin. ¹⁰ And Jacob said: 'Me have ye bereaved of my children! Joseph is not and Simeon also is not, and ye will take Benjamin away. On me has your wickedness come. ¹¹ 'And he said: 'My son will not go down with you lest perchance he fall sick; for their mother gave birth to two sons, and one has perished, and this one also ye will take from me. If perchance he took a fever on the road, ye would bring down my old age with sorrow unto death.' ¹² For he saw that their money had been returned to every man in his sack, and for this reason he feared to send him. ¹³ And the famine increased and became sore in the land of Canaan, and in all lands save in the land of Egypt, for many of the children of the Egyptians had stored up their seed for food from the time when they saw Joseph gathering seed together and putting it in storehouses and preserving it for the years of famine. ¹⁴ And the people of Egypt fed themselves thereon during the first year of their famine. ¹⁵ But when Israel saw that the famine was very sore in the land, and that there was no deliverance, he said unto his sons: 'Go again, and procure food for us that we die not.' ¹⁶ And they said: 'We shall not go; unless our youngest brother go with us, we shall not go.' ¹⁷ And Israel saw that if he did not send him with them, they should all perish by reason of the famine ¹⁸ And Reuben said: 'Give him into my hand, and if I do not bring him back to thee, slay my two sons instead of his soul.' ¹⁹ And he said unto him: 'He shall not go with thee.' And Judah came near and said: 'Send him with me, and if I do not bring him back to thee, let me bear the blame before thee all the days of my life.' ²⁰ And he sent him with them in the second year of this week on the [2172 A.m.] first day of the month, and they came to the land of Egypt with all those who went, and (they had) presents in their hands, stacte and almonds and terebinth nuts and pure honey. ²¹ And they went and stood before Joseph, and he saw Benjamin his brother, and he knew him, and said unto them: Is this your youngest brother?' And they said unto him: 'It is he.' And he said The Lord be gracious to thee, my son!' ²² And he sent him into his house and he brought forth Simeon unto them and he made a feast for them, and they presented to him the gift which they had brought in their hands. ²³ And they eat before him and he gave them all a portion, but the portion of Benjamin was seven times larger than that of any of theirs. ²⁴ And they eat and drank and arose and remained with their asses. ²⁵ And

Joseph devised a plan whereby he might learn their thoughts as to whether thoughts of peace prevailed amongst them, and he said to the steward who was over his house: 'Fill all their sacks with food, and return their money unto them into their vessels, and my cup, the silver cup out of which I drink, put it in the sack of the youngest, and send them away.'

Jub. 43

Joseph's plan to stay his brethren, 1-10. Judah's supplication, 11-13. Joseph makes himself known to his brethren and sends them back for his father, 14-24. (Cf. Gen. xliv.3-10, 12-18, 27-8, 30-2; xlv.1-2, 5-9, 12, 18, 20-1, 23, 25-8.) ¹ And he did as Joseph had told him, and filled all their sacks for them with food and put their money in their sacks, and put the cup in Benjamin's sack. ² And early in the morning they departed, and it came to pass that, when they had gone from thence, Joseph said unto the steward of his house: 'Pursue them, run and seize them, saying, "For good ye have requited me with evil; you have stolen from me the silver cup out of which my lord drinks." And bring back to me their youngest brother, and fetch (him) quickly before I go forth to my seat of judgment.' ³ And he ran after them and said unto them according to these words. ⁴ And they said unto him: 'God forbid that thy servants should do this thing, and steal from the house of thy lord any utensil, and the money also which we found in our sacks the first time, we thy servants brought back from the land of Canaan. ⁵ How then should we steal any utensil? Behold here are we and our sacks search, and wherever thou findest the cup in the sack of any man amongst us, let him be slain, and we and our asses will serve thy lord.' ⁶ And he said unto them: 'Not so, the man with whom I find, him only shall I take as a servant, and ye shall return in peace unto your house.' ⁷ And as he was searching in their vessels, beginning with the eldest and ending with the youngest, it was found in Benjamin's sack. ⁸ And they rent their garments, and laded their asses, and returned to the city and came to the house of Joseph, and they all bowed themselves on their faces to the ground before him. ⁹ And Joseph said unto them: 'Ye have done evil.' And they said: 'What shall we say and how shall we defend ourselves? Our lord hath discovered the transgression of his servants; behold we are the servants of our lord, and our asses also. ¹⁰ 'And Joseph said unto them: 'I too fear the Lord; as for you, go ye to your homes and let your brother be my servant, for ye have done evil. Know ye not that a man delights in his cup as I with this cup? And yet ye have stolen it from me.' ¹¹ And Judah said: 'O my lord, let thy servant, I pray thee, speak a word in my lord's ear two brothers did thy servant's mother bear to our father: one went away and was lost, and hath not been found, and he alone is left of his mother, and thy servant our father loves him, and his life also is bound up with the life of this (lad). ¹² And it will come to pass, when we go to thy servant our father, and the lad is not with us, that he will die, and we shall bring down our father with sorrow unto death. ¹³ Now rather let me, thy servant, abide instead of the boy as a bondsman unto my lord, and let the lad go with his brethren, for I became surety for him at the hand of thy servant our father, and if I do not bring him back, thy servant will hear the blame to our father for ever.' ¹⁴ And Joseph saw that they were all accordant in goodness one with another, and he could not refrain himself, and he told them that he was Joseph. ¹⁵ And he conversed with them in the Hebrew tongue and fell on their neck and wept. ¹⁶ But they knew him not and they began to weep. And he said unto them: 'Weep not over me, but hasten and bring my father to me; and ye see that it is my mouth that speaketh and the eyes of my brother Benjamin see. ¹⁷ For behold this is the second year of the famine, and there are still five years without harvest or fruit of trees or ploughing. ¹⁸ Come down quickly ye and your households, so that ye perish not through the famine, and do not be grieved for your possessions, for the Lord sent me before you to set things in order that many people might live. 19 And tell my father that I am still alive, and ye, behold, ye see that the Lord has made me as a father to Pharaoh, and ruler over his house and over all the land of Egypt. 20 And tell my father of all my glory, and all the riches and glory that the Lord hath given me.' 21 And by the command of the mouth of Pharaoh he gave them chariots and provisions for the way, and he gave them all many-coloured raiment and silver. 22 And to their father he sent raiment and silver and ten asses which carried corn, and he sent them away. 23 And they went up and told their father that Joseph was alive, and was measuring out corn to all the nations of the earth, and that he was ruler over all the land of Egypt. 24 And their father did not believe it, for he was beside himself in his mind; but when he saw the wagons which Joseph had sent, the life of his spirit revived, and he said: 'It is enough for me if Joseph lives; I will go down and see him before I die.'

Jub. 44

Jacob celebrates the feast of firstfruits, and encouraged by a vision goes down to Egypt, 1-10. Names of his descendants, 11-34. (Cf. Gen. xlvi.1-28.) 1 And Israel took his journey from Haran from his house on the new moon of the third month, and he went on the way of the Well of the Oath, and he offered a sacrifice to the God of his father Isaac on the seventh of this month. 2 And Jacob remembered the dream that he had seen at Bethel, and he feared to go down into Egypt. 3 And while he was thinking of sending word to Joseph to come to him, and that he would not go down, he remained there seven days, if perchance he could see a vision as to whether he should remain or go down. 4 And he celebrated the harvest festival of the first-fruits with old grain, for in all the land of Canaan there was not a handful of seed [in the land], for the famine was over all the beasts and cattle and birds, and also over man. 5 And on the sixteenth the Lord appeared unto him, and said unto him, 'Jacob, Jacob'; and he said, 'Here am I.' And He said unto him: 'I am the God of thy fathers, the God of Abraham and Isaac; fear not to go down into Egypt, for I will there make of thee a great nation I will go down with thee, and I will bring thee up (again), and in this land shalt thou be buried, and Joseph shall put his hands upon thy eyes. 6 Fear not; go down into Egypt.' 7 And his sons rose up, and his sons' sons, and they placed their father and their possessions upon wagons. 8 And Israel rose up from the Well of the Oath on the sixteenth of this third month, and he went to the land of Egypt. 9 And Israel sent Judah before him to his son Joseph to examine the Land of Goshen, for Joseph had told his brothers that they should come and dwell there that they might be near him. 10 And this was the goodliest (land) in the land of Egypt, and near to him, for all (of them) and also for the cattle. 11 And these are the names of the sons of Jacob who went into Egypt with Jacob their father. 12 Reuben, the First-born of Israel; and these are the names of his sons Enoch, and Pallu, and Hezron and Carmi-five. 13 Simeon and his sons; and these are the names of his sons: Jemuel, and Jamin, and Ohad, and Jachin, and Zohar, and Shaul, the son of the Zephathite woman-seven. 14 Levi and his sons; and these are the names of his sons: Gershon, and Kohath, and Merari-four. 15 Judah and his sons; and these are the names of his sons: Shela, and Perez, and Zerah-four. 16 Issachar and his sons; and these are the names of his sons: Tola, and Phua, and Jasub, and Shimron-five. 17 Zebulon and his sons; and these are the names of his sons: Sered, and Elon, and Jahleel-four. 18 And these are the sons of Jacob and their sons whom Leah bore to Jacob in Mesopotamia, six, and their one sister, Dinah and all the souls of the sons of Leah, and their sons, who went with Jacob their father into Egypt, were twenty-nine, and Jacob their father being with them,

162

they were thirty. 19 And the sons of Zilpah, Leah's handmaid, the wife of Jacob, who bore unto Jacob Gad and Ashur. 20 And these are the names of their sons who went with him into Egypt. The sons of Gad: Ziphion, and Haggi, and Shuni, and Ezbon, , and Areli, and Arodi-eight. 21 And the sons of Asher: Imnah, and Ishvah, , and Beriah, and Serah, their one sister-six. 22 All the souls were fourteen, and all those of Leah were forty-four. 23 And the sons of Rachel, the wife of Jacob: Joseph and Benjamin. 24 And there were born to Joseph in Egypt before his father came into Egypt, those whom Asenath, daughter of Potiphar priest of Heliopolis bare unto him, Manasseh, and Ephraim-three. 25 And the sons of Benjamin: Bela and Becher and Ashbel, Gera, and Naaman, and Ehi, and Rosh, and Muppim, and Huppim, and Ard-eleven. 26 And all the souls of Rachel were fourteen. 27 And the sons of Bilhah, the handmaid of Rachel, the wife of Jacob, whom she bare to Jacob, were Dan and Naphtali. 28 And these are the names of their sons who went with them into Egypt. And the sons of Dan were Hushim, and Samon, and Asudi. and 'Ijaka, and Salomon-six. 29 And they died the year in which they entered into Egypt, and there was left to Dan Hushim alone. 30 And these are the names of the sons of Naphtali Jahziel, and Guni and Jezer, and Shallum, and 'Iv. 31 And 'Iv, who was born after the years of famine, died in Egypt. 32 And all the souls of Rachel were twenty-six. 33 And all the souls of Jacob which went into Egypt were seventy souls. These are his children and his children's children, in all seventy, but five died in Egypt before Joseph, and had no children. 34 And in the land of Canaan two sons of Judah died, Er and Onan, and they had no children, and the children of Israel buried those who perished, and they were reckoned among the seventy Gentile nations.

Jub. 45

Joseph receives Jacob, and gives him Goshen, 1-7. Joseph acquires all the land and its inhabitants for Pharaoh, 8-12. Jacob dies and is buried in Hebron, 13-15. His books given to Levi, 16. (Cf. Gen. xlvi.28-30; xlvii.11-13, 19, 20, 23, 24, 28; l.13.) 1 And Israel went into the country of Egypt, into the land of Goshen, on the new moon of the fourth [2172 A.M]. month, in the second year of the third week of the forty-fifth jubilee. 2 And Joseph went to meet his father Jacob, to the land of Goshen, and he fell on his father's neck and wept. 3 And Israel said unto Joseph: 'Now let me die since I have seen thee, and now may the Lord God of Israel be blessed the God of Abraham and the God of Isaac who hath not withheld His mercy and His grace from His servant Jacob. 4 It is enough for me that I have seen thy face whilst I am yet alive; yea, true is the vision which I saw at Bethel. Blessed be the Lord my God for ever and ever, and blessed be His name.' 5 And Joseph and his brothers eat bread before their father and drank wine, and Jacob rejoiced with exceeding great joy because he saw Joseph eating with his brothers and drinking before him, and he blessed the Creator of all things who had preserved him, and had preserved for him his twelve sons. 6 And Joseph had given to his father and to his brothers as a gift the right of dwelling in the land of Goshen and in Rameses and all the region round about, which he ruled over before Pharaoh. And Israel and his sons dwelt in the land of Goshen, the best part of the land of Egypt and Israel was one hundred and thirty years old when he came into Egypt. 7 And Joseph nourished his father and his brethren and also their possessions with bread as much as sufficed them for the seven years of the famine. 8 And the land of Egypt suffered by reason of the famine, and Joseph acquired all the land of Egypt for Pharaoh in return for food, and he got possession of the people and their cattle and everything for Pharaoh. 9 And the years of the famine were accomplished, and Joseph gave to the people in the land seed and food that they might sow (the land) in the eighth year, for the river had overflowed all the land of Egypt. ¹⁰ For in the seven years of the famine it had (not) overflowed and had irrigated only a few places on the banks of the river, but now it overflowed and the Egyptians sowed the land, and it bore much corn that year. ¹¹ And this was the first year of [2178 A.M.] the fourth week of the forty-fifth jubilee. ¹² And Joseph took of the corn of the harvest the fifth part for the king and left four parts for them for food and for seed, and Joseph made it an ordinance for the land of Egypt until this day. ¹³ And Israel lived in the land of Egypt seventeen years, and all the days which he lived were three jubilees, one hundred and forty-seven years, and he died in the fourth [2188 A.M.] year of the fifth week of the forty-fifth jubilee. ¹⁴ And Israel blessed his sons before he died and told them everything that would befall them in the land of Egypt; and he made known to them what would come upon them in the last days, and blessed them and gave to Joseph two portions in the land. ¹⁵ And he slept with his fathers, and he was buried in the double cave in the land of Canaan, near Abraham his father in the grave which he dug for himself in the double cave in the land of Hebron. ¹⁶ And he gave all his books and the books of his fathers to Levi his son that he might preserve them and renew them for his children until this day.

Jub. 46

Prosperity of Israel in Egypt, 1-2. Death of Joseph, 3-5. War between Egypt and Canaan during which the bones of all the sons of Jacob except Joseph are buried at Hebron, 6-11. Egypt oppresses Israel, 12-16. (Cf. Gen. l.22, 25-6; Exod. i.6-14.) ¹ And it came to pass that after Jacob died the children of Israel multiplied in the land of Egypt, and they became a great nation, and they were of one accord in heart, so that brother loved brother and every man helped his brother, and they increased abundantly and multiplied exceedingly, ten [2242 A.M.] weeks of years, all the days of the life of Joseph. ² And there was no Satan nor any evil all the days of the life of Joseph which he lived after his father Jacob, for all the Egyptians honoured the children of Israel all the days of the life of Joseph. ³ And Joseph died being a hundred and ten years old; seventeen years he lived in the land of Canaan, and ten years he was a servant, and three years in prison, and eighty years he was under the king, ruling all the land of Egypt. ⁴ And he died and all his brethren and all that generation. ⁵ And he commanded the children of Israel before he died that they should carry his bones with them when they went forth from the land of Egypt. ⁶ And he made them swear regarding his bones, for he knew that the Egyptians would not again bring forth and bury him in the land of Canaan, for Makamaron, king of Canaan, while dwelling in the land of Assyria, fought in the valley with the king of Egypt and slew him there, and pursued after the Egyptians to the gates of 'Ermon. ⁷ But he was not able to enter, for another, a new king, had become king of Egypt, and he was stronger than he, and he returned to the land of Canaan, and the gates of Egypt were closed, and none went out and none came into Egypt. ⁸ And Joseph died in the forty-sixth jubilee, in the sixth week, in the second year, and they buried him in the land of Egypt, and [2242 A.M.] all his brethren died after him. ⁹ And the king of Egypt went forth to war with the king of Canaan [2263 A.M.] in the forty-seventh jubilee, in the second week in the second year, and the children of Israel brought forth all the bones of the children of Jacob save the bones of Joseph, and they buried them in the field in the double cave in the mountain. ¹⁰ And the most (of them) returned to Egypt, but a few of them remained in the mountains of Hebron, and Amram thy father remained with them. ¹¹ And the king of Canaan was victorious over the king of Egypt, and he closed the gates of Egypt. ¹² And he devised an evil device against the children of Israel of afflicting them and he said unto the people of Egypt: 'Behold the people of the children of

163

Israel have increased and multiplied more than we. ¹³ Come and let us deal wisely with them before they become too many, and let us afflict them with slavery before war come upon us and before they too fight against us; else they will join themselves unto our enemies and get them up out of our land, for their hearts and faces are towards the land of Canaan.' ¹⁴ And he set over them taskmasters to afflict them with slavery; and they built strong cities for Pharaoh, Pithom, and Raamses and they built all the walls and all the fortifications which had fallen in the cities of Egypt. ¹⁵ And they made them serve with rigour, and the more they dealt evilly with them, the more they increased and multiplied. ¹⁶ And the people of Egypt abominated the children of Israel

Jub. 47

Birth of Moses, 1-4. Adopted by Pharaoh's daughter, 5-9. Slays an Egyptian and flees (into Midian), 10-12. (Cf. Exod. i.22; ii. 2-15.) ¹ And in the seventh week, in the seventh year, in the forty-seventh jubilee, thy father went forth [2303 A.M.] from the land of Canaan, and thou wast born in the fourth week, in the sixth year thereof, in the [2330 A.M.] forty-eighth jubilee; this was the time of tribulation on the children of Israel. ² And Pharaoh, king of Egypt, issued a command regarding them that they should cast all their male children which were born into the river. ³ And they cast them in for seven months until the day that thou wast born ⁴ And thy mother hid thee for three months, and they told regarding her. And she made an ark for thee, and covered it with pitch and asphalt, and placed it in the flags on the bank of the river, and she placed thee in it seven days, and thy mother came by night and suckled thee, and by day Miriam, thy sister, guarded thee from the birds. ⁵ And in those days Tharmuth, the daughter of Pharaoh, came to bathe in the river, and she heard thy voice crying, and she told her maidens to bring thee forth, and they brought thee unto her. ⁶ And she took thee out of the ark, and she had compassion on thee. ⁷ And thy sister said unto her: 'Shall I go and call unto thee one of the Hebrew women to nurse and suckle this babe for thee?' ⁸ And she said : 'Go.' And she went and called thy mother Jochebed, and she gave her wages, and she nursed thee. ⁹ And afterwards, when thou wast grown up, they brought thee unto the daughter of Pharaoh, and thou didst become her son, and Amram thy father taught thee writing, and after thou hadst completed three weeks they brought thee into the royal court. ¹⁰ And thou wast three weeks of years at court until the time [2351-] when thou didst go forth from the royal court and didst see an Egyptian smiting thy friend who was [2372 A.M.] of the children of Israel, and thou didst slay him and hide him in the sand. ¹¹ And on the second day thou didst and two of the children of Israel striving together, and thou didst say to him who was doing the wrong: 'Why dost thou smite thy brother?' ¹² And he was angry and indignant, and said: 'Who made thee a prince and a judge over us? Thinkest thou to kill me as thou killedst the Egyptian yesterday?' And thou didst fear and flee on account of these words.

Jub. 48

Moses returns from Midian to Egypt. Mastêmâ seeks to slay him on the way, 1-3. The ten plagues, 4-11. Israel goes forth out of Egypt: the destruction of the Egyptians on the Red Sea, 12-19. (Cf. Exod. ii.15; iv.19, 24; vii. seqq.) ¹ And in the sixth year of the third week of the forty-ninth jubilee thou didst depart and dwell , five weeks and one year. And thou didst return into Egypt in the second week in the second year in the fiftieth jubilee. ² And thou thyself knowest what He spake unto thee on [2410 A.M.] Mount Sinai, and what prince Mastêmâ desired to do with thee when thou wast returning into Egypt . ³ Did he not with all his power seek to slay thee and deliver the Egyptians out of thy hand when he saw that thou wast sent to execute judgment and vengeance on the Egyptians? ⁴ And I delivered thee out of his hand,

and thou didst perform the signs and wonders which thou wast sent to perform in Egypt against Pharaoh, and against all his house, and against his servants and his people. 5 And the Lord executed a great vengeance on them for Israel's sake, and smote them through (the plagues of) blood and frogs, lice and dog-flies, and malignant boils breaking forth in blains; and their cattle by death; and by hail-stones, thereby He destroyed everything that grew for them; and by locusts which devoured the residue which had been left by the hail, and by darkness; and of the first-born of men and animals, and on all their idols the Lord took vengeance and burned them with fire. 6 And everything was sent through thy hand, that thou shouldst declare (these things) before they were done, and thou didst speak with the king of Egypt before all his servants and before his people. 7 And everything took place according to thy words; ten great and terrible judgments came on the land of Egypt that thou mightest execute vengeance on it for Israel. 8 And the Lord did everything for Israel's sake, and according to His covenant, which he had ordained with Abraham that He would take vengeance on them as they had brought them by force into bondage. 9 And the prince Mastêmâ stood up against thee, and sought to cast thee into the hands of Pharaoh, and he helped the Egyptian sorcerers, 10 and they stood up and wrought before thee the evils indeed we permitted them to work, but the remedies we did not allow to be wrought by their hands. 11 And the Lord smote them with malignant ulcers, and they were not able to stand, for we destroyed them so that they could not perform a single sign. 12 And notwithstanding all (these) signs and wonders the prince Mastêmâ was not put to shame because he took courage and cried to the Egyptians to pursue after thee with all the powers of the Egyptians, with their chariots, and with their horses, and with all the hosts of the peoples of Egypt. 13 And I stood between the Egyptians and Israel, and we delivered Israel out of his hand, and out of the hand of his people, and the Lord brought them through the midst of the sea as if it were dry land. 14 And all the peoples whom he brought to pursue after Israel, the Lord our God cast them into the midst of the sea, into the depths of the abyss beneath the children of Israel, even as the people of Egypt had cast their children into the river He took vengeance on 1,000,000 of them, and one thousand strong and energetic men were destroyed on account of one suckling of the children of thy people which they had thrown into the river. 15 And on the fourteenth day and on the fifteenth and on the sixteenth and on the seventeenth and on the eighteenth the prince Mastêmâ was bound and imprisoned behind the children of Israel that he might not accuse them. 16 And on the nineteenth we let them loose that they might help the Egyptians and pursue the children of Israel. 17 And he hardened their hearts and made them stubborn, and the device was devised by the Lord our God that He might smite the Egyptians and cast them into the sea. 18 And on the fourteenth we bound him that he might not accuse the children of Israel on the day when they asked the Egyptians for vessels and garments, vessels of silver, and vessels of gold, and vessels of bronze, in order to despoil the Egyptians in return for the bondage in which they had forced them to serve. 19 And we did not lead forth the children of Israel from Egypt empty handed.

Jub. 49

The Passover: regulations regarding its celebration. (Cf. Exod. xii.6, 9, 11, 13, 22-3, 30, 46; xv.22.) 1 Remember the commandment which the Lord commanded thee concerning the passover, that thou shouldst celebrate it in its season on the fourteenth of the first month, that thou shouldst kill it before it is evening, and that they should eat it by night on the evening of the fifteenth from the time of the setting of the sun. 2 For on this night -the beginning of the festival and the beginning of the joy- ye were eating the passover in Egypt, when all the powers of Mastêmâ had been let loose to slay all the first-born in the land of Egypt, from the first-born of Pharaoh to the first-born of the captive maid-servant in the mill, and to the cattle. 3 And this is the sign which the Lord gave them: Into every house on the lintels of which they saw the blood of a lamb of the first year, into (that) house they should not enter to slay, but should pass by (it), that all those should be saved that were in the house because the sign of the blood was on its lintels. 4 And the powers of the Lord did everything according as the Lord commanded them, and they passed by all the children of Israel, and the plague came not upon them to destroy from amongst them any soul either of cattle, or man, or dog. 5 And the plague was very grievous in Egypt, and there was no house in Egypt where there was not one dead, and weeping and lamentation. 6 And all Israel was eating the flesh of the paschal lamb, and drinking the wine, and was lauding, and blessing, and giving thanks to the Lord God of their fathers, and was ready to go forth from under the yoke of Egypt, and from the evil bondage. 7 And remember thou this day all the days of thy life, and observe it from year to year all the days of thy life, once a year, on its day, according to all the law thereof, and do not adjourn (it) from day to day, or from month to month. 8 For it is an eternal ordinance, and engraven on the heavenly tablets regarding all the children of Israel that they should observe it every year on its day once a year, throughout all their generations; and there is no limit of days, for this is ordained for ever. 9 And the man who is free from uncleanness, and does not come to observe it on occasion of its day, so as to bring an acceptable offering before the Lord, and to eat and to drink before the Lord on the day of its festival, that man who is clean and close at hand shall be cut off: because he offered not the oblation of the Lord in its appointed season, he shall take the guilt upon himself. 10 Let the children of Israel come and observe the passover on the day of its fixed time, on the fourteenth day of the first month, between the evenings, from the third part of the day to the third part of the night, for two portions of the day are given to the light, and a third part to the evening. 11 This is that which the Lord commanded thee that thou shouldst observe it between the evenings. 12 And it is not permissible to slay it during any period of the light, but during the period bordering on the evening, and let them eat it at the time of the evening, until the third part of the night, and whatever is left over of all its flesh from the third part of the night and onwards, let them burn it with fire. 13 And they shall not cook it with water, nor shall they eat it raw, but roast on the fire: they shall eat it with diligence, its head with the inwards thereof and its feet they shall roast with fire, and not break any bone thereof; for of the children of Israel no bone shall be crushed. 14 For this reason the Lord commanded the children of Israel to observe the passover on the day of its fixed time, and they shall not break a bone thereof; for it is a festival day, and a day commanded, and there may be no passing over from day to day, and month to month, but on the day of its festival let it be observed. 15 And do thou command the children of Israel to observe the passover throughout their days, every year, once a year on the day of its fixed time, and it shall come for a memorial well pleasing before the Lord, and no plague shall come upon them to slay or to smite in that year in which they celebrate the passover in its season in every respect according to His command. 16 And they shall not eat it outside the sanctuary of the Lord, but before the sanctuary of the Lord, and all the people of the congregation of Israel shall celebrate it in its appointed season. 17 And every man who has come upon its day shall eat it in the sanctuary of your God before the Lord from twenty years old and upward; for thus is it written and ordained that they should eat it in the sanctuary of the Lord. [18] And when the children of Israel come into the land which they are to possess, into the land of Canaan, and set up the tabernacle of the Lord in the midst of the land in one of their tribes until the sanctuary of the Lord has been built in the land, let them come and celebrate the passover in the midst of the tabernacle of the Lord, and let them slay it before the Lord from year to year. [19] And in the days when the house has been built in the name of the Lord in the land of their inheritance, they shall go there and slay the passover in the evening, at sunset, at the third part of the day. [20] And they shall offer its blood on the threshold of the altar, and shall place its fat on the fire which is upon the altar, and they shall eat its flesh roasted with fire in the court of the house which has been sanctified in the name of the Lord. [21] And they may not celebrate the passover in their cities, nor in any place save before the tabernacle of the Lord, or before His house where His name hath dwelt; and they shall not go astray from the Lord. [22] And do thou, Moses, command the children of Israel to observe the ordinances of the passover, as it was commanded unto thee; declare thou unto them every year and the day of its days, and the festival of unleavened bread, that they should eat unleavened bread seven days, (and) that they should observe its festival, and that they bring an oblation every day during those seven days of joy before the Lord on the altar of your God. [23] For ye celebrated this festival with haste when ye went forth from Egypt till ye entered into the wilderness of Shur; for on the shore of the sea ye completed it.

Jub. 50

Laws regarding the jubilees, 1-5, and the Sabbath, 6-13. [1] And after this law I made known to thee the days of the Sabbaths in the desert of Sin[ai], which is between Elim and Sinai. [2] And I told thee of the Sabbaths of the land on Mount Sinai, and I told thee of the jubilee years in the sabbaths of years: but the year thereof have I not told thee till ye enter the land which ye are to possess. [3] And the land also shall keep its sabbaths while they dwell upon it, and they shall know the jubilee year. [4] Wherefore I have ordained for thee the year-weeks and the years and the jubilees: there are forty-nine jubilees from the days of Adam until this day, [2410 A.M.] and one week and two years: and there are yet forty years to come (lit. 'distant') for learning the [2450 A.M.] commandments of the Lord, until they pass over into the land of Canaan, crossing the Jordan to the west. [5] And the jubilees shall pass by, until Israel is cleansed from all guilt of fornication, and uncleanness, and pollution, and sin, and error, and dwells with confidence in all the land, and there shall be no more a Satan or any evil one, and the land shall be clean from that time for evermore. [6] And behold the commandment regarding the Sabbaths -I have written (them) down for thee- and all the judgments of its laws. [7] Six days shalt thou labour, but on the seventh day is the Sabbath of the Lord your God. In it ye shall do no manner of work, ye and your sons, and your men- servants and your maid-servants, and all your cattle and the sojourner also who is with you. [8] And the man that does any work on it shall die: whoever desecrates that day, whoever lies with (his) wife, or whoever says he will do something on it, that he will set out on a journey thereon in regard to any buying or selling: and whoever draws water thereon which he had not prepared for himself on the sixth day, and whoever takes up any burden to carry it out of his tent or out of his house shall die. [9] Ye shall do no work whatever on the Sabbath day save what ye have prepared for yourselves on the sixth day, so as to eat, and drink, and rest, and keep Sabbath from all work on that day, and to bless the Lord your God, who has given you a day of festival and a holy day: and a day of the holy kingdom for all Israel is this day among their days for ever. [10] For great is the honour which the Lord has given to

Israel that they should eat and drink and be satisfied on this festival day, and rest thereon from all labour which belongs to the labour of the children of men save burning frankincense and bringing oblations and sacrifices before the Lord for days and for Sabbaths. [11] This work alone shall be done on the Sabbath-days in the sanctuary of the Lord your God; that they may atone for Israel with sacrifice continually from day to day for a memorial well-pleasing before the Lord, and that He may receive them always from day to day according as thou hast been commanded. [12] And every man who does any work thereon, or goes a journey, or tills (his) farm, whether in his house or any other place, and whoever lights a fire, or rides on any beast, or travels by ship on the sea, and whoever strikes or kills anything, or slaughters a beast or a bird, or whoever catches an animal or a bird or a fish, or whoever fasts or makes war on the Sabbaths: [13] The man who does any of these things on the Sabbath shall die, so that the children of Israel shall observe the Sabbaths according to the commandments regarding the Sabbaths of the land, as it is written in the tablets, which He gave into my hands that I should write out for thee the laws of the seasons, and the seasons according to the division of their days. Herewith is completed the account of the division of the days.

Enoch 1 – The Ethiopian Book of Enoch

The Book of the Watchers
1Enoch 1

[1] The words of the blessing of Enoch, wherewith he blessed the elect and righteous, who will be [2] living in the day of tribulation, when all the wicked and godless are to be removed. And he took up his parable and said -Enoch a righteous man, whose eyes were opened by God, saw the vision of the Holy One in the heavens, which the angels showed me, and from them I heard everything, and from them I understood as I saw, but not for this generation, but for a remote one which is for to come. [3] Concerning the elect I said, and took up my parable concerning them: The Holy Great One will come forth from His dwelling, [4] And the eternal God will tread upon the earth, (even) on Mount Sinai, [And appear from His camp] And appear in the strength of His might from the heaven of heavens. [5] And all shall be smitten with fear And the Watchers shall quake, And great fear and trembling shall seize them unto the ends of the earth. [6] And the high mountains shall be shaken, And the high hills shall be made low, And shall melt like wax before the flame [7] And the earth shall be wholly rent in sunder, And all that is upon the earth shall perish, And there shall be a judgement upon all (men). [8] But with the righteous He will make peace. And will protect the elect, And mercy shall be upon them. And they shall all belong to God, And they shall be prospered, And they shall all be blessed. And He will help them all, And light shall appear unto them, And He will make peace with them'. [9] And behold! He cometh with ten thousands of His holy ones To execute judgement upon all, And to destroy all the ungodly: And to convict all flesh Of all the works of their ungodliness which they have ungodly committed, And of all the hard things which ungodly sinners have spoken against Him.

1Enoch 2

[1] Observe ye everything that takes place in the heaven, how they do not change their orbits, and the luminaries which are in the heaven, how they all rise and set in order each in its season, and [2] transgress not against their appointed order. Behold ye the earth, and give heed to the things which take place upon it from first to last, how steadfast they are, how none of the things upon earth [3] change, but all the works of God appear to you. Behold the summer and the winter, how the whole earth is filled with water, and clouds and dew and rain lie upon it.

1Enoch 3

[1] Observe and see how (in the winter) all the trees seem as though they had withered and shed all their leaves, except fourteen trees, which do not lose their foliage but retain the old foliage from two to three years till the new comes.

1Enoch 4

[1] And again, observe ye the days of summer how the sun is above the earth over against it. And you seek shade and shelter by reason of the heat of the sun, and the earth also burns with growing heat, and so you cannot tread on the earth, or on a rock by reason of its heat.

1Enoch 5

[1] Observe ye how the trees cover themselves with green leaves and bear fruit: wherefore give ye heed and know with regard to all His works, and recognize how He that liveth for ever hath made them so. [2] and all His works go on thus from year to year for ever, and all the tasks which they accomplish for Him, and their tasks change not, but according as God hath ordained so is it done. [3] And behold how the sea and the rivers in like manner accomplish and change not their tasks from His commandments'. [4] But ye -ye have not been steadfast, nor done the commandments of the Lord, But ye have turned away and spoken proud and hard words With your impure mouths against His greatness. Oh, ye hard-hearted, ye shall find no peace. [5] Therefore shall ye execrate your days, And the years of your life shall perish, And the years of your destruction shall be multiplied in eternal execration, And ye shall find no mercy. 6a In those days ye shall make your names an eternal execration unto all the righteous, 6b And by you shall all who curse, curse, And all the sinners and godless shall imprecate by you, 6c And for you the godless there shall be a curse. 6d And all the . . . shall rejoice, 6e And there shall be forgiveness of sins, 6f And every mercy and peace and forbearance: 6g There shall be salvation unto them, a goodly light. 6h And for all of you sinners there shall be no salvation, 6i But on you all shall abide a curse. 7a But for the elect there shall be light and joy and peace, 7b And they shall inherit the earth. [8] And then there shall be bestowed upon the elect wisdom, And they shall all live and never again sin, Either through ungodliness or through pride: But they who are wise shall be humble. [9] And they shall not again transgress, Nor shall they sin all the days of their life, Nor shall they die of (the divine) anger or wrath, But they shall complete the number of the days of their life. And their lives shall be increased in peace, And the years of their joy shall be multiplied, In eternal gladness and peace, All the days of their life.

1Enoch 6

[1] And it came to pass when the children of men had multiplied that in those days were born unto them beautiful and comely daughters. [2] And the angels, the children of the heaven, saw and lusted after them, and said to one another: 'Come, let us choose us wives from among the children of men [3] and beget us children.' And Semjaza, who was their leader, said unto them: 'I fear ye will not [4] indeed agree to do this deed, and I alone shall have to pay the penalty of a great sin.' And they all answered him and said: 'Let us all swear an oath, and all bind ourselves by mutual imprecations [5] not to abandon this plan but to do this thing.' Then sware they all together and bound themselves [6] by mutual imprecations upon it. And they were in all two hundred; who descended in the days of Jared on the summit of Mount Hermon, and they called it Mount Hermon, because they had sworn [7] and bound themselves by mutual imprecations upon it. And these are the names of their leaders: Samlazaz, their leader, Araklba, Rameel, Kokablel, Tamlel, Ramlel, Danel, Ezeqeel, Baraqijal, [8] Asael, Armaros, Batarel, Ananel, Zaq1el,

Samsapeel, Satarel, Turel, Jomjael, Sariel. These are their chiefs of tens.

1Enoch 7

[1] And all the others together with them took unto themselves wives, and each chose for himself one, and they began to go in unto them and to defile themselves with them, and they taught them charms 2and enchantments, and the cutting of roots, and made them acquainted with plants. And they [3] became pregnant, and they bare great giants, whose height was three thousand ells: Who consumed [4] all the acquisitions of men. And when men could no longer sustain them, the giants turned against [5] them and devoured mankind. And they began to sin against birds, and beasts, and reptiles, and [6] fish, and to devour one another's flesh, and drink the blood. Then the earth laid accusation against the lawless ones.

1Enoch 8

[1] And Azazel taught men to make swords, and knives, and shields, and breastplates, and made known to them the metals of the earth and the art of working them, and bracelets, and ornaments, and the use of antimony, and the beautifying of the eyelids, and all kinds of costly stones, and all [2] colouring tinctures. And there arose much godlessness, and they committed fornication, and they [3] were led astray, and became corrupt in all their ways. Semjaza taught enchantments, and root-cuttings, 'Armaros the resolving of enchantments, Baraqijal (taught) astrology, Kokabel the constellations, Ezeqeel the knowledge of the clouds, Araqiel the signs of the earth, Shamsiel the signs of the sun, and Sariel the course of the moon. And as men perished, they cried, and their cry went up to heaven . . .

1Enoch 9

[1] And then Michael, Uriel, Raphael, and Gabriel looked down from heaven and saw much blood being [2] shed upon the earth, and all lawlessness being wrought upon the earth. And they said one to another: "The earth made without inhabitant cries the voice of their cryingst up to the gates of heaven. [3] And now to you, the holy ones of heaven, the souls of men make their suit, saying, "Bring our cause [4] before the Most High."' And they said to the Lord of the ages: 'Lord of lords, God of gods, King of kings, and God of the ages, the throne of Thy glory (standeth) unto all the generations of the [5] ages, and Thy name holy and glorious and blessed unto all the ages! Thou hast made all things, and power over all things hast Thou: and all things are naked and open in Thy sight, and Thou seest all [6] things, and nothing can hide itself from Thee. Thou seest what Azazel hath done, who hath taught all unrighteousness on earth and revealed the eternal secrets which were (preserved) in heaven, which [7] men were striving to learn: And Semjaza, to whom Thou hast given authority to bear rule over his associates. And they have gone to the daughters of men upon the earth, and have slept with the [9] women, and have defiled themselves, and revealed to them all kinds of sins. And the women have [10] borne giants, and the whole earth has thereby been filled with blood and unrighteousness. And now, behold, the souls of those who have died are crying and making their suit to the gates of heaven, and their lamentations have ascended: and cannot cease because of the lawless deeds which are [11] wrought on the earth. And Thou knowest all things before they come to pass, and Thou seest these things and Thou dost suffer them, and Thou dost not say to us what we are to do to them in regard to these.'

1Enoch 10

[1] Then said the Most High, the Holy and Great One spake, and sent Uriel to the son of Lamech, [2] and said to him: Go to Noah and tell him in my name "Hide thyself!" and reveal to him the end that is approaching: that the whole earth will be destroyed, and a deluge is

about to come [3] upon the whole earth, and will destroy all that is on it. And now instruct him that he may escape [4] and his seed may be preserved for all the generations of the world. And again the Lord said to Raphael: Bind Azazel hand and foot, and cast him into the darkness: and make an opening [5] in the desert, which is in Dudael, and cast him therein. And place upon him rough and jagged rocks, and cover him with darkness, and let him abide there for ever, and cover his face that he may 6,[7] not see light. And on the day of the great judgement he shall be cast into the fire. And heal the earth which the angels have corrupted, and proclaim the healing of the earth, that they may heal the plague, and that all the children of men may not perish through all the secret things that the [8] Watchers have disclosed and have taught their sons. And the whole earth has been corrupted [9] through the works that were taught by Azazel: to him ascribe all sin. And to Gabriel said the Lord: Proceed against the bastards and the reprobates, and against the children of fornication: and destroy [the children of fornication and] the children of the Watchers from amongst men [and cause them to go forth]: send them one against the other that they may destroy each other in [10] battle: for length of days shall they not have. And no request that they (i.e. their fathers) make of thee shall be granted unto their fathers on their behalf; for they hope to live an eternal life, and [11] that each one of them will live five hundred years. And the Lord said unto Michael: Go, bind Semjaza and his associates who have united themselves with women so as to have defiled themselves [12] with them in all their uncleanness. And when their sons have slain one another, and they have seen the destruction of their beloved ones, bind them fast for seventy generations in the valleys of the earth, till the day of their judgement and of their consummation, till the judgement that is [13] for ever and ever is consummated. In those days they shall be led off to the abyss of fire: and [14] to the torment and the prison in which they shall be confined for ever. And whosoever shall be condemned and destroyed will from thenceforth be bound together with them to the end of all [15] generations. And destroy all the spirits of the reprobate and the children of the Watchers, because [16] they have wronged mankind. Destroy all wrong from the face of the earth and let every evil work come to an end: and let the plant of righteousness and truth appear: and it shall prove a blessing; the works of righteousness and truth shall be planted in truth and joy for evermore. [17] And then shall all the righteous escape, And shall live till they beget thousands of children, And all the days of their youth and their old age Shall they complete in peace. [18] And then shall the whole earth be tilled in righteousness, and shall all be planted with trees and [19] be full of blessing. And all desirable trees shall be planted on it, and they shall plant vines on it: and the vine which they plant thereon shall yield wine in abundance, and as for all the seed which is sown thereon each measure (of it) shall bear a thousand, and each measure of olives shall yield [20] ten presses of oil. And cleanse thou the earth from all oppression, and from all unrighteousness, and from all sin, and from all godlessness: and all the uncleanness that is wrought upon the earth [21] destroy from off the earth. And all the children of men shall become righteous, and all nations [22] shall offer adoration and shall praise Me, and all shall worship Me. And the earth shall be cleansed from all defilement, and from all sin, and from all punishment, and from all torment, and I will never again send (them) upon it from generation to generation and for ever.

1Enoch 11

[1] And in those days I will open the store chambers of blessing which are in the heaven, so as to send [2] them down upon the earth over the work and labour of the children of men. And truth and peace shall be associated together throughout all the days of the world and throughout all the generations of men.

1Enoch 12

[1] Before these things Enoch was hidden, and no one of the children of men knew where he was [2] hidden, and where he abode, and what had become of him. And his activities had to do with the Watchers, and his days were with the holy ones. [3] And I Enoch was blessing the Lord of majesty and the King of the ages, and lo! the Watchers 4called me -Enoch the scribe- and said to me: 'Enoch, thou scribe of righteousness, go, declare to the Watchers of the heaven who have left the high heaven, the holy eternal place, and have defiled themselves with women, and have done as the children of earth do, and have taken unto themselves 5wives: "Ye have wrought great destruction on the earth: And ye shall have no peace nor forgiveness [6] of sin: and inasmuch as they delight themselves in their children, The murder of their beloved ones shall they see, and over the destruction of their children shall they lament, and shall make supplication unto eternity, but mercy and peace shall ye not attain."

1Enoch 13

[1] And Enoch went and said: Azazel, thou shalt have no peace: a severe sentence has gone forth [2] against thee to put thee in bonds: And thou shalt not have toleration nor request granted to thee, because of the unrighteousness which thou hast taught, and because of all the works of godlessness [3] and unrighteousness and sin which thou hast shown to men. Then I went and spoke to them all [4] together, and they were all afraid, and fear and trembling seized them. And they besought me to draw up a petition for them that they might find forgiveness, and to read their petition in the presence [5] of the Lord of heaven. For from thenceforward they could not speak (with Him) nor lift up their [6] eyes to heaven for shame of their sins for which they had been condemned. Then I wrote out their petition, and the prayer in regard to their spirits and their deeds individually and in regard to their [7] requests that they should have forgiveness and length. And I went off and sat down at the waters of Dan, in the land of Dan, to the south of the west of Hermon: I read their petition till I fell [8] asleep. And behold a dream came to me, and visions fell down upon me, and I saw visions of chastisement, and a voice came bidding (me) I to tell it to the sons of heaven, and reprimand them. [9] And when I awaked, I came unto them, and they were all sitting gathered together, weeping in [10] Abelsjail, which is between Lebanon and Seneser, with their faces covered. And I recounted before them all the visions which I had seen in sleep, and I began to speak the words of righteousness, and to reprimand the heavenly Watchers.

1Enoch 14

[1] The book of the words of righteousness, and of the reprimand of the eternal Watchers in accordance [2] with the command of the Holy Great One in that vision. I saw in my sleep what I will now say with a tongue of flesh and with the breath of my mouth: which the Great One has given to men to [3] converse therewith and understand with the heart. As He has created and given to man the power of understanding the word of wisdom, so hath He created me also and given me the power of reprimanding [4] the Watchers, the children of heaven. I wrote out your petition, and in my vision it appeared thus, that your petition will not be granted unto you throughout all the days of eternity, and that judgement [5] has been finally passed upon you: yea (your petition) will not be granted unto you. And from henceforth you shall not ascend into heaven unto all eternity, and in bonds of the earth the decree [6] has gone forth to bind you for all the days of the world. And (that) previously you shall have seen the destruction of your beloved sons and ye shall have no pleasure in them, but they shall fall before [7] you by the sword. And your petition

on their behalf shall not be granted, nor yet on your own: even though you weep and pray and speak all the words contained in the writing which I have [8] written. And the vision was shown to me thus: Behold, in the vision clouds invited me and a mist summoned me, and the course of the stars and the lightnings sped and hastened me, and the winds in [9] the vision caused me to fly and lifted me upward, and bore me into heaven. And I went in till I drew nigh to a wall which is built of crystals and surrounded by tongues of fire: and it began to affright [10] me. And I went into the tongues of fire and drew nigh to a large house which was built of crystals: and the walls of the house were like a tesselated floor (made) of crystals, and its groundwork was [11] of crystal. Its ceiling was like the path of the stars and the lightnings, and between them were [12] fiery cherubim, and their heaven was (clear as) water. A flaming fire surrounded the walls, and its [13] portals blazed with fire. And I entered into that house, and it was hot as fire and cold as ice: there [14] were no delights of life therein: fear covered me, and trembling got hold upon me. And as I quaked [15] and trembled, I fell upon my face. And I beheld a vision, And lo! there was a second house, greater [16] than the former, and the entire portal stood open before me, and it was built of flames of fire. And in every respect it so excelled in splendour and magnificence and extent that I cannot describe to [17] you its splendour and its extent. And its floor was of fire, and above it were lightnings and the path 18of the stars, and its ceiling also was flaming fire. And I looked and saw therein a lofty throne: its appearance was as crystal, and the wheels thereof as the shining sun, and there was the vision of [19] cherubim. And from underneath the throne came streams of flaming fire so that I could not look [20] thereon. And the Great Glory sat thereon, and His raiment shone more brightly than the sun and [21] was whiter than any snow. None of the angels could enter and could behold His face by reason [22] of the magnificence and glory and no flesh could behold Him. The flaming fire was round about Him, and a great fire stood before Him, and none around could draw nigh Him: ten thousand times [23] ten thousand (stood) before Him, yet He needed no counselor. And the most holy ones who were [24] nigh to Him did not leave by night nor depart from Him. And until then I had been prostrate on my face, trembling: and the Lord called me with His own mouth, and said to me: ' Come hither, [25] Enoch, and hear my word.' And one of the holy ones came to me and waked me, and He made me rise up and approach the door: and I bowed my face downwards.

1Enoch 15

[1] And He answered and said to me, and I heard His voice: 'Fear not, Enoch, thou righteous [2] man and scribe of righteousness: approach hither and hear my voice. And go, say to the Watchers of heaven, who have sent thee to intercede for them: "You should intercede" for men, and not men [3] for you: Wherefore have ye left the high, holy, and eternal heaven, and lain with women, and defiled yourselves with the daughters of men and taken to yourselves wives, and done like the children [4] of earth, and begotten giants (as your) sons? And though ye were holy, spiritual, living the eternal life, you have defiled yourselves with the blood of women, and have begotten (children) with the blood of flesh, and, as the children of men, have lusted after flesh and blood as those also do who die [5] and perish. Therefore have I given them wives also that they might impregnate them, and beget [6] children by them, that thus nothing might be wanting to them on earth. But you were formerly [7] spiritual, living the eternal life, and immortal for all generations of the world. And therefore I have not appointed wives for you; for as for the spiritual ones of the heaven, in heaven is their dwelling. [8] And now, the giants, who are produced from the spirits and flesh, shall be called evil spirits upon [9] the earth, and on the earth shall be their dwelling. Evil

spirits have proceeded from their bodies; because they are born from men and from the holy Watchers is their beginning and primal origin; [10] they shall be evil spirits on earth, and evil spirits shall they be called. [As for the spirits of heaven, in heaven shall be their dwelling, but as for the spirits of the earth which were born upon the earth, on the earth shall be their dwelling.] [11] And the spirits of the giants afflict, oppress, destroy, attack, do battle, and work destruction on the earth, and cause trouble: they take no food, but nevertheless [12] hunger and thirst, and cause offences. And these spirits shall rise up against the children of men and against the women, because they have proceeded from them.

1Enoch 16

[1] From the days of the slaughter and destruction and death of the giants, from the souls of whose flesh the spirits, having gone forth, shall destroy without incurring judgement -thus shall they destroy until the day of the consummation, the great judgement in which the age shall be [2] consummated, over the Watchers and the godless, yea, shall be wholly consummated." And now as to the Watchers who have sent thee to intercede for them, who had been aforetime in heaven, say to them: [3] "You have been in heaven, but all the mysteries had not yet been revealed to you, and you knew worthless ones, and these in the hardness of your hearts you have made known to the women, and through these mysteries women and men work much evil on earth." [4] Say to them therefore: " You have no peace.'"

1Enoch 17

[1] And they took and brought me to a place in which those who were there were like flaming fire, [2] and, when they wished, they appeared as men. And they brought me to the place of darkness, and to a mountain the point of whose summit reached to heaven. [3] And I saw the places of the luminaries and the treasuries of the stars and of the thunder and in the uttermost depths, where were [4] a fiery bow and arrows and their quiver, and a fiery sword and all the lightnings. And they took [5] me to the living waters, and to the fire of the west, which receives every setting of the sun. And I came to a river of fire in which the fire flows like water and discharges itself into the great sea towards [6] the west. I saw the great rivers and came to the great river and to the great darkness, and went [7] to the place where no flesh walks. I saw the mountains of the darkness of winter and the place [8] whence all the waters of the deep flow. I saw the mouths of all the rivers of the earth and the mouth of the deep.

1Enoch 18

[1] I saw the treasuries of all the winds: I saw how He had furnished with them the whole creation [2] and the firm foundations of the earth. And I saw the corner-stone of the earth: I saw the four [3] winds which bear [the earth and] the firmament of the heaven. And I saw how the winds stretch out the vaults of heaven, and have their station between heaven and earth: these are the pillars [4] of the heaven. I saw the winds of heaven which turn and bring the circumference of the sun and [5] all the stars to their setting. I saw the winds on the earth carrying the clouds: I saw the paths [6] of the angels. I saw at the end of the earth the firmament of the heaven above. And I proceeded and saw a place which burns day and night, where there are seven mountains of magnificent stones, [7] three towards the east, and three towards the south. And as for those towards the east, was of coloured stone, and one of pearl, and one of jacinth, and those towards the south of red stone. [8] But the middle one reached to heaven like the throne of God, of alabaster, and the summit of the 9,10 throne was of sapphire. And I saw a flaming fire. And beyond these mountains Is a region the end of the great earth: there the heavens were completed. [11] And I saw a deep abyss, with columns of heavenly fire, and among them I saw columns of fire fall, which were beyond measure alike towards [12] the height and towards the

depth. And beyond that abyss I saw a place which had no firmament of the heaven above, and no firmly founded earth beneath it: there was no water upon it, and no [13] birds, but it was a waste and horrible place. I saw there seven stars like great burning mountains, [14] and to me, when I inquired regarding them, The angel said: 'This place is the end of heaven and earth: this has become a prison for the stars and the host of heaven. 15And the stars which roll over the fire are they which have transgressed the commandment of the Lord in the beginning of [16] their rising, because they did not come forth at their appointed times. And He was wroth with them, and bound them till the time when their guilt should be consummated (even) for ten thousand years.'

1Enoch 19

[1] And Uriel said to me: 'Here shall stand the angels who have connected themselves with women, and their spirits assuming many different forms are defiling mankind and shall lead them astray into sacrificing to demons as gods, (here shall they stand,) till the day of the great judgement in [2] which they shall be judged till they are made an end of. And the women also of the angels who [3] went astray shall become sirens.' And I, Enoch, alone saw the vision, the ends of all things: and no man shall see as I have seen.

1Enoch 20

[1,2] And these are the names of the holy angels who watch. Uriel, one of the holy angels, who is [3] over the world and over Tartarus. Raphael, one of the holy angels, who is over the spirits of men. [4,5] Raguel, one of the holy angels who takes vengeance on the world of the luminaries. Michael, one [6] of the holy angels, to wit, he that is set over the best part of mankind and over chaos. Saraqael, [7] one of the holy angels, who is set over the spirits, who sin in the spirit. Gabriel, one of the holy [8] angels, who is over Paradise and the serpents and the Cherubim. Remiel, one of the holy angels, whom God set over those who rise.

1Enoch 21

[1,2] And I proceeded to where things were chaotic. And I saw there something horrible: I saw neither [3] a heaven above nor a firmly founded earth, but a place chaotic and horrible. And there I saw [4] seven stars of the heaven bound together in it, like great mountains and burning with fire. Then [5] I said: 'For what sin are they bound, and on what account have they been cast in hither?' Then said Uriel, one of the holy angels, who was with me, and was chief over them, and said: 'Enoch, why [6] dost thou ask, and why art thou eager for the truth? These are of the number of the stars of heaven, which have transgressed the commandment of the Lord, and are bound here till ten thousand years, [7] the time entailed by their sins, are consummated.' And from thence I went to another place, which was still more horrible than the former, and I saw a horrible thing: a great fire there which burnt and blazed, and the place was cleft as far as the abyss, being full of great descending columns of [8] fire: neither its extent or magnitude could I see, nor could I conjecture. Then I said: 'How [9] fearful is the place and how terrible to look upon!' Then Uriel answered me, one of the holy angels who was with me, and said unto me: 'Enoch, why hast thou such fear and affright?' And [10] I answered: 'Because of this fearful place, and because of the spectacle of the pain.' And he said unto me: "This place is the prison of the angels, and here they will be imprisoned for ever.'

1Enoch 22

[1] And thence I went to another place, and he mountain [and] of hard rock. [2] And there was in it four hollow places, deep and wide and very smooth. How smooth are the hollow places and deep and dark to look at. [3] Then Raphael answered, one of the holy angels who was with me, and said unto me: "These hollow places have been created

169

for this very purpose, that the spirits of the souls of the dead should [4] assemble therein, yea that all the souls of the children of men should assemble here. And these places have been made to receive them till the day of their judgement and till their appointed period [till the period appointed], till the great judgement (comes) upon them.' I saw (the spirit of) a dead man making suit, [5] and his voice went forth to heaven and made suit. And I asked Raphael the angel who was [6] with me, and I said unto him: "This spirit which maketh suit, whose is it, whose voice goeth forth and maketh suit to heaven ?' [7] And he answered me saying: "This is the spirit which went forth from Abel, whom his brother Cain slew, and he makes his suit against him till his seed is destroyed from the face of the earth, and his seed is annihilated from amongst the seed of men.' [8] The I asked regarding it, and regarding all the hollow places: 'Why is one separated from the other?' [9] And he answered me and said unto me: 'These three have been made that the spirits of the dead might be separated. And such a division has been make (for) the spirits of the righteous, in which there is the bright spring of [10] water. And such has been made for sinners when they die and are buried in the earth and judgement has not been executed on them in their [11] lifetime. Here their spirits shall be set apart in this great pain till the great day of judgement and punishment and torment of those who curse for ever and retribution for their spirits. There [12] He shall bind them for ever. And such a division has been made for the spirits of those who make their suit, who make disclosures concerning their destruction, when they were slain in the days [13] of the sinners. Such has been made for the spirits of men who were not righteous but sinners, who were complete in transgression, and of the transgressors they shall be companions: but their spirits shall not be slain in the day of judgement nor shall they be raised from thence.' [14] The I blessed the Lord of glory and said: 'Blessed be my Lord, the Lord of righteousness, who ruleth for ever.'

1Enoch 23

[1,2] From thence I went to another place to the west of the ends of the earth. And I saw a burning [3] fire which ran without resting, and paused not from its course day or night but (ran) regularly. And [4] I asked saying: 'What is this which rests not?' Then Raguel, one of the holy angels who was with me, answered me and said unto me: "This course of fire which thou hast seen is the fire in the west which persecutes all the luminaries of heaven.'

1Enoch 24

[1] And from thence I went to another place of the earth, and he showed me a mountain range of [2] fire which burnt day and night. And I went beyond it and saw seven magnificent mountains all differing each from the other, and the stones (thereof) were magnificent and beautiful, magnificent as a whole, of glorious appearance and fair exterior: three towards the east, one founded on the other, and three towards the south, one upon the other, and deep rough ravines, no one of which [3] joined with any other. And the seventh mountain was in the midst of these, and it excelled them [4] in height, resembling the seat of a throne: and fragrant trees encircled the throne. And amongst them was a tree such as I had never yet smelt, neither was any amongst them nor were others like it: it had a fragrance beyond all fragrance, and its leaves and blooms and wood wither not for ever: [5] and its fruit is beautiful, and its fruit n resembles the dates of a palm. Then I said: 'How beautiful is this tree, and fragrant, and its leaves are fair, and its blooms very delightful in appearance.' [6] Then answered Michael, one of the holy and honoured angels who was with me, and was their leader.

1Enoch 25

[1] And he said unto me: 'Enoch, why dost thou ask me regarding the fragrance of the tree, [2] and why dost thou wish to learn the truth?'

Then I answered him saying: 'I wish to [3] know about everything, but especially about this tree.' And he answered saying: "This high mountain which thou hast seen, whose summit is like the throne of God, is His throne, where the Holy Great One, the Lord of Glory, the Eternal King, will sit, when He shall come down to visit [4] the earth with goodness. And as for this fragrant tree no mortal is permitted to touch it till the great judgement, when He shall take vengeance on all and bring (everything) to its consummation [5] for ever. It shall then be given to the righteous and holy. Its fruit shall be for food to the elect: it shall be transplanted to the holy place, to the temple of the Lord, the Eternal King. [6] Then shall they rejoice with joy and be glad, And into the holy place shall they enter; And its fragrance shall be in their bones, And they shall live a long life on earth, Such as thy fathers lived: And in their days shall no sorrow or plague Or torment or calamity touch them.' [7] Then blessed I the God of Glory, the Eternal King, who hath prepared such things for the righteous, and hath created them and promised to give to them.

1Enoch 26

[1] And I went from thence to the middle of the earth, and I saw a blessed place in which there were [2] trees with branches abiding and blooming [of a dismembered tree]. And there I saw a holy mountain, [3] and underneath the mountain to the east there was a stream and it flowed towards the south. And I saw towards the east another mountain higher than this, and between them a deep and narrow [4] ravine: in it also ran a stream underneath the mountain. And to the west thereof there was another mountain, lower than the former and of small elevation, and a ravine deep and dry between them: and another deep and dry ravine was at the extremities of the three mountains. [5] And all the ravines were deep rand narrow, (being formed) of hard rock, and trees were not planted upon [6] them. And I marveled at the rocks, and I marveled at the ravine, yea, I marveled very much.

1Enoch 27

[1] Then said I: 'For what object is this blessed land, which is entirely filled with trees, and this [2] accursed valley between?' Then Uriel, one of the holy angels who was with me, answered and said: "This accursed valley is for those who are accursed for ever: Here shall all the accursed be gathered together who utter with their lips against the Lord unseemly words and of His glory speak hard things. Here shall they be gathered together, and here [3] shall be their place of judgement. In the last days there shall be upon them the spectacle of righteous judgement in the presence of the righteous for ever: here shall the merciful bless the Lord of glory, the Eternal King. [4] In the days of judgement over the former, they shall bless Him for the mercy in accordance with [5] which He has assigned them (their lot).' Then I blessed the Lord of Glory and set forth His glory and lauded Him gloriously.

1Enoch 28

[1] And thence I went towards the east, into the midst of the mountain range of the desert, and [2] I saw a wilderness and it was solitary, full of trees and plants. And water gushed forth from [3] above. Rushing like a copious watercourse [which flowed] towards the north-west it caused clouds and dew to ascend on every side.

1Enoch 29

[1] And thence I went to another place in the desert, and approached to the east of this mountain range. [2] And there I saw aromatic trees exhaling the fragrance of frankincense and myrrh, and the trees also were similar to the almond tree.

1Enoch 30

[1,2] And beyond these, I went afar to the east, and I saw another place, a valley (full) of water. And [3] therein there was a tree, the colour (?) of fragrant trees such as the mastic. And on the sides of those valleys I saw fragrant cinnamon. And beyond these I proceeded to the east.

1Enoch 31

[1] And I saw other mountains, and amongst them were groves of trees, and there flowed forth from [2] them nectar, which is named sarara and galbanum. And beyond these mountains I saw another mountain to the east of the ends of the earth, whereon were aloe-trees, and all the trees were full [3] of stacte, being like almond-trees. And when one burnt it, it smelt sweeter than any fragrant odour.

1Enoch 32

[1] And after these fragrant odours, as I looked towards the north over the mountains I saw seven mountains full of choice nard and fragrant trees and cinnamon and pepper. [2] And thence I went over the summits of all these mountains, far towards the east of the earth, and passed above the Erythraean sea and went far from it, and passed over the angel Zotiel. And I came to the Garden of Righteousness, [3] I and from afar off trees more numerous than I these trees and great-two trees there, very great, beautiful, and glorious, and magnificent, and the tree of knowledge, whose holy fruit they eat and know great wisdom. [4] That tree is in height like the fir, and its leaves are like (those of) the Carob tree: and its fruit [5] is like the clusters of the vine, very beautiful: and the fragrance of the tree penetrates afar. Then [6] I said: 'How beautiful is the tree, and how attractive is its look!' Then Raphael the holy angel, who was with me, answered me and said: "This is the tree of wisdom, of which thy father old (in years) and thy aged mother, who were before thee, have eaten, and they learnt wisdom and their eyes were opened, and they knew that they were naked and they were driven out of the garden.'

1Enoch 33

[1] And from thence I went to the ends of the earth and saw there great beasts, and each differed from the other; and (I saw) birds also differing in appearance and beauty and voice, the one differing from the other. And to the east of those beasts I saw the ends of the earth whereon the heaven [2] rests, and the portals of the heaven open. And I saw how the stars of heaven come forth, and [3] I counted the portals out of which they proceed, and wrote down all their outlets, of each individual star by itself, according to their number and their names, their courses and their positions, and their [4] times and their months, as Uriel the holy angel who was with me showed me. He showed all things to me and wrote them down for me: also their names he wrote for me, and their laws and their companies.

1Enoch 34

[1] And from thence I went towards the north to the ends of the earth, and there I saw a great and [2] glorious device at the ends of the whole earth. And here I saw three portals of heaven open in the heaven: through each of them proceed north winds: when they blow there is cold, hail, frost, [3] snow, dew, and rain. And out of one portal they blow for good: but when they blow through the other two portals, it is with violence and affliction on the earth, and they blow with violence.

1Enoch 35

[1] And from thence I went towards the west to the ends of the earth, and saw there three portals of the heaven open such as I had seen in the east, the same number of portals, and the same number of outlets.

1Enoch 36

[1] And from thence I went to the south to the ends of the earth, and saw there three open portals [2] of the heaven: and thence there come dew, rain, and wind. And from thence I went to the east to the ends of the heaven, and saw here the three eastern portals of heaven open and small portals [3] above them. Through each of these small portals

pass the stars of heaven and run their course to the west on the path which is shown to them. And as often as I saw I blessed always the Lord of Glory, and I continued to bless the Lord of Glory who has wrought great and glorious wonders, to show the greatness of His work to the angels and to spirits and to men, that they might praise His work and all His creation: that they might see the work of His might and praise the great work of His hands and bless Him for ever.

The Book of Parables

1Enoch 37

[1] The second vision which he saw, the vision of wisdom -which Enoch the son of Jared, the son [2] of Mahalalel, the son of Cainan, the son of Enos, the son of Seth, the son of Adam, saw. And this is the beginning of the words of wisdom which I lifted up my voice to speak and say to those which dwell on earth: Hear, ye men of old time, and see, ye that come after, the words of the Holy [3] One which I will speak before the Lord of Spirits. It were better to declare (them only) to the men of old time, but even from those that come after we will not withhold the beginning of wisdom. [4] Till the present day such wisdom has never been given by the Lord of Spirits as I have received according to my insight, according to the good pleasure of the Lord of Spirits by whom the lot of [5] eternal life has been given to me. Now three Parables were imparted to me, and I lifted up my voice and recounted them to those that dwell on the earth.

1Enoch 38

[1] The first Parable. When the congregation of the righteous shall appear, And sinners shall be judged for their sins, And shall be driven from the face of the earth: [2] And when the Righteous One shall appear before the eyes of the righteous, Whose elect works hang upon the Lord of Spirits, And light shall appear to the righteous and the elect who dwell on the earth, Where then will be the dwelling of the sinners, And where the resting-place of those who have denied the Lord of Spirits? It had been good for them if they had not been born. [3] When the secrets of the righteous shall be revealed and the sinners judged, And the godless driven from the presence of the righteous and elect, [4] From that time those that possess the earth shall no longer be powerful and exalted: And they shall not be able to behold the face of the holy, For the Lord of Spirits has caused His light to appear On the face of the holy, righteous, and elect. [5] Then shall the kings and the mighty perish And be given into the hands of the righteous and holy. [6] And thenceforward none shall seek for themselves mercy from the Lord of Spirits For their life is at an end.

1Enoch 39

[1] And it shall come to pass in those days that elect and holy children will descend from the [2] high heaven, and their seed will become one with the children of men. And in those days Enoch received books of zeal and wrath, and books of disquiet and expulsion. And mercy shall not be accorded to them, saith the Lord of Spirits. [3] And in those days a whirlwind carried me off from the earth, And set me down at the end of the heavens. [4] And there I saw another vision, the dwelling-places of the holy, And the resting-places of the righteous. [5] Here mine eyes saw their dwellings with His righteous angels, And their resting-places with the holy. And they petitioned and interceded and prayed for the children of men, And righteousness flowed before them as water, And mercy like dew upon the earth: Thus it is amongst them for ever and ever. 6a And in that place mine eyes saw the Elect One of righteousness and of faith, And I saw his dwelling-place under the wings of the Lord of Spirits. 6b And righteousness shall prevail in his days, And the righteous and elect shall be without number before Him for ever and ever. [7] And all the righteous and elect before Him shall be strong

as fiery lights, And their mouth shall be full of blessing, And their lips extol the name of the Lord of Spirits, And righteousness before Him shall never fail, [And uprightness shall never fail before Him.] [8] There I wished to dwell, And my spirit longed for that dwelling-place: And there heretofore hath been my portion, For so has it been established concerning me before the Lord of Spirits. [9] In those days I praised and extolled the name of the Lord of Spirits with blessings and praises, because He hath destined me for blessing and glory according to the good pleasure of the Lord of [10] Spirits. For a long time my eyes regarded that place, and I blessed Him and praised Him, saying: Blessed is He, and may He be blessed from the beginning and for evermore. And before Him there is no ceasing. He knows before the world was created what is for ever and what will be from [11] generation unto generation. Those who sleep not bless Thee: they stand before Thy glory and bless, praise, and extol, saying: "Holy, holy, holy, is the Lord of Spirits: He filleth the earth with [12] spirits." And here my eyes saw all those who sleep not: they stand before Him and bless and say: Blessed be Thou, and blessed be the name of the Lord for ever and ever. And my face was changed; for I could no longer behold.

1Enoch 40

[1] And after that I saw thousands of thousands and ten thousand times ten thousand, I saw a multitude [2] beyond number and reckoning, who stood before the Lord of Spirits. And on the four sides of the Lord of Spirits I saw four presences, different from those that sleep not, and I learnt their names: for the angel that went with me made known to me their names, and showed me all the hidden things. [3] And I heard the voices of those four presences as they uttered praises before the Lord of glory. 4,5 The first voice blesses the Lord of Spirits for ever and ever. And the second voice I heard blessing [6] the Elect One and the elect ones who hang upon the Lord of Spirits. And the third voice I heard pray and intercede for those who dwell on the earth and supplicate in the name of the Lord of Spirits. [7] And I heard the fourth voice fending off the Satans and forbidding them to come before the Lord [8] of Spirits to accuse them who dwell on the earth. After that I asked the angel of peace who went with me, who showed me everything that is hidden: Who are these four presences which I have [9] seen and whose words I have heard and written down? And he said to me: This first is Michael, the merciful and long-suffering: and the second, who is set over all the diseases and all the wounds of the children of men, is Raphael: and the third, who is set over all the powers, is Gabriel: and the fourth, who is set over the repentance unto hope of those who inherit eternal life, is named Phanuel. [10] And these are the four angels of the Lord of Spirits and the four voices I heard in those days.

1Enoch 41

[1] And after that I saw all the secrets of the heavens, and how the kingdom is divided, and how the [2] actions of men are weighed in the balance. And there I saw the mansions of the elect and the mansions of the holy, and mine eyes saw there all the sinners being driven from thence which deny the name of the Lord of Spirits, and being dragged off: and they could not abide because of the punishment which proceeds from the Lord of Spirits. [3] And there mine eyes saw the secrets of the lightning and of the thunder, and the secrets of the winds, how they are divided to blow over the earth, and the secrets of the clouds and dew, and these [4] I saw from whence they proceed in that place and from whence they saturate the dusty earth. And there I saw closed chambers out of which the winds are divided, the chamber of the hail and winds, the chamber of the mist, and of the clouds, and the cloud thereof hovers over the earth from the [5] beginning of the world. And I saw the chambers of the sun and moon, whence they proceed and whither they come again, and their

glorious return, and how one is superior to the other, and their stately orbit, and how they do not leave their orbit, and they add nothing to their orbit and they take nothing from it, and they keep faith with each other, in accordance with the oath by which they [6] are bound together. And first the sun goes forth and traverses his path according to the commandment [7] of the Lord of Spirits, and mighty is His name for ever and ever. And after that I saw the hidden and the visible path of the moon, and she accomplishes the course of her path in that place by day and by night-the one holding a position opposite to the other before the Lord of Spirits. And they give thanks and praise and rest not; For unto them is their thanksgiving rest. [8] For the sun changes oft for a blessing or a curse, And the course of the path of the moon is light to the righteous And darkness to the sinners in the name of the Lord, Who made a separation between the light and the darkness, And divided the spirits of men, And strengthened the spirits of the righteous, In the name of His righteousness. [9] For no angel hinders and no power is able to hinder; for He appoints a judge for them all and He judges them all before Him.

1Enoch 42

[1] Wisdom found no place where she might dwell; Then a dwelling-place was assigned her in the heavens. [2] Wisdom went forth to make her dwelling among the children of men, And found no dwelling-place: Wisdom returned to her place, And took her seat among the angels. [3] And unrighteousness went forth from her chambers: Whom she sought not she found, And dwelt with them, As rain in a desert And dew on a thirsty land.

1Enoch 43

[1] And I saw other lightnings and the stars of heaven, and I saw how He called them all by their [2] names and they hearkened unto Him. And I saw how they are weighed in a righteous balance according to their proportions of light: (I saw) the width of their spaces and the day of their appearing, and how their revolution produces lightning: and (I saw) their revolution according to the [3] number of the angels, and (how) they keep faith with each other. And I asked the angel who went [4] with me who showed me what was hidden: What are these? And he said to me: The Lord of Spirits hath showed thee their parabolic meaning (lit. their parable): these are the names of the holy who dwell on the earth and believe in the name of the Lord of Spirits for ever and ever.

1Enoch 44

Also another phenomenon I saw in regard to the lightnings: how some of the stars arise and become lightnings and cannot part with their new form.

1Enoch 45

[1] And this is the second Parable concerning those who deny the name of the dwelling of the holy ones and the Lord of Spirits. [2] And into the heaven they shall not ascend, And on the earth they shall not come: Such shall be the lot of the sinners Who have denied the name of the Lord of Spirits, Who are thus preserved for the day of suffering and tribulation. [3] On that day Mine Elect One shall sit on the throne of glory And shall try their works, And their places of rest shall be innumerable. And their souls shall grow strong within them when they see Mine Elect Ones, And those who have called upon My glorious name: [4] Then will I cause Mine Elect One to dwell among them. And I will transform the heaven and make it an eternal blessing and light [5] And I will transform the earth and make it a blessing: And I will cause Mine elect ones to dwell upon it: But the sinners and evil-doers shall not set foot thereon. [6] For I have provided and satisfied with peace My righteous ones And have caused them to dwell before Me: But for the sinners there is

judgement impending with Me, So that I shall destroy them from the face of the earth.

1Enoch 46

[1] And there I saw One who had a head of days, And His head was white like wool, And with Him was another being whose countenance had the appearance of a man, And his face was full of graciousness, like one of the holy angels. [2] And I asked the angel who went with me and showed me all the hidden things, concerning that [3] Son of Man, who he was, and whence he was, (and) why he went with the Head of Days? And he answered and said unto me: This is the son of Man who hath righteousness, With whom dwelleth righteousness, And who revealeth all the treasures of that which is hidden, Because the Lord of Spirits hath chosen him, And whose lot hath the pre-eminence before the Lord of Spirits in uprightness for ever. [4] And this Son of Man whom thou hast seen Shall raise up the kings and the mighty from their seats, [And the strong from their thrones] And shall loosen the reins of the strong, And break the teeth of the sinners. 5[And he shall put down the kings from their thrones and kingdoms] Because they do not extol and praise Him, Nor humbly acknowledge whence the kingdom was bestowed upon them. [6] And he shall put down the countenance of the strong, And shall fill them with shame. And darkness shall be their dwelling, And worms shall be their bed, And they shall have no hope of rising from their beds, Because they do not extol the name of the Lord of Spirits. [7] And these are they who judge the stars of heaven, [And raise their hands against the Most High], And tread upon the earth and dwell upon it. And all their deeds manifest unrighteousness, And their power rests upon their riches, And their faith is in the gods which they have made with their hands, And they deny the name of the Lord of Spirits, [8] And they persecute the houses of His congregations, And the faithful who hang upon the name of the Lord of Spirits.

1Enoch 47

[1] And in those days shall have ascended the prayer of the righteous, And the blood of the righteous from the earth before the Lord of Spirits. [2] In those days the holy ones who dwell above in the heavens Shall unite with one voice And supplicate and pray and praise, And give thanks and bless the name of the Lord of Spirits On behalf of the blood of the righteous which has been shed, And that the prayer of the righteous may not be in vain before the Lord of Spirits, That judgement may be done unto them, And that they may not have to suffer for ever. [3] In those days I saw the Head of Days when He seated himself upon the throne of His glory, And the books of the living were opened before Him: And all His host which is in heaven above and His counselors stood before Him, [4] And the hearts of the holy were filled with joy; Because the number of the righteous had been offered, And the prayer of the righteous had been heard, And the blood of the righteous been required before the Lord of Spirits.

1Enoch 48

[1] And in that place I saw the fountain of righteousness Which was inexhaustible: And around it were many fountains of wisdom: And all the thirsty drank of them, And were filled with wisdom, And their dwellings were with the righteous and holy and elect. [2] And at that hour that Son of Man was named In the presence of the Lord of Spirits, And his name before the Head of Days. [3] Yea, before the sun and the signs were created, Before the stars of the heaven were made, His name was named before the Lord of Spirits. [4] He shall be a staff to the righteous whereon to stay themselves and not fall, And he shall be the light of the Gentiles, And the hope of those who are troubled of heart. [5] All who dwell on earth shall fall down and worship before him, And will praise and bless and celebrate with song the Lord of Spirits. [6] And for this reason hath he been chosen

and hidden before Him, Before the creation of the world and for evermore. [7] And the wisdom of the Lord of Spirits hath revealed him to the holy and righteous; For he hath preserved the lot of the righteous, Because they have hated and despised this world of unrighteousness, And have hated all its works and ways in the name of the Lord of Spirits: For in his name they are saved, And according to his good pleasure hath it been in regard to their life. [8] In these days downcast in countenance shall the kings of the earth have become, And the strong who possess the land because of the works of their hands, For on the day of their anguish and affliction they shall not (be able to) save themselves. And I will give them over into the hands of Mine elect: 9As straw in the fire so shall they burn before the face of the holy: As lead in the water shall they sink before the face of the righteous, And no trace of them shall any more be found. [10] And on the day of their affliction there shall be rest on the earth, And before them they shall fall and not rise again: And there shall be no one to take them with his hands and raise them: For they have denied the Lord of Spirits and His Anointed. The name of the Lord of Spirits be blessed.

1Enoch 49

[1] For wisdom is poured out like water, And glory faileth not before him for evermore. [2] For he is mighty in all the secrets of righteousness, And unrighteousness shall disappear as a shadow, And have no continuance; Because the Elect One standeth before the Lord of Spirits, And his glory is for ever and ever, And his might unto all generations. [3] And in him dwells the spirit of wisdom, And the spirit which gives insight, And the spirit of understanding and of might, And the spirit of those who have fallen asleep in righteousness. [4] And he shall judge the secret things, And none shall be able to utter a lying word before him; For he is the Elect One before the Lord of Spirits according to His good pleasure.

1Enoch 50

[1] And in those days a change shall take place for the holy and elect, And the light of days shall abide upon them, And glory and honour shall turn to the holy, [2] On the day of affliction on which evil shall have been treasured up against the sinners. And the righteous shall be victorious in the name of the Lord of Spirits: And He will cause the others to witness (this) That they may repent And forgo the works of their hands. [3] They shall have no honour through the name of the Lord of Spirits, Yet through His name shall they be saved, And the Lord of Spirits will have compassion on them, For His compassion is great. [4] And He is righteous also in His judgement, And in the presence of His glory unrighteousness also shall not maintain itself: At His judgement the unrepentant shall perish before Him. [5] And from henceforth I will have no mercy on them, saith the Lord of Spirits.

1Enoch 51

[1] And in those days shall the earth also give back that which has been entrusted to it, And Sheol also shall give back that which it has received, And hell shall give back that which it owes. For in those days the Elect One shall arise, [2] And he shall choose the righteous and holy from among them: For the day has drawn nigh that they should be saved. [3] And the Elect One shall in those days sit on My throne, And his mouth shall pour forth all the secrets of wisdom and counsel: For the Lord of Spirits hath given (them) to him and hath glorified him. [4] And in those days shall the mountains leap like rams, And the hills also shall skip like lambs satisfied with milk, And the faces of [all] 5a the angels in heaven shall be lighted up with joy. 5b And the earth shall rejoice, 5c And the righteous shall dwell upon it, 5d And the elect shall walk thereon.

1Enoch 52

[1] And after those days in that place where I had seen all the visions of that which is hidden, for [2] I had been carried off in a whirlwind and they had borne me towards the west-There mine eyes saw all the secret things of heaven that shall be, a mountain of iron, and a mountain of copper, and a mountain of silver, and a mountain of gold, and a mountain of soft metal, and a mountain of lead. [3] And I asked the angel who went with me, saying, What things are these which I have seen in [4] secret? And he said unto me: All these things which thou hast seen shall serve the dominion of His Anointed that he may be potent and mighty on the earth. [5] And that angel of peace answered, saying unto me: Wait a little, and there shall be revealed unto thee all the secret things which surround the Lord of Spirits. [6] And these mountains which thine eyes have seen, The mountain of iron, and the mountain of copper, and the mountain of silver, And the mountain of gold, and the mountain of soft metal, and the mountain of lead, All these shall be in the presence of the Elect One As wax: before the fire, And like the water which streams down from above [upon those mountains], And they shall become powerless before his feet. [7] And it shall come to pass in those days that none shall be saved, Either by gold or by silver, And none be able to escape. [8] And there shall be no iron for war, Nor shall one clothe oneself with a breastplate. Bronze shall be of no service, And tin [shall be of no service and] shall not be esteemed, And lead shall not be desired. [9] And all these things shall be [denied and] destroyed from the surface of the earth, When the Elect One shall appear before the face of the Lord of Spirits.

1Enoch 53

[1] There mine eyes saw a deep valley with open mouths, and all who dwell on the earth and sea and islands shall bring to him gifts and presents and tokens of homage, but that deep valley shall not become full. [2] And their hands commit lawless deeds, And the sinners devour all whom they lawlessly oppress: Yet the sinners shall be destroyed before the face of the Lord of Spirits, And they shall be banished from off the face of His earth, And they shall perish for ever and ever. [3] For I saw all the angels of punishment abiding (there) and preparing all the instruments of Satan. [4] And I asked the angel of peace who went with me: For whom are they preparing these Instruments? [5] And he said unto me: They prepare these for the kings and the mighty of this earth, that they may thereby be destroyed. [6] And after this the Righteous and Elect One shall cause the house of his congregation to appear: henceforth they shall be no more hindered in the name of the Lord of Spirits. [7] And these mountains shall not stand as the earth before his righteousness, But the hills shall be as a fountain of water, And the righteous shall have rest from the oppression of sinners.

1Enoch 54

[1] And I looked and turned to another part of the earth, and saw there a deep valley with burning [2] fire. And they brought the kings and the mighty, and began to cast them into this deep valley. [3] And there mine eyes saw how they made these their instruments, iron chains of immeasurable weight. [4] And I asked the angel of peace who went with me, saying: For whom are these chains being prepared ? And he said unto me: These are being prepared for the hosts of Azazel, so that they may take them and cast them into the abyss of complete condemnation, and they shall cover their jaws with rough stones as the Lord of Spirits commanded. [6] And Michael, and Gabriel, and Raphael, and Phanuel shall take hold of them on that great day, and cast them on that day into the burning furnace, that the Lord of Spirits may take vengeance on them for their unrighteousness in becoming subject to Satan and leading astray those who dwell on the earth. [7] And in those days shall punishment come from the Lord of Spirits, and he will open all the chambers of waters which are

above the heavens, and of the fountains which are beneath the earth. [8] And all the waters shall be joined with the waters: that which is above the heavens is the masculine, [9] and the water which is beneath the earth is the feminine. And they shall destroy all who dwell [10] on the earth and those who dwell under the ends of the heaven. And when they have recognized their unrighteousness which they have wrought on the earth, then by these shall they perish.

1Enoch 55

[1] And after that the Head of Days repented and said: In vain have I destroyed all who dwell [2] on the earth. And He sware by His great name: Henceforth I will not do so to all who dwell on the earth, and I will set a sign in the heaven: and this shall be a pledge of good faith between Me and them for ever, so long as heaven is above the earth. And this is in accordance with My command. [3] When I have desired to take hold of them by the hand of the angels on the day of tribulation and pain because of this, I will cause My chastisement and My wrath to abide upon them, saith [4] God, the Lord of Spirits. Ye mighty kings who dwell on the earth, ye shall have to behold Mine Elect One, how he sits on the throne of glory and judges Azazel, and all his associates, and all his hosts in the name of the Lord of Spirits.

1Enoch 56

[1] And I saw there the hosts of the angels of punishment going, and they held scourges and chains [2] of iron and bronze. And I asked the angel of peace who went with me, saying: To whom are [3] these who hold the scourges going ? And he said unto me: To their elect and beloved ones, that they may be cast into the chasm of the abyss of the valley. [4] And then that valley shall be filled with their elect and beloved, And the days of their lives shall be at an end, And the days of their leading astray shall not thenceforward be reckoned. [5] And in those days the angels shall return And hurl themselves to the east upon the Parthians and Medes: They shall stir up the kings, so that a spirit of unrest shall come upon them, And they shall rouse them from their thrones, That they may break forth as lions from their lairs, And as hungry wolves among their flocks. [6] And they shall go up and tread under foot the land of His elect ones [And the land of His elect ones shall be before them a threshing-floor and a highway :] [7] But the city of my righteous shall be a hindrance to their horses. And they shall begin to fight among themselves, And their right hand shall be strong against themselves, And a man shall not know his brother, Nor a son his father or his mother, Till there be no number of the corpses through their slaughter, And their punishment be not in vain. [8] In those days Sheol shall open its jaws, And they shall be swallowed up therein And their destruction shall be at an end; Sheol shall devour the sinners in the presence of the elect.

1Enoch 57

[1] And it came to pass after this that I saw another host of wagons, and men riding thereon, and [2] coming on the winds from the east, and from the west to the south. And the noise of their wagons was heard, and when this turmoil took place the holy ones from heaven remarked it, and the pillars of the earth were moved from their place, and the sound thereof was heard from the one end of heaven [3] to the other, in one day. And they shall all fall down and worship the Lord of Spirits. And this is the end of the second Parable.

1Enoch 58

[1] And I began to speak the third Parable concerning the righteous and elect. [2] Blessed are ye, ye righteous and elect, For glorious shall be your lot. [3] And the righteous shall be in the light of the sun. And the elect in the light of eternal life: The days of their life shall be unending, And the days of the holy without number. [4] And they shall

seek the light and find righteousness with the Lord of Spirits: There shall be peace to the righteous in the name of the Eternal Lord. [5] And after this it shall be said to the holy in heaven That they should seek out the secrets of righteousness, the heritage of faith: For it has become bright as the sun upon earth, And the darkness is past. [6] And there shall be a light that never endeth, And to a limit (lit. number) of days they shall not come, For the darkness shall first have been destroyed, [And the light established before the Lord of Spirits] And the light of uprightness established for ever before the Lord of Spirits.

1Enoch 59

[1] In those days mine eyes saw the secrets of the lightnings, and of the lights, and the judgements they execute (lit. their judgement): and they lighten for a blessing or a curse as the Lord of [2] Spirits willeth. And there I saw the secrets of the thunder, and how when it resounds above in the heaven, the sound thereof is heard, and he caused me to see the judgements executed on the earth, whether they be for well-being and blessing, or for a curse according to the word of the Lord of Spirits. [3] And after that all the secrets of the lights and lightnings were shown to me, and they lighten for blessing and for satisfying.

1Enoch 60

A Fragment of the Book of Noah [1] In the year 500, in the seventh month, on the fourteenth day of the month in the life of Enoch. In that Parable I saw how a mighty quaking made the heaven of heavens to quake, and the host of the Most High, and the angels, a thousand thousands and ten thousand times ten thousand, were [2] disquieted with a great disquiet. And the Head of Days sat on the throne of His glory, and the angels and the righteous stood around Him. [3] And a great trembling seized me, And fear took hold of me, And my loins gave way, And dissolved were my reins, And I fell upon my face. [4] And Michael sent another angel from among the holy ones and he raised me up, and when he had raised me up my spirit returned; for I had not been able to endure the look of this host, and the [5] commotion and the quaking of the heaven. And Michael said unto me: Why art thou disquieted with such a vision ? Until this day lasted the day of His mercy; and He hath been merciful and [6] long-suffering towards those who dwell on the earth. And when the day, and the power, and the punishment, and the judgement come, which the Lord of Spirits hath prepared for those who worship not the righteous law, and for those who deny the righteous judgement, and for those who take His name in vain-that day is prepared, for the elect a covenant, but for sinners an inquisition. [7] When the punishment of the Lord of Spirits shall rest upon them, it shall rest in order that the punishment of the Lord of Spirits may not come, in vain, and it shall slay the children with their mothers and the children with their fathers. Afterwards the judgement shall take place according to His mercy and His patience. [7] And on that day were two monsters parted, a female monster named Leviathan, to dwell in the [8] abysses of the ocean over the fountains of the waters. But the male is named Behemoth, who occupied with his breast a waste wilderness named Duidain, on the east of the garden where the elect and righteous dwell, where my grandfather was taken up, the seventh from Adam, the first [9] man whom the Lord of Spirits created. And I besought the other angel that he should show me the might of those monsters, how they were parted on one day and cast, the one into the abysses [10] of the sea, and the other unto the dry land of the wilderness. And he said to me: Thou son of man, herein thou dost seek to know what is hidden. [11] And the other angel who went with me and showed me what was hidden told me what is first and last in the heaven in the height, and beneath the earth in the depth, and at the ends of the [12] heaven, and on the foundation of the heaven. And the chambers of the winds, and how the winds are divided, and how they are weighed, and (how) the portals of the winds are reckoned, each according to the power of the wind, and the power of the lights of the moon, and according to the power that is fitting: and the divisions of the stars according to their names, and how all the divisions [13] are divided. And the thunders according to the places where they fall, and all the divisions that are made among the lightnings that it may lighten, and their host that they may at once obey. [14] For the thunder has places of rest (which) are assigned (to it) while it is waiting for its peal; and the thunder and lightning are inseparable, and although not one and undivided, they both go together [15] through the spirit and separate not. For when the lightning lightens, the thunder utters its voice, and the spirit enforces a pause during the peal, and divides equally between them; for the treasury of their peals is like the sand, and each one of them as it peals is held in with a bridle, and turned back by the power of the spirit, and pushed forward according to the many quarters of the earth. [16] And the spirit of the sea is masculine and strong, and according to the might of his strength he draws it back with a rein, and in like manner it is driven forward and disperses amid all the mountains [17] of the earth. And the spirit of the hoar-frost is his own angel, and the spirit of the hail is a good [18] angel. And the spirit of the snow has forsaken his chambers on account of his strength - There is a special spirit therein, and that which ascends from it is like smoke, and its name is frost. 19And the spirit of the mist is not united with them in their chambers, but it has a special chamber; for its course is glorious both in light and in darkness, and in winter and in summer, and in its chamber is an angel. [20] And the spirit of the dew has its dwelling at the ends of the heaven, and is connected with the chambers of the rain, and its course is in winter and summer: and its clouds and the clouds of the [21] mist are connected, and the one gives to the other. And when the spirit of the rain goes forth from its chamber, the angels come and open the chamber and lead it out, and when it is diffused over the whole earth it unites with the water on the earth. And whensoever it unites with the water on [22] the earth . . . For the waters are for those who dwell on the earth; for they are nourishment for the earthfrom the Most High who is in heaven: therefore there is a measure for the rain, andthe angels take it in charge. And these things I saw towards the Garden of the Righteous. [23] And the angel of peace who was with me said to me: These two monsters, prepared conformably to the greatness of God, shall feed . . .

1Enoch 61

[1] And I saw in those days how long cords were given to those angels, and they took to themselves wings and flew, and they went towards the north. [2] And I asked the angel, saying unto him: Why have those (angels) taken these cords and gone off ? And he said unto me: They have gone to measure. [3] And the angel who went with me said unto me: These shall bring the measures of the righteous, And the ropes of the righteous to the righteous, That they may stay themselves on the name of the Lord of Spirits for ever and ever. [4] The elect shall begin to dwell with the elect, And those are the measures which shall be given to faith And which shall strengthen righteousness. [5] And these measures shall reveal all the secrets of the depths of the earth, And those who have been destroyed by the desert, And those who have been devoured by the beasts, And those who have been devoured by the fish of the sea, That they may return and stay themselves On the day of the Elect One; For none shall be destroyed before the Lord of Spirits, And none can be destroyed. [6] And all who dwell above in the heaven received a command and power and one voice and one light like unto

fire. [7] And that One (with) their first words they blessed, And extolled and lauded with wisdom, And they were wise in utterance and in the spirit of life. [8] And the Lord of Spirits placed the Elect one on the throne of glory. And he shall judge all the works of the holy above in the heaven, And in the balance shall their deeds be weighed

1Enoch 62

[1] And thus the Lord commanded the kings and the mighty and the exalted, and those who dwell on the earth, and said: Open your eyes and lift up your horns if ye are able to recognize the Elect One. [2] And the Lord of Spirits seated him on the throne of His glory, And the spirit of righteousness was poured out upon him, And the word of his mouth slays all the sinners, And all the unrighteous are destroyed from before his face. [3] And there shall stand up in that day all the kings and the mighty, And the exalted and those who hold the earth, And they shall see and recognize How he sits on the throne of his glory, And righteousness is judged before him, And no lying word is spoken before him. [4] Then shall pain come upon them as on a woman in travail, [And she has pain in bringing forth] When her child enters the mouth of the womb, And she has pain in bringing forth. 5And one portion of them shall look on the other, And they shall be terrified, And they shall be downcast of countenance, And pain shall seize them, When they see that Son of Man Sitting on the throne of his glory. [6] And the kings and the mighty and all who possess the earth shall bless and glorify and extol him who rules over all, who was hidden. [7] For from the beginning the Son of Man was hidden, And the Most High preserved him in the presence of His might, And revealed him to the elect. [8] And the congregation of the elect and holy shall be sown, And all the elect shall stand before him on that day. [9] And all the kings and the mighty and the exalted and those who rule the earth Shall fall down before him on their faces, And worship and set their hope upon that Son of Man, And petition him and supplicate for mercy at his hands. [10] Nevertheless that Lord of Spirits will so press them That they shall hastily go forth from His presence, And their faces shall be filled with shame, And the darkness grow deeper on their faces. [11] And He will deliver them to the angels for punishment, To execute vengeance on them because they have oppressed His children and His elect [12] And they shall be a spectacle for the righteous and for His elect: They shall rejoice over them, Because the wrath of the Lord of Spirits resteth upon them, And His sword is drunk with their blood. [13] And the righteous and elect shall be saved on that day, And they shall never thenceforward see the face of the sinners and unrighteous. [14] And the Lord of Spirits will abide over them, And with that Son of Man shall they eat And lie down and rise up for ever and ever. [15] And the righteous and elect shall have risen from the earth, And ceased to be of downcast countenance. And they shall have been clothed with garments of glory, [16] And these shall be the garments of life from the Lord of Spirits: And your garments shall not grow old, Nor your glory pass away before the Lord of Spirits.

1Enoch 63

[1] In those days shall the mighty and the kings who possess the earth implore (Him) to grant them a little respite from His angels of punishment to whom they were delivered, that they might fall [2] down and worship before the Lord of Spirits, and confess their sins before Him. And they shall bless and glorify the Lord of Spirits, and say: Blessed is the Lord of Spirits and the Lord of kings, And the Lord of the mighty and the Lord of the rich, And the Lord of glory and the Lord of wisdom, [3] And splendid in every secret thing is Thy power from generation to generation, And Thy glory for ever and ever: Deep are all Thy secrets and innumerable, And Thy righteousness is beyond reckoning. [4] We have now learnt that we

should glorify And bless the Lord of kings and Him who is king over all kings. [5] And they shall say: Would that we had rest to glorify and give thanks And confess our faith before His glory ! [6] And now we long for a little rest but find it not: We follow hard upon and obtain (it) not: And light has vanished from before us, And darkness is our dwelling-place for ever and ever: [7] For we have not believed before Him Nor glorified the name of the Lord of Spirits, [nor glorified our Lord] But our hope was in the sceptre of our kingdom, And in our glory. [8] And in the day of our suffering and tribulation He saves us not, And we find no respite for confession That our Lord is true in all His works, and in His judgements and His justice, And His judgements have no respect of persons. And we pass away from before His face on account of our works, And all our sins are reckoned up in righteousness. [10] Now they shall say unto themselves: Our souls are full of unrighteous gain, but it does not prevent us from descending from the midst thereof into the burden of Sheol. [11] And after that their faces shall be filled with darkness And shame before that Son of Man, And they shall be driven from his presence, And the sword shall abide before his face in their midst. [12] Thus spake the Lord of Spirits: This is the ordinance and judgement with respect to the mighty and the kings and the exalted and those who possess the earth before the Lord of Spirits.

1Enoch 64

[1,2] And other forms I saw hidden in that place. I heard the voice of the angel saying: These are the angels who descended to the earth, and revealed what was hidden to the children of men and seduced the children of men into committing sin.

1Enoch 65

[1, 2] And in those days Noah saw the earth that it had sunk down and its destruction was nigh. And he arose from thence and went to the ends of the earth, and cried aloud to his grandfather Enoch: [3] and Noah said three times with an embittered voice: Hear me, hear me, hear me. And I said unto him: Tell me what it is that is falling out on the earth that the earth is in such evil plight [4] and shaken, lest perchance I shall perish with it ? And thereupon there was a great commotion , on the earth, and a voice was heard from heaven, and I fell on my face. [5] And Enoch my grandfather came and stood by me, and said unto me: Why hast thou cried unto me with a bitter cry and weeping [6] And a command has gone forth from the presence of the Lord concerning those who dwell on the earth that their ruin is accomplished because they have learnt all the secrets of the angels, and all the violence of the Satans, and all their powers -the most secret ones- and all the power of those who practice sorcery, and the power of witchcraft, and the power of those who make molten images [7] for the whole earth: And how silver is produced from the dust of the earth, and how soft metal [8] originates in the earth. For lead and tin are not produced from the earth like the first: it is a fountain [9] that produces them, and an angel stands therein, and that angel is pre-eminent. And after that my grandfather Enoch took hold of me by my hand and raised me up, and said unto me: Go, for I have [10] asked the Lord of Spirits as touching this commotion on the earth. And He said unto me: " Because of their unrighteousness their judgement has been determined upon and shall not be withheld by Me for ever. Because of the sorceries which they have searched out and learnt, the earth and those [11] who dwell upon it shall be destroyed." And these-they have no place of repentance for ever, because they have shown them what was hidden, and they are the damned: but as for thee, my son, the Lord of Spirits knows that thou art pure, and guiltless of this reproach concerning the secrets. [12] And He has destined thy name to be among the holy, And will preserve thee amongst those who dwell on the earth, And has destined thy righteous seed both for kingship and for great honours, And from

thy seed shall proceed a fountain of the righteous and holy without number for ever.

1Enoch 66

[1] And after that he showed me the angels of punishment who are prepared to come and let loose all the powers of the waters which are beneath in the earth in order to bring judgement and destruction [2] on all who [abide and] dwell on the earth. And the Lord of Spirits gave commandment to the angels who were going forth, that they should not cause the waters to rise but should hold them [3] in check; for those angels were over the powers of the waters. And I went away from the presence of Enoch.

1Enoch 67

[1] And in those days the word of God came unto me, and He said unto me: Noah, thy lot has come [2] Up before Me, a lot without blame, a lot of love and uprightness. And now the angels are making a wooden (building), and when they have completed that task I will place My hand upon it and preserve it, and there shall come forth from it the seed of life, and a change shall set in so that the [3] earth will not remain without inhabitant. And I will make fast thy seed before me for ever and ever, and I will spread abroad those who dwell with thee: it shall not be unfruitful on the face of the earth, but it shall be blessed and multiply on the earth in the name of the Lord. [4] And He will imprison those angels, who have shown unrighteousness, in that burning valley which my grandfather Enoch had formerly shown to me in the west among the mountains of gold [5] and silver and iron and soft metal and tin. And I saw that valley in which there was a great [6] convulsion and a convulsion of the waters. And when all this took place, from that fiery molten metal and from the convulsion thereof in that place, there was produced a smell of sulphur, and it was connected with those waters, and that valley of the angels who had led astray (mankind) burned [7] beneath that land. And through its valleys proceed streams of fire, where these angels are punished who had led astray those who dwell upon the earth. [8] But those waters shall in those days serve for the kings and the mighty and the exalted, and those who dwell on the earth, for the healing of the body, but for the punishment of the spirit; now their spirit is full of lust, that they may be punished in their body, for they have denied the Lord of Spirits [9] and see their punishment daily, and yet believe not in His name. And in proportion as the burning of their bodies becomes severe, a corresponding change shall take place in their spirit for ever and ever; [10] for before the Lord of Spirits none shall utter an idle word. For the judgement shall come upon them, [11] because they believe in the lust of their body and deny the Spirit of the Lord. And those same waters will undergo a change in those days; for when those angels are punished in these waters, these water-springs shall change their temperature, and when the angels ascend, this water of the [12] springs shall change and become cold. And I heard Michael answering and saying: This judgement wherewith the angels are judged is a testimony for the kings and the mighty who possess the [13] earth. Because these waters of judgement minister to the healing of the body of the kings and the lust of their body; therefore they will not see and will not believe that those waters will change and become a fire which burns for ever.

1Enoch 68

[1] And after that my grandfather Enoch gave me the teaching of all the secrets in the book in the Parables which had been given to him, and he put them together for me in the words of the book [2] of the Parables. And on that day Michael answered Raphael and said: The power of the spirit transports and makes me to tremble because of the severity of the judgement of the secrets, the judgement of the angels: who can endure the severe judgement which has been

executed, and before [3] which they melt away ? And Michael answered again, and said to Raphael: Who is he whose heart is not softened concerning it, and whose reins are not troubled by this word of judgement [4] (that) has gone forth upon them because of those who have thus led them out ? And it came to pass when he stood before the Lord of Spirits, Michael said thus to Raphael: I will not take their part under the eye of the Lord; for the Lord of Spirits has been angry with them because they do [5] as if they were the Lord. Therefore all that is hidden shall come upon them for ever and ever; for neither angel nor man shall have his portion (in it), but alone they have received their judgement for ever and ever.

1Enoch 69

[1] And after this judgement they shall terrify and make them to tremble because they have shown this to those who dwell on the earth. [2] And behold the names of those angels [and these are their names: the first of them is Samjaza, the second Artaqifa, and the third Armen, the fourth Kokabel, the fifth Turael, the sixth Rumjal, the seventh Danjal, the eighth Neqael, the ninth Baraqel, the tenth Azazel, the eleventh Armaros, the twelfth Batarjal, the thirteenth Busasejal, the fourteenth Hananel, the fifteenth Turel, and the sixteenth Simapesiel, the seventeenth Jetrel, the eighteenth Tumael, the nineteenth Turel, [3] the twentieth Rumael, the twenty-first Azazel. And these are the chiefs of their angels and their names, and their chief ones over hundreds and over fifties and over tens. [4] The name of the first Jeqon: that is, the one who led astray [all] the sons of God, and brought them [5] down to the earth, and led them astray through the daughters of men. And the second was named Asbeel: he imparted to the holy sons of God evil counsel, and led them astray so that they defiled [6] their bodies with the daughters of men. And the third was named Gadreel: he it is who showed the children of men all the blows of death, and he led astray Eve, and showed [the weapons of death to the sons of men] the shield and the coat of mail, and the sword for battle, and all the weapons [7] of death to the children of men. And from his hand they have proceeded against those who dwell [8] on the earth from that day and for evermore. And the fourth was named Penemue: he taught the [9] children of men the bitter and the sweet, and he taught them all the secrets of their wisdom. And he instructed mankind in writing with ink and paper, and thereby many sinned from eternity to [10] eternity and until this day. For men were not created for such a purpose, to give confirmation [11] to their good faith with pen and ink. For men were created exactly like the angels, to the intent that they should continue pure and righteous, and death, which destroys everything, could not have taken hold of them, but through this their knowledge they are perishing, and through this power [12] it is consuming me. And the fifth was named Kasdeja: this is he who showed the children of men all the wicked smitings of spirits and demons, and the smitings of the embryo in the womb, that it may pass away, and [the smitings of the soul] the bites of the serpent, and the smitings [13] which befall through the noontide heat, the son of the serpent named Tabaet. And this is the task of Kasbeel, the chief of the oath which he showed to the holy ones when he dwelt high [14] above in glory, and its name is Biqa. This (angel) requested Michael to show him the hidden name, that he might enunciate it in the oath, so that those might quake before that name and oath who revealed all that was in secret to the children of men. And this is the power of this oath, for it is powerful and strong, and he placed this oath Akae in the hand of Michael. [16] And these are the secrets of this oath . . . And they are strong through his oath: And the heaven was suspended before the world was created, And for ever. [17] And through it the earth was founded upon the water, And from the secret recesses of the mountains come beautiful waters, From the creation of the world

177

and unto eternity. [18] And through that oath the sea was created, And as its foundation He set for it the sand against the time of (its) anger, And it dare not pass beyond it from the creation of the world unto eternity. [19] And through that oath the depths are made fast, And abide and stir not from their place from eternity to eternity. [20] And through that oath the sun and moon complete their course, And deviate not from their ordinance from eternity to eternity. [21] And through that oath the stars complete their course, And He calls them by their names, And they answer Him from eternity to eternity. [22] [And in like manner the spirits of the water, and of the winds, and of all zephyrs, and(their) paths [23] from all the quarters of the winds. And there are preserved the voices of the thunder and the light of the lightnings: and there are preserved the chambers of the hail and the chambers of the [24] hoarfrost, and the chambers of the mist, and the chambers of the rain and the dew. And all these believe and give thanks before the Lord of Spirits, and glorify (Him) with all their power, and their food is in every act of thanksgiving: they thank and glorify and extol the name of the Lord of Spirits for ever and ever.] [25] And this oath is mighty over them And through it [they are preserved and] their paths are preserved, And their course is not destroyed. [26] And there was great joy amongst them, And they blessed and glorified and extolled Because the name of that Son of Man had been revealed unto them. [27] And he sat on the throne of his glory, And the sum of judgement was given unto the Son of Man, And he caused the sinners to pass away and be destroyed from off the face of the earth, And those who have led the world astray. [28] With chains shall they be bound, And in their assemblage-place of destruction shall they be imprisoned, And all their works vanish from the face of the earth. [29] And from henceforth there shall be nothing corruptible; For that Son of Man has appeared, And has seated himself on the throne of his glory, And all evil shall pass away before his face, And the word of that Son of Man shall go forth And be strong before the Lord of Spirits.

1Enoch 70

[1] And it came to pass after this that his name during his lifetime was raised aloft to that Son of [2] Man and to the Lord of Spirits from amongst those who dwell on the earth. And he was raised aloft [3] on the chariots of the spirit and his name vanished among them. And from that day I was no longer numbered amongst them: and he set me between the two winds, between the North and the [4] West, where the angels took the cords to measure for me the place for the elect and righteous. And there I saw the first fathers and the righteous who from the beginning dwell in that place.

1Enoch 71

[1] And it came to pass after this that my spirit was translated And it ascended into the heavens: And I saw the holy sons of God. They were stepping on flames of fire: Their garments were white [and their raiment] , And their faces shone like snow. [2] And I saw two streams of fire, And the light of that fire shone like hyacinth, And I fell on my face before the Lord of Spirits. [3] And the angel Michael[one of the archangels] seized me by my right hand, And lifted me up and led me forth into all the secrets, And he showed me all the secrets of righteousness. [4] And he showed me all the secrets of the ends of the heaven, And all the chambers of all the stars, and all the luminaries, Whence they proceed before the face of the holy ones. [5] And he translated my spirit into the heaven of heavens, And I saw there as it were a structure built of crystals, And between those crystals tongues of living fire. [6] And my spirit saw the girdle which girt that house of fire, And on its four sides were streams full of living fire, And they girt that house. [7] And round about were Seraphin, Cherubic, and Ophannin: And these are they who sleep not And guard the throne of His glory. [8] And I saw angels

who could not be counted, A thousand thousands, and ten thousand times ten thousand, Encircling that house. And Michael, and Raphael, and Gabriel, and Phanuel, And the holy angels who are above the heavens, Go in and out of that house. [9] And they came forth from that house, And Michael and Gabriel, Raphael and Phanuel, And many holy angels without number. [10] And with them the Head of Days, His head white and pure as wool, And His raiment indescribable. [11] And I fell on my face, And my whole body became relaxed, And my spirit was transfigured; And I cried with a loud voice, . . . with the spirit of power, And blessed and glorified and extolled. [12] And these blessings which went forth out of my mouth were well pleasing before that Head of Days. And that Head of Days came with Michael and Gabriel, Raphael and Phanuel, thousands and ten thousands of angels without number. [Lost passage wherein the Son of Man was described as accompanying the Head of Days, and Enoch asked one of the angels (as in xlvi. 3) concerning the Son of Man as to who he was.] [14] And he (i.e. the angel) came to me and greeted me with His voice, and said unto me This is the Son of Man who is born unto righteousness, And righteousness abides over him, And the righteousness of the Head of Days forsakes him not. [15] And he said unto me: He proclaims unto thee peace in the name of the world to come; For from hence has proceeded peace since the creation of the world, And so shall it be unto thee for ever and for ever and ever. [16] And all shall walk in his ways since righteousness never forsaketh him: With him will be their dwelling-places, and with him their heritage, And they shall not be separated from him for ever and ever and ever. And so there shall be length of days with that Son of Man, And the righteous shall have peace and an upright way In the name of the Lord of Spirits for ever and ever.

The Astronomical Book
1Enoch 72

[1] The book of the courses of the luminaries of the heaven, the relations of each, according to their classes, their dominion and their seasons, according to their names and places of origin, and according to their months, which Uriel, the holy angel, who was with me, who is their guide, showed me; and he showed me all their laws exactly as they are, and how it is with regard to all the years of the world [2] and unto eternity, till the new creation is accomplished which dureth till eternity. And this is the first law of the luminaries: the luminary the Sun has its rising in the eastern portals of the heaven, [3] and its setting in the western portals of the heaven. And I saw six portals in which the sun rises, and six portals in which the sun sets and the moon rises and sets in these portals, and the leaders of the stars and those whom they lead: six in the east and six in the west, and all following each other [4] in accurately corresponding order: also many windows to the right and left of these portals. And first there goes forth the great luminary, named the Sun, and his circumference is like the [5] circumference of the heaven, and he is quite filled with illuminating and heating fire. The chariot on which he ascends, the wind drives, and the sun goes down from the heaven and returns through the north in order to reach the east, and is so guided that he comes to the appropriate (lit. that) portal and [6] shines in the face of the heaven. In this way he rises in the first month in the great portal, which [7] is the fourth [those six portals in the east]. And in that fourth portal from which the sun rises in the first month are twelve window-openings, from which proceed a flame when they are opened in [8] their season. When the sun rises in the heaven, he comes forth through that fourth portal thirty, [9] mornings in succession, and sets accurately in the fourth portal in the west of the heaven. And during this period the day becomes daily longer and the night nightly shorter to the thirtieth [10] morning. On that day the

day is longer than the night by a ninth part, and the day amounts exactly to ten parts and the night to eight parts. And the sun rises from that fourth portal, and sets in the fourth and returns to the fifth portal of the east thirty mornings, and rises from it and sets in the fifth [12] portal. And then the day becomes longer by two parts and amounts to eleven parts, and the night [13] becomes shorter and amounts to seven parts. And it returns to the east and enters into the sixth [14] portal, and rises and sets in the sixth portal one-and-thirty mornings on account of its sign. On that day the day becomes longer than the night, and the day becomes double the night, and the day [15] becomes twelve parts, and the night is shortened and becomes six parts. And the sun mounts up to make the day shorter and the night longer, and the sun returns to the east and enters into the [16] sixth portal, and rises from it and sets thirty mornings. And when thirty mornings are accomplished, [17] the day decreases by exactly one part, and becomes eleven parts, and the night seven. And the sun goes forth from that sixth portal in the west, and goes to the east and rises in the fifth portal for [18] thirty mornings, and sets in the west again in the fifth western portal. On that day the day decreases by two parts, and amounts to ten parts and the night to eight parts. [19] And the sun goes forth from that fifth portal and sets in the fifth portal of the west, and rises in the fourth portal for one- [20] and-thirty mornings on account of its sign, and sets in the west. On that day the day is equalized with the night, [and becomes of equal length], and the night amounts to nine parts and the day to [21] nine parts. And the sun rises from that portal and sets in the west, and returns to the east and rises [22] thirty mornings in the third portal and sets in the west in the third portal. And on that day the night becomes longer than the day, and night becomes longer than night, and day shorter than day till thhe thirtieth morning, and the night amounts exactly to ten parts and the day to eight [23] parts. And the sun rises from that third portal and sets in the third portal in the west and returns to the east, and for thirty mornings rises [24] in the second portal in the east, and in like manner sets in the second portal in the west of the heaven. And on that day the night amounts to eleven [25] parts and the day to seven parts. And the sun rises on that day from that second portal and sets in the west in the second portal, and returns to the east into the first portal for one-and-thirty [26] mornings, and sets in the first portal in the west of the heaven. And on that day the night becomes longer and amounts to the double of the day: and the night amounts exactly to twelve parts and [27] the day to six. And the sun has (therewith) traversed the divisions of his orbit and turns again on those divisions of his orbit, and enters that portal thirty mornings and sets also in the west [28] opposite to it. And on that night has the night decreased in length by a ninth part, and the night [29] has become eleven parts and the day seven parts. And the sun has returned and entered into the second portal in the east, and returns on those his divisions of his orbit for thirty mornings, rising [30] and setting. And on that day the night decreases in length, and the night amounts to ten parts [31] and the day to eight. And on that day the sun rises from that portal, and sets in the west, and returns to the east, and rises in the third portal for one-and-thirty mornings, and sets in the west of the heaven. [32] On that day the night decreases and amounts to nine parts, and the day to nine parts, and the night [33] is equal to the day and the year is exactly as to its days three hundred and sixty-four. And the length of the day and of the night, and the shortness of the day and of the night arise-through the course [34] of the sun these distinctions are made (lit. they are separated). So it comes that its course becomes [35] daily longer, and its course nightly shorter. And this is the law and the course of the sun, and his return as often as he returns sixty times and rises, i.e. the great luminary which is named the sun, for ever and ever. 36 And that which (thus) rises is the great luminary, and is so named according to 37 its appearance, according as the Lord commanded. As he rises, so he sets and decreases not, and rests not, but runs day and night, and his light is sevenfold brighter than that of the moon; but as regards size they are both equal.

1Enoch 73

1 And after this law I saw another law dealing with the smaller luminary, which is named the Moon. 2 And her circumference is like the circumference of the heaven, and her chariot in which she rides is driven by the wind, and light is given to her in (definite) measure. And her rising and setting change every month: 3and her days are like the days of the sun, and when her light is uniform (i.e. full) it amounts to the seventh part of the light of the sun. 4 And thus she rises. And her first phase in the east comes forth on the thirtieth morning: and on that day she becomes visible, and constitutes for you the first phase of the moon on the thirtieth day together with the sun in the portal where the sun rises. 5 And the one half of her goes forth by a seventh part, and her whole circumference is empty, without light, with the exception of one-seventh part of it, (and) the 6 fourteenth part of her light. And when she receives one-seventh part of the half of her light, her light 7 amounts to one-seventh part and the half thereof. And she sets with the sun, and when the sun rises the moon rises with him and receives the half of one part of light, and in that night in the beginning of her morning in the commencement of the lunar day the moon sets with the sun, and 8 is invisible that night with the fourteen parts and the half of one of them. And she rises on that day with exactly a seventh part, and comes forth and recedes from the rising of the sun, and in her remaining days she becomes bright in the (remaining) thirteen parts.

1Enoch 74

1 And I saw another course, a law for her, (and) how according to that law she performs her monthly 2 revolution. And all these Uriel, the holy angel who is the leader of them all,showed to me, and their positions, and I wrote down their positions as he showed them to me, and I wrote down their months 3 as they were, and the appearance of their lights till fifteen days were accomplished. In single seventh parts she accomplishes all her light in the east, and in single seventh parts accomplishes all her 4 darkness in the west. And in certain months she alters her settings, and in certain months she pursues 5 her own peculiar course. In two months the moon sets with the sun: in those two middle portals the 6 third and the fourth. She goes forth for seven days, and turns about and returns again through the portal where the sun rises, and accomplishes all her light: and she recedes from the sun, and in eight 7 days enters the sixth portal from which the sun goes forth. And when the sun goes forth from the fourth portal she goes forth seven days, until she goes forth from the fifth and turns back again in seven days into the fourth portal and accomplishes all her light: and she recedes and enters into the 8 first portal in eight days.And she returns again in seven days into the fourth portal from which the 9, 10 sun goes forth. Thus I saw their position -how the moons rose and the sun set in those days. And if five years are added together the sun has an overplus of thirty days, and all the days which accrue 11 to it for one of those five years, when they are full, amount to 364 days. And the overplus of the sun and of the stars amounts to six days: in 5 years 6 days every year come to 30 days: and the 12 moon falls behind the sun and stars to the number of 30 days. And the sun and the stars bring in all the years exactly, so that they do not advance or delay their position by a single day unto eternity; but complete the years with perfect justice in 364 days. 13 In 3 years there are 1,092 days, and in 5 years 1,820 days, so that in 8 years there are 2,912 days. 14 For

179

the moon alone the days amount in 3 years to 1,062 days, and in 5 years she falls 50 days behind:i.e. to the sum (of 1,770) there is 5 to be added (1,000 and) 62 days. 15 And in 5 years there are 1,770 days, so that for the moon the days 6 in 8 years amount to 21,832 days. 16 For in 8 years she falls behind to the amount of 80 days, all the 17 days she falls behind in 8 years are 80. And the year is accurately completed in conformity with their world-stations and the stations of the sun, which rise from the portals through which it (the sun) rises and sets 30 days.

1Enoch 75

1 And the leaders of the heads of the thousands, who are placed over the whole creation and over all the stars, have also to do with the four intercalary days, being inseparable from their office, according to the reckoning of the year, and these render service on the four days which are not 2 reckoned in the reckoning of the year. And owing to them men go wrong therein, for those luminaries truly render service on the world-stations, one in the first portal, one in the third portal of the heaven, one in the fourth portal, and one in the sixth portal, and the exactness of the year is 3 accomplished through its separate three hundred and sixty-four stations. For the signs and the times and the years and the days the angel Uriel showed to me, whom the Lord of glory hath set for ever over all the luminaries of the heaven, in the heaven and in the world, that they should rule on the face of the heaven and be seen on the earth, and be leaders for the day and the night, i.e. the sun, moon, and stars, and all the ministering creatures which make their revolution in all the chariots 4 of the heaven. In like manner twelve doors Uriel showed me, open in the circumference of the suns chariot in the heaven, through which the rays of the sun break forth: and from them is warmth 5 diffused over the earth, when they are opened at their appointed seasons.And for the winds and 6 the spirit of the dew when they are opened, standing open in the heavens at the ends. As for the twelve portals in the heaven, at the ends of the earth, out of which go forth the sun, moon, and stars, 7 and all the works of heaven in the east and in the west, There are many windows open to the left and right of them, and one window at its (appointed) season produces warmth, corresponding (as these do) to those doors from which the stars come forth according as He has commanded them, 8 and wherein they set corresponding to their number. And I saw chariots in the heaven, running 9 in the world, above those portals in which revolve the stars that never set. And one is larger than all the rest, and it is that that makes its course through the entire world.

1Enoch 76

1 And at the ends of the earth I saw twelve portals open to all the quarters (of the heaven), from 2 which the winds go forth and blow over the earth. Three of them are open on the face (i.e. the east) of the heavens, and three in the west, and three on the right (i.e. the south) of the heaven, and 3 three on the left (i.e. the north). And the three first are those of the east, and three are of the 4 north, and threeafter those on the left of the south, and three of the west. Through four of these come winds of blessing and prosperity, and from those eight come hurtful winds: when they are sent, they bring destruction on all the earth and on the water upon it, and on all who dwell thereon, and on everything which is in the water and on the land. 5 And the first wind from those portals, called the east wind, comes forth through the first portal which is in the east, inclining towards the south: from it come forth desolation, drought, heat, 6 and destruction. And through the second portal in the middle comes what is fitting, and from it there come rain and fruitfulness and prosperity and dew; and through the third portal which lies toward the north come cold and drought. 7 And after these come forth the south winds through three portals: through the first portal

of [8] them inclining to the east comes forth a hot wind. And through the middle portal next to it there [9] come forth fragrant smells, and dew and rain, and prosperity and health. And through the third portal lying to the west come forth dew and rain, locusts and desolation. [10] And after these the north winds: from the seventh portal in the east come dew and rain, locusts and desolation. [11] And from the middle portal come in a direct direction health and rain and dew and prosperity; and through the third portal in the west come cloud and hoar-frost, and snow and rain, and dew and locusts. [12] And after these four are the west winds: through the first portal adjoining the north come forth dew and hoar-frost, and cold and snow and frost. And from the middle portal come forth dew and rain, and prosperity and blessing; and through the last portal which adjoins the south come forth drought and desolation, and burning and destruction. And the twelve portals of the four quarters of the heaven are therewith completed, and all their laws and all their plagues and all their benefactions have I shown to thee, my son Methuselah.

1Enoch 77

[1] And the first quarter is called the east, because it is the first: and the second, the south, because the Most High will descend there, yea, there in quite a special sense will He who is blessed for ever [2] descend. And the west quarter is named the diminished, because there all the luminaries of the [3] heaven wane and go down. And the fourth quarter, named the north, is divided into three parts: the first of them is for the dwelling of men: and the second contains seas of water, and the abysses and forests and rivers, and darkness and clouds; and the third part contains the garden of righteousness. [4] I saw seven high mountains, higher than all the mountains which are on the earth: and thence [5] comes forth hoar-frost, and days, seasons, and years pass away. I saw seven rivers on the earth larger than all the rivers: one of them coming from the west pours its waters into the Great Sea. [6] And these two come from the north to the sea and pour their waters into the Erythraean Sea in the [7] east. And the remaining, four come forth on the side of the north to their own sea, two of them to the Erythraean Sea, and two into the Great Sea and discharge themselves there and some say: [8] into the desert. Seven great islands I saw in the sea and in the mainland: two in the mainland and five in the Great Sea.

1Enoch 78

[1,2] And the names of the sun are the following: the first Orjares, and the second Tomas. And the moon has four names: the first name is Asonja, the second Ebla, the third Benase, and the fourth [3] Erae. These are the two great luminaries: their circumference is like the circumference of the [4] heaven, and the size of the circumference of both is alike. In the circumference of the sun there are seven portions of light which are added to it more than to the moon, and in definite measures it is s transferred till the seventh portion of the sun is exhausted. [5] And they set and enter the portals of the west, and make their revolution by the north, and come forth through the eastern portals [6] on the face of the heaven. And when the moon rises one-fourteenth part appears in the heaven: 7the light becomes full in her : on the fourteenth day she accomplishes her light. [7] And fifteen parts of light are transferred to her till the fifteenth day (when) her light is accomplished, according to the sign of the year, and she becomes fifteen parts, and the moon grows by (the addition of) fourteenth [8] parts. And in her waning (the moon) decreases on the first day to fourteen parts of her light, on the second to thirteen parts of light, on the third to twelve, on the fourth to eleven, on the fifth to ten, on the sixth to nine, on the seventh to eight, on the eighth to seven, on the ninth to six, on the tenth to five, on the eleventh to four, on the twelfth to three, on the thirteenth to two,

on the [9] fourteenth to the half of a seventh, and all her remaining light disappears wholly on the fifteenth. And [10] in certain months the month has twenty-nine days and once twenty-eight. And Uriel showed me another law: when light is transferred to the moon, and on which side it is transferred to her by the sun. [11] During all the period during which the moon is growing in her light, she is transferring it to herself when opposite to the sun during fourteen days her light is accomplished in the heaven, [12] and when she is illumined throughout, her light is accomplished full in the heaven. And on the first [13] day she is called the new moon, for on that day the light rises upon her. She becomes full moon exactly on the day when the sun sets in the west, and from the east she rises at night, and the moon shines the whole night through till the sun rises over against her and the moon is seen over against the sun. [14] On the side whence the light of the moon comes forth, there again she wanes till all the light vanishes and all the days of the month are at an end, and her circumference is empty, void of [15] light. And three months she makes of thirty days, and at her time she makes three months of twenty- nine days each, in which she accomplishes her waning in the first period of time, and in the first [16] portal for one hundred and seventy-seven days. And in the time of her going out she appears for three months (of) thirty days each, and for three months she appears (of) twenty-nine each. At night she appears like a man for twenty days each time, and by day she appears like the heaven, and there is nothing else in her save her light.

1Enoch 79

[1] And now, my son, I have shown thee everything, and the law of all the stars of the heaven is [2] completed. And he showed me all the laws of these for every day, and for every season of bearing rule, and for every year, and for its going forth, and for the order prescribed to it every month [3] and every week: And the waning of the moon which takes place in the sixth portal: for in this [4] sixth portal her light is accomplished, and after that there is the beginning of the waning: (And the waning) which takes place in the first portal in its season, till one hundred and seventy-seven [5] days are accomplished: reckoned according to weeks, twenty-five (weeks) and two days. She falls behind the sun and the order of the stars exactly five days in the course of one period, and when [6] this place which thou seest has been traversed. Such is the picture and sketch of every luminary which Uriel the archangel, who is their leader, showed unto me.

1Enoch 80

[1] And in those days the angel Uriel answered and said to me: Behold, I have shown thee everything, Enoch, and I have revealed everything to thee that thou shouldst see this sun and this moon, and the leaders of the stars of the heaven and all those who turn them, their tasks and times and departures. [2] And in the days of the sinners the years shall be shortened, And their seed shall be tardy on their lands and fields, And all things on the earth shall alter, And shall not appear in their time: And the rain shall be kept back And the heaven shall withhold (it). [3] And in those times the fruits of the earth shall be backward, And shall not grow in their time, And the fruits of the trees shall be withheld in their time. [4] And the moon shall alter her order, And not appear at her time. 5And in those days the sun shall be seen and he shall journey in the evening on the extremity of the great chariot in the west And shall shine more brightly than accords with the order of light. [6] And many chiefs of the stars shall transgress the order (prescribed). And these shall alter their orbits and tasks, And not appear at the seasons prescribed to them. [7] And the whole order of the stars shall be concealed from the sinners, And the thoughts of those on the earth shall err concerning them, And they shall be altered from all their ways, Yea, they shall

err and take them to be gods. [8] And evil shall be multiplied upon them, And punishment shall come upon them So as to destroy all.

1Enoch 81

[1] And he said unto me: Observe, Enoch, these heavenly tablets, And read what is written thereon, And mark every individual fact. [2] And I observed the heavenly tablets, and read everything which was written (thereon) and understood everything, and read the book of all the deeds of mankind, and of all the children of flesh [3] that shall be upon the earth to the remotest generations. And forthwith I blessed the great Lord the King of glory for ever, in that He has made all the works of the world, And I extolled the Lord because of His patience, And blessed Him because of the children of men. [4] And after that I said: Blessed is the man who dies in righteousness and goodness, Concerning whom there is no book of unrighteousness written, And against whom no day of judgement shall be found. [5] And those seven holy ones brought me and placed me on the earth before the door of my house, and said to me: Declare everything to thy son Methuselah, and show to all thy children that no [6] flesh is righteous in the sight of the Lord, for He is their Creator. One year we will leave thee with thy son, till thou givest thy (last) commands, that thou mayest teach thy children and record (it) for them, and testify to all thy children; and in the second year they shall take thee from their midst. [7] Let thy heart be strong, For the good shall announce righteousness to the good; The righteous with the righteous shall rejoice, And shall offer congratulation to one another. [8] But the sinners shall die with the sinners, And the apostate go down with the apostate. [9] And those who practice righteousness shall die on account of the deeds of men, And be taken away on account of the doings of the godless. [10] And in those days they ceased to speak to me, and I came to my people, blessing the Lord of the world.

1Enoch 82

[1] And now, my son Methuselah, all these things I am recounting to thee and writing down for thee! and I have revealed to thee everything, and given thee books concerning all these: so preserve, my son Methuselah, the books from thy fathers hand, and (see) that thou deliver them to the generations of the world. [2] I have given Wisdom to thee and to thy children, And thy children that shall be to thee, That they may give it to their children for generations, This wisdom (namely) that passeth their thought. [3] And those who understand it shall not sleep, But shall listen with the ear that they may learn this wisdom, And it shall please those that eat thereof better than good food. [4] Blessed are all the righteous, blessed are all those who walk In the way of righteousness and sin not as the sinners, in the reckoning of all their days in which the sun traverses the heaven, entering into and departing from the portals for thirty days with the heads of thousands of the order of the stars, together with the four which are intercalated which divide the four portions of the year, which [5] lead them and enter with them four days. Owing to them men shall be at fault and not reckon them in the whole reckoning of the year: yea, men shall be at fault, and not recognize them [6] accurately. For they belong to the reckoning of the year and are truly recorded (thereon) for ever, one in the first portal and one in the third, and one in the fourth and one in the sixth, and the year is completed in three hundred and sixty-four days. [7] And the account thereof is accurate and the recorded reckoning thereof exact; for the luminaries, and months and festivals, and years and days, has Uriel shown and revealed to me, to whom the [8] Lord of the whole creation of the world hath subjected the host of heaven. And he has power over night and day in the heaven to cause the light to give light to men -sun, moon, and stars, [9] and all the powers of the heaven which revolve in their circular chariots. And these are the orders of the

stars, which set in their places, and in their seasons and festivals and months. [10] And these are the names of those who lead them, who watch that they enter at their times, in their orders, in their seasons, in their months, in their periods of dominion, and in their positions. Their four leaders who divide the four parts of the year enter first; and after them the twelve leaders of the orders who divide the months; [11] and for the three hundred and sixty (days) there are heads over thousands who divide the days; and for the four intercalary days there are the leaders which sunder [12] the four parts of the year. And these heads over thousands are intercalated between [13] leader and leader, each behind a station, but their leaders make the division. And these are the names of the leaders who divide the four parts of the year which are ordained: Milkiel, Helemmelek, and Melejal, [14] and Narel. And the names of those who lead them: Adnarel, and Ijasusael, and Elomeel- these three follow the leaders of the orders, [15] and there is one that follows the three leaders of the orders which follow those leaders of stations that divide the four parts of the year. In the beginning of the year Melkejal rises first and rules, who is named Tamaini and sun, and [16] all the days of his dominion whilst he bears rule are ninety-one days. And these are the signs of the days which are to be seen on earth in the days of his dominion: sweat, and heat, and calms; and all the trees bear fruit, and leaves are produced on all the trees, and the harvest of wheat, and the rose-flowers, and all the flowers which come forth in the field, [17] but the trees of the winter season become withered. And these are the names of the leaders which are under them: Berkael, Zelebsel, and another who is added a head of a thousand, called Hilujaseph: and the days of the dominion of this (leader) are at an end. [18] The next leader after him is Helemmelek, whom one names the shining sun, and all the days [19] of his light are ninety-one days. And these are the signs of (his) days on the earth: glowing heat and dryness, and the trees ripen their fruits and produce all their fruits ripe and ready, and the sheep pair and become pregnant, and all the fruits of the earth are gathered in, and everything that is [20] in the fields, and the winepress: these things take place in the days of his dominion. These are the names, and the orders, and the leaders of those heads of thousands: Gidaljal, Keel, and Heel, and the name of the head of a thousand which is added to them, Asfael: and the days of his dominion are at an end.

The Book of Dreams
1Enoch 83

[1] And now, my son Methuselah, I will show thee all my visions which I have seen, recounting [2] them before thee. Two visions I saw before I took a wife, and the one was quite unlike the other: the first when I was learning to write: the second before I took thy mother, (when) I saw a terrible [3] vision. And regarding them I prayed to the Lord. I had laid me down in the house of my grandfather Mahalalel, (when) I saw in a vision how the heaven collapsed and was borne off and fell to [4] the earth. And when it fell to the earth I saw how the earth was swallowed up in a great abyss, and mountains were suspended on mountains, and hills sank down on hills, and high trees were rent [5] from their stems, and hurled down and sunk in the abyss. And thereupon a word fell into my mouth, [6] and I lifted up (my voice) to cry aloud, and said: The earth is destroyed. And my grandfather Mahalalel waked me as I lay near him, and said unto me: Why dost thou cry so, my son, and why [7] dost thou make such lamentation? And I recounted to him the whole vision which I had seen, and he said unto me: A terrible thing hast thou seen, my son, and of grave moment is thy dream- vision as to the secrets if all the sin of the earth: it must sink into the abyss and be destroyed with [8] a great destruction. And now, my son, arise and make petition to the Lord of glory, since thou art a believer, that a remnant may remain on the

earth, and that He may not destroy the whole [9] earth. My son, from heaven all this will come upon the earth, and upon the earth there will be great [10] destruction. After that I arose and prayed and implored and besought, and wrote down my prayer for the generations of the world, and I will show everything to thee, my son Methuselah. And when I had gone forth below and seen the heaven, and the sun rising in the east, and the moon setting in the west, and a few stars, and the whole earth, and everything as He had known it in the beginning, then I blessed the Lord of judgement and extolled Him because He had made the sun to go forth from the windows of the east, and he ascended and rose on the face of the heaven, and set out and kept traversing the path shown unto him.

1Enoch 84

[1] And I lifted up my hands in righteousness and blessed the Holy and Great One, and spake with the breath of my mouth, and with the tongue of flesh, which God has made for the children of the flesh of men, that they should speak therewith, and He gave them breath and a tongue and a mouth that they should speak therewith: [2] Blessed be Thou, O Lord, King, Great and mighty in Thy greatness, Lord of the whole creation of the heaven, King of kings and God of the whole world. And Thy power and kingship and greatness abide for ever and ever, And throughout all generations Thy dominion; And all the heavens are Thy throne for ever, And the whole earth Thy footstool for ever and ever. [3] For Thou hast made and Thou rulest all things, And nothing is too hard for Thee, Wisdom departs not from the place of Thy throne, Nor turns away from Thy presence. And Thou knowest and seest and hearest everything, And there is nothing hidden from Thee for Thou seest everything. [4] And now the angels of Thy heavens are guilty of trespass, And upon the flesh of men abideth Thy wrath until the great day of judgement. [5] And now, O God and Lord and Great King, I implore and beseech Thee to fulfil my prayer, To leave me a posterity on earth, And not destroy all the flesh of man, And make the earth without inhabitant, So that there should be an eternal destruction. [6] And now, my Lord, destroy from the earth the flesh which has aroused Thy wrath, But the flesh of righteousness and uprightness establish as a plant of the eternal seed, And hide not Thy face from the prayer of Thy servant, O Lord.

1Enoch 85

[1,2] And after this I saw another dream, and I will show the whole dream to thee, my son. And Enoch lifted up (his voice) and spake to his son Methuselah: To thee, my son, will I speak: hear my words-incline thine ear to the dream-vision of thy father. [3] Before I took thy mother Edna, I saw in a vision on my bed, and behold a bull came forth from the earth, and that bull was white; and after it came forth a heifer, and along with this (latter) came forth two bulls, one of them black and [4] the other red. And that black bull gored the red one and pursued him over the earth, and thereupon [5] I could no longer see that red bull. But that black bull grew and that heifer went with him, and [6] I saw that many oxen proceeded from him which resembled and followed him. And that cow, that first one, went from the presence of that first bull in order to seek that red one, but found him [7] not, and lamented with a great lamentation over him and sought him. And I looked till that first [8] bull came to her and quieted her, and from that time onward she cried no more. And after that she bore another white bull, and after him she bore many bulls and black cows. [9] And I saw in my sleep that white bull likewise grow and become a great white bull, and from Him proceeded many white bulls, and they resembled him. And they began to beget many white bulls, which resembled them, one following the other, (even) many.

1Enoch 86

[1] And again I saw with mine eyes as I slept, and I saw the heaven above, and behold a star fell [2] from heaven, and it arose and eat and pastured amongst those oxen. And after that I saw the large and the black oxen, and behold they all changed their stalls and pastures and their cattle, and began [3] to live with each other. And again I saw in the vision, and looked towards the heaven, and behold I saw many stars descend and cast themselves down from heaven to that first star, and they became [4] bulls amongst those cattle and pastured with them amongst them. And I looked at them and saw, and behold they all let out their privy members, like horses, and began to cover the cows of the oxen, [5] and they all became pregnant and bare elephants, camels, and asses. And all the oxen feared them and were affrighted at them, and began to bite with their teeth and to devour, and to gore with their [6] horns. And they began, moreover, to devour those oxen; and behold all the children of the earth began to tremble and quake before them and to flee from them.

1Enoch 87

[1] And again I saw how they began to gore each other and to devour each other, and the earth [2] began to cry aloud. And I raised mine eyes again to heaven, and I saw the vision, and behold there came forth from heaven beings who were like white men: and four went forth from that place [3] and three with them. And those three that had last come forth grasped me by my hand and took me up, away from the generations of the earth, and raised me up to a lofty place, and showed me [4] a tower raised high above the earth, and all the hills were lower. And one said unto me: Remain here till thou seest everything that befalls those elephants, camels, and asses, and the stars and the oxen, and all of them.

1Enoch 88

[1] And I saw one of those four who had come forth first, and he seized that first star which had fallen from the heaven, and bound it hand and foot and cast it into an abyss: now that abyss was [2] narrow and deep, and horrible and dark. And one of them drew a sword, and gave it to those elephants and camels and asses: then they began to smite each other, and the whole earth quaked [3] because of them. And as I was beholding in the vision, lo, one of those four who had come forth stoned (them) from heaven, and gathered and took all the great stars whose privy members were like those of horses, and bound them all hand and foot, and cast them in an abyss of the earth.

1Enoch 89

[1] And one of those four went to that white bull and instructed him in a secret, without his being terrified: he was born a bull and became a man, and built for himself a great vessel and dwelt thereon; [2] and three bulls dwelt with him in that vessel and they were covered in. And again I raised mine eyes towards heaven and saw a lofty roof, with seven water torrents thereon, and those torrents [3] flowed with much water into an enclosure. And I saw again, and behold fountains were opened on the surface of that great enclosure, and that water began to swell and rise upon the surface, [4] and I saw that enclosure till all its surface was covered with water. And the water, the darkness, and mist increased upon it; and as I looked at the height of that water, that water had risen above the height of that enclosure, and was streaming over that enclosure, and it stood upon the earth. [5] And all the cattle of that enclosure were gathered together until I saw how they sank and were [6] swallowed up and perished in that water. But that vessel floated on the water, while all the oxen and elephants and camels and asses sank to the bottom with all the animals, so that I could no longer see them, [7] and they were not able to escape, (but) perished and sank into the depths. And again I saw in the vision till those water torrents were removed from that high roof, and the chasms [8] of the earth were leveled up and other abysses were opened. Then the water began to run down

into these, till the earth became visible; but that vessel settled on the earth, and the darkness [9] retired and light appeared. But that white bull which had become a man came out of that vessel, and the three bulls with him, and one of those three was white like that bull, and one of them was red as blood, and one black: and that white bull departed from them. [10] And they began to bring forth beasts of the field and birds, so that there arose different genera: lions, tigers, wolves, dogs, hyenas, wild boars, foxes, squirrels, swine, falcons, vultures, kites, eagles, and ravens; [11] and among them was born a white bull. And they began to bite one another; but that white bull which was born amongst them begat a wild ass and a white bull with it, and the [12] wild asses multiplied. But that bull which was born from him begat a black wild boar and a white [13] sheep; and the former begat many boars, but that sheep begat twelve sheep. And when those twelve sheep had grown, they gave up one of them to the asses, and those asses again gave up that sheep to the wolves, [14] and that sheep grew up among the wolves. And the Lord brought the eleven sheep to live with it and to pasture with it among the wolves: and they multiplied and became many flocks of sheep. 15And the wolves began to fear them, and they oppressed them until they destroyed [16] cry aloud on account of their little ones, and to complain unto their Lord. And a sheep which had been saved from the wolves fled and escaped to the wild asses; and I saw the sheep how they lamented and cried, and besought their Lord with all their might, till that Lord of the sheep descended at the voice of the sheep from a lofty abode, and came to them and pastured them. [17] And He called that sheep which had escaped the wolves, and spake with it concerning the wolves that it should [18] admonish them not to touch the sheep. And the sheep went to the wolves according to the word of the Lord, and another sheep met it and went with it, and the two went and entered together into the assembly of those wolves, and spake with them and admonished them not to touch the [19] sheep from henceforth. And thereupon I saw the wolves, and how they oppressed the sheep [20] exceedingly with all their power; and the sheep cried aloud. And the Lord came to the sheep and they began to smite those wolves: and the wolves began to make lamentation; but the sheep became [21] quiet and forthwith ceased to cry out. And I saw the sheep till they departed from amongst the wolves; but the eyes of the wolves were blinded, and those wolves departed in pursuit of the sheep [22] with all their power. And the Lord of the sheep went with them, as their leader, and all His sheep [23] followed Him: and his face was dazzling and glorious and terrible to behold. But the wolves [24] began to pursue those sheep till they reached a sea of water. And that sea was divided, and the water stood on this side and on that before their face, and their Lord led them and placed Himself between [25] them and the wolves. And as those wolves did not yet see the sheep, they proceeded into the midst of that sea, and the wolves followed the sheep, and those wolves ran after them into that sea. [26] And when they saw the Lord of the sheep, they turned to flee before His face, but that sea gathered itself together, and became as it had been created, and the water swelled and rose till it covered [27] those wolves. And I saw till all the wolves who pursued those sheep perished and were drowned. [28] But the sheep escaped from that water and went forth into a wilderness, where there was no water and no grass; and they began to open their eyes and to see; and I saw the Lord of the sheep [29] pasturing them and giving them water and grass, and that sheep going and leading them. And that [30] sheep ascended to the summit of that lofty rock, and the Lord of the sheep sent it to them. And after that I saw the Lord of the sheep who stood before them, and His appearance was great and [31] terrible and majestic, and all those sheep saw Him and were afraid before His face. And they all feared and trembled because of

183

Him, and they cried to that sheep with them which was amongst [32] them: We are not able to stand before our Lord or to behold Him. And that sheep which led them again ascended to the summit of that rock, but the sheep began to be blinded and to wander [33] from the way which he had showed them, but that sheep wot not thereof. And the Lord of the sheep was wrathful exceedingly against them, and that sheep discovered it, and went down from the summit of the rock, and came to the sheep, and found the greatest part of them blinded and fallen [34] away. And when they saw it they feared and trembled at its presence, and desired to return to their [35] folds. And that sheep took other sheep with it, and came to those sheep which had fallen away, and began to slay them; and the sheep feared its presence, and thus that sheep brought back those [36] sheep that had fallen away, and they returned to their folds. And I saw in this vision till that sheep became a man and built a house for the Lord of the sheep, and placed all the sheep in that house. [37] And I saw till this sheep which had met that sheep which led them fell asleep: and I saw till all the great sheep perished and little ones arose in their place, and they came to a pasture, and [38] approached a stream of water. Then that sheep, their leader which had become a man, withdrew [39] from them and fell asleep, and all the sheep sought it and cried over it with a great crying. And I saw till they left off crying for that sheep and crossed that stream of water, and there arose the two sheep as leaders in the place of those which had led them and fallen asleep (lit. had fallen asleep and led [40] them). And I saw till the sheep came to a goodly place, and a pleasant and glorious land, and I saw till those sheep were satisfied; and that house stood amongst them in the pleasant land. [41] And sometimes their eyes were opened, and sometimes blinded, till another sheep arose and led them and brought them all back, and their eyes were opened. [42] And the dogs and the foxes and the wild boars began to devour those sheep till the Lord of the sheep raised up another sheep a ram from their [43] midst, which led them. And that ram began to butt on either side those dogs, foxes, and wild [44] boars till he had destroyed them all. And that sheep whose eyes were opened saw that ram, which was amongst the sheep, till it forsook its glory and began to butt those sheep, and trampled upon them, and behaved itself [45] unseemly. And the Lord of the sheep sent the lamb to another lamb and raised it to being a ram and leader of the sheep instead of that [46] ram which had forsaken its glory. And it went to it and spake to it alone, and raised it to being a ram, and made it the prince and leader of the sheep; but during all these things those dogs [47] oppressed the sheep. And the first ram pursued that second ram, and that second ram arose and fled before it; and I saw till those dogs pulled [48] down the first ram. And that second ram arose 48b and led the little sheep. And those sheep grew and multiplied; but all the dogs, and foxes, and wild boars feared and fled before it, and that ram butted and killed the wild beasts, and those wild beasts had no longer any power among the 49sheep and robbed them no more of ought. And that ram begat many sheep and fell asleep; and a little sheep became ram in its stead, and became prince and leader of those sheep [50] And that house became great and broad, and it was built for those sheep: (and) a tower lofty and great was built on the house for the Lord of the sheep, and that house was low, but the tower was elevated and lofty, and the Lord of the sheep stood on that tower and they offered a full table before Him. [51] And again I saw those sheep that they again erred and went many ways, and forsook that their house, and the Lord of the sheep called some from amongst the sheep and sent them to the sheep, [52] but the sheep began to slay them. And one of them was saved and was not slain, and it sped away and cried aloud over the sheep; and they sought to slay it, but the Lord of the sheep saved it from [53] the sheep, and brought it up to me, and caused it to dwell there. And many other sheep He sent to those sheep to testify unto them and lament over them. 54 And after that I saw that when they forsook the house of the Lord and His tower they fell away entirely, and their eyes were blinded; and I saw the Lord of the sheep how He wrought much slaughter amongst them in their herds until 55 those sheep invited that slaughter and betrayed His place. And He gave them over into the hands of the lions and tigers, and wolves and hyenas, and into the hand of the foxes, and to all the wild 56 beasts, and those wild beasts began to tear in pieces those sheep. And I saw that He forsook that their house and their tower and gave them all into the hand of the lions, to tear and devour them, 57 into the hand of all the wild beasts. And I began to cry aloud with all my power, and to appeal to the Lord of the sheep, and to represent to Him in regard to the sheep that they were devoured 58 by all the wild beasts. But He remained unmoved, though He saw it, and rejoiced that they were devoured and swallowed and robbed, and left them to be devoured in the hand of all the beasts. 59 And He called seventy shepherds, and cast those sheep to them that they might pasture them, and He spake to the shepherds and their companions: Let each individual of you pasture the sheep 60 henceforward, and everything that I shall command you that do ye. And I will deliver them over unto you duly numbered, and tell you which of them are to be destroyed-and them destroy ye. And 61 He gave over unto them those sheep. And He called another and spake unto him: Observe and mark everything that the shepherds will do to those sheep; for they will destroy more of them than 62 I have commanded them. And every excess and the destruction which will be wrought through the shepherds, record (namely) how many they destroy according to my command, and how many according to their own caprice: record against every individual shepherd all the destruction he 63 effects. And read out before me by number how many they destroy, and how many they deliver over for destruction, that I may have this as a testimony against them, and know every deed of the shepherds, that I may comprehend and see what they do, whether or not they abide by my 64 command which I have commanded them. But they shall not know it, and thou shalt not declare it to them, nor admonish them, but only record against each individual all the destruction which 65 the shepherds effect each in his time and lay it all before me. And I saw till those shepherds pastured in their season, and they began to slay and to destroy more than they were bidden, and they delivered 66 those sheep into the hand of the lions. And the lions and tigers eat and devoured the greater part of those sheep, and the wild boars eat along with them; and they burnt that tower and demolished 67 that house. And I became exceedingly sorrowful over that tower because that house of the sheep was demolished, and afterwards I was unable to see if those sheep entered that house. 68 And the shepherds and their associates delivered over those sheep to all the wild beasts, to devour them, and each one of them received in his time a definite number: it was written by the other 69 in a book how many each one of them destroyed of them. And each one slew and destroyed many 70 more than was prescribed; and I began to weep and lament on account of those sheep. And thus in the vision I saw that one who wrote, how he wrote down every one that was destroyed by those shepherds, day by day, and carried up and laid down and showed actually the whole book to the Lord of the sheep-(even) everything that they had done, and all that each one of them had made 71 away with, and all that they had given over to destruction. And the book was read before the Lord of the sheep, and He took the book from his hand and read it and sealed it and laid it down. 72 And forthwith I saw how the shepherds pastured for twelve hours, and behold three of those sheep turned

back and came and entered and began to build up all that had fallen down of that 73 house; but the wild boars tried to hinder them, but they were not able. And they began again to build as before, and they reared up that tower, and it was named the high tower; and they began again to place a table before the tower, but all the bread on it was polluted and not pure. 74 And as touching all this the eyes of those sheep were blinded so that they saw not, and (the eyes of) their shepherds likewise; and they delivered them in large numbers to their shepherds for 75 destruction, and they trampled the sheep with their feet and devoured them. And the Lord of the sheep remained unmoved till all the sheep were dispersed over the field and mingled with them (the beasts), 76 and they (the shepherds) did not save them out of the hand of the beasts. And this one who wrote the book carried it up, and showed it and read it before the Lord of the sheep, and implored Him on their account, and besought Him on their account as he showed Him all the doings 77 of the shepherds, and gave testimony before Him against all the shepherds. And he took the actual book and laid it down beside Him and departed.

1Enoch 90

1 And I saw till that in this manner thirty-five shepherds undertook the pasturing (of the sheep), and they severally completed their periods as did the first; and others receive them into their 2 hands, to pasture them for their period, each shepherd in his own period. And after that I saw in my vision all the birds of heaven coming, the eagles, the vultures, the kites, the ravens; but the eagles led all the birds; and they began to devour those sheep, and to pick out their eyes and to 3 devour their flesh. And the sheep cried out because their flesh was being devoured by the birds, 4 and as for me I looked and lamented in my sleep over that shepherd who pastured the sheep. And I saw until those sheep were devoured by the dogs and eagles and kites, and they left neither flesh nor skin nor sinew remaining on them till only their bones stood there: and their bones too fell 5 to the earth and the sheep became few. And I saw until that twenty-three had undertaken the pasturing and completed in their several periods fifty-eight times. 6 But behold lambs were borne by those white sheep, and they began to open their eyes and to see, 7 and to cry to the sheep. Yea, they cried to them, but they did not hearken to what they said to 8 them, but were exceedingly deaf, and their eyes were very exceedingly blinded. And I saw in the vision how the ravens flew upon those lambs and took one of those lambs, and dashed the sheep 9 in pieces and devoured them. And I saw till horns grew upon those lambs, and the ravens cast down their horns; and I saw till there sprouted a great horn of one of those sheep, and their eyes 10 were opened. And it looked at themand their eyes opened, and it cried to the sheep, and the 11 rams saw it and all ran to it. 12And notwithstanding all this those eagles and vultures and ravens and kites 13 still kept tearing the sheep and swooping down upon them 14and devouring them: still the sheep remained silent, but the rams lamented and cried out. 15 And those ravens fought and battled with it and sought to lay low its horn, but they had no power over it. 16 All the eagles and vultures and ravens and kites were gathered together, 17 and there came with them all the sheep of the field, 18 yea, they all came together, and helped each other to break that horn of the ram. 19 And I saw till a great sword was given to the sheep, and the sheep proceeded against all the beasts of the field to slay them, and all the beasts and the birds of the heaven fled before their face. And I saw that man, who wrote the book according to the command of the Lord, till he opened that book concerning the destruction which those twelve last shepherds had wrought, and showed that they had destroyed much more than their predecessors, before the Lord of the sheep. And I saw till the Lord of the sheep came unto them and took in His hand the staff of His wrath, and smote the

earth, and the earth clave asunder, and all the beasts and all the birds of the heaven fell from among those sheep, and were swallowed up in the earth and it covered them. [20] And I saw till a throne was erected in the pleasant land, and the Lord of the sheep sat Himself thereon, and the other took the sealed books and opened those books before the Lord of the sheep. [21] And the Lord called those men the seven first white ones, and commanded that they should bring before Him, beginning with the first star which led the way, all the stars whose privy members [22] were like those of horses, and they brought them all before Him. And He said to that man who wrote before Him, being one of those seven white ones, and said unto him: Take those seventy shepherds to whom I delivered the sheep, and who taking them on their own authority slew more [23] than I commanded them. And behold they were all bound, I saw, and they all stood before Him. [24] And the judgement was held first over the stars, and they were judged and found guilty, and went to the place of condemnation, and they were cast into an abyss, full of fire and flaming, and full [25] of pillars of fire. And those seventy shepherds were judged and found guilty, and they were cast [26] into that fiery abyss. And I saw at that time how a like abyss was opened in the midst of the earth, full of fire, and they brought those blinded sheep, and they were all judged and found guilty and [27] cast into this fiery abyss, and they burned; now this abyss was to the right of that house. And I saw those sheep burning and their bones burning. [28] And I stood up to see till they folded up that old house; and carried off all the pillars, and all the beams and ornaments of the house were at the same time folded up with it, and they carried [29] it off and laid it in a place in the south of the land. And I saw till the Lord of the sheep brought a new house greater and loftier than that first, and set it up in the place of the first which had beer folded up: all its pillars were new, and its ornaments were new and larger than those of the first, the old one which He had taken away, and all the sheep were within it. [30] And I saw all the sheep which had been left, and all the beasts on the earth, and all the birds of the heaven, falling down and doing homage to those sheep and making petition to and obeying [31] them in every thing. And thereafter those three who were clothed in white and had seized me by my handwho had taken me up before, and the hand of that ram also seizing hold of me, they [32] took me up and set me down in the midst of those sheep before the judgement took place. And those [33] sheep were all white, and their wool was abundant and clean. And all that had been destroyed and dispersed, and all the beasts of the field, and all the birds of the heaven, assembled in that house, and the Lord of the sheep rejoiced with great joy because they were all good and had returned to [34] His house. And I saw till they laid down that sword, which had been given to the sheep, and they brought it back into the house, and it was sealed before the presence of the Lord, and all the sheep [35] were invited into that house, but it held them not. And the eyes of them all were opened, and they [36] saw the good, and there was not one among them that did not see. And I saw that that house was large and broad and very full. [37] And I saw that a white bull was born, with large horns and all the beasts of the field and all the [38] birds of the air feared him and made petition to him all the time. of And I saw till all their generations were transformed, and they all became white bulls; and the first among them became a lamb, and that lamb became a great animal and had great black horns on its head; and the Lord of the sheep [39] rejoiced over it and over all the oxen. And I slept in their midst: and I awoke and saw everything. [40] This is the vision which I saw while I slept, and I awoke and blessed the Lord of righteousness and [41] gave Him glory. Then I wept with a great weeping and my tears stayed not till I could no longer endure it: when I saw, they flowed on account of what I had seen; for

185

everything shall come and [42] be fulfilled, and all the deeds of men in their order were shown to me. On that night I remembered the first dream, and because of it I wept and was troubled-because I had seen that vision.

The Epistle of Enoch
1Enoch 91

[1] And now, my son Methuselah, call to me all thy brothers And gather together to me all the sons of thy mother; For the word calls me, And the spirit is poured out upon me, That I may show you everything That shall befall you for ever. [2] And there upon Methuselah went and summoned to him all his brothers and assembled his relatives. [3] And he spake unto all the children of righteousness and said: Hear, ye sons of Enoch, all the words of your father, And hearken aright to the voice of my mouth; For I exhort you and say unto you, beloved: [4] Love uprightness and walk therein. And draw not nigh to uprightness with a double heart, And associate not with those of a double heart, But walk in righteousness, my sons. And it shall guide you on good paths, And righteousness shall be your companion. [5] For I know that violence must increase on the earth, And a great chastisement be executed on the earth, And all unrighteousness come to an end: Yea, it shall be cut off from its roots, And its whole structure be destroyed. [6] And unrighteousness shall again be consummated on the earth, And all the deeds of unrighteousness and of violence And transgression shall prevail in a twofold degree. [7] And when sin and unrighteousness and blasphemy And violence in all kinds of deeds increase, And apostasy and transgression and uncleanness increase, A great chastisement shall come from heaven upon all these, And the holy Lord will come forth with wrath and chastisement To execute judgement on earth. [8] In those days violence shall be cut off from its roots, And the roots of unrighteousness together with deceit, And they shall be destroyed from under heaven. [9] And all the idols of the heathen shall be abandoned, And the temples burned with fire, And they shall remove them from the whole earth, And they (the heathen) shall be cast into the judgement of fire, And shall perish in wrath and in grievous judgement for ever. [10] And the righteous shall arise from their sleep, And wisdom shall arise and be given unto them. [11] And after that the roots of unrighteousness shall be cut off, and the sinners shall bedestroyed by the sword and the blasphemers destroyed in every place, [12] and those who plan violence and those who commit blasphemy shall perish by the sword. [13] And now I tell you, my sons, and show you The paths of righteousness and the paths of violence. Yea, I will show them to you again That ye may know what will come to pass. [14] And now, hearken unto me, my sons, And walk in the paths of righteousness, And walk not in the paths of violence; For all who walk in the paths of unrighteousness shall perish for ever.

1Enoch 92

[1] The book written by Enoch-Enoch indeed wrote this complete doctrine of wisdom, (which is) praised of all men and a judge of all the earth for all my children who shall dwell on the earth. And for the future generations who shall observe uprightness and peace. [2] Let not your spirit be troubled on account of the times; For the Holy and Great One has appointed days for all things. [3] And the righteous one shall arise from sleep, Shall arise and walk in the paths of righteousness, And all his path and conversation shall be in eternal goodness and grace. [4] He will be gracious to the righteous and give him eternal uprightness, And He will give him power so that he shall be (endowed) with goodness and righteousness. And he shall walk in eternal light. [5] And sin shall perish in darkness for ever, And shall no more be seen from that day for evermore.

1Enoch 93

[1,2] And after that Enoch both gave and began to recount from the books. And Enoch said: Concerning the children of righteousness and concerning the elect of the world, And concerning the plant of uprightness, I will speak these things, Yea, I Enoch will declare (them) unto you, my sons: According to that which appeared to me in the heavenly vision, And which I have known through the word of the holy angels, And have learnt from the heavenly tablets. [3] And Enoch began to recount from the books and said: I was born the seventh in the first week, While judgement and righteousness still endured. [4] And after me there shall arise in the second week great wickedness, And deceit shall have sprung up; And in it there shall be the first end. And in it a man shall be saved; And after it is ended unrighteousness shall grow up, And a law shall be made for the sinners. And after that in the third week at its close A man shall be elected as the plant of righteous judgement, And his posterity shall become the plant of righteousness for evermore. [6] And after that in the fourth week, at its close, Visions of the holy and righteous shall be seen, And a law for all generations and an enclosure shall be made for them. [7] And after that in the fifth week, at its close, The house of glory and dominion shall be built for ever. [8] And after that in the sixth week all who live in it shall be blinded, And the hearts of all of them shall godlessly forsake wisdom. And in it a man shall ascend; And at its close the house of dominion shall be burnt with fire, And the whole race of the chosen root shall be dispersed. [9] And after that in the seventh week shall an apostate generation arise, And many shall be its deeds, And all its deeds shall be apostate. [10] And at its close shall be elected The elect righteous of the eternal plant of righteousness, To receive sevenfold instruction concerning all His creation. 11For who is there of all the children of men that is able to hear the voice of the Holy One without being troubled ? And who can think His thoughts ? and who is there that can behold all the works [12] of heaven ? And how should there be one who could behold the heaven, and who is there that could understand the things of heaven and see a soul or a spirit and could tell thereof, or ascend and see [13] all their ends and think them or do like them ? And who is there of all men that could know what is the breadth and the length of the earth, and to whom has been shown the measure of all of them ? [14] Or is there any one who could discern the length of the heaven and how great is its height, and upon what it is founded, and how great is the number of the stars, and where all the luminaries rest ?

1Enoch 94

[1] And now I say unto you, my sons, love righteousness and walk therein; For the paths of righteousness are worthy of acceptation, But the paths of unrighteousness shall suddenly be destroyed and vanish. [2] And to certain men of a generation shall the paths of violence and of death be revealed, And they shall hold themselves afar from them, And shall not follow them. [3] And now I say unto you the righteous: Walk not in the paths of wickedness, nor in the paths of death, And draw not nigh to them, lest ye be destroyed. [4] But seek and choose for yourselves righteousness and an elect life, And walk in the paths of peace, And ye shall live and prosper. [5] And hold fast my words in the thoughts of your hearts, And suffer them not to be effaced from your hearts; For I know that sinners will tempt men to evilly-entreat wisdom, So that no place may be found for her, And no manner of temptation may minish. [6] Woe to those who build unrighteousness and oppression And lay deceit as a foundation; For they shall be suddenly overthrown, And they shall have no peace. [7] Woe to those who build their houses with sin; For from all their foundations shall they be overthrown, And by the sword shall they fall. And those who acquire gold and silver in judgement suddenly shall perish. [8] Woe to

you, ye rich, for ye have trusted in your riches, And from your riches shall ye depart, Because ye have not remembered the Most High in the days of your riches. [9] Ye have committed blasphemy and unrighteousness, And have become ready for the day of slaughter, And the day of darkness and the day of the great judgement. [10] Thus I speak and declare unto you: He who hath created you will overthrow you, And for your fall there shall be no compassion, And your Creator will rejoice at your destruction. [11] And your righteous ones in those days shall be A reproach to the sinners and the godless.

1Enoch 95

[1] Oh that mine eyes were a cloud of waters That I might weep over you, And pour down my tears as a cloud of waters: That so I might rest from my trouble of heart! [2] who has permitted you to practice reproaches and wickedness ? And so judgement shall overtake you, sinners. [3] Fear not the sinners, ye righteous; For again will the Lord deliver them into your hands, That ye may execute judgement upon them according to your desires. [4] Woe to you who fulminate anathemas which cannot be reversed: Healing shall therefore be far from you because of your sins. [5] Woe to you who requite your neighbour with evil; For ye shall be requited according to your works. [6] Woe to you, lying witnesses, And to those who weigh out injustice, For suddenly shall ye perish. [7] Woe to you, sinners, for ye persecute the righteous; For ye shall be delivered up and persecuted because of injustice, And heavy shall its yoke be upon you.

1Enoch 96

[1] Be hopeful, ye righteous; for suddenly shall the sinners perish before you, And ye shall have lordship over them according to your desires. [2] And in the day of the tribulation of the sinners, Your children shall mount and rise as eagles, And higher than the vultures will be your nest, And ye shall ascend and enter the crevices of the earth, And the clefts of the rock for ever as coneys before the unrighteous, And the sirens shall sigh because of you-and weep [3] Wherefore fear not, ye that have suffered; For healing shall be your portion, And a bright light shall enlighten you, And the voice of rest ye shall hear from heaven. [4] Woe unto you, ye sinners, for your riches make you appear like the righteous, But your hearts convict you of being sinners, And this fact shall be a testimony against you for a memorial of (your) evil deeds. [5] Woe to you who devour the finest of the wheat, And drink wine in large bowls, And tread under foot the lowly with your might. [6] Woe to you who drink water from every fountain, For suddenly shall ye be consumed and wither away, Because ye have forsaken the fountain of life. [7] Woe to you who work unrighteousness And deceit and blasphemy: It shall be a memorial against you for evil. [8] Woe to you, ye mighty, Who with might oppress the righteous; For the day of your destruction is coming. In those days many and good days shall come to the righteous-in the day of your judgement.

1Enoch 97

[1] Believe, ye righteous, that the sinners will become a shame And perish in the day of unrighteousness. [2] Be it known unto you (ye sinners) that the Most High is mindful of your destruction, And the angels of heaven rejoice over your destruction. [3] What will ye do, ye sinners, And whither will ye flee on that day of judgement, When ye hear the voice of the prayer of the righteous ? [4] Yea, ye shall fare like unto them, Against whom this word shall be a testimony: " Ye have been companions of sinners." [5] And in those days the prayer of the righteous shall reach unto the Lord, And for you the days of your judgement shall come. [6] And all the words of your unrighteousness shall be read out before the Great Holy One, And your faces shall be covered with shame, And He will reject every work which is grounded on unrighteousness. [7] Woe to you, ye sinners, who live on the mid ocean and on the dry land, Whose remembrance is evil

against you. [8] Woe to you who acquire silver and gold in unrighteousness and say: " We have become rich with riches and have possessions; And have acquired everything we have desired. [9] And now let us do what we purposed: For we have gathered silver, 9c And many are the husbandmen in our houses." 9d And our granaries are (brim) full as with water, [10] Yea and like water your lies shall flow away; For your riches shall not abide But speedily ascend from you; For ye have acquired it all in unrighteousness, And ye shall be given over to a great curse.

1Enoch 98

[1] And now I swear unto you, to the wise and to the foolish, For ye shall have manifold experiences on the earth. [2] For ye men shall put on more adornments than a woman, And coloured garments more than a virgin: In royalty and in grandeur and in power, And in silver and in gold and in purple, And in splendour and in food they shall be poured out as water. [3] Therefore they shall be wanting in doctrine and wisdom, And they shall perish thereby together with their possessions; And with all their glory and their splendour, And in shame and in slaughter and in great destitution, Their spirits shall be cast into the furnace of fire. [4] I have sworn unto you, ye sinners, as a mountain has not become a slave, And a hill does not become the handmaid of a woman, Even so sin has not been sent upon the earth, But man of himself has created it, And under a great curse shall they fall who commit it. [5] And barrenness has not been given to the woman, But on account of the deeds of her own hands she dies without children. [6] I have sworn unto you, ye sinners, by the Holy Great One, That all your evil deeds are revealed in the heavens, And that none of your deeds of oppression are covered and hidden. [7] And do not think in your spirit nor say in your heart that ye do not know and that ye do not see [8] that every sin is every day recorded in heaven in the presence of the Most High. From henceforth ye know that all your oppression wherewith ye oppress is written down every day till the day of your judgement . [9] Woe to you, ye fools, for through your folly shall ye perish: and ye transgress against the wise, [10] and so good hap shall not be your portion. And now, know ye that ye are prepared for the day of destruction: wherefore do not hope to live, ye sinners, but ye shall depart and die; for ye know no ransom; for ye are prepared for the day of the great judgement, for the day of tribulation and great shame for your spirits. [11] Woe to you, ye obstinate of heart, who work wickedness and eat blood: Whence have ye good things to eat and to drink and to be filled ? From all the good things which the Lord the Most High has placed in abundance on the earth; therefore ye shall have no peace. [12] Woe to you who love the deeds of unrighteousness: wherefore do ye hope for good hap unto yourselves? know that ye shall be delivered into the hands of the righteous, and they shall cut [3] off your necks and slay you, and have no mercy upon you. Woe to you who rejoice in the tribulation of the righteous; for no grave shall be dug for you. Woe to you who set at nought the words of [5] the righteous; for ye shall have no hope of life. Woe to you who write down lying and godless words; for they write down their lies that men may hear them and act godlessly towards (their) [6] neighbour. Therefore they shall have no peace but die a sudden death.

1Enoch 99

[1] Woe to you who work godlessness, And glory in lying and extol them: Ye shall perish, and no happy life shall be yours. [2] Woe to them who pervert the words of uprightness, And transgress the eternal law, And transform themselves into what they were notinto sinners : They shall be trodden under foot upon the earth. [3] In those days make ready, ye righteous, to raise your prayers as a memorial, And place them as a testimony before the angels, That they may place the sin of the sinners for a memorial before the Most High. [4] In those days the nations shall be stirred up, And the families of the nations shall arise on the day of destruction. [5] And in those days the destitute shall go forth and carry off their children, And they shall abandon them, so that their children shall perish through them: Yea, they shall abandon their children (that are still) sucklings, and not return to them, And shall have no pity on their beloved ones. 6,[7] And again I swear to you, ye sinners, that sin is prepared for a day of unceasing bloodshed. And they who worship stones, and grave images of gold and silver and wood (and stone) and clay, and those who worship impure spirits and demons, and all kinds of idols not according to knowledge, shall get no manner of help from them. [8] And they shall become godless by reason of the folly of their hearts, And their eyes shall be blinded through the fear of their hearts And through visions in their dreams. [9] Through these they shall become godless and fearful; For they shall have wrought all their work in a lie, And shall have worshiped a stone: Therefore in an instant shall they perish. [10] But in those days blessed are all they who accept the words of wisdom, and understand them, And observe the paths of the Most High, and walk in the path of His righteousness, And become not godless with the godless; For they shall be saved. [11] Woe to you who spread evil to your neighbours; For you shall be slain in Sheol. [12] Woe to you who make deceitful and false measures, And (to them) who cause bitterness on the earth; For they shall thereby be utterly consumed. [13] Woe to you who build your houses through the grievous toil of others, And all their building materials are the bricks and stones of sin; I tell you ye shall have no peace. [14] Woe to them who reject the measure and eternal heritage of their fathers And whose souls follow after idols; For they shall have no rest. [15] Woe to them who work unrighteousness and help oppression, And slay their neighbours until the day of the great judgement. [16] For He shall cast down your glory, And bring affliction on your hearts, And shall arouse His fierce indignation And destroy you all with the sword; And all the holy and righteous shall remember your sins.

1Enoch 100

[1] And in those days in one place the fathers together with their sons shall be smitten And brothers one with another shall fall in death Till the streams flow with their blood. [2] For a man shall not withhold his hand from slaying his sons and his sons sons, And the sinner shall not withhold his hand from his honoured brother: From dawn till sunset they shall slay one another. [3] And the horse shall walk up to the breast in the blood of sinners, And the chariot shall be submerged to its height. [4] In those days the angels shall descend into the secret places And gather together into one place all those who brought down sin And the Most High will arise on that day of judgement To execute great judgement amongst sinners. [5] And over all the righteous and holy He will appoint guardians from amongst the holy angels To guard them as the apple of an eye, Until He makes an end of all wickedness and all sin, And though the righteous sleep a long sleep, they have nought to fear. [6] And (then) the children of the earth shall see the wise in security, And shall understand all the words of this book, And recognize that their riches shall not be able to save them In the overthrow of their sins. [7] Woe to you, Sinners, on the day of strong anguish, Ye who afflict the righteous and burn them with fire: Ye shall be requited according to your works. [8] Woe to you, ye obstinate of heart, Who watch in order to devise wickedness: Therefore shall fear come upon you And there shall be none to help you. [9] Woe to you, ye sinners, on account of the words of your mouth, And on account of the deeds of your hands which your godlessness as wrought, In blazing flames burning worse than fire shall ye burn. [10] And now, know ye that from the angels He will inquire as to your deeds in heaven, from the sun and from the moon

and from the stars in reference to your sins because upon the earth ye execute [11] judgement on the righteous. And He will summon to testify against you every cloud and mist and dew and rain; for they shall all be withheld because of you from descending upon you, and they [12] shall be mindful of your sins. And now give presents to the rain that it be not withheld from descending upon you, nor yet the dew, when it has received gold and silver from you that it may descend. When the hoar-frost and snow with their chilliness, and all the snow-storms with all their plagues fall upon you, in those days ye shall not be able to stand before them.

1Enoch 101

[1] Observe the heaven, ye children of heaven, and every work of the Most High, and fear ye Him [2] and work no evil in His presence. If He closes the windows of heaven, and withholds the rain and [3] the dew from descending on the earth on your account, what will ye do then? And if He sends His anger upon you because of yoour deeds, ye cannot petition Him; for ye spake proud and insolent [4] words against His righteousness: therefore ye shall have no peace. And see ye not the sailors of the ships, how their ships are tossed to and fro by the waves, and are shaken by the winds, and are [5] in sore trouble ? And therefore do they fear because all their goodly possessions go upon the sea with them, and they have evil forebodings of heart that the sea will swallow them and they will [6] perish therein. Are not the entire sea and all its waters, and all its movements, the work of the Most [7] High, and has He not set limits to its doings, and confined it throughout by the sand ? And at His reproof it is afraid and dries up, and all its fish die and all that is in it; But ye sinners that are [8] on the earth fear Him not. Has He not made the heaven and the earth, and all that is therein ? Who has given understanding and wisdom to everything that moves on the earth and in the sea. [9] Do not the sailors of the ships fear the sea ? Yet sinners fear not the Most High.

1Enoch 102

[1] In those days when He hath brought a grievous fire upon you, Whither will ye flee, and where will ye find deliverance ? And when He launches forth His Word against you Will you not be affrighted and fear ? [2] And all the luminaries shall be affrighted with great fear, And all the earth shall be affrighted and tremble and be alarmed. [3] And all the angels shall execute their commandst And shall seek to hide themselves from the presence of the Great Glory, And the children of earth shall tremble and quake; And ye sinners shall be cursed for ever, And ye shall have no peace. [4] Fear ye not, ye souls of the righteous, And be hopeful ye that have died in righteousness. [5] And grieve not if your soul into Sheol has descended in grief, And that in your life your body fared not according to your goodness, But wait for the day of the judgement of sinners And for the day of cursing and chastisement. [6] And yet when ye die the sinners speak over you: " As we die, so die the righteous, And what benefit do they reap for their deeds ? [7] Behold, even as we, so do they die in grief and darkness, And what have they more than we ? From henceforth we are equal. [8] And what will they receive and what will they see for ever ? Behold, they too have died, And henceforth for ever shall they see no light." [9] I tell you, ye sinners, ye are content to eat and drink, and rob and sin, and strip men naked, and [10] acquire wealth and see good days. Have ye seen the righteous how their end falls out, that no manner [11] of violence is found in them till their death ? " Nevertheless they perished and became as though they had not been, and their spirits descended into Sheol in tribulation."

1Enoch 103

[1] Now, therefore, I swear to you, the righteous, by the glory of the Great and Honoured and [2] Mighty One in dominion, and by His greatness I swear to you. I know a mystery And have read the heavenly tablets, And have seen the holy books, And have found

written therein and inscribed regarding them: [3] That all goodness and joy and glory are prepared for them, And written down for the spirits of those who have died in righteousness, And that manifold good shall be given to you in recompense for your labours, And that your lot is abundantly beyond the lot of the living. [4] And the spirits of you who have died in righteousness shall live and rejoice, And their spirits shall not perish, nor their memorial from before the face of the Great One Unto all the generations of the world: wherefore no longer fear their contumely. [5] Woe to you, ye sinners, when ye have died, If ye die in the wealth of your sins, And those who are like you say regarding you: Blessed are the sinners: they have seen all their days. [6] And how they have died in prosperity and in wealth, And have not seen tribulation or murder in their life; And they have died in honour, And judgement has not been executed on them during their life." [7] Know ye, that their souls will be made to descend into Sheol And they shall be wretched in their great tribulation. [8] And into darkness and chains and a burning flame where there is grievous judgement shall your spirits enter; And the great judgement shall be for all the generations of the world. Woe to you, for ye shall have no peace. [9] Say not in regard to the righteous and good who are in life: " In our troubled days we have toiled laboriously and experienced every trouble, And met with much evil and been consumed, And have become few and our spirit small. [10] And we have been destroyed and have not found any to help us even with a word: We have been torturedand destroyed, and not hoped to see life from day to day. [11] We hoped to be the head and have become the tail: We have toiled laboriously and had no satisfaction in our toil; And we have become the food of the sinners and the unrighteous, And they have laid their yoke heavily upon us. [12] They have had dominion over us that hated us and smote us; And to those that hated us we have bowed our necks But they pitied us not. [13] We desired to get away from them that we might escape and be at rest, But found no place whereunto we should flee and be safe from them. [14] And are complained to the rulers in our tribulation, And cried out against those who devoured us, But they did not attend to our cries And would not hearken to our voice. [15] And they helped those who robbed us and devoured us and those who made us few; and they concealed their oppression, and they did not remove from us the yoke of those that devoured us and dispersed us and murdered us, and they concealed their murder, and remembered not that they had lifted up their hands against us.

1Enoch 104

[1] I swear unto you, that in heaven the angels remember you for good before the glory of the Great [2] One: and your names are written before the glory of the Great One. Be hopeful; for aforetime ye were put to shame through ill and affliction; but now ye shall shine as the lights of heaven, [3] ye shall shine and ye shalll be seen, and the portals of heaven shall be opened to you. And in your cry, cry for judgement, and it shall appear to you; for all your tribulation shall be visited on the [4] rulers, and on all who helped those who plundered you. Be hopeful, and cast not away your hopes for ye shall have great joy as the angels of heaven. [5] What shall ye be obliged to do ? Ye shall not have to hide on the day of the great judgement and ye shall not be found as sinners, and the eternal [6] judgement shall be far from you for all the generations of the world. And now fear not, ye righteous, when ye see the sinners growing strong and prospering in their ways: be not companions with them, [7] but keep afar from their violence; for ye shall become companions of the hosts of heaven. And, although ye sinners say: " All our sins shall not be searched out and be written down," nevertheless [8] they shall write down all your sins every day. And now I show unto you that light and darkness, [9] day and night, see all your sins. Be not godless in your

hearts, and lie not and alter not the words of uprightness, nor charge with lying the words of the Holy Great One, nor take account of your [10] idols; for all your lying and all your godlessness issue not in righteousness but in great sin. And now I know this mystery, that sinners will alter and pervert the words of righteousness in many ways, and will speak wicked words, and lie, and practice great deceits, and write books concerning [11] their words. But when they write down truthfully all my words in their languages, and do not change or minish ought from my words but write them all down truthfully -all that I first testified [12] concerning them. Then, I know another mystery, that books will be given to the righteous and the [13] wise to become a cause of joy and uprightness and much wisdom. And to them shall the books be given, and they shall believe in them and rejoice over them, and then shall all the righteous who have learnt therefrom all the paths of uprightness be recompensed.

1Enoch 105

[1] In those days the Lord bade (them) to summon and testify to the children of earth concerning their wisdom: Show (it) unto them; for ye are their guides, and a recompense over the whole earth. [2] For I and My son will be united with them for ever in the paths of uprightness in their lives; and ye shall have peace: rejoice, ye children of uprightness. Amen.

1Enoch 106

[1] And after some days my son Methuselah took a wife for his son Lamech, and she became [2] pregnant by him and bore a son. And his body was white as snow and red as the blooming of a rose, and the hair of his head and his long locks were white as wool, and his eyes beautiful. And when he opened his eyes, he lighted up the whole house like the sun, and the whole house [3] was very bright. And thereupon he arose in the hands of the midwife, opened his mouth, and conversed with the Lord of righteousness. [4] And his father Lamech was afraid of him and [5] fled, and came to his father Methuselah. And he said unto him: I have begotten a strange son, diverse from and unlike man, and resembling the sons of the God of heaven; and his nature is different and he is not like us, and his eyes are as the rays of the sun, and his [6] countenance is glorious. And it seems to me that he is not sprung from me but from the angels, and I fear that in his days a wonder may be [7] wrought on the earth. And now, my father, I am here to petition thee and implore thee that thou mayest go to Enoch, our father, and learn from him the truth, for his dwelling-place is [8] amongst the angels. And when Methuselah heard the words of his son, he came to me to the ends of the earth; for he had heard that [9] I was there, and he cried aloud, and I heard his voice and I came to him. And I said unto him: Behold, here am I, my son, wherefore hast thou come to me ? And he answered and said: Because of a great cause of anxiety have I come to thee, and because of a disturbing vision [10] have I approached. And now, my father, hear me: unto Lamech my son there hath been born a son, the like of whom there is none, and his nature is not like mans nature, and the colour of his body is whiter than snow and redder than the bloom of a rose, and the hair of his head is whiter than white wool, and his eyes are like the rays of the sun, and he opened his eyes and [11] thereupon lighted up the whole house. And he arose in the hands of the midwife, and opened [12] his mouth and blessed the Lord of heaven. And his father Lamech became afraid and fled to me, and did not believe that he was sprung from him, but that he was in the likeness of the angels of heaven; and behold I have come to thee that thou mayest make known to me the truth. [13] And I, Enoch, answered and said unto him: The Lord will do a new thing on the earth, and this I have already seen in a vision, and make known to thee that in the generation of my father Jared some of the angels of heaven transgressed the word of

the Lord. [14] And behold they commit sin and transgress the law, and have united themselves with women and commit sin with them, and have married some of them, and have begot children by them. [15] And they shall produce on the earth giants not according to the spirit, but according to the flesh, and there shall be a great punishment on the earth, and the earth shall be cleansed from all impurity. Yea, there shall come a great destruction over the whole earth, and there shall be a deluge and [16] a great destruction for one year. And this son who has been born unto you shall be left on the earth, and his three children shall be saved with him: when all mankind that are on the earth [17] shall diehe and his sons shall be saved. And now make known to thy son Lamech that he who has been born is in truth his son, and call his name Noah; for he shall be left to you, and he and his sons shall be saved from the destruction, which shall come upon the earth on account of all the sin and all the unrighteousness, which shall be consummated on the earth in his days. And after that there shall be still more unrighteousness than that which was first consummated on the earth; for I know the mysteries of the holy ones; for He, the Lord, has showed me and informed me, and I have read (them) in the heavenly tablets.

1Enoch 107

[1] And I saw written on them that generation upon generation shall transgress, till a generation of righteousness arises, and transgression is destroyed and sin passes away from the earth, and all [2] manner of good comes upon it. And now, my son, go and make known to thy son Lamech that this [3] son, which has been born, is in truth his son, and that (this) is no lie. And when Methuselah had heard the words of his father Enoch-for he had shown to him everything in secret- he returned and showed (them) to him and called the name of that son Noah; for he will comfort the earth after all the destruction.

1Enoch 108

[1] Another book which Enoch wrote for his son Methuselah and for those who will come after him, [2] and keep the law in the last days. Ye who have done good shall wait for those days till an end is made of those who work evil; and an end of the might of the transgressors. And wait ye indeed till sin has passed away, [3] for their names shall be blotted out of the book of life and out of the holy books, and their seed shall be destroyed for ever, [4] and their spirits shall be slain, and they shall cry and make lamentation in a place that is a chaotic wilderness, and in the fire shall they burn; for there is no earth there. And I saw there something like an invisible cloud; for by reason of its depth I could not look over, and I saw a flame of fire blazing brightly, and things like shining [5] mountains circling and sweeping to and fro. And I asked one of the holy angels who was with me and said unto him: What is this shining thing? for it is not a heaven but only the flame of a blazing [6] fire, and the voice of weeping and crying and lamentation and strong pain. And he said unto me: This place which thou seest-here are cast the spirits of sinners and blasphemers, and of those who work wickedness, and of those who pervert everything that the Lord hath spoken through the mouth [7] of the prophets-(even) the things that shall be. For some of them are written and inscribed above in the heaven, in order that the angels may read them and know that which shall befall the sinners, and the spirits of the humble, and of those who have afflicted their bodies, and been recompensed [8] by God; and of those who have been put to shame by wicked men: Who love God and loved neither gold nor silver nor any of the good things which are in the world, but gave over their bodies to torture. [9] Who, since they came into being, longed not after earthly food, but regarded everything as a passing breath, and lived accordingly, and the Lord tried them much, and their spirits were [10] found pure so that they should bless His name.

And all the blessings destined for them I have recounted in the books. And he hath assigned them their recompense, because they have been found to be such as loved heaven more than their life in the world, and though they were trodden under foot of wicked men, and experienced abuse and reviling from them and were put to shame, [11] yet they blessed Me. And now I will summon the spirits of the good who belong to the generation of light, and I will transform those who were born in darkness, who in the flesh were not recompensed [12] with such honour as their faithfulness deserved. And I will bring forth in shining light those who [13] have loved My holy name, and I will seat each on the throne of his honour. And they shall be resplendent for times without number; for righteousness is the judgement of God; for to the faithful [14] He will give faithfulness in the habitation of upright paths. And they shall see those who were, [15] born in darkness led into darkness, while the righteous shall be resplendent. And the sinners shall cry aloud and see them resplendent, and they indeed will go where days and seasons are prescribed for them.

Enoch 2 – The Slavonic Secrets of Enoch

2Enoch 1

[1] There was a wise man, a great artificer, and the Lord conceived love for him and received him, that he should behold the uppermost dwellings and be an eye-witness of the wise and great and inconceivable and immutable realm of God Almighty, of the very wonderful and glorious and bright and many-eyed station of the Lord's servants, and of the inaccessible throne of the Lord, and of the degrees and manifestations of the incorporeal hosts, and of the ineffable ministration of the multitude of the elements, and of the various apparition and inexpressible singing of the host of Cherubim, and of the boundless light. [2] At that time, he said, when my one hundred and sixty-fifth year was completed, I begat my son Mathusal (Methuselah). [3] After this too I lived two hundred years and completed of all the years of my life three hundred and sixty-five years. [4] On the first day of the month I was in my house alone and was resting on my bed and slept. [5] And when I was asleep, great distress came up into my heart, and I was weeping with my eyes in sleep, and I could not understand what this distress was, or what would happen to me. [6] And there appeared to me two men, exceeding big, so that I never saw such on earth; their faces were shining like the sun, their eyes too (were) like a burning light, and from their lips was fire coming forth with clothing and singing of various kinds in appearance purple, their wings (were)brighter than gold, their hands whiter than snow. [7] They were standing at the head of my bed and began to call me by my name. [8] And I arose from my sleep and saw clearly those two men standing in front of me. [9] And I saluted them and was seized with fear and the appearance of my face was changed from terror, and those men said to me: [10] Have courage, Enoch, do not fear; the eternal God sent us to you, and lo! You shalt to-day ascend with us into heaven, and you shall tell your sons and all your household all that they shall do without you on earth in your house, and let no one seek you till the Lord return you to them. [11] And I made haste to obey them and went out from my house, and made to the doors, as it was ordered me, and summoned my sons Mathusal (Methuselah) and Regim and Gaidad and made known to them all the marvels those (men) had told me.

2Enoch 2

[1] Listen to me, my children, I know not whither I go, or what will befall me; now therefore, my children, I tell you: turn not from God before the face of the vain, who made not Heaven and earth, for these shall perish and those who worship them, and may the Lord make confident your hearts in the fear of him. And now, my children, let no one think to seek me, until the Lord return me to you.

2Enoch 3

[1] It came to pass, when Enoch had told his sons, that the angels took him on to their wings and bore him up on to the first heaven and placed him on the clouds. And there I looked, and again I looked higher, and saw the ether, and they placed me on the first heaven and showed me a very great Sea, greater than the earthly sea.

2Enoch 4

[1] They brought before my face the elders and rulers of the stellar orders, and showed me two hundred angels, who rule the stars and (their) services to the heavens, and fly with their wings and come round all those who sail.

2Enoch 5

[1] And here I looked down and saw the treasure-houses of the snow, and the angels who keep their terrible store-houses, and the clouds whence they come out and into which they go.

2Enoch 6

[1] They showed me the treasure-house of the dew, like oil of the olive, and the appearance of its form, as of all the flowers of the earth; further many angels guarding the treasure-houses of these (things), and how they are made to shut and open.

2Enoch 7

[1] And those men took me and led me up on to the second heaven, and showed me darkness, greater than earthly darkness, and there I saw prisoners hanging, watched, awaiting the great and boundless judgment, and these angels (spirits) were dark-looking, more than earthly darkness, and incessantly making weeping through all hours. [2] And I said to the men who were with me: Wherefore are these incessantly tortured? They answered me: These are God's apostates, who obeyed not God's commands, but took counsel with their own will, and turned away with their prince, who also (is) fastened on the fifth heaven. [3] And I felt great pity for them, and they saluted me, and said to me: Man of God, pray for us to the Lord; and I answered to them: Who am I, a mortal man, that I should pray for angels (spirits)? Who knows whither I go, or what will befall me? Or who will pray for me?

2Enoch 8

[1] And those men took me thence, and led me up on to the third heaven, and placed me there; and I looked downwards, and saw the produce of these places, such as has never been known for goodness. [2] And I saw all the sweet-flowering trees and beheld their fruits, which were sweet-smelling, and all the foods borne (by them) bubbling with fragrant exhalation. [3] And in the midst of the trees that of life, in that place whereon the Lord rests, when he goes up into paradise; and this tree is of ineffable goodness and fragrance, and adorned more than every existing thing; and on all sides (it is) in form gold-looking and vermilion and fire-like and covers all, and it has produce from all fruits. [4] Its root is in the garden at the earth's end. [5] And paradise is between corruptibility and incorruptibility. [6] And two springs come out which send forth honey and milk, and their springs send forth oil and wine, and they separate into four parts, and go round with quiet course, and go down into the PARADISE OF EDEN, between corruptibility and incorruptibility. [7] And thence they go forth along the earth, and have a revolution to their circle even as other elements. [8] And here there is no unfruitful tree, and every place is blessed. [9] And (there are) three hundred angels very bright, who keep the garden, and with incessant sweet singing and never-silent voices serve the Lord throughout all days and hours. [10] And I said: How very sweet is this place, and those men said to me:

2Enoch 9

[1] This place, O Enoch, is prepared for the righteous, who endure all manner of offence from those that exasperate their souls, who avert their eyes from iniquity, and make righteous judgment, and give bread to the hungering, and cover the naked with clothing, and raise up the fallen, and help injured orphans, and who walk without fault before the face of the Lord, and serve him alone, and for them is prepared this place for eternal inheritance.

2Enoch 10

1 And those two men led me up on to the Northern side, and showed me there a very terrible place, and (there were) all manner of tortures in that place: cruel darkness and unillumined gloom, and there is no light there, but murky fire constantly flaming aloft, and (there is) a fiery river coming forth, and that whole place is everywhere fire, and everywhere (there is) frost and ice, thirst and shivering, while the bonds are very cruel, and the angels (spirits) fearful and merciless, bearing angry weapons, merciless torture, and I said:2 Woe, woe, how very terrible is this place.3 And those men said to me: This place, O Enoch, is prepared for those who dishonour God, who on earth practice sin against nature, which is child-corruption after the sodomitic fashion, magic-making, enchantments and devilish witchcrafts, and who boast of their wicked deeds, stealing, lies, calumnies, envy, rancour, fornication, murder, and who, accursed, steal the souls of men, who, seeing the poor take away their goods and themselves wax rich, injuring them for other men's goods; who being able to satisfy the empty, made the hungering to die; being able to clothe, stripped the naked; and who knew not their creator, and bowed to the soulless (and lifeless) gods, who cannot see nor hear, vain gods, (who also) built hewn images and bow down to unclean handiwork, for all these is prepared this place among these, for eternal inheritance.

2Enoch 11

[1] Those men took me, and led me up on to the fourth heaven, and showed me all the successive goings, and all the rays of the light of sun and moon.[2] And I measure their goings, and compared their light, and saw that the sun's light is greater than the moon's.[3] Its circle and the wheels on which it goes always, like the wind going past with very marvellous speed, and day and night it has no rest.[4] Its passage and return (are accompanied by) four great stars, (and) each star has under it a thousand stars, to the right of the sun's wheel, (and by) four to the left, each having under it a thousand stars, altogether eight thousand, issuing with the sun continually.[5] And by day fifteen myriads of angels attend it, and by night A thousand.[6] And six-winged ones issue with the angels before the sun's wheel into the fiery flames, and a hundred angels kindle the sun and set it alight.

2Enoch 12

[1] And I looked and saw other flying elements of the sun, whose names (are) Phoenixes and Chalkydri, marvellous and wonderful, with feet and tails in the form of a lion, and a crocodile's head, their appearance (is) empurpled, like the rainbow; their size (is) nine hundred measures, their wings (are like) those of angels, each (has) twelve, and they attend and accompany the sun, bearing heat and dew, as it is ordered them from God.[2] Thus (the sun) revolves and goes, and rises under the heaven, and its course goes under the earth with the light of its rays incessantly.

2Enoch 13

[1] Those men bore me away to the east, and placed me at the sun's gates, where the sun goes forth according to the regulation of the seasons and the circuit of the months of the whole year, and the number of the hours day and night.[2] And I saw six gates open, each gate having sixty-one stadia and A quarter of one stadium, and I measured (them) truly, and understood their size (to be) so much, through which the sun goes forth, and goes to the west, and is made even, and rises throughout all the months, and turns back again from the six gates according to the succession of the seasons; thus (the period) of the whole year is finished after the returns of the four seasons.

2Enoch 14

[1] And again those men led me away to the western parts, and showed me six great gates open corresponding to the eastern gates, opposite to where the sun sets, according to the number of the days three hundred and sixty-five and A quarter.[2] Thus again it goes down to the western gates, (and) draws away its light, the greatness of its brightness, under the earth; for since the crown of its shining is in heaven with the Lord, and guarded by four hundred angels, while the sun goes round on wheel under the earth, and stands seven great hours in night, and spends half (its course) under the earth, when it comes to the eastern approach in the eighth hour of the night, it brings its lights, and the crown of shining, and the sun flames forth more than fire.

2Enoch 15

[1] Then the elements of the sun, called Phoenixes and Chalkydri break into song, therefore every bird flutters with its wings, rejoicing at the giver of light, and they broke into song at the command of the Lord.[2] The giver of light comes to give brightness to the whole world, and the morning guard takes shape, which is the rays of the sun, and the sun of the earth goes out, and receives its brightness to light up the whole face of the earth, and they showed me this calculation of the sun's going.[3] And the gates which it enters, these are the great gates of the calculation of the hours of the year; for this reason the sun is a great creation, whose circuit (lasts) twenty-eight years, and begins again from the beginning.

2Enoch 16

[1] Those men showed me the other course, that of the moon, twelve great gates, crowned from west to east, by which the moon goes in and out of the customary times.[2] It goes in at the first gate to the western places of the sun, by the first gates with (thirty)-one (days) exactly, by the second gates with thirty-one days exactly, by the third with thirty days exactly, by the fourth with thirty days exactly, by the fifth with thirty-one days exactly, by the sixth with thirty-one days exactly, by the seventh with thirty days exactly, by the eighth with thirty-one days perfectly, by the ninth with thirty-one days exactly, by the tenth with thirty days perfectly, by the eleventh with thirty-one days exactly, by the twelfth with twenty-eight days exactly.[3] And it goes through the western gates in the order and number of the eastern, and accomplishes the three hundred and sixty-five and a quarter days of the solar year, while the lunar year has three hundred fifty-four, and there are wanting (to it) twelve days of the solar circle, which are the lunar epacts of the whole year.[4] Thus, too, the great circle contains five hundred and thirty-two years.[5] The quarter (of a day) is omitted for three years, the fourth fulfills it exactly.[6] Therefore they are taken outside of heaven for three years and are not added to the number of days, because they change the time of the years to two new months towards completion, to two others towards diminution.[7] And when the western gates are finished, it returns and goes to the eastern to the lights, and goes thus day and night about the heavenly circles, lower than all circles, swifter than the heavenly winds, and spirits and elements and angels flying; each angel has six wings.[8] It has a sevenfold course in nineteen years.

2Enoch 17

[1] In the midst of the heavens I saw armed soldiers, serving the Lord, with tympana and organs, with incessant voice, with sweet voice, with sweet and incessant (voice) and various singing, which it is

impossible to describe, and (which) astonishes every mind, so wonderful and marvellous is the singing of those angels, and I was delighted listening to it.

2Enoch 18

[1] The men took me on to the fifth heaven and placed me, and there I saw many and countless soldiers, called Grigori, of human appearance, and their size (was) greater than that of great giants and their faces withered, and the silence of their mouths perpetual, and their was no service on the fifth heaven, and I said to the men who were with me:[2] Wherefore are these very withered and their faces melancholy, and their mouths silent, and (wherefore) is there no service on this heaven?[3] And they said to me: These are the Grigori, who with their prince Satanail (Satan) rejected the Lord of light, and after them are those who are held in great darkness on the second heaven, and three of them went down on to earth from the Lord's throne, to the place Ermon, and broke through their vows on the shoulder of the hill Ermon and saw the daughters of men how good they are, and took to themselves wives, and befouled the earth with their deeds, who in all times of their age made lawlessness and mixing, and giants are born and marvellous big men and great enmity.[4] And therefore God judged them with great judgment, and they weep for their brethren and they will be punished on the Lord's great day.[5] And I said to the Grigori: I saw your brethren and their works, and their great torments, and I prayed for them, but the Lord has condemned them (to be) under earth till (the existing) heaven and earth shall end for ever.[6] And I said: Wherefore do you wait, brethren, and do not serve before the Lord's face, and have not put your services before the Lord's face, lest you anger your Lord utterly?[7] And they listened to my admonition, and spoke to the four ranks in heaven, and lo! As I stood with those two men four trumpets trumpeted together with great voice, and the Grigori broke into song with one voice, and their voice went up before the Lord pitifully and affectingly.

2Enoch 19

[1] And thence those men took me and bore me up on to the sixth heaven, and there I saw seven bands of angels, very bright and very glorious, and their faces shining more than the sun's shining, glistening, and there is no difference in their faces, or behaviour, or manner of dress; and these make the orders, and learn the goings of the stars, and the alteration of the moon, or revolution of the sun, and the good government of the world.[2] And when they see evildoing they make commandments and instruction, and sweet and loud singing, and all (songs) of praise.[3] These are the archangels who are above angels, measure all life in heaven and on earth, and the angels who are (appointed) over seasons and years, the angels who are over rivers and sea, and who are over the fruits of the earth, and the angels who are over every grass, giving food to all, to every living thing, and the angels who write all the souls of men, and all their deeds, and their lives before the Lord's face; in their midst are six Phoenixes and six Cherubim and six six-winged ones continually with one voice singing one voice, and it is not possible to describe their singing, and they rejoice before the Lord at his footstool.

2Enoch 20

[1] And those two men lifted me up thence on to the seventh heaven, and I saw there a very great light, and fiery troops of great archangels, incorporeal forces, and dominions, orders and governments, Cherubim and seraphim, thrones and many-eyed ones, nine regiments, the Ioanit stations of light, and I became afraid, and began to tremble with great terror, and those men took me, and led me after them, and said to me:[2] Have courage, Enoch, do not fear, and showed me the Lord from afar, sitting on His very high throne. For what is there on the tenth heaven, since the Lord

dwells there?[3] On the tenth heaven is God, in the Hebrew tongue he is called Aravat.[4] And all the heavenly troops would come and stand on the ten steps according to their rank, and would bow down to the Lord, and would again go to their places in joy and felicity, singing songs in the boundless light with small and tender voices, gloriously serving him.

2Enoch 21

[1] And the Cherubim and seraphim standing about the throne, the six-winged and many-eyed ones do not depart, standing before the Lord's face doing his will, and cover his whole throne, singing with gentle voice before the Lord's face: Holy, holy, holy, Lord Ruler of Sabaoth, heavens and earth are full of Your glory.[2] When I saw all these things, those men said to me: Enoch, thus far is it commanded us to journey with you, and those men went away from me and thereupon I saw them not.[3] And I remained alone at the end of the seventh heaven and became afraid, and fell on my face and said to myself: Woe is me, what has befallen me?[4] And the Lord sent one of his glorious ones, the archangel Gabriel, and (he) said to me: Have courage, Enoch, do not fear, arise before the Lord's face into eternity, arise, come with me.[5] And I answered him, and said in myself: My Lord, my soul is departed from me, from terror and trembling, and I called to the men who led me up to this place, on them I relied, and (it is) with them I go before the Lord's face.[6] And Gabriel caught me up, as a leaf caught up by the wind, and placed me before the Lord's face.[7] And I saw the eighth heaven, which is called in the Hebrew tongue Muzaloth, changer of the seasons, of drought, and of wet, and of the twelve constellations of the circle of the firmament, which are above the seventh heaven.[8] And I saw the ninth heaven, which is called in Hebrew Kuchavim, where are the heavenly homes of the twelve constellations of the circle of the firmament.

2Enoch 22

[1] On the tenth heaven, (which is called) Aravoth, I saw the appearance of the Lord's face, like iron made to glow in fire, and brought out, emitting sparks, and it burns.[2] Thus (in a moment of eternity) I saw the Lord's face, but the Lord's face is ineffable, marvellous and very awful, and very, very terrible.[3] And who am I to tell of the Lord's unspeakable being, and of his very wonderful face? And I cannot tell the quantity of his many instructions, and various voices, the Lord's throne (is) very great and not made with hands, nor the quantity of those standing round him, troops of Cherubim and seraphim, nor their incessant singing, nor his immutable beauty, and who shall tell of the ineffable greatness of his glory.[4] And I fell prone and bowed down to the Lord, and the Lord with his lips said to me:[5] Have courage, Enoch, do not fear, arise and stand before my face into eternity.[6] And the archistratege Michael lifted me up, and led me to before the Lord's face.[7] And the Lord said to his servants tempting them: Let Enoch stand before my face into eternity, and the glorious ones bowed down to the Lord, and said: Let Enoch go according to Your word.[8] And the Lord said to Michael: Go and take Enoch from out (of) his earthly garments, and anoint him with my sweet ointment, and put him into the garments of My glory.[9] And Michael did thus, as the Lord told him. He anointed me, and dressed me, and the appearance of that ointment is more than the great light, and his ointment is like sweet dew, and its smell mild, shining like the sun's ray, and I looked at myself, and (I) was like (transfigured) one of his glorious ones.[10] And the Lord summoned one of his archangels by name Pravuil, whose knowledge was quicker in wisdom than the other archangels, who wrote all the deeds of the Lord; and the Lord said to Pravuil: Bring out the books from my store-houses, and a reed of quick-writing,

and give (it) to Enoch, and deliver to him the choice and comforting books out of your hand.

2Enoch 23

[1] And he was telling me all the works of heaven, earth and sea, and all the elements, their passages and goings, and the thunderings of the thunders, the sun and moon, the goings and changes of the stars, the seasons, years, days, and hours, the risings of the wind, the numbers of the angels, and the formation of their songs, and all human things, the tongue of every human song and life, the commandments, instructions, and sweet-voiced singings, and all things that it is fitting to learn.[2] And Pravuil told me: All the things that I have told you, we have written. Sit and write all the souls of mankind, however many of them are born, and the places prepared for them to eternity; for all souls are prepared to eternity, before the formation of the world.[3] And all double thirty days and thirty nights, and I wrote out all things exactly, and wrote three hundred and sixty-six books.

2Enoch 24

[1] And the Lord summoned me, and said to me: Enoch, sit down on my left with Gabriel.[2] And I bowed down to the Lord, and the Lord spoke to me: Enoch, beloved, all (that) you see, all things that are standing finished I tell to you even before the very beginning, all that I created from non-being, and visible (physical) things from invisible (spiritual).[3] Hear, Enoch, and take in these my words, for not to My angels have I told my secret, and I have not told them their rise, nor my endless realm, nor have they understood my creating, which I tell you to-day.[4] For before all things were visible (physical), I alone used to go about in the invisible (spiritual) things, like the sun from east to west, and from west to east.[5] But even the sun has peace in itself, while I found no peace, because I was creating all things, and I conceived the thought of placing foundations, and of creating visible (physical) creation.

2Enoch 25

[1] I commanded in the very lowest (parts), that visible (physical) things should come down from invisible (spiritual), and Adoil came down very great, and I beheld him, and lo! He had a belly of great light.[2] And I said to him: Become undone, Adoil, and let the visible (physical) (come) out of you.[3] And he came undone, and a great light came out. And I (was) in the midst of the great light, and as there is born light from light, there came forth a great age, and showed all creation, which I had thought to create.[4] And I saw that (it was) good.[5] And I placed for myself a throne, and took my seat on it, and said to the light: Go thence up higher and fix yourself high above the throne, and be A foundation to the highest things.[6] And above the light there is nothing else, and then I bent up and looked up from my throne.

2Enoch 26

[1] And I summoned the very lowest a second time, and said: Let Archas come forth hard, and he came forth hard from the invisible (spiritual).[2] And Archas came forth, hard, heavy, and very red.[3] And I said: Be opened, Archas, and let there be born from you, and he came undone, an age came forth, very great and very dark, bearing the creation of all lower things, and I saw that (it was) good and said to him:[4] Go thence down below, and make yourself firm, and be a foundation for the lower things, and it happened and he went down and fixed himself, and became the foundation for the lower things, and below the darkness there is nothing else.

2Enoch 27

[1] And I commanded that there should be taken from light and darkness, and I said: Be thick, and it became thus, and I spread it out with the light, and it became water, and I spread it out over the darkness, below the light, and then I made firm the waters, that is to say the bottomless, and I made foundation of light around the water, and created seven circles from inside, and imaged (the water) like crystal wet and dry, that is to say like glass, (and) the circumcession of the waters and the other elements, and I showed each one of them its road, and the seven stars each one of them in its heaven, that they go thus, and I saw that it was good.[2] And I separated between light and between darkness, that is to say in the midst of the water hither and thither, and I said to the light, that it should be the day, and to the darkness, that it should be the night, and there was evening and there was morning the first day.

2Enoch 28

[1] And then I made firm the heavenly circle, and (made) that the lower water which is under heaven collect itself together, into one whole, and that the chaos become dry, and it became so.[2] Out of the waves I created rock hard and big, and from the rock I piled up the dry, and the dry I called earth, and the midst of the earth I called abyss, that is to say the bottomless, I collected the sea in one place and bound it together with a yoke.[3] And I said to the sea: Behold I give you (your) eternal limits, and you shalt not break loose from your component parts.[4] Thus I made fast the firmament. This day I called me the first-created [Sunday].

2Enoch 29

[1] And for all the heavenly troops I imaged the image and essence of fire, and my eye looked at the very hard, firm rock, and from the gleam of my eye the lightning received its wonderful nature, (which) is both fire in water and water in fire, and one does not put out the other, nor does the one dry up the other, therefore the lightning is brighter than the sun, softer than water and firmer than hard rock.[2] And from the rock I cut off a great fire, and from the fire I created the orders of the incorporeal ten troops of angels, and their weapons are fiery and their raiment a burning flame, and I commanded that each one should stand in his order.[3] And one from out the order of angels, having turned away with the order that was under him, conceived an impossible thought, to place his throne higher than the clouds above the earth, that he might become equal in rank to my power.[4] And I threw him out from the height with his angels, and he was flying in the air continuously above the bottomless.

2Enoch 30

[1] On the third day I commanded the earth to make grow great and fruitful trees, and hills, and seed to sow, and I planted Paradise, and enclosed it, and placed as armed (guardians) flaming angels, and thus I created renewal.[2] Then came evening, and came morning the fourth day.[3] [Wednesday]. On the fourth day I commanded that there should be great lights on the heavenly circles.[4] On the first uppermost circle I placed the stars, Kruno, and on the second Aphrodit, on the third Aris, on the fifth Zoues, on the sixth Ermis, on the seventh lesser the moon, and adorned it with the lesser stars.[5] And on the lower I placed the sun for the illumination of day, and the moon and stars for the illumination of night.[6] The sun that it should go according to each constellation, twelve, and I appointed the succession of the months and their names and lives, their thunderings, and their hour-markings, how they should succeed.[7] Then evening came and morning came the fifth day.[8] [Thursday]. On the fifth day I commanded the sea, that it should bring forth fishes, and feathered birds of many varieties, and all animals creeping over the earth, going forth over the earth on four legs, and soaring in the air, male sex and female, and every soul breathing the spirit of life.[9] And there came evening, and there came morning the sixth day.[10] [Friday]. On the sixth day I commanded my wisdom to create man from seven consistencies: one, his flesh from the earth; two, his blood from the dew; three, his eyes from the sun;

four, his bones from stone; five, his intelligence from the swiftness of the angels and from cloud; six, his veins and his hair from the grass of the earth; seven, his soul from my breath and from the wind.[11] And I gave him seven natures: to the flesh hearing, the eyes for sight, to the soul smell, the veins for touch, the blood for taste, the bones for endurance, to the intelligence sweetness [enjoyment].[12] I conceived a cunning saying to say, I created man from invisible (spiritual) and from visible (physical) nature, of both are his death and life and image, he knows speech like some created thing, small in greatness and again great in smallness, and I placed him on earth, a second angel, honourable, great and glorious, and I appointed him as ruler to rule on earth and to have my wisdom, and there was none like him of earth of all my existing creatures.[13] And I appointed him a name, from the four component parts, from east, from west, from south, from north, and I appointed for him four special stars, and I called his name Adam, and showed him the two ways, the light and the darkness, and I told him:[14] This is good, and that bad, that I should learn whether he has love towards me, or hatred, that it be clear which in his race love me.[15] For I have seen his nature, but he has not seen his own nature, therefore (through) not seeing he will sin worse, and I said After sin (what is there) but death?[16] And I put sleep into him and he fell asleep. And I took from him A rib, and created him a wife, that death should come to him by his wife, and I took his last word and called her name mother, that is to say, Eva (Eve).

2Enoch 31

[1] Adam has life on earth, and I created a garden in Eden in the east, that he should observe the testament and keep the command.[2] I made the heavens open to him, that he should see the angels singing the song of victory, and the gloomless light.[3] And he was continuously in paradise, and the devil understood that I wanted to create another world, because Adam was lord on earth, to rule and control it.[4] The devil is the evil spirit of the lower places, as a fugitive he made Sotona from the heavens as his name was Satanail (Satan), thus he became different from the angels, (but his nature) did not change (his) intelligence as far as (his) understanding of righteous and sinful (things).[5] And he understood his condemnation and the sin which he had sinned before, therefore he conceived thought against Adam, in such form he entered and seduced Eva (Eve), but did not touch Adam.[6] But I cursed ignorance, but what I had blessed previously, those I did not curse, I cursed not man, nor the earth, nor other creatures, but man's evil fruit, and his works.

2Enoch 32

[1] I said to him: Earth you are, and into the earth whence I took you you shalt go, and I will not ruin you, but send you whence I took you.[2] Then I can again receive you at My second presence.[3] And I blessed all my creatures visible (physical) and invisible (spiritual). And Adam was five and half hours in paradise.[4] And I blessed the seventh day, which is the Sabbath, on which he rested from all his works.

2Enoch 33

[1] And I appointed the eighth day also, that the eighth day should be the first-created after my work, and that (the first seven) revolve in the form of the seventh thousand, and that at the beginning of the eighth thousand there should be a time of not-counting, endless, with neither years nor months nor weeks nor days nor hours.[2] And now, Enoch, all that I have told you, all that you have understood, all that you have seen of heavenly things, all that you have seen on earth, and all that I have written in books by my great wisdom, all these things I have devised and created from the uppermost foundation to the lower and to the end, and there is no counsellor nor inheritor to my creations.[3] I am self-eternal, not made with hands, and without change.[4] My thought is my counsellor, my wisdom and my word are made, and my eyes observe all things how they stand here and tremble with terror.[5] If I turn away my face, then all things will be destroyed.[6] And apply your mind, Enoch, and know him who is speaking to you, and take thence the books which you yourself have written.[7] And I give you Samuil and Raguil, who led you up, and the books, and go down to earth, and tell your sons all that I have told you, and all that you have seen, from the lower heaven up to my throne, and all the troops.[8] For I created all forces, and there is none that resists me or that does not subject himself to me. For all subject themselves to my monarchy, and labour for my sole rule.[9] Give them the books of the handwriting, and they will read (them) and will know me for the creator of all things, and will understand how there is no other God but me.[10] And let them distribute the books of your handwriting–children to children, generation to generation, nations to nations.[11] And I will give you, Enoch, my intercessor, the archistratege Michael, for the handwritings of your fathers Adam, Seth, Enos, Cainan, Mahaleleel, and Jared your father.

2Enoch 34

[1] They have rejected my commandments and my yoke, worthless seed has come up, not fearing God, and they would not bow down to me, but have begun to bow down to vain gods, and denied my unity, and have laden the whole earth with untruths, offences, abominable lecheries, namely one with another, and all manner of other unclean wickedness, which are disgusting to relate.[2] And therefore I will bring down a deluge upon the earth and will destroy all men, and the whole earth will crumble together into great darkness.

2Enoch 35

[1] Behold from their seed shall arise another generation, much afterwards, but of them many will be very insatiate.[2] He who raises that generation, (shall) reveal to them the books of your handwriting, of your fathers, (to them) to whom he must point out the guardianship of the world, to the faithful men and workers of my pleasure, who do not acknowledge my name in vain.[3] And they shall tell another generation, and those (others) having read shall be glorified thereafter, more than the first.

2Enoch 36

[1] Now, Enoch, I give you the term of thirty days to spend in your house, and tell your sons and all your household, that all may hear from my face what is told them by you, that they may read and understand, how there is no other God but me.[2] And that they may always keep my commandments, and begin to read and take in the books of your handwriting.[3] And after thirty days I shall send my angel for you, and he will take you from earth and from your sons to me.

2Enoch 37

[1] And the Lord called upon one of the older angels, terrible and menacing, and placed him by me, in appearance white as snow, and his hands like ice, having the appearance of great frost, and he froze my face, because I could not endure the terror of the Lord, just as it is not possible to endure A stove's fire and the sun's heat, and the frost of the air.[2] And the Lord said to me: Enoch, if your face be not frozen here, no man will be able to behold your face.

2Enoch 38

[1] And the Lord said to those men who first led me up: Let Enoch go down on to earth with you, and await him till the determined day.[2] And they placed me by night on my bed.[3] And Mathusal (Methuselah) expecting my coming, keeping watch by day and by night at my bed, was filled with awe when he heard my coming, and

I told him, Let all my household come together, that I tell them everything.

2Enoch 39

[1] Oh my children, my beloved ones, hear the admonition of your father, as much as is according to the Lord's will.[2] I have been let come to you to-day, and announce to you, not from my lips, but from the Lord's lips, all that is and was and all that is now, and all that will be till judgment-day.[3] For the Lord has let me come to you, you hear therefore the words of my lips, of a man made big for you, but I am one who has seen the Lord's face, like iron made to glow from fire it sends forth sparks and burns.[4] You look now upon my eyes, (the eyes) of a man big with meaning for you, but I have seen the Lord's eyes, shining like the sun's rays and filling the eyes of man with awe.[5] You see now, my children, the right hand of a man that helps you, but I have seen the Lord's right hand filling heaven as he helped me.[6] You see the compass of my work like your own, but I have seen the Lord's limitless and perfect compass, which has no end.[7] You hear the words of my lips, as I heard the words of the Lord, like great thunder incessantly with hurling of clouds.[8] And now, my children, hear the discourses of the father of the earth, how fearful and awful it is to come before the face of the ruler of the earth, how much more terrible and awful it is to come before the face of the ruler of heaven, the controller (judge) of quick and dead, and of the heavenly troops. Who can endure that endless pain?

2Enoch 40

[1] And now, my children, I know all things, for this (is) from the Lord's lips, and this my eyes have seen, from beginning to end.[2] I know all things, and have written all things into books, the heavens and their end, and their plenitude, and all the armies and their marchings.[3] I have measured and described the stars, the great countless multitude (of them).[4] What man has seen their revolutions, and their entrances? For not even the angels see their number, while I have written all their names.[5] And I measured the sun's circle, and measured its rays, counted the hours, I wrote down too all things that go over the earth, I have written the things that are nourished, and all seed sown and unsown, which the earth produces and all plants, and every grass and every flower, and their sweet smells, and their names, and the dwelling-places of the clouds, and their composition, and their wings, and how they bear rain and raindrops.[6] And I investigated all things, and wrote the road of the thunder and of the lightning, and they showed me the keys and their guardians, their rise, the way they go; it is let out (gently) in measure by a chain, lest by A heavy chain and violence it hurl down the angry clouds and destroy all things on earth.[7] I wrote the treasure-houses of the snow, and the store-houses of the cold and the frosty airs, and I observed their season's key-holder, he fills the clouds with them, and does not exhaust the treasure-houses.[8] And I wrote the resting-places of the winds and observed and saw how their key-holders bear weighing-scales and measures; first, they put them in (one) weighing-scale, then in the other the weights and let them out according to measure cunningly over the whole earth, lest by heavy breathing they make the earth to rock.[9] And I measured out the whole earth, its mountains, and all hills, fields, trees, stones, rivers, all existing things I wrote down, the height from earth to the seventh heaven, and downwards to the very lowest hell, and the judgment-place, and the very great, open and weeping hell.[10] And I saw how the prisoners are in pain, expecting the limitless judgment.[11] And I wrote down all those being judged by the judge, and all their judgment (and sentences) and all their works.

2Enoch 41

[1] And I saw all forefathers from (all) time with Adam and Eva (Eve), and I sighed and broke into tears and said of the ruin of their

dishonour:[2] Woe is me for my infirmity and (for that) of my forefathers, and thought in my heart and said:[3] Blessed (is) the man who has not been born or who has been born and shall not sin before the Lord's face, that he come not into this place, nor bring the yoke of this place.

2Enoch 42

[1] I saw the key-holders and guards of the gates of hell standing, like great serpents, and their faces like extinguishing lamps, and their eyes of fire, their sharp teeth, and I saw all the Lord's works, how they are right, while the works of man are some (good), and others bad, and in their works are known those who lie evilly.

2Enoch 43

[1] I, my children, measured and wrote out every work and every measure and every righteous judgment.[2] As (one) year is more honourable than another, so is (one) man more honourable than another, some for great possessions, some for wisdom of heart, some for particular intellect, some for cunning, one for silence of lip, another for cleanliness, one for strength, another for comeliness, one for youth, another for sharp wit, one for shape of body, another for sensibility, let it be heard everywhere, but there is none better than he who fears God, he shall be more glorious in time to come.

2Enoch 44

[1] The Lord with his hands having created man, in the likeness of his own face, the Lord made him small and great.[2] Whoever reviles the ruler's face, and abhors the Lord's face, has despised the Lord's face, and he who vents anger on any man without injury, the Lord's great anger will cut him down, he who spits on the face of man reproachfully, will be cut down at the Lord's great judgment.[3] Blessed is the man who does not direct his heart with malice against any man, and helps the injured and condemned, and raises the broken down, and shall do charity to the needy, because on the day of the great judgment every weight, every measure and every makeweight (will be) as in the market, that is to say (they are) hung on scales and stand in the market, (and every one) shall learn his own measure, and according to his measure shall take his reward.

2Enoch 45

[1] Whoever hastens to make offerings before the Lord's face, the Lord for his part will hasten that offering by granting of his work.[2] But whoever increases his lamp before the Lord's face and make not true judgment, the Lord will (not) increase his treasure in the realm of the highest.[3] When the Lord demands bread, or candles, or (the)flesh (of beasts), or any other sacrifice, then that is nothing; but God demands pure hearts, and with all that (only) tests the heart of man.

2Enoch 46

[1] Hear, my people, and take in the words of my lips.[2] If any one bring any gifts to an earthly ruler, and have disloyal thoughts in his heart, and the ruler know this, will he not be angry with him, and not refuse his gifts, and not give him over to judgment?[3] Or (if) one man make himself appear good to another by deceit of tongue, but (have) evil in his heart, then will not (the other) understand the treachery of his heart, and himself be condemned, since his untruth was plain to all?[4] And when the Lord shall send a great light, then there will be judgment for the just and the unjust, and there no one shall escape notice.

2Enoch 47

[1] And now, my children, lay thought on your hearts, mark well the words of your father, which are all (come) to you from the Lord's lips.[2] Take these books of your father's handwriting and read them.[3] For the books are many, and in them you will learn all the Lord's works, all that has been from the beginning of creation, and will be till the end of time.[4] And if you will observe my handwriting,

you will not sin against the Lord; because there is no other except the Lord, neither in heaven, nor in earth, nor in the very lowest (places), nor in the (one) foundation.[5] The Lord has placed the foundations in the unknown, and has spread forth heavens visible (physical) and invisible (spiritual); he fixed the earth on the waters, and created countless creatures, and who has counted the water and the foundation of the unfixed, or the dust of the earth, or the sand of the sea, or the drops of the rain, or the morning dew, or the wind's breathings? Who has filled earth and sea, and the indissoluble winter?[6] I cut the stars out of fire, and decorated heaven, and put it in their midst.

2Enoch 48

[1] That the sun go along the seven heavenly circles, which are the appointment of one hundred and eighty-two thrones, that it go down on a short day, and again one hundred and eighty-two, that it go down on a big day, and he has two thrones on which he rests, revolving hither and thither above the thrones of the months, from the seventeenth day of the month Tsivan it goes down to the month Thevan, from the seventeenth of Thevan it goes up.[2] And thus it goes close to the earth, then the earth is glad and makes grow its fruits, and when it goes away, then the earth is sad, and trees and all fruits have no florescence.[3] All this he measured, with good measurement of hours, and fixed A measure by his wisdom, of the visible (physical) and the invisible (spiritual).[4] From the invisible (spiritual) he made all things visible (physical), himself being invisible (spiritual).[5] Thus I make known to you, my children, and distribute the books to your children, into all your generations, and amongst the nations who shall have the sense to fear God, let them receive them, and may they come to love them more than any food or earthly sweets, and read them and apply themselves to them.[6] And those who understand not the Lord, who fear not God, who accept not, but reject, who do not receive the (books), a terrible judgment awaits these.[7] Blessed is the man who shall bear their yoke and shall drag them along, for he shall be released on the day of the great judgment.

2Enoch 49

[1] I swear to you, my children, but I swear not by any oath, neither by heaven nor by earth, nor by any other creature which God created.[2] The Lord said: There is no oath in me, nor injustice, but truth.[3] If there is no truth in men, let them swear by the words, Yea, yea, or else, Nay, nay.[4] And I swear to you, yea, yea, that there has been no man in his mother's womb, (but that) already before, even to each one there is a place prepared for the repose of that soul, and a measure fixed how much it is intended that a man be tried in this world.[5] Yea, children, deceive not yourselves, for there has been previously prepared a place for every soul of man.

2Enoch 50

[1] I have put every man's work in writing and none born on earth can remain hidden nor his works remain concealed.[2] I see all things.[3] Now therefore, my children, in patience and meekness spend the number of your days, that you inherit endless life.[4] Endure for the sake of the Lord every wound, every injury, every evil word and attack.[5] If ill-requitals befall you, return (them) not either to neighbour or enemy, because the Lord will return (them) for you and be your avenger on the day of great judgment, that there be no avenging here among men.[6] Whoever of you spends gold or silver for his brother's sake, he will receive ample treasure in the world to come.[7] Injure not widows nor orphans nor strangers, lest God's wrath come upon you.

2Enoch 51

[1] Stretch out your hands to the poor according to your strength.[2] Hide not your silver in the earth.[3] Help the faithful man

in affliction, and affliction will not find you in the time of your trouble.[4] And every grievous and cruel yoke that come upon you bear all for the sake of the Lord, and thus you will find your reward in the day of judgment.[5] It is good to go morning, midday, and evening into the Lord's dwelling, for the glory of your creator.[6] Because every breathing (thing) glorifies him, and every creature visible (physical) and invisible (spiritual) returns him praise.

2Enoch 52

[1] Blessed is the man who opens his lips in praise of God of Sabaoth and praises the Lord with his heart.[2] Cursed every man who opens his lips for the bringing into contempt and calumny of his neighbour, because he brings God into contempt.[3] Blessed is he who opens his lips blessing and praising God.[4] Cursed is he before the Lord all the days of his life, who opens his lips to curse and abuse.[5] Blessed is he who blesses all the Lord's works.[6] Cursed is he who brings the Lord's creation into contempt.[7] Blessed is he who looks down and raises the fallen.[8] Cursed is he who looks to and is eager for the destruction of what is not his.[9] Blessed is he who keeps the foundations of his fathers made firm from the beginning.[10] Cursed is he who perverts the decrees of his forefathers.[11] Blessed is he who imparts peace and love.[12] Cursed is he who disturbs those that love their neighbours.[13] Blessed is he who speaks with humble tongue and heart to all.[14] Cursed is he who speaks peace with his tongue, while in his heart there is no peace but a sword.[15] For all these things will be laid bare in the weighing-scales and in the books, on the day of the great judgment.

2Enoch 53

[1] And now, my children, do not say: Our father is standing before God, and is praying for our sins, for there is there no helper of any man who has sinned.[2] You see how I wrote all works of every man, before his creation, (all) that is done amongst all men for all time, and none can tell or relate my handwriting, because the Lord see all imaginings of man, how they are vain, where they lie in the treasure-houses of the heart.[3] And now, my children, mark well all the words of your father, that I tell you, lest you regret, saying: Why did our father not tell us?

2Enoch 54

[1] At that time, not understanding this let these books which I have given you be for an inheritance of your peace.[2] Hand them to all who want them, and instruct them, that they may see the Lord's very great and marvellous works.

2Enoch 55

[1] My children, behold, the day of my term and time have approached.[2] For the angels who shall go with me are standing before me and urge me to my departure from you; they are standing here on earth, awaiting what has been told them.[3] For to-morrow I shall go up on to heaven, to the uppermost Jerusalem to my eternal inheritance.[4] Therefore I bid you do before the Lord's face all (his) good pleasure.

2Enoch 56

[1] Mathosalam having answered his father Enoch, said: What is agreeable to your eyes, father, that I may make before your face, that you may bless our dwellings, and your sons, and that your people may be made glorious through you, and then (that) you may depart thus, as the Lord said?[2] Enoch answered to his son Mathosalam (and) said: Hear, child, from the time when the Lord anointed me with the ointment of his glory, (there has been no) food in me, and my soul remembers not earthly enjoyment, neither do I want anything earthly.

2Enoch 57

[1] My child Methosalam, summon all your brethren and all your household and the elders of the people, that I may talk to them and

depart, as is planned for me.[2] And Methosalam made haste, and summoned his brethren, Regim, Riman, Uchan, Chermion, Gaidad, and all the elders of the people before the face of his father Enoch; and he blessed them, (and) said to them:

2Enoch 58

[1] Listen to me, my children, to-day.[2] In those days when the Lord came down on to earth for Adam's sake, and visited all his creatures, which he created himself, after all these he created Adam, and the Lord called all the beasts of the earth, all the reptiles, and all the birds that soar in the air, and brought them all before the face of our father Adam.[3] And Adam gave the names to all things living on earth.[4] And the Lord appointed him ruler over all, and subjected to him all things under his hands, and made them dumb and made them dull that they be commanded of man, and be in subjection and obedience to him.[5] Thus also the Lord created every man lord over all his possessions.[6] The Lord will not judge a single soul of beast for man's sake, but adjudges the souls of men to their beasts in this world; for men have a special place.[7] And as every soul of man is according to number, similarly beasts will not perish, nor all souls of beasts which the Lord created, till the great judgment, and they will accuse man, if he feed them ill.

2Enoch 59

[1] Whoever defiles the soul of beasts, defiles his own soul.[2] For man brings clean animals to make sacrifice for sin, that he may have cure of his soul.[3] And if they bring for sacrifice clean animals, and birds, man has cure, he cures his soul.[4] All is given you for food, bind it by the four feet, that is to make good the cure, he cures his soul.[5] But whoever kills beast without wounds, kills his own souls and defiles his own flesh.[6] And he who does any beast any injury whatsoever, in secret, it is evil practice, and he defiles his own soul.

2Enoch 60

[1] He who works the killing of a man's soul, kills his own soul, and kills his own body, and there is no cure for him for all time.[2] He who puts a man in any snare, shall stick in it himself, and there is no cure for him for all time.[3] He who puts a man in any vessel, his retribution will not be wanting at the great judgment for all time.[4] He who works crookedly or speaks evil against any soul, will not make justice for himself for all time.

2Enoch 61

[1] And now, my children, keep your hearts from every injustice, which the Lord hates. Just as a man asks something for his own soul from God, so let him do to every living soul, because I know all things, how in the great time to come there is much inheritance prepared for men, good for the good, and bad for the bad, without number many.[2] Blessed are those who enter the good houses, for in the bad houses there is no peace nor return from them.[3] Hear, my children, small and great! When man puts a good thought in his heart, brings gifts from his labours before the Lord's face and his hands made them not, then the Lord will turn away his face from the labour of his hand, and (that) man cannot find the labour of his hands.[4] And if his hands made it, but his heart murmur, and his heart cease not making murmur incessantly, he has not any advantage.

2Enoch 62

[1] Blessed is the man who in his patience brings his gifts with faith before the Lord's face, because he will find forgiveness of sins.[2] But if he take back his words before the time, there is no repentance for him; and if the time pass and he do not of his own will what is promised, there is no repentance after death.[3] Because every work which man does before the time, is all deceit before men, and sin before God.

2Enoch 63

[1] When man clothes the naked and fills the hungry, he will find reward from God.[2] But if his heart murmur, he commits a double evil; ruin of himself and of that which he gives; and for him there will be no finding of reward on account of that.[3] And if his own heart is filled with his food and his own flesh, clothed with his own clothing, he commits contempt, and will forfeit all his endurance of poverty, and will not find reward of his good deeds.[4] Every proud and magniloquent man is hateful to the Lord, and every false speech, clothed in untruth; it will be cut with the blade of the sword of death, and thrown into the fire, and shall burn for all time.

2Enoch 64

[1] When Enoch had spoken these words to his sons, all people far and near heard how the Lord was calling Enoch. They took counsel together:[2] Let us go and kiss Enoch, and two thousand men came together and came to the place Achuzan where Enoch was, and his sons.[3] And the elders of the people, the whole assembly, came and bowed down and began to kiss Enoch and said to him:[4] Our father Enoch, (may) you (be) blessed of the Lord, the eternal ruler, and now bless your sons and all the people, that we may be glorified to-day before your face.[5] For you shalt be glorified before the Lord's face for all time, since the Lord chose you, rather than all men on earth, and designated you writer of all his creation, visible (physical) and invisible (spiritual), and redeemed of the sins of man, and helper of your household.

2Enoch 65

[1] And Enoch answered all his people saying: Hear, my children, before that all creatures were created, the Lord created the visible (physical) and invisible (spiritual) things.[2] And as much time as there was and went past, understand that after all that he created man in the likeness of his own form, and put into him eyes to see, and ears to hear, and heart to reflect, and intellect wherewith to deliberate.[3] And the Lord saw all man's works, and created all his creatures, and divided time, from time he fixed the years, and from the years he appointed the months, and from the months he appointed the days, and of days he appointed seven.[4] And in those he appointed the hours, measured them out exactly, that man might reflect on time and count years, months, and hours, (their) alternation, beginning, and end, and that he might count his own life, from the beginning until death, and reflect on his sin and write his work bad and good; because no work is hidden before the Lord, that every man might know his works and never transgress all his commandments, and keep my handwriting from generation to generation.[5] When all creation visible (physical) and invisible (spiritual), as the Lord created it, shall end, then every man goes to the great judgment, and then all time shall perish, and the years, and thenceforward there will be neither months nor days nor hours, they will be adhered together and will not be counted.[6] There will be one aeon, and all the righteous who shall escape the Lord's great judgment, shall be collected in the great aeon, for the righteous the great aeon will begin, and they will live eternally, and then too there will be amongst them neither labour, nor sickness, nor humiliation, nor anxiety, nor need, nor brutality, nor night, nor darkness, but great light.[7] And they shall have a great indestructible wall, and a paradise bright and incorruptible (eternal), for all corruptible (mortal) things shall pass away, and there will be eternal life.

2Enoch 66

[1] And now, my children, keep your souls from all injustice, such as the Lord hates.[2] Walk before his face with terror and trembling and serve him alone.[3] Bow down to the true God, not to dumb idols, but bow down to his similitude, and bring all just offerings before the Lord's face. The Lord hates what is unjust.[4] For the Lord sees all things; when man takes thought in his heart, then he counsels the

intellects, and every thought is always before the Lord, who made firm the earth and put all creatures on it.[5] If you look to heaven, the Lord is there; if you take thought of the sea's deep and all the under-earth, the Lord is there.[6] For the Lord created all things. Bow not down to things made by man, leaving the Lord of all creation, because no work can remain hidden before the Lord's face.[7] Walk, my children, in long-suffering, in meekness, honesty, in provocation, in grief, in faith and in truth, in (reliance on) promises, in illness, in abuse, in wounds, in temptation, in nakedness, in privation, loving one another, till you go out from this age of ills, that you become inheritors of endless time.[8] Blessed are the just who shall escape the great judgment, for they shall shine forth more than the sun sevenfold, for in this world the seventh part is taken off from all, light, darkness, food, enjoyment, sorrow, paradise, torture, fire, frost, and other things; he put all down in writing, that you might read and understand.

2Enoch 67

[1] When Enoch had talked to the people, the Lord sent out darkness on to the earth, and there was darkness, and it covered those men standing with Enoch, and they took Enoch up on to the highest heaven, where the Lord (is); and he received him and placed him before his face, and the darkness went off from the earth, and light came again.[2] And the people saw and understood not how Enoch had been taken, and glorified God, and found a roll in which was traced The Invisible (spiritual) God; and all went to their dwelling places.

2Enoch 68

[1] Enoch was born on the sixth day of the month Tsivan, and lived three hundred and sixty-five years.[2] He was taken up to heaven on the first day of the month Tsivan and remained in heaven sixty days.[3] He wrote all these signs of all creation, which the Lord created, and wrote three hundred and sixty-six books, and handed them over to his sons and remained on earth thirty days, and was again taken up to heaven on the sixth day of the month Tsivan, on the very day and hour when he was born.[4] As every man's nature in this life is dark, so are also his conception, birth, and departure from this life.[5] At what hour he was conceived, at that hour he was born, and at that hour too he died.[6] Methosalam and his brethren, all the sons of Enoch, made haste, and erected an altar at that place called Achuzan, whence and where Enoch had been taken up to heaven.[7] And they took sacrificial oxen and summoned all people and sacrificed the sacrifice before the Lord's face.[8] All people, the elders of the people and the whole assembly came to the feast and brought gifts to the sons of Enoch.[9] And they made a great feast, rejoicing and making merry three days, praising God, who had given them such a sign through Enoch, who had found favour with him, and that they should hand it on to their sons from generation to generation, from age to age.[10] Amen.

Enoch 3 – The Hebrew Book of Enoch

3Enoch 1

Introduction: R. Ishmael ascends to heaven to behold the vision of the Merkaba and is given in charge to Metatron AND ENOCH WALKED WITH GOD: AND HE WAS NOT ; FOR GOD TOOK HIM (Gen. V. 24)
Rabbi Ishmael said : [1] When I ascended on high to behold the vision of the Merkaba and had entered the six Halls, one within the other: [2] as soon as I reached the door of the seventh Hall I stood still in prayer before the Holy One, blessed be He, and, lifting up my eyes on high (i.e. towards the Divine Majesty), I said : [3] " Lord of the Universe, I pray thee, that the merit of Aaron, the son of Amram, the lover of peace and pursuer of peace, who received the crown of priesthood from Thy Glory on the mount of Sinai, be valid for me in this hour, so that Qafsiel*, the prince, and the angels with him may not get power over me nor throw me down from the heavens ". [4] Forthwith the Holy One, blessed be He, sent to me Metatron, his Servant ('Ebed) the angel, the Prince of the Presence, and he, spreading his wings, with great joy came to meet me so as to save me from their hand. [5] And he took me by his hand in their sight, saying to me: "Enter in peace before the high and exalted King3 and behold the picture of the Merkaba". [6] Then I entered the seventh Hall, and he led me to the camp(s) of Shekina and placed me before 6the Holy One, blessed be He, to behold the Merkaba. [7] As soon as the princes of the Merkaba and the flaming Seraphim perceived me, they fixed their eyes upon me. Instantly trembling and shuddering seized me and I fell down and was benumbed by the radiant image of their eyes and the splendid appearance of their faces; until the Holy One, blessed be He, rebuked them, saying: [8] "My servants, my Seraphim, my Kerubim and my 'Ophanniml Cover ye your eyes before Ishmael, my son, my friend, my beloved one and my glory, that he tremble not nor shudder ! " [9] Forthwith Metatron the Prince of the Presence, came and restored my spiritand put me upon my feet. [10] After that (moment) there was notin me strength enough to say a song before the Throne of Glory of the glorious King, the mightiest of all kings, the most excellent of all princes, until after the hour had passed. [11] After one hour (had passed) the Holy One, blessed be He, opened to me the gates of Shekina, the gates of Peace, the gates of Wisdom, the gates of Strength, the gates of Power, the gates of Speech (Dibbur), the gates of Song, the gates of Qedushsha, the gates of Chant. [12] And he enlightened my eyes and my heart by words of psalm, song, praise, exaltation, thanksgiving, extolment, glorification, hymn and eulogy. And as I opened my mouth, uttering a song before the Holy One, blessed be He, the Holy Chayyoth beneath and above the Throne of Glory answered and said : "HOLY " and "BLESSED BE THE GLORY OF YHWH FROM HIS PLACE !" (i.e. chanted the Qedushsha).

3Enoch 2

The highest classes of angels make inquiries about R. Ishmael which are answered by Metatron R. Ishmael said; [1] In that hour the eagles of the Merkaba, the flaming 'Ophannim and the Seraphim of consuming fire asked Metatron, saying to him: [2] "Youth ! Why sufferest thou one born of woman to enter and behold the Merkaba? From which nation, from which tribe is this one? What is his character?" [3] Metatron answered and said to them : "From the nation of Israel whom the Holy One, blessed be He, chose for his people from among seventy tongues (nations), from the tribe of Levi, whom he set aside as a contribution to his name and from the seed of Aaron whom the Holy One, blessed be He, did choose for his servant and put upon him the crown of priesthood on Sinai". [4] Forthwith they spake and said : "Indeed, this one is worthy to behold the Merkaba ". And they said: "Happy is the people that is in such a case!".

3Enoch 3

Metatron has 70 names, but God calls him ' Youth ' R. Ishmael said: [1] In that hourl I asked Metatron, the angel, the Prince of the Presence: "What is thy name?" [2] He answered me: "I have seventy names, corresponding to the seventy tongues of the world and all of them are based upon the name Metatron, angel of the Presence; but my King calls me Youth' (Na'ar)"

3Enoch 4

Metatron is identical with Enoch who was translated to heaven at the time of the Deluge R. Ishmael said : [1] I asked Metatron and said to him: "Why art thou called by the name of thy Creator, by seventy names? Thou art greater than all the princes, higher than all the angels, beloved more than all the servants, honoured above all the mighty ones in kingship, greatness and glory : why do they call thee ' Youth ' in the high heavens ?" [2] He answered and said to me: " Because I am Enoch, the son of Jared. [3] For when the generation of the flood sinned and were confounded in their deeds, saying unto God: 'Depart from us, for we desire not the knowledge of thy ways' (Job xxi. 14), then the Holy One, blessed be He, removed me from their midst to be a witness against them in the high heavens to all the inhabitants of the world, that they may not say: 'The Merciful One is cruel". [4] What sinned all those multitudes, their wives, their sons and their, daughters, their horses, their mules and their cattle and their property, and all the birds of the world, all of which the Holy One, blessed be He, destroyed from the world together with them in the waters of the flood? [5] Hence the Holy One, blessed be He, lifted me up in their lifetime before their eyes to be a witness against them to the future world. And the Holy One, blessed be He, assigned me for a prince and a ruler among the ministering angels. [6] In that hour three of the ministering angels, 'UZZA, 'AZZA and 'AZZAEL came forth and brought charges against me in the high heavens, saying before the Holy One, blessed be He: "Said not the Ancient Ones (First Ones) rightly before Thee: < Do not create man! ' " The Holy One, blessed be He, answered and said unto them: "I have made and I will bear, yea, I will carry and will deliver". (Is. xlvi. 4.) [7] As soon as they saw me, they said before Him: "Lord of the Universe ! What is this one that he should ascend to the height of heights? Is not he one from among the sons of [the sons of] those who perished in the days of the Flood? "What doeth he in the Raqia'?" [8] Again, the Holy One, blessed be He, answered and said to them: "What are ye, that ye enter and speak in my presence? I delight in this one more than in all of you, and hence he shall be a prince and a ruler over you in the high heavens." [9] Forthwith all stood up and went out to meet me, prostrated themselves before me and said: "Happy art thou and happy is thy father for thy Creator doth favour thee". [10] And because I am small and a youth among them in days, months and years, therefore they call me "Youth" (Na'ar).

3Enoch 5

The idolatry of the generation of Enosh causes God to remove the Shekina from earth. The idolatry inspired by 'Azza, 'Uzza and 'Azziel R.Ishmael said; Metatron, the Prince of the Presence, said to me; [1] From the day when the Holy One, blessed be He, expelled the first Adam from the Garden of Eden (and onwards), Shekina was dwelling upon a Kerub under the Tree of Life. [2] And the ministering angels were gathering together and going down from heaven in parties, from the Raqia in companies and from the heavens in camps to do His will in the whole world. [3] And the first man and his generation were sitting outside the gate of the Garden to behold the radiant appearance of the Shekina. [4] For the silendour of the Shekina traversed the world from one end to the other (with a splendour) 365,000 times (that) of the globe of the sun. And everyone who made use of the splendour of the Shekina, on him no flies and no gnats did rest, neither was he ill nor suffered he any pain. No demons got power over him, neither were they able to injure him. [5] When the Holy One, blessed be He, went out and went in; from the Garden to Eden, from Eden to the Garden, from the Garden to Raqia and from Raqia to the Garden of Eden then all and everyone beheld the splendour of His Shekina and they were not injured; [6] until uthe time of the generation of Enosh who was the head of all idol worshippers of the world. [7] And what did the generation of Enosh do? They went from one end of the world to the other, and each one brought silver, gold, precious stones and pearls in heaps like unto mountains and hills making idols out of

them throughout all the world. And they erected the idols in every quarter of the world: the size of each idol was 1000 parasangs. [8] And they brought down the sun, the moon, planets and constellations, and placed them before the idols on their right hand and on their left, to attend them even as they attend the Holy One, blessed be He, as it is written (1 Kings xxii. 19): "And all the host of heaven was standing by him on his right hand and on his left". [9] What power was in them that they were able to bring them down? They would not have been able to bring them down but for 'Uzza, 'Azza and 'Azziel who taught them sorceries whereby they brought them down and made use of them [10] In that time the ministering angels brought charges (against them) before the Holy One, blessed be He, saying before him: "Master of the World! What hast thou to do with the children of men? As it is written (Ps. viii. 4) 'What is man (Enosh) that thou art mindful of him?' 'Mah Adam' is not written here, but 'Mah Enosh', for he (Enosh) is the head of the idol worshippers. [11] Why hast thou left the highest of the high heavens, the abode of thy glorious Name, and the high and exalted Throne in 'Araboth Raqia' in the highest and art gone and dwellest with the children of men who worship idols and equal thee to the idols. [12] Now thou art on earth and the idols likewise. What hast thou to do with the inhabitants of the earth who worship idols?" [13] Forthwith the Holy One, blessed be He, lifted up His Shekina from the earth, from their midst. [14] In that moment came the ministering angels, the troops of hosts and the armies of 'Araboth in thousand camps and ten thousand hosts : they fetched trumpets and took the horns in their hands and surrounded the Shekina with all kinds of songs.And He ascended to the high heavens, as it is written (Ps. xlvii. 5): "God is gone up with a shout, the Lord with the sound of a trumpet ".

3Enoch 6

Enoch lifted up to heaven together with the Shekina. Angels protests answered by God R. Ishmael said: Metatron, the Angel, the Prince of the Presence, said to me : [1] When the Holy One, blessed be He, desired to lift me up on high, He first sent 'Anaphiel H (H = Tetragrammaton) the Prince, and he took me from their midst in their sight and carried me in great glory upon a a fiery chariot with fiery horses, servants of glory. And he lifted me up to the high heavens together with the Shekina. [2] As soon as I reached the high heavens, the Holy Chayyoth, the 'Ophannim, the Seraphim, the Kerubim, the Wheels of the Merkaba (the Galgallim), and the ministers of the consuming fire, perceiving my smell from a distance of 365,000 myriads of parasangs, said: "What smell of one born of woman and what taste of a white drop (is this) that ascends on high, and, (lo, he is merely) a gnat among those who 'divide flames (of fire)'?" [3] The Holy One, blessed be He, answered and spake unto them: "My servants, my hosts, my Kerubim, my 'Ophannim, my Seraphim! Be ye not displeased on account of this! Since all the children of men have denied me and my great Kingdom and are gone worshipping idols, I have removed my Shekina from among them and have lifted it up on high. But this one whom I have taken from among them is an ELECT ONE among (the inhabitants of) the world and he is equal to all of them in faith, righteousness and perfection of deed and I have taken him for (as) a tribute from my world under all the heavens".

3Enoch 7

Enoch raised upon the wings of the Shekina to the place of the Throne, the Merkaba and the angehc hosts R. Ishmael said: Metatron, the Angel, the Prince of the Presence, said to me; [1] When the Holy One, blessed be He, took me away from the generation of the Flood, he lifted me on the wings of the wind of Shekina to the highest heaven and brought me into the great palaces of the

'Araboth Raqia' on high, where are the glorious Throne of Shekina, the Merkaba, the troops of anger, the armies of vehemence, the fiery Shin'anim', the flaming Kerubim, and the burning 'Ophannim, the flaming servants, the flashing Chashmattim and the lightening Seraphim. And he placed me (there) to attend the Throne of Glory day after day.

3Enoch 8

The gates (of the treasuries of heaven) opened to Metatron R. Ishmael said : Metatron, the Prince of the Presence, said to me : [1] Before He appointed me to attend the Throne of Glory, the Holy One, blessed be He, opened to me three hundred thousand gates of Understanding three hundred thousand gates of Subtlety three hundred thousand gates of Life three hundred thousand gates of grace and loving-kindness three hundred thousand gates of love three hundred thousand gates of Tora three hundred thousand gates of meekness three hundred thousand gates of maintenance three hundred thousand gates' of mercy three hundred thousand gates of fear of heaven [2] In that hour the Holy One, blessed be He, added in me wisdom unto wisdom, understanding unto understanding, subtlety unto subtlety, knowledge unto knowledge, mercy unto mercy, instruction unto instruction, love unto love, loving-kindness unto loving-kindness, goodness unto goodness, meekness unto meekness, power unto power, strength unto strength, might unto might, brilliance unto brilliance, beauty unto beauty, splendour unto splendour, and I was honoured and adorned with all these good and praiseworthy things more than all the children of heaven.

3Enoch 9

Enoch receives blessings from the Most High and is adorned with angelic attributes R. Ishmael said : Metatron, the Prince of the Presence, said to me : [1] After all these things the Holy One, blessed be He, put His hand upon me and blessed me with 5360 blessings. [2] And I was raised and enlarged to the size of the length and width of the world. [3] And He caused 72 wings to grow on me, 36 on each side. And each wing was as the whole world. [4] And He fixed on me 365 eyes : each eye was as the great luminary. [5] And He left no kind of splendour, brilliance, radiance, beauty in (of) all the lights of the universe that He did not fix on me.

3Enoch 10

God places Metatron on a throne at the door of the seventh Hall and announces through the Herald, that Metatron henceforth is God's representative and ruler over all the princes of kingdoms and all the children of heaven, save the eight high princes called YHWH by the name of their King R. Ishmael said : Metatron, the Prince of the Presence, said to me ; [1] All these things the Holy One, blessed be He, made for me:He made me a Throne, similar to the Throne of Glory. And He spread over me a curtain of splendour and brilliant appearance, of beauty, grace and mercy, similar to the curtain of the Throne of Glory; and on it were fixed all kinds of lights in the universe. [2] And He placed it at the door of the Seventh Hall and seated me on it. [3] And the herald went forth into every heaven, saying:This is Metatron, my servant. I have made him into a prince and a ruler over all the princes of my kingdoms and over all the children of heaven, except the eight great princes, the honoured and revered ones who are called YHWH, by the name of their King. [4] And every angel and every prince who has a word to speak in my presence (before me) shall go into his presence (before him) and shall speak to him (instead). [5]And every command that he utters to you in my name do ye observe and fulfil. For the Prince of Wisdom and the Prince of Understanding have I committed to him to instruct him in the wisdom of heavenly things and of earthly things, in the wisdom of this world and of the world to come. [6] Moreover, I have set him over all the treasuries of the

palapes of Araboih and over all the stores of life that I have in the high heavens.

3Enoch 11

God reveals all mysteries and secrets to Metatron R. Ishmael said : Metatron, the angel, the Prince of the Presence, said to me: [1] Henceforth the Holy One, blessed be He, revealed to me all the mysteries of Tora and all the secrets of wisdom and all the depths of the Perfect Law; and all living beings' thoughts of heart and all the secrets of the universe and all the secrets of Creation were revealed unto me even as they are revealed unto the Maker of Creation. [2] And I watched intently to behold the secrets of the depth and the wonderful mystery. Before a man did think in secret, I saw (it) and before a man made a thing I beheld it. [3] And there was no thing on high nor in the deep hidden from me.

3Enoch 12

God clothes Metatron in a garment of glory, puts a royal crown on his head and calls him "the Lesser YHWH" R. Ishmael said: Metatron, the Prince of the Presence, said to me: [1] By reason of the love with which the Holy One, blessed be He, loved me more than all the children of heaven. He made me a garment of glory on which were fixed all kinds of lights, and He clad me in it. [2]And He made me a robe of honour on which were fixed all kinds of beauty, splendour, brilliance and majesty. [3] And he made me a royal crown in which were fixed forty-nine costly stones like unto the light of the globe of the sun. [4] For its splendour went forth in the four quarters of the Araboth Raqia', and in (through) the seven heavens, and in the four quarters of the world. And he put it on my head. [5] And He called me THE LESSER YHWH in the presence of all His heavenly household; as it is written (Ex. xxiii. 21): "For my name is in him".

3Enoch 13

God writes with a flaming style on Metatron's crown the cosmic letters by which heaven and earth were created R. Ishmael said : Metatron, the angel, the Prince of the Presence, the Glory of all heavens, said to me : [1] Because of the great love and mercy with which the Holy One, blessed be He, loved and cherished me more than all the children of heaven. He wrote with his ringer with a flaming style upon the crown on my head the letters by which were created heaven and earth, the seas and rivers, the mountains and hills, the planets and constellations, the Ughtnings, winds, earthquakes and voices (thunders), the snow and hail, the storm-wind and the tempest ; the letters by which were created all the needs of the world and all the orders of Creation. [2] And every single letter sent forth time after time as it were lightnings, time after time as it were torches, time after time as it were flames of fire, time after time (rays) like [as] the rising of the sun and the moon and the planets.

3Enoch 14

All the highest princes, the elementary angels and the planetary and sideric angels fear and tremble at the sight of Metatron crowned R. Ishmael said: Metatron, the Angel, the Prince of the Presence, said to me : [1] When the Holy One, blessed be He, put this crown on my head, (then) trembled before me all the Princes of Kingdoms who are in the height of Araboth Raqiaf and all the hosts of every heaven; and even the princes (of) the 'Elim, the princes (of) the 'Er'ellim and the princes (of) the Tafsarim, who are greater than all the ministering angels who minister before the Throne of Glory, shook, feared and trembled before me when they beheld me. [2] Even Sammael, the Prince of the Accusers, who is greater than all the princes of kingdoms on high; feared and trembled before me. [3] And even the angel of fire, and the angel of hail, and the angel of the wind, and the angel of the lightning, and the angel of anger, and the angel of the thunder, and the angel of the snow, and the angel of the rain ; and the angel of the day, and the angel of the night, and the angel of the sun and the angel of the moon, and the angel of the planets and the angel of the constellations who rule the world under their hands, feared and trembled and were affrighted before me, when they beheld me. [4] These are the names of the rulers of the world: Gabriel, the angel of the fire, Baradiel, the angel of the hail, Ruchiel who is appointed over the wind, Baraqiel who is appointed over the lightnings, Za'amiel who is appointed over the vehemence, Ziqiel who is appointed over the sparks, Zi'iel who is appointed over the commotion, Zdaphiel who is appointed over the storm-wind, Ra'amiel who is appointed over the thunders, Rctashiel who is appointed over the earthquake, Shalgiel who is appointed over the snow, Matariel who is appointed over the rain, Shimshiel who is appointed over the day, Lailiel who is appointed over the night, Galgalliel who is appointed over the globe of the sun, 'Ophanniel who is appointed over the globe of the moon, Kokbiel who is appointed over the planets, Rahatiel who is appointed over the constellations. [5] And they all fell prostrate, when they saw me. And they were not able to behold me because of the majestic glory and beauty of the appearance of the shining light of the crown of glory upon my head.

3Enoch 15

Metatron transformed into fire R. Ishmael said : Metatron, the angel, the Prince of the Presence, the Glory of all heavens, said to me : [1] As soon as the Holy One, blessed be He, took me in (His) service to attend the Throne of Glory and the Wheels (Galgallim) of the Merkaba and the needs of Shekina, forthwith my flesh was changed into flames, my sinews into flaming fire, my bones into coals of burning juniper, the light of my eye-lids into splendour of lightnings, my eye-balls into fire-brands, the hair of my head into dot flames, all my limbs into wings of burning fire and the whole of my body into glowing fire. [2] And on my right were divisions 6 of fiery flames, on my left fire-brands were burning, round about me stormwind and tempest were blowing and in front of me and behind me was roaring of thunder with earthquake. FRAGMENT OF 'ASCENSION OF MOSES' [1] R. Ishmael said: Said to me Metatron, the Prince of the Presence and the prince over all the princes and he stands befote Him who is greater than all the Elohim. And he goes in under the Throne of Glory. And he has a great tabernacle of light on high. And he brings forth the fire of deafness and puts (it) into the ears of the Holy Chayyoth, that they may not hear the voice of the Word (Dibbur) that goes forth from the mouth of the Divine Majesty. [2] And when Moses ascended on high, he fasted 121 fasts, till the habitations of the chashmal were opened to him; and he saw the heart within the heart of the Lion and he saw the innumerable companies of the hosts Around about him. And they desired to burn him. But Moses prayed for mercy, first for Israel and after that for himself: and He who sitteth on the Merkaba opened the windows that are above the heads of the Kerubim. And a host of 1800 advocates and the Prince of the Presence, Metatron, with them went forth to meet Moses. And they took the prayers of Israel and put them as a crown on the head of the Holy One, blessed be He. [3] And they said (Deut. vi. 4): "Hear, O Israel; the Lord our God is one Lord"and their face shone and rejoiced over Shekinaand they said to Metatron: "What are these? And to whom do they give all this honour and glory?" And they answered: "To the Glorious Lord of Israel". And they spake: "Hear, O Israel: the Lord, our God, is one Lord. To whom shall be given abundance of honour and majesty but to Thee YHWH, the Divine Majesty, the King, living and eternal". [4] In that moment spake Akatriel Yah Yehod Sebaoth and said to Metatron, the Prince of the Presence: "Let no prayer that he prayeth before me return (to him) void. Hear thou his prayer and fulfil his desire whether (it be) great or small". [5] Forthwith Metatron,

the Prince of the Presence, said to Moses: "Son of Amram! Fear not, for now God delights in thee. And ask thou u thy desire of the Glory and Majesty. For thy face shines from one end of the world to the other". But Moses answered him: "(I fear) lest I bring guiltiness upon myself". Metatron said to him: "Receive the letters of the oath, in (by) which there is no breaking the covenant" (which precludes any breach of the covenant).

3Enoch 16

[1]Probably additional Metatron divested of his privilege of presiding on a Tlirone of his own on account of Acher's misapprehension in taking him for a second Divine Power R. Ishmael said: Metatron, the Angel, the Prince of the Presence, the Glory of all heaven, said to me; [1] At first I was sitting upon a great Throne at the door of the Seventh Hall ; and I was judging the children of heaven, the household on high by authority of the Holy One, blessed be He. And I divided Greatness, Kingship, Dignity, Rulership, Honour and Praise, and Diadem and Crown of Glory unto all the princes of kingdoms, while I was presiding (lit. sitting) in the Celestial Court (Yeshiba), and the princes of kingdoms were standing before me, on my right and on my left by authority of the Holy One, blessed be He. [2] But when Acher came to behold the vision of the Merkaba and fixed his eyes on me, he feared and trembled before me and his soul was affrighted even unto departing from him, because of fear, horror and dread of me, when he beheld me sitting upon a throne like a king with all the ministering angels standing by me as my servants and all the princes of kingdoms adorned with crowns surrounding me: [3] in that moment he opened his mouth and said: "Indeed, there are two Divine Powers in heaven!" [4] Forthwith Bath Qol (the Divine Voice) went forth from heaven from before the Shekina and said: "Return, ye backsliding children (Jer. iii. 22), except Acher!" [5] Then came 'Aniyel, the Prince, the honoured, glorified, beloved, wonderful, revered and fearful one, in commission from the Holy One, blessed be He and gave me sixty strokes with lashes of fire and made me stand on my feet.

3Enoch 17

The princes of the seven heavens, of the sun, moon, planets and constellations and their suites of angels R. Ishmael said : Metatron, the angel, the Prince of the Presence, the glory of all heavens, said to me: [1] Seven (are the) princes, the great, beautiful, revered, wonderful and honoured ones who are appointed over the seven heavens. And these are they : MIKAEL, GABRIEL, SHATQIEL, SHACHAQIEL, BAKARIEL, BAD ARIEL, PACHRIEL. [2] And every one of them is the prince of the host of (one) heaven. And each one of them is accompanied by 496,000 myriads of ministering angels. [3] MIKAEL, the great prince, is appointed over the seventh heaven, the highest one, which is in the 'Araboth. GABRIEL, the prince of the host, is appointed over the sixth heaven which is in Makon. SHATAQIEL, prince of the host, is appointed over the fifth heaven which is in Ma'on. SHAHAQi'EL, prince of the host, is appointed over the fourth heaven which is in Zebul. BAD ARIEL, prince of the host, is appointed over the third heaven which is in Shehaqim. BARAKIEL, prince of the host, is appointed over the second heaven which is in the height of (Merom) Raqia. PAZRIEL, prince of the host, is appointed over the first heaven which is in Wilon, which is in Shamayim. [4] Under them is GALGALLIEL, the prince who is appointed over the globe (galgal) of the sun, and with him are 96 great and honoured angels who move the sun in Raqia'. [5]Under them is 'OPHANNIEL, the prince who is set over the globe ('ophari) of the moon. And with him are 88 angels who move the globe of the moon 354 thousand parasangs every night at the time when the moon stands in the East at its turning point. And when is the moon sitting in the East at its turning point? Answer: in the fifteenth day of every month. [6] Under them is RAHATIEL, the prince who is appointed over the constellations. And he is accompanied by 72 great and honoured angels. And why is he called RAHATIEL? Because he makes the stars run (marhit) in their orbits and courses 339 thousand parasangs every night from the East to the West, and from the West to the East. For the Holy One, blessed be He, has made a tent for all of them, for the sun, the moon, the planets and the stars in which they travel at night from the West to the East. [7] Under them is KOKBIEL, the prince who is appointed over all the planets. And with him are 365,000 myriads of ministering angels, great and honoured ones who move the planets from city to city and from province to province in the Raqia' of heavens. [8] And over them are SEVENTY-TWO PRINCES OF KINGDOMS on high corresponding to the 72 tongues of the world. And all of them are crowned with royal crowns and clad in royal garments and wrapped in royal cloaks. And all of them are riding on royal horses and they are holding royal sceptres in their hands. And before each one of them when he is travelling in Raqia', royal servants are running with great glory and majesty even as on earth they (princes) are travelling in chariot(s) with horsemen and great armies and in glory and greatness with praise, song and honour.

3Enoch 18

The order of ranks of the angels and the homage received by the higher ranks from the lower ones R. Ishmael said: Metatron, the Angel, the Prince of the Presence, the glory of all heaven, said to me: [1] THE ANGELS OF THE FIRST HEAVEN, when(ever) they see their prince, they dismount from their horses and fall on their faces. And THE PRINCE OF THE FIRST HEAVEN, when he sees the prince of the second heaven, he dismounts, removes the crown of glory from his head and falls on his face. And THE PRINCE OF THE SECOND HEAVEN, when he sees the Prince of the third heaven, he removes the crown of glory from his head and falls on his face. And THE PRINCE OF THE THIRD HEAVEN, when he sees the prince of the fourth heaven, he removes the crown of glory from his head and falls on his face. And THE PRINCE OF THE FOURTH HEAVEN, when he sees the prince of the fifth heaven, he removes the crown of glory from his head and falls on his face. xAnd THE PRINCE OF THE FIFTH HEAVEN, when he sees the prince of the sixth heaven, he removes the crown of glory from his head and falls on his face. And THE PRINCE OF THE SIXTH HEAVEN, when he sees the prince of the seventh heaven, he removes the crown of glory from his head and falls on his face. [2] And THE PRINCE OF THE SEVENTH HEAVEN, when he sees THE SEVENTY-TWO PRINCES OF KINGDOMS, he removes the crown of glory from his head and falls on his face. 2 [3] And the seventy-two princes of kingdoms, when they see THE DOOR KEEPERS OF THE FIRST HALL IN THE ARABOTH RAQIA in the highest, they remove the royal crown from their head and fall on their faces. 3And THE DOOR KEEPERS OF THE FIRST HALL, when they see the door keepers of the second Hall, they remove the crown of glory from their head and fall on their faces. And THE DOOR KEEPERS OF THE SECOND HALL, when they see the door keepers of the third Hall, they remove the crown of glory from their head and fall on their faces. And THE DOOR KEEPERS OF THE THIRD HALL, when they see the door keepers of the fourth Hall, they remove the crown of glory from their head and fall on their faces. And THE DOOR KEEPERS OF THE FOURTH HALL, when they see the door keepers of the fifth Hall, they remove the crown of glory from their head and fall on their faces. And THE DOOR KEEPERS OF THE FIFTH HALL, when they see the door keepers of the sixth Hall, they remove the crown of glory from their head and fall on

their faces. And THE DOOR KEEPERS OF THE SIXTH HALL, when they see the DOOR KEEPERS OF THE SEVENTH HALL, they remove the crown of glory from their head and fall on their faces. [4] And the door keepers of the seventh Hall, when they see THE FOUR GREAT PRINCES, the honoured ones, WHO ARE APPOINTED OVER THE FOUR CAMPS OF SHEKINA, they remove the crown(s) of glory from their head and fall on their faces. [5] And the four great princes, when they see TAG'AS, the prince, great and honoured with song (and) praise, at the head of all thechildren of heaven, they remove the crown of glory from their head and fall on their faces. [6] And Tag' as, the great and honoured prince, when he sees BARATTIEL, the great prince of three fingers in the height of 'Araboth, the highest heaven, he removes the crown of glory from his head and falls on his face. [7] And Barattiel, the great prince, when he sees HAMON, the great prince, the fearful and honoured, pleasant and terrible one who maketh all the children of heaven to tremble, when the time draweth nigh (that is set) for the saying of the '(Thrice) Holy', as it is written (Isa. xxxiii. 3): "At the noise of the tumult (hamon) the peoples are fled; at the lifting up of thyself the nations are scattered" he removes the crown of glory from his head and falls on his face. [8] And Hamon, the great prince, when he sees TUTRESIEL, the great prince, he removes the crown of glory from his head and falls on his face. [9] And Tutresiel H', the great prince, when he sees ATRUGIEL, the great prince, he removes the crown of glory from his head and falls on his face. [10] And Atrugiel the great prince, when he sees NA'ARIRIEL H', the great prince, he removes the crown of glory from his head and falls on his face. (n) And Na'aririel H', the great prince, when he sees SASNIGIEL H', the great prince, he removes the crown of glory from his head and falls on his face. [12] And Sasnigiel H', when he sees ZAZRIEL H', the great prince, he removes the crown of glory from his head and falls on his face. [13] And Zazriel H', the prince, when he sees GEBURATIEL H', the prince, he removes the crown of glory from his head and falls on his face. [14] And Geburatiel H', the prince, when he sees 'ARAPHIEL H', the prince, he removes the crown of glory from his head and falls on his face. [15] And 'Araphiel H', the prince, when he sees 'ASHRUYLU, the prince, who presides in all the sessions of the children of heaven, he removes the crown of glory from his head and falls on his face. [16] And Ashruylu H, the prince, when he sees GALLISUR H', THE PRINCE, WHO REVEALS ALL THE SECRETS OF THE LAW (Tora), he removes the crown of glory from his head and falls on his face. [17] And Gallisur H', the prince, when he sees ZAKZAKIEL H', the prince who is appointed to write down the merits of Israel on the Throne of Glory, he removes the crown of glory from his head and falls on his face. [18] And Zakzakiel H', the great prince, when he sees 'ANAPHIEL H', the prince who keeps the keys of the heavenly Halls, he removes the crown of glory from his head and falls on his face. Why is he called by the name of 'Anaphiel ? Because the bough of his honour and majesty and his crown and his splendour and his brilliance covers (overshadows) all the chambers of 'Araboth Raqia on high even as the Maker of the World (doth overshadow them). Just as it is written with regard to the Maker of the World (Hab. iii. 3): "His glory covered the heavens, and the earth was full of his praise", even so do the honour and majesty of 'Anaphiel cover all the glories of 'Araboth the highest. [19] And when he sees SOTHER 'ASHIEL H', the prince, the great, fearful and honoured one, he removes the crown of glory from his head and falls on his face. Why is he called Sother Ashiel? Because he is appointed over the four heads of the fiery river over against the Throne of Glory; and every single prince who goes out or enters before the Shekina, goes out or enters only by his permission. For the seals of the fiery river are entrusted to him. And furthermore, his height is 7000 myriads of parasangs. And he stirs up the fire of the river ; and he goes out and enters before the Shekina to expound what is written (recorded) concerning the inhabitants of the world. According as it is written (Dan. vii. 10) : "the judgement was set, and the books were opened". ²⁰ And Sother 'Ashiel the prince, when he sees SHOQED CHOZI, the great prince, the mighty, terrible and honoured one, he removes the crown of glory from his head and falls upon his face. And why is he called Shoqed Chozi? Because he weighs all the merits (of man) in a balance in the presence of the Holy One, blessed be He. ²¹ And when he sees ZEHANPURYU H',the great prince, the mighty and terrible one, honoured, glorified and feared in all the heavenly household, he removes the crown of glory from his head and falls on his face. Why is he called Zehanpuryu? Because he rebukes the fiery river and pushes it back to its place. ²² And when he sees 'AZBUGA H', the great prince, glorified, revered, honoured, adorned, wonderful, exalted, beloved and feared among all the great princes who know the mystery of the Throne of Glory, he removes the crown of glory from his head and falls on his face. Why is he called 'Azbuga? Because in the future he will gird (clothe) the righteous and pious of the world with the garments of life and wrap them in the cloak of life, that they may live in them an eternal life. ²³ And when he sees the two great princes, the strong and glorified ones who are standing above him, he removes the crown of glory from his head and falls on his face. And these are the names of the two princes: SOPHERIEL H' (WHO) KILLETH, (Sopheriel H' the Killer), the great prince, the honoured, glorified, blameless, venerable, ancient and mighty one; (and) SOPHERIEL H' (WHO) MAKETH ALIVE (Sopheriel H' the Lifegiver), the great prince, the honoured, glorified, blameless, ancient and mighty one. ²⁴ Why is he called Sopheriel H' who killeth (Sopheriel H' the Killer)? Because he is appointed over the books of the dead : [so that] everyone, when the day of his death draws nigh, he writes him in the books of the dead. Why is he called Sopheriel H' who maketh alive (Sopheriel H' the Lifegiver)? Because he is appointed over the books of the living (of life), so that every one whom the Holy One, blessed be He, will bring into life, he writes him in the book of the living (of life), by authority of MAQOM. Thou might perhaps say: "Since the Holy One, blessed be He, is sitting on a throne, they also are sitting when writing". (Answer): The Scripture teaches us (1 Kings xxii. 19, 2 Chron. xviii. 18) : "And all the host of heaven are standing by him ". "The host of heaven " (it is said) in order to show us, that even the Great Princes, none like whom there is in the high heavens, do not fulfil the requests of the Shekina otherwise than standing. But how is it (possible that) they (are able to) write, when they are standing? It is like this : ²⁵ One is standing on the wheels of the tempest and the other is standing on the wheels of the storm-wind. The one is clad in kingly garments, the other is clad in kingly garments. The one is wrapped in a mantle of majesty and the other is wrapped in a mantle of majesty. The one is crowned with a royal crown, and the other is crowned with a royal crown. The one's body is full of eyes, and the other's body is full of eyes. The appearance of one is like unto the appearance of lightnings, and the appearance of the other is like unto the appearance of lightnings. The eyes of the one are like the sun in its might, and the eyes of the other are like the sun in its might. The one's height is like the height of the seven heavens, and the other's height is like the height of the seven heavens. The wings of the one are as (many as) the days of the year, and the wings of the other are as (many as) the days of the year. The wings of the one extend over the breadth of Raqia', and the wings of the other extend over the breadth of Raqia. The lips of the one, are as the gates of the East,

and the lips of the other are as the gates of the East. The tongue of the one is as high as the waves of the sea, and the tongue of the other is as high as the waves of the sea. From the mouth of the one a flame goes forth, and from the mouth of the other a flame goes forth. From the mouth of the one there go forth lightnings and from the mouth of the other there go forth lightnings. From the sweat of the one fire is kindled, and from the perspiration of the other fire is kindled. From the one's tongue a torch is burning, and from the tongue of the other a torch is burning. On the head of the one there is a sapphire stone, and upon the head of the other there is a sapphire stone. On the shoulders of the one there is a wheel of a swift cherub, and on the shoulders of the other there is a wheel of a swift cherub. One has in his hand a burning scroll, the other has in his hand a burning scroll. The one has in his hand a flaming style, the other has in his hand a flaming style. The length of the scroll is 3000 myriads of parasangs ; the size of the style is 3000 myriads of parasangs; the size of every single letter that they write is 365 parasangs.

3 Enoch 19
Rikbiel, the prince of the wheels of the Merkaba. The surroundings of the Merkaba. The commotion among the angelic hosts at the time of the Qedushsha R. Ishmael said: Metatron, the Angel, the Prince of the Presence, said to me : ¹ Above ² these three angels, these great princes there is one Prince, distinguished, honoured, noble, glorified, adorned, fearful, valiant, strong, great, magnified, glorious, crowned, wonderful, exalted, blameless, beloved, lordly, high and lofty, ancient and mighty, like unto whom there is none among the princes. His name is RIKBIEL H', the great and revered Prince who is standing by the Merkaba. ² And why is he called RIKBIEL? Because he is appointed over the wheels of the Merkaba, and they are given in his charge. ³ And how many are the wheels? Eight; two in each direction. And there are four winds compassing them round about. And these are their names: "the Storm-Wind", "the Tempest", "the Strong Wind", and "the Wind of Earthquake". ⁴ And under them four fiery rivers are continually running, one fiery river on each side. And round about them, between the rivers, four clouds are planted (placed), and these they are: "clouds of fire", "clouds of lamps", "clouds of coal", "clouds of brimstone" and they are standing over against [their] wheels. ⁵ And the feet of the Chayyoth are resting upon the wheels. And between one wheel and the other earthquake is roaring and thunder is thundering. ⁶ And when the time draws nigh for the recital of the Song, (then) the multitudes of wheels are moved, the multitude of clouds tremble, all the chieftains (shallishim) are made afraid, all the horsemen (parashim) do rage, all the mighty ones (gibborim) are excited, all the hosts (seba'im) are afrighted, all the troops (gedudim) are in fear, all the appointed ones (memunnim) haste away, all the princes (sarim) and armies (chayyelim) are dismayed, all the servants (mesharetim) do faint and all the angels (mal'akim) and divisions (degalim) travail with pain. ⁷ And one wheel makes a sound to be heard to the other and one Kerub to another, one Chayya. to another, one Seraph to another (saying) (Ps. lxviii. 5) "Extol to him that rideth in 'Araboth, by his name Jah and rejoice before him!"

3 Enoch 20
CHAYYLIEL, the prince of the Chayyoth R. Ishmael said: Metatron, the angel, the Prince of the Presence, said to me : ¹ Above these there is one great and mighty prince. His name is CHAYYLIEL H', a noble and revered prince, a glorious and mighty prince, a great and revered prince, a prince before whom all the children of heaven do tremble, a prince who is able to swallow up the whole earth in one moment (at a mouthful). ² And why is he called CHAYYLIEL H'? Because he is appointed over the Holy

Chayyoth and smites the Chayyoth with lashes of fire: and glorifies them, when they give praise and glory and rejoicing and he causes them to make haste to say "Holy" and "Blessed be the Glory of H' from his place!" (i.e. the Qedushshd).

3Enoch 21

The Chayyoth R. Ishmael said: Metatron, the angel, the Prince of the Presence, said to me : ¹ Four (are) the Chayyoth corresponding to the four winds. Each Chayya is as the space of the whole world. And each one has four faces ; and each face is as the face of the East. ² Each one has four wings and each wing is like the cover (roof) of the universe. ³ And each one has faces in the middle of faces and wings in the middle of wings. The size of the faces is (as the size of) 248 faces, and the size of the wings is (as the size of) 365 wings. ⁴ And every one is crowned with 2000 crowns on his head. And each crown is like unto the bow in the cloud. And its splendour is like unto the splendour of the globe of the sun. And the sparks that go forth from every one are like the splendour of the morning star (planet Venus) in the East.

3Enoch 22

¹ KERUBIEL, the Prince of the Kembim. Description of the Kerubim R. Ishmael said; Metatron, the angel, the Prince of the Presence, said to me : ¹ Above these la there is one prince, noble, wonderful, strong, and praised with all kinds of praise. His name is KERUBIEL H', a mighty prince, full of power and strength a prince of highness, and Highness (is) with him, a righteous prince, and righteousness (is) with him, a holy prince, and holiness (is) with him, a prince glorified in (by) thousand hosts, exalted by ten thousand armies. ² At his wrath the earth trembles, at his anger the camps are moved, from fear of him the foundations are shaken, at his rebuke the Araboth do tremble. ³ His stature is full of (burning) coals. The height of his stature is as the height of the seven heavens the breadth of his stature is as the wideness of the seven heavens and the thickness of his stature is as the seven heavens. ⁴ The opening of his mouth is like a lamp of fire. His tongue is a consuming fire. His eyebrows are like unto the splendour of the lightning. His eyes are like sparks of brilliance. His countenance is like a burning fire. ⁵ And there is a crown of holiness upon his head on which (crown) the Explicit Name is graven, and hghtnings go forth from it. And the bow of Shekina is between his shoulders. ⁶ And his sword is like unto a lightning; and upon his loins there are arrows like unto a flame, and upon his armour and shield there is a consuming fire, and upon his neck there are coals of burning juniper and (also) round about him (there are coals of burning juniper). ⁷ And the splendour of Shekina is on his face ; and the horns of majesty on his wheels; and a royal diadem upon his skull. ⁸ And his body is full of eyes. And wings are covering the whole of his high stature (lit. the height of his stature is all wings). ⁹ On his right hand a flame is burning, and on his left a fire is glowing; and coals are burning from it. And firebrands go forth from his body. And hghtnings are cast forth from his face. With him there is alway thunder upon (in) thunder, by his side there is ever earthquake upon (in) earthquake. ¹⁰ And the two princes of the Merkaba are together with him. ¹¹ Why is he called KERUBIEL H', the Prince. Because he is appointed over the chariot of the Kerubim. And the mighty Kerubim are given in his charge. And he adorns the crowns on their heads and polishes the diadem upon their skull. ¹²He magnifies the glory of their appearance. And he glorifies the beauty of their majesty. And he increases the greatness of their honour. He causes the song of their praise to be sung. He intensifies their beautiful strength. He causes the brilliance of their glory to shine forth. He beautifies their goodly mercy and lovingkindness. He frames the fairness of their radiance. He makes their merciful beauty even more beautiful. He glorifies

204

their upright majesty. He extols the order of their praise, to stablish the dwellingplace of him "who dwelleth on the Kerubim". ¹³ And the Kerubim are standing by the Holy Chayyoth, and their wings are raised up to their heads (lit. are as the height of their heads) and Shekina is (resting) upon them and the brillianceof the Glory is upon their faces and song and praise in their mouth and their hands are under their wings and their feet are covered by their wings and horns of glory are upon their heads and the splendour of Shekina on their face and Shekina is (resting) upon them and sapphire stones are round about them and columns of fire on their four sides and columns of firebrands beside them. ¹⁴ There is one sapphire on one side and another sapphire on another side and under the sapphires there are coals of burning juniper. ¹⁵ And one Kerub is standing in each direction but the wings of the Kerubim compass each other above their skulls in glory; and they spread them to sing with them a song to him that inhabiteth the clouds and to praise with them the fearful majesty of the king of kings. ¹⁶ And KERUB lEL H', the prince who is appointed over them, he arrays them in comely, beautiful and pleasant orders and he exalts them in all manner of exaltation, dignity and glory. And he hastens them in glory and might to do the will of their Creator every moment. For above their lofty heads abides continually the glory of the high king "who dwelleth on the Kerubim".

3Enoch 22-b

¹ And there is a court before the Throne of Glory, ² which no seraph nor angel can enter, and it is 36,000 myriads of parasangs, as it is written (Is.vi.2): "and the Seraphim are standing above him" (the last word of the scriptural passage being 'Lamech-Vav' [numerical value: 36]). ³ As the numerical value Lamech-Vav 36 the number of the bridges there. ⁴ And there are 24 myriads of wheels of fire. And the ministering angels are 12,000 myriads. And there are 12,000 rivers of hail, and 12,000 treasuries of snow. And in the seven Halls are chariots of fire and flames, without reckoning, or end or searching. R. Ishmael said to me: Metatron, the angel, the Prince of the Presence, said to me: ¹ How are the angels standing on high? Pie said: Like a bridge that is placed over a river so that every one can pass over it, likewise a bridge is placed from the beginning of the entry to the end. ² And three ministering angels surround it and utter a song before YHWH, the God of Israel. And there are standing before it lords of dread and captains of fear, thousand times thousand and ten thousand times ten thousand in number and they sing praise and hymns before YHWH, the God of Israel. ³ Numerous bridges are there: bridges of fire and numerous bridges of hail. Also numerous rivers of hail, numerous treasuries of snow and numerous wheels offire. ⁴ And how many are the ministering angels? 12,000 myriads: six (thousand myriads) above and six (thousand myriads] below. And 12,000 are the treasuries of snow, six above and six below. And 24 myriads of wheels of fire, 12 (myriads] above and 12 (myriads] below. And they surround the bridges and the rivers of fire and the rivers of hail. And there are numerous ministering angels, forming entries, for all the creatures that are standing in the midst thereof, corresponding to (over against) the paths of Raqia Shamayim. ⁵ What doeth YHWH, the God of Israel, the King of Glory? The Great and Fearful God, mighty in strength, doth cover his face. ⁶ In Araboth are 660,000 myriads of angels of glory standing over against the Throne of Glory and the divisions offlaming fire. And the King of Glory doth cover His face; for else the (Araboth Raqia 1 would be rent asunder in its midst because of the majesty, splendour, beauty, radiance, loveliness, brilliancy, brightness and excellency of the appearance of (the Holy One,) blessed be He. ⁷ There are numerous ministering angelsperforming his will, numerous kings, numerous princes in the

'Araboth of his delight, angels who are revered among the rulers in heaven, distinguished, adorned with song and bringing love to remembrance: (who) are affrighted by the splendour of the Shekina, and their eyes are dazzled by the shining beauty of their King, their faces grow black and their strength doth fail. 8 There go forth rivers ofjoy, streams of gladness, rivers of rejoicing, streams of triumph, rivers of love, streams of friendship (another reading:) of commotion and they flow over and go forth before the Throne of Glory and wax great and go through the gates of the paths of 'Araboth Raqia at the voice of the shouting and musick of the CHAYYOTH, at the voice of the rejoicing of the timbrels of his 'OPHANNIM and at the melody of the cymbals of His Kerubim. And they wax great and go forth with commotion with the sound of the hymn: "HOLY, HOLY, HOLY, IS THE LORD OF HOSTS; THE WHOLE EARTH IS FULL OF HIS GLORY!"

3Enoch 22-c

R. Ishmael said: Metatron, the Prince of the Presence said to me: 1 What is the distance between one bridge and another? 12 myriads ofparasangs. Their ascent is 12 myriads of parasangs, and their descent 12 myriads ofparasangs. 2 (The distance) between the rivers of dread and the rivers offear is 22 myriads of parasangs; between the rivers of hail and the rivers of darkness 36 myriads of parasangs; between the chambers of lightnings and the clouds of compassion 42 myriads of parasangs; between the clouds of compassion and the Merkaba 84 myriads ofparasangs; between the Merkaba and the Kerubim 148 myriads of parasangs; between the Kerubim and the 'Ophannim 24 myriads of parasangs; between the Ophannim and the chambers of chambers 24 myriads of parasangs; between the chambers of chambers and the Holy Chayyoth 40,000 myriads ofparasangs; between one wing (of the Chayyoth) and another 12 myriads of parasangs; and the breadth of each one wing is of that same measure; and the distance between the Holy Chayyoth and the Throne of Glory is 30,000 myriads ofparasangs. 3 And from the foot of the Throne to the seat there are 40,000 myriads of parasangs. And the name of Him that sitteth on it: let the name be sanctified! 4 And the arches of the Bow are set above the 'Araboth, and they are 1000 thousands and 10,000 times ten thousands (of parasangs) high. Their measure is after the measure of the 'Irin and Qaddishin (Watchers and Holy Ones). As it is written (Gen. ix. 13) "My bow I have set in the cloud". It is not written here "I will set" but "I have set", (i.e.) already; clouds that surround the Throne of Glory. As His clouds pass by, the angels of hail (turn into) burning coal. 5 And a fire of the voice goes down from by the Holy Chayyoth. And because of the breath of that voice they "run" (Ezek. i. 14) to another place, fearing lest it command them to go; and they "return" lest it injure them from the other side. Therefore "they run and return" (Ezek. i. 14). 6 And these arches of the Bow are more beautiful and radiant than the radiance of the sun during the summer solstice. And they are whiter than a flaming fire and they are great and beautiful. 7 Above the arches of the Bow are the wheels of the 'Ophannim. Their height is 1000 thousand and 10,000 times 10,000 units of measure after the measure of the Seraphim and the Troops (Gedudim).

3Enoch 23

The winds blowing under the wings of the Kembim R. Ishmael said; Metatron, the Angel, the Prince of the Presence, said to me : 1 There are numerous winds blowing under the wings of the Kerubim. There blows "the Brooding Wind", as it is written (Gen. i. 2): " and the wind of God was brooding upon the face of the waters ". 2 There blows "the Strong Wind", as it is said (Ex. xiv. 21): "and the Lord caused the sea to go back by a strong east wind all that night". 3 There blows "the East Wind"as it is written (Ex. x. 13): "the

east wind brought the locusts". 4 There blows "the Wind of Quails" as it is written (Num. xi. 31): "And there went forth a wind from the Lord and brought quails". 5 There blows "the Wind of Jealousy" as it is written (Num. v. 14): "And the wind of jealousy came upon him". 6 There blows the "Wind of Earthquake" as it is written (i Kings .xix. 1 1): "and after that the wind of the earthquake ; but the Lord was not in the earthquake". 7 There blows the "Wind of H' " as it is written (Ex. xxxvii. i) : "and he carried me out by the wind of H' and set me down". 8 There blows the "Evil Wind " as it is written (i Sam. xvi. 23): "and the evil wind departed from him". 9 There blow the "Wind of Wisdom" Sand the "Wind of Understanding" and the "Wind of Knowledge" and the "Wind of the Fear of H'" as it is written (Is. xi. 2): "And the wind of H'shall rest upon him; the wind of wisdom and understanding, the wind of counsel and might, the wind of knowledge and of the fear. 10 There blows the "Wind of Rain", as it is written (Prov. xxv. 23): "the north wind bringeth forth rain". 11 There blows the "Wind of Lightnings ", as it is written (Jer.x.l3, li. 16): "he maketh lightnings for the rain and bringeth forth the wind out of his treasuries ". 12There blows the "Wind, Breaking the Rocks", as it is written (i Kings xix. n): "the Lord passed by and a great and strong wind (rent the mountains and brake in pieces the rocks before the Lord)". 13 There blows the "Wind of Assuagement of the Sea", as it is written (Gen. viii. i): "and God made a wind to pass over the earth, and the waters assuaged". 14 There blows the "Wind of Wrath", as it is written (Job i. 19) : "and behold there came a great wind from the wilderness and smote the four corners of the house and it fell". 15 There blows the " Storm-Wind ", as it is written (Ps. cxlviii. 8) : "Storm-wind, fulfilling his word". 16 And Satan is standing among these winds, for "storm-wind " is nothing else but "Satan", and all these winds do not blow but under the wings of the Kerubim, as it is written (Ps. xviii. n) : "and he rode upon a cherub and did fly, yea, and he flew swiftly upon the wings of the wind". 17 And whither go all these winds? The Scripture teaches us, that they go out from under the wings of the Kerubim and descend on the globe of the sun, as it is written (Eccl. i. 6) : " The wind goeth toward the south and turneth about unto the north ; it tumeth about continually in its course and the wind 14 returneth again to its circuits ". And from the globe of the sun they return and descend upon the rivers and the seas, upon] the mountains and upon the hills, as it is written (Am.iv.13): "For lo, he that formeth the mountains and createth the wind". 18 And from the mountains and the hills they return and descend to the seas and the rivers ; and from the seas and the rivers they return and descend upon (the) cities and provinces ; and from the cities and provinces they return and descend into the Garden, and from the Garden they return and descend to Eden, as it is written (Gen.iii. 8): "walking in the Garden in the wind of day". And in the midst of the Garden they join together and blow from one side to the other and are perfumed with the spices of the Garden even from \ts remotest parts, until they separate from each other, and, filled with the scent of the pure spices, they bring the odour from the remotest parts of Eden and the spices of the Garden to the righteous and godly who in the time to come shall inherit the Garden of Eden and the Tree of Life, as it is written (Cant. iv. 16) : "Awake, O north wind; and come thou south; blow upon my garden, that the spices thereof may flow out. Let my beloved come into his garden and eat his precious fruits".

3Enoch 24

The different chariots of the Holy One, blessed be He R. Ishmael said: Metatron, the Angel, the Prince of the Presence, the glory of all heaven, said to me : 1 Numerous chariots has the Holy One, blessed be He: He has the "Chariots of (the) Kerubim", as it is written (Ps.xviii.ll, 2 Sam.xxii.ll): "And he rode upon a cherub and did fly". [2] He has the "Chariots of Wind", as it is written (ib.) : "and he flew swiftly upon the wings of the wind ". [3] He has the "Chariots of (the) Swift Cloud", as it is written (Is. xix. i): "Behold, the Lord rideth upon a swift cloud". [4] He has "the Chariots of Clouds", as it is written (Ex. xix. 9): "Lo, I come unto thee in a cloud". [5] He has the "Chariots of the Altar", as it is written (Am. ix. i) :"I saw the Lord standing upon the Altar". [6] He has the "Chariots of Ribbotaim", as it is written (Ps.lxviii. 18) : "The chariots of God are Ribbotaim ; thousands of angels ". [7] He has the "Chariots of the Tent", as it is written (Deut.xxxi. 15) : "And the Lord appeared in the Tent in a pillar of cloud ". [8] He has the "Chariots of the Tabernacle", as it is written (Lev. i. 1): "And the Lord spake unto him out of the tabernacle". [9] He has the "Chariots of the Mercy-Seat", as it is written (Num. vii. 89): "then he heard the Voice speaking unto him from upon the mercy-seat". [10] He has the "Chariots of Sapphire Stone", as it is written (Ex. xxiv. 10) : "and there was under his feet as it were a paved work of sapphire stone". [11] He has the "Chariots of Eagles ", as it is written (Ex. xix. 4) :"I bare you on eagles' wings". Eagles literally are not meant here but "they that fly swiftly as eagles". [12] He has the "chariots of Shout", as it is written (Ps. xlvii. 6) :"God is gone up with a shout". [13] He has the "Chariots of Araboth", as it is written (Ps.lxviii. 5): "Extol Him that rideth upon the Araboth". [14] He has the "Chariots of Thick Clouds", as it is written (Ps. civ. 3): "who maketh the thick clouds His chariot". [15] He has the "Chariots of the Chayyoth", as it is written (Ezek. i. 14) : "and the Chayyoth ran and returned". They run by permission and return by permission, for Shekina is above their heads. [16] He has the "Chariots of Wheels (Galgallim)", as it is written (Ezek. x. 2): "And he said: Go in between the whirling wheels". [17] lie has the "Chariots of a Swift Kerub", as it is written (Ps.xviii.lO & Is.xix.l): "riding on a swift cherub". And at the time when He rides on a swift kerub, as he sets one of His feet upon him, before he sets the other foot upon his back, he looks through eighteen thousand worlds at one glance. And he discerns and sees into them all and knows what is in all of them and then he sets down the other foot upon him, according as it is written (Ezek. xlviii. 35): "Round about eighteen thousand". Whence do we know that He looks through every one of them every day? It is written (Ps. xiv. 2): "He looked down from heaven upon the children of men to see if there were any that did understand, that did seek after God". [18] He has the "Chariots of the 'Ophannim", as it is written (Ezek. X. 12): "and the 'Ophannim were full of eyes round about". 12 [19] He has the "Chariots of His Holy Throne", as it is written (Ps. xlvii. 8) :" God sitteth upon his holy throne ". [20] He has the "chariots of the Throne of Yah", as it is written (Ex. xvii. 16) : "Because a hand is lifted up upon the Throne of Jah". [21] He has the "Chariots of the Throne of Judgement", as it is written (Is. v. 16): "but the Lord of hosts shall be exalted in judgment". [22] He has the "Chariots of the Throne of Glory ", as it is written (Jer. xvii. 12) : "The Throne of Glory, set on high from the beginning, is the place of our sanctuary". [23] He has the "Chariots of the High and Exalted Throne", as it is written (Is. vi. i): "I saw the Lord sitting upon the high and exalted throne".

3Enoch 25

'Ophphanniel, the prince of the 'Ophannim. Description of the 'Ophannim R. Ishmael said: Metatron, the Angel, the Prince of the Presence, said to me : [1] Above these there is one great prince, revered, high, lordly, fearful, ancient and strong. 'OPHPHANNIEL H is his name. [2] He has sixteen faces, four faces on each side, (also) hundred wings on each side. And he has 8466 eyes, corresponding to the days of the year. [2190 -and some say 2116- on each side.] [2191 /2196 and sixteen on each side.] [3] And those two eyes of his

206

face, in each one of them lightnings are flashing, and from each one of them firebrands are burning ; and no creature is able to behold them : for anyone who looks at them is burnt instantly. [4] His height is (as) the distance of 2500 years' journey. No eye can behold and no mouth can tell the mighty power of his strength save the King of kings, the Holy One, blessed be He, alone. [5] Why is he called 'OPHPHANNIEL ? Because he is appointed over the 'Ophannim and the 'Ophannimare given in his charge. He stands every day and attends and beautifies them. And he exalts and orders their apartment and polishes their standing-place and makes bright their dwellings, makes their corners even and cleanses their seats. And he waits upon them early and late, by day and by night, to increase their beauty, to make great their dignity and to make them "diligent in praise of their Creator. [6] And all the 'Ophannim are full of eyes, and they are all full of brightness; seventy two sapphire stones are fixed on their garments on their right side and seventy two sapphire stones are fixed on their garments on their left side. [7] And four carbuncle stones are fixed on the crown of every single one, the splendour of which proceeds in the four directions of 'Araboth even as the splendour of the globe of the sun proceeds in all the directions of the universe. And why is it called Carbuncle (Bareqet)? Because its splendour is like the appearance of a lightning (Baraq). And tents of splendour, tents of brilliance, tents of brightness as of sapphire and carbuncle inclose them because of the shining appearance of their eyes.

3Enoch 26

SERAPHIEL, the Prince of the Seraphim. Description of the Seraphim R. Ishmael said: Metatron, the Angel, the Prince of the Presence, said to me : [1] Above these there is one prince, wonderful, noble, great, honourable, mighty, terrible, a chief and leader 1 and a swift scribe, glorified, honoured and beloved. [2] He is altogether filled with splendour, full of praise and shining; and he is wholly full of brilliance, of light and of beauty; and the whole of him is filled with goodliness and greatness. [3] His countenance is altogether like (that of) angels, but his body is like an eagle's body. [4] His splendour is like unto lightnings, his appearance like fire brands, his beauty like unto sparks, his honour like fiery coals, his majesty like chashmals, his radiance like the light of the planet Venus. The image of him is like unto the Greater Light. His height is as the seven heavens. The light from his eyebrows is like the sevenfold light. [5] The sapphire stone upon his head is as great as the whole universe and like unto the splendour of the very heavens in radiance. [6] His body is full of eyes like the stars of the sky, innumerable and unsearchable. Every eye is like the planet Venus. Yet, there are some of them like the Lesser Light and some of them like unto the Greater Light. From his ankles to his knees (they are) like unto stars of lightning, from his knees to his thighs like unto the planet Venus, from his thighs to his loins like unto the moon, from his loins to his neck like the sun, from his neck to his skull like unto the Light Imperishable. (Cf. Zeph. iii. 5.) [7] The crown on his head is like unto the splendour of the Throne of Glory. The measure of the crown is the distance of 502 years' journey. There is no kind of splendour, no kind of brilliance, no kind of radiance, no kind of light in the universe but is fixed on that crown. [8] The name of that prince is SERAPHIEL H". And the crown on his head, its name is "the Prince of Peace". And why is he called by the name of SERAPHIEL '? Because he is appointed over the Seraphim. And the flaming Seraphim are given in his charge. And he presides over them by day and by night and teaches them song, praise, proclamation of beauty, might and majesty; that they may proclaim the beauty of their King in all manner of Praise and Sanctification (Qedushsha). [9] How many are the Seraphim? Four, corresponding to the four winds of the world.

And how many wings have they each one of them? Six, corresponding to the six days of Creation. And how many faces have they? Each one of them four faces. 10 The measure of the Seraphim and the height of each one of them correspond to the height of the seven heavens. The size of each wing is like the measure of all Raqia' . The size of each face is like that of the face of the East. 11 And each one of them gives forth light like unto the splendour of the Throne of Glory: so that not even the Holy Chayyoth, the honoured 'Ophannim, nor the majestic KeruUm are able to behold it. For everyone who beholds it, his eyes are darkened because of its great splendour. 12 Why are they called Seraphim? Because they burn (saraph) the writing tables of Satan : Every day Satan is sitting, together with SAMMAEL, the Prince of Rome, and with DUBBIEL, the Prince of Persia, and they write the iniquities of Israel on writing tables which they hand over to the Seraphim, in order that they may present them before the Holy One, blessed be He, so that He may destroy Israel from the world. But the Seraphim know from the secrets of the Holy One, blessed be He, that he desires not, that this people Israel should perish. What do the Seraphim? Every day do they receive (accept) them from the hand of Satan and bum them in the burning fire over against the high and exalted Throne in order that they may not come before the Holy One, blessed be He, at the time when he is sitting upon the Throne of Judgement, judging the whole world in truth.

3Enoch 27
RADWERIEL, the keeper of the Book of Records R. Ishmael said: Metatron, the Angel of H' , the Prince of the Presence, said to me : 1 Above the Seraphim there is one prince, exalted above all the princes, wondrous more than all the servants. His name is RADWERIEL H' who is appointed over the treasuries of the books. 2 He fetches forth the Case of Writings (with) the Book of Records in it, and brings it before the Holy One, blessed be He. And he breaks the seals of the case, opens it, takes out the books and delivers them before the Holy One, blessed be He. And the Holy One, blessed be He, receives them of his hand and gives them in his sight to the Scribes, that they may read them in the Great Beth Din (The court of justice) in the height of 'Araboth Raqia', before the heavenly household. 3 And why is he called RADWERIEL? Because out of every word that goes forth from his mouth an angel is created : and he stands in the songs (in the singing company) of the ministering angels and utters a song before the Holy One, blessed be He when the time draws nigh for the recitation of the (Thrice) Holy.

3Enoch 28
The 'Irin and Qaddishin R. Ishmael said : Metatron, the Angel, the Prince of the Presence, said to me : 1 Above all these there are four great princes, Irin and Qaddishin by name; high, honoured, revered, beloved, wonderful and glorious ones, greater than all the children of heaven. There is none like unto them among all the celestial princes and none their equal among all the Servants. For each one of them is equal to all the rest together. 2 And their dwelling is over against the Throne of Glory, and their standing place over against the Holy One, blessed be He, so that the briUiance of their dwelling is a reflection of the brilliance of the Throne of Glory. And the splendour of their countenance is a reflection of the splendour of Shekina. 3 And they are glorified by the glory of 4the Divine Majesty (Gebura) and praised by (through) the praise of Shekina. 4 And not only that, but the Holy One, blessed be He, does nothing in his world without first consulting them, but after that he doeth it. As it is written (Dan. iv. 17) : "The sentence is by the decree of the Irin and the demand by the word of the Qaddishin." 5 The Urin are two and the Qaddishin are two. And how are they standing before the

207

Holy One, blessed be He? It is to be understood, that one 'Ir is standing on one side and the other 'Ir on the other side, and one Qaddish is standing on one side and the other on the other side. 6 And ever do they exalt the humble, and they abase to the ground those that are proud, and they exalt to the height those that are humble. 7 And every day, as the Holy One, blessed be He, is sitting upon the Throne of Judgement and judges the whole world, and the Books of the Living and the Books of the Dead are opened before Him, then all the children of heaven are standing before him in fear, dread, awe and trembling. At that time, (when) the Holy One, blessed be He, is sitting upon the Throne of Judgement to execute judgement, his garment is white as snow, the hair on his head as pure wool and the whole of his cloak is like the shining light. And he is covered with righteousness all over as with a coat of mail. 8 And those Irm and Qaddishin are standing before him like court officers before the judge. And they raise and argue every case and close the case that comes before the Holy One, blessed be He, in judgement, according as it is written (Dan. iv. 17) : "The sentence is by the decree of the Irm and the demand by the word of the Qaddishin" 9 Some of them argue and others pass the sentence in the Great Beth Din in 'Araboth. Some of them make the requests from before uthe Divine Majesty and some close the cases before the Most High. Others finish by going down and (confirming) executing the sentences on earth below. According as it is written (Dan. iv. 13 , 14) : " Behold an Ir and a Qaddishcame down from heaven and cried aloud and said thus. Hew down the tree, and cut off his branches, shake off his leaves, and scatter his fruit: let the beasts get away from under it, and the fowls from his branches ". 10 Why are they called 'Irin and Qaddishint By reason that they sanctify the body and the spirit with lashes of fire on the third day of the judgement, as it is written (Hos. vi. 2): "After two days will he revive us : on the third he will raise us up, and we shall live before him."

3Enoch 29
Description of a class of angels R. Ishmael said: Metatron, the Angel, the Prince of the Presence, said to me: 1 Each one of them has seventy names corresponding to the seventy tongues of the world. And all of them are (based) upon the name of the Holy One, blessed be He. And every several name is written with a flaming style upon the Fearful Crown (Keiher Nora) which is on the head of the high and exalted King. 2 And from each one of them there go forth sparks and lightnings. And each one of them is beset with horns of splendour round about. From each one lights are shining forth, and each one is surrounded by tents of brilliance so that not even the Seraphim and the Chayyoth who are greater than all the children of heaven are able to behold them.

3Enoch 30
The 72 princes of Kingdoms and the Prince of the World officiating at the Great Sanhedrin in heaven R. Ishmael said: Metatron, the Angel, the Prince of the Presence, said to me: 1 Whenever the Great Beth Din is seated in the Araboth Raqia' on high there is no opening of the mouth for anyone in the world save those great princes who are called H' by the name of the Holy One, blessed be He. 2 How many are those princes? Seventy-two princes of the kingdoms of the world besides the Prince of the World who speaks (pleads) in favour of the world before the Holy One, blessed be He, every day, at the hour when the book is opened in which are recorded all the doings of the world, according as it is written (Dan.vii.lO) : "The judgement was set and the books were opened."

3Enoch 31
(The attributes of) Justice, Mercy and Truth by the Throne of Judgement R. Ishmael said: Metatron, the Angel, the Prince of the

Presence, said to me : [1] At the time when the Holy One, blessed be He, is sitting on the Throne, of Judgement, (then) Justice is standing on His right and Mercy on His left and Truth before His face. [2] And when man enters before Him to judgement, (then) there comes forth from the splendour of the Mercy towards him as (it were) a staff and stands in front of him. Forthwith man falls upon his face, (and) all the angels of destruction fear and tremble before him, according as it is written (Is.xvi. 5): "And with mercy shall the throne be established, and he shall sit upon it in truth."

3Enoch 32

The execution of judgement on the wicked. God's sword R. Ishmael said: Metatron, the Angel, the Prince of the Presence, said to me : [1] When the Holy One, blessed be He, opens the Book half of which is fire and half flame, (then) they go out from before Him in every moment to execute the judgement on the wicked by His sword (that is) drawn forth out of its sheath and the splendour of which shines like a lightning and pervades the world from one end to the other, as it is written (Is. Ixvi. 16): "For by fire will the Lord plead (and by his sword with all flesh)." [2] And all the inhabitants of the world (lit. those who come into the world) fear and tremble before Him, when they behold His sharpened sword like unto a hghtning from one end of the world to the other, and sparks and flashes of the size of the stars of Raqia' going out from it; according as it is written (Deut. xxxii. 41):" If I whet the hghtning of my sword".

3Enoch 33

The angels of Mercy, of Peace and of Destruction by the Throne of Judgement. The scribes, (vss. i, 2) The angels by the Throne of Glory and the fiery rivers under it. (vss. 3-5) R. Ishmael said: Metatron, the Angel, the Prince of the Presence, said to me : [1] At the time that the Holy One, blessed be He, is sitting on the Throne of Judgement, (then) the angels of Mercy are standing on His right, the angels of Peace are standing on His left and the angels of Destruction are standing in front of Him. [2] And one scribe is standing beneath Him, and another scribe above Him. [3] And the glorious Seraphim surround the Throne on its four sides with walls of lightnings, and the 'Ophannim. surround them with fire-brands round about the Throne of Glory. And clouds of fire and clouds of flames compass them to the right and to the left; and the Holy Chayyoth carry the Throne of Glory from below: each one with three fingers. The measure of the fingers of each one is 800,000 and 700 times hundred, (and) 66,000 parasangs. [4] And underneath the feet of the Chayyoth seven fiery rivers are running and flowing. And the breadth of each river is 365 thousand parasangs and its depth is 248 thousand myriads of parasangs. Its length is unsearchable and immeasureable. [5] And each river turns round in a bow in the four directions of 'Araboth Raqict , and (from there) it falls down to Ma'on and is stayed, and from Mai on to Zebul, from Zebul to Shechaqim, from Shechaqim to Raqia' , from Raqia' to Shamayim and from Shamayim upon the heads of the wicked who are in Gehenna, as it is written (Jer. xxiii. 19): "Behold a whirlwind of the Lord, even his fury, is gone, yea, a whirling tempest; it shall burst upon the head of the wicked".

3Enoch 34

The different concentric circles round the Chayyoth, consisting of fire, water, hailstones etc. and of the angels uttering the Qedushsha responsorium R. Ishmael said: Metatron; the Angel, the Prince of the Presence, said to me : [1] The hoofs of the Chayyoth are surrounded by seven clouds of burning coals. The clouds of burning coals are surrounded on the outside by seven walls of flame(s). The seven walls of flame(s) are surrounded on the outside by seven walls of hailstones (stones of 'Et-gabish, Ezek. xiii. 11,13, xxviii. 22). The hailstones are surrounded on the outside by xstones of hail (stone

208

of Barad). The stones of hail are surrounded on the outside by stones of "the wings of the tempest ". The stones of "the wings of the tempest" are surrounded on the outside by flames of fire. The flames of fire are surrounded by the chambers of the whirlwind. The chambers of the whirlwind are surrounded on the outside by the fire and the water. [2] Round about the fire and the water are those who utter the "Holy". Round about those who utter the "Holy" are those who utter the "Blessed"'. Round about those who utter the "Blessed" are the bright clouds. The bright clouds are surrounded on the outside by coals of burning jumper ; and on the outside surrounding the coals of burning juniper there are thousand camps of fire and ten thousand hosts of flame(s). And between every several camp and every several host there is a cloud, so that they may not be burnt by the fire.

3Enoch 35

The camps of angels in 'Araboth Raqia: angels, performing the Qedushsha [1] R. Ishmael said: Metatron, the Angel, the Prince of the Presence, said to me : [1] 506 thousand myriads of camps has the Holy One, blessed be He, in the height of Araboth Raqia. And each camp is (composed of) 496 thousand angels. [2] And every single angel, the height of his stature is as the great sea; and the appearance of their countenance as the appearance of the lightning, and their eyes as lamps of fire, and their arms and their feet like in colour to polished brass and the roaring voice of their words like the voice of a multitude. [3] And they are all standing before the Throne of Glory in four rows. And the princes of the army are standing at the head of each row. [4] And some of them utter the "Holy" and others utter the "Blessed", some of them run as messengers, others are standing in attendance, according as it is written (Dan. vii. 10): "Thousand thousands ministered unto him, and ten thousand times ten thousand stood before him : the judgment was set and the books were opened ". [5] And in the hour, when the time draws nigh for to say the "Holy", (then) first there goes forth a whirlwind from before the Holy One, blessed be He, and bursts upon the camp of Shekina and there arises a great commotion among them, as it is written (Jer.xxx. 23): "Behold, the whirlwind of the Lord goeth forth with fury, a continuing commotion". [6] At that moment 4thousand thousands of them are changed into sparks, thousand thousands of them into firebrands, thousand thousands into flashes, thousand thousands into flames, thousand thousands into males, thousand thousands into females, thousand thousands into winds, thousand thousands into burning fires, thousand thousands into flames, thousand thousands into sparks, thousand thousands into chashmals of light; until they take upon themselves the yoke of the kingdom of heaven, the high and lifted up, of the Creator of them all with fear, dread, awe and trembling, with commotion, anguish, terror and trepidation. Then they are changed again into their former shape to have the fear of their King before them alway, as they have set their hearts on saying the Song continually, as it is written (Is. vi. 3): "And one cried unto another and said (Holy, Holy, Holy, etc.)".

3Enoch 36

The angels bathe in the fiery river before reciting the 'Song' R. Ishmael said: Metatron, the Angel, the Prince of the Presence, said to me ; [1] At the time when the ministering angels desire to say (the) Song, (then) Nehar di-Nur (the fiery stream) rises with many thousand thousands and myriads of myriads" (of angels) of power and strength of fire and it runs and passes under the Throne of Glory, between the camps of the ministering angels and the troops of Araboth. [2] And all the ministering angels first go down into Nehar di-Nur, and they dip themselves in the fire and dip their tongue and their mouth seven times ; and after that they go up and put on the garment of 'Machaqe Samal' and cover themselves with cloaks of chashmal and stand in four rows over against the Throne of Glory, in all the heavens.

3Enoch 37

The four camps of Shekina and their surroundings R. Ishmael said: Metatron, the Angel, the Prince of the Presence, said to me : [1] In the seven Halls there are standing four chariots of Shekina, and before each one are standing the four camps of Shekina. Between each camp a river of fire is continually flowing. [2] Between each river there are bright clouds [surrounding them], and between each cloud there are put up pillars of brimstone. Between one pillar and another there are standing flaming wheels, surrounding them. And between one wheel and another there are flames of fire round about. Between one flame and another there are treasuries of lightnings; behind the treasuries of lightnings are the wings of the stormwind. Behind the wings of the storm-wind are the chambers of the tempest; behind the chambers of the tempest there are winds, voices, thunders, sparks [upon] sparks and earthquakes [upon] earthquakes.

3Enoch 38

The fear that befalls all the heavens at the sound of the 'Holy? esp. the heavenly bodies. These appeased by the Prince of the World R. Ishmael said: Metatron, the Angel, the Prince of the Presence, said to me : [1] At the time, when the ministering angels utter (the Thrice) Holy, then all the pillars of the heavens and their sockets do tremble, and the gates of the Halls of Araboth Raqia' are shaken and the foundations of Shechaqim and the Universe (Tebel) are moved, and the orders of Ma'on and the chambers of Makon quiver, and all the orders of Raqia and the constellations and the planets are dismayed, and the globes of the sun and the moon haste away and flee out of their courses and run 12,000 parasangs and seek to throw themselves down from heaven, [2] by reason of the roaring voice of their chant, and the noise of their praise and the sparks and lightnings that go forth from their faces; as it is written (Ps. lxxvii. 18): "The voice of thy thunder was in the heaven (the lightnings lightened the world, the earth trembled and shook) ". [3] Until the prince of the world calls them, saying: "Be ye quiet in your place ! Fear not because of the ministering angels who sing the Song before the Holy One, blessed be He". As it is written (Job.xxxviii. 7): "When the morning stars sang together and all the children of heaven shouted for joy".

3Enoch 39

The explicit names fly offfrom the Throne and all the various angelic hosts prostrate themselves before it at the time of the Qedushsha R. Ishmael said: Metatron, the Angel, the Prince of the Presence, said to me : [1] When the ministering angels utter the "Holy" then all the explicit names that are graven with a flaming style on the Throne of Glory fly off like eagles, with sixteen wings. And they surround and compass the Holy One, blessed be He, on the four sides of the place of His Shekinal . [2] And the angels of the host, and the flaming Servants, and the mighty 'Ophannim, and the Kerubim of the Shekina, and the Holy Chayyoth, and the Seraphim, and the 'Er'ellim, and the Taphsarim and the troops of consuming fire, and the fiery armies, and the flaming hosts, and the holy princes, adorned with crowns, clad in kingly majesty, wrapped in glory, girt with loftiness, 4 fall upon their faces three times, saying: "Blessed be the name of His glorious kingdom for ever and ever".

3Enoch 40

The ministering angels rewarded with crowns, when uttering the" Holy ' ' in its right order, andpunished by consumingfire if not. New ones created in the stead of the consumed angels R. Ishmael said: Metatron, the Angel, the Prince of the Presence, said to me : [1] When the ministering angels say "Holy" before the Holy One, blessed be He, in the proper way, then the servants of His Throne, the attendants of His Glory, go forth with great mirth from under the

Throne of Glory. [2] And they all carry in their hands, each one of them thousand thousand and ten thousand times ten thousand crowns of stars, similar in appearance to the planet Venus, and put them on the ministering angels and the great princes who utter the "Holy". Three crowns they put on each one of them: one crown because they say "Holy", another crown, because they say "Holy, Holy", and a third crown because they say "Holy, Holy, Holy, is the Lord of Hosts" . [3] And in the moment that they do not utter the "Holy" in the right order, a consuming fire goes forth from the little finger of the Holy One, blessed be He, and falls down in the midst of their ranksand is divided into 496 thousand parts corresponding to the four camps of the ministering angels, and consumes them in one moment, as it is written (Ps. xcvii. 3): "A fire goeth before him and burneth up his adversaries round about". [4] After that the Holy One, blessed be He, opens His mouth and speaks one word and creates others in their stead, new ones like them. And each one stands before His Throne of Glory, uttering the "Holy", as it is written (Lam. iii. 23): "They are new every morning; great is thy faithfulness".

3Enoch 41

Metatron shows R. Ishmael the letters engraved on the Throne of Glory by which letters everything in heaven and earth has been created R. Ishmael said: Metatron, the Angel, the Prince of the Presence, said to me : [1] Come and behold the letters by which the heaven and theearth were created, the letters by which were created the mountains and hills, the letters by which were created the seas and rivers, the letters by which were created the trees and herbs, the letters by which were created the planets and the constellations, the letters by which were created the globe of the moon and the globe of the sun, Orion, the Pleiades and all the different luminaries of Raqia' . [2] the letters by which were created the Throne of Glory and the Wheels of the Merkaba, the letters by which were created the necessities of the worlds, [3] the letters by which were created wisdom, understanding, knowledge, prudence, meekness and righteousness by which the whole world is sustained. [4] And I walked by his side and he took me by his hand and raised me upon his wings and showed me those letters, all of them, that are graven with a flaming style on the Throne of Glory : and sparks go forth from them and cover all the chambers of 'Araboth.

3Enoch 42

Instances of polar opposites kept in balance by several Divine Names and other similar wonders R. Ishmael said: Metatron, the Angel, the Prince of the Presence, said to me : [1] Come and I will show thee, where the waters are suspended in the highest, where fire is burning in the midst of hail, where lightnings lighten out of the midst of snowy mountains, where thunders are roaring in the celestial heights, where a flame is burning in the midst of the burning fire and where voices make themselves heard in the midst of thunder and earthquake. [2] Then I went by his side and he took me by his hand and hfted me up on his wings and showed me all those things. I beheld the waters suspended on high in Araboth Raqia' by (force of) the name YAH 'EHYE ASHER 'EHYE (Jah, I am that I am). And their fruits going down from heaven and watering the face of the world, as it is written (Ps.civ.13): "(He watereth the mountains from his chambers :) the earth is satisfied with the fruit of thy work". [3] And I saw fire and snow and hailstone that were mingled together within each other and yet were undamaged, by (force of) the name 'ESH 'OKELA (consuming fire), as it is written (Deut. iv. 24) : "For the Lord, thy God, is a consuming fire". [4] And I saw lightnings that were hghtening out of mountains of snow and yet were not damaged (quenched), by (force of) the name YAH SUR 'OLAMIM (Jah, the everlasting rock), as it is written (Is. xxvi. 4):

"For in Jah, YHWH, the everlasting rock". 5 And I saw thunders and voices that were roaring in the midst of fiety flames and were not damaged (silenced), by (force of) the name 'EL-SHADDAI RABBA (the Great God Almighty) as it is written (Gen. xvii. i): "I am God Almighty". 6 And I beheld a flame (and) a glow (glowing flames) that were flaming and glowing in the midst of burning fire, and yet were not damaged (devoured), by (force of) the name YAD 'AL KES YAH (the hand upon the Throne of the Lord) as it is written (Ex. xvii. 16) : " And he said: for the hand is upon the Throne of the Lord ". 7 And I beheld rivers of fire in the midst of rivers of water and they were not damaged (quenched) by (force of) the name 'OSE SHALOM (Maker of Peace) as it is written (Job xxv. 2): "He maketh peace in his high places". For he makes peace between the fire and the water, between the hail and the fire, between the wind and the cloud, between the earthquake and the sparks.

3Enoch 43

Metatron shows R. Ishmael the abode of the unborn spirits and of the spirits of the righteous dead R. Ishmael said: Metatron said to me: 1 Come and I will show thee Iwhere arel the spirits of the righteous that have been created and have returned, and the spirits of the righteous that have not yet been created. 2 And he lifted me up to his side, took me by his hand and hfted me up near the Throne of Glory by the place of the Shekina ; and he revealed the Throne of Glory to me, and he showed me the spirits that have been created and had returned : and they were flying above the Throne of Glory before the Holy One, blessed be He. 3 After that I went to interpret the following verse of Scripture and I found in what is written (Isa.Ivii. 16): "for the spirit clothed itself before me, and the souls I have made" that ("for the spirit was clothed before me") means the spirits that have been created in the chamber of creation of the righteous and that have returned before the Holy One, blessed be He; (and the words:) "and the souls I have made" refer to the spirits 4 of the righteous that have not yet been created in the chamber (GUPH).

3Enoch 44

Metatron shows R. Ishmael the abode of the wicked and the intermediate in Sheol. (vss. 1-6) The Patriarchs pray for the deliverance of Israel (vss. 7-10) R. Ishmael said: Metatron, x the Angel, the Prince of the Presence, said to me : 1 Come and I will show thee the spirits of the wicked and the spirits of the intermediate where they are standing, and the spirits of the intermediate, whither they go down, 3and the spirits of the wicked, where they go down. 2 And he said to me : The spirits of the wicked go down to She'ol by the hands of two angels of destruction: ZAAPHIEL and SIMKIEL are their names. 3 SIMKIEL is appointed over the intermediate to support them and purify them because of the great mercy of the Prince of the Place (Maqom). ZAAPHIEL is appointed over the spirits of the wicked in order to cast them down from the presence of the Holy One, blessed be He, and from the splendour of the Shekina to She'ol, to be punished in the fire of Gehenna with staves of burning coal. 4 And I went by his side, and he took me by his hand and showed me all of them with his fingers. 5 And I beheld the appearance of their faces (and, lo, it was) as the appearance of children of men, and their bodies like eagles. And not only that but (furthermore) the colour of the countenance of the intermediate was like pale grey on account of their deeds, for there are stains upon them until they have become cleaned from their iniquity in the fire. 6 And the colour of the wicked was like the bottom of a pot on account of the wickedness of their doings. 7 And I saw the spirits of the Patriarchs Abraham Isaac and Jacob and the rest of the righteous whom they have brought up out of their graves and who have ascended to the Heaven (Raqirf). And they were praying before the

210

Holy One, blessed be He, saying intheir prayer: "Lord of the Universe! How long wilt thou sit upon (thy) Throne like a mourner in the days of his mourning with thy right hand behind thee 7and notV deliver thy children and reveal thy Kingdom in the world? And for how long wilt thou have no pity upon thy children who are made slaves among the nations of the world? Nor upon thy right hand that is behind thee wherewith thou didst stretch out the heavens and the earth and the heavens of heavens? When wilt thou have compassion?" 8 Then the Holy One, blessed be He, answered every one of them, saying: "Since these wicked do sin so and so, and transgress with such and such transgressions against me, how could I deliver my great Right Hand in the downfall by their hands (caused by them). 9 In that moment Metatron called me and spake to me: "My servant! Take the books, and read their evil doings!" Forthwith I took the books and read their doings and there were to be found 36 transgressions (written down) with regard to each wicked one and besides, that they have transgressed all the letters in the Tora, as it is written (Dan. ix. u) : "Yea, all Israel have transgressed thy Law". It is not written 'al torateka but 'et (JIN) torateka, for they have transgressed from 'Aleph to Taw, 40 statutes have they transgressed for each letter. 10 Forthwith Abraham, Isaac and Jacob wept. Then said to them the Holy One, blessed be He: "Abraham, my beloved, Isaac, my Elect one, Jacob, my firstborn! How can I now deliver them from among the nations of the world?" And forthwith MIKAEL, the Prince of Israel, cried and wept with a loud voice and said (Ps. x. i) : "Why standest thou afar off, O Lord?".

3Enoch 45

Metatron shows R. Ishmael past andfuture events recorded on the Curtain of the Throne R. Ishmael said: Metatron said to me: 1 Come, and I will show thee the Curtain of MAQOM (the Divine Majesty) which is spread before the Holy One, blessed be He, (and) whereon are graven all the generations of the world and all their doings, both what they have done and what they will do until the end of all generations. 2 And I went, and he showed it to me pointing it out with his fingers Mike a father who teaches his children the letters of Tora. And I saw each generation, the rulers of each generation, and the heads of each generation, the shepherds of each generation, the oppressors (drivers) of each generation, the keepers of each generation, the scourgers of each generation, the overseers of each generation, the judges of each generation, the court officers of each generation , the teachers of each generation, the supporters of each generation, the chiefs of each generation, the presidents of academies of each generation, the magistrates of each generation, the princes of each generation, the counsellors of each generation, the nobles of each generation, and the men of might of each generation, the elders of each generation, and the guides of each generation. 3 And I saw Adam, his generation, their doings and their thoughts,Noah and his generation, their doings and their thoughts, and the generation of the flood, their doings and their thoughts, Shem and his generation, their doings and their thoughts, Nimrod and the generation of the confusion of tongues, and his generation, their doings and their thoughts, Abraham and his generation, their doings and their thoughts, Isaac and his generation, their doings and their thoughts, Ishmael and his generation, their doings and their thoughts, Jacob and his generation, their doings and their thoughts, Joseph and his generation, their doings and their thoughts, the tribes and their generation, their doings and their thoughts, Amram and his generation, their doings and their thoughts, Moses and his generation, their doings and their thoughts, 4 Aaron and Mirjam their works and their doings, the princes and the elders, their works and doings, Joshua and his generation, their works and doings, the judges and their generation, their works and doings, Eli and his generation, their works and doings, "Phinehas, their works and doings, Elkanah and his generation, their works and their doings, Samuel and his generation, their works and doings, the kings of Judah with their generations, their works and their doings, the kings of Israel and their generations, their works and their doings, the princes of Israel, their works and their doings; the princes of the nations of the world, their works and their doings, the heads of the councils of Israel, their works and their doings ; the heads of (the councils in) the nations of the world, their generations, their works and their doings; the rulers of Israel and their generation, their works and their doings ; the nobles of Israel and their generation, their works and their doings ; the nobles of the nations of the world and their generation(s), their works and their doings; the men of reputation in Israel, their generation, their works and their doings ; the judges of Israel, their generation, their works and their doings ; the judges of the nations of the world and their generation, their works and their doings ; the teachers of children in Israel, their generations, their works and their doings ; the teachers of children in the nations of the world, their generations, their works and their doings; the counsellors (interpreters) of Israel, their generation, their works and their doings ; the counsellors (interpreters) of the nations of the world, their generation, their works and their doings ; all the prophets of Israel, their generation, their works and their doings ; all the prophets of the nations of the world, their generation, their works and their doings ; [5] and all the fights and wars that the nations [16] of the world wrought against the people of Israel in the time of their kingdom. And I saw Messiah, son of Joseph, and his generation "and their" works and their doings that they will do against the nations of the world. And I saw Messiah, son of David, and his generation, and all the fights and wars, and their works and their doings that they will do with Israel both for good and evil. And I saw all the fights and wars that Gog and Magog will fight in the days of Messiah, and all that the Holy One, blessed be He, will do with them in the time to come. [6]And all the rest of all the leaders of the generations and all the works of the generations both in Israel and in the nations of the world, both what is done and what will be done hereafter to all generations until the end of time, (all) were graven on the Curtain of MAQOM. And I saw all these things with my eyes; and after I had seen it, I opened my mouth in praise of MAQOM (the Divine Majesty) (saying thus, Eccl. viii. 4, 5): "For the King's word hath power (and who may say unto him: What doest thou?) Whoso keepeth the commandments shall know no evil thing". And I said: (Ps. civ. 24) "O Lord, how manifold are thy works!".

3Enoch 46
The place of the stars shown to R. Ishmael R. Ishmael said : Metatron said to me : [1] (Come and I will show thee) the space of the stars a that are standing in Raqia' night by night in fear of the Almighty (MAQOM) and (I will show thee) where they go and where they stand. [2] I walked by his side, and he took me by his hand and pointed out all to me with his fingers. And they were standing on sparks of flames round the Merkaba of the Almighty (MAQOM). What did Metatron do? At that moment he clapped his hands and chased them off from their place. Forthwith they flew off on flaming wings, rose and fled from the four sides of the Throne of the Merkaba, and (as they flew) he told me the names of every single one. As it is written (Ps. cxlvii. 4) :" He telleth the number of the stars ; he giveth them all their names", teaching, that the Holy One, blessed be He, has given a name to each one of them. [3] And they all enter in counted order under the guidance of (lit. through, by the hands of) RAHATIEL to Raqia' ha-shSHamayim to serve the world. And they go out in counted order to praise the Holy One, blessed be He, with songs and hymns, according as it is written (Ps. xix. i):

211

"The heavens declare the glory of God". [4] But in the time to come the Holy One, blessed be He, will create them anew, as it is written (Lam. iii. 23): "They are new every morning". And they open their mouth and utter a song. Which is the song that they utter? (Ps. viii. 3): "When I consider thy heavens".

3Enoch 47
Metatron shows R. Ishmael the spirits of the punished angels R. Ishmael said; Metatron said to me; [1] Come and I will show thee the souls of the angels and the spirits of the ministering servants whose bodies have been burnt in the fire of MAQOM (the Almighty) that goes forth from his little finger. And they have been made into fiery coals in the midst of the fiery river (Nehar di-Nur). But their spirits and their souls are standing behind the Shekina. [2] Whenever the ministering angels utter a song at a wrong timeor as not appointed to be sung they are burnt and consumed by the fire of their Creator and by a flame from their Maker, in the places (chambers) of the whirlwind, for it blows upon them and drives them into the Nehar di-Nur; and there they are made into numerous mountains of burning coal. But their spirit and their soul return to their Creator, and all are standing behind their Master. [3] And I went by his side and he took me by his hand ; and he showed me all the souls of the angels and the spirits of the ministering servants who were standing behind the Shekina upon wings of the whirlwind and walls of fire surrounding them. [4] At that moment Metatron opened to me the gates of the walls within which they were standing behind the Shekina, And I lifted up my eyes and saw them, and behold, the likeness of every one was as (that of) angels and their wings hke birds' (wings), made out of flames, the work of burning fire. In that moment I opened my mouth in praise of MAQOM and said (Ps. xcii. 5): "How great are thy works, O Lord ".

3Enoch 48-a
Metatron shows R. Ishmael the Right Hand of the Most High, now inactive behind Him, but in the future destined to work the deliverance of Israel R. Ishmael said ; Metatron said to me ; [1] Come, and I will show thee the Right Hand of MAQOM, laid behind (Him) because of the destruction of the Holy Temple ; from which all kinds of splendour and light shine forth and by which the 955 heavens were created ; and whom not even the Seraphim and the 'Ophannim are permitted (to behold), until the day of salvation shall arrive. [2] And I went by his side and he took me by his hand and showed me (the Right Hand of MAQOM), with all manner of praise, rejoicing and song: and no mouth can tell its praise, and no eye can behold it, because of its greatness, dignity, majesty, glory and beauty. [3]And not only that, but all the souls of the righteous who are counted worthy to behold the joy of Jerusalem, they are standing by it, praising and praying before it three times every day, saying (Is.li.9): "Awake, awake, put on strength, arm of the Lord" according as it is written (Is. Ixiii. 12): "He caused his glorious arm to go at the right hand of Moses". [4] In that moment the Right Hand of MAQOM was weeping. And there went forth from its five fingers five rivers of tears and fell down into the great sea and shook the whole world, according as it is written (Is. xxiv. 19, 20): "The earth is utterly broken [1], the earth is clean dissolved [2], the earth is moved exceedingly [3], the earth shall stagger like a drunken man [4] and shall be moved to and fro like a hut [5]", five times corresponding to the fingers of his Great Right Hand. [5] But when the Holy One, blessed be He, sees, that there is no righteous man in the generation, and no pious man (Chasid] on earth, and no justice in the hands of men ; and (that there is) no man like unto Moses, and no intercessor as Samuel who could pray before MAQOM for the salvation and for the deliverance, and for His Kingdom, that it be revealed in the whole world; and for His great Right Hand that He put it before

Himself again to work great salvation by it for Israel, [6] then forthwith will the Holy One, blessed be He, remember His own justice, favour, mercy and grace : and He will dehver His great Arm by himself, and His righteousness will support Him. According as it is written (Is. lix. 16): "And he saw, that there was no man" (that is:) like unto Moses who prayed countless times for Israel in the desert and averted the (Divine) decrees from them" and he wondered, that there was no intercessor" like unto Samuel who intreated the Holy One, blessed be He, and called unto Him and he answered him and fulfilled his desire, even if it was not fit (in accordance with the Divine plan), according as it is written (i Sam. xii. 17) : "Is it not wheat-harvest to-day? I will call unto the Lord". [7] And not only that, but He joined fellowship with Moses in every place, as it is written (Ps.xcix.6): "Moses and Aaron among His priests." And again it is written (Jer. xv. i): "Though Moses and Samuel stood before me" (Is. Ixiii. 5): "Mine own arm brought salvation unto me". [8] Said the Holy One, blessed be He in that hour: " How long shall I wait for the children of men to work salvation according to their righteousness for my arm? For my own sake and for the sake of my merit and righteousness will I deliver my arm and by it redeem my children from among the nations of the world. As it is written (Is. xlviii. n): "For my own sake will I do it. For how should my name be profaned". [9] In that moment will the Holy One, blessed be He, reveal His Great Arm and show it to the nations of the world: for its length is as the length of the world and its breadth is as the width of the world. And the appearance of its splendour is like unto the splendour of the sunshine in its might, in the summer solstice. [10] Forthwith Israel will be saved from among the nations of the world. And Messiah will appear unto them and He will bring them up to Jerusalem with great joy. And not only that but Israel will come from the four quarters of the World and eat with Messiah. But the nations of the world shall not eat with them, as it is written (Is. Hi. 10): "The Lord hath made bare his holy arm in the eyes of all the nations ; and all the ends of the earth shall see the salvation of our God". And again (Deut. xxxii. 12): "The Lord alone did lead him, and there was no strange god with him". (Zech. xiv. 9) : "And the Lord shall be king over all the earth".

3Enoch 48-b

The Divine Names that go forth from the Throne of Glory, crowned and escorted by numerous angelic hosts through the heavens and back again to the Throne the angels sing the 'Holy' and the 'Blessed' These are the seventy-two names written on the heart of the Holy One, blessed be He: SS, SeDeQ {righteousness), SaHPeL SUR {Is. xxvi. 4}, SBI, SaDdlQ{righteous}, STh, SHN, SeBa'oTh {Lord ofHostsKShaDdaY {God Almighty}, 'eLoHIM {God},YHWH, SH, DGUL, W'DOM, SSS", 'YW, 'F, 'HW, HB, YaH, HW, WWW, SSS, PPP, NN, HH, HaY {living}, HaY, ROKeB 'aRaBOTh {riding upon the 'Araboth', Ps. Ixviii. 5}, YH, HH, WH, MMM, NNN, HWW, YH, YHH, HPhS, H'S, 1, W, S", Z', "', QQQ {Holy, Holy, Holy}, QShR, BW, ZK, GINUR, GINURYa', Y', YOD, 'aLePh, H'N, P'P, R'W, YYWy YYW, BBS, DDD, TTT, KKK, KLL, SYS, 'XT', BShKMLW { = blessed be the Name of His glorious kingdom for ever and ever}, completed for MeLeK HalOLaM {the King of the Universe], JBRH LB' {the beginning of Wisdom for the children of men}, BNLK W" Y {blessed be He who gives strength to the weary and increaseth strength to them that have no might. Is. xl. 29}that go forth (adorned) with numerous crowns of fire with numerous crowns of flame, with numerous crowns of chashmal, with numerous crowns of lightning from before the Throne of Glory. And with them (there are) thousand hundreds of power (i.e. powerful angels) who escort them like a king with trembling and dread, with awe and shivering, with honour and majesty andfear, with terror, with greatness and dignity, with glory and strength, with understanding and knowledge and with a pillar of fire and a pillar of flame and lightning and their light is as lightnings of light and with the likeness of the chashmal. [2] And they give glory unto them and they answer and cry before them: Holy, Holy, Holy. And they roll (convoy) them through every heaven as mighty and honoured princes. And when they bring them all back to the place of the Throne of Glory, then all the Chayyoth by the Merkaba open their mouth in praise of His glorious name, saying: "Blessed be the name of His glorious kingdom for ever and ever".

3Enoch 48-c

An Enoch-Metatron piece ALTl [1] "I seized him, and I took him and I appointed him" that is Enoch, the son of Jared, whose name is Metatron [2] and I took him from among the children of men [5] and made him a Throne over against my Throne. Which is the size of that Throne? Seventy thousand parasangs (all) of fire. [9] I committed unto him 70 angels corresponding to the nations (of the world) and I gave into his charge all the household above and below. [7] And I committed to him Wisdom and Intelligence more than (to) all the angels. And I called his name "the LESSER YAH", whose name is by Gematria 71. And I arranged for him all the works of Creation. And I made his power to transcend (lit. I made for him power more than) all the ministering angels. ALT 2 [3] He committed unto Metatron that is Enoch, the son of Jared all treasuries. And I appointed him over all the stores that I have in every heaven. And I committed into his hands the keys of each heavenly store. [4] I made (of) him the prince over all the princes, and I made (of) him a minister of my Throne of Glory, to provide for and arrange the Holy Chayyoth, to wreathe crowns for them (to crown them with crowns), to clothe them with honour and majesty to prepare for them a seat when he is sitting on his throne to magnify his glory in the height. [5] The height of his stature among all those (that are) of high stature (is) seventy thousand parasangs. And I made his glory great as the majesty of my glory. [6] and the brilliance of his eyes as the splendour of the Throne of Glory. [7] his garment honour and majesty, his royal crown 500 by 500 parasangs. ALTS [1] Alephl I made him strong, I took him, I appointed him: (namely) Metatron, my servant who is one (unique) among all the children of heaven. I made him strong in the generation of the first Adam. But when I beheld the men of the generation of the flood, that they were corrupt, then I went and removed my Shekina from among them. And 1 lifted it up on high with the sound of a trumpet and with a shout, as it is written (Ps.xlvii. 6): "God is gone up with a shout, the Lord with the sound of a trumpet". [2] "And I took him": (that is) Enoch, the son of Jared, from among them. And I lifted him up with the sound of a trumpet and with a tera'a (shout) to the high heavens, to be my witness together with the Chayyoth by the Merkaba in the world to come. [3] I appointed him over all the treasuries and stores that I have in every heaven. And I committed into his hand the keys of every several one. [4] I made (of) him the prince over all the princes and a minister of the Throne of Glory (and) the Halls of 'Araboth: to open their doors to me, and (of) the Throne of Glory, to exalt an arrange it; (and I appointed him over) the Holy Chayyot to wreathe crowns upon their heads; the majestic 'Ophannim, to crown them with strength and glory; the; honoured Kerubim, to clothe: them in majesty; over the radiant sparks, to make them to shine with splendour and brilliance; over the flaming Seraphim, to cover them with highness; the Chashmallim of light, to make them radiant with Light and to prepare the seat for me every morning as I sit upon the Throne of Glory. And to extol and magnify my glory inthe height of my power; (and I have committed unto him) the secrets of above and the secrets of below (heavenly secrets and earthly secrets). [5] I made him higher than all. The height of his stature, in the midst of all (who are) high of stature (I made) seventy thousand parasangs. I made his Throne great by the majesty of my Throne. And I increased its glory by the honour of my glory. [6] I transformed his flesh into torches of fire, and all the bones of his body into fiery coals; and I made the appearance of his eyes as the lightning, and the light of his eyebrows as the imperishable light. I made his face bright as the splendour of the sun, and his eyes as the splendour of the Throne of Glory. [7] I made honour and majesty his clothing, beauty and highness his covering cloak and a royal crown of 500 by (times) 500 parasangs (his) diadem. And I put upon him of my honour, my majesty and the splendour, of my glory that is upon my Throne of Glory. I called him the LESSER YHWH, the Prince of the Presence, the Knower of Secrets: for every secret did I reveal to him as a father and all mysteries declared I unto him in uprightness. [8] I set up his throne at the door of my Hall that he may sit and judge the heavenly household on high. And I placed every prince before him, to receive authority from him, to perform his will. [9] Seventy names did I take from (my) names and called him by them to enhance his glory. Seventy princes gave I into his hand, to command unto them my precepts and my words in every language: to abase by his word the proud to the ground, and to exalt by the utterance of his lips the humble to the height ; to smite kings by his speech, to turn kings away from their paths, to set up(the) rulers over their dominion as it is written (Dan.ii. 21): "and he changeth the times and the seasons, and to give wisdom unto all the setwise of the world and understanding (and) knowledge to all who understand knowledge, as it is griten (Dan. ii. 21): " and knowledge to them that know understanding", to reveal to them the secrets of my words and to teach the decree of my righteous judgement, [10] as it is written (Is.Iv. n): "so shall my word be that goeth forth out of my mouth; it shall not return unto me void but shall accomplish (that which I please)". 'E'eseh' (I shall accomplish) is not written here, but 'asdh' (he shall accomplish), meaning, that whatever word and whatever utterance goes forth from before the Holy One, blessed be He, Metatron stands and carries it out. And he establishes the decrees of the Holy One, blessed be He.

3Enoch 48-d
The names of Metatron. The treasuries of Wisdom opened to Moses on mount Sinai. The angels protest against Metatron for revealing the secrets to Moses and are answered and rebuked by God. The chain of tradition and the power of the transmitted mysteries to heal diseases [1] Seventy names has Metatron which the Holy One, blessed be He, took from his own name and put upon him. And these they are: YeHOEL, YaH, YeHOEL, YOPHIEL and Yophphiel, and APHPHIEL and MaRGeZIEL, GIPpUYEL, Pa'aZIEL, 'A'aH, PeRIEL, TaTRIEL, TaBKIEL,'W, YHWH, DH, WHYH, 'eBeD, DiBbURIEL, 'aPh'aPIEL, SPPIEL, PaSPaSIEL, SeNeGRON, MeTaTRON, SOGDIN, ADRIGON, ASUM, SaQPaM, SaQTaM, MIGON MITTON, MOTTRON, ROSPHIM, QINOTh, ChaTaTYaH, DeGaZYaH, PSPYaH, BSKNYH, MZRG, BaRaD.., MKRKK, MSPRD, ChShG, ChShB, MNRTTT, BSYRYM, MITMON, TITMON, PiSQON, SaPhSaPhYaH, ZRCh, ZRChYaH, B', BeYaH, HBH BeYaH, PeLeT, PLTYaH, RaBRaBYaH, ChaS, ChaSYaH, TaPhTaPhYaH, TaMTaMYaH, SeHaSYaH, IRURYaH, 'aL'aLYaH, BaZRIDYaH, SaTSaTKYaH, SaSDYaH, RaZRaZYaH, BaZRaZYaH, 'aRIMYaH, SBHYaH, SBIBKHYH, SiMKaM, YaHSeYaH, SSBIBYaH, SaBKaSBeYaH, QeLILaQaLYaH, fKIHHH, HHYH, WH, WHYH, ZaKklKYaH, TUTRISYaH, SURYaH, ZeH, PeNIRHYaH, ZIZ'H, GaL RaZaYYa, MaMLIKYaH, TTYaH, eMeQ, QaMYaH, MeKaPpeRYaH, PeRISHYaH, SePhaM, GBIR, GiBbORYaH,

GOR, GORYaH, ZIW, 'OKBaR, the LESSER YHWH, after the name of his Master, (Ex. xxiii. 21) "for my name is in him", RaBIBIEL, TUMIEL, Segansakkiel ('Sagnezagiel' / 'Neganzegael), the Prince of Wisdom. [2] And why is he called by the name Sagnesakiel? Because all the treasuries of wisdom are committed in his hand. [3] And all of them were opened to Moses on Sinai, so that he learnt them during the forty days, while he was standing (remaining}: the Torah in the seventy aspects of the seventy tongues, the Prophets in the seventy aspects of the seventy tongues, the Writings in the seventy aspects of the seventy tongues, "the Halakas in the seventy aspects of the seventy tongues, the Traditions in the seventy aspects of the seventy tongues, the Haggadas in the seventy aspects of the seventy tongues and the Toseftas in the seventy aspects of the seventy tongues'. [4] But as soon as the forty days were ended, he forgot all of them in one moment. Then the Holy One, blessed be He, called Yephiphyah, the Prince of the Law, and (through him) they were given to Moses as a gift. As it is written (Deut. x. 4): "and the Lord gave them unto me". And after that it remained with him. And whence do we know, that it remained (in his memory) ? Because it is written (Mai. iv. 4): " Remember ye the Law of Moses my servant which I commanded unto him in Horeb for all Israel, even my statutes and judgements". The Law of Moses': that is the Tora, the Prophets and the Writings, 'statutes': that is the Halakas and Traditions, 'judgements'; that is the Haggadas and the Toseftas. And all of them were given to Moses on high on Sinai. [5] These seventy names (are) a reflection of the Explicit Name(s) on the Merkaba which are graven upon the Throne of Glory. For the Holy One, blessed be He, took from His Explicit Name(s) and put upon the name of Metatron: Seventy Names of His by which the ministering angels call the King of the kings of kings, blessed be He, in the high heavens, and twenty-two letters that are on the ring upon his finger with which are sealed the destinies of the princes of kingdoms on high in greatness and power and with which are sealed the lots of the Angel of Death, and the destinies of every nation and tongue. [6] Said Metatron, the Angel, the Prince of the Presence; the Angel, the Prince of the Wisdom; the Angel, the Prince of the Understanding; the Angel, the Prince of the Kings; the Angel, the Prince of the Rulers; the angel, the Prince of the Glory; the angel, the Prince of the high ones, and of the princes, the exalted, great and honoured ones, in heaven and on earth: [7] "H, the God of Israel, is my witness in this thing, (that] when I revealed this secret to Moses, then all the hosts in every heaven on high raged against me and said to me: [8] Why dost thou reveal this secret to son of man, born of woman, tainted and unclean, a man of a putrefying drop, the secret by which were created heaven and earth, the sea and the dry land, the mountains and hills, the rivers and springs, Gehenna of fire and hail, the Garden of Eden and the Tree of Life; and by which were formed Adam and Eve, and the cattle, and the wild beasts, and the fowl of the air, and the fish of the sea, and Behemoth and Leviathan, and the creeping things, the worms, the dragons of the sea, and the creeping things of the deserts; and the Tora and Wisdom and Knowledge and Thought and the Gnosis of things above and the fear of heaven. Why dost thou reveal this to flesh and blood? I answered them: Because the Holy One, blessed be He, has given me authority. And furthermore, I have obtained permission from the high and exalted Throne, from which all the Explicit Names go forth with lightnings of fire and flaming chashmallim. [9] But they were not appeased, until the Holy One, blessed be He, rebuked them and drove them away with rebuke from before him, saying to them: "I delight in, and have set my love on, and have entrusted and committed unto Metatron, my Servant, alone, for he is One (unique) among all the children of heaven. [10] And Metatron brought them out from his house of treasuries and committed them to Moses, and Moses to Joshua, and Joshua to the elders, and the elders to the prophets and the prophets to the men of the Great Synagogue, and the men of the Great Synagogue to Ezra and Ezra the Scribe to Hillel the elder, and Hillel the elder to R. Abbahu and R. Abbahu to R. Zera, and R. Zera to the men of faith, and the men of faith (committed them) to give warning and to heal by them all diseases that rage in the world, as it is written (Ex. xv. 26): "If thou wilt diligently hearken to the voice of the Lord, thy God, and wilt do that which is right in his eyes, and wilt give ear to his commandments, and keep all his statutes, I will put none of the diseases upon thee, which I have put upon the Egyptians : for I am the Lord, that healeth thee". (Ended and finished. Praise be unto the Creator of the World.).

Book of Jasher

Jash.1

[1] And God said, Let us make man in our image, after our likeness, and God created man in his own image. [2] And God formed man from the ground, and he blew into his nostrils the breath of life, and man became a living soul endowed with speech. [3] And the Lord said, It is not good for man to be alone; I will make unto him a helpmeet. [4] And the Lord caused a deep sleep to fall upon Adam, and he slept, and he took away one of his ribs, and he built flesh upon it, and formed it and brought it to Adam, and Adam awoke from his sleep, and behold a woman was standing before him. [5] And he said, This is a bone of my bones and it shall be called woman, for this has been taken from man; and Adam called her name Eve, for she was the mother of all living. [6] And God blessed them and called their names Adam and Eve in the day that he created them, and the Lord God said, Be fruitful and multiply and fill the earth. [7] And the Lord God took Adam and his wife, and he placed them in the garden of Eden to dress it and to keep it; and he commanded them and said unto them, From every tree of the garden you may eat, but from the tree of the knowledge of good and evil you shall not eat, for in the day that you eat thereof you shall surely die. [8] And when God had blessed and commanded them, he went from them, and Adam and his wife dwelt in the garden according to the command which the Lord had commanded them. [9] And the serpent, which God had created with them in the earth, came to them to incite them to transgress the command of God which he had commanded them. [10] And the serpent enticed and persuaded the woman to eat from the tree of knowledge, and the woman hearkened to the voice of the serpent, and she transgressed the word of God, and took from the tree of the knowledge of good and evil, and she ate, and she took from it and gave also to her husband and he ate. [11] And Adam and his wife transgressed the command of God which he commanded them, and God knew it, and his anger was kindled against them and he cursed them. [12] And the Lord God drove them that day from the garden of Eden, to till the ground from which they were taken, and they went and dwelt at the east of the garden of Eden; and Adam knew his wife Eve and she bore two sons and three daughters. [13] And she called the name of the first born Cain, saying, I have obtained a man from the Lord, and the name of the other she called Abel, for she said, In vanity we came into the earth, and in vanity we shall be taken from it. [14] And the boys grew up and their father gave them a possession in the land; and Cain was a tiller of the ground, and Abel a keeper of sheep. [15] And it was at the expiration of a few years, that they brought an approximating offering to the Lord, and Cain brought from the fruit of the ground, and Abel brought from the firstlings of his flock from the fat thereof, and God turned and inclined to Abel and his offering, and

a fire came down from the Lord from heaven and consumed it. [16] And unto Cain and his offering the Lord did not turn, and he did not incline to it, for he had brought from the inferior fruit of the ground before the Lord, and Cain was jealous against his brother Abel on account of this, and he sought a pretext to slay him. [17] And in some time after, Cain and Abel his brother, went one day into the field to do their work; and they were both in the field, Cain tilling and ploughing his ground, and Abel feeding his flock; and the flock passed that part which Cain had ploughed in the ground, and it sorely grieved Cain on this account. [18] And Cain approached his brother Abel in anger, and he said unto him, What is there between me and thee, that thou comest to dwell and bring thy flock to feed in my land? [19] And Abel answered his brother Cain and said unto him, What is there between me and thee, that thou shalt eat the flesh of my flock and clothe thyself with their wool? [20] And now therefore, put off the wool of my sheep with which thou hast clothed thyself, and recompense me for their fruit and flesh which thou hast eaten, and when thou shalt have done this, I will then go from thy land as thou hast said? [21] And Cain said to his brother Abel, Surely if I slay thee this day, who will require thy blood from me? [22] And Abel answered Cain, saying, Surely God who has made us in the earth, he will avenge my cause, and he will require my blood from thee shouldst thou slay me, for the Lord is the judge and arbiter, and it is he who will requite man according to his evil, and the wicked man according to the wickedness that he may do upon earth. [23] And now, if thou shouldst slay me here, surely God knoweth thy secret views, and will judge thee for the evil which thou didst declare to do unto me this day. [24] And when Cain heard the words which Abel his brother had spoken, behold the anger of Cain was kindled against his brother Abel for declaring this thing. [25] And Cain hastened and rose up, and took the iron part of his ploughing instrument, with which he suddenly smote his brother and he slew him, and Cain spilt the blood of his brother Abel upon the earth, and the blood of Abel streamed upon the earth before the flock. [26] And after this Cain repented having slain his brother, and he was sadly grieved, and he wept over him and it vexed him exceedingly. [27] And Cain rose up and dug a hole in the field, wherein he put his brother's body, and he turned the dust over it. [28] And the Lord knew what Cain had done to his brother, and the Lord appeared to Cain and said unto him, Where is Abel thy brother that was with thee? [29] And Cain dissembled, and said, I do not know, am I my brother's keeper? And the Lord said unto him, What hast thou done? The voice of thy brother's blood crieth unto me from the ground where thou hast slain him. [30] For thou hast slain thy brother and hast dissembled before me, and didst imagine in thy heart that I saw thee not, nor knew all thy actions. [31] But thou didst this thing and didst slay thy brother for naught and because he spoke rightly to thee, and now, therefore, cursed be thou from the ground which opened its mouth to receive thy brother's blood from thy hand, and wherein thou didst bury him. [32] And it shall be when thou shalt till it, it shall no more give thee its strength as in the beginning, for thorns and thistles shall the ground produce, and thou shalt be moving and wandering in the earth until the day of thy death. [33] And at that time Cain went out from the presence of the Lord, from the place where he was, and he went moving and wandering in the land toward the east of Eden, he and all belonging to him. [34] And Cain knew his wife in those days, and she conceived and bare a son, and he called his name Enoch, saying, In that time the Lord began to give him rest and quiet in the earth. [35] And at that time Cain also began to build a city: and he built the city and he called the name of the city Enoch, according to the name of his son; for in those days the Lord had given him rest upon the earth, and he did not move about and wander as in the beginning. [36] And Irad was born to Enoch, and Irad begat Mechuyael and Mechuyael begat Methusael.

Jash.2

[1] And it was in the hundred and thirtieth year of the life of Adam upon the earth, that he again knew Eve his wife, and she conceived and bare a son in his likeness and in his image, and she called his name Seth, saying, Because God has appointed me another seed in the place of Abel, for Cain has slain him. [2] And Seth lived one hundred and five years, and he begat a son; and Seth called the name of his son Enosh, saying, Because in that time the sons of men began to multiply, and to afflict their souls and hearts by transgressing and rebelling against God. [3] And it was in the days of Enosh that the sons of men continued to rebel and transgress against God, to increase the anger of the Lord against the sons of men. [4] And the sons of men went and they served other gods, and they forgot the Lord who had created them in the earth: and in those days the sons of men made images of brass and iron, wood and stone, and they bowed down and served them. [5] And every man made his god and they bowed down to them, and the sons of men forsook the Lord all the days of Enosh and his children; and the anger of the Lord was kindled on account of their works and abominations which they did in the earth. [6] And the Lord caused the waters of the river Gihon to overwhelm them, and he destroyed and consumed them, and he destroyed the third part of the earth, and notwithstanding this, the sons of men did not turn from their evil ways, and their hands were yet extended to do evil in the sight of the Lord. [7] And in those days there was neither sowing nor reaping in the earth; and there was no food for the sons of men and the famine was very great in those days. [8] And the seed which they sowed in those days in the ground became thorns, thistles and briers; for from the days of Adam was this declaration concerning the earth, of the curse of God, which he cursed the earth, on account of the sin which Adam sinned before the Lord. [9] And it was when men continued to rebel and transgress against God, and to corrupt their ways, that the earth also became corrupt. [10] And Enosh lived ninety years and he begat Cainan; [11] And Cainan grew up and he was forty years old, and he became wise and had knowledge and skill in all wisdom, and he reigned over all the sons of men, and he led the sons of men to wisdom and knowledge; for Cainan was a very wise man and had understanding in all wisdom, and with his wisdom he ruled over spirits and demons; [12] And Cainan knew by his wisdom that God would destroy the sons of men for having sinned upon earth, and that the Lord would in the latter days bring upon them the waters of the flood. [13] And in those days Cainan wrote upon tablets of stone, what was to take place in time to come, and he put them in his treasures. [14] And Cainan reigned over the whole earth, and he turned some of the sons of men to the service of God. [15] And when Cainan was seventy years old, he begat three sons and two daughters. [16] And these are the names of the children of Cainan; the name of the first born Mahlallel, the second Enan, and the third Mered, and their sisters were Adah and Zillah; these are the five children of Cainan that were born to him. [17] And Lamech, the son of Methusael, became related to Cainan by marriage, and he took his two daughters for his wives, and Adah conceived and bare a son to Lamech, and she called his name Jabal. [18] And she again conceived and bare a son, and called his name Jubal; and Zillah, her sister, was barren in those days and had no offspring. [19] For in those days the sons of men began to trespass against God, and to transgress the commandments which he had commanded to Adam, to be fruitful and multiply in the earth. [20] And some of the sons of men caused their wives to drink a draught that would render them barren, in order that they might retain their figures and whereby their beautiful appearance might not fade. [21] And when the sons of men caused some of their wives to drink, Zillah drank with them. [22] And the child-bearing women appeared abominable in the sight of their husbands as widows, whilst their husbands lived, for to the barren ones only they were attached. [23] And in the end of days and years, when Zillah became old, the Lord opened her womb. [24] And she conceived and bare a son and she called his name Tubal Cain, saying, After I had withered away have I obtained him from the Almighty God. [25] And she conceived again and bare a daughter, and she called her name Naamah, for she said, After I had withered away have I obtained pleasure and delight. [26] And Lamech was old and advanced in years, and his eyes were dim that he could not see, and Tubal Cain, his son, was leading him and it was one day that Lamech went into the field and Tubal Cain his son was with him, and whilst they were walking in the field, Cain the son of Adam advanced towards them; for Lamech was very old and could not see much, and Tubal Cain his son was very young. [27] And Tubal Cain told his father to draw his bow, and with the arrows he smote Cain, who was yet far off, and he slew him, for he appeared to them to be an animal. [28] And the arrows entered Cain's body although he was distant from them, and he fell to the ground and died. [29] And the Lord requited Cain's evil according to his wickedness, which he had done to his brother Abel, according to the word of the Lord which he had spoken. [30] And it came to pass when Cain had died, that Lamech and Tubal went to see the animal which they had slain, and they saw, and behold Cain their grandfather was fallen dead upon the earth. [31] And Lamech was very much grieved at having done this, and in clapping his hands together he struck his son and caused his death. [32] And the wives of Lamech heard what Lamech had done, and they sought to kill him. [33] And the wives of Lamech hated him from that day, because he slew Cain and Tubal Cain, and the wives of Lamech separated from him, and would not hearken to him in those days. [34] And Lamech came to his wives, and he pressed them to listen to him about this matter. [35] And he said to his wives Adah and Zillah, Hear my voice O wives of Lamech, attend to my words, for now you have imagined and said that I slew a man with my wounds, and a child with my stripes for their having done no violence, but surely know that I am old and grey-headed, and that my eyes are heavy through age, and I did this thing unknowingly. [36] And the wives of Lamech listened to him in this matter, and they returned to him with the advice of their father Adam, but they bore no children to him from that time, knowing that God's anger was increasing in those days against the sons of men, to destroy them with the waters of the flood for their evil doings. [37] And Mahlallel the son of Cainan lived sixty-five years and he begat Jared; and Jared lived sixty-two years and he begat Enoch.

Jash.3

[1] And Enoch lived sixty-five years and he begat Methuselah; and Enoch walked with God after having begot Methuselah, and he served the Lord, and despised the evil ways of men. [2] And the soul of Enoch was wrapped up in the instruction of the Lord, in knowledge and in understanding; and he wisely retired from the sons of men, and secreted himself from them for many days. [3] And it was at the expiration of many years, whilst he was serving the Lord, and praying before him in his house, that an angel of the Lord called to him from Heaven, and he said, Here am I. [4] And he said, Rise, go forth from thy house and from the place where thou dost hide thyself, and appear to the sons of men, in order that thou mayest teach them the way in which they should go and the work which they must accomplish to enter in the ways of God. [5] And Enoch rose up according to the word of the Lord, and went forth from his house, from his place and from the chamber in which he was

concealed; and he went to the sons of men and taught them the ways of the Lord, and at that time assembled the sons of men and acquainted them with the instruction of the Lord. 6 And he ordered it to be proclaimed in all places where the sons of men dwelt, saying, Where is the man who wishes to know the ways of the Lord and good works? let him come to Enoch. 7 And all the sons of men then assembled to him, for all who desired this thing went to Enoch, and Enoch reigned over the sons of men according to the word of the Lord, and they came and bowed to him and they heard his word. 8 And the spirit of God was upon Enoch, and he taught all his men the wisdom of God and his ways, and the sons of men served the Lord all the days of Enoch, and they came to hear his wisdom. 9 And all the kings of the sons of men, both first and last, together with their princes and judges, came to Enoch when they heard of his wisdom, and they bowed down to him, and they also required of Enoch to reign over them, to which he consented. 10 And they assembled in all, one hundred and thirty kings and princes, and they made Enoch king over them and they were all under his power and command. 11 And Enoch taught them wisdom, knowledge, and the ways of the Lord; and he made peace amongst them, and peace was throughout the earth during the life of Enoch. 12 And Enoch reigned over the sons of men two hundred and forty-three years, and he did justice and righteousness with all his people, and he led them in the ways of the Lord. 13 And these are the generations of Enoch, Methuselah, Elisha, and Elimelech, three sons; and their sisters were Melca and Nahmah, and Methuselah lived eighty-seven years and he begat Lamech. 14 And it was in the fifty-sixth year of the life of Lamech when Adam died; nine hundred and thirty years old was he at his death, and his two sons, with Enoch and Methuselah his son, buried him with great pomp, as at the burial of kings, in the cave which God had told him. 15 And in that place all the sons of men made a great mourning and weeping on account of Adam; it has therefore become a custom among the sons of men to this day. 16 And Adam died because he ate of the tree of knowledge; he and his children after him, as the Lord God had spoken. 17 And it was in the year of Adam's death which was the two hundred and forty-third year of the reign of Enoch, in that time Enoch resolved to separate himself from the sons of men and to secret himself as at first in order to serve the Lord. 18 And Enoch did so, but did not entirely secret himself from them, but kept away from the sons of men three days and then went to them for one day. 19 And during the three days that he was in his chamber, he prayed to, and praised the Lord his God, and the day on which he went and appeared to his subjects he taught them the ways of the Lord, and all they asked him about the Lord he told them. 20 And he did in this manner for many years, and he afterward concealed himself for six days, and appeared to his people one day in seven; and after that once in a month, and then once in a year, until all the kings, princes and sons of men sought for him, and desired again to see the face of Enoch, and to hear his word; but they could not, as all the sons of men were greatly afraid of Enoch, and they feared to approach him on account of the Godlike awe that was seated upon his countenance; therefore no man could look at him, fearing he might be punished and die. 21 And all the kings and princes resolved to assemble the sons of men, and to come to Enoch, thinking that they might all speak to him at the time when he should come forth amongst them, and they did so. 22 And the day came when Enoch went forth and they all assembled and came to him, and Enoch spoke to them the words of the Lord and he taught them wisdom and knowledge, and they bowed down before him and they said, May the king live! May the king live! 23 And in some time after, when the kings and princes and the sons of men were speaking

to Enoch, and Enoch was teaching them the ways of God, behold an angel of the Lord then called unto Enoch from heaven, and wished to bring him up to heaven to make him reign there over the sons of God, as he had reigned over the sons of men upon earth. 24 When at that time Enoch heard this he went and assembled all the inhabitants of the earth, and taught them wisdom and knowledge and gave them divine instructions, and he said to them, I have been required to ascend into heaven, I therefore do not know the day of my going. 25 And now therefore I will teach you wisdom and knowledge and will give you instruction before I leave you, how to act upon earth whereby you may live; and he did so. 26 And he taught them wisdom and knowledge, and gave them instruction, and he reproved them, and he placed before them statutes and judgments to do upon earth, and he made peace amongst them, and he taught them everlasting life, and dwelt with them some time teaching them all these things. 27 And at that time the sons of men were with Enoch, and Enoch was speaking to them, and they lifted up their eyes and the likeness of a great horse descended from heaven, and the horse paced in the air; 28 And they told Enoch what they had seen, and Enoch said to them, On my account does this horse descend upon earth; the time is come when I must go from you and I shall no more be seen by you. 29 And the horse descended at that time and stood before Enoch, and all the sons of men that were with Enoch saw him. 30 And Enoch then again ordered a voice to be proclaimed, saying, Where is the man who delighteth to know the ways of the Lord his God, let him come this day to Enoch before he is taken from us. 31 And all the sons of men assembled and came to Enoch that day; and all the kings of the earth with their princes and counsellors remained with him that day; and Enoch then taught the sons of men wisdom and knowledge, and gave them divine instruction; and he bade them serve the Lord and walk in his ways all the days of their lives, and he continued to make peace amongst them. 32 And it was after this that he rose up and rode upon the horse; and he went forth and all the sons of men went after him, about eight hundred thousand men; and they went with him one day's journey. 33 And the second day he said to them, Return home to your tents, why will you go? perhaps you may die; and some of them went from him, and those that remained went with him six day's journey; and Enoch said to them every day, Return to your tents, lest you may die; but they were not willing to return, and they went with him. 34 And on the sixth day some of the men remained and clung to him, and they said to him, We will go with thee to the place where thou goest; as the Lord liveth, death only shall separate us. 35 And they urged so much to go with him, that he ceased speaking to them; and they went after him and would not return; 36 And when the kings returned they caused a census to be taken, in order to know the number of remaining men that went with Enoch; and it was upon the seventh day that Enoch ascended into heaven in a whirlwind, with horses and chariots of fire. 37 And on the eighth day all the kings that had been with Enoch sent to bring back the number of men that were with Enoch, in that place from which he ascended into heaven. 38 And all those kings went to the place and they found the earth there filled with snow, and upon the snow were large stones of snow, and one said to the other, Come, let us break through the snow and see, perhaps the men that remained with Enoch are dead, and are now under the stones of snow, and they searched but could not find him, for he had ascended into heaven.

Jash.4

1 And all the days that Enoch lived upon earth, were three hundred and sixty-five years. 2 And when Enoch had ascended into heaven, all the kings of the earth rose and took Methuselah his son and

anointed him, and they caused him to reign over them in the place of his father. 3 And Methuselah acted uprightly in the sight of God, as his father Enoch had taught him, and he likewise during the whole of his life taught the sons of men wisdom, knowledge and the fear of God, and he did not turn from the good way either to the right or to the left. 4 But in the latter days of Methuselah, the sons of men turned from the Lord, they corrupted the earth, they robbed and plundered each other, and they rebelled against God and they transgressed, and they corrupted their ways, and would not hearken to the voice of Methuselah, but rebelled against him. 5 And the Lord was exceedingly wroth against them, and the Lord continued to destroy the seed in those days, so that there was neither sowing nor reaping in the earth. 6 For when they sowed the ground in order that they might obtain food for their support, behold, thorns and thistles were produced which they did not sow. 7 And still the sons of men did not turn from their evil ways, and their hands were still extended to do evil in the sight of God, and they provoked the Lord with their evil ways, and the Lord was very wroth, and repented that he had made man. 8 And he thought to destroy and annihilate them and he did so. 9 In those days when Lamech the son of Methuselah was one hundred and sixty years old, Seth the son of Adam died. 10 And all the days that Seth lived, were nine hundred and twelve years, and he died. 11 And Lamech was one hundred and eighty years old when he took Ashmua, the daughter of Elishaa the son of Enoch his uncle, and she conceived. 12 And at that time the sons of men sowed the ground, and a little food was produced, yet the sons of men did not turn from their evil ways, and they trespassed and rebelled against God. 13 And the wife of Lamech conceived and bare him a son at that time, at the revolution of the year. 14 And Methuselah called his name Noah, saying, The earth was in his days at rest and free from corruption, and Lamech his father called his name Menachem, saying, This one shall comfort us in our works and miserable toil in the earth, which God had cursed. 15 And the child grew up and was weaned, and he went in the ways of his father Methuselah, perfect and upright with God. 16 And all the sons of men departed from the ways of the Lord in those days as they multiplied upon the face of the earth with sons and daughters, and they taught one another their evil practices and they continued sinning against the Lord. 17 And every man made unto himself a god, and they robbed and plundered every man his neighbor as well as his relative, and they corrupted the earth, and the earth was filled with violence. 18 And their judges and rulers went to the daughters of men and took their wives by force from their husbands according to their choice, and the sons of men in those days took from the cattle of the earth, the beasts of the field and the fowls of the air, and taught the mixture of animals of one species with the other, in order therewith to provoke the Lord; and God saw the whole earth and it was corrupt, for all flesh had corrupted its ways upon earth, all men and all animals. 19 And the Lord said, I will blot out man that I created from the face of the earth, yea from man to the birds of the air, together with cattle and beasts that are in the field for I repent that I made them. 20 And all men who walked in the ways of the Lord, died in those days, before the Lord brought the evil upon man which he had declared, for this was from the Lord, that they should not see the evil which the Lord spoke of concerning the sons of men. 21 And Noah found grace in the sight of the Lord, and the Lord chose him and his children to raise up seed from them upon the face of the whole earth.

Jash.5

1 And it was in the eighty-fourth year of the life of Noah, that Enoch the son of Seth died, he was nine hundred and five years old at his death. 2 And in the one hundred and seventy ninth year of the life of Noah, Cainan the son of Enosh died, and all the days of Cainan were nine hundred and ten years, and he died. 3 And in the two hundred and thirty fourth year of the life of Noah, Mahlallel the son of Cainan died, and the days of Mahlallel were eight hundred and ninety-five years, and he died. 4 And Jared the son of Mahlallel died in those days, in the three hundred and thirty-sixth year of the life of Noah; and all the days of Jared were nine hundred and sixty-two years, and he died. 5 And all who followed the Lord died in those days, before they saw the evil which God declared to do upon earth. 6 And after the lapse of many years, in the four hundred and eightieth year of the life of Noah, when all those men, who followed the Lord had died away from amongst the sons of men, and only Methuselah was then left, God said unto Noah and Methuselah, saying, 7 Speak ye, and proclaim to the sons of men, saying, Thus saith the Lord, return from your evil ways and forsake your works, and the Lord will repent of the evil that he declared to do to you, so that it shall not come to pass. 8 For thus saith the Lord, Behold I give you a period of one hundred and twenty years; if you will turn to me and forsake your evil ways, then will I also turn away from the evil which I told you, and it shall not exist, saith the Lord. 9 And Noah and Methuselah spoke all the words of the Lord to the sons of men, day after day, constantly speaking to them. 10 But the sons of men would not hearken to them, nor incline their ears to their words, and they were stiffnecked. 11 And the Lord granted them a period of one hundred and twenty years, saying, If they will return, then will God repent of the evil, so as not to destroy the earth. 12 Noah the son of Lamech refrained from taking a wife in those days, to beget children, for he said, Surely now God will destroy the earth, wherefore then shall I beget children? 13 And Noah was a just man, he was perfect in his generation, and the Lord chose him to raise up seed from his seed upon the face of the earth. 14 And the Lord said unto Noah, Take unto thee a wife, and beget children, for I have seen thee righteous before me in this generation. 15 And thou shalt raise up seed, and thy children with thee, in the midst of the earth; and Noah went and took a wife, and he chose Naamah the daughter of Enoch, and she was five hundred and eighty years old. 16 And Noah was four hundred and ninety-eight years old, when he took Naamah for a wife. 17 And Naamah conceived and bare a son, and he called his name Japheth, saying, God has enlarged me in the earth; and she conceived again and bare a son, and he called his name Shem, saying, God has made me a remnant, to raise up seed in the midst of the earth. 18 And Noah was five hundred and two years old when Naamah bare Shem, and the boys grew up and went in the ways of the Lord, in all that Methuselah and Noah their father taught them. 19 And Lamech the father of Noah, died in those days; yet verily he did not go with all his heart in the ways of his father, and he died in the hundred and ninety-fifth year of the life of Noah. 20 And all the days of Lamech were seven hundred and seventy years, and he died. 21 And all the sons of men who knew the Lord, died in that year before the Lord brought evil upon them; for the Lord willed them to die, so as not to behold the evil that God would bring upon their brothers and relatives, as he had so declared to do. 22 In that time, the Lord said to Noah and Methuselah, Stand forth and proclaim to the sons of men all the words that I spoke to you in those days, peradventure they may turn from their evil ways, and I will then repent of the evil and will not bring it. 23 And Noah and Methuselah stood forth, and said in the ears of the sons of men, all that God had spoken concerning them. 24 But the sons of men would not hearken, neither would they incline their ears to all their declarations. 25 And it was after this that the Lord said to Noah, The end of all flesh is come before me, on account of their evil deeds, and behold I will destroy the earth. 26 And do thou take unto thee gopher wood, and go to a

certain place and make a large ark, and place it in that spot. 27 And thus shalt thou make it; three hundred cubits its length, fifty cubits broad and thirty cubits high. 28 And thou shalt make unto thee a door, open at its side, and to a cubit thou shalt finish above, and cover it within and without with pitch. 29 And behold I will bring the flood of waters upon the earth, and all flesh be destroyed, from under the heavens all that is upon earth shall perish. 30 And thou and thy household shall go and gather two couple of all living things, male and female, and shall bring them to the ark, to raise up seed from them upon earth. 31 And gather unto thee all food that is eaten by all the animals, that there may be food for thee and for them. 32 And thou shalt choose for thy sons three maidens, from the daughters of men, and they shall be wives to thy sons. 33 And Noah rose up, and he made the ark, in the place where God had commanded him, and Noah did as God had ordered him. 34 In his five hundred and ninety-fifth year Noah commenced to make the ark, and he made the ark in five years, as the Lord had commanded. 35 Then Noah took the three daughters of Eliakim, son of Methuselah, for wives for his sons, as the Lord had commanded Noah. 36 And it was at that time Methuselah the son of Enoch died, nine hundred and sixty years old was he, at his death.

Jash.6

1 At that time, after the death of Methuselah, the Lord said to Noah, Go thou with thy household into the ark; behold I will gather to thee all the animals of the earth, the beasts of the field and the fowls of the air, and they shall all come and surround the ark. 2 And thou shalt go and seat thyself by the doors of the ark, and all the beasts, the animals, and the fowls, shall assemble and place themselves before thee, and such of them as shall come and crouch before thee, shalt thou take and deliver into the hands of thy sons, who shall bring them to the ark, and all that will stand before thee thou shalt leave. 3 And the Lord brought this about on the next day, and animals, beasts and fowls came in great multitudes and surrounded the ark. 4 And Noah went and seated himself by the door of the ark, and of all flesh that crouched before him, he brought into the ark, and all that stood before him he left upon earth. 5 And a lioness came, with her two whelps, male and female, and the three crouched before Noah, and the two whelps rose up against the lioness and smote her, and made her flee from her place, and she went away, and they returned to their places, and crouched upon the earth before Noah. 6 And the lioness ran away, and stood in the place of the lions. 7 And Noah saw this, and wondered greatly, and he rose and took the two whelps, and brought them into the ark. 8 And Noah brought into the ark from all living creatures that were upon earth, so that there was none left but which Noah brought into the ark. 9 Two and two came to Noah into the ark, but from the clean animals, and clean fowls, he brought seven couples, as God had commanded him. 10 And all the animals, and beasts, and fowls, were still there, and they surrounded the ark at every place, and the rain had not descended till seven days after. 11 And on that day, the Lord caused the whole earth to shake, and the sun darkened, and the foundations of the world raged, and the whole earth was moved violently, and the lightning flashed, and the thunder roared, and all the fountains in the earth were broken up, such as was not known to the inhabitants before; and God did this mighty act, in order to terrify the sons of men, that there might be no more evil upon earth. 12 And still the sons of men would not return from their evil ways, and they increased the anger of the Lord at that time, and did not even direct their hearts to all this. 13 And at the end of seven days, in the six hundredth year of the life of Noah, the waters of the flood were upon the earth. 14 And all the fountains of the deep were broken up, and the windows of heaven were opened, and the rain

was upon the earth forty days and forty nights. 15 And Noah and his household, and all the living creatures that were with him, came into the ark on account of the waters of the flood, and the Lord shut him in. 16 And all the sons of men that were left upon the earth, became exhausted through evil on account of the rain, for the waters were coming more violently upon the earth, and the animals and beasts were still surrounding the ark. 17 And the sons of men assembled together, about seven hundred thousand men and women, and they came unto Noah to the ark. 18 And they called to Noah, saying, Open for us that we may come to thee in the ark--and wherefore shall we die? 19 And Noah, with a loud voice, answered them from the ark, saying, Have you not all rebelled against the Lord, and said that he does not exist? and therefore the Lord brought upon you this evil, to destroy and cut you off from the face of the earth. 20 Is not this the thing that I spoke to you of one hundred and twenty years back, and you would not hearken to the voice of the Lord, and now do you desire to live upon earth? 21 And they said to Noah, We are ready to return to the Lord; only open for us that we may live and not die. 22 And Noah answered them, saying, Behold now that you see the trouble of your souls, you wish to return to the Lord; why did you not return during these hundred and twenty years, which the Lord granted you as the determined period? 23 But now you come and tell me this on account of the troubles of your souls, now also the Lord will not listen to you, neither will he give ear to you on this day, so that you will not now succeed in your wishes. 24 And the sons of men approached in order to break into the ark, to come in on account of the rain, for they could not bear the rain upon them. 25 And the Lord sent all the beasts and animals that stood round the ark. And the beasts overpowered them and drove them from that place, and every man went his way and they again scattered themselves upon the face of the earth. 26 And the rain was still descending upon the earth, and it descended forty days and forty nights, and the waters prevailed greatly upon the earth; and all flesh that was upon the earth or in the waters died, whether men, animals, beasts, creeping things or birds of the air, and there only remained Noah and those that were with him in the ark. 27 And the waters prevailed and they greatly increased upon the earth, and they lifted up the ark and it was raised from the earth. 28 And the ark floated upon the face of the waters, and it was tossed upon the waters so that all the living creatures within were turned about like pottage in a cauldron. 29 And great anxiety seized all the living creatures that were in the ark, and the ark was like to be broken. 30 And all the living creatures that were in the ark were terrified, and the lions roared, and the oxen lowed, and the wolves howled, and every living creature in the ark spoke and lamented in its own language, so that their voices reached to a great distance, and Noah and his sons cried and wept in their troubles; they were greatly afraid that they had reached the gates of death. 31 And Noah prayed unto the Lord, and cried unto him on account of this, and he said, O Lord help us, for we have no strength to bear this evil that has encompassed us, for the waves of the waters have surrounded us, mischievous torrents have terrified us, the snares of death have come before us; answer us, O Lord, answer us, light up thy countenance toward us and be gracious to us, redeem us and deliver us. 32 And the Lord hearkened to the voice of Noah, and the Lord remembered him. 33 And a wind passed over the earth, and the waters were still and the ark rested. 34 And the fountains of the deep and the windows of heaven were stopped, and the rain from heaven was restrained. 35 And the waters decreased in those days, and the ark rested upon the mountains of Ararat. 36 And Noah then opened the windows of the ark, and Noah still called out to the Lord at that time and he said, O Lord, who didst form the earth and the heavens and all that are therein, bring forth our souls from this confinement, and from the prison wherein thou hast placed us, for I am much wearied with sighing. 37 And the Lord hearkened to the voice of Noah, and said to him, When though shalt have completed a full year thou shalt then go forth. 38 And at the revolution of the year, when a full year was completed to Noah's dwelling in the ark, the waters were dried from off the earth, and Noah put off the covering of the ark. 39 At that time, on the twenty-seventh day of the second month, the earth was dry, but Noah and his sons, and those that were with him, did not go out from the ark until the Lord told them. 40 And the day came that the Lord told them to go out, and they all went out from the ark. 41 And they went and returned every one to his way and to his place, and Noah and his sons dwelt in the land that God had told them, and they served the Lord all their days, and the Lord blessed Noah and his sons on their going out from the ark. 42 And he said to them, Be fruitful and fill all the earth; become strong and increase abundantly in the earth and multiply therein.

Jash.7

1 And these are the names of the sons of Noah: Japheth, Ham and Shem; and children were born to them after the flood, for they had taken wives before the flood. 2 These are the sons of Japheth; Gomer, Magog, Madai, Javan, Tubal, Meshech, and Tiras, seven sons. 3 And the sons of Gomer were Askinaz, Rephath and Tegarmah. 4 And the sons of Magog were Elichanaf and Lubal. 5 And the children of Madai were Achon, Zeelo, Chazoni and Lot. 6 And the sons of Javan were Elisha, Tarshish, Chittim and Dudonim. 7 And the sons of Tubal were Ariphi, Kesed and Taari. 8 And the sons of Meshech were Dedon, Zaron and Shebashni. 9 And the sons of Tiras were Benib, Gera, Lupirion and Gilak; these are the sons of Japheth according to their families, and their numbers in those days were about four hundred and sixty men. 10 And these are the sons of Ham; Cush, Mitzraim, Phut and Canaan, four sons; and the sons of Cush were Seba, Havilah, Sabta, Raama and Satecha, and the sons of Raama were Sheba and Dedan. 11 And the sons of Mitzraim were Lud, Anom and Pathros, Chasloth and Chaphtor. 12 And the sons of Phut were Gebul, Hadan, Benah and Adan. 13 And the sons of Canaan were Zidon, Heth, Amori, Gergashi, Hivi, Arkee, Seni, Arodi, Zimodi and Chamothi. 14 These are the sons of Ham, according to their families, and their numbers in those days were about seven hundred and thirty men. 15 And these are the sons of Shem; Elam, Ashur, Arpachshad, Lud and Aram, five sons; and the sons of Elam were Shushan, Machul and Harmon. 16 And the sons of Ashar were Mirus and Mokil, and the sons of Arpachshad were Shelach, Anar and Ashcol. 17 And the sons of Lud were Pethor and Bizayon, and the sons of Aram were Uz, Chul, Gather and Mash. 18 These are the sons of Shem, according to their families; and their numbers in those days were about three hundred men. 19 These are the generations of Shem; Shem begat Arpachshad and Arpachshad begat Shelach, and Shelach begat Eber and to Eber were born two children, the name of one was Peleg, for in his days the sons of men were divided, and in the latter days, the earth was divided. 20 And the name of the second was Yoktan, meaning that in his day the lives of the sons of men were diminished and lessened. 21 These are the sons of Yoktan; Almodad, Shelaf, Chazarmoveth, Yerach, Hadurom, Ozel, Diklah, Obal, Abimael, Sheba, Ophir, Havilah and Jobab; all these are the sons of Yoktan. 22 And Peleg his brother begat Yen, and Yen begat Serug, and Serug begat Nahor and Nahor begat Terah, and Terah was thirty-eight years old, and he begat Haran and Nahor. 23 And Cush the son of Ham, the son of Noah, took a wife in those days in his old age, and she bare a son, and they called his name Nimrod, saying, At that time the sons of men again began to rebel and

transgress against God, and the child grew up, and his father loved him exceedingly, for he was the son of his old age. 24 And the garments of skin which God made for Adam and his wife, when they went out of the garden, were given to Cush. 25 For after the death of Adam and his wife, the garments were given to Enoch, the son of Jared, and when Enoch was taken up to God, he gave them to Methuselah, his son. 26 And at the death of Methuselah, Noah took them and brought them to the ark, and they were with him until he went out of the ark. 27 And in their going out, Ham stole those garments from Noah his father, and he took them and hid them from his brothers. 28 And when Ham begat his first born Cush, he gave him the garments in secret, and they were with Cush many days. 29 And Cush also concealed them from his sons and brothers, and when Cush had begotten Nimrod, he gave him those garments through his love for him, and Nimrod grew up, and when he was twenty years old he put on those garments. 30 And Nimrod became strong when he put on the garments, and God gave him might and strength, and he was a mighty hunter in the earth, yea, he was a mighty hunter in the field, and he hunted the animals and he built altars, and he offered upon them the animals before the Lord. 31 And Nimrod strengthened himself, and he rose up from amongst his brethren, and he fought the battles of his brethren against all their enemies round about. 32 And the Lord delivered all the enemies of his brethren in his hands, and God prospered him from time to time in his battles, and he reigned upon earth. 33 Therefore it became current in those days, when a man ushered forth those that he had trained up for battle, he would say to them, Like God did to Nimrod, who was a mighty hunter in the earth, and who succeeded in the battles that prevailed against his brethren, that he delivered them from the hands of their enemies, so may God strengthen us and deliver us this day. 34 And when Nimrod was forty years old, at that time there was a war between his brethren and the children of Japheth, so that they were in the power of their enemies. 35 And Nimrod went forth at that time, and he assembled all the sons of Cush and their families, about four hundred and sixty men, and he hired also from some of his friends and acquaintances about eighty men, and be gave them their hire, and he went with them to battle, and when he was on the road, Nimrod strengthened the hearts of the people that went with him. 36 And he said to them, Do not fear, neither be alarmed, for all our enemies will be delivered into our hands, and you may do with them as you please. 37 And all the men that went were about five hundred, and they fought against their enemies, and they destroyed them, and subdued them, and Nimrod placed standing officers over them in their respective places. 38 And he took some of their children as security, and they were all servants to Nimrod and to his brethren, and Nimrod and all the people that were with him turned homeward. 39 And when Nimrod had joyfully returned from battle, after having conquered his enemies, all his brethren, together with those who knew him before, assembled to make him king over them, and they placed the regal crown upon his head. 40 And he set over his subjects and people, princes, judges, and rulers, as is the custom amongst kings. 41 And he placed Terah the son of Nahor the prince of his host, and he dignified him and elevated him above all his princes. 42 And whilst he was reigning according to his heart's desire, after having conquered all his enemies around, he advised with his counselors to build a city for his palace, and they did so. 43 And they found a large valley opposite to the east, and they built him a large and extensive city, and Nimrod called the name of the city that he built Shinar, for the Lord had vehemently shaken his enemies and destroyed them. 44 And Nimrod dwelt in Shinar, and he reigned securely, and he fought with his enemies and he subdued them, and he prospered in all his battles, and his kingdom became very great. 45 And all nations and tongues heard of his fame, and they gathered themselves to him, and they bowed down to the earth, and they brought him offerings, and he became their lord and king, and they all dwelt with him in the city at Shinar, and Nimrod reigned in the earth over all the sons of Noah, and they were all under his power and counsel. 46 And all the earth was of one tongue and words of union, but Nimrod did not go in the ways of the Lord, and he was more wicked than all the men that were before him, from the days of the flood until those days. 47 And he made gods of wood and stone, and he bowed down to them, and he rebelled against the Lord, and taught all his subjects and the people of the earth his wicked ways; and Mardon his son was more wicked than his father. 48 And every one that heard of the acts of Mardon the son of Nimrod would say, concerning him, From the wicked goeth forth wickedness; therefore it became a proverb in the whole earth, saying, From the wicked goeth forth wickedness, and it was current in the words of men from that time to this. 49 And Terah the son of Nahor, prince of Nimrod's host, was in those days very great in the sight of the king and his subjects, and the king and princes loved him, and they elevated him very high. 50 And Terah took a wife and her name was Amthelo the daughter of Cornebo; and the wife of Terah conceived and bare him a son in those days. 51 Terah was seventy years old when he begat him, and Terah called the name of his son that was born to him Abram, because the king had raised him in those days, and dignified him above all his princes that were with him.

Jash.8

1 And it was in the night that Abram was born, that all the servants of Terah, and all the wise men of Nimrod, and his conjurors came and ate and drank in the house of Terah, and they rejoiced with him on that night. 2 And when all the wise men and conjurors went out from the house of Terah, they lifted up their eyes toward heaven that night to look at the stars, and they saw, and behold one very large star came from the east and ran in the heavens, and he swallowed up the four stars from the four sides of the heavens. 3 And all the wise men of the king and his conjurors were astonished at the sight, and the sages understood this matter, and they knew its import. 4 And they said to each other, This only betokens the child that has been born to Terah this night, who will grow up and be fruitful, and multiply, and possess all the earth, he and his children for ever, and he and his seed will slay great kings, and inherit their lands. 5 And the wise men and conjurors went home that night, and in the morning all these wise men and conjurors rose up early, and assembled in an appointed house. 6 And they spoke and said to each other, Behold the sight that we saw last night is hidden from the king, it has not been made known to him. 7 And should this thing get known to the king in the latter days, he will say to us, Why have you concealed this matter from me, and then we shall all suffer death; therefore, now let us go and tell the king the sight which we saw, and the interpretation thereof, and we shall then remain clear. 8 And they did so, and they all went to the king and bowed down to him to the ground, and they said, May the king live, may the king live. 9 We heard that a son was born to Terah the son of Nahor, the prince of thy host, and we yesternight came to his house, and we ate and drank and rejoiced with him that night. 10 And when thy servants went out from the house of Terah, to go to our respective homes to abide there for the night, we lifted up our eyes to heaven, and we saw a great star coming from the east, and the same star ran with great speed, and swallowed up four great stars, from the four sides of the heavens. 11 And thy servants were astonished at the sight which we saw, and were greatly terrified, and

we made our judgment upon the sight, and knew by our wisdom the proper interpretation thereof, that this thing applies to the child that is born to Terah, who will grow up and multiply greatly, and become powerful, and kill all the kings of the earth, and inherit all their lands, he and his seed forever. 12 And now our lord and king, behold we have truly acquainted thee with what we have seen concerning this child. 13 If it seemeth good to the king to give his father value for this child, we will slay him before he shall grow up and increase in the land, and his evil increase against us, that we and our children perish through his evil. 14 And the king heard their words and they seemed good in his sight, and he sent and called for Terah, and Terah came before the king. 15 And the king said to Terah, I have been told that a son was yesternight born to thee, and after this manner was observed in the heavens at his birth. 16 And now therefore give me the child, that we may slay him before his evil springs up against us, and I will give thee for his value, thy house full of silver and gold. 17 And Terah answered the king and said to him: My Lord and king, I have heard thy words, and thy servant shall do all that his king desireth. 18 But my lord and king, I will tell thee what happened to me yesternight, that I may see what advice the king will give his servant, and then I will answer the king upon what he has just spoken; and the king said, Speak. 19 And Terah said to the king, Ayon, son of Mored, came to me yesternight, saying, 20 Give unto me the great and beautiful horse that the king gave thee, and I will give thee silver and gold, and straw and provender for its value; and I said to him, Wait till I see the king concerning thy words, and behold whatever the king saith, that will I do. 21 And now my lord and king, behold I have made this thing known to thee, and the advice which my king will give unto his servant, that will I follow. 22 And the king heard the words of Terah, and his anger was kindled and he considered him in the light of a fool. 23 And the king answered Terah, and he said to him, Art thou so silly, ignorant, or deficient in understanding, to do this thing, to give thy beautiful horse for silver and gold or even for straw and provender? 24 Art thou so short of silver and gold, that thou shouldst do this thing, because thou canst not obtain straw and provender to feed thy horse? and what is silver and gold to thee, or straw and provender, that thou shouldst give away that fine horse which I gave thee, like which there is none to be had on the whole earth? 25 And the king left off speaking, and Terah answered the king, saying, Like unto this has the king spoken to his servant; 26 I beseech thee, my lord and king, what is this which thou didst say unto me, saying, Give thy son that we may slay him, and I will give thee silver and gold for his value; what shall I do with silver and gold after the death of my son? who shall inherit me? surely then at my death, the silver and gold will return to my king who gave it. 27 And when the king heard the words of Terah, and the parable which he brought concerning the king, it grieved him greatly and he was vexed at this thing, and his anger burned within him. 28 And Terah saw that the anger of the king was kindled against him, and he answered the king, saying, All that I have is in the king's power; whatever the king desireth to do to his servant, that let him do, yea, even my son, he is in the king's power, without value in exchange, he and his two brothers that are older than he. 29 And the king said to Terah, No, but I will purchase thy younger son for a price. 30 And Terah answered the king, saying, I beseech thee my lord and king to let thy servant speak a word before thee, and let the king hear the word of his servant, and Terah said, Let my king give me three days' time till I consider this matter within myself, and consult with my family concerning the words of my king; and he pressed the king greatly to agree to this. 31 And the king hearkened to Terah, and he did so and he gave him three days' time, and Terah went out from the king's presence, and he came home to his family and spoke to them all the words of the king; and the people were greatly afraid. 32 And it was in the third day that the king sent to Terah, saying, Send me thy son for a price as I spoke to thee; and shouldst thou not do this, I will send and slay all thou hast in thy house, so that thou shalt not even have a dog remaining. 33 And Terah hastened, (as the thing was urgent from the king), and he took a child from one of his servants, which his handmaid had born to him that day, and Terah brought the child to the king and received value for him. 34 And the Lord was with Terah in this matter, that Nimrod might not cause Abram's death, and the king took the child from Terah and with all his might dashed his head to the ground, for he thought it had been Abram; and this was concealed from him from that day, and it was forgotten by the king, as it was the will of Providence not to suffer Abram's death. 35 And Terah took Abram his son secretly, together with his mother and nurse, and he concealed them in a cave, and he brought them their provisions monthly. 36 And the Lord was with Abram in the cave and he grew up, and Abram was in the cave ten years, and the king and his princes, soothsayers and sages, thought that the king had killed Abram.

Jash.9

1 And Haran, the son of Terah, Abram's oldest brother, took a wife in those days. 2 Haran was thirty-nine years old when he took her; and the wife of Haran conceived and bare a son, and he called his name Lot. 3 And she conceived again and bare a daughter, and she called her name Milca; and she again conceived and bare a daughter, and she called her name Sarai. 4 Haran was forty-two years old when he begat Sarai, which was in the tenth year of the life of Abram; and in those days Abram and his mother and nurse went out from the cave, as the king and his subjects had forgotten the affair of Abram. 5 And when Abram came out from the cave, he went to Noah and his son Shem, and he remained with them to learn the instruction of the Lord and his ways, and no man knew where Abram was, and Abram served Noah and Shem his son for a long time. 6 And Abram was in Noah's house thirty-nine years, and Abram knew the Lord from three years old, and he went in the ways of the Lord until the day of his death, as Noah and his son Shem had taught him; and all the sons of the earth in those days greatly transgressed against the Lord, and they rebelled against him and they served other gods, and they forgot the Lord who had created them in the earth; and the inhabitants of the earth made unto themselves, at that time, every man his god; gods of wood and stone which could neither speak, hear, nor deliver, and the sons of men served them and they became their gods. 7 And the king and all his servants, and Terah with all his household were then the first of those that served gods of wood and stone.

8 And Terah had twelve gods of large size, made of wood and stone, after the twelve months of the year, and he served each one monthly, and every month Terah would bring his meat offering and drink offering to his gods; thus did Terah all the days. 9 And all that generation were wicked in the sight of the Lord, and they thus made every man his god, but they forsook the Lord who had created them. 10 And there was not a man found in those days in the whole earth, who knew the Lord (for they served each man his own God) except Noah and his household, and all those who were under his counsel knew the Lord in those days. 11 And Abram the son of Terah was waxing great in those days in the house of Noah, and no man knew it, and the Lord was with him. 12 And the Lord gave Abram an understanding heart, and he knew all the works of that generation were vain, and that all their gods were vain and were of no avail. 13 And Abram saw the sun shining upon the earth, and Abram said unto himself Surely now this sun that shines upon the

earth is God, and him will I serve. 14 And Abram served the sun in that day and he prayed to him, and when evening came the sun set as usual, and Abram said within himself, Surely this cannot be God? 15 And Abram still continued to speak within himself, Who is he who made the heavens and the earth? who created upon earth? where is he? 16 And night darkened over him, and he lifted up his eyes toward the west, north, south, and east, and he saw that the sun had vanished from the earth, and the day became dark. 17 And Abram saw the stars and moon before him, and he said, Surely this is the God who created the whole earth as well as man, and behold these his servants are gods around him: and Abram served the moon and prayed to it all that night. 18 And in the morning when it was light and the sun shone upon the earth as usual, Abram saw all the things that the Lord God had made upon earth. 19 And Abram said unto himself Surely these are not gods that made the earth and all mankind, but these are the servants of God, and Abram remained in the house of Noah and there knew the Lord and his ways' and he served the Lord all the days of his life, and all that generation forgot the Lord, and served other gods of wood and stone, and rebelled all their days. 20 And king Nimrod reigned securely, and all the earth was under his control, and all the earth was of one tongue and words of union. 21 And all the princes of Nimrod and his great men took counsel together; Phut, Mitzraim, Cush and Canaan with their families, and they said to each other, Come let us build ourselves a city and in it a strong tower, and its top reaching heaven, and we will make ourselves famed, so that we may reign upon the whole world, in order that the evil of our enemies may cease from us, that we may reign mightily over them, and that we may not become scattered over the earth on account of their wars. 22 And they all went before the king, and they told the king these words, and the king agreed with them in this affair, and he did so. 23 And all the families assembled consisting of about six hundred thousand men, and they went to seek an extensive piece of ground to build the city and the tower, and they sought in the whole earth and they found none like one valley at the east of the land of Shinar, about two days' walk, and they journeyed there and they dwelt there. 24 And they began to make bricks and burn fires to build the city and the tower that they had imagined to complete. 25 And the building of the tower was unto them a transgression and a sin, and they began to build it, and whilst they were building against the Lord God of heaven, they imagined in their hearts to war against him and to ascend into heaven. 26 And all these people and all the families divided themselves in three parts; the first said We will ascend into heaven and fight against him; the second said, We will ascend to heaven and place our own gods there and serve them; and the third part said, We will ascend to heaven and smite him with bows and spears; and God knew all their works and all their evil thoughts, and he saw the city and the tower which they were building. 27 And when they were building they built themselves a great city and a very high and strong tower; and on account of its height the mortar and bricks did not reach the builders in their ascent to it, until those who went up had completed a full year, and after that, they reached to the builders and gave them the mortar and the bricks; thus was it done daily. 28 And behold these ascended and others descended the whole day; and if a brick should fall from their hands and get broken, they would all weep over it, and if a man fell and died, none of them would look at him. 29 And the Lord knew their thoughts, and it came to pass when they were building they cast the arrows toward the heavens, and all the arrows fell upon them filled with blood, and when they saw them they said to each other, Surely we have slain all those that are in heaven. 30 For this was from the Lord in order to cause them to err, and in order; to destroy them from off the face of the ground. 31 And they built the tower and the city, and they did this thing daily until many days and years were elapsed. 32 And God said to the seventy angels who stood foremost before him, to those who were near to him, saying, Come let us descend and confuse their tongues, that one man shall not understand the language of his neighbor, and they did so unto them. 33 And from that day following, they forgot each man his neighbor's tongue, and they could not understand to speak in one tongue, and when the builder took from the hands of his neighbor lime or stone which he did not order, the builder would cast it away and throw it upon his neighbor, that he would die. 34 And they did so many days, and they killed many of them in this manner. 35 And the Lord smote the three divisions that were there, and he punished them according to their works and designs; those who said, We will ascend to heaven and serve our gods, became like apes and elephants; and those who said, We will smite the heaven with arrows, the Lord killed them, one man through the hand of his neighbor; and the third division of those who said, We will ascend to heaven and fight against him, the Lord scattered them throughout the earth. 36 And those who were left amongst them, when they knew and understood the evil which was coming upon them, they forsook the building, and they also became scattered upon the face of the whole earth. 37 And they ceased building the city and the tower; therefore he called that place Babel, for there the Lord confounded the Language of the whole earth; behold it was at the east of the land of Shinar. 38 And as to the tower which the sons of men built, the earth opened its mouth and swallowed up one third part thereof, and a fire also descended from heaven and burned another third, and the other third is left to this day, and it is of that part which was aloft, and its circumference is three days' walk. 39 And many of the sons of men died in that tower, a people without number.

Jash.10

1 And Peleg the son of Eber died in those days, in the forty-eighth year of the life of Abram son of Terah, and all the days of Peleg were two hundred and thirty-nine years. 2 And when the Lord had scattered the sons of men on account of their sin at the tower, behold they spread forth into many divisions, and all the sons of men were dispersed into the four corners of the earth. 3 And all the families became each according to its language, its land, or its city. 4 And the sons of men built many cities according to their families, in all the places where they went, and throughout the earth where the Lord had scattered them. 5 And some of them built cities in places from which they were afterward extirpated, and they called these cities after their own names, or the names of their children, or after their particular occurrences. 6 And the sons of Japheth the son of Noah went and built themselves cities in the places where they were scattered, and they called all their cities after their names, and the sons of Japheth were divided upon the face of the earth into many divisions and languages. 7 And these are the sons of Japheth according to their families, Gomer, Magog, Medai, Javan, Tubal, Meshech and Tiras; these are the children of Japheth according to their generations. 8 And the children of Gomer, according to their cities, were the Francum, who dwell in the land of Franza, by the river Franza, by the river Senah. 9 And the children of Rephath are the Bartonim, who dwell in the land of Bartonia by the river Ledah, which empties its waters in the great sea Gihon, that is, oceanus. 10 And the children of Tugarma are ten families, and these are their names: Buzar, Parzunac, Balgar, Elicanum, Ragbib, Tarki, Bid, Zebuc, Ongal and Tilmaz; all these spread and rested in the north and built themselves cities. 11 And they called their cities after their own names, those are they who abide by the rivers Hithlah and Italac unto this day. 12 But the families of Angoli, Balgar and Parzunac, they dwell by the great river Dubnee; and the names of their cities are also according to their own names. 13 And the children of Javan are the Javanim who dwell in the land of Makdonia, and the children of Medaiare are the Orelum that dwell in the land of Curson, and the children of Tubal are those that dwell in the land of Tuskanah by the river Pashiah. 14 And the children of Meshech are the Shibashni and the children of Tiras are Rushash, Cushni, and Ongolis; all these went and built themselves cities; those are the cities that are situate by the sea Jabus by the river Cura, which empties itself in the river Tragan. 15 And the children of Elishah are the Almanim, and they also went and built themselves cities; those are the cities situate between the mountains of Job and Shibathmo; and of them were the people of Lumbardi who dwell opposite the mountains of Job and Shibathmo, and they conquered the land of Italia and remained there unto this day. 16 And the children of Chittim are the Romim who dwell in the valley of Canopia by the river Tibreu. 17 And the children of Dudonim are those who dwell in the cities of the sea Gihon, in the land of Bordna. 18 These are the families of the children of Japheth according to their cities and languages, when they were scattered after the tower, and they called their cities after their names and occurrences; and these are the names of all their cities according to their families, which they built in those days after the tower. 19 And the children of Ham were Cush, Mitzraim, Phut and Canaan according to their generation and cities. 20 All these went and built themselves cities as they found fit places for them, and they called their cities after the names of their fathers Cush, Mitzraim, Phut and Canaan. 21 And the children of Mitzraim are the Ludim, Anamim, Lehabim, Naphtuchim, Pathrusim, Casluchim and Caphturim, seven families. 22 All these dwell by the river Sihor, that is the brook of Egypt, and they built themselves cities and called them after their own names. 23 And the children of Pathros and Casloch intermarried together, and from them went forth the Pelishtim, the Azathim, and the Gerarim, the Githim and the Ekronim, in all five families; these also built themselves cities, and they called their cities after the names of their fathers unto this day. 24 And the children of Canaan also built themselves cities, and they called their cities after their names, eleven cities and others without number. 25 And four men from the family of Ham went to the land of the plain; these are the names of the four men, Sodom, Gomorrah, Admah and Zeboyim. 26 And these men built themselves four cities in the land of the plain, and they called the names of their cities after their own names. 27 And they and their children and all belonging to them dwelt in those cities, and they were fruitful and multiplied greatly and dwelt peaceably. 28 And Seir the son of Hur, son of Hivi, son of Canaan, went and found a valley opposite to Mount Paran, and he built a city there, and he and his seven sons and his household dwelt there, and he called the city which he built Seir, according to his name; that is the land of Seir unto this day. 29 These are the families of the children of Ham, according to their languages and cities, when they were scattered to their countries after the tower. 30 And some of the children of Shem son of Noah, father of all the children of Eber, also went and built themselves cities in the places wherein they were scattered, and they called their cities after their names. 31 And the sons of Shem were Elam, Ashur, Arpachshad, Lud and Aram, and they built themselves cities and called the names of all their cities after their names. 32 And Ashur son of Shem and his children and household went forth at that time, a very large body of them, and they went to a distant land that they found, and they met with a very extensive valley in the land that they went to, and they built themselves four cities, and they called them after their own names and occurrences. 33 And these are the names of the cities which the children of Ashur built, Ninevah, Resen, Calach and Rehobother;

and the children of Ashur dwell there unto this day. [34] And the children of Aram also went and built themselves a city, and they called the name of the city Uz after their eldest brother, and they dwell therein; that is the land of Uz to this day. [35] And in the second year after the tower a man from the house of Ashur, whose name was Bela, went from the land of Ninevah to sojourn with his household wherever he could find a place; and they came until opposite the cities of the plain against Sodom, and they dwelt there. [36] And the man rose up and built there a small city, and called its name Bela, after his name; that is the land of Zoar unto this day. [37] And these are the families of the children of Shem according to their language and cities, after they were scattered upon the earth after the tower. [38] And every kingdom, city, and family of the families of the children of Noah built themselves many cities after this. [39] And they established governments in all their cities, in order to be regulated by their orders; so did all the families of the children of Noah forever.

Jash.11

[1] And Nimrod son of Cush was still in the land of Shinar, and he reigned over it and dwelt there, and he built cities in the land of Shinar. [2] And these are the names of the four cities which he built, and he called their names after the occurrences that happened to them in the building of the tower. [3] And he called the first Babel, saying, Because the Lord there confounded the language of the whole earth; and the name of the second he called Erech, because from there God dispersed them. [4] And the third he called Eched, saying there was a great battle at that place; and the fourth he called Calnah, because his princes and mighty men were consumed there, and they vexed the Lord, they rebelled and transgressed against him. [5] And when Nimrod had built these cities in the land of Shinar, he placed in them the remainder of his people, his princes and his mighty men that were left in his kingdom. [6] And Nimrod dwelt in Babel, and he there renewed his reign over the rest of his subjects, and he reigned securely, and the subjects and princes of Nimrod called his name Amraphel, saying that at the tower his princes and men fell through his means. [7] And notwithstanding this, Nimrod did not return to the Lord, and he continued in wickedness and teaching wickedness to the sons of men; and Mardon, his son, was worse than his father, and continued to add to the abominations of his father. [8] And he caused the sons of men to sin, therefore it is said, From the wicked goeth forth wickedness. [9] At that time there was war between the families of the children of Ham, as they were dwelling in the cities which they had built. [10] And Chedorlaomer, king of Elam, went away from the families of the children of Ham, and he fought with them and he subdued them, and he went to the five cities of the plain and he fought against them and he subdued them, and they were under his control. [11] And they served him twelve years, and they gave him a yearly tax. [12] At that time died Nahor, son of Serug, in the forty-ninth year of the life of Abram son of Terah. [13] And in the fiftieth year of the life of Abram son of Terah, Abram came forth from the house of Noah, and went to his father's house. [14] And Abram knew the Lord, and he went in his ways and instructions, and the Lord his God was with him. [15] And Terah his father was in those days, still captain of the host of king Nimrod, and he still followed strange gods. [16] And Abram came to his father's house and saw twelve gods standing there in their temples, and the anger of Abram was kindled when he saw these images in his father's house. [17] And Abram said, As the Lord liveth these images shall not remain in my father's house; so shall the Lord who created me do unto me if in three days' time I do not break them all. [18] And Abram went from them, and his anger burned within him. And Abram hastened and went from the chamber to his

father's outer court, and he found his father sitting in the court, and all his servants with him, and Abram came and sat before him. [19] And Abram asked his father, saying, Father, tell me where is God who created heaven and earth, and all the sons of men upon earth, and who created thee and me. And Terah answered his son Abram and said, Behold those who created us are all with us in the house. [20] And Abram said to his father, My lord, shew them to me I pray thee; and Terah brought Abram into the chamber of the inner court, and Abram saw, and behold the whole room was full of gods of wood and stone, twelve great images and others less than they without number. [21] And Terah said to his son, Behold these are they which made all thou seest upon earth, and which created me and thee, and all mankind. [22] And Terah bowed down to his gods, and he then went away from them, and Abram, his son, went away with him. [23] And when Abram had gone from them he went to his mother and sat before her, and he said to his mother, Behold, my father has shown me those who made heaven and earth, and all the sons of men. [24] Now, therefore, hasten and fetch a kid from the flock, and make of it savory meat, that I may bring it to my father's gods as an offering for them to eat; perhaps I may thereby become acceptable to them. [25] And his mother did so, and she fetched a kid, and made savory meat thereof, and brought it to Abram, and Abram took the savory meat from his mother and brought it before his father's gods, and he drew nigh to them that they might eat; and Terah his father, did not know of it. [26] And Abram saw on the day when he was sitting amongst them, that they had no voice, no hearing, no motion, and not one of them could stretch forth his hand to eat. [27] And Abram mocked them, and said, Surely the savory meat that I prepared has not pleased them, or perhaps it was too little for them, and for that reason they would not eat; therefore tomorrow I will prepare fresh savory meat, better and more plentiful than this, in order that I may see the result. [28] And it was on the next day that Abram directed his mother concerning the savory meat, and his mother rose and fetched three fine kids from the flock, and she made of them some excellent savory meat, such as her son was fond of, and she gave it to her son Abram; and Terah his father did not know of it. [29] And Abram took the savory meat from his mother, and brought it before his father's gods into the chamber; and he came nigh unto them that they might eat, and he placed it before them, and Abram sat before them all day, thinking perhaps they might eat. [30] And Abram viewed them, and behold they had neither voice nor hearing, nor did one of them stretch forth his hand to the meat to eat. [31] And in the evening of that day in that house Abram was clothed with the spirit of God. [32] And he called out and said, Wo unto my father and this wicked generation, whose hearts are all inclined to vanity, who serve these idols of wood and stone which can neither eat, smell, hear nor speak, who have mouths without speech, eyes without sight, ears without hearing, hands without feeling, and legs which cannot move; like them are those that made them and that trust in them. [33] And when Abram saw all these things his anger was kindled against his father, and he hastened and took a hatchet in his hand, and came unto the chamber of the gods, and he broke all his father's gods. [34] And when he had done breaking the images, he placed the hatchet in the hand of the great god which was there before them, and he went out; and Terah his father came home, for he had heard at the door the sound of the striking of the hatchet; so Terah came into the house to know what this was about. [35] And Terah, having heard the noise of the hatchet in the room of images, ran to the room to the images, and he met Abram going out. [36] And Terah entered the room and found all the idols fallen down and broken, and the hatchet in the hand of the largest, which was not broken, and the savory meat which Abram his son had made was still before them. 37 And when Terah saw this his anger was greatly kindled, and he hastened and went from the room to Abram. 38 And he found Abram his son still sitting in the house; and he said to him, What is this work thou hast done to my gods? 39 And Abram answered Terah his father and he said, Not so my lord, for I brought savory meat before them, and when I came nigh to them with the meat that they might eat, they all at once stretched forth their hands to eat before the great one had put forth his hand to eat. 40 And the large one saw their works that they did before him, and his anger was violently kindled against them, and he went and took the hatchet that was in the house and came to them and broke them all, and behold the hatchet is yet in his hand as thou seest. 41 And Terah's anger was kindled against his son Abram, when he spoke this; and Terah said to Abram his son in his anger, What is this tale that thou hast told? Thou speakest lies to me. 42 Is there in these gods spirit, soul or power to do all thou hast told me? Are they not wood and stone, and have I not myself made them, and canst thou speak such lies, saying that the large god that was with them smote them? It is thou that didst place the hatchet in his hands, and then sayest he smote them all. 43 And Abram answered his father and said to him, And how canst thou then serve these idols in whom there is no power to do any thing? Can those idols in which thou trustest deliver thee? can they hear thy prayers when thou callest upon them? can they deliver thee from the hands of thy enemies, or will they fight thy battles for thee against thy enemies, that thou shouldst serve wood and stone which can neither speak nor hear? 44 And now surely it is not good for thee nor for the sons of men that are connected with thee, to do these things; are you so silly, so foolish or so short of understanding that you will serve wood and stone, and do after this manner? 45 And forget the Lord God who made heaven and earth, and who created you in the earth, and thereby bring a great evil upon your souls in this matter by serving stone and wood? 46 Did not our fathers in days of old sin in this matter, and the Lord God of the universe brought the waters of the flood upon them and destroyed the whole earth? 47 And how can you continue to do this and serve gods of wood and stone, who cannot hear, or speak, or deliver you from oppression, thereby bringing down the anger of the God of the universe upon you? 48 Now therefore my father refrain from this, and bring not evil upon thy soul and the souls of thy household. 49 And Abram hastened and sprang from before his father, and took the hatchet from his father's largest idol, with which Abram broke it and ran away. 50 And Terah, seeing all that Abram had done, hastened to go from his house, and he went to the king and he came before Nimrod and stood before him, and he bowed down to the king; and the king said, What dost thou want? 51 And he said, I beseech thee my lord, to hear me--Now fifty years back a child was born to me, and thus has he done to my gods and thus has he spoken; and now therefore, my lord and king, send for him that he may come before thee, and judge him according to the law, that we may be delivered from his evil. 52 And the king sent three men of his servants, and they went and brought Abram before the king. And Nimrod and all his princes and servants were that day sitting before him, and Terah sat also before them. 53 And the king said to Abram, What is this that thou hast done to thy father and to his gods? And Abram answered the king in the words that he spoke to his father, and he said, The large god that was with them in the house did to them what thou hast heard. 54 And the king said to Abram, Had they power to speak and eat and do as thou hast said? And Abram answered the king, saying, And if there be no power in them why dost thou serve them and cause the sons of men to err through thy follies? 55 Dost thou imagine that they can deliver thee or do anything small or great, that

224

thou shouldst serve them? And why wilt thou not sense the God of the whole universe, who created thee and in whose power it is to kill and keep alive? 56 0 foolish, simple, and ignorant king, woe unto thee forever. 57 I thought thou wouldst teach thy servants the upright way, but thou hast not done this, but hast filled the whole earth with thy sins and the sins of thy people who have followed thy ways. 58 Dost thou not know, or hast thou not heard, that this evil which thou doest, our ancestors sinned therein in days of old, and the eternal God brought the waters of the flood upon them and destroyed them all, and also destroyed the whole earth on their account? And wilt thou and thy people rise up now and do like unto this work, in order to bring down the anger of the Lord God of the universe, and to bring evil upon thee and the whole earth? 59 Now therefore put away this evil deed which thou doest, and serve the God of the universe, as thy soul is in his hands, and then it will be well with thee. 60 And if thy wicked heart will not hearken to my words to cause thee to forsake thy evil ways, and to serve the eternal God, then wilt thou die in shame in the latter days, thou, thy people and all who are connected with thee, hearing thy words or walking in thy evil ways. 61 And when Abram had ceased speaking before the king and princes, Abram lifted up his eyes to the heavens, and he said, The Lord seeth all the wicked, and he will judge them.

Jash.12

1 And when the king heard the words of Abram he ordered him to be put into prison; and Abram was ten days in prison. 2 And at the end of those days the king ordered that all the kings, princes and governors of different provinces and the sages should come before him, and they sat before him, and Abram was still in the house of confinement. 3 And the king said to the princes and sages, Have you heard what Abram, the son of Terah, has done to his father? Thus has he done to him, and I ordered him to be brought before me, and thus has he spoken; his heart did not misgive him, neither did he stir in my presence, and behold now he is confined in the prison. 4 And therefore decide what judgment is due to this man who reviled the king; who spoke and did all the things that you heard. 5 And they all answered the king saying, The man who revileth the king should be hanged upon a tree; but having done all the things that he said, and having despised our gods, he must therefore be burned to death, for this is the law in this matter. 6 If it pleaseth the king to do this, let him order his servants to kindle a fire both night and day in thy brick furnace, and then we will cast this man into it. And the king did so, and he commanded his servants that they should prepare a fire for three days and three nights in the king's furnace, that is in Casdim; and the king ordered them to take Abram from prison and bring him out to be burned. 7 And all the king's servants, princes, lords, governors, and judges, and all the inhabitants of the land, about nine hundred thousand men, stood opposite the furnace to see Abram. 8 And all the women and little ones crowded upon the roofs and towers to see what was doing with Abram, and they all stood together at a distance; and there was not a man left that did not come on that day to behold the scene. 9 And when Abram was come, the conjurors of the king and the sages saw Abram, and they cried out to the king, saying, Our sovereign lord, surely this is the man whom we know to have been the child at whose birth the great star swallowed the four stars, which we declared to the king now fifty years since. 10 And behold now his father has also transgressed thy commands, and mocked thee by bringing thee another child, which thou didst kill. 11 And when the king heard their words, he was exceedingly wroth, and he ordered Terah to be brought before him. 12 And the king said, Hast thou heard what the conjurors have spoken? Now tell me truly, how didst thou; and if thou shalt speak truth thou shalt be acquitted. 13 And seeing that the king's anger was

so much kindled, Terah said to the king, My lord and king, thou hast heard the truth, and what the sages have spoken is right. And the king said, How couldst thou do this thing, to transgress my orders and to give me a child that thou didst not beget, and to take value for him? 14 And Terah answered the king, Because my tender feelings were excited for my son, at that time, and I took a son of my handmaid, and I brought him to the king. 15 And the king said Who advised thee to this? Tell me, do not hide aught from me, and then thou shalt not die. 16 And Terah was greatly terrified in the king's presence, and he said to the king, It was Haran my eldest son who advised me to this; and Haran was in those days that Abram was born, two and thirty years old. 17 But Haran did not advise his father to anything, for Terah said this to the king in order to deliver his soul from the king, for he feared greatly; and the king said to Terah, Haran thy son who advised thee to this shall die through fire with Abram; for the sentence of death is upon him for having rebelled against the king's desire in doing this thing. 18 And Haran at that time felt inclined to follow the ways of Abram, but he kept it within himself. 19 And Haran said in his heart, Behold now the king has seized Abram on account of these things which Abram did, and it shall come to pass, that if Abram prevail over the king I will follow him, but if the king prevail I will go after the king. 20 And when Terah had spoken this to the king concerning Haran his son, the king ordered Haran to be seized with Abram. 21 And they brought them both, Abram and Haran his brother, to cast them into the fire; and all the inhabitants of the land and the king's servants and princes and all the women and little ones were there, standing that day over them. 22 And the king's servants took Abram and his brother, and they stripped them of all their clothes excepting their lower garments which were upon them. 23 And they bound their hands and feet with linen cords, and the servants of the king lifted them up and cast them both into the furnace. 24 And the Lord loved Abram and he had compassion over him, and the Lord came down and delivered Abram from the fire and he was not burned. 25 But all the cords with which they bound him were burned, while Abram remained and walked about in the fire. 26 And Haran died when they had cast him into the fire, and he was burned to ashes, for his heart was not perfect with the Lord; and those men who cast him into the fire, the flame of the fire spread over them, and they were burned, and twelve men of them died. 27 And Abram walked in the midst of the fire three days and three nights, and all the servants of the king saw him walking in the fire, and they came and told the king, saying, Behold we have seen Abram walking about in the midst of the fire, and even the lower garments which are upon him are not burned, but the cord with which he was bound is burned. 28 And when the king heard their words his heart fainted and he would not believe them; so he sent other faithful princes to see this matter, and they went and saw it and told it to the king; and the king rose to go and see it, and he saw Abram walking to and fro in the midst of the fire, and he saw Haran's body burned, and the king wondered greatly. 29 And the king ordered Abram to be taken out from the fire; and his servants approached to take him out and they could not, for the fire was round about and the flame ascending toward them from the furnace. 30 And the king's servants fled from it, and the king rebuked them, saying, Make haste and bring Abram out of the fire that you shall not die. 31 And the servants of the king again approached to bring Abram out, and the flames came upon them and burned their faces so that eight of them died. 32 And when the king saw that his servants could not approach the fire lest they should be burned, the king called to Abram, O servant of the God who is in heaven, go forth from amidst the fire and come hither before me; and Abram hearkened to the voice of the king, and he went forth from the fire

and came and stood before the king. 33 And when Abram came out the king and all his servants saw Abram coming before the king, with his lower garments upon him, for they were not burned, but the cord with which he was bound was burned. 34 And the king said to Abram, How is it that thou wast not burned in the fire? 35 And Abram said to the king, The God of heaven and earth in whom I trust and who has all in his power, he delivered me from the fire into which thou didst cast me. 36 And Haran the brother of Abram was burned to ashes, and they sought for his body, and they found it consumed. 37 And Haran was eighty-two years old when he died in the fire of Casdim. And the king, princes, and inhabitants of the land, seeing that Abram was delivered from the fire, they came and bowed down to Abram. 38 And Abram said to them, Do not bow down to me, but bow down to the God of the world who made you, and serve him, and go in his ways for it is he who delivered me from out of this fire, and it is he who created the souls and spirits of all men, and formed man in his mother's womb, and brought him forth into the world, and it is he who will deliver those who trust in him from all pain. 39 And this thing seemed very wonderful in the eyes of the king and princes, that Abram was saved from the fire and that Haran was burned; and the king gave Abram many presents and he gave him his two head servants from the king's house; the name of one was Oni and the name of the other was Eliezer. 40 And all the kings, princes and servants gave Abram many gifts of silver and gold and pearl, and the king and his princes sent him away, and he went in peace. 41 And Abram went forth from the king in peace; and many of the king's servants followed him, and about three hundred men joined him. 42 And Abram returned on that day and went to his father's house, he and the men that followed him, and Abram served the Lord his God all the days of his life, and he walked in his ways and followed his law. 43 And from that day forward Abram inclined the hearts of the sons of men to serve the Lord. 44 And at that time Nahor and Abram took unto themselves wives, the daughters of their brother Haran; the wife of Nahor was Milca and the name of Abram's wife was Sarai. And Sarai, wife of Abram, was barren; she had no offspring in those days. 45 And at the expiration of two years from Abram's going out of the fire, that is in the fifty-second year of his life, behold king Nimrod sat in Babel upon the throne, and the king fell asleep and dreamed that he was standing with his troops and hosts in a valley opposite the king's furnace. 46 And he lifted up his eyes and saw a man in the likeness of Abram coming forth from the furnace, and that he came and stood before the king with his drawn sword, and then sprang to the king with his sword, when the king fled from the man, for he was afraid; and while he was running, the man threw an egg upon the king's head, and the egg became a great river. 47 And the king dreamed that all his troops sank in that river and died, and the king took flight with three men who were before him and he escaped. 48 And the king looked at these men and they were clothed in princely dresses as the garments of kings, and had the appearance and majesty of kings. 49 And while they were running, the river again turned to an egg before the king, and there came forth from the egg a young bird which came before the king, and flew at his head and plucked out the king's eye. 50 And the king was grieved at the sight, and he awoke out of his sleep and his spirit was agitated; and he felt a great terror. 51 And in the morning the king rose from his couch in fear, and he ordered all the wise men and magicians to come before him, when the king related his dream to them. 52 And a wise servant of the king, whose name was Anuki, answered the king, saying, This is nothing else but the evil of Abram and his seed which will spring up against my Lord and king in the latter days. 53 And behold the day will come when Abram and his seed and the children of his household will war with my king, and they will smite all the king's hosts and his troops. 54 And as to what thou hast said concerning three men which thou didst see like unto thyself, and which did escape, this means that only thou wilt escape with three kings from the kings of the earth who will be with thee in battle. 55 And that which thou sawest of the river which turned to an egg as at first, and the young bird plucking out thine eye, this means nothing else but the seed of Abram which will slay the king in latter days. 56 This is my king's dream, and this is its interpretation, and the dream is true, and the interpretation which thy servant has given thee is right. 57 Now therefore my king, surely thou knowest that it is now fifty-two years since thy sages saw this at the birth of Abram, and if my king will suffer Abram to live in the earth it will be to the injury of my lord and king, for all the days that Abram liveth neither thou nor thy kingdom will be established, for this was known formerly at his birth; and why will not my king slay him, that his evil may be kept from thee in latter days? 58 And Nimrod hearkened to the voice of Anuki, and he sent some of his servants in secret to go and seize Abram, and bring him before the king to suffer death. 59 And Eliezer, Abram's servant whom the king had given him, was at that time in the presence of the king, and he heard what Anuki had advised the king, and what the king had said to cause Abram's death. 60 And Eliezer said to Abram, Hasten, rise up and save thy soul, that thou mayest not die through the hands of the king, for thus did he see in a dream concerning thee, and thus did Anuki interpret it, and thus also did Anuki advise the king concerning thee. 61 And Abram hearkened to the voice of Eliezer, and Abram hastened and ran for safety to the house of Noah and his son Shem, and he concealed himself there and found a place of safety; and the king's servants came to Abram's house to seek him, but they could not find him, and they searched through out the country and he was not to be found, and they went and searched in every direction and he was not to be met with. 62 And when the king's servants could not find Abram they returned to the king, but the king's anger against Abram was stilled, as they did not find him, and the king drove from his mind this matter concerning Abram. 63 And Abram was concealed in Noah's house for one month, until the king had forgotten this matter, but Abram was still afraid of the king; and Terah came to see Abram his son secretly in the house of Noah, and Terah was very great in the eyes of the king. 64 And Abram said to his father, Dost thou not know that the king thinketh to slay me, and to annihilate my name from the earth by the advice of his wicked counsellors? 65 Now whom hast thou here and what hast thou in this land? Arise, let us go together to the land of Canaan, that we may be delivered from his hand, lest thou perish also through him in the latter days. 66 Dost thou not know or hast thou not heard, that it is not through love that Nimrod giveth thee all this honor, but it is only for his benefit that he bestoweth all this good upon thee? 67 And if he do unto thee greater good than this, surely these are only vanities of the world, for wealth and riches cannot avail in the day of wrath and anger. 68 Now therefore hearken to my voice, and let us arise and go to the land of Canaan, out of the reach of injury from Nimrod; and serve thou the Lord who created thee in the earth and it will be well with thee; and cast away all the vain things which thou pursuest. 69 And Abram ceased to speak, when Noah and his son Shem answered Terah, saying, True is the word which Abram hath said unto thee. 70 And Terah hearkened to the voice of his son Abram, and Terah did all that Abram said, for this was from the Lord, that the king should not cause Abram's death.

Jash.13

1 And Terah took his son Abram and his grandson Lot, the son of Haran, and Sarai his daughter-in-law, the wife of his son Abram, and

all the souls of his household and went with them from Ur Casdim to go to the land of Canaan. And when they came as far as the land of Haran they remained there, for it was exceedingly good land for pasture, and of sufficient extent for those who accompanied them. 2 And the people of the land of Haran saw that Abram was good and upright with God and men, and that the Lord his God was with him, and some of the people of the land of Haran came and joined Abram, and he taught them the instruction of the Lord and his ways; and these men remained with Abram in his house and they adhered to him. 3 And Abram remained in the land three years, and at the expiration of three years the Lord appeared to Abram and said to him; I am the Lord who brought thee forth from Ur Casdim, and delivered thee from the hands of all thine enemies. 4 And now therefore if thou wilt hearken to my voice and keep my commandments, my statutes and my laws, then will I cause thy enemies to fall before thee, and I will multiply thy seed like the stars of heaven, and I will send my blessing upon all the works of thy hands, and thou shalt lack nothing. 5 Arise now, take thy wife and all belonging to thee and go to the land of Canaan and remain there, and I will there be unto thee for a God, and I will bless thee. And Abram rose and took his wife and all belonging to him, and he went to the land of Canaan as the Lord had told him; and Abram was fifty years old when he went from Haran. 6 And Abram came to the land of Canaan and dwelt in the midst of the city, and he there pitched his tent amongst the children of Canaan, inhabitants of the land. 7 And the Lord appeared to Abram when he came to the land of Canaan, and said to him, This is the land which I gave unto thee and to thy seed after thee forever, and I will make thy seed like the stars of heaven, and I will give unto thy seed for an inheritance all the lands which thou seest. 8 And Abram built an altar in the place where God had spoken to him, and Abram there called upon the name of the Lord. 9 At that time, at the end of three years of Abram's dwelling in the land of Canaan, in that year Noah died, which was the fifty-eighth year of the life of Abram; and all the days that Noah lived were nine hundred and fifty years and he died. 10 And Abram dwelt in the land of Canaan, he, his wife, and all belonging to him, and all those that accompanied him, together with those that joined him from the people of the land; but Nahor, Abram's brother, and Terah his father, and Lot the son of Haran and all belonging to them dwelt in Haran. 11 In the fifth year of Abram's dwelling in the land of Canaan the people of Sodom and Gomorrah and all the cities of the plain revolted from the power of Chedorlaomer, king of Elam; for all the kings of the cities of the plain had served Chedorlaomer for twelve years, and given him a yearly tax, but in those days in the thirteenth year, they rebelled against him. 12 And in the tenth year of Abram's dwelling in the land of Canaan there was war between Nimrod king of Shinar and Chedorlaomer king of Elam, and Nimrod came to fight with Chedorlaomer and to subdue him. 13 For Chedorlaomer was at that time one of the princes of the hosts of Nimrod, and when all the people at the tower were dispersed and those that remained were also scattered upon the face of the earth, Chedorlaomer went to the land of Elam and reigned over it and rebelled against his lord. 14 And in those days when Nimrod saw that the cities of the plain had rebelled, he came with pride and anger to war with Chedorlaomer, and Nimrod assembled all his princes and subjects, about seven hundred thousand men, and went against Chedorlaomer, and Chedorlaomer went out to meet him with five thousand men, and they prepared for battle in the valley of Babel which is between Elam and Shinar. 15 And all those kings fought there, and Nimrod and his people were smitten before the people of Chedorlaomer, and there fell from Nimrod's men about six hundred thousand, and Mardon the king's son fell amongst them. ¹⁶ And Nimrod fled and returned in shame and disgrace to his land, and he was under subjection to Chedorlaomer for a long time, and Chedorlaomer returned to his land and sent princes of his host to the kings that dwelt around him, to Arioch king of Elasar, and to Tidal king of Goyim, and made a covenant with them, and they were all obedient to his commands. ¹⁷ And it was in the fifteenth year of Abram's dwelling in the land of Canaan, which is the seventieth year of the life of Abram, and the Lord appeared to Abram in that year and he said to him, I am the Lord who brought thee out from Ur Casdim to give thee this land for an inheritance. ¹⁸ Now therefore walk before me and be perfect and keep my commands, for to thee and to thy seed I will give this land for an inheritance, from the river Mitzraim unto the great river Euphrates. ¹⁹ And thou shalt come to thy fathers in peace and in good age, and the fourth generation shall return here in this land and shall inherit it forever; and Abram built an altar, and he called upon the name of the Lord who appeared to him, and he brought up sacrifices upon the altar to the Lord. ²⁰ At that time Abram returned and went to Haran to see his father and mother, and his father's household, and Abram and his wife and all belonging to him returned to Haran, and Abram dwelt in Haran five years. ²¹ And many of the people of Haran, about seventy-two men, followed Abram and Abram taught them the instruction of the Lord and his ways, and he taught them to know the Lord. ²² In those days the Lord appeared to Abram in Haran, and he said to him, Behold, I spoke unto thee these twenty years back saying, ²³ Go forth from thy land, from thy birth-place and from thy father's house, to the land which I have shown thee to give it to thee and to thy children, for there in that land will I bless thee, and make thee a great nation, and make thy name great, and in thee shall the families of the earth be blessed. ²⁴ Now therefore arise, go forth from this place, thou, thy wife, and all belonging to thee, also every one born in thy house and all the souls thou hast made in Haran, and bring them out with thee from here, and rise to return to the land of Canaan. ²⁵ And Abram arose and took his wife Sarai and all belonging to him and all that were born to him in his house and the souls which they had made in Haran, and they came out to go to the land of Canaan. ²⁶ And Abram went and returned to the land of Canaan, according to the word of the Lord. And Lot the son of his brother Haran went with him, and Abram was seventy-five years old when he went forth from Haran to return to the land of Canaan. ²⁷ And he came to the land of Canaan according to the word of the Lord to Abram, and he pitched his tent and he dwelt in the plain of Mamre, and with him was Lot his brother's son, and all belonging to him. ²⁸ And the Lord again appeared to Abram and said, To thy seed will I give this land; and he there built an altar to the Lord who appeared to him, which is still to this day in the plains of Mamre.

Jash.14

¹ In those days there was in the land of Shinar a wise man who had understanding in all wisdom, and of a beautiful appearance, but he was poor and indigent; his name was Rikayon and he was hard set to support himself. ² And he resolved to go to Egypt, to Oswiris the son of Anom king of Egypt, to show the king his wisdom; for perhaps he might find grace in his sight, to raise him up and give him maintenance; and Rikayon did so. ³ And when Rikayon came to Egypt he asked the inhabitants of Egypt concerning the king, and the inhabitants of Egypt told him the custom of the king of Egypt, for it was then the custom of the king of Egypt that he went from his royal palace and was seen abroad only one day in the year, and after that the king would return to his palace to remain there. ⁴ And on the day when the king went forth he passed judgment in the land, and every one having a suit came before the king that day to obtain

his request. ⁵ And when Rikayon heard of the custom in Egypt and that he could not come into the presence of the king, he grieved greatly and was very sorrowful. ⁶ And in the evening Rikayon went out and found a house in ruins, formerly a bake house in Egypt, and he abode there all night in bitterness of soul and pinched with hunger, and sleep was removed from his eyes. ⁷ And Rikayon considered within himself what he should do in the town until the king made his appearance, and how he might maintain himself there. ⁸ And he rose in the morning and walked about, and met in his way those who sold vegetables and various sorts of seed with which they supplied the inhabitants. ⁹ And Rikayon wished to do the same in order to get a maintenance in the city, but he was unacquainted with the custom of the people, and he was like a blind man among them. ¹⁰ And he went and obtained vegetables to sell them for his support, and the rabble assembled about him and ridiculed him, and took his vegetables from him and left him nothing. ¹¹ And he rose up from there in bitterness of soul, and went sighing to the bake house in which he had remained all the night before, and he slept there the second night. ¹² And on that night again he reasoned within himself how he could save himself from starvation, and he devised a scheme how to act. ¹³ And he rose up in the morning and acted ingeniously, and went and hired thirty strong men of the rabble, carrying their war instruments in their hands, and he led them to the top of the Egyptian sepulchre, and he placed them there. ¹⁴ And he commanded them, saying, Thus saith the king, Strengthen yourselves and be valiant men, and let no man be buried here until two hundred pieces of silver be given, and then he may be buried; and those men did according to the order of Rikayon to the people of Egypt the whole of that year. ¹⁵ And in eight months time Rikayon and his men gathered great riches of silver and gold, and Rikayon took a great quantity of horses and other animals, and he hired more men, and he gave them horses and they remained with him. ¹⁶ And when the year came round, at the time the king went forth into the town, all the inhabitants of Egypt assembled together to speak to him concerning the work of Rikayon and his men. ¹⁷ And the king went forth on the appointed day, and all the Egyptians came before him and cried unto him, saying, ¹⁸ May the king live forever. What is this thing thou doest in the town to thy servants, not to suffer a dead body to be buried until so much silver and gold be given? Was there ever the like unto this done in the whole earth, from the days of former kings yea even from the days of Adam, unto this day, that the dead should not be buried only for a set price? ¹⁹ We know it to be the custom of kings to take a yearly tax from the living, but thou dost not only do this, but from the dead also thou exactest a tax day by day. ²⁰ Now, O king, we can no more bear this, for the whole city is ruined on this account, and dost thou not know it? ²¹ And when the king heard all that they had spoken he was very wroth, and his anger burned within him at this affair, for he had known nothing of it. ²² And the king said, Who and where is he that dares to do this wicked thing in my land without my command? Surely you will tell me. ²³ And they told him all the works of Rikayon and his men, and the king's anger was aroused, and he ordered Rikayon and his men to be brought before him. ²⁴ And Rikayon took about a thousand children, sons and daughters, and clothed them in silk and embroidery, and he set them upon horses and sent them to the king by means of his men, and he also took a great quantity of silver and gold and precious stones, and a strong and beautiful horse, as a present for the king, with which he came before the king and bowed down to the earth before him; and the king, his servants and all the inhabitants of Egypt wondered at the work of Rikayon, and they saw his riches and the present that he had brought to the king. ²⁵ And it greatly pleased the king and he wondered at it; and when Rikayon sat before him the king asked him concerning all his works, and Rikayon spoke all his words wisely before the king, his servants and all the inhabitants of Egypt. 26 And when the king heard the words of Rikayon and his wisdom, Rikayon found grace in his sight, and he met with grace and kindness from all the servants of the king and from all the inhabitants of Egypt, on account of his wisdom and excellent speeches, and from that time they loved him exceedingly. 27 And the king answered and said to Rikayon, Thy name shall no more be called Rikayon but Pharaoh shall be thy name, since thou didst exact a tax from the dead; and he called his name Pharaoh. 28 And the king and his subjects loved Rikayon for his wisdom, and they consulted with all the inhabitants of Egypt to make him prefect under the king. 29 And all the inhabitants of Egypt and its wise men did so, and it was made a law in Egypt. 30 And they made Rikayon Pharaoh prefect under Oswiris king of Egypt, and Rikayon Pharaoh governed over Egypt, daily administering justice to the whole city, but Oswiris the king would judge the people of the land one day in the year, when he went out to make his appearance. 31 And Rikayon Pharaoh cunningly usurped the government of Egypt, and he exacted a tax from all the inhabitants of Egypt. 32 And all the inhabitants of Egypt greatly loved Rikayon Pharaoh, and they made a decree to call every king that should reign over them and their seed in Egypt, Pharaoh. 33 Therefore all the kings that reigned in Egypt from that time forward were called Pharaoh unto this day.

Jash.15

1 And in that year there was a heavy famine throughout the land of Canaan, and the inhabitants of the land could not remain on account of the famine for it was very grievous. 2 And Abram and all belonging to him rose and went down to Egypt on account of the famine, and when they were at the brook Mitzraim they remained there some time to rest from the fatigue of the road. 3 And Abram and Sarai were walking at the border of the brook Mitzraim, and Abram beheld his wife Sarai that she was very beautiful. 4 And Abram said to his wife Sarai, Since God has created thee with such a beautiful countenance, I am afraid of the Egyptians lest they should slay me and take thee away, for the fear of God is not in these places. 5 Surely then thou shalt do this, Say thou art my sister to all that may ask thee, in order that it may be well with me, and that we may live and not be put to death. 6 And Abram commanded the same to all those that came with him to Egypt on account of the famine; also his nephew Lot he commanded, saying, If the Egyptians ask thee concerning Sarai say she is the sister of Abram. 7 And yet with all these orders Abram did not put confidence in them, but he took Sarai and placed her in a chest and concealed it amongst their vessels, for Abram was greatly concerned about Sarai on account of the wickedness of the Egyptians. 8 And Abram and all belonging to him rose up from the brook Mitzraim and came to Egypt; and they had scarcely entered the gates of the city when the guards stood up to them saying, Give tithe to the king from what you have, and then you may come into the town; and Abram and those that were with him did so. 9 And Abram with the people that were with him came to Egypt, and when they came they brought the chest in which Sarai was concealed and the Egyptians saw the chest. 10 And the king's servants approached Abram, saying, What hast thou here in this chest which we have not seen? Now open thou the chest and give tithe to the king of all that it contains. 11 And Abram said, This chest I will not open, but all you demand upon it I will give. And Pharaoh's officers answered Abram, saying, It is a chest of precious stones, give us the tenth thereof. 12 Abram said, All that you desire I will give, but you must not open the chest. 13 And the king's officers pressed Abram, and they reached the chest and opened it with force,

and they saw, and behold a beautiful woman was in the chest. 14 And when the officers of the king beheld Sarai they were struck with admiration at her beauty, and all the princes and servants of Pharaoh assembled to see Sarai, for she was very beautiful. And the king's officers ran and told Pharaoh all that they had seen, and they praised Sarai to the king; and Pharaoh ordered her to be brought, and the woman came before the king. 15 And Pharaoh beheld Sarai and she pleased him exceedingly, and he was struck with her beauty, and the king rejoiced greatly on her account, and made presents to those who brought him the tidings concerning her. 16 And the woman was then brought to Pharaoh's house, and Abram grieved on account of his wife, and he prayed to the Lord to deliver her from the hands of Pharaoh. 17 And Sarai also prayed at that time and said, O Lord God thou didst tell my Lord Abram to go from his land and from his father's house to the land of Canaan, and thou didst promise to do well with him if he would perform thy commands; now behold we have done that which thou didst command us, and we left our land and our families, and we went to a strange land and to a people whom we have not known before. 18 And we came to this land to avoid the famine, and this evil accident has befallen me; now therefore, O Lord God, deliver us and save us from the hand of this oppressor, and do well with me for the sake of thy mercy. 19 And the Lord hearkened to the voice of Sarai, and the Lord sent an angel to deliver Sarai from the power of Pharaoh. 20 And the king came and sat before Sarai and behold an angel of the Lord was standing over them, and he appeared to Sarai and said to her, Do not fear, for the Lord has heard thy prayer. 21 And the king approached Sarai and said to her, What is that man to thee who brought thee hither? and she said, He is my brother. 22 And the king said, It is incumbent upon us to make him great, to elevate him and to do unto him all the good which thou shalt command us; and at that time the king sent to Abram silver and gold and precious stones in abundance, together with cattle, men servants and maid servants; and the king ordered Abram to be brought, and he sat in the court of the king's house, and the king greatly exalted Abram on that night. 23 And the king approached to speak to Sarai, and he reached out his hand to touch her, when the angel smote him heavily, and he was terrified and he refrained from reaching to her. 24 And when the king came near to Sarai, the angel smote him to the ground, and acted thus to him the whole night, and the king was terrified. 25 And the angel on that night smote heavily all the servants of the king, and his whole household, on account of Sarai, and there was a great lamentation that night amongst the people of Pharaoh's house. 26 And Pharaoh, seeing the evil that befell him, said, Surely on account of this woman has this thing happened to me, and he removed himself at some distance from her and spoke pleasing words to her. 27 And the king said to Sarai, Tell me I pray thee concerning the man with whom thou camest here; and Sarai said, This man is my husband, and I said to thee that he was my brother for I was afraid, lest thou shouldst put him to death through wickedness. 28 And the king kept away from Sarai, and the plagues of the angel of the Lord ceased from him and his household; and Pharaoh knew that he was smitten on account of Sarai, and the king was greatly astonished at this. 29 And in the morning the king called for Abram and said to him, What is this thou hast done to me? Why didst thou say, She is my sister, owing to which I took her unto me for a wife, and this heavy plague has therefore come upon me and my household. 30 Now therefore here is thy wife, take her and go from our land lest we all die on her account. And Pharaoh took more cattle, men servants and maid servants, and silver and gold, to give to Abram, and he returned unto him Sarai his wife. 31 And the king took a maiden whom he begat by his concubines, and he gave her to Sarai for a handmaid. 32 And the king said to his daughter, It is better for thee my daughter to be a handmaid in this man's house than to be mistress in my house, after we have beheld the evil that befell us on account of this woman. 33 And Abram arose, and he and all belonging to him went away from Egypt; and Pharaoh ordered some of his men to accompany him and all that went with him. 34 And Abram returned to the land of Canaan, to the place where he had made the altar, where he at first had pitched his tent. 35 And Lot the son of Haran, Abram's brother, had a heavy stock of cattle, flocks and herds and tents, for the Lord was bountiful to them on account of Abram. 36 And when Abram was dwelling in the land the herdsmen of Lot quarrelled with the herdsmen of Abram, for their property was too great for them to remain together in the land, and the land could not bear them on account of their cattle. 37 And when Abram's herdsmen went to feed their flock they would not go into the fields of the people of the land, but the cattle of Lot's herdsmen did otherwise, for they were suffered to feed in the fields of the people of the land. 38 And the people of the land saw this occurrence daily, and they came to Abram and quarrelled with him on account of Lot's herdsmen. 39 And Abram said to Lot, What is this thou art doing to me, to make me despicable to the inhabitants of the land, that thou orderest thy herdsman to feed thy cattle in the fields of other people? Dost thou not know that I am a stranger in this land amongst the children of Canaan, and why wilt thou do this unto me? 40 And Abram quarrelled daily with Lot on account of this, but Lot would not listen to Abram, and he continued to do the same and the inhabitants of the land came and told Abram. 41 And Abram said unto Lot, How long wilt thou be to me for a stumbling block with the inhabitants of the land? Now I beseech thee let there be no more quarrelling between us, for we are kinsmen. 42 But I pray thee separate from me, go and choose a place where thou mayest dwell with thy cattle and all belonging to thee, but Keep thyself at a distance from me, thou and thy household. 43 And be not afraid in going from me, for if any one do an injury to thee, let me know and I will avenge thy cause from him, only remove from me. 44 And when Abram had spoken all these words to Lot, then Lot arose and lifted up his eyes toward the plain of Jordan. 45 And he saw that the whole of this place was well watered, and good for man as well as affording pasture for the cattle. 46 And Lot went from Abram to that place, and he there pitched his tent and he dwelt in Sodom, and they were separated from each other. 47 And Abram dwelt in the plain of Mamre, which is in Hebron, and he pitched his tent there, and Abram remained in that place many years.

Jash.16

1 At that time Chedorlaomer king of Elam sent to all the neighboring kings, to Nimrod, king of Shinar who was then under his power, and to Tidal, king of Goyim, and to Arioch, king of Elasar, with whom he made a covenant, saying, Come up to me and assist me, that we may smite all the towns of Sodom and its inhabitants, for they have rebelled against me these thirteen years. 2 And these four kings went up with all their camps, about eight hundred thousand men, and they went as they were, and smote every man they found in their road. 3 And the five kings of Sodom and Gomorrah, Shinab king of Admah, Shemeber king of Zeboyim, Bera king of Sodom, Bersha king of Gomorrah, and Bela king of Zoar, went out to meet them, and they all joined together in the valley of Siddim. 4 And these nine kings made war in the valley of Siddim; and the kings of Sodom and Gomorrah were smitten before the kings of Elam. 5 And the valley of Siddim was full of lime pits and the kings of Elam pursued the kings of Sodom, and the kings of Sodom with their camps fled and fell into the lime pits, and all that remained went to the mountain for safety, and the five kings of Elam came after them and pursued

229

them to the gates of Sodom, and they took all that there was in Sodom. 6 And they plundered all the cities of Sodom and Gomorrah, and they also took Lot, Abram's brother's son, and his property, and they seized all the goods of the cities of Sodom, and they went away; and Unic, Abram's servant, who was in the battle, saw this, and told Abram all that the kings had done to the cities of Sodom, and that Lot was taken captive by them. 7 And Abram heard this, and he rose up with about three hundred and eighteen men that were with him, and he that night pursued these kings and smote them, and they all fell before Abram and his men, and there was none remaining but the four kings who fled, and they went each his own road. 8 And Abram recovered all the property of Sodom, and he also recovered Lot and his property, his wives and little ones and all belonging to him, so that Lot lacked nothing. 9 And when he returned from smiting these kings, he and his men passed the valley of Siddim where the kings had made war together. 10 And Bera king of Sodom, and the rest of his men that were with him, went out from the lime pits into which they had fallen, to meet Abram and his men. 11 And Adonizedek king of Jerusalem, the same was Shem, went out with his men to meet Abram and his people, with bread and wine, and they remained together in the valley of Melech. 12 And Adonizedek blessed Abram, and Abram gave him a tenth from all that he had brought from the spoil of his enemies, for Adonizedek was a priest before God. 13 And all the kings of Sodom and Gomorrah who were there, with their servants, approached Abram and begged of him to return them their servants whom he had made captive, and to take unto himself all the property. 14 And Abram answered the kings of Sodom, saying, As the Lord liveth who created heaven and earth, and who redeemed my soul from all affliction, and who delivered me this day from my enemies, and gave them into my hand, I will not take anything belonging to you, that you may not boast tomorrow, saying, Abram became rich from our property that he saved. 15 For the Lord my God in whom I trust said unto me, Thou shalt lack nothing, for I will bless thee in all the works of thy hands. 16 And now therefore behold, here is all belonging to you, take it and go; as the Lord liveth I will not take from you from a living soul down to a shoetie or thread, excepting the expense of the food of those who went out with me to battle, as also the portions of the men who went with me, Anar, Ashcol, and Mamre, they and their men, as well as those also who had remained to watch the baggage, they shall take their portion of the spoil. 17 And the kings of Sodom gave Abram according to all that he had said, and they pressed him to take of whatever he chose, but he would not. 18 And he sent away the kings of Sodom and the remainder of their men, and he gave them orders about Lot, and they went to their respective places. 19 And Lot, his brother's son, he also sent away with his property, and he went with them, and Lot returned to his home, to Sodom, and Abram and his people returned to their home to the plains of Mamre, which is in Hebron. 20 At that time the Lord again appeared to Abram in Hebron, and he said to him, Do not fear, thy reward is very great before me, for I will not leave thee, until I shall have multiplied thee, and blessed thee and made thy seed like the stars in heaven, which cannot be measured nor numbered. 21 And I will give unto thy seed all these lands that thou seest with thine eyes, to them will I give them for an inheritance forever, only be strong and do not fear, walk before me and be perfect. 22 And in the seventy-eighth year of the life of Abram, in that year died Reu, the son of Peleg, and all the days of Reu were two hundred and thirty-nine years, and he died. 23 And Sarai, the daughter of Haran, Abram's wife, was still barren in those days; she did not bear to Abram either son or daughter. 24 And when she saw that she bare no children she took her handmaid Hagar, whom

Pharaoh had given her, and she gave her to Abram her husband for a wife. 25 For Hagar learned all the ways of Sarai as Sarai taught her, she was not in any way deficient in following her good ways. 26 And Sarai said to Abram, Behold here is my handmaid Hagar, go to her that she may bring forth upon my knees, that I may also obtain children through her. 27 And at the end of ten years of Abram's dwelling in the land of Canaan, which is the eighty-fifth year of Abram's life, Sarai gave Hagar unto him. 28 And Abram hearkened to the voice of his wife Sarai, and he took his handmaid Hagar and Abram came to her and she conceived. 29 And when Hagar saw that she had conceived she rejoiced greatly, and her mistress was despised in her eyes, and she said within herself, This can only be that I am better before God than Sarai my mistress, for all the days that my mistress has been with my lord, she did not conceive, but me the Lord has caused in so short a time to conceive by him. 30 And when Sarai saw that Hagar had conceived by Abram, Sarai was jealous of her handmaid, and Sarai said within herself, This is surely nothing else but that she must be better than I am. 31 And Sarai said unto Abram, My wrong be upon thee, for at the time when thou didst pray before the Lord for children why didst thou not pray on my account, that the Lord should give me seed from thee? 32 And when I speak to Hagar in thy presence, she despiseth my words, because she has conceived, and thou wilt say nothing to her; may the Lord judge between me and thee for what thou hast done to me. 33 And Abram said to Sarai, Behold thy handmaid is in thy hand, do unto her as it may seem good in thy eyes; and Sarai afflicted her, and Hagar fled from her to the wilderness. 34 And an angel of the Lord found her in the place where she had fled, by a well, and he said to her, Do not fear, for I will multiply thy seed, for thou shalt bear a son and thou shalt call his name Ishmael; now then return to Sarai thy mistress, and submit thyself under her hands. 35 And Hagar called the place of that well Beer-lahai-roi, it is between Kadesh and the wilderness of Bered. 36 And Hagar at that time returned to her master's house, and at the end of days Hagar bare a son to Abram, and Abram called his name Ishmael; and Abram was eighty-six years old when he begat him.

Jash.17

1 And in those days, in the ninety-first year of the life of Abram, the children of Chittim made war with the children of Tubal, for when the Lord had scattered the sons of men upon the face of the earth, the children of Chittim went and embodied themselves in the plain of Canopia, and they built themselves cities there and dwelt by the river Tibreu. 2 And the children of Tubal dwelt in Tuscanah, and their boundaries reached the river Tibreu, and the children of Tubal built a city in Tuscanan, and they called the name Sabinah, after the name of Sabinah son of Tubal their father, and they dwelt there unto this day. 3 And it was at that time the children of Chittim made war with the children of Tubal, and the children of Tubal were smitten before the children of Chittim, and the children of Chittim caused three hundred and seventy men to fall from the children of Tubal. 4 And at that time the children of Tubal swore to the children of Chittim, saying, You shall not intermarry amongst us, and no man shall give his daughter to any of the sons of Chittim. 5 For all the daughters of Tubal were in those days fair, for no women were then found in the whole earth so fair as the daughters of Tubal. 6 And all who delighted in the beauty of women went to the daughters of Tubal and took wives from them, and the sons of men, kings and princes, who greatly delighted in the beauty of women, took wives in those days from the daughters of Tubal. 7 And at the end of three years after the children of Tubal had sworn to the children of Chittim not to give them their daughters for wives, about twenty men of the children of Chittim went to take some of the daughters of Tubal, but they found none. 8 For the children of Tubal kept their oaths not to intermarry with them, and they would not break their oaths. 9 And in the days of harvest the children of Tubal went into their fields to get in their harvest, when the young men of Chittim assembled and went to the city of Sabinah, and each man took a young woman from the daughters of Tubal, and they came to their cities. 10 And the children of Tubal heard of it and they went to make war with them, and they could not prevail over them, for the mountain was exceedingly high from them, and when they saw they could not prevail over them they returned to their land. 11 And at the revolution of the year the children of Tubal went and hired about ten thousand men from those cities that were near them, and they went to war with the children of Chittim. 12 And the children of Tubal went to war with the children of Chittim, to destroy their land and to distress them, and in this engagement the children of Tubal prevailed over the children of Chittim, and the children of Chittim, seeing that they were greatly distressed, lifted up the children which they had had by the daughters of Tubal, upon the wall which had been built, to be before the eyes of the children of Tubal. 13 And the children of Chittim said to them, Have you come to make war with your own sons and daughters, and have we not been considered your flesh and bones from that time till now? 14 And when the children of Tubal heard this they ceased to make war with the children of Chittim, and they went away. 15 And they returned to their cities, and the children of Chittim at that time assembled and built two cities by the sea, and they called one Purtu and the other Ariza. 16 And Abram the son of Terah was then ninety-nine years old. 17 At that time the Lord appeared to him and he said to him, I will make my covenant between me and thee, and I will greatly multiply thy seed, and this is the covenant which I make between me and thee, that every male child be circumcised, thou and thy seed after thee. 18 At eight days old shall it be circumcised, and this covenant shall be in your flesh for an everlasting covenant. 19 And now therefore thy name shall no more be called Abram but Abraham, and thy wife shall no more be called Sarai but Sarah. 20 For I will bless you both, and I will multiply your seed after you that you shall become a great nation, and kings shall come forth from you.

Jash.18

1 And Abraham rose and did all that God had ordered him, and he took the men of his household and those bought with his money, and he circumcised them as the Lord had commanded him. 2 And there was not one left whom he did not circumcise, and Abraham and his son Ishmael were circumcised in the flesh of their foreskin; thirteen years old was Ishmael when he was circumcised in the flesh of his foreskin. 3 And in the third day Abraham went out of his tent and sat at the door to enjoy the heat of the sun, during the pain of his flesh. 4 And the Lord appeared to him in the plain of Mamre, and sent three of his ministering angels to visit him, and he was sitting at the door of the tent, and he lifted his eyes and saw, and lo three men were coming from a distance, and he rose up and ran to meet them, and he bowed down to them and brought them into his house. 5 And he said to them, If now I have found favor in your sight, turn in and eat a morsel of bread; and he pressed them, and they turned in and he gave them water and they washed their feet, and he placed them under a tree at the door of the tent. 6 And Abraham ran and took a calf, tender and good, and he hastened to kill it, and gave it to his servant Eliezer to dress. 7 And Abraham came to Sarah into the tent, and he said to her, Make ready quickly three measures of fine meal, knead it and make cakes to cover the pot containing the meat, and she did so. 8 And Abraham hastened and brought before them butter and milk, beef and mutton, and gave it before them to eat before the flesh of the calf was sufficiently

done, and they did eat. ⁹ And when they had done eating one of them said to him, I will return to thee according to the time of life, and Sarah thy wife shall have a son. ¹⁰ And the men afterward departed and went their ways, to the places to which they were sent. ¹¹ In those days all the people of Sodom and Gomorrah, and of the whole five cities, were exceedingly wicked and sinful against the Lord and they provoked the Lord with their abominations, and they strengthened in aging abominably and scornfully before the Lord, and their wickedness and crimes were in those days great before the Lord. ¹² And they had in their land a very extensive valley, about half a day's walk, and in it there were fountains of water and a great deal of herbage surrounding the water. ¹³ And all the people of Sodom and Gomorrah went there four times in the year, with their wives and children and all belonging to them, and they rejoiced there with timbrels and dances. ¹⁴ And in the time of rejoicing they would all rise and lay hold of their neighbor's wives, and some, the virgin daughters of their neighbors, and they enjoyed them, and each man saw his wife and daughter in the hands of his neighbor and did not say a word. ¹⁵ And they did so from morning to night, and they afterward returned home each man to his house and each woman to her tent; so they always did four times in the year. ¹⁶ Also when a stranger came into their cities and brought goods which he had purchased with a view to dispose of there, the people of these cities would assemble, men, women and children, young and old, and go to the man and take his goods by force, giving a little to each man until there was an end to all the goods of the owner which he had brought into the land. ¹⁷ And if the owner of the goods quarreled with them, saying, What is this work which you have done to me, then they would approach to him one by one, and each would show him the little which he took and taunt him, saying, I only took that little which thou didst give me; and when he heard this from them all, he would arise and go from them in sorrow and bitterness of soul, when they would all arise and go after him, and drive him out of the city with great noise and tumult. ¹⁸ And there was a man from the country of Elam who was leisurely going on the road, seated upon his ass, which carried a fine mantle of divers colors, and the mantle was bound with a cord upon the ass. ¹⁹ And the man was on his journey passing through the street of Sodom when the sun set in the evening, and he remained there in order to abide during the night, but no one would let him into his house; and at that time there was in Sodom a wicked and mischievous man, one skillful to do evil, and his name was Hedad. ²⁰ And he lifted up his eyes and saw the traveler in the street of the city, and he came to him and said, Whence comest thou and whither dost thou go? ²¹ And the man said to him, I am traveling from Hebron to Elam where I belong, and as I passed the sun set and no one would suffer me to enter his house, though I had bread and water and also straw and provender for my ass, and am short of nothing. ²² And Hedad answered and said to him, All that thou shalt want shall be supplied by me, but in the street thou shalt not abide all night. ²³ And Hedad brought him to his house, and he took off the mantle from the ass with the cord, and brought them to his house, and he gave the ass straw and provender whilst the traveler ate and drank in Hedad's house, and he abode there that night. ²⁴ And in the morning the traveler rose up early to continue his journey, when Hedad said to him, Wait, comfort thy heart with a morsel of bread and then go, and the man did so; and he remained with him, and they both ate and drank together during the day, when the man rose up to go. ²⁵ And Hedad said to him, Behold now the day is declining, thou hadst better remain all night that thy heart may be comforted; and he pressed him so that he tarried there all night, and on the second day he rose up early to go away, when Hedad pressed him, saying, Comfort thy

231

heart with a morsel of bread and then go, and he remained and ate with him also the second day, and then the man rose up to continue his journey. ²⁶ And Hedad said to him, Behold now the day is declining, remain with me to comfort thy heart and in the morning rise up early and go thy way. ²⁷ And the man would not remain, but rose and saddled his ass, and whilst he was saddling his ass the wife of Hedad said to her husband, Behold this man has remained with us for two days eating and drinking and he has given us nothing, and now shall he go away from us without giving anything? and Hedad said to her, Be silent. ²⁸ And the man saddled his ass to go, and he asked Hedad to give him the cord and mantle to tie it upon the ass. ²⁹ And Hedad said to him, What sayest thou? And he said to him, That thou my lord shalt give me the cord and the mantle made with divers colors which thou didst conceal with thee in thy house to take care of it. ³⁰ And Hedad answered the man, saying, This is the interpretation of thy dream, the cord which thou didst see, means that thy life will be lengthened out like a cord, and having seen the mantle colored with all sorts of colors, means that thou shalt have a vineyard in which thou wilt plant trees of all fruits. ³¹ And the traveler answered, saying, Not so my lord, for I was awake when I gave thee the cord and also a mantle woven with different colors, which thou didst take off the ass to put them by for me; and Hedad answered and said, Surely I have told thee the interpretation of thy dream and it is a good dream, and this is the interpretation thereof. ³² Now the sons of men give me four pieces of silver, which is my charge for interpreting dreams, and of thee only I require three pieces of silver. ³³ And the man was provoked at the words of Hedad, and he cried bitterly, and he brought Hedad to Serak judge of Sodom. ³⁴ And the man laid his cause before Serak the judge, when Hedad replied, saying, It is not so, but thus the matter stands; and the judge said to the traveler, This man Hedad telleth thee truth, for he is famed in the cities for the accurate interpretation of dreams. ³⁵ And the man cried at the word of the judge, and he said, Not so my Lord, for it was in the day that I gave him the cord and mantle which was upon the ass, in order to put them by in his house; and they both disputed before the judge, the one saying, Thus the matter was, and the other declaring otherwise. ³⁶ And Hedad said to the man, Give me four pieces of silver that I charge for my interpretations of dreams; I will not make any allowance; and give me the expense of the four meals that thou didst eat in my house. ³⁷ And the man said to Hedad, Truly I will pay thee for what I ate in thy house, only give me the cord and mantle which thou didst conceal in thy house. ³⁸ And Hedad replied before the judge and said to the man, Did I not tell thee the interpretation of thy dream? the cord means that thy days shall be prolonged like a cord, and the mantle, that thou wilt have a vineyard in which thou wilt plant all kinds of fruit trees. ³⁹ This is the proper interpretation of thy dream, now give me the four pieces of silver that I require as a compensation, for I will make thee no allowance. ⁴⁰ And the man cried at the words of Hedad and they both quarreled before the judge, and the judge gave orders to his servants, who drove them rashly from the house. ⁴¹ And they went away quarreling from the judge, when the people of Sodom heard them, and they gathered about them and they exclaimed against the stranger, and they drove him rashly from the city. ⁴² And the man continued his journey upon his ass with bitterness of soul, lamenting and weeping. ⁴³ And whilst he was going along he wept at what had happened to him in the corrupt city of Sodom.

Jash.19

¹ And the cities of Sodom had four judges to four cities, and these were their names, Serak in the city of Sodom, Sharkad in Gomorrah, Zabnac in Admah, and Menon in Zeboyim. ² And Eliezer

Abraham's servant applied to them different names, and he converted Serak to Shakra, Sharkad to Shakrura, Zebnac to Kezobim, and Menon to Matzlodin. 3 And by desire of their four judges the people of Sodom and Gomorrah had beds erected in the streets of the cities, and if a man came to these places they laid hold of him and brought him to one of their beds, and by force made him to lie in them. 4 And as he lay down, three men would stand at his head and three at his feet, and measure him by the length of the bed, and if the man was less than the bed these six men would stretch him at each end, and when he cried out to them they would not answer him. 5 And if he was longer than the bed they would draw together the two sides of the bed at each end, until the man had reached the gates of death. 6 And if he continued to cry out to them, they would answer him, saying, Thus shall it be done to a man that cometh into our land. 7 And when men heard all these things that the people of the cities of Sodom did, they refrained from coming there. 8 And when a poor man came to their land they would give him silver and gold, and cause a proclamation in the whole city not to give him a morsel of bread to eat, and if the stranger should remain there some days, and die from hunger, not having been able to obtain a morsel of bread, then at his death all the people of the city would come and take their silver and gold which they had given to him. 9 And those that could recognize the silver or gold which they had given him took it back, and at his death they also stripped him of his garments, and they would fight about them, and he that prevailed over his neighbor took them. 10 They would after that carry him and bury him under some of the shrubs in the deserts; so they did all the days to any one that came to them and died in their land. 11 And in the course of time Sarah sent Eliezer to Sodom, to see Lot and inquire after his welfare. 12 And Eliezer went to Sodom, and he met a man of Sodom fighting with a stranger, and the man of Sodom stripped the poor man of all his clothes and went away. 13 And this poor man cried to Eliezer and supplicated his favor on account of what the man of Sodom had done to him. 14 And he said to him, Why dost thou act thus to the poor man who came to thy land? 15 And the man of Sodom answered Eliezer, saying, Is this man thy brother, or have the people of Sodom made thee a judge this day, that thou speakest about this man? 16 And Eliezer strove with the man of Sodom on account of the poor man, and when Eliezer approached to recover the poor man's clothes from the man of Sodom, he hastened and with a stone smote Eliezer in the forehead. 17 And the blood flowed copiously from Eliezer's forehead, and when the man saw the blood he caught hold of Eliezer, saying, Give me my hire for having rid thee of this bad blood that was in thy forehead, for such is the custom and the law in our land. 18 And Eliezer said to him, Thou hast wounded me and requirest me to pay thee thy hire; and Eliezer would not hearken to the words of the man of Sodom. 19 And the man laid hold of Eliezer and brought him to Shakra the judge of Sodom for judgment. 20 And the man spoke to the judge, saying, I beseech thee my lord, thus has this man done, for I smote him with a stone that the blood flowed from his forehead, and he is unwilling to give me my hire. 21 And the judge said to Eliezer, This man speaketh truth to thee, give him his hire, for this is the custom in our land; and Eliezer heard the words of the judge, and he lifted up a stone and smote the judge, and the stone struck on his forehead, and the blood flowed copiously from the forehead of the judge, and Eliezer said, If this then is the custom in your land give thou unto this man what I should have given him, for this has been thy decision, thou didst decree it. 22 And Eliezer left the man of Sodom with the judge, and he went away. 23 And when the kings of Elam had made war with the kings of Sodom, the kings of Elam captured all the property of Sodom, and they took Lot captive, with his property, and when it was told to Abraham he went and made war with the kings of Elam, and he recovered from their hands all the property of Lot as well as the property of Sodom. 24 At that time the wife of Lot bare him a daughter, and he called her name Paltith, saying, Because God had delivered him and his whole household from the kings of Elam; and Paltith daughter of Lot grew up, and one of the men of Sodom took her for a wife. 25 And a poor man came into the city to seek a maintenance, and he remained in the city some days, and all the people of Sodom caused a proclamation of their custom not to give this man a morsel of bread to eat, until he dropped dead upon the earth, and they did so. 26 And Paltith the daughter of Lot saw this man lying in the streets starved with hunger, and no one would give him any thing to keep him alive, and he was just upon the point of death. 27 And her soul was filled with pity on account of the man, and she fed him secretly with bread for many days, and the soul of this man was revived. 28 For when she went forth to fetch water she would put the bread in the water pitcher, and when she came to the place where the poor man was, she took the bread from the pitcher and gave it him to eat; so she did many days. 29 And all the people of Sodom and Gomorrah wondered how this man could bear starvation for so many days. 30 And they said to each other, This can only be that he eats and drinks, for no man can bear starvation for so many days or live as this man has, without even his countenance changing; and three men concealed themselves in a place where the poor man was stationed, to know who it was that brought him bread to eat. 31 And Paltith daughter of Lot went forth that day to fetch water, and she put bread into her pitcher of water, and she went to draw water by the poor man's place, and she took out the bread from the pitcher and gave it to the poor man and he ate it. 32 And the three men saw what Paltith did to the poor man, and they said to her, It is thou then who hast supported him, and therefore has he not starved, nor changed in appearance nor died like the rest. 33 And the three men went out of the place in which they were concealed, and they seized Paltith and the bread which was in the poor man's hand. 34 And they took Paltith and brought her before their judges, and they said to them, Thus did she do, and it is she who supplied the poor man with bread, therefore did he not die all this time; now therefore declare to us the punishment due to this woman for having transgressed our law. 35 And the people of Sodom and Gomorrah assembled and kindled a fire in the street of the city, and they took the woman and cast her into the fire and she was burned to ashes. 36 And in the city of Admah there was a woman to whom they did the like. 37 For a traveler came into the city of Admah to abide there all night, with the intention of going home in the morning, and he sat opposite the door of the house of the young woman's father, to remain there, as the sun had set when be had reached that place; and the young woman saw him sitting by the door of the house. 38 And he asked her for a drink of water and she said to him, Who art thou? and he said to her, I was this day going on the road, and reached here when the sun set, so I will abide here all night, and in the morning I will arise early and continue my journey. 39 And the young woman went into the house and fetched the man bread and water to eat and drink. 40 And this affair became known to the people of Admah, and they assembled and brought the young woman before the judges, that they should judge her for this act. 41 And the judge said, The judgment of death must pass upon this woman because she transgressed our law, and this therefore is the decision concerning her. 42 And the people of those cities assembled and brought out the young woman, and anointed her with honey from head to foot, as the judge had decreed, and they placed her before a swarm of bees which were then in their hives, and the bees flew upon her and stung her that her whole body was swelled. 43 And the young woman cried out on account of the bees, but no one took notice of her or pitied her, and her cries ascended to heaven. 44 And the Lord was provoked at this and at all the works of the cities of Sodom, for they had abundance of food, and had tranquility amongst them, and still would not sustain the poor and the needy, and in those days their evil doings and sins became great before the Lord. 45 And the Lord sent for two of the angels that had come to Abraham's house, to destroy Sodom and its cities. 46 And the angels rose up from the door of Abraham's tent, after they had eaten and drunk, and they reached Sodom in the evening, and Lot was then sitting in the gate of Sodom, and when he saw them he rose to meet them, and he bowed down to the ground. 47 And he pressed them greatly and brought them into his house, and he gave them victuals which they ate, and they abode all night in his house. 48 And the angels said to Lot, Arise, go forth from this place, thou and all belonging to thee, lest thou be consumed in the iniquity of this city, for the Lord will destroy this place. 49 And the angels laid hold upon the hand of Lot and upon the hand of his wife, and upon the hands of his children, and all belonging to him, and they brought him forth and set him without the cities. 50 And they said to Lot, Escape for thy life, and he fled and all belonging to him. 51 Then the Lord rained upon Sodom and upon Gomorrah and upon all these cities brimstone and fire from the Lord out of heaven. 52 And he overthrew these cities, all the plain and all the inhabitants of the cities, and that which grew upon the ground; and Ado the wife of Lot looked back to see the destruction of the cities, for her compassion was moved on account of her daughters who remained in Sodom, for they did not go with her. 53 And when she looked back she became a pillar of salt, and it is yet in that place unto this day. 54 And the oxen which stood in that place daily licked up the salt to the extremities of their feet, and in the morning it would spring forth afresh, and they again licked it up unto this day. 55 And Lot and two of his daughters that remained with him fled and escaped to the cave of Adullam, and they remained there for some time. 56 And Abraham rose up early in the morning to see what had been done to the cities of Sodom; and he looked and beheld the smoke of the cities going up like the smoke of a furnace. 57 And Lot and his two daughters remained in the cave, and they made their father drink wine, and they lay with him, for they said there was no man upon earth that could raise up seed from them, for they thought that the whole earth was destroyed. 58 And they both lay with their father, and they conceived and bare sons, and the first born called the name of her son Moab, saying, From my father did I conceive him; he is the father of the Moabites unto this day. 59 And the younger also called her son Benami; he is the father of the children of Ammon unto this day. 60 And after this Lot and his two daughters went away from there, and he dwelt on the other side of the Jordan with his two daughters and their sons, and the sons of Lot grew up, and they went and took themselves wives from the land of Canaan, and they begat children and they were fruitful and multiplied.

Jash.20

1 And at that time Abraham journeyed from the plain of Mamre, and he went to the land of the Philistines, and he dwelt in Gerar; it was in the twenty-fifth year of Abraham's being in the land of Canaan, and the hundredth year of the life of Abraham, that he came to Gerar in the land of the Philistines. 2 And when they entered the land he said to Sarah his wife, Say thou art my sister, to any one that shall ask thee, in order that we may escape the evil of the inhabitants of the land. 3 And as Abraham was dwelling in the land of the Philistines, the servants of Abimelech, king of the Philistines, saw that Sarah was exceedingly beautiful, and they asked Abraham

concerning her, and he said, She is my sister. 4 And the servants of Abimelech went to Abimelech, saying, A man from the land of Canaan is come to dwell in the land, and he has a sister that is exceeding fair. 5 And Abimelech heard the words of his servants who praised Sarah to him, and Abimelech sent his officers, and they brought Sarah to the king. 6 And Sarah came to the house of Abimelech, and the king saw that Sarah was beautiful, and she pleased him exceedingly. 7 And he approached her and said to her, What is that man to thee with whom thou didst come to our land? and Sarah answered and said He is my brother, and we came from the land of Canaan to dwell wherever we could find a place. 8 And Abimelech said to Sarah, Behold my land is before thee, place thy brother in any part of this land that pleases thee, and it will be our duty to exalt and elevate him above all the people of the land since he is thy brother. 9 And Abimelech sent for Abraham, and Abraham came to Abimelech. 10 And Abimelech said to Abraham, Behold I have given orders that thou shalt be honored as thou desirest on account of thy sister Sarah. 11 And Abraham went forth from the king, and the king's present followed him. 12 As at evening time, before men lie down to rest, the king was sitting upon his throne, and a deep sleep fell upon him, and he lay upon the throne and slept till morning. 13 And he dreamed that an angel of the Lord came to him with a drawn sword in his hand, and the angel stood over Abimelech, and wished to slay him with the sword, and the king was terrified in his dream, and said to the angel, In what have I sinned against thee that thou comest to slay me with thy sword? 14 And the angel answered and said to Abimelech, Behold thou diest on account of the woman which thou didst yesternight bring to thy house, for she is a married woman, the wife of Abraham who came to thy house; now therefore return that man his wife, for she is his wife; and shouldst thou not return her, know that thou wilt surely die, thou and all belonging to thee. 15 And on that night there was a great outcry in the land of the Philistines, and the inhabitants of the land saw the figure of a man standing with a drawn sword in his hand, and he smote the inhabitants of the land with the sword, yea he continued to smite them. 16 And the angel of the Lord smote the whole land of the Philistines on that night, and there was a great confusion on that night and on the following morning. 17 And every womb was closed, and all their issues, and the hand of the Lord was upon them on account of Sarah, wife of Abraham, whom Abimelech had taken. 18 And in the morning Abimelech rose with terror and confusion and with a great dread, and he sent and had his servants called in, and he related his dream to them, and the people were greatly afraid. 19 And one man standing amongst the servants of the king answered the king, saying, O sovereign king, restore this woman to her husband, for he is her husband, for the like happened to the king of Egypt when this man came to Egypt. 20 And he said concerning his wife, She is my sister, for such is his manner of doing when he cometh to dwell in the land in which he is a stranger. 21 And Pharaoh sent and took this woman for a wife and the Lord brought upon him grievous plagues until he returned the woman to her husband. 22 Now therefore, O sovereign king, know what happened yesternight to the whole land, for there was a very great consternation and great pain and lamentation, and we know that it was on account of the woman which thou didst take. 23 Now, therefore, restore this woman to her husband, lest it should befall us as it did to Pharaoh king of Egypt and his subjects, and that we may not die; and Abimelech hastened and called and had Sarah called for, and she came before him, and he had Abraham called for, and he came before him. 24 And Abimelech said to them, What is this work you have been doing in saying you are brother and sister, and I took this woman for a wife? 25 And Abraham said, Because I thought I should suffer death on account of my wife; and Abimelech took flocks and herds, and men servants and maid servants, and a thousand pieces of silver, and he gave them to Abraham, and he returned Sarah to him. 26 And Abimelech said to Abraham, Behold the whole land is before thee, dwell in it wherever thou shalt choose. 27 And Abraham and Sarah, his wife, went forth from the king's presence with honor and respect, and they dwelt in the land, even in Gerar. 28 And all the inhabitants of the land of the Philistines and the king's servants were still in pain, through the plague which the angel had inflicted upon them the whole night on account of Sarah. 29 And Abimelech sent for Abraham, saying, Pray now for thy servants to the Lord thy God, that he may put away this mortality from amongst us. 30 And Abraham prayed on account of Abimelech and his subjects, and the Lord heard the prayer of Abraham, and he healed Abimelech and all his subjects.

Jash.21

1 And it was at that time at the end of a year and four months of Abraham's dwelling in the land of the Philistines in Gerar, that God visited Sarah, and the Lord remembered her, and she conceived and bare a son to Abraham. 2 And Abraham called the name of the son which was born to him, which Sarah bare to him, Isaac. 3 And Abraham circumcised his son Isaac at eight days old, as God had commanded Abraham to do unto his seed after him; and Abraham was one hundred, and Sarah ninety years old, when Isaac was born to them. 4 And the child grew up and he was weaned, and Abraham made a great feast upon the day that Isaac was weaned. 5 And Shem and Eber and all the great people of the land, and Abimelech king of the Philistines, and his servants, and Phicol, the captain of his host, came to eat and drink and rejoice at the feast which Abraham made upon the day of his son Isaac's being weaned. 6 Also Terah, the father of Abraham, and Nahor his brother, came from Haran, they and all belonging to them, for they greatly rejoiced on hearing that a son had been born to Sarah. 7 And they came to Abraham, and they ate and drank at the feast which Abraham made upon the day of Isaac's being weaned. 8 And Terah and Nahor rejoiced with Abraham, and they remained with him many days in the land of the Philistines. 9 At that time Serug the son of Reu died, in the first year of the birth of Isaac son of Abraham. 10 And all the days of Serug were two hundred and thirty-nine years, and he died. 11 And Ishmael the son of Abraham was grown up in those days; he was fourteen years old when Sarah bare Isaac to Abraham. 12 And God was with Ishmael the son of Abraham, and he grew up, and he learned to use the bow and became an archer. 13 And when Isaac was five years old he was sitting with Ishmael at the door of the tent. 14 And Ishmael came to Isaac and seated himself opposite to him, and he took the bow and drew it and put the arrow in it, and intended to slay Isaac. 15 And Sarah saw the act which Ishmael desired to do to her son Isaac, and it grieved her exceedingly on account of her son, and she sent for Abraham, and said to him, Cast out this bondwoman and her son, for her son shall not be heir with my son, for thus did he seek to do unto him this day. 16 And Abraham hearkened to the voice of Sarah, and he rose up early in the morning, and he took twelve loaves and a bottle of water which he gave to Hagar, and sent her away with her son, and Hagar went with her son to the wilderness, and they dwelt in the wilderness of Paran with the inhabitants of the wilderness, and Ishmael was an archer, and he dwelt in the wilderness a long time. 17 And he and his mother afterward went to the land of Egypt, and they dwelt there, and Hagar took a wife for her son from Egypt, and her name was Meribah. 18 And the wife of Ishmael conceived and bare four sons and two daughters, and Ishmael and his mother and his wife and children afterward went and returned to the wilderness. 19 And they made themselves tents in the wilderness, in which they dwelt, and they continued to travel and then to rest monthly and yearly. 20 And God gave Ishmael flocks and herds and tents on account of Abraham his father, and the man increased in cattle. 21 And Ishmael dwelt in deserts and in tents, traveling and resting for a long time, and he did not see the face of his father. 22 And in some time after, Abraham said to Sarah his wife, I will go and see my son Ishmael, for I have a desire to see him, for I have not seen him for a long time. 23 And Abraham rode upon one of his camels to the wilderness to seek his son Ishmael, for he heard that he was dwelling in a tent in the wilderness with all belonging to him. 24 And Abraham went to the wilderness, and he reached the tent of Ishmael about noon, and he asked after Ishmael, and he found the wife of Ishmael sitting in the tent with her children, and Ishmael her husband and his mother were not with them. 25 And Abraham asked the wife of Ishmael, saying, Where has Ishmael gone? and she said, He has gone to the field to hunt, and Abraham was still mounted upon the camel, for he would not get off to the ground as he had sworn to his wife Sarah that he would not get off from the camel. 26 And Abraham said to Ishmael's wife, My daughter, give me a little water that I may drink, for I am fatigued from the journey. 27 And Ishmael's wife answered and said to Abraham, We have neither water nor bread, and she continued sitting in the tent and did not notice Abraham, neither did she ask him who he was. 28 But she was beating her children in the tent, and she was cursing them, and she also cursed her husband Ishmael and reproached him, and Abraham heard the words of Ishmael's wife to her children, and he was very angry and displeased. 29 And Abraham called to the woman to come out to him from the tent, and the woman came and stood opposite to Abraham, for Abraham was still mounted upon the camel. 30 And Abraham said to Ishmael's wife, When thy husband Ishmael returneth home say these words to him, 31 A very old man from the land of the Philistines came hither to seek thee, and thus was his appearance and figure; I did not ask him who he was, and seeing thou wast not here he spoke unto me and said, When Ishmael thy husband returneth tell him thus did this man say, When thou comest home put away this nail of the tent which thou hast placed here, and place another nail in its stead. 32 And Abraham finished his instructions to the woman, and he turned and went off on the camel homeward. 33 And after that Ishmael came from the chase he and his mother, and returned to the tent, and his wife spoke these words to him, 34 A very old man from the land of the Philistines came to seek thee, and thus was his appearance and figure; I did not ask him who he was, and seeing thou wast not at home he said to me, When thy husband cometh home tell him, thus saith the old man, Put away the nail of the tent which thou hast placed here and place another nail in its stead. 35 And Ishmael heard the words of his wife, and he knew that it was his father, and that his wife did not honor him. 36 And Ishmael understood his father's words that he had spoken to his wife, and Ishmael hearkened to the voice of his father, and Ishmael cast off that woman and she went away. 37 And Ishmael afterward went to the land of Canaan, and he took another wife and he brought her to his tent to the place where he then dwelt. 38 And at the end of three years Abraham said, I will go again and see Ishmael my son, for I have not seen him for a long time. 39 And he rode upon his camel and went to the wilderness, and he reached the tent of Ishmael about noon. 40 And he asked after Ishmael, and his wife came out of the tent and she said, He is not here my lord, for he has gone to hunt in the fields, and to feed the camels, and the woman said to Abraham, Turn in my lord into the tent, and eat a morsel of bread, for thy soul must be wearied on account of the journey. 41 And Abraham said to her, I will not stop for I am in haste

to continue my journey, but give me a little water to drink, for I have thirst; and the woman hastened and ran into the tent and she brought out water and bread to Abraham, which she placed before him and she urged him to eat, and he ate and drank and his heart was comforted and he blessed his son Ishmael. 42 And he finished his meal and he blessed the Lord, and he said to Ishmael's wife, When Ishmael cometh home say these words to him, 43 A very old man from the land of the Philistines came hither and asked after thee, and thou wast not here; and I brought him out bread and water and he ate and drank and his heart was comforted. 44 And he spoke these words to me: When Ishmael thy husband cometh home, say unto him, The nail of the tent which thou hast is very good, do not put it away from the tent. 45 And Abraham finished commanding the woman, and he rode off to his home to the land of the Philistines; and when Ishmael came to his tent his wife went forth to meet him with joy and a cheerful heart. 46 And she said to him, An old man came here from the land of the Philistines and thus was his appearance, and he asked after thee and thou wast not here, so I brought out bread and water, and he ate and drank and his heart was comforted. 47 And he spoke these words to me, When Ishmael thy husband cometh home say to him, The nail of the tent which thou hast is very good, do not put it away from the tent. 48 And Ishmael knew that it was his father, and that his wife had honored him, and the Lord blessed Ishmael.

Jash.22

1 And Ishmael then rose up and took his wife and his children and his cattle and all belonging to him, and he journeyed from there and he went to his father in the land of the Philistines. 2 And Abraham related to Ishmael his son the transaction with the first wife that Ishmael took, according to what she did. 3 And Ishmael and his children dwelt with Abraham many days in that land, and Abraham dwelt in the land of the Philistines a long time. 4 And the days increased and reached twenty six years, and after that Abraham with his servants and all belonging to him went from the land of the Philistines and removed to a great distance, and they came near to Hebron, and they remained there, and the servants of Abraham dug wells of water, and Abraham and all belonging to him dwelt by the water, and the servants of Abimelech king of the Philistines heard the report that Abraham's servants had dug wells of water in the borders of the land. 5 And they came and quarreled with the servants of Abraham, and they robbed them of the great well which they had dug. 6 And Abimelech king of the Philistines heard of this affair, and he with Phicol the captain of his host and twenty of his men came to Abraham, and Abimelech spoke to Abraham concerning his servants, and Abraham rebuked Abimelech concerning the well of which his servants had robbed him. 7 And Abimelech said to Abraham, As the Lord liveth who created the whole earth, I did not hear of the act which my servants did unto thy servants until this day. 8 And Abraham took seven ewe lambs and gave them to Abimelech, saying, Take these, I pray thee, from my hands that it may be a testimony for me that I dug this well. 9 And Abimelech took the seven ewe lambs which Abraham had given to him, for he had also given him cattle and herds in abundance, and Abimelech swore to Abraham concerning the well, therefore he called that well Beersheba, for there they both swore concerning it. 10 And they both made a covenant in Beersheba, and Abimelech rose up with Phicol the captain of his host and all his men, and they returned to the land of the Philistines, and Abraham and all belonging to him dwelt in Beersheba and he was in that land a long time. 11 And Abraham planted a large grove in Beersheba, and he made to it four gates facing the four sides of the earth, and he planted a vineyard in it, so that if a traveler came to Abraham he entered any gate which

235

was in his road, and remained there and ate and drank and satisfied himself and then departed. 12 For the house of Abraham was always open to the sons of men that passed and repassed, who came daily to eat and drink in the house of Abraham. 13 And any man who had hunger and came to Abraham's house, Abraham would give him bread that he might eat and drink and be satisfied, and any one that came naked to his house he would clothe with garments as he might choose, and give him silver and gold and make known to him the Lord who had created him in the earth; this did Abraham all his life. 14 And Abraham and his children and all belonging to him dwelt in Beersheba, and he pitched his tent as far as Hebron. 15 And Abraham's brother Nahor and his father and all belonging to them dwelt in Haran, for they did not come with Abraham to the land of Canaan. 16 And children were born to Nahor which Milca the daughter of Haran, and sister to Sarah, Abraham's wife, bare to him. 17 And these are the names of those that were born to him, Uz, Buz, Kemuel, Kesed, Chazo, Pildash, Tidlaf, and Bethuel, being eight sons, these are the children of Milca which she bare to Nahor, Abraham's brother. 18 And Nahor had a concubine and her name was Reumah, and she also bare to Nahor, Zebach, Gachash, Tachash and Maacha, being four sons. 19 And the children that were born to Nahor were twelve sons besides his daughters, and they also had children born to them in Haran. 20 And the children of Uz the first born of Nahor were Abi, Cheref, Gadin, Melus, and Deborah their sister. 21 And the sons of Buz were Berachel, Naamath, Sheva, and Madonu. 22 And the sons of Kemuel were Aram and Rechob. 23 And the sons of Kesed were Anamlech, Meshai, Benon and Yifi; and the sons of Chazo were Pildash, Mechi and Opher. 24 And the sons of Pildash were Arud, Chamum, Mered and Moloch. 25 And the sons of Tidlaf were Mushan, Cushan and Mutzi. 26 And the children of Bethuel were Sechar, Laban and their sister Rebecca. 27 These are the families of the children of Nahor, that were born to them in Haran; and Aram the son of Kemuel and Rechob his brother went away from Haran, and they found a valley in the land by the river Euphrates. 28 And they built a city there, and they called the name of the city after the name of Pethor the son of Aram, that is Aram Naharayim unto this day. 29 And the children of Kesed also went to dwell where they could find a place, and they went and they found a valley opposite to the land of Shinar, and they dwelt there. 30 And they there built themselves a city, and they called the name at the city Kesed after the name of their father, that is the land Kasdim unto this day, and the Kasdim dwelt in that land and they were fruitful and multiplied exceedingly. 31 And Terah, father of Nahor and Abraham, went and took another wife in his old age, and her name was Pelilah, and she conceived and bare him a son and he called his name Zoba. 32 And Terah lived twenty-five years after he begat Zoba. 33 And Terah died in that year, that is in the thirty-fifth year of the birth of Isaac son of Abraham. 34 And the days of Terah were two hundred and five years, and he was buried in Haran. 35 And Zoba the son of Terah lived thirty years and he begat Aram, Achlis and Merik. 36 And Aram son of Zoba son of Terah, had three wives and he begat twelve sons and three daughters; and the Lord gave to Aram the son of Zoba, riches and possessions, and abundance of cattle, and flocks and herds, and the man increased greatly. 37 And Aram the son of Zoba and his brother and all his household journeyed from Haran, and they went to dwell where they should find a place, for their property was too great to remain in Haran; for they could not stop in Haran together with their brethren the children of Nahor. 38 And Aram the son of Zoba went with his brethren, and they found a valley at a distance toward the eastern country and they dwelt there. 39 And they also built a city there, and they called the name thereof Aram, after the name of their eldest brother; that is Aram Zoba to this day. 40 And Isaac the son of Abraham was growing up in those days, and Abraham his father taught him the way of the Lord to know the Lord, and the Lord was with him. 41 And when Isaac was thirty-seven years old, Ishmael his brother was going about with him in the tent. 42 And Ishmael boasted of himself to Isaac, saying, I was thirteen years old when the Lord spoke to my father to circumcise us, and I did according to the word of the Lord which he spoke to my father, and I gave my soul unto the Lord, and I did not transgress his word which he commanded my father. 43 And Isaac answered Ishmael, saying, Why dost thou boast to me about this, about a little bit of thy flesh which thou didst take from thy body, concerning which the Lord commanded thee? 44 As the Lord liveth, the God of my father Abraham, if the Lord should say unto my father, Take now thy son Isaac and bring him up an offering before me, I would not refrain but I would joyfully accede to it. 45 And the Lord heard the word that Isaac spoke to Ishmael, and it seemed good in the sight of the Lord, and he thought to try Abraham in this matter. 46 And the day arrived when the sons of God came and placed themselves before the Lord, and Satan also came with the sons of God before the Lord. 47 And the Lord said unto Satan, Whence comest thou? and Satan answered the Lord and said, From going to and fro in the earth, and from walking up and down in it. 48 And the Lord said to Satan, What is thy word to me concerning all the children of the earth? and Satan answered the Lord and said, I have seen all the children of the earth who serve thee and remember thee when they require anything from thee. 49 And when thou givest them the thing which they require from thee, they sit at their ease, and forsake thee and they remember thee no more. 50 Hast thou seen Abraham the son of Terah, who at first had no children, and he served thee and erected altars to thee wherever he came, and he brought up offerings upon them, and he proclaimed thy name continually to all the children of the earth. 51 And now that his son Isaac is born to him, he has forsaken thee, he has made a great feast for all the inhabitants of the land, and the Lord he has forgotten. 52 For amidst all that he has done he brought thee no offering; neither burnt offering nor peace offering, neither ox, lamb nor goat of all that he killed on the day that his son was weaned. 53 Even from the time of his son's birth till now, being thirty-seven years, he built no altar before thee, nor brought any offering to thee, for he saw that thou didst give what he requested before thee, and he therefore forsook thee. 54 And the Lord said to Satan, Hast thou thus considered my servant Abraham? for there is none like him upon earth, a perfect and an upright man before me, one that feareth God and avoideth evil; as I live, were I to say unto him, Bring up Isaac thy son before me, he would not withhold him from me, much more if I told him to bring up a burnt offering before me from his flock or herds. 55 And Satan answered the Lord and said, Speak then now unto Abraham as thou hast said, and thou wilt see whether he will not this day transgress and cast aside thy words.

Jash.23

1 At that time the word of the Lord came to Abraham, and he said unto him, Abraham, and he said, Here I am. 2 And he said to him, Take now thy son, thine only son whom thou lovest, even Isaac, and go to the land of Moriah, and offer him there for a burnt offering upon one of the mountains which shall be shown to thee, for there wilt thou see a cloud and the glory of the Lord. 3 And Abraham said within himself, How shall I separate my son Isaac from Sarah his mother, in order to bring him up for a burnt offering before the Lord? 4 And Abraham came into the tent, and he sat before Sarah his wife, and he spoke these words to her, 5 My son Isaac is grown up and he has not for some time studied the service of his God, now

tomorrow I will go and bring him to Shem, and Eber his son, and there he will learn the ways of the Lord, for they will teach him to know the Lord as well as to know that when he prayeth continually before the Lord, he will answer him, therefore there he will know the way of serving the Lord his God. 6 And Sarah said, Thou hast spoken well, go my lord and do unto him as thou hast said, but remove him not at a great distance from me, neither let him remain there too long, for my soul is bound within his soul. 7 And Abraham said unto Sarah, My daughter, let us pray to the Lord our God that he may do good with us. 8 And Sarah took her son Isaac and he abode all that night with her, and she kissed and embraced him, and gave him instructions till morning. 9 And she said to him, O my son, how can my soul separate itself from thee? And she still kissed him and embraced him, and she gave Abraham instructions concerning him. 10 And Sarah said to Abraham, O my lord, I pray thee take heed of thy son, and place thine eyes over him, for I have no other son nor daughter but him. 11 O forsake him not. If he be hungry give him bread, and if he be thirsty give him water to drink; do not let him go on foot, neither let him sit in the sun. 12 Neither let him go by himself in the road, neither force him from whatever he may desire, but do unto him as he may say to thee. 13 And Sarah wept bitterly the whole night on account of Isaac, and she gave him instructions till morning. 14 And in the morning Sarah selected a very fine and beautiful garment from those garments which she had in the house, that Abimelech had given to her. 15 And she dressed Isaac her son therewith, and she put a turban upon his head, and she enclosed a precious stone in the top of the turban, and she gave them provision for the road, and they went forth, and Isaac went with his father Abraham, and some of their servants accompanied them to see them off the road. 16 And Sarah went out with them, and she accompanied them upon the road to see them off, and they said to her, Return to the tent. 17 And when Sarah heard the words of her son Isaac she wept bitterly, and Abraham her husband wept with her, and their son wept with them a great weeping; also those who went with them wept greatly. 18 And Sarah caught hold of her son Isaac, and she held him in her arms, and she embraced him and continued to weep with him, and Sarah said, Who knoweth if after this day I shall ever see thee again? 19 And they still wept together, Abraham, Sarah and Isaac, and all those that accompanied them on the road wept with them, and Sarah afterward turned away from her son, weeping bitterly, and all her men servants and maid servants returned with her to the tent. 20 And Abraham went with Isaac his son to bring him up as an offering before the Lord, as He had commanded him. 21 And Abraham took two of his young men with him, Ishmael the son of Hagar and Eliezer his servant, and they went together with them, and whilst they were walking in the road the young men spoke these words to themselves, 22 And Ishmael said to Eliezer, Now my father Abraham is going with Isaac to bring him up for a burnt offering to the Lord, as He commanded him. 23 Now when he returneth he will give unto me all that he possesses, to inherit after him, for I am his first born. 24 And Eliezer answered Ishmael and said, Surely Abraham did cast thee away with thy mother, and swear that thou shouldst not inherit any thing of all he possesses, and to whom will he give all that he has, with all his treasures, but unto me his servant, who has been faithful in his house, who has served him night and day, and has done all that he desired me? to me will he bequeath at his death all that he possesses. 25 And whilst Abraham was proceeding with his son Isaac along the road, Satan came and appeared to Abraham in the figure of a very aged man, humble and of contrite spirit, and he approached Abraham and said to him, Art thou silly or brutish, that thou goest to do this thing this day to thine only son? 26 For God gave thee a son in thy latter days, in thy old age, and wilt thou go and slaughter him this day because he committed no violence, and wilt thou cause the soul of thine only son to perish from the earth? 27 Dost thou not know and understand that this thing cannot be from the Lord? for the Lord cannot do unto man such evil upon earth to say to him, Go slaughter thy child. 28 And Abraham heard this and knew that it was the word of Satan who endeavored to draw him aside from the way of the Lord, but Abraham would not hearken to the voice of Satan, and Abraham rebuked him so that he went away. 29 And Satan returned and came to Isaac; and he appeared unto Isaac in the figure of a young man comely and well favored. 30 And he approached Isaac and said unto him, Dost thou not know and understand that thy old silly father bringeth thee to the slaughter this day for naught? 31 Now therefore, my son, do not listen nor attend to him, for he is a silly old man, and let not thy precious soul and beautiful figure be lost from the earth. 32 And Isaac heard this, and said unto Abraham, Hast thou heard, my father, that which this man has spoken? even thus has he spoken. 33 And Abraham answered his son Isaac and said to him, Take heed of him and do not listen to his words, nor attend to him, for he is Satan, endeavoring to draw us aside this day from the commands of God. 34 And Abraham still rebuked Satan, and Satan went from them, and seeing he could not prevail over them he hid himself from them, and he went and passed before them in the road; and he transformed himself to a large brook of water in the road, and Abraham and Isaac and his two young men reached that place, and they saw a brook large and powerful as the mighty waters. 35 And they entered the brook and passed through it, and the waters at first reached their legs. 36 And they went deeper in the brook and the waters reached up to their necks, and they were all terrified on account of the water; and whilst they were going over the brook Abraham recognized that place, and he knew that there was no water there before. 37 And Abraham said to his son Isaac, I know this place in which there was no brook nor water, now therefore it is this Satan who does all this to us, to draw us aside this day from the commands of God. 38 And Abraham rebuked him and said unto him, The Lord rebuke thee, O Satan, begone from us for we go by the commands of God. 39 And Satan was terrified at the voice of Abraham, and he went away from them, and the place again became dry land as it was at first. 40 And Abraham went with Isaac toward the place that God had told him. 41 And on the third day Abraham lifted up his eyes and saw the place at a distance which God had told him of. 42 And a pillar of fire appeared to him that reached from the earth to heaven, and a cloud of glory upon the mountain, and the glory of the Lord was seen in the cloud. 43 And Abraham said to Isaac, My son, dost thou see in that mountain, which we perceive at a distance, that which I see upon it? 44 And Isaac answered and said unto his father, I see and lo a pillar of fire and a cloud, and the glory of the Lord is seen upon the cloud. 45 And Abraham knew that his son Isaac was accepted before the Lord for a burnt offering. 46 And Abraham said unto Eliezer and unto Ishmael his son, Do you also see that which we see upon the mountain which is at a distance? 47 And they answered and said, We see nothing more than like the other mountains of the earth. And Abraham knew that they were not accepted before the Lord to go with them, and Abraham said to them, Abide ye here with the ass whilst I and Isaac my son will go to yonder mount and worship there before the Lord and then return to you. 48 And Eliezer and Ishmael remained in that place, as Abraham had commanded. 49 And Abraham took wood for a burnt offering and placed it upon his son Isaac, and he took the fire and the knife, and they both went to that place. 50 And when they were going along Isaac said to his father, Behold, I see here the fire and wood, and where then is the lamb

237

that is to be the burnt offering before the Lord? 51 And Abraham answered his son Isaac, saying, The Lord has made choice of thee my son, to be a perfect burnt offering instead of the lamb. 52 And Isaac said unto his father, I will do all that the Lord spoke to thee with joy and cheerfulness of heart. 53 And Abraham again said unto Isaac his son, Is there in thy heart any thought or counsel concerning this, which is not proper? tell me my son, I pray thee, O my son conceal it not from me. 54 And Isaac answered his father Abraham and said unto him, O my father, as the Lord liveth and as thy soul liveth, there is nothing in my heart to cause me to deviate either to the right or to the left from the word that he has spoken to thee. 55 Neither limb nor muscle has moved or stirred at this, nor is there in my heart any thought or evil counsel concerning this. 56 But I am of joyful and cheerful heart in this matter, and I say, Blessed is the Lord who has this day chosen me to be a burnt offering before Him. 57 And Abraham greatly rejoiced at the words of Isaac, and they went on and came together to that place that the Lord had spoken of. 58 And Abraham approached to build the altar in that place, and Abraham was weeping, and Isaac took stones and mortar until they had finished building the altar. 59 And Abraham took the wood and placed it in order upon the altar which he had built. 60 And he took his son Isaac and bound him in order to place him upon the wood which was upon the altar, to slay him for a burnt offering before the Lord. 61 And Isaac said to his father, Bind me securely and then place me upon the altar lest I should turn and move, and break loose from the force of the knife upon my flesh and thereof profane the burnt offering; and Abraham did so. 62 And Isaac still said to his father, O my father, when thou shalt have slain me and burnt me for an offering, take with thee that which shall remain of my ashes to bring to Sarah my mother, and say to her, This is the sweet smelling savor of Isaac; but do not tell her this if she should sit near a well or upon any high place, lest she should cast her soul after me and die. 63 And Abraham heard the words of Isaac, and he lifted up his voice and wept when Isaac spake these words; and Abraham's tears gushed down upon Isaac his son, and Isaac wept bitterly, and he said to his father, Hasten thou, O my father, and do with me the will of the Lord our God as He has commanded thee. 64 And the hearts of Abraham and Isaac rejoiced at this thing which the Lord had commanded them; but the eye wept bitterly whilst the heart rejoiced. 65 And Abraham bound his son Isaac, and placed him on the altar upon the wood, and Isaac stretched forth his neck upon the altar before his father, and Abraham stretched forth his hand to take the knife to slay his son as a burnt offering before the Lord. 66 At that time the angels of mercy came before the Lord and spake to him concerning Isaac, saying, 67 0 Lord, thou art a merciful and compassionate King over all that thou hast created in heaven and in earth, and thou supportest them all; give therefore ransom and redemption instead of thy servant Isaac, and pity and have compassion upon Abraham and Isaac his son, who are this day performing thy commands. 68 Hast thou seen, O Lord, how Isaac the son of Abraham thy servant is bound down to the slaughter like an animal? now therefore let thy pity be roused for them, O Lord. 69 At that time the Lord appeared unto Abraham, and called to him, from heaven, and said unto him, Lay not thine hand upon the lad, neither do thou any thing unto him, for now I know that thou fearest God in performing this act, and in not withholding thy son, thine only son, from me. 70 And Abraham lifted up his eyes and saw, and behold, a ram was caught in a thicket by his horns; that was the ram which the Lord God had created in the earth in the day that he made earth and heaven. 71 For the Lord had prepared this ram from that day, to be a burnt offering instead of Isaac. 72 And this ram was advancing to Abraham when Satan caught hold of him and entangled his horns in the thicket, that he might not advance to Abraham, in order that Abraham might slay his son. [73] And Abraham, seeing the ram advancing to him and Satan withholding him, fetched him and brought him before the altar, and he loosened his son Isaac from his binding, and he put the ram in his stead, and Abraham killed the ram upon the altar, and brought it up as an offering in the place of his son Isaac. [74] And Abraham sprinkled some of the blood of the ram upon the altar, and he exclaimed and said, This is in the place of my son, and may this be considered this day as the blood of my son before the Lord. [75] And all that Abraham did on this occasion by the altar, he would exclaim and say, This is in the room of my son, and may it this day be considered before the Lord in the place of my son; and Abraham finished the whole of the service by the altar, and the service was accepted before the Lord, and was accounted as if it had been Isaac; and the Lord blessed Abraham and his seed on that day. [76] And Satan went to Sarah, and he appeared to her in the figure of an old man very humble and meek, and Abraham was yet engaged in the burnt offering before the Lord. [77] And he said unto her, Dost thou not know all the work that Abraham has made with thine only son this day? for he took Isaac and built an altar, and killed him, and brought him up as a sacrifice upon the altar, and Isaac cried and wept before his father, but he looked not at him, neither did he have compassion over him. [78] And Satan repeated these words, and he went away from her, and Sarah heard all the words of Satan, and she imagined him to be an old man from amongst the sons of men who had been with her son, and had come and told her these things. [79] And Sarah lifted up her voice and wept and cried out bitterly on account of her son; and she threw herself upon the ground and she cast dust upon her head, and she said, O my son, Isaac my son, O that I had this day died instead of thee. And she continued to weep and said, It grieves me for thee, O my son, my son Isaac, O that I had died this day in thy stead. [80] And she still continued to weep, and said, It grieves me for thee after that I have reared thee and have brought thee up; now my joy is turned into mourning over thee, I that had a longing for thee, and cried and prayed to God till I bare thee at ninety years old; and now hast thou served this day for the knife and the fire, to be made an offering. [81] But I console myself with thee, my son, in its being the word of the Lord, for thou didst perform the command of thy God; for who can transgress the word of our God, in whose hands is the soul of every living creature? [82] Thou art just, O Lord our God, for all thy works are good and righteous; for I also am rejoiced with thy word which thou didst command, and whilst mine eye weepeth bitterly my heart rejoiceth. [83] And Sarah laid her head upon the bosom of one of her handmaids, and she became as still as a stone. [84] She afterward rose up and went about making inquiries till she came to Hebron, and she inquired of all those whom she met walking in the road, and no one could tell her what had happened to her son. [85] And she came with her maid servants and men servants to Kireath-arba, which is Hebron, and she asked concerning her Son, and she remained there while she sent some of her servants to seek where Abraham had gone with Isaac; they went to seek him in the house of Shem and Eber, and they could not find him, and they sought throughout the land and he was not there. [86] And behold, Satan came to Sarah in the shape of an old man, and he came and stood before her, and he said unto her, I spoke falsely unto thee, for Abraham did not kill his son and he is not dead; and when she heard the word her joy was so exceedingly violent on account of her son, that her soul went out through joy; she died and was gathered to her people. [87] And when Abraham had finished his service he returned with his son Isaac to his young men, and they rose up and went together to Beersheba, and they came

238

home. [88] And Abraham sought for Sarah, and could not find her, and he made inquiries concerning her, and they said unto him, She went as far as Hebron to seek you both where you had gone, for thus was she informed. [89] And Abraham and Isaac went to her to Hebron, and when they found that she was dead they lifted up their voices and wept bitterly over her; and Isaac fell upon his mother's face and wept over her, and he said, O my mother, my mother, how hast thou left me, and where hast thou gone? O how, how hast thou left me! [90] And Abraham and Isaac wept greatly and all their servants wept with them on account of Sarah, and they mourned over her a great and heavy mourning.

Jash.24

[1] And the life of Sarah was one hundred and twenty-seven years, and Sarah died; and Abraham rose up from before his dead to seek a burial place to bury his wife Sarah; and he went and spoke to the children of Heth, the inhabitants of the land, saying, [2] I am a stranger and a sojourner with you in your land; give me a possession of a burial place in your land, that I may bury my dead from before me. [3] And the children of Heth said unto Abraham, behold the land is before thee, in the choice of our sepulchers bury thy dead, for no man shall withhold thee from burying thy dead. [4] And Abraham said unto them, If you are agreeable to this go and entreat for me to Ephron, the son of Zochar, requesting that he may give me the cave of Machpelah, which is in the end of his field, and I will purchase it of him for whatever he desire for it. [5] And Ephron dwelt among the children of Heth, and they went and called for him, and he came before Abraham, and Ephron said unto Abraham, Behold all thou requirest thy servant will do; and Abraham said, No, but I will buy the cave and the field which thou hast for value, In order that it may be for a possession of a burial place for ever. [6] And Ephron answered and said, Behold the field and the cave are before thee, give whatever thou desirest; and Abraham said, Only at full value will I buy it from thy hand, and from the hands of those that go in at the gate of thy city, and from the hand of thy seed for ever. [7] And Ephron and all his brethren heard this, and Abraham weighed to Ephron four hundred shekels of silver in the hands of Ephron and in the hands of all his brethren; and Abraham wrote this transaction, and he wrote it and testified it with four witnesses. [8] And these are the names of the witnesses, Amigal son of Abishna the Hittite, Adichorom son of Ashunach the Hivite, Abdon son of Achiram the Gomerite, Bakdil the son of Abudish the Zidonite. [9] And Abraham took the book of the purchase, and placed it in his treasures, and these are the words that Abraham wrote in the book, namely: [10] That the cave and the field Abraham bought from Ephron the Hittite, and from his seed, and from those that go out of his city, and from their seed for ever, are to be a purchase to Abraham and to his seed and to those that go forth from his loins, for a possession of a burial place for ever; and he put a signet to it and testified it with witnesses. [11] And the field and the cave that was in it and all that place were made sure unto Abraham and unto his seed after him, from the children of Heth; behold it is before Mamre in Hebron, which is in the land of Canaan. [12] And after this Abraham buried his wife Sarah there, and that place and all its boundary became to Abraham and unto his seed for a possession of a burial place. [13] And Abraham buried Sarah with pomp as observed at the interment of kings, and she was buried in very fine and beautiful garments. [14] And at her bier was Shem, his sons Eber and Abimelech, together with Anar, Ashcol and Mamre, and all the grandees of the land followed her bier. [15] And the days of Sarah were one hundred and twenty-seven years and she died, and Abraham made a great and heavy mourning, and he performed the rites of mourning for seven days. [16] And all the inhabitants of the land comforted Abraham and

Isaac his son on account of Sarah. [17] And when the days of their mourning passed by Abraham sent away his son Isaac, and he went to the house of Shem and Eber, to learn the ways of the Lord and his instructions, and Abraham remained there three years. [18] At that time Abraham rose up with all his servants, and they went and returned homeward to Beersheba, and Abraham and all his servants remained in Beersheba. [19] And at the revolution of the year Abimelech king of the Philistines died in that year; he was one hundred and ninety-three years old at his death; and Abraham went with his people to the land of the Philistines, and they comforted the whole household and all his servants, and he then turned and went home. [20] And it was after the death of Abimelech that the people of Gerar took Benmalich his son, and he was only twelve years old, and they made him lying in the place of his father. [21] And they called his name Abimelech after the name of his father, for thus was it their custom to do in Gerar, and Abimelech reigned instead of Abimelech his father, and he sat upon his throne. [22] And Lot the son of Haran also died in those days, in the thirty-ninth year of the life of Isaac, and all the days that Lot lived were one hundred and forty years and he died. [23] And these are the children of Lot, that were born to him by his daughters, the name of the first born was Moab, and the name of the second was Benami. [24] And the two sons of Lot went and took themselves wives from the land of Canaan, and they bare children to them, and the children of Moab were Ed, Mayon, Tarsus, and Kanvil, four sons, these are fathers to the children of Moab unto this day. [25] And all the families of the children of Lot went to dwell wherever they should light upon, for they were fruitful and increased abundantly. [26] And they went and built themselves cities in the land where they dwelt, and they called the names of the cities which they built after their own names. [27] And Nahor the son of Terah, brother to Abraham, died in those days in the fortieth year of the life of Isaac, and all the days of Nahor were one hundred and seventy-two years and he died and was buried in Haran. [28] And when Abraham heard that his brother was dead he grieved sadly, and he mourned over his brother many days. [29] And Abraham called for Eliezer his head servant, to give him orders concerning his house, and he came and stood before him. [30] And Abraham said to him, Behold I am old, I do not know the day of my death; for I am advanced in days; now therefore rise up, go forth and do not take a wife for my son from this place and from this land, from the daughters of the Canaanites amongst whom we dwell. [31] But go to my land and to my birthplace, and take from thence a wife for my son, and the Lord God of Heaven and earth who took me from my father's house and brought me to this place, and said unto me, To thy seed will I give this land for an inheritance for ever, he will send his angel before thee and prosper thy way, that thou mayest obtain a wife for my son from my family and from my father's house. [32] And the servant answered his master Abraham and said, Behold I go to thy birthplace and to thy father's house, and take a wife for thy son from there; but if the woman be not willing to follow me to this land, shall I take thy son back to the land of thy birthplace? [33] And Abraham said unto him, Take heed that thou bring not my son hither again, for the Lord before whom I have walked he will send his angel before thee and prosper thy way. [34] And Eliezer did as Abraham ordered him, and Eliezer swore unto Abraham his master upon this matter; and Eliezer rose up and took ten camels of the camels of his master, and ten men from his master's servants with him, and they rose up and went to Haran, the city of Abraham and Nahor, in order to fetch a wife for Isaac the son of Abraham; and whilst they were gone Abraham sent to the house of Shem and Eber, and they brought from thence his son Isaac. [35] And Isaac came home to his father's house to Beersheba,

whilst Eliezer and his men came to Haran; and they stopped in the city by the watering place, and he made his camels to kneel down by the water and they remained there. [36] And Eliezer, Abraham's servant, prayed and said, O God of Abraham my master; send me I pray thee good speed this day and show kindness unto my master, that thou shalt appoint this day a wife for my master's son from his family. [37] And the Lord hearkened to the voice of Eliezer, for the sake of his servant Abraham, and he happened to meet with the daughter of Bethuel, the son of Milcah, the wife of Nahor, brother to Abraham, and Eliezer came to her house. [38] And Eliezer related to them all his concerns, and that he was Abraham's servant, and they greatly rejoiced at him. [39] And they all blessed the Lord who brought this thing about, and they gave him Rebecca, the daughter of Bethuel, for a wife for Isaac. [40] And the young woman was of very comely appearance, she was a virgin, and Rebecca was ten years old in those days. [41] And Bethuel and Laban and his children made a feast on that night, and Eliezer and his men came and ate and drank and rejoiced there on that night. [42] And Eliezer rose up in the morning, he and the men that were with him, and he called to the whole household of Bethuel, saying, Send me away that I may go to my master; and they rose up and sent away Rebecca and her nurse Deborah, the daughter of Uz, and they gave her silver and gold, men servants and maid servants, and they blessed her. [43] And they sent Eliezer away with his men; and the servants took Rebecca, and he went and returned to his master to the land of Canaan. [44] And Isaac took Rebecca and she became his wife, and he brought her into the tent. [45] And Isaac was forty years old when he took Rebecca, the daughter of his uncle Bethuel, for a wife.

Jash.25

[1] And it was at that time that Abraham again took a wife in his old age, and her name was Keturah, from the land of Canaan. [2] And she bare unto him Zimran, Jokshan, Medan, Midian, Ishbak and Shuach, being six sons. And the children of Zimran were Abihen, Molich and Narim. [3] And the sons of Jokshan were Sheba and Dedan, and the sons of Medan were Amida, Joab, Gochi, Elisha and Nothach; and the sons of Midian were Ephah, Epher, Chanoch, Abida and Eldaah. [4] And the sons of Ishbak were Makiro, Beyodua and Tator. [5] And the sons of Shuach were Bildad, Mamdad, Munan and Meban; all these are the families of the children of Keturah the Canaanitish woman which she bare unto Abraham the Hebrew. [6] And Abraham sent all these away, and he gave them gifts, and they went away from his son Isaac to dwell wherever they should find a place. [7] And all these went to the mountain at the east, and they built themselves six cities in which they dwelt unto this day. [8] But the children of Sheba and Dedan, children of Jokshan, with their children, did not dwell with their brethren in their cities, and they journeyed and encamped in the countries and wildernesses unto this day. [9] And the children of Midian, son of Abraham, went to the east of the land of Cush, and they there found a large valley in the eastern country, and they remained there and built a city, and they dwelt therein, that is the land of Midian unto this day. [10] And Midian dwelt in the city which he built, he and his five sons and all belonging to him. [11] And these are the names of the sons of Midian according to their names in their cities, Ephah, Epher, Chanoch, Abida and Eldaah. [12] And the sons of Ephah were Methach, Meshar, Avi and Tzanua, and the sons of Epher were Ephron, Zur, Alirun and Medin, and the sons of Chanoch were Reuel, Rekem, Azi, Alyoshub and Alad. [13] And the sons of Abida were Chur, Melud, Kerury, Molchi; and the sons of Eldaah were Miker, and Reba, and Malchiyah and Gabol; these are the names of the Midianites according to their families; and afterward the families of Midian spread throughout the land of Midian. [14] And these are the

generations of Ishmael the son Abraham, whom Hagar, Sarah's handmaid, bare unto Abraham. 15 And Ishmael took a wife from the land of Egypt, and her name was Ribah, the same is Meribah. 16 And Ribah bare unto Ishmael Nebayoth, Kedar, Adbeel, Mibsam and their sister Bosmath. 17 And Ishmael cast away his wife Ribah, and she went from him and returned to Egypt to the house of her father, and she dwelt there, for she had been very bad in the sight of Ishmael, and in the sight of his father Abraham. 18 And Ishmael afterward took a wife from the land of Canaan, and her name was Malchuth, and she bare unto him Nishma, Dumah, Masa, Chadad, Tema, Yetur, Naphish and Kedma. 19 These are the sons of Ishmael, and these are their names, being twelve princes according to their nations; and the families of Ishmael afterward spread forth, and Ishmael took his children and all the property that he had gained, together with the souls of his household and all belonging to him, and they went to dwell where they should find a place. 20 And they went and dwelt near the wilderness of Paran, and their dwelling was from Havilah unto Shur, that is before Egypt as thou comest toward Assyria. 21 And Ishmael and his sons dwelt in the land, and they had children born to them, and they were fruitful and increased abundantly. 22 And these are the names of the sons of Nebayoth the first born of Ishmael; Mend, Send, Mayon; and the sons of Kedar were Alyon, Kezem, Chamad and Eli. 23 And the sons of Adbeel were Chamad and Jabin; and the sons of Mibsam were Obadiah, Ebedmelech and Yeush; these are the families of the children of Ribah the wife of Ishmael. 24 And the sons of Mishma the son of Ishmael were Shamua, Zecaryon and Obed; and the sons of Dumah were Kezed, Eli, Machmad and Amed. 25 And the sons of Masa were Melon, Mula and Ebidadon; and the sons of Chadad were Azur, Minzar and Ebedmelech; and the sons of Tema were Seir, Sadon and Yakol. 26 And the sons of Yetur were Merith, Yaish, Alyo, and Pachoth; and the sons of Naphish were Ebed-Tamed, Abiyasaph and Mir; and the sons of Kedma were Calip, Tachti, and Omir; these were the children of Malchuth the wife of Ishmael according to their families. 27 All these are the families of Ishmael according to their generations, and they dwelt in those lands wherein they had built themselves cities unto this day. 28 And Rebecca the daughter of Bethuel, the wife of Abraham's son Isaac, was barren in those days, she had no offspring; and Isaac dwelt with his father in the land of Canaan; and the Lord was with Isaac; and Arpachshad the son of Shem the son of Noah died in those days, in the forty-eighth year of the life of Isaac, and all the days that Arpachshad lived were four hundred and thirty-eight years, and he died.

Jash.26

1 And in the fifty-ninth year of the life of Isaac the son of Abraham, Rebecca his wife was still barren in those days. 2 And Rebecca said unto Isaac, Truly I have heard, my lord, that thy mother Sarah was barren in her days until my Lord Abraham, thy father, prayed for her and she conceived by him. 3 Now therefore stand up, pray thou also to God and he will hear thy prayer and remember us through his mercies. 4 And Isaac answered his wife Rebecca, saying, Abraham has already prayed for me to God to multiply his seed, now therefore this barrenness must proceed to us from thee. 5 And Rebecca said unto him, But arise now thou also and pray, that the Lord may hear thy prayer and grant me children, and Isaac hearkened to the words of his wife, and Isaac and his wife rose up and went to the land of Moriah to pray there and to seek the Lord, and when they had reached that place Isaac stood up and prayed to the Lord on account of his wife because she was barren. 6 And Isaac said, O Lord God of heaven and earth, whose goodness and mercies fill the earth, thou who didst take my father from his father's house and from his birthplace, and didst bring him unto this land, and didst

say unto him, To thy seed will I give the land, and thou didst promise him and didst declare unto him, I will multiply thy seed as the stars of heaven and as the sand of the sea, now may thy words be verified which thou didst speak unto my father. 7 For thou art the Lord our God, our eyes are toward thee to give us seed of men, as thou didst promise us, for thou art the Lord our God and our eyes are directed toward thee only. 8 And the Lord heard the prayer of Isaac the son of Abraham, and the Lord was entreated of him and Rebecca his wife conceived. 9 And in about seven months after the children struggled together within her, and it pained her greatly that she was wearied on account of them, and she said to all the women who were then in the land, Did such a thing happen to you as it has to me? and they said unto her, No. 10 And she said unto them, Why am I alone in this amongst all the women that were upon earth? and she went to the land of Moriah to seek the Lord on account of this; and she went to Shem and Eber his son to make inquiries of them in this matter, and that they should seek the Lord in this thing respecting her. 11 And she also asked Abraham to seek and inquire of the Lord about all that had befallen her. 12 And they all inquired of the Lord concerning this matter, and they brought her word from the Lord and told her, Two children are in thy womb, and two nations shall rise from them; and one nation shall be stronger than the other, and the greater shall serve the younger. 13 And when her days to be delivered were completed, she knelt down, and behold there were twins in her womb, as the Lord had spoken to her. 14 And the first came out red all over like a hairy garment, and all the people of the land called his name Esau, saying, That this one was made complete from the womb. 15 And after that came his brother, and his hand took hold of Esau's heel, therefore they called his name Jacob. 16 And Isaac, the son of Abraham, was sixty years old when he begat them. 17 And the boys grew up to their fifteenth year, and they came amongst the society of men. Esau was a designing and deceitful man, and an expert hunter in the field, and Jacob was a man perfect and wise, dwelling in tents, feeding flocks and learning the instructions of the Lord and the commands of his father and mother. 18 And Isaac and the children of his household dwelt with his father Abraham in the land of Canaan, as God had commanded them. 19 And Ishmael the son of Abraham went with his children and all belonging to them, and they returned there to the land of Havilah, and they dwelt there. 20 And all the children of Abraham's concubines went to dwell in the land of the east, for Abraham had sent them away from his son, and had given them presents, and they went away. 21 And Abraham gave all that he had to his son Isaac, and he also gave him all his treasures. 22 And he commanded him saying, Dost thou not know and understand the Lord is God in heaven and in earth, and there is no other beside him? 23 And it was he who took me from my father's house, and from my birth place, and gave me all the delights upon earth; who delivered me from the counsel of the wicked, for in him did I trust. 24 And he brought me to this place, and he delivered me from Ur Casdim; and he said unto me, To thy seed will I give all these lands, and they shall inherit them when they keep my commandments, my statutes and my judgments that I have commanded thee, and which I shall command them. 25 Now therefore my son, hearken to my voice, and keep the commandments of the Lord thy God, which I commanded thee, do not turn from the right way either to the right or to the left, in order that it may be well with thee and thy children after thee forever. 26 And remember the wonderful works of the Lord, and his kindness that he has shown toward us, in having delivered us from the hands of our enemies, and the Lord our God caused them to fall into our hands; and now therefore keep all that I have commanded thee, and turn not away from the commandments of thy God, and serve none beside him, in order that it may be well with thee and thy seed after thee. 27 And teach thou thy children and thy seed the instructions of the Lord and his commandments, and teach them the upright way in which they should go, in order that it may be well with them forever. 28 And Isaac answered his father and said unto him, That which my Lord has commanded that will I do, and I will not depart from the commands of the Lord my God, I will keep all that he commanded me; and Abraham blessed his son Isaac, and also his children; and Abraham taught Jacob the instruction of the Lord and his ways. 29 And it was at that time that Abraham died, in the fifteenth year of the life of Jacob and Esau, the sons of Isaac, and all the days of Abraham were one hundred and seventy-five years, and he died and was gathered to his people in good old age, old and satisfied with days, and Isaac and Ishmael his sons buried him. 30 And when the inhabitants of Canaan heard that Abraham was dead, they all came with their kings and princes and all their men to bury Abraham. 31 And all the inhabitants of the land of Haran, and all the families of the house of Abraham, and all the princes and grandees, and the sons of Abraham by the concubines, all came when they heard of Abraham's death, and they requited Abraham's kindness, and comforted Isaac his son, and they buried Abraham in the cave which he bought from Ephron the Hittite and his children, for the possession of a burial place. 32 And all the inhabitants of Canaan, and all those who had known Abraham, wept for Abraham a whole year, and men and women mourned over him. 33 And all the little children, and all the inhabitants of the land wept on account of Abraham, for Abraham had been good to them all, and because he had been upright with God and men. 34 And there arose not a man who feared God like unto Abraham, for he had feared his God from his youth, and had served the Lord, and had gone in all his ways during his life, from his childhood to the day of his death. 35 And the Lord was with him and delivered him from the counsel of Nimrod and his people, and when he made war with the four kings of Elam he conquered them. 36 And he brought all the children of the earth to the service of God, and he taught them the ways of the Lord, and caused them to know the Lord. 37 And he formed a grove and he planted a vineyard therein, and he had always prepared in his tent meat and drink to those that passed through the land, that they might satisfy themselves in his house. 38 And the Lord God delivered the whole earth on account of Abraham. 39 And it was after the death of Abraham that God blessed his son Isaac and his children, and the Lord was with Isaac as he had been with his father Abraham, for Isaac kept all the commandments of the Lord as Abraham his father had commanded him; he did not turn to the right or to the left from the right path which his father had commanded him.

Jash.27

1 And Esau at that time, after the death of Abraham, frequently went in the field to hunt. 2 And Nimrod king of Babel, the same was Amraphel, also frequently went with his mighty men to hunt in the field, and to walk about with his men in the cool of the day. 3 And Nimrod was observing Esau all the days, for a jealousy was formed in the heart of Nimrod against Esau all the days. 4 And on a certain day Esau went in the field to hunt, and he found Nimrod walking in the wilderness with his two men. 5 And all his mighty men and his people were with him in the wilderness, but they removed at a distance from him, and they went from him in different directions to hunt, and Esau concealed himself for Nimrod, and he lurked for him in the wilderness. 6 And Nimrod and his men that were with him did not know him, and Nimrod and his men frequently walked about in the field at the cool of the day, and to know where his men were hunting in the field. 7 And Nimrod and two of his men that were

with him came to the place where they were, when Esau started suddenly from his lurking place, and drew his sword, and hastened and ran to Nimrod and cut off his head. 8 And Esau fought a desperate fight with the two men that were with Nimrod, and when they called out to him, Esau turned to them and smote them to death with his sword. 9 And all the mighty men of Nimrod, who had left him to go to the wilderness, heard the cry at a distance, and they knew the voices of those two men, and they ran to know the cause of it, when they found their king and the two men that were with him lying dead in the wilderness. 10 And when Esau saw the mighty men of Nimrod coming at a distance, he fled, and thereby escaped; and Esau took the valuable garments of Nimrod, which Nimrod's father had bequeathed to Nimrod, and with which Nimrod prevailed over the whole land, and he ran and concealed them in his house. 11 And Esau took those garments and ran into the city on account of Nimrod's men, and he came unto his father's house wearied and exhausted from fight, and he was ready to die through grief when he approached his brother Jacob and sat before him. 12 And he said unto his brother Jacob, Behold I shall die this day, and wherefore then do I want the birthright? And Jacob acted wisely with Esau in this matter, and Esau sold his birthright to Jacob, for it was so brought about by the Lord. 13 And Esau's portion in the cave of the field of Machpelah, which Abraham had bought from the children of Heth for the possession of a burial ground, Esau also sold to Jacob, and Jacob bought all this from his brother Esau for value given. 14 And Jacob wrote the whole of this in a book, and he testified the same with witnesses, and he sealed it, and the book remained in the hands of Jacob. 15 And when Nimrod the son of Cush died, his men lifted him up and brought him in consternation, and buried him in his city, and all the days that Nimrod lived were two hundred and fifteen years and he died. 16 And the days that Nimrod reigned upon the people of the land were one hundred and eighty-five years; and Nimrod died by the sword of Esau in shame and contempt, and the seed of Abraham caused his death as he had seen in his dream. 17 And at the death of Nimrod his kingdom became divided into many divisions, and all those parts that Nimrod reigned over were restored to the respective kings of the land, who recovered them after the death of Nimrod, and all the people of the house of Nimrod were for a long time enslaved to all the other kings of the land.

Jash.28

1 And in those days, after the death of Abraham, in that year the Lord brought a heavy famine in the land, and whilst the famine was raging in the land of Canaan, Isaac rose up to go down to Egypt on account of the famine, as his father Abraham had done. 2 And the Lord appeared that night to Isaac and he said to him, Do not go down to Egypt but rise and go to Gerar, to Abimelech king of the Philistines, and remain there till the famine shall cease. 3 And Isaac rose up and went to Gerar, as the Lord commanded him, and he remained there a full year. 4 And when Isaac came to Gerar, the people of the land saw that Rebecca his wife was of a beautiful appearance, and the people of Gerar asked Isaac concerning his wife, and he said, She is my sister, for he was afraid to say she was his wife lest the people of the land should slay him on account of her. 5 And the princes of Abimelech went and praised the woman to the king, but he answered them not, neither did he attend to their words. 6 But he heard them say that Isaac declared her to be his sister, so the king reserved this within himself. 7 And when Isaac had remained three months in the land, Abimelech looked out at the window, and he saw, and behold Isaac was sporting with Rebecca his wife, for Isaac dwelt in the outer house belonging to the king, so that the house of Isaac was opposite the house of the king. 8 And the

king said unto Isaac, What is this thou hast done to us in saying of thy wife, She is my sister? how easily might one of the great men of the people have lain with her, and thou wouldst then have brought guilt upon us.[9] And Isaac said unto Abimelech, Because I was afraid lest I die on account of my wife, therefore I said, She is my sister.[10] At that time Abimelech gave orders to all his princes and great men, and they took Isaac and Rebecca his wife and brought them before the king.[11] And the king commanded that they should dress them in princely garments, and make them ride through the streets of the city, and proclaim before them throughout the land, saying, This is the man and this is his wife; whoever toucheth this man or his wife shall surely die. And Isaac returned with his wife to the king's house, and the Lord was with Isaac and he continued to wax great and lacked nothing.[12] And the Lord caused Isaac to find favor in the sight of Abimelech, and in the sight of all his subjects, and Abimelech acted well with Isaac, for Abimelech remembered the oath and the covenant that existed between his father and Abraham.[13] And Abimelech said unto Isaac, Behold the whole earth is before thee; dwell wherever it may seem good in thy sight until thou shalt return to thy land; and Abimelech gave Isaac fields and vineyards and the best part of the land of Gerar, to sow and reap and eat the fruits of the ground until the days of the famine should have passed by.[14] And Isaac sowed in that land, and received a hundred-fold in the same year, and the Lord blessed him.[15] And the man waxed great, and he had possession of flocks and possession of herds and great store of servants.[16] And when the days of the famine had passed away the Lord appeared to Isaac and said unto him, Rise up, go forth from this place and return to thy land, to the land of Canaan; and Isaac rose up and returned to Hebron which is in the land of Canaan, he and all belonging to him as the Lord commanded him.[17] And after this Shelach the son at Arpachshad died in that year, which is the eighteenth year of the lives of Jacob and Esau; and all the days that Shelach lived were four hundred and thirty-three years and he died.[18] At that time Isaac sent his younger son Jacob to the house of Shem and Eber, and he learned the instructions of the Lord, and Jacob remained in the house of Shem and Eber for thirty-two years, and Esau his brother did not go, for he was not willing to go, and he remained in his father's house in the land of Canaan.[19] And Esau was continually hunting in the fields to bring home what he could get, so did Esau all the days.[20] And Esau was a designing and deceitful man, one who hunted after the hearts of men and inveigled them, and Esau was a valiant man in the field, and in the course of time went as usual to hunt; and he came as far as the field of Seir, the same is Edom.[21] And he remained in the land of Seir hunting in the field a year and four months.[22] And Esau there saw in the land of Seir the daughter of a man of Canaan, and her name was Jehudith, the daughter of Beeri, son of Epher, from the families of Heth the son of Canaan.[23] And Esau took her for a wife, and he came unto her; forty years old was Esau when he took her, and he brought her to Hebron, the land of his father's dwelling place, and he dwelt there.[24] And it came to pass in those days, in the hundred and tenth year of the life of Isaac, that is in the fiftieth year of the life of Jacob, in that year died Shem the son of Noah; Shem was six hundred years old at his death.[25] And when Shem died Jacob returned to his father to Hebron which is in the land of Canaan.[26] And in the fifty-sixth year of the life of Jacob, people came from Haran, and Rebecca was told concerning her brother Laban the son of Bethuel.[27] For the wife of Laban was barren in those days, and bare no children, and also all his handmaids bare none to him.[28] And the Lord afterward remembered Adinah the wife of Laban, and she conceived and bare twin daughters, and Laban called the names of his daughters, the name of the elder Leah, and the name of the younger Rachel.[29] And those people came and told these things to Rebecca, and Rebecca rejoiced greatly that the Lord had visited her brother and that he had got children.

Jash.29

[1] And Isaac the son of Abraham became old and advanced in days, and his eyes became heavy through age; they were dim and could not see.[2] At that time Isaac called unto Esau his son, saying, Get I pray thee thy weapons, thy quiver and thy bow, rise up and go forth into the field and get me some venison, and make me savory meat and bring it to me, that I may eat in order that I may bless thee before my death, as I have now become old and gray-headed.[3] And Esau did so; and he took his weapon and went forth into the field to hunt for venison, as usual, to bring to his father as he had ordered him, so that he might bless him.[4] And Rebecca heard all the words that Isaac had spoken unto Esau, and she hastened and called her son Jacob, saying, Thus did thy father speak unto thy brother Esau, and thus did I hear, now therefore hasten thou and make that which I shall tell thee.[5] Rise up and go, I pray thee, to the flock and fetch me two fine kids of the goats, and I will get the savory meat for thy father, and thou shalt bring the savory meat that he may eat before thy brother shall have come from the chase, in order that thy father may bless thee.[6] And Jacob hastened and did as his mother had commanded him, and he made the savory meat and brought it before his father before Esau had come from his chase.[7] And Isaac said unto Jacob, Who art thou, my son? And he said, I am thy first born Esau, I have done as thou didst order me, now therefore rise up I pray thee, and eat of my hunt, in order that thy soul may bless me as thou didst speak unto me.[8] And Isaac rose up and he ate and he drank, and his heart was comforted, and he blessed Jacob and Jacob went away from his father; and as soon as Isaac had blessed Jacob and he had gone away from him, behold Esau came from his hunt from the field, and he also made savory meat and brought it to his father to eat thereof and to bless him.[9] And Isaac said unto Esau, And who was he that has taken venison and brought it me before thou camest and whom I did bless? And Esau knew that his brother Jacob had done this, and the anger of Esau was kindled against his brother Jacob that he had acted thus toward him.[10] And Esau said, Is he not rightly called Jacob? for he has supplanted me twice, he took away my birthright and now he has taken away my blessing; and Esau wept greatly; and when Isaac heard the voice of his son Esau weeping, Isaac said unto Esau, What can I do, my son, thy brother came with subtlety and took away thy blessing; and Esau hated his brother Jacob on account of the blessing that his father had given him, and his anger was greatly roused against him.[11] And Jacob was very much afraid of his brother Esau, and he rose up and fled to the house of Eber the son of Shem, and he concealed himself there on account of his brother, and Jacob was sixty-three years old when he went forth from the land of Canaan from Hebron, and Jacob was concealed in Eber's house fourteen years on account of his brother Esau, and he there continued to learn the ways of the Lord and his commandments.[12] And when Esau saw that Jacob had fled and escaped from him, and that Jacob had cunningly obtained the blessing, then Esau grieved exceedingly, and he was also vexed at his father and mother; and he also rose up and took his wife and went away from his father and mother to the land of Seir, and he dwelt there; and Esau saw there a woman from amongst the daughters of Heth whose name was Bosmath, the daughter of Elon the Hittite, and he took her for a wife in addition to his first wife, and Esau called her name Adah, saying the blessing had in that time passed from him.[13] And Esau dwelt in the land of Seir six months without seeing his father and mother, and afterward Esau took his wives and rose up and returned to the land of Canaan, and Esau

placed his two wives in his father's house in Hebron. [14] And the wives of Esau vexed and provoked Isaac and Rebecca with their works, for they walked not in the ways of the Lord, but served their father's gods of wood and stone as their father had taught them, and they were more wicked than their father. [15] And they went according to the evil desires of their hearts, and they sacrificed and burnt incense to the Baalim, and Isaac and Rebecca became weary of them. [16] And Rebecca said, I am weary of my life because of the daughters of Heth; if Jacob take a wife of the daughters of Heth, such as these which are of the daughters of the land, what good then is life unto me? [17] And in those days Adah the wife of Esau conceived and bare him a son, and Esau called the name of the son that was born unto him Eliphaz, and Esau was sixty-five years old when she bare him. [18] And Ishmael the son of Abraham died in those days, in the sixty-forth year of the life of Jacob, and all the days that Ishmael lived were one hundred and thirty-seven years and he died. [19] And when Isaac heard that Ishmael was dead he mourned for him, and Isaac lamented over him many days. [20] And at the end of fourteen years of Jacob's residing in the house of Eber, Jacob desired to see his father and mother, and Jacob came to the house of his father and mother to Hebron, and Esau had in those days forgotten what Jacob had done to him in having taken the blessing from him in those days. [21] And when Esau saw Jacob coming to his father and mother he remembered what Jacob had done to him, and he was greatly incensed against him and he sought to slay him. [22] And Isaac the son of Abraham was old and advanced in days, and Esau said, Now my father's time is drawing nigh that he must die, and when he shall die I will slay my brother Jacob. [23] And this was told to Rebecca, and she hastened and sent and called for Jacob her son, and she said unto him, Arise, go and flee to Haran to my brother Laban, and remain there for some time, until thy brother's anger be turned from thee and then shalt thou come back. [24] And Isaac called unto Jacob and said unto him, Take not a wife from the daughters of Canaan, for thus did our father Abraham command us according to the word of the Lord which he had commanded him, saying, Unto thy seed will I give this land; if thy children keep my covenant that I have made with thee, then will I also perform to thy children that which I have spoken unto thee and I will not forsake them. [25] Now therefore my son hearken to my voice, to all that I shall command thee, and refrain from taking a wife from amongst the daughters of Canaan; arise, go to Haran to the house of Bethuel thy mother's father, and take unto thee a wife from there from the daughters of Laban thy mother's brother. [26] Therefore take heed lest thou shouldst forget the Lord thy God and all his ways in the land to which thou goest, and shouldst get connected with the people of the land and pursue vanity and forsake the Lord thy God. [27] But when thou comest to the land serve there the Lord, do not turn to the right or to the left from the way which I commanded thee and which thou didst learn. [28] And may the Almighty God grant thee favor in the sight of the people of the earth, that thou mayest take there a wife according to thy choice; one who is good and upright in the ways of the Lord. [29] And may God give unto thee and thy seed the blessing of thy father Abraham, and make thee fruitful and multiply thee, and mayest thou become a multitude of people in the land whither thou goest, and may God cause thee to return to this land, the land of thy father's dwelling, with children and with great riches, with joy and with pleasure. [30] And Isaac finished commanding Jacob and blessing him, and he gave him many gifts, together with silver and gold, and he sent him away; and Jacob hearkened to his father and mother; he kissed them and arose and went to Padan-aram; and Jacob was seventy-seven years old when he went out from the land of Canaan from Beersheba. [31] And when Jacob went away to go to

Haran Esau called unto his son Eliphaz, and secretly spoke unto him, saying, Now hasten, take thy sword in thy hand and pursue Jacob and pass before him in the road, and lurk for him, and slay him with thy sword in one of the mountains, and take all belonging to him and come back. [32] And Eliphaz the son of Esau was an active man and expert with the bow as his father had taught him, and he was a noted hunter in the field and a valiant man. [33] And Eliphaz did as his father had commanded him, and Eliphaz was at that time thirteen years old, and Eliphaz rose up and went and took ten of his mother's brothers with him and pursued Jacob. [34] And he closely followed Jacob, and he lurked for him in the border of the land of Canaan opposite to the city of Shechem. [35] And Jacob saw Eliphaz and his men pursuing him, and Jacob stood still in the place in which he was going, in order to know what this was, for he did not know the thing; and Eliphaz drew his sword and he went on advancing, he and his men, toward Jacob; and Jacob said unto them, What is to do with you that you have come hither, and what meaneth it that you pursue with your swords. [36] And Eliphaz came near to Jacob and he answered and said unto him, Thus did my father command me, and now therefore I will not deviate from the orders which my father gave me; and when Jacob saw that Esau had spoken to Eliphaz to employ force, Jacob then approached and supplicated Eliphaz and his men, saying to him, [37] Behold all that I have and which my father and mother gave unto me, that take unto thee and go from me, and do not slay me, and may this thing be accounted unto thee a righteousness. [38] And the Lord caused Jacob to find favor in the sight of Eliphaz the son of Esau, and his men, and they hearkened to the voice of Jacob, and they did not put him to death, and Eliphaz and his men took all belonging to Jacob together with the silver and gold that he had brought with him from Beersheba; they left him nothing. [39] And Eliphaz and his men went away from him and they returned to Esau to Beersheba, and they told him all that had occurred to them with Jacob, and they gave him all that they had taken from Jacob. [40] And Esau was indignant at Eliphaz his son, and at his men that were with him, because they had not put Jacob to death. [41] And they answered and said unto Esau, Because Jacob supplicated us in this matter not to slay him, our pity was excited toward him, and we took all belonging to him and brought it unto thee; and Esau took all the silver and gold which Eliphaz had taken from Jacob and he put them by in his house. [42] At that time when Esau saw that Isaac had blessed Jacob, and had commanded him, saying, Thou shalt not take a wife from amongst the daughters of Canaan, and that the daughters of Canaan were bad in the sight of Isaac and Rebecca, [43] Then he went to the house of Ishmael his uncle, and in addition to his older wives he took Machlath the daughter of Ishmael, the sister of Nebayoth, for a wife.

Jash.30

[1] And Jacob went forth continuing his road to Haran, and he came as far as mount Moriah, and he tarried there all night near the city of Luz; and the Lord appeared there unto Jacob on that night, and he said unto him, I am the Lord God of Abraham and the God of Isaac thy father; the land upon which thou liest I will give unto thee and thy seed. [2] And behold I am with thee and will keep thee wherever thou goest, and I will multiply thy seed as the stars of Heaven, and I will cause all thine enemies to fall before thee; and when they shall make war with thee they shall not prevail over thee, and I will bring thee again unto this land with joy, with children, and with great riches. [3] And Jacob awoke from his sleep and he rejoiced greatly at the vision which he had seen; and he called the name of that place Bethel. [4] And Jacob rose up from that place quite rejoiced, and when he walked his feet felt light to him for joy, and he went from there to the land of the children of the East, and he returned

to Haran and he set by the shepherd's well.[5] And he there found some men; going from Haran to feed their flocks, and Jacob made inquiries of them, and they said, We are from Haran.[6] And he said unto them, Do you know Laban, the son of Nahor? and they said, We know him, and behold his daughter Rachel is coming along to feed her father's flock.[7] Whilst he was yet speaking with them, Rachel the daughter of Laban came to feed her father's sheep, for she was a shepherdess.[8] And when Jacob saw Rachel, the daughter of Laban, his mother's brother, he ran and kissed her, and lifted up his voice and wept.[9] And Jacob told Rachel that he was the son of Rebecca, her father's sister, and Rachel ran and told her father, and Jacob continued to cry because he had nothing with him to bring to the house of Laban.[10] And when Laban heard that his sister's son Jacob had come, he ran and kissed him and embraced him and brought him into the house and gave him bread, and he ate.[11] And Jacob related to Laban what his brother Esau had done to him, and what his son Eliphaz had done to him in the road.[12] And Jacob resided in Laban's house for one month, and Jacob ate and drank in the house of Laban, and afterward Laban said unto Jacob, Tell me what shall be thy wages, for how canst thou serve me for nought?[13] And Laban had no sons but only daughters, and his other wives and handmaids were still barren in those days; and these are the names of Laban's daughters which his wife Adinah had borne unto him; the name of the elder was Leah and the name of the younger was Rachel; and Leah was tender-eyed, but Rachel was beautiful and well favored, and Jacob loved her.[14] And Jacob said unto Laban, I will serve thee seven years for Rachel thy younger daughter; and Laban consented to this and Jacob served Laban seven years for his daughter Rachel.[15] And in the second year of Jacob's dwelling in Haran, that is in the seventy ninth year of the life of Jacob, in that year died Eber the son of Shem, he was four hundred and sixty-four years old at his death.[16] And when Jacob heard that Eber was dead he grieved exceedingly, and he lamented and mourned over him many days.[17] And in the third year of Jacob's dwelling in Haran, Bosmath, the daughter of Ishmael, the wife of Esau, bare unto him a son, and Esau called his name Reuel.[18] And in the fourth year of Jacob's residence in the house of Laban, the Lord visited Laban and remembered him on account of Jacob, and sons were born unto him, and his first born was Beor, his second was Alib, and the third was Chorash.[19] And the Lord gave Laban riches and honor, sons and daughters, and the man increased greatly on account of Jacob.[20] And Jacob in those days served Laban in all manner of work, in the house and in the field, and the blessing of the Lord was in all that belonged to Laban in the house and in the field.[21] And in the fifth year died Jehudith, the daughter of Beeri, the wife of Esau, in the land of Canaan, and she had no sons but daughters only.[22] And these are the names of her daughters which she bare to Esau, the name of the elder was Marzith, and the name of the younger was Puith.[23] And when Jehudith died, Esau rose up and went to Seir to hunt in the field, as usual, and Esau dwelt in the land of Seir for a long time.[24] And in the sixth year Esau took for a wife, in addition to his other wives, Ahlibamah, the daughter of Zebeon the Hivite, and Esau brought her to the land of Canaan.[25] And Ahlibamah conceived and bare unto Esau three sons, Yeush, Yaalan, and Korah.[26] And in those days, in the land of Canaan, there was a quarrel between the herdsmen of Esau and the herdsmen of the inhabitants of the land of Canaan, for Esau's cattle and goods were too abundant for him to remain in the land of Canaan, in his father's house, and the land of Canaan could not bear him on account of his cattle.[27] And when Esau saw that his quarreling increased with the inhabitants of the land of Canaan, he rose up and took his wives and his sons and his daughters, and all

244

belonging to him, and the cattle which he possessed, and all his property that he had acquired in the land of Canaan, and he went away from the inhabitants of the land to the land of Seir, and Esau and all belonging to him dwelt in the land of Seir.[28] But from time to time Esau would go and see his father and mother in the land of Canaan, and Esau intermarried with the Horites, and he gave his daughters to the sons of Seir, the Horite.[29] And he gave his elder daughter Marzith to Anah, the son of Zebeon, his wife's brother, and Puith he gave to Azar, the son of Bilhan the Horite; and Esau dwelt in the mountain, he and his children, and they were fruitful and multiplied.

Jash.31

[1] And in the seventh year, Jacob's service which he served Laban was completed, and Jacob said unto Laban, Give me my wife, for the days of my service are fulfilled; and Laban did so, and Laban and Jacob assembled all the people of that place and they made a feast.[2] And in the evening Laban came to the house, and afterward Jacob came there with the people of the feast, and Laban extinguished all the lights that were there in the house.[3] And Jacob said unto Laban, Wherefore dost thou do this thing unto us? and Laban answered, Such is our custom to act in this land.[4] And afterward Laban took his daughter Leah, and he brought her to Jacob, and he came to her and Jacob did not know that she was Leah.[5] And Laban gave his daughter Leah his maid Zilpah for a handmaid.[6] And all the people at the feast knew what Laban had done to Jacob, but they did not tell the thing to Jacob.[7] And all the neighbors came that night to Jacob's house, and they ate and drank and rejoiced, and played before Leah upon timbrels, and with dances, and they responded before Jacob, Heleah, Heleah.[8] And Jacob heard their words but did not understand their meaning, but he thought such might be their custom in this land.[9] And the neighbors spoke these words before Jacob during the night, and all the lights that were in the house Laban had that night extinguished.[10] And in the morning, when daylight appeared, Jacob turned to his wife and he saw, and behold it was Leah that had been lying in his bosom, and Jacob said, Behold now I know what the neighbors said last night, Heleah, they said, and I knew it not.[11] And Jacob called unto Laban, and said unto him, What is this that thou didst unto me? Surely I served thee for Rachel, and why didst thou deceive me and didst give me Leah?[12] And Laban answered Jacob, saying, Not so is it done in our place to give the younger before the elder now therefore if thou desirest to take her sister likewise, take her unto thee for the service which thou wilt serve me for another seven years.[13] And Jacob did so, and he also took Rachel for a wife, and he served Laban seven years more, and Jacob also came to Rachel, and he loved Rachel more than Leah, and Laban gave her his maid Bilhah for a handmaid.[14] And when the Lord saw that Leah was hated, the Lord opened her womb, and she conceived and bare Jacob four sons in those days.[15] And these are their names, Reuben Simeon, Levi, and Judah, and she afterward left bearing.[16] And at that time Rachel was barren, and she had no offspring, and Rachel envied her sister Leah, and when Rachel saw that she bare no children to Jacob, she took her handmaid Bilhah, and she bare Jacob two sons, Dan and Naphtali.[17] And when Leah saw that she had left bearing, she also took her handmaid Zilpah, and she gave her to Jacob for a wife, and Jacob also came to Zilpah, and she also bare Jacob two sons, Gad and Asher.[18] And Leah again conceived and bare Jacob in those days two sons and one daughter, and these are their names, Issachar, Zebulon, and their sister Dinah.[19] And Rachel was still barren in those days, and Rachel prayed unto the Lord at that time, and she said, O Lord God remember me and visit me, I beseech thee, for now my husband will cast me off, for I have borne

him no children. [20] Now O Lord God, hear my supplication before thee, and see my affliction, and give me children like one of the handmaids, that I may no more bear my reproach. [21] And God heard her and opened her womb, and Rachel conceived and bare a son, and she said, The Lord has taken away my reproach, and she called his name Joseph, saying, May the Lord add to me another son; and Jacob was ninety-one years old when she bare him. [22] At that time Jacob's mother, Rebecca, sent her nurse Deborah the daughter of Uz, and two of Isaac's servants unto Jacob. [23] And they came to Jacob to Haran and they said unto him, Rebecca has sent us to thee that thou shalt return to thy father's house to the land of Canaan; and Jacob hearkened unto them in this which his mother had spoken. [24] At that time, the other seven years which Jacob served Laban for Rachel were completed, and it was at the end of fourteen years that he had dwelt in Haran that Jacob said unto Laban, give me my wives and send me away, that I may go to my land, for behold my mother did send unto me from the land at Canaan that I should return to my father's house. [25] And Laban said unto him, Not so I pray thee; if I have found favor in thy sight do not leave me; appoint me thy wages and I will give them, and remain with me. [26] And Jacob said unto him, This is what thou shalt give me for wages, that I shall this day pass through all thy flock and take away from them every lamb that is speckled and spotted and such as are brown amongst the sheep, and amongst the goats, and if thou wilt do this thing for me I will return and feed thy flock and keep them as at first. [27] And Laban did so, and Laban removed from his flock all that Jacob had said and gave them to him. [28] And Jacob placed all that he had removed from Laban's flock in the hands of his sons, and Jacob was feeding the remainder of Laban's flock. [29] And when the servants of Isaac which he had sent unto Jacob saw that Jacob would not then return with them to the land of Canaan to his father, they then went away from him, and they returned home to the land of Canaan. [30] And Deborah remained with Jacob in Haran, and she did not return with the servants of Isaac to the land of Canaan, and Deborah resided with Jacob's wives and children in Haran. [31] And Jacob served Laban six years longer, and when the sheep brought forth, Jacob removed from them such as were speckled and spotted, as he had determined with Laban, and Jacob did so at Laban's for six years, and the man increased abundantly and he had cattle and maid servants and men servants, camels, and asses. [32] And Jacob had two hundred drove of cattle, and his cattle were of large size and of beautiful appearance and were very productive, and all the families of the sons of men desired to get some of the cattle of Jacob, for they were exceedingly prosperous. [33] And many of the sons of men came to procure some of Jacob's flock, and Jacob gave them a sheep for a man servant or a maid servant or for an ass or a camel, or whatever Jacob desired from them they gave him. [34] And Jacob obtained riches and honor and possessions by means of these transactions with the sons of men, and the children of Laban envied him of this honor. [35] And in the course of time he heard the words of Laban's sons, saying, Jacob has taken away all that was our father's, and of that which was our father's has he acquired all this glory. [36] And Jacob beheld the countenance of Laban and of his children, and behold it was not toward him in those days as it had been before. [37] And the Lord appeared to Jacob at the expiration of the six years, and said unto him, Arise, go forth out of this land, and return to the land of thy birthplace and I will be with thee. [38] And Jacob rose up at that time and he mounted his children and wives and all belonging to him upon camels, and he went forth to go to the land of Canaan to his father Isaac. [39] And Laban did not know that Jacob had gone from him, for Laban had been that day sheep-shearing. [40] And Rachel stole her father's images, and she took them

and she concealed them upon the camel upon which she sat, and she went on. [41] And this is the manner of the images; in taking a man who is the first born and slaying him and taking the hair off his head, and taking salt and salting the head and anointing it in oil, then taking a small tablet of copper or a tablet of gold and writing the name upon it, and placing the tablet under his tongue, and taking the head with the tablet under the tongue and putting it in the house, and lighting up lights before it and bowing down to it. [42] And at the time when they bow down to it, it speaketh to them in all matters that they ask of it, through the power of the name which is written in it. [43] And some make them in the figures of men, of gold and silver, and go to them in times known to them, and the figures receive the influence of the stars, and tell them future things, and in this manner were the images which Rachel stole from her father. [44] And Rachel stole these images which were her father's, in order that Laban might not know through them where Jacob had gone. [45] And Laban came home and he asked concerning Jacob and his household, and he was not to be found, and Laban sought his images to know where Jacob had gone, and could not find them, and he went to some other images, and he inquired of them and they told him that Jacob had fled from him to his father's, to the land of Canaan. [46] And Laban then rose up and he took his brothers and all his servants, and he went forth and pursued Jacob, and he overtook him in mount Gilead. [47] And Laban said unto Jacob, What is this thou hast done to me to flee and deceive me, and lead my daughters and their children as captives taken by the sword? [48] And thou didst not suffer me to kiss them and send them away with joy, and thou didst steal my gods and didst go away. [49] And Jacob answered Laban, saying, Because I was afraid lest thou wouldst take thy daughters by force from me; and now with whomsoever thou findest thy gods he shall die. [50] And Laban searched for the images and he examined in all Jacob's tents and furniture, but could not find them. [51] And Laban said unto Jacob, We will make a covenant together and it shall be a testimony between me and thee; if thou shalt afflict my daughters, or shalt take other wives besides my daughters, even God shall be a witness between me and thee in this matter. [52] And they took stones and made a heap, and Laban said, This heap is a witness between me and thee, therefore he called the name thereof Gilead. [53] And Jacob and Laban offered sacrifice upon the mount, and they ate there by the heap, and they tarried in the mount all night, and Laban rose up early in the morning, and he wept with his daughters and he kissed them, and he returned unto his place. [54] And he hastened and sent off his son Beor, who was seventeen years old, with Abichorof the son of Uz, the son of Nahor, and with them were ten men. [55] And they hastened and went and passed on the road before Jacob, and they came by another road to the land of Seir. [56] And they came unto Esau and said unto him, Thus saith thy brother and relative, thy mother's brother Laban, the son of Bethuel, saying, [57] Hast thou heard what Jacob thy brother has done unto me, who first came to me naked and bare, and I went to meet him, and brought him to my house with honor, and I made him great, and I gave him my two daughters for wives and also two of my maids. [58] And God blessed him on my account, and he increased abundantly, and had sons, daughters and maid servants. [59] He has also an immense stock of flocks and herds, camels and asses, also silver and gold in abundance; and when he saw that his wealth increased, he left me whilst I went to shear my sheep, and he rose up and fled in secrecy. [60] And he lifted his wives and children upon camels, and he led away all his cattle and property which he acquired in my land, and he lifted up his countenance to go to his father Isaac, to the land of Canaan. [61] And he did not suffer me to kiss my daughters and their children, and he led my daughters as captives taken by the sword, and he also stole my gods and he fled.[62] And now I have left him in the mountain of the brook of Jabuk, him and all belonging to him; he lacketh nothing.[63] If it be thy wish to go to him, go then and there wilt thou find him, and thou canst do unto him as thy soul desireth; and Laban's messengers came and told Esau all these things.[64] And Esau heard all the words of Laban's messengers, and his anger was greatly kindled against Jacob, and he remembered his hatred, and his anger burned within him.[65] And Esau hastened and took his children and servants and the souls of his household, being sixty men, and he went and assembled all the children of Seir the Horite and their people, being three hundred and forty men, and took all this number of four hundred men with drawn swords, and he went unto Jacob to smite him.[66] And Esau divided this number into several parts, and he took the sixty men of his children and servants and the souls of his household as one head, and gave them in care of Eliphaz his eldest son.[67] And the remaining heads he gave to the care of the six sons of Seir the Horite, and he placed every man over his generations and children.[68] And the whole of this camp went as it was, and Esau went amongst them toward Jacob, and he conducted them with speed.[69] And Laban's messengers departed from Esau and went to the land of Canaan, and they came to the house of Rebecca the mother of Jacob and Esau.[70] And they told her saying, Behold thy son Esau has gone against his brother Jacob with four hundred men, for he heard that he was coming, and he is gone to make war with him, and to smite him and to take all that he has.[71] And Rebecca hastened and sent seventy two men from the servants of Isaac to meet Jacob on the road; for she said, Peradventure, Esau may make war in the road when he meets him.[72] And these messengers went on the road to meet Jacob, and they met him in the road of the brook on the opposite side of the brook Jabuk, and Jacob said when he saw them, This camp is destined to me from God, and Jacob called the name of that place Machnayim.[73] And Jacob knew all his father's people, and he kissed them and embraced them and came with them, and Jacob asked them concerning his father and mother, and they said, They were well.[74] And these messengers said unto Jacob, Rebecca thy mother has sent us to thee, saying, I have heard, my son, that thy brother Esau has gone forth against thee on the road with men from the children of Seir the Horite.[75] And therefore, my son, hearken to my voice and see with thy counsel what thou wilt do, and when he cometh up to thee, supplicate him, and do not speak rashly to him, and give him a present from what thou possessest, and from what God has favored thee with.[76] And when he asketh thee concerning thy affairs, conceal nothing from him, perhaps he may turn from his anger against thee and thou wilt thereby save thy soul, thou and all belonging to thee, for it is thy duty to honor him, for he is thy elder brother.[77] And when Jacob heard the words of his mother which the messengers had spoken to him, Jacob lifted up his voice and wept bitterly, and did as his mother then commanded him.

Jash.32

[1] And at that time Jacob sent messengers to his brother Esau toward the land of Seir, and he spoke to him words of supplication.[2] And he commanded them, saying, Thus shall ye say to my lord, to Esau, Thus saith thy servant Jacob, Let not my lord imagine that my father's blessing with which he did bless me has proved beneficial to me.[3] For I have been these twenty years with Laban, and he deceived me and changed my wages ten times, as it has all been already told unto my lord.[4] And I served him in his house very laboriously, and God afterward saw my affliction, my labor and the work of my hands, and he caused me to find grace and favor in his sight.[5] And I afterward through God's great mercy and kindness acquired oxen and asses and cattle, and men servants and maid servants.[6] And now

246

I am coming to my land and my home to my father and mother, who are in the land of Canaan; and I have sent to let my lord know all this in order to find favor in the sight of my lord, so that he may not imagine that I have of myself obtained wealth, or that the blessing with which my father blessed me has benefited me.[7] And those messengers went to Esau, and found him on the borders of the land of Edom going toward Jacob, and four hundred men of the children of Seir the Horite were standing with drawn swords.[8] And the messengers of Jacob told Esau all the words that Jacob had spoken to them concerning Esau.[9] And Esau answered them with pride and contempt, and said unto them, Surely I have heard and truly it has been told unto me what Jacob has done to Laban, who exalted him in his house and gave him his daughters for wives, and he begat sons and daughters, and abundantly increased in wealth and riches in Laban's house through his means.[10] And when he saw that his wealth was abundant and his riches great he fled with all belonging to him, from Laban's house, and he led Laban's daughters away from the face of their father, as captives taken by the sword without telling him of it.[11] And not only to Laban has Jacob done thus but also unto me has he done so and has twice supplanted me, and shall I be silent?[12] Now therefore I have this day come with my camps to meet him, and I will do unto him according to the desire of my heart.[13] And the messengers returned and came to Jacob and said unto him, We came to thy brother, to Esau, and we told him all thy words, and thus has he answered us, and behold he cometh to meet thee with four hundred men.[14] Now then know and see what thou shalt do, and pray before God to deliver thee from him.[15] And when he heard the words of his brother which he had spoken to the messengers of Jacob, Jacob was greatly afraid and he was distressed.[16] And Jacob prayed to the Lord his God, and he said, O Lord God of my fathers, Abraham and Isaac, thou didst say unto me when I went away from my father's house, saying,[17] I am the Lord God of thy father Abraham and the God of Isaac, unto thee do I give this land and thy seed after thee, and I will make thy seed as the stars of heaven, and thou shalt spread forth to the four sides of heaven, and in thee and in thy seed shall all the families of the earth be blessed.[18] And thou didst establish thy words, and didst give unto me riches and children and cattle, as the utmost wishes of my heart didst thou give unto thy servant; thou didst give unto me all that I asked from thee, so that I lacked nothing.[19] And thou didst afterward say unto me, Return to thy parents and to thy birth place and I will still do well with thee.[20] And now that I have come, and thou didst deliver me from Laban, I shall fall in the hands of Esau who will slay me, yea, together with the mothers of my children.[21] Now therefore, O Lord God, deliver me, I pray thee, also from the hands of my brother Esau, for I am greatly afraid of him.[22] And if there is no righteousness in me, do it for the sake of Abraham and my father Isaac.[23] For I know that through kindness and mercy have I acquired this wealth; now therefore I beseech thee to deliver me this day with thy kindness and to answer me.[24] And Jacob ceased praying to the Lord, and he divided the people that were with him with the flocks and cattle into two camps, and he gave the half to the care of Damesek, the son of Eliezer, Abraham's servant, for a camp, with his children, and the other half he gave to the care of his brother Elianus the son of Eliezer, to be for a camp with his children.[25] And he commanded them, saying, Keep yourselves at a distance with your camps, and do not come too near each other, and if Esau come to one camp and slay it, the other camp at a distance from it will escape him.[26] And Jacob tarried there that night, and during the whole night he gave his servants instructions concerning the forces and his children.[27] And the Lord heard the prayer of Jacob on that day, and the Lord then delivered Jacob from the hands of his brother Esau.[28] And the Lord sent three angels of the angels of heaven, and they went before Esau and came to him.[29] And these angels appeared unto Esau and his people as two thousand men, riding upon horses furnished with all sorts of war instruments, and they appeared in the sight of Esau and all his men to be divided into four camps, with four chiefs to them.[30] And one camp went on and they found Esau coming with four hundred men toward his brother Jacob, and this camp ran toward Esau and his people and terrified them, and Esau fell off the horse in alarm, and all his men separated from him in that place, for they were greatly afraid.[31] And the whole of the camp shouted after them when they fled from Esau, and all the warlike men answered, saying,[32] Surely we are the servants of Jacob, who is the servant of God, and who then can stand against us? And Esau said unto them, O then, my lord and brother Jacob is your lord, whom I have not seen for these twenty years, and now that I have this day come to see him, do you treat me in this manner?[33] And the angels answered him saying, As the Lord liveth, were not Jacob of whom thou speaketh thy brother, we had not let one remaining from thee and thy people, but only on account of Jacob we will do nothing to them.[34] And this camp passed from Esau and his men and it went away, and Esau and his men had gone from them about a league when the second camp came toward him with all sorts of weapons, and they also did unto Esau and his men as the first camp had done to them.[35] And when they had left it to go on, behold the third camp came toward him and they were all terrified, and Esau fell off the horse, and the whole camp cried out, and said, Surely we are the servants of Jacob, who is the servant of God, and who can stand against us?[36] And Esau again answered them saying, O then, Jacob my lord and your lord is my brother, and for twenty years I have not seen his countenance and hearing this day that he was coming, I went this day to meet him, and do you treat me in this manner?[37] And they answered him, and said unto him, As the Lord liveth, were not Jacob thy brother as thou didst say, we had not left a remnant from thee and thy men, but on account of Jacob of whom thou speakest being thy brother, we will not meddle with thee or thy men.[38] And the third camp also passed from them, and he still continued his road with his men toward Jacob, when the fourth camp came toward him, and they also did unto him and his men as the others had done.[39] And when Esau beheld the evil which the four angels had done to him and to his men, he became greatly afraid of his brother Jacob, and he went to meet him in peace.[40] And Esau concealed his hatred against Jacob, because he was afraid of his life on account of his brother Jacob, and because he imagined that the four camps that he had lighted upon were Jacob's servants.[41] And Jacob tarried that night with his servants in their camps, and he resolved with his servants to give unto Esau a present from all that he had with him, and from all his property; and Jacob rose up in the morning, he and his men, and they chose from amongst the cattle a present for Esau.[42] And this is the amount of the present which Jacob chose from his flock to give unto his brother Esau: and he selected two hundred and forty head from the flocks, and he selected from the camels and asses thirty each, and of the herds he chose fifty kine.[43] And he put them all in ten droves, and he placed each sort by itself, and he delivered them into the hands of ten of his servants, each drove by itself.[44] And he commanded them, and said unto them, Keep yourselves at a distance from each other, and put a space between the droves, and when Esau and those who are with him shall meet you and ask you, saying, Whose are you, and whither do you go, and to whom belongeth all this before you, you shall say unto them, We are the servants of Jacob, and we come to meet Esau in peace, and behold Jacob cometh behind us.[45] And that which is before us is a present sent from Jacob to his brother Esau.[46] And if they shall say unto you, Why doth he delay behind you, from coming to meet his brother and to see his face, then you shall say unto them, Surely he cometh joyfully behind us to meet his brother, for he said, I will appease him with the present that goeth to him, and after this I will see his face, peradventure he will accept of me.[47] So the whole present passed on in the hands of his servants, and went before him on that day, and he lodged that night with his camps by the border of the brook of Jabuk, and he rose up in the midst of the night, and he took his wives and his maid servants, and all belonging to him, and he that night passed them over the ford Jabuk.[48] And when he passed all belonging to him over the brook, Jacob was left by himself, and a man met him, and he wrestled with him that night until the breaking of the day, and the hollow of Jacob's thigh was out of joint through wrestling with him.[49] And at the break of day the man left Jacob there, and he blessed him and went away, and Jacob passed the brook at the break of day, and he halted upon his thigh.[50] And the sun rose upon him when he had passed the brook, and he came up to the place of his cattle and children.[51] And they went on till midday, and whilst they were going the present was passing on before them.[52] And Jacob lifted up his eyes and looked, and behold Esau was at a distance, coming along with many men, about four hundred, and Jacob was greatly afraid of his brother.[53] And Jacob hastened and divided his children unto his wives and his handmaids, and his daughter Dinah he put in a chest, and delivered her into the hands of his servants.[54] And he passed before his children and wives to meet his brother, and he bowed down to the ground, yea he bowed down seven times until he approached his brother, and God caused Jacob to find grace and favor in the sight of Esau and his men, for God had heard the prayer of Jacob.[55] And the fear of Jacob and his terror fell upon his brother Esau, for Esau was greatly afraid of Jacob for what the angels of God had done to Esau, and Esau's anger against Jacob was turned into kindness.[56] And when Esau saw Jacob running toward him, he also ran toward him and he embraced him, and he fell upon his neck, and they kissed and they wept.[57] And God put fear and kindness toward Jacob in the hearts of the men that came with Esau, and they also kissed Jacob and embraced him.[58] And also Eliphaz, the son of Esau, with his four brothers, sons of Esau, wept with Jacob, and they kissed him and embraced him, for the fear of Jacob had fallen upon them all.[59] And Esau lifted up his eyes and saw the women with their offspring, the children of Jacob, walking behind Jacob and bowing along the road to Esau.[60] And Esau said unto Jacob, Who are these with thee, my brother? are they thy children or thy servants? and Jacob answered Esau and said, They are my children which God hath graciously given to thy servant.[61] And whilst Jacob was speaking to Esau and his men, Esau beheld the whole camp, and he said unto Jacob, Whence didst thou get the whole of the camp that I met yesternight? and Jacob said, To find favor in the sight of my lord, it is that which God graciously gave to thy servant.[62] And the present came before Esau, and Jacob pressed Esau, saying, Take I pray thee the present that I have brought to my lord, and Esau said, Wherefore is this my purpose? keep that which thou hast unto thyself.[63] And Jacob said, It is incumbent upon me to give all this, since I have seen thy face, that thou still livest in peace.[64] And Esau refused to take the present, and Jacob said unto him, I beseech thee my lord, if now I have found favor in thy sight, then receive my present at my hand, for I have therefore seen thy face, as though I had seen a god-like face, because thou wast pleased with me.[65] And Esau took the present, and Jacob also gave unto Esau silver and gold and bdellium, for he pressed him so much that he took them.[66] And Esau divided the cattle that were in the camp, and he gave the half to the men who had come with him, for they had come on hire, and the other half he delivered unto the hands of his children.[67] And the silver and gold and bdellium he gave in the hands of Eliphaz his eldest son, and Esau said unto Jacob, Let us remain with thee, and we will go slowly along with thee until thou comest to my place with me, that we may dwell there together.[68] And Jacob answered his brother and said, I would do as my lord speaketh unto me, but my lord knoweth that the children are tender, and the flocks and herds with their young who are with me, go but slowly, for if they went swiftly they would all die, for thou knowest their burdens and their fatigue.[69] Therefore let my lord pass on before his servant, and I will go on slowly for the sake of the children and the flock, until I come to my lord's place to Seir.[70] And Esau said unto Jacob, I will place with thee some of the people that are with me to take care of thee in the road, and to bear thy fatigue and burden, and he said, What needeth it my lord, if I may find grace in thy sight?[71] Behold I will come unto thee to Seir to dwell there together as thou hast spoken, go thou then with thy people for I will follow thee.[72] And Jacob said this to Esau in order to remove Esau and his men from him, so that Jacob might afterward go to his father's house to the land of Canaan.[73] And Esau hearkened to the voice of Jacob, and Esau returned with the four hundred men that were with him on their road to Seir, and Jacob and all belonging to him went that day as far as the extremity of the land of Canaan in its borders, and he remained there some time.

Jash.33

[1] And in some time after Jacob went away from the borders of the land, and he came to the land of Shalem, that is the city of Shechem, which is in the land of Canaan, and he rested in front of the city.[2] And he bought a parcel of the field which was there, from the children of Hamor the people of the land, for five shekels.[3] And Jacob there built himself a house, and he pitched his tent there, and he made booths for his cattle, therefore he called the name of that place Succoth.[4] And Jacob remained in Succoth a year and six months.[5] At that time some of the women of the inhabitants of the land went to the city of Shechem to dance and rejoice with the daughters of the people of the city, and when they went forth then Rachel and Leah the wives of Jacob with their families also went to behold the rejoicing of the daughters of the city.[6] And Dinah the daughter of Jacob also went along with them and saw the daughters of the city, and they remained there before these daughters whilst all the people of the city were standing by them to behold their rejoicings, and all the great people of the city were there.[7] And Shechem the son of Hamor, the prince of the land was also standing there to see them.[8] And Shechem beheld Dinah the daughter of Jacob sitting with her mother before the daughters of the city, and the damsel pleased him greatly, and he there asked his friends and his people, saying, Whose daughter is that sitting amongst the women, whom I do not know in this city?[9] And they said unto him, Surely this is the daughter of Jacob the son of Isaac the Hebrew, who has dwelt in this city for some time, and when it was reported that the daughters of the land were going forth to rejoice she went with her mother and maid servants to sit amongst them as thou seest.[10] And Shechem beheld Dinah the daughter of Jacob, and when he looked at her his soul became fixed upon Dinah.[11] And he sent and had her taken by force, and Dinah came to the house of Shechem and he seized her forcibly and lay with her and humbled her, and he loved her exceedingly and placed her in his house.[12] And they came and told the thing unto Jacob, and when Jacob heard that Shechem had defiled his daughter Dinah, Jacob sent twelve of his servants to fetch Dinah from the house of Shechem, and they went and came to the house of Shechem to take away Dinah from

there.[13] And when they came Shechem went out to them with his men and drove them from his house, and he would not suffer them to come before Dinah, but Shechem was sitting with Dinah kissing and embracing her before their eyes.[14] And the servants of Jacob came back and told him, saying, When we came, he and his men drove us away, and thus did Shechem do unto Dinah before our eyes.[15] And Jacob knew moreover that Shechem had defiled his daughter, but he said nothing, and his sons were feeding his cattle in the field, and Jacob remained silent till their return.[16] And before his sons came home Jacob sent two maidens from his servants' daughters to take care of Dinah in the house of Shechem, and to remain with her, and Shechem sent three of his friends to his father Hamor the son of Chiddekem, the son of Pered, saying, Get me this damsel for a wife.[17] And Hamor the son of Chiddekem the Hivite came to the house of Shechem his son, and he sat before him, and Hamor said unto his son, Shechem, Is there then no woman amongst the daughters of thy people that thou wilt take an Hebrew woman who is not of thy people?[18] And Shechem said to him, Her only must thou get for me, for she is delightful in my sight; and Hamor did according to the word of his son, for he was greatly beloved by him.[19] And Hamor went forth to Jacob to commune with him concerning this matter, and when he had gone from the house of his son Shechem, before he came to Jacob to speak unto him, behold the sons of Jacob had come from the field, as soon as they heard the thing that Shechem the son of Hamor had done.[20] And the men were very much grieved concerning their sister, and they all came home fired with anger, before the time of gathering in their cattle.[21] And they came and sat before their father and they spoke unto him kindled with wrath, saying, Surely death is due to this man and to his household, because the Lord God of the whole earth commanded Noah and his children that man shall never rob, nor commit adultery; now behold Shechem has both ravaged and committed fornication with our sister, and not one of all the people of the city spoke a word to him.[22] Surely thou knowest and understandest that the judgment of death is due to Shechem, and to his father, and to the whole city on account of the thing which he has done.[23] And whilst they were speaking before their father in this matter, behold Hamor the father of Shechem came to speak to Jacob the words of his son concerning Dinah, and he sat before Jacob and before his sons.[24] And Hamor spoke unto them, saying, The soul of my son Shechem longeth for your daughter; I pray you give her unto him for a wife and intermarry with us; give us your daughters and we will give you our daughters, and you shall dwell with us in our land and we will be as one people in the land.[25] For our land is very extensive, so dwell ye and trade therein and get possessions in it, and do therein as you desire, and no one shall prevent you by saying a word to you.[26] And Hamor ceased speaking unto Jacob and his sons, and behold Shechem his son had come after him, and he sat before them.[27] And Shechem spoke before Jacob and his sons, saying, May I find favor in your sight that you will give me your daughter, and whatever you say unto me that will I do for her.[28] Ask me for abundance of dowry and gift, and I will give it, and whatever you shall say unto me that will I do, and whoever he be that will rebel against your orders, he shall die; only give me the damsel for a wife.[29] And Simeon and Levi answered Hamor and Shechem his son deceitfully, saying, All you have spoken unto us we will do for you.[30] And behold our sister is in your house, but keep away from her until we send to our father Isaac concerning this matter, for we can do nothing without his consent.[31] For he knoweth the ways of our father Abraham, and whatever he sayeth unto us we will tell you, we will conceal nothing from you.[32] And Simeon and Levi spoke this unto Shechem and his father in order to find a pretext, and to seek counsel what was to be done to Shechem and to his city in this matter.³³ And when Shechem and his father heard the words of Simeon and Levi, it seemed good in their sight, and Shechem and his father came forth to go home.³⁴ And when they had gone, the sons of Jacob said unto their father, saying, Behold, we know that death is due to these wicked ones and to their city, because they transgressed that which God had commanded unto Noah and his children and his seed after them.³⁵ And also because Shechem did this thing to our sister Dinah in defiling her, for such vileness shall never be done amongst us.³⁶ Now therefore know and see what you will do, and seek counsel and pretext what is to be done to them, in order to kill all the inhabitants of this city.³⁷ And Simeon said to them, Here is a proper advice for you: tell them to circumcise every male amongst them as we are circumcised, and if they do not wish to do this, we shall take our daughter from them and go away.³⁸ And if they consent to do this and will do it, then when they are sunk down with pain, we will attack them with our swords, as upon one who is quiet and peaceable, and we will slay every male person amongst them.³⁹ And Simeon's advice pleased them, and Simeon and Levi resolved to do unto them as it was proposed.⁴⁰ And on the next morning Shechem and Hamor his father came again unto Jacob and his sons, to speak concerning Dinah, and to hear what answer the sons of Jacob would give to their words.⁴¹ And the sons of Jacob spoke deceitfully to them, saying, We told our father Isaac all your words, and your words pleased him.⁴² But he spoke unto us, saying, Thus did Abraham his father command him from God the Lord of the whole earth, that any man who is not of his descendants that should wish to take one of his daughters, shall cause every male belonging to him to be circumcised, as we are circumcised, and then we may give him our daughter for a wife.⁴³ Now we have made known to you all our ways that our father spoke unto us, for we cannot do this of which you spoke unto us, to give our daughter to an uncircumcised man, for it is a disgrace to us.⁴⁴ But herein will we consent to you, to give you our daughter, and we will also take unto ourselves your daughters, and will dwell amongst you and be one people as you have spoken, if you will hearken to us, and consent to be like us, to circumcise every male belonging to you, as we are circumcised.⁴⁵ And if you will not hearken unto us, to have every male circumcised as we are circumcised, as we have commanded, then we will come to you, and take our daughter from you and go away.⁴⁶ And Shechem and his father Hamor heard the words of the sons of Jacob, and the thing pleased them exceedingly, and Shechem and his father Hamor hastened to do the wishes of the sons of Jacob, for Shechem was very fond of Dinah, and his soul was riveted to her.⁴⁷ And Shechem and his father Hamor hastened to the gate of the city, and they assembled all the men of their city and spoke unto them the words of the sons of Jacob, saying,⁴⁸ We came to these men, the sons of Jacob, and we spoke unto them concerning their daughter, and these men will consent to do according to our wishes, and behold our land is of great extent for them, and they will dwell in it, and trade in it, and we shall be one people; we will take their daughters, and our daughters we will give unto them for wives.⁴⁹ But only on this condition will these men consent to do this thing, that every male amongst us be circumcised as they are circumcised, as their God commanded them, and when we shall have done according to their instructions to be circumcised, then will they dwell amongst us, together with their cattle and possessions, and we shall be as one people with them.⁵⁰ And when all the men of the city heard the words of Shechem and his father Hamor, then all the men of their city were agreeable to this proposal, and they obeyed to be circumcised, for Shechem and his father Hamor were greatly esteemed by them, being the princes of the land.⁵¹ And on the next day, Shechem and Hamor his father rose up early in the morning, and they assembled all the men of their city into the middle of the city, and they called for the sons of Jacob, who circumcised every male belonging to them on that day and the next.⁵² And they circumcised Shechem and Hamor his father, and the five brothers of Shechem, and then every one rose up and went home, for this thing was from the Lord against the city of Shechem, and from the Lord was Simeon's counsel in this matter, in order that the Lord might deliver the city of Shechem into the hands of Jacob's two sons.

Jash.34

¹ And the number of all the males that were circumcised, were six hundred and forty-five men, and two hundred and forty-six children.² But Chiddekem, son of Pered, the father of Hamor, and his six brothers, would not listen unto Shechem and his father Hamor, and they would not be circumcised, for the proposal of the sons of Jacob was loathsome in their sight, and their anger was greatly roused at this, that the people of the city had not hearkened to them.³ And in the evening of the second day, they found eight small children who had not been circumcised, for their mothers had concealed them from Shechem and his father Hamor, and from the men of the city.⁴ And Shechem and his father Hamor sent to have them brought before them to be circumcised, when Chiddekem and his six brothers sprang at them with their swords, and sought to slay them.⁵ And they sought to slay also Shechem and his father Hamor and they sought to slay Dinah with them on account of this matter.⁶ And they said unto them, What is this thing that you have done? are there no women amongst the daughters of your brethren the Canaanites, that you wish to take unto yourselves daughters of the Hebrews, whom ye knew not before, and will do this act which your fathers never commanded you?⁷ Do you imagine that you will succeed through this act which you have done? and what will you answer in this affair to your brethren the Canaanites, who will come tomorrow and ask you concerning this thing?⁸ And if your act shall not appear just and good in their sight, what will you do for your lives, and me for our lives, in your not having hearkened to our voices?⁹ And if the inhabitants of the land and all your brethren the children of Ham, shall hear of your act, saying,¹⁰ On account of a Hebrew woman did Shechem and Hamor his father, and all the inhabitants of their city, do that with which they had been unacquainted and which their ancestors never commanded them, where then will you fly or where conceal your shame, all your days before your brethren, the inhabitants of the land of Canaan?¹¹ Now therefore we cannot bear up against this thing which you have done, neither can we be burdened with this yoke upon us, which our ancestors did not command us.¹² Behold tomorrow we will go and assemble all our brethren, the Canaanitish brethren who dwell in the land, and we will all come and smite you and all those who trust in you, that there shall not be a remnant left from you or them.¹³ And when Hamor and his son Shechem and all the people of the city heard the words of Chiddekem and his brothers, they were terribly afraid of their lives at their words, and they repented of what they had done.¹⁴ And Shechem and his father Hamor answered their father Chiddekem and his brethren, and they said unto them, All the words which you spoke unto us are true.¹⁵ Now do not say, nor imagine in your hearts that on account of the love of the Hebrews we did this thing that our ancestors did not command us.¹⁶ But because we saw that it was not their intention and desire to accede to our wishes concerning their daughter as to our taking her, except on this condition, so we hearkened to their voices and did this act which you saw, in order to obtain our desire from them.¹⁷ And when we shall have obtained our request from them, we will then return to them and do unto them that which you say unto us.¹⁸ We beseech

you then to wait and tarry until our flesh shall be healed and we again become strong, and we will then go together against them, and do unto them that which is in your hearts and in ours.[19] And Dinah the daughter of Jacob heard all these words which Chiddekem and his brothers had spoken, and what Hamor and his son Shechem and the people of their city had answered them.[20] And she hastened and sent one of her maidens, that her father had sent to take care of her in the house of Shechem, to Jacob her father and to her brethren, saying:[21] Thus did Chiddekem and his brothers advise concerning you, and thus did Hamor and Shechem and the people of the city answer them.[22] And when Jacob heard these words he was filled with wrath, and he was indignant at them, and his anger was kindled against them.[23] And Simeon and Levi swore and said, As the Lord liveth, the God of the whole earth, by this time tomorrow, there shall not be a remnant left in the whole city.[24] And twenty young men had concealed themselves who were not circumcised, and these young men fought against Simeon and Levi, and Simeon and Levi killed eighteen of them, and two fled from them and escaped to some lime pits that were in the city, and Simeon and Levi sought for them, but could not find them.[25] And Simeon and Levi continued to go about in the city, and they killed all the people of the city at the edge of the sword, and they left none remaining.[26] And there was a great consternation in the midst of the city, and the cry of the people of the city ascended to heaven, and all the women and children cried aloud.[27] And Simeon and Levi slew all the city; they left not a male remaining in the whole city.[28] And they slew Hamor and Shechem his son at the edge of the sword, and they brought away Dinah from the house of Shechem and they went from there.[29] And the sons of Jacob went and returned, and came upon the slain, and spoiled all their property which was in the city and the field.[30] And whilst they were taking the spoil, three hundred men stood up and threw dust at them and struck them with stones, when Simeon turned to them and he slew them all with the edge of the sword, and Simeon turned before Levi, and came into the city.[31] And they took away their sheep and their oxen and their cattle, and also the remainder of the women and little ones, and they led all these away, and they opened a gate and went out and came unto their father Jacob with vigor.[32] And when Jacob saw all that they had done to the city, and saw the spoil that they took from them, Jacob was very angry at them, and Jacob said unto them, What is this that you have done to me? behold I obtained rest amongst the Canaanitish inhabitants of the land, and none of them meddled with me.[33] And now you have done to make me obnoxious to the inhabitants of the land, amongst the Canaanites and the Perizzites, and I am but of a small number, and they will all assemble against me and slay me when they hear of your work with their brethren, and I and my household will be destroyed.[34] And Simeon and Levi and all their brothers with them answered their father Jacob and said unto him, Behold we live in the land, and shall Shechem do this to our sister? why art thou silent at all that Shechem has done? and shall he deal with our sister as with a harlot in the streets?[35] And the number of women whom Simeon and Levi took captives from the city of Shechem, whom they did not slay, was eighty-five who had not known man.[36] And amongst them was a young damsel of beautiful appearance and well favored, whose name was Bunah, and Simeon took her for a wife, and the number of the males which they took captives and did not slay, was forty-seven men, and the rest they slew.[37] And all the young men and women that Simeon and Levi had taken captives from the city of Shechem, were servants to the sons of Jacob and to their children after them, until the day of the sons of Jacob going forth from the land of Egypt.[38] And when Simeon and Levi had gone forth from the city, the two young men that were

left, who had concealed themselves in the city, and did not die amongst the people of the city, rose up, and these young men went into the city and walked about in it, and found the city desolate without man, and only women weeping, and these young men cried out and said, Behold, this is the evil which the sons of Jacob the Hebrew did to this city in their having this day destroyed one of the Canaanitish cities, and were not afraid of their lives of all the land of Canaan.[39] And these men left the city and went to the city of Tapnach, and they came there and told the inhabitants of Tapnach all that had befallen them, and all that the sons of Jacob had done to the city of Shechem.[40] And the information reached Jashub king of Tapnach, and he sent men to the city of Shechem to see those young men, for the king did not believe them in this account, saying, How could two men lay waste such a large town as Shechem?[41] And the messengers of Jashub came back and told him, saying, We came unto the city, and it is destroyed, there is not a man there; only weeping women; neither is any flock or cattle there, for all that was in the city the sons of Jacob took away.[42] And Jashub wondered at this, saying, How could two men do this thing, to destroy so large a city, and not one man able to stand against them?[43] For the like has not been from the days of Nimrod, and not even from the remotest time, has the like taken place; and Jashub, king of Tapnach, said to his people, Be courageous and we will go and fight against these Hebrews, and do unto them as they did unto the city, and we will avenge the cause of the people of the city.[44] And Jashub, king of Tapnach, consulted with his counsellors about this matter, and his advisers said unto him, Alone thou wilt not prevail over the Hebrews, for they must be powerful to do this work to the whole city.[45] If two of them laid waste the whole city, and no one stood against them, surely if thou wilt go against them, they will all rise against us and destroy us likewise.[46] But if thou wilt send to all the kings that surround us, and let them come together, then we will go with them and fight against the sons of Jacob; then wilt thou prevail against them.[47] And Jashub heard the words of his counsellors, and their words pleased him and his people, and he did so; and Jashub king of Tapnach sent to all the kings of the Amorites that surrounded Shechem and Tapnach, saying,[48] Go up with me and assist me, and we will smite Jacob the Hebrew and all his sons, and destroy them from the earth, for thus did he do to the city of Shechem, and do you not know of it?[49] And all the kings of the Amorites heard the evil that the sons of Jacob had done to the city of Shechem, and they were greatly astonished at them.[50] And the seven kings of the Amorites assembled with all their armies, about ten thousand men with drawn swords, and they came to fight against the sons of Jacob; and Jacob heard that the kings of the Amorites had assembled to fight against his sons, and Jacob was greatly afraid, and it distressed him.[51] And Jacob exclaimed against Simeon and Levi, saying, What is this act that you did? why have you injured me, to bring against me all the children of Canaan to destroy me and my household? for I was at rest, even I and my household, and you have done this thing to me, and provoked the inhabitants of the land against me by your proceedings.[52] And Judah answered his father, saying, Was it for naught my brothers Simeon and Levi killed all the inhabitants of Shechem? Surely it was because Shechem had humbled our sister, and transgressed the command of our God to Noah and his children, for Shechem took our sister away by force, and committed adultery with her.[53] And Shechem did all this evil and not one of the inhabitants of his city interfered with him, to say, Why wilt thou do this? surely for this my brothers went and smote the city, and the Lord delivered it into their hands, because its inhabitants had transgressed the commands of our God. Is it then for naught that they have done all this?[54] And now why art thou afraid or distressed, and why art thou displeased at my brothers, and why is thine anger kindled against them?[55] Surely our God who delivered into their hand the city of Shechem and its people, he will also deliver into our hands all the Canaanitish kings who are coming against us, and we will do unto them as my brothers did unto Shechem.[56] Now be tranquil about them and cast away thy fears, but trust in the Lord our God, and pray unto him to assist us and deliver us, and deliver our enemies into our hands.[57] And Judah called to one of his father's servants, Go now and see where those kings, who are coming against us, are situated with their armies.[58] And the servant went and looked far off, and went up opposite Mount Sihon, and saw all the camps of the kings standing in the fields, and he returned to Judah and said, Behold the kings are situated in the field with all their camps, a people exceedingly numerous, like unto the sand upon the sea shore.[59] And Judah said unto Simeon and Levi, and unto all his brothers, Strengthen yourselves and be sons of valor, for the Lord our God is with us, do not fear them.[60] Stand forth each man, girt with his weapons of war, his bow and his sword, and we will go and fight against these uncircumcised men; the Lord is our God, He will save us.[61] And they rose up, and each girt on his weapons of war, great and small, eleven sons of Jacob, and all the servants of Jacob with them.[62] And all the servants of Isaac who were with Isaac in Hebron, all came to them equipped in all sorts of war instruments, and the sons of Jacob and their servants, being one hundred and twelve men, went towards these kings, and Jacob also went with them.[63] And the sons of Jacob sent unto their father Isaac the son of Abraham to Hebron, the same is Kireath-arba, saying,[64] Pray we beseech thee for us unto the Lord our God, to protect us from the hands of the Canaanites who are coming against us, and to deliver them into our hands.[65] And Isaac the son of Abraham prayed unto the Lord for his sons, and he said, O Lord God, thou didst promise my father, saying, I will multiply thy seed as the stars of heaven, and thou didst also promise me, and establish thou thy word, now that the kings of Canaan are coming together, to make war with my children because they committed no violence.[66] Now therefore, O Lord God, God of the whole earth, pervert, I pray thee, the counsel of these kings that they may not fight against my sons.[67] And impress the hearts of these kings and their people with the terror of my sons and bring down their pride, and that they may turn away from my sons.[68] And with thy strong hand and outstretched arm deliver my sons and their servants from them, for power and might are in thy hands to do all this.[69] And the sons of Jacob and their servants went toward these kings, and they trusted in the Lord their God, and whilst they were going, Jacob their father also prayed unto the Lord and said, O Lord God, powerful and exalted God, who has reigned from days of old, from thence till now and forever;[70] Thou art He who stirreth up wars and causeth them to cease, in thy hand are power and might to exalt and to bring down; O may my prayer be acceptable before thee that thou mayest turn to me with thy mercies, to impress the hearts of these kings and their people with the terror of my sons, and terrify them and their camps, and with thy great kindness deliver all those that trust in thee, for it is thou who canst bring people under us and reduce nations under our power.

Jash.35

[1] And all the kings of the Amorites came and took their stand in the field to consult with their counsellors what was to be done with the sons of Jacob, for they were still afraid of them, saying, Behold, two of them slew the whole of the city of Shechem.[2] And the Lord heard the prayers of Isaac and Jacob, and he filled the hearts of all these kings' advisers with great fear and terror that they unanimously exclaimed,[3] Are you silly this day, or is there no understanding in

you, that you will fight with the Hebrews, and why will you take a delight in your own destruction this day?[4] Behold two of them came to the city of Shechem without fear or terror, and they killed all the inhabitants of the city, that no man stood up against them, and how will you be able to fight with them all?[5] Surely you know that their God is exceedingly fond of them, and has done mighty things for them, such as have not been done from days of old, and amongst all the gods of nations, there is none can do like unto his mighty deeds.[6] Surely he delivered their father Abraham, the Hebrew, from the hand of Nimrod, and from the hand of all his people who had many times sought to slay him.[7] He delivered him also from the fire in which king Nimrod had cast him, and his God delivered him from it.[8] And who else can do the like? surely it was Abraham who slew the five kings of Elam, when they had touched his brother's son who in those days dwelt in Sodom.[9] And took his servant that was faithful in his house and a few of his men, and they pursued the kings of Elam in one night and killed them, and restored to his brother's son all his property which they had taken from him.[10] And surely you know the God of these Hebrews is much delighted with them, and they are also delighted with him, for they know that he delivered them from all their enemies.[11] And behold through his love toward his God, Abraham took his only and precious son and intended to bring him up as a burnt offering to his God, and had it not been for God who prevented him from doing this, he would then have done it through his love to his God.[12] And God saw all his works, and swore unto him, and promised him that he would deliver his sons and all his seed from every trouble that would befall them, because he had done this thing, and through his love to his God stifled his compassion for his child.[13] And have you not heard what their God did to Pharaoh king of Egypt, and to Abimelech king of Gerar, through taking Abraham's wife, who said of her, She is my sister, lest they might slay him on account of her, and think of taking her for a wife? and God did unto them and their people all that you heard of.[14] And behold, we ourselves saw with our eyes that Esau, the brother of Jacob, came to him with four hundred men, with the intention of slaying him, for he called to mind that he had taken away from him his father's blessing.[15] And he went to meet him when he came from Syria, to smite the mother with the children, and who delivered him from his hands but his God in whom he trusted? he delivered him from the hand of his brother and also from the hands of his enemies, and surely he again will protect them.[16] Who does not know that it was their God who inspired them with strength to do to the town of Shechem the evil which you heard of?[17] Could it then be with their own strength that two men could destroy such a large city as Shechem had it not been for their God in whom they trusted? he said and did unto them all this to slay the inhabitants of the city in their city.[18] And can you then prevail over them who have come forth together from your city to fight with the whole of them, even if a thousand times as many more should come to your assistance?[19] Surely you know and understand that you do not come to fight with them, but you come to war with their God who made choice of them, and you have therefore all come this day to be destroyed.[20] Now therefore refrain from this evil which you are endeavoring to bring upon yourselves, and it will be better for you not to go to battle with them, although they are but few in numbers, because their God is with them.[21] And when the kings of the Amorites heard all the words of their advisers, their hearts were filled with terror, and they were afraid of the sons of Jacob and would not fight against them.[22] And they inclined their ears to the words of their advisers, and they listened to all their words, and the words of the counsellors greatly pleased the kings, and they did so.[23] And the kings turned and refrained from the sons of Jacob, for they durst not approach them to make war with them, for they were greatly afraid of them, and their hearts melted within them from their fear of them.[24] For this proceeded from the Lord to them, for he heard the prayers of his servants Isaac and Jacob, for they trusted in him; and all these kings returned with their camps on that day, each to his own city, and they did not at that time fight with the sons of Jacob.[25] And the sons of Jacob kept their station that day till evening opposite mount Sihon, and seeing that these kings did not come to fight against them, the sons of Jacob returned home.

Jash.36

[1] At that time the Lord appeared unto Jacob saying, Arise, go to Bethel and remain there, and make there an altar to the Lord who appeareth unto thee, who delivered thee and thy sons from affliction.[2] And Jacob rose up with his sons and all belonging to him, and they went and came to Bethel according to the word of the Lord.[3] And Jacob was ninety-nine years old when he went up to Bethel, and Jacob and his sons and all the people that were with him, remained in Bethel in Luz, and he there built an altar to the Lord who appeared unto him, and Jacob and his sons remained in Bethel six months.[4] At that time died Deborah the daughter of Uz, the nurse of Rebecca, who had been with Jacob; and Jacob buried her beneath Bethel under an oak that was there.[5] And Rebecca the daughter of Bethuel, the mother of Jacob, also died at that time in Hebron, the same is Kireath-arba, and she was buried in the cave of Machpelah which Abraham had bought from the children of Heth.[6] And the life of Rebecca was one hundred and thirty-three years, and she died and when Jacob heard that his mother Rebecca was dead he wept bitterly for his mother, and made a great mourning for her, and for Deborah her nurse beneath the oak, and he called the name of that place Allon-bachuth.[7] And Laban the Syrian died in those days, for God smote him because he transgressed the covenant that existed between him and Jacob.[8] And Jacob was a hundred years old when the Lord appeared unto him, and blessed him and called his name Israel, and Rachel the wife of Jacob conceived in those days.[9] And at that time Jacob and all belonging to him journeyed from Bethel to go to his father's house, to Hebron.[10] And whilst they were going on the road, and there was yet but a little way to come to Ephrath, Rachel bare a son and she had hard labor and she died.[11] And Jacob buried her in the way to Ephrath, which is Bethlehem, and he set a pillar upon her grave, which is there unto this day; and the days of Rachel were forty-five years and she died.[12] And Jacob called the name of his son that was born to him, which Rachel bare unto him, Benjamin, for he was born to him in the land on the right hand.[13] And it was after the death of Rachel, that Jacob pitched his tent in the tent of her handmaid Bilhah.[14] And Reuben was jealous for his mother Leah on account of this, and he was filled with anger, and he rose up in his anger and went and entered the tent of Bilhah and he thence removed his father's bed.[15] At that time the portion of birthright, together with the kingly and priestly offices, was removed from the sons of Reuben, for he had profaned his father's bed, and the birthright was given unto Joseph, the kingly office to Judah, and the priesthood unto Levi, because Reuben had defiled his father's bed.[16] And these are the generations of Jacob who were born to him in Padan-aram, and the sons of Jacob were twelve.[17] The sons of Leah were Reuben the first born, and Simeon, Levi, Judah, Issachar, Zebulun, and their sister Dinah; and the sons of Rachel were Joseph and Benjamin.[18] The sons of Zilpah, Leah's handmaid, were Gad and Asher, and the sons of Bilhah, Rachel's handmaid, were Dan and Naphtali; these are the sons of Jacob which were born to him in Padan-aram.[19] And Jacob and his sons and all belonging to him journeyed and came to Mamre, which is Kireath-arba, that is in

Hebron, where Abraham and Isaac sojourned, and Jacob with his sons and all belonging to him, dwelt with his father in Hebron.[20] And his brother Esau and his sons, and all belonging to him went to the land of Seir and dwelt there, and had possessions in the land of Seir, and the children of Esau were fruitful and multiplied exceedingly in the land of Seir.[21] And these are the generations of Esau that were born to him in the land of Canaan, and the sons of Esau were five.[22] And Adah bare to Esau his first born Eliphaz, and she also bare to him Reuel, and Ahlibamah bare to him Jeush, Yaalam and Korah.[23] These are the children of Esau who were born to him in the land of Canaan; and the sons of Eliphaz the son of Esau were Teman, Omar, Zepho, Gatam, Kenaz and Amalex, and the sons of Reuel were Nachath, Zerach, Shamah and Mizzah.[24] And the sons of Jeush were Timnah, Alvah, Jetheth; and the sons of Yaalam were Alah, Phinor and Kenaz.[25] And the sons of Korah were Teman, Mibzar, Magdiel and Eram; these are the families of the sons of Esau according to their dukedoms in the land of Seir.[26] And these are the names of the sons of Seir the Horite, inhabitants of the land of Seir, Lotan, Shobal, Zibeon, Anah, Dishan, Ezer and Dishon, being seven sons.[27] And the children of Lotan were Hori, Heman and their sister Timna, that is Timna who came to Jacob and his sons, and they would not give ear to her, and she went and became a concubine to Eliphaz the son of Esau, and she bare to him Amalek.[28] And the sons of Shobal were Alvan, Manahath, Ebal, Shepho, and Onam, and the sons of Zibeon were Ajah, and Anah, this was that Anah who found the Yemim in the wilderness when he fed the asses of Zibeon his father.[29] And whilst he was feeding his father's asses he led them to the wilderness at different times to feed them.[30] And there was a day that he brought them to one of the deserts on the sea shore, opposite the wilderness of the people, and whilst he was feeding them, behold a very heavy storm came from the other side of the sea and rested upon the asses that were feeding there, and they all stood still.[31] And afterward about one hundred and twenty great and terrible animals came out from the wilderness at the other side of the sea, and they all came to the place where the asses were, and they placed themselves there.[32] And those animals, from their middle downward, were in the shape of the children of men, and from their middle upward, some had the likeness of bears, and some the likeness of the keephas, with tails behind them from between their shoulders reaching down to the earth, like the tails of the ducheephath, and these animals came and mounted and rode upon these asses, and led them away, and they went away unto this day.[33] And one of these animals approached Anah and smote him with his tail, and then fled from that place.[34] And when he saw this work he was exceedingly afraid of his life, and he fled and escaped to the city.[35] And he related to his sons and brothers all that had happened to him, and many men went to seek the asses but could not find them, and Anah and his brothers went no more to that place from that day following, for they were greatly afraid of their lives.[36] And the children of Anah the son of Seir, were Dishon and his sister Ahlibamah, and the children of Dishon were Hemdan, Eshban, Ithran and Cheran, and the children of Ezer were Bilhan, Zaavan and Akan, and the children of Dishon were Uz and Aran.[37] These are the families of the children of Seir the Horite, according to their dukedoms in the land of Seir.[38] And Esau and his children dwelt in the land of Seir the Horite, the inhabitant of the land, and they had possessions in it and were fruitful and multiplied exceedingly, and Jacob and his children and all belonging to them, dwelt with their father Isaac in the land of Canaan, as the Lord had commanded Abraham their father.

Jash.37

[1] And in the one hundred and fifth year of the life of Jacob, that is the ninth year of Jacob's dwelling with his children in the land of Canaan, he came from Padan-aram.[2] And in those days Jacob journeyed with his children from Hebron, and they went and returned to the city of Shechem, they and all belonging to them, and they dwelt there, for the children of Jacob obtained good and fat pasture land for their cattle in the city of Shechem, the city of Shechem having then been rebuilt, and there were in it about three hundred men and women.[3] And Jacob and his children and all belonging to him dwelt in the part of the field which Jacob had bought from Hamor the father of Shechem, when he came from Padan-aram before Simeon and Levi had smitten the city.[4] And all those kings of the Canaanites and Amorites that surrounded the city of Shechem, heard that the sons of Jacob had again come to Shechem and dwelt there.[5] And they said, Shall the sons of Jacob the Hebrew again come to the city and dwell therein, after that they have smitten its inhabitants and driven them out? shall they now return and also drive out those who are dwelling in the city or slay them?[6] And all the kings of Canaan again assembled, and they came together to make war with Jacob and his sons.[7] And Jashub king of Tapnach sent also to all his neighboring kings, to Elan king of Gaash, and to Ihuri king of Shiloh, and to Parathon king of Chazar, and to Susi king of Sarton, and to Laban king of Bethchoran, and to Shabir king of Othnay-mah, saying,[8] Come up to me and assist me, and let us smite Jacob the Hebrew and his sons, and all belonging to him, for they are again come to Shechem to possess it and to slay its inhabitants as before.[9] And all these kings assembled together and came with all their camps, a people exceedingly plentiful like the sand upon the sea shore, and they were all opposite to Tapnach.[10] And Jashub king of Tapnach went forth to them with all his army, and he encamped with them opposite to Tapnach without the city, and all these kings they divided into seven divisions, being seven camps against the sons of Jacob.[11] And they sent a declaration to Jacob and his son, saying, Come you all forth to us that we may have an interview together in the plain, and revenge the cause of the men of Shechem whom you slew in their city, and you will now again return to the city of Shechem and dwell therein, and slay its inhabitants as before.[12] And the sons of Jacob heard this and their anger was kindled exceedingly at the words of the kings of Canaan, and ten of the sons of Jacob hastened and rose up, and each of them girt on his weapons of war; and there were one hundred and two of their servants with them equipped in battle array.[13] And all these men, the sons of Jacob with their servants, went toward these kings, and Jacob their father was with them, and they all stood upon the heap of Shechem.[14] And Jacob prayed to the Lord for his sons, and he spread forth his hands to the Lord, and he said, O God, thou art an Almighty God, thou art our father, thou didst form us and we are the works of thine hands; I pray thee deliver my sons through thy mercy from the hand of their enemies, who are this day coming to fight with them and save them from their hand, for in thy hand is power and might, to save the few from the many.[15] And give unto my sons, thy servants, strength of heart and might to fight with their enemies, to subdue them, and make their enemies fall before them, and let not my sons and their servants die through the hands of the children of Canaan.[16] But if it seemeth good in thine eyes to take away the lives of my sons and their servants, take them in thy great mercy through the hands of thy ministers, that they may not perish this day by the hands of the kings of the Amorites.[17] And when Jacob ceased praying to the Lord the earth shook from its place, and the sun darkened, and all these kings were terrified and a great consternation seized them.[18] And the Lord hearkened to the prayer of Jacob, and the Lord impressed the hearts of all the kings and their

hosts with the terror and awe of the sons of Jacob.[19] For the Lord caused them to hear the voice of chariots, and the voice of mighty horses from the sons of Jacob, and the voice of a great army accompanying them.[20] And these kings were seized with great terror at the sons of Jacob, and whilst they were standing in their quarters, behold the sons of Jacob advanced upon them, with one hundred and twelve men, with a great and tremendous shouting.[21] And when the kings saw the sons of Jacob advancing toward them, they were still more panic struck, and they were inclined to retreat from before the sons of Jacob as at first, and not to fight with them.[22] But they did not retreat, saying, It would be a disgrace to us thus twice to retreat from before the Hebrews.[23] And the sons of Jacob came near and advanced against all these kings and their armies, and they saw, and behold it was a very mighty people, numerous as the sand of the sea.[24] And the sons of Jacob called unto the Lord and said, Help us O Lord, help us and answer us, for we trust in thee, and let us not die by the hands of these uncircumcised men, who this day have come against us.[25] And the sons of Jacob girt on their weapons of war, and they took in their hands each man his shield and his javelin, and they approached to battle.[26] And Judah, the son of Jacob, ran first before his brethren, and ten of his servants with him, and he went toward these kings.[27] And Jashub, king of Tapnach, also came forth first with his army before Judah, and Judah saw Jashub and his army coming toward him, and Judah's wrath was kindled, and his anger burned within him, and he approached to battle in which Judah ventured his life.[28] And Jashub and all his army were advancing toward Judah, and he was riding upon a very strong and powerful horse, and Jashub was a very valiant man, and covered with iron and brass from head to foot.[29] And whilst he was upon the horse, he shot arrows with both hands from before and behind, as was his manner in all his battles, and he never missed the place to which he aimed his arrows.[30] And when Jashub came to fight with Judah, and was darting many arrows against Judah, the Lord bound the hand of Jashub, and all the arrows that he shot rebounded upon his own men.[31] And notwithstanding this, Jashub kept advancing toward Judah, to challenge him with the arrows, but the distance between them was about thirty cubits, and when Judah saw Jashub darting forth his arrows against him, he ran to him with his wrath-excited might.[32] And Judah took up a large stone from the ground, and its weight was sixty shekels, and Judah ran toward Jashub, and with the stone struck him on his shield, that Jashub was stunned with the blow, and fell off from his horse to the ground.[33] And the shield burst asunder out of the hand of Jashub, and through the force of the blow sprang to the distance of about fifteen cubits, and the shield fell before the second camp.[34] And the kings that came with Jashub saw at a distance the strength of Judah, the son of Jacob, and what he had done to Jashub, and they were terribly afraid of Judah.[35] And they assembled near Jashub's camp, seeing his confusion, and Judah drew his sword and smote forty-two men of the camp of Jashub, and the whole of Jashub's camp fled before Judah, and no man stood against him, and they left Jashub and fled from him, and Jashub was still prostrate upon the ground.[36] And Jashub seeing that all the men of his camp had fled from him, hastened and rose up with terror against Judah, and stood upon his legs opposite Judah.[37] And Jashub had a single combat with Judah, placing shield toward shield, and Jashub's men all fled, for they were greatly afraid of Judah.[38] And Jashub took his spear in his hand to strike Judah upon his head, but Judah had quickly placed his shield to his head against Jashub's spear, so that the shield of Judah received the blow from Jashub's spear, and the shield was split in too.[39] And when Judah saw that his shield was split, he hastily drew his sword and smote Jashub at his ankles, and cut off his feet that

Jashub fell upon the ground, and the spear fell from his hand.[40] And Judah hastily picked up Jashub's spear, with which he severed his head and cast it next to his feet.[41] And when the sons of Jacob saw what Judah had done to Jashub, they all ran into the ranks of the other kings, and the sons of Jacob fought with the army of Jashub, and the armies of all the kings that were there.[42] And the sons of Jacob caused fifteen thousand of their men to fall, and they smote them as if smiting at gourds, and the rest fled for their lives.[43] And Judah was still standing by the body of Jashub, and stripped Jashub of his coat of mail.[44] And Judah also took off the iron and brass that was about Jashub, and behold nine men of the captains of Jashub came along to fight against Judah.[45] And Judah hastened and took up a stone from the ground, and with it smote one of them upon the head, and his skull was fractured, and the body also fell from the horse to the ground.[46] And the eight captains that remained, seeing the strength of Judah, were greatly afraid and they fled, and Judah with his ten men pursued them, and they overtook them and slew them.[47] And the sons of Jacob were still smiting the armies of the kings, and they slew many of them, but those kings daringly kept their stand with their captains, and did not retreat from their places, and they exclaimed against those of their armies that fled from before the sons of Jacob, but none would listen to them, for they were afraid of their lives lest they should die.[48] And all the sons of Jacob, after having smitten the armies of the kings, returned and came before Judah, and Judah was still slaying the eight captains of Jashub, and stripping off their garments.[49] And Levi saw Elon, king of Gaash, advancing toward him, with his fourteen captains to smite him, but Levi did not know it for certain.[50] And Elon with his captains approached nearer, and Levi looked back and saw that battle was given him in the rear, and Levi ran with twelve of his servants, and they went and slew Elon and his captains with the edge of the sword.

Jash.38

[1] And Ihuri king of Shiloh came up to assist Elon, and he approached Jacob, when Jacob drew his bow that was in his hand and with an arrow struck Ihuri which caused his death.[2] And when Ihuri king of Shiloh was dead, the four remaining kings fled from their station with the rest of the captains, and they endeavored to retreat, saying, We have no more strength with the Hebrews after their having killed the three kings and their captains who were more powerful than we are.[3] And when the sons of Jacob saw that the remaining kings had removed from their station, they pursued them, and Jacob also came from the heap of Shechem from the place where he was standing, and they went after the kings and they approached them with their servants.[4] And the kings and the captains with the rest of their armies, seeing that the sons of Jacob approached them, were afraid of their lives and fled till they reached the city of Chazar.[5] And the sons of Jacob pursued them to the gate of the city of Chazar, and they smote a great smiting amongst the kings and their armies, about four thousand men, and whilst they were smiting the army of the kings, Jacob was occupied with his bow confining himself to smiting the kings, and he slew them all.[6] And he slew Parathon king of Chazar at the gate of the city of Chazar, and he afterward smote Susi king of Sarton, and Laban king of Bethchorin, and Shabir king of Machnaymah, and he slew them all with arrows, an arrow to each of them, and they died.[7] And the sons of Jacob seeing that all the kings were dead and that they were broken up and retreating, continued to carry on the battle with the armies of the kings opposite the gate of Chazar, and they still smote about four hundred of their men.[8] And three men of the servants of Jacob fell in that battle, and when Judah saw that three of his servants had died, it grieved him greatly, and his anger burned within

him against the Amorites.[9] And all the men that remained of the armies of the kings were greatly afraid of their lives, and they ran and broke the gate of the walls of the city of Chazar, and they all entered the city for safety.[10] And they concealed themselves in the midst of the city of Chazar, for the city of Chazar was very large and extensive, and when all these armies had entered the city, the sons of Jacob ran after them to the city.[11] And four mighty men, experienced in battle, went forth from the city and stood against the entrance of the city, with drawn swords and spears in their hands, and they placed themselves opposite the sons of Jacob, and would not suffer them to enter the city.[12] And Naphtali ran and came between them and with his sword smote two of them, and cut off their heads at one stroke.[13] And he turned to the other two, and behold they had fled, and he pursued them, overtook them, smote them and slew them.[14] And the sons of Jacob came to the city and saw, and behold there was another wall to the city, and they sought for the gate of the wall and could not find it, and Judah sprang upon the top of the wall, and Simeon and Levi followed him, and they all three descended from the wall into the city.[15] And Simeon and Levi slew all the men who ran for safety into the city, and also the inhabitants of the city with their wives and little ones, they slew with the edge of the sword, and the cries of the city ascended up to heaven.[16] And Dan and Naphtali sprang upon the wall to see what caused the noise of lamentation, for the sons of Jacob felt anxious about their brothers, and they heard the inhabitants of the city speaking with weeping and supplications, saying, Take all that we possess in the city and go away, only do not put us to death.[17] And when Judah, Simeon, and Levi had ceased smiting the inhabitants of the city, they ascended the wall and called to Dan and Naphtali, who were upon the wall, and to the rest of their brothers, and Simeon and Levi informed them of the entrance into the city, and all the sons of Jacob came to fetch the spoil.[18] And the sons of Jacob took the spoil of the city of Chazar, the flocks and herds, and the property, and they took all that could be captured, and went away that day from the city.[19] And on the next day the sons of Jacob went to Sarton, for they heard that the men of Sarton who had remained in the city were assembling to fight with them for having slain their king, and Sarton was a very high and fortified city, and it had a deep rampart surrounding the city.[20] And the pillar of the rampart was about fifty cubits and its breadth forty cubits, and there was no place for a man to enter the city on account of the rampart, and the sons of Jacob saw the rampart of the city, and they sought an entrance in it but could not find it.[21] For the entrance to the city was at the rear, and every man that wished to come into the city came by that road and went around the whole city, and he afterwards entered the city.[22] And the sons of Jacob seeing they could not find the way into the city, their anger was kindled greatly, and the inhabitants of the city seeing that the sons of Jacob were coming to them were greatly afraid of them, for they had heard of their strength and what they had done to Chazar.[23] And the inhabitants of the city of Sarton could not go out toward the sons of Jacob after having assembled in the city to fight against them, lest they might thereby get into the city, but when they saw that they were coming toward them, they were greatly afraid of them, for they had heard of their strength and what they had done to Chazar.[24] So the inhabitants of Sarton speedily took away the bridge of the road of the city, from its place, before the sons of Jacob came, and they brought it into the city.[25] And the sons of Jacob came and sought the way into the city, and could not find it and the inhabitants of the city went up to the top of the wall, and saw, and behold the sons of Jacob were seeking an entrance into the city.[26] And the inhabitants of the city reproached the sons of Jacob from the top of the wall, and they cursed them, and the sons of Jacob heard the reproaches, and they were greatly incensed, and their anger burned within them.[27] And the sons of Jacob were provoked at them, and they all rose and sprang over the rampart with the force of their strength, and through their might passed the forty cubits' breadth of the rampart.[28] And when they had passed the rampart they stood under the wall of the city, and they found all the gates of the city enclosed with iron doors.[29] And the sons of Jacob came near to break open the doors of the gates of the city, and the inhabitants did not let them, for from the top of the wall they were casting stones and arrows upon them.[30] And the number of the people that were upon the wall was about four hundred men, and when the sons of Jacob saw that the men of the city would not let them open the gates of the city, they sprang and ascended the top of the wall, and Judah went up first to the east part of the city.[31] And Gad and Asher went up after him to the west corner of the city, and Simeon and Levi to the north, and Dan and Reuben to the south.[32] And the men who were on the top of the wall, the inhabitants of the city, seeing that the sons of Jacob were coming up to them, they all fled from the wall, descended into the city, and concealed themselves in the midst of the city.[33] And Issachar and Naphtali that remained under the wall approached and broke the gates of the city, and kindled a fire at the gates of the city, that the iron melted, and all the sons of Jacob came into the city, they and all their men, and they fought with the inhabitants of the city of Sarton, and smote them with the edge of the sword, and no man stood up before them.[34] And about two hundred men fled from the city, and they all went and hid themselves in a certain tower in the city, and Judah pursued them to the tower and he broke down the tower, which fell upon the men, and they all died.[35] And the sons of Jacob went up the road of the roof of that tower, and they saw, and behold there was another strong and high tower at a distance in the city, and the top of it reached to heaven, and the sons of Jacob hastened and descended, and went with all their men to that tower, and found it filled with about three hundred men, women and little ones.[36] And the sons of Jacob smote a great smiting amongst those men in the tower and they ran away and fled from them.[37] And Simeon and Levi pursued them, when twelve mighty and valiant men came out to them from the place where they had concealed themselves.[38] And those twelve men maintained a strong battle against Simeon and Levi, and Simeon and Levi could not prevail over them, and those valiant men broke the shields of Simeon and Levi, and one of them struck at Levi's head with his sword, when Levi hastily placed his hand to his head, for he was afraid of the sword, and the sword struck Levi's hand, and it wanted but little to the hand of Levi being cut off.[39] And Levi seized the sword of the valiant man in his hand, and took it forcibly from the man, and with it he struck at the head of the powerful man, and he severed his head.[40] And eleven men approached to fight with Levi, for they saw that one of them was killed, and the sons of Jacob fought, but the sons of Jacob could not prevail over them, for those men were very powerful.[41] And the sons of Jacob seeing that they could not prevail over them, Simeon gave a loud and tremendous shriek, and the eleven powerful men were stunned at the voice of Simeon's shrieking.[42] And Judah at a distance knew the voice of Simeon's shouting, and Naphtali and Judah ran with their shields to Simeon and Levi, and found them fighting with those powerful men, unable to prevail over them as their shields were broken.[43] And Naphtali saw that the shields of Simeon and Levi were broken, and he took two shields from his servants and brought them to Simeon and Levi.[44] And Simeon, Levi and Judah on that day fought all three against the eleven mighty men until the time of sunset, but they could not prevail over them.[45] And this was told unto Jacob, and he

255

was sorely grieved, and he prayed unto the Lord, and he and Naphtali his son went against these mighty men.[46] And Jacob approached and drew his bow, and came nigh unto the mighty men, and slew three of their men with the bow, and the remaining eight turned back, and behold, the war waged against them in the front and rear, and they were greatly afraid of their lives, and could not stand before the sons of Jacob, and they fled from before them.[47] And in their flight they met Dan and Asher coming toward them, and they suddenly fell upon them, and fought with them, and slew two of them, and Judah and his brothers pursued them, and smote the remainder of them, and slew them.[48] And all the sons of Jacob returned and walked about the city, searching if they could find any men, and they found about twenty young men in a cave in the city, and Gad and Asher smote them all, and Dan and Naphtali lighted upon the rest of the men who had fled and escaped from the second tower, and they smote them all.[49] And the sons of Jacob smote all the inhabitants of the city of Sarton, but the women and little ones they left in the city and did not slay them.[50] And all the inhabitants of the city of Sarton were powerful men, one of them would pursue a thousand, and two of them would not flee from ten thousand of the rest of men.[51] And the sons of Jacob slew all the inhabitants of the city of Sarton with the edge of the sword, that no man stood up against them, and they left the women in the city.[52] And the sons of Jacob took all the spoil of the city, and captured what they desired, and they took flocks and herds and property from the city, and the sons of Jacob did unto Sarton and its inhabitants as they had done to Chazar and its inhabitants, and they turned and went away.

Jash.39

[1] And when the sons of Jacob went from the city of Sarton, they had gone about two hundred cubits when they met the inhabitants of Tapnach coming toward them, for they went out to fight with them, because they had smitten the king of Tapnach and all his men.[2] So all that remained in the city of Tapnach came out to fight with the sons of Jacob, and they thought to retake from them the booty and the spoil which they had captured from Chazar and Sarton.[3] And the rest of the men of Tapnach fought with the sons of Jacob in that place, and the sons of Jacob smote them, and they fled before them, and they pursued them to the city of Arbelan, and they all fell before the sons of Jacob.[4] And the sons of Jacob returned and came to Tapnach, to take away the spoil of Tapnach, and when they came to Tapnach they heard that the people of Arbelan had gone out to meet them to save the spoil of their brethren, and the sons of Jacob left ten of their men in Tapnach to plunder the city, and they went out toward the people of Arbelan.[5] And the men of Arbelan went out with their wives to fight with the sons of Jacob, for their wives were experienced in battle, and they went out, about four hundred men and women.[6] And all the sons of Jacob shouted with a loud voice, and they all ran toward the inhabitants of Arbelan, and with a great and tremendous voice.[7] And the inhabitants of Arbelan heard the noise of the shouting of the sons of Jacob, and their roaring like the noise of lions and like the roaring of the sea and its waves.[8] And fear and terror possessed their hearts on account of the sons of Jacob, and they were terribly afraid of them, and they retreated and fled before them into the city, and the sons of Jacob pursued them to the gate of the city, and they came upon them in the city.[9] And the sons of Jacob fought with them in the city, and all their women were engaged in slinging against the sons of Jacob, and the combat was very severe amongst them the whole of that day till evening.[10] And the sons of Jacob could not prevail over them, and the sons of Jacob had almost perished in that battle, and the sons of Jacob cried unto the Lord and greatly gained strength toward evening, and the sons

of Jacob smote all the inhabitants of Arbelan by the edge of the sword, men, women and little ones.[11] And also the remainder of the people who had fled from Sarton, the sons of Jacob smote them in Arbelan, and the sons of Jacob did unto Arbelan and Tapnach as they had done to Chazar and Sarton, and when the women saw that all the men were dead, they went upon the roofs of the city and smote the sons of Jacob by showering down stones like rain.[12] And the sons of Jacob hastened and came into the city and seized all the women and smote them with the edge of the sword, and the sons of Jacob captured all the spoil and booty, flocks and herds and cattle.[13] And the sons of Jacob did unto Machnaymah as they had done to Tapnach, to Chazar and to Shiloh, and they turned from there and went away.[14] And on the fifth day the sons of Jacob heard that the people of Gaash had gathered against them to battle, because they had slain their king and their captains, for there had been fourteen captains in the city of Gaash, and the sons of Jacob had slain them all in the first battle.[15] And the sons of Jacob that day girt on their weapons of war, and they marched to battle against the inhabitants of Gaash, and in Gaash there was a strong and mighty people of the people of the Amorites, and Gaash was the strongest and best fortified city of all the cities of the Amorites, and it had three walls.[16] And the sons of Jacob came to Gaash and they found the gates of the city locked, and about five hundred men standing at the top of the outer-most wall, and a people numerous as the sand upon the sea shore were in ambush for the sons of Jacob from without the city at the rear thereof.[17] And the sons of Jacob approached to open the gates of the city, and whilst they were drawing nigh, behold those who were in ambush at the rear of the city came forth from their places and surrounded the sons of Jacob.[18] And the sons of Jacob were enclosed between the people of Gaash, and the battle was both to their front and rear, and all the men that were upon the wall, were casting from the wall upon them, arrows and stones.[19] And Judah, seeing that the men of Gaash were getting too heavy for them, gave a most piercing and tremendous shriek and all the men of Gaash were terrified at the voice of Judah's cry, and men fell from the wall at his powerful shriek, and all those that were from without and within the city were greatly afraid of their lives.[20] And the sons of Jacob still came nigh to break the doors of the city, when the men of Gaash threw stones and arrows upon them from the top of the wall, and made them flee from the gate.[21] And the sons of Jacob returned against the men of Gaash who were with them from without the city, and they smote them terribly, as striking against gourds, and they could not stand against the sons of Jacob, for fright and terror had seized them at the shriek of Judah.[22] And the sons of Jacob slew all those men who were without the city, and the sons of Jacob still drew nigh to effect an entrance into the city, and to fight under the city walls, but they could not for all the inhabitants of Gaash who remained in the city had surrounded the walls of Gaash in every direction, so that the sons of Jacob were unable to approach the city to fight with them.[23] And the sons of Jacob came nigh to one corner to fight under the wall, the inhabitants of Gaash threw arrows and stones upon them like showers of rain, and they fled from under the wall.[24] And the people of Gaash who were upon the wall, seeing that the sons of Jacob could not prevail over them from under the wall, reproached the sons of Jacob in these words, saying,[25] What is the matter with you in the battle that you cannot prevail? can you then do unto the mighty city of Gaash and its inhabitants as you did to the cities of the Amorites that were not so powerful? Surely to those weak ones amongst us you did those things, and slew them in the entrance of the city, for they had no strength when they were terrified at the sound of your shouting.[26] And will you now then be

able to fight in this place? Surely here you will all die, and we will avenge the cause of those cities that you have laid waste.[27] And the inhabitants of Gaash greatly reproached the sons of Jacob and reviled them with their gods, and continued to cast arrows and stones upon them from the wall.[28] And Judah and his brothers heard the words of the inhabitants of Gaash and their anger was greatly roused, and Judah was jealous of his God in this matter, and he called out and said, O Lord, help, send help to us and our brothers.[29] And he ran at a distance with all his might, with his drawn sword in his hand, and he sprang from the earth and by dint of his strength, mounted the wall, and his sword fell from his hand.[30] And Judah shouted upon the wall, and all the men that were upon the wall were terrified, and some of them fell from the wall into the city and died, and those who were yet upon the wall, when they saw Judah's strength, they were greatly afraid and fled for their lives into the city for safety.[31] And some were emboldened to fight with Judah upon the wall, and they came nigh to slay him when they saw there was no sword in Judah's hand, and they thought of casting him from the wall to his brothers, and twenty men of the city came up to assist them, and they surrounded Judah and they all shouted over him, and approached him with drawn swords, and they terrified Judah, and Judah cried out to his brothers from the wall.[32] And Jacob and his sons drew the bow from under the wall, and smote three of the men that were upon the top of the wall, and Judah continued to cry and he exclaimed, O Lord help us, O Lord deliver us, and he cried out with a loud voice upon the wall, and the cry was heard at a great distance.[33] And after this cry he again repeated to shout, and all the men who surrounded Judah on the top of the wall were terrified, and they each threw his sword from his hand at the sound of Judah's shouting and his tremor, and fled.[34] And Judah took the swords which had fallen from their hands, and Judah fought with them and slew twenty of their men upon the wall.[35] And about eighty men and women still ascended the wall from the city and they all surrounded Judah, and the Lord impressed the fear of Judah in their hearts, that they were unable to approach him.[36] And Jacob and all who were with him drew the bow from under the wall, and they slew ten men upon the wall, and they fell below the wall, before Jacob and his sons.[37] And the people upon the wall seeing that twenty of their men had fallen, they still ran toward Judah with drawn swords, but they could not approach him for they were greatly terrified at Judah's strength.[38] And one of their mighty men whose name was Arud approached to strike Judah upon the head with his sword, when Judah hastily put his shield to his head, and the sword hit the shield, and it was split in two.[39] And this mighty man after he had struck Judah ran for his life, at the fear of Judah, and his feet slipped upon the wall and he fell amongst the sons of Jacob who were below the wall, and the sons of Jacob smote him and slew him.[40] And Judah's head pained him from the blow of the powerful man, and Judah had nearly died from it.[41] And Judah cried out upon the wall owing to the pain produced by the blow, when Dan heard him, and his anger burned within him, and he also rose up and went at a distance and ran and sprang from the earth and mounted the wall with his wrath-excited strength.[42] And when Dan came upon the wall near unto Judah all the men upon the wall fled, who had stood against Judah, and they went up to the second wall, and they threw arrows and stones upon Dan and Judah from the second wall, and endeavored to drive them from the wall.[43] And the arrows and stones struck Dan and Judah, and they had nearly been killed upon the wall, and wherever Dan and Judah fled from the wall, they were attacked with arrows and stones from the second wall.[44] And Jacob and his sons were still at the entrance of the city below the first wall, and they were not able to draw their bow against the inhabitants of the city, as they could not be seen by them, being upon the second wall.⁴⁵ And Dan and Judah when they could no longer bear the stones and arrows that fell upon them from the second wall, they both sprang upon the second wall near the people of the city, and when the people of the city who were upon the second wall saw that Dan and Judah had come to them upon the second wall, they all cried out and descended below between the walls.⁴⁶ And Jacob and his sons heard the noise of the shouting from the people of the city, and they were still at the entrance of the city, and they were anxious about Dan and Judah who were not seen by them, they being upon the second wall.⁴⁷ And Naphtali went up with his wrath-excited might and sprang upon the first wall to see what caused the noise of shouting which they had heard in the city, and Issachar and Zebulun drew nigh to break the doors of the city, and they opened the gates of the city and came into the city.⁴⁸ And Naphtali leaped from the first wall to the second, and came to assist his brothers, and the inhabitants of Gaash who were upon the wall, seeing that Naphtali was the third who had come up to assist his brothers, they all fled and descended into the city, and Jacob and all his sons and all their young men came into the city to them.⁴⁹ And Judah and Dan and Naphtali descended from the wall into the city and pursued the inhabitants of the city, and Simeon and Levi were from without the city and knew not that the gate was opened, and they went up from there to the wall and came down to their brothers into the city.⁵⁰ And the inhabitants of the city had all descended into the city, and the sons of Jacob came to them in different directions, and the battle waged against them from the front and the rear, and the sons of Jacob smote them terribly, and slew about twenty thousand of them men and women, not one of them could stand up against the sons of Jacob.⁵¹ And the blood flowed plentifully in the city, and it was like a brook of water, and the blood flowed like a brook to the outer part of the city, and reached the desert of Bethchorin.⁵² And the people of Bethchorin saw at a distance the blood flowing from the city of Gaash, and about seventy men from amongst them ran to see the blood, and they came to the place where the blood was.⁵³ And they followed the track of the blood and came to the wall of the city of Gaash, and they saw the blood issue from the city, and they heard the voice of crying from the inhabitants of Gaash, for it ascended unto heaven, and the blood was continuing to flow abundantly like a brook of water.⁵⁴ And all the sons of Jacob were still smiting the inhabitants of Gaash, and were engaged in slaying them till evening, about twenty thousand men and women, and the people of Chorin said, Surely this is the work of the Hebrews, for they are still carrying on war in all the cities of the Amorites.⁵⁵ And those people hastened and ran to Bethchorin, and each took his weapons of war, and they cried out to all the inhabitants of Bethchorin, who also girt on their weapons of war to go and fight with the sons of Jacob.⁵⁶ And when the sons of Jacob had done smiting the inhabitants of Gaash, they walked about the city to strip all the slain, and coming in the innermost part of the city and farther on they met three very powerful men, and there was no sword in their hand.⁵⁷ And the sons of Jacob came up to the place where they were, and the powerful men ran away, and one of them had taken Zebulun, who he saw was a young lad and of short stature, and with his might dashed him to the ground.⁵⁸ And Jacob ran to him with his sword and Jacob smote him below his loins with the sword, and cut him in two, and the body fell upon Zebulun.⁵⁹ And the second one approached and seized Jacob to fell him to the ground, and Jacob turned to him and shouted to him, whilst Simeon and Levi ran and smote him on the hips with the sword and felled him to the ground.⁶⁰ And the powerful man rose up from the ground with wrath-excited might, and Judah came to him before he had gained

257

his footing, and struck him upon the head with the sword, and his head was split and he died.⁶¹ And the third powerful man, seeing that his companions were killed, ran from before the sons of Jacob, and the sons of Jacob pursued him in the city; and whilst the powerful man was fleeing he found one of the swords of the inhabitants of the city, and he picked it up and turned to the sons of Jacob and fought them with that sword.⁶² And the powerful man ran to Judah to strike him upon the head with the sword, and there was no shield in the hand of Judah; and whilst he was aiming to strike him, Naphtali hastily took his shield and put it to Judah's head, and the sword of the powerful man hit the shield of Naphtali and Judah escaped the sword.⁶³ And Simeon and Levi ran upon the powerful man with their swords and struck at him forcibly with their swords, and the two swords entered the body of the powerful man and divided it in two, length-wise.⁶⁴ And the sons of Jacob smote the three mighty men at that time, together with all the inhabitants of Gaash, and the day was about to decline.⁶⁵ And the sons of Jacob walked about Gaash and took all the spoil of the city, even the little ones and women they did not suffer to live, and the sons of Jacob did unto Gaash as they had done to Sarton and Shiloh.

Jash.40

¹ And the sons of Jacob led away all the spoil of Gaash, and went out of the city by night.² They were going out marching toward the castle of Bethchorin, and the inhabitants of Bethchorin were going to the castle to meet them, and on that night the sons of Jacob fought with the inhabitants of Bethchorin, in the castle of Bethchorin.³ And all the inhabitants of Bethchorin were mighty men, one of them would not flee from before a thousand men, and they fought on that night upon the castle, and their shouts were heard on that night from afar, and the earth quaked at their shouting.⁴ And all the sons of Jacob were afraid of those men, as they were not accustomed to fight in the dark, and they were greatly confounded, and the sons of Jacob cried unto the Lord, saying, Give help to us O Lord, deliver us that we may not die by the hands of these uncircumcised men.⁵ And the Lord hearkened to the voice of the sons of Jacob, and the Lord caused great terror and confusion to seize the people of Bethchorin, and they fought amongst themselves the one with the other in the darkness of night, and smote each other in great numbers.⁶ And the sons of Jacob, knowing that the Lord had brought a spirit of perverseness amongst those men, and that they fought each man with his neighbor, went forth from among the bands of the people of Bethchorin and went as far as the descent of the castle of Bethchorin, and farther, and they tarried there securely with their young men on that night.⁷ And the people of Bethchorin fought the whole night, one man with his brother, and the other with his neighbor, and they cried out in every direction upon the castle, and their cry was heard at a distance, and the whole earth shook at their voice, for they were powerful above all the people of the earth.⁸ And all the inhabitants of the cities of the Canaanites, the Hittites, the Amorites, the Hivites and all the kings of Canaan, and also those who were on the other side of the Jordan, heard the noise of the shouting on that night.⁹ And they said, Surely these are the battles of the Hebrews who are fighting against the seven cities, who came nigh unto them; and who can stand against those Hebrews?¹⁰ And all the inhabitants of the cities of the Canaanites, and all those who were on the other side of the Jordan, were greatly afraid of the sons of Jacob, for they said, Behold the same will be done to us as was done to those cities, for who can stand against their mighty strength?¹¹ And the cries of the Chorinites were very great on that night, and continued to increase; and they smote each other till morning, and numbers of them were killed.¹² And the morning appeared, and all the sons of Jacob rose

up at daybreak and went up to the castle, and they smote those who remained of the Chorinites in a terrible manner, and they were all killed in the castle.[13] And the sixth day appeared, and all the inhabitants of Canaan saw at a distance all the people of Bethchorin lying dead in the castle of Bethchorin, and strewed about as the carcasses of lambs and goats.[14] And the sons of Jacob led all the spoil which they had captured from Gaash and went to Bethchorin, and they found the city full of people like the sand of the sea, and they fought with them, and the sons of Jacob smote them there till evening time.[15] And the sons of Jacob did unto Bethchorin as they had done to Gaash and Tapnach, and as they had done to Chazar, to Sarton and to Shiloh.[16] And the sons of Jacob took with them the spoil of Bethchorin and all the spoil of the cities, and on that day they went home to Shechem.[17] And the sons of Jacob came home to the city of Shechem, and they remained without the city, and they then rested there from the war, and tarried there all night.[18] And all their servants together with all the spoil that they had taken from the cities, they left without the city, and they did not enter the city, for they said, Peradventure there may be yet more fighting against us, and they may come to besiege us in Shechem.[19] And Jacob and his sons and their servants remained on that night and the next day in the portion of the field which Jacob had purchased from Hamor for five shekels, and all that they had captured was with them.[20] And all the booty which the sons of Jacob had captured, was in the portion of the field, immense as the sand upon the sea shore.[21] And the inhabitants of the land observed them from afar, and all the inhabitants of the land were afraid of the sons of Jacob who had done this thing, for no king from the days of old had ever done the like.[22] And the seven kings of the Canaanites resolved to make peace with the sons of Jacob, for they were greatly afraid of their lives, on account of the sons of Jacob.[23] And on that day, being the seventh day, Japhia king of Hebron sent secretly to the king of Ai, and to the king of Gibeon, and to the king of Shalem, and to the king of Adulam, and to the king of Lachish, and to the king of Chazar, and to all the Canaanitish kings who were under their subjection, saying,[24] Go up with me, and come to me that we may go to the sons of Jacob, and I will make peace with them, and form a treaty with them, lest all your lands be destroyed by the swords of the sons of Jacob, as they did to Shechem and the cities around it, as you have heard and seen.[25] And when you come to me, do not come with many men, but let every king bring his three head captains, and every captain bring three of his officers.[26] And come all of you to Hebron, and we will go together to the sons of Jacob, and supplicate them that they shall form a treaty of peace with us.[27] And all those kings did as the king of Hebron had sent to them, for they were all under his counsel and command, and all the kings of Canaan assembled to go to the sons of Jacob, to make peace with them; and the sons of Jacob returned and went to the portion of the field that was in Shechem, for they did not put confidence in the kings of the land.[28] And the sons of Jacob returned and remained in the portion of the field ten days, and no one came to make war with them.[29] And when the sons of Jacob saw that there was no appearance of war, they all assembled and went to the city of Shechem, and the sons of Jacob remained in Shechem.[30] And at the expiration of forty days, all the kings of the Amorites assembled from all their places and came to Hebron, to Japhia, king of Hebron.[31] And the number of kings that came to Hebron, to make peace with the sons of Jacob, was twenty-one kings, and the number of captains that came with them was sixty-nine, and their men were one hundred and eighty-nine, and all these kings and their men rested by Mount Hebron.[32] And the king of Hebron went out with his three captains and nine men, and these kings resolved to go to the sons of Jacob

to make peace.[33] And they said unto the king of Hebron, Go thou before us with thy men, and speak for us unto the sons of Jacob, and we will come after thee and confirm thy words, and the king of Hebron did so.[34] And the sons of Jacob heard that all the kings of Canaan had gathered together and rested in Hebron, and the sons of Jacob sent four of their servants as spies, saying, Go and spy these kings, and search and examine their men whether they are few or many, and if they are but few in number, number them all and come back.[35] And the servants of Jacob went secretly to these kings, and did as the sons of Jacob had commanded them, and on that day they came back to the sons of Jacob, and said unto them, We came unto those kings, and they are but few in number, and we numbered them all, and behold, they were two hundred and eighty-eight, kings and men.[36] And the sons of Jacob said, They are but few in number, therefore we will not all go out to them; and in the morning the sons of Jacob rose up and chose sixty two of their men, and ten of the sons of Jacob went with them; and they girt on their weapons of war, for they said, They are coming to make war with us, for they knew not that they were coming to make peace with them.[37] And the sons of Jacob went with their servants to the gate of Shechem, toward those kings, and their father Jacob was with them.[38] And when they had come forth, behold, the king of Hebron and his three captains and nine men with him were coming along the road against the sons of Jacob, and the sons of Jacob lifted up their eyes, and saw at a distance Japhia, king of Hebron, with his captains, coming toward them, and the sons of Jacob took their stand at the place of the gate of Shechem, and did not proceed.[39] And the king of Hebron continued to advance, he and his captains, until he came nigh to the sons of Jacob, and he and his captains bowed down to them to the ground, and the king of Hebron sat with his captains before Jacob and his sons.[40] And the sons of Jacob said unto him, What has befallen thee, O king of Hebron? why hast thou come to us this day? what dost thou require from us? and the king of Hebron said unto Jacob, I beseech thee my lord, all the kings of the Canaanites have this day come to make peace with you.[41] And the sons of Jacob heard the words of the king of Hebron, and they would not consent to his proposals, for the sons of Jacob had no faith in him, for they imagined that the king of Hebron had spoken deceitfully to them.[42] And the king of Hebron knew from the words of the sons of Jacob, that they did not believe his words, and the king of Hebron approached nearer to Jacob, and said unto him, I beseech thee, my lord, to be assured that all these kings have come to you on peaceable terms, for they have not come with all their men, neither did they bring their weapons of war with them, for they have come to seek peace from my lord and his sons.[43] And the sons of Jacob answered the king of Hebron, saying, Send thou to all these kings, and if thou speakest truth unto us, let them each come singly before us, and if they come unto us unarmed, we shall then know that they seek peace from us.[44] And Japhia, king of Hebron, sent one of his men to the kings, and they all came before the sons of Jacob, and bowed down to them to the ground, and these kings sat before Jacob and his sons, and they spoke unto them, saying,[45] We have heard all that you did unto the kings of the Amorites with your sword and exceedingly mighty arm, so that no man could stand up before you, and we were afraid of you for the sake of our lives, lest it should befall us as it did to them.[46] So we have come unto you to form a treaty of peace between us, and now therefore contract with us a covenant of peace and truth, that you will not meddle with us, inasmuch as we have not meddled with you.[47] And the sons of Jacob knew that they had really come to seek peace from them, and the sons of Jacob listened to them, and formed a covenant with them.[48] And the sons of Jacob swore unto them that they would not meddle with them, and all the kings of the Canaanites swore also to them, and the sons of Jacob made them tributary from that day forward.[49] And after this all the captains of these kings came with their men before Jacob, with presents in their hands for Jacob and his sons, and they bowed down to him to the ground.[50] And these kings then urged the sons of Jacob and begged of them to return all the spoil they had captured from the seven cities of the Amorites, and the sons of Jacob did so, and they returned all that they had captured, the women, the little ones, the cattle and all the spoil which they had taken, and they sent them off, and they went away each to his city.[51] And all these kings again bowed down to the sons of Jacob, and they sent or brought them many gifts in those days, and the sons of Jacob sent off these kings and their men, and they went peaceably away from them to their cities, and the sons of Jacob also returned to their home, to Shechem.[52] And there was peace from that day forward between the sons of Jacob and the kings of the Canaanites, until the children of Israel came to inherit the land of Canaan.

Jash.41

[1] And at the revolution of the year the sons of Jacob journeyed from Shechem, and they came to Hebron, to their father Isaac, and they dwelt there, but their flocks and herds they fed daily in Shechem, for there was there in those days good and fat pasture, and Jacob and his sons and all their household dwelt in the valley of Hebron.[2] And it was in those days, in that year, being the hundred and sixth year of the life of Jacob, in the tenth year of Jacob's coming from Padan-aram, that Leah the wife of Jacob died; she was fifty-one years old when she died in Hebron.[3] And Jacob and his sons buried her in the cave of the field of Machpelah, which is in Hebron, which Abraham had bought from the children of Heth, for the possession of a burial place.[4] And the sons of Jacob dwelt with their father in the valley of Hebron, and all the inhabitants of the land knew their strength and their fame went throughout the land.[5] And Joseph the son of Jacob, and his brother Benjamin, the sons of Rachel, the wife of Jacob, were yet young in those days, and did not go out with their brethren during their battles in all the cities of the Amorites.[6] And when Joseph saw the strength of his brethren, and their greatness, he praised them and extolled them, but he ranked himself greater than them, and extolled himself above them; and Jacob, his father, also loved him more than any of his sons, for he was a son of his old age, and through his love toward him, he made him a coat of many colors.[7] And when Joseph saw that his father loved him more than his brethren, he continued to exalt himself above his brethren, and he brought unto his father evil reports concerning them.[8] And the sons of Jacob seeing the whole of Joseph's conduct toward them, and that their father loved him more than any of them, they hated him and could not speak peaceably to him all the days.[9] And Joseph was seventeen years old, and he was still magnifying himself above his brethren, and thought of raising himself above them.[10] At that time he dreamed a dream, and he came unto his brothers and told them his dream, and he said unto them, I dreamed a dream, and behold we were all binding sheaves in the field, and my sheaf rose and placed itself upon the ground and your sheaves surrounded it and bowed down to it.[11] And his brethren answered him and said unto him, What meaneth this dream that thou didst dream? dost thou imagine in thy heart to reign or rule over us?[12] And he still came, and told the thing to his father Jacob, and Jacob kissed Joseph when he heard these words from his mouth, and Jacob blessed Joseph.[13] And when the sons of Jacob saw that their father had blessed Joseph and had kissed him, and that he loved him exceedingly, they became jealous of him and hated him the more.[14] And after this Joseph dreamed another dream and related

259

the dream to his father in the presence of his brethren, and Joseph said unto his father and brethren, Behold I have again dreamed a dream, and behold the sun and the moon and the eleven stars bowed down to me.[15] And his father heard the words of Joseph and his dream, and seeing that his brethren hated Joseph on account of this matter, Jacob therefore rebuked Joseph before his brethren on account of this thing, saying, What meaneth this dream which thou hast dreamed, and this magnifying thyself before thy brethren who are older than thou art?[16] Dost thou imagine in thy heart that I and thy mother and thy eleven brethren will come and bow down to thee, that thou speakest these things?[17] And his brethren were jealous of him on account of his words and dreams, and they continued to hate him, and Jacob reserved the dreams in his heart.[18] And the sons of Jacob went one day to feed their father's flock in Shechem, for they were still herdsmen in those days; and whilst the sons of Jacob were that day feeding in Shechem they delayed, and the time of gathering in the cattle was passed, and they had not arrived.[19] And Jacob saw that his sons were delayed in Shechem, and Jacob said within himself, Peradventure the people of Shechem have risen up to fight against them, therefore they have delayed coming this day.[20] And Jacob called Joseph his son and commanded him, saying, Behold thy brethren are feeding in Shechem this day, and behold they have not yet come back; go now therefore and see where they are, and bring me word back concerning the welfare of thy brethren and the welfare of the flock.[21] And Jacob sent his son Joseph to the valley of Hebron, and Joseph came for his brothers to Shechem, and could not find them, and Joseph went about the field which was near Shechem, to see where his brothers had turned, and he missed his road in the wilderness, and knew not which way he should go.[22] And an angel of the Lord found him wandering in the road toward the field, and Joseph said unto the angel of the Lord, I seek my brethren; hast thou not heard where they are feeding? and the angel of the Lord said unto Joseph, I saw thy brethren feeding here, and I heard them say they would go to feed in Dothan.[23] And Joseph hearkened to the voice of the angel of the Lord, and he went to his brethren in Dothan and he found them in Dothan feeding the flock.[24] And Joseph advanced to his brethren, and before he had come nigh unto them, they had resolved to slay him.[25] And Simeon said to his brethren, Behold the man of dreams is coming unto us this day, and now therefore come and let us kill him and cast him in one of the pits that are in the wilderness, and when his father shall seek him from us, we will say an evil beast has devoured him.[26] And Reuben heard the words of his brethren concerning Joseph, and he said unto them, You should not do this thing, for how can we look up to our father Jacob? Cast him into this pit to die there, but stretch not forth a hand upon him to spill his blood; and Reuben said this in order to deliver him from their hand, to bring him back to his father.[27] And when Joseph came to his brethren he sat before them, and they rose upon him and seized him and smote him to the earth, and stripped the coat of many colors which he had on.[28] And they took him and cast him into a pit, and in the pit there was no water, but serpents and scorpions. And Joseph was afraid of the serpents and scorpions that were in the pit. And Joseph cried out with a loud voice, and the Lord hid the serpents and scorpions in the sides of the pit, and they did no harm unto Joseph.[29] And Joseph called out from the pit to his brethren, and said unto them, What have I done unto you, and in what have I sinned? why do you not fear the Lord concerning me? am I not of your bones and flesh, and is not Jacob your father, my father? why do you do this thing unto me this day, and how will you be able to look up to our father Jacob?[30] And he continued to cry out and call unto his brethren from the pit, and he said, O Judah,

Simeon, and Levi, my brethren, lift me up from the place of darkness in which you have placed me, and come this day to have compassion on me, ye children of the Lord, and sons of Jacob my father. And if I have sinned unto you, are you not the sons of Abraham, Isaac, and Jacob? if they saw an orphan they had compassion over him, or one that was hungry, they gave him bread to eat, or one that was thirsty, they gave him water to drink, or one that was naked, they covered him with garments! 31 And how then will you withhold your pity from your brother, for I am of your flesh and bones, and if I have sinned unto you, surely you will do this on account of my father! 32 And Joseph spoke these words from the pit, and his brethren could not listen to him, nor incline their ears to the words of Joseph, and Joseph was crying and weeping in the pit. 33 And Joseph said, O that my father knew, this day, the act which my brothers have done unto me, and the words which they have this day spoken unto me. 34 And all his brethren heard his cries and weeping in the pit, and his brethren went and removed themselves from the pit, so that they might not hear the cries of Joseph and his weeping in the pit.

Jash.42

1 And they went and sat on the opposite side, about the distance of a bow-shot, and they sat there to eat bread, and whilst they were eating, they held counsel together what was to be done with him, whether to slay him or to bring him back to his father. 2 They were holding the counsel, when they lifted up their eyes, and saw, and behold there was a company of Ishmaelites coming at a distance by the road of Gilead, going down to Egypt. 3 And Judah said unto them, What gain will it be to us if we slay our brother? peradventure God will require him from us; this then is the counsel proposed concerning him, which you shall do unto him: Behold this company of Ishmaelites going down to Egypt, 4 Now therefore, come let us dispose of him to them, and let not our hand be upon him, and they will lead him along with them, and he will be lost amongst the people of the land, and we will not put him to death with our own hands. And the proposal pleased his brethren and they did according to the word of Judah. 5 And whilst they were discoursing about this matter, and before the company of Ishmaelites had come up to them, seven trading men of Midian passed by them, and as they passed they were thirsty, and they lifted up their eyes and saw the pit in which Joseph was immured, and they looked, and behold every species of bird was upon him. 6 And these Midianites ran to the pit to drink water, for they thought that it contained water, and on coming before the pit they heard the voice of Joseph crying and weeping in the pit, and they looked down into the pit, and they saw and behold there was a youth of comely appearance and well favored. 7 And they called unto him and said, Who art thou and who brought thee hither, and who placed thee in this pit, in the wilderness? and they all assisted to raise up Joseph and they drew him out, and brought him up from the pit, and took him and went away on their journey and passed by his brethren. 8 And these said unto them, Why do you do this, to take our servant from us and to go away? surely we placed this youth in the pit because he rebelled against us, and you come and bring him up and lead him away; now then give us back our servant. 9 And the Midianites answered and said unto the sons of Jacob, Is this your servant, or does this man attend you? peradventure you are all his servants, for he is more comely and well favored than any of you, and why do you all speak falsely unto us? 10 Now therefore we will not listen to your words, nor attend to you, for we found the youth in the pit in the wilderness, and we took him; we will therefore go on. 11 And all the sons of Jacob approached them and rose up to them and said unto them, Give us back our servant, and why will you all die by the edge of the sword? And the Midianites cried out

against them, and they drew their swords, and approached to fight with the sons of Jacob. 12 And behold Simeon rose up from his seat against them, and sprang upon the ground and drew his sword and approached the Midianites and he gave a terrible shout before them, so that his shouting was heard at a distance, and the earth shook at Simeon's shouting. 13 And the Midianites were terrified on account of Simeon and the noise of his shouting, and they fell upon their faces, and were excessively alarmed. 14 And Simeon said unto them, Verily I am Simeon, the son of Jacob the Hebrew, who have, only with my brother, destroyed the city of Shechem and the cities of the Amorites; so shall God moreover do unto me, that if all your brethren the people of Midian, and also the kings of Canaan, were to come with you, they could not fight against me. 15 Now therefore give us back the youth whom you have taken, lest I give your flesh to the birds of the skies and the beasts of the earth. 16 And the Midianites were more afraid of Simeon, and they approached the sons of Jacob with terror and fright, and with pathetic words, saying, 17 Surely you have said that the young man is your servant, and that he rebelled against you, and therefore you placed him in the pit; what then will you do with a servant who rebels against his master? Now therefore sell him unto us, and we will give you all that you require for him; and the Lord was pleased to do this in order that the sons of Jacob should not slay their brother. 18 And the Midianites saw that Joseph was of a comely appearance and well-favored; they desired him in their hearts and were urgent to purchase him from his brethren. 19 And the sons of Jacob hearkened to the Midianites and they sold their brother Joseph to them for twenty pieces of silver, and Reuben their brother was not with them, and the Midianites took Joseph and continued their journey to Gilead. 20 They were going along the road, and the Midianites repented of what they had done, in having purchased the young man, and one said to the other, What is this thing that we have done, in taking this youth from the Hebrews, who is of comely appearance and well favored. 21 Perhaps this youth is stolen from the land of the Hebrews, and why then have we done this thing? and if he should be sought for and found in our hands we shall die through him. 22 Now surely hardy and powerful men have sold him to us, the strength of one of whom you saw this day; perhaps they stole him from his land with their might and with their powerful arm, and have therefore sold him to us for the small value which we gave unto them. 23 And whilst they were thus discoursing together, they looked, and behold the company of Ishmaelites which was coming at first, and which the sons of Jacob saw, was advancing toward the Midianites, and the Midianites said to each other, Come let us sell this youth to the company of Ishmaelites who are coming toward us, and we will take for him the little that we gave for him, and we will be delivered from his evil. 24 And they did so, and they reached the Ishmaelites, and the Midianites sold Joseph to the Ishmaelites for twenty pieces of silver which they had given for him to his brethren. 25 And the Midianites went on their road to Gilead, and the Ishmaelites took Joseph and they let him ride upon one of the camels, and they were leading him to Egypt. 26 And Joseph heard that the Ishmaelites were proceeding to Egypt, and Joseph lamented and wept at this thing that he was to be so far removed from the land of Canaan, from his father, and he wept bitterly whilst he was riding upon the camel, and one of their men observed him, and made him go down from the camel and walk on foot, and notwithstanding this Joseph continued to cry and weep, and he said, O my father, my father. 27 And one of the Ishmaelites rose up and smote Joseph upon the cheek, and still he continued to weep; and Joseph was fatigued in the road, and was unable to proceed on account of the bitterness of his soul, and they all smote him and afflicted him in the road, and they terrified him in order that he might cease from weeping. 28 And the Lord saw the ambition of Joseph and his trouble, and the Lord brought down upon those men darkness and confusion, and the hand of every one that smote him became withered. 29 And they said to each other, What is this thing that God has done to us in the road? and they knew not that this befell them on account of Joseph. And the men proceeded on the road, and they passed along the road of Ephrath where Rachel was buried. 30 And Joseph reached his mother's grave, and Joseph hastened and ran to his mother's grave, and fell upon the grave and wept. 31 And Joseph cried aloud upon his mother's grave, and he said, O my mother, my mother, O thou who didst give me birth, awake now, and rise and see thy son, how he has been sold for a slave, and no one to pity him. 32 O rise and see thy son, weep with me on account of my troubles, and see the heart of my brethren. 33 Arouse my mother, arouse, awake from thy sleep for me, and direct thy battles against my brethren. O how have they stripped me of my coat, and sold me already twice for a slave, and separated me from my father, and there is no one to pity me. 34 Arouse and lay thy cause against them before God, and see whom God will justify in the judgment, and whom he will condemn. 35 Rise, O my mother, rise, awake from thy sleep and see my father how his soul is with me this day, and comfort him and ease his heart. 36 And Joseph continued to speak these words, and Joseph cried aloud and wept bitterly upon his mother's grave; and he ceased speaking, and from bitterness of heart he became still as a stone upon the grave. 37 And Joseph heard a voice speaking to him from beneath the ground, which answered him with bitterness of heart, and with a voice of weeping and praying in these words: 38 My son, my son Joseph, I have heard the voice of thy weeping and the voice of thy lamentation; I have seen thy tears; I know thy troubles, my son, and it grieves me for thy sake, and abundant grief is added to my grief. 39 Now therefore my son, Joseph my son, hope to the Lord, and wait for him and do not fear, for the Lord is with thee, he will deliver thee from all trouble. 40 Rise my son, go down unto Egypt with thy masters, and do not fear, for the Lord is with thee, my son. And she continued to speak like unto these words unto Joseph, and she was still. 41 And Joseph heard this, and he wondered greatly at this, and he continued to weep; and after this one of the Ishmaelites observed him crying and weeping upon the grave, and his anger was kindled against him, and he drove him from there, and he smote him and cursed him. 42 And Joseph said unto the men, May I find grace in your sight to take me back to my father's house, and he will give you abundance of riches. 43 And they answered him, saying, Art thou not a slave, and where is thy father? and if thou hadst a father thou wouldst not already twice have been sold for a slave for so little value; and their anger was still roused against him, and they continued to smite him and to chastise him, and Joseph wept bitterly. 44 And the Lord saw Joseph's affliction, and Lord again smote these men, and chastised them, and the Lord caused darkness to envelope them upon the earth, and the lightning flashed and the thunder roared, and the earth shook at the voice of the thunder and of the mighty wind, and the men were terrified and knew not where they should go. 45 And the beasts and camels stood still, and they led them, but they would not go, they smote them, and they crouched upon the ground; and the men said to each other, What is this that God has done to us? what are our transgressions, and what are our sins that this thing has thus befallen us? 46 And one of them answered and said unto them, Perhaps on account of the sin of afflicting this slave has this thing happened this day to us; now therefore implore him strongly to forgive us, and then we shall know on whose account this evil befalleth us, and if God shall have

compassion over us, then we shall know that all this cometh to us on account of the sin of afflicting this slave. 47 And the men did so, and they supplicated Joseph and pressed him to forgive them; and they said, We have sinned to the Lord and to thee, now therefore vouchsafe to request of thy God that he shall put away this death from amongst us, for we have sinned to him. 48 And Joseph did according to their words, and the Lord hearkened to Joseph, and the Lord put away the plague which he had inflicted upon those men on account of Joseph, and the beasts rose up from the ground and they conducted them, and they went on, and the raging storm abated and the earth became tranquilized, and the men proceeded on their journey to go down to Egypt, and the men knew that this evil had befallen them on account of Joseph. 49 And they said to each other, Behold we know that it was on account of his affliction that this evil befell us; now therefore why shall we bring this death upon our souls? Let us hold counsel what to do to this slave. 50 And one answered and said, Surely he told us to bring him back to his father; now therefore come, let us take him back and we will go to the place that he will tell us, and take from his family the price that we gave for him and we will then go away. 51 And one answered again and said, Behold this counsel is very good, but we cannot do so for the way is very far from us, and we cannot go out of our road. 52 And one more answered and said unto them, This is the counsel to be adopted, we will not swerve from it; behold we are this day going to Egypt, and when we shall have come to Egypt, we will sell him there at a high price, and we will be delivered from his evil. 53 And this thing pleased the men and they did so, and they continued their journey to Egypt with Joseph.

Jash.43

1 And when the sons of Jacob had sold their brother Joseph to the Midianites, their hearts were smitten on account of him, and they repented of their acts, and they sought for him to bring him back, but could not find him. 2 And Reuben returned to the pit in which Joseph had been put, in order to lift him out, and restore him to his father, and Reuben stood by the pit, and he heard not a word, and he called out Joseph! Joseph! and no one answered or uttered a word. 3 And Reuben said, Joseph has died through fright, or some serpent has caused his death; and Reuben descended into the pit, and he searched for Joseph and could not find him in the pit, and he came out again. 4 And Reuben tore his garments and he said, The child is not there, and how shall I reconcile my father about him if he be dead? and he went to his brethren and found them grieving on account of Joseph, and counseling together how to reconcile their father about him, and Reuben said unto his brethren, I came to the pit and behold Joseph was not there, what then shall we say unto our father, for my father will only seek the lad from me. 5 And his brethren answered him saying, Thus and thus we did, and our hearts afterward smote us on account of this act, and we now sit to seek a pretext how we shall reconcile our father to it. 6 And Reuben said unto them, What is this you have done to bring down the grey hairs of our father in sorrow to the grave? the thing is not good, that you have done. 7 And Reuben sat with them, and they all rose up and swore to each other not to tell this thing unto Jacob, and they all said, The man who will tell this to our father or his household, or who will report this to any of the children of the land, we will all rise up against him and slay him with the sword. 8 And the sons of Jacob feared each other in this matter, from the youngest to the oldest, and no one spoke a word, and they concealed the thing in their hearts. 9 And they afterward sat down to determine and invent something to say unto their father Jacob concerning all these things. 10 And Issachar said unto them, Here is an advice for you if it seem good in your eyes to do this thing, take the coat which

belongeth to Joseph and tear it, and kill a kid of the goats and dip it in its blood. [11] And send it to our father and when he seeth it he will say an evil beast has devoured him, therefore tear ye his coat and behold his blood will be upon his coat, and by your doing this we shall be free of our father's murmurings. [12] And Issachar's advice pleased them, and they hearkened unto him and they did according to the word of Issachar which he had counselled them. [13] And they hastened and took Joseph's coat and tore it, and they killed a kid of the goats and dipped the coat in the blood of the kid, and then trampled it in the dust, and they sent the coat to their father Jacob by the hand of Naphtali, and they commanded him to say these words: [14] We had gathered in the cattle and had come as far as the road to Shechem and farther, when we found this coat upon the road in the wilderness dipped in blood and in dust; now therefore know whether it be thy son's coat or not. [15] And Naphtali went and he came unto his father and he gave him the coat, and he spoke unto him all the words which his brethren had commanded him. [16] And Jacob saw Joseph's coat and he knew it and he fell upon his face to the ground, and became as still as a stone, and he afterward rose up and cried out with a loud and weeping voice and he said, It is the coat of my son Joseph! [17] And Jacob hastened and sent one of his servants to his sons, who went to them and found them coming along the road with the flock. [18] And the sons of Jacob came to their father about evening, and behold their garments were torn and dust was upon their heads, and they found their father crying out and weeping with a loud voice. [19] And Jacob said unto his sons, Tell me truly what evil have you this day suddenly brought upon me? and they answered their father Jacob, saying, We were coming along this day after the flock had been gathered in, and we came as far as the city of Shechem by the road in the wilderness, and we found this coat filled with blood upon the ground, and we knew it and we sent unto thee if thou couldst know it. [20] And Jacob heard the words of his sons and he cried out with a loud voice, and he said, It is the coat of my son, an evil beast has devoured him; Joseph is rent in pieces, for I sent him this day to see whether it was well with you and well with the flocks and to bring me word again from you, and he went as I commanded him, and this has happened to him this day whilst I thought my son was with you. [21] And the sons of Jacob answered and said, He did not come to us, neither have we seen him from the time of our going out from thee until now. [22] And when Jacob heard their words he again cried out aloud, and he rose up and tore his garments, and he put sackcloth upon his loins, and he wept bitterly and he mourned and lifted up his voice in weeping and exclaimed and said these words, [23] Joseph my son, O my son Joseph, I sent thee this day after the welfare of thy brethren, and behold thou hast been torn in pieces; through my hand has this happened to my son. [24] It grieves me for thee Joseph my son, it grieves me for thee; how sweet wast thou to me during life, and now how exceedingly bitter is thy death to me. [25] 0 that I had died in thy stead Joseph my son, for it grieves me sadly for thee my son, O my son, my son. Joseph my son, where art thou, and where hast thou been drawn? arouse, arouse from thy place, and come and see my grief for thee, O my son Joseph. [26] Come now and number the tears gushing from my eyes down my cheeks, and bring them up before the Lord, that his anger may turn from me. [27] 0 Joseph my son, how didst thou fall, by the hand of one by whom no one had fallen from the beginning of the world unto this day; for thou hast been put to death by the smiting of an enemy, inflicted with cruelty, but surely I know that this has happened to thee, on account of the multitude of my sins. [28] Arouse now and see how bitter is my trouble for thee my son, although I did not rear thee, nor fashion thee, nor give thee breath and soul, but it was God who formed thee and built thy bones

and covered them with flesh, and breathed in thy nostrils the breath of life, and then he gave thee unto me. [29] Now truly God who gave thee unto me, he has taken thee from me, and such then has befallen thee [30] And Jacob continued to speak like unto these words concerning Joseph, and he wept bitterly; he fell to the ground and became still. [31] And all the sons of Jacob seeing their father's trouble, they repented of what they had done, and they also wept bitterly. [32] And Judah rose up and lifted his father's head from the ground, and placed it upon his lap, and he wiped his father's tears from his cheeks, and Judah wept an exceeding great weeping, whilst his father's head was reclining upon his lap, still as a stone. [33] And the sons of Jacob saw their father's trouble, and they lifted up their voices and continued to weep, and Jacob was yet lying upon the ground still as a stone. [34] And all his sons and his servants and his servant's children rose up and stood round him to comfort him, and he refused to be comforted. [35] And the whole household of Jacob rose up and mourned a great mourning on account of Joseph and their father's trouble, and the intelligence reached Isaac, the son of Abraham, the father of Jacob, and he wept bitterly on account of Joseph, he and all his household, and he went from the place where he dwelt in Hebron, and his men with him, and he comforted Jacob his son, and he refused to be comforted. [36] And after this, Jacob rose up from the ground, and his tears were running down his cheeks, and he said unto his sons, Rise up and take your swords and your bows, and go forth into the field, and seek whether you can find my son's body and bring it unto me that I may bury it. [37] Seek also, I pray you, among the beasts and hunt them, and that which shall come the first before you seize and bring it unto me, perhaps the Lord will this day pity my affliction, and prepare before you that which did tear my son in pieces, and bring it unto me, and I will avenge the cause of my son. [38] And his sons did as their father had commanded them, and they rose up early in the morning, and each took his sword and his bow in his hand, and they went forth into the field to hunt the beasts. [39] And Jacob was still crying aloud and weeping and walking to and fro in the house, and smiting his hands together, saying, Joseph my son, Joseph my son. [40] And the sons of Jacob went into the wilderness to seize the beasts, and behold a wolf came toward them, and they seized him, and brought him unto their father, and they said unto him, This is the first we have found, and we have brought him unto thee as thou didst command us, and thy son's body we could not find. [41] And Jacob took the beast from the hands of his sons, and he cried out with a loud and weeping voice, holding the beast in his hand, and he spoke with a bitter heart unto the beast, Why didst thou devour my son Joseph, and how didst thou have no fear of the God of the earth, or of my trouble for my son Joseph? [42] And thou didst devour my son for naught, because he committed no violence, and didst thereby render me culpable on his account, therefore God will require him that is persecuted. [43] And the Lord opened the mouth of the beast in order to comfort Jacob with its words, and it answered Jacob and spoke these words unto him, [44] As God liveth who created us in the earth, and as thy soul liveth, my lord, I did not see thy son, neither did I tear him to pieces, but from a distant land I also came to seek my son who went from me this day, and I know not whether he be living or dead. [45] And I came this day into the field to seek my son, and your sons found me, and seized me and increased my grief, and have this day brought me before thee, and I have now spoken all my words to thee. [46] And now therefore, O son of man, I am in thy hands, and do unto me this day as it may seem good in thy sight, but by the life of God who created me, I did not see thy son, nor did I tear him to pieces, neither has the flesh of man entered my mouth all the days of my life. [47] And when Jacob heard the words of the beast he was greatly astonished, and sent forth the beast from his hand, and she went her way. ⁴⁸ And Jacob was still crying aloud and weeping for Joseph day after day, and he mourned for his son many days.

Jash.44

¹ And the sons of Ishmael who had bought Joseph from the Midianites, who had bought him from his brethren, went to Egypt with Joseph, and they came upon the borders of Egypt, and when they came near unto Egypt, they met four men of the sons of Medan the son of Abraham, who had gone forth from the land of Egypt on their journey. ² And the Ishmaelites said unto them, Do you desire to purchase this slave from us? and they said, Deliver him over to us, and they delivered Joseph over to them, and they beheld him, that he was a very comely youth and they purchased him for twenty shekels. ³ And the Ishmaelites continued their journey to Egypt and the Medanim also returned that day to Egypt, and the Medanim said to each other, Behold we have heard that Potiphar, an officer of Pharaoh, captain of the guard, seeketh a good servant who shall stand before him to attend him, and to make him overseer over his house and all belonging to him. ⁴ Now therefore come let us sell him to him for what we may desire, if he be able to give unto us that which we shall require for him. ⁵ And these Medanim went and came to the house of Potiphar, and said unto him, We have heard that thou seekest a good servant to attend thee, behold we have a servant that will please thee, if thou canst give unto us that which we may desire, and we will sell him unto thee. ⁶ And Potiphar said, Bring him before me, and I will see him, and if he please me I will give unto you that which you may require for him. ⁷ And the Medanim went and brought Joseph and placed him before Potiphar, and he saw him, and he pleased him exceedingly, and Potiphar said unto them, Tell me what you require for this youth? ⁸ And they said, Four hundred pieces of silver we desire for him, and Potiphar said, I will give it you if you bring me the record of his sale to you, and will tell me his history, for perhaps he may be stolen, for this youth is neither a slave, nor the son of a slave, but I observe in him the appearance of a goodly and handsome person. ⁹ And the Medanim went and brought unto him the Ishmaelites who had sold him to them, and they told him, saying, He is a slave and we sold him to them. ¹⁰ And Potiphar heard the words of the Ishmaelites in his giving the silver unto the Medanim, and the Medanim took the silver and went on their journey, and the Ishmaelites also returned home. ¹¹ And Potiphar took Joseph and brought him to his house that he might serve him, and Joseph found favor in the sight of Potiphar, and he placed confidence in him, and made him overseer over his house, and all that belonged to him he delivered over into his hand. ¹² And the Lord was with Joseph and he became a prosperous man, and the Lord blessed the house of Potiphar for the sake of Joseph. ¹³ And Potiphar left all that he had in the hand of Joseph, and Joseph was one that caused things to come in and go out, and everything was regulated by his wish in the house of Potiphar. ¹⁴ And Joseph was eighteen years old, a youth with beautiful eyes and of comely appearance, and like unto him was not in the whole land of Egypt. ¹⁵ At that time whilst he was in his master's house, going in and out of the house and attending his master, Zelicah, his master's wife, lifted up her eyes toward Joseph and she looked at him, and behold he was a youth comely and well favored. ¹⁶ And she coveted his beauty in her heart, and her soul was fixed upon Joseph, and she enticed him day after day, and Zelicah persuaded Joseph daily, but Joseph did not lift up his eyes to behold his master's wife. ¹⁷ And Zelicah said unto him, How goodly are thy appearance and form, truly I have looked at all the slaves, and have not seen so beautiful a slave as thou art; and Joseph said unto her,

Surely he who created me in my mother's womb created all mankind. ¹⁸ And she said unto him, How beautiful are thine eyes, with which thou hast dazzled all the inhabitants of Egypt, men and women; and he said unto her, How beautiful they are whilst we are alive, but shouldst thou behold them in the grave, surely thou wouldst move away from them. ¹⁹ And she said unto him, How beautiful and pleasing are all thy words; take now, I pray thee, the harp which is in the house, and play with thy hands and let us hear thy words. ²⁰ And he said unto her, How beautiful and pleasing are my words when I speak the praise of my God and his glory; and she said unto him, How very beautiful is the hair of thy head, behold the golden comb which is in the house, take it I pray thee, and curl the hair of thy head. ²¹ And he said unto her, How long wilt thou speak these words? cease to utter these words to me, and rise and attend to thy domestic affairs. ²² And she said unto him, There is no one in my house, and there is nothing to attend to but to thy words and to thy wish; yet notwithstanding all this, she could not bring Joseph unto her, neither did he place his eye upon her, but directed his eyes below to the ground. ²³ And Zelicah desired Joseph in her heart, that he should lie with her, and at the time that Joseph was sitting in the house doing his work, Zelicah came and sat before him, and she enticed him daily with her discourse to lie with her, or ever to look at her, but Joseph would not hearken to her. ²⁴ And she said unto him, If thou wilt not do according to my words, I will chastise thee with the punishment of death, and put an iron yoke upon thee. ²⁵ And Joseph said unto her, Surely God who created man looseth the fetters of prisoners, and it is he who will deliver me from thy prison and from thy judgment. ²⁶ And when she could not prevail over him, to persuade him, and her soul being still fixed upon him, her desire threw her into a grievous sickness. ²⁷ And all the women of Egypt came to visit her, and they said unto her, Why art thou in this declining state? thou that lackest nothing; surely thy husband is a great and esteemed prince in the sight of the king, shouldst thou lack anything of what thy heart desireth? ²⁸ And Zelicah answered them, saying, This day it shall be made known to you, whence this disorder springs in which you see me, and she commanded her maid servants to prepare food for all the women, and she made a banquet for them, and all the women ate in the house of Zelicah. ²⁹ And she gave them knives to peel the citrons to eat them, and she commanded that they should dress Joseph in costly garments, and that he should appear before them, and Joseph came before their eyes and all the women looked on Joseph, and could not take their eyes from off him, and they all cut their hands with the knives that they had in their hands, and all the citrons that were in their hands were filled with blood. ³⁰ And they knew not what they had done but they continued to look at the beauty of Joseph, and did not turn their eyelids from him. ³¹ And Zelicah saw what they had done, and she said unto them, What is this work that you have done? behold I gave you citrons to eat and you have all cut your hands. ³² And all the women saw their hands, and behold they were full of blood, and their blood flowed down upon their garments, and they said unto her, this slave in your house has overcome us, and we could not turn our eyelids from him on account of his beauty. ³³ And she said unto them, Surely this happened to you in the moment that you looked at him, and you could not contain yourselves from him; how then can I refrain when he is constantly in my house, and I see him day after day going in and out of my house? how then can I keep from declining or even from perishing on account of this? ³⁴ And they said unto her, the words are true, for who can see this beautiful form in the house and refrain from him, and is he not thy slave and attendant in thy house, and why dost thou not tell him that which is in thy heart, and sufferest thy soul to perish through this matter? 35 And she said unto them, I am daily endeavoring to persuade him, and he will not consent to my wishes, and I promised him everything that is good, and yet I could meet with no return from him; I am therefore in a declining state as you see. 36 And Zelicah became very ill on account of her desire toward Joseph, and she was desperately lovesick on account of him, and all the people of the house of Zelicah and her husband knew nothing of this matter, that Zelicah was ill on account of her love to Joseph. 37 And all the people of her house asked her, saying, Why art thou ill and declining, and lackest nothing? and she said unto them, I know not this thing which is daily increasing upon me. 38 And all the women and her friends came daily to see her, and they spoke with her, and she said unto them, This can only be through the love of Joseph; and they said unto her, Entice him and seize him secretly, perhaps he may hearken to thee, and put off this death from thee. 39 And Zelicah became worse from her love to Joseph, and she continued to decline, till she had scarce strength to stand. 40 And on a certain day Joseph was doing his master's work in the house, and Zelicah came secretly and fell suddenly upon him, and Joseph rose up against her, and he was more powerful than she, and he brought her down to the ground. 41 And Zelicah wept on account of the desire of her heart toward him, and she supplicated him with weeping, and her tears flowed down her cheeks, and she spoke unto him in a voice of supplication and in bitterness of soul, saying, 42 Hast thou ever heard, seen or known of so beautiful a woman as I am, or better than myself, who speak daily unto thee, fall into a decline through love for thee, confer all this honor upon thee, and still thou wilt not hearken to my voice? 43 And if it be through fear of thy master lest he punish thee, as the king liveth no harm shall come to thee from thy master through this thing; now, therefore pray listen to me, and consent for the sake of the honor which I have conferred upon thee, and put off this death from me, and why should I die for thy sake? and she ceased to speak. 44 And Joseph answered her, saying, Refrain from me, and leave this matter to my master; behold my master knoweth not what there is with me in the house, for all that belongeth to him he has delivered into my hand, and how shall I do these things in my master's house? 45 For he hath also greatly honored me in his house, and he hath also made me overseer over his house, and he hath exalted me, and there is no one greater in this house than I am, and my master hath refrained nothing from me, excepting thee who art his wife, how then canst thou speak these words unto me, and how can I do this great evil and sin to God and to thy husband? 46 Now therefore refrain from me, and speak no more such words as these, for I will not hearken to thy words. But Zelicah would not hearken to Joseph when he spoke these words unto her, but she daily enticed him to listen to her. 47 And it was after this that the brook of Egypt was filled above all its sides, and all the inhabitants of Egypt went forth, and also the king and princes went forth with timbrels and dances, for it was a great rejoicing in Egypt, and a holiday at the time of the inundation of the sea Sihor, and they went there to rejoice all the day. 48 And when the Egyptians went out to the river to rejoice, as was their custom, all the people of the house of Potiphar went with them, but Zelicah would not go with them, for she said, I am indisposed, and she remained alone in the house, and no other person was with her in the house. 49 And she rose up and ascended to her temple in the house, and dressed herself in princely garments, and she placed upon her head precious stones of onyx stones, inlaid with silver and gold, and she beautified her face and skin with all sorts of women's purifying liquids, and she perfumed the temple and the house with cassia and frankincense, and she spread myrrh and aloes, and she afterward sat in the entrance of the temple, in the passage of the

264

house, through which Joseph passed to do his work, and behold Joseph came from the field, and entered the house to do his master's work. 50 And he came to the place through which he had to pass, and he saw all the work of Zelicah, and he turned back. 51 And Zelicah saw Joseph turning back from her, and she called out to him, saying What aileth thee Joseph? come to thy work, and behold I will make room for thee until thou shalt have passed to thy seat. 52 And Joseph returned and came to the house, and passed from thence to the place of his seat, and he sat down to do his master's work as usual and behold Zelicah came to him and stood before him in princely garments, and the scent from her clothes was spread to a distance. 53 And she hastened and caught hold of Joseph and his garments, and she said unto him, As the king liveth if thou wilt not perform my request thou shalt die this day, and she hastened and stretched forth her other hand and drew a sword from beneath her garments, and she placed it upon Joseph's neck, and she said, Rise and perform my request, and if not thou diest this day. 54 And Joseph was afraid of her at her doing this thing, and he rose up to flee from her, and she seized the front of his garments, and in the terror of his flight the garment which Zelicah seized was torn, and Joseph left the garment in the hand of Zelicah, and he fled and got out, for he was in fear. 55 And when Zelicah saw that Joseph's garment was torn, and that he had left it in her hand, and had fled, she was afraid of her life, lest the report should spread concerning her, and she rose up and acted with cunning, and put off the garments in which she was dressed, and she put on her other garments. 56 And she took Joseph's garment, and she laid it beside her, and she went and seated herself in the place where she had sat in her illness, before the people of her house had gone out to the river, and she called a young lad who was then in the house, and she ordered him to call the people of the house to her. 57 And when she saw them she said unto them with a loud voice and lamentation, See what a Hebrew your master has brought to me in the house, for he came this day to lie with me. 58 For when you had gone out he came to the house, and seeing that there was no person in the house, he came unto me, and caught hold of me, with intent to lie with me. 59 And I seized his garments and tore them and called out against him with a loud voice, and when I had lifted up my voice he was afraid of his life and left his garment before me, and fled. 60 And the people of her house spoke nothing, but their wrath was very much kindled against Joseph, and they went to his master and told him the words of his wife. 61 And Potiphar came home enraged, and his wife cried out to him, saying, What is this thing that thou hast done unto me in bringing a He. brew servant into my house, for he came unto me this day to sport with me; thus did he do unto me this day. 62 And Potiphar heard the words of his wife, and he ordered Joseph to be punished with severe stripes, and they did so to him. 63 And whilst they were smiting him, Joseph called out with a loud voice, and he lifted up his eyes to heaven, and he said, O Lord God, thou knowest that I am innocent of all these things, and why shall I die this day through falsehood, by the hand of these uncircumcised wicked men, whom thou knowest? 64 And whilst Potiphar's men were beating Joseph, he continued to cry out and weep, and there was a child there eleven months old, and the Lord opened the mouth of the child, and he spake these words before Potiphar's men, who were smiting Joseph, saying, 65 What do you want of this man, and why do you do this evil unto him? my mother speaketh falsely and uttereth lies; thus was the transaction. 66 And the child told them accurately all that happened, and all the words of Zelicah to Joseph day after day did he declare unto them. 67 And all the men heard the words of the child and they wondered greatly at the child's words, and the child ceased to speak and became still. 68 And Potiphar was very much ashamed at the words of his son, and he commanded his men not to beat Joseph any more, and the men ceased beating Joseph. 69 And Potiphar took Joseph and ordered him to be brought to justice before the priests, who were judges belonging to the king, in order to judge him concerning this affair. 70 And Potiphar and Joseph came before the priests who were the king's judges, and he said unto them, Decide I pray you, what judgment is due to a servant, for thus has he done. 71 And the priests said unto Joseph, Why didst thou do this thing to thy master? and Joseph answered them, saying, Not so my lords, thus was the matter; and Potiphar said unto Joseph, Surely I entrusted in thy hands all that belonged to me, and I withheld nothing from thee but my wife, and how couldst thou do this evil? 72 And Joseph answered saying, Not so my lord, as the Lord liveth, and as thy soul liveth, my lord, the word which thou didst hear from thy wife is untrue, for thus was the affair this day. 73 A year has elapsed to me since I have been in thy house; hast thou seen any iniquity in me, or any thing which might cause thee to demand my life? 74 And the priests said unto Potiphar, Send, we pray thee, and let them bring before us Joseph's torn garment, and let us see the tear in it, and if it shall be that the tear is in front of the garment, then his face must have been opposite to her and she must have caught hold of him, to come to her, and with deceit did thy wife do all that she has spoken. 75 And they brought Joseph's garment before the priests who were judges, and they saw and behold the tear was in front of Joseph, and all the judging priests knew that she had pressed him, and they said, The judgment of death is not due to this slave for he has done nothing, but his judgment is, that he be placed in the prison house on account of the report, which through him has gone forth against thy wife. 76 And Potiphar heard their words, and he placed him in the prison house, the place where the king's prisoners are confined, and Joseph was in the house of confinement twelve years. 77 And notwithstanding this, his master's wife did not turn from him, and she did not cease from speaking to him day after day to hearken to her, and at the end of three months Zelicah continued going to Joseph to the house of confinement day by day, and she enticed him to hearken to her, and Zelicah said unto Joseph, How long wilt thou remain in this house? but hearken now to my voice, and I will bring thee out of this house. 78 And Joseph answered her, saying, It is better for me to remain in this house than to hearken to thy words, to sin against God; and she said unto him, If thou wilt not perform my wish, I will pluck out thine eyes, add fetters to thy feet, and will deliver thee into the hands of them whom thou didst not know before. 79 And Joseph answered her and said, Behold the God of the whole earth is able to deliver me from all that thou canst do unto me, for he openeth the eyes of the blind, and looseth those that are bound, and preserveth all strangers who are unacquainted with the land. 80 And when Zelicah was unable to persuade Joseph to hearken to her, she left off going to entice him; and Joseph was still confined in the house of confinement. And Jacob the father of Joseph, and all his brethren who were in the land of Canaan still mourned and wept in those days on account of Joseph, for Jacob refused to be comforted for his son Joseph, and Jacob cried aloud, and wept and mourned all those days.

Jash.45

1 And it was at that time in that year, which is the year of Joseph's going down to Egypt after his brothers had sold him, that Reuben the son of Jacob went to Timnah and took unto him for a wife Eliuram, the daughter of Avi the Canaanite, and he came to her. 2 And Eliuram the wife of Reuben conceived and bare him Hanoch, Palu, Chetzron and Carmi, four sons; and Simeon his brother took his sister Dinah for a wife, and she bare unto him

Memuel, Yamin, Ohad, Jachin and Zochar, five sons. 3 And he afterward came to Bunah the Canaanitish woman, the same is Bunah whom Simeon took captive from the city of Shechem, and Bunah was before Dinah and attended upon her, and Simeon came to her, and she bare unto him Saul. 4 And Judah went at that time to Adulam, and he came to a man of Adulam, and his name was Hirah, and Judah saw there the daughter of a man from Canaan, and her name was Aliyath, the daughter of Shua, and he took her, and came to her, and Aliyath bare unto Judah, Er, Onan and Shiloh; three sons. 5 And Levi and Issachar went to the land of the east, and they took unto themselves for wives the daughters of Jobab the son of Yoktan, the son of Eber; and Jobab the son of Yoktan had two daughters; the name of the elder was Adinah, and the name of the younger was Aridah. 6 And Levi took Adinah, and Issachar took Aridah, and they came to the land of Canaan, to their father's house, and Adinah bare unto Levi, Gershon, Kehath and Merari; three sons. 7 And Aridah bare unto Issachar Tola, Puvah, Job and Shomron, four sons; and Dan went to the land of Moab and took for a wife Aphlaleth, the daughter of Chamudan the Moabite, and he brought her to the land of Canaan. 8 And Aphlaleth was barren, she had no offspring, and God afterward remembered Aphlaleth the wife of Dan, and she conceived and bare a son, and she called his name Chushim. 9 And Gad and Naphtali went to Haran and took from thence the daughters of Amuram the son of Uz, the son of Nahor, for wives. 10 And these are the names of the daughters of Amuram; the name of the elder was Merimah, and the name of the younger Uzith; and Naphtali took Merimah, and Gad took Uzith; and brought them to the land of Canaan, to their father's house. 11 And Merimah bare unto Naphtali Yachzeel, Guni, Jazer and Shalem, four sons; and Uzith bare unto Gad Zephion, Chagi, Shuni, Ezbon, Eri, Arodi and Arali, seven sons. 12 And Asher went forth and took Adon the daughter of Aphlal, the son of Hadad, the son of Ishmael, for a wife, and he brought her to the land of Canaan. 13 And Adon the wife of Asher died in those days: she had no offspring; and it was after the death of Adon that Asher went to the other side of the river and took for a wife Hadurah the daughter of Abimael, the son of Eber, the son of Shem. 14 And the young woman was of a comely appearance, and a woman of sense, and she had been the wife of Malkiel the son of Elam, the son of Shem. 15 And Hadurah bare a daughter unto Malkiel, and he called her name Serach, and Malkiel died after this, and Hadurah went and remained in her father's house. 16 And after the death of the wife at Asher he went and took Hadurah for a wife, and brought her to the land of Canaan, and Serach her daughter he also brought with them, and she was three years old, and the damsel was brought up in Jacob's house. 17 And the damsel was of a comely appearance, and she went in the sanctified ways of the children of Jacob; she lacked nothing, and the Lord gave her wisdom and understanding. 18 And Hadurah the wife of Asher conceived and bare unto him Yimnah, Yishvah, Yishvi and Beriah; four sons. 19 And Zebulun went to Midian, and took for a wife Merishah the daughter of Molad, the son of Abida, the son of Midian, and brought her to the land of Canaan. 20 And Merushah bare unto Zebulun Sered, Elon and Yachleel; three sons. 21 And Jacob sent to Aram, the son of Zoba, the son of Terah, and he took for his son Benjamin Mechalia the daughter of Aram, and she came to the land of Canaan to the house of Jacob; and Benjamin was ten years old when he took Mechalia the daughter of Aram for a wife. 22 And Mechalia conceived and bare unto Benjamin Bela, Becher, Ashbel, Gera and Naaman, five sons; and Benjamin went afterward and took for a wife Aribath, the daughter of Shomron, the son of Abraham, in addition to his first wife, and he was eighteen years old; and Aribath bare unto Benjamin

Achi, Vosh, Mupim, Chupim, and Ord; five sons. 23 And in those days Judah went to the house of Shem and took Tamar the daughter of Elam, the son of Shem, for a wife for his first born Er. 24 And Er came to his wife Tamar, and she became his wife, and when he came to her he outwardly destroyed his seed, and his work was evil in the sight of the Lord, and the Lord slew him. 25 And it was after the death of Er, Judah's first born, that Judah said unto Onan, go to thy brother's wife and marry her as the next of kin, and raise up seed to thy brother. 26 And Onan took Tamar for a wife and he came to her, and Onan also did like unto the work of his brother, and his work was evil in the sight of the Lord, and he slew him also. 27 And when Onan died, Judah said unto Tamar, Remain in thy father's house until my son Shiloh shall have grown up, and Judah did no more delight in Tamar, to give her unto Shiloh, for he said, Peradventure he will also die like his brothers. 28 And Tamar rose up and went and remained in her father's house, and Tamar was in her father's house for some time. 29 And at the revolution of the year, Aliyath the wife of Judah died; and Judah was comforted for his wife, and after the death of Aliyath, Judah went up with his friend Hirah to Timnah to shear their sheep. 30 And Tamar heard that Judah had gone up to Timnah to shear the sheep, and that Shiloh was grown up, and Judah did not delight in her. 31 And Tamar rose up and put off the garments of her widowhood, and she put a vail upon her, and she entirely covered herself, and she went and sat in the public thoroughfare, which is upon the road to Timnah. 32 And Judah passed and saw her and took her and he came to her, and she conceived by him, and at the time of being delivered, behold, there were twins in her womb, and he called the name of the first Perez, and the name of the second Zarah.

Jash.46

1 In those days Joseph was still confined in the prison house in the land of Egypt. 2 At that time the attendants of Pharaoh were standing before him, the chief of the butlers and the chief of the bakers which belonged to the king of Egypt. 3 And the butler took wine and placed it before the king to drink, and the baker placed bread before the king to eat, and the king drank of the wine and ate of the bread, he and his servants and ministers that ate at the king's table. 4 And whilst they were eating and drinking, the butler and the baker remained there, and Pharaoh's ministers found many flies in the wine, which the butler had brought, and stones of nitre were found in the baker's bread. 5 And the captain of the guard placed Joseph as an attendant on Pharaoh's officers, and Pharaoh's officers were in confinement one year. 6 And at the end of the year, they both dreamed dreams in one night, in the place of confinement where they were, and in the morning Joseph came to them to attend upon them as usual, and he saw them, and behold their countenances were dejected and sad. 7 And Joseph asked them, Why are your countenances sad and dejected this day? and they said unto him, We dreamed a dream, and there is no one to interpret it; and Joseph said unto them, Relate, I pray you, your dream unto me, and God shall give you an answer of peace as you desire. 8 And the butler related his dream unto Joseph, and he said, I saw in my dream, and behold a large vine was before me, and upon that vine I saw three branches, and the vine speedily blossomed and reached a great height, and its clusters were ripened and became grapes. 9 And I took the grapes and pressed them in a cup, and placed it in Pharaoh's hand and he drank; and Joseph said unto him, The three branches that were upon the vine are three days. 10 Yet within three days, the king will order thee to be brought out and he will restore thee to thy office, and thou shalt give the king his wine to drink as at first when thou wast his butler; but let me find favor in thy sight, that thou shalt remember me to Pharaoh when it will be well with thee, and do

kindness unto me, and get me brought forth from this prison, for I was stolen away from the land of Canaan and was sold for a slave in this place. 11 And also that which was told thee concerning my master's wife is false, for they placed me in this dungeon for naught; and the butler answered Joseph, saying, If the king deal well with me as at first, as thou last interpreted to me, I will do all that thou desirest, and get thee brought out of this dungeon. 12 And the baker, seeing that Joseph had accurately interpreted the butler's dream, also approached, and related the whole of his dream to Joseph. 13 And he said unto him, In my dream I saw and behold three white baskets upon my head, and I looked, and behold there were in the uppermost basket all manner of baked meats for Pharaoh, and behold the birds were eating them from off my head. 14 And Joseph said unto him, The three baskets which thou didst see are three days, yet within three days Pharaoh will take off thy head, and hang thee upon a tree, and the birds will eat thy flesh from off thee, as thou sawest in thy dream. 15 In those days the queen was about to be delivered, and upon that day she bare a son unto the king of Egypt, and they proclaimed that the king had gotten his first born son and all the people of Egypt together with the officers and servants of Pharaoh rejoiced greatly. 16 And upon the third day of his birth Pharaoh made a feast for his officers and servants, for the hosts of the land of Zoar and of the land of Egypt. 17 And all the people of Egypt and the servants of Pharaoh came to eat and drink with the king at the feast of his son, and to rejoice at the king's rejoicing. 18 And all the officers of the king and his servants were rejoicing at that time for eight days at the feast, and they made merry with all sorts of musical instruments, with timbrels and with dances in the king's house for eight days. 19 And the butler, to whom Joseph had interpreted his dream, forgot Joseph, and he did not mention him to the king as he had promised, for this thing was from the Lord in order to punish Joseph because he had trusted in man. 20 And Joseph remained after this in the prison house two years, until he had completed twelve years.

Jash.47

1 And Isaac the son of Abraham was still living in those days in the land of Canaan; he was very aged, one hundred and eighty years old, and Esau his son, the brother of Jacob, was in the land of Edom, and he and his sons had possessions in it amongst the children of Seir. 2 And Esau heard that his father's time was drawing nigh to die, and he and his sons and household came unto the land of Canaan, unto his father's house, and Jacob and his sons went forth from the place where they dwelt in Hebron, and they all came to their father Isaac, and they found Esau and his sons in the tent. 3 And Jacob and his sons sat before his father Isaac, and Jacob was still mourning for his son Joseph. 4 And Isaac said unto Jacob, Bring me hither thy sons and I will bless them; and Jacob brought his eleven children before his father Isaac. 5 And Isaac placed his hands upon all the sons of Jacob, and he took hold of them and embraced them, and kissed them one by one, and Isaac blessed them on that day, and he said unto them, May the God of your fathers bless you and increase your seed like the stars of heaven for number. 6 And Isaac also blessed the sons of Esau, saying, May God cause you to be a dread and a terror to all that will behold you, and to all your enemies. 7 And Isaac called Jacob and his sons, and they all came and sat before Isaac, and Isaac said unto Jacob, The Lord God of the whole earth said unto me, Unto thy seed will I give this land for an inheritance if thy children keep my statutes and my ways, and I will perform unto them the oath which I swore unto thy father Abraham. 8 Now therefore my son, teach thy children and thy children's children to fear the Lord, and to go in the good way which will please the Lord thy God, for if you keep the ways of the Lord and his statutes the

Lord will also keep unto you his covenant with Abraham, and will do well with you and your seed all the days. 9 And when Isaac had finished commanding Jacob and his children, he gave up the ghost and died, and was gathered unto his people. 10 And Jacob and Esau fell upon the face of their father Isaac, and they wept, and Isaac was one hundred and eighty years old when he died in the land of Canaan, in Hebron, and his sons carried him to the cave of Machpelah, which Abraham had bought from the children of Heth for a possession of a burial place. 11 And all the kings of the land of Canaan went with Jacob and Esau to bury Isaac, and all the kings of Canaan showed Isaac great honor at his death. 12 And the sons of Jacob and the sons of Esau went barefooted round about, walking and lamenting until they reached Kireath-arba. 13 And Jacob and Esau buried their father Isaac in the cave of Machpelah, which is in Kireath-arba in Hebron, and they buried him with very great honor, as at the funeral of kings. 14 And Jacob and his sons, and Esau and his sons, and all the kings of Canaan made a great and heavy mourning, and they buried him and mourned for him many days. 15 And at the death of Isaac, he left his cattle and his possessions and all belonging to him to his sons; and Esau said unto Jacob, Behold I pray thee, all that our father has left we will divide it in two parts, and I will have the choice, and Jacob said, We will do so. 16 And Jacob took all that Isaac had left in the land of Canaan, the cattle and the property, and he placed them in two parts before Esau and his sons, and he said unto Esau, Behold all this is before thee, choose thou unto thyself the half which thou wilt take. 17 And Jacob said unto Esau, Hear thou I pray thee what I will speak unto thee, saying, The Lord God of heaven and earth spoke unto our fathers Abraham and Isaac, saying, Unto thy seed will I give this land for an inheritance forever. 18 Now therefore all that our father has left is before thee, and behold all the land is before thee; choose thou from them what thou desirest. 19 If thou desirest the whole land take it for thee and thy children forever, and I will take this riches, and it thou desirest the riches take it unto thee, and I will take this land for me and for my children to inherit it forever. 20 And Nebayoth, the son of Ishmael, was then in the land with his children, and Esau went on that day and consulted with him, saying. 21 Thus has Jacob spoken unto me, and thus has he answered me, now give thy advice and we will hear. 22 And Nebayoth said, What is this that Jacob hath spoken unto thee? behold all the children of Canaan are dwelling securely in their land, and Jacob sayeth he will inherit it with his seed all the days. 23 Go now therefore and take all thy father's riches and leave Jacob thy brother in the land, as he has spoken. 24 And Esau rose up and returned to Jacob, and did all that Nebayoth the son of Ishmael had advised; and Esau took all the riches that Isaac had left, the souls, the beasts, the cattle and the property, and all the riches; he gave nothing to his brother Jacob; and Jacob took all the land of Canaan, from the brook of Egypt unto the river Euphrates, and he took it for an everlasting possession, and for his children and for his seed after him forever. 25 Jacob also took from his brother Esau the cave of Machpelah, which is in Hebron, which Abraham had bought from Ephron for a possession of a burial place for him and his seed forever. 26 And Jacob wrote all these things in the book of purchase, and he signed it, and he testified all this with four faithful witnesses. 27 And these are the words which Jacob wrote in the book, saying: The land of Canaan and all the cities of the Hittites, the Hivites, the Jebusites, the Amorites, the Perizzites, and the Gergashites, all the seven nations from the river of Egypt unto the river Euphrates. 28 And the city of Hebron Kireath-arba, and the cave which is in it, the whole did Jacob buy from his brother Esau for value, for a possession and for an inheritance for his seed after him forever. 29 And Jacob took the book of purchase and the

signature, the command and the statutes and the revealed book, and he placed them in an earthen vessel in order that they should remain for a long time, and he delivered them into the hands of his children. 30 Esau took all that his father had left him after his death from his brother Jacob, and he took all the property, from man and beast, camel and ass, ox and lamb, silver and gold, stones and bdellium, and all the riches which had belonged to Isaac the son of Abraham; there was nothing left which Esau did not take unto himself, from all that Isaac had left after his death. 31 And Esau took all this, and he and his children went home to the land of Seir the Horite, away from his brother Jacob and his children. 32 And Esau had possessions amongst the children of Seir, and Esau returned not to the land of Canaan from that day forward. 33 And the whole land of Canaan became an inheritance to the children of Israel for an everlasting inheritance, and Esau with all his children inherited the mountain of Seir.

Jash.48

1 In those days, after the death of Isaac, the Lord commanded and caused a famine upon the whole earth. 2 At that time Pharaoh king of Egypt was sitting upon his throne in the land of Egypt, and lay in his bed and dreamed dreams, and Pharaoh saw in his dream that he was standing by the side of the river of Egypt. 3 And whilst he was standing he saw and behold seven fat fleshed and well favored kine came up out of the river. 4 And seven other kine, lean fleshed and ill favored, came up after them, and the seven ill favored ones swallowed up the well favored ones, and still their appearance was ill as at first. 5 And he awoke, and he slept again and he dreamed a second time, and he saw and behold seven ears of corn came up upon one stalk, rank and good, and seven thin ears blasted with the east wind sprang, up after them, and the thin ears swallowed up the full ones, and Pharaoh awoke out of his dream. 6 And in the morning the king remembered his dreams, and his spirit was sadly troubled on account of his dreams, and the king hastened and sent and called for all the magicians of Egypt, and the wise men, and they came and stood before Pharaoh. 7 And the king said unto them, I have dreamed dreams, and there is none to interpret them; and they said unto the king, relate thy dreams to thy servants and let us hear them. 8 And the king related his dreams to them, and they all answered and said with one voice to the king, may the king live forever; and this is the interpretation of thy dreams. 9 The seven good kine which thou didst see denote seven daughters that will be born unto thee in the latter days, and the seven kine which thou sawest come up after them, and swallowed them up, are for a sign that the daughters which will be born unto thee will all die in the life-time of the king. 10 And that which thou didst see in the second dream of seven full good ears of corn coming up upon one stalk, this is their interpretation, that thou wilt build unto thyself in the latter days seven cities throughout the land of Egypt; and that which thou sawest of the seven blasted ears of corn springing up after them and swallowing them up whilst thou didst behold them with thine eyes, is for a sign that the cities which thou wilt build will all be destroyed in the latter days, in the life-time of the king. 11 And when they spoke these words the king did not incline his ear to their words, neither did he fix his heart upon them, for the king knew in his wisdom that they did not give a proper interpretation of the dreams; and when they had finished speaking before the king, the king answered them, saying, What is this thing that you have spoken unto me? surely you have uttered falsehood and spoken lies; therefore now give the proper interpretation of my dreams, that you may not die. 12 And the king commanded after this, and he sent and called again for other wise men, and they came and stood before the king, and the king related his dreams to them, and they all answered

him according to the first interpretation, and the king's anger was kindled and he was very wroth, and the king said unto them, Surely you speak lies and utter falsehood in what you have said. 13 And the king commanded that a proclamation should be issued throughout the land of Egypt, saying, It is resolved by the king and his great men, that any wise man who knoweth and understandeth the interpretation of dreams, and will not come this day before the king, shall die. 14 And the man that will declare unto the king the proper interpretation of his dreams, there shall be given unto him all that he will require from the king. And all the wise men of the land of Egypt came before the king, together with all the magicians and sorcerers that were in Egypt and in Goshen, in Rameses, in Tachpanches, in Zoar, and in all the places on the borders of Egypt, and they all stood before the king. 15 And all the nobles and the princes, and the attendants belonging to the king, came together from all the cities of Egypt, and they all sat before the king, and the king related his dreams before the wise men, and the princes, and all that sat before the king were astonished at the vision. 16 And all the wise men who were before the king were greatly divided in their interpretation of his dreams; some of them interpreted them to the king, saying, The seven good kine are seven kings, who from the king's issue will be raised over Egypt. 17 And the seven bad kine are seven princes, who will stand up against them in the latter days and destroy them; and the seven ears of corn are the seven great princes belonging to Egypt, who will fall in the hands of the seven less powerful princes of their enemies, in the wars of our lord the king. 18 And some of them interpreted to the king in this manner, saying, The seven good kine are the strong cities of Egypt, and the seven bad kine are the seven nations of the land of Canaan, who will come against the seven cities of Egypt in the latter days and destroy them. 19 And that which thou sawest in the second dream, of seven good and bad ears of corn, is a sign that the government of Egypt will again return to thy seed as at first. 20 And in his reign the people of the cities of Egypt will turn against the seven cities of Canaan who are stronger than they are, and will destroy them, and the government of Egypt will return to thy seed. 21 And some of them said unto the king, This is the interpretation of thy dreams; the seven good kine are seven queens, whom thou wilt take for wives in the latter days, and the seven bad kine denote that those women will all die in the lifetime of the king. 22 And the seven good and bad ears of corn which thou didst see in the second dream are fourteen children, and it will be in the latter days that they will stand up and fight amongst themselves, and seven of them will smite the seven that are more powerful. 23 And some of them said these words unto the king, saying, The seven good kine denote that seven children will be born to thee, and they will slay seven of thy children's children in the latter days; and the seven good ears of corn which thou didst see in the second dream, are those princes against whom seven other less powerful princes will fight and destroy them in the latter days, and avenge thy children's cause, and the government will again return to thy seed. 24 And the king heard all the words of the wise men of Egypt and their interpretation of his dreams, and none of them pleased the king. 25 And the king knew in his wisdom that they did not altogether speak correctly in all these words, for this was from the Lord to frustrate the words of the wise men of Egypt, in order that Joseph might go forth from the house of confinement, and in order that he should become great in Egypt. 26 And the king saw that none amongst all the wise men and magicians of Egypt spoke correctly to him, and the king's wrath was kindled, and his anger burned within him. 27 And the king commanded that all the wise men and magicians should go out from before him, and they all went out from before the king with shame and disgrace. 28 And

268

the king commanded that a proclamation be sent throughout Egypt to slay all the magicians that were in Egypt, and not one of them should be suffered to live. 29 And the captains of the guards belonging to the king rose up, and each man drew his sword, and they began to smite the magicians of Egypt, and the wise men. 30 And after this Merod, chief butler to the king, came and bowed down before the king and sat before him. 31 And the butler said unto the king, May the king live forever, and his government be exalted in the land. 32 Thou wast angry with thy servant in those days, now two years past, and didst place me in the ward, and I was for some time in the ward, I and the chief of the bakers. 33 And there was with us a Hebrew servant belonging to the captain of the guard, his name was Joseph, for his master had been angry with him and placed him in the house of confinement, and he attended us there. 34 And in some time after when we were in the ward, we dreamed dreams in one night, I and the chief of the bakers; we dreamed, each man according to the interpretation of his dream. 35 And we came in the morning and told them to that servant, and he interpreted to us our dreams, to each man according to his dream, did he correctly interpret. 36 And it came to pass as he interpreted to us, so was the event; there fell not to the ground any of his words. 37 And now therefore my lord and king do not slay the people of Egypt for naught; behold that slave is still confined in the house by the captain of the guard his master, in the house of confinement. 38 If it pleaseth the king let him send for him that he may come before thee and he will make known to thee, the correct interpretation of the dream which thou didst dream. 39 And the king heard the words of the chief butler, and the king ordered that the wise men of Egypt should not be slain. 40 And the king ordered his servants to bring Joseph before him, and the king said unto them, Go to him and do not terrify him lest he be confused and will not know to speak properly. 41 And the servants of the king went to Joseph, and they brought him hastily out of the dungeon, and the king's servants shaved him, and he changed his prison garment and he came before the king. 42 And the king was sitting upon his royal throne in a princely dress girt around with a golden ephod, and the fine gold which was upon it sparkled, and the carbuncle and the ruby and the emerald, together with all the precious stones that were upon the king's head, dazzled the eye, and Joseph wondered greatly at the king. 43 And the throne upon which the king sat was covered with gold and silver, and with onyx stones, and it had seventy steps. 44 And it was their custom throughout the land of Egypt, that every man who came to speak to the king, if he was a prince or one that was estimable in the sight of the king, he ascended to the king's throne as far as the thirty-first step, and the king would descend to the thirty-sixth step, and speak with him. 45 If he was one of the common people, he ascended to the third step, and the king would descend to the fourth and speak to him, and their custom was, moreover, that any man who understood to speak in all the seventy languages, he ascended the seventy steps, and went up and spoke till he reached the king. 46 And any man who could not complete the seventy, he ascended as many steps as the languages which he knew to speak in. 47 And it was customary in those days in Egypt that no one should reign over them, but who understood to speak in the seventy languages. 48 And when Joseph came before the king he bowed down to the ground before the king, and he ascended to the third step, and the king sat upon the fourth step and spoke with Joseph. 49 And the king said unto Joseph, I dreamed a dream, and there is no interpreter to interpret it properly, and I commanded this day that all the magicians of Egypt and the wise men thereof, should come before me, and I related my dreams to them, and no one has properly interpreted them to me. 50 And after this I this day heard concerning thee, that thou art a wise man, and canst correctly interpret every dream that thou hearest. ⁵¹ And Joseph answered Pharaoh, saying, Let Pharaoh relate his dreams that he dreamed; surely the interpretations belong to God; and Pharaoh related his dreams to Joseph, the dream of the kine, and the dream of the ears of corn, and the king left off speaking. ⁵² And Joseph was then clothed with the spirit of God before the king, and he knew all the things that would befall the king from that day forward, and he knew the proper interpretation of the king's dream, and he spoke before the king. ⁵³ And Joseph found favor in the sight of the king, and the king inclined his ears and his heart, and he heard all the words of Joseph. And Joseph said unto the king, Do not imagine that they are two dreams, for it is only one dream, for that which God has chosen to do throughout the land he has shown to the king in his dream, and this is the proper interpretation of thy dream: ⁵⁴ The seven good kine and ears of corn are seven years, and the seven bad kine and ears of corn are also seven years; it is one dream. ⁵⁵ Behold the seven years that are coming there will be a great plenty throughout the land, and after that the seven years of famine will follow them, a very grievous famine; and all the plenty will be forgotten from the land, and the famine will consume the inhabitants of the land. ⁵⁶ The king dreamed one dream, and the dream was therefore repeated unto Pharaoh because the thing is established by God, and God will shortly bring it to pass. ⁵⁷ Now therefore I will give thee counsel and deliver thy soul and the souls of the inhabitants of the land from the evil of the famine, that thou seek throughout thy kingdom for a man very discreet and wise, who knoweth all the affairs of government, and appoint him to superintend over the land of Egypt. ⁵⁸ And let the man whom thou placest over Egypt appoint officers under him, that they gather in all the food of the good years that are coming, and let them lay up corn and deposit it in thy appointed stores. ⁵⁹ And let them keep that food for the seven years of famine, that it may be found for thee and thy people and thy whole land, and that thou and thy land be not cut off by the famine. ⁶⁰ Let all the inhabitants of the land be also ordered that they gather in, every man the produce of his field, of all sorts of food, during the seven good years, and that they place it in their stores, that it may be found for them in the days of the famine and that they may live upon it. ⁶¹ This is the proper interpretation of thy dream, and this is the counsel given to save thy soul and the souls of all thy subjects. ⁶² And the king answered and said unto Joseph, Who sayeth and who knoweth that thy words are correct? And he said unto the king, This shall be a sign for thee respecting all my words, that they are true and that my advice is good for thee. ⁶³ Behold thy wife sitteth this day upon the stool of delivery, and she will bear thee a son and thou wilt rejoice with him; when thy child shall have gone forth from his mother's womb, thy first born son that has been born these two years back shall die, and thou wilt be comforted in the child that will be born unto thee this day. ⁶⁴ And Joseph finished speaking these words to the king, and he bowed down to the king and he went out, and when Joseph had gone out from the king's presence, those signs which Joseph had spoken unto the king came to pass on that day. ⁶⁵ And the queen bare a son on that day and the king heard the glad tidings about his son, and he rejoiced, and when the reporter had gone forth from the king's presence, the king's servants found the first born son of the king fallen dead upon the ground. ⁶⁶ And there was great lamentation and noise in the king's house, and the king heard it, and he said, What is the noise and lamentation that I have heard in the house? and they told the king that his first born son had died; then the king knew that all Joseph's words that he had spoken were correct, and the king was consoled

for his son by the child that was born to him on that day as Joseph had spoken.

Jash.49

¹ After these things the king sent and assembled all his officers and servants, and all the princes and nobles belonging to the king, and they all came before the king. ² And the king said unto them, Behold you have seen and heard all the words of this Hebrew man, and all the signs which he declared would come to pass, and not any of his words have fallen to the ground. ³ You know that he has given a proper interpretation of the dream, and it will surely come to pass, now therefore take counsel, and know what you will do and how the land will be delivered from the famine. ⁴ Seek now and see whether the like can be found, in whose heart there is wisdom and knowledge, and I will appoint him over the land. ⁵ For you have heard what the Hebrew man has advised concerning this to save the land therewith from the famine, and I know that the land will not be delivered from the famine but with the advice of the Hebrew man, him that advised me. ⁶ And they all answered the king and said, The counsel which the Hebrew has given concerning this is good; now therefore, our lord and king, behold the whole land is in thy hand, do that which seemeth good in thy sight. ⁷ Him whom thou chooses, and whom thou in thy wisdom knowest to be wise and capable of delivering the land with his wisdom, him shall the king appoint to be under him over the land. ⁸ And the king said to all the officers: I have thought that since God has made known to the Hebrew man all that he has spoken, there is none so discreet and wise in the whole land as he is; if it seem good in your sight I will place him over the land, for he will save the land with his wisdom. ⁹ And all the officers answered the king and said, But surely it is written in the laws of Egypt, and it should not be violated, that no man shall reign over Egypt, nor be the second to the king, but one who has knowledge in all the languages of the sons of men. ¹⁰ Now therefore our lord and king, behold this Hebrew man can only speak the Hebrew language, and how then can he be over us the second under government, a man who not even knoweth our language? ¹¹ Now we pray thee send for him, and let him come before thee, and prove him in all things, and do as thou see fit. ¹² And the king said, It shall be done tomorrow, and the thing that you have spoken is good; and all the officers came on that day before the king. ¹³ And on that night the Lord sent one of his ministering angels, and he came into the land of Egypt unto Joseph, and the angel of the Lord stood over Joseph, and behold Joseph was lying in the bed at night in his master's house in the dungeon, for his master had put him back into the dungeon on account of his wife. ¹⁴ And the angel roused him from his sleep, and Joseph rose up and stood upon his legs, and behold the angel of the Lord was standing opposite to him; and the angel of the Lord spoke with Joseph, and he taught him all the languages of man in that night, and he called his name Jehoseph. ¹⁵ And the angel of the Lord went from him, and Joseph returned and lay upon his bed, and Joseph was astonished at the vision which he saw. ¹⁶ And it came to pass in the morning that the king sent for all his officers and servants, and they all came and sat before the king, and the king ordered Joseph to be brought, and the king's servants went and brought Joseph before Pharaoh. ¹⁷ And the king came forth and ascended the steps of the throne, and Joseph spoke unto the king in all languages, and Joseph went up to him and spoke unto the king until he arrived before the king in the seventieth step, and he sat before the king. ¹⁸ And the king greatly rejoiced on account of Joseph, and all the king's officers rejoiced greatly with the king when they heard all the words of Joseph. ¹⁹ And the thing seemed good in the sight of the king and the officers, to appoint Joseph to be second to the king over the whole land of Egypt, and

the king spoke to Joseph, saying, 20 Now thou didst give me counsel to appoint a wise man over the land of Egypt, in order with his wisdom to save the land from the famine; now therefore, since God has made all this known to thee, and all the words which thou hast spoken, there is not throughout the land a discreet and wise man like unto thee. 21 And thy name no more shall be called Joseph, but Zaphnath Paaneah shall be thy name; thou shalt be second to me, and according to thy word shall be all the affairs of my government, and at thy word shall my people go out and come in. 22 Also from under thy hand shall my servants and officers receive their salary which is given to them monthly, and to thee shall all the people of the land bow down; only in my throne will I be greater than thou. 23 And the king took off his ring from his hand and put it upon the hand of Joseph, and the king dressed Joseph in a princely garment, and he put a golden crown upon his head, and he put a golden chain upon his neck. 24 And the king commanded his servants, and they made him ride in the second chariot belonging to the king, that went opposite to the king's chariot, and he caused him to ride upon a great and strong horse from the king's horses, and to be conducted through the streets of the land of Egypt. 25 And the king commanded that all those that played upon timbrels, harps and other musical instruments should go forth with Joseph; one thousand timbrels, one thousand mecholoth, and one thousand nebalim went after him. 26 And five thousand men, with drawn swords glittering in their hands, and they went marching and playing before Joseph, and twenty thousand of the great men of the king girt with girdles of skin covered with gold, marched at the right hand of Joseph, and twenty thousand at his left, and all the women and damsels went upon the roofs or stood in the streets playing and rejoicing at Joseph, and gazed at the appearance of Joseph and at his beauty. 27 And the king's people went before him and behind him, perfuming the road with frankincense and with cassia, and with all sorts of fine perfume, and scattered myrrh and aloes along the road, and twenty men proclaimed these words before him throughout the land in a loud voice: 28 Do you see this man whom the king has chosen to be his second? all the affairs of government shall be regulated by him, and he that transgresses his orders, or that does not bow down before him to the ground, shall die, for he rebels against the king and his second. 29 And when the heralds had ceased proclaiming, all the people of Egypt bowed down to the ground before Joseph and said, May the king live, also may his second live; and all the inhabitants of Egypt bowed down along the road, and when the heralds approached them, they bowed down, and they rejoiced with all sorts of timbrels, mechol and nebal before Joseph. 30 And Joseph upon his horse lifted up his eyes to heaven, and called out and said, He raiseth the poor man from the dust, He lifteth up the needy from the dunghill. O Lord of Hosts, happy is the man who trusteth in thee. 31 And Joseph passed throughout the land of Egypt with Pharaoh's servants and officers, and they showed him the whole land of Egypt and all the king's treasures. 32 And Joseph returned and came on that day before Pharaoh, and the king gave unto Joseph a possession in the land of Egypt, a possession of fields and vineyards, and the king gave unto Joseph three thousand talents of silver and one thousand talents of gold, and onyx stones and bdellium and many gifts. 33 And on the next day the king commanded all the people of Egypt to bring unto Joseph offerings and gifts, and that he that violated the command of the king should die; and they made a high place in the street of the city, and they spread out garments there, and whoever brought anything to Joseph put it into the high place. 34 And all the people of Egypt cast something into the high place, one man a golden ear-ring, and the other rings and ear-rings, and different vessels of gold and silver

270

work, and onyx stones and bdellium did he cast upon the high place; every one gave something of what he possessed. 35 And Joseph took all these and placed them in his treasuries, and all the officers and nobles belonging to the king exalted Joseph, and they gave him many gifts, seeing that the king had chosen him to be his second. 36 And the king sent to Potiphera, the son of Ahiram priest of On, and he took his young daughter Osnath and gave her unto Joseph for a wife. 37 And the damsel was very comely, a virgin, one whom man had not known, and Joseph took her for a wife; and the king said unto Joseph, I am Pharaoh, and beside thee none shall dare to lift up his hand or his foot to regulate my people throughout the land of Egypt. 38 And Joseph was thirty years old when he stood before Pharaoh, and Joseph went out from before the king, and he became the king's second in Egypt. 39 And the king gave Joseph a hundred servants to attend him in his house, and Joseph also sent and purchased many servants and they remained in the house of Joseph. 40 Joseph then built for himself a very magnificent house like unto the houses of kings, before the court of the king's palace, and he made in the house a large temple, very elegant in appearance and convenient for his residence; three years was Joseph in erecting his house. 41 And Joseph made unto himself a very elegant throne of abundance of gold and silver, and he covered it with onyx stones and bdellium, and he made upon it the likeness of the whole land of Egypt, and the likeness of the river of Egypt that watereth the whole land of Egypt; and Joseph sat securely upon his throne in his house and the Lord increased Joseph's wisdom. 42 And all the inhabitants of Egypt and Pharaoh's servants and his princes loved Joseph exceedingly, for this thing was from the Lord to Joseph. 43 And Joseph had an army that made war, going out in hosts and troops to the number of forty thousand six hundred men, capable of bearing arms to assist the king and Joseph against the enemy, besides the king's officers and his servants and inhabitants of Egypt without number. 44 And Joseph gave unto his mighty men, and to all his host, shields and javelins, and caps and coats of mail and stones for slinging.

Jash.50

1 At that time the children of Tarshish came against the sons of Ishmael, and made war with them, and the children of Tarshish spoiled the Ishmaelites for a long time. 2 And the children of Ishmael were small in number in those days, and they could not prevail over the children of Tarshish, and they were sorely oppressed. 3 And the old men of the Ishmaelites sent a record to the king of Egypt, saying, Send I pray thee unto thy servants officers and hosts to help us to fight against the children of Tarshish, for we have been consuming away for a long time. 4 And Pharaoh sent Joseph with the mighty men and host which were with him, and also his mighty men from the king's house. 5 And they went to the land of Havilah to the children of Ishmael, to assist them against the children of Tarshish, and the children of Ishmael fought with the children of Tarshish, and Joseph smote the Tarshishites and he subdued all their land, and the children of Ishmael dwell therein unto this day. 6 And when the land of Tarshish was subdued, all the Tarshishites ran away, and came on the border of their brethren the children of Javan, and Joseph with all his mighty men and host returned to Egypt, not one man of them missing. 7 And at the revolution of the year, in the second year of Joseph's reigning over Egypt, the Lord gave great plenty throughout the land for seven years as Joseph had spoken, for the Lord blessed all the produce of the earth in those days for seven years, and they ate and were greatly satisfied. 8 And Joseph at that time had officers under him, and they collected all the food of the good years, and heaped corn year by year, and they placed it in the treasuries of Joseph. 9 And at any time

when they gathered the food Joseph commanded that they should bring the corn in the ears, and also bring with it some of the soil of the field, that it should not spoil. ¹⁰ And Joseph did according to this year by year, and he heaped up corn like the sand of the sea for abundance, for his stores were immense and could not be numbered for abundance. ¹¹ And also all the inhabitants of Egypt gathered all sorts of food in their stores in great abundance during the seven good years, but they did not do unto it as Joseph did. ¹² And all the food which Joseph and the Egyptians had gathered during the seven years of plenty, was secured for the land in stores for the seven years of famine, for the support of the whole land. ¹³ And the inhabitants of Egypt filled each man his store and his concealed place with corn, to be for support during the famine. ¹⁴ And Joseph placed all the food that he had gathered in all the cities of Egypt, and he closed all the stores and placed sentinels over them. ¹⁵ And Joseph's wife Osnath the daughter of Potiphera bare him two sons, Manasseh and Ephraim, and Joseph was thirty-four years old when he begat them. ¹⁶ And the lads grew up and they went in his ways and in his instructions, they did not deviate from the way which their father taught them, either to the right or left. ¹⁷ And the Lord was with the lads, and they grew up and had understanding and skill in all wisdom and in all the affairs of government, and all the king's officers and his great men of the inhabitants of Egypt exalted the lads, and they were brought up amongst the king's children. ¹⁸ And the seven years of plenty that were throughout the land were at an end, and the seven years of famine came after them as Joseph had spoken, and the famine was throughout the land. ¹⁹ And all the people of Egypt saw that the famine had commenced in the land of Egypt, and all the people of Egypt opened their stores of corn for the famine prevailed over them. ²⁰ And they found all the food that was in their stores, full of vermin and not fit to eat, and the famine prevailed throughout the land, and all the inhabitants of Egypt came and cried before Pharaoh, for the famine was heavy upon them. ²¹ And they said unto Pharaoh, Give food unto thy servants, and wherefore shall we die through hunger before thy eyes, even we and our little ones? ²² And Pharaoh answered them, saying, And wherefore do you cry unto me? did not Joseph command that the corn should be laid up during the seven years of plenty for the years of famine? and wherefore did you not hearken to his voice? ²³ And the people of Egypt answered the king, saying, As thy soul liveth, our lord, thy servants have done all that Joseph ordered, for thy servants also gathered in all the produce of their fields during the seven years of plenty and laid it in the stores unto this day. ²⁴ And when the famine prevailed over thy servants we opened our stores, and behold all our produce was filled with vermin and was not fit for food. ²⁵ And when the king heard all that had befallen the inhabitants of Egypt, the king was greatly afraid on account of the famine, and he was much terrified; and the king answered the people of Egypt, saying, Since all this has happened unto you, go unto Joseph, do whatever he shall say unto you, transgress not his commands. ²⁶ And all the people of Egypt went forth and came unto Joseph, and said unto him, Give unto us food, and wherefore shall we die before thee through hunger? for we gathered in our produce during the seven years as thou didst command, and we put it in store, and thus has it befallen us. ²⁷ And when Joseph heard all the words of the people of Egypt and what had befallen them, Joseph opened all his stores of the produce and he sold it unto the people of Egypt. ²⁸ And the famine prevailed throughout the land, and the famine was in all countries, but in the land of Egypt there was produce for sale. ²⁹ And all the inhabitants of Egypt came unto Joseph to buy corn, for the famine prevailed over them, and all their corn was spoiled, and Joseph daily sold it to all the people of Egypt. ³⁰ And all

the inhabitants of the land of Canaan and the Philistines, and those beyond the Jordan, and the children of the east and all the cities of the lands far and nigh heard that there was corn in Egypt, and they all came to Egypt to buy corn, for the famine prevailed over them. ³¹ And Joseph opened the stores of corn and placed officers over them, and they daily stood and sold to all that came. ³² And Joseph knew that his brethren also would come to Egypt to buy corn, for the famine prevailed throughout the earth. And Joseph commanded all his people that they should cause it to be proclaimed throughout the land of Egypt, saying, ³³ It is the pleasure of the king, of his second and of their great men, that any person who wishes to buy corn in Egypt shall not send his servants to Egypt to purchase, but his sons, and also any Egyptian or Canaanite, who shall come from any of the stores from buying corn in Egypt, and shall go and sell it throughout the land, he shall die, for no one shall buy but for the support of his household. ³⁴ And any man leading two or three beasts shall die, for a man shall only lead his own beast. ³⁵ And Joseph placed sentinels at the gates of Egypt, and commanded them, saying, Any person who may come to buy corn, suffer him not to enter until his name, and the name of his father, and the name of his father's father be written down, and whatever is written by day, send their names unto me in the evening that I may know their names. ³⁶ And Joseph placed officers throughout the land of Egypt, and he commanded them to do all these things. ³⁷ And Joseph did all these things, and made these statutes, in order that he might know when his brethren should come to Egypt to buy corn; and Joseph's people caused it daily to be proclaimed in Egypt according to these words and statutes which Joseph had commanded. ³⁸ And all the inhabitants of the east and west country, and of all the earth, heard of the statutes and regulations which Joseph had enacted in Egypt, and the inhabitants of the extreme parts of the earth came and they bought corn in Egypt day after day, and then went away. ³⁹ And all the officers of Egypt did as Joseph had commanded, and all that came to Egypt to buy corn, the gate keepers would write their names, and their fathers' names, and daily bring them in the evening before Joseph.

Jash.51

¹ And Jacob afterward heard that there was corn in Egypt, and he called unto his sons to go to Egypt to buy corn, for upon them also did the famine prevail, and he called unto his sons, saying, ² Behold I hear that there is corn in Egypt, and all the people of the earth go there to purchase, now therefore why will you show yourselves satisfied before the whole earth? go you also down to Egypt and buy us a little corn amongst those that come there, that we may not die. ³ And the sons of Jacob hearkened to the voice of their father, and they rose up to go down to Egypt in order to buy corn amongst the rest that came there. ⁴ And Jacob their father commanded them, saying, When you come into the city do not enter together in one gate, on account of the inhabitants of the land. ⁵ And the sons of Jacob went forth and they went to Egypt, and the sons of Jacob did all as their father had commanded them, and Jacob did not send Benjamin, for he said, Lest an accident might befall him on the road like his brother; and ten of Jacob's sons went forth. ⁶ And whilst the sons of Jacob were going on the road, they repented of what they had done to Joseph, and they spoke to each other, saying, We know that our brother Joseph went down to Egypt, and now we will seek him where we go, and if we find him we will take him from his master for a ransom, and if not, by force, and we will die for him. ⁷ And the sons of Jacob agreed to this thing and strengthened themselves on account of Joseph, to deliver him from the hand of his master, and the sons of Jacob went to Egypt; and when they came near to Egypt they separated from each other, and they came

through ten gates of Egypt, and the gate keepers wrote their names on that day, and brought them to Joseph in the evening. 8 And Joseph read the names from the hand of the gate-keepers of the city, and he found that his brethren had entered at the ten gates of the city, and Joseph at that time commanded that it should be proclaimed throughout the land of Egypt, saying, 9 Go forth all ye store guards, close all the corn stores and let only one remain open, that those who come may purchase from it. 10 And all the officers of Joseph did so at that time, and they closed all the stores and left only one open. 11 And Joseph gave the written names of his brethren to him that was set over the open store, and he said unto him, Whosoever shall come to thee to buy corn, ask his name, and when men of these names shall come before thee, seize them and send them, and they did so. 12 And when the sons of Jacob came into the city, they joined together in the city to seek Joseph before they bought themselves corn. 13 And they went to the walls of the harlots, and they sought Joseph in the walls of the harlots for three days, for they thought that Joseph would come in the walls of the harlots, for Joseph was very comely and well favored, and the sons of Jacob sought Joseph for three days, and they could not find him. 14 And the man who was set over the open store sought for those names which Joseph had given him, and he did not find them. 15 And he sent to Joseph, saying, These three days have passed, and those men whose names thou didst give unto me have not come; and Joseph sent servants to seek the men in all Egypt, and to bring them before Joseph. 16 And Joseph's servants went and came into Egypt and could not find them, and went to Goshen and they were not there, and then went to the city of Rameses and could not find them. 17 And Joseph continued to send sixteen servants to seek his brothers, and they went and spread themselves in the four corners of the city, and four of the servants went into the house of the harlots, and they found the ten men there seeking their brother. 18 And those four men took them and brought them before him, and they bowed down to him to the ground, and Joseph was sitting upon his throne in his temple, clothed with princely garments, and upon his head was a large crown of gold, and all the mighty men were sitting around him. 19 And the sons of Jacob saw Joseph, and his figure and comeliness and dignity of countenance seemed wonderful in their eyes, and they again bowed down to him to the ground. 20 And Joseph saw his brethren, and he knew them, but they knew him not, for Joseph was very great in their eyes, therefore they knew him not. 21 And Joseph spoke to them, saying, From whence come ye? and they all answered and said, Thy servants have come from the land of Canaan to buy corn, for the famine prevails throughout the earth, and thy servants heard that there was corn in Egypt, so they have come amongst the other comers to buy corn for their support. 22 And Joseph answered them, saying, If you have come to purchase as you say, why do you come through ten gates of the city? it can only be that you have come to spy through the land. 23 And they all together answered Joseph, and said, Not so my lord, we are right, thy servants are not spies, but we have come to buy corn, for thy servants are all brothers, the sons of one man in the land of Canaan, and our father commanded us, saying, When you come to the city do not enter together at one gate on account of the inhabitants of the land. 24 And Joseph again answered them and said, That is the thing which I spoke unto you, you have come to spy through the land, therefore you all came through ten gates of the city; you have come to see the nakedness of the land. 25 Surely every one that cometh to buy corn goeth his way, and you are already three days in the land, and what do you do in the walls of harlots in which you have been for these three days? surely spies do like unto these things. 26 And they said unto Joseph, Far be it from our lord

to speak thus, for we are twelve brothers, the sons of our father Jacob, in the land of Canaan, the son of Isaac, the son of Abraham, the Hebrew, and behold the youngest is with our father this day in the land of Canaan, and one is not, for he was lost from us, and we thought perhaps he might be in this land, so we are seeking him throughout the land, and have come even to the houses of harlots to seek him there. 27 And Joseph said unto them, And have you then sought him throughout the earth, that there only remained Egypt for you to seek him in? And what also should your brother do in the houses of harlots, although he were in Egypt? have you not said, That you are from the sons of Isaac, the son of Abraham, and what shall the sons of Jacob do then in the houses of harlots? 28 And they said unto him, Because we heard that Ishmaelites stole him from us, and it was told unto us that they sold him in Egypt, and thy servant, our brother, is very comely and well favored, so we thought he would surely be in the houses of harlots, therefore thy servants went there to seek him and give ransom for him. 29 And Joseph still answered them, saying, Surely you speak falsely and utter lies, to say of yourselves that you are the sons of Abraham; as Pharaoh liveth you are spies, therefore have you come to the houses of harlots that you should not be known. 30 And Joseph said unto them, And now if you find him, and his master requireth of you a great price, will you give it for him? and they said, It shall be given. 31 And he said unto them, And if his master will not consent to part with him for a great price, what will you do unto him on his account? and they answered him, saying, If he will not give him unto us we will slay him, and take our brother and go away. 32 And Joseph said unto them, That is the thing which I have spoken to you; you are spies, for you are come to slay the inhabitants of the land, for we heard that two of your brethren smote all the inhabitants of Shechem, in the land of Canaan, on account of your sister, and you now come to do the like in Egypt on account of your brother. 33 Only hereby shall I know that you are true men; if you will send home one from amongst you to fetch your youngest brother from your father, and to bring him here unto me, and by doing this thing I will know that you are right. 34 And Joseph called to seventy of his mighty men, and he said unto them, Take these men and bring them into the ward. 35 And the mighty men took the ten men, they laid hold of them and put them into the ward, and they were in the ward three days. 36 And on the third day Joseph had them brought out of the ward, and he said unto them, Do this for yourselves if you be true men, so that you may live, one of your brethren shall be confined in the ward whilst you go and take home the corn for your household to the land of Canaan, and fetch your youngest brother, and bring him here unto me, that I may know that you are true men when you do this thing. 37 And Joseph went out from them and came into the chamber, and wept a great weeping, for his pity was excited for them, and he washed his face, and returned to them again, and he took Simeon from them and ordered him to be bound, but Simeon was not willing to be done so, for he was a very powerful man and they could not bind him. 38 And Joseph called unto his mighty men and seventy valiant men came before him with drawn swords in their hands, and the sons of Jacob were terrified at them. 39 And Joseph said unto them, Seize this man and confine him in prison until his brethren come to him, and Joseph's valiant men hastened and they all laid hold of Simeon to bind him, and Simeon gave a loud and terrible shriek and the cry was heard at a distance. 40 And all the valiant men of Joseph were terrified at the sound of the shriek, that they fell upon their faces, and they were greatly afraid and fled. 41 And all the men that were with Joseph fled, for they were greatly afraid of their lives, and only Joseph and Manasseh his son remained there, and Manassah the son of Joseph saw the strength of Simeon, and he was exceedingly wroth. ⁴² And Manassah the son of Joseph rose up to Simeon, and Manassah smote Simeon a heavy blow with his fist against the back of his neck, and Simeon was stilled of his rage. ⁴³ And Manassah laid hold of Simeon and he seized him violently and he bound him and brought him into the house of confinement, and all the sons of Jacob were astonished at the act of the youth. ⁴⁴ And Simeon said unto his brethren, None of you must say that this is the smiting of an Egyptian, but it is the smiting of the house of my father. ⁴⁵ And after this Joseph ordered him to be called who was set over the storehouse, to fill their sacks with corn as much as they could carry, and to restore every man's money into his sack, and to give them provision for the road, and thus did he unto them. ⁴⁶ And Joseph commanded them, saying, Take heed lest you transgress my orders to bring your brother as I have told you, and it shall be when you bring your brother hither unto me, then will I know that you are true men, and you shall traffic in the land, and I will restore unto you your brother, and you shall return in peace to your father. ⁴⁷ And they all answered and said, According as our lord speaketh so will we do, and they bowed down to him to the ground. ⁴⁸ And every man lifted his corn upon his ass, and they went out to go to the land of Canaan to their father; and they came to the inn and Levi spread his sack to give provender to his ass, when he saw and behold his money in full weight was still in his sack. ⁴⁹ And the man was greatly afraid, and he said unto his brethren, My money is restored, and lo, it is even in my sack, and the men were greatly afraid, and they said, What is this that God hath done unto us? ⁵⁰ And they all said, And where is the Lord's kindness with our fathers, with Abraham, Isaac, end Jacob, that the Lord has this day delivered us into the hands of the king of Egypt to contrive against us? ⁵¹ And Judah said unto them, Surely we are guilty sinners before the Lord our God in having sold our brother, our own flesh, and wherefore do you say, Where is the Lord's kindness with our fathers? ⁵² And Reuben said unto them, Said I not unto you, do not sin against the lad, and you would not listen to me? now God requireth him from us, and how dare you say, Where is the Lord's kindness with our fathers, whilst you have sinned unto the Lord? ⁵³ And they tarried over night in that place, and they rose up early in the morning and laded their asses with their corn, and they led them and went on and came to their father's house in the land of Canaan. ⁵⁴ And Jacob and his household went out to meet his sons, and Jacob saw and behold their brother Simeon was not with them, and Jacob said unto his sons, Where is your brother Simeon, whom I do not see? and his sons told him all that had befallen them in Egypt.

Jash.52

¹ And they entered their house, and every man opened his sack and they saw and behold every man's bundle of money was there, at which they and their father were greatly terrified. ² And Jacob said unto them, What is this that you have done to me? I sent your brother Joseph to inquire after your welfare and you said unto me. A wild beast did devour him. ³ And Simeon went with you to buy food and you say the king of Egypt hath confined him in prison, and you wish to take Benjamin to cause his death also, and bring down my grey hairs with sorrow to the grave on account of Benjamin and his brother Joseph. ⁴ Now therefore my son shall not go down with you, for his brother is dead and he is left alone, and mischief may befall him by the way in which you go, as it befell his brother. ⁵ And Reuben said unto his father, Thou shalt slay my two sons if I do not bring thy son and place him before thee; and Jacob said unto his sons, Abide ye here and do not go down to Egypt, for my son shall not go down with you to Egypt, nor die like his brother. ⁶ And Judah said unto them, refrain ye from him until the corn is finished, and

he will then say, Take down your brother, when he will find his own life and the life of his household in danger from the famine. ⁷ And in those days the famine was sore throughout the land, and all the people of the earth went and came to Egypt to buy food, for the famine prevailed greatly amongst them, and the sons of Jacob remained in Canaan a year and two months until their corn was finished. ⁸ And it came to pass after their corn was finished, the whole household of Jacob was pinched with hunger, and all the infants of the sons of Jacob came together and they approached Jacob, and they all surrounded him, and they said unto him, Give unto us bread, and wherefore shall we all perish through hunger in thy presence? ⁹ Jacob heard the words of his son's children, and he wept a great weeping, and his pity was roused for them, and Jacob called unto his sons and they all came and sat before him. ¹⁰ And Jacob said unto them, And have you not seen how your children have been weeping over me this day, saying, Give unto us bread, and there is none? now therefore return and buy for us a little food. ¹¹ And Judah answered and said unto his father, If thou wilt send our brother with us we will go down and buy corn for thee, and if thou wilt not send him then we will not go down, for surely the king of Egypt particularly enjoined us, saying, You shall not see my face unless your brother be with you, for the king of Egypt is a strong and mighty king, and behold if we shall go to him without our brother we shall all be put to death. ¹² Dost thou not know and hast thou not heard that this king is very powerful and wise, and there is not like unto him in all the earth? behold we have seen all the kings of the earth and we have not seen one like that king, the king of Egypt; surely amongst all the kings of the earth there is none greater than Abimelech king of the Philistines, yet the king of Egypt is greater and mightier than he, and Abimelech can only be compared to one of his officers. ¹³ Father, thou hast not seen his palace and his throne, and all his servants standing before him; thou hast not seen that king upon his throne in his pomp and royal appearance, dressed in his kingly robes with a large golden crown upon his head; thou hast not seen the honor and glory which God has given unto him, for there is not like unto him in all the earth. ¹⁴ Father, thou hast not seen the wisdom, the understanding and the knowledge which God has given in his heart, nor heard his sweet voice when he spake unto us. ¹⁵ We know not, father, who made him acquainted with our names and all that befell us, yet he asked also after thee, saying, Is your father still living, and is it well with him? ¹⁶ Thou hast not seen the affairs of the government of Egypt regulated by him, without inquiring of Pharaoh his lord; thou hast not seen the awe and fear which he impressed upon all the Egyptians. ¹⁷ And also when we went from him, we threatened to do unto Egypt like unto the rest of the cities of the Amorites, and we were exceedingly wroth against all his words which he spoke concerning us as spies, and now when we shall again come before him his terror will fall upon us all, and not one of us will be able to speak to him either a little or a great thing. ¹⁸ Now therefore father, send we pray thee the lad with us, and we will go down and buy thee food for our support, and not die through hunger. And Jacob said, Why have you dealt so ill with me to tell the king you had a brother? what is this thing that you have done unto me? ¹⁹ And Judah said unto Jacob his father, Give the lad into my care and we will rise up and go down to Egypt and buy corn, and then return, and it shall be when we return if the lad be not with us, then let me bear thy blame forever. ²⁰ Hast thou seen all our infants weeping over thee through hunger and there is no power in thy hand to satisfy them? now let thy pity be roused for them and send our brother with us and we will go. ²¹ For how will the Lord's kindness to our ancestors be manifested to thee when thou sayest that the king of Egypt will take away thy son? as the Lord liveth I will not leave him until I bring him and place him before thee; but pray for us unto the Lord, that he may deal kindly with us, to cause us to be received favorably and kindly before the king of Egypt and his men, for had we not delayed surely now we had returned a second time with thy son. 22 And Jacob said unto his sons, I trust in the Lord God that he may deliver you and give you favor in the sight of the king of Egypt, and in the sight of all his men. 23 Now therefore rise up and go to the man, and take for him in your hands a present from what can be obtained in the land and bring it before him, and may the Almighty God give you mercy before him that he may send Benjamin and Simeon your brethren with you. 24 And all the men rose up, and they took their brother Benjamin, and they took in their hands a large present of the best of the land, and they also took a double portion of silver. 25 And Jacob strictly commanded his sons concerning Benjamin, Saying, Take heed of him in the way in which you are going, and do not separate yourselves from him in the road, neither in Egypt. 26 And Jacob rose up from his sons and spread forth his hands and he prayed unto the Lord on account of his sons, saying, O Lord God of heaven and earth, remember thy covenant with our father Abraham, remember it with my father Isaac and deal kindly with my sons and deliver them not into the hands of the king of Egypt; do it I pray thee O God for the sake of thy mercies and redeem all my children and rescue them from Egyptian power, and send them their two brothers. 27 And all the wives of the sons of Jacob and their children lifted up their eyes to heaven and they all wept before the Lord, and cried unto him to deliver their fathers from the hand of the king of Egypt. 28 And Jacob wrote a record to the king of Egypt and gave it into the hand of Judah and into the hands of his sons for the king of Egypt, saying, 29 From thy servant Jacob, son of Isaac, son of Abraham the Hebrew, the prince of God, to the powerful and wise king, the revealer of secrets, king of Egypt, greeting. 30 Be it known to my lord the king of Egypt, the famine was sore upon us in the land of Canaan, and I sent my sons to thee to buy us a little food from thee for our support. 31 For my sons surrounded me and I being very old cannot see with my eyes, for my eyes have become very heavy through age, as well as with daily weeping for my son, for Joseph who was lost from before me, and I commanded my sons that they should not enter the gates of the city when they came to Egypt, on account of the inhabitants of the land. 32 And I also commanded them to go about Egypt to seek for my son Joseph, perhaps they might find him there, and they did so, and thou didst consider them as spies of the land. 33 Have we not heard concerning thee that thou didst interpret Pharaoh's dream and didst speak truly unto him? how then dost thou not know in thy wisdom whether my sons are spies or not? 34 Now therefore, my lord and king, behold I have sent my son before thee, as thou didst speak unto my sons; I beseech thee to put thy eyes upon him until he is returned to me in peace with his brethren. 35 For dost thou not know, or hast thou not heard that which our God did unto Pharaoh when he took my mother Sarah, and what he did unto Abimelech king of the Philistines on account of her, and also what our father Abraham did unto the nine kings of Elam, how he smote them all with a few men that were with him? 36 And also what my two sons Simeon and Levi did unto the eight cities of the Amorites, how they destroyed them on account of their sister Dinah? 37 And also on account of their brother Benjamin they consoled themselves for the loss of his brother Joseph; what will they then do for him when they see the hand of any people prevailing over them, for his sake? 38 Dost thou not know, O king of Egypt, that the power of God is with us, and that also God ever heareth our prayers and forsaketh us not all the days? 39 And when my sons told me of thy

dealings with them, I called not unto the Lord on account of thee, for then thou wouldst have perished with thy men before my son Benjamin came before thee, but I thought that as Simeon my son was in thy house, perhaps thou mightest deal kindly with him, therefore I did not this thing unto thee. 40 Now therefore behold Benjamin my son cometh unto thee with my sons, take heed of him and put thy eyes upon him, and then will God place his eyes over thee and throughout thy kingdom. 41 Now I have told thee all that is in my heart, and behold my sons are coming to thee with their brother, examine the face of the whole earth for their sake and send them back in peace with their brethren. 42 And Jacob gave the record to his sons into the care of Judah to give it unto the king of Egypt.

Jash.53

1 And the sons of Jacob rose up and took Benjamin and the whole of the presents, and they went and came to Egypt and they stood before Joseph. 2 And Joseph beheld his brother Benjamin with them and he saluted them, and these men came to Joseph's house. 3 And Joseph commanded the superintendent of his house to give to his brethren to eat, and he did so unto them. 4 And at noon time Joseph sent for the men to come before him with Benjamin, and the men told the superintendent of Joseph's house concerning the silver that was returned in their sacks, and he said unto them, It will be well with you, fear not, and he brought their brother Simeon unto them. 5 And Simeon said unto his brethren, The lord of the Egyptians has acted very kindly unto me, he did not keep me bound, as you saw with your eyes, for when you went out from the city he let me free and dealt kindly with me in his house. 6 And Judah took Benjamin by the hand, and they came before Joseph, and they bowed down to him to the ground. 7 And the men gave the present unto Joseph and they all sat before him, and Joseph said unto them, Is it well with you, is it well with your children, is it well with your aged father? and they said, It is well, and Judah took the record which Jacob had sent and gave it into the hand of Joseph. 8 And Joseph read the letter and knew his father's writing, and he wished to weep and he went into an inner room and he wept a great weeping; and he went out. 9 And he lifted up his eyes and beheld his brother Benjamin, and he said, Is this your brother of whom you spoke unto me? And Benjamin approached Joseph, and Joseph placed his hand upon his head and he said unto him, May God be gracious unto thee my son. 10 And when Joseph saw his brother, the son of his mother, he again wished to weep, and he entered the chamber, and he wept there, and he washed his face, and went out and refrained from weeping, and he said, Prepare food. 11 And Joseph had a cup from which he drank, and it was of silver beautifully inlaid with onyx stones and bdellium, and Joseph struck the cup in the sight of his brethren whilst they were sitting to eat with him. 12 And Joseph said unto the men, I know by this cup that Reuben the first born, Simeon and Levi and Judah, Issachar and Zebulun are children from one mother, seat yourselves to eat according to your births. 13 And he also placed the others according to their births, and he said, I know that this your youngest brother has no brother, and I, like him, have no brother, he shall therefore sit down to eat with me. 14 And Benjamin went up before Joseph and sat upon the throne, and the men beheld the acts of Joseph, and they were astonished at them; and the men ate and drank at that time with Joseph, and he then gave presents unto them, and Joseph gave one gift unto Benjamin, and Manasseh and Ephraim saw the acts of their father, and they also gave presents unto him, and Osnath gave him one present, and they were five presents in the hand of Benjamin. 15 And Joseph brought them out wine to drink, and they would not drink, and they said, From the day on which Joseph was lost we have not drunk wine, nor eaten any delicacies. 16 And Joseph

swore unto them, and he pressed them hard, and they drank plentifully with him on that day, and Joseph afterward turned to his brother Benjamin to speak with him, and Benjamin was still sitting upon the throne before Joseph. 17 And Joseph said unto him, Hast thou begotten any children? and he said, Thy servant has ten sons, and these are their names, Bela, Becher, Ashbal, Gera, Naaman, Achi, Rosh, Mupim, Chupim, and Ord, and I called their names after my brother whom I have not seen. 18 And he ordered them to bring before him his map of the stars, whereby Joseph knew all the times, and Joseph said unto Benjamin, I have heard that the Hebrews are acquainted with all wisdom, dost thou know anything of this? 19 And Benjamin said, Thy servant is knowing also in all the wisdom which my father taught me, and Joseph said unto Benjamin, Look now at this instrument and understand where thy brother Joseph is in Egypt, who you said went down to Egypt. 20 And Benjamin beheld that instrument with the map of the stars of heaven, and he was wise and looked therein to know where his brother was, and Benjamin divided the whole land of Egypt into four divisions, and he found that he who was sitting upon the throne before him was his brother Joseph, and Benjamin wondered greatly, and when Joseph saw that his brother Benjamin was so much astonished, he said unto Benjamin, What hast thou seen, and why art thou astonished? 21 And Benjamin said unto Joseph, I can see by this that Joseph my brother sitteth here with me upon the throne, and Joseph said unto him, I am Joseph thy brother, reveal not this thing unto thy brethren; behold I will send thee with them when they go away, and I will command them to be brought back again into the city, and I will take thee away from them. 22 And if they dare their lives and fight for thee, then shall I know that they have repented of what they did unto me, and I will make myself known to them, and if they forsake thee when I take thee, then shalt thou remain with me, and I will wrangle with them, and they shall go away, and I will not become known to them. 23 At that time Joseph commanded his officer to fill their sacks with food, and to put each man's money into his sack, and to put the cup in the sack of Benjamin, and to give them provision for the road, and they did so unto them. 24 And on the next day the men rose up early in the morning, and they loaded their asses with their corn, and they went forth with Benjamin, and they went to the land of Canaan with their brother Benjamin. 25 They had not gone far from Egypt when Joseph commanded him that was set over his house, saying, Rise, pursue these men before they get too far from Egypt, and say unto them, Why have you stolen my master's cup? 26 And Joseph's officer rose up and he reached them, and he spoke unto them all the words of Joseph; and when they heard this thing they became exceedingly wroth, and they said, He with whom thy master's cup shall be found shall die, and we will also become slaves. 27 And they hastened and each man brought down his sack from his ass, and they looked in their bags and the cup was found in Benjamin's bag, and they all tore their garments and they returned to the city, and they smote Benjamin in the road, continually smiting him until he came into the city, and they stood before Joseph. 28 And Judah's anger was kindled, and he said, This man has only brought me back to destroy Egypt this day. 29 And the men came to Joseph's house, and they found Joseph sitting upon his throne, and all the mighty men standing at his right and left. 30 And Joseph said unto them, What is this act that you have done, that you took away my silver cup and went away? but I know that you took my cup in order to know thereby in what part of the land your brother was. 31 And Judah said, What shall we say to our lord, what shall we speak and how shall we justify ourselves, God has this day found the iniquity of all thy servants, therefore has he done this thing to us this day. 32 And Joseph rose

up and caught hold of Benjamin and took him from his brethren with violence, and he came to the house and locked the door at them, and Joseph commanded him that was set over his house that he should say unto them, Thus saith the king, Go in peace to your father, behold I have taken the man in whose hand my cup was found.

Jash.54

1 And when Judah saw the dealings of Joseph with them, Judah approached him and broke open the door, and came with his brethren before Joseph. 2 And Judah said unto Joseph, Let it not seem grievous in the sight of my lord, may thy servant I pray thee speak a word before thee? and Joseph said unto him, Speak. 3 And Judah spoke before Joseph, and his brethren were there standing before them; and Judah said unto Joseph, Surely when we first came to our lord to buy food, thou didst consider us as spies of the land, and we brought Benjamin before thee, and thou still makest sport of us this day. 4 Now therefore let the king hear my words, and send I pray thee our brother that he may go along with us to our father, lest thy soul perish this day with all the souls of the inhabitants of Egypt. 5 Dost thou not know what two of my brethren, Simeon and Levi, did unto the city of Shechem, and unto seven cities of the Amorites, on account of our sister Dinah, and also what they would do for the sake of their brother Benjamin? 6 And I with my strength, who am greater and mightier than both of them, come this day upon thee and thy land if thou art unwilling to send our brother. 7 Hast thou not heard what our God who made choice of us did unto Pharaoh on account of Sarah our mother, whom he took away from our father, that he smote him and his household with heavy plagues, that even unto this day the Egyptians relate this wonder to each other? so will our God do unto thee on account of Benjamin whom thou hast this day taken from his father, and on account of the evils which thou this day heapest over us in thy land; for our God will remember his covenant with our father Abraham and bring evil upon thee, because thou hast grieved the soul of our father this day. 8 Now therefore hear my words that I have this day spoken unto thee, and send our brother that he may go away lest thou and the people of thy land die by the sword, for you cannot all prevail over me. 9 And Joseph answered Judah, saying, Why hast thou opened wide thy mouth and why dost thou boast over us, saying, Strength is with thee? as Pharaoh liveth, if I command all my valiant men to fight with you, surely thou and these thy brethren would sink in the mire. 10 And Judah said unto Joseph, Surely it becometh thee and thy people to fear me; as the Lord liveth if I once draw my sword I shall not sheathe it again until I shall this day have slain all Egypt, and I will commence with thee and finish with Pharaoh thy master. 11 And Joseph answered and said unto him, Surely strength belongeth not alone to thee; I am stronger and mightier than thou, surely if thou drawest thy sword I will put it to thy neck and the necks of all thy brethren. 12 And Judah said unto him, Surely if I this day open my mouth against thee I would swallow thee up that thou be destroyed from off the earth and perish this day from thy kingdom. And Joseph said, Surely if thou openest thy mouth I have power and might to close thy mouth with a stone until thou shalt not be able to utter a word; see how many stones are before us, truly I can take a stone, and force it into thy mouth and break thy jaws. 13 And Judah said, God is witness between us, that we have not hitherto desired to battle with thee, only give us our brother and we will go from thee; and Joseph answered and said, As Pharaoh liveth, if all the kings of Canaan came together with you, you should not take him from my hand. 14 Now therefore go your way to your father, and your brother shall be unto me for a slave, for he has robbed the king's house. And Judah said, What is it to thee or to the

character of the king, surely the king sendeth forth from his house, throughout the land, silver and gold either in gifts or expenses, and thou still talkest about thy cup which thou didst place in our brother's bag and sayest that he has stolen it from thee? 15 God forbid that our brother Benjamin or any of the seed of Abraham should do this thing to steal from thee, or from any one else, whether king, prince, or any man. 16 Now therefore cease this accusation lest the whole earth hear thy words, saying, For a little silver the king of Egypt wrangled with the men, and he accused them and took their brother for a slave. 17 And Joseph answered and said, Take unto you this cup and go from me and leave your brother for a slave, for it is the judgment of a thief to be a slave. 18 And Judah said, Why art thou not ashamed of thy words, to leave our brother and to take thy cup? Surely if thou givest us thy cup, or a thousand times as much, we will not leave our brother for the silver which is found in the hand of any man, that we will not die over him. 19 And Joseph answered, And why did you forsake your brother and sell him for twenty pieces of silver unto this day, and why then will you not do the same to this your brother? 20 And Judah said, the Lord is witness between me and thee that we desire not thy battles; now therefore give us our brother and we will go from thee without quarreling. 21 And Joseph answered and said, If all the kings of the land should assemble they will not be able to take your brother from my hand; and Judah said, What shall we say unto our father, when he seeth that our brother cometh not with us, and will grieve over him? 22 And Joseph answered and said, This is the thing which you shall tell unto your father, saying, The rope has gone after the bucket. 23 And Judah said, Surely thou art a king, and why speakest thou these things, giving a false judgment? woe unto the king who is like unto thee. 24 And Joseph answered and said, There is no false judgment in the word that I spoke on account of your brother Joseph, for all of you sold him to the Midianites for twenty pieces of silver, and you all denied it to your father and said unto him, An evil beast has devoured him, Joseph has been torn to pieces. 25 And Judah said, Behold the fire of Shem burneth in my heart, now I will burn all your land with fire; and Joseph answered and said, Surely thy sister-in-law Tamar, who killed your sons, extinguished the fire of Shechem. 26 And Judah said, If I pluck out a single hair from my flesh, I will fill all Egypt with its blood. 27 And Joseph answered and said, Such is your custom to do as you did to your brother whom you sold, and you dipped his coat in blood and brought it to your father in order that he might say an evil beast devoured him and here is his blood. 28 And when Judah heard this thing he was exceedingly wroth and his anger burned within him, and there was before him in that place a stone, the weight of which was about four hundred shekels, and Judah's anger was kindled and he took the stone in one hand and cast it to the heavens and caught it with his left hand. 29 And he placed it afterward under his legs, and he sat upon it with all his strength and the stone was turned into dust from the force of Judah. 30 And Joseph saw the act of Judah and he was very much afraid, but he commanded Manassah his son and he also did with another stone like unto the act of Judah, and Judah said unto his brethren, Let not any of you say, this man is an Egyptian, but by his doing this thing he is of our father's family. 31 And Joseph said, Not to you only is strength given, for we are also powerful men, and why will you boast over us all? and Judah said unto Joseph, Send I pray thee our brother and ruin not thy country this day. 32 And Joseph answered and said unto them, Go and tell your father, an evil beast hath devoured him as you said concerning your brother Joseph. 33 And Judah spoke to his brother Naphtali, and he said unto him, Make haste, go now and number all the streets of Egypt and come and tell me; and Simeon said unto him, Let not this thing be a trouble to thee; now I will go to the mount and take up one large stone from the mount and level it at every one in Egypt, and kill all that are in it. 34 And Joseph heard all these words that his brethren spoke before him, and they did not know that Joseph understood them, for they imagined that he knew not to speak Hebrew. 35 And Joseph was greatly afraid at the words of his brethren lest they should destroy Egypt, and he commanded his son Manasseh, saying, Go now make haste and gather unto me all the inhabitants of Egypt, and all the valiant men together, and let them come to me now upon horseback and on foot and with all sorts of musical instruments, and Manasseh went and did so. 36 And Naphtali went as Judah had commanded him, for Naphtali was lightfooted as one of the swift stags, and he would go upon the ears of corn and they would not break under him. 37 And he went and numbered all the streets of Egypt, and found them to be twelve, and he came hastily and told Judah, and Judah said unto his brethren, Hasten you and put on every man his sword upon his loins and we will come over Egypt, and smite them all, and let not a remnant remain. 38 And Judah said, Behold, I will destroy three of the streets with my strength, and you shall each destroy one street; and when Judah was speaking this thing, behold the inhabitants of Egypt and all the mighty men came toward them with all sorts of musical instruments and with loud shouting. 39 And their number was five hundred cavalry and ten thousand infantry, and four hundred men who could fight without sword or spear, only with their hands and strength. 40 And all the mighty men came with great storming and shouting, and they all surrounded the sons of Jacob and terrified them, and the ground quaked at the sound of their shouting. 41 And when the sons of Jacob saw these troops they were greatly afraid of their lives, and Joseph did so in order to terrify the sons of Jacob to become tranquilized. 42 And Judah, seeing some of his brethren terrified, said unto them, Why are you afraid whilst the grace of God is with us? and when Judah saw all the people of Egypt surrounding them at the command of Joseph to terrify them, only Joseph commanded them, saying, Do not touch any of them. 43 Then Judah hastened and drew his sword, and uttered a loud and bitter scream, and he smote with his sword, and he sprang upon the ground and he still continued to shout against all the people. 44 And when he did this thing the Lord caused the terror of Judah and his brethren to fall upon the valiant men and all the people that surrounded them. 45 And they all fled at the sound of the shouting, and they were terrified and fell one upon the other, and many of them died as they fell, and they all fled from before Judah and his brethren and from before Joseph. 46 And whilst they were fleeing, Judah and his brethren pursued them unto the house of Pharaoh, and they all escaped, and Judah again sat before Joseph and roared at him like a lion, and gave a great and tremendous shriek at him. 47 And the shriek was heard at a distance, and all the inhabitants of Succoth heard it, and all Egypt quaked at the sound of the shriek, and also the walls of Egypt and of the land of Goshen fell in from the shaking of the earth, and Pharaoh also fell from his throne upon the ground, and also all the pregnant women of Egypt and Goshen miscarried when they heard the noise of the shaking, for they were terribly afraid. 48 And Pharaoh sent word, saying, What is this thing that has this day happened in the land of Egypt? and they came and told him all the things from beginning to end, and Pharaoh was alarmed and he wondered and was greatly afraid. 49 And his fright increased when he heard all these things, and he sent unto Joseph, saying, Thou hast brought unto me the Hebrews to destroy all Egypt; what wilt thou do with that thievish slave? send him away and let him go with his brethren, and let us not perish through their evil, even we, you and all Egypt. 50 And if thou desirest not to do this thing, cast off from thee all my valuable things, and go with them to their land, if thou delightest in it, for they will this day destroy my whole country and slay all my people; even all the women of Egypt have miscarried through their screams; see what they have done merely by their shouting and speaking, moreover if they fight with the sword, they will destroy the land; now therefore choose that which thou desirest, whether me or the Hebrews, whether Egypt or the land of the Hebrews. 51 And they came and told Joseph all the words of Pharaoh that he had said concerning him, and Joseph was greatly afraid at the words of Pharaoh and Judah and his brethren were still standing before Joseph indignant and enraged, and all the sons of Jacob roared at Joseph, like the roaring of the sea and its waves. 52 And Joseph was greatly afraid of his brethren and on account of Pharaoh, and Joseph sought a pretext to make himself known unto his brethren, lest they should destroy all Egypt. 53 And Joseph commanded his son Manasseh, and Manasseh went and approached Judah, and placed his hand upon his shoulder, and the anger of Judah was stilled. 54 And Judah said unto his brethren, Let no one of you say that this is the act of an Egyptian youth for this is the work of my father's house. 55 And Joseph seeing and knowing that Judah's anger was stilled, he approached to speak unto Judah in the language of mildness. 56 And Joseph said unto Judah, Surely you speak truth and have this day verified your assertions concerning your strength, and may your God who delighteth in you, increase your welfare; but tell me truly why from amongst all thy brethren dost thou wrangle with me on account of the lad, as none of them have spoken one word to me concerning him. 57 And Judah answered Joseph, saying, Surely thou must know that I was security for the lad to his father, saying, If I brought him not unto him I should bear his blame forever. 58 Therefore have I approached thee from amongst all my brethren, for I saw that thou wast unwilling to suffer him to go from thee; now therefore may I find grace in thy sight that thou shalt send him to go with us, and behold I will remain as a substitute for him, to serve thee in whatever thou desirest, for wheresoever thou shalt send me I will go to serve thee with great energy. 59 Send me now to a mighty king who has rebelled against thee, and thou shalt know what I will do unto him and unto his land; although he may have cavalry and infantry or an exceeding mighty people, I will slay them all and bring the king's head before thee. 60 Dost thou not know or hast thou not heard that our father Abraham with his servant Eliezer smote all the kings of Elam with their hosts in one night, they left not one remaining? and ever since that day our father's strength was given unto us for an inheritance, for us and our seed forever. 61 And Joseph answered and said, You speak truth, and falsehood is not in your mouth, for it was also told unto us that the Hebrews have power and that the Lord their God delighteth much in them, and who then can stand before them? 62 However, on this condition will I send your brother, if you will bring before me his brother the son of his mother, of whom you said that he had gone from you down to Egypt; and it shall come to pass when you bring unto me his brother I will take him in his stead, because not one of you was security for him to your father, and when he shall come unto me, I will then send with you his brother for whom you have been security. 63 And Judah's anger was kindled against Joseph when he spoke this thing, and his eyes dropped blood with anger, and he said unto his brethren, How doth this man this day seek his own destruction and that of all Egypt! 64 And Simeon answered Joseph, saying, Did we not tell thee at first that we knew not the particular spot to which he went, and whether he be dead or alive, and wherefore speaketh my lord like unto these things? 65 And Joseph observing the countenance of Judah discerned that his anger began to kindle when he spoke unto him, saying, Bring unto me your

other brother instead of this brother. 66 And Joseph said unto his brethren, Surely you said that your brother was either dead or lost, now if I should call him this day and he should come before you, would you give him unto me instead of his brother? 67 And Joseph began to speak and call out, Joseph, Joseph, come this day before me, and appear to thy brethren and sit before them. 68 And when Joseph spoke this thing before them, they looked each a different way to see from whence Joseph would come before them. 69 And Joseph observed all their acts, and said unto them, Why do you look here and there? I am Joseph whom you sold to Egypt, now therefore let it not grieve you that you sold me, for as a support during the famine did God send me before you. 70 And his brethren were terrified at him when they heard the words of Joseph, and Judah was exceedingly terrified at him. 71 And when Benjamin heard the words of Joseph he was before them in the inner part of the house, and Benjamin ran unto Joseph his brother, and embraced him and fell upon his neck, and they wept. 72 And when Joseph's brethren saw that Benjamin had fallen upon his brother's neck and wept with him, they also fell upon Joseph and embraced him, and they wept a great weeping with Joseph. 73 And the voice was heard in the house of Joseph that they were Joseph's brethren, and it pleased Pharaoh exceedingly, for he was afraid of them lest they should destroy Egypt. 74 And Pharaoh sent his servants unto Joseph to congratulate him concerning his brethren who had come to him, and all the captains of the armies and troops that were in Egypt came to rejoice with Joseph, and all Egypt rejoiced greatly about Joseph's brethren. 75 And Pharaoh sent his servants to Joseph, saying, Tell thy brethren to fetch all belonging to them and let them come unto me, and I will place them in the best part of the land of Egypt, and they did so. 76 And Joseph commanded him that was set over his house to bring out to his brethren gifts and garments, and he brought out to them many garments being robes of royalty and many gifts, and Joseph divided them amongst his brethren. 77 And he gave unto each of his brethren a change of garments of gold and silver, and three hundred pieces of silver, and Joseph commanded them all to be dressed in these garments, and to be brought before Pharaoh. 78 And Pharaoh seeing that all Joseph's brethren were valiant men, and of beautiful appearance, he greatly rejoiced. 79 And they afterward went out from the presence of Pharaoh to go to the land of Canaan, to their father, and their brother Benjamin was with them. 80 And Joseph rose up and gave unto them eleven chariots from Pharaoh, and Joseph gave unto them his chariot, upon which he rode on the day of his being crowned in Egypt, to fetch his father to Egypt; and Joseph sent to all his brothers' children, garments according to their numbers, and a hundred pieces of silver to each of them, and he also sent garments to the wives of his brethren from the garments of the king's wives, and he sent them. 81 And he gave unto each of his brethren ten men to go with them to the land of Canaan to serve them, to serve their children and all belonging to them in coming to Egypt. 82 And Joseph sent by the hand of his brother Benjamin ten suits of garments for his ten sons, a portion above the rest of the children of the sons of Jacob. 83 And he sent to each fifty pieces of silver, and ten chariots on the account of Pharaoh, and he sent to his father ten asses laden with all the luxuries of Egypt, and ten she asses laden with corn and bread and nourishment for his father, and to all that were with him as provisions for the road. 84 And he sent to his sister Dinah garments of silver and gold, and frankincense and myrrh, and aloes and women's ornaments in great plenty, and he sent the same from the wives of Pharaoh to the wives of Benjamin. 85 And he gave unto all his brethren, also to their wives, all sorts of onyx stones and bdellium, and from all the valuable things amongst the great people of Egypt, nothing of all the costly things was left but what Joseph sent of to his father's household. 86 And he sent his brethren away, and they went, and he sent his brother Benjamin with them. 87 And Joseph went out with them to accompany them on the road unto the borders of Egypt, and he commanded them concerning his father and his household, to come to Egypt. 88 And he said unto them, Do not quarrel on the road, for this thing was from the Lord to keep a great people from starvation, for there will be yet five years of famine in the land. 89 And he commanded them, saying, When you come unto the land of Canaan, do not come suddenly before my father in this affair, but act in your wisdom. 90 And Joseph ceased to command them, and he turned and went back to Egypt, and the sons of Jacob went to the land of Canaan with joy and cheerfulness to their father Jacob. 91 And they came unto the borders of the land, and they said to each other, What shall we do in this matter before our father, for if we come suddenly to him and tell him the matter, he will be greatly alarmed at our words and will not believe us. 92 And they went along until they came nigh unto their houses, and they found Serach, the daughter of Asher, going forth to meet them, and the damsel was very good and subtle, and knew how to play upon the harp. 93 And they called unto her and she came before them, and she kissed them, and they took her and gave unto her a harp, saying, Go now before our father, and sit before him, and strike upon the harp, and speak these words. 94 And they commanded her to go to their house, and she took the harp and hastened before them, and she came and sat near Jacob. 95 And she played well and sang, and uttered in the sweetness of her words, Joseph my uncle is living, and he ruleth throughout the land of Egypt, and is not dead. 96 And she continued to repeat and utter these words, and Jacob heard her words and they were agreeable to him. 97 He listened whilst she repeated them twice and thrice, and joy entered the heart of Jacob at the sweetness of her words, and the spirit of God was upon him, and he knew all her words to be true. 98 And Jacob blessed Serach when she spoke these words before him, and he said unto her, My daughter, may death never prevail over thee, for thou hast revived my spirit; only speak yet before me as thou hast spoken, for thou hast gladdened me with all thy words. 99 And she continued to sing these words, and Jacob listened and it pleased him, and he rejoiced, and the spirit of God was upon him. 100 Whilst he was yet speaking with her, behold his sons came to him with horses and chariots and royal garments and servants running before them. 101 And Jacob rose up to meet them, and saw his sons dressed in royal garments and he saw all the treasures that Joseph had sent to them. 102 And they said unto him, Be informed that our brother Joseph is living, and it is he who ruleth throughout the land of Egypt, and it is he who spoke unto us as we told thee. 103 And Jacob heard all the words of his sons, and his heart palpitated at their words, for he could not believe them until he saw all that Joseph had given them and what he had sent him, and all the signs which Joseph had spoken unto them. 104 And they opened out before him, and showed him all that Joseph had sent, they gave unto each what Joseph had sent him, and he knew that they had spoken the truth, and he rejoiced exceedingly an account of his son. 105 And Jacob said, It is enough for me that my son Joseph is still living, I will go and see him before I die. 106 And his sons told him all that had befallen them, and Jacob said, I will go down to Egypt to see my son and his offspring. 107 And Jacob rose up and put on the garments which Joseph had sent him, and after he had washed, and shaved his hair, he put upon his head the turban which Joseph had sent him. 108 And all the people of Jacob's house and their wives put on the garments which Joseph had sent to them, and they greatly rejoiced at Joseph that he was still living and that he was ruling in

Egypt, 109 And all the inhabitants of Canaan heard of this thing, and they came and rejoiced much with Jacob that he was still living. 110 And Jacob made a feast for them for three days, and all the kings of Canaan and nobles of the land ate and drank and rejoiced in the house of Jacob.

Jash.55

1 And it came to pass after this that Jacob said, I will go and see my son in Egypt and will then come back to the land of Canaan of which God had spoken unto Abraham, for I cannot leave the land of my birth-place. 2 Behold the word of the Lord came unto him, saying, Go down to Egypt with all thy household and remain there, fear not to go down to Egypt for I will there make thee a great nation. 3 And Jacob said within himself, I will go and see my son whether the fear of his God is yet in his heart amidst all the inhabitants of Egypt. 4 And the Lord said unto Jacob, Fear not about Joseph, for he still retaineth his integrity to serve me, as will seem good in thy sight, and Jacob rejoiced exceedingly concerning his son. 5 At that time Jacob commanded his sons and household to go to Egypt according to the word of the Lord unto him, and Jacob rose up with his sons and all his household, and he went out from the land of Canaan from Beersheba, with joy and gladness of heart, and they went to the land of Egypt. 6 And it came to pass when they came near Egypt, Jacob sent Judah before him to Joseph that he might show him a situation in Egypt, and Judah did according to the word of his father, and he hastened and ran and came to Joseph, and they assigned for them a place in the land of Goshen for all his household, and Judah returned and came along the road to his father. 7 And Joseph harnessed the chariot, and he assembled all his mighty men and his servants and all the officers of Egypt in order to go and meet his father Jacob, and Joseph's mandate was proclaimed in Egypt, saying, All that do not go to meet Jacob shall die. 8 And on the next day Joseph went forth with all Egypt a great and mighty host, all dressed in garments of fine linen and purple and with instruments of silver and gold and with their instruments of war with them. 9 And they all went to meet Jacob with all sorts of musical instruments, with drums and timbrels, strewing myrrh and aloes all along the road, and they all went after this fashion, and the earth shook at their shouting. 10 And all the women of Egypt went upon the roofs of Egypt and upon the walls to meet Jacob, and upon the head of Joseph was Pharaoh's regal crown, for Pharaoh had sent it unto him to put on at the time of his going to meet his father. 11 And when Joseph came within fifty cubits of his father, he alighted from the chariot and he walked toward his father, and when all the officers of Egypt and her nobles saw that Joseph had gone on foot toward his father, they also alighted and walked on foot toward Jacob. 12 And when Jacob approached the camp of Joseph, Jacob observed the camp that was coming toward him with Joseph, and it gratified him and Jacob was astonished at it. 13 And Jacob said unto Judah, Who is that man whom I see in the camp of Egypt dressed in kingly robes with a very red garment upon him and a royal crown upon his head, who has alighted from his chariot and is coming toward us? and Judah answered his father, saying, He is thy son Joseph the king; and Jacob rejoiced in seeing the glory of his son. 14 And Joseph came nigh unto his father and he bowed to his father, and all the men of the camp bowed to the ground with him before Jacob. 15 And behold Jacob ran and hastened to his son Joseph and fell upon his neck and kissed him, and they wept, and Joseph also embraced his father and kissed him, and they wept and all the people of Egypt wept with them. 16 And Jacob said unto Joseph, Now I will die cheerfully after I have seen thy face, that thou art still living and with glory. 17 And the sons of Jacob and their wives and their children and their servants, and all the household of

Jacob wept exceedingly with Joseph, and they kissed him and wept greatly with him. [18] And Joseph and all his people returned afterward home to Egypt, and Jacob and his sons and all the children of his household came with Joseph to Egypt, and Joseph placed them in the best part of Egypt, in the land of Goshen. [19] And Joseph said unto his father and unto his brethren, I will go up and tell Pharaoh, saying, My brethren and my father's household and all belonging to them have come unto me, and behold they are in the land of Goshen. [20] And Joseph did so and took from his brethren Reuben, Issachar Zebulun and his brother Benjamin and he placed them before Pharaoh. [21] And Joseph spoke unto Pharaoh, saying, My brethren and my father's household and all belonging to them, together with their flocks and cattle have come unto me from the land of Canaan, to sojourn in Egypt; for the famine was sore upon them. [22] And Pharaoh said unto Joseph, Place thy father and brethren in the best part of the land, withhold not from them all that is good, and cause them to eat of the fat of the land. [23] And Joseph answered, saying, Behold I have stationed them in the land of Goshen, for they are shepherds, therefore let them remain in Goshen to feed their flocks apart from the Egyptians. [24] And Pharaoh said unto Joseph, Do with thy brethren all that they shall say unto thee; and the sons of Jacob bowed down to Pharaoh, and they went forth from him in peace, and Joseph afterward brought his father before Pharaoh. [25] And Jacob came and bowed down to Pharaoh, and Jacob blessed Pharaoh, and he then went out; and Jacob and all his sons, and all his household dwelt in the land of Goshen. [26] In the second year, that is in the hundred and thirtieth year of the life of Jacob, Joseph maintained his father and his brethren, and all his father's household, with bread according to their little ones, all the days of the famine; they lacked nothing. [27] And Joseph gave unto them the best part of the whole land; the best of Egypt had they all the days of Joseph; and Joseph also gave unto them and unto the whole of his father's household, clothes and garments year by year; and the sons of Jacob remained securely in Egypt all the days of their brother. [28] And Jacob always ate at Joseph's table, Jacob and his sons did not leave Joseph's table day or night, besides what Jacob's children consumed in their houses. [29] And all Egypt ate bread during the days of the famine from the house of Joseph, for all the Egyptians sold all belonging to them on account of the famine. [30] And Joseph purchased all the lands and fields of Egypt for bread on the account of Pharaoh, and Joseph supplied all Egypt with bread all the days of the famine, and Joseph collected all the silver and gold that came unto him for the corn which they bought throughout the land, and he accumulated much gold and silver, besides an immense quantity of onyx stones, bdellium and valuable garments which they brought unto Joseph from every part of the land when their money was spent. [31] And Joseph took all the silver and gold that came into his hand, about seventy two talents of gold and silver, and also onyx stones and bdellium in great abundance, and Joseph went and concealed them in four parts, and he concealed one part in the wilderness near the Red sea, and one part by the river Perath, and the third and fourth part he concealed in the desert opposite to the wilderness of Persia and Media. [32] And he took part of the gold and silver that was left, and gave it unto all his brothers and unto all his father's household, and unto all the women of his father's household, and the rest he brought to the house of Pharaoh, about twenty talents of gold and silver. [33] And Joseph gave all the gold and silver that was left unto Pharaoh, and Pharaoh placed it in the treasury, and the days of the famine ceased after that in the land, and they sowed and reaped in the whole land, and they obtained their usual quantity year by year; they lacked nothing. [34] And Joseph dwelt securely in Egypt, and the whole land was under his advice, and his father and all his brethren dwelt in the land of Goshen and took possession of it. [35] And Joseph was very aged, advanced in days, and his two sons, Ephraim and Manasseh, remained constantly in the house of Jacob, together with the children of the sons of Jacob their brethren, to learn the ways of the Lord and his law. [36] And Jacob and his sons dwelt in the land of Egypt in the land of Goshen, and they took possession in it, and they were fruitful and multiplied in it.

Jash.56

[1] And Jacob lived in the land of Egypt seventeen years, and the days of Jacob, and the years of his life were a hundred and forty seven years. [2] At that time Jacob was attacked with that illness of which he died and he sent and called for his son Joseph from Egypt, and Joseph his son came from Egypt and Joseph came unto his father. [3] And Jacob said unto Joseph and unto his sons, Behold I die, and the God of your ancestors will visit you, and bring you back to the land, which the Lord sware to give unto you and unto your children after you, now therefore when I am dead, bury me in the cave which is in Machpelah in Hebron in the land of Canaan, near my ancestors. [4] And Jacob made his sons swear to bury him in Machpelah, in Hebron, and his sons swore unto him concerning this thing. [5] And he commanded them, saying, Serve the Lord your God, for he who delivered your fathers will also deliver you from all trouble. [6] And Jacob said, Call all your children unto me, and all the children of Jacob's sons came and sat before him, and Jacob blessed them, and he said unto them, The Lord God of your fathers shall grant you a thousand times as much and bless you, and may he give you the blessing of your father Abraham; and all the children of Jacob's sons went forth on that day after he had blessed them. [7] And on the next day Jacob again called for his sons, and they all assembled and came to him and sat before him, and Jacob on that day blessed his sons before his death, each man did he bless according to his blessing; behold it is written in the book of the law of the Lord appertaining to Israel. [8] And Jacob said unto Judah, I know my son that thou art a mighty man for thy brethren; reign over them, and thy sons shall reign over their sons forever. [9] Only teach thy sons the bow and all the weapons of war, in order that they may fight the battles of their brother who will rule over his enemies. [10] And Jacob again commanded his sons on that day, saying, Behold I shall be this day gathered unto my people; carry me up from Egypt, and bury me in the cave of Machpelah as I have commanded you. [11] Howbeit take heed I pray you that none of your sons carry me, only yourselves, and this is the manner you shall do unto me, when you carry my body to go with it to the land of Canaan to bury me, [12] Judah, Issachar and Zebulun shall carry my bier at the eastern side; Reuben, Simeon and Gad at the south, Ephraim, Manasseh and Benjamin at the west, Dan, Asher and Naphtali at the north. [13] Let not Levi carry with you, for he and his sons will carry the ark of the covenant of the Lord with the Israelites in the camp, neither let Joseph my son carry, for as a king so let his glory be; howbeit, Ephraim and Manasseh shall be in their stead. [14] Thus shall you do unto me when you carry me away; do not neglect any thing of all that I command you; and it shall come to pass when you do this unto me, that the Lord will remember you favorably and your children after you forever. [15] And you my sons, honor each his brother and his relative, and command your children and your children's children after you to serve the Lord God of your ancestors all the days. [16] In order that you may prolong your days in the land, you and your children and your children's children for ever, when you do what is good and upright in the sight of the Lord your God, to go in all his ways. [17] And thou, Joseph my son, forgive I pray thee the prongs of thy brethren and all their misdeeds in the injury that

279

they heaped upon thee, for God intended it for thine and thy children's benefit. [18] And O my son leave not thy brethren to the inhabitants of Egypt, neither hurt their feelings, for behold I consign them to the hand of God and in thy hand to guard them from the Egyptians; and the sons of Jacob answered their father saying, O, our father, all that thou hast commanded us, so will we do; may God only be with us. [19] And Jacob said unto his sons, So may God be with you when you keep all his ways; turn not from his ways either to the right or the left in performing what is good and upright in his sight. [20] For I know that many and grievous troubles will befall you in the latter days in the land, yea your children and children's children, only serve the Lord and he will save you from all trouble. [21] And it shall come to pass when you shall go after God to serve him and will teach your children after you, and your children's children, to know the Lord, then will the Lord raise up unto you and your children a servant from amongst your children, and the Lord will deliver you through his hand from all affliction, and bring you out of Egypt and bring you back to the land of your fathers to inherit it securely. [22] And Jacob ceased commanding his sons, and he drew his feet into the bed, he died and was gathered to his people. [23] And Joseph fell upon his father and he cried out and wept over him and he kissed him, and he called out in a bitter voice, and he said, O my father, my father. [24] And his son's wives and all his household came and fell upon Jacob, and they wept over him, and cried in a very loud voice concerning Jacob. [25] And all the sons of Jacob rose up together, and they tore their garments, and they all put sackcloth upon their loins, and they fell upon their faces, and they cast dust upon their heads toward the heavens. [26] And the thing was told unto Osnath Joseph's wife, and she rose up and put on a sack and she with all the Egyptian women with her came and mourned and wept for Jacob. [27] And also all the people of Egypt who knew Jacob came all on that day when they heard this thing, and all Egypt wept for many days. [28] And also from the land of Canaan did the women come unto Egypt when they heard that Jacob was dead, and they wept for him in Egypt for seventy days. [29] And it came to pass after this that Joseph commanded his servants the doctors to embalm his father with myrrh and frankincense and all manner of incense and perfume, and the doctors embalmed Jacob as Joseph had commanded them. [30] And all the people of Egypt and the elders and all the inhabitants of the land of Goshen wept and mourned over Jacob, and all his sons and the children of his household lamented and mourned over their father Jacob many days. [31] And after the days of his weeping had passed away, at the end of seventy days, Joseph said unto Pharaoh, I will go up and bury my father in the land of Canaan as he made me swear, and then I will return. [32] And Pharaoh sent Joseph, saying, Go up and bury thy father as he said, and as he made thee swear; and Joseph rose up with all his brethren to go to the land of Canaan to bury their father Jacob as he had commanded them. [33] And Pharaoh commanded that it should be proclaimed throughout Egypt, saying, Whoever goeth not up with Joseph and his brethren to the land of Canaan to bury Jacob, shall die. [34] And all Egypt heard of Pharaoh's proclamation, and they all rose up together, and all the servants of Pharaoh, and the elders of his house, and all the elders of the land of Egypt went up with Joseph, and all the officers and nobles of Pharaoh went up as the servants of Joseph, and they went to bury Jacob in the land of Canaan. [35] And the sons of Jacob carried the bier upon which he lay; according to all that their father commanded them, so did his sons unto him. [36] And the bier was of pure gold, and it was inlaid round about with onyx stones and bdellium; and the covering of the bier was gold woven work, joined with threads, and over them were hooks of onyx stones and bdellium. [37] And Joseph placed upon the

280

head of his father Jacob a large golden crown, and he put a golden scepter in his hand, and they surrounded the bier as was the custom of kings during their lives. [38] And all the troops of Egypt went before him in this array, at first all the mighty men of Pharaoh, and the mighty men of Joseph, and after them the rest of the inhabitants of Egypt, and they were all girded with swords and equipped with coats of mail, and the trappings of war were upon them. [39] And all the weepers and mourners went at a distance opposite to the bier, going and weeping and lamenting, and the rest of the people went after the bier. [40] And Joseph and his household went together near the bier barefooted and weeping, and the rest of Joseph's servants went around him; each man had his ornaments upon him, and they were all armed with their weapons of war. [41] And fifty of Jacob's servants went in front of the bier, and they strewed along the road myrrh and aloes, and all manner of perfume, and all the sons of Jacob that carried the bier walked upon the perfumery, and the servants of Jacob went before them strewing the perfume along the road. [42] And Joseph went up with a heavy camp, and they did after this manner every day until they reached the land of Canaan, and they came to the threshing floor of Atad, which was on the other side of Jordan, and they mourned an exceeding great and heavy mourning in that place. [43] And all the kings of Canaan heard of this thing and they all went forth, each man from his house, thirty-one kings of Canaan, and they all came with their men to mourn and weep over Jacob. [44] And all these kings beheld Jacob's bier, and behold Joseph's crown was upon it, and they also put their crowns upon the bier, and encircled it with crowns. [45] And all these kings made in that place a great and heavy mourning with the sons of Jacob and Egypt over Jacob, for all the kings of Canaan knew the valor of Jacob and his sons. [46] And the report reached Esau, saying, Jacob died in Egypt, and his sons and all Egypt are conveying him to the land of Canaan to bury him. [47] And Esau heard this thing, and he was dwelling in mount Seir, and he rose up with his sons and all his people and all his household, a people exceedingly great, and they came to mourn and weep over Jacob. [48] And it came to pass, when Esau came he mourned for his brother Jacob, and all Egypt and all Canaan again rose up and mourned a great mourning with Esau over Jacob in that place [49] And Joseph and his brethren brought their father Jacob from that place, and they went to Hebron to bury Jacob in the cave by his fathers. [50] And they came unto Kireath-arba, to the cave, and as they came Esau stood with his sons against Joseph and his brethren as a hindrance in the cave, saying, Jacob shall not be buried therein, for it belongeth to us and to our father. [51] And Joseph and his brethren heard the words of Esau's sons, and they were exceedingly wroth, and Joseph approached unto Esau, saying, What is this thing which they have spoken? surely my father Jacob bought it from thee for great riches after the death of Isaac, now five and twenty years ago, and also all the land of Canaan he bought from thee and from thy sons, and thy seed after thee. [52] And Jacob bought it for his sons and his seed after him for an inheritance for ever, and why speakest thou these things this day? [53] And Esau answered, saying, Thou speakest falsely and utterest lies, for I sold not anything belonging to me in all this land, as thou sayest, neither did my brother Jacob buy aught belonging to me in this land. [54] And Esau spoke these things in order to deceive Joseph with his words, for Esau knew that Joseph was not present in those days when Esau sold all belonging to him in the land of Canaan to Jacob. [55] And Joseph said unto Esau, Surely my father inserted these things with thee in the record of purchase, and testified the record with witnesses, and behold it is with us in Egypt. [56] And Esau answered, saying unto him, Bring the record, all that thou wilt find in the record, so will we do. [57] And Joseph called unto Naphtali his brother, and he said, Hasten quickly, stay not, and run I pray thee to Egypt and bring all the records; the record of the purchase, the sealed record and the open record, and also all the first records in which all the transactions of the birth-right are written, fetch thou. 58 And thou shalt bring them unto us hither, that we may know from them all the words of Esau and his sons which they spoke this day. 59 And Naphtali hearkened to the voice of Joseph and he hastened and ran to go down to Egypt, and Naphtali was lighter on foot than any of the stags that were upon the wilderness, for he would go upon ears of corn without crushing them. 60 And when Esau saw that Naphtali had gone to fetch the records, he and his sons increased their resistance against the cave, and Esau and all his people rose up against Joseph and his brethren to battle. 61 And all the sons of Jacob and the people of Egypt fought with Esau and his men, and the sons of Esau and his people were smitten before the sons of Jacob, and the sons of Jacob slew of Esau's people forty men. 62 And Chushim the son of Dan, the son of Jacob, was at that time with Jacob's sons, but he was about a hundred cubits distant from the place of battle, for he remained with the children of Jacob's sons by Jacob's bier to guard it. 63 And Chushim was dumb and deaf, still he understood the voice of consternation amongst men. 64 And he asked, saying, Why do you not bury the dead, and what is this great consternation? and they answered him the words of Esau and his sons; and he ran to Esau in the midst of the battle, and he slew Esau with a sword, and he cut off his head, and it sprang to a distance, and Esau fell amongst the people of the battle. 65 And when Chushim did this thing the sons of Jacob prevailed over the sons of Esau, and the sons of Jacob buried their father Jacob by force in the cave, and the sons of Esau beheld it. 66 And Jacob was buried in Hebron, in the cave of Machpelah which Abraham had bought from the sons of Heth for the possession of a burial place, and he was buried in very costly garments. 67 And no king had such honor paid him as Joseph paid unto his father at his death, for he buried him with great honor like unto the burial of kings. 68 And Joseph and his brethren made a mourning of seven days for their father.

Jash.57

1 And it was after this that the sons of Esau waged war with the sons of Jacob, and the sons of Esau fought with the sons of Jacob in Hebron, and Esau was still lying dead, and not buried. 2 And the battle was heavy between them, and the sons of Esau were smitten before the sons of Jacob, and the sons of Jacob slew of the sons of Esau eighty men, and not one died of the people of the sons of Jacob; and the hand of Joseph prevailed over all the people of the sons of Esau, and he took Zepho, the son of Eliphaz, the son of Esau, and fifty of his men captive, and he bound them with chains of iron, and gave them into the hand of his servants to bring them to Egypt. 3 And it came to pass when the sons of Jacob had taken Zepho and his people captive, all those that remained were greatly afraid of their lives from the house of Esau, lest they should also be taken captive, and they all fled with Eliphaz the son of Esau and his people, with Esau's body, and they went on their road to Mount Seir. 4 And they came unto Mount Seir and they buried Esau in Seir, but they had not brought his head with them to Seir, for it was buried in that place where the battle had been in Hebron. 5 And it came to pass when the sons of Esau had fled from before the sons of Jacob, the sons of Jacob pursued them unto the borders of Seir, but they did not slay a single man from amongst them when they pursued them, for Esau's body which they carried with them excited their confusion, so they fled and the sons of Jacob turned back from them and came up to the place where their brethren were in Hebron, and they remained there on that day, and on the next day until they

rested from the battle. 6 And it came to pass on the third day they assembled all the sons of Seir the Horite, and they assembled all the children of the east, a multitude of people like the sand of the sea, and they went and came down to Egypt to fight with Joseph and his brethren, in order to deliver their brethren. 7 And Joseph and all the sons of Jacob heard that the sons of Esau and the children of the east had come upon them to battle in order to deliver their brethren. 8 And Joseph and his brethren and the strong men of Egypt went forth and fought in the city of Rameses, and Joseph and his brethren dealt out a tremendous blow amongst the sons of Esau and the children of the east. 9 And they slew of them six hundred thousand men, and they slew amongst them all the mighty men of the children of Seir the Horite; there were only a few of them left, and they slew also a great many of the children of the east, and of the children of Esau; and Eliphaz the son of Esau, and the children of the east all fled before Joseph and his brethren. 10 And Joseph and his brethren pursued them until they came unto Succoth, and they yet slew of them in Succoth thirty men, and the rest escaped and they fled each to his city. 11 And Joseph and his brethren and the mighty men of Egypt turned back from them with joy and cheerfulness of heart, for they had smitten all their enemies. 12 And Zepho the son of Eliphaz and his men were still slaves in Egypt to the sons of Jacob, and their pains increased. 13 And when the sons of Esau and the sons of Seir returned to their land, the sons of Seir saw that they had all fallen into the hands of the sons of Jacob, and the people of Egypt, on account of the battle of the sons of Esau. 14 And the sons of Seir said unto the sons of Esau, You have seen andtherefore you know that this camp was on your account, and not one mighty man or an adept in war remaineth. 15 Now therefore go forth from our land, go from us to the land of Canaan to the land of the dwelling of your fathers; wherefore shall your children inherit the effects of our children in latter days? 16 And the children of Esau would not listen to the children of Seir, and the children of Seir considered to make war with them. 17 And the children of Esau sent secretly to Angeas king of Africa, the same is Dinhabah, saying, 18 Send unto us some of thy men and let them come unto us, and we will fight together with the children of Seir the Horite, for they have resolved to fight with us to drive us away from the land. 19 And Angeas king of Dinhabah did so, for he was in those days friendly to the children of Esau, and Angeas sent five hundred valiant infantry to the children of Esau, and eight hundred cavalry. 20 And the children of Seir sent unto the children of the east and unto the children of Midian, saying, You have seen what the children of Esau have done unto us, upon whose account we are almost all destroyed, in their battle with the sons of Jacob. 21 Now therefore come unto us and assist us, and we will fight them together, and we will drive them from the land and be avenged of the cause of our brethren who died for their sakes in their battle with their brethren the sons of Jacob. 22 And all the children of the east listened to the children of Seir, and they came unto them about eight hundred men with drawn swords, and the children of Esau fought with the children of Seir at that time in the wilderness of Paran. 23 And the children of Seir prevailed then over the sons of Esau, and the children of Seir slew on that day of the children of Esau in that battle about two hundred men of the people of Angeas king of Dinhabah. 24 And on the second day the children of Esau came again to fight a second time with the children of Seir, and the battle was sore upon the children of Esau this second time, and it troubled them greatly on account of the children of Seir. 25 And when the children of Esau saw that the children of Seir were more powerful than they were, some men of the children of Esau turned and assisted the children of Seir their enemies. 26 And there fell yet of the people of the children of Esau in the second battle fifty-eight men of the people at Angeas king of Dinhabah. 27 And on the third day the children of Esau heard that some of their brethren had turned from them to fight against them in the second battle; and the children of Esau mourned when they heard this thing. 28 And they said, What shall we do unto our brethren who turned from us to assist the children of Seir our enemies? and the children of Esau again sent to Angeas king of Dinhabah, saying, 29 Send unto us again other men that with them we may fight with the children of Seir, for they have already twice been heavier than we were. 30 And Angeas again sent to the children of Esau about six hundred valiant men, and they came to assist the children of Esau. 31 And in ten days' time the children of Esau again waged war with the children of Seir in the wilderness of Paran, and the battle was very severe upon the children of Seir, and the children of Esau prevailed at this time over the children of Seir, and the children of Seir were smitten before the children of Esau, and the children of Esau slew from them about two thousand men. 32 And all the mighty men of the children of Seir died in this battle, and there only remained their young children that were left in their cities. 33 And all Midian and the children of the east betook themselves to flight from the battle, and they left the children of Seir and fled when they saw that the battle was severe upon them, and the children of Esau pursued all the children of the east until they reached their land. 34 And the children of Esau slew yet of them about two hundred and fifty men and from the people of the children of Esau there fell in that battle about thirty men, but this evil came upon them through their brethren turning from them to assist the children of Seir the Horite, and the children of Esau again heard of the evil doings of their brethren, and they again mourned on account of this thing. 35 And it came to pass after the battle, the children of Esau turned back and came home unto Seir, and the children of Esau slew those who had remained in the land of the children of Seir; they slew also their wives and little ones, they left not a soul alive except fifty young lads and damsels whom they suffered to live, and the children of Esau did not put them to death, and the lads became their slaves, and the damsels they took for wives. 36 And the children of Esau dwelt in Seir in the place of the children of Seir, and they inherited their land and took possession of it. 37 And the children of Esau took all belonging in the land to the children of Seir, also their flocks, their bullocks and their goods, and all belonging to the children of Seir, did the children of Esau take, and the children of Esau dwelt in Seir in the place of the children of Seir unto this day, and the children of Esau divided the land into divisions to the five sons of Esau, according to their families. 38 And it came to pass in those days, that the children of Esau resolved to crown a king over them in the land of which they became possessed. And they said to each other, Not so, for he shall reign over us in our land, and we shall be under his counsel and he shall fight our battles, against our enemies, and they did so. 39 And all the children of Esau swore, saying, That none of their brethren should ever reign over them, but a strange man who is not of their brethren, for the souls of all the children of Esau were embittered every man against his son, brother and friend, on account of the evil they sustained from their brethren when they fought with the children of Seir. 40 Therefore the sons of Esau swore, saying, From that day forward they would not choose a king from their brethren, but one from a strange land unto this day. 41 And there was a man there from the people of Angeas king of Dinhabah; his name was Bela the son of Beor, who was a very valiant man, beautiful and comely and wise in all wisdom, and a man of sense and counsel; and there was none of the people of Angeas like unto him. 42 And all the children of Esau took him and anointed him and they crowned him

282

for a king, and they bowed down to him, and they said unto him, May the king live, may the king live. 43 And they spread out the sheet, and they brought him each man earrings of gold and silver or rings or bracelets, and they made him very rich in silver and in gold, in onyx stones and bdellium, and they made him a royal throne, and they placed a regal crown upon his head, and they built a palace for him and he dwelt therein, and he became king over all the children of Esau. 44 And the people of Angeas took their hire for their battle from the children of Esau, and they went and returned at that time to their master in Dinhabah. 45 And Bela reigned over the children of Esau thirty years, and the children of Esau dwelt in the land instead of the children of Seir, and they dwelt securely in their stead unto this day.

Jash.58

1 And it came to pass in the thirty-second year of the Israelites going down to Egypt, that is in the seventy-first year of the life of Joseph, in that year died Pharaoh king of Egypt, and Magron his son reigned in his stead. 2 And Pharaoh commanded Joseph before his death to be a father to his son, Magron, and that Magron should be under the care of Joseph and under his counsel. 3 And all Egypt consented to this thing that Joseph should be king over them, for all the Egyptians loved Joseph as of heretofore, only Magron the son of Pharaoh sat upon, his father's throne, and he became king in those days in his father's stead. 4 Magron was forty-one years old when he began to reign, and forty years he reigned in Egypt, and all Egypt called his name Pharaoh after the name of his father, as it was their custom to do in Egypt to every king that reigned over them. 5 And it came to pass when Pharaoh reigned in his father's stead, he placed the laws of Egypt and all the affairs of government in the hand of Joseph, as his father had commanded him. 6 And Joseph became king over Egypt, for he superintended over all Egypt, and all Egypt was under his care and under his counsel, for all Egypt inclined to Joseph after the death of Pharaoh, and they loved him exceedingly to reign over them. 7 But there were some people amongst them, who did not like him, saying, No stranger shall reign over us; still the whole government of Egypt devolved in those days upon Joseph, after the death of Pharaoh, he being the regulator, doing as he liked throughout the land without any one interfering. 8 And all Egypt was under the care of Joseph, and Joseph made war with all his surrounding enemies, and he subdued them; also all the land and all the Philistines, unto the borders of Canaan, did Joseph subdue, and they were all under his power and they gave a yearly tax unto Joseph. 9 And Pharaoh king of Egypt sat upon his throne in his father's stead, but he was under the control and counsel of Joseph, as he was at first under the control of his father. 10 Neither did he reign but in the land of Egypt only, under the counsel of Joseph, but Joseph reigned over the whole country at that time, from Egypt unto the great river Perath. 11 And Joseph was successful in all his ways, and the Lord was with him, and the Lord gave Joseph additional wisdom, and honor, and glory, and love toward him in the hearts of the Egyptians and throughout the land, and Joseph reigned over the whole country forty years. 12 And all the countries of the Philistines and Canaan and Zidon, and on the other side of Jordan, brought presents unto Joseph all his days, and the whole country was in the hand of Joseph, and they brought unto him a yearly tribute as it was regulated, for Joseph had fought against all his surrounding enemies and subdued them, and the whole country was in the hand of Joseph, and Joseph sat securely upon his throne in Egypt. 13 And also all his brethren the sons of Jacob dwelt securely in the land, all the days of Joseph, and they were fruitful and multiplied exceedingly in the land, and they served the Lord all their days, as their father Jacob had commanded them. 14 And it came to pass at the end of

many days and years, when the children of Esau were dwelling quietly in their land with Bela their king, that the children of Esau were fruitful and multiplied in the land, and they resolved to go and fight with the sons of Jacob and all Egypt, and to deliver their brother Zepho, the son of Eliphaz, and his men, for they were yet in those days slaves to Joseph. 15 And the children of Esau sent unto all the children of the east, and they made peace with them, and all the children of the east came unto them to go with the children of Esau to Egypt to battle. 16 And there came also unto them of the people of Angeas, king of Dinhabah, and they also sent unto the children of Ishmael and they also came unto them. 17 And all this people assembled and came unto Seir to assist the children of Esau in their battle, and this camp was very large and heavy with people, numerous as the sand of the sea, about eight hundred thousand men, infantry and cavalry, and all these troops went down to Egypt to fight with the sons of Jacob, and they encamped by Rameses. 18 And Joseph went forth with his brethren with the mighty men of Egypt, about six hundred men, and they fought with them in the land of Rameses; and the sons of Jacob at that time again fought with the children of Esau, in the fiftieth year of the sons of Jacob going down to Egypt, that is the thirtieth year of the reign of Bela over the children of Esau in Seir. 19 And the Lord gave all the mighty men of Esau and the children of the east into the hand of Joseph and his brethren, and the people of the children of Esau and the children of the east were smitten before Joseph. 20 And of the people of Esau and the children of the east that were slain, there fell before the sons of Jacob about two hundred thousand men, and their king Bela the son of Beor fell with them in the battle, and when the children of Esau saw that their king had fallen in battle and was dead, their hands became weak in the combat. 21 And Joseph and his brethren and all Egypt were still smiting the people of the house of Esau, and all Esau's people were afraid of the sons of Jacob and fled from before them. 22 And Joseph and his brethren and all Egypt pursued them a day's journey, and they slew yet from them about three hundred men, continuing to smite them in the road; and they afterward turned back from them. 23 And Joseph and all his brethren returned to Egypt, not one man was missing from them, but of the Egyptians there fell twelve men. 24 And when Joseph returned to Egypt he ordered Zepho and his men to be additionally bound, and they bound them in irons and they increased their grief. 25 And all the people of the children of Esau, and the children of the east, returned in shame each unto his city, for all the mighty men that were with them had fallen in battle. 26 And when the children of Esau saw that their king had died in battle they hastened and took a man from the people of the children of the east; his name was Jobab the son of Zarach, from the land of Botzrah, and they caused him to reign over them instead of Bela their king. 27 And Jobab sat upon the throne of Bela as king in his stead, and Jobab reigned in Edom over all the children of Esau ten years, and the children of Esau went no more to fight with the sons of Jacob from that day forward, for the sons of Esau knew the valor of the sons of Jacob, and they were greatly afraid of them. 28 But from that day forward the children of Esau hated the sons of Jacob, and the hatred and enmity were very strong between them all the days, unto this day. 29 And it came to pass after this, at the end of ten years, Jobab, the son of Zarach, from Botzrah, died, and the children of Esau took a man whose name was Chusham, from the land of Teman, and they made him king over them instead of Jobab, and Chusham reigned in Edom over all the children of Esau for twenty years. 30 And Joseph, king of Egypt, and his brethren, and all the children of Israel dwelt securely in Egypt in those days, together with all the children of Joseph and his brethren, having no hindrance or evil accident and

the land of Egypt was at that time at rest from war in the days of Joseph and his brethren.

Jash.59

1 And these are the names of the sons of Israel who dwelt in Egypt, who had come with Jacob, all the sons of Jacob came unto Egypt, every man with his household. 2 The children of Leah were Reuben, Simeon, Levi, Judah, Issachar and Zebulun, and their sister Dinah. 3 And the sons of Rachel were Joseph and Benjamin. 4 And the sons of Zilpah, the handmaid of Leah, were Gad and Asher. 5 And the sons of Bilhah, the handmaid of Rachel, were Dan and Naphtali. 6 And these were their offspring that were born unto them in the land of Canaan, before they came to Egypt with their father Jacob. 7 The sons of Reuben were Chanoch, Pallu, Chetzron and Carmi. 8 And the sons of Simeon were Jemuel, Jamin, Ohad, Jachin, Zochar and Saul, the son of the Canaanitish woman. 9 And the children of Levi were Gershon, Kehath and Merari, and their sister Jochebed, who was born unto them in their going down to Egypt. 10 And the sons of Judah were Er, Onan, Shelah, Perez and Zarach. 11 And Er and Onan died in the land of Canaan; and the sons of Perez were Chezron and Chamul. 12 And the sons of Issachar were Tola, Puvah, Job and Shomron. 13 And the sons of Zebulun were Sered, Elon and Jachleel, and the son of Dan was Chushim. 14 And the sons of Naphtali were Jachzeel, Guni, Jetzer and Shilam. 15 And the sons of Gad were Ziphion, Chaggi, Shuni, Ezbon, Eri, Arodi and Areli. 16 And the children of Asher were Jimnah, Jishvah, Jishvi, Beriah and their sister Serach; and the sons of Beriah were Cheber and Malchiel. 17 And the sons of Benjamin were Bela, Becher, Ashbel, Gera, Naaman, Achi, Rosh, Mupim, Chupim and Ord. 18 And the sons of Joseph, that were born unto him in Egypt, were Manasseh and Ephraim. 19 And all the souls that went forth from the loins of Jacob, were seventy souls; these are they who came with Jacob their father unto Egypt to dwell there: and Joseph and all his brethren dwelt securely in Egypt, and they ate of the best of Egypt all the days of the life of Joseph. 20 And Joseph lived in the land of Egypt ninety-three years, and Joseph reigned over all Egypt eighty years. 21 And when the days of Joseph drew nigh that he should die, he sent and called for his brethren and all his father's household, and they all came together and sat before him. 22 And Joseph said unto his brethren and unto the whole of his father's household, Behold I die, and God will surely visit you and bring you up from this land to the land which he swore to your fathers to give unto them. 23 And it shall be when God shall visit you to bring you up from here to the land of your fathers, then bring up my bones with you from here. 24 And Joseph made the sons of Israel to swear for their seed after them, saying, God will surely visit you and you shall bring up my bones with you from here. 25 And it came to pass after this that Joseph died in that year, the seventy-first year of the Israelites going down to Egypt. 26 And Joseph was one hundred and ten years old when he died in the land of Egypt, and all his brethren and all his servants rose up and they embalmed Joseph, as was their custom, and his brethren and all Egypt mourned over him for seventy days. 27 And they put Joseph in a coffin filled with spices and all sorts of perfume, and they buried him by the side of the river, that is Sihor, and his sons and all his brethren, and the whole of his father's household made a seven day's mourning for him. 28 And it came to pass after the death of Joseph, all the Egyptians began in those days to rule over the children of Israel, and Pharaoh, king of Egypt, who reigned in his father's stead, took all the laws of Egypt and conducted the whole government of Egypt under his counsel, and he reigned securely over his people.

Jash.60

1 And when the year came round, being the seventy-second year from the Israelites going down to Egypt, after the death of Joseph, Zepho, the son of Eliphaz, the son of Esau, fled from Egypt, he and his men, and they went away. 2 And he came to Africa, which is Dinhabah, to Angeas king of Africa, and Angeas received them with great honor, and he made Zepho the captain of his host. 3 And Zepho found favor in the sight of Angeas and in the sight of his people, and Zepho was captain of the host to Angeas king of Africa for many days. 4 And Zepho enticed Angeas king of Africa to collect all his army to go and fight with the Egyptians, and with the sons of Jacob, and to avenge of them the cause of his brethren. 5 But Angeas would not listen to Zepho to do this thing, for Angeas knew the strength of the sons of Jacob, and what they had done to his army in their warfare with the children of Esau. 6 And Zepho was in those days very great in the sight of Angeas and in the sight of all his people, and he continually enticed them to make war against Egypt, but they would not. 7 And it came to pass in those days there was in the land of Chittim a man in the city of Puzimna, whose name was Uzu, and he became degenerately deified by the children of Chittim, and the man died and had no son, only one daughter whose name was Jania. 8 And the damsel was exceedingly beautiful, comely and intelligent, there was none seen like unto her for beauty and wisdom throughout the land. 9 And the people of Angeas king of Africa saw her and they came and praised her unto him, and Angeas sent to the children of Chittim, and he requested to take her unto himself for a wife, and the people of Chittim consented to give her unto him for a wife. 10 And when the messengers of Angeas were going forth from the land of Chittim to take their journey, behold the messengers of Turnus king of Bibentu came unto Chittim, for Turnus king of Bibentu also sent his messengers to request Jania for him, to take unto himself for a wife, for all his men had also praised her to him, therefore he sent all his servants unto her. 11 And the servants of Turnus came to Chittim, and they asked for Jania, to be taken unto Turnus their king for a wife. 12 And the people of Chittim said unto them, We cannot give her, because Angeas king of Africa desired her to take her unto him for a wife before you came, and that we should give her unto him, and now therefore we cannot do this thing to deprive Angeas of the damsel in order to give her unto Turnus. 13 For we are greatly afraid of Angeas lest he come in battle against us and destroy us, and Turnus your master will not be able to deliver us from his hand. 14 And when the messengers of Turnus heard all the words of the children of Chittim, they turned back to their master and told him all the words of the children of Chittim. 15 And the children of Chittim sent a memorial to Angeas, saying, Behold Turnus has sent for Jania to take her unto him for a wife, and thus have we answered him; and we heard that he has collected his whole army to go to war against thee, and he intends to pass by the road of Sardunia to fight against thy brother Lucus, and after that he will come to fight against thee. 16 And Angeas heard the words of the children of Chittim which they sent to him in the record, and his anger was kindled and he rose up and assembled his whole army and came through the islands of the sea, the road to Sardunia, unto his brother Lucus king of Sardunia. 17 And Niblos, the son of Lucus, heard that his uncle Angeas was coming, and he went out to meet him with a heavy army, and he kissed him and embraced him, and Niblos said unto Angeas, When thou askest my father after his welfare, when I shall go with thee to fight with Turnus, ask of him to make me captain of his host, and Angeas did so, and he came unto his brother and his brother came to meet him, and he asked him after his welfare. 18 And Angeas asked his brother Lucus after his welfare, and to make his son Niblos captain of his host, and Lucus did so, and Angeas and his brother Lucus rose up

284

and they went toward Turnus to battle, and there was with them a great army and a heavy people. 19 And he came in ships, and they came into the province of Ashtorash, and behold Turnus came toward them, for he went forth to Sardunia, and intended to destroy it and afterward to pass on from there to Angeas to fight with him. 20 And Angeas and Lucus his brother met Turnus in the valley of Canopia, and the battle was strong and mighty between them in that place. 21 And the battle was severe upon Lucus king of Sardunia, and all his army fell, and Niblos his son fell also in that battle. 22 And his uncle Angeas commanded his servants and they made a golden coffin for Niblos and they put him into it, and Angeas again waged battle toward Turnus, and Angeas was stronger than he, and he slew him, and he smote all his people with the edge of the sword, and Angeas avenged the cause of Niblos his brother's son and the cause of the army of his brother Lucus. 23 And when Turnus died, the hands of those that survived the battle became weak, and they fled from before Angeas and Lucus his brother. 24 And Angeas and his brother Lucus pursued them unto the highroad, which is between Alphanu and Romah, and they slew the whole army of Turnus with the edge of the sword. 25 And Lucus king of Sardunia commanded his servants that they should make a coffin of brass, and that they should place therein the body of his son Niblos, and they buried him in that place. 26 And they built upon it a high tower there upon the highroad, and they called its name after the name of Niblos unto this day, and they also buried Turnus king of Bibentu there in that place with Niblos. 27 And behold upon the highroad between Alphanu and Romah the grave of Niblos is on one side and the grave of Turnus on the other, and a pavement between them unto this day. 28 And when Niblos was buried, Lucus his father returned with his army to his land Sardunia, and Angeas his brother king of Africa went with his people unto the city of Bibentu, that is the city of Turnus. 29 And the inhabitants of Bibentu heard of his fame and they were greatly afraid of him, and they went forth to meet him with weeping and supplication, and the inhabitants of Bibentu entreated of Angeas not to slay them nor destroy their city; and he did so, for Bibentu was in those days reckoned as one of the cities of the children of Chittim; therefore he did not destroy the city. 30 But from that day forward the troops of the king of Africa would go to Chittim to spoil and plunder it, and whenever they went, Zepho the captain of the host of Angeas would go with them. 31 And it was after this that Angeas turned with his army and they came to the city of Puzimna, and Angeas took thence Jania the daughter of Uzu for a wife and brought her unto his city unto Africa.

Jash.61

1 And it came to pass at that time Pharaoh king of Egypt commanded all his people to make for him a strong palace in Egypt. 2 And he also commanded the sons of Jacob to assist the Egyptians in the building, and the Egyptians made a beautiful and elegant palace for a royal habitation, and he dwelt therein and he renewed his government and he reigned securely. 3 And Zebulun the son of Jacob died in that year, that is the seventy-second year of the going down of the Israelites to Egypt, and Zebulun died a hundred and fourteen years old, and was put into a coffin and given into the hands of his children. 4 And in the seventy-fifth year died his brother Simeon, he was a hundred and twenty years old at his death, and he was also put into a coffin and given into the hands of his children. 5 And Zepho the son of Eliphaz the son of Esau, captain of the host to Angeas king of Dinhabah, was still daily enticing Angeas to prepare for battle to fight with the sons of Jacob in Egypt, and Angeas was unwilling to do this thing, for his servants had related to him all the might of the sons of Jacob, what they had done unto them in their battle with the children of Esau. 6 And Zepho

was in those days daily enticing Angeas to fight with the sons of Jacob in those days. 7 And after some time Angeas hearkened to the words of Zepho and consented to him to fight with the sons of Jacob in Egypt, and Angeas got all his people in order, a people numerous as the sand which is upon the sea shore, and he formed his resolution to go to Egypt to battle. 8 And amongst the servants of Angeas was a youth fifteen years old, Balaam the son of Beor was his name and the youth was very wise and understood the art of witchcraft. 9 And Angeas said unto Balaam, Conjure for us, I pray thee, with the witchcraft, that we may know who will prevail in this battle to which we are now proceeding. 10 And Balaam ordered that they should bring him wax, and he made thereof the likeness of chariots and horsemen representing the army of Angeas and the army of Egypt, and he put them in the cunningly prepared waters that he had for that purpose, and he took in his hand the boughs of myrtle trees, and he exercised his cunning, and he joined them over the water, and there appeared unto him in the water the resembling images of the hosts of Angeas falling before the resembling images of the Egyptians and the sons of Jacob. 11 And Balaam told this thing to Angeas, and Angeas despaired and did not arm himself to go down to Egypt to battle, and he remained in his city. 12 And when Zepho the son of Eliphaz saw that Angeas despaired of going forth to battle with the Egyptians, Zepho fled from Angeas from Africa, and he went and came unto Chittim. 13 And all the people of Chittim received him with great honor, and they hired him to fight their battles all the days, and Zepho became exceedingly rich in those days, and the troops of the king of Africa still spread themselves in those days, and the children of Chittim assembled and went to Mount Cuptizia on account of the troops of Angeas king of Africa, who were advancing upon them. 14 And it was one day that Zepho lost a young heifer, and he went to seek it, and he heard it lowing round about the mountain. 15 And Zepho went and he saw and behold there was a large cave at the bottom of the mountain, and there was a great stone there at the entrance of the cave, and Zepho split the stone and he came into the cave and he looked and behold, a large animal was devouring the ox; from the middle upward it resembled a man, and from the middle downward it resembled an animal, and Zepho rose up against the animal and slew it with his swords. 16 And the inhabitants of Chittim heard of this thing, and they rejoiced exceedingly, and they said, What shall we do unto this man who has slain this animal that devoured our cattle? 17 And they all assembled to consecrate one day in the year to him, and they called the name thereof Zepho after his name, and they brought unto him drink offerings year after year on that day, and they brought unto him gifts. 18 At that time Jania the daughter of Uzu wife of king Angeas became ill, and her illness was heavily felt by Angeas and his officers, and Angeas said unto his wise men, What shall I do to Jania and how shall I heal her from her illness? And his wise men said unto him, Because the air of our country is not like the air of the land of Chittim, and our water is not like their water, therefore from this has the queen become ill. 19 For through the change of air and water she became ill, and also because in her country she drank only the water which came from Purmah, which her ancestors had brought up with bridges. 20 And Angeas commanded his servants, and they brought unto him in vessels of the waters of Purmah belonging to Chittim, and they weighed those waters with all the waters of the land of Africa, and they found those waters lighter than the waters of Africa. 21 And Angeas saw this thing, and he commanded all his officers to assemble the hewers of stone in thousands and tens of thousands, and they hewed stone without number, and the builders came and they built an exceedingly strong bridge, and they conveyed the spring of water from the land

285

of Chittim unto Africa, and those waters were for Jania the queen and for all her concerns, to drink from and to bake, wash and bathe therewith, and also to water therewith all seed from which food can be obtained, and all fruit of the ground. 22 And the king commanded that they should bring of the soil of Chittim in large ships, and they also brought stones to build therewith, and the builders built palaces for Jania the queen, and the queen became healed of her illness. 23 And at the revolution of the year the troops of Africa continued coming to the land of Chittim to plunder as usual, and Zepho son of Eliphaz heard their report, and he gave orders concerning them and he fought with them, and they fled before him, and he delivered the land of Chittim from them. 24 And the children of Chittim saw the valor of Zepho, and the children of Chittim resolved and they made Zepho king over them, and he became king over them, and whilst he reigned they went to subdue the children of Tubal, and all the surrounding islands. 25 And their king Zepho went at their head and they made war with Tubal and the islands, and they subdued them, and when they returned from the battle they renewed his government for him, and they built for him a very large palace for his royal habitation and seat, and they made a large throne for him, and Zepho reigned over the whole land of Chittim and over the land of Italia fifty years.

Jash.62

1 In that year, being the seventy-ninth year of the Israelites going down to Egypt, died Reuben the son of Jacob, in the land of Egypt; Reuben was a hundred and twenty-five years old when he died, and they put him into a coffin, and he was given into the hands of his children. 2 And in the eightieth year died his brother Dan; he was a hundred and twenty years at his death, and he was also put into a coffin and given into the hands of his children. 3 And in that year died Chusham king of Edom, and after him reigned Hadad the son of Bedad, for thirty-five years; and in the eighty-first year died Issachar the son of Jacob, in Egypt, and Issachar was a hundred and twenty-two years old at his death, and he was put into a coffin in Egypt, and given into the hands of his children. 4 And in the eighty-second year died Asher his brother, he was a hundred and twenty-three years old at his death, and he was placed in a coffin in Egypt, and given into the hands of his children. 5 And in the eighty-third year died Gad, he was a hundred and twenty-five years old at his death, and he was put into a coffin in Egypt, and given into the hands of his children. 6 And it came to pass in the eighty-fourth year, that is the fiftieth year of the reign of Hadad, son of Bedad, king of Edom, that Hadad assembled all the children of Esau, and he got his whole army in readiness, about four hundred thousand men, and he directed his way to the land of Moab, and he went to fight with Moab and to make them tributary to him. 7 And the children of Moab heard this thing, and they were very much afraid, and they sent to the children of Midian to assist them in fighting with Hadad, son of Bedad, king of Edom. 8 And Hadad came unto the land of Moab, and Moab and the children of Midian went out to meet him, and they placed themselves in battle array against him in the field of Moab. 9 And Hadad fought with Moab, and there fell of the children of Moab and the children of Midian many slain ones, about two hundred thousand men. 10 And the battle was very severe upon Moab, and when the children of Moab saw that the battle was sore upon them, they weakened their hands and turned their backs, and left the children of Midian to carry on the battle. 11 And the children of Midian knew not the intentions of Moab, but they strengthened themselves in battle and fought with Hadad and all his host, and all Midian fell before him. 12 And Hadad smote all Midian with a heavy smiting, and he slew them with the edge of the sword, he left none remaining of those who came to assist Moab. 13 And when all the

children of Midian had perished in battle, and the children at Moab had escaped, Hadad made all Moab at that time tributary to him, and they became under his hand, and they gave a yearly tax as it was ordered, and Hadad turned and went back to his land. 14 And at the revolution of the year, when the rest of the people of Midian that were in the land heard that all their brethren had fallen in battle with Hadad for the sake of Moab, because the children of Moab had turned their backs in battle and left Midian to fight, then five of the princes of Midian resolved with the rest of their brethren who remained in their land, to fight with Moab to avenge the cause of their brethren. 15 And the children of Midian sent to all their brethren the children of the east, and all their brethren, all the children of Keturah came to assist Midian to fight with Moab. 16 And the children of Moab heard this thing, and they were greatly afraid that all the children of the east had assembled together against them for battle, and they the children of Moab sent a memorial to the land of Edom to Hadad the son of Bedad, saying, 17 Come now unto us and assist us and we will smite Midian, for they all assembled together and have come against us with all their brethren the children of the east to battle, to avenge the cause of Midian that fell in battle. 18 And Hadad, son of Bedad, king of Edom, went forth with his whole army and went to the land of Moab to fight with Midian, and Midian and the children of the east fought with Moab in the field of Moab, and the battle was very fierce between them. 19 And Hadad smote all the children of Midian and the children of the east with the edge of the sword, and Hadad at that time delivered Moab from the hand of Midian, and those that remained of Midian and of the children of the east fled before Hadad and his army, and Hadad pursued them to their land, and smote them with a very heavy slaughter, and the slain fell in the road. 20 And Hadad delivered Moab from the hand of Midian, for all the children of Midian had fallen by the edge of the sword, and Hadad turned and went back to his land. 21 And from that day forth, the children of Midian hated the children of Moab, because they had fallen in battle for their sake, and there was a great and mighty enmity between them all the days. 22 And all that were found of Midian in the road of the land of Moab perished by the sword of Moab, and all that were found of Moab in the road of the land of Midian, perished by the sword of Midian; thus did Midian unto Moab and Moab unto Midian for many days. 23 And it came to pass at that time that Judah the son of Jacob died in Egypt, in the eighty-sixth year of Jacob's going down to Egypt, and Judah was a hundred and twenty-nine years old at his death, and they embalmed him and put him into a coffin, and he was given into the hands of his children. 24 And in the eighty-ninth year died Naphtali, he was a hundred and thirty-two years old, and he was put into a coffin and given into the hands of his children. 25 And it came to pass in the ninety-first year of the Israelites going down to Egypt, that is in the thirtieth year of the reign of Zepho the son of Eliphaz, the son of Esau, over the children of Chittim, the children of Africa came upon the children of Chittim to plunder them as usual, but they had not come upon them for these thirteen years. 26 And they came to them in that year, and Zepho the son of Eliphaz went out to them with some of his men and smote them desperately, and the troops of Africa fled from before Zepho and the slain fell before him, and Zepho and his men pursued them, going on and smiting them until they were near unto Africa. 27 And Angeas king of Africa heard the thing which Zepho had done, and it vexed him exceedingly, and Angeas was afraid of Zepho all the days.

Jash.63

1 And in the ninety-third year died Levi, the son of Jacob, in Egypt, and Levi was a hundred and thirty-seven years old when he died,

and they put him into a coffin and he was given into the hands of his children. 2 And it came to pass after the death of Levi, when all Egypt saw that the sons of Jacob the brethren of Joseph were dead, all the Egyptians began to afflict the children of Jacob, and to embitter their lives from that day unto the day of their going forth from Egypt, and they took from their hands all the vineyards and fields which Joseph had given unto them, and all the elegant houses in which the people of Israel lived, and all the fat of Egypt, the Egyptians took all from the sons of Jacob in those days. 3 And the hand of all Egypt became more grievous in those days against the children of Israel, and the Egyptians injured the Israelites until the children of Israel were wearied of their lives on account of the Egyptians. 4 And it came to pass in those days, in the hundred and second year of Israel's going down to Egypt, that Pharaoh king of Egypt died, and Melol his son reigned in his stead, and all the mighty men of Egypt and all that generation which knew Joseph and his brethren died in those days. 5 And another generation rose up in their stead, which had not known the sons of Jacob and all the good which they had done to them, and all their might in Egypt. 6 Therefore all Egypt began from that day forth to embitter the lives of the sons of Jacob, and to afflict them with all manner of hard labor, because they had not known their ancestors who had delivered them in the days of the famine. 7 And this was also from the Lord, for the children of Israel, to benefit them in their latter days, in order that all the children of Israel might know the Lord their God. 8 And in order to know the signs and mighty wonders which the Lord would do in Egypt on account of his people Israel, in order that the children of Israel might fear the Lord God of their ancestors, and walk in all his ways, they and their seed after them all the days. 9 Melol was twenty years old when he began to reign, and he reigned ninety-four years, and all Egypt called his name Pharaoh after the name of his father, as it was their custom to do to every king who reigned over them in Egypt. 10 At that time all the troops of Angeas king of Africa went forth to spread along the land of Chittim as usual for plunder. 11 And Zepho the son of Eliphaz the son of Esau heard their report, and he went forth to meet them with his army, and he fought them there in the road. 12 And Zepho smote the troops of the king of Africa with the edge of the sword, and left none remaining of them, and not even one returned to his master in Africa. 13 And Angeas heard of this which Zepho the son of Eliphaz had done to all his troops, that he had destroyed them, and Angeas assembled all his troops, all the men of the land of Africa, a people numerous like the sand by the sea shore. 14 And Angeas sent to Lucus his brother, saying, Come to me with all thy men and help me to smite Zepho and all the children of Chittim who have destroyed my men, and Lucus came with his whole army, a very great force, to assist Angeas his brother to fight with Zepho and the children of Chittim. 15 And Zepho and the children of Chittim heard this thing, and they were greatly afraid and a great terror fell upon their hearts. 16 And Zepho also sent a letter to the land of Edom to Hadad the son of Bedad king of Edom and to all the children of Esau, saying, 17 I have heard that Angeas king of Africa is coming to us with his brother for battle against us, and we are greatly afraid of him, for his army is very great, particularly as he comes against us with his brother and his army likewise. 18 Now therefore come you also up with me and help me, and we will fight together against Angeas and his brother Lucus, and you will save us out of their hands, but if not, know ye that we shall all die. 19 And the children of Esau sent a letter to the children of Chittim and to Zepho their king, saying, We cannot fight against Angeas and his people for a covenant of peace has been between us these many years, from the days of Bela the first king, and from the days of Joseph the son of

Jacob king of Egypt, with whom we fought on the other side of Jordan when he buried his father. 20 And when Zepho heard the words of his brethren the children of Esau he refrained from them, and Zepho was greatly afraid of Angeas. 21 And Angeas and Lucus his brother arrayed all their forces, about eight hundred thousand men, against the children of Chittim. 22 And all the children of Chittim said unto Zepho, Pray for us to the God of thy ancestors, peradventure he may deliver us from the hand of Angeas and his army, for we have heard that he is a great God and that he delivers all who trust in him. 23 And Zepho heard their words, and Zepho sought the Lord and he said, 24 0 Lord God of Abraham and Isaac my ancestors, this day I know that thou art a true God, and all the gods of the nations are vain and useless. 25 Remember now this day unto me thy covenant with Abraham our father, which our ancestors related unto us, and do graciously with me this day for the sake of Abraham and Isaac our fathers, and save me and the children of Chittim from the hand of the king of Africa who comes against us for battle. 26 And the Lord hearkened to the voice of Zepho, and he had regard for him on account of Abraham and Isaac, and the Lord delivered Zepho and the children of Chittim from the hand of Angeas and his people. 27 And Zepho fought Angeas king of Africa and all his people on that day, and the Lord gave all the people of Angeas into the hands of the children of Chittim. 28 And the battle was severe upon Angeas, and Zepho smote all the men of Angeas and Lucus his brother, with the edge of the sword, and there fell from them unto the evening of that day about four hundred thousand men. 29 And when Angeas saw that all his men perished, he sent a letter to all the inhabitants of Africa to come to him, to assist him in the battle, and he wrote in the letter, saying, All who are found in Africa let them come unto me from ten years old and upward; let them all come unto me, and behold if he comes not he shall die, and all that he has, with his whole household, the king will take. 30 And all the rest of the inhabitants of Africa were terrified at the words of Angeas, and there went out of the city about three hundred thousand men and boys, from ten years upward, and they came to Angeas. 31 And at the end of ten days Angeas renewed the battle against Zepho and the children of Chittim, and the battle was very great and strong between them. 32 And from the army of Angeas and Lucus, Zepho sent many of the wounded unto his hand, about two thousand men, and Sosiphtar the captain of the host of Angeas fell in that battle. 33 And when Sosiphtar had fallen, the African troops turned their backs to flee, and they fled, and Angeas and Lucus his brother were with them. 34 And Zepho and the children of Chittim pursued them, and they smote them still heavily on the road, about two hundred men, and they pursued Azdrubal the son of Angeas who had fled with his father, and they smote twenty of his men in the road, and Azdrubal escaped from the children of Chittim, and they did not slay him. 35 And Angeas and Lucus his brother fled with the rest of their men, and they escaped and came into Africa with terror and consternation, and Angeas feared all the days lest Zepho the son of Eliphaz should go to war with him.

Jash.64

1 And Balaam the son of Beor was at that time with Angeas in the battle, and when he saw that Zepho prevailed over Angeas, he fled from there and came to Chittim. 2 And Zepho and the children of Chittim received him with great honor, for Zepho knew Balaam's wisdom, and Zepho gave unto Balaam many gifts and he remained with him. 3 And when Zepho had returned from the war, he commanded all the children of Chittim to be numbered who had gone into battle with him, and behold not one was missed. 4 And Zepho rejoiced at this thing, and he renewed his kingdom, and he made a feast to all his subjects. 5 But Zepho remembered not the Lord and considered not that the Lord had helped him in battle, and that he had delivered him and his people from the hand of the king of Africa, but still walked in the ways of the children of Chittim and the wicked children of Esau, to serve other gods which his brethren the children of Esau had taught him; it is therefore said, From the wicked goes forth wickedness. 6 And Zepho reigned over all the children of Chittim securely, but knew not the Lord who had delivered him and all his people from the hand of the king of Africa; and the troops of Africa came no more to Chittim to plunder as usual, for they knew of the power of Zepho who had smitten them all at the edge of the sword, so Angeas was afraid of Zepho the son of Eliphaz, and of the children of Chittim all the days. 7 At that time when Zepho had returned from the war, and when Zepho had seen how he prevailed over all the people of Africa and had smitten them in battle at the edge of the sword, then Zepho advised with the children of Chittim, to go to Egypt to fight with the sons of Jacob and with Pharaoh king of Egypt. 8 For Zepho heard that the mighty men of Egypt were dead and that Joseph and his brethren the sons at Jacob were dead, and that all their children the children of Israel remained in Egypt. 9 And Zepho considered to go to fight against them and all Egypt, to avenge the cause of his brethren the children of Esau, whom Joseph with his brethren and all Egypt had smitten in the land of Canaan, when they went up to bury Jacob in Hebron. 10 And Zepho sent messengers to Hadad, son of Bedad, king of Edom, and to all his brethren the children of Esau, saying, 11 Did you not say that you would not fight against the king of Africa for he is a member of your covenant? behold I fought with him and smote him and all his people. 12 Now therefore I have resolved to fight against Egypt and the children of Jacob who are there, and I will be revenged of them for what Joseph, his brethren and ancestors did to us in the land of Canaan when they went up to bury their father in Hebron. 13 Now then if you are willing to come to me to assist me in fighting against them and Egypt, then shall we avenge the cause of our brethren. 14 And the children of Esau hearkened to the words of Zepho, and the children of Esau gathered themselves together, a very great people, and they went to assist Zepho and the children of Chittim in battle. 15 And Zepho sent to all the children of the east and to all the children of Ishmael with words like unto these, and they gathered themselves and came to the assistance of Zepho and the children of Chittim in the war upon Egypt. 16 And all these kings, the king of Edom and the children of the east, and all the children of Ishmael, and Zepho the king of Chittim went forth and arrayed all their hosts in Hebron. 17 And the camp was very heavy, extending in length a distance of three days' journey, a people numerous as the sand upon the sea shore which can not be counted. 18 And all these kings and their hosts went down and came against all Egypt in battle, and encamped together in the valley of Pathros. 19 And all Egypt heard their report, and they also gathered themselves together, all the people of the land of Egypt, and of all the cities belonging to Egypt, about three hundred thousand men. 20 And the men of Egypt sent also to the children of Israel who were in those days in the land of Goshen, to come to them in order to go and fight with these kings. 21 And the men of Israel assembled and were about one hundred and fifty men, and they went into battle to assist the Egyptians. 22 And the men of Israel and of Egypt went forth, about three hundred thousand men and one hundred and fifty men, and they went toward these kings to battle, and they placed themselves from without the land of Goshen opposite Pathros. 23 And the Egyptians believed not in Israel to go with them in their camps together for battle, for all the Egyptians said, Perhaps the children of Israel will deliver us into the hand of

the children of Esau and Ishmael, for they are their brethren. 24 And all the Egyptians said unto the children of Israel, Remain you here together in your stand and we will go and fight against the children of Esau and Ishmael, and if these kings should prevail over us, then come you altogether upon them and assist us, and the children of Israel did so. 25 And Zepho the son of Eliphaz the son of Esau king of Chittim, and Hadad the son of Bedad king of Edom, and all their camps, and all the children of the east, and children of Ishmael, a people numerous as sand, encamped together in the valley of Pathros opposite Tachpanches. 26 And Balaam the son of Beor the Syrian was there in the camp of Zepho, for he came with the children of Chittim to the battle, and Balaam was a man highly honored in the eyes of Zepho and his men. 27 And Zepho said unto Balaam, Try by divination for us that we may know who will prevail in the battle, we or the Egyptians. 28 And Balaam rose up and tried the art of divination, and he was skillful in the knowledge of it, but he was confused and the work was destroyed in his hand. 29 And he tried it again but it did not succeed, and Balaam despaired of it and left it and did not complete it, for this was from the Lord, in order to cause Zepho and his people to fall into the hand of the children of Israel, who had trusted in the Lord, the God of their ancestors, in their war. 30 And Zepho and Hadad put their forces in battle array, and all the Egyptians went alone against them, about three hundred thousand men, and not one man of Israel was with them. 31 And all the Egyptians fought with these kings opposite Pathros and Tachpanches, and the battle was severe against the Egyptians. 32 And the kings were stronger than the Egyptians in that battle, and about one hundred and eighty men of Egypt fell on that day, and about thirty men of the forces of the kings, and all the men of Egypt fled from before the kings, so the children of Esau and Ishmael pursued the Egyptians, continuing to smite them unto the place where was the camp of the children of Israel. 33 And all the Egyptians cried unto the children of Israel, saying, Hasten to us and assist us and save us from the hand of Esau, Ishmael and the children of Chittim. 34 And the hundred and fifty men of the children of Israel ran from their station to the camps of these kings, and the children of Israel cried unto the Lord their God to deliver them. 35 And the Lord hearkened to Israel, and the Lord gave all the men of the kings into their hand, and the children of Israel fought against these kings, and the children of Israel smote about four thousand of the kings' men. 36 And the Lord threw a great consternation in the camp of the kings, so that the fear of the children of Israel fell upon them. 37 And all the hosts of the kings fled from before the children of Israel and the children of Israel pursued them continuing to smite them unto the borders of the land of Cush. 38 And the children of Israel slew of them in the road yet two thousand men, and of the children of Israel not one fell. 39 And when the Egyptians saw that the children of Israel had fought with such few men with the kings, and that the battle was so very severe against them, 40 All the Egyptians were greatly afraid of their lives on account of the strong battle, and all Egypt fled, every man hiding himself from the arrayed forces, and they hid themselves in the road, and they left the Israelites to fight. 41 And the children of Israel inflicted a terrible blow upon the kings' men, and they returned from them after they had driven them to the border of the land of Cush. 42 And all Israel knew the thing which the men of Egypt had done to them, that they had fled from them in battle, and had left them to fight alone. 43 So the children of Israel also acted with cunning, and as the children of Israel returned from battle, they found some of the Egyptians in the road and smote them there. 44 And whilst they slew them, they said unto them these words: 45 Wherefore did you go from us and leave us, being a few

288

people, to fight against these kings who had a great people to smite us, that you might thereby deliver your own souls? 46 And of some which the Israelites met on the road, they the children of Israel spoke to each other, saying, Smite, smite, for he is an Ishmaelite, or an Edomite, or from the children of Chittim, and they stood over him and slew him, and they knew that he was an Egyptian. 47 And the children of Israel did these things cunningly against the Egyptians, because they had deserted them in battle and had fled from them. 48 And the children of Israel slew of the men of Egypt in the road in this manner, about two hundred men. 49 And all the men of Egypt saw the evil which the children of Israel had done to them, so all Egypt feared greatly the children of Israel, for they had seen their great power, and that not one man of them had fallen. 50 So all the children of Israel returned with joy on their road to Goshen, and the rest of Egypt returned each man to his place.

Jash.65

1 And it came to pass after these things, that all the counsellors of Pharaoh, king of Egypt, and all the elders of Egypt assembled and came before the king and bowed down to the ground, and they sat before him. 2 And the counsellors and elders of Egypt spoke unto the king, saying, 3 Behold the people of the children of Israel is greater and mightier than we are, and thou knowest all the evil which they did to us in the road when we returned from battle. 4 And thou hast also seen their strong power, for this power is unto them from their fathers, for but a few men stood up against a people numerous as the sand, and smote them at the edge of the sword, and of themselves not one has fallen, so that if they had been numerous they would then have utterly destroyed them. 5 Now therefore give us counsel what to do with them, until we gradually destroy them from amongst us, lest they become too numerous for us in the land. 6 For if the children of Israel should increase in the land, they will become an obstacle to us, and if any war should happen to take place, they with their great strength will join our enemy against us, and fight against us, destroy us from the land and go away from it. 7 So the king answered the elders of Egypt and said unto them, This is the plan advised against Israel, from which we will not depart, 8 Behold in the land are Pithom and Rameses, cities unfortified against battle, it behooves you and us to build them, and to fortify them. 9 Now therefore go you also and act cunningly toward them, and proclaim a voice in Egypt and in Goshen at the command of the king, saying, 10 All ye men of Egypt, Goshen, Pathros and all their inhabitants! the king has commanded us to build Pithom and Rameses, and to fortify them for battle; who amongst you of all Egypt, of the children of Israel and of all the inhabitants of the cities, are willing to build with us, shall each have his wages given to him daily at the king's order; so go you first and do cunningly, and gather yourselves and come to Pithom and Rameses to build. 11 And whilst you are building, cause a proclamation of this kind to be made throughout Egypt every day at the command of the king. 12 And when some of the children of Israel shall come to build with you, you shall give them their wages daily for a few days. 13 And after they shall have built with you for their daily hire, drag yourselves away from them daily one by one in secret, and then you shall rise up and become their task-masters and officers, and you shall leave them afterward to build without wages, and should they refuse, then force them with all your might to build. 14 And if you do this it will be well with us to strengthen our land against the children of Israel, for on account of the fatigue of the building and the work, the children of Israel will decrease, because you will deprive them from their wives day by day. 15 And all the elders of Egypt heard the counsel of the king, and the counsel seemed good in their eyes and in the eyes of the servants of Pharaoh,

and in the eyes of all Egypt, and they did according to the word of the king. 16 And all the servants went away from the king, and they caused a proclamation to be made in all Egypt, in Tachpanches and in Goshen, and in all the cities which surrounded Egypt, saying, 17 You have seen what the children of Esau and Ishmael did to us, who came to war against us and wished to destroy us. 18 Now therefore the king commanded us to fortify the land, to build the cities Pithom and Rameses, and to fortify them for battle, if they should again come against us. 19 Whosoever of you from all Egypt and from the children of Israel will come to build with us, he shall have his daily wages given by the king, as his command is unto us. 20 And when Egypt and all the children of Israel heard all that the servants of Pharaoh had spoken, there came from the Egyptians, and the children of Israel to build with the servants of Pharaoh, Pithom and Rameses, but none of the children of Levi came with their brethren to build. 21 And all the servants of Pharaoh and his princes came at first with deceit to build with all Israel as daily hired laborers, and they gave to Israel their daily hire at the beginning. 22 And the servants of Pharaoh built with all Israel, and were employed in that work with Israel for a month. 23 And at the end of the month, all the servants of Pharaoh began to withdraw secretly from the people of Israel daily. 24 And Israel went on with the work at that time, but they then received their daily hire, because some of the men of Egypt were yet carrying on the work with Israel at that time; therefore the Egyptians gave Israel their hire in those days, in order that they, the Egyptians their fellow-workmen, might also take the pay for their labor. 25 And at the end of a year and four months all the Egyptians had withdrawn from the children of Israel, so that the children of Israel were left alone engaged in the work. 26 And after all the Egyptians had withdrawn from the children of Israel they returned and became oppressors and officers over them, and some of them stood over the children of Israel as task masters, to receive from them all that they gave them for the pay of their labor. 27 And the Egyptians did in this manner to the children of Israel day by day, in order to afflict in their work. 28 And all the children of Israel were alone engaged in the labor, and the Egyptians refrained from giving any pay to the children of Israel from that time forward. 29 And when some of the men of Israel refused to work on account of the wages not being given to them, then the exactors and the servants of Pharaoh oppressed them and smote them with heavy blows, and made them return by force, to labor with their brethren; thus did all the Egyptians unto the children of Israel all the days. 30 And all the children of Israel were greatly afraid of the Egyptians in this matter, and all the children of Israel returned and worked alone without pay. 31 And the children of Israel built Pithom and Rameses, and all the children of Israel did the work, some making bricks, and some building, and the children of Israel built and fortified all the land of Egypt and its walls, and the children of Israel were engaged in work for many years, until the time came when the Lord remembered them and brought them out of Egypt. 32 But the children of Levi were not employed in the work with their brethren of Israel, from the beginning unto the day of their going forth from Egypt. 33 For all the children of Levi knew that the Egyptians had spoken all these words with deceit to the Israelites, therefore the children of Levi refrained from approaching to the work with their brethren. 34 And the Egyptians did not direct their attention to make the children of Levi work afterward, since they had not been with their brethren at the beginning, therefore the Egyptians left them alone. 35 And the hands of the men of Egypt were directed with continued severity against the children of Israel in that work, and the Egyptians made the children of Israel work with rigor. 36 And the Egyptians embittered the lives of the children

of Israel with hard work, in mortar and bricks, and also in all manner of work in the field. 37 And the children of Israel called Melol the king of Egypt "Meror, king of Egypt," because in his days the Egyptians had embittered their lives with all manner of work. 38 And all the work wherein the Egyptians made the children of Israel labor, they exacted with rigor, in order to afflict the children of Israel, but the more they afflicted them, the more they increased and grew, and the Egyptians were grieved because of the children of Israel.

Jash.66

1 At that time died Hadad the son of Bedad king of Edom, and Samlah from Mesrekah, from the country of the children of the east, reigned in his place. 2 In the thirteenth year of the reign of Pharaoh king of Egypt, which was the hundred and twenty-fifth year of the Israelites going down into Egypt, Samlah had reigned over Edom eighteen years. 3 And when he reigned, he drew forth his hosts to go and fight against Zepho the son of Eliphaz and the children of Chittim, because they had made war against Angeas king of Africa, and they destroyed his whole army. 4 But he did not engage with him, for the children of Esau prevented him, saying, He was their brother, so Samlah listened to the voice of the children of Esau, and turned back with all his forces to the land of Edom, and did not proceed to fight against Zepho the son of Eliphaz. 5 And Pharaoh king of Egypt heard this thing, saying, Samlah king of Edom has resolved to fight the children of Chittim, and afterward he will come to fight against Egypt. 6 And when the Egyptians heard this matter, they increased the labor upon the children of Israel, lest the Israelites should do unto them as they did unto them in their war with the children of Esau in the days of Hadad. 7 So the Egyptians said unto the children of Israel, Hasten and do your work, and finish your task, and strengthen the land, lest the children of Esau your brethren should come to fight against us, for on your account will they come against us. 8 And the children of Israel did the work of the men of Egypt day by day, and the Egyptians afflicted the children of Israel in order to lessen them in the land. 9 But as the Egyptians increased the labor upon the children of Israel, so did the children of Israel increase and multiply, and all Egypt was filled with the children of Israel. 10 And in the hundred and twenty-fifth year of Israel's going down into Egypt, all the Egyptians saw that their counsel did not succeed against Israel, but that they increased and grew, and the land of Egypt and the land of Goshen were filled with the children of Israel. 11 So all the elders of Egypt and its wise men came before the king and bowed down to him and sat before him. 12 And all the elders of Egypt and the wise men thereof said unto the king, May the king live forever; thou didst counsel us the counsel against the children of Israel, and we did unto them according to the word of the king. 13 But in proportion to the increase of the labor so do they increase and grow in the land, and behold the whole country is filled with them. 14 Now therefore our lord and king, the eyes of all Egypt are upon thee to give them advice with thy wisdom, by which they may prevail over Israel to destroy them, or to diminish them from the land; and the king answered them saying, Give you counsel in this matter that we may know what to do unto them. 15 And an officer, one of the king's counsellors, whose name was Job, from Mesopotamia, in the land of Uz, answered the king, saying, 16 If it please the king, let him hear the counsel of his servant; and the king said unto him, Speak. 17 And Job spoke before the king, the princes, and before all the elders of Egypt, saying, 18 Behold the counsel of the king which he advised formerly respecting the labor of the children of Israel is very good, and you must not remove from them that labor forever. 19 But this is the advice counselled by which you may lessen them, if it seems good to the king to afflict them. 20 Behold we have feared war for a long time, and we said,

When Israel becomes fruitful in the land, they will drive us from the land if a war should take place. 21 If it please the king, let a royal decree go forth, and let it be written in the laws of Egypt which shall not be revoked, that every male child born to the Israelites, his blood shall be spilled upon the ground. 22 And by your doing this, when all the male children of Israel shall have died, the evil of their wars will cease; let the king do so and send for all the Hebrew midwives and order them in this matter to execute it; so the thing pleased the king and the princes, and the king did according to the word of Job. 23 And the king sent for the Hebrew midwives to be called, of which the name of one was Shephrah, and the name of the other Puah. 24 And the midwives came before the king, and stood in his presence. 25 And the king said unto them, When you do the office of a midwife to the Hebrew women, and see them upon the stools, if it be a son, then you shall kill him, but if it be a daughter, then she shall live. 26 But if you will not do this thing, then will I burn you up and all your houses with fire. 27 But the midwives feared God and did not hearken to the king of Egypt nor to his words, and when the Hebrew women brought forth to the midwife son or daughter, then did the midwife do all that was necessary to the child and let it live; thus did the midwives all the days. 28 And this thing was told to the king, and he sent and called for the midwives and he said to them, Why have you done this thing and have saved the children alive? 29 And the midwives answered and spoke together before the king, saying, 30 Let not the king think that the Hebrew women are as the Egyptian women, for all the children of Israel are hale, and before the midwife comes to them they are delivered, and as for us thy handmaids, for many days no Hebrew woman has brought forth upon us, for all the Hebrew women are their own midwives, because they are hale. 31 And Pharaoh heard their words and believed them in this matter, and the midwives went away from the king, and God dealt well with them, and the people multiplied and waxed exceedingly.

Jash.67

1 There was a man in the land of Egypt of the seed of Levi, whose name was Amram, the son of Kehath, the son of Levi, the son of Israel. 2 And this man went and took a wife, namely Jochebed the daughter of Levi his father's sister, and she was one hundred and twenty-six years old, and he came unto her. 3 And the woman conceived and bare a daughter, and she called her name Miriam, because in those days the Egyptians had embittered the lives of the children of Israel. 4 And she conceived again and bare a son and she called his name Aaron, for in the days of her conception, Pharaoh began to spill the blood of the male children of Israel. 5 In those days died Zepho the son of Eliphaz, son of Esau, king of Chittim, and Janeas reigned in his stead. 6 And the time that Zepho reigned over the children of Chittim was fifty years, and he died and was buried in the city of Nabna in the land of Chittim. 7 And Janeas, one of the mighty men of the children of Chittim, reigned after him and he reigned fifty years. 8 And it was after the death of the king of Chittim that Balaam the son of Beor fled from the land of Chittim, and he went and came to Egypt to Pharaoh king of Egypt. 9 And Pharaoh received him with great honor, for he had heard of his wisdom, and he gave him presents and made him for a counsellor, and aggrandized him. 10 And Balaam dwelt in Egypt, in honor with all the nobles of the king, and the nobles exalted him, because they all coveted to learn his wisdom. 11 And in the hundred and thirtieth year of Israel's going down to Egypt, Pharaoh dreamed that he was sitting upon his kingly throne, and lifted up his eyes and saw an old man standing before him, and there were scales in the hands of the old man, such scales as are used by merchants. 12 And the old man took the scales and hung them before Pharaoh. 13 And the old man

took all the elders of Egypt and all its nobles and great men, and he tied them together and put them in one scale. 14 And he took a milk kid and put it into the other scale, and the kid preponderated over all. 15 And Pharaoh was astonished at this dreadful vision, why the kid should preponderate over all, and Pharaoh awoke and behold it was a dream. 16 And Pharaoh rose up early in the morning and called all his servants and related to them the dream, and the men were greatly afraid. 17 And the king said to all his wise men, Interpret I pray you the dream which I dreamed, that I may know it. 18 And Balaam the son of Beor answered the king and said unto him, This means nothing else but a great evil that will spring up against Egypt in the latter days. 19 For a son will be born to Israel who will destroy all Egypt and its inhabitants, and bring forth the Israelites from Egypt with a mighty hand. 20 Now therefore, O king, take counsel upon this matter, that you may destroy the hope of the children of Israel and their expectation, before this evil arise against Egypt. 21 And the king said unto Balaam, And what shall we do unto Israel? surely after a certain manner did we at first counsel against them and could not prevail over them. 22 Now therefore give you also advice against them by which we may prevail over them. 23 And Balaam answered the king, saying, Send now and call thy two counsellors, and we will see what their advice is upon this matter and afterward thy servant will speak. 24 And the king sent and called his two counsellors Reuel the Midianite and Job the Uzite, and they came and sat before the king. 25 And the king said to them, Behold you have both heard the dream which I have dreamed, and the interpretation thereof; now therefore give counsel and know and see what is to be done to the children of Israel, whereby we may prevail over them, before their evil shall spring up against us. 26 And Reuel the Midianite answered the king and said, May the king live, may the king live forever. 27 If it seem good to the king, let him desist from the Hebrews and leave them, and let him not stretch forth his hand against them. 28 For these are they whom the Lord chose in days of old, and took as the lot of his inheritance from amongst all the nations of the earth and the kings of the earth; and who is there that stretched his hand against them with impunity, of whom their God was not avenged? 29 Surely thou knowest that when Abraham went down to Egypt, Pharaoh, the former king of Egypt, saw Sarah his wife, and took her for a wife, because Abraham said, She is my sister, for he was afraid, lest the men of Egypt should slay him on account of his wife. 30 And when the king of Egypt had taken Sarah then God smote him and his household with heavy plagues, until he restored unto Abraham his wife Sarah, then was he healed. 31 And Abimelech the Gerarite, king of the Philistines, God punished on account of Sarah wife of Abraham, in stopping up every womb from man to beast. 32 When their God came to Abimelech in the dream of night and terrified him in order that he might restore to Abraham Sarah whom he had taken, and afterward all the people of Gerar were punished on account of Sarah, and Abraham prayed to his God for them, and he was entreated of him, and he healed them. 33 And Abimelech feared all this evil that came upon him and his people, and he returned to Abraham his wife Sarah, and gave him with her many gifts. 34 He did so also to Isaac when he had driven him from Gerar, and God had done wonderful things to him, that all the water courses of Gerar were dried up, and their productive trees did not bring forth. 35 Until Abimelech of Gerar, and Ahuzzath one of his friends, and Pichol the captain of his host, went to him and they bent and bowed down before him to the ground. 36 And they requested of him to supplicate for them, and he prayed to the Lord for them, and the Lord was entreated of him and he healed them. 37 Jacob also, the plain man, was delivered through his integrity from the hand of his brother Esau, and the hand of Laban the Syrian his mother's brother, who had sought his life; likewise from the hand of all the kings of Canaan who had come together against him and his children to destroy them, and the Lord delivered them out of their hands, that they turned upon them and smote them, for who had ever stretched forth his hand against them with impunity? 38 Surely Pharaoh the former, thy father's father, raised Joseph the son of Jacob above all the princes of the land of Egypt, when he saw his wisdom, for through his wisdom he rescued all the inhabitants of the land from the famine. 39 After which he ordered Jacob and his children to come down to Egypt, in order that through their virtue, the land of Egypt and the land of Goshen might be delivered from the famine. 40 Now therefore if it seem good in thine eyes, cease from destroying the children of Israel, but if it be not thy will that they shall dwell in Egypt, send them forth from here, that they may go to the land of Canaan, the land where their ancestors sojourned. 41 And when Pharaoh heard the words of Jethro he was very angry with him, so that he rose with shame from the king's presence, and went to Midian, his land, and took Joseph's stick with him. 42 And the king said to Job the Uzite, What sayest thou Job, and what is thy advice respecting the Hebrews? 43 So Job said to the king, Behold all the inhabitants of the land are in thy power, let the king do as it seems good in his eyes. 44 And the king said unto Balaam, What dost thou say, Balaam, speak thy word that we may hear it. 45 And Balaam said to the king, Of all that the king has counselled against the Hebrews will they be delivered, and the king will not be able to prevail over them with any counsel. 46 For if thou thinkest to lessen them by the flaming fire, thou canst not prevail over them, for surely their God delivered Abraham their father from Ur of the Chaldeans; and if thou thinkest to destroy them with a sword, surely Isaac their father was delivered from it, and a ram was placed in his stead. 47 And if with hard and rigorous labor thou thinkest to lessen them, thou wilt not prevail even in this, for their father Jacob served Laban in all manner of hard work, and prospered. 48 Now therefore, O King, hear my words, for this is the counsel which is counselled against them, by which thou wilt prevail over them, and from which thou shouldst not depart. 49 If it please the king let him order all their children which shall be born from this day forward, to be thrown into the water, for by this canst thou wipe away their name, for none of them, nor of their fathers, were tried in this manner. 50 And the king heard the words of Balaam, and the thing pleased the king and the princes, and the king did according to the word of Balaam. 51 And the king ordered a proclamation to be issued and a law to be made throughout the land of Egypt, saying, Every male child born to the Hebrews from this day forward shall be thrown into the water. 52 And Pharaoh called unto all his servants, saying, Go now and seek throughout the land of Goshen where the children of Israel are, and see that every son born to the Hebrews shall be cast into the river, but every daughter you shall let live. 53 And when the children of Israel heard this thing which Pharaoh had commanded, to cast their male children into the river, some of the people separated from their wives and others adhered to them. 54 And from that day forward, when the time of delivery arrived to those women of Israel who had remained with their husbands, they went to the field to bring forth there, and they brought forth in the field, and left their children upon the field and returned home. 55 And the Lord who had sworn to their ancestors to multiply them, sent one of his ministering angels which are in heaven to wash each child in water, to anoint and swathe it and to put into its hands two smooth stones from one of which it sucked milk and from the other honey, and he caused its hair to grow to its knees, by which it might cover itself; to comfort it and to cleave to it, through his compassion for it. 56 And when God had compassion

291

over them and had desired to multiply them upon the face of the land, he ordered his earth to receive them to be preserved therein till the time of their growing up, after which the earth opened its mouth and vomited them forth and they sprouted forth from the city like the herb of the earth, and the grass of the forest, and they returned each to his family and to his father's house, and they remained with them. 57 And the babes of the children of Israel were upon the earth like the herb of the field, through God's grace to them. 58 And when all the Egyptians saw this thing, they went forth, each to his field with his yoke of oxen and his ploughshare, and they ploughed it up as one ploughs the earth at seed time. 59 And when they ploughed they were unable to hurt the infants of the children of Israel, so the people increased and waxed exceedingly. 60 And Pharaoh ordered his officers daily to go to Goshen to seek for the babes of the children of Israel. 61 And when they had sought and found one, they took it from its mother's bosom by force, and threw it into the river, but the female child they left with its mother; thus did the Egyptians do to the Israelites all the days.

Jash.68

1 And it was at that time the spirit of God was upon Miriam the daughter of Amram the sister of Aaron, and she went forth and prophesied about the house, saying, Behold a son will be born unto us from my father and mother this time, and he will save Israel from the hands of Egypt. 2 And when Amram heard the words of his daughter, he went and took his wife back to the house, after he had driven her away at the time when Pharaoh ordered every male child of the house of Jacob to be thrown into the water. 3 So Amram took Jochebed his wife, three years after he had driven her away, and he came to her and she conceived. 4 And at the end of seven months from her conception she brought forth a son, and the whole house was filled with great light as of the light of the sun and moon at the time of their shining. 5 And when the woman saw the child that it was good and pleasing to the sight, she hid it for three months in an inner room. 6 In those days the Egyptians conspired to destroy all the Hebrews there. 7 And the Egyptian women went to Goshen where the children of Israel were, and they carried their young ones upon their shoulders, their babes who could not yet speak. 8 And in those days, when the women of the children of Israel brought forth, each woman had hidden her son from before the Egyptians, that the Egyptians might not know of their bringing forth, and might not destroy them from the land. 9 And the Egyptian women came to Goshen and their children who could not speak were upon their shoulders, and when an Egyptian woman came into the house of a Hebrew woman her babe began to cry. 10 And when it cried the child that was in the inner room answered it, so the Egyptian women went and told it at the house of Pharaoh. 11 And Pharaoh sent his officers to take the children and slay them; thus did the Egyptians to the Hebrew women all the days. 12 And it was at that time, about three months from Jochebed's concealment of her son, that the thing was known in Pharaoh's house. 13 And the woman hastened to take away her son before the officers came, and she took for him an ark of bulrushes, and daubed it with slime and with pitch, and put the child therein, and she laid it in the flags by the river's brink. 14 And his sister Miriam stood afar off to know what would be done to him, and what would become of her words. 15 And God sent forth at that time a terrible heat in the land of Egypt, which burned up the flesh of man like the sun in his circuit, and it greatly oppressed the Egyptians. 16 And all the Egyptians went down to bathe in the river, on account of the consuming heat which burned up their flesh. 17 And Bathia, the daughter of Pharaoh, went also to bathe in the river, owing to the consuming heat, and her maidens walked at the river side, and all the women of Egypt as well. 18 And Bathia

lifted up her eyes to the river, and she saw the ark upon the water, and sent her maid to fetch it. 19 And she opened it and saw the child, and behold the babe wept, and she had compassion on him, and she said, This is one of the Hebrew children. 20 And all the women of Egypt walking on the river side desired to give him suck, but he would not suck, for this thing was from the Lord, in order to restore him to his mother's breast. 21 And Miriam his sister was at that time amongst the Egyptian women at the river side, and she saw this thing and she said to Pharaoh's daughter, Shall I go and fetch a nurse of the Hebrew women, that she may nurse the child for thee? 22 And Pharaoh's daughter said to her, Go, and the young woman went and called the child's mother. 23 And Pharaoh's daughter said to Jochebed, Take this child away and suckle it for me, and I will pay thee thy wages, two bits of silver daily; and the woman took the child and nursed it. 24 And at the end of two years, when the child grew up, she brought him to the daughter of Pharaoh, and he was unto her as a son, and she called his name Moses, for she said, Because I drew him out of the water. 25 And Amram his father called his name Chabar, for he said, It was for him that he associated with his wife whom he had turned away. 26 And Jochebed his mother called his name Jekuthiel, Because, she said, I have hoped for him to the Almighty, and God restored him unto me. 27 And Miriam his sister called him Jered, for she descended after him to the river to know what his end would be. 28 And Aaron his brother called his name Abi Zanuch, saying, My father left my mother and returned to her on his account. 29 And Kehath the father of Amram called his name Abigdor, because on his account did God repair the breach of the house of Jacob, that they could no longer throw their male children into the water. 30 And their nurse called him Abi Socho, saying, In his tabernacle was he hidden for three months, on account of the children of Ham. 31 And all Israel called his name Shemaiah, son of Nethanel, for they said, In his days has God heard their cries and rescued them from their oppressors. 32 And Moses was in Pharaoh's house, and was unto Bathia, Pharaoh's daughter, as a son, and Moses grew up amongst the king's children.

Jash.69

1 And the king of Edom died in those days, in the eighteenth year of his reign, and was buried in his temple which he had built for himself as his royal residence in the land of Edom. 2 And the children of Esau sent to Pethor, which is upon the river, and they fetched from there a young man of beautiful eyes and comely aspect, whose name was Saul, and they made him king over them in the place of Samlah. 3 And Saul reigned over all the children of Esau in the land of Edom for forty years. 4 And when Pharaoh king of Egypt saw that the counsel which Balaam had advised respecting the children of Israel did not succeed, but that still they were fruitful, multiplied and increased throughout the land of Egypt, 5 Then Pharaoh commanded in those days that a proclamation should be issued throughout Egypt to the children of Israel, saying, No man shall diminish any thing of his daily labor. 6 And the man who shall be found deficient in his labor which he performs daily, whether in mortar or in bricks, then his youngest son shall be put in their place. 7 And the labor of Egypt strengthened upon the children of Israel in those days, and behold if one brick was deficient in any man's daily labor, the Egyptians took his youngest boy by force from his mother, and put him into the building in the place of the brick which his father had left wanting. 8 And the men of Egypt did so to all the children of Israel day by day, all the days for a long period. 9 But the tribe of Levi did not at that time work with the Israelites their brethren, from the beginning, for the children of Levi knew the cunning of the Egyptians which they exercised at first toward the Israelites.

Jash.70

1 And in the third year from the birth of Moses, Pharaoh was sitting at a banquet, when Alparanith the queen was sitting at his right and Bathia at his left, and the lad Moses was lying upon her bosom, and Balaam the son of Beor with his two sons, and all the princes of the kingdom were sitting at table in the king's presence. 2 And the lad stretched forth his hand upon the king's head, and took the crown from the king's head and placed it on his own head. 3 And when the king and princes saw the work which the boy had done, the king and princes were terrified, and one man to his neighbor expressed astonishment. 4 And the king said unto the princes who were before him at table, What speak you and what say you, O ye princes, in this matter, and what is to be the judgment against the boy on account of this act? 5 And Balaam the son of Beor the magician answered before the king and princes, and he said, Remember now, O my lord and king, the dream which thou didst dream many days since, and that which thy servant interpreted unto thee. 6 Now therefore this is a child from the Hebrew children, in whom is the spirit of God, and let not my lord the king imagine that this youngster did this thing without knowledge. 7 For he is a Hebrew boy, and wisdom and understanding are with him, although he is yet a child, and with wisdom has he done this and chosen unto himself the kingdom of Egypt. 8 For this is the manner of all the Hebrews to deceive kings and their nobles, to do all these things cunningly, in order to make the kings of the earth and their men tremble. 9 Surely thou knowest that Abraham their father acted thus, who deceived the army of Nimrod king of Babel, and Abimelech king of Gerar, and that he possessed himself of the land of the children of Heth and all the kingdoms of Canaan. 10 And that he descended into Egypt and said of Sarah his wife, she is my sister, in order to mislead Egypt and her king. 11 His son Isaac also did so when he went to Gerar and dwelt there, and his strength prevailed over the army of Abimelech king of the Philistines. 12 He also thought of making the kingdom of the Philistines stumble, in saying that Rebecca his wife was his sister. 13 Jacob also dealt treacherously with his brother, and took from his hand his birthright and his blessing. 14 He went then to Padan-aram to the house of Laban his mother's brother, and cunningly obtained from him his daughter, his cattle, and all belonging to him, and fled away and returned to the land of Canaan to his father. 15 His sons sold their brother Joseph, who went down into Egypt and became a slave, and was placed in the prison house for twelve years. 16 Until the former Pharaoh dreamed dreams, and withdrew him from the prison house, and magnified him above all the princes in Egypt on account of his interpreting his dreams to him. 17 And when God caused a famine throughout the land he sent for and brought his father and all his brothers, and the whole of his father's household, and supported them without price or reward, and bought the Egyptians for slaves. 18 Now therefore my lord king behold this child has risen up in their stead in Egypt, to do according to their deeds and to trifle with every king, prince and judge. 19 If it please the king, let us now spill his blood upon the ground, lest he grow up and take away the government from thy hand, and the hope of Egypt perish after he shall have reigned. 20 And Balaam said to the king, Let us moreover call for all the judges of Egypt and the wise men thereof, and let us know if the judgment of death is due to this boy as thou didst say, and then we will slay him. 21 And Pharaoh sent and called for all the wise men of Egypt and they came before the king, and an angel of the Lord came amongst them, and he was like one of the wise men of Egypt. 22 And the king said to the wise men, Surely you have heard what this Hebrew boy who is in the house has done, and thus has Balaam judged in the matter. 23 Now judge you also and see what is due to the boy for the

act he has committed. 24 And the angel, who seemed like one of the wise men of Pharaoh, answered and said as follows, before all the wise men of Egypt and before the king and the princes: 25 If it please the king let the king send for men who shall bring before him an onyx stone and a coal of fire, and place them before the child, and if the child shall stretch forth his hand and take the onyx stone, then shall we know that with wisdom has the youth done all that he has done, and we must slay him. 26 But if he stretch forth his hand upon the coal, then shall we know that it was not with knowledge that he did this thing, and he shall live. 27 And the thing seemed good in the eyes of the king and the princes, so the king did according to the word of the angel of the Lord. 28 And the king ordered the onyx stone and coal to be brought and placed before Moses. 29 And they placed the boy before them, and the lad endeavored to stretch forth his hand to the onyx stone, but the angel of the Lord took his hand and placed it upon the coal, and the coal became extinguished in his hand, and he lifted it up and put it into his mouth, and burned part of his lips and part of his tongue, and he became heavy in mouth and tongue. 30 And when the king and princes saw this, they knew that Moses had not acted with wisdom in taking off the crown from the king's head. 31 So the king and princes refrained from slaying the child, so Moses remained in Pharaoh's house, growing up, and the Lord was with him. 32 And whilst the boy was in the king's house, he was robed in purple and he grew amongst the children of the king. 33 And when Moses grew up in the king's house, Bathia the daughter of Pharaoh considered him as a son, and all the household of Pharaoh honored him, and all the men of Egypt were afraid of him. 34 And he daily went forth and came into the land of Goshen, where his brethren the children of Israel were, and Moses saw them daily in shortness of breath and hard labor. 35 And Moses asked them, saying, Wherefore is this labor meted out unto you day by day? 36 And they told him all that had befallen them, and all the injunctions which Pharaoh had put upon them before his birth. 37 And they told him all the counsels which Balaam the son of Beor had counselled against them, and what he had also counselled against him in order to slay him when he had taken the king's crown from off his head. 38 And when Moses heard these things his anger was kindled against Balaam, and he sought to kill him, and he was in ambush for him day by day. 39 And Balaam was afraid of Moses, and he and his two sons rose up and went forth from Egypt, and they fled and delivered their souls and betook themselves to the land of Cush to Kikianus, king of Cush. 40 And Moses was in the king's house going out and coming in, the Lord gave him favor in the eyes of Pharaoh, and in the eyes of all his servants, and in the eyes of all the people of Egypt, and they loved Moses exceedingly. 41 And the day arrived when Moses went to Goshen to see his brethren, that he saw the children of Israel in their burdens and hard labor, and Moses was grieved on their account. 42 And Moses returned to Egypt and came to the house of Pharaoh, and came before the king, and Moses bowed down before the king. 43 And Moses said unto Pharaoh, I pray thee my lord, I have come to seek a small request from thee, turn not away my face empty; and Pharaoh said unto him, Speak. 44 And Moses said unto Pharaoh, Let there be given unto thy servants the children of Israel who are in Goshen, one day to rest therein from their labor. 45 And the king answered Moses and said, Behold I have lifted up thy face in this thing to grant thy request. 46 And Pharaoh ordered a proclamation to be issued throughout Egypt and Goshen, saying, 47 To you, all the children of Israel, thus says the king, for six days you shall do your work and labor, but on the seventh day you shall rest, and shall not preform any work, thus shall you do all the days, as the king and Moses the son of Bathia have commanded. 48 And Moses rejoiced at this thing

which the king had granted to him, and all the children of Israel did as Moses ordered them. 49 For this thing was from the Lord to the children of Israel, for the Lord had begun to remember the children of Israel to save them for the sake of their fathers. 50 And the Lord was with Moses and his fame went throughout Egypt. 51 And Moses became great in the eyes of all the Egyptians, and in the eyes of all the children of Israel, seeking good for his people Israel and speaking words of peace regarding them to the king.

Jash.71

1 And when Moses was eighteen years old, he desired to see his father and mother and he went to them to Goshen, and when Moses had come near Goshen, he came to the place where the children of Israel were engaged in work, and he observed their burdens, and he saw an Egyptian smiting one of his Hebrew brethren. 2 And when the man who was beaten saw Moses he ran to him for help, for the man Moses was greatly respected in the house of Pharaoh, and he said to him, My lord attend to me, this Egyptian came to my house in the night, bound me, and came to my wife in my presence, and now he seeks to take my life away. 3 And when Moses heard this wicked thing, his anger was kindled against the Egyptian, and he turned this way and the other, and when he saw there was no man there he smote the Egyptian and hid him in the sand, and delivered the Hebrew from the hand of him that smote him. 4 And the Hebrew went to his house, and Moses returned to his home, and went forth and came back to the king's house. 5 And when the man had returned home, he thought of repudiating his wife, for it was not right in the house of Jacob, for any man to come to his wife after she had been defiled. 6 And the woman went and told her brothers, and the woman's brothers sought to slay him, and he fled to his house and escaped. 7 And on the second day Moses went forth to his brethren, and saw, and behold two men were quarreling, and he said to the wicked one, Why dost thou smite thy neighbor? 8 And he answered him and said to him, Who has set thee for a prince and judge over us? dost thou think to slay me as thou didst slay the Egyptian? and Moses was afraid and he said, Surely the thing is known? 9 And Pharaoh heard of this affair, and he ordered Moses to be slain, so God sent his angel, and he appeared unto Pharaoh in the likeness of a captain of the guard. 10 And the angel of the Lord took the sword from the hand of the captain of the guard, and took his head off with it, for the likeness of the captain of the guard was turned into the likeness of Moses. 11 And the angel of the Lord took hold of the right hand of Moses, and brought him forth from Egypt, and placed him from without the borders of Egypt, a distance of forty days' journey. 12 And Aaron his brother alone remained in the land of Egypt, and he prophesied to the children of Israel, saying, 13 Thus says the Lord God of your ancestors, Throw away, each man, the abominations of his eyes, and do not defile yourselves with the idols of Egypt. 14 And the children of Israel rebelled and would not hearken to Aaron at that time. 15 And the Lord thought to destroy them, were it not that the Lord remembered the covenant which he had made with Abraham, Isaac and Jacob. 16 In those days the hand of Pharaoh continued to be severe against the children of Israel, and he crushed and oppressed them until the time when God sent forth his word and took notice of them.

Jash.72

1 And it was in those days that there was a great war between the children of Cush and the children of the east and Aram, and they rebelled against the king of Cush in whose hands they were. 2 So Kikianus king of Cush went forth with all the children of Cush, a people numerous as the sand, and he went to fight against Aram and the children of the east, to bring them under subjection. 3 And when Kikianus went out, he left Balaam the magician, with his two sons,

to guard the city, and the lowest sort of the people of the land. 4 So Kikianus went forth to Aram and the children of the east, and he fought against them and smote them, and they all fell down wounded before Kikianus and his people. 5 And he took many of them captives and he brought them under subjection as at first, and he encamped upon their land to take tribute from them as usual. 6 And Balaam the son of Beor, when the king of Cush had left him to guard the city and the poor of the city, he rose up and advised with the people of the land to rebel against king Kikianus, not to let him enter the city when he should come home. 7 And the people of the land hearkened to him, and they swore to him and made him king over them, and his two sons for captains of the army. 8 So they rose up and raised the walls of the city at the two corners, and they built an exceeding strong building. 9 And at the third corner they dug ditches without number, between the city and the river which surrounded the whole land of Cush, and they made the waters of the river burst forth there. 10 At the fourth corner they collected numerous serpents by their incantations and enchantments, and they fortified the city and dwelt therein, and no one went out or in before them. 11 And Kikianus fought against Aram and the children of the east and he subdued them as before, and they gave him their usual tribute, and he went and returned to his land. 12 And when Kikianus the king of Cush approached his city and all the captains of the forces with him, they lifted up their eyes and saw that the walls of the city were built up and greatly elevated, so the men were astonished at this. 13 And they said one to the other, It is because they saw that we were delayed, in battle, and were greatly afraid of us, therefore have they done this thing and raised the city walls and fortified them so that the kings of Canaan might not come in battle against them. 14 So the king and the troops approached the city door and they looked up and behold, all the gates of the city were closed, and they called out to the sentinels, saying, Open unto us, that we may enter the city. 15 But the sentinels refused to open to them by the order of Balaam the magician, their king, they suffered them not to enter their city. 16 So they raised a battle with them opposite the city gate, and one hundred and thirty men of the army at Kikianus fell on that day. 17 And on the next day they continued to fight and they fought at the side of the river; they endeavored to pass but were not able, so some of them sank in the pits and died. 18 So the king ordered them to cut down trees to make rafts, upon which they might pass to them, and they did so. 19 And when they came to the place of the ditches, the waters revolved by mills, and two hundred men upon ten rafts were drowned. 20 And on the third day they came to fight at the side where the serpents were, but they could not approach there, for the serpents slew of them one hundred and seventy men, and they ceased fighting against Cush, and they besieged Cush for nine years, no person came out or in. 21 At that time that the war and the siege were against Cush, Moses fled from Egypt from Pharaoh who sought to kill him for having slain the Egyptian. 22 And Moses was eighteen years old when he fled from Egypt from the presence of Pharaoh, and he fled and escaped to the camp of Kikianus, which at that time was besieging Cush. 23 And Moses was nine years in the camp of Kikianus king of Cush, all the time that they were besieging Cush, and Moses went out and came in with them. 24 And the king and princes and all the fighting men loved Moses, for he was great and worthy, his stature was like a noble lion, his face was like the sun, and his strength was like that of a lion, and he was counsellor to the king. 25 And at the end of nine years, Kikianus was seized with a mortal disease, and his illness prevailed over him, and he died on the seventh day. 26 So his servants embalmed him and carried him and buried him opposite the city gate to the north of the land of Egypt. 27 And they built over

him an elegant strong and high building, and they placed great stones below. 28 And the king's scribes engraved upon those stones all the might of their king Kikianus, and all his battles which he had fought, behold they are written there at this day. 29 Now after the death of Kikianus king of Cush it grieved his men and troops greatly on account of the war. 30 So they said one to the other, Give us counsel what we are to do at this time, as we have resided in the wilderness nine years away from our homes. 31 If we say we will fight against the city many of us will fall wounded or killed, and if we remain here in the siege we shall also die. 32 For now all the kings of Aram and of the children of the east will hear that our king is dead, and they will attack us suddenly in a hostile manner, and they will fight against us and leave no remnant of us. 33 Now therefore let us go and make a king over us, and let us remain in the siege until the city is delivered up to us. 34 And they wished to choose on that day a man for king from the army of Kikianus, and they found no object of their choice like Moses to reign over them. 35 And they hastened and stripped off each man his garments and cast them upon the ground, and they made a great heap and placed Moses thereon. 36 And they rose up and blew with trumpets and called out before him, and said, May the king live, may the king live! 37 And all the people and nobles swore unto him to give him for a wife Adoniah the queen, the Cushite, wife of Kikianus, and they made Moses king over them on that day. 38 And all the people of Cush issued a proclamation on that day, saying, Every man must give something to Moses of what is in his possession. 39 And they spread out a sheet upon the heap, and every man cast into it something of what he had, one a gold earring and the other a coin. 40 Also of onyx stones, bdellium, pearls and marble did the children of Cush cast unto Moses upon the heap, also silver and gold in great abundance. 41 And Moses took all the silver and gold, all the vessels, and the bdellium and onyx stones, which all the children of Cush had given to him, and he placed them amongst his treasures. 42 And Moses reigned over the children of Cush on that day, in the place of Kikianus king of Cush.

Jash.73

1 In the fifty-fifth year of the reign of Pharaoh king of Egypt, that is in the hundred and fifty-seventh year of the Israelites going down into Egypt, reigned Moses in Cush. 2 Moses was twenty-seven years old when he began to reign over Cush, and forty years did he reign. 3 And the Lord granted Moses favor and grace in the eyes of all the children of Cush, and the children of Cush loved him exceedingly, so Moses was favored by the Lord and by men. 4 And in the seventh day of his reign, all the children of Cush assembled and came before Moses and bowed down to him to the ground. 5 And all the children spoke together in the presence of the king, saying, Give us counsel that we may see what is to be done to this city. 6 For it is now nine years that we have been besieging round about the city, and have not seen our children and our wives. 7 So the king answered them, saying, If you will hearken to my voice in all that I shall command you, then will the Lord give the city into our hands and we shall subdue it. 8 For if we fight with them as in the former battle which we had with them before the death of Kikianus, many of us will fall down wounded as before. 9 Now therefore behold here is counsel for you in this matter; if you will hearken to my voice, then will the city be delivered into our hands. 10 So all the forces answered the king, saying, All that our lord shall command that will we do. 11 And Moses said unto them, Pass through and proclaim a voice in the whole camp unto all the people, saying, 12 Thus says the king, Go into the forest and bring with you of the young ones of the stork, each man a young one in his hand. 13 And any person transgressing the word of the king, who shall not bring his young one, he shall die, and the king will take all

belonging to him. ¹⁴ And when you shall bring them they shall be in your keeping, you shall rear them until they grow up, and you shall teach them to dart upon, as is the way of the young ones of the hawk. ¹⁵ So all the children of Cush heard the words of Moses, and they rose up and caused a proclamation to be issued throughout the camp, saying, ¹⁶ Unto you, all the children of Cush, the king's order is, that you go all together to the forest, and catch there the young storks each man his young one in his hand, and you shall bring them home. ¹⁷ And any person violating the order of the king shall die, and the king will take all that belongs to him. ¹⁸ And all the people did so, and they went out to the wood and they climbed the fir trees and caught, each man a young one in his hand, all the young of the storks, and they brought them into the desert and reared them by order of the king, and they taught them to dart upon, similar to the young hawks. ¹⁹ And after the young storks were reared, the king ordered them to be hungered for three days, and all the people did so. ²⁰ And on the third day, the king said unto them, strengthen yourselves and become valiant men, and put on each man his armor and gird on his sword upon him, and ride each man his horse and take each his young stork in his hand. ²¹ And we will rise up and fight against the city at the place where the serpents are; and all the people did as the king had ordered. ²² And they took each man his young one in his hand, and they went away, and when they came to the place of the serpents the king said to them, Send forth each man his young stork upon the serpents. ²³ And they sent forth each man his young stork at the king's order, and the young storks ran upon the serpents and they devoured them all and destroyed them out of that place. ²⁴ And when the king and people had seen that all the serpents were destroyed in that place, all the people set up a great shout. ²⁵ And they approached and fought against the city and took it and subdued it, and they entered the city. ²⁶ And there died on that day one thousand and one hundred men of the people of the city, all that inhabited the city, but of the people besieging not one died. ²⁷ So all the children of Cush went each to his home, to his wife and children and to all belonging to him. ²⁸ And Balaam the magician, when he saw that the city was taken, he opened the gate and he and his two sons and eight brothers fled and returned to Egypt to Pharaoh king of Egypt. ²⁹ They are the sorcerers and magicians who are mentioned in the book of the law, standing against Moses when the Lord brought the plagues upon Egypt. ³⁰ So Moses took the city by his wisdom, and the children of Cush placed him on the throne instead of Kikianus king of Cush. ³¹ And they placed the royal crown upon his head, and they gave him for a wife Adoniah the Cushite queen, wife of Kikianus. ³² And Moses feared the Lord God of his fathers, so that he came not to her, nor did he turn his eyes to her. ³³ For Moses remembered how Abraham had made his servant Eliezer swear, saying unto him, Thou shalt not take a woman from the daughters of Canaan for my son Isaac. ³⁴ Also what Isaac did when Jacob had fled from his brother, when he commanded him, saying, Thou shalt not take a wife from the daughters of Canaan, nor make alliance with any of the children of Ham. ³⁵ For the Lord our God gave Ham the son of Noah, and his children and all his seed, as slaves to the children of Shem and to the children of Japheth, and unto their seed after them for slaves, forever. ³⁶ Therefore Moses turned not his heart nor his eyes to the wife of Kikianus all the days that he reigned over Cush. ³⁷ And Moses feared the Lord his God all his life, and Moses walked before the Lord in truth, with all his heart and soul, he turned not from the right way all the days of his life; he declined not from the way either to the right or to the left, in which Abraham, Isaac and Jacob had walked. ³⁸ And Moses strengthened himself in the kingdom of the children of Cush, and he guided the children of Cush with his usual

wisdom, and Moses prospered in his kingdom. ³⁹ And at that time Aram and the children of the east heard that Kikianus king of Cush had died, so Aram and the children of the east rebelled against Cush in those days. ⁴⁰ And Moses gathered all the children of Cush, a people very mighty, about thirty thousand men, and he went forth to fight with Aram and the children of the east. ⁴¹ And they went at first to the children of the east, and when the children of the east heard their report, they went to meet them, and engaged in battle with them. ⁴² And the war was severe against the children of the east, so the Lord gave all the children of the east into the hand of Moses, and about three hundred men fell down slain. ⁴³ And all the children of the east turned back and retreated, so Moses and the children of Cush followed them and subdued them, and put a tax upon them, as was their custom. ⁴⁴ So Moses and all the people with him passed from there to the land of Aram for battle. ⁴⁵ And the people of Aram also went to meet them, and they fought against them, and the Lord delivered them into the hand of Moses, and many of the men of Aram fell down wounded. ⁴⁶ And Aram also were subdued by Moses and the people of Cush, and also gave their usual tax. ⁴⁷ And Moses brought Aram and the children of the east under subjection to the children of Cush, and Moses and all the people who were with him, turned to the land of Cush. ⁴⁸ And Moses strengthened himself in the kingdom of the children of Cush, and the Lord was with him, and all the children of Cush were afraid of him.

Jash.74

¹ In the end of years died Saul king of Edom, and Baal Chanan the son of Achbor reigned in his place. ² In the sixteenth year of the reign of Moses over Cush, Baal Chanan the son of Achbor reigned in the land of Edom over all the children of Edom for thirty-eight years. ³ In his days Moab rebelled against the power of Edom, having been under Edom since the days of Hadad the son of Bedad, who smote them and Midian, and brought Moab under subjection to Edom. ⁴ And when Baal Chanan the son of Achbor reigned over Edom, all the children of Moab withdrew their allegiance from Edom. ⁵ And Angeas king of Africa died in those days, and Azdrubal his son reigned in his stead. ⁶ And in those days died Janeas king of the children of Chittim, and they buried him in his temple which he had built for himself in the plain of Canopia for a residence, and Latinus reigned in his stead. ⁷ In the twenty-second year of the reign of Moses over the children of Cush, Latinus reigned over the children of Chittim forty-five years. ⁸ And he also built for himself a great and mighty tower, and he built therein an elegant temple for his residence, to conduct his government, as was the custom. ⁹ In the third year of his reign he caused a proclamation to be made to all his skilful men, who made many ships for him. ¹⁰ And Latinus assembled all his forces, and they came in ships, and went therein to fight with Azdrubal son of Angeas king of Africa, and they came to Africa and engaged in battle with Azdrubal and his army. ¹¹ And Latinus prevailed over Azdrubal, and Latinus took from Azdrubal the aqueduct which his father had brought from the children of Chittim, when he took Janiah the daughter of Uzi for a wife, so Latinus overthrew the bridge of the aqueduct, and smote the whole army of Azdrubal a severe blow. ¹² And the remaining strong men of Azdrubal strengthened themselves, and their hearts were filled with envy, and they courted death, and again engaged in battle with Latinus king of Chittim. ¹³ And the battle was severe upon all the men of Africa, and they all fell wounded before Latinus and his people, and Azdrubal the king also fell in that battle. ¹⁴ And the king Azdrubal had a very beautiful daughter, whose name was Ushpezena, and all the men of Africa embroidered her likeness on their garments, on account of her great beauty and comely appearance. ¹⁵ And the men of Latinus saw Ushpezena, the daughter

of Azdrubal, and praised her unto Latinus their king. 16 And Latinus ordered her to be brought to him, and Latinus took Ushpezena for a wife, and he turned back on his way to Chittim. 17 And it was after the death of Azdrubal son of Angeas, when Latinus had turned back to his land from the battle, that all the inhabitants of Africa rose up and took Anibal the son of Angeas, the younger brother of Azdrubal, and made him king instead at his brother over the whole land at Africa. 18 And when he reigned, he resolved to go to Chittim to fight with the children of Chittim, to avenge the cause of Azdrubal his brother, and the cause of the inhabitants of Africa, and he did so. 19 And he made many ships, and he came therein with his whole army, and he went to Chittim. 20 So Anibal fought with the children of Chittim, and the children of Chittim fell wounded before Anibal and his army, and Anibal avenged his brother's cause. 21 And Anibal continued the war for eighteen years with the children of Chittim, and Anibal dwelt in the land of Chittim and encamped there for a long time. 22 And Anibal smote the children of Chittim very severely, and he slew their great men and princes, and of the rest of the people he smote about eighty thousand men. 23 And at the end of days and years, Anibal returned to his land of Africa, and he reigned securely in the place of Azdrubal his brother.

Jash.75

1 At that time, in the hundred and eightieth year of the Israelites going down into Egypt, there went forth from Egypt valiant men, thirty thousand on foot, from the children of Israel, who were all of the tribe of Joseph, of the children of Ephraim the son of Joseph. 2 For they said the period was completed which the Lord had appointed to the children of Israel in the times of old, which he had spoken to Abraham. 3 And these men girded themselves, and they put each man his sword at his side, and every man his armor upon him, and they trusted to their strength, and they went out together from Egypt with a mighty hand. 4 But they brought no provision for the road, only silver and gold, not even bread for that day did they bring in their hands, for they thought of getting their provision for pay from the Philistines, and if not they would take it by force. 5 And these men were very mighty and valiant men, one man could pursue a thousand and two could rout ten thousand, so they trusted to their strength and went together as they were. 6 And they directed their course toward the land of Gath, and they went down and found the shepherds of Gath feeding the cattle of the children of Gath. 7 And they said to the shepherds, Give us some of the sheep for pay, that we may eat, for we are hungry, for we have eaten no bread this day. 8 And the shepherds said, Are they our sheep or cattle that we should give them to you even for pay? so the children of Ephraim approached to take them by force. 9 And the shepherds of Gath shouted over them that their cry was heard at a distance, so all the children of Gath went out to them. 10 And when the children of Gath saw the evil doings of the children of Ephraim, they returned and assembled the men of Gath, and they put on each man his armor, and came forth to the children of Ephraim for battle. 11 And they engaged with them in the valley of Gath, and the battle was severe, and they smote from each other a great many on that day. 12 And on the second day the children of Gath sent to all the cities of the Philistines that they should come to their help, saying, 13 Come up unto us and help us, that we may smite the children of Ephraim who have come forth from Egypt to take our cattle, and to fight against us without cause. 14 Now the souls of the children of Ephraim were exhausted with hunger and thirst, for they had eaten no bread for three days. And forty thousand men went forth from the cities of the Philistines to the assistance of the men of Gath. 15 And these men were engaged in battle with the children of Ephraim, and the Lord delivered the children of Ephraim into

296

the hands of the Philistines. 16 And they smote all the children of Ephraim, all who had gone forth from Egypt, none were remaining but ten men who had run away from the engagement. 17 For this evil was from the Lord against the children of Ephraim, for they transgressed the word of the Lord in going forth from Egypt, before the period had arrived which the Lord in the days of old had appointed to Israel. 18 And of the Philistines also there fell a great many, about twenty thousand men, and their brethren carried them and buried them in their cities. 19 And the slain of the children of Ephraim remained forsaken in the valley of Gath for many days and years, and were not brought to burial, and the valley was filled with men's bones. 20 And the men who had escaped from the battle came to Egypt, and told all the children of Israel all that had befallen them. 21 And their father Ephraim mourned over them for many days, and his brethren came to console him. 22 And he came unto his wife and she bare a son, and he called his name Beriah, for she was unfortunate in his house.

Jash.76

1 And Moses the son of Amram was still king in the land of Cush in those days, and he prospered in his kingdom, and he conducted the government of the children of Cush in justice, in righteousness, and integrity. 2 And all the children of Cush loved Moses all the days that he reigned over them, and all the inhabitants of the land of Cush were greatly afraid of him. 3 And in the fortieth year of the reign of Moses over Cush, Moses was sitting on the royal throne whilst Adoniah the queen was before him, and all the nobles were sitting around him. 4 And Adoniah the queen said before the king and the princes, What is this thing which you, the children of Cush, have done for this long time? 5 Surely you know that for forty years that this man has reigned over Cush he has not approached me, nor has he served the gods of the children of Cush. 6 Now therefore hear, O ye children of Cush, and let this man no more reign over you as he is not of our flesh. 7 Behold Menacrus my son is grown up, let him reign over you, for it is better for you to serve the son of your lord, than to serve a stranger, slave of the king of Egypt. 8 And all the people and nobles of the children of Cush heard the words which Adoniah the queen had spoken in their ears. 9 And all the people were preparing until the evening, and in the morning they rose up early and made Menacrus, son of Kikianus, king over them. 10 And all the children of Cush were afraid to stretch forth their hand against Moses, for the Lord was with Moses, and the children of Cush remembered the oath which they swore unto Moses, therefore they did no harm to him. 11 But the children of Cush gave many presents to Moses, and sent him from them with great honor. 12 So Moses went forth from the land of Cush, and went home and ceased to reign over Cush, and Moses was sixty-six years old when he went out of the land of Cush, for the thing was from the Lord, for the period had arrived which he had appointed in the days of old, to bring forth Israel from the affliction of the children of Ham. 13 So Moses went to Midian, for he was afraid to return to Egypt on account of Pharaoh, and he went and sat at a well of water in Midian. 14 And the seven daughters of Reuel the Midianite went out to feed their father's flock. 15 And they came to the well and drew water to water their father's flock. 16 So the shepherds of Midian came and drove them away, and Moses rose up and helped them and watered the flock. 17 And they came home to their father Reuel, and told him what Moses did for them. 18 And they said, An Egyptian man has delivered us from the hands of the shepherds, he drew up water for us and watered the flock. 19 And Reuel said to his daughters, And where is he? wherefore have you left the man? 20 And Reuel sent for him and fetched him and brought him home, and he ate bread with him. 21 And Moses related

to Reuel that he had fled from Egypt and that he reigned forty years over Cush, and that they afterward had taken the government from him, and had sent him away in peace with honor and with presents. 22 And when Reuel had heard the words of Moses, Reuel said within himself, I will put this man into the prison house, whereby I shall conciliate the children of Cush, for he has fled from them. 23 And they took and put him into the prison house, and Moses was in prison ten years, and whilst Moses was in the prison house, Zipporah the daughter of Reuel took pity over him, and supported him with bread and water all the time. 24 And all the children of Israel were yet in the land of Egypt serving the Egyptians in all manner of hard work, and the hand of Egypt continued in severity over the children of Israel in those days. 25 At that time the Lord smote Pharaoh king of Egypt, and he afflicted with the plague of leprosy from the sole of his foot to the crown of his head; owing to the cruel treatment of the children of Israel was this plague at that time from the Lord upon Pharaoh king of Egypt. 26 For the Lord had hearkened to the prayer of his people the children of Israel, and their cry reached him on account of their hard work. 27 Still his anger did not turn from them, and the hand of Pharaoh was still stretched out against the children of Israel, and Pharaoh hardened his neck before the Lord, and he increased his yoke over the children of Israel, and embittered their lives with all manner of hard work. 28 And when the Lord had inflicted the plague upon Pharaoh king of Egypt, he asked his wise men and sorcerers to cure him. 29 And his wise men and sorcerers said unto him, That if the blood of little children were put into the wounds he would be healed. 30 And Pharaoh hearkened to them, and sent his ministers to Goshen to the children of Israel to take their little children. 31 And Pharaoh's ministers went and took the infants of the children of Israel from the bosoms of their mothers by force, and they brought them to Pharaoh daily, a child each day, and the physicians killed them and applied them to the plague; thus did they all the days. 32 And the number of the children which Pharaoh slew was three hundred and seventy-five. 33 But the Lord hearkened not to the physicians of the king of Egypt, and the plague went on increasing mightily. 34 And Pharaoh was ten years afflicted with that plague, still the heart of Pharaoh was more hardened against the children of Israel. 35 And at the end of ten years the Lord continued to afflict Pharaoh with destructive plagues. 36 And the Lord smote him with a bad tumor and sickness at the stomach, and that plague turned to a severe boil. 37 At that time the two ministers of Pharaoh came from the land of Goshen where all the children of Israel were, and went to the house of Pharaoh and said to him, We have seen the children of Israel slacken in their work and negligent in their labor. 38 And when Pharaoh heard the words of his ministers, his anger was kindled against the children of Israel exceedingly, for he was greatly grieved at his bodily pain. 39 And he answered and said, Now that the children of Israel know that I am ill, they turn and scoff at us, now therefore harness my chariot for me, and I will betake myself to Goshen and will see the scoff of the children of Israel with which they are deriding me; so his servants harnessed the chariot for him. 40 And they took and made him ride upon a horse, for he was not able to ride of himself; 41 And he took with him ten horsemen and ten footmen, and went to the children of Israel to Goshen. 42 And when they had come to the border of Egypt, the king's horse passed into a narrow place, elevated in the hollow part of the vineyard, fenced on both sides, the low, plain country being on the other side. 43 And the horses ran rapidly in that place and pressed each other, and the other horses pressed the king's horse. 44 And the king's horse fell into the low plain whilst the king was riding upon it, and when he fell the chariot turned over the

king's face and the horse lay upon the king, and the king cried out, for his flesh was very sore. 45 And the flesh of the king was torn from him, and his bones were broken and he could not ride, for this thing was from the Lord to him, for the Lord had heard the cries of his people the children of Israel and their affliction. 46 And his servants carried him upon their shoulders, a little at a time, and they brought him back to Egypt, and the horsemen who were with him came also back to Egypt. 47 And they placed him in his bed, and the king knew that his end was come to die, so Aparanith the queen his wife came and cried before the king, and the king wept a great weeping with her. 48 And all his nobles and servants came on that day and saw the king in that affliction, and wept a great weeping with him. 49 And the princes of the king and all his counselors advised the king to cause one to reign in his stead in the land, whomsoever he should choose from his sons. 50 And the king had three sons and two daughters which Aparanith the queen his wife had borne to him, besides the king's children of concubines. 51 And these were their names, the firstborn Othri, the second Adikam, and the third Morion, and their sisters, the name of the elder Bathia and of the other Acuzi. 52 And Othri the first born of the king was an idiot, precipitate and hurried in his words. 53 But Adikam was a cunning and wise man and knowing in all the wisdom of Egypt, but of unseemly aspect, thick in flesh, and very short in stature; his height was one cubit. 54 And when the king saw Adikam his son intelligent and wise in all things, the king resolved that he should be king in his stead after his death. 55 And he took for him a wife Gedudah daughter of Abilot, and he was ten years old, and she bare unto him four sons. 56 And he afterward went and took three wives and begat eight sons and three daughters. 57 And the disorder greatly prevailed over the king, and his flesh stank like the flesh of a carcass cast upon the field in summer time, during the heat of the sun. 58 And when the king saw that his sickness had greatly strengthened itself over him, he ordered his son Adikam to be brought to him, and they made him king over the land in his place. 59 And at the end of three years, the king died, in shame, disgrace, and disgust, and his servants carried him and buried him in the sepulcher of the kings of Egypt in Zoan Mizraim. 60 But they embalmed him not as was usual with kings, for his flesh was putrid, and they could not approach to embalm him on account of the stench, so they buried him in haste. 61 For this evil was from the Lord to him, for the Lord had requited him evil for the evil which in his days he had done to Israel. 62 And he died with terror and with shame, and his son Adikam reigned in his place.<

Jash.77

1 Adikam was twenty years old when he reigned over Egypt, he reigned four years. 2 In the two hundred and sixth year of Israel's going down to Egypt did Adikam reign over Egypt, but he continued not so long in his reign over Egypt as his fathers had continued their reigns. 3 For Melol his father reigned ninety-four years in Egypt, but he was ten years sick and died, for he had been wicked before the Lord. 4 And all the Egyptians called the name of Adikam Pharaoh like the name of his fathers, as was their custom to do in Egypt. 5 And all the wise men of Pharaoh called the name of Adikam Ahuz, for short is called Ahuz in the Egyptian language. 6 And Adikam was exceedingly ugly, and he was a cubit and a span and he had a great beard which reached to the soles of his feet. 7 And Pharaoh sat upon his father's throne to reign over Egypt, and he conducted the government of Egypt in his wisdom. 8 And whilst he reigned he exceeded his father and all the preceding kings in wickedness, and he increased his yoke over the children of Israel. 9 And he went with his servants to Goshen to the children of Israel, and he strengthened the labor over them and he

said unto them, Complete your work, each day's task, and let not your hands slacken from our work from this day forward as you did in the days of my father. ¹⁰ And he placed officers over them from amongst the children of Israel, and over these officers he placed taskmasters from amongst his servants. ¹¹ And he placed over them a measure of bricks for them to do according to that number, day by day, and he turned back and went to Egypt. ¹² At that time the task-masters of Pharaoh ordered the officers of the children of Israel according to the command of Pharaoh, saying, ¹³ Thus says Pharaoh, Do your work each day, and finish your task, and observe the daily measure of bricks; diminish not anything. ¹⁴ And it shall come to pass that if you are deficient in your daily bricks, I will put your young children in their stead. ¹⁵ And the task-masters of Egypt did so in those days as Pharaoh had ordered them. ¹⁶ And whenever any deficiency was found in the children of Israel's measure of their daily bricks, the task-masters of Pharaoh would go to the wives of the children of Israel and take infants of the children of Israel to the number of bricks deficient, they would take them by force from their mother's laps, and put them in the building instead of the bricks; ¹⁷ Whilst their fathers and mothers were crying over them and weeping when they heard the weeping voices of their infants in the wall of the building. ¹⁸ And the task-masters prevailed over Israel, that the Israelites should place their children in the building, so that a man placed his son in the wall and put mortar over him, whilst his eyes wept over him, and his tears ran down upon his child. ¹⁹ And the task-masters of Egypt did so to the babes of Israel for many days, and no one pitied or had compassion over the babes of the children of Israel. ²⁰ And the number of all the children killed in the building was two hundred and seventy, some whom they had built upon instead of the bricks which had been left deficient by their fathers, and some whom they had drawn out dead from the building. ²¹ And the labor imposed upon the children of Israel in the days of Adikam exceeded in hardship that which they performed in the days of his father. ²² And the children of Israel sighed every day on account of their heavy work, for they had said to themselves, Behold when Pharaoh shall die, his son will rise up and lighten our work! ²³ But they increased the latter work more than the former, and the children of Israel sighed at this and their cry ascended to God on account of their labor. ²⁴ And God heard the voice of the children of Israel and their cry, in those days, and God remembered to them his covenant which he had made with Abraham, Isaac and Jacob. ²⁵ And God saw the burden of the children of Israel, and their heavy work in those days, and he determined to deliver them. ²⁶ And Moses the son of Amram was still confined in the dungeon in those days, in the house of Reuel the Midianite, and Zipporah the daughter of Reuel did support him with food secretly day by day. ²⁷ And Moses was confined in the dungeon in the house of Reuel for ten years. ²⁸ And at the end of ten years which was the first year of the reign of Pharaoh over Egypt, in the place of his father, ²⁹ Zipporah said to her father Reuel, No person inquires or seeks after the Hebrew man, whom thou didst bind in prison now ten years. ³⁰ Now therefore, if it seem good in thy sight, let us send and see whether he is living or dead, but her father knew not that she had supported him. ³¹ And Reuel her father answered and said to her, Has ever such a thing happened that a man should be shut up in a prison without food for ten years, and that he should live? ³² And Zipporah answered her father, saying, Surely thou hast heard that the God of the Hebrews is great and awful, and does wonders for them at all times. ³³ He it was who delivered Abraham from Ur of the Chaldeans, and Isaac from the sword of his father, and Jacob from the angel of the Lord who wrestled with him at the ford of Jabbuk. ³⁴ Also with this man has he done many things, he

298

delivered him from the river in Egypt and from the sword of Pharaoh, and from the children of Cush, so also can he deliver him from famine and make him live. ³⁵ And the thing seemed good in the sight of Reuel, and he did according to the word of his daughter, and sent to the dungeon to ascertain what became of Moses. ³⁶ And he saw, and behold the man Moses was living in the dungeon, standing upon his feet, praising and praying to the God of his ancestors. ³⁷ And Reuel commanded Moses to be brought out of the dungeon, so they shaved him and he changed his prison garments and ate bread. ³⁸ And afterward Moses went into the garden of Reuel which was behind the house, and he there prayed to the Lord his God, who had done mighty wonders for him. ³⁹ And it was that whilst he prayed he looked opposite to him, and behold a sapphire stick was placed in the ground, which was planted in the midst of the garden. ⁴⁰ And he approached the stick and he looked, and behold the name of the Lord God of hosts was engraved thereon, written and developed upon the stick. ⁴¹ And he read it and stretched forth his hand and he plucked it like a forest tree from the thicket, and the stick was in his hand. ⁴² And this is the stick with which all the works of our God were performed, after he had created heaven and earth, and all the host of them, seas, rivers and all their fishes. ⁴³ And when God had driven Adam from the garden of Eden, he took the stick in his hand and went and tilled the ground from which he was taken. ⁴⁴ And the stick came down to Noah and was given to Shem and his descendants, until it came into the hand of Abraham the Hebrew. ⁴⁵ And when Abraham had given all he had to his son Isaac, he also gave to him this stick. ⁴⁶ And when Jacob had fled to Padan-aram, he took it into his hand, and when he returned to his father he had not left it behind him. ⁴⁷ Also when he went down to Egypt he took it into his hand and gave it to Joseph, one portion above his brethren, for Jacob had taken it by force from his brother Esau. ⁴⁸ And after the death of Joseph, the nobles of Egypt came into the house of Joseph, and the stick came into the hand of Reuel the Midianite, and when he went out of Egypt, he took it in his hand and planted it in his garden. ⁴⁹ And all the mighty men of the Kinites tried to pluck it when they endeavored to get Zipporah his daughter, but they were unsuccessful. ⁵⁰ So that stick remained planted in the garden of Reuel, until he came who had a right to it and took it. ⁵¹ And when Reuel saw the stick in the hand of Moses, he wondered at it, and he gave him his daughter Zipporah for a wife.

Jash.78

¹ At that time died Baal Channan son of Achbor, king of Edom, and was buried in his house in the land of Edom. ² And after his death the children of Esau sent to the land of Edom, and took from there a man who was in Edom, whose name was Hadad, and they made him king over them in the place of Baal Channan, their king. ³ And Hadad reigned over the children of Edom forty-eight years. ⁴ And when he reigned he resolved to fight against the children of Moab, to bring them under the power of the children of Esau as they were before, but he was not able, because the children of Moab heard this thing, and they rose up and hastened to elect a king over them from amongst their brethren. ⁵ And they afterward gathered together a great people, and sent to the children of Ammon their brethren for help to fight against Hadad king of Edom. ⁶ And Hadad heard the thing which the children of Moab had done, and was greatly afraid of them, and refrained from fighting against them. ⁷ In those days Moses, the son of Amram, in Midian, took Zipporah, the daughter of Reuel the Midianite, for a wife. ⁸ And Zipporah walked in the ways of the daughters of Jacob, she was nothing short of the righteousness of Sarah, Rebecca, Rachel and Leah. ⁹ And Zipporah conceived and bare a son and he called his

name Gershom, for he said, I was a stranger in a foreign land; but he circumcised not his foreskin, at the command of Reuel his father-in-law. [10] And she conceived again and bare a son, but circumcised his foreskin, and called his name Eliezer, for Moses said, Because the God of my fathers was my help, and delivered me from the sword of Pharaoh. [11] And Pharaoh king of Egypt greatly increased the labor of the children of Israel in those days, and continued to make his yoke heavier upon the children of Israel. [12] And he ordered a proclamation to be made in Egypt, saying, Give no more straw to the people to make bricks with, let them go and gather themselves straw as they can find it. [13] Also the tale of bricks which they shall make let them give each day, and diminish nothing from them, for they are idle in their work. [14] And the children of Israel heard this, and they mourned and sighed, and they cried unto the Lord on account of the bitterness of their souls. [15] And the Lord heard the cries of the children of Israel, and saw the oppression with which the Egyptians oppressed them. [16] And the Lord was jealous of his people and his inheritance, and heard their voice, and he resolved to take them out of the affliction of Egypt, to give them the land of Canaan for a possession.

Jash.79

[1] And in those days Moses was feeding the flock of Reuel the Midianite his father-in-law, beyond the wilderness of Sin, and the stick which he took from his father-in-law was in his hand. [2] And it came to pass one day that a kid of goats strayed from the flock, and Moses pursued it and it came to the mountain of God to Horeb. [3] And when he came to Horeb, the Lord appeared there unto him in the bush, and he found the bush burning with fire, but the fire had no power over the bush to consume it. [4] And Moses was greatly astonished at this sight, wherefore the bush was not consumed, and he approached to see this mighty thing, and the Lord called unto Moses out of the fire and commanded him to go down to Egypt, to Pharaoh king of Egypt, to send the children of Israel from his service. [5] And the Lord said unto Moses, Go, return to Egypt, for all those men who sought thy life are dead, and thou shalt speak unto Pharaoh to send forth the children of Israel from his land. [6] And the Lord showed him to do signs and wonders in Egypt before the eyes of Pharaoh and the eyes of his subjects, in order that they might believe that the Lord had sent him. [7] And Moses hearkened to all that the Lord had commanded him, and he returned to his father-in-law and told him the thing, and Reuel said to him, Go in peace. [8] And Moses rose up to go to Egypt, and he took his wife and sons with him, and he was at an inn in the road, and an angel of God came down, and sought an occasion against him. [9] And he wished to kill him on account of his first born son, because he had not circumcised him, and had transgressed the covenant which the Lord had made with Abraham. [10] For Moses had hearkened to the words of his father-in-law which he had spoken to him, not to circumcise his first born son, therefore he circumcised him not. [11] And Zipporah saw the angel of the Lord seeking an occasion against Moses, and she knew that this thing was owing to his not having circumcised her son Gershom. [12] And Zipporah hastened and took of the sharp rock stones that were there, and she circumcised her son, and delivered her husband and her son from the hand of the angel of the Lord. [13] And Aaron the son of Amram, the brother of Moses, was in Egypt walking at the river side on that day. [14] And the Lord appeared to him in that place, and he said to him, Go now toward Moses in the wilderness, and he went and met him in the mountain of God, and he kissed him. [15] And Aaron lifted up his eyes, and saw Zipporah the wife of Moses and her children, and he said unto Moses, Who are these unto thee? [16] And Moses said unto him, They are my wife and sons, which

God gave to me in Midian; and the thing grieved Aaron on account of the woman and her children. [17] And Aaron said to Moses, Send away the woman and her children that they may go to her father's house, and Moses hearkened to the words of Aaron, and did so. [18] And Zipporah returned with her children, and they went to the house of Reuel, and remained there until the time arrived when the Lord had visited his people, and brought them forth from Egypt from the hand at Pharaoh. [19] And Moses and Aaron came to Egypt to the community of the children of Israel, and they spoke to them all the words of the Lord, and the people rejoiced an exceeding great rejoicing. [20] And Moses and Aaron rose up early on the next day, and they went to the house of Pharaoh, and they took in their hands the stick of God. [21] And when they came to the king's gate, two young lions were confined there with iron instruments, and no person went out or came in from before them, unless those whom the king ordered to come, when the conjurors came and withdrew the lions by their incantations, and this brought them to the king. [22] And Moses hastened and lifted up the stick upon the lions, and he loosed them, and Moses and Aaron came into the king's house. [23] The lions also came with them in joy, and they followed them and rejoiced as a dog rejoices over his master when he comes from the field. [24] And when Pharaoh saw this thing he was astonished at it, and he was greatly terrified at the report, for their appearance was like the appearance of the children of God. [25] And Pharaoh said to Moses, What do you require? and they answered him, saying, The Lord God of the Hebrews has sent us to thee, to say, Send forth my people that they may serve me. [26] And when Pharaoh heard their words he was greatly terrified before them, and he said to them, Go today and come back to me tomorrow, and they did according to the word of the king. [27] And when they had gone Pharaoh sent for Balaam the magician and to Jannes and Jambres his sons, and to all the magicians and conjurors and counsellors which belonged to the king, and they all came and sat before the king. [28] And the king told them all the words which Moses and his brother Aaron had spoken to him, and the magicians said to the king, But how came the men to thee, on account of the lions which were confined at the gate? [29] And the king said, Because they lifted up their rod against the lions and loosed them, and came to me, and the lions also rejoiced at them as a dog rejoices to meet his master. [30] And Balaam the son of Beor the magician answered the king, saying, These are none else than magicians like ourselves. [31] Now therefore send for them, and let them come and we will try them, and the king did so. [32] And in the morning Pharaoh sent for Moses and Aaron to come before the king, and they took the rod of God, and came to the king and spoke to him, saying, [33] Thus said the Lord God of the Hebrews, Send my people that they may serve me. [34] And the king said to them, But who will believe you that you are the messengers of God and that you come to me by his order? [35] Now therefore give a wonder or sign in this matter, and then the words which you speak will be believed. [36] And Aaron hastened and threw the rod out of his hand before Pharaoh and before his servants, and the rod turned into a serpent. [37] And the sorcerers saw this and they cast each man his rod upon the ground and they became serpents. [38] And the serpent of Aaron's rod lifted up its head and opened its mouth to swallow the rods of the magicians. [39] And Balaam the magician answered and said, This thing has been from the days of old, that a serpent should swallow its fellow, and that living things devour each other. [40] Now therefore restore it to a rod as it was at first, and we will also restore our rods as they were at first, and if thy rod shall swallow our rods, then shall we know that the spirit of God is in thee, and if not, thou art only an artificer like unto ourselves. [41] And Aaron hastened and stretched forth his hand and caught hold of the serpent's tail and it became a rod in his hand, and the sorcerers did the like with their rods, and they got hold, each man of the tail of his serpent, and they became rods as at first. 42 And when they were restored to rods, the rod of Aaron swallowed up their rods. 43 And when the king saw this thing, he ordered the book of records that related to the kings of Egypt, to be brought, and they brought the book of records, the chronicles of the kings of Egypt, in which all the idols of Egypt were inscribed, for they thought of finding therein the name of Jehovah, but they found it not. 44 And Pharaoh said to Moses and Aaron, Behold I have not found the name of your God written in this book, and his name I know not. 45 And the counsellors and wise men answered the king, We have heard that the God of the Hebrews is a son of the wise, the son of ancient kings. 46 And Pharaoh turned to Moses and Aaron and said to them, I know not the Lord whom you have declared, neither will I send his people. 47 And they answered and said to the king, The Lord God of Gods is his name, and he proclaimed his name over us from the days of our ancestors, and sent us, saying, Go to Pharaoh and say unto him, Send my people that they may serve me. 48 Now therefore send us, that we may take a journey for three days in the wilderness, and there may sacrifice to him, for from the days of our going down to Egypt, he has not taken from our hands either burnt offering, oblation or sacrifice, and if thou wilt not send us, his anger will be kindled against thee, and he will smite Egypt either with the plague or with the sword. 49 And Pharaoh said to them, Tell me now his power and his might; and they said to him, He created the heaven and the earth, the seas and all their fishes, he formed the light, created the darkness, caused rain upon the earth and watered it, and made the herbage and grass to sprout, he created man and beast and the animals of the forest, the birds of the air and the fish of the sea, and by his mouth they live and die. 50 Surely he created thee in thy mother's womb, and put into thee the breath of life, and reared thee and placed thee upon the royal throne of Egypt, and he will take thy breath and soul from thee, and return thee to the ground whence thou wast taken. 51 And the anger of the king was kindled at their words, and he said to them, But who amongst all the Gods of nations can do this? my river is mine own, and I have made it for myself. 52 And he drove them from him, and he ordered the labor upon Israel to be more severe than it was yesterday and before. 53 And Moses and Aaron went out from the king's presence, and they saw the children of Israel in an evil condition for the task-masters had made their labor exceedingly heavy. 54 And Moses returned to the Lord and said, Why hast thou ill treated thy people? for since I came to speak to Pharaoh what thou didst send me for, he has exceedingly ill used the children of Israel. 55 And the Lord said to Moses, Behold thou wilt see that with an outstretched hand and heavy plagues, Pharaoh will send the children of Israel from his land. 56 And Moses and Aaron dwelt amongst their brethren the children of Israel in Egypt. 57 And as for the children of Israel the Egyptians embittered their lives, with the heavy work which they imposed upon them.

Jash.80

1 And at the end of two years, the Lord again sent Moses to Pharaoh to bring forth the children of Israel, and to send them out of the land of Egypt. 2 And Moses went and came to the house of Pharaoh, and he spoke to him the words of the Lord who had sent him, but Pharaoh would not hearken to the voice of the Lord, and God roused his might in Egypt upon Pharaoh and his subjects, and God smote Pharaoh and his people with very great and sore plagues. 3 And the Lord sent by the hand of Aaron and turned all the waters of Egypt into blood, with all their streams and rivers. 4 And when an Egyptian came to drink and draw water, he looked into his pitcher, and behold all the water was turned into blood; and when he came to drink from his cup the water in the cup became blood. 5 And when a woman kneaded her dough and cooked her victuals, their appearance was turned to that of blood. 6 And the Lord sent again and caused all their waters to bring forth frogs, and all the frogs came into the houses of the Egyptians. 7 And when the Egyptians drank, their bellies were filled with frogs and they danced in their bellies as they dance when in the river. 8 And all their drinking water and cooking water turned to frogs, also when they lay in their beds their perspiration bred frogs. 9 Notwithstanding all this the anger of the Lord did not turn from them, and his hand was stretched out against all the Egyptians to smite them with every heavy plague. 10 And he sent and smote their dust to lice, and the lice became in Egypt to the height of two cubits upon the earth. 11 The lice were also very numerous, in the flesh of man and beast, in all the inhabitants of Egypt, also upon the king and queen the Lord sent the lice, and it grieved Egypt exceedingly on account of the lice. 12 Notwithstanding this, the anger of the Lord did not turn away, and his hand was still stretched out over Egypt. 13 And the Lord sent all kinds of beasts of the field into Egypt, and they came and destroyed all Egypt, man and beast, and trees, and all things that were in Egypt. 14 And the Lord sent fiery serpents, scorpions, mice, weasels, toads, together with others creeping in dust. 15 Flies, hornets, fleas, bugs and gnats, each swarm according to its kind. 16 And all reptiles and winged animals according to their kind came to Egypt and grieved the Egyptians exceedingly. 17 And the fleas and flies came into the eyes and ears of the Egyptians. 18 And the hornet came upon them and drove them away, and they removed from it into their inner rooms, and it pursued them. 19 And when the Egyptians hid themselves on account of the swarm of animals, they locked their doors after them, and God ordered the Sulanuth which was in the sea, to come up and go into Egypt. 20 And she had long arms, ten cubits in length of the cubit of a man. 21 And she went upon the roofs and uncovered the raftering and flooring and cut them, and stretched forth her arm into the house and removed the lock and the bolt, and opened the houses of Egypt. 22 Afterward came the swarm of animals into the houses of Egypt, and the swarm of animals destroyed the Egyptians, and it grieved them exceedingly. 23 Notwithstanding this the anger of the Lord did not turn away from the Egyptians, and his hand was yet stretched forth against them. 24 And God sent the pestilence, and the pestilence pervaded Egypt, in the horses and asses, and in the camels, in herds of oxen and sheep and in man. 25 And when the Egyptians rose up early in the morning to take their cattle to pasture they found all their cattle dead. 26 And there remained of the cattle of the Egyptians only one in ten, and of the cattle belonging to Israel in Goshen not one died. 27 And God sent a burning inflammation in the flesh of the Egyptians, which burst their skins, and it became a severe itch in all the Egyptians from the soles of their feet to the crowns of their heads. 28 And many boils were in their flesh, that their flesh wasted away until they became rotten and putrid. 29 Notwithstanding this the anger of the Lord did not turn away, and his hand was still stretched out over all Egypt. 30 And the Lord sent a very heavy hail, which smote their vines and broke their fruit trees and dried them up that they fell upon them. 31 Also every green herb became dry and perished, for a mingling fire descended amidst the hail, therefore the hail and the fire consumed all things. 32 Also men and beasts that were found abroad perished of the flames of fire and of the hail, and all the young lions were exhausted. 33 And the Lord sent and brought numerous locusts into Egypt, the Chasel, Salom, Chargol, and Chagole, locusts each of its kind, which devoured all that the hail had left remaining. 34 Then the

Egyptians rejoiced at the locusts, although they consumed the produce of the field, and they caught them in abundance and salted them for food. 35 And the Lord turned a mighty wind of the sea which took away all the locusts, even those that were salted, and thrust them into the Red Sea; not one locust remained within the boundaries of Egypt. 36 And God sent darkness upon Egypt, that the whole land of Egypt and Pathros became dark for three days, so that a man could not see his hand when he lifted it to his mouth. 37 At that time died many of the people of Israel who had rebelled against the Lord and who would not hearken to Moses and Aaron, and believed not in them that God had sent them. 38 And who had said, We will not go forth from Egypt lest we perish with hunger in a desolate wilderness, and who would not hearken to the voice of Moses. 39 And the Lord plagued them in the three days of darkness, and the Israelites buried them in those days, without the Egyptians knowing of them or rejoicing over them. 40 And the darkness was very great in Egypt for three days, and any person who was standing when the darkness came, remained standing in his place, and he that was sitting remained sitting, and he that was lying continued lying in the same state, and he that was walking remained sitting upon the ground in the same spot; and this thing happened to all the Egyptians, until the darkness had passed away. 41 And the days of darkness passed away, and the Lord sent Moses and Aaron to the children of Israel, saying, Celebrate your feast and make your Passover, for behold I come in the midst of the night amongst all the Egyptians, and I will smite all their first born, from the first born of a man to the first born of a beast, and when I see your Passover, I will pass over you. 42 And the children of Israel did according to all that the Lord had commanded Moses and Aaron, thus did they in that night. 43 And it came to pass in the middle of the night, that the Lord went forth in the midst of Egypt, and smote all the first born of the Egyptians, from the first born of man to the first born of beast. 44 And Pharaoh rose up in the night, he and all his servants and all the Egyptians, and there was a great cry throughout Egypt in that night, for there was not a house in which there was not a corpse. 45 Also the likenesses of the first born of Egypt, which were carved in the walls at their houses, were destroyed and fell to the ground. 46 Even the bones of their first born who had died before this and whom they had buried in their houses, were raked up by the dogs of Egypt on that night and dragged before the Egyptians and cast before them. 47 And all the Egyptians saw this evil which had suddenly come upon them, and all the Egyptians cried out with a loud voice. 48 And all the families of Egypt wept upon that night, each man for his son and each man for his daughter, being the first born, and the tumult of Egypt was heard at a distance on that night. 49 And Bathia the daughter of Pharaoh went forth with the king on that night to seek Moses and Aaron in their houses, and they found them in their houses, eating and drinking and rejoicing with all Israel. 50 And Bathia said to Moses, Is this the reward for the good which I have done to thee, who have reared thee and stretched thee out, and thou hast brought this evil upon me and my father's house? 51 And Moses said to her, Surely ten plagues did the Lord bring upon Egypt; did any evil accrue to thee from any of them? did one of them affect thee? and she said, No. 52 And Moses said to her, Although thou art the first born to thy mother, thou shalt not die, and no evil shall reach thee in the midst of Egypt. 53 And she said, What advantage is it to me, when I see the king, my brother, and all his household and subjects in this evil, whose first born perish with all the first born of Egypt? 54 And Moses said to her, Surely thy brother and his household, and subjects, the families of Egypt, would not hearken to the words of the Lord, therefore did this evil come upon them. 55 And Pharaoh king of Egypt approached Moses

and Aaron, and some of the children of Israel who were with them in that place, and he prayed to them, saying, 56 Rise up and take your brethren, all the children of Israel who are in the land, with their sheep and oxen, and all belonging to them, they shall leave nothing remaining, only pray for me to the Lord your God. 57 And Moses said to Pharaoh, Behold though thou art thy mother's first born, yet fear not, for thou wilt not die, for the Lord has commanded that thou shalt live, in order to show thee his great might and strong stretched out arm. 58 And Pharaoh ordered the children of Israel to be sent away, and all the Egyptians strengthened themselves to send them, for they said, We are all perishing. 59 And all the Egyptians sent the Israelites forth, with great riches, sheep and oxen and precious things, according to the oath of the Lord between him and our Father Abraham. 60 And the children of Israel delayed going forth at night, and when the Egyptians came to them to bring them out, they said to them, Are we thieves, that we should go forth at night? 61 And the children of Israel asked of the Egyptians, vessels of silver, and vessels of gold, and garments, and the children of Israel stripped the Egyptians. 62 And Moses hastened and rose up and went to the river of Egypt, and brought up from thence the coffin of Joseph and took it with him. 63 The children of Israel also brought up, each man his father's coffin with him, and each man the coffins of his tribe.

Jash.81

1 And the children of Israel journeyed from Rameses to Succoth, about six hundred thousand men on foot, besides the little ones and their wives. 2 Also a mixed multitude went up with them, and flocks and herds, even much cattle. 3 And the sojourning of the children of Israel, who dwelt in the land of Egypt in hard labor, was two hundred and ten years. 4 And at the end of two hundred and ten years, the Lord brought forth the children of Israel from Egypt with a strong hand. 5 And the children of Israel traveled from Egypt and from Goshen and from Rameses, and encamped in Succoth on the fifteenth day of the first month. 6 And the Egyptians buried all their first born whom the Lord had smitten, and all the Egyptians buried their slain for three days. 7 And the children of Israel traveled from Succoth and encamped in Ethom, at the end of the wilderness. 8 And on the third day after the Egyptians had buried their first born, many men rose up from Egypt and went after Israel to make them return to Egypt, for they repented that they had sent the Israelites away from their servitude. 9 And one man said to his neighbor, Surely Moses and Aaron spoke to Pharaoh, saying, We will go a three days' journey in the wilderness and sacrifice to the Lord our God. 10 Now therefore let us rise up early in the morning and cause them to return, and it shall be that if they return with us to Egypt to their masters, then shall we know that there is faith in them, but if they will not return, then will we fight with them, and make them come back with great power and a strong hand. 11 And all the nobles of Pharaoh rose up in the morning, and with them about seven hundred thousand men, and they went forth from Egypt on that day, and came to the place where the children of Israel were. 12 And all the Egyptians saw and behold Moses and Aaron and all the children of Israel were sitting before Pi-hahiroth, eating and drinking and celebrating the feast of the Lord. 13 And all the Egyptians said to the children of Israel, Surely you said, We will go a journey for three days in the wilderness and sacrifice to our God and return. 14 Now therefore this day makes five days since you went, why do you not return to your masters? 15 And Moses and Aaron answered them, saying, Because the Lord our God has testified in us, saying, You shall no more return to Egypt, but we will betake ourselves to a land flowing with milk and honey, as the Lord our God had sworn to our ancestors to give to us. 16 And when the

nobles of Egypt saw that the children of Israel did not hearken to them, to return to Egypt, they girded themselves to fight with Israel. 17 And the Lord strengthened the hearts of the children of Israel over the Egyptians, that they gave them a severe beating, and the battle was sore upon the Egyptians, and all the Egyptians fled from before the children of Israel, for many of them perished by the hand of Israel. 18 And the nobles of Pharaoh went to Egypt and told Pharaoh, saying, The children of Israel have fled, and will no more return to Egypt, and in this manner did Moses and Aaron speak to us. 19 And Pharaoh heard this thing, and his heart and the hearts of all his subjects were turned against Israel, and they repented that they had sent Israel; and all the Egyptians advised Pharaoh to pursue the children of Israel to make them come back to their burdens. 20 And they said each man to his brother, What is this which we have done, that we have sent Israel from our servitude? 21 And the Lord strengthened the hearts of all the Egyptians to pursue the Israelites, for the Lord desired to overthrow the Egyptians in the Red Sea. 22 And Pharaoh rose up and harnessed his chariot, and he ordered all the Egyptians to assemble, not one man was left excepting the little ones and the women. 23 And all the Egyptians went forth with Pharaoh to pursue the children of Israel, and the camp of Egypt was an exceedingly large and heavy camp, about ten hundred thousand men. 24 And the whole of this camp went and pursued the children of Israel to bring them back to Egypt, and they reached them encamping by the Red Sea. 25 And the children of Israel lifted up their eyes, and beheld all the Egyptians pursuing them, and the children of Israel were greatly terrified at them, and the children of Israel cried to the Lord. 26 And on account of the Egyptians, the children of Israel divided themselves into four divisions, and they were divided in their opinions, for they were afraid of the Egyptians, and Moses spoke to each of them. 27 The first division was of the children of Reuben, Simeon, and Issachar, and they resolved to cast themselves into the sea, for they were exceedingly afraid of the Egyptians. 28 And Moses said to them, Fear not, stand still and see the salvation of the Lord which He will effect this day for you. 29 The second division was of the children of Zebulun, Benjamin and Naphtali, and they resolved to go back to Egypt with the Egyptians. 30 And Moses said to them, Fear not, for as you have seen the Egyptians this day, so shall you see them no more for ever. 31 The third division was of the children of Judah and Joseph, and they resolved to go to meet the Egyptians to fight with them. 32 And Moses said to them, Stand in your places, for the Lord will fight for you, and you shall remain silent. 33 And the fourth division was of the children of Levi, Gad, and Asher, and they resolved to go into the midst of the Egyptians to confound them, and Moses said to them, Remain in your stations and fear not, only call unto the Lord that he may save you out of their hands. 34 After this Moses rose up from amidst the people, and he prayed to the Lord and said, 35 O Lord God of the whole earth, save now thy people whom thou didst bring forth from Egypt, and let not the Egyptians boast that power and might are theirs. 36 So the Lord said to Moses, Why dost thou cry unto me? speak to the children of Israel that they shall proceed, and do thou stretch out thy rod upon the sea and divide it, and the children of Israel shall pass through it. 37 And Moses did so, and he lifted up his rod upon the sea and divided it. 38 And the waters of the sea were divided into twelve parts, and the children of Israel passed through on foot, with shoes, as a man would pass through a prepared road. 39 And the Lord manifested to the children of Israel his wonders in Egypt and in the sea by the hand of Moses and Aaron. 40 And when the children of Israel had entered the sea, the Egyptians came after them, and the waters of the sea resumed upon them, and they all sank in the water,

and not one man was left excepting Pharaoh, who gave thanks to the Lord and believed in him, therefore the Lord did not cause him to perish at that time with the Egyptians. 41 And the Lord ordered an angel to take him from amongst the Egyptians, who cast him upon the land of Ninevah and he reigned over it for a long time. 42 And on that day the Lord saved Israel from the hand of Egypt, and all the children of Israel saw that the Egyptians had perished, and they beheld the great hand of the Lord, in what he had performed in Egypt and in the sea. 43 Then sang Moses and the children of Israel this song unto the Lord, on the day when the Lord caused the Egyptians to fall before them. 44 And all Israel sang in concert, saying, I will sing to the Lord for He is greatly exalted, the horse and his rider has he cast into the sea; behold it is written in the book of the law of God. 45 After this the children of Israel proceeded on their journey, and encamped in Marah, and the Lord gave to the children of Israel statutes and judgments in that place in Marah, and the Lord commanded the children of Israel to walk in all his ways and to serve him. 46 And they journeyed from Marah and came to Elim, and in Elim were twelve springs of water and seventy date trees, and the children encamped there by the waters. 47 And they journeyed from Elim and came to the wilderness of Sin, on the fifteenth day of the second month after their departure from Egypt. 48 At that time the Lord gave the manna to the children of Israel to eat, and the Lord caused food to rain from heaven for the children of Israel day by day. 49 And the children of Israel ate the manna for forty years, all the days that they were in the wilderness, until they came to the land of Canaan to possess it. 50 And they proceeded from the wilderness of Sin and encamped in Alush. 51 And they proceeded from Alush and encamped in Rephidim. 52 And when the children of Israel were in Rephidim, Amalek the son of Eliphaz, the son of Esau, the brother of Zepho, came to fight with Israel. 53 And he brought with him eight hundred and one thousand men, magicians and conjurers, and he prepared for battle with Israel in Rephidim. 54 And they carried on a great and severe battle against Israel, and the Lord delivered Amalek and his people into the hands of Moses and the children of Israel, and into the hand of Joshua, the son of Nun, the Ephrathite, the servant of Moses. 55 And the children of Israel smote Amalek and his people at the edge of the sword, but the battle was very sore upon the children of Israel. 56 And the Lord said to Moses, Write this thing as a memorial for thee in a book, and place it in the hand of Joshua, the son of Nun, thy servant, and thou shalt command the children of Israel, saying, When thou shalt come to the land of Canaan, thou shalt utterly efface the remembrance of Amalek from under heaven. 57 And Moses did so, and he took the book and wrote upon it these words, saying, 58 Remember what Amalek has done to thee in the road when thou wentest forth from Egypt. 59 Who met thee in the road and smote thy rear, even those that were feeble behind thee when thou wast faint and weary. 60 Therefore it shall be when the Lord thy God shall have given thee rest from all thine enemies round about in the land which the Lord thy God giveth thee for an inheritance, to possess it, that thou shalt blot out the remembrance of Amalek from under heaven, thou shalt not forget it. 61 And the king who shall have pity on Amalek, or upon his memory or upon his seed, behold I will require it of him, and I will cut him off from amongst his people. 62 And Moses wrote all these things in a book, and he enjoined the children of Israel respecting all these matters.

Jash.82

1 And the children of Israel proceeded from Rephidim and they encamped in the wilderness of Sinai, in the third month from their going forth from Egypt. 2 At that time came Reuel the Midianite, the father-in-law of Moses, with Zipporah his daughter and her two

sons, for he had heard of the wonders of the Lord which he had done to Israel, that he had delivered them from the hand of Egypt. 3 And Reuel came to Moses to the wilderness where he was encamped, where was the mountain of God. 4 And Moses went forth to meet his father-in-law with great honor, and all Israel was with him. 5 And Reuel and his children remained amongst the Israelites for many days, and Reuel knew the Lord from that day forward. 6 And in the third month from the children of Israel's departure from Egypt, on the sixth day thereof, the Lord gave to Israel the ten commandments on Mount Sinai. 7 And all Israel heard all these commandments, and all Israel rejoiced exceedingly in the Lord on that day. 8 And the glory of the Lord rested upon Mount Sinai, and he called to Moses, and Moses came in the midst of a cloud and ascended the mountain. 9 And Moses was upon the mount forty days and forty nights; he ate no bread and drank no water, and the Lord instructed him in the statutes and judgments in order to teach the children of Israel. 10 And the Lord wrote the ten commandments which he had commanded the children of Israel upon two tablets of stone, which he gave to Moses to command the children of Israel. 11 And at the end of forty days and forty nights, when the Lord had finished speaking to Moses on Mount Sinai, then the Lord gave to Moses the tablets of stone, written with the finger of God. 12 And when the children of Israel saw that Moses tarried to come down from the mount, they gathered round Aaron, and said, As for this man Moses we know not what has become of him. 13 Now therefore rise up, make unto us a god who shall go before us, so that thou shalt not die. 14 And Aaron was greatly afraid of the people, and he ordered them to bring him gold and he made it into a molten calf for the people. 15 And the Lord said to Moses, before he had come down from the mount, Get thee down, for thy people whom thou didst bring forth from Egypt have corrupted themselves. 16 They have made to themselves a molten calf, and have bowed down to it, now therefore leave me, that I may consume them from off the earth, for they are a stiffnecked people. 17 And Moses besought the countenance of the Lord, and he prayed to the Lord for the people on account of the calf which they had made, and he afterward descended from the mount and in his hands were the two tablets of stone, which God had given him to command the Israelites. 18 And when Moses approached the camp and saw the calf which the people had made, the anger of Moses was kindled and he broke the tablets under the mount. 19 And Moses came to the camp and he took the calf and burned it with fire, and ground it till it became fine dust, and strewed it upon the water and gave it to the Israelites to drink. 20 And there died of the people by the swords of each other about three thousand men who had made the calf. 21 And on the morrow Moses said to the people, I will go up to the Lord, peradventure I may make atonement for your sins which you have sinned to the Lord. 22 And Moses again went up to the Lord, and he remained with the Lord forty days and forty nights. 23 And during the forty days did Moses entreat the Lord in behalf of the children of Israel, and the Lord hearkened to the prayer of Moses, and the Lord was entreated of him in behalf of Israel. 24 Then spake the Lord to Moses to hew two stone tablets and to bring them up to the Lord, who would write upon them the ten commandments. 25 Now Moses did so, and he came down and hewed the two tablets and went up to Mount Sinai to the Lord, and the Lord wrote the ten commandments upon the tablets. 26 And Moses remained yet with the Lord forty days and forty nights, and the Lord instructed him in statutes and judgments to impart to Israel. 27 And the Lord commanded him respecting the children of Israel that they should make a sanctuary for the Lord, that his name might rest therein, and the Lord showed him the likeness of the sanctuary and the likeness

of all its vessels. 28 And at the end of the forty days, Moses came down from the mount and the two tablets were in his hand. 29 And Moses came to the children of Israel and spoke to them all the words of the Lord, and he taught them laws, statutes and judgments which the Lord had taught him. 30 And Moses told the children of Israel the word of the Lord, that a sanctuary should be made for him, to dwell amongst the children of Israel. 31 And the people rejoiced greatly at all the good which the Lord had spoken to them, through Moses, and they said, We will do all that the Lord has spoken to thee. 32 And the people rose up like one man and they made generous offerings to the sanctuary of the Lord, and each man brought the offering of the Lord for the work of the sanctuary, and for all its service. 33 And all the children of Israel brought each man of all that was found in his possession for the work of the sanctuary of the Lord, gold, silver and brass, and every thing that was serviceable for the sanctuary. 34 And all the wise men who were practiced in work came and made the sanctuary of the Lord, according to all that the Lord had commanded, every man in the work in which he had been practiced; and all the wise men in heart made the sanctuary, and its furniture and all the vessels for the holy service, as the Lord had commanded Moses. 35 And the work of the sanctuary of the tabernacle was completed at the end of five months, and the children of Israel did all that the Lord had commanded Moses. 36 And they brought the sanctuary and all its furniture to Moses; like unto the representation which the Lord had shown to Moses, so did the children of Israel. 37 And Moses saw the work, and behold they did it as the Lord had commanded him, so Moses blessed them.

Jash.83

1 And in the twelfth month, in the twenty-third day of the month, Moses took Aaron and his sons, and he dressed them in their garments, and anointed them and did unto them as the Lord had commanded him, and Moses brought up all the offerings which the Lord had on that day commanded him. 2 Moses afterward took Aaron and his sons and said to them, For seven days shall you remain at the door of the tabernacle, for thus am I commanded. 3 And Aaron and his sons did all that the Lord had commanded them through Moses, and they remained for seven days at the door of the tabernacle. 4 And on the eighth day, being the first day of the first month, in the second year from the Israelites' departure from Egypt, Moses erected the sanctuary, and Moses put up all the furniture of the tabernacle and all the furniture of the sanctuary, and he did all that the Lord had commanded him. 5 And Moses called to Aaron and his sons, and they brought the burnt offering and the sin offering for themselves and the children of Israel, as the Lord had commanded Moses. 6 On that day the two sons of Aaron, Nadab and Abihu, took strange fire and brought it before the Lord who had not commanded them, and a fire went forth from before the Lord, and consumed them, and they died before the Lord on that day. 7 Then on the day when Moses had completed to erect the sanctuary, the princes of the children of Israel began to bring their offerings before the Lord for the dedication of the altar. 8 And they brought up their offerings each prince for one day, a prince each day for twelve days. 9 And all the offerings which they brought, each man in his day, one silver charger weighing one hundred and thirty shekels, one silver bowl of seventy shekels after the shekel of the sanctuary, both of them full of fine flour, mingled with oil for a meat offering. 10 One spoon, weighing ten shekels of gold, full of incense. 11 One young bullock, one ram, one lamb of the first year for a burnt offering. 12 And one kid of the goats for a sin offering. 13 And for a sacrifice of peace offering, two oxen, five rams, five he-goats, five lambs of a year old. 14 Thus did the twelve

princes of Israel day by day, each man in his day. ¹⁵ And it was after this, in the thirteenth day of the month, that Moses commanded the children of Israel to observe the Passover. ¹⁶ And the children of Israel kept the Passover in its season in the fourteenth day of the month, as the Lord had commanded Moses, so did the children of Israel. ¹⁷ And in the second month, on the first day thereof, the Lord spoke unto Moses, saying, ¹⁸ Number the heads of all the males of the children of Israel from twenty years old and upward, thou and thy brother Aaron and the twelve princes of Israel. ¹⁹ And Moses did so, and Aaron came with the twelve princes of Israel, and they numbered the children of Israel in the wilderness of Sinai. ²⁰ And the numbers of the children of Israel by the houses of their fathers, from twenty years old and upward, were six hundred and three thousand, five hundred and fifty. ²¹ But the children of Levi were not numbered amongst their brethren the children of Israel. ²² And the number of all the males of the children of Israel from one month old and upward, was twenty-two thousand, two hundred and seventy-three. ²³ And the number of the children of Levi from one month old and above, was twenty-two thousand. ²⁴ And Moses placed the priests and the Levites each man to his service and to his burden to serve the sanctuary of the tabernacle, as the Lord had commanded Moses. ²⁵ And on the twentieth day of the month, the cloud was taken away from the tabernacle of testimony. ²⁶ At that time the children of Israel continued their journey from the wilderness of Sinai, and they took a journey of three days, and the cloud rested upon the wilderness of Paran; there the anger of the Lord was kindled against Israel, for they had provoked the Lord in asking him for meat, that they might eat. ²⁷ And the Lord hearkened to their voice, and gave them meat which they ate for one month. ²⁸ But after this the anger of the Lord was kindled against them, and he smote them with a great slaughter, and they were buried there in that place. ²⁹ And the children of Israel called that place Kebroth Hattaavah, because there they buried the people that lusted flesh. ³⁰ And they departed from Kebroth Hattaavah and pitched in Hazeroth, which is in the wilderness of Paran. ³¹ And whilst the children of Israel were in Hazeroth, the anger of the Lord was kindled against Miriam on account of Moses, and she became leprous, white as snow. ³² And she was confined without the camp for seven days, until she had been received again after her leprosy. ³³ The children of Israel afterward departed from Hazeroth, and pitched in the end of the wilderness of Paran. ³⁴ At that time, the Lord spoke to Moses to send twelve men from the children of Israel, one man to a tribe, to go and explore the land of Canaan. ³⁵ And Moses sent the twelve men, and they came to the land of Canaan to search and examine it, and they explored the whole land from the wilderness of Sin to Rechob as thou comest to Chamoth. ³⁶ And at the end of forty days they came to Moses and Aaron, and they brought him word as it was in their hearts, and ten of the men brought up an evil report to the children of Israel, of the land which they had explored, saying, It is better for us to return to Egypt than to go to this land, a land that consumes its inhabitants. ³⁷ But Joshua the son of Nun, and Caleb the son of Jephuneh, who were of those that explored the land, said, The land is exceedingly good. ³⁸ If the Lord delight in us, then he will bring us to this land and give it to us, for it is a land flowing with milk and honey. ³⁹ But the children of Israel would not hearken to them, and they hearkened to the words of the ten men who had brought up an evil report of the land. ⁴⁰ And the Lord heard the murmurings of the children of Israel and he was angry and swore, saying, ⁴¹ Surely not one man of this wicked generation shall see the land from twenty years old and upward excepting Caleb the son of Jephuneh and Joshua the son of Nun. ⁴² But surely this wicked generation shall

perish in this wilderness, and their children shall come to the land and they shall possess it; so the anger of the Lord was kindled against Israel, and he made them wander in the wilderness for forty years until the end of that wicked generation, because they did not follow the Lord. ⁴³ And the people dwelt in the wilderness of Paran a long time, and they afterward proceeded to the wilderness by the way of the Red Sea.

Jash.84

¹ At that time Korah the son of Jetzer the son of Kehath the son of Levi, took many men of the children of Israel, and they rose up and quarreled with Moses and Aaron and the whole congregation. ² And the Lord was angry with them, and the earth opened its mouth, and swallowed them up, with their houses and all belonging to them, and all the men belonging to Korah. ³ And after this God made the people go round by the way of Mount Seir for a long time. ⁴ At that time the Lord said unto Moses, Provoke not a war against the children of Esau, for I will not give to you of any thing belonging to them, as much as the sole of the foot could tread upon, for I have given Mount Seir for an inheritance to Esau. ⁵ Therefore did the children of Esau fight against the children of Seir in former times, and the Lord had delivered the children of Seir into the hands of the children of Esau, and destroyed them from before them, and the children of Esau dwelt in their stead unto this day. ⁶ Therefore the Lord said to the children of Israel, Fight not against the children of Esau your brethren, for nothing in their land belongs to you, but you may buy food of them for money and eat it, and you may buy water of them for money and drink it. ⁷ And the children of Israel did according to the word of the Lord. ⁸ And the children of Israel went about the wilderness, going round by the way of Mount Sinai for a long time, and touched not the children of Esau, and they continued in that district for nineteen years. ⁹ At that time died Latinus king of the children of Chittim, in the forty-fifth year of his reign, which is the fourteenth year of the children of Israel's departure from Egypt. ¹⁰ And they buried him in his place which he had built for himself in the land of Chittim, and Abimnas reigned in his place for thirty-eight years. ¹¹ And the children of Israel passed the boundary of the children of Esau in those days, at the end of nineteen years, and they came and passed the road of the wilderness of Moab. ¹² And the Lord said to Moses, besiege not Moab, and do not fight against them, for I will give you nothing of their land. ¹³ And the children of Israel passed the road of the wilderness of Moab for nineteen years, and they did not fight against them. ¹⁴ And in the thirty-sixth year of the children of Israel's departing from Egypt the Lord smote the heart of Sihon, king of the Amorites, and he waged war, and went forth to fight against the children of Moab. ¹⁵ And Sihon sent messengers to Beor the son of Janeas, the son of Balaam, counsellor to the king of Egypt, and to Balaam his son, to curse Moab, in order that it might be delivered into the hand of Sihon. ¹⁶ And the messengers went and brought Beor the son of Janeas, and Balaam his son, from Pethor in Mesopotamia, so Beor and Balaam his son came to the city of Sihon and they cursed Moab and their king in the presence of Sihon king of the Amorites. ¹⁷ So Sihon went out with his whole army, and he went to Moab and fought against them, and he subdued them, and the Lord delivered them into his hands, and Sihon slew the king of Moab. ¹⁸ And Sihon took all the cities of Moab in the battle; he also took Heshbon from them, for Heshbon was one of the cities of Moab, and Sihon placed his princes and his nobles in Heshbon, and Heshbon belonged to Sihon in those days. ¹⁹ Therefore the parable speakers Beor and Balaam his son uttered these words, saying, Come unto Heshbon, the city of Sihon will be built and established. ²⁰ Woe unto thee Moab! thou art lost, O people of Kemosh! behold it is

written upon the book of the law of God. 21 And when Sihon had conquered Moab, he placed guards in the cities which he had taken from Moab, and a considerable number of the children of Moab fell in battle into the hand of Sihon, and he made a great capture of them, sons and daughters, and he slew their king; so Sihon turned back to his own land. 22 And Sihon gave numerous presents of silver and gold to Beor and Balaam his son, and he dismissed them, and they went to Mesopotamia to their home and country. 23 At that time all the children of Israel passed from the road of the wilderness of Moab, and returned and surrounded the wilderness of Edom. 24 So the whole congregation came to the wilderness of Sin in the first month of the fortieth year from their departure from Egypt, and the children of Israel dwelt there in Kadesh, of the wilderness of Sin, and Miriam died there and she was buried there. 25 At that time Moses sent messengers to Hadad king of Edom, saying, Thus says thy brother Israel, Let me pass I pray thee through thy land, we will not pass through field or vineyard, we will not drink the water of the well; we will walk in the king's road. 26 And Edom said to him, Thou shalt not pass through my country, and Edom went forth to meet the children of Israel with a mighty people. 27 And the children of Esau refused to let the children of Israel pass through their land, so the Israelites removed from them and fought not against them. 28 For before this the Lord had commanded the children of Israel, saying, You shall not fight against the children of Esau, therefore the Israelites removed from them and did not fight against them. 29 So the children of Israel departed from Kadesh, and all the people came to Mount Hor. 30 At that time the Lord said to Moses, Tell thy brother Aaron that he shall die there, for he shall not come to the land which I have given to the children of Israel. 31 And Aaron went up, at the command of the Lord, to Mount Hor, in the fortieth year, in the fifth month, in the first day of the month. 32 And Aaron was one hundred and twenty-three years old when he died in Mount Hor

Jash.85

1 And king Arad the Canaanite, who dwelt in the south, heard that the Israelites had come by the way of the spies, and he arranged his forces to fight against the Israelites. 2 And the children of Israel were greatly afraid of him, for he had a great and heavy army, so the children of Israel resolved to return to Egypt. 3 And the children of Israel turned back about the distance of three days' journey unto Maserath Beni Jaakon, for they were greatly afraid on account of the king Arad. 4 And the children of Israel would not get back to their places, so they remained in Beni Jaakon for thirty days. 5 And when the children of Levi saw that the children of Israel would not turn back, they were jealous for the sake of the Lord, and they rose up and fought against the Israelites their brethren, and slew of them a great body, and forced them to turn back to their place, Mount Hor. 6 And when they returned, king Arad was still arranging his host for battle against the Israelites. 7 And Israel vowed a vow, saying, If thou wilt deliver this people into my hand, then I will utterly destroy their cities. 8 And the Lord hearkened to the voice of Israel, and he delivered the Canaanites into their hand, and he utterly destroyed them and their cities, and he called the name of the place Hormah. 9 And the children of Israel journeyed from Mount Hor and pitched in Oboth, and they journeyed from Oboth and they pitched at Ije-abarim, in the border of Moab. 10 And the children of Israel sent to Moab, saying, Let us pass now through thy land into our place, but the children of Moab would not suffer the children of Israel to pass through their land, for the children of Moab were greatly afraid lest the children of Israel should do unto them as Sihon king of the Amorites had done to them, who had taken their land and had slain many of them. 11 Therefore Moab would not suffer

the Israelites to pass through his land, and the Lord commanded the children of Israel, saying, That they should not fight against Moab, so the Israelites removed from Moab. 12 And the children of Israel journeyed from the border of Moab, and they came to the other side of Arnon, the border of Moab, between Moab and the Amorites, and they pitched in the border of Sihon, king of the Amorites, in the wilderness of Kedemoth. 13 And the children of Israel sent messengers to Sihon, king of the Amorites, saying, 14 Let us pass through thy land, we will not turn into the fields or into the vineyards, we will go along by the king's highway until we shall have passed thy border, but Sihon would not suffer the Israelites to pass. 15 So Sihon collected all the people of the Amorites and went forth into the wilderness to meet the children of Israel, and he fought against Israel in Jahaz. 16 And the Lord delivered Sihon king of the Amorites into the hand of the children of Israel, and Israel smote all the people of Sihon with the edge of the sword and avenged the cause of Moab. 17 And the children of Israel took possession of the land of Sihon from Aram unto Jabuk, unto the children of Ammon, and they took all the spoil of the cities. 18 And Israel took all these cities, and Israel dwelt in all the cities of the Amorites. 19 And all the children of Israel resolved to fight against the children of Ammon, to take their land also. 20 So the Lord said to the children of Israel, Do not besiege the children of Ammon, neither stir up battle against them, for I will give nothing to you of their land, and the children of Israel hearkened to the word of the Lord, and did not fight against the children of Ammon. 21 And the children of Israel turned and went up by the way of Bashan to the land of Og, king of Bashan, and Og the king of Bashan went out to meet the Israelites in battle, and he had with him many valiant men, and a very strong force from the people of the Amorites. 22 And Og king of Bashan was a very powerful man, but Naaron his son was exceedingly powerful, even stronger than he was. 23 And Og said in his heart, Behold now the whole camp of Israel takes up a space of three parsa, now will I smite them at once without sword or spear. 24 And Og went up Mount Jahaz, and took therefrom one large stone, the length of which was three parsa, and he placed it on his head, and resolved to throw it upon the camp of the children of Israel, to smite all the Israelites with that stone. 25 And the angel of the Lord came and pierced the stone upon the head of Og, and the stone fell upon the neck of Og that Og fell to the earth on account of the weight of the stone upon his neck. 26 At that time the Lord said to the children of Israel, Be not afraid of him, for I have given him and all his people and all his land into your hand, and you shall do to him as you did to Sihon. 27 And Moses went down to him with a small number of the children of Israel, and Moses smote Og with a stick at the ankles of his feet and slew him. 28 The children of Israel afterward pursued the children of Og and all his people, and they beat and destroyed them till there was no remnant left of them. 29 Moses afterward sent some of the children of Israel to spy out Jaazer, for Jaazer was a very famous city. 30 And the spies went to Jaazer and explored it, and the spies trusted in the Lord, and they fought against the men of Jaazer. 31 And these men took Jaazer and its villages, and the Lord delivered them into their hand, and they drove out the Amorites who had been there. 32 And the children of Israel took the land of the two kings of the Amorites, sixty cities which were on the other side of Jordan, from the brook of Arnon unto Mount Herman. 33 And the children of Israel journeyed and came into the plain of Moab which is on this side of Jordan, by Jericho. 34 And the children of Moab heard all the evil which the children of Israel had done to the two kings of the Amorites, to Sihon and Og, so all the men of Moab greatly afraid of the Israelites. 35 And the elders of Moab said, Behold the two kings of the Amorites, Sihon and Og, who were more powerful than all the kings of the earth, could not stand against the children of Israel, how then can we stand before them? 36 Surely they sent us a message before now to pass through our land on their way, and we would not suffer them, now they will turn upon us with their heavy swords and destroy us; and Moab was distressed on account of the children of Israel, and they were greatly afraid of them, and they counselled together what was to be done to the children of Israel. 37 And the elders of Moab resolved and took one of their men, Balak the son of Zippor the Moabite, and made him king over them at that time, and Balak was a very wise man. 38 And the elders of Moab rose up and sent to the children of Midian to make peace with them, for a great battle and enmity had been in those days between Moab and Midian, from the days of Hadad the son of Bedad king of Edom, who smote Midian in the field of Moab, unto these days. 39 And the children of Moab sent to the children of Midian, and they made peace with them, and the elders of Midian came to the land of Moab to make peace in behalf of the children of Midian. 40 And the elders of Moab counselled with the elders of Midian what to do in order to save their lives from Israel. 41 And all the children of Moab said to the elders of Midian, Now therefore the children of Israel lick up all that are round about us, as the ox licks up the grass of the field, for thus did they do to the two kings of the Amorites who are stronger than we are. 42 And the elders of Midian said to Moab, We have heard that at the time when Sihon king of the Amorites fought against you, when he prevailed over you and took your land, he had sent to Beor the son of Janeas and to Balaam his son from Mesopotamia, and they came and cursed you; therefore did the hand of Sihon prevail over you, that he took your land. 43 Now therefore send you also to Balaam his son, for he still remains in his land, and give him his hire, that he may come and curse all the people of whom you are afraid; so the elders of Moab heard this thing, and it pleased them to send to Balaam the son of Beor. 44 So Balak the son of Zippor king of Moab sent messengers to Balaam, saying, 45 Behold there is a people come out from Egypt, behold they cover the face of the earth, and they abide over against me. 46 Now therefore come and curse this people for me, for they are too mighty for me, peradventure I shall prevail to fight against them, and drive them out, for I heard that he whom thou blessest is blessed, and whom thou cursest is cursed. 47 So the messengers of Balak went to Balaam and brought Balaam to curse the people to fight against Moab. 48 And Balaam came to Balak to curse Israel, and the Lord said to Balaam, Curse not this people for it is blessed. 49 And Balak urged Balaam day by day to curse Israel, but Balaam hearkened not to Balak on account of the word of the Lord which he had spoken to Balaam. 50 And when Balak saw that Balaam would not accede to his wish, he rose up and went home, and Balaam also returned to his land and he went from there to Midian. 51 And the children of Israel journeyed from the plain of Moab, and pitched by Jordan from Beth-jesimoth even unto Abel-shittim, at the end of the plains of Moab. 52 And when the children of Israel abode in the plain of Shittim, they began to commit whoredom with the daughters of Moab. 53 And the children of Israel approached Moab, and the children of Moab pitched their tents opposite to the camp of the children of Israel. 54 And the children of Moab were afraid of the children of Israel, and the children of Moab took all their daughters and their wives of beautiful aspect and comely appearance, and dressed them in gold and silver and costly garments. 55 And the children of Moab seated those women at the door of their tents, in order that the children of Israel might see them and turn to them, and not fight against Moab. 56 And all the children of Moab did this thing to the children of Israel, and every man placed his wife and

306

daughter at the door of his tent, and all the children of Israel saw the act of the children of Moab, and the children of Israel turned to the daughters of Moab and coveted them, and they went to them. 57 And it came to pass that when a Hebrew came to the door of the tent of Moab, and saw a daughter of Moab and desired her in his heart, and spoke with her at the door of the tent that which he desired, whilst they were speaking together the men of the tent would come out and speak to the Hebrew like unto these words: 58 Surely you know that we are brethren, we are all the descendants of Lot and the descendants of Abraham his brother, wherefore then will you not remain with us, and wherefore will you not eat our bread and our sacrifice? 59 And when the children of Moab had thus overwhelmed him with their speeches, and enticed him by their flattering words, they seated him in the tent and cooked and sacrificed for him, and he ate of their sacrifice and of their bread. 60 They then gave him wine and he drank and became intoxicated, and they placed before him a beautiful damsel, and he did with her as he liked, for he knew not what he was doing, as he had drunk plentifully of wine. 61 Thus did the children of Moab to Israel in that place, in the plain of Shittim, and the anger of the Lord was kindled against Israel on account of this matter, and he sent a pestilence amongst them, and there died of the Israelites twenty-four thousand men. 62 Now there was a man of the children of Simeon whose name was Zimri, the son of Salu, who connected himself with the Midianite Cosbi, the daughter of Zur, king of Midian, in the sight of all the children of Israel. 63 And Phineas the son of Elazer, the son of Aaron the priest, saw this wicked thing which Zimri had done, and he took a spear and rose up and went after them, and pierced them both and slew them, and the pestilence ceased from the children of Israel.

Jash.86

1 At that time after the pestilence, the Lord said to Moses, and to Elazer the son of Aaron the priest, saying, 2 Number the heads of the whole community of the children of Israel, from twenty years old and upward, all that went forth in the army. 3 And Moses and Elazer numbered the children of Israel after their families, and the number of all Israel was seven hundred thousand, seven hundred and thirty. 4 And the number of the children of Levi, from one month old and upward, was twenty-three thousand, and amongst these there was not a man of those numbered by Moses and Aaron in the wilderness of Sinai. 5 For the Lord had told them that they would die in the wilderness, so they all died, and not one had been left of them excepting Caleb the son of Jephuneh, and Joshua the son of Nun. 6 And it was after this that the Lord said to Moses, Say unto the children of Israel to avenge upon Midian the cause of their brethren the children of Israel. 7 And Moses did so, and the children of Israel chose from amongst them twelve thousand men, being one thousand to a tribe, and they went to Midian. 8 And the children of Israel warred against Midian, and they slew every male, also the five princes of Midian, and Balaam the son of Beor did they slay with the sword. 9 And the children of Israel took the wives of Midian captive, with their little ones and their cattle, and all belonging to them. 10 And they took all the spoil and all the prey, and they brought it to Moses and to Elazer to the plains of Moab. 11 And Moses and Elazer and all the princes of the congregation went forth to meet them with joy. 12 And they divided all the spoil of Midian, and the children of Israel had been revenged upon Midian for the cause of their brethren the children of Israel.

Jash.87

1 At that time the Lord said to Moses, Behold thy days are approaching to an end, take now Joshua the son of Nun thy servant and place him in the tabernacle, and I will command him, and Moses

did so. 2 And the Lord appeared in the tabernacle in a pillar of cloud, and the pillar of cloud stood at the entrance of the tabernacle. 3 And the Lord commanded Joshua the son of Nun and said unto him, Be strong and courageous, for thou shalt bring the children of Israel to the land which I swore to give them, and I will be with thee. 4 And Moses said to Joshua, Be strong and courageous, for thou wilt make the children of Israel inherit the land, and the Lord will be with thee, he will not leave thee nor forsake thee, be not afraid nor disheartened. 5 And Moses called to all the children of Israel and said to them, You have seen all the good which the Lord your God has done for you in the wilderness. 6 Now therefore observe all the words of this law, and walk in the way of the Lord your God, turn not from the way which the Lord has commanded you, either to the right or to the left. 7 And Moses taught the children of Israel statutes and judgments and laws to do in the land as the Lord had commanded him. 8 And he taught them the way of the Lord and his laws; behold they are written upon the book of the law of God which he gave to the children of Israel by the hand of Moses. 9 And Moses finished commanding the children of Israel, and the Lord said to him, saying, Go up to the Mount Abarim and die there, and be gathered unto thy people as Aaron thy brother was gathered. 10 And Moses went up as the Lord had commanded him, and he died there in the land of Moab by the order of the Lord, in the fortieth year from the Israelites going forth from the land of Egypt. 11 And the children of Israel wept for Moses in the plains of Moab for thirty days, and the days of weeping and mourning for Moses were completed.

Jash.88

1 And it was after the death of Moses that the Lord said to Joshua the son of Nun, saying, 2 Rise up and pass the Jordan to the land which I have given to the children of Israel, and thou shalt make the children of Israel inherit the land. 3 Every place upon which the sole of your feet shall tread shall belong to you, from the wilderness of Lebanon unto the great river the river of Perath shall be your boundary. 4 No man shall stand up against thee all the days of thy life; as I was with Moses, so will I be with thee, only be strong and of good courage to observe all the law which Moses commanded thee, turn not from the way either to the right or to the left, in order that thou mayest prosper in all that thou doest. 5 And Joshua commanded the officers of Israel, saying, Pass through the camp and command the people, saying, Prepare for yourselves provisions, for in three days more you will pass the Jordan to possess the land. 6 And the officers of the children of Israel did so, and they commanded the people and they did all that Joshua had commanded. 7 And Joshua sent two men to spy out the land of Jericho, and the men went and spied out Jericho. 8 And at the end of seven days they came to Joshua in the camp and said to him, The Lord has delivered the whole land into our hand, and the inhabitants thereof are melted with fear because of us. 9 And it came to pass after that, that Joshua rose up in the morning and all Israel with him, and they journeyed from Shittim, and Joshua and all Israel with him passed the Jordan; and Joshua was eighty-two years old when he passed the Jordan with Israel. 10 And the people went up from Jordan on the tenth day of the first month, and they encamped in Gilgal at the eastern corner of Jericho. 11 And the children of Israel kept the Passover in Gilgal, in the plains of Jericho, on the fourteenth day at the month, as it is written in the law of Moses. 12 And the manna ceased at that time on the morrow of the Passover, and there was no more manna for the children of Israel, and they ate of the produce of the land of Canaan. 13 And Jericho was entirely closed against the children of Israel, no one came out or went in. 14 And it was in the second month, on the first day of

the month, that the Lord said to Joshua, Rise up, behold I have given Jericho into thy hand with all the people thereof; and all your fighting men shall go round the city, once each day, thus shall you do for six days. 15 And the priests shall blow upon trumpets, and when you shall hear the sound of the trumpet, all the people shall give a great shouting, that the walls of the city shall fall down; all the people shall go up every man against his opponent. 16 And Joshua did so according to all that the Lord had commanded him. 17 And on the seventh day they went round the city seven times, and the priests blew upon trumpets. 18 And at the seventh round, Joshua said to the people, Shout, for the Lord has delivered the whole city into our hands. 19 Only the city and all that it contains shall be accursed to the Lord, and keep yourselves from the accursed thing, lest you make the camp of Israel accursed and trouble it. 20 But all the silver and gold and brass and iron shall be consecrated to the Lord, they shall come into the treasury of the Lord. 21 And the people blew upon trumpets and made a great shouting, and the walls of Jericho fell down, and all the people went up, every man straight before him, and they took the city and utterly destroyed all that was in it, both man and woman, young and old, ox and sheep and ass, with the edge of the sword. 22 And they burned the whole city with fire; only the vessels of silver and gold, and brass and iron, they put into the treasury of the Lord. 23 And Joshua swore at that time, saying, Cursed be the man who builds Jericho; he shall lay the foundation thereof in his first-born, and in his youngest son shall he set up the gates thereof. 24 And Achan the son of Carmi, the son of Zabdi, the son of Zerah, son of Judah, dealt treacherously in the accursed thing, and he took of the accursed thing and hid it in the tent, and the anger of the Lord was kindled against Israel. 25 And it was after this when the children of Israel had returned from burning Jericho, Joshua sent men to spy out also Ai, and to fight against it. 26 And the men went up and spied out Ai, and they returned and said, Let not all the people go up with thee to Ai, only let about three thousand men go up and smite the city, for the men thereof are but few. 27 And Joshua did so, and there went up with him of the children of Israel about three thousand men, and they fought against the men of Ai. 28 And the battle was severe against Israel, and the men of Ai smote thirty-six men of Israel, and the children of Israel fled from before the men of Ai. 29 And when Joshua saw this thing, he tore his garments and fell upon his face to the ground before the Lord, he, with the elders of Israel, and they put dust upon their heads. 30 And Joshua said, Why O Lord didst thou bring this people over the Jordan? what shall I say after the Israelites have turned their backs against their enemies? 31 Now therefore all the Canaanites, inhabitants of the land, will hear this thing, and surround us and cut off our name. 32 And the Lord said to Joshua, Why dost thou fall upon thy face? rise, get thee off, for the Israelites have sinned, and taken of the accursed thing; I will no more be with them unless they destroy the accursed thing from amongst them. 33 And Joshua rose up and assembled the people, and brought the Urim by the order of the Lord, and the tribe of Judah was taken, and Achan the son of Carmi was taken. 34 And Joshua said to Achan, Tell me my son, what hast thou done, and Achan said, I saw amongst the spoil a goodly garment of Shinar and two hundred shekels of silver, and a wedge of gold of fifty shekels weight; I coveted them and took them, and behold they are all hid in the earth in the midst of the tent. 35 And Joshua sent men who went and took them from the tent of Achan, and they brought them to Joshua. 36 And Joshua took Achan and these utensils, and his sons and daughters and all belonging to him, and they brought them into the valley of Achor. 37 And Joshua burned them there with fire, and all the Israelites stoned Achan with stones, and they raised over him a heap of stones, therefore did he call that place the valley of Achor, so the Lord's anger was appeased, and Joshua afterward came to the city and fought against it. 38 And the Lord said to Joshua, Fear not, neither be thou dismayed, behold I have given into thy hand Ai, her king and her people, and thou shalt do unto them as thou didst to Jericho and her king, only the spoil thereof and the cattle thereof shall you take for a prey for yourselves; lay an ambush for the city behind it. 39 So Joshua did according to the word of the Lord, and he chose from amongst the sons of war thirty thousand valiant men, and he sent them, and they lay in ambush for the city. 40 And he commanded them, saying, When you shall see us we will flee before them with cunning, and they will pursue us, you shall then rise out of the ambush and take the city, and they did so. 41 And Joshua fought, and the men of the city went out toward Israel, not knowing that they were lying in ambush for them behind the city. 42 And Joshua and all the Israelites feigned themselves wearied out before them, and they fled by the way of the wilderness with cunning. 43 And the men of Ai gathered all the people who were in the city to pursue the Israelites, and they went out and were drawn away from the city, not one remained, and they left the city open and pursued the Israelites. 44 And those who were lying in ambush rose up out of their places, and hastened to come to the city and took it and set it on fire, and the men of Ai turned back, and behold the smoke of the city ascended to the skies, and they had no means of retreating either one way or the other. 45 And all the men of Ai were in the midst of Israel, some on this side and some on that side, and they smote them so that not one of them remained. 46 And the children of Israel took Melosh king of Ai alive, and they brought him to Joshua, and Joshua hanged him on a tree and he died. 47 And the children of Israel returned to the city after having burned it, and they smote all those that were in it with the edge of the sword. 48 And the number of those that had fallen of the men of Ai, both man and woman, was twelve thousand; only the cattle and the spoil of the city they took to themselves, according to the word of the Lord to Joshua. 49 And all the kings on this side Jordan, all the kings of Canaan, heard of the evil which the children of Israel had done to Jericho and to Ai, and they gathered themselves together to fight against Israel. 50 Only the inhabitants of Gibeon were greatly afraid of fighting against the Israelites lest they should perish, so they acted cunningly, and they came to Joshua and to all Israel, and said unto them, We have come from a distant land, now therefore make a covenant with us. 51 And the inhabitants of Gibeon over-reached the children of Israel, and the children of Israel made a covenant with them, and they made peace with them, and the princes of the congregation swore unto them, but afterward the children of Israel knew that they were neighbors to them and were dwelling amongst them. 52 But the children of Israel slew them not; for they had sworn to them by the Lord, and they became hewers of wood and drawers of water. 53 And Joshua said to them, Why did you deceive me, to do this thing to us? and they answered him, saying, Because it was told to thy servants all that you had done to all the kings of the Amorites, and we were greatly afraid of our lives, and we did this thing. 54 And Joshua appointed them on that day to hew wood and to draw water, and he divided them for slaves to all the tribes of Israel. 55 And when Adonizedek king of Jerusalem heard all that the children of Israel had done to Jericho and to Ai, he sent to Hoham king of Hebron and to Piram king at Jarmuth, and to Japhia king of Lachish and to Deber king of Eglon, saying, 56 Come up to me and help me, that we may smite the children of Israel and the inhabitants of Gibeon who have made peace with the children of Israel. 57 And they gathered themselves together and the five kings of the Amorites went up with all their camps, a mighty people numerous as the sand of the sea shore. 58 And all these kings came and encamped before Gibeon, and they began to fight against the inhabitants of Gibeon, and all the men of Gibeon sent to Joshua, saying, Come up quickly to us and help us, for all the kings of the Amorites have gathered together to fight against us. 59 And Joshua and all the fighting people went up from Gilgal, and Joshua came suddenly to them, and smote these five kings with a great slaughter. 60 And the Lord confounded them before the children at Israel, who smote them with a terrible slaughter in Gibeon, and pursued them along the way that goes up to Beth Horon unto Makkedah, and they fled from before the children of Israel. 61 And whilst they were fleeing, the Lord sent upon them hailstones from heaven, and more of them died by the hailstones, than by the slaughter of the children of Israel. 62 And the children of Israel pursued them, and they still smote them in the road, going on and smiting them. 63 And when they were smiting, the day was declining toward evening, and Joshua said in the sight of all the people, Sun, stand thou still upon Gibeon, and thou moon in the valley of Ajalon, until the nation shall have revenged itself upon its enemies. 64 And the Lord hearkened to the voice of Joshua, and the sun stood still in the midst of the heavens, and it stood still six and thirty moments, and the moon also stood still and hastened not to go down a whole day. 65 And there was no day like that, before it or after it, that the Lord hearkened to the voice of a man, for the Lord fought for Israel.

Jash.89

1 Then spoke Joshua this song, on the day that the Lord had given the Amorites into the hand of Joshua and the children of Israel, and he said in the sight of all Israel, 2 Thou hast done mighty things, O Lord, thou hast performed great deeds; who is like unto thee? my lips shall sing to thy name. 3 My goodness and my fortress, my high tower, I will sing a new song unto thee, with thanksgiving will I sing to thee, thou art the strength of my salvation. 4 All the kings of the earth shall praise thee, the princes of the world shall sing to thee, the children of Israel shall rejoice in thy salvation, they shall sing and praise thy power. 5 To thee, O Lord, did we confide; we said thou art our God, for thou wast our shelter and strong tower against our enemies. 6 To thee we cried and were not ashamed, in thee we trusted and were delivered; when we cried unto thee, thou didst hear our voice, thou didst deliver our souls from the sword, thou didst show unto us thy grace, thou didst give unto us thy salvation, thou didst rejoice our hearts with thy strength. 7 Thou didst go forth for our salvation, with thine arm thou didst redeem thy people; thou didst answer us from the heavens of thy holiness, thou didst save us from ten thousands of people. 8 The sun and moon stood still in heaven, and thou didst stand in thy wrath against our oppressors and didst command thy judgments over them. 9 All the princes of the earth stood up, the kings of the nations had gathered themselves together, they were not moved at thy presence, they desired thy battles. 10 Thou didst rise against them in thine anger, and didst bring down thy wrath upon them; thou didst destroy them in thine anger, and cut them off in thine heart. 11 Nations have been consumed with thy fury, kingdoms have declined because of thy wrath, thou didst wound kings in the day of thine anger. 12 Thou didst pour out thy fury upon them, thy wrathful anger took hold of them; thou didst turn their iniquity upon them, and didst cut them off in their wickedness. 13 They did spread a trap, they fell therein, in the net they hid, their foot was caught. 14 Thine hand was ready for all thine enemies who said, Through their sword they possessed the land, through their arm they dwelt in the city; thou didst fill their faces with shame, thou didst bring their horns down to the ground, thou didst terrify them in thy wrath, and didst destroy them in thine anger. 15 The earth trembled and shook at the sound of thy storm

over them, thou didst not withhold their souls from death, and didst bring down their lives to the grave. 16 Thou didst pursue them in thy storm, thou didst consume them in thy whirlwind, thou didst turn their rain into hail, they fell in deep pits so that they could not rise. 17 Their carcasses were like rubbish cast out in the middle of the streets. 18 They were consumed and destroyed in thine anger, thou didst save thy people with thy might. 19 Therefore our hearts rejoice in thee, our souls exalt in thy salvation. 20 Our tongues shall relate thy might, we will sing and praise thy wondrous works. 21 For thou didst save us from our enemies, thou didst deliver us from those who rose up against us, thou didst destroy them from before us and depress them beneath our feet. 22 Thus shall all thine enemies perish O Lord, and the wicked shall be like chaff driven by the wind, and thy beloved shall be like trees planted by the waters. 23 So Joshua and all Israel with him returned to the camp in Gilgal, after having smitten all the kings, so that not a remnant was left of them. 24 And the five kings fled alone on foot from battle, and hid themselves in a cave, and Joshua sought for them in the field of battle, and did not find them. 25 And it was afterward told to Joshua, saying, The kings are found and behold they are hidden in a cave. 26 And Joshua said, Appoint men to be at the mouth of the cave, to guard them, lest they take themselves away; and the children of Israel did so. 27 And Joshua called to all Israel and said to the officers of battle, Place your feet upon the necks of these kings, and Joshua said, So shall the Lord do to all your enemies. 28 And Joshua commanded afterward that they should slay the kings and cast them into the cave, and to put great stones at the mouth of the cave. 29 And Joshua went afterward with all the people that were with him on that day to Makkedah, and he smote it with the edge of the sword. 30 And he utterly destroyed the souls and all belonging to the city, and he did to the king and people thereof as he had done to Jericho. 31 And he passed from there to Libnah and he fought against it, and the Lord delivered it into his hand, and Joshua smote it with the edge of the sword, and all the souls thereof, and he did to it and to the king thereof as he had done to Jericho. 32 And from there he passed on to Lachish to fight against it, and Horam king of Gaza went up to assist the men of Lachish, and Joshua smote him and his people until there was none left to him. 33 And Joshua took Lachish and all the people thereof, and he did to it as he had done to Libnah. 34 And Joshua passed from there to Eglon, and he took that also, and he smote it and all the people thereof with the edge of the sword. 35 And from there he passed to Hebron and fought against it and took it and utterly destroyed it, and he returned from there with all Israel to Debir and fought against it and smote it with the edge of the sword. 36 And he destroyed every soul in it, he left none remaining, and he did to it and the king thereof as he had done to Jericho. 37 And Joshua smote all the kings of the Amorites from Kadesh-barnea to Azah, and he took their country at once, for the Lord had fought for Israel. 38 And Joshua with all Israel came to the camp to Gilgal. 39 When at that time Jabin king of Chazor heard all that Joshua had done to the kings of the Amorites, Jabin sent to Jobat king of Midian, and to Laban king of Shimron, to Jephal king of Achshaph, and to all the kings of the Amorites, saying, 40 Come quickly to us and help us, that we may smite the children of Israel, before they come upon us and do unto us as they have done to the other kings of the Amorites. 41 And all these kings hearkened to the words of Jabin, king of Chazor, and they went forth with all their camps, seventeen kings, and their people were as numerous as the sand on the sea shore, together with horses and chariots innumerable, and they came and pitched together at the waters of Merom, and they were met together to fight against Israel. 42 And the Lord said to Joshua, Fear them not, for tomorrow about this

time I will deliver them up all slain before you, thou shalt hough their horses and burn their chariots with fire. 43 And Joshua with all the men of war came suddenly upon them and smote them, and they fell into their hands, for the Lord had delivered them into the hands of the children of Israel. 44 So the children of Israel pursued all these kings with their camps, and smote them until there was none left of them, and Joshua did to them as the Lord had spoken to him. 45 And Joshua returned at that time to Chazor and smote it with the sword and destroyed every soul in it and burned it with fire, and from Chazor, Joshua passed to Shimron and smote it and utterly destroyed it. 46 From there he passed to Achshaph and he did to it as he had done to Shimron. 47 From there he passed to Adulam and he smote all the people in it, and he did to Adulam as he had done to Achshaph and to Shimron. 48 And he passed from them to all the cities of the kings which he had smitten, and he smote all the people that were left of them and he utterly destroyed them. 49 Only their booty and cattle the Israelites took to themselves as a prey, but every human being they smote, they suffered not a soul to live. 50 As the Lord had commanded Moses so did Joshua and all Israel, they failed not in anything. 51 So Joshua and all the children of Israel smote the whole land of Canaan as the Lord had commanded them, and smote all their kings, being thirty and one kings, and the children of Israel took their whole country. 52 Besides the kingdoms of Sihon and Og which are on the other side Jordan, of which Moses had smitten many cities, and Moses gave them to the Reubenites and the Gadites and to half the tribe of Manasseh. 53 And Joshua smote all the kings that were on this side Jordan to the west, and gave them for an inheritance to the nine tribes and to the half tribe of Israel. 54 For five years did Joshua carry on the war with these kings, and he gave their cities to the Israelites, and the land became tranquil from battle throughout the cities of the Amorites and the Canaanites.

Jash.90

1 At that time in the fifth year after the children of Israel had passed over Jordan, after the children of Israel had rested from their war with the Canaanites, at that time great and severe battles arose between Edom and the children of Chittim, and the children of Chittim fought against Edom. 2 And Abianus king of Chittim went forth in that year, that is in the thirty-first year of his reign, and a great force with him of the mighty men of the children of Chittim, and he went to Seir to fight against the children of Esau. 3 And Hadad the king of Edom heard of his report, and he went forth to meet him with a heavy people and strong force, and engaged in battle with him in the field of Edom. 4 And the hand of Chittim prevailed over the children of Esau, and the children of Chittim slew of the children of Esau, two and twenty thousand men, and all the children of Esau fled from before them. 5 And the children of Chittim pursued them and they reached Hadad king of Edom, who was running before them and they caught him alive, and brought him to Abianus king of Chittim. 6 And Abianus ordered him to be slain, and Hadad king of Edom died in the forty-eighth year of his reign. 7 And the children of Chittim continued their pursuit of Edom, and they smote them with a great slaughter and Edom became subject to the children of Chittim. 8 And the children of Chittim ruled over Edom, and Edom became under the hand of the children of Chittim and became one kingdom from that day. 9 And from that time they could no more lift up their heads, and their kingdom became one with the children of Chittim. 10 And Abianus placed officers in Edom and all the children of Edom became subject and tributary to Abianus, and Abianus turned back to his own land, Chittim. 11 And when he returned he renewed his government and built for himself a spacious and fortified palace for a royal residence, and reigned securely over the children of Chittim

and over Edom. [12] In those days, after the children of Israel had driven away all the Canaanites and the Amorites, Joshua was old and advanced in years. [13] And the Lord said to Joshua, Thou art old, advanced in life, and a great part of the land remains to be possessed. [14] Now therefore divide this land for an inheritance to the nine tribes and to the half tribe of Manasseh, and Joshua rose up and did as the Lord had spoken to him. [15] And he divided the whole land to the tribes of Israel as an inheritance according to their divisions. [16] But to the tribe at Levi he gave no inheritance, the offerings of the Lord are their inheritance as the Lord had spoken of them by the hand of Moses. [17] And Joshua gave Mount Hebron to Caleb the son of Jephuneh, one portion above his brethren, as the Lord had spoken through Moses. [18] Therefore Hebron became an inheritance to Caleb and his children unto this day. [19] And Joshua divided the whole land by lots to all Israel for an inheritance, as the Lord had commanded him. [20] And the children of Israel gave cities to the Levites from their own inheritance, and suburbs for their cattle, and property, as the Lord had commanded Moses so did the children of Israel, and they divided the land by lot whether great or small. [21] And they went to inherit the land according to their boundaries, and the children of Israel gave to Joshua the son of Nun an inheritance amongst them. [22] By the word of the Lord did they give to him the city which he required, Timnath-serach in Mount Ephraim, and he built the city and dwelt therein. [23] These are the inheritances which Elazer the priest and Joshua the son of Nun and the heads of the fathers of the tribes portioned out to the children of Israel by lot in Shiloh, before the Lord, at the door of the tabernacle, and they left off dividing the land. [24] And the Lord gave the land to the Israelites, and they possessed it as the Lord had spoken to them, and as the Lord had sworn to their ancestors. [25] And the Lord gave to the Israelites rest from all their enemies around them, and no man stood up against them, and the Lord delivered all their enemies into their hands, and not one thing failed of all the good which the Lord had spoken to the children of Israel, yea the Lord performed every thing. [26] And Joshua called to all the children of Israel and he blessed them, and commanded them to serve the Lord, and he afterward sent them away, and they went each man to his city, and each man to his inheritance. [27] And the children of Israel served the Lord all the days of Joshua, and the Lord gave them rest from all around them, and they dwelt securely in their cities. [28] And it came to pass in those days, that Abianus king of Chittim died, in the thirty-eighth year of his reign, that is the seventh year of his reign over Edom, and they buried him in his place which he had built for himself, and Latinus reigned in his stead fifty years. [29] And during his reign he brought forth an army, and he went and fought against the inhabitants of Britannia and Kernania, the children of Elisha son of Javan, and he prevailed over them and made them tributary. [30] He then heard that Edom had revolted from under the hand of Chittim, and Latinus went to them and smote them and subdued them, and placed them under the hand of the children of Chittim, and Edom became one kingdom with the children of Chittim all the days. [31] And for many years there was no king in Edom, and their government was with the children of Chittim and their king. [32] And it was in the twenty-sixth year after the children of Israel had passed the Jordan, that is the sixty-sixth year after the children of Israel had departed from Egypt, that Joshua was old, advanced in years, being one hundred and eight years old in those days. [33] And Joshua called to all Israel, to their elders, their judges and officers, after the Lord had given to all the Israelites rest from all their enemies round about, and Joshua said to the elders of Israel, and to their judges, Behold I am old, advanced in years, and you have seen what the Lord has done to all the nations

whom he has driven away from before you, for it is the Lord who has fought for you. [34] Now therefore strengthen yourselves to keep and to do all the words of the law of Moses, not to deviate from it to the right or to the left, and not to come amongst those nations who are left in the land; neither shall you make mention of the name of their gods, but you shall cleave to the Lord your God, as you have done to this day. [35] And Joshua greatly exhorted the children of Israel to serve the Lord all their days. [36] And all the Israelites said, We will serve the Lord our God all our days, we and our children, and our children's children, and our seed for ever. [37] And Joshua made a covenant with the people on that day, and he sent away the children of Israel, and they went each man to his inheritance and to his city. [38] And it was in those days, when the children of Israel were dwelling securely in their cities, that they buried the coffins of the tribes of their ancestors, which they had brought up from Egypt, each man in the inheritance of his children, the twelve sons of Jacob did the children of Israel bury, each man in the possession of his children. [39] And these are the names of the cities wherein they buried the twelve sons of Jacob, whom the children of Israel had brought up from Egypt. [40] And they buried Reuben and Gad on this side Jordan, in Romia, which Moses had given to their children. [41] And Simeon and Levi they buried in the city Mauda, which he had given to the children of Simeon, and the suburb of the city was for the children of Levi. [42] And Judah they buried in the city of Benjamin opposite Bethlehem. [43] And the bones of Issachar and Zebulun they buried in Zidon, in the portion which fell to their children. [44] And Dan was buried in the city of his children in Eshtael, and Naphtali and Asher they buried in Kadesh-naphtali, each man in his place which he had given to his children. [45] And the bones of Joseph they buried in Shechem, in the part of the field which Jacob had purchased from Hamor, and which became to Joseph for an inheritance. [46] And they buried Benjamin in Jerusalem opposite the Jebusite, which was given to the children of Benjamin; the children of Israel buried their fathers each man in the city of his children. [47] And at the end of two years, Joshua the son of Nun died, one hundred and ten years old, and the time which Joshua judged Israel was twenty-eight years, and Israel served the Lord all the days of his life. [48] And the other affairs of Joshua and his battles and his reproofs with which he reproved Israel, and all which he had commanded them, and the names of the cities which the children of Israel possessed in his days, behold they are written in the book of the words of Joshua to the children of Israel, and in the book of the wars of the Lord, which Moses and Joshua and the children of Israel had written. [49] And the children of Israel buried Joshua in the border of his inheritance, in Timnath-serach, which was given to him in Mount Ephraim. [50] And Elazer the son of Aaron died in those days, and they buried him in a hill belonging to Phineas his son, which was given him in Mount Ephraim.

Jash.91

[1] At that time, after the death of Joshua, the children of the Canaanites were still in the land, and the Israelites resolved to drive them out. [2] And the children of Israel asked of the Lord, saying, Who shall first go up for us to the Canaanites to fight against them? and the Lord said, Judah shall go up. [3] And the children of Judah said to Simeon, Go up with us into our lot, and we will fight against the Canaanites and we likewise will go up with you, in your lot, so the children of Simeon went with the children of Judah. [4] And the children of Judah went up and fought against the Canaanites, so the Lord delivered the Canaanites into the hands of the children of Judah, and they smote them in Bezek, ten thousand men. [5] And they fought with Adonibezek in Bezek, and he fled from before them, and they pursued him and caught him, and they took hold of him

and cut off his thumbs and great toes. ⁶ And Adonibezek said, Three score and ten kings having their thumbs and great toes cut off, gathered their meat under my table, as I have done, so God has requited me, and they brought him to Jerusalem and he died there. ⁷ And the children of Simeon went with the children of Judah, and they smote the Canaanites with the edge of the sword. ⁸ And the Lord was with the children of Judah, and they possessed the mountain, and the children of Joseph went up to Bethel, the same is Luz, and the Lord was with them. ⁹ And the children of Joseph spied out Bethel, and the watchmen saw a man going forth from the city, and they caught him and said unto him, Show us now the entrance of the city and we will show kindness to thee. ¹⁰ And that man showed them the entrance of the city, and the children of Joseph came and smote the City with the edge of the sword. ¹¹ And the man with his family they sent away, and he went to the Hittites and he built a city, and he called the name thereof Luz, so all the Israelites dwelt in their cities, and the children at Israel dwelt in their cities, and the children of Israel served the Lord all the days of Joshua, and all the days of the elders, who had lengthened their days after Joshua, and saw the great work of the Lord, which he had performed for Israel. ¹² And the elders judged Israel after the death of Joshua for seventeen years. ¹³ And all the elders also fought the battles of Israel against the Canaanites and the Lord drove the Canaanites from before the children of Israel, in order to place the Israelites in their land. ¹⁴ And he accomplished all the words which he had spoken to Abraham, Isaac, and Jacob, and the oath which he had sworn, to give to them and to their children, the land of the Canaanites. ¹⁵ And the Lord gave to the children of Israel the whole land of Canaan, as he had sworn to their ancestors, and the Lord gave them rest from those around them, and the children of Israel dwelt securely in their cities. ¹⁶ Blessed be the Lord for ever, amen, and amen. ¹⁷ Strengthen yourselves, and let the hearts of all you that trust in the Lord be of good courage. THE END

Life of Adam and Eve

I ¹ When they were driven out from paradise, they made themselves a booth, and spent seven days mourning and lamenting in great grief. **II** ¹ But after seven days, they began to be hungry and started to look for victual to eat, and they ² found it not. Then Eve said to Adam: 'My lord, I am hungry. Go, look for (something) for us to eat. Perchance the Lord God will look back and pity us and recall us to the place in which we were before. **III** I And Adam arose and walked seven days over all that land, and found no victual such as they ² used to have in paradise. And Eve said to Adam: 'Wilt thou slay me? that I may die, and perchance God the Lord will bring thee into paradise, for on my account hast thou been driven thence.' ³ Adam answered: 'Forbear, Eve, from such words, that peradventure God bring not some other curse upon us. How is it possible that I should stretch forth my hand against my own flesh? Nay, let us arise and look for something for us to live on, that we fail not.' **IV** ¹ And they walked about and searched for nine days, and they found none such as they were used to have in paradise, but found only animals' ² food. And Adam said to Eve: 'This hath the Lord provided for animals and brutes to eat; ³ but we used to have angels' food. But it is just and right that we lament before the sight of God who made us. Let us repent with a great penitence: perchance the Lord will be gracious to us and will pity us and give us a share of something for our living.' **V** ¹ And Eve said to Adam: 'What is penitence? Tell me, what sort of penitence am I to do? Let us not put too great a labour on ourselves, which we cannot endure, so that the Lord will not hearken to our prayers: and will turn away His countenance from us, because we have not ³ fulfilled what we

promised. My lord, how much penitence hast thou thought (to do) for I have brought trouble and anguish upon thee?' **VI** ¹ And Adam said to Eve: 'Thou canst not do so much as I, but do only so much as thou hast strength for. For I will spend forty days fasting, but do thou arise and go to the river Tigris and lift up a stone and stand on it in the water up to thy neck in the deep of the river. And let no speech proceed out of thy mouth, since we are unworthy to address the Lord, for our lips are unclean from the unlawful and forbidden tree. ² And do thou stand in the water of the river thirty-seven days. But I will spend forty days in the water of Jordan, perchance the Lord God will take pity upon us.' **VII** ¹ And Eve walked to the river Tigris and did ² as Adam had told her. Likewise, Adam walked to the river Jordan and stood on a stone up to his neck in water. **VIII** ¹ And Adam said: 'I tell thee, water of Jordan, grieve with me, and assemble to me all swimming (creatures), which are in thee, and let them surround me and mourn in company with me. Not for themselves let them lament, but for me; for it is not they that have sinned, but I.' ³ Forthwith, all living things came and surrounded him, and, from that hour, the water of Jordan stood (still) and its current was stayed.' **IX** ¹ And eighteen days passed by; then Satan was wroth and transformed himself into the brightness of angels, and went away to the river ² Tigris to Eve, and found her weeping, and the devil himself pretended to grieve with her, and he began to weep and said to her: 'Come out of the river and lament no more. Cease now from sorrow and moans. Why art thou anxious ³ and thy husband Adam? The Lord God hath heard your groaning and hath accepted your penitence, and all we angels have entreated on your behalf, and made supplication to the Lord; ⁴ and he hath sent me to bring you out of the water and give you the nourishment which you had in paradise, and for which you are crying ⁵ out. Now come out of the water and I will conduct you to the place where your victual hath been made ready.' **X** ¹ But Eve heard and believed and went out of the water of the river, and her flesh was (trembling) ² like grass, from the chill of the water. And when she had gone out, she fell on the earth and the devil raised her up and led her to Adam. ³ But when Adam had seen her and the devil with her, he wept and cried aloud and said: 'O Eve, Eve, where is the labour of thy penitence? ⁴ How hast thou been again ensnared by our adversary, by whose means we have been estranged from our abode in paradise and spiritual joy?' **XI** ¹ And when she heard this, Eve understood that (it was) the devil (who) had persuaded her to go out of the river; and she fell on her face on the earth and her sorrow and groaning and wailing ² was redoubled. And she cried out and said: 'Woe unto thee, thou devil. Why dost thou attack us for no cause? What hast thou to do with us? What have we done to thee? for thou pursuest us with craft? Or why doth thy malice ³ assail us? Have we taken away thy glory and caused thee to be without honour? Why dost thou harry us, thou enemy (and persecute us) to the death in wickedness and envy?' **XII** ¹ And with a heavy sigh, the devil spake: 'O Adam! all my hostility, envy, and sorrow is for thee, since it is for thee that I have been expelled from my glory, which I possessed in the heavens ² in the midst of the angels and for thee was I cast out in the earth.' Adam answered, 'What dost ³ thou tell me? What have I done to thee or what is my fault against thee? Seeing that thou hast received no harm or injury from us, why dost thou pursue us?' **XIII** ¹ The devil replied, 'Adam, what dost thou tell me? It is for thy sake that I have been hurled ² from that place. When thou wast formed. I was hurled out of the presence of God and banished from the company of the angels. When God blew into thee the breath of life and thy face and likeness was made in the image of God, Michael also brought thee and made (us) worship thee in the sight of God; and God the Lord spake: Here is Adam. I have made thee in our image and likeness.' **XIV** [1] And Michael went out and called all the angels saying: 'Worship the image of God as the Lord God hath commanded.' And Michael himself worshipped first; then he called me and said: 'Worship the image of God [3] the Lord.' And I answered, 'I have no (need) to worship Adam.' And since Michael kept urging me to worship, I said to him, 'Why dost thou urge me? I will not worship an inferior and younger being (than I). I am his senior in the Creation, before he was made was I already made. It is his duty to worship me.' **XV** [1,2] When the angels, who were under me, heard this, they refused to worship him. And Michael saith, 'Worship the image of God, but if thou wilt not worship him, the Lord God will be wrath [3] with thee.' And I said, 'If He be wrath with me, I will set my seat above the stars of heaven and will be like the Highest.' **XVI** [1] And God the Lord was wrath with me and banished me and my angels from our glory; and on [2] thy account were we expelled from our abodes into this world and hurled on the earth. And [3] straightway we were overcome with grief, since we had been spoiled of so great glory. And we [4] were grieved when we saw thee in such joy and luxury. And with guile I cheated thy wife and caused thee to be expelled through her (doing) from thy joy and luxury, as I have been driven out of my glory. **XVII** [1] When Adam heard the devil say this, he cried out and wept and spake: 'O Lord my God, my life is in thy hands. Banish this Adversary far from me, who seeketh to destroy my soul, and give [2,3] me his glory which he himself hath lost.' And at that moment, the devil vanished before him. But Adam endured in his penance, standing for forty days (on end) in the water of Jordan. **XVIII** [1] And Eve said to Adam: 'Live thou, my Lord, to thee life is granted, since thou hast committed neither the first nor the second error. But I have erred and been led astray for I have not kept the commandment of God; and now banish me from the light of thy life and I will go to the sunsetting, [2] and there will I be, until I die.' And she began to walk towards the western parts and to mourn [3] and to weep bitterly and groan aloud. And she made there a booth, while she had in her womb offspring of three months old. **XIX** [1] And when the time of her bearing approached, she began to be distressed with pains, and she [2] cried aloud to the Lord and said: 'Pity me, O Lord, assist me.' And she was not heard and the [3] mercy of God did not encircle her. And she said to herself: 'Who shall tell my lord Adam? I implore you, ye luminaries of heaven, what time ye return to the east, bear a message to my lord Adam.' **XX** [1] But in that hour, Adam said: 'The complaint of Eve hath come to me. Perchance, once more hath the serpent fought with her.' [2] And he went and found her in great distress. And Eve said: 'From the moment I saw thee, my lord, my grief-laden soul was refreshed. And now entreat the Lord God on my behalf to [3] hearken unto thee and look upon me and free me from my awful pains.' And Adam entreated the Lord for Eve. **XXI** [1] And behold, there came twelve angels and two 'virtues', standing on the right and on the left [2] of Eve; and Michael was standing on the right; and he stroked her on the face as far as to the breast and said to Eve: 'Blessed art thou, Eve, for Adam's sake. Since his prayers and intercessions are great, I have been sent that thou mayst receive our help. Rise up now, and [3] prepare thee to bear. And she bore a son and he was shining; and at once the babe rose up and ran and bore a blade of grass in his hands, and gave it to his mother, and his name was called Cain. **XXII** [1] And Adam carried Eve and the boy and led [2] them to the East. And the Lord God sent divers seeds by Michael the archangel and gave to Adam and showed him how to work and till the ground, that they might have fruit by which they and all their generations might live. [3] For thereafter Eve conceived and bare a son, whose name was Abel; and Cain and Abel used to stay together. [4] And Eve said to Adam: 'My lord, while I slept, I saw a vision, as it were the blood of our son Abel in the hand of Cain, who was gulping it down in his mouth. Therefore I have sorrow.' [5] And Adam said, 'Alas if Cain slew Abel. Yet let us separate them from each other mutually, and let us make for each of them separate dwellings.' **XXIII** [1] And they made Cain an husbandman, (but) Abel they made a shepherd; in order that in this wise they might be mutually separated. [2] And thereafter, Cain slew Abel, but Adam was then one hundred and thirty years old, but Abel was slain when he was one hundred and twenty-two years. And thereafter Adam knew his wife and he begat a son and called his name Seth. **XXIV** [1] And Adam said to Eve, 'Behold, I have begotten a son, in place of Abel, whom Cain slew.' [2] And after Adam had begotten Seth, he lived eight hundred years and begat thirty sons and thirty daughters; in all sixty-three children. And they were increased over the face of the earth in their nations. **XXV** [1] And Adam said to Seth, 'Hear, my son Seth, that I may relate to thee what I heard and [2] saw after your mother and I had been driven out of paradise. When we were at prayer, there [3] came to me Michael the archangel, a messenger of God. And I saw a chariot like the wind and its wheels were fiery and I was caught up into the Paradise of righteousness, and I saw the Lord sitting and his face was flaming fire that could not be endured. And many thousands of angels were on the right and the left of that chariot. **XXVI** [1] When I saw this, I was confounded, and terror seized me and I bowed myself down before [2] God with my face to the earth. And God said to me, 'Behold thou diest, since thou hast transgressed the commandment of God, for thou didst hearken rather to the voice of thy wife, whom I gave into thy power, that thou mightst hold her to thy will. Yet thou didst listen to her and didst pass by My words.' **XXVII** [1] And when I heard these words of God, I fell prone on the earth and worshipped the Lord and said, 'My Lord, All powerful and merciful God, Holy and Righteous One, let not the name that is mindful of Thy majesty be blotted out, but convert my soul, for I die and my [2] breath will go out of my mouth. Cast me not out from Thy presence, (me) whom Thou didst form of the clay of the earth. Do not banish from Thy favour him whom Thou didst nourish.' [3] And lo! a word concerning thee came upon me and the Lord said to me, 'Since thy days were fashioned, thou hast been created with a love of knowledge; therefore there shall not be taken from thy seed for ever the (right) to serve Me.' **XXVIII** [1] And when I heard these words. I threw myself on the earth and adored the Lord God and said, 'Thou art the eternal and supreme God; and all creatures give thee honour and praise. [2] 'Thou art the true Light gleaming above all light(s), the Living Life, infinite mighty Power. To Thee, the spiritual powers give honour and praise. Thou workest on the race of men the abundance of Thy mercy.' [3] After I had worshipped the Lord, straightway Michael, God's archangel, seized my hand and [4] cast me out of the paradise of 'vision' and of God's command. And Michael held a rod in his hand, and he touched the waters, which were round about paradise, and they froze hard. **XXIX** [1] And I went across, and Michael the archangel went across with me, and he led me back to [2] the place whence he had caught me up. Hearken, my son Seth, even to the rest of the secrets [and sacraments] that shall be, which were revealed to me, when I had eaten of the tree of the [3] knowledge, and knew and perceived what will come to pass in this age; [what God intends to do [4] to his creation of the race of men. The Lord will appear in a flame of fire (and) from the mouth of His majesty He will give commandments and statutes [from His mouth will proceed a two-edged sword] and they will sanctify Him in the house of the habitation of His majesty. [5] And He will show them the marvellous place of His majesty. And then they will build a house to the Lord their God in the land which He shall prepare for them and there they will transgress His statutes and their sanctuary will be burnt up and their land will be deserted and they [6] themselves will be dispersed; because they have kindled the wrath of God. And once more He will cause them to come back from their dispersion; and again they will build the house of God; [7] and in the last time the house of God will be exalted greater than of old. And once more iniquity will exceed righteousness. And thereafter God will dwell with men on earth [in visible form]; and then, righteousness will begin to shine. And the house of God will be honoured in the age and their enemies will no more be able to hurt the men, who are believing in God; and God will stir up for Himself a faithful people, whom He shall save for eternity, and the impious shall be punished [8] by God their king, the men who refused to love His law. Heaven and earth, nights and days, and all creatures shall obey Him, and not overstep His commandment. Men shall not change their [9] works, but they shall be changed from forsaking the law of the Lord. Therefore the Lord shall repel from Himself the wicked, and the just shall shine like the sun, in the sight of God. And [10] in that time, shall men be purified by water from their sins. But those who are unwilling to be purified by water shall be condemned. And happy shall the man be, who hath ruled his soul, when the Judgement shall come to pass and the greatness of God be seen among men and their deeds be inquired into by God the just judge. **XXX** [1] After Adam was nine hundred and thirty years old, since he knew that his days were coming to an end, he said: 'Let all my sons assemble themselves to me, that I may bless them before I die, and speak with them.' [2] And they were assembled in three parts, before his sight, in the house of prayer, where they used [3] to worship the Lord God. And they asked him (saying): 'What concerns thee, Father, that thou shouldst assemble us, and why dost thou lie on [4] thy bed? 'Then Adam answered and said: 'My sons, I am sick and in pain.' And all his sons said to him: 'What does it mean, father, this illness and pain?' **XXXI** [1] Then said Seth his son: 'O (my) lord, perchance thou hast longed after the fruit of paradise, which thou wast wont to eat, and therefore thou liest in sadness? Tell me and I will go to the nearest gates of paradise and put dust on my head and throw myself down on the earth before the gates of paradise and lament and make entreaty to God with loud lamentation; perchance he will hearken to me and send his angel to bring me the fruit, for which thou hast longed.' [2] Adam answered and said: 'No, my son, I do not long (for this), but I feel weakness and great [3] pain in my body.' Seth answered, 'What is pain, my lord father? I am ignorant; but hide it not from us, but tell us (about it).' **XXXII** [1]And Adam answered and said: 'Hear me, my sons. When God made us, me and your mother, and placed us in paradise and gave us every tree bearing fruit to eat, he laid a prohibition on us concerning the tree of knowledge of good and evil, which is in the midst of paradise; (saying) [2] 'Do not eat of it.' But God gave a part of paradise to me and (a part) to your mother: the trees of the eastern part and the north, which is over against Aquilo he gave to me, and to your mother he gave the part of the south and the western part. **XXXIII** [1] (Moreover) God the Lord gave us two angels [2] to guard us. The hour came when the angels had ascended to worship in the sight of God; forthwith the adversary [the devil] found an opportunity while the angels were absent and the devil led your mother astray to eat of the [3] unlawful and forbidden tree. And she did eat and gave to me. **XXXIV** [1] And immediately, the Lord God was wrath with us, and the Lord said to me: 'In that thou hast left behind my commandment and hast not kept my word, which I confirmed to thee; behold, I will bring upon thy body, seventy blows; with divers griefs, shalt thou be tormented, beginning at thy head and thine eyes and thine ears down to thy nails on thy toes, and in every [2] separate limb. These hath God

313

appointed for chastisement. All these things hath the Lord sent to me and to all our race.' **XXXV** [1] Thus spake Adam to his sons, and he was seized with violent pains, and he cried out with a loud voice, 'What shall I do? I am in distress. So cruel are the pains with which I am beset.' And when Eve had seen him weeping, she also began to weep herself, and said: 'O Lord my God, hand over to me his pain, for it is I who sinned.' [3] And Eve said to Adam: 'My lord, give me a part of thy pains, for this hath come to thee from fault of mine.' **XXXVI** [1] And Adam said to Eve: 'Rise up and go with my son Seth to the neighbourhood of paradise, and put dust on your heads and throw yourselves on the ground and lament in the sight of [2] God. Perchance He will have pity (upon you) and send His angel across to the tree of His mercy, whence floweth the oil of life, and will give you a drop of it, to anoint me with it, that I may have rest from these pains, by which I am being consumed.' **XXXVII** [1]Then Seth and his mother went off towards the gates of paradise. And while they were walking, lo! suddenly there came a beast [2] [a serpent] and attacked and bit Seth. And as soon as Eve saw it, she wept and said: 'Alas, wretched woman that I am. I am accursed since I have not kept the commandment of God.' [3] And Eve said to the serpent in a loud voice: 'Accursed beast! how (is it that) thou hast not feared to let thyself loose against the image of God, but hast dared to fight with it?' **XXXVIII** [1] The beast answered in the language of men: 'Is it not against you, Eve, that our malice (is directed)? Are not ye the objects of our rage? [2] Tell me, Eve, how was thy mouth opened to eat of the fruit? But now if I shall begin to reprove thee thou canst not bear it.' **XXXIX** [1] Then said Seth to the beast: 'God the Lord revile thee. Be silent, be dumb, shut thy mouth, accursed enemy of Truth, confounder and destroyer. Avaunt from the image of God till the day when the Lord God shall order thee to be brought to the ordeal.' And the beast said to Seth: 'See, I leave the presence of the image of God, as thou hast said.' Forthwith he left Seth, wounded by his teeth. **XL** [1] But Seth and his mother walked to the regions of paradise for the oil of mercy to anoint the sick Adam: and they arrived at the gates of paradise, (and) they took dust from the earth and placed it on their heads, and bowed themselves with their faces to the earth and began to lament and [2] make loud moaning, imploring the Lord God to pity Adam in his pains and to send His angel to give them the oil from the 'tree of His mercy'. **XLI** [1] But when they had been praying and imploring for many hours, behold, the angel Michael ap- [2] peared to them and said: 'I have been sent to you from the Lord -I am set by God over the [3] bodies of men- I tell thee, Seth, (thou) man of God, weep not nor pray and entreat on account of the oil of the tree of mercy to anoint thy father Adam for the pains of his body. **XLII** [1] 'For I tell thee that in no wise wilt thou be able to receive thereof save in the last days.' [2] [When five thousand five hundred years have been fulfilled, then will come upon earth the most beloved king Christ, the son of God, to revive the body of Adam and with him to revive [3] the bodies of the dead. He Himself, the Son of God, when He comes will be baptized in the river of Jordan, and when He hath come out of the water of Jordan, then He will anoint from the [4] oil of mercy all that believe in Him. And the oil of mercy shall be for generation to generation for those who are ready to be born again of [5] water and the Holy Spirit to life eternal. Then the most beloved Son of God, Christ, descending on earth shall lead thy father Adam to Paradise to the tree of mercy.] **XLIII** [1] 'But do thou, Seth, go to thy father Adam, since the time of his life is fulfilled. Six days hence, his soul shall go off his body and when it shall have gone out, thou shalt see great marvels in the heaven and in the earth and the [2] luminaries of heaven. With these words, straightway Michael departed from Seth. [3] And Eve and Seth returned bearing with them herbs of fragrance, i.e. nard and crocus and calamus and cinnamon. **XLIV** [1] And when Seth and his mother had reached Adam, they told him, how the beast [the serpent] [2] bit Seth. And Adam said to Eve: 'What hast thou done? A great plague hast thou brought upon us, transgression and sin for all our generations: and this which thou hast done, tell thy [3] children after my death, [for those who arise from us shall toil and fail but they shall be [4] wanting and curse us (and) say, All evils have our parents brought upon us, who were at the [5] beginning].' When Eve heard these words, she began to weep and moan. **XLV** [1] And just as Michael the archangel had fore- [2] told, after six days came Adam's death. When Adam perceived that the hour of his death was at hand, he said to all his sons: 'Behold, I am nine hundred and thirty years old, and if I die, [3] bury me towards the sunrising in the field of yonder dwelling.' And it came to pass that when he had finished all his discourse, he gave up the ghost. (Then) was the sun darkened and the moon **XLVI** [1] and the stars for seven days, and Seth in his mourning embraced from above the body of his father, and Eve was looking on the ground with hands folded over her head, and all her children wept most bitterly. And behold, there appeared [2] Michael the angel and stood at the head of Adam and said to Seth: 'Rise up from the body of thy [3] father and come to me and see what is the doom of the Lord God concerning him. His creature is he, and God hath pitied him.' And all angels blew their trumpets, and cried: **XLVII** [1] 'Blessed art thou, O Lord, for thou hast had pity on Thy creature.' **XLVIII** [1] Then Seth saw the hand of God stretched out holding Adam and he handed him over to [2] Michael, saying: 'Let him be in thy charge till the day of Judgement in punishment, till the last years when I will convert his sorrow into joy. [3] Then shall he sit on the throne of him who hath been his supplanter.' [4] And the Lord said again to the angels Michael and Uriel: 'Bring me three linen clothes of byssus and spread them out over Adam and other linen clothes over Abel his son and bury Adam and Abel his son.' [5] And all the 'powers' of angels marched before Adam, and the sleep of the dead was [6] consecrated. And the angels Michael and Uriel buried Adam and Abel in the parts of Paradise, before the eyes of Seth and his mother [7] [and no one else], and Michael and Uriel said: 'Just as ye have seen, in like manner, bury your dead.' **XLIX** [1] Six days after, Adam died; and Eve perceived that she would die, (so) she assembled all her sons [2] and daughters, Seth with thirty brothers and thirty sisters, and Eve said to all, 'Hear me, my children, and I will tell you what the archangel Michael said to us when I and your father transgressed the command of God [3] On account of your transgression, Our Lord will bring upon your race the anger of his judgement, first by water, the second time by fire; by these two, will the Lord judge the whole human race **L** [1] But hearken unto me, my children. Make ye then tables of stone and others of clay, and write [2] on them, all my life and your father's (all) that ye have heard and seen from us. If by water the Lord judge our race, the tables of clay will be dissolved and the tables of stone will remain; but if by fire, the tables of stone will be broken up and the tables of clay will be baked (hard).' [3] When Eve had said all this to her children, she spread out her hands to heaven in prayer, and bent her knees to the earth, and while she worshipped the Lord and gave him thanks, she gave up the ghost. Thereafter, all her children buried her with loud lamentation. **LI** [1] When they had been mourning four days, (then) Michael the archangel appeared and said [2] to Seth: 'Man of God, mourn not for thy dead more than six days, for on the seventh day is the sign of the resurrection and the rest of the age to come; on the seventh day the Lord rested from all His works.' [3] Thereupon Seth made the tables.

Book of Creation (Sefer Yetzirah)

314

Creation 1

[1] In thirty-two mysterious paths of Wisdom, Yah, Eternal of Hosts [Yod-Vav- Yod], God of Israel, Living Elohim, Almighty God, High and Extolled, Dwelling in Eternity, Holy Be His Name, engraved and created His world in three Sefarim: in writing, number and word. Ten Sefirot out of nothing, twenty-two foundation letters, three mothers, seven doubles and twelve simples. [2] Ten Sefirot out of nothing according to the number of the ten digits [fingers and toes], which are five against five and a single covenant to be determined in the center. In word and tongue and mouth, they are ten extending beyond limit: depth of beginning, depth of end, depth of good, depth of evil, depth above and depth below, depth of east and depth of west, depth of north and depth of south, and the sole Master and lofty King faithfully governs them all from his Holy dwelling in Eternity forever. [3] Twenty-two foundation letters: three mothers, seven doubles and twelve simples. Three mothers: Alef, Mem, Shin: their basis is a scale of innocence and a scale of guilt and a tongue ordained to balance between the two. Seven doubles: Bet, Gimel, Dalet, Kaf, Peh, Resh, Tav. Their foundation is life and peace, wisdom and wealth, fruitfulness, grace and government. Twelve simples: He, Vav, Zayin; Chet, Tet, Yod; Lamed, Nun, Samech; Ayin, Tsadeh, Qof. Their foundation is seeing, hearing, smelling, swallowing, copulating, acting, walking, raging, laughing, thinking, and sleeping. [4] By means of these media, Yah, Eternal of Hosts, God of Israel, Living Elohim, Almighty God, High and Extolled, Dwelling in Eternity, Holy Be His Name traced out [carved] three fathers and their posterity, seven conquerors and their hosts, and twelve diagonal boundaries. The proof of this is revealed in the universe, the year, and the soul, which rule ten, three, seven and twelve. Over them rule Tali (the dragon), the wheel, and the heart.

Creation 2

[1] Ten Sefirot out of nothing. Ten and not nine, ten and not eleven. Understand in Wisdom and be wise in Understanding. Examine them, investigate them, think clearly and form. Place the word above its creator and reinstate a Creator upon His foundation; and they are ten extending beyond limit. Observe them: they appear like a flash. Their boundary has no limit for His word is with them: "and they ran and returned." And they pursue His saying like a whirlwind [vortex]; and they prostrate themselves [bend] themselves before His throne. [2] Twenty-two foundation letters: three mothers, seven doubles, and twelve simples. Three mothers: Alef, Mem, Shin: a great mystery, concealed, marvelous and magnificent whence emerge fire, wind [air, spirit, breath] and water, whence everything was created. Seven doubles: Bet, Gimel, Dalet, Kaf, Peh, Resh, Tav, which are to be pronounced in two tongues: Bet, Vayt, Gimel, Ghimel, Dalet, Dhalet, Kaf, Khaf, Peh, Feh, Resh, Rhesh, Tav, Thav, a pattern of hard and soft, strong and weak. The doubles represent the contraries [syzygies]. The opposite of life is death, the opposite of peace is evil [or 'harm'], the opposite of wisdom is foolishness, the opposite of wealth is poverty, the opposite of fruitfulness is barrenness, the opposite of grace is ugliness, the opposite of dominion is slavery. [3] Seven doubles: Bet, Gimel, Dalet, Kaf, Peh, Resh, Tav. Seven and not six, seven and not eight. Six sides in the six directions, and the Holy Palace [Heikhal] ruling in the center. Blessed is the Eternal [Yod-Vav-Yod] in His dwelling. He is the place of the universe and the universe is not His place. [4] Twelve simples: He, Vav, Zayin; Het, Tet, Yod; Lamed, Nun, Samech; Ayin, Tsadeh, Qof. Twelve and not eleven, twelve and not thirteen. Twelve diagonal boundaries divide the directions and separate the different sides: the extremity of the northeast, the extremity of the eastern height, the extremity of the eastern depth,

the extremity of the northwest, the extremity of the northern height, the extremity of the northern depth, the extremity of the southwest, the extremity of the western height, the extremity of the western depth, the extremity of the southeast, the extremity of the southern height, the extremity of the southern depth. [5] By these means, Yah, Eternal of Hosts, God of Israel, Living Elohim, Almighty God, High and Extolled, Dwelling in Eternity, Holy Be His Name traced twenty-two letters and fixed them upon a wheel. He turns the wheel forwards and backwards, and as a sign of this, nothing is better than to ascend in delight [Ayin-Nun-Gimel], and nothing is worse than to descend with the plague [Nun-Gimel-Ayin]. [6] The proof of this is revealed in the universe, the year and the soul. The universe is calculated according to ten: the three are fire, air, and water; the seven are the seven planets; the twelve are the twelve signs of the zodiac; the year is computed by ten: the three are winter, summer and the seasons between; the seven are the seven days of creation; the twelve are the twelve months; the living soul is calculated according to ten: three are the head, chest and stomach; seven are the seven apertures of the body; the twelve are the twelve leading organs.

Creation 3

[1] Ten Sefirot out of nothing. Stop your mouth from speaking, stop your heart from thinking, and if your heart runs (to think) return to a place of which it is said "they ran and returned"; and concerning this thing the covenant was made; and they are ten in extent beyond limit. Their end is infused with their beginning, and their beginning with their end like a flame attached to a glowing ember. Know, think [reflect, meditate] and imagine that the Creator is One and there is nothing apart from Him, and before One what do you count? [2] Twenty-two foundation letters: three mothers, seven doubles, and twelve simples. Three mothers: Alef, Mem, Shin are fire, wind [air] and water. The nature of the heavens is fire, the nature of air is wind [ruach], the nature of earth is water. Fire ascends and water descends and wind balances between the two. Mem is silent, Shin is sibilant, and Alef balances between the two. Alef, Mem, Shin are signed in six rings and enveloped in male and female. Know, meditate and imagine that the fire supports water. [3] Seven doubles: Bet, Gimel, Dalet, Kaf, Peh, Resh, Tav which are to be pronounced in two tongues: Bet, Vet, Gimel, Ghimel, Dalet, Dhalet, Kaf, Khaf, Peh, Feh, Resh, Rhesh, Tav, Thav, a pattern of hard and soft, strong and weak. The doubles represent the contraries. The opposite of life is death, the opposite of peace is evil, the opposite of wisdom is foolishness, the opposite of wealth is poverty, the opposite of fruitfulness is barrenness, the opposite of grace is ugliness, the opposite of dominion is slavery. [4] Twelve simples: He, Vav, Zayin; Het, Tet, Yod; Lamed, Nun, Samech; Ayin, Tsadeh, Qof. He engraved them, hewed them, tested them, weighed them, and exchanged them. How did He combine them? Two stones build two houses. Three stones build six houses. Four stones build twenty-four houses. Five stones build one hundred twenty houses. Six stones build seven hundred twenty houses. Seven stones build five thousand forty houses. Thenceforth, go out and calculate what the mouth is unable to say and what the ear is unable to hear. [5] Through these media, Yah, Eternal of Hosts, God of Israel, Living Elohim, Almighty Master, Lofty and Extolled, Dwelling in Eternity, Holy Be His Name traced [carved] (His universe). Yah [Yod-He] is composed of two letters; YHVH [Yod-He-Vav-He] is composed of four letters; Hosts [Tsvaot]: it is like a signal [sign, ot] in his army [tsava]; God of Israel: Israel is a prince [Sar] before God [El]; Living Elohim: three things are called living, Living Elohim, the water of life and the Tree of Life; El [Alef-Lamed]: strength, Shaddai [Shin-Dalet-Yod]: He is sufficient to this point; Lofty [Ram]: because He

dwells in the heights of the universe and is above all elevated being; Extolled [Nisah]: because He carries and maintains the height and depth whilst the bearers are below and their burden is above. He carries and maintains the entire creation; Dwelling in Eternity [Shochen ahd]: because His reign is eternal and uninterrupted; Holy Be His Name[Qadosh Shmo]: because He and His servants are sacred and they declare unto Him every day: Holy, Holy, Holy. [6] The proof of this is revealed in the universe, the year and the soul. The twelve are below, the seven are above them, and the three are above the seven. Of the three, He has formed His sanctuary and all are attached to the One: a sign of the One who has no second, a solitary King in His Universe is One, and His Name is One.

Creation 4

[1] Ten Sefirot out of nothing. One: Spirit-wind of the Living Elohim, Life of the Universe, whose throne strengthens all eternity, Blessed and Beneficent Be His Name, constant and eternal: this is the Holy Spirit. [2] Spirit from Spirit engraved and hewed: He cut the four dimensions of Heaven: the east, the west, the north and the south, and there is a wind for each direction. [3] Twenty-two foundation letters: three mothers, seven doubles, and twelve simples. He hewed them in spirit, carved them in voice, fixed them in the mouth in five place: Alef, He, Het, Ayin [ahacha]; Bet, Vav, Mem, Feh [bumaf]; Gimel, Yod, Khaf, Qof [gikhaq]; Dalet, Tet, Lamed, Nun, Tav [datlanat]; Zayin, Samech, Tsadeh, Resh, Shin [zsats'ras]. Alef, He, Het, Ayin are pronounced at the end of the tongue at the place of swallowing; Bet, Vav, Mem, Feh between the teeth with the tip of the tongue; Gimel, Yod, Khaf, Qof on the palate; Dalet, Tet, Lamed, Nun, Tav on the middle of the tongue and pronounced with the voice; Zayin, Samech, Tsadeh, Resh, Shin between the teeth with the tongue at rest. [4] Twenty-two letters: He carved them, hewed them, refined them, weighed them, and combined them, and He made of them the entire creation and everything to be created in the future. How did He test them? Alef with all and all with Alef, Bet with all and all with Bet, Gimel with all and all with Gimel, and they all return again and again, and they emanate through two hundred and thirty-one gates. All the words and all the creatures emanate from One Name. [5] He created reality from Tohu [Tav-He-Vav] and made His existence out of His nothingness, and He hewed great pillars from the intangible air. [6] Three: water of spirit carved and hewed of it Tohu [Tav-He-Vav] and Bohu [Bet-He-Vav], mud and clay. He made them like a garden bed, put them into position like a wall and covered them like a fortification; he poured water upon them and made dust, for He saith to the snow: be earth. Tohu: this is the green line which encircles the entire world; Bohu: this refers to the rocks split and submerged in the abyss where the water has its source. As it is said: He spread out the line of Tohu and the rocks of Bohu upon it [the water]. [7] Four: fire from water, He engraved and hewed from it a throne of glory and the host dwelling in the heights, as it is written: Who maketh the winds His messengers, the flames of fire His ministers. [8] Five: He chose three simples and fixed them to His great Name, and with them He sealed six extremities. He sealed the height, turning upwards and sealed it with Yod-He-Vav. Six: He sealed the depth and He turned below and sealed it with Yod-Vav-He. Seven: he sealed the east and turned forwards, and sealed it with He-Vav-Yod. Eight: He sealed the west and turned backwards and sealed it with He-Yod-Vav. Nine: He sealed the south and turned to His right and sealed it with Vav-Yod-He. Ten: He sealed the north and turned to His left and sealed it with Vav-He-Yod. These are the ten Sefirot out of nothing, One: Spirit of the Living Elohim; two: wind of the spirit; three: water of the wind; four: fire from the water, height and depth, east and west, north and south.

Creation 5

[1] He made the letter Alef King in Spirit and bound to it a crown and tested this one with this one, and formed of it: air in the universe, abundant moisture in the year, and body in the soul, male and female; with the male: Alef, Mem, Shin, and with the female: Alef, Shin, Mem. [2] He made the letter Mem King in Spirit and bound to it a crown and tested this one with this one, and formed of it: earth in the universe, cold in the year, and belly in the soul (male and female). [3] He made the letter Shin King in Spirit and bound to it a crown and tested this one with this one, and formed of it: Heaven in the universe, heat in the year, and head in the soul, male and female. How did He combine them? Alef-Mem-Shin, Alef-Shin-Mem, Mem-Shin-Alef, Mem-Alef-Shin, Shin-Alef-Mem, Shin-Mem-Alef. Heaven is from fire, the atmosphere is from air, the earth is from water. The head of Adam is fire, his heart is of the spirit-wind, and his stomach is from water. [4] Seven doubles: Bet, Gimel, Dalet, Kaf, Peh, Resh, Tav. He carved them, hewed them, tested them, weighed them, and combined them. He made of them: the planets, the days (of the week), and the apertures (of the head). [5] He made the letter Bet King and bound to it a crown and tested this one with this one, and formed of it: Saturn in the universe, the Sabbath in the year, and the mouth in the soul. [6] He made the letter Gimel King and bound to it a crown and tested this one with this one, and formed of it: Jupiter in the universe, Sunday in the year, and the right eye of the soul. [7] He made the letter Dalet King and bound to it a crown and tested this one with this one, and formed of it: Mars in the universe, Monday in the year, and the left eye of the soul. [8] He made the letter Kaf King and bound to it a crown and tested this one with this one, and formed of it: Sun in the universe, Tuesday in the year, and the right nostril of the soul. [9] He made the letter Peh King and bound to it a crown and tested this one with this one, and formed of it: Venus in the universe, Wednesday in the year, and the left nostril of the soul. [10] He made the letter Resh King and bound to it a crown and tested this one with this one, and formed of it: Mercury in the universe, Thursday in the year, and the right ear of the soul. [11] He made the letter Tav King and bound to it a crown and tested this one with this one, and formed of it: Moon in the universe, Friday in the year, and the left ear of the soul. [12] He separated the witnesses and He bestowed a portion to each of them: a portion to the universe, a portion to the year, and a portion to the soul.

Creation 6

Twelve simples: He, Vav, Zayin; Het, Tet, Yod; Lamed, Nun, Samech; Ayin, Tsadeh, Qof. He carved them, hewed them, tested them, weighed them, and combined them. He formed of them: the signs of the zodiac, the months [of the year], and the leading organs of the body; two are agitated, two are tranquil, two are advising, and two are joyous (these are the two intestines), the two hands, and the two feet. [1] He made them like contenders and set them up like a kind of war; Elohim made them one against the other. [2] Three, to each a portion; seven divided into three above, three [below], and the one rules as a balance between the two. Twelve are arranged in battle: three are friends, three are enemies, three are murderers, and three are resurrectors; and they all are attached one to another. As a sign of this thing, twenty-two inclinations and one body. [3] How did He combine them? He, Vav, Vav, He; Zayin, Het, Het, Zayin; Tet, Yod, Yod, Tet; Lamed, Nun, Nun, Lamed; Samech, Ayin, Ayin, Samech; Tsadeh, Qof, Qof, Tsadeh. [4] He made the letter He King and bound to it a crown and tested this one with this one, and formed of it: Aries in the universe, Nisan in the year, and the liver of the soul. [5] He made the letter Vav King and bound to it a crown and tested this one with this one, and formed of it: Taurus in the universe, Iyyar in

the year, and the gall-bladder of the soul. [6] He made the letter Zayin King and bound to it a crown and tested this one with this one, and formed of it: Gemini in the universe, Sivan in the year, and the spleen in the soul. [7] He made the letter Het King and bound to it a crown and tested this one with this one, and formed of it: Cancer in the universe, Tammuz in the year, and the intestine in the soul. [8] He made the letter Tet King and bound to it a crown and tested this one with this one, and formed of it: Leo in the universe, Ab in the year, and the right kidney in the soul. [9] He made the letter Yod King and bound to it a crown and tested this one with this one, and formed of it: Virgo in the universe, Elul in the year, and the left kidney in the soul. [10] He made the letter Lamed King and bound to it a crown and tested this one with this one, and formed of it: Libra in the universe, Tishri in the year, and the intestines in the soul. [11] He made the letter Nun King and bound to it a crown and tested this one with this one, and formed of it: Scorpio in the universe, Marheshvan in the year, and the stomach in the soul. [12] He made the letter Samech King and bound to it a crown and tested this one with this one, and formed of it: Sagittarius in the universe, Kislev in the year, and the right hand of the soul. [13] He made the letter Ayin King and bound to it a crown and tested this one with this one, and formed of it: Capricorn in the universe, Tevet in the year, and the left hand of the soul. [14] He made the letter Tsadeh King and bound to it a crown and tested this one with this one, and formed of it: Aquarius in the universe, Shvat in the year, and the right foot of the soul. [15] He made the letter Qof King and bound to it a crown and tested this one with this one, and formed of it: Pisces in the universe, Adar in the year, and the left foot of the soul. [16] He divided the witnesses and bestowed a portion to each of them: a portion to the universe, a portion to the year, and a portion to the soul.

Creation 7

[1] Air, between seasons ["abundant moisture"], trunk [i.e. torso]. — Earth, cold, belly. — Heaven, heat [summer], the head: these are Alef, Mem and Shin. [2] Saturn, Sabbath, the mouth. — Jupiter, Sunday, right eye. — Mars, Monday, left eye. — The Sun, Tuesday, right nostril. — Venus, Wednesday, left nostril. — Mercury, Thursday, right ear. —Moon, Friday, left ear: these are Bet, Gimel, Dalet, Kaf, Peh, Resh and Tav. [3] Aries, Nisan, liver. —Taurus, Iyyar, gall-bladder. —Gemini, Sivan, spleen. — Cancer, Tammuz, intestine. — Leo, Ab, right kidney. — Virgo, Elul, left kidney. — Libra, Tishri, intestines. — Scorpio, Marheshvan, stomach. — Sagittarius, Kislev, right hand. — Capricorn, Tevet, left hand. — Aquarius, Shvat, right foot. — Pisces, Adar, left foot: and these are He, Vav, Zayin; Het, Tet, Yod; Lamed, Nun, Samech; Ayin, Tsadeh, Qof.

Creation 8

With Alef have been formed: the spirit-wind, air, the between seasons, the chest, the tongue. With Mem have been formed: water, earth, cold, belly, and the balance of guilt. With Shin have been formed: fire, Heaven, heat, the head, and the balance of innocence. With Bet have been formed: Saturn, the Sabbath, life and death. With Gimel have been formed: Jupiter, Sunday, the right eye, peace and harm. With Dalet have been formed: Mars, Monday, the left eye, wisdom and foolishness. With Kaf have been formed: the Sun, Tuesday, the right nostril, wealth and poverty. With Peh have been formed: Venus, Wednesday, the left nostril, fertility and desolation [barrenness]. With Resh have been formed: Mercury, Thursday, the right ear, grace and ugliness. With Tav have been formed: the Moon, Friday, the left ear, dominion and slavery. With He have been formed: Aries, Nisan, the liver, vision and blindness. With Vav have been formed: Taurus, Iyyar, the spleen, hearing and deafness. With Zayin have been formed: Gemini, Sivan, the gall, odor and odorlessness. With Het have been formed: Cancer, Tammuz, the intestine, the word and silence. With Tet have been formed: Leo, Ab, the right kidney, eating and hunger. With Yod have been formed: Virgo, Elul, the left kidney, copulating and castration. With Lamed have been formed: Libra, Tishri, the intestines, acting and impotence. With Nun have been formed: Scorpio, Marheshvan, the gullet, walking and limping. With Samech have been formed: Sagittarius, Kislev, the right hand, rage and loss of faith. With Ayin have been formed: Capricorn, Tevet, the left hand, laughing and the loss of spleen. With Tsadeh have been formed: Aquarius, Shvat, the right foot, thinking and loss of heart. With Qof have been formed: Pisces, Adar, the left foot, sleeping and languor. And they are all fixed to the Dragon [Tali], the wheel, and the heart. Tali in the universe is like a king upon his throne, the wheel in the year is like a king in his empire, and the heart in the body is like a king at war. To recapitulate: some reunited with the others, and those reunited with the former. These are opposed to those and those are opposed to these. These are the contrary of those and those are the contrary of these. If these are not, those are not. And if those are not, these are not; and they are all fixed to Tali [the Dragon], the wheel and the heart. And when Abraham our father had formed and combined and investigated and reckoned and succeeded, then He-Qof-Bet-He, "The Holy One Blessed Be He" was revealed unto him, and unto Abraham He called this convocation: "Before I formed thee in the belly, I knew thee, and before thou left the womb, I sanctified thee, and I placed thee like a prophet amidst the nations." And He made Abraham a beloved friend, and cut a covenant with him and his seed forever and ever.

The Testament of Abraham.

Version I.

Test. Abr. I. 1. Abraham lived the measure of his life, nine hundred and ninety-five years, and having lived all the years of his life in quietness, gentleness, and righteousness, the righteous one was exceeding hospitable; for, pitching his tent in the cross-ways at the oak of Mamre, he received every one, both rich and poor, kings and rulers, the maimed and the helpless, friends and strangers, neighbors and travelers, all alike did the devout, all-holy, righteous, and hospitable Abraham entertain. Even upon him, however, there came the common, inexorable, bitter lot of death, and the uncertain end of life. Therefore the Lord God, summoning his archangel Michael, said to him: Go down, chief-captain Michael, to Abraham and speak to him concerning his death, that he may set his affairs in order, for I have blessed him as the stars of heaven, and as the sand by the sea-shore, and he is in abundance of long life and many possessions, and is becoming exceeding rich. Beyond all men, moreover, he is righteous in every goodness, hospitable and loving to the end of his life; but do thou, archangel Michael, go to Abraham, my beloved friend, and announce to him his death and assure him thus: Thou shalt at this time depart from this vain world, and shalt quit the body, and go to thine own Lord among the good.

Test. Abr. I. 2. And the chief-captain departed from before the face of God, and went down to Abraham to the oak of Mamre, and found the righteous Abraham in the field close by, sitting beside yokes of oxen for ploughing, together with the sons of Masek and other servants, to the number of twelve. And behold the chief-captain came to him, and Abraham, seeing the chief-captain Michael coming from afar, like to a very comely warrior, arose and met him as was his custom, meeting and entertaining all strangers. And the chief-captain saluted him and said: Hail, most honored father, righteous soul chosen of God, true son of the heavenly one. Abraham said to the chief-captain: Hail, most honored warrior,

bright as the sun and most beautiful above all the sons of men; thou art welcome; therefore I beseech thy presence, tell me whence the youth of thy age has come; teach me, thy suppliant, whence and from what army and from what journey thy beauty has come hither. The chief-captain said: I, O righteous Abraham, come from the great city. I have been sent by the great king to take the place of a good friend of his, for the king has summoned him. And Abraham said, Come, my Lord, go with me as far as my field. The chief-captain said: I come; and going into the field of the ploughing, they sat down beside the company. And Abraham said to his servants, the sons of Masek: Go ye to the herd of horses, and bring two horses, quiet, and gentle and tame, so that I and this stranger may sit thereon. But the chief-captain said, Nay, my Lord, Abraham, let them not bring horses, for I abstain from ever sitting upon any four-footed beast. Is not my king rich in much merchandise, having power both over men and all kinds of cattle? but I abstain from ever sitting upon any four-footed beast. Let us go, then, O righteous soul, walking lightly until we reach thy house. And Abraham said, Amen, be it so.

Test. Abr. I. 3. And as they went on from the field toward his house, beside that way there stood a cypress tree, and by the command of the Lord the tree cried out with a human voice, saying, Holy, holy, holy is the Lord God that calls himself to those that love him; but Abraham hid the mystery, thinking that the chief-captain had not heard the voice of the tree. And coming nigh to the house they sat down in the court, and Isaac seeing the face of the angel said to Sarah his mother, My lady mother, behold, the man sitting with my father Abraham is not a son of the race of those that dwell on the earth. And Isaac ran, and saluted him, and fell at the feet of the Incorporeal, and the Incorporeal blessed him and said, The Lord God will grant thee his promise that he made to thy father Abraham and to his seed, and will also grant thee the precious prayer of thy father and thy mother. Abraham said to Isaac his son, My son Isaac, draw water from the well, and bring it me in the vessel, that we may wash the feet of this stranger, for he is tired, having come to us from off a long journey. And Isaac ran to the well and drew water in the vessel and brought it to them, and Abraham went up and washed the feet of the chief captain Michael, and the heart of Abraham was moved, and he wept over the stranger. And Isaac, seeing his father weeping, wept also, and the chief captain, seeing them weeping, also wept with them, and the tears of the chief captain fell upon the vessel into the water of the basin and became precious stones. And Abraham seeing the marvel, and being astonished, took the stones secretly, and hid the mystery, keeping it by himself in his heart.

Test. Abr. I. 4. And Abraham said to Isaac his son: Go, my beloved son, into the inner chamber of the house and beautify it. Spread for us there two couches, one for me and one for this man that is guest with us this day. Prepare for us there a seat and a candlestick and a table with abundance of every good thing. Beautify the chamber, my son, and spread under us linen and purple and fine linen. Burn there every precious and excellent incense, and bring sweet-smelling plants from the garden and fill our house with them. Kindle seven lamps full of oil, so that we may rejoice, for this man that is our guest this day is more glorious than kings or rulers, and his appearance surpasses all the sons of men. And Isaac prepared all things well, and Abraham taking the archangel Michael went into the chamber, and they both sat down upon the couches, and between them he placed a table with abundance of every good thing. Then the chief captain arose and went out, as if by constraint of his belly to make issue of water, and ascended to heaven in the twinkling of an eye, and stood before the Lord, and said to him: Lord and Master, let thy power know that I am unable to remind that righteous man of his death, for I have not seen upon the earth a man like him, pitiful, hospitable, righteous, truthful, devout, refraining from every evil deed. And now know, Lord, that I cannot remind him of his death. And the Lord said: Go down, chief-captain Michael, to my friend Abraham, and whatever he say to thee, that do thou also, and whatever he eat, eat thou also with him. And I will send my Holy Spirit upon his son Isaac, and will put the remembrance of his death into the heart of Isaac, so that even he in a dream may see the death of his father, and Isaac will relate the dream, and thou shalt interpret it, and he himself will know his end. And the chief-captain said, Lord, all the heavenly spirits are incorporeal, and neither eat nor drink, and this man has set before me a table with abundance of all good things earthly and corruptible. Now, Lord, what shall I do? How shall I escape him, sitting at one table with him? The Lord said: Go down to him, and take no thought for this, for when thou sittest down with him, I will send upon thee a devouring spirit, and it will consume out of thy hands and through thy mouth all that is on the table. Rejoice together with him in everything, only thou shalt interpret well the things of the vision, that Abraham may know the sickle of death and the uncertain end of life, and may make disposal of all his possessions, for I have blessed him above the sand of the sea and as the stars of heaven.

Test. Abr. I. 5. Then the chief captain went down to the house of Abraham, and sat down with him at the table, and Isaac served them. And when the supper was ended, Abraham prayed after his custom, and the chief-captain prayed together with him, and each lay down to sleep upon his couch. And Isaac said to his father, Father, I too would fain sleep with you in this chamber, that I also may hear your discourse, for I love to hear the excellence of the conversation of this virtuous man. Abraham said, Nay, my son, but go to thy own chamber and sleep on thy own couch, lest we be troublesome to this man. Then Isaac, having received the prayer from them, and having blessed them, went to his own chamber and lay down upon his couch. But the Lord cast the thought of death into the heart of Isaac as in a dream, and about the third hour of the night Isaac awoke and rose up from his couch, and came running to the chamber where his father was sleeping together with the archangel. Isaac, therefore, on reaching the door cried out, saying, My father Abraham, arise and open to me quickly, that I may enter and hang upon thy neck, and embrace thee before they take thee away from me. Abraham therefore arose and opened to him, and Isaac entered and hung upon his neck, and began to weep with a loud voice. Abraham therefore being moved at heart, also wept with a loud voice, and the chief-captain, seeing them weeping, wept also. Sarah being in her room, heard their weeping, and came running to them, and found them embracing and weeping. And Sarah said with weeping, My Lord Abraham, what is this that ye weep? Tell me, my Lord, has this brother that has been entertained by us this day brought thee tidings of Lot, thy brother's son, that he is dead? is it for this that ye grieve thus? The chief-captain answered and said to her, Nay, my sister Sarah, it is not as thou sayest, but thy son Isaac, methinks, beheld a dream, and came to us weeping, and we seeing him were moved in our hearts and wept.

Test. Abr. I. 6. Then Sarah, hearing the excellence of the conversation of the chief-captain, straightway knew that it was an angel of the Lord that spoke. Sarah therefore signified to Abraham to come out towards the door, and said to him, My Lord Abraham, knowest thou who this man is? Abraham said, I know not. Sarah said, Thou knowest, my Lord, the three men from heaven that were entertained by us in our tent beside the oak of Mamre, when thou didst kill the kid without blemish, and set a table before them. After the flesh had been eaten, the kid rose again, and sucked its mother with great joy. Knowest thou not, my Lord Abraham, that by

promise they gave to us Isaac as the fruit of the womb? Of these three holy men this is one. Abraham said, O Sarah, in this thou speakest the truth. Glory and praise from our God and the Father. For late in the evening when I washed his feet in the basin I said in my heart, These are the feet of one of the three men that I washed then; and his tears that fell into the basin then became precious stones. And shaking them out from his lap he gave them to Sarah, saying, If thou believest me not, look now at these. And Sarah receiving them bowed down and saluted and said, Glory be to God that showeth us wonderful things. And now know, my Lord Abraham, that there is among us the revelation of some thing, whether it be evil or good!

Test. Abr. I. 7. And Abraham left Sarah, and went into the chamber, and said to Isaac, Come hither, my beloved son, tell me the truth, what it was thou sawest and what befell thee that thou camest so hastily to us. And Isaac answering began to say, I saw, my Lord, in this night the sun and the moon above my head, surrounding me with its rays and giving me light. As I gazed at this and rejoiced, I saw the heaven opened, and a man bearing light descend from it, shining more than seven suns. And this man like the sun came and took away the sun from my head, and went up into the heavens from whence he came, but I was greatly grieved that he took away the sun from me. After a little, as I was still sorrowing and sore troubled, I saw this man come forth from heaven a second time, and he took away from me the moon also from off my head, and I wept greatly and called upon that man of light, and said, Do not, my Lord, take away my glory from me; pity me and hear me, and if thou takest away the sun from me, then leave the moon to me. He said, Suffer them to be taken up to the king above, for he wishes them there. And he took them away from me, but he left the rays upon me. The chief-captain said, Hear, O righteous Abraham; the sun which thy son saw is thou his father, and the moon likewise is Sarah his mother. The man bearing light who descended from heaven, this is the one sent from God who is to take thy righteous soul from thee. And now know, O most honored Abraham, that at this time thou shalt leave this worldly life, and remove to God. Abraham said to the chief captain O strangest of marvels! and now art thou he that shall take my soul from me? The chief-captain said to him, I am the chief-captain Michael, that stands before the Lord, and I was sent to thee to remind thee of thy death, and then I shall depart to him as I was commanded. Abraham said, Now I know that thou art an angel of the Lord, and wast sent to take my soul, but I will not go with thee; but do thou whatever thou art commanded.

Test. Abr. I. 8. The chief-captain hearing these words immediately vanished, and ascending into heaven stood before God, and told all that he had seen in the house of Abraham; and the chief-captain said this also to his Lord, Thus says thy friend Abraham, I will not go with thee, but do thou whatever thou art commanded; and now, O Lord Almighty, doth thy glory and immortal kingdom order aught? God said to the chief-captain Michael, Go to my friend Abraham yet once again, and speak to him thus, Thus saith the Lord thy God, he that brought thee into the land of promise, that blessed thee above the sand of the sea and above the stars of heaven, that opened the womb of barrenness of Sarah, and granted thee Isaac as the fruit of the womb in old age, Verily I say unto thee that blessing I will bless thee, and multiplying I will multiply thy seed, and I will give thee all that thou shalt ask from me, for I am the Lord thy God, and besides me there is no other. Tell me why thou hast rebelled against me, and why there is grief in thee, and why thou rebelled against my archangel Michael? Knowest thou not that all who have come from Adam and Eve have died, and that none of the prophets has escaped death? None of those that rule as kings is immortal; none of thy forefathers has escaped the mystery of death. They have all died, they have all departed into Hades, they are all gathered by the sickle of death. But upon thee I have not sent death, I have not suffered any deadly disease to come upon thee, I have not permitted the sickle of death to meet thee, I have not allowed the nets of Hades to enfold thee, I have never wished thee to meet with any evil. But for good comfort I have sent my chief-captain Michael to thee, that thou mayst know thy departure from the world, and set thy house in order, and all that belongs to thee, and bless Isaac thy beloved son. And now know that I have done this not wishing to grieve thee. Wherefore then hast thou said to my chief-captain, I will not go with thee? Wherefore hast thou spoken thus? Knowest thou not that if I give leave to death and he comes upon thee, then I should see whether thou wouldst come or not?

Test. Abr. I. 9. And the chief-captain receiving the exhortations of the Lord went down to Abraham, and seeing him the righteous one fell upon his face to the ground as one dead, and the chief-captain told him all that he had heard from the Most High. Then the holy and just Abraham rising with many tears fell at the feet of the Incorporeal, and besought him, saying, I beseech thee, chief-captain of the hosts above, since thou hast wholly deigned to come thyself to me a sinner and in all things thy unworthy servant, I beseech thee even now, O chief-captain, to carry my word yet again to the Most High, and thou shalt say to him, Thus saith Abraham thy servant, Lord, Lord, in every work and word which I have asked of thee thou hast heard me, and hast fulfilled all my counsel. Now, Lord, I resist not thy power, for I too know that I am not immortal but mortal. Since therefore to thy command all things yield, and fear and tremble at the face of thy power, I also fear, but I ask one request of thee, and now, Lord and Master, hear my prayer, for while still in this body I desire to see all the inhabited earth, and all the creations which thou didst establish by one word, and when I see these, then if I shall depart from life I shall be without sorrow. So the chief-captain went back again, and stood before God, and told him all, saying, Thus saith thy friend Abraham, I desired to behold all the earth in my lifetime before I died. And the Most High hearing this, again commanded the chief-captain Michael, and said to him, Take a cloud of light, and the angels that have power over the chariots, and go down, take the righteous Abraham upon a chariot of the cherubim, and exalt him into the air of heaven that he may behold all the earth.

Test. Abr. I. 10. And the archangel Michael went down and took Abraham upon a chariot of the cherubim, and exalted him into the air of heaven, and led him upon the cloud together with sixty angels, and Abraham ascended upon the chariot over all the earth. And Abraham saw the world as it was in that day, some ploughing, others driving wains, in one place men herding flocks, and in another watching them by night, and dancing and playing and harping, in another place men striving and contending at law, elsewhere men weeping and having the dead in remembrance. He saw also the newly-wedded received with honor, and in a word he saw all things that are done in the world, both good and bad. Abraham therefore passing over them saw men bearing swords, wielding in their hands sharpened swords, and Abraham asked the chief-captain, Who are these? The chief-captain said, These are thieves, who intend to commit murder, and to steal and burn and destroy. Abraham said, Lord, Lord, hear my voice, and command that wild beasts may come out of the wood and devour them. And even as he spoke there came wild beasts out of the wood and devoured them. And he saw in another place a man with a woman committing fornication with each other, and said, Lord, Lord, command that the earth may open

and swallow them, and straightway the earth was cleft and swallowed them. And he saw in another place men digging through a house, and carrying away other men's possessions, and he said, Lord, Lord, command that fire may come down from heaven and consume them. And even as he spoke, fire came down from heaven and consumed them. And straightway there came a voice from heaven to the chief-captain, saying thus, O chief-captain Michael, command the chariot to stop, and turn Abraham away that he may not see all the earth, for if he behold all that live in wickedness, he will destroy all creation. For behold, Abraham has not sinned, and has no pity on sinners, but I have made the world, and desire not to destroy any one of them, but wait for the death of the sinner, till he be converted and live. But take Abraham up to the first gate of heaven, that he may see there the judgments and recompenses, and repent of the souls of the sinners that he has destroyed.

Test. Abr. I. 11. So Michael turned the chariot and brought Abraham to the east, to the first gate of heaven; and Abraham saw two ways, the one narrow and contracted, the other broad and spacious, and there he saw two gates, the one broad on the broad way, and the other narrow on the narrow way. And outside the two gates there he saw a man sitting upon a gilded throne, and the appearance of that man was terrible, as of the Lord. And they saw many souls driven by angels and led in through the broad gate, and other souls, few in number, that were taken by the angels through the narrow gate. And when the wonderful one who sat upon the golden throne saw few entering through the narrow gate, and many entering through the broad one, straightway that wonderful one tore the hairs of his head and the sides of his beard, and threw himself on the ground from his throne, weeping and lamenting. But when he saw many souls entering through the narrow gate, then he arose from the ground and sat upon his throne in great joy, rejoicing and exulting. And Abraham asked the chief-captain, My Lord chief-captain, who is this most marvelous man, adorned with such glory, and sometimes he weeps and laments, and sometimes he rejoices and exults? The incorporeal one said: This is the first-created Adam who is in such glory, and he looks upon the world because all are born from him, and when he sees many souls going through the narrow gate, then he arises and sits upon his throne rejoicing and exulting in joy, because this narrow gate is that of the just, that leads to life, and they that enter through it go into Paradise. For this, then, the first-created Adam rejoices, because he sees the souls being saved. But when he sees many souls entering through the broad gate, then he pulls out the hairs of his head, and casts himself on the ground weeping and lamenting bitterly, for the broad gate is that of sinners, which leads to destruction and eternal punishment. And for this the first-formed Adam falls from his throne weeping and lamenting for the destruction of sinners, for they are many that are lost, and they are few that are saved, for in seven thousand there is scarcely found one soul saved, being righteous and undefiled.

Test. Abr. I. 12. While he was yet saying these things to me, behold two angels, fiery in aspect, and pitiless in mind, and severe in look, and they drove on thousands of souls, pitilessly lashing them with fiery thongs. The angel laid hold of one soul, and they drove all the souls in at the broad gate to destruction. So we also went along with the angels, and came within that broad gate, and between the two gates stood a throne terrible of aspect, of terrible crystal, gleaming as fire, and upon it sat a wondrous man bright as the sun, like to the Son of God. Before him stood a table like crystal, all of gold and fine linen, and upon the table there was lying a book, the thickness of it six cubits, and the breadth of it ten cubits, and on the right and left of it stood two angels holding paper and ink and pen. Before the table sat an angel of light, holding in his hand a balance, and on his left sat an angel all fiery, pitiless, and severe, holding in his hand a trumpet, having within it all-consuming fire with which to try the sinners. The wondrous man who sat upon the throne himself judged and sentenced the souls, and the two angels on the right and on the left wrote down, the one on the right the righteousness and the one on the left the wickedness. The one before the table, who held the balance, weighed the souls, and the fiery angel, who held the fire, tried the souls. And Abraham asked the chief-captain Michael, What is this that we behold? And the chief-captain said, These things that thou seest, holy Abraham, are the judgment and recompense. And behold the angel holding the soul in his hand, and he brought it before the judge, and the judge said to one of the angels that served him, Open me this book, and find me the sins of this soul. And opening the book he found its sins and its righteousness equally balanced, and he neither gave it to the tormentors, nor to those that were saved, but set it in the midst.

Test. Abr. I. 13. And Abraham said, My Lord chief-captain, who is this most wondrous judge? and who are the angels that write down? and who is the angel like the sun, holding the balance? and who is the fiery angel holding the fire? The chief-captain said, "Seest thou, most holy Abraham, the terrible man sitting upon the throne? This is the son of the first created Adam, who is called Abel, whom the wicked Cain killed, and he sits thus to judge all creation, and examines righteous men and sinners. For God has said, I shall not judge you, but every man born of man shall be judged. Therefore he has given to him judgment, to judge the world until his great and glorious coming, and then, O righteous Abraham, is the perfect judgment and recompense, eternal and unchangeable, which no one can alter. For every man has come from the first-created, and therefore they are first judged here by his son, and at the second coming they shall be judged by the twelve tribes of Israel, every breath and every creature. But the third time they shall be judged by the Lord God of all, and then, indeed, the end of that judgment is near, and the sentence terrible, and there is none to deliver. And now by three tribunals the judgment of the world and the recompense is made, and for this reason a matter is not finally confirmed by one or two witnesses, but by three witnesses shall everything be established. The two angels on the right hand and on the left, these are they that write down the sins and the righteousness, the one on the right hand writes down the righteousness, and the one on the left the sins. The angel like the sun, holding the balance in his hand, is the archangel, Dokiel the just weigher, and he weighs the righteousnesses and sins with the righteousness of God. The fiery and pitiless angel, holding the fire in his hand, is the archangel Puruel, who has power over fire, and tries the works of men through fire, and if the fire consume the work of any man, the angel of judgment immediately seizes him, and carries him away to the place of sinners, a most bitter place of punishment. But if the fire approves the work of anyone, and does not seize upon it, that man is justified, and the angel of righteousness takes him and carries him up to be saved in the lot of the just. And thus, most righteous Abraham, all things in all men are tried by fire and the balance."

Test. Abr. I. 14. And Abraham said to the chief-captain, My Lord the chief-captain, the soul which the angel held in his hand, why was it adjudged to be set in the midst? The chief-captain said, Listen, righteous Abraham. Because the judge found its sins. and its righteousnesses equal, he neither committed it to judgment nor to be saved, until the judge of all shall come. Abraham said to the chief-captain, And what yet is wanting for the soul to be saved? The chief-captain said, If it obtains one righteousness above its sins, it enters into salvation. Abraham said to the chief-captain, Come

hither, chief-captain Michael, let us make prayer for this soul, and see whether God will hear us. The chief-captain said, Amen, be it so; and they made prayer and entreaty for the soul, and God heard them, and when they rose up from their prayer they did not see the soul standing there. And Abraham said to the angel, Where is the soul that thou didst hold in the midst? And the angel answered, It has been saved by thy righteous prayer, and behold an angel of light has taken it and carried it up into Paradise. Abraham said, I glorify the name of God, the Most High, and his immeasurable mercy. And Abraham said to the chief-captain, I beseech thee, archangel, hearken to my prayer, and let us yet call upon the Lord, and supplicate his compassion, and entreat his mercy for the souls of the sinners whom I formerly, in my anger, cursed and destroyed, whom the earth devoured, and the wild beasts tore in pieces, and the fire consumed through my words. Now I know that I have sinned before the Lord our God. Come then, O Michael, chief-captain of the hosts above, come, let us call upon God with tears that he may forgive me my sin, and grant them to me. And the chief-captain heard him, and they made entreaty before the Lord, and when they had called upon him for a long space, there came a voice from heaven saying, Abraham, Abraham, I have hearkened to thy voice and thy prayer, and forgive thee thy sin, and those whom thou thinkest that I destroyed I have called up and brought them into life by my exceeding kindness, because for a season I have requited them in judgment, and those whom I destroy living upon earth, I will not requite in death.

Test. Abr. I. 15. And the voice of the Lord said also to the chief-captain Michael, Michael, my servant, turn back Abraham to his house, for behold his end has come nigh, and the measure of his life is fulfilled, that he may set all things in order, and then take him and bring him to me. So the chief-captain, turning the chariot and the cloud, brought Abraham to his house, and going into his chamber he sat upon his couch. And Sarah his wife came and embraced the feet of the Incorporeal, and spoke humbly, saying, I give thee thanks, my Lord, that thou hast brought my Lord Abraham, for behold we thought he had been taken up from us. And his son Isaac also came and fell upon his neck, and in the same way all his men-slaves and women-slaves surrounded Abraham and embraced him, glorifying God. And the Incorporeal one said to them, Hearken, righteous Abraham. Behold thy wife Sarah, behold also thy beloved son Isaac, behold also all thy men-servants and maid-servants round about thee. Make disposition of all that thou hast, for the day has come nigh in which thou shalt depart from the body and go to the Lord once for all. Abraham said, Has the Lord said it, or sayest thou this of thyself? The chief-captain answered, Hearken, righteous Abraham. The Lord has commanded, and I tell it thee. Abraham said, I will not go with thee. The chief-captain, hearing these words, straightway went forth from the presence of Abraham, and went up into the heavens, and stood before God the Most High, and said, Lord Almighty, behold I have hearkened to Thy friend Abraham in all he has said to Thee, and have fulfilled his requests. I have shown to him Thy power, and all the earth and sea that is under heaven. I have shown to him judgment and recompense by means of cloud and chariots, and again he says, I will not go with thee. And the Most High said to the angel, Does my friend Abraham say thus again, I will not go with thee? The archangel said, Lord Almighty, he says thus, and I refrain from laying hands on him, because from the beginning he is Thy friend, and has done all things pleasing in Thy sight. There is no man like him on earth, not even Job the wondrous man, and therefore I refrain from laying hands on him. Command, therefore, Immortal King, what shall be done.

Test. Abr. I. 16. Then the Most High said, Call me hither Death that is called the shameless countenance and the pitiless look. And Michael the Incorporeal went and said to Death, Come hither; the Lord of creation, the immortal king, calls thee. And Death, hearing this, shivered and trembled, being possessed with great terror, and coming with great fear it stood before the invisible father, shivering, groaning and trembling, awaiting the command of the Lord. Therefore the invisible God said to Death, Come hither, thou bitter and fierce name of the world, hide thy fierceness, cover thy corruption, and cast away thy bitterness from thee, and put on thy beauty and all thy glory, and go down to Abraham my friend, and take him and bring him to me. But now also I tell thee not to terrify him, but bring him with fair speech, for he is my own friend. Having heard this, Death went out from the presence of the Most High, and put on a robe of great brightness, and made his appearance like the sun, and became fair and beautiful above the sons of men, assuming the form of an archangel, having his cheeks flaming with fire, and he departed to Abraham. Now the righteous Abraham went out of his chamber, and sat under the trees of Mamre, holding his chin in his hand, and awaiting the coming of the archangel Michael. And behold, a smell of sweet odor came to him, and a flashing of light, and Abraham turned and saw Death coming towards him in great glory and beauty. And Abraham arose and went to meet him, thinking that it was the chief-captain of God, and Death beholding him saluted him, saying, Rejoice, precious Abraham, righteous soul, true friend of the Most High God, and companion of the holy angels. Abraham said to Death, Hail thou of appearance and form like the sun, most glorious helper, bringer of light, wondrous man, from whence does thy glory come to us, and who art thou, and whence comest thou? Then Death said, Most righteous Abraham, behold I tell thee the truth. I am the bitter lot of death. Abraham said to him, Nay, but thou art the comeliness of the world, thou art the glory and beauty of angels and men, thou art fairer in form than every other, and sayest thou, I am the bitter lot of death, and not rather, I am fairer than every good thing. Death said, I tell thee the truth. What the Lord has named me, that also I tell thee. Abraham said, For what art thou come hither? Death said, For thy holy soul am I come. Then Abraham said, I know what thou meanest, but I will not go with thee; and Death was silent and answered him not a word.

Test. Abr. I. 17. Then Abraham arose, and went into his house, and Death also accompanied him thither. And Abraham went up into his chamber, and Death went up with him. And Abraham lay down upon his couch, and Death came and sat by his feet. Then Abraham said, Depart, depart from me, for I desire to rest upon my couch. Death said, I will not depart until I take thy spirit from thee. Abraham said to him, By the immortal God I charge thee to tell me the truth. Art thou death? Death said to him, I am Death. I am the destroyer of the world. Abraham said, I beseech thee, since thou art Death, tell me if thou comest thus to all in such fairness and glory and beauty? Death said, Nay, my Lord Abraham, for thy righteousnesses, and the boundless sea of thy hospitality, and the greatness of thy love towards God has become a crown upon my head, and in beauty and great peace and gentleness I approach the righteous, but to sinners I come in great corruption and fierceness and the greatest bitterness and with fierce and pitiless look. Abraham said, I beseech thee, hearken to me, and show me thy fierceness and all thy corruption and bitterness. And Death said, Thou canst not behold my fierceness, most righteous Abraham. Abraham said, Yes, I shall be able to behold all thy fierceness by means of the name of the living God, for the might of my God that is in heaven is with me. Then Death put off all his comeliness and

beauty, and all his glory and the form like the sun with which he was clothed, and put upon himself a tyrant's robe, and made his appearance gloomy and fiercer than all kind of wild beasts, and more unclean than all uncleanness. And he showed to Abraham seven fiery heads of serpents and fourteen faces, (one) of flaming fire and of great fierceness, and a face of darkness, and a most gloomy face of a viper, and a face of a most terrible precipice, and a face fiercer than an asp, and a face of a terrible lion, and a face of a cerastes and basilisk. He showed him also a face of a fiery scimitar, and a sword-bearing face, and a face of lightning, lightening terribly, and a noise of dreadful thunder. He showed him also another face of a fierce stormy sea, and a fierce rushing river, and a terrible three-headed serpent, and a cup mingled with poisons, and in short he showed to him great fierceness and unendurable bitterness, and every mortal disease as of the odor of Death. And from the great bitterness and fierceness there died servants and maid-servants in number about seven thousand, and the righteous Abraham came into indifference of death so that his spirit failed him.

Test. Abr. I. 18. And the all-holy Abraham, seeing these things thus, said to Death, I beseech thee, all-destroying Death, hide thy fierceness, and put on thy beauty and the shape which thou hadst before. And straightway Death hid his fierceness, and put on his beauty which he had before. And Abraham said to Death, Why hast thou done this, that thou hast slain all my servants and maidservants? Has God sent thee hither for this end this day? Death said, Nay, my Lord Abraham, it is not as thou sayest, but on thy account was I sent hither. Abraham said to Death, How then have these died? Has the Lord not spoken it? Death said, Believe thou, most righteous Abraham, that this also is wonderful, that thou also wast not taken away with them. Nevertheless I tell thee the truth, for if the right hand of God had not been with thee at that time, thou also wouldst have had to depart from this life. The righteous Abraham said, Now I know that I have come into indifference of death, so that my spirit fails, but I beseech thee, all-destroying Death, since my servants have died before their time, come let us pray to the Lord our God that he may hear us and raise up those who died by thy fierceness before their time. And Death said, Amen, be it so. Therefore Abraham arose and fell upon the face of the ground in prayer, and Death together with him, and the Lord sent a spirit of life upon those that were dead and they were made alive again. Then the righteous Abraham gave glory to God.

Test. Abr. I. 19. And going up into his chamber he lay down, and Death came and stood before him. And Abraham said to him, Depart from me, for I desire to rest, because my p. 200 spirit is in indifference. Death said, I will not depart from thee until I take thy soul. And Abraham with an austere countenance and angry look said to Death, Who has ordered thee to say this? Thou sayest these words of thyself boastfully, and I will not go with thee until the chief-captain Michael come to me, and I shall go with him. But this also I tell thee, if thou desirest that I shall accompany thee, explain to me all thy changes, the seven fiery heads of serpents and what the face of the precipice is, and what the sharp sword, and what the loud-roaring river, and what the tempestuous sea that rages so fiercely. Teach me also the unendurable thunder, and the terrible lightning, and the evil-smelling cup mingled with poisons. Teach me concerning all these. And Death answered, Listen, righteous Abraham. For seven ages I destroy the world and lead all down to Hades, kings and rulers, rich and poor, slaves and free men, I convoy to the bottom of Hades, and for this I showed thee the seven heads of serpents. The face of fire I showed thee because many die consumed by fire, and behold death through a face of fire. The face of the precipice I showed thee, because many men die descending from the tops of trees or terrible precipices and losing their life, and see death in the shape of a terrible precipice. The face of the sword I showed thee because many are slain in wars by the sword, and see death as a sword. The face of the great rushing river I showed thee because many are drowned and perish snatched away by the crossing of many waters and carried off by great rivers, and see death before their time. The face of the angry raging sea I showed thee because many in the sea falling into great surges and becoming shipwrecked are swallowed up and behold death as the sea. The unendurable thunder and the terrible lightning I showed thee because many men in the moment of anger meet with unendurable thunder and terrible lightning coming to seize upon men, and see death thus. I showed thee also the poisonous wild beasts, asps and basilisks, leopards and lions and lions' whelps, bears and vipers, and in short the face of every wild beast I showed thee, most righteous one, because many men are destroyed by wild beasts, and others by poisonous snakes, serpents and asps and cerastes and basilisks and vipers, breathe out their life and die. I showed thee also the destroying cups mingled with poison, because many men being given poison to drink by other men straightway depart unexpectedly.

Test. Abr. I. 20. Abraham said, I beseech thee, is there also an unexpected death? Tell me. Death said, Verily, verily, I tell thee in the truth of God that there are seventy-two deaths. One is the just death, buying its fixed time, and many men in one hour enter into death being given over to the grave. Behold, I have told thee all that thou hast asked, now I tell thee, most righteous Abraham, to dismiss all counsel, and cease from asking anything once for all, and come, go with me, as the God and judge of all has commanded me. Abraham said to Death, Depart from me yet a little, that I may rest on my couch, for I am very faint at heart, for since I have seen thee with my eyes my strength has failed me, all the limbs of my flesh seem to me a weight as of lead, and my spirit is distressed exceedingly. Depart for a little; for I have said I cannot bear to see thy shape. Then Isaac his son came and fell upon his breast weeping, and his wife Sarah came and embraced his feet, lamenting bitterly. There came also his men slaves and women slaves and surrounded his couch, lamenting greatly. And Abraham came into indifference of death, and Death said to Abraham, Come, take my right hand, and may cheerfulness and life and strength come to thee. For Death deceived Abraham, and he took his right hand, and straightway his soul adhered to the hand of Death. And immediately the archangel Michael came with a multitude of angels and took up his precious soul in his hands in a divinely woven linen cloth, and they tended the body of the just Abraham with divine ointments and perfumes until the third day after his death, and buried him in the land of promise, the oak of Mamre, but the angels received his precious soul, and ascended into heaven, singing the hymn of "thrice holy" to the Lord the God of all, and they set it there to worship the God and Father. And after great praise and glory had been given to the Lord, and Abraham bowed down to worship, there came the undefiled voice of the God and Father saying thus, Take therefore my friend Abraham into Paradise, where are the tabernacles of my righteous ones, and the abodes of my saints Isaac and Jacob in his bosom, where there is no trouble, nor grief, nor sighing, but peace and rejoicing and life unending. (And let us, too, my beloved brethren, imitate the hospitality of the patriarch Abraham, and attain to his virtuous way of life, that we may be thought worthy of the life eternal, glorifying the Father, Son and Holy Ghost; to whom be glory and power forever. Amen.).

Version II

Test. Abr. II. 1. It came to pass, when the days of the death of Abraham drew near, that the Lord said to Michael: Arise and go to Abraham, my servant, and say to him, Thou shalt depart from life, for lo! the days of thy temporal life are fulfilled: so that he may set his house in order before he die.

Test. Abr. II. 2. And Michael went and came to Abraham, and found him sitting before his oxen for ploughing, and he was exceeding old in appearance, and had his son in his arms. Abraham, therefore, seeing the archangel Michael, rose from the ground and saluted him, not knowing who he was, and said to him: The Lord preserve thee. May thy journey be prosperous with thee. And Michael answered him: Thou art kind, good father. Abraham answered and said to him: Come, draw near to me, brother, and sit down a little while, that I may order a beast to be brought that we may go to my house, and thou mayest rest with me, for it is toward evening, and in the morning arise and go whithersoever thou wilt, lest some evil beast meet thee and do thee hurt. And Michael enquired of Abraham, saying: Tell me thy name, before I enter thy house, lest I be burdensome to thee. Abraham answered and said, My parents called me Abram, and the Lord named me Abraham, saying: Arise and depart from thy house, and from thy kindred, and go into the land which I shall show unto thee. And when I went away into the land which the Lord showed me, he said to me: Thy name shall no more be called Abram, but thy name shall be Abraham. Michael answered and said to him: Pardon me, my father, experienced man of God, for I am a stranger, and I have heard of thee that thou didst go forty furlongs and didst bring a goat and slay it, entertaining angels in thy house, that they might rest there. Thus speaking together, they arose and went towards the house. And Abraham called one of his servants, and said to him: Go, bring me a beast that the stranger may sit upon it, for he is wearied with his journey. And Michael said: Trouble not the youth, but let us go lightly until we reach the house, for I love thy company.

Test. Abr. II. 3. And arising they went on, and as they drew nigh to the city, about three furlongs from it, they found a great tree having three hundred branches, like to a tamarisk tree. And they heard a voice from its branches singing, "Holy art thou, because thou hast kept the purpose for which thou wast sent." And Abraham heard the voice, and hid the mystery in his heart, saying within himself, What is the mystery that I have heard? As he came into the house, Abraham said to his servants, Arise, go out to the flocks, and bring three sheep, and slay them quickly, and make them ready that we may eat and drink, for this day is a feast for us. And the servants brought the sheep, and Abraham called his son Isaac, and said to him, My son Isaac, arise and put water in the vessel that we may wash the feet of this stranger. And he brought it as he was commanded, and Abraham said, I perceive, and so it shall be, that in this basin I shall never again wash the feet of any man coming to us as a guest. And Isaac hearing his father say this wept, and said to him, My father what is this that thou sayest, This is my last time to wash the feet of a stranger? And Abraham seeing his son weeping, also wept exp. 187 ceedingly, and Michael seeing them weeping, wept also, and the tears of Michael fell upon the vessel and became a precious stone.

Test. Abr. II. 4. When Sarah, being inside in her house, heard their weeping, she came out and said to Abraham, Lord, why is it that ye thus weep? Abraham answered, and said to her, It is no evil. Go into thy house, and do thy own work, lest we be troublesome to the man. And Sarah went away, being about to prepare the supper. And the sun came near to setting, and Michael went out of the house, and was taken up into the heavens to worship before God, for at sunset all the angels worship God and Michael himself is the first of the angels. And they all worshipped him, and went each to his own place, but Michael spoke before the Lord and said, Lord, command me to be questioned before thy holy glory! And the Lord said to Michael, Announce whatsoever thou wilt! And the Archangel answered and said, Lord, thou didst send me to Abraham to say to him, Depart from thy body, and leave this world; the Lord calls thee; and I dare not, Lord, reveal myself to him, for he is thy friend, and a righteous man, and one that receives strangers. But I beseech thee, Lord, command the remembrance of the death of Abraham to enter into his own heart, and bid not me tell it him, for it is great abruptness to say, Leave the world, and especially to leave one's own body, for thou didst create him from the beginning to have pity on the souls of all men. Then the Lord said to Michael, Arise and go to Abraham, and lodge with him, and whatever thou seest him eat, eat thou also, and wherever he shall sleep, sleep thou there also. For I will cast the thought of the death of Abraham into the heart of Isaac his son in a dream.

Test. Abr. II. 5. Then Michael went into the house of Abraham on that evening, and found them preparing the supper, and they ate and drank and were merry. And Abraham said to his son Isaac, Arise, my son, and spread the man's couch that he may sleep, and set the lamp upon the stand. And Isaac did as his father commanded him, and Isaac said to his father, I too am coming to sleep beside you. Abraham answered him, Nay, my son, lest we be troublesome to this man, but go to thy own chamber and sleep. And Isaac not wishing to disobey his father's command, went away and slept in his own chamber.

Test. Abr. II. 6. And it happened about the seventh hour of the night Isaac awoke, and came to the door of his father's chamber, crying out and saying, Open, father, that I may touch thee before they take thee away from me. Abraham arose and opened to him, and Isaac entered and hung upon his father's neck weeping, and kissed him with lamentations. And Abraham wept together with his son, and Michael saw them weeping and wept likewise. And Sarah hearing them weeping called from her bed-chamber, saying, My Lord Abraham, why is this weeping? Has the stranger told thee of thy brother's son Lot that he is dead? or has aught else befallen us? Michael answered and said to Sarah, Nay, Sarah, I have brought no tidings of Lot, but I knew of all your kindness of heart, that therein ye excel all men upon earth, and the Lord has remembered you. Then Sarah said to Abraham, How durst thou weep when the man of God has come in to thee, and why have thy eyes 3993 shed tears for today there is great rejoicing? Abraham said to her, How knowest thou that this is a man of God? Sarah answered and said, Because I say and declare that this is one of the three men who were entertained by us at the oak of Mamre, when one of the servants went and brought a kid and thou didst kill it, and didst say to me, Arise, make ready that we may eat with these men in our house. Abraham answered and said, Thou has perceived well, O woman, for I too, when I washed his feet knew in my heart that these were the feet which I had washed at the oak of Mamre, and when I began to enquire concerning his journey, he said to me, I go to preserve Lot thy brother from the men of Sodom, and then I knew the mystery.

Test. Abr. II. 7. And Abraham said to Michael, Tell me, man of God, and show to me why thou hast come hither. And Michael said, Thy son Isaac will show thee. And Abraham said to his son, My beloved son, tell me what thou hast seen in thy dream today, and wast frightened. Relate it to me. Isaac answered his father, I saw in my dream the sun and the moon, and there was a crown upon my head, and there came from heaven a man of great size, and shining as the light that is called the father of light. He took the sun from my head, and yet left the rays behind with me. And I wept and said, I beseech thee, my Lord, take not away the glory of my head, and

the light of my house, and all my glory. And the sun and the moon and the stars lamented, saying, Take not away the glory of our power. And that shining man answered and said to me, Weep not that I take the light of thy house, for it is taken up from troubles into rest, from a low estate to a high one; they lift him up from a narrow to a wide place; they raise him from darkness to light. And I said to him, I beseech thee, Lord, take also the rays with it. He said to me, There are twelve hours of the day, and then I shall take all the rays. As the shining man said this, I saw the sun of my house ascending into heaven, but that crown I saw no more, and that sun was like thee my father. And Michael said to Abraham, Thy son Isaac has spoken truth, for thou shalt go, and be taken up into the heavens, but thy body shall remain on earth, until seven thousand ages are fulfilled, for then all flesh shall arise. Now therefore, Abraham, set thy house in order, and thy children, for thou hast heard fully what is decreed concerning thee. Abraham answered and said to Michael, I beseech thee, Lord, if I shall depart from my body, I have desired to be taken up in my body that I may see the creatures that the Lord my God has created in heaven and on earth. Michael answered and said, This is not for me to do, but I shall go and tell the Lord of this, and if I am commanded I shall show thee all these things.

Test. Abr. II. 8. And Michael went up into heaven, and spoke before the Lord concerning Abraham, and the Lord answered Michael, Go and take up Abraham in the body, and show him all things, and whatsoever he shall say to thee do to him as to my friend. So Michael went forth and took up Abraham in the body on a cloud, and brought him to the river of Ocean. And after Abraham had seen the place of judgment, the cloud took him down upon the firmament below, and Abraham, looking down upon the earth, saw a man committing adultery with a wedded woman. And Abraham turning said to Michael, Seest thou this wickedness? but, Lord, send fire from heaven to consume them. And straightway there came down fire and consumed them, for the Lord had said to Michael, Whatsoever Abraham shall ask thee to do for him, do thou. Abraham looked again, and saw other men railing at their companions, and said, Let the earth open and swallow them, and as he spoke the earth swallowed them alive. Again the cloud led him to another place, and Abraham saw some going into a desert place to commit murder, and he said to Michael, Seest thou this wickedness? but let wild beasts come out of the desert, and tear them in pieces, and that same hour wild beasts came out of the desert, and devoured them. Then the Lord God spoke to Michael saying, Turn away Abraham to his own house, and let him not go round all the creation that I have made, because he has no compassion on sinners, but I have compassion on sinners that they may turn and live, and repent of their sins and be saved. And Abraham looked and saw two gates, the one small and the other large, and between the two gates sat a man upon a throne of great glory, and a multitude of angels round about him, and he was weeping, and again laughing, but his weeping exceeded his laughter seven-fold. And Abraham said to Michael, Who is this that sits between the two gates in great glory; sometimes he laughs, and sometimes he weeps, and his weeping exceeds his laughter seven-fold? And Michael said to Abraham, Knowest thou not who it is? And he said, No, Lord. And Michael said to Abraham, Seest thou these two gates, the small and the great? These are they which lead to life and to destruction. This man that sits between them is Adam, the first man whom the Lord created, and set him in this place to see every soul that departs from the body, seeing that all are from him. When, therefore, thou seest him weeping, know that he has seen many souls being led to destruction, but when thou seest him laughing, he has seen many souls being led into life. Seest thou how his weeping exceeds his laughter? Since he sees the greater part of the world being led away through the broad gate to destruction, therefore his weeping exceeds his laughter seven-fold.

Test. Abr. II. 9. And Abraham said, And he that cannot enter through the narrow gate, can he not enter into life? Then Abraham wept, saying, Woe is me, what shall I do? for I am a man broad of body, and how shall I be able to enter by the narrow gate, by which a boy of fifteen years cannot enter? Michael answered and said to Abraham, Fear not, father, nor grieve, for thou shalt enter by it unhindered, and all those who are like thee. And as Abraham stood and marveled, behold an angel of the Lord driving sixty thousand souls of sinners to destruction. And Abraham said to Michael, Do all these go into destruction? And Michael said to him, Yea, but let us go and search among these souls, if there is among them even one righteous. And when they went, they found an angel holding in his hand one soul of a woman from among these sixty thousand, because he had found her sins weighing equally with all her works, and they were neither in motion nor at rest, but in a state between; but the other souls he led away to destruction. Abraham said to Michael, Lord, is this the angel that removes the souls from the body or not? Michael answered and said, This is death, and he leads them into the place of judgment, that the judge may try them.

Test. Abr. II. 10. And Abraham said, My Lord, I beseech thee to lead me to the place of judgment so that I too may see how they are judged. Then Michael took Abraham upon a cloud, and led him into Paradise, and when he came to the place where the judge was, the angel came and gave that soul to the judge. And the soul said, Lord have mercy on me. And the judge said, How shall I have mercy upon thee, when thou hadst no mercy upon thy daughter which thou hadst, the fruit of thy womb? Wherefore didst thou slay her? It answered, Nay, Lord, slaughter has not been done by me, but my daughter has lied upon me. But the judge commanded him to come that wrote down the records, and behold cherubim carrying two books. And there was with them a man of exceeding great stature, having on his head three crowns, and the one crown was higher than the other two. These are called the crowns of witness. And the man had in his hand a golden pen, and the judge said to him, Exhibit the sin of this soul. And that man, opening one of the books of the cherubim, sought out the sin of the woman's soul and found it. And the judge said, O wretched soul, why sayest thou that thou hast not done murder? Didst thou not, after the death of thy husband, go and commit adultery with thy daughter's husband, and kill her? And he convicted her also of her other sins, whatsoever she had done from her youth. Hearing these things the woman cried out, saying, Woe is me, all the sins that I did in the world I forgot, but here they were not forgotten. Then they took her away also and gave her over to the tormentors.

Test. Abr. II. 11. And Abraham said to Michael, Lord, who is this judge, and who is the other, who convicts the sins? And Michael said to Abraham, Seest thou the judge? This is Abel, who first testified, and God brought him hither to judge, and he that bears witness here is the teacher of heaven and earth, and the scribe of righteousness, Enoch, for the Lord sent them hither to write down the sins and righteousnesses of each one. Abraham said, And how can Enoch bear the weight of the souls, not having seen death? or how can he give sentence to all the souls? Michael said, If he gives sentence concerning the souls, it is not permitted; but Enoch himself does not give sentence, but it is the Lord who does so, and he has no more to do than only to write. For Enoch prayed to the Lord saying, I desire not, Lord, to give sentence on the souls, lest I be grievous to anyone; and the Lord said to Enoch, I shall command thee to write down the sins of the soul that makes atonement and it shall enter into life, and if the soul make not atonement and repent, thou shalt find its sins written down and it shall be cast into punishment. And about the ninth hour Michael brought Abraham back to his house. But Sarah his wife, not seeing what had become of Abraham, was consumed with grief, and gave up the ghost, and after the return of Abraham he found her dead, and buried her.

Test. Abr. II. 12. But when the day of the death of Abraham drew nigh, the Lord God said to Michael, Death will not dare to go near to take away the soul of my servant, because he is my friend, but go thou and adorn Death with great beauty, and send him thus to Abraham, that he may see him with his eyes. And Michael straightway, as he was commanded, adorned Death with great beauty, and sent him thus to Abraham that he might see him. And he sat down near to Abraham, and Abraham seeing Death sitting near to him was afraid with a great fear. And Death said to Abraham, Hail, holy soul! hail, friend of the Lord God! hail, consolation and entertainment of travelers! And Abraham said, Thou art welcome, servant of the Most High. God. I beseech thee, tell me who thou art; and entering into my house partake of food and drink, and depart from me, for since I have seen thee sitting near to me my soul has been troubled. For I am not at all worthy to come near thee, for thou art an exalted spirit and I am flesh and blood, and therefore I cannot bear thy glory, for I see that thy beauty is not of this world. And Death said to Abraham, I tell thee, in all the creation that God has made, there has not been found one like thee, for even the Lord himself by searching has not found such an one upon the whole earth. And Abraham said to Death, How durst thou lie? for I see that thy beauty is not of this world. And Death said to Abraham, Think not, Abraham, that this beauty is mine, or that I come thus to every man. Nay, but if any one is righteous like thee, I thus take crowns and come to him, but if it is a sinner I come in great corruption, and out of their sin I make a crown for my head, and I shake them with great fear, so that they are dismayed. Abraham therefore said to him, And whence comes thy beauty? And Death said, There is none other more full of corruption than I am. Abraham said to him, And art thou indeed he that is called Death? He answered him and said, I am the bitter name. I am weeping....

Test. Abr. II. 15. And Abraham said to Death, Show us thy corruption. And Death made manifest his corruption; and he had two heads, the one had the face of a serpent and by it some die at once by asps, and the other head was like a sword; by it some die by the sword as by bows. In that day the servants of Abraham died through fear of Death, and Abraham seeing them prayed to the Lord, and he raised them up. But God returned and removed the soul of Abraham as in a dream, and the archangel Michael took it up into the heavens. And Isaac buried his father beside his mother Sarah, glorifying and praising God, for to him is due glory, honor and worship, of the Father, Son and Holy Ghost, now and always and to all eternity. Amen.

Testament of Isaac

[1] Now Isaac the patriarch writes his testament and addresses his words of instruction to his son Jacob and to all those gathered round him. The blessings of the patriarch will be on those who come after us, even thos who listen to these words, to these words of instruction and these medicines of life, so that the grace of God may be with all those who believe. This is the end of obedience, as it is weitten. You have heard a word, let it abide with you – which means that a man should strive patiently with what he hears. God gives grace to those who believe: he who believes the words of God and of his saints will be an inheritor of the Kingdom of God. God has been with the generations gone by, which have passed away, because

of their innocence and their faith towards God. He will be with the generations to come also

2. Now it came to pass, when the time had come for the Patriarch Isaac to go forth from the body, God sent to him the angel of his father Abraham at dawn on the twentysecond of Mesore. He said to him. Hail, son of promise! (Now it was the daily custom of the righteous old man Isaac to converse with the angels.) He lifted his face up to the face of the angel: he saw him assuming the likeness of his father Abraham; and he opened his mouth and raised his voice and cried out in great joy, I have seen your face like someone who has seen the lace of God. The angel said to him. Listen, my beloved Isaac: [1] havee been sent for you by God to take you to the heavens and set you beside your father Abraham, so that you can see all the saints; for your father is expecting you and is coming for you himself. Behold, a throne has been set up for you close to your father Abraham, and your lot and your beloved son Jacob's lot will surpass that of all others in the whole of God's creation that is why you have been given for evermore the name of Patriarch and Father of the World. But the God-loviig old man Isaac said to the angel, 'I am astonished by you, for you are my father'.The angel answered. my beloved Isaac, I am the angel that ministers to your father Abraham. But rejoice now, for I am to take you out of sorrow into gladness, out of suffering to rest for ever. I am to transport you from prison to a place where you can range at will — to a place of joy and gladness: I am to take you to where there is light and merriment and rejoicing and abundance that never fails. So then, draw up your testament and a statement for your household. for I am to translate you to rest for all eternity. Blessed is your father who begot you: blessed are you also: blessed is your son Jacob; and blessed are your descendants that will come after you. 3. Now Jacob heard them talking together, but he said nothing. Our father Isaac said to the angel with a heavy heart. What shall I do about the light of my eyes, my beloved son Jacob? For I am afraid of what Esau might do to him - you know the situation. The angel said to him: 'My beloved Isaac, if all the nations on earth were gathered together, they would not be able to bring these blessings pronounced over Jacob to nothing. When you blessed him, the Father and the Son and the Holy Spirit blessed him; and Michael and Giabriel and all the angels and all the heavenly ones and the spirits ol all the righteous and your father Abraham all answered Amen. The sword therefore, shall not touch his body; but he shall be held in high honour and grow great and spread far and wide, and twelve thrones shall spring from him'. Our father Isaac said to the angel: 'You have given me much comfort, but do not let Jacob know in case he is distressed'. The angel said to him: 'My beloved Isaac, blessed is everv righteous man who goes forth from the body: blessed are they when they meet with God. Woe. woe, woe, three times woe to the sinner, because he has been born into this world: great sufferings will come to him. Isaac, beloved of God. give these instructions, therefore, to your sons, and the instructions your father has given you. Hide nothing from Jacob, so that he can write them as instructions for the generations that will come after you. and those who love God may live their lives in accordance with them. And take care that I am able to fetch you with Joy. without delay. The peace of my Lord that he has given me. I give to you, as I go to him who sent me'. 4. And when the angel had said this, he rose from the bed on which Isaac was sleeping. He went back to the worlds on high while our father Isaac watched him go, astonished at the vision he had seen. And he said: ' I shall not see daylight before I am sent for'. And while he was thinking this, behold, Jacob got up and came to the door of the room. The angel had cast a sleep over him so that he should not hear them; and he got up and ran to where his father slept and said to him: 'My father,

whom have you been talking to?', Our father Isaac said to him: 'You have heard, my son: your aged father has been sent for to be taken from you', and Jacob put his arms round his father's neck and wept, saying: 'Ah me! My strength has left me: today you have made me an orphan, my father'. Our father Isaac embraced his son Jacob and wept; and both wept together until they could weep no more .And Jacob said: 'Take me with you, father Isaac'. But Isaac replied: 'I would not have it so, my son; wait until you arc sent for, my loved one. I remember on the day when the whole earth was shaken from end to end talking to my lord and father Abraham, and I had no strenght to do anything. What god has ordained, he has ordained for each one by sure authority: his ordinances are immutable. But I know, and I am glad that I am to go to God, and I am strengthened by a guiding spirit; for this is a way that no one can escape. Listen, my son, Whcrc is the first creation of the hands of God - our father Adam and our mother Eve? Where is Abel, and after him Mahalalel, and Jared, and our father Enoch, and Methuselah, and our father Noah, and his sons Shem, Ham, and Japheth? .After these Arpachshad, and Cainan, and Shelah, and Eber, and Reu, and Serug, and Nahor, and Terah, and my blessed father Abraham, and Lot his brother? All these experienced death except the perfect one, our father Enoch.' .After these, forty-two generations more shall pass until Christ comes, born of a pure virgin called Mary. He will spend thirty years preaching in the world. At the end of all this, he will choose twelve men and reveal to them his mysteries and teach them about the archetype of his body and his true blood by means of bread and wine: and the bread will become the body of God and the wine will become the blood of God. And then he will ascend the tree of the cross and die for the whole creation, and rise on the third day and despoil hell, and deliver all mankind from the enemy. The generations to come will be saved by his body and by his blood until the end of time. The sacrifices of Christians will not cease until the end of time, whether offered secretly or openly; and the Antichrist will not appear so long as they offer up their sacrilice. Blessed is every man who performs that service and believes in it, because the archetypal service is in the heavens; and they shall celebrate with the Son of God in his kingdom'. 5. While the God-loving old man, our father Isaac, was saying this, all his household gathered round him and wept. His son told all his relations, and they came to him in tears. Now our father Isaac had made for himself a bedroom in his house; and when his sight began to fail he withdrew into it and remained there for a hundred years, fasting daily until evening, and offering for himself and his household a young animal for their soul. And he spent half the night in prayer and praise of Giod. Thus he lived an ascetic life for a hundred years. And he kept three periods of forty days as fasts each year, neither drinking wine nor eating fruit nor sleeping on his bed. And he prayed and gave thanks to God continually. 6. Now when it became generally known that the man of God had regained his sight, people gathered to him from everywhere, listening to his words of life; for they realized that a holy spirit of God was speaking in him. The great ones who came said to him: 'You can now see clearly enough: how comes it that after your sight had failed you have now regained it?' The God-Ioving old man smiled and said to them: 'My sons and brothers, the God of my father Abraham has brought this about to comfort me in my old age. But the priest of God said to him: 'Tell me what I ought to do, my father Isaac'. Our father Isaac said to him: 'Keep your body holy, for the temple of God is set in it. Do not engage in controversy with other men in case an angry word escapes your mouth. Be on your guard against evil-speaking, against vainglory, and against uttering any thoughtless word; and see that your hands do not reach out after what is not yours. Do not offer a sacrifice with a blemish in it; and wash yourself with water when you approach the altar. Do not mix the thoughts of the world with the thoughts of God when you stand before him. Do your utmost to be at peace with everyone. When you stand before God and offer your sacrifice. when you come to offer it on the altar, you should recite privately a hundred prayers to God and make this confession to God saying: 'Oh God, the incomprehensible, the unfathomable, the unattainable, the pure treasure, purify me in love; for I am flesh and blood and I run defiled to thee, that thou mayest purify me. I come burdened, and I ask that thou mayest lighten my burden: a fire will burn wood, and thy mercy will take away mine iniquities. Forgive me, me that am a sinner: I forgive the whole creation that thou hast made, [1] have no complaint against anyone: I am at peace with all that is made in thine image: I am unmoved by all the evil reasonings that have been brought before me. I am thy servant and the son of thy maidservant: [1] am the one who sins, thou art the one who forgives: forgive me and enable me to stand in thy holy place. Let my sacrifice be acceptable before thee: do not reject me because of my sins; but receive me unto thee, in spite of my many sins, like a sheep that has gone astray. God who hast been with our father Adam, and Abel. and Noah, and our father Abraham, and his son Isaac, who hast been with Jacob, be thou with me also, and receive my sacrilice from my hand'. As you recite all this, take your sacrifice and offer it; and strive heavenwards because of the sacrifice of God, so that you do not displease him. For the work of the priest is no small thing. 7. Every priest today (and till the end of time) must be temperate as regards his food and drink and sleep; neither should he talk about events connected with this world, nor listen to anyone who is talking about them. Rather should he spend his whole life occupied with prayer and vigils and recitation until our God sends for him in peace. Every man on earth, be he priest or monk (for after a long time they will love the life of holy retreat), must renounce the world and all its evil cares and join in the holy service the angels render in purity to God. And they will be honoured before God and his angels because of their holy sacrifices and their angelic service, which is like the archetype that is rendered in the heavens. And the angels will be their friends, because of their perfect faith and their purity; and great is their honour before God.In a word, whether great or small, sinlessness is required of us. The chief sins worthy of repentance are these: You shall not kill with the sword; You shall not kill with the tongue either: You shall not commit fornication with your body; You shall not commit fornication with your thoughts; You shall not go in to the young to defile them; You shall not be envious; You shall not be angry until the sun has set; You shall not be proud in dispositon; You shall not rejoice over your neighbour's fall: You shall not slander; You shall not look at a woman with a lustful eye; and. Do not readily listen to slander. We need to beware of these things, and of others like them, till each one of us is secure from the wrath that shall be revealed from heaven. 8. Now when the people gathered about him heard him, they cried out aloud saying. This is meet and right..Amen. But the Godloving old man was silent: he drew up his blanket: he covered his face.And the people and the priest were silent, so that he could rest himself a little. But the angel of his father .Abraham came to him and took him up into the heavens. He saw terrors and tumults spread abroad on this side and on that; and it was a terror and a tumult fearful to behold. Some had the face of a camel, others had the face of a lion: some had the face of a dog, others had but one eye and had tongs in their hands, three ells long, all of iron. I looked, and behold, a man was brought, and those who brought him went with him. When they reached the beasts, those who went with him withdrew to one side: the lion advanced towards him, tore him apart into little pieces, and

swallowed him; it then vomited him up, and he became like himself again; and the next beast treated him in just the same way. In short, they passed him on from one to the other; each one would tear him into pieces, swallow him, and then vomit him up; and he would become like himself again. I said to the angel: What sin has this man committed, my lord, that all this is done to him? The angel said to me: 'This man you are looking at now had a quarrel with his neighbour, and he died without their being reconciled. See, he has been handed over to five chief tormentors: they spend a year tormenting him for every hour he spent Quarreling with his neighbour'. The angel also said to me: 'My beloved Isaac, do you think these are the only ones? Believe me Isaac. beloved of God, there are six hundred thousand tormentors. They spend a year tormenting a man for every hour that he spends sinning – if he did not repent, that is, before he went forth From the body. 9. He led me on and brought me to a fiery river. the waters of wich were an ell high, and its noise like the noise of heaven's thunder. And [1] saw a host of souls submerged in it; and those who were in that river cried out and wept aloud, and there was a great commotion and much groaning. But it is a discerning fire that does not touch the righteous, yet burns up sinners and boils them in the stench that surrounds them. I saw also the pit of the abyss, the smoke of which went up in clouds; I saw men sunk in it grinding their teeth, crying out and wailing, and each one was groaning. The angel said to me. Look and see these others too. And when I had looked at them. the angel said to me," These are those who have committed the sin of Sodom; these are indeed in great distress. I saw also pits full of worms that do not sleep; I saw Abdemerouchos who is in charge of the punishments, made all of fire, threatening the tormentors in hell and saying. Beat them initil they know that God is. I saw a house built of fiery stone, and there were grown men underneath it, crying out and wailing. The angel said to me. Look with your eyes and contemplate the Punishments. I said to the angel, .My eyes could not endure it; for how long must These punishmenls go on? He said to me. Until the merciful God has pity. 10. After this the angel took me up into the heavens; I saw my father, Abraham and I made obeisance to him. He saluted me, with all the saints, and the saints honoured me because of my father; I they walked with me and took me to my Father, I worshipped him with all the saints. Songs of praise rang out, Thou art holy, thou art holy, thou art holy. King, Lord Sabaoth: the heavens and the earth are full of thy holy glory. The Lord said to my father from the holy place, 'Is good that you have come, Abraham, your righteous root and faithful saint: it is good that you have come to our city. Whatever you may want to ask now, make your requests in the name of your beloved son Isaac, and they shall be yours indeed'. My father Abraham said. 'Thine is the power, Oh Lord Almighty'. The Lord said to Abraham, 'As for all those who are given the name of my beloved Isaac, let each one of them copy out his testament and honour it, and feed a poor man with bread in the name of my beloved Isaac on the day of his holy commemoration; to you will I grant them as sons in my kingdom'. Abraham said. 'My Lord Almighty, if a man cannot copy out his testament,' can'st thou not in thy mercy accept him, for thou art merciful and compassionate?' The Lord said to Abraham: 'Let him feed a poor man with bread, and I will give him to you as a gift and as a son in my kingdom, and he shall come with you to the first hour of the thousand years. Abraham said, 'Suppose he is poor and has no means of getting bread?' The Lord said, 'Let him spend the night of my beloved Isaac's commemoration without sleep, and I will give him to you as a gift and an inheritor in my kingdom'. My father Abraham said 'Suppose he is weak and has no strength, can'st thou not in thy mercy accept him in love?'. The Lord said to him. 'Let him offer up a little incense in the name of your beloved son Isaac, and I will give him to you as a son in my kingdom. If he has no means of getting incense, let him seek out a copy of his testament and read it on my beloved Isaac's day. If he cannot read it, let him go and listen to others who can. If he is unable to do any of these things, let him go into his house and say a hundred Prayers, and I will give him to you as a son in my kingdom. But the most essential thing of all is that he should offer a sacrifice in my beloved Isaac's name, For his body was offered as a sacrifice.'Yet not only will I give you everyone called by my beloved Isaac's name as a son in my Kingdom; I will give you also everyone who does one of the things I have mentioned. And i will give you everyone who concerns himself about Isaac'slife and his testament, or does any compassionate act. such as giving someone a cup of water to drink, or who copies out his testament with his own hand, and those who read it with all their heart in faith, believing everything that I have said. .My power and the power of my beloved Son and the Holy Spirit shall be with them, and I will give them to you as sons in my kingdom. Peace to all of you, all my saints'. 11. Now when he had said this, songs of praise rang out. Thou art holy, thou art holy, thou art holy. King. Lord. Sabaoth; the heavens and the earth are full of thy holy glory. The Father said to Michael from the holy place: 'Michael, my steward, go quickly and gather together the angels and all the saints, so that they may come and meet my beloved Isaac. And Michael sounded the trumpet at once. All the saints gathered with the angels and came to the couch of our father Isaac:'the Lord mounted his chariot, and the seraphim were in front of him with the angels.And when they came to our father Isaac's couch, our father Isaac beheld our Lord's face immediately turned towards him full of joy. He cried out: 'It is good that thou hast come, my Lord, and thy great archangel Michael: it is good that you have come, tny father Abraham, and all the saints. 12. Now when he had said this, Jacob embraced his Father; he kissed his mouth and wept. Our father Isaac fixed his eyes on him and motioned to him to be silent. Our father Isaac said to the Lord: 'Remember my beloved Jacob'. The Lord said to him: 'My power shall be with him; and when the time comes and I become man and die and rise from the dead on the third day, I will put your name in everyone's mind, and they will invoke you as their father.' Isaac said to Jacob: 'My beloved son, this is the last commandment I give you today; keep a sharp eye on yourself Do not dishonour the image of God; for what you do to the image of man, you do to the image of God, and God will do it to you too in the place where you will meet him. This is the beginning and the end. Now when he had said this, our Lord brought his soul out of his body, and it was white as snow. He greeted it: he set it on the chariot with him: he took it up into the heavens, with the seraphim making music before him, and all the angels and the saints. He freely granted him the good things of his kingdom for ever, and all the requests our father Abraham had asked of the Lord he freely granted him as a covenant for ever. 13. This is the going forth from the body of our father Isaac, the patriarch, on the twenty-fourth of the month Mesore.And the day on which his father Abraham offered him as a sacrifice is the eighteenth of Mechir.(12 February) The heavens and the earth were full of the soothing odour of our father Isaac, like choice silver: this is the sacrifice of our father Isaac the patriarch. When Abraham offered him as a sacrifice to God, the soothing odour of Isaac's sacrifice went up into the heavens. Blessed is every man who performs an act of mercy in the name of these patriarchs, for they will be their sons in the kingdom of the heavens. For our Lord has made with them a covenant for ever, that everyone who performs an act of mercy on the day of their commemoration shall be given to them as a son in the kingdom of the heavens forever.

And they shall come to the first hour of the thousand years, in accordance with the promise of our Lord, even our God and our Saviour Jesus Christ, through whom every glory is due to him and his good Father and the Holy Spirit, the giver of life to all creation and one in being with the Father and the Son, now and always, for ever and ever. Amen"

Testament of Jacob

1. Now it came to pass when the time had come lijr our beloved father Jacob the patriarch, the son of Isaac, the son of Abraham, to go forth from the body (and the God-loving Jacob was well on in years), the Lord sent Michael the archangel to him .And he said to him, Israel, my beloved, you righteous root, write your words of instruction for your sons, and draw up your testament for them, and concern yourself about those of your household, for the time has come for you to go to your fathers and rejoice with them for ever. And when the God-loving Jacob heard this from the angel, he answered and said to him. My lord - For it was his daily custom to talk to angels. He said to him. May the will of the Lord be done. 2. And God blessed our father Jacob. He made for himsell a place apart, to which he withdrew and offered his prayers to God day and night, while the angels visited him and guarded him and kept him safe and gave him strength in everything. God blessed him; and his people increased greatly in numbers in the land of Egypt. For at the time he went down to Egypt to his son Joseph, his sight was failing as a result of continual weeping and worrying over his son Joseph; but after he arrived in Egypt and had seen his son Joseph's face, he saw everything clearly again. And Jacob Israel flung on his son Joseph's neck; he greeted him with tears and said: 'Now let me die, for I have seen your face once more while you are still alive, my beloved'. And Joseph ruled over the whole of Egypt. Jacob lived in the land of Gashen for seventeen years. He became very old and attained a great age: he kept all the commandments and lived always in the fear of the Lord: and his sight failed so that he could see no one because of extreme old age. 3. He lifted his eyes towards the radiance of the angel who was speaking to him, who was in appearance and in face like his father Isaac: he was afraid and troubled. The angel said to him. Do not be afraid, Jacob: I am the angel who has been with you from your youth. I chose you to receive your father Isaac's blessing, and your mother Rebecca's. I am with you, Israel, in everything you do and everything you have seen. It was I who delivered you from Laban when he pursued you; I blessed you, and all your wives, and your sons, and all your cattle. It was I too who rescued you from Esau. It was I too who brought you down into the land of Egypt, Israel; and I have spread you out far and wide. Blessed is your father Abraham, for he became a friend of the Most High God because of his hospitality. Blessed is your lather Isaac who gave you life, for his sacrifice was perfect and pleasing to God. Blessed are you too, Jacob, for you saw God face to face and beheld the host of the angels of the Most High God. You saw the ladder set up on the earth with its top reaching to heaven. You also saw the Lord set on the top of it in power too great for words. You cried out saying: 'This is the house of God, and this is the gate of heaven. Blessed are you, for you have found strength in God and are strong among men. Now, therefore, do not be troubled, beloved of God. Blessed are you, Israel, and blessed are all your descendants, for you shall be called patriarchs until the end of this age; for you are my people, and you are the root of the servants of God. Blessed is every nation which emulates your purity, and your virtues, and your righteousness, and your good works. Blessed is the man who commemorates you on your honoured festival. Blessed is he who does a charitable deed in your name, or gives a man a cup of cold

water, or brings a perfect offering to your place, or to any place, in your name, or receives a stranger, or visits the sick, or comforts an orphan, or clothes someone who is naked, in your name. He shall lack no good thing in this world; and in the world to come he shall have eternal life. And further, whoever writes an account of your life with its labours, or whoever makes a copy of it with his hands, or whoever reads it attentively, and whoever listens to it with faith and a resolute heart, and whoever emulates your manner of life -they shall be forgiven all their sins, and they shall be freely granted you in the kingdom of the heavens. So get up now, for you are to exchange trouble and sorrow for eternal rest, and you are to be borne away to a repose that never ceases, to a rest that never ends, and to a light that never sets, and to pleasure and gladness and spiritual joy. So now, give your commands to your sons, and peace be with you; for I am about to go to him who sent me'. 4. And when he had said this to him, the angel left him in peace and returned to the heavens, while Jacob gazed after him. .And those who were in the house heard him giving thanks to the Lord and glorifying him with praises. And all his sons gathered round him, from the youngest to the eldest of them, all in tears and in great distress, saying. He is about to go away and leave us. And they said to him. What shall we do, beloved father, For we are aliens in a foreign land?. And Jacob said to them. Do not be afraid, for God appeared to me in Mesopotamia saying: 'I am the God of your fathers: do not be afraid: I am with you for ever, and with your descendants that shall come after you for ever: the land on which you are standing I will give to you and your descendants for ever. And again he said to me, Do not be afraid to go down into Egypt; I will go with you down to Egypt; and I will increase your numbers, and your descendants shall flourish for ever, and Joseph shall lay his hands upon your eyes. And your people shall increase greatly in Egypt; and then they shall return to me here, and I will do them good because of you. But now you must leave this place. 5. And after this the time drew near for Jacob Israel to go forth from the body. He called Joseph and spoke to him as follows: 'If I have found favour with you, then put your blessed hand upon my thigh and swear to me on oath before the Lord to lay my body in my fathers grave. And Joseph said to him, I will do as you ask, my God-loving father. His father said to him. I would have you swear; and Joseph swore the oath to Jacob his father that he would take his body to his fathers grave. And Jacob bowed himself upon his son's neck. 6. Now after this it was reported to Joseph. Behold, your father is in a sorry state. He took his two sons, Ephraim and Manasseh and came to his father Israel. When Israel saw them, he said to Joseph,: 'Who are these, my son?' Joseph said to his father Jacob Israel: 'These are my sons that God has given me in the land of my humiliation'. Israel said: 'Bring them near to me'. Now Israel's sight had failed because of his great age, and he could hardly see. .And Joseph' brought them close to him; and he kissed them. When Israel had embraced them, he said, God will add to your descendants; And Joseph made his two sons, Ephraim and .Manasseh, do obeisance to him on the ground: Joseph put Manasseh under his right hand and Ephraim under his left hand. But Israel changed his hands: he laid his right hand on Ephraim's head and his left hand on Manasseh's head. And he blessed them; he gave them their patrimony, saying: 'The God who approved my fathers Abraham and Isaac, The God who has looked after me from my childhood till today. The angel who rescues me from all my tribulations. Bless these lads who are my sons. With whom is left my name. And the name of my holy fathers Abraham and Isaac. They shall multiply; they shall increase; They shall become a great people on the earth. Afterwards Israel said to Joseph: 'I am dying: but you will return to the land of your fathers, and God will be with you. Behold, you have

been more favoured than your brothers, for I have taken the Amorites with my bow and my sword'. 7. Jacob called all his sons and said to them, Come to me. all of you, so that I can tell you what will happen to you. and also what will happen to each one of you at the end of time. All Israel's sons gathered round him, from the youngest to the eldest of them. Jacob Israel answered and said to his sons: 'Listen, sons of Jacob, listen to Israel your father, from Reuben my first-born unto Benjamin'. He told his sons what would happen to all twelve of them, name by name and tribe by tribe, with heaven's blessing. Then all kept silence so that he might rest a little. 8. He was taken up into the heavens to visit the resting-places. And behold, a host of tormentors came out. The appearance of each one was different; and they were ready to torment the sinners - that is the fornicators, and the harlots, and the catamites, and the sodomites, and the adulterers, and those who have corrupted God's creation, and the magicians, and the sorcerers, and the unrighteous, and the idolworshippers, and the astrologers, and the slanderers and the doubletongued. In short, many are the punishments for all the sins we have mentioned; the unquenchable fire, the outer darkness, the place where there shall be weeping and grinding of teeth, and the worm that does not sleep. And it is a terrible thing for you to be brought before the judge, and it is a terrible thing to come into the hands o f the living God. Woe to all sinful men for whom these tortures and these tormentors are prepared. And again afterwards he took me and showed me the place where my fathers Abraham and Isaac were, a place that was all light; and they were glad and rejoiced in the kingdom of the heavens, in the city of the beloved. And he showed me all the restingplaces and all the good things prepared for the righteous, and the things that eye has not seen nor ear heard, and have not come into the heart of men. that God has prepared for those who love him and do his will on earth (for if they end well, they do his will). 9 After this, Jacob said to his sons: 'Behold I am about to be taken away and laid to rest with my people; lay my body with my people in the double grave in the field of Ephron the Hittite, where Abraham and his wife .Sarah were buried, where Isaac was buried, in the path of the field and the grave that is in it, which was bought from the sons of Heth'. And when Jacob had finished saying this, he drew his feet up on to his bed; he went forth from the body like; every man. And the Lord came from heaven with Michael and Gabriel accompanying him, and many legions of angels singing before him. They took the soul of Jacob Israel to abodes of light with his holy fathers Abraham and Isaac. Such was the life of Jacob Israel the patriarch. Joseph presented him to Pharaoh when he was a hundred and thirty years old and he spent another seventeen years in Egypt; together this makes a hundred and forty-seven years. He went to his rest in a ripe old age, perfect in every virtue and spiritual grace; and he glorified God in all his ways, in the peace of God. Amen. 10. Joseph threw himself upon his father, kissing him and weeping for him. And Joseph instructed his servants, the embalmers, saying: 'Embalm my father in accordance with the best Egyptian practice'. They spent forty days embalming Israel; and when the forts days of Israel's embalming were over, they spent another eights days mourning for him. And when the days of Pharaoh's mourning were over (for he had been weeping for Jacob because of his love for Joseph). Joseph spoke with Pharaoh's great ones and said to them: 'If I may claim this favour from you, speak on my behalf to Pharaoh the king saying: My father made me take an oath when he was about to go forth from the body, saying: Bury my body in my fathers grave in the land of Canaan. .So now I ask to be allowed to go and bury my father there and come back again'. Pharaoh the king said to Joseph the wise: 'Go in peace and bury your lather as he made you swear to do; take with you chariots and wagons, and all the great ones of my kingdom, and as many of my servants as you need'. Joseph worshipped God in Pharaoh's presence and went out from him. And Joseph set out to bury his father. Many of Pharaoh's servants went with him. and the elders of Egipt as well as all Joseph's household, and his brothers, and the whole of Israel's household. And there went up with him chariots and horsemen; they were a very great company. And they stopped at the threshing floor of Gadad. wich is on the bank on the other side of Jordan. They mourned for him there with a great and bitter mourning; and they mourned for him for seven days. Those in the lowland heard the mourning at the threshing-floor of Gadad, and they said: 'This great mourning is a mourning of the Egyptians, so that that place is called The Mourning of Egypt to this day'. They took Israel and buried him in the land of Canaan in the double grave that Abraham had bought as a burial-place for silver from Ephron the Hittite, opposite Mamre. And Joseph returned to Egypt together with his brothers and the party from Pharaoh's household. After his father's death Joseph lived for many more years and was king over Egipt. But Jacob Israel died and was laid with his people. [11]. Behold now, we have told you these things as best we could in order to instruct you about the going forth from the body of our father the patriarch Jacob Israel. 'It is written in the divinely inspired scriptures and the ancient books of our fathers the apostles, even I, Athanasius your father. If you want confirmation of this testament of the patriarch Jacob, take the book Genesis of the prophet Moses, the lawgiver, and read what is in it: your mind will be enlightened: you will find this, and more, written about it. And again, you will find mention of God and his angels, for God was a friend to the patriarchs while they were yet in the body and spoke with them many times in many passages of scripture. And you will find that he spoke too in many passages in scripture with the patriarch Jacob, saying. I will bless your descendants and make them as many as the stars of heaven. And again, Jacob spoke with his son Joseph saying, My God appeared to me in the land of Canaan at Luz: he blessed me saying: 'I will bless you and make you too many to be counted, and peoples and nations shall spring from you; I will give this land to your descendants after you as a possession for all time'. [12]. See then, my beloved, we have heard these things about our fathers the patriarchs. Let us therefore emulate their deeds and their virtues, and their love of God and their love of men, and their hospitality, that we may be worthy to become their sons in the kingdom of the heavens, and that they may pray for us to God that he may save us from punishments in hell which the holy patriarch Jacob spoke about in his words full of all sweetness, when he taught his sons about the punishments and called them the sword of the Lord God. These are the river of fire that is prepared, and which engulfs sinners in its waves and those that have defiled themselves. These are the things the patriarch Jacob revealed when he taught the rest of his sons, that those that love instruction should listen to him and do what is good at all times, and love one another, and strive after love and pity. For pity triumphs over judgement and love covers a multitude of sins; and again. He who has pity on a poor man lends on usury to God. [13]. So now. my sons, let neither prayer nor fasting (be lacking), and persist in them continually; for they drive away the demons. My sons, keep yourselves from fornication, and anger, and adultery, and every evil thing, and especially from violence, and blasphemy, and theft. For no man of violence will inherit the kingdom of the heavens, neither will any fornicator, nor catamite, nor sodomite, nor blasphemer, nor covetous man. nor curser, nor anyone who is defiled. In short, these and the others we have mentioned will not inherit the kingdom of God. My sons, honour the saints, for it is they who pray for you, that your descendants may prosper and that the land may be yours as an inheritance for ever. My sons, be hospitable, that you may share the lot of our father Abraham, the great patriarch. My sons, love the poor, that as you do to the poor man here, so God may give you the bread of eternal life in the heavens unto the end. He who feeds a poor man with bread here, God will feed him from the tree of life. Clothe the poor man who is naked here on earth, that God may put on you a robe of glory in the heavens, and so you may become a true son of our holy fathers the patriarchs. Abraham and Isaae and Jacob, in the heavens for ever. Call to mind the word of God here and remember the saints, and take care that copies of their memoirs and their hymns are made for the encouragement of those who hear them, so that your name also may be written in the book of life in the heavens, and you too may be numbered with the number of God's saints who have pleased him in their generation, and take part in the chorus with the angels in the land of the living. We commemorate the saints, our fathers the patriarchs, at this very time every year; our father Abraham the patriarch on the twenty-eighth of Mesore, also our father Isaac the patriarch on the twentyeighth of Mesore, and again our father Jacob on the twenty-eighth of this same month Mesore, as we have found it written in the ancient books of our holy fathers who were pleasing unto God. Through their supplication and their prayers may all of us together be granted to share their lot in the kingdom of our Lord and our God and our Saviour Jesus Christ, through whom is the glory of the Father with him and the Holy life-giving Spirit now and always and for ever. Amen. Remember me, that God may forgive me all my sins and giv e me understanding and give me stability without sin. Amen.

The Ladder of Jacob

Lad. Jacob 1

Jacob then went to Laban his uncle. He found a place and, laying his head on a stone, he slept there, for the son had gone down. He had a dream. And behold, a ladder was fixed on the earth, whose top reached to heaven. And the top of the ladder was the face as of a man, carved out of fire. There were twelve steps leading to the top of the ladder, and on each step to the top there were two human faces, on the right and on the left, twenty-four faces (or busts) including their chests. And the face in the middle was higher than all that I saw, the one of fire, including the shoulders and arms, exceedingly terrifying, more than those twenty-four faces. And while I was still looking at it, behold, angels of God ascended and descended on it. And God was standing above its highest face, and he called to me from there, saying "Jacob, Jacob!" And I said, "Here I sm Lord!" And he said to me, "The land on which you are sleeping, to you will I give it, and to your seed after you. And I will multiply your seed as the stars of heaven and the sand of the sea. And through your seed all the earth and those living on it in the last times of the years of completion shall be blessed, My blessing with which I have blessed you shall flow from you unto the last generation, the East and the west all shall be full of your tribe."

Lad. Jacob 2

And when I heard (this) from on high, awe and trembling fell upon me. And I rose up from my dream and, the voice still being in my ears, I said, "How fearful is this place! This is none other than the house of God and this is the gate of heave." And I set up the stone which had been my pillow as a pillar, and I poured olive oil on the top of it, and I called the name of that place the House of God. And I stood and began to sing, and I said,

"Lord God of Adam your creature and
Lord God of Abraham and Isaac my fathers
and of all who have walked before you in justice!

You who sit firmly on the cherubim and the fiery throne of glory
...and the many-eyed (ones) just as I saw in my dream,
holding the four-faced cherubim,
bearing also the many-eyed seraphim,
carrying the whole world under your arm,
yet not bing borne by anyone;
you who have made the skies firm for the glory of your name,
stretching out on two heavenly clouds the heaven which gleams under you,
that beneath it you may cause the sun to course and conceal it during the night so that it might not seem a god;
(you) who made on them a way for the moon and the stars;
and you make the moon wax and wane, and destine the stars to pass on so that they too might not seen gods.
Before the face of your glory the six winged seraphim are afraid, and they cover their feet and faces with their wings, while flying with their other (wings), and they sing unceasingly a hymn:
...whom I now in sanctifying a new (song)...
Twelve-topped, twelve-faced, many-named, fiery one!
Lightning-eyed holy one!
Holy, Holy, Holy, Yao, Yaova, Yaoil, Yao,
Kados, Chavod, Savaoth,
Omlemlech il avir amismi varich,
eternal king, mighty, powerful, most great,
patient, blessed one!"
you who fill heaven and earth, the sea and abysses
and all the ages with your glory,
hear my song which I have sung you and grant me the request I ask of you,
and tell me the interpretation of my dream,
for you are a god who is mighty, powerful and glorious,
a god who is holy; my Lord and Lord of my fathers."

Lad. Jacob 3

And while I was still saying this prayer, behold, a voice came before my face saying, "Sariel, leader of the beguiled, you who are in charge of dreams, go and make Jacob understand the meaning of the dream he has had and explain to him everything he saw' but first bless him." And Sariel the archangel came to me and I saw (him), and his appearance was very beautiful and awesome. But I was not astonished by his appearance, for the vision which I had seen in my dream was more terrible than he. And I did not fear the vision of the angel.

Lad. Jacob 4

And the angel said to me, "What is your name?" And I said, "Jacob." (He announced), "Your name shall no longer be called Jacob, but your name shall be similar to my name, Israel." And when I was going from Phandana of Syria to meet Esau my brother, he came to me and blessed me and called me Israel. And he would not tell me his name until I adjured him. And then he said to me. "As you were kep zul..."

Lad. Jacob 5

Thus he said to me: "You have seen a ladder with twelve steps, each step having two human faces which kept changing their appearance. The ladder is this age, and the twelve steps are the periods of this age. But the twenty-four faces are the kings of the ungodly nations of this age. Under these kings the children of you children and the generations of your sons will be interrogated. These will rise up against the iniquity of you grandsons. And this place will be made desolate by the four ascents...through the sins of your grandsons. And around the property of your forefathers a palace will be built, a temple in the name of your God and of (the God) of your fathers, and in the provocations of your children it will becomes deserted by the four ascents of this age. For you saw the first four busts which were striking against the steps...angels ascending and descending, and the busts amid the steps. The Most High will raise up kings from

the grandsons of your brother Esau, and they will receive all the nobles of the tribes of the earth who will have maltreated your seed. And they will be delivered into his hands and he will be vexed by them. And he will hold them by force and rule over them, and they will not be able to oppose him until the day when his thought will go out against them to serve idols and (to offer) sacrifices of the dead... (He will) do violence to all those in his tribe and kfalkonagargailyuya. Know, Jacob that your descendants shall be exiles in a strange land, and they will afflict them with slavery and inflict wounds on them every day. But the Lord will judge the people for whom they slave.

Lad. Jacob 6

"And when the king arises, judgment too will come upon that place. Then your seed, Israel, will go out of slavery to the nations who hold them by force and they will be free from any rebuke of your enemies. For this king is the head of all revenge and retaliation against those who have done evil to you, Israel, and the end of the age. For bitter ones will rise; they will cry out, and the Lord will hear them and accept their plea. And the Mighty One will repent because of their sufferings. For the angels and archangels will hurl their bolts of lightning before them for the sake of the salvation of your tribe. And you will gain the mercy of the Most High. Then their wives will bear many children. And afterward the Lord will fight for your tribe through great and terrible signs against those who made them slaves. He filled their storehouses, and they will be found empty. Their land swarmed with reptiles and all sorts of deadly things. There will be earthquakes and much destruction. And the Lord will pour out his wrath against Leviathan the sea-dragon; he will kill the lawless Falkon with the sword, because he will raise the wrath of the God of gods by his pride. And then your justice will be revealed, Jacob, and that of your children who are to be after you (and) who will walk in your justice. And then your seed will sound the horn and all the kingdom of Edom will perish together with all the peoples of Moab.

Lad. Jacob 7

"And as for the angels you saw descending and ascending the ladder, in the last years there will be a man from the Most High, and he will desire to join the upper (things) with the lower. And before his coming your sons and daughters will tell about him and your young men will have visions about his. Such will be the signs at the time of his coming: A tree cut with an ax will bleed; three-month-old babes will speak understanding; a baby in the womb of his mother will speak of his way; a youth will be like an old man. And then the expected one will come, whose path will not be noticed by anyone. "Then the earth will be glorified, receiving heavenly glory. What was above will be below also. And from your seed will bloom a root of kings; it will emerge and overthrow the power of evil. And he himself will be the Savior for every land and rest for those who toil, and a cloud shading the whole world from the burning heat, For otherwise the uncontrolled will not be controlled. If he does not come, the lower (things) cannot be joined with the upper. At his coming the idols of brass, stone, and any sort of carving will give voice for three days. They will give wise men news of him and let them know what will be on earth. By a star, those who wish to see on earth him whom the angels do not see above will find the way to him. Then the Almighty will be on earth in body, and, embraced by corporeal arms, he will restore human matter. And he will revive Eve, who died by the fruit of the tree. Then the deceit of the impious will be exposed and all the idols will fall face down. For they will be put to shame by a dignitary. For because (they were) lying by means of hallucinations, henceforth they will not be able to rule or to prophesy. Honor will be taken from them and they will remain without glory.

"For he who comes will take power and might and will give Abraham the truth which he previously told him. Everything sharp he will make dull, and the rough will be smooth. And he will cast all the iniquitous into the depths of the sea. He will work wonders in heaven and on earth. And he will be wounded in the midst of his beloved house. And when he is wounded, then salvation will be ready, and the end to all perdition. For those who have wounded him will themselves receive a wound which will not be cured in them forever. And all creation will bow to him who was wounded, and many will trust in him. And he will become known everywhere in all lands, and those who acknowledged his name will not be ashamed, His own dominion and years will be unending forever."

The Testament of Moses

[1] The Testament of Moses even the things which he commanded in the one hundred and twentieth year of his life, that is the two thousand five hundredth year from the creation of the world: [But according to oriental reckoning the two thousand and seven hundredth, and the four hundredth after the departure from Phoenicia], when the people had gone forth after the Exodus that was made by Moses to Amman beyond the Jordan, in the prophecy that was made by Moses in the book Deuteronomy: and he called to him Joshua the son of Nun, a man approved of the Lord, that he might be the minister of the people and of the tabernacle of the testimony with all its holy things, and that he might bring the people into the land given to their fathers, that it should be given to them according to the covenant and the oath, which He spoke in the tabernacle to give (it) by Joshua: saying to Joshua these words: '(Be strong) and of a good courage so as to do with thy might all that has been commanded that you may be blameless unto God.' So says the Lord of the world. For He has created the world on behalf of His people. But He was not pleased to manifest this purpose of creation from the foundation of the world, in order that the Gentiles might thereby be convicted, yea to their own humiliation might by (their) arguments convict one another. Accordingly He designed and devised me, and He prepared me before the foundation of the world, that I should be the mediator of His covenant. And now I declare unto you that the time of the years of my life is fulfilled and I am passing away to sleep with my fathers even in the presence of all the people And receive this writing that you may know how to preserve the books which I shall deliver unto you: and you shall set these in order and anoint them with oil of cedar and put them away in earthen vessels in the place which He made from the beginning of the creation of the world, that His name should be called upon until the day of repentance in the visitation wherewith the Lord will visit them in the consummation of the end of the days. [2] And now they shall go by means of you into the land which He determined and promised to give to their fathers, in the which you shall bless and give to them individually and confirm unto them their inheritance in me and establish for them the kingdom, and you shall appoint them local magistrates according to the good pleasure of their Lord in judgment and righteousness. And five years after they enter into the land, that thereafter they shall be ruled by chiefs and kings for eighteen years, and during nineteen years the ten tribes shall break away. And the twelve tribes shall go down and transfer the tabernacle of the testimony. Then the God of heaven will make the court of His tabernacle and the tower of His sanctuary, and the two holy tribes shall be (there) established: but the ten tribes shall establish kingdoms for themselves according to their own ordinances. And they shall offer sacrifices throughout twenty years: and seven shall entrench the walls, and I will protect nine, but four shall transgress the covenant of the Lord, and profane the oath which the Lord made with them. And they shall sacrifice their sons to strange gods, and they shall set up idols in the sanctuary, to worship them. And in the house of the Lord they shall work impiety and engrave every form of beast, even many abominations. [3] And in those days a king from the east shall come against them and his cavalry shall cover their land. And he shall burn their colony with fire together with the holy temple of the Lord, and he shall carry away all the holy vessels. And he shall cast forth all the people, and he shall take them to the land of his nativity, yea he shall take the two tribes with him. Then the two tribes shall call upon the ten tribes, and shall march as a lioness on the dusty plains, being hungry and thirsty. And they shall cry aloud: 'Righteous and holy is the Lord, for, inasmuch as ye have sinned, we too, in like manner, have been carried away with you, together with our children.' Then the ten tribes shall mourn on hearing the reproaches of the two tribes, and they shall say: 'What have we done unto you, brethren? Has not this tribulation come on all the house of Israel?' And all the tribes shall mourn, crying unto heaven and saying: 'God of Abraham God of Isaac and God of Jacob, remember Thy covenant which You made with them, and the oath which You didst swear unto them by Yourself, that their seed should never fail from the land which You hast given them.' Then they shall remember me, saying, in that day, tribe unto tribe and each man unto his neighbor: 'Is not this that which Moses did then declare unto us in prophecies, who suffered many things in Egypt and in the Red Sea and in the wilderness during forty years: and assuredly called heaven and earth to witness against us, that we should not transgress His commandments, in the which he was a mediator unto us? Behold these things have befallen us after his death according to his declaration, as he declared to us at that time, yes, behold these have taken place even to our being carried away captive into the country of the east.' Who shall be also in bondage for about seventy and seven years. [4] Then there shall enter one who is over them, and he shall spread forth his hands, and kneel upon his knees and pray on their behalf saying: 'Lord of all, King on the lofty throne, who rules the world, and did will that this people should be Your elect people, then (indeed) You didst will that You should be called their God, according to the covenant which You didst make with their fathers. [3] And yet they have gone in captivity in another land with their wives and their children, and around the gates of strange peoples and where there is great vanity. Regard and have compassion on them, O Lord of heaven.' Then God will remember them on account of the covenant which He made with their fathers. and He will manifest His compassion in those times also. And He will put it into the mind of a king to have compassion on them, and he shall send them off to their land and country. Then some portions of the tribes shall go up and they shall come to their appointed place, and they shall anew surround the place with walls. And the two tribes shall continue in their prescribed faith, sad and lamenting because they will not be able to offer sacrifices to the Lord of their fathers. And the ten tribes shall increase and multiply among the Gentiles during the time of their captivity. [5] And when the times of chastisement draw nigh and vengeance arises through the kings who share in their guilt and punish them, they themselves also shall be divided as to the truth. Wherefore it hath been said: "They shall turn aside from righteousness and approach iniquity, and they shall defile with pollutions the house of their worship,' and [because] 'they shall prostitute themselves with strange gods.' For they shall not follow the truth of God, but some shall pollute the altar with the (very) gifts which they offer to the Lord, who are not priests but slaves, sons of slaves. And many in those times shall have respect unto desirable persons and receive gifts, and pervert judgment [on receiving

presents]. And on this account the colony and the borders of their habitation shall be filled with lawless deeds and iniquities: those who wickedly depart from the Lord shall be judges: they shall be ready to judge for money as each may wish. 6 Then there shall be raised up unto them kings bearing rule, and they shall call themselves priests of the Most High God: they shall assuredly work iniquity in the holy of holies. And an insolent king shall succeed them, who will not be of the race of the priests, a man bold and shameless, and he shall judge them as they shall deserve. And he shall cut off their chief men with the sword, and shall destroy them in secret places, so that no one may know where their bodies are. He shall slay the old and the young, and he shall not spare. Then the fear of him shall be bitter unto them in their land. And he shall execute judgments on them as the Egyptians executed upon them, during thirty and four years, and he shall punish them. And he shall beget children, (who) succeeding him shall rule for shorter periods. Into their parts cohorts and a powerful king of the west shall come, who shall conquer them: and he shall take them captive, and burn a part of their temple with fire, (and) shall crucify some around their colony. 7 And when this is done the times shall be ended, in a moment the (second) course shall be (ended), the four hours shall come. They shall be forced. . . And, in the time of these, destructive and impious men shall rule, saying that they are just. And these shall stir up the poison of their minds, being treacherous men, self-pleasers, dissemblers in all their own affairs and lovers of banquets at every hour of the day. gluttons, gourmands.... Devourers of the goods of the (poor) saying that they do so on the ground of their justice, but in reality to destroy them, complainers, deceitful, concealing themselves lest they should be recognized, impious, filled with lawlessness and iniquity from sunrise to sunset: saying: 'We shall have feastings and luxury, eating and drinking, and we shall esteem ourselves as princes.' And though their hands and their minds touch unclean things, yet their mouth shall speak great things, and they shall say furthermore: 'Do not touch me lest you should pollute me in the place (where I stand') . . . 8 And there shall come upon them a second visitation and wrath, such as has not befallen them from the beginning until that time, in which He will stir up against them the king of the kings of the earth and one that rules with great power, who shall crucify those who confess to their circumcision: and those who conceal (it) he shall torture and deliver them up to be bound and led into prison. And their wives shall be given to the gods among the Gentiles, and their young sons shall be operated on by the physicians in order to bring forward their foreskin. And others amongst them shall be punished by tortures and fire and sword, and they shall be forced to bear in public their idols, polluted as they are like those who keep. them. And they shall likewise be forced by those who torture them to enter their inmost sanctuary, and they shall be forced by goads to blaspheme with insolence the word, finally after these things the laws and what they had above their altar. 9 Then in that day there shall be a man of the tribe of Levi, whose name shall be Taxo, who having seven sons shall speak to them exhorting (them): 'Observe, my sons, behold a second ruthless (and) unclean visitation has come upon the people, and a punishment merciless and far exceeding the first. For what nation or what region or what people of those who are impious towards the Lord, who have done many abominations, have suffered as great calamities as have befallen us? Now, therefore, my sons, hear me: for observe and know that neither did the fathers nor their forefathers tempt God, so as to transgress His commands. And you know that this is our strength, and thus we will do. Let us fast for the space of three days and on the fourth let us go into a cave which is in the field, and let us die rather than transgress the commands of the Lord of Lords, the God of our fathers. For if we

do this and die, our blood shall be avenged before the Lord. 10 And then His kingdom shall appear throughout all His creation, And then Satan shall be no more, And sorrow shall depart with him. Then the hands of the angel shall be filled Who has been appointed chief, And he shall forthwith avenge them of their enemies. For the Heavenly One will arise from His royal throne, And He will go forth from His holy habitation With indignation and wrath on account of His sons. And the earth shall tremble: to its confines shall it be shaken: And the high mountains shall be made low And the hills shall be shaken and fall. And the horns of the sun shall be broken and he shall be turned into darkness; And the moon shall not give her light, and be turned wholly into blood. And the circle of the stars shall be disturbed. And the sea shall retire into the abyss, And the fountains of waters shall fail, And the rivers shall dry up. For the Most High will arise, the Eternal God alone, And He will appear to punish the Gentiles, And He will destroy all their idols. Then you, O Israel, shall be happy, And you shall mount upon the necks and wings of the eagle, And they shall be ended. And God will exalt you, And He will cause you to approach to the heaven of the stars, In the place of their habitation. And you will look from on high and see your enemies in Ge(henna) And you shall recognize them and rejoice, And you shall give thanks and confess thy Creator. And do you; Joshua (the son of) Nun, keep these words and this book; For from my death [assumption] until His advent there shall be 250 times [= year-weeks = 1750 years]. And this is the course of the times which they shall pursue till they are consummated. And I shall go to sleep with my fathers. Wherefore, Joshua you (son of) Nun, (be strong and) be of good courage; (for) God has chosen (you) to be minister in the same covenant. 11 And when Joshua had heard the words of Moses that were so written in his writing all that he had before said, he rent his clothes and cast himself at Moses' feet. And Moses comforted him and wept with him. And Joshua answered him and said: 'Why do you comfort me, (my) lord Moses ? And how shall I be comforted in regard to the bitter word which you hast spoken which has gone forth from thy mouth, which is full of tears and lamentation, in that you depart from this people? (But now) what place shall receive you? Or what shall be the sign that marks (your) sepulcher? Or who shall dare to move your body from there as that of a mere man from place to place? For all men when they die have according to their age their sepulchers on earth; but your sepulcher is from the rising to the setting sun, and from the south to the confines of the north: all the world is your sepulcher. My lord, you are departing, and who shall feed this people? Or who is there that shall have compassion on them and who shall be their guide by the way? Or who shall pray for them, not omitting a single day, in order that I may lead them into the land of their forefathers? How therefore am I to foster this people as a father (his) only son, or as a mistress her daughter, a virgin who is being prepared to be given to the husband whom she will revere, while she guards her person from the sun and (takes care) that her feet are not unshod for running upon the ground. (And how) shall I supply them with food and drink according to the pleasure of their will? For of them, there shall be 600,000 (men), for these have multiplied to this degree through your prayers, (my) lord Moses. And what wisdom or understanding have I that I should judge or answer by word in the house (of the Lord)? And the kings of the Amorites also when they hear that we are attacking them, believing that there is no longer among them the holy spirit who was worthy of the Lord, manifold and incomprehensible, the lord of the word, who was faithful in all things, God's chief prophet throughout the earth, the most perfect teacher in the world, [that he is no longer among them], shall say "Let us go against them. If the enemy have but once wrought impiously against their Lord, they have no advocate to offer prayers on their behalf to the Lord, like Moses the great messenger, who every hour day and night had his knees fixed to the earth, praying and looking for help to Him that rules all the world with compassion and righteousness, reminding Him of the covenant of the fathers and propitiating the Lord with the oath." For they shall say: "He is not with them: let us go therefore and destroy them from off the face of the earth." What shall then become of this people, my lord Moses?' 12 And when Joshua had finished (these) words, he cast himself again at the feet of Moses. And Moses took his hand and raised him into the seat before him, and answered and said unto him: Joshua, do not despise yourself; but set your mind at ease, and hear my words. All the nations which are in the earth God has created and us, He has foreseen them and us from the beginning of the creation of the earth unto the end of the age, and nothing has been neglected by Him even to the least thing, but all things He hath foreseen and caused all to come forth. (Yes) all things which are to be in this earth the Lord has foreseen and, look, they are brought forward (into the light. . . . The Lord,) has on their behalf appointed me to (pray) for their sins and (make intercession) for them. For not for any virtue or strength of mine, but of His good pleasure have His compassion and longsuffering fallen to my lot. For I say unto you, Joshua: it is not on account of the godliness of this people that you shall root out the nations. The lights of the heaven, the foundations of the earth have been made and approved by God and are under the signet ring of His right hand. Those, therefore, who do and fulfill the commandments of God shall increase and be prospered: but those who sin and set at naught the commandments shall be without the blessings before mentioned, and they shall be punished with many torments by the nations. But wholly to root out and destroy them is not permitted. For God will go forth who has foreseen all things for ever, and His covenant has been established and by the oath which . . .

Testament of Solomon

1. Testament of Solomon, son of David, who was king in Jerusalem, and mastered and controlled all spirits of the air, on the earth and under the earth... By means of them also he wrought all the transcendent works of the Temple. Telling also of the authorities they wield against men, and by what angels these demons are brought to naught Of the sage Solomon. Blessed art thou, Lord God, who didst give to Solomon such authority. Glory to thee and might unto the ages. Amen. 2. And behold, when the Temple of the city of Jerusalem was being builded, and the artificers were working thereat, Ornias the demon came among them toward sunset; and he took away the half of the pay of the chief-deviser's little boy, as well as half his food. He also continued to suck the thumb of his right hand every day. And the child grew thin although he was very much loved by the king. 3. So King Solomon called the boy one day, and questioned him, saying: "Do I not love thee more than all the artisans who are working in the Temple of God? Do I not give thee double wages and a double supply of food? How is it that day by day and hour by hour thou growest thinner?" 4. But the child said to the king: "I pray thee, O king. Listen to what has befallen all that thy child hath. After we are all released from our work on the Temple of God, after sunset, when I lie down to rest, one of the evil demons comes and takes away from me the half of my pay and half of my food. Then he also takes hold of my right hand and sucks my thumb. And lo, my soul is oppressed, and so my body waxes thinner every day." 5. Now when I Solomon heard this, I entered the Temple of God, and prayed with all my soul, night and day, that the demon might be delivered into my hands, and that I might gain authority

over him. And it came about through my prayer that grace was given to me from the Lord Sabaôth by Michael his archangel. [He brought me] a little ring, having a seal consisting of an engraved stone, and said to me: "Take, O Solomon, king, son of David, the gift which the Lord God has sent thee, the highest Sabaôth. With it thou shalt lock up all the demons of the earth, male and female; and with their help thou shalt build up Jerusalem. [But] thou [must] wear this seal of God. And this engraving of the seal of the ring sent thee is a Pentalpha." 6. And I Solomon was overjoyed, and praised and glorified the God of heaven and earth. And on the morrow I called the boy, and gave him the ring, and said to him: "Take this, and at the hour in which the demon shall come unto thee, throw this ring at the chest of the demon, and say to him: 'In the name of God, King Solomon calls thee hither.' And then do thou come running to me, without having any misgivings or fear in respect of aught thou mayest hear on the part of the demon." 7. So the child took the ring, and went off; and behold, at the customary hour Ornias, the fierce demon, came like a burning fire to take the pay from the child. But the child, according to the instructions received from the king, threw the ring at the chest of the demon, and said: "King Solomon calls thee hither." And then he went off at a run to the king. But the demon cried out aloud, saying: "Child, why hast thou done this to me? Take the ring off me, and I will render to thee the gold of the earth. Only take this off me, and forbear to lead me away to Solomon." 8. But the child said to the demon: "As the Lord God of Israel liveth, I will not brook thee. So come hither." And the child came at a run, rejoicing, to the king, and said: "I have brought the demon, O king, as thou didst command me, O my master. And behold, he stands before the gates of the court of thy palace, crying out, and supplicating with a loud voice; offering me the silver and gold of the earth if I will only not bring him unto thee." 9. And when Solomon heard this, he rose up from his throne, and went outside into the vestibule of the court of his palace; and there he saw the demon, shuddering and trembling. And he said to him: "Who art thou?" And the demon answered: "I am called Ornias." 10. And Solomon said to him: "Tell me, O demon, to what zodiacal sign thou art subject." And he answered: "To the Water-pourer. And those who are consumed with desire for noble virgins upon earth . . . , these I strangle. But in case there is no disposition to sleep, I am changed into three forms. Whenever men come to be enamoured of women, I metamorphose myself into a comely female; and I take hold of the men in their sleep, and play with them. And after a while I again take to my wings, and hie me to heavenly regions. I also appear as a lion[21], and I am commande by all the demons. I am offspring of the archangel Uriel, the power of God." 11. I Solomon, having heard the name of the archangel, prayed and glorified God, the Lord of heaven and earth. And I sealed the demon and set him to work at stone-cutting, so that he might cut the stones in the Temple, which, lying along the shore, had been brought by the Sea of Arabia. But he, fearful of the iron, continued and said to me: "I pray thee, King Solomon, let me go free; and I will bring you all the demons." And as he was not willing to be subject to me, I prayed the archangel Uriel to come and succour me; and I forthwith beheld the archangel Uriel coming down to me from the heavens. 12, And the angel bade the whales of the sea come out of the abyss. And he cast his destiny upon the ground, and that [destiny] made subject [to him] the great demon. And he commanded the great demon and bold, Ornias, to cut stones at the Temple. And accordingly I Solomon glorified the God of heaven and Maker of the earth. And he bade Ornias come with his destiny, and I gave him the seal, saying: "Away with thee, and bring me hither the prince of all the demons." 13. So Ornias took the finger-ring, and went off to

Beelzeboul, who has kingship over the demons. He said to him: "Hither! Solomon calls thee." But Beelzeboul, having heard, said to him: "Tell me, who is this Solomon of whom thou speakest to me?" Then Ornias threw the ring at the chest of Beelzeboul, saying: "Solomon the king calls thee." But Beelzeboul cried aloud with a mighty voice, and shot out a great burning flame of fire; and he arose, and followed Ornias, and came to Solomon. 14. And when I saw the prince of demons, I glorified the Lord God, Maker of heaven and earth, and I said: "Blessed art thou, Lord God Almighty, who hast given to Solomon thy servant wisdom, the assessor of the wise, and hast subjected unto me all the power of the devil." 15. And I questioned him, and said: "Who art thou?" The demon replied: "I am Beelzeboul, the exarch of the demons. And all the demons have their chief seats close to me. And I it is who make manifest the apparition of each demon." And he promised to bring to me in bonds all the unclean spirits. And I again glorified the God of heaven and earth, as I do always give thanks to him. 16. I then asked of the demon if there were females among them. And when he told me that there were, I said that I desired to see them. So Beelzeboul went off at high speed, and brought unto me Onoskelis, that had a very pretty shape, and the skin of a fair-hued woman; and she tossed her head. 17. And when she was come, I said to her: "Tell me, who art thou?" But she said to me: "I am called Onoskelis, a spirit wrought …, lurking upon the earth. There is a golden cave where I lie. But I have a place that ever shifts. At one time I strangle men with a noose; at another, I creep up from the nature to the arms. But my most frequent dwelling-places are the precipices, caves, ravines. Oftentimes, however, do I consort with men in the semblance of a woman, and above all with those of a dark skin. For they share my star with me; since they it is who privily or openly worship my star, without knowing that they harm themselves, and but whet my appetite for further mischief. For they wish to provide money by means of memory, but I supply a little to those who worship me fairly." 18. And I Solomon questioned her about her birth, and she replied: "I was born of a voice untimely, the so-called echo of a man's ordure dropped in a wood." 19. And I said to her: "Under what star dost thou pass?" And she answered me: "Under the star of the full moon, for the reason that the moon travels over most things." Then I said to her: "And what angel is it that frustrates thee?" And she said to me: "He that in thee is reigning." And I thought that she mocked me, and bade a soldier strike her. But she cried aloud, and said: "I am [subjected] to thee, O king, by the wisdom of God given to thee, and by the angel Joel." 20. So I commanded her to spin the hemp for the ropes used in the building of the house of God; and accordingly, when I had sealed and bound her, she was so overcome and brought to naught as to stand night and day spinning the hemp. 21. And I at once bade another demon to be led unto me; and instantly there approached me the demon Asmodeus, bound, and I asked him: "Who art thou?" But he shot on me a glance of anger and rage, and said: "And who art thou?" And I said to him: "Thus punished as thou art, answerest thou me?" But he, with rage, said to me: "But how shall I answer thee, for thou art a son of man; whereas I was born an angel's seed by a daughter of man, so that no word of our heavenly kind addressed to the earthborn can be overweening. Wherefore also my star is bright in heaven, and men call it, some the Wain, and some the dragon's-child. I keep near unto this star. So ask me not many things; for thy kingdom also after a little time is to be disrupted, and thy glory is but for a season. And short will be thy tyranny over us; and then we shall again have free range over mankind, so as that they shall revere us as if we were gods, not knowing, men that they are, the names of the angels set over us." 22. And I Solomon, on hearing this, bound him more carefully, and

334

ordered him to be flogged with thongs of ox-hide, and to tell me humbly what was his name and what his business. And he answered me thus: "I am called Asmodeus among mortals, and my business is to plot against the newly wedded, so that they may not know one another. And I sever them utterly by many calamities, and I waste away the beauty of virgin women, and estrange their hearts." 23. And I said to him: "Is this thy only business?" And he answered me: "I transport men into fits of madness and desire, when they have wives of their own, so that they leave them, and go off by night and day to others that belong to other men; with the result that they commit sin, and fall into murderous deeds." 24. And I adjured him by the name of the Lord Sabaóth, saying: "Fear God, Asmodeus, and tell me by what angel thou art frustrated." But he said: "By Raphael, the archangel that stands before the throne of God. But the liver and gall of a fish put me to flight, when smoked over ashes of the tamarisk." I again asked him, and said: "Hide not aught from me. For I am Solomon, son of David, King of Israel. Tell me the name of the fish which thou reverest." And he answered: "It is the Glanos by name, and is found in the rivers of Assyria; wherefore it is that I roam about in those parts." 25. And I said to him: "Hast thou nothing else about thee, Asmodeus?" And he answered: "The power of God knoweth, which hath bound me with the indissoluble bonds of yonder one's seal, that whatever I have told thee is true. I pray thee, King Solomon, condemn me not to [go into] water." But I smiled, and said to him: "As the Lord God of my fathers liveth, I will lay iron on thee to wear. But thou shalt also make the clay for the entire construction of the Temple, treading it down with thy feet." And I ordered them to give him ten water-jars to carry water in. And the demon groaned terribly, and did the work I ordered him to do. And this I did, because that fierce demon Asmodeus knew even the future. And I Solomon glorified God, who gave wisdom to me, Solomon his servant. And the liver of the fish and its gall I hung on the spike of a reed, and burned it over Asmodeus, because of his being so strong, and his unbearable malice was thus frustrated. 26. And I summoned again to stand before me Beelzeboul, the prince of demons, and I sat him down on a raised seat of honour, and said to him: "Why art thou alone, prince of the demons?" And he said to me: "Because I alone am left of the angels of heaven that came down. For I was first angel in the first heaven, being entitled Beelzeboul. And now I control all those who are bound in Tartarus. But I too have a child, and he haunts the Red Sea. And on any suitable occasion he comes up to me again, being subject to me; and reveals to me what he has done, and I support him. 27. I Solomon said unto him: "Beelzeboul, what is thy employment?" And he answered me: "I destroy kings. I ally myself with foreign tyrants. And my own demons I set on to men, in order that the latter may believe in them and be lost. And the chosen servants of God, priests and faithful men, I excite unto desires for wicked sins, and evil heresies, and lawless deeds; and they obey me, and I bear them on to destruction. And I inspire men with envy, and [desire for] murder, and for wars and sodomy, and other evil things. And I will destroy the world." 28. So I said to him: "Bring to me thy child, who is, as thou sayest, in the Red Sea." But he said to me: "I will not bring him to thee. But there shall come to me another demon, called Ephippas. Him will I bind, and he will bring him up from the deep unto me." And I said to him: "How comes thy son to be in the depth of the sea, and what is his name?" And he answered me: "Ask me not, for thou canst not learn from me. However, he will come to thee by my command, and will tell thee openly." 29. I said to him: "Tell me by what angel thou art frustrated." And he answered: "By the holy and precious name of the Almighty God, called by the Hebrews by a row of numbers, of which the sum is 644, and among the Greeks it is

Emmanue¹. And if one of the Romans adjure me by the great name of the power Eleêth, I disappear at once." ³⁰. I Solomon was astounded when I heard this; and I ordered him to saw up Theban marbles. And when he began to saw the marbles, the other demons cried out with a loud voice, howling because of their king Beelzeboul. ³¹. But I Solomon questioned him, saying: "If thou wouldst gain a respite, discourse to me about the things in heaven." And Beelzeboul said: "Hear, O king, if thou burn gum, and incense, and bulbs of the sea, with nard and saffron, and light seven lamps in an earthquake, thou wilt firmly fix thy house. And if, being pure, thou light them at dawn in the sun alight, then wilt thou see the heavenly dragons, how they wind themselves along and drag the chariot of the sun." ³². And I Solomon, having heard this, rebuked him, and said: "Silence for this present, and continue to saw the marbles as I commanded thee." And I Solomon praised God, and commanded another demon to present himself to me. And one came before me who carried his face high up in the air, but the rest of the spirit curled away like a snail. And it broke through the few soldiers, and raised also a terrible dust on the ground, and carried it upwards; and then again hurled it back to frighten us, and asked what questions I could ask as a rule. And I stood up, and spat on the ground in that spot, and sealed with the ring of God. And forthwith the dust-wind stopped. Then I asked him, saying: "Who art thou, wind?" Then he once more shook up a dust, and answered me: "What wouldst thou have, King Solomon?" I answered him: "Tell me what thou art called, and I would fain ask thee a question. But so far I give thanks to God who has made me wise to answer their evil plots." ³³. But [the demon] answered me: "I am the spirit of the ashes (Tephras)." And I said to him: "What is thy pursuit?" And he said: "I bring darkness on men, and set fire to fields; and I bring homesteads to naught. But most busy am I in summer. However, when I get an opportunity, I creep into corners of the wall, by night and day. For I am offspring of the great one, and nothing less." Accordingly I said to him: "Under what star dost thou lie?" And he answered: "In the very tip of the moon's horn, when it is found in the south. There is my star. For I have been bidden to restrain the convulsions of the hemitertian fever; and this is why many men pray to the hemitertian fever, using these three names: Bultala, Thallal, Melchal. And I heal them." And I said to him: "I am Solomon; when therefore thou wouldst do harm, by whose aid dost thou do it?" But he said to me: " By the angel's, by whom also the third day's fever is lulled to rest." So I questioned him, and said: " And by what name'?" And he answered: "That of the archangel Azael." And I summoned the archangel Azael, and set a seal on the demon, and commanded him to seize great stones, and toss them up to the workmen on the higher parts of the Temple. And, being compelled, the demon began to do what he was bidden to do. ³⁴. And I glorified God afresh who gave me this authority, and ordered another demon to come before me. And there came seven spirits ^ females, bound and woven together, fair in appearance and comely. And I Solomon, seeing them, questioned them and said: "Who are ye?" But they, with one accord, said with one voice': "We are of the thirty-three elements of the cosmic ruler of the darkness*." And the first said: "I am Deception." The second: "I am Strife." The third: " I am Klothod, which is battle." The fourth: "I am Jealousy." The fifth: "I am Power." The sixth: "I am Error." The seventh: " I am the worst of all, and our stars are in heaven. Seven stars humble in sheen, and all together. And we are called as it were goddesses. We change our place all together, and together we live, sometimes in Lydia, sometimes in Olympus, sometimes in a great mountain." ³⁵. So I Solomon questioned them one by one, beginning with the fii-st, and going down to the seventh. The first said: "I am Deception, I deceive

335

and weave snares here and there. I whet and excite heresies. But I have an angel who frustrates me, LamechalaV³⁶. Likewise also the second said: " I am Strife, strife of strifes. I bring timbers, stones, hangers, my weapons on the spot. But I have an angel who frustrates me, Baruchiachel." ³⁷. Likewise also the third said: " I am called Kloihod S which is battle, and I cause the well-behaved to scatter and fall foul one of the other. And why do I say so much? I have an angel that frustrates me, Marmarath." ³⁸. Likewise also the fourth said: "I cause men to forget their sobriety and moderation. I part them and split them into parties; for Strife follows me hand in hand. I rend the husband from the sharer of his bed, and children from parents, and brothers from sisters. But why tell so much to my despite? I have an angel that frustrates me, the great Balthial." ³⁹. Likewise also the fifth said: " I am Power. By power I raise up tyrants and tear down kings. To all rebels I furnish power. I have an angel that frustrates me, Asteradth." ⁴⁰. Likewise also the sixth said: " I am Error King Solomon. And I will make thee to err, as I have before made thee to err, when I caused thee to slay thy own brother '. I will lead you into error, so as to pry into graves *; and I teach them that dig, and I lead errant souls away from all piety, and many other evil traits are mine. But I have an angel that frustrates me, Uriel." ⁴¹. Likewise also the seventh said: "I am the worst, and I make thee worse off than thou wast; because I will impose the bonds of Artemis °. But the locust ° will set me free, for by means thereof is it fated that thou shalt achieve my desire For if one were wise, he would not turn his steps toward me." ⁴². So I Solomon, having heard and wondered, sealed them with my ring; and since they were so considerable, I bade them dig the foundations of the Temple of God. For the length of it was ²⁵⁰ cubits. And I bade them be industrious, and with one murmur of joint protest they began to perform the tasks enjoined.⁴³. But I Solomon glorified the Lord, and bade another demon come before me. And there was brought to me a demon having all the limbs of a man, but without a head. And I, seeing him, said to him: " Tell me, who art thou? " And he answered: " I am a demon." So I said to him: " Which? " And he answered me: " I am called Envy. For I delight to devour heads, being desirous to secure for myself a head; but I do not eat enough, but am anxious to have such a head as thou hast." ⁴⁴. I Solomon, on hearing this, sealed him, stretching out my hand against his chest. Whereon the demon leapt up, and threw himself down, and gave a groan, saying: " Woe is me! where am I come to? O traitor Ornias, I cannot see! " So I said to him: " I am Solomon. Tell me then how thou dost manage to see." And he answered me: "By means of my feelings." I then, Solomon, having heard his voice come up to me, asked him how he managed to speak. And he answered me: " I, King Solomon, am wholly voice, for I have inherited the voices of many men. For in the case of all men who are called dumb, I it is who smashed their heads, when they were children and had reached their eighth day. Then when a child is crying in the night, I become a spirit, and glide by means of his voice. ... In the crossways^ also I have many services to render, and my encounter is fraught with harm. For I grasp in an instant a man's head, and with my hands, as with a sword, I cut it off, and put it on to myself. And in this way, by means of the fire which is in me, through my neck it is swallowed up. I it is that sends grave mutilations and incurable on men's feet, and inflict sores." ⁴⁵. And I Solomon, on hearing this, said to him: " Tell me how thou dost discharge forth the fire? Out of what sources dost thou emit it?" And the spirit said to me: " From the Day-star^ For here hath not yet been found that Elburion, to whom men offer prayers and kindle lights. And his name is invoked by the seven demons before me. And he cherishes them." ⁴⁶. But I said to him: " Tell me his name." But he answered: "I cannot tell thee. For if I tell his name, I render myself incurable. But he will come in response to his name." And on hearing this, I Solomon said to him: "Tell me then, by what angel thou art frustrated?" And he answered: "By the fiery flash of lightning." And I bowed myself before the Lord God of Israel, and bade bim remain in the keeping of Beelzehoul until lax'^ should come. 47. Then I ordered another demon to come before me, and there came into my presence a hound, having a very large shape, and it spoke vsrith a loud voice, and said, " Hail, Lord, King Solomon! " And I Solomon was astounded. I said to it: " Who art thou, hound? " And it answered: " I do indeed seem to thee to be a hound, but before thou wast, King Solomon, I was a man, that wrought many unholy deeds on earth. I was surpassingly learned in letters, and was so mighty that I could hold the stars of heaven back. And many divine works did I prepare. For I do harm to men who follow after our star, and turn them to .... '^ And I seize the frenzied men by the larynx, and so destroy them." 48. And I Solomon said to him: " What is thy name? " And he answered: "Staff*" (Rabdos). And I said to him: "What is thine employment? And what results canst thou achieve? " And he replied: " Give me thy man. and I will lead him away into a mountainous spot, and will show him a green * stone, tossed to and fro ', with which thou mayest adorn the Temple of the Lord God." 49. And I Solomon, on hearing this, ordered my servant to set off with him, and to take the finger-ring bearing the seal of God with him. And I said to him: "Whoever shall show thee the green stone, seal him with this finger-ring. And mark the spot with care, and bring me the demon hither. And the demon showed him the green stone, and he sealed it, and brought the demon to me. And I Solomon decided to confine with my seal on my right hand the two, the headless demon, likewise the hound, that was so huge ^; he should be bound as well. And I bade the hound keep safe the fiery spirit, so that lamps as it were might by day and night cast their light through its maw on the artisans at work. 50. And I Solomon took from the mine of that stone shekels for the supports of the table of incense, which was similar in appearance. And I Solomon glorified the Lord God, and then closed round the treasure of that stone. And I ordered afresh the demons to cut marble for the construction of the house of God. And I Solomon prayed to the Lord, and asked the hound, saying: " By what angel art thou frustrated? " And the demon replied: " By the great Brieus ^" 51. And I praised the Lord God of heaven and earth, and bade another demon come forward to me; and there came before me one in the form of a lion roaring. And he stood and answered me, saying: "O king, in the form which I have, I am a spirit quite incapable of being perceived. Upon all men who lie prostrate with sickness I leap, coming stealthily along; and I render the man weak, so that his habit of body is enfeebled. But I have also another glory, O king. I cast out demons, and I have legions under my control. And I am capable of being received^ in my dwelling-places, along with all the demons belonging to the legions under me," But I Solomon, on hearing this, asked him: "What is thy name?" But he answered: "Lion-bearer, Rath" in kind." And I said to him: " How art thou to be frustrated along with thy legions? What angel is it that frustrates thee? " And he answered: " If I tell thee my name, I bind not myself alone, but also the legion of demons under me." 52. So I said to him: " I adjure thee in the name of the God SabaSth, to tell me by what name thou art frustrated along with thy host." And the spirit answered me: " The ' great among men,' who is to suffer many things at the hands of men, whose name is the figure 644, which is Emmanuel; he it is who has bound us, and who will then come and plunge us from the steep ° under water. He is noised abroad in the three letters which bring him down^." 53. And I Solomon, on hearing this, glorified God, and condemned his legion to carry wood from the thicket. And I

condemned the lion-shaped one himself to saw up the wood small with his teeth, for burning in the unquenchable furnace for the Temple of God. 54. And I worshipped the Lord God of Israel, and bade another demon come forward. And there came before me a dragon, threeheaded, of fearful hue. And I questioned him: "Who art thou?" And he answered me: " I am a caltrop-like spirit ^, whose activity is in three lines. But I blind children in women's wombs, and twirl their ears round. And I make them deaf ^ and mute. And I have again in my third head means of slipping in'. And I smite men in the limbless * part of the body, and cause them to fall down, and foam, and grind their teeth. But I have my own way of being frustrated, Jerusalem being signified in writing, unto the place called ' of the head ' For there is fore-appointed the angel of the great counsel, and now he will openly dwell on the cross. He doth frastrate me, and to him am I subject." 55. " But in the place where thou sittest, King Solomon, standeth a column in the air, of purple. . . . ° The demon called EpMppas hath brought [it] up from the Red Sea, from inner Arabia. He it is that shall be shut up in a skin-bottle and brought before thee. But at the entrance of the Temple, which thou hast begun to build, King Solomon, lies stored much gold, which dig thou up and carry off." And I Solomon sent my servant, and found it to be as the demon told me. And I sealed him with my ring, and praised the Lord God. 56. So I said to him: " What art thou called? " And the demon said: " I am the crest ' of dragons." And I bade him make bricks in the Temple. He had human hands. 57. And I adored the Lord God of Israel, and bade another demon present himself. And there came before me a spirit in woman's form, that had a head without any limbs ', and her hair was dishevelled. And I said to her: "Who art thou?" But she answered: "Nay, who art thou? And why dost thou want to hear concerning me? But, as thou wouldst learn, here I stand bound before thj' face. Go then into thy royal storehouses and wash thy hands. Then sit down afresh before thy tribunal, and ask me questions; and thou shalt learn, king, who I am." 58. And I Solomon did as she enjoined me, and restrained myself because of the wisdom dwelling in me '; in order that I might hear of her deeds, and reprehend them, and manifest them to men. And I sat down, and said to the demon: " Who art thou? " And she said: " I am called among men Obizuth; and by night I sleep not, but go my rounds over all the world, and visit women in childbirth. And divining the hour I take my stand '; and if I am lucky, I strangle the child. But if not, I retire to another place. For I cannot for a single night retire unsuccessful. For I am a fierce ' spirit, of myriad names and many shapes. And now hither, now thither I roam. And to westering parts I go my rounds. But as it now is, though thou hast sealed me round with the ring of God, thou hast done nothing. ¹ am not standing before thee, and thou wilt not be able to command me. For I have no work other than the destruction of children, and the making their ears to be deaf, and the working of evil to their eyes, and the binding their mouths with a bond, and the ruin of their minds, and paining of their bodies." 59. When I Solomon heard this, I marvelled at her appearance, for I beheld all her body to be in darkness. But her glance was altogether bright and greeny, and her hair was tossed wildly like a dragon's; and the whole of her limbs were invisible. And her voice was very clear as it came to me. And I cunningly said: " Tell me by what angel thou art frustrated, evil spirit? " But she answered me: "By the angel of God called Afardf, which is interpreted Raphael, by whom I am frustrated now and for all time. His name, if any man know it, and write the same on a woman in childbirth, then I shall not be able to enter her. Of this name the number is 640 *." And I Solomon having heard this, and having glorified the Lord, ordered her hair to be bound, and that she should be hung up in front of the Temple of God; that all the children of Israel, as they passed, might see it, and glorify the Lord God of Israel, who had given me this authority, with wisdom and power from God, by means of this signet.[60]. And I again ordered another demon to come before me. And there came, rolling itself along, one in appearance like to a dragon, but having the face and hands of a man. And all its limbs, except its feet, were those of a dragon; and it had wings on its back. And when I beheld it, I was astonied, and said: " Who art thou, demon, and what art thou called? And whence hast thou come? Tell me." [61]. And the spirit answered and said: " This is the first time I have stood before thee, King Solomon. I am a spirit made into a god among men, but now brought to naught by the ring and wisdom vouchsafed to thee by God. Now I am the so-called winged dragon', and I chamber not with many women, but only with a few that are of fair shape, which possess the name of xull, of this star. And I pair with them in the guise of a spirit winged in form, coitnm hahens per nates. And she on whom I have leapt goes heavy with child, and that which is born of her becomes eros. But since such offspring cannot be carried by men, the woman in question breaks wind. Such is my role. Suppose then only that I am satisfied, and all the other demons molested and disturbed by thee will speak the whole truth. But those composed of fire ^ will cause to be burned up by fire the material of the logs which is to be collected by them for the building in the Temple." [62]. And as the demon said this, I saw the spirit going forth from his mouth, and it consumed the wood of the frankincense-tree, and burned up all the logs which we had placed in the Temple of God. And I Solomon saw what the spirit had done, and I marvelled. [63]. And, having glorified God, I asked the dragon-shaped demon, and said: " Tell me, by what angel art thou frustrated '? " And he answered: " By the great angel which has its seat in the second heaven, which is called in Hebrew Bazazath. And I Solomon, having heard this, and having invoked his angel, condemned him to saw up marbles for the building of the Temple of God; and I praised God, and commanded another demon to come before me. [64]. And there came before my face another spirit, as it were a woman in the form she had. But on her shoulders she had two other heads with hands. And I asked her, and said: " Tell me, who art thou? " And she said to me: " I am EnSpsigos, who also have a myriad names." And I said to her: " By what angel art thou frustrated? " But she said to me: " What seekest, what askest thou? I undergo changes, like the goddess I am called. And I change again, and pass into possession of another shape. And be not desirous therefore to know all that concerns me. But since thou art before me for this much, hearken. I have my abode in the moon, and for that reason I possess three forms. At times I am magically ' invoked by the wise as Kronos. At other times, in connexion with those who bring me down, I come down and appear in another shape. The measure of the element '^ is inexplicable and indefinable, and not to be frustrated. I then, changing into these three forms, come down and become such as thou seest me; but I am frustrated by the angel Bathanael, who sits in the third heaven. This then is why I speak to thee. Yonder temple cannot contain ' me." [65]. I therefore Solomon prayed to my God, and I invoked the angel of whom Enepsigos spoke to me, and used my seal. And I sealed her with a triple chain, and (placed) beneath her the fastening of the chain. I used the seal of God, and the spirit prophesied to me, saying: "This is what thou, King Solomon, doest to us. But after a time thy kingdom shall be broken, and again in season this Temple shall be riven asunder*; and all Jerusalem shall be undone by the King of the Persians and Medes and Chaldaeans. And the vessels of this Temple, which thou makest, shall be put to servile uses of the gods; and along with them all the jars, in which thou dost shut us up, shall be broken by the hands of men. And then

we shall go forth in great power hither and thither, and be disseminated all over the world. And we shall lead astray the inhabited world for a long season, until the Son of God is stretched upon the cross. For never before doth arise a king like unto him, one frustrating us all, whose mother shall not have contact with man. Who else can receive such authority over spirits, except he, whom the first devil will seek to tempt, but will not prevail over? The number of his name is [644] which is Emmanuel. Wherefore, King Solomon, thy time is evil, and thy years short and evil, and to thy servant shall thy kingdom be given *." [66]. And I Solomon, having heard this, glorified God. And though I marvelled at the apology of the demons, I did not credit it until it came true. And I did not believe their words; but when they were realized, then I understood, and at my death I wrote this Testament to the children of Israel, and gave it to them, so that they might know the powers of the demons and their shapes, and the names of their angels, by which these angels are frustrated. And I glorified the Lord God of Israel, and commanded the spirit to be bound with bonds indissoluble. [67]. And having praised God, I commanded another spirit to come before me; and there came before my face another demon, having in front the shape of ahorse, but behind of a fish. And he had a mighty voice, and said to me: " King Solomon, I am a fierce spirit of the sea, and I am greedy of gold and silver. I am such a spirit as rounds itself and comes over the expanses of the water of the sea, and I trip up the men who sail thereon. For I round myself into a wave ', and transform myself, and then throw myself on ships and come right in on them. And that is my business, and my way of getting hold of money and men. For I take the men, and whirl them round with myself, and hurl the men out of the sea. For I am not covetous of men's bodies, but cast them up out of the sea so far. But since Beelzebotd, ruler of the spirits of air and of those under the earth, and lord of earthly ones, hath a joint kingship with us in respect of the deeds of each one of us, therefore I went up from the sea, to get a certain outlook ^ in his company. [68]. "But I also have another character and rdle. I metamorphose myself into waves ^, and come up from the sea. And I show myself to men, so that those on earth call me Kunolsl-paston *, because I assume the human form. And my name is a true one. For by my passage up into men, I send forth a certain nausea. I came then to take counsel with the prince Beeleeboul; and he bound me and delivered me into thy hands. And I am here before thee because of this seal, and thou dost now torment me ^. Behold now, in two or three days the spirit that converseth with thee will fail, because I shall have no water." [69]. And I said to him: " Tell me by what angel thou art frus trated." And he answered: " By Iameth." And I glorified God. I commanded the spirit to be thrown into a phial along with ten jugs of sea- water of two measures each And I sealed them round above with marbles and asphalt and pitch in the mouth of the vesseP. And having sealed it with my ring, I ordered it to be deposited in the Temple of God. And I ordered another spirit to come before me. [70]. And there came before my face another enslaved' spirit, having obscurely the form of a man, with gleaming eyes, and bearing in his hand a blade. And I asked: " Who art thou? " But he answered: "I am a lascivious* spirit, engendered of a giant man who died in the massacre in the time of the giants." I said to him: " Tell me what thou art employed on upon earth, and where thou hast thy dwelling." [71]. Andhe said: "My dwelling is in fruitful places, but my procedure is this. I seat myself beside the men who pass along among the tombs, and in untimely season I assume the form of the dead; and if I catch any one, I at once destroy him with my sword. But if I cannot destroy him, I cause him to be possessed with a demon, and to devour his own flesh, and the hair to fall off his chin." But I said to him: " Do thou then be in fear of the God of heaven and of earth, and tell me by what angel thou art frustrated." And he answered: " He destroys me who is to become Saviour, a man whose number °, if any one shall write it on his forehead % he will defeat me, and in fear I shall quickly retreat. And, indeed, if any one write this sign on him, I shall be in fear." And I Solomon, on hearing this, and having glorified the Lord God, shut up this demon like the rest. 72. And I commanded another demon to come before me. And there came before my face thirty-six spirits, their heads shapeless like dogs, but in themselves they were human in form; with faces of asses, faces of oxen, and faces of birds. And I Solomon, on hearing and seeing them, wondered, and I asked them and said: " Who are you?" But they, of one accord with one voice, said ': " We are the thirtysix elements, the world-rulers " of this darkness. But, King Solomon, thou wilt not wrong us nor imprison us, nor lay command on us; but since the Lord God has given thee authority over every spirit, in the air, and on the earth, and under the earth, therefore do we also present ourselves before thee like the other spirits, from ram and bull, from both twin and crab, lion and virgin, scales and scorpion, archer, goat-homed, water-pourer, and fish. 73. Then I Solomon invoked the name of the Lord Sahadth, and questioned each in turn as to what was its character. And I bade each one come forward and tell of its actions. Then the first one came foi-ward, and said: "I am the first decanus^ of the zodiacal circle, and I am called the ram, and with me are these two." So I put to them the question: "Who are ye called?" The first said: "¹, Lord, am called Ruax, and I cause the heads of men to be idle, and I pillage their brows. But let me only hear the words, 'Michael, imprison Ruax,' and at once I retreat." 74. And the second said: " I am called Barsafael, and I cause those who are subject to my hour * to feel the pain of migrain '. If only I hear the words, ' Gabriel, imprison Barsafael,' at once I retreat." 75. The third said: " I am called ArStosael. I do harm to eyes, and grievously injure them. Only let me hear the words, ' Uriel, imprison AraiosaeV {sic), at once I retreat " 76. The fifth said: " I am called Iitdal, and I bring about a block in the ears and deafness of hearing. If I hear, ' Uruel Ivdal,' I at once retreat." 77. The sixth said: "I am called Sphendonael. I cause tumours of the parotid gland, and inflammations of the tonsils, and tetanic recurvation. If I hear, ' Sabrael, imprison SphendonaSl,' at once I retreat." 78. And the seventh said: " I am called SphandSr, and I weaken the strength of the shoulders, and cause them to tremble; and I paralyze the nerves of the hands, and I break and bruise the bones of the neck. And I, I suck out the marrow. But if I hear the words, 'Arail, imprison Sphanddr,' I at once retreat." 79. And the eighth said: " I am called Belhel. I distort the hearts and minds of men. If I hear the words, 'AraSl, imprison Belhel,' I at once retreat." 80. And the ninth said: " I am called Kurtael. I send colics in the bowels. I induce pains. If I hear the words, 'ladth, imprison Kurtail,' I at once retreat." 81. The tenth said: "I am called Metaihiax. I cause the reins to ache. If I hear the words, 'AddnaSl, imprison Metathiax,' I at once retreat." 82. The eleventh said: " I am called KatanikotaSl. I create strife and wrongs in men's homes, and send on them hard temper. If any one would be at peace in his home, let him write on seven leaves of laurel the names of the angel that frustrates me, along with these names: lae, led, sons of Sabadth, in the name of the great God let him shut up Katanikotall. Then let him wash the laurel-leaves in water, and sprinkle his house with the water, from within to the outside. And at once I retreat." 83. The twelfth said: " I am called SaphathoraM, and I inspire partisanship in men, and delight in causing them to stumble. If any one will write on paper these names of angels, laed, leald, Idelet, Sabadth, Ithoih, Bae, and having folded it up, wear it round his neck or against his ear, I at once retreat and dissipate the drunken fit." 84. The thirteenth said: " I am called Bobil {sic), and I cause nervous illness by my assaults. If I hear the name of the great ' Adonael, imprison BoihoihM, I at once retreat." 85. The fourteenth said: "I am called KumeatSl, and I inflict shivering fits and torpor. If only I hear the words: 'ZdroSl, imprison Kumentael,' I at once retreat." 86. The fifteenth said: " I am called Roeled. I cause cold and frost and pain in the stomach. Let me only hear the words: '⁷a a;, bide not, be not warmed, for Solomon is fairer than eleven fathers,' I at retreat." 87. The sixteenth said: " I am called Atrax. I inflict upon men fevers, irremediable and harmful. If you would imprison me, chop up coriander' and smear it on the lips, reciting the following charm: ' The fever which is from dirt. I exorcise the e by the throne of the most high God, retreat from dirt and retreat from the creature fashioned by God.' And at once I retreat." 88. The seventeenth said: " I am called Ieropael. On the stomach of men I sit, and cause convulsions in the bath and in the road; and wherever I be found, or find a man, I throw him down. But if any one will say to the afflicted into their ear these names, three times over, into the right ear: ' ludarizi, Sabuni, DendS,^ I at once retreat." 89. The eighteenth said: " I am called Buldumich. I separate wife from husband and bring about a grudge between them. If any one write down the names of thy sires, Solomon, on paper and place it in the ante-chamber of his house, I retreat thence. And the legend written shall be as follows: ' The God of Abram, and the God of Isaac, and the God of Jacob commands thee—retire from this house in peace.' And I at once retire."90. The nineteenth said: " I am called Na⁶th, and I take my seat on the knees of men. If any one write on paper: ' Phnunohoeol, depart Nathath, and touch thou not the neck,' I at once retreat." 91. The twentieth said: "I am called Marderd. I send on men incurable fever. If any one write on the leaf of a book: ' Sphener, Rafael, retire, drag me not about, flay me not, and tie it round his neck,' I at once retreat." 92. The twenty-first said: "I am called Alath, and I cause coughing and hard-breathing in children. If any one write on paper: ' Eorex, do thou pursue Alath,' and fasten it round his neck, ¹ at once retire . . . ' " 93. The twenty-third said: " I am called Nefthada. ¹ cause the reins to ache, and I bring about dysury. If any one write on a plate of tin the words: ' lathdth, TJruel, Nephthada, and iasten it round the loins, I at once retreat." 94. The twenty-fourth said: " I am called Akton. I cause ribs and lumbic muscles to ache. If one engrave on copper material, taken from a ship which has missed its anchorage, this: ' Marmaraoth, Sabadth, pursue Akton,' and fasten it round the loin, I at once retreat." 95. The twenty-fifth said: " I am called Anatreih, and I send burnings and fevers into the entrails. But if I hear: ' Arara, Charara,' instantly do I retreat." 96. The twenty-sixth said: " I am called Enenuth. I steal away men's minds, and change their hearts, and make a man toothless. If one write: ' Allazool, pursue Enenuth,^ and tie the paper round him, I at once retreat." 97. The twenty-seventh said: "I am called Pheth. I make men consumptive and cause hemorrhagia. If one exorcise me in wine, sweet-smelling and unmixed by the eleventh aeon'^, and say: ' I exorcise thee by the eleventh aeon to stop, I demand, Pheth (Axidpheth),' then give it to the patient to drink, and I at once retreat." 98. The twenty-eighth said: " I am called Harpax, and I send sleeplessness on men. If one vrrite ' Kokphnedismos,' and bind it round the temples, I at once retire." 99. The twenty-ninth said: " I am called Anoster. ¹ engender uterine mania and pains in the bladder. If one powder into pure oil three seeds of laurel and smear it on, saying: ' I exorcise thee, Anoster. Stop by Marmarad,' at once I retreat." 100. The thirtieth said: " I am called AUeborifh. If in eating fish one has swallowed a bone, then he must take a bone from the fish and cough, and at once I retreat." 101. The thirty-first said: "I am called Hephesikirefh, and cause lingering disease. If you throw salt, rubbed in the hand, into oil and smear it on the patient, saying: ' Seraphim, Cherubim, help me! ' I at once retire." 102. The thirty-second said: " I am called Ichthion. I paralyze muscles and contuse them. If I hear: ' Adonaeth, help! ' I at once retire." 103. The thirty-third said: " I am called Agehonidn. I lie among swaddling-clothes and in the precipice. And if any one write on fig-leaves ' Li/curgos,' taking away one letter at a time, and write it, reversing the letters, I retire at once. ' Lycurgos, yeurgos, kurgos, yrgos, gos, os ^.' " 104. The thirty-fourth said: " I am called Autothith. I cause grudges and fighting. Therefore I am frustrated by Alpha and Omega, if written down." 105. The thirty-fifth said: " I am called Phthenoth. ¹ cast evil eye on every man. Therefore, the eye much-suifering, if it be drawn, frustrates me." 106. The thirty-sixth said: "I am called Bianakith. I have a grudge against the body. I lay waste houses, I cause flesh to decay, and all else that is similar. If a man write on the front-door of his house: 'Meltd, Ardu, Anaath,' I flee from that place." 107. And I Solomon, when I heard this, glorified the God of heaven and earth. And I commanded them to fetch water in the Temple of God. And I furthermore prayed to the Lord God to cause the demons without, that hamper humanity, to be bound and made to approach the Temple of God. Some of these demons I condemned to do the heavy work of the construction of the Temple of God. Others I shut up in prisons. Others I ordered to wrestle with fire in (the making of) gold and silver, sitting down by lead and spoon. And to make readj' places for the other demons in which they should be confined. 108. And I Solomon had much quiet in all the earth, and spent my life in profound peace, honoured by all men and by all under heaven. And I built the entire Temple of the Lord God. And my kingdom was prosperous, and my army was with me. And for the rest the city of Jerusalem had repose, rejoicing and delighted. And all the kings of the earth came to me from the ends of the earth to behold the Temple which I builded to the Lord God. And having heard of the wisdom given to me, they did homage to me in the Temple, bringing gold and silver and precious stones, many and divers, and bronze, and iron, and lead, and cedar logs. And woods that decay not they brought me, for the equipment of the Temple of God. 109. And among them also the queen of the south, being a witch ', came in great concern and bowed low before me to the earth. And having heard my wisdom, she glorified the God of Israel, and she made formal trial of all my wisdom, of all the love in which I instructed her, according to the wisdom imparted to me. And all the sons of Israel glorified God. 110. And behold, in those days one of the workmen, of ripe old age, threw himself down before me, and said: " King Solomon, pity me, because I am old." So I bade him stand up, and said: " Tell me, old man, all you will." And he answered: " I beseech you, king, I have an only-bom son, and he insults and beats me openly, and plucks out the hair of my head, and threatens me with a painful death. Therefore I beseech you, avenge me." 111. And I Solomon, on hearing this, felt compunction as I looked at his old age; and I bade the child be brought to me. And when he was brought I questioned him whether it were true. And the youth said: "I was not so filled with madness as to strike my father with my hand. Be kind to me, king. For I have not dared to commit such impiety, poor wretch that I am." But I Solomon, on hearing this from the youth, exhorted the old man to reflect on the matter, and accept his son's apology. However, he would not, but said he would rather let him die. And as the old man would not yield, I was about to pronounce sentence on the youth, when I saw Ornias the demon laughing. I was very angry at the demon's laughing in my presence; and I ordered my men to remove the other parties, and bring forward Ornias before my tribunal. And when he was brought before me, I said to him: " Accursed one, why didst thou look at me

and laugh? " And the demon answered: "Prithee, king, it was not because of thee I laughed, but because of this ill-starred old man and the wretched youth, his son. For after three days his son will die untimely; and lo, the old man desires to foully make away with him." 112. But I Solomon, having heard this, said to the demon: " Is that true that thou speakest?" And he answered: "It is true, king." And I, on hearing that, bade them remove the demon, and that they should again bring before me the old man with his son. I bade them make friends with one another again, and I supplied them with food. And then I told the old man after three days to bring his son again to me here; " and," said I, "I will. attend to him." And they saluted me, and went their way. 113. And when they were gone I ordered Omias to be brought forward, and said to him: " Tell me how you know this; " and he answered: " We demons ascend into the firmament of heaven, and fly about among the stars. And we hear the sentences which go forth upon the souls of men, and forthwith we come, and whether by force of influence *, or by fire, or by sword, or by some accident, we veil our act of destruction; and if a man does not die by some untimely disaster or by violence, then we demons transform ourselves in such a way as to appear to men and be worshipped in our human nature." 114. I therefore, having heard this, glorified the Lord God, and again I questioned the demon, saying: " Tell me how ye can ascend into heaven, being demons, and amidst the stars and holy angels intermingle." And he answered: "Just as things are fulfilled in heaven, so also on earth (are fulfilled) the types * of all of them. For there are principalities, authorities, world -rulers', and we demons fly about in the air; and we hear the voices of the heavenly beings, and survey all the powers. And as having no ground (basis) on which to alight and rest, we lose strength and fall off like leaves from trees. And men seeing us imagine that the stars are falling from heaven. But it is not really so, king; but we fall because of our weakness, and because we have nowhere anything to lay hold of; and so we fall down like lightnings* in the depth of night and suddenly. And we set cities in flames and fire the fields. For the stars have firm foundations in the heaven, like the sun and the moon." 115. And I Solomon, having heard this, ordered the demon to be guarded for five days. And after the five days I recalled the old man, and was about to question him. But he came to me in grief and with black face. And I said to him: " Tell me, old man, where is thy son? And what means this garb? " And he answered: " Lo, I am become childless, and sit by my son's grave in despair. For it is already two days that he is dead." But I Solomon, on hearing that, and knowing that the demon Omias had told me the truth, glorified the God of Israel. 116. And the queen of the south saw all this, and marvelled, glorifying the God of Israel; and she beheld the Temple of the Lord being builded. And she gave a siklos of gold and one hundred myriads of silver and choice bronze, and she went into the Temple. And (she beheld) the altar of incense and the brazen supports of this altar, and the gems of the lamps flashing forth of different colours, and of the lamp-stand of stone, and of emerald, and hyacinth, and sapphire; and she beheld the vessels of gold, and silver, and bronze, and wood, and the folds of skins dyed red with madder. And she saw the bases of the pillars of the Temple of the Lord. All were of one gold . . . . apart from the demons whom I condemned to labour. And there was peace in the circle of my kingdom and over all the earth. 117. And it came to pass, while I was in my kingdom, the King of the Arabians, Adares, sent me a letter, and the writing of the letter was written as follows: — " To King Solomon, all hail! Lo, we have heard, and it hath been heard unto all the ends of the earth, concerning the wisdom vouchsafed in thee, and that thou art a man merciful from the Lord. And understanding hath been granted thee over all the spirits of the air, and on earth, and under the earth. Now, forasmuch as there is present in the land of Arabia a spirit of the following kind: at early dawn there begins to blow a certain wind until the third hour. And its blast is harsh and terrible, and it slays man and beast. And no spirit can live upon earth against this demon. I pray thee then, forasmuch as the spirit is a wind, contrive something according to the wisdom given in thee by the Lord thy God, and deign to send a man able to capture it. And behold, King Solomon, I and my people and all my land will serve thee unto death. And all Arabia shall be at peace with thee, if thou wilt perform this act of righteousness for us. Wherefore we pray thee, contemn not our humble prayer, and suffer not to be utterly brought to naught the eparchy subordinated to thy authority. Because we are thy suppliants, both I and my people and all my land. Farewell to my Lord. All health! " [118]. And I Solomon read this epistle; and I folded it up and gave it to my people, and said to them: " After seven days shalt thou remind me of this epistle. And Jerusalem was built, and the Temple was being completed. And there was a stone ', the end stone of the comer lying there, great, chosen out, one which I desired to lay in the head of the corner of the completion of the Temple. And all the workmen, and all the demons helping them, came to the same place to bring up the stone and lay it on the pinnacle ^ of the holy Temple, and were not strong enough to stir it, and lay it upon the corner allotted to it. For that stone was exceedingly great and useful for the comer of the Temple." [119]. And after seven days, being reminded of the epistle oi Adares, King of Arabia, I called my servant and said to him: " Order thy camel and take for thyself a leather flask, and take also this seal. And go away into Arabia to the place in which the evil spirit blows; and there take the flask, and the signet-ring in front of the mouth of the flask, and (hold them) towards the blast of the spirit. And when the flask is blown out, thou wilt understand that the demon is (in it). Then hastily tie up the mouth of the flask, and seal it securely with the seal-ring, and lay it carefully on the camel and bring it me hither. And if on the way it offer thee gold or silver or treasure in return for letting it go, see that thou be not persuaded. But arrange without using oath to release it. And then if it point out to the places where are gold or silver, mark the places and seal them with this seal. And bring the demon to me. And now depart, and fare thee well." [120]. Then the youth did as was bidden him. And he ordered his camel, and laid on it a flask, and set off into Arabia. And the men of that region would not believe that he would be able to catch the evil spirit. And when it was dawn, the servant stood before the spirit's blast, and laid the flask on the ground, and the finger-ring on the mouth of the flask. And the demon blew through the middle of the finger-ring into the mouth of the flask, and going in blew out the flask. But the man promptly stood up to it and drew tight with his hand the mouth of the flask, in the name of the Lord God of Sabadth. And the demon remained within the flask. And after that the youth remained in that land three days to make trial. And the spirit no longer blew against that city. And all the Arabs knew that he had safely shut in the spirit. [121]. Then the youth fastened the flask on the camel, and the Arabs sent him forth on his way with much honour and precious gifts, praising and magnifying the God of Israel. But the youth brought in the bag and laid it in the middle of the Temple. And on the next day, I King Solomon, went into the Temple of God and sat in deep distress about the stone of the end of the corner. And when I entered the Temple, the flask stood up and walked around some seven steps, and then fell on its mouth and did homage to me. And I marvelled that even along with the bottle the demon still had power and could walk about; and I commanded it to stand up. And the flask stood up, and stood on its feet all blown out. And I questioned him, saying: " Tell me, who art thou? " And

the spirit within said: "I am the demon called Ephippas, that is in Arabia." And I said to him: " Is this thy name? " And he answered: " Yes; wheresoever I will, I alight and set fire and do to death." [122]. And I said to him: " By what angel art thou frustrated?" And he answered: " By the only-ruling God, that hath authority over me even to be heard. He that is to be bom of a virgin and crucified by the Jews on a cross. Whom the angels and archangels worship. He doth frustrate me, and enfeeble me of my great strength, which has been given me by my father the devil." And I said to him: "What canst thou do? " And he answered: " I am able to remove * mountains, to overthrow the oaths of kings. I wither trees and make their leaves to fall off." And I said to him: " Canst thou raise this stone, and lay it for the beginning of this comer which exists in the fair plan of the Temple ? " And he said: " Not only raise this, king; but also, with the help of the demon who presides over the Red Sea, I will bring up the pillar of air', and will stand it where thou wilt in Jerusalem. [123]. Saying this, I laid stress on him, and the flask became as if depleted of air. And I placed it under the stone, and (the spirit) girded himself up, and lifted it up top of the flask. And the flask went up the steps, carrying the stone, and laid it down at the end of the entrance of the Temple. And I Solomon, beholding the stone raised aloft and placed on a foundation, said: " Truly the Scripture is fulfilled, which says: ' The stone which the builders rejected on trial, that same is become the head of the comer.' For this it is not mine to grant, but God's, that the demon should be strong enough to lift up so great a stone and deposit it in the place I wished." [124]. And Ephippas led the demon of the Red Sea with the column. And they both took the column and raised it aloft from the earth. And I outwitted * these two spirits, so that they could not shake the entire earth in a moment of time. And then I sealed round with my ring on this side and that, and said: "Watch." And the spirits have remained upholding it until this day, for proof of the wisdom vouchsafed to me. And there the pillar was hanging, of enormous size, in mid air, supported by the winds. And thus the spirits appeared underneath, like air, supporting it. And if one looks fixedly, the pillar is a little oblique, being supported by the spirits; and it is so to this day. [125]. And I Solomon questioned the other spirit, which came up with the pillar from the depth of the Red Sea. And I said to him: "Who art thou, and what calls thee? And what is thy business? For I hear many things about thee." And the demon answered: "I, O King Solomon, am called Abezithibod. I am a descendant of the archangel. Once as I sat in the first heaven, of which the name is Ameleouth—I then am a fierce spirit and winged, and with a single wing, plotting against every spirit under heaven. I was present when Moses went in before Pharaoh, king of Egypt, and I hardened his heart. I am he whom Iannes and Iambres invoked homing with Moses in Egypt. I am he who fought against Moses with wonders with signs." [126]. I said therefore to him: "How wast thou found in the Red Sea?" And he answered: "In the exodus of the sons of Israel I hardened the heart of Pharaoh. And I excited his heart and that of his ministers. And I caused them to pursue after the children of Israel. And Pharaoh followed with (me) and all the Egyptians. Then I was present there, and we followed together. And we all came up upon the Red Sea. And it came to pass when the children of Israel had crossed over, the water returned and hid all the host of the Egyptians and all their might. And I remained in the sea, being kept under this pillar. But when Ephippas came, being sent by thee, shut up in the vessel of a flask, he fetched me up to thee." [127]. I, therefore, Solomon, having heard this, glorified God and adjured the demons not to disobey me, but to remain supporting the pillar. And they both sware, saying: "The Lord thy God liveth, we will not let go this pillar until the world's end. But on whatever day this stone fall, then shall be the end of the world. [128]. And I Solomon glorified God, and adorned the Temple of the Lord with all fair-seeming. And I was glad in spirit in my kingdom, and there was peace in my days. And I took wives of my own from every land, who were numberless. And I marched against the Jebusaeans, and there I saw a Jebusaean, daughter of a man; and fell violently in love with her, and desired to take her to wife along with my other wives. And I said to their priests: "Give me the Sonmanites (i.e. Shunammite) to wife." But the priests of Moloch said to me: "If thou lovest this maiden, go in and worship our gods, the great god Raphan and the god called Moloch." I therefore was in fear of the glory of God, and did not follow to worship. And I said to them: "I will not worship a strange god. What is this proposal, that ye compel me to do so much?" But they said: "… by our fathers." [129]. And when I answered that I would on no account worship strange gods, they told the maiden not to sleep with me until I complied and sacrificed to the gods. I then was moved, but crafty Eros brought and laid by her for me five grasshoppers, saying: "Take these grasshoppers, and crush them together in the name of the god Moloch; and then will I sleep with you." And this I actually did. And at once the Spirit of God departed from me, and I became weak as well as foolish in my words. And after that I was obliged by her to build a temple of idols to Baal, and to Rapha, and to Moloch, and to the other idols. [130]. I then, wretch that I am, followed her advice, and the glory of God quite departed from me; and my spirit was darkened, and I became the sport of idols and demons. Wherefore I wrote out this Testament, that ye who get possession of it may pray, and attend to the last things, and not to the first. So that ye may find grace for ever and ever. Amen.

The Psalms of Solomon

Ps. Sol. 1. The Ancient Pseudepigraphal Book

[1] I cried unto the Lord when I was in distress [ ], Unto God when sinners assailed. [2] Suddenly the alarm of war was heard before me; (I said), He will hearken to me, for I am full of righteousness. [3] I thought in my heart that I was full of righteousness, Because I was well off and had become rich in children. [4] Their wealth spread to the whole earth, And their glory unto the end of the earth. [5] They were exalted unto the stars; They said they would never fall. [6] But they became insolent in their prosperity, And they were without understanding, [7] Their sins were in secret, And even I had no knowledge (of them). [8] Their transgressions (went) beyond those of the heathen before them; They utterly polluted the holy things of the Lord.

Ps. Sol. 2. A Psalm Of Solomon. Concerning Jerusalem

[2] [1] When the sinner waxed proud, with a battering-ram he cast down fortified walls, And Thou didst not restrain (him). [2] Alien nations ascended Thine altar, They trampled (it) proudly with their sandals; [3] Because the sons of Jerusalem had defiled the holy things of the Lord, Had profaned with iniquities the offerings of God. [4] Therefore He said: Cast them far from Me; [5] It was set at naught before God, It was utterly dishonoured; [6] The sons and the daughters were in grievous captivity, Sealed (?) (was) their neck, branded (?) (was it) among the nations. [7] According to their sins hath He done unto them, For He hath left them in the hands of them that prevailed. [8] He hath turned away His face from pitying them, Young and old and their children together; [9] For they had done evil one and all, in not hearkening. [10] And the heavens were angry, And the earth abhorred them; [11] For no man upon it had done what they did, [12] And the earth recognized all Thy righteous judgements, O God. [13] They set the sons of Jerusalem to be mocked at in return for (the) harlots in her; Every wayfarer entered in in the full light of day. [14] They made mock with their transgressions, as they themselves were wont to do; In the full light of day they revealed their iniquities. And the daughters of Jerusalem were defiled in accordance with Thy judgement, [15] Because they had defiled themselves with unnatural intercourse. I am pained in my bowels and my inward parts for these things. (And yet) I will justify Thee, O God, in uprightness of heart, For in Thy judgements is Thy righteousness (displayed), O God. [17] For Thou hast rendered to the sinners according to their deeds, Yea according to their sins, which were very wicked. [18] Thou hast uncovered their sins, that Thy judgement might be manifest; [19] Thou hast wiped out their memorial from the earth. God is a righteous judge, And He is no respecter of persons. [20] For the nations reproached Jerusalem, trampling it down; Her beauty was dragged down from the throne of glory. [21] She girded on sackcloth instead of comely raiment, A rope (was) about her head instead of a crown. [22] She put off the glorious diadem which God had set upon her, [23] In dishonour was her beauty cast upon the ground. [24] And I saw and entreated the Lord and said, Long enough, O Lord, has Thine hand been heavy on Israel, in bringing the nations upon (them). [25] For they have made sport unsparingly in wrath and fierce anger; [26] And they will make an utter end, unless Thou, O Lord, rebuke them in Thy wrath. [27] For they have done it not in zeal, but in lust of soul, [28] Pouring out their wrath upon us with a view to rapine. [29] Delay not, O God, to recompense them on (their) heads, To turn the pride of the dragon into dishonour. [30] And I had not long to wait before God showed me the insolent one Slain on the mountains of Egypt, Esteemed of less account than the least on land and sea; [31] His body, (too,) borne hither and thither on the billows with much insolence, With none to bury (him), because He had rejected him with dishonour. He reflected not that he was man. [32] And reflected not on the latter end; [33] He said: I will be lord of land and sea; And he recognized not that it is God who is great, Mighty in His great strength. [34] He is king over the heavens, And judgeth kings and kingdoms. [35] (It is He) who setteth me up in glory, And bringeth down the proud to eternal destruction in dishonour, Because they knew Him not. [36] And now behold, ye princes of the earth, the judgement of the Lord, For a great king and righteous (is He), judging (all) that is under heaven. [37] Bless God, ye that fear the Lord with wisdom, For the mercy of the Lord will be upon them that fear Him, in the Judgement; [38] So that He will distinguish between the righteous and the sinner, (And) recompense the sinners for ever according to their deeds; [39] And have mercy on the righteous, (delivering him) from the affliction of the sinner, And recompensing the sinner for what he hath done to the righteous. [40] For the Lord is good to them that call upon Him in patience, Doing according to His mercy to His pious ones, Establishing (them) at all times before Him in strength. [41] Blessed be the Lord for ever before His servants.

Ps. Sol. 3. A Psalm Of Solomon. Concerning the righteous.

[3] [1] Why sleepest thou, O my soul, And blessest not the Lord? [2] Sing a new song, Unto God who is worthy to be praised. Sing and be wakeful against His awaking, For good is a psalm (sung) to God from a glad heart. [3] The righteous remember the Lord at all times, With thanksgiving and declaration of the righteousness of the Lord's judgements [4] The righteous despiseth not the chastening of the Lord; His will is always before the Lord. [5] The righteous stumbleth and holdeth the Lord righteous: He falleth and looketh out for what God will do to him; [6] He seeketh out whence his deliverance will come. [7] The steadfastness of the righteous is from God their deliverer; There lodgeth not in the house of the righteous sin upon sin. [8] The righteous continually searcheth his house, To remove utterly (all) iniquity (done) by him in error. [9] He maketh atonement

for (sins of) ignorance by fasting and afflicting his soul, [10] And the Lord counteth guiltless every pious man and his house. [11] The sinner stumbleth and curseth his life, The day when he was begotten, and his mother's travail. [12] He addeth sins to sins, while he liveth (?); [13] He falleth -verily grievous is his fall- and riseth no more. The destruction of the sinner is for ever, [14] And he shall not be remembered, when the righteous is visited. [15] This is the portion of sinners for ever. [16] But they that fear the Lord shall rise to life eternal, And their life (shall be) in the light of the Lord, and shall come to an end no more.

Ps. Sol. 4. A Conversation of Solomon with the Men-pleasers.

[4] [1] Wherefore sittest thou, O profane (man), in the council of the pious, Seeing that thy heart is far removed from the Lord, Provoking with transgressions the God of Israel? [2] Extravagant in speech, extravagant in outward seeming beyond all (men), Is he that is severe of speech in condemning sinners in judgement. [3] And his hand is first upon him as (though he acted) in zeal, And (yet) he is himself guilty in respect of manifold sins and of wantonness. [4] His eyes are upon every woman without distinction; His tongue lieth when he maketh contract with an oath. [5] By night and in secret he sinneth as though unseen, With his eyes he talketh to every woman of evil compacts. [6] He is swift to enter every house with cheerfulness as though guileless. [7] Let God remove those that live in hypocrisy in the company of the pious, (Even) the life of such an one with corruption of his flesh and penury. [8] Let God reveal the deeds of the men-pleasers, The deeds of such an one with laughter and derision; [9] That the pious may count righteous the judgement of their God, When sinners are removed from before the righteous, [10] (Even the) man- pleaser who uttereth law guilefully. [11] And their eyes (are fixed) upon any man's house that is (still) secure, That they may, like (the) Serpent, destroy the wisdom of… with words of transgressors, [12] His words are deceitful that (he) may accomplish (his) wicked desire. [13] He never ceaseth from scattering (families) as though (they were) orphans, Yea, he layeth waste a house on account of (his) lawless desire. [14] He deceiveth with words, (saying,) There is none that seeth, or judgeth. [15] He fills one (house) with lawlessness, And (then) his eyes (are fixed) upon the next house, To destroy it with words that give wing to (desire). (Yet) with all these his soul, like Sheol, is not sated. [16] Let his portion, O Lord, be dishonoured before thee; Let him go forth groaning and come home cursed. [17] Let his life be (spent) in anguish, and penury, and want, O Lord; Let his sleep be (beset) with pains and his awaking with perplexities. [18] Let sleep be withdrawn from his eyelids at night; Let him fail dishonorably in every work of his hands. [19] Let him come home empty-handed to his house, And his house be void of everything wherewith he could sate his appetite. [20] (Let) his old age (be spent) in childless loneliness until his removal (by death). [21] Let the flesh of the men-pleasers be rent by wild beasts, And (let) the bones of the lawless (lie) dishonoured in the sight of the sun. [22] Let ravens peck out the eyes of the hypocrites. [23] For they have laid waste many houses of men, in dishonour, And scattered (them) in (their) lust; [24] And they have not remembered God, Nor feared God in all these things; [25] But they have provoked God's anger and vexed Him. May He remove them from off the earth, Because with deceit they beguiled the souls of the flawless. [26] Blessed are they that fear the Lord in their flawlessness; [27] The Lord shall deliver them from guileful men and sinners, And deliver us from every stumbling-block of the lawless (men). [28] Let God destroy them that insolently work all unrighteousness, For a great and mighty judge is the Lord our God in righteousness. [29] Let Thy mercy, O Lord, be upon all them that love Thee.

Ps. Sol. 5. A Psalm Of Solomon

[5] [1] O Lord God, I will praise Thy name with joy, In the midst of them that know Thy righteous judgements. [2] For Thou art good and merciful, the refuge of the poor; [3] When I cry to Thee, do not silently disregard me. [4] For no man taketh spoil from a mighty man; [5] Who, then, can take aught of all that Thou hast made, except Thou Thyself givest? [6] For man and his portion (lie) before Thee in the balance; He cannot add to, so as to enlarge, what has been prescribed by Thee. O God, [7] when we are in distress we call upon Thee for help, And Thou dost not turn back our petition, for Thou art our God. [8] Cause not Thy hand to be heavy upon us, Lest through necessity we sin. [9] Even though Thou restore us not, we will not keep away; But unto Thee will we come. [10] For if I hunger, unto Thee will I cry, O God; And Thou wilt give to me. [11] Birds and fish dost Thou nourish, In that Thou givest rain to the steppes that green grass may spring up, (So) to prepare fodder in the steppe for every living thing; [12] And if they hunger, unto Thee do they lift up their face. [13] Kings and rulers and peoples Thou dost nourish, O God; And who is the help of the poor and needy, if not Thou, O Lord? [14] And Thou wilt hearken -for who is good and gentle but Thou?- Making glad the soul of the humble by opening Thine hand in mercy. [15] Man's goodness is (bestowed) grudgingly and …, And if he repeat (it) without murmuring, even that is marvellous. [16] But Thy gift is great in goodness and wealth, And he whose hope is (set) on Thee shall have no lack of gifts. [17] Upon the whole earth is Thy mercy, O Lord, in goodness. [18] Happy is he whom God remembereth in (granting to him) a due sufficiency; [19] If a man abound over much, he sinneth. [20] Sufficient are moderate means with righteousness, And hereby the blessing of the Lord (becomes) abundance with righteousness. [21] They that fear the Lord rejoice in good (gifts), And Thy goodness is upon Israel in Thy kingdom. Blessed is the glory of the Lord for He is our king.

Ps. Sol. 6. In Hope. Of Solomon

[6] [1] Happy is the man whose heart is fixed to call upon the name of the Lord; [2] When he remembereth the name of the Lord, he will be saved. [3] His ways are made even by the Lord, And the works of his hands are preserved by the Lord his God. [4] At what he sees in his bad dreams, his soul shall not be troubled; [5] When he passes through rivers and the tossing of the seas, he shall not be dismayed. [6] He ariseth from his sleep, and blesseth the name of the Lord: [7] When his heart is at peace, he singeth to the name of his God, And he entreateth the Lord for all his house. [8] And the Lord heareth the prayer of every one that feareth God, And every request of the soul that hopes for Him doth the Lord accomplish. [9] Blessed is the Lord, who showeth mercy to those who love Him in sincerity.

Ps. Sol. 7. Of Solomon. Of turning

[7] [1] Make not Thy dwelling afar from us, O God; Lest they assail us that hate us without cause. [2] For Thou hast rejected them, O God; Let not their foot trample upon Thy holy inheritance. [3] Chasten us Thyself in Thy good pleasure; But give (us) not up to the nations; [4] For, if Thou sendest pestilence, Thou Thyself givest it charge concerning us; For Thou art merciful, And wilt not be angry to the point of consuming us. [5] While Thy name dwelleth in our midst, we shall find mercy; [6] And the nations shall not prevail against us. For Thou art our shield, [7] And when we call upon Thee, Thou hearkenest to us; [8] For Thou wilt pity the seed of Israel for ever And Thou wilt not reject (them): But we (shall be) under Thy yoke for ever, And (under) the rod of Thy chastening. [9] Thou wilt establish us in the time that Thou helpest us, Showing mercy to the house of Jacob on the day wherein Thou didst promise (to help them).

Ps. Sol. 8. Of Solomon Of the chief Musician

8 ¹ Distress and the sound of war hath my ear heard; The sound of a trumpet announcing slaughter and calamity, ² The sound of much people as of an exceeding high wind, As a tempest with mighty fire sweeping through the Negeb. ³ And I said in my heart; Surely (?) God judgeth us; ⁴ A sound I hear (moving) towards Jerusalem, the holy city. ⁵ My loins were broken at what I heard, my knees tottered: ⁶ My heart was afraid, my bones were dismayed like flax. ⁷ I said: They establish their ways in righteousness. I thought upon the judgements of God since the creation of heaven and earth; I held God righteous in His judgements which have been from of old. ⁸ God laid bare their sins in the full light of day; All the earth came to know the righteous judgements of God. ⁹ In secret places underground their iniquities (were committed) to provoke (Him) to anger; ¹⁰ They wrought confusion, son with mother and father with daughter; ¹¹ They committed adultery, every man with his neighbour's wife. They concluded covenants with one another with an oath touching these things; ¹² They plundered the sanctuary of God, as though there was no avenger. ¹³ They trode the altar of the Lord, (coming straight) from all manner of uncleanness; And with menstrual blood they defiled the sacrifices, as (though these were) common flesh. ¹⁴ They left no sin undone, wherein they surpassed not the heathen. ¹⁵ Therefore God mingled for them a spirit of wandering; And gave them to drink a cup of undiluted wine, that they might become drunken. ¹⁶ He brought him that is from the end of the earth, that smiteth mightily; ¹⁷ He decreed (?) war against Jerusalem, and against her land. ¹⁸ The princes of the land went to meet him with joy: they said unto him: Blessed be thy way! Come ye, enter ye in with peace. ¹⁹ They made the rough ways even, before his entering in; They opened the gates to Jerusalem, they crowned its walls. ²⁰ As a father (entereth) the house of his sons, (so) he entered (Jerusalem) in peace; He established his feet (there) in great safety. ²¹ He captured her fortresses and the wall of Jerusalem; ²² For God Himself led him in safety, while they wandered. ²³ He destroyed their princes and every one wise in counsel; He poured out the blood of the inhabitants of Jerusalem, like the water of uncleanness. ²⁴ He led away their sons and daughters, whom they had begotten in defilement. ²⁵ They did according to their uncleanness, even as their fathers (had done): ²⁶ They defiled Jerusalem and the things that had been hallowed to the name of God. ²⁷ (But) God hath shown Himself righteous in His judgements upon the nations of the earth; ²⁸ And the pious (servants) of God are like innocent lambs in their midst. ²⁹ Worthy to be praised is the Lord that judgeth the whole earth in His righteousness. ³⁰ Behold, now, O God, Thou hast shown us Thy judgement in Thy righteousness; ³¹ Our eyes have seen Thy judgements, O God. We have justified Thy name that is honoured for ever; ³² For Thou art the God of righteousness, judging Israel with chastening. ³³ Turn, O God, Thy mercy upon us, and have pity upon us; ³⁴ Gather together the dispersed of Israel, with mercy and goodness; ³⁵ For Thy faithfulness is with us. And (though) we have stiffened our neck, yet Thou art our chastener; ³⁶ Overlook us not, O our God, lest the nations swallow us up, as though there were none to deliver. ³⁷ But Thou art our God from the beginning, And upon Thee is our hope (set), O Lord; ³⁸ And we will not depart from Thee, For good are Thy judgements upon us. ³⁹ Ours and our children's be Thy good pleasure for ever O Lord our Saviour, we shall never more be moved. ⁴⁰ The Lord is worthy to be praised for His judgements with the mouth of His pious ones; And blessed be Israel of the Lord for ever

Ps. Sol. 9. Of Solomon. For rebuke

⁹ ¹ When Israel was led away captive into a strange land, When they fell away from the Lord who redeemed them, ² They were cast away from the inheritance, which Lord had given them. A mong every nation (were) the dispersed of Israel according to the word of God, ³ That Thou mightest be justified, O God, in Thy righteousness by reason of our transgressions: ⁴ For Thou art a just judge over all the peoples of the earth. ⁵ For from Thy knowledge none that doeth unjustly is hidden, ⁶ And the righteous deeds of Thy pious ones (are) before Thee, O Lord, Where, then, can a man hide himself from Thy knowledge, O God? ⁷ Our works are subject to our own choice and power To do right or wrong in the works of our hands ⁸ And in Thy righteousness Thou visitest the sons of men. ⁹ He that doeth righteousness layeth up life for himself with the Lord; And he that doeth wrongly forfeits his life to destruction; ¹⁰ For the judgements of the Lord are (given) in righteousness to (every) man and (his) house. Unto whom art Thou good, O God, except to them that call upon the Lord? ¹² He cleanseth from sins a soul when it maketh confession, when it maketh acknowledgement; ¹³ For shame is upon us and upon our faces on account of all these things. ¹⁴ And to whom doth He forgive sins, except to them that have sinned? ¹⁵ Thou blessest the righteous, and dost not reprove them for the sins that they have committed; And Thy goodness is upon them that sin, when they repent. ¹⁶ And, now, Thou art our God, and we the people whom Thou hast loved: Behold and show pity, O God of Israel, for we are Thine; And remove not Thy mercy from us, lest they assail us. ¹⁷ For Thou didst choose the seed of Abraham before all the nations, And didst set Thy name upon us, O Lord, ¹⁸ And Thou wilt not reject (us) for ever. Thou madest a covenant with our fathers concerning us; ¹⁹ And we hope in Thee, when our soul turneth (unto Thee). The mercy of the Lord be upon the house of Israel for ever and ever.

Ps. Sol. 10. A Hymn Of Solomon

¹⁰ ¹ Happy is the man whom the Lord remembereth with reproving, And whom He restraineth from the way of evil with strokes, That he may be cleansed from sin, that it may not be multiplied. ² He that maketh ready his back for strokes shall be cleansed, For the Lord is good to them that endure chastening. ³ For He maketh straight the ways of the righteous, And doth not pervert (them) by His chastening. ⁴ And the mercy of the Lord (is) upon them that love Him in truth, And the Lord remembereth His servants in mercy. ⁵ For the testimony (is) in the law of the eternal covenant, The testimony of the Lord (is) on the ways of men in (His) visitation. ⁶ Just and kind is our Lord in His judgements for ever, And Israel shall praise the name of the Lord in gladness. ⁷ And the pious shall give thanks in the assembly of the people; And on the poor shall God have mercy in the gladness (?) of Israel; ⁸ For good and merciful is God for ever, And the assemblies of Israel shall glorify the name of the Lord. The salvation of the Lord be upon house of Israel unto everlasting gladness!

Ps. Sol. 11. Of Solomon. Unto expectation

¹¹ ¹ Blow ye in Zion on the trumpet to summon (the) saints, ² Cause ye to be heard in Jerusalem the voice of him that bringeth good tidings; For God hath had pity on Israel in visiting them. ³ Stand on the height, O Jerusalem, and behold thy children, From the East and the West, gathered together by the Lord; ⁴ From the North they come in the gladness of their God, From the isles afar off God hath gathered them. ⁵ High mountains hath He abased into a plain for them; ⁶ The hills fled at their entrance. The woods gave them shelter as they passed by; ⁷ Every sweet-smelling tree God caused to spring up for them, That Israel might pass by in the visitation of the glory of their God. ⁸ Put on, O Jerusalem, thy glorious garments; Make ready thy holy robe; For God hath spoken good concerning Israel, for ever and ever. ⁹ Let the Lord do what He hath spoken concerning Israel and Jerusalem; Let the Lord raise up Israel by His

glorious name. The mercy of the Lord be upon Israel for ever and ever.

Ps. Sol. 12. Of Solomon. Against the tongue of transgressors

12 1 O Lord, deliver my soul from (the) lawless and wicked man, From the tongue that is lawless and slanderous, and speaketh lies and deceit. 2 Manifoldly twisted (?) are the words of the tongue of the wicked man, Even as among a people a fire that burneth up their beauty. 3 So he delights to fill houses with a lying tongue, To cut down the trees of gladness which setteth on fire transgressors, 4 To involve households in warfare by means of slanderous lips. May God remove far from the innocent the lips of transgressors by (bringing them to) want And may the bones of slanderers be scattered (far) away from them that fear the Lord! 5 In flaming fire perish the slanderous tongue (far) away from the pious! 6 May the Lord preserve the quiet soul that hateth the unrighteous; And may the Lord establish the man that followeth peace at home. 7 The salvation of the Lord be upon Israel His servant for ever; And let the sinners perish together at the presence of the Lord; But let the Lord's pious ones inherit the promises of the Lord.

Ps. Sol. 13. Of Solomon. A Psalm. Comfort for the righteous

13 1 The right hand of the Lord hath covered me; The right hand of the Lord hath spared us. 2 The arm of the Lord hath saved us from the sword that passed through, From famine and the death of sinners. 3 Noisome beasts ran upon them: With their teeth they tore their flesh, And with their molars crushed their bones. But from all these things the Lord delivered us, 4 The righteous was troubled on account of his errors, Lest he should be taken away along with the sinners; 5 For terrible is the overthrow of the sinner; But not one of all these things toucheth the righteous. For not alike are the chastening of the righteous (for sins done) in ignorance, And the overthrow of the sinners 7 Secretly (?) is the righteous chastened, Lest the sinner rejoice over the righteous. 8 For He correcteth the righteous as a beloved son, And his chastisement is as that of a firstborn. 9 10) For the Lord spareth His pious ones, And blotteth out their errors by His chastening. For the life of the righteous shall be for ever; 10 But sinners shall be taken away into destruction, And their memorial shall be found no more. 11 But upon the pious is the mercy of the Lord, And upon them that fear Him His mercy.

Ps. Sol. 14. A Hymn. Of Solomon

14 1 Faithful is the Lord to them that love Him in truth, To them that endure His chastening, To them that walk in the righteousness of His commandments, In the law which He commanded us that we might live. 2 The pious of the Lord shall live by it for ever; The Paradise of the Lord, the trees of life, are His pious ones. 3 Their planting is rooted for ever; They shall not be plucked up all the days of heaven: For the portion and the inheritance of God is Israel. 4 But not so are the sinners and transgressors, Who love (the brief) day (spent) in companionship with their sin; Their delight is in fleeting corruption, 5 And they remember not God. For the ways of men are known before Him at all times, And He knoweth the secrets of the heart before they come to pass. 6 Therefore their inheritance is Sheol and darkness and destruction, And they shall not be found in the day when the righteous obtain mercy; 7 But the pious of the Lord shall inherit life in gladness.

Ps. Sol. 15. A Psalm. Of Solomon. With a Song

15 1 When I was in distress I called upon the name of the Lord, I hoped for the help of the God of Jacob and was saved; 2 For the hope and refuge of the poor art Thou, O God. 3 (a) For who, O God, is strong except to give thanks unto Thee in truth? 4 And wherein is a man powerful except in giving thanks to Thy name? 5 A new psalm with song in gladness of heart, The fruit of the lips with the well-tuned instrument of the tongue, The firstfruits of the lips

from a pious and righteous heart– 6 He that offereth these things shall never be shaken by evil; The flame of fire and the wrath against the unrighteous shall not touch him, 7 When it goeth forth from the face of the Lord against sinners, To destroy all the substance of sinners, 8 For the mark of God is upon the righteous that they .may be saved. Famine and sword and pestilence (shall be) far from the righteous, 9 For they shall flee away from the pious as men pursued in war; But they shall pursue sinners and overtake (them), And they that do lawlessness shall not escape the judgement of God; As by enemies experienced (in war) shall they be overtaken, 10 For the mark of destruction is upon their forehead. 11 And the inheritance of sinners is destruction and darkness, And their iniquities shall pursue them unto Sheol beneath. 12 Their inheritance shall not be found of their children, 13 For sins shall lay waste the houses of sinners. And sinners shall perish for ever in the day of the Lord's judgement, 14 When God visiteth the earth with His judgement. 15 But they that fear the Lord shall find mercy therein, And shall live by the compassion of their God; But sinners shall perish for ever.

Ps. Sol. 16. A Hymn. Of Solomon. For Help to the Pious

16 1 When my soul slumbered (being afar) from the Lord, I had all but slipped down to the pit, When (I was) far from God, 2 my soul had been well nigh poured out unto death, (I had been) nigh unto the gates of Sheol with thesinner, 3 when my soul departed from the Lord God of Israel– Had not the Lord helped me with His everlasting mercy. 4 He pricked me, as a horse is pricked, that I might serve Him, My saviour and helper at all times saved me. 5 I will give thanks unto Thee, O God, for Thou hast helped me to (my) salvation; And hast not counted me with sinners to (my) destruction. 6 Remove not Thy mercy from me, O God, Nor Thy memorial from my heart until I die. 7 Rule me, O God, (keeping me back) from wicked sin, And from every wicked woman that causeth the simple to stumble. 8 And let not the beauty of a lawless woman beguile me, Nor any one that is subject to (?) unprofitable sin. 9 Establish the works of my hands before Thee, And preserve my goings in the remembrance of Thee. 10 Protect my tongue and my lips with words of truth; Anger and unreasoning wrath put far from me. 11 Murmuring, and impatience in affliction, remove far from me, When, if I sin, Thou chastenest me that I may return (unto Thee). 12 But with goodwill and cheerfulness support my soul; When Thou strengthenest my soul, what is given (to me) will be sufficient for me. 13 For if Thou givest not strength, Who can endure chastisement with poverty? 14 When a man is rebuked by means of his corruption, Thy testing (of him) is in his flesh and in the affliction of poverty. 15 If the righteous endureth in all these (trials), he shall receive mercy from the Lord.

Ps. Sol. 17. A Psalm. Of Solomon. With Song. Of the King

17 1 O Lord, Thou art our King for ever and ever, For in Thee, O God, doth our soul glory. 2 How long are the days of man's life upon the earth? As are his days, so is the hope (set) upon him. 3 But we hope in God, our deliverer; For the might of our God is for ever with mercy, 4 And the kingdom of our God is for ever over the nations in judgement. 5 Thou, O Lord, didst choose David (to be) king over Israel, And swaredst to him touching his seed that never should his kingdom fail before Thee. 6 But, for our sins, sinners rose up against us; They assailed us and thrust us out; What Thou hadst not promised to them, they took away (from us) with violence. 7 They in no wise glorified Thy honourable name; They set a (worldly) monarchy in place of (that which was) their excellency; 8 They laid waste the throne of David in tumultuous arrogance. But Thou, O God, didst cast them down and remove their seed from the earth, 9 In that there rose up against them a man

that was alien to our race. [10] According to their sins didst Thou recompense them, O God; So that it befell them according to their deeds. [11] God showed them no pity; He sought out their seed and let not one of them go free. [12] Faithful is the Lord in all His judgements Which He doeth upon the earth. [13] The lawless one laid waste our land so that none inhabited it, They destroyed young and old and their children together. [14] In the heat of His anger He sent them away even unto the west, And (He exposed) the rulers of the land unsparingly to derision. [15] Being an alien the enemy acted proudly, And his heart was alien from our God. [16] And all things whatsoever he did in Jerusalem, As also the nations in the cities to their gods. [17] And the children of the covenant in the midst of the mingled peoples surpassed them in evil. There was not among them one that wrought in the midst of Jerusalem mercy and truth. [18] They that loved the synagogues of the pious fled from them, As sparrows that fly from their nest. [19] They wandered in deserts that their lives might be saved from harm, And precious in the eyes of them that lived abroad was any that escaped alive from them. [20] Over the whole earth were they scattered by lawless (men). [21] For the heavens withheld the rain from dropping upon the earth, Springs were stopped (that sprang) perennial(ly) out of the deeps, (that ran down) from lofty mountains. For there was none among them that wrought righteousness and justice; From the chief of them to the least (of them) all were sinful; [22] The king was a transgressor, and the judge disobedient, and the people sinful. [23] Behold, O Lord, and raise up unto them their king, the son of David, At the time in the which Thou seest, O God, that he may reign over Israel Thy servant [24] And gird him with strength, that he may shatter unrighteous rulers, [25] And that he may purge Jerusalem from nations that trample (her) down to destruction. Wisely, righteously [26] he shall thrust out sinners from (the) inheritance, He shall destroy the pride of the sinner as a potter's vessel. With a rod of iron he shall break in pieces all their substance, [21] He shall destroy the godless nations with the word of his mouth; At his rebuke nations shall flee before him, And he shall reprove sinners for the thoughts of their heart. [28] And he shall gather together a holy people, whom he shall lead in righteousness, And he shall judge the tribes of the people that has been sanctified by the Lord his God. [29] And he shall not suffer unrighteousness to lodge any more in their midst, Nor shall there dwell with them any man that knoweth wickedness, [30] For he shall know them, that they are all sons of their God. And he shall divide them according to their tribes upon the land, [31] And neither sojourner nor alien shall sojourn with them any more. He shall judge peoples and nations in the wisdom of his righteousness. Selah. [32] And he shall have the heathen nations to serve him under his yoke; And he shall glorify the Lord in a place to be seen of (?) all the earth; [33] And he shall purge Jerusalem, making it holy as of old: [34] So that nations shall come from the ends of the earth to see his glory, Bringing as gifts her sons who had fainted, [35] And to see the glory of the Lord, wherewith God hath glorified her. And he (shall be) a righteous king, taught of God, over them, [36] And there shall be no unrighteousness in his days in their midst, For all shall be holy and their king the anointed of the Lord. [37] For he shall not put his trust in horse and rider and bow, Nor shall he multiply for himself gold and silver for war, Nor shall he gather confidence from (?) a multitude (?) for the day of battle. [38] The Lord Himself is his king, the hope of him that is mighty through (his) hope in God. All nations (shall be) in fear before him, [39] For he will smite the earth with the word of his mouth for ever. [40] He will bless the people of the Lord with wisdom and gladness, [41] And he himself (will be) pure from sin, so that he may rule a great people. He will rebuke rulers, and remove sinners by the might of his word; [42] And (relying) upon

his God, throughout his days he will not stumble; For God will make him mighty by means of (His) holy spirit, And wise by means of the spirit of understanding, with strength and righteousness. [43] And the blessing of the Lord (will be) with him: he will be strong and stumble not; [44] His hope (will be) in the Lord: who then can prevail against him? (He will be) mighty in his works, and strong in the fear of God, [45] (He will be) shepherding the flock of the Lord faithfully and righteously, And will suffer none among them to stumble in their pasture. [46] He will lead them all aright, And there will be no pride among them that any among them should be oppressed. [47] This (will be) the majesty of the king of Israel whom God knoweth; He will raise him up over the house of Israel to correct him. [48] His words (shall be) more refined than costly gold, the choicest; In the assemblies he will judge the peoples, the tribes of the sanctified. [49] His words (shall be) like the words of the holy ones in the midst of sanctified peoples. [50] Blessed be they that shall be in those days, In that they shall see the good fortune of Israel which God shall bring to pass in the gathering together of the tribes. [51] May the Lord hasten His mercy upon Israel! May He deliver us from the uncleanness of unholy enemies! The Lord Himself is our king for ever and ever.

Ps. Sol. 18. A Psalm. Of Solomon. Again of the Anointed of the Lord.

[18] [1] Lord, Thy mercy is over the works of Thy hands for ever; Thy goodness is over Israel with a rich gift. [2] Thine eyes look upon them, so that none of them suffers want; [3] Thine ears listen to the hopeful prayer of the poor. Thy judgements (are executed) upon the whole earth in mercy; [4] And Thy love (is) toward the seed of Abraham, the children of Israel. Thy chastisement is upon us as (upon) a first-born, only-begotten son, [5] To turn back the obedient soul from folly (that is wrought) in ignorance. [6] May God cleanse Israel against the day of mercy and blessing, Against the day of choice when He bringeth back His anointed. [7] Blessed shall they be that shall be in those days, In that they shall see the goodness of the Lord which He shall perform for the generation that is to come, [8] Under the rod of chastening of the Lord's anointed in the fear of his God, In the spirit of wisdom and righteousness and strength; [9] That he may direct (every} man in the works of righteousness by the fear of God, That he may establish them all before the Lord, [10] A good generation (living) in the fear of God in the days of mercy. Selah. [11] Great is our God and glorious, dwelling in the highest. [12] (It is He) who hath established in (their) courses the lights (of heaven) for determining seasons from year to year, And they have not turned aside from the way which He appointed them [13] In the fear of God (they pursue) their path every day, From the day God created them and for evermore. [14] And they have erred not since the day He created them. Since the generations of old they have not withdrawn from their path, Unless God commanded them (so to do) by the command of His servants.

The Words of Gad the Seer

Gad, the ninth son of Jacob and Zilpah. Shepherd and strong man but a murderer at heart. Verse 25 is a notable definition of hatred.

Gad, spoke to his sons in the one hundred and twenty-fifth year of his life, telling them:

[2] Hearken, my children, I was the ninth son born to Jacob, and I was valiant in keeping the flocks. [3] Accordingly I guarded at night the flock; and whenever the lion came, or the wolf, or any wild beast against the fold, I pursued it, and overtaking it I seized its foot with my hand and hurled it about a stone's throw, and so killed it. [4] Now Joseph my brother was feeding the flock with us for upwards of thirty days, and being young, he fell sick by reason of the heat. [5] And

he returned to Hebron to our father, who made him lie down near him, because he loved him greatly. 6 And Joseph told our father that the sons of Zilpah and Bilhah were slaying the best of the flock and eating them against the judgement of Reuben and Judah. 7 For he saw that I had delivered a lamb out of the mouth of a bear, and put the bear to death; but had slain the lamb, being grieved concerning it that it could not live, and that we had eaten it. 8 And regarding this matter I was wroth with Joseph until the day that he was sold. 9 And the spirit of hatred was in me, and I wished not either to hear of Joseph with the ears, or see him with the eyes, because he rebuked us to our faces saying that we were eating of the flock without Judah. 10 For whatsoever things he told our father, he believed him. 11 I confess now my gin, my children, that oftentimes I wished to kill him, because I hated him from my heart. 12 Moreover, I hated him yet more for his dreams; and I wished to lick 1 him out of the land of the living, even as an ox licketh up the grass of the field. 13 And Judah sold him secretly to the Ishmaelites. 14 Thus the God of our fathers delivered him from our hands, that we should not work great lawlessness in Israel. 15 And now, my children, hearken to the words of truth to work righteousness, and all the law of the Most High, and go not astray through the spirit of hatred, for it is evil in all the doings of men. 16 Whatsoever a man doeth the hater abominateth him: and though a man worketh the law of the Lord, he praiseth him not; though a man feareth the Lord, and taketh pleasure in that which is righteous, he loveth him not. 17 He dispraiseth the truth, he envieth him that prospereth, he welcometh evil-speaking, he loveth arrogance, for hatred blindeth his soul; as I also then looked on Joseph. 18 Beware, therefore, my children of hatred, for it worketh lawlessness even against the Lord Himself. 19 For it will not hear the words of His commandments concerning the loving of one's--neighbour, and it sinneth against God. 20 For if a brother stumble, it delighteth immediately to proclaim it to all men, and is urgent that he should be judged for it, and be punished and be put to death. 21 And if it be a servant it stirreth him up against his master, and with every affliction it deviseth against him, if possibly he can be put to death. 22 For hatred worketh with envy also against them that prosper: so long as it heareth of or seeth their success it always languisheth. 23 For as love would quicken even the dead, and would call back them that are condemned to die, so hatred would slay the living, and those that had sinned venially it would not suffer to live. 24 For the spirit of hatred worketh together with Satan, through hastiness of spirits, in all things to men's death; but the spirit of love worketh together with the law of God in long-suffering unto the salvation of men. 25 Hatred, therefore, is evil, for it constantly mateth with lying, speaking against the truth; and it maketh small things to be great, and causeth the light to be darkness, and calleth the sweet bitter, and teacheth slander, and kindleth wrath, and stirreth up war, and violence and all covetousness; it filleth the heart with evils and devilish poison. 26 These things, therefore, I say to you from experience, my children, that ye may drive forth hatred, which is of the devil, and cleave to the love of God. 27 Righteousness casteth out hatred, humility destroyeth envy. 28 For he that is just and humble is ashamed to do what is unjust, being reproved not of another, but of his own heart, because the Lord looketh on his inclination. 29 He speaketh not against a holy man, because the fear of God overcometh hatred. 30 For fearing lest he should offend the Lord, he will not do wrong to any man, even in thought. 31 These things I learnt at last, after I had repented concerning Joseph. 32 For true repentance after a godly sort destroyeth ignorance, and driveth away the darkness, and enlighteneth the eyes, and giveth knowledge to the soul, and leadeth the mind to salvation. 33 And those things

which it hath not learnt from man, it knoweth through repentance. 34 For God brought upon me a disease of the liver; and had not the prayers of Jacob my father succoured me, it had hardly failed but my spirit had departed. 35 For by what things a man transgresseth by the same also is he punished. 36 Since, therefore, my liver was set mercilessly against Joseph, in my liver too I suffered mercilessly, and was judged for eleven months, for so long a time as I had been angry against Joseph.

AND now, my children, I exhort you, love ye each one his brother, and put away hatred from your hearts, love one another in deed, and in word, and in the inclination of the soul.

2 For in the presence of my father I spake peaceably to Joseph; and when I had gone out, the spirit of hatred darkened my mind, and stirred up my soul to slay him. 3 Love ye one another from the heart; and if a man sin against thee, speak peaceably to him, and in thy soul hold not guile; and if he repent and confess, forgive him. 4 But if he deny it, do not get into a passion with him, lest catching the poison from thee he take to swearing and so thou sin doubly. 5 Let not another man hear thy secrets when engaged in legal strife, lest he come to hate thee and become thy enemy, and commit a great sin against thee; for ofttimes he addresseth thee guilefully or busieth himself about thee with wicked intent. 6 And though he deny it and yet have a sense of shame when reproved, give over reproving him. 7 For he who denieth may repent so as not again to wrong thee; yea, he may also honour thee, and fear and be at peace with thee. 8 And if he be shameless and persist in his wrong-doing, even so forgive him from the heart, and leave to God the avenging. 9 If a man prospereth more than you, do not be vexed, but pray also for him, that he may have perfect prosperity. 10 for so it is expedient for you. 11 And if he be further exalted, be not envious of him, remembering that all flesh shall die; and offer praise to God, who giveth things good and profitable to all men. 12 Seek out the judgments of the Lord, and thy mind will rest and be at peace. 13 And though a man become rich by evil means, even as Esau, the brother of my father, be not jealous; but wait for the end of the Lord. 14 For if he taketh away from a man wealth gotten by evil means He forgiveth him if he repent, but the unrepentant is reserved for eternal punishment. 15 For the poor man, if free from envy he pleaseth the Lord in all things, is blessed beyond all men, because he hath not the travail of vain men. 16 Put away, therefore, jealousy from your souls, and love one another with uprightness of heart. 17 Do ye also therefore tell these things to your children, that they honour Judah and Levi, for from them shall the Lord raise up salvation to Israel. 18 For I know that at the last your children shall depart from Him, and shall walk in O wickedness, and affliction and corruption before the Lord. 19 And when he had rested for a little while, he said again; My children, obey your father, and bury me near to my fathers. 20 And he drew up his feet, and fell asleep in peace. 21 And after five years they carried him up to Hebron, and laid him with his fathers.

The Ascension of Isaiah

Asc. Isa. 1 - AND it came to pass in the twenty-sixth year of the reign of Hezediah king of Judah that he called Manasseh his son. Now he was his only one. 2. And he called him into the presence of Isaiah the son of Amoz the prophet, and into the presence of Josab the son of Isaiah, in order to deliver unto him the words of righteousness which the king himself had seen: 3. And of the eternal judgments and torments of Gehenna, and of the prince of this world, and of his angels, and his authorities and his powers. 4. And the words of the faith of the Beloved which he himself had seen in the fifteenth year of his reign during his illness. 5. And he delivered unto him the written words which Samnas the scribe had written, and also those which Isaiah, the son of Amoz, had given to him, and also to the prophets, that they might write and store up with him what he himself had seen in the king's house regarding the judgment of the angels, and the destruction of this world, and regarding the garments of the saints and their going forth, and regarding their transformation and the persecution and ascension of the Beloved. 6. In the twentieth year of the reign of Hezekiah, Isaiah had seen the words of this prophecy and had delivered them to Josab his son. And whilst he (Hezekiah) gave commands, Josab the son of Isaiah standing by. 7. Isaiah said to Hezekiah the king, but not in the presence of Manasseh only did he say unto him: `As the Lord liveth, and the Spirit which speaketh in me liveth, all these commands and these words will be made of none effect by Manasseh thy son, and through the agency of his hands I shall depart mid the torture of my body. 8. And Sammael Malchira will serve Manasseh, and execute all his desire, and he will become a follower of Beliar rather than of me: 9. And many in Jerusalem and in Judea he will cause to abandon the true faith, and Beliar will dwell in Manasseh, and by his hands I shall be sawn asunder.' 10. And when Hezekiah heard these words he wept very bitterly, and rent his garments, and placed earth upon his head, and fell on his face. 11. And Isaiah said unto him: `The counsel of Sammael against Manasseh is consummated: nought will avail thee." 12. And on that day Hezekiah resolved in his heart to slay Manasseh his son. 13. And Isaiah said to Hezekiah: `The Beloved hath made of none effect thy design, and the purpose of thy heart will not be accomplished, for with this calling have I been called and I shall inherit the heritage of the Beloved.'

Asc. Isa. 2 - AND it came to pass after that Hezekiah died and Manasseh became king, that he did not remember the commands of Hezekiah his father, but forgat them, and Sammael abode in Manasseh and clung fast to him. 2. And Manasseh forsook the service of the God of his father, and he served Satan and his angels and his powers. 3. And he turned aside the house of his father, which had been before the face of Hezekiah (from) the words of wisdom and from the service of God. 4. And Manasseh turned aside his heart to serve Beliar; for the angel of lawlessness, who is the ruler of this world, is Beliar, whose name is Mantanbuchus. and he delighted in Jerusalem because of Manasseh, and he made him strong in apostatizing (Israel) and in the lawlessness which were spread abroad in Jerusalem. 5. And witchcraft and magic increased and divination and auguration, and fornication, a [and adultery], and the persecution of the righteous by Manasseh and [Belachira, and] Tobia the Canaanite, and John of Anathoth, an by (Zadok) the chief of the works. 6. And the rest of the acts, behold they are written in the book of the Kings of Judah and Israel. 7. And, when Isaiah, the son of Amoz, saw the lawlessness which was being perpetrated in Jerusalem and the worship of Satan and his wantonness, he withdrew from Jerusalem and settled in Bethlehem of Judah. 8. And there also there was much lawlessness, and withdrawing from Bethlehem he settled on a mountain in a desert place. 9. And Micaiah the prophet, and the aged Ananias, and Joel and Habakkuk, and his son Josab, and many of the faithful who believed in the ascension into heaven, withdrew and settled on the mountain. 10. They were all clothed with garments of hair, and they were all prophets. And they had nothing with them but were naked, and they all lamented with a great lamentation because of the going astray of Israel. 11. And these eat nothing save wild herbs which they gathered on the mountains, and having cooked them, they lived thereon together with Isaiah the prophet. And they spent two years of days on the mountains and hills. 12. And after this, whilst they were in the desert, there was a certain man in Samaria named Belchira, of the family of

Zedekiah, the son of Chenaan, a false prophet, whose dwelling was in Bethlehem. Now Hezekiah the son of Chanani, who was the brother of his father, and in the days of Ahab, king of Israel, had been the teacher of the 400. prophets of Baal, had himself smitten and reproved Micaiah the son of Amada the prophet. 13. And he, Micaiah, had been reproved by Ahab and cast into prison. (And he was) with Zedekiah the prophet: they were with Ahaziah the son of Ahab, king in Samaria. 14. And Elijah the prophet of Tebon of Gilead was reproving Ahaziah and Samaria, and prophesied regarding Ahaziah that he should die on his bed of sickness, and that Samaria should be delivered into the had of Leba Nasr because he had slain the prophets of God. 15. And when the false prophets, who were with Ahaziah the son of Ahab and their teacher Jalerjas of Mount Joel, had heard- 16. Now he was a brother of Zedekiah - when they persuaded Ahaziah the king of Aguaron and (slew) Micaiah.

Asc. Isa. 3 - AND Belchira recognized and saw the place of Isaiah and the prophets who were with him; for he dwelt in the region of Bethlehem, and was an adherent of Manasseh. And he prophesied falsely in Jerusalem, and many belonging to Jerusalem were confederate with him, and he was a Samaritan. 2. And it came to pass when Alagar Zagar, king of Assyria, had come and captive, and led them away to the mountains of the medes and the rivers of Tazon; 3. This (Belchira), whilst still a youth, had escaped and come to Jerusalem in the days of Hezekiah king of Judah, but he walked not in the ways of his father of Samaria; for he feared Hezekiah. 4. And he was found in the days of Hezekiah speaking words of lawlessness in Jerusalem. 5. And the servants of Hezekiah accused him, and he made his escape to the region of Bethlehem. And they persuaded... 6. And Belchira accused Isaiah and the prophets who were with him, saying: `Isaiah and those who are with him prophesy against Jerusalem and against the cities of Judah that they shall be laid waste and (against the children of Judah and) Benjamin also that they shall go into captivity, and also against thee, O lord the king, that thou shalt go (bound) with hooks and iron chains': 7. But they prophesy falsely against Israel and Judah. 8. And Isaiah himself hath said: `I see more than Moses the prophet.' 9. But Moses said: `No man can see God and live'; and Isaiah hath said: `I have seen God and behold I live.' 10. Know, therefore, O king, that he is lying. And Jerusalem also he hath called Sodom, and the princes of Judah and Jerusalem he hath declared to be the people of Gomorrah. And he brought many accusations against Isaiah and the prophets before Manasseh. 11. But Beliar dwelt in the heart of Manasseh and in the heart of the princes of Judah and Benjamin and of the eunuchs and of the councillors of the king. 12. And the words of Belchira pleased him [exceedingly], and he sent and seized Isaiah. 13. For Beliar was in great wrath against Isaiah by reason of the vision, and because of the exposure wherewith he had exposed Sammael, and because through him the going forth of the Beloved from the seventh heaven had been made known, and His transformation and His descent and the likeness into which He should be transformed (that is) the likeness of man, and the persecution wherewith he should be persecuted, and the torturers wherewith the children of Israel should torture Him, and the coming of His twelve disciples, and the teaching, and that He should before the sabbath be crucified upon the tree, and should be crucified together with wicked men, and that He should be buried in the sepulchre, 14. And the twelve who were with Him should be offended because of Him: and the watch of those who watched the sepulchre: 15. And the descent of the angel of the Christian Church, which is in the heavens, whom He will summon in the last days. 16. And that (Gabriel) the angel of the Holy Spirit, and Michael, the chief of the holy angels, on the third day will open the sepulchre: 17. And the Beloved sitting on their shoulders will come forth and send out His twelve disciples; 18. And they will teach all the nations and every tongue of the resurrection of the Beloved, and those who believe in His cross will be saved, and in His ascension into the seventh heaven whence He came: 19. And that many who believe in Him will speak through the Holy Spirit: 20. And many signs and wonders will be wrought in those days. 21. And afterwards, on the eve of His approach, His disciples will forsake the teachings of the Twelve Apostles, and their faith, and their love and their purity. 22. And there will be much contention on the eve of [His advent and] His approach. 23. And in those days many will love office, though devoid of wisdom. 24. And there will be many lawless elders, and shepherds dealing wrongly by their own sheep, and they will ravage (them) owing to their not having holy shepherds. 25. And many will change the honour of the garments of the saints for the garments of the covetous, and there will be much respect of persons in those days and lovers of the honour of this world. 26. And there will be much slander and vainglory at the approach of the Lord, and the Holy Spirit will withdraw from many. 27. And there will not be in those days many prophets, nor those who speak trustworthy words, save one here and there in divers places, 28. On account of the spirit of error and fornication and of vainglory, and of covetousness, which shall be in those, who will be called servants of that One and in those who will receive that One. 29. And there will be great hatred in the shepherds and elders towards each other. 30. For there will be great jealousy in the last days; for every one will say what is pleasing in his own eyes. 31. And they will make of none effect the prophecy of the prophets which were before me, and these my visions also will they make of none effect, in order to speak after the impulse of their own hearts.

Asc. Isa. 4 - AND now Hezekiah and Josab my son, these are the days of the completion of the world. 2. After it is consummated, Beliar the great ruler, the king of this world, will descend, who hath ruled it since it came into being; yea, he will descent from his firmament in the likeness of a man, a lawless king, the slayer of his mother: who himself (even) this king. 3. Will persecute the plant which the Twelve Apostles of the Beloved have planted. Of the Twelve one will be delivered into his hands. 4. This ruler in the form of that king will come and there will come and there will come with him all the powers of this world, and they will hearken unto him in all that he desires. 5. And at his word the sun will rise at night and he will make the moon to appear at the sixth hour. 6. And all that he hath desired he will do in the world: he will do and speak like the Beloved and he will say: "I am God and before me there has been none." 7. And all the people in the world will believe in him. 8. And they will sacrifice to him and they will serve him saying: "This is God and beside him there is no other." 9. And they greater number of those who shall have been associated together in order to receive the Beloved, he will turn aside after him. 10. And there will be the power of his miracles in every city and region. 11. And he will set up his image before him in every city. 12. And he shall bear sway three years and seven months and twenty-seven days. 13. And many believers and saints having seen Him for whom they were hoping, who was crucified, Jesus the Lord Christ, [after that I, Isaiah, had seen Him who was crucified and ascended] and those also who were believers in Him - of these few in those days will be left as His servants, while they flee from desert to desert, awaiting the coming of the Beloved. 14. And after (one thousand) three hundred and thirty-two days the Lord will come with His angels and with the armies of the holy ones from the seventh heaven with the glory of the seventh heaven, and He will drag Beliar into Gehenna and also his armies. 15. And He will give rest of the godly whom He shall find in the body in this world, [and the sun wil be ashamed]: 16. And to

all who because of (their) faith in Him have execrated Beliar and his kings. But the saints will come with the Lord with their garments which are (now) stored up on high in the seventh heaven: with the Lord they will come, whose spirits are clothed, they will descend and be present in the world, and He will strengthen those, who have been found in the body, together with the saints, in the garments of the saints, and the Lord will minister to those who have kept watch in this world. 17. And afterwards they will turn themselves upward in their garments, and their body will be left in the world. 18. Then the voice of the Beloved will in wrath rebuke the things of heaven and the things of earth and the things of earth and the mountains and the hills and the cities and the desert and the forests and the angel of the sun and that of the moon, and all things wherein Beliar manifested himself and acted openly in this world, and there will be [a resurrection and] a judgment in their midst in those days, and the Beloved will cause fire to go forth from Him, and it will consume all the godless, and they will be as though they had not been created. 19. And the rest of the words of the vision is written in the vision of Babylon. 20. And the rest of the vision regarding the Lord, behold, it is written in three parables according to my words which are written in the book which I publicly prophesied. 21. And the descent of the Beloved into Sheol, behold, it is written in the section, where the Lord says: "Behold my Son will understand." And all these things, behold they are written [in the Psalms] in the parables of David, the son of Jesse, and in the Proverbs of Solomon his son, and in the words of Korah, and Ethan the Israelite, and in the words of Asaph, and in the rest of the Psalms also which the angel of the Spirit inspired. 22. (Namely) in those which have not the name written, and in the words of my father Amos, and of Hosea the prophet, and of Micah and Joel and Nahum and Jonah and Obadiah and Habakkuk and Haggai and Malachi, and in the words of Joseph the Just and in the words of Daniel.

Asc. Isa. 5 - ON account of these visions, therefore, Beliar was wroth with Isaiah, and he dwelt in the heart of Manasseh and he sawed him in sunder with a wooden saw. 2. And when Isaiah was being sawn in sunder, Belchira stood up, accusing him, and all the false prophets stood up, laughing and rejoicing because of Isaiah. 3. And Belchira, with the aid of Mechembechus, stood up before Isaiah, [laughing] deriding; 4. And Belchira said to Isaiah: 'Say, "I have lied in all that I have spoken, and likewise the ways of Manasseh are good and right. 5. And the ways also of Belchira and of his associates are good." 6. And this he said to him when he began to be sawn in sunder. 7. But Isaiah was (absorbed) in a vision of the Lord, and though his eyes were open, he saw them (not). 8. And Belchira spake thus to Isaiah: "Say what I say unto thee and I will turn their hearts, and I will compel Manasseh and the princes of Judah and the people and all Jerusalem to reverence thee. 9. And Isaiah answered and said: "So far as I have utterance (I say): Damned and accused be thou and all they powers and all thy house. 10. For thou canst not take (from me) aught save the skin of my body." 11. And they seized and sawed in sunder Isaiah, the son of Amoz, with a wooden saw. 12. And Manasseh and Belchira and the false prophets and the princes and the people [and] all stood looking on. 13. And to the prophets who were with him he said before he had been sawn in sunder: "Go ye to the region of Tyre and Sidon; for for me only hath God mingled the cup." 14. And when Isaiah was being sawn in sunder, he neither cried aloud nor wept, but his lips spake with the Holy Spirit until he was sawn in twain. 15. This, Beliar did to Isaiah through Belchira and Manasseh; for Sammael was very wrathful against Isaiah from the days of Hezekiah, king of Judah, on account of the things which he had seen regarding the Beloved. 16. And on account of the destruction of Sammael, which he had seen through the Lord, while Hezekiah his father was still king. And he did according to the will of Satan.

Asc. Isa. 6 - The Vision Which Isaiah the Son of Amoz Saw: In the twentieth year of the reign of Hezekiah, king of Judah, came Isaiah the son of Amoz, and Josab the son of Isaiah to Hezekiah to Jerusalem from Galgala. 2. And (having entered) he sat down on the couch of the king, and they brought him a seat, but he would not sit (thereon). 3. And when Isaiah began to speak the words of faith and truth with King Hezekiah, all the princes of Israel were seated and the eunuchs and the councillors of the king. And there were there forty prophets and sons of the prophets: they had come from the villages and from the mountains and the plains when they had heard that Isaiah was coming from Galgala to Hezekiah. 4. And they had come to salute him and to hear his words. 5. And that he might place his hands upon them, and that they might prophesy and that he might hear their prophecy: and they were all before Isaiah. 6. And when Isaiah was speaking to Hezekiah the words of truth and faith, they all heard a door which one had opened and the voice of the Holy Spirit. 7. And the king summoned all the prophets and all the people who were found there, and they came. and Macaiah and the aged Ananias and Joel and Josab sat on his right hand (and on the left). 8. And it came to pass when they had all heard the voice of the Holy Spirit, they all worshipped on their knees, and glorified the God of truth, the Most High who is in the upper world and who sits on High the Holy One and who rest among His holy ones. 9. And they gave glory to Him who had thus bestowed a door in an alien world had bestowed (it) on a man. 10. And as he was speaking in the Holy Spirit in the hearing of all, he became silent and his mind was taken up from him and he saw not the men that stood before him. 11. Though his eyes indeed were open. Moreover his lips were silent and the mind in his body was taken up from him. 12. But his breath was in him; for he was seeing a vision. 13. And the angel who was sent to make him see was not of this firmament, nor was he of the angels of glory of this world, but he had come from the seventh heaven. 14. And the people who stood near did (not) think, but the circle of the prophets (did), that the holy Isaiah had been taken up. 15. And the vision which the holy Isaiah saw was not from this world but from the world which is hidden from the flesh. 16. And after Isaiah had seen this vision, he narrated it to Hezekiah, and to Josab his son and to the other prophets who had come. 17. But the leaders and the eunuchs and the people did not hear, but only Samna the scribe, and Ijoaqem, and Asaph the recorder; for these also were doers of righteousness, and the sweet smell of the Spirit was upon them. But the people had not heard; for Micaiah and Josab his son had caused them to go forth, when the wisdom of this world had been taken form him and he became as one dead.

Asc. Isa. 7 - AND the vision which Isaiah saw, he told to Hezekiah and Josab his son and Micaiah and the rest of the prophets, (and) said: 2. At this moment, when I prophesied according to the (words) heard which ye heard, I saw a glorious angel not like unto the glory of the angels which I used always to see, but possessing such glory ad position that I cannot describe the glory of that angel. 3. And having seized me by my hand he raised me on high, and I said unto him: "Who art thou, and what is thy name, and whither art thou raising me on high? for strength was given me to speak with him." 4. And he said unto me: "When I have raised thee on high [though the (various) degrees] and made thee see the vision, on account of which I have been sent, then thou wilt understand who I am: but my name thou dost not know. 5. Because thou wilt return into this thy body, but whither I am raising thee on high, thou wilt see; for for this purpose have I been sent." 6. And I rejoiced because he spake courteously to me. 7. And he said unto me: "Hast thou rejoiced

349

because I have spoken courteously to thee?" And he said: "And thou wilt see how a grater also that I am will speak courteously and peaceably with thee." 8. And His Father also who is greater thou wilt see; for for this purpose have I been sent from the seventh heaven in order to explain all these things unto thee." 9. And we ascended to the firmament, I and he, and there I saw Sammael and his hosts, and there was great fighting therein and the angels of Satan were envying one another. 10. And as above so on the earth also; for the likeness of that which is in the firmament is here ont he earth. 11. And I said unto the angel (who was with me): "(What is this war and) what is this envying?" 12. And he said unto me: "So has it been since this world was made until now, and this war (will continue) till He, whom thou shalt see will come and destroy him." 13. And afterwards he caused me to ascend (to that which is) above the firmament: which is the (first) heaven. 14. And there I saw a throne in the midst, and on his right and on his left were angels. 15. And (the angels on the left were) not like unto the angels who stood on the right, but those who stood on the right had the greater glory, and they all praised with one voice, and there was a throne in the midst, and those who were out he left gave praise after them; but their voice was not such as the voice of those on the right, nor their praise like the praise of those. 16. And I asked the angel who conducted me, and I said unto him: "To whom is this praise sent?" 17. And he said unto me: "(it is sent) to the praise of (Him who sitteth in) the seventh heaven: to Him who rests in the holy world, and to His Beloved, whence I have been sent to thee. [Thither is it sent.]" 18. And again, he made me to ascend to the second heaven. now the height of that heaven is the same as from the haven to the earth [and to the firmament]. 19. And (I saw there, as) in the first heaven, angels on the right and on the left, and a throne in the midst, and the praise of the angels in the second heaven; and he who sat on the throne in the second heaven was more glorious than all (the rest). 20. And there was great glory in the second heaven, and the praise also was not like the praise of those who were in the first heaven. 21. And I fell on my face to worship him, but he angel who conducted me did not permit me, but said unto me: "Worship neither throne nor angel which belongs to the six heavens - for for this cause I was sent to conduct thee j- until I tell thee in the seventh heaven. 22. For above all the heavens and their angels has thy throne been placed, and thy garments and thy crown which thou shalt see." 23. And I rejoiced with great joy, that those who love the Most High and His Beloved will afterwards ascend thither by the angel of the Holy Spirit. 24. And he raise me to the third heaven, and in like manner I saw those upon the right and upon the left, and there was a throne there in the midst; but the memorial of this world is there unheard of. 25. And I said to the angel who was with me; for the glory of my appearance was undergoing transformation as I ascended to each heaven in turn: "Nothing of the vanity of that world is here named." 26. And he answered me, and said unto me: "Nothing is named on account of its weakness, and nothing is hidden there of what is done." 27. And I wished to learn how it is know, and he answered me saying: "When I have raised thee to the seventh heaven whence I was sent, to that which is above these, then thou shalt know that there is nothing hidden from the thrones and from those who dwell in the heavens and from the angels. And the praise wherewith they praised and glory of him who sat on the throne was great, and the glory of the angels on the right hand and on the left was beyond that of the heaven which was below them. 28. And again he raised me to the fourth heaven, and the height from the third to the height from the third to the forth heaven was greater than from the earth to the firmament. 29. And there again I saw those who were on the right hand and those who were on the left, and him who sat on the throne was in the midst, and there also they were praising. 30. And the praise and glory of the angels on the right was greater than that of those on the left. 31. And again the glory of him who sat on the throne was greater than that of the angels on the right, and their glory was beyond that of those who were below. 32. And he raised me to the fifth heaven. 33. And again I saw those upon the right hand and on the left, and him who sat on the throne possessing greater glory that those of the forth heaven. 34. And the glory of those on the right hand was greater than that of those on the left [from the third to the fourth]. 35. And the glory of him who was on the throne was greater than that of the angels on the right hand. 36. And their praise was more glorious than that of the fourth heaven. 37. And I praised Him, who is not named and the Only-begotten who dwelleth in the heavens, whose name is not known to any flesh, who has bestowed such glory on the several heaves, and who makes great the glory of the angels, and more excellent the glory of Him who sitteth on the throne.

Asc. Isa. 8 - AND again he raised me into the air of the sixth heaven, and I saw such glory as I had not seen in the five heavens. 2. For I saw angels possessing great glory. 3. And the praise there was holy and wonderful. 4. And I said to the angel who conducted me: "What is this which I see, my Lord?" 5. And he said: "I am not thy lord, but thy fellow servant." 6. And again I asked him, and I said unto him: "Why are there not angelic fellow servants (on the left)?" 7. And he said: "From the sixth heaven there are no longer angels on the left, nor a throne set in the midst, but (they are directed) by the power of the seventh heaven, where dwelleth He that is not named and the Elect One, whose name has not been made known, and none of the heavens can learn His name. 8. For it is He alone to whose voice all the heavens and thrones give answer. I have therefore been empowered and sent to raise thee here that thou mayest see this glory. 9. And that thou mayest see the Lord of all those heavens and these thrones. 10. Undergoing (successive) transformation until He resembles your form and likeness. 11. I indeed say unto thee, Isaiah; No man about to return into a body of that world has ascended or seen what thou seest or perceived what thou hast perceived and what thou wilt see. 12. For it has been permitted to thee in the lot of the Lord to come hither. [And from thence comes the power of the sixth heaven and of the air]." 13. And I magnified my Lord with praise, in that through His lot I should come hither. 14. And he said: "Hear, furthermore, therefore, this also from thy fellow servant: when from the body by the will of God thou hast ascended hither, then thou wilt receive the garment which thou seest, and likewise other numbered garments laid up (there) thou wilt see. 15. And then thou wilt become equal to the angels of the seventh heaven. 16. And he raised me up into the sixth heaven, and there were no (angels) on the left, nor a throne in the midst, but all had one appearance and their (power of) praise was equal. 17. And (power) was given to me also, and I also praised along with them and that angel also, and our praise was like theirs. 18. And there they all named the primal Father and His Beloved, the Christ, and the Holy Spirit, all with one voice.19 And (their voice) was not like the voice of the angels in the five heavens. 20. [Nor like their discourse] but the voice was different there, and there was much light there. 21. And then, when I was in the sixth heaven I thought the light which I had seen in the five heavens to be but darkness. 22. And I rejoiced and praised Him who hath bestowed such lights on those who wait for His promise. 23. And I besought the angel who conducted me that I should not henceforth return to the carnal world. 24. I say indeed unto you, Hezekiah and Josab my son and Micaiah, that there is much darkness here. 25. And the angel who conducted me discovered what I thought and said: "If in this light thou dost rejoice,

how much more wilt thou rejoice, when in the seventh heaven thou seest the light where is the Lord and His Beloved [whence I have been sent, who is to be called "Son" in this world. 26. Not (yet) hath been manifested he shall be in the corruptible world] and the garments, and the thrones, and the crowns which are laid up for the righteous, for those who trust in that Lord who will descend in your form. For the light which is there is great and wonderful. 27. And as concerning thy not returning into the body thy days are not yet fulfilled for coming here." 28. And when I heard (that) I was troubled, and he said: "Do not be troubled."

Asc. Isa. 9 - AND he took me into the air of the seventh heaven, and moreover I heard a voice saying: "How far will he ascend that dwelleth in the flesh?" And I feared and trembled. 2. And when I trembled, behold, I heard from hence another voice being sent forth, and saying: "It is permitted to the holy Isaiah to ascend hither; for here is his garment." 3. And I asked the angel who was with me and said: "Who is he who forbade me and who is he who permitted me to ascend?" 4. And he said unto me: "He who forbade thee, is he who is over the praise-giving of the sixth heaven. 5. And He who permitted thee, this is thy Lord God, the Lord Christ, who will be called "Jesus" in the world, but His name thou canst not hear till thou hast ascended out of thy body." 6. And he raised me up into the seventh heaven, and I saw there a wonderful light and angels innumerable. 7. And there I saw the holy Abel and all the righteous. 8. And there I saw Enoch and all who were with him, stript of the garments of the flesh, and I saw them in their garments of the upper world, and they were like angels, standing there in great glory. 9. And there I saw Enoch and all who were with him, stript of the garments of the flesh, and I saw them in their garments of the upper world, and they were like angels, standing there in great glory. 10. But they sat not on their thrones, nor were their crowns of glory on them. 11. And I asked the angel who was with me: "How is it that they have received the garments, but have not the thrones and the crowns?" 12. And he said unto me: "Crowns and thrones of glory they do not receive, till the Beloved will descent in the form in which you will see Him descent [will descent, I say] into the world in the last days the Lord, who will be called Christ. 13. Nevertheless they see and know whose will be thrones, and whose the crowns when He has descended and been made in your form, and they will think that He is flesh and is a man. 14. And the god of that world will stretch forth his hand against the Son, and they will crucify Him on a tree, and will slay Him not knowing who He is. 15. And thus His descent, as you will see, will be hidden even from the heavens, so that it will not be known who He is. 16. And when He hath plundered the angel of death, He will ascend on the third day, [and he will remain in that world five hundred and forty-five days]. 17. And then many of the righteous will ascend with Him, whose spirits do not receive their garments till the Lord Christ ascend and they ascend with Him. 18. Then indeed they will receive their [garments and] thrones and crowns, when He has ascended into the seventh heaven." 19. And I said unto him that which I had asked him in the third heaven: 20. "Show me how everything which is done in that world is here made known." 21. And whilst I was still speaking with him, behold one of the angels who stood nigh, more glorious than the glory of that angel, who had raised me up from the world. 22. Showed me a book, [but not as a book of this world] and he opened it, and the book was written, but not as a book of this world. And he gave (it) to me and I read it, and lo! the deeds of the children of Israel were written therein, and the deeds of those whom I know (not), my son Josab. 23. And I said: "In truth, there is nothing hidden in the seventh heaven, which is done in this world." 24. And I saw there many garments laid up, and many thrones and many crowns. 25. And I said to the angel: "Whose are these garments and thrones and crowns?" 26. And he said unto me: "These garments many from that world will receive, believing in the words of That One, who shall be named as I told thee, and they will observe those things, and believe in them, and believe in His cross: for them are these laid up." 27. And I saw a certain One standing, whose glory surpassed that of all, and His glory was great and wonderful. 28. And after I had seen Him, all the righteous whom I had seen and also the angels whom I had seen came to Him. And Adam and Abel and Seth and all the righteous first drew near and worshipped Him, and they all praised Him with one voice, and I myself also gave praise with them, and my giving of praise was as theirs. 29. And then all the angels drew nigh and worshipped and gave praise. 30. And I was (again) transformed and became like an angel. 31. And thereupon the angel who conducted me said to me: "Worship this One," and I worshipped and praised. 32. And the angel said unto me: "This is the Lord of all the praise-givings which thou hast seen." 33. And whilst he was still speaking, I saw another Glorious One who was like Him, and the righteous drew nigh and worshipped and praised, and I praised together with them. But my glory was not transformed into accordance with their form. 34. And thereupon the angels drew near and worshipped Him. 35. And I saw the Lord and the second angel, and they were standing. 36. And the second whom I saw was on he left of my Lord. And I asked: "Who is this?" and he said unto me: "Worship Him, for He is the angel of the Holy Spirit, who speaketh in thee and the rest of the righteous." 37. And I saw the great glory, the eyes of my spirit being open, and I could not thereupon see, nor yet could the angel who was with me, nor all the angels whom I had seen worshipping my Lord. 38. But I saw the righteous beholding with great power the glory of that One. 39. And my Lord drew nigh to me and the angel of the Spirit and He said: "See how it is given to thee to see God, and on thy account power is given to the angel who is with thee." 40. And I saw how my Lord and the angel of the Spirit worshipped, and they both together praised God. 41. And thereupon all the righteous drew near and worshipped. 42. And the angels drew near and worshipped and all the angels praised.

Asc. Isa. 10 - AND thereupon I heard the voices and the giving of praise, which I had heard in each of the six heavens, ascending and being heard there: 2. And all were being sent up to that Glorious One whose glory I could not behold. 3. And I myself was hearing and beholding the praise (which was given) to Him. 4. And the Lord and the angel of the Spirit were beholding all and hearing all. 5. And all the praises which are sent up from the six heavens are not only heard, but seen. 6. And I heard the angel who conducted me and he said: "This is the Most High of the high ones, dwelling in the holy world, and resting in His holy ones, who will be called by the Holy Spirit through the lips of the righteous the Father of the Lord." 7. And I heard the voice of the Most High, the Father of my Lord, saying to my Lord Christ who will be called Jesus: 8. "Go forth and descent through all the heavens, and thou wilt descent to the firmament and that world: to the angel in Sheol thou wilt descend, but to Haguel thou wilt not go. 9. And thou wilt become like unto the likeness of all who are in the five heavens. 10. And thou wilt be careful to become like the form of the angels of the firmament [and the angels also who are in Sheol]. 11. And none of the angels of that world shall know that Thou art with Me of the seven heavens and of their angels. 12. And they shall not know that Thou art with Me, till with a loud voice I have called (to) the heavens, and their angels and their lights, (even) unto the sixth heaven, in order that you mayest judge and destroy the princes and angels and gods of that world, and the world that is dominated by them: 13. For they have denied Me and said: "We alone are and there is none beside us." 14.

351

And afterwards from the angels of death Thou wilt ascend to Thy place. And Thou wilt not be transformed in each heaven, but in glory wilt Thou ascend and sit on My right hand. 15. And thereupon the princes and powers of that world will worship Thee." 16. These commands I heard the Great Glory giving to my Lord. 17. And so I saw my Lord go forth from the seventh heaven into the sixth heaven. 18. And the angel who conducted me [from this world was with me and] said unto me: "Understand, Isaiah, and see the transformation and descent of the Lord will appear." 19. And I saw, and when the angels saw Him, thereupon those in the sixth heaven praised and lauded Him; for He had not been transformed after the shape of the angels there, and they praised Him and I also praised with them. 20. And I saw when He descended into the fifth heaven, that in the fifth heaven He made Himself like unto the form of the angels there, and they did not praise Him (nor worship Him); for His form was like unto theirs. 21. And then He descended into the forth heaven, and made Himself like unto the form of the angels there. 22. And when they saw Him, they did not praise or laud Him; for His form was like unto their form. 23. And again I saw when He descended into the third heaven, and He made Himself like unto the form of the angels in the third heaven. 24. And those who kept the gate of the (third) heaven demanded the password, and the Lord gave (it) to them in order that He should not be recognized. And when they saw Him, they did not praise or laud Him; for His form was like unto their form. 25. And again I saw when He descended into the second heaven, and again He gave the password there; those who kept the gate proceeded to demand and the Lord to give. 26. And I saw when He made Himself like unto the form of the angels in the second heaven, and they saw Him and they did not praise Him; for His form was like unto their form. 27. And again I saw when He descended into the first heaven, and there also He gave the password to those who kept the gate, and He made Himself like unto the form of the angels who were on the left of that throne, and they neither praised nor lauded Him; for His form was like unto their form. 28. But as for me no one asked me on account of the angel who conducted me. 29. And again He descended into the firmament where dwelleth the ruler of this world, and He gave the password to those on the left, and His form was like theirs, and they did not praise Him there; but they were envying one another and fighting; for here there is a power of evil and envying about trifles. 30. And I saw when He descended and made Himself like unto the angels of the air, and He was like one of them. 31. And He gave no password; for one was plundering and doing violence to another.

Asc. Isa. 11 - AFTER this I saw, and the angel who spoke with me, who conducted me, said unto me: "Understand, Isaiah son of Amoz; for for this purpose have I been sent from God." 2. And I indeed saw a woman of the family of David the prophet, named Mary, and Virgin, and she was espoused to a man named Joseph, a carpenter, and he also was of the seed and family of the righteous David of Bethlehem Judah. 3. And he came into his lot. And when she was espoused, she was found with child, and Joseph the carpenter was desirous to put her away. 4. But the angel of the Spirit appeared in this world, and after that Joseph did not put her away, but kept Mary and did not reveal this matter to any one. 5. And he did not approach May, but kept her as a holy virgin, though with child. 6. And he did not live with her for two months. 7. And after two months of days while Joseph was in his house, and Mary his wife, but both alone. 8. It came to pass that when they were alone that Mary straight-way looked with her eyes and saw a small babe, and she was astonished. 9. And after she had been astonished, her womb was found as formerly before she had conceived. 10. And when her husband Joseph said unto her: "What has astonished thee?" his eyes were opened and he saw the infant and praised God, because into his portion God had come. [11]. And a voice came to them: "Tell this vision to no one." [12]. And the story regarding the infant was noised broad in Bethlehem. [13]. Some said: "The Virgin Mary hath borne a child, before she was married two months." [14]. And many said: "She has not borne a child, nor has a midwife gone up (to her), nor have we heard the cries of (labour) pains." And they were all blinded respecting Him and they all knew regarding Him, though they knew not whence He was. [15]. And they took Him, and went to Nazareth in Galilee. [16]. And I saw, O Hezekiah and Josab my son, and I declare to the other prophets also who are standing by, that (this) hath escaped all the heavens and all the princes and all the gods of this world. [17]. And I saw: In Nazareth He sucked the breast as a babe and as is customary in order that He might not be recognized. [18]. And when He had grown up he worked great signs and wonders in the land of Israel and of Jerusalem. [19]. And after this the adversary envied Him and roused the children of Israel against Him, not knowing who He was, and they delivered Him to the king, and crucified Him, and He descended to the angel (of Sheol). [20]. In Jerusalem indeed I was Him being crucified on a tree: [21]. And likewise after the third day rise again and remain days. [22]. And the angel who conducted me said: "Understand, Isaiah": and I saw when He sent out the Twelve Apostles and ascended. [23]. And I saw Him, and He was in the firmament, but He had not changed Himself into their form, and all the angels of the firmament and the Satans saw Him and they worshipped. [24]. And there was much sorrow there, while they said: "How did our Lord descend in our midst, and we perceived not the glory [which has been upon Him], which we see has been upon Him from the sixth heaven?" [25]. And He ascended into the second heaven, and He did not transform Himself, but all the angels who were on the right and on the left and the throne in the midst. [26]. Both worshiped Him and praised Him and said: "How did our Lord escape us whilst descending, and we perceived not?" [27]. And in like manner He ascended into the third heaven, and they praised and said in like manner. [28]. And in the fourth heaven and in the fifth also they said precisely after the same manner. [29]. But there was one glory, and from it He did not change Himself. [30]. And I saw when He ascended into the sixth heaven, and they worshipped and glorified Him. [31]. But in all the heavens the praise increased (in volume). [32]. And I saw how He ascended into the seventh heaven, and all the righteous and all the angels praised Him. And then I saw Him sit down on the right hand of that Great Glory whose glory I told you that I could not behold. [33]. And also the angel of the Holy Spirit I saw sitting on the left hand. [34]. And this angel said unto me: "Isaiah, son of Amoz, it is enough for thee;... for thou hast seen what no child of flesh has seen. [35]. And thou wilt return into thy garment (of the flesh) until thy days are completed. Then thou wilt come hither." [36]. These things Isaiah saw and told unto all that stood before him, and they praised. And he spake to Hezekiah the King and said: "I have spoken these things." [37]. Both the end of this world; [38]. And all this vision will be consummated in the last generations. [39]. And Isaiah made him swear that he would not tell (it) to the people of Israel, nor give these words to any man to transcribe. [40]. ...such things ye will read. and watch ye in the Holy Spirit in order they ye may receive your garments and thrones and crowns of glory which are laid up in the seventh heaven. [41]. On account of these visions and prophecies Sammael Satan sawed in sunder Isaiah the son of Amoz, the prophet, by the hand of Manasseh. [42]. And all these things Hezekiah delivered to Manasseh in the twenty-sixth year. [43]. But Manasseh did not remember them nor place these things in his heart, but becoming the servant of Satan

he was destroyed. Here endeth the vision of Isaiah the prophet with his ascension.

Early Christian Writings and New Testament Apocrypha

Introduction

This section encompasses a collection of influential texts that illuminate the beliefs, practices, and theological discussions of early Christian communities. These writings, while not included in the canonical New Testament, provide invaluable insights into the diversity and development of early Christian thought and offer perspectives on issues central to the faith during its formative centuries.

Historical Context - The texts in this section were written from the late first century to the mid-second century CE, a period marked by rapid expansion and doctrinal formulation within the Christian movement. These writings reflect the theological diversity of early Christianity, addressing pastoral care, ecclesiastical discipline, theological controversies, and eschatological expectations. They were often highly revered by many early Christians but did not achieve canonical status for various reasons, including their late composition, limited geographical spread, or divergence from emerging orthodox doctrines.

Theological Significance - The "Early Christian Writings and New Testament Apocrypha" offer profound insights into the spiritual and doctrinal life of early Christian communities. Among these, five texts stand out for their historical importance and theological depth:

- **Didache:** Also known as "The Teaching of the Twelve Apostles," this text is one of the earliest known written catechisms, providing instructions on Christian ethics, practices such as baptism and fasting, and Church organization. It reflects the transitional phase from Jewish Christian sects to a gentile Christian church.

- **1 Clement**: An epistle written by Clement of Rome, this document addresses the authority of church leaders and the need for church unity. It is notable for its early assertion of Roman primacy in ecclesiastical matters.

- **The Shepherd of Hermas**: A Christian literary work of the 2nd century, composed of visions, mandates, and parables. It was very popular in the early Church and was even considered scriptural by some early Christian fathers.

- **Epistle of Barnabas**: This epistle sheds light on the way early Christians viewed their relationship with Judaism, interpreting the Old Testament in a distinctly Christian way that emphasizes the idea of the new covenant.

- **Revelation of Peter:** An apocalyptic text that offers a graphic description of heaven and hell, it was influential in shaping early Christian views on the afterlife.

Rationale for Inclusion - These texts were introduced into early Christian literature to instruct, unify, and define communities amidst the theological diversity of the time. They were tools for pastoral care, doctrinal instruction, and community formation. Their exclusion from the canon typically stemmed from the formalization of the New Testament canon in the fourth century, which sought to solidify the doctrinal foundations of the church.

The inclusion of these writings in "Apocrypha Complete" enriches our understanding of early Christian theology, ecclesiology, and eschatology. They illuminate the historical context of early Christian practices and beliefs and demonstrate the complex and dynamic nature of early Christian identity and community life. Through their study, we gain a richer, more nuanced picture of early Christianity, providing depth to our understanding of the historical and theological development of the Christian faith.

Embarking on the exploration of these texts within "Complete Apocrypha," we might appreciate the depth and breadth of early Christian literature. Each document, whether doctrinal, instructive or visionary, contributes uniquely to the tapestry of Christian history, offering insights that challenge and enrich our understanding of the early Church. This collection, therefore, not only enhances our understanding of Christian historical and doctrinal development, but also connects us more deeply to the spiritual and communal life of our early predecessors in the faith.

The Didache

The Lord's Teaching Through the Twelve Apostles to the Nations.

Did. 1. The Two Ways and the First Commandment. There are two ways, one of life and one of death, but a great difference between the two ways. The way of life, then, is this: First, you shall love God who made you; second, love your neighbor as yourself, and do not do to another what you would not want done to you. And of these sayings the teaching is this: Bless those who curse you, and pray for your enemies, and fast for those who persecute you. For what reward is there for loving those who love you? Do not the Gentiles do the same? But love those who hate you, and you shall not have an enemy. Abstain from fleshly and worldly lusts. If someone strikes your right cheek, turn to him the other also, and you shall be perfect. If someone impresses you for one mile, go with him two. If someone takes your cloak, give him also your coat. If someone takes from you what is yours, ask it not back, for indeed you are not able. Give to every one who asks you, and ask it not back; for the Father wills that to all should be given of our own blessings (free gifts). Happy is he who gives according to the commandment, for he is guiltless. Woe to him who receives; for if one receives who has need, he is guiltless; but he who receives not having need shall pay the penalty, why he received and for what. And coming into confinement, he shall be examined concerning the things which he has done, and he shall not escape from there until he pays back the last penny. And also concerning this, it has been said, Let your alms sweat in your hands, until you know to whom you should give.

Did. 2. The Second Commandment: Grave Sin Forbidden. And the second commandment of the Teaching; You shall not commit murder, you shall not commit adultery, you shall not commit pederasty, you shall not commit fornication, you shall not steal, you shall not practice magic, you shall not practice witchcraft, you shall not murder a child by abortion nor kill that which is born. You shall not covet the things of your neighbor, you shall not swear, you shall not bear false witness, you shall not speak evil, you shall bear no grudge. You shall not be double-minded nor double-tongued, for to be double-tongued is a snare of death. Your speech shall not be false, nor empty, but fulfilled by deed. You shall not be covetous, nor rapacious, nor a hypocrite, nor evil disposed, nor haughty. You shall not take evil counsel against your neighbor. You shall not hate any man; but some you shall reprove, and concerning some you shall pray, and some you shall love more than your own life.

Did. 3. Other Sins Forbidden. My child, flee from every evil thing, and from every likeness of it. Be not prone to anger, for anger leads to murder. Be neither jealous, nor quarrelsome, nor of hot temper, for out of all these murders are engendered. My child, be not a lustful one. for lust leads to fornication. Be neither a filthy talker, nor of lofty eye, for out of all these adulteries are engendered. My child, be

not an observer of omens, since it leads to idolatry. Be neither an enchanter, nor an astrologer, nor a purifier, nor be willing to took at these things, for out of all these idolatry is engendered. My child, be not a liar, since a lie leads to theft. Be neither money-loving, nor vainglorious, for out of all these thefts are engendered. My child, be not a murmurer, since it leads the way to blasphemy. Be neither self-willed nor evil-minded, for out of all these blasphemies are engendered.

Rather, be meek, since the meek shall inherit the earth. Be long-suffering and pitiful and guileless and gentle and good and always trembling at the words which you have heard. You shall not exalt yourself, nor give over-confidence to your soul. Your soul shall not be joined with lofty ones, but with just and lowly ones shall it have its intercourse. Accept whatever happens to you as good, knowing that apart from God nothing comes to pass.

Did. 4. Various Precepts. My child, remember night and day him who speaks the word of God to you, and honor him as you do the Lord. For wherever the lordly rule is uttered, there is the Lord. And seek out day by day the faces of the saints, in order that you may rest upon their words. Do not long for division, but rather bring those who contend to peace. Judge righteously, and do not respect persons in reproving for transgressions. You shall not be undecided whether or not it shall be. Be not a stretcher forth of the hands to receive and a drawer of them back to give. If you have anything, through your hands you shall give ransom for your sins. Do not hesitate to give, nor complain when you give; for you shall know who is the good repayer of the hire. Do not turn away from him who is in want; rather, share all things with your brother, and do not say that they are your own. For if you are partakers in that which is immortal, how much more in things which are mortal? Do not remove your hand from your son or daughter; rather, teach them the fear of God from their youth. Do not enjoin anything in your bitterness upon your bondman or maidservant, who hope in the same God, lest ever they shall fear not God who is over both; for he comes not to call according to the outward appearance, but to them whom the Spirit has prepared. And you bondmen shall be subject to your masters as to a type of God, in modesty and fear. You shall hate all hypocrisy and everything which is not pleasing to the Lord. Do not in any way forsake the commandments of the Lord; but keep what you have received, neither adding thereto nor taking away therefrom. In the church you shall acknowledge your transgressions, and you shall not come near for your prayer with an evil conscience. This is the way of life.

Did. 5. Against False Teachers, and Food Offered to Idols. See that no one causes you to err from this way of the Teaching, since apart from God it teaches you. For if you are able to bear the entire yoke of the Lord, you will be perfect; but if you are not able to do this, do what you are able. And concerning food, bear what you are able; but against that which is sacrificed to idols be exceedingly careful; for it is the service of dead gods.

Did. 6. Concerning Baptism. And concerning baptism, baptize this way: Having first said all these things, baptize into the name of the Father, and of the Son, and of the Holy Spirit, in living water. But if you have no living water, baptize into other water; and if you cannot do so in cold water, do so in warm. But if you have neither, pour out water three times upon the head into the name of Father and Son and Holy Spirit. But before the baptism let the baptizer fast, and the baptized, and whoever else can; but you shall order the baptized to fast one or two days before.

Did. 7. Fasting and Prayer (the Lord's Prayer). But let not your fasts be with the hypocrites, for they fast on the second and fifth day of the week. Rather, fast on the fourth day and the Preparation

(Friday). Do not pray like the hypocrites, but rather as the Lord commanded in His Gospel, like this:

Our Father who art in heaven, hallowed be Thy name. Thy kingdom come. Thy will be done on earth, as it is in heaven. Give us today our daily (needful) bread, and forgive us our debt as we also forgive our debtors. And bring us not into temptation, but deliver us from the evil one (or, evil); for Thine is the power and the glory for ever.. Pray this three times each day.

Did. 8. The Eucharist. Now concerning the Eucharist, give thanks this way. First, concerning the cup:

We thank thee, our Father, for the holy vine of David Thy servant, which You madest known to us through Jesus Thy Servant; to Thee be the glory for ever..

And concerning the broken bread:

We thank Thee, our Father, for the life and knowledge which You madest known to us through Jesus Thy Servant; to Thee be the glory for ever. Even as this broken bread was scattered over the hills, and was gathered together and became one, so let Thy Church be gathered together from the ends of the earth into Thy kingdom; for Thine is the glory and the power through Jesus Christ for ever..

But let no one eat or drink of your Eucharist, unless they have been baptized into the name of the Lord; for concerning this also the Lord has said, "Give not that which is holy to the dogs."

Did. 9. Prayer after Communion. But after you are filled, give thanks this way: We thank Thee, holy Father, for Thy holy name which You didst cause to tabernacle in our hearts, and for the knowledge and faith and immortality, which You modest known to us through Jesus Thy Servant; to Thee be the glory for ever. Thou, Master almighty, didst create all things for Thy name's sake; You gavest food and drink to men for enjoyment, that they might give thanks to Thee; but to us You didst freely give spiritual food and drink and life eternal through Thy Servant. Before all things we thank Thee that You are mighty; to Thee be the glory for ever. Remember, Lord, Thy Church, to deliver it from all evil and to make it perfect in Thy love, and gather it from the four winds, sanctified for Thy kingdom which Thou have prepared for it; for Thine is the power and the glory for ever. Let grace come, and let this world pass away. Hosanna to the God (Son) of David! If any one is holy, let him come; if any one is not so, let him repent. Maranatha. Amen. But permit the prophets to make Thanksgiving as much as they desire.

Did. 10. Concerning Teachers, Apostles, and Prophets. Whosoever, therefore, comes and teaches you all these things that have been said before, receive him. But if the teacher himself turns and teaches another doctrine to the destruction of this, hear him not. But if he teaches so as to increase righteousness and the knowledge of the Lord, receive him as the Lord. But concerning the apostles and prophets, act according to the decree of the Gospel. Let every apostle who comes to you be received as the Lord. But he shall not remain more than one day; or two days, if there's a need. But if he remains three days, he is a false prophet. And when the apostle goes away, let him take nothing but bread until he lodges. If he asks for money, he is a false prophet. And every prophet who speaks in the Spirit you shall neither try nor judge; for every sin shall be forgiven, but this sin shall not be forgiven. But not every one who speaks in the Spirit is a prophet; but only if he holds the ways of the Lord. Therefore from their ways shall the false prophet and the prophet be known. And every prophet who orders a meal in the Spirit does not eat it, unless he is indeed a false prophet. And every prophet who teaches the truth, but does not do what he teaches, is a false prophet. And every prophet, proved true, working unto the mystery of the Church in

354

the world, yet not teaching others to do what he himself does, shall not be judged among you, for with God he has his judgment; for so did also the ancient prophets. But whoever says in the Spirit, Give me money, or something else, you shall not listen to him. But if he tells you to give for others' sake who are in need, let no one judge him.

Did. 11. Reception of Christians. But receive everyone who comes in the name of the Lord, and prove and know him afterward; for you shall have understanding right and left. If he who comes is a wayfarer, assist him as far as you are able; but he shall not remain with you more than two or three days, if need be. But if he wants to stay with you, and is an artisan, let him work and eat. But if he has no trade, according to your understanding, see to it that, as a Christian, he shall not live with you idle. But if he wills not to do, he is a Christ-monger. Watch that you keep away from such.

Did. 12. Support of Prophets. But every true prophet who wants to live among you is worthy of his support. So also a true teacher is himself worthy, as the workman, of his support. Every first-fruit, therefore, of the products of wine-press and threshing-floor, of oxen and of sheep, you shall take and give to the prophets, for they are your high priests. But if you have no prophet, give it to the poor. If you make a batch of dough, take the first-fruit and give according to the commandment. So also when you open a jar of wine or of oil, take the first-fruit and give it to the prophets; and of money (silver) and clothing and every possession, take the first-fruit, as it may seem good to you, and give according to the commandment.

Did. 13. Christian Assembly on the Lord's Day. But every Lord's day gather yourselves together, and break bread, and give thanksgiving after having confessed your transgressions, that your sacrifice may be pure. But let no one who is at odds with his fellow come together with you, until they be reconciled, that your sacrifice may not be profaned. For this is that which was spoken by the Lord: "In every place and time offer to me a pure sacrifice; for I am a great King, says the Lord, and my name is wonderful among the nations."

Did. 14. Bishops and Deacons; Christian Reproof. Appoint, therefore, for yourselves, bishops and deacons worthy of the Lord, men meek, and not lovers of money, and truthful and proved; for they also render to you the service of prophets and teachers. Therefore do not despise them, for they are your honored ones, together with the prophets and teachers. And reprove one another, not in anger, but in peace, as you have it in the Gospel. But to anyone that acts amiss against another, let no one speak, nor let him hear anything from you until he repents. But your prayers and alms and all your deeds so do, as you have it in the Gospel of our Lord.

Did. 15. Watchfulness; the Coming of the Lord. Watch for your life's sake. Let not your lamps be quenched, nor your loins unloosed; but be ready, for you know not the hour in which our Lord will come. But come together often, seeking the things which are befitting to your souls: for the whole time of your faith will not profit you, if you are not made perfect in the last time. For in the last days false prophets and corrupters shall be multiplied, and the sheep shall be turned into wolves, and love shall be turned into hate; for when lawlessness increases, they shall hate and persecute and betray one another, and then shall appear the world-deceiver as Son of God, and shall do signs and wonders, and the earth shall be delivered into his hands, and he shall do iniquitous things which have never yet come to pass since the beginning. Then shall the creation of men come into the fire of trial, and many shall be made to stumble and shall perish; but those who endure in their faith shall be saved from under the curse itself. And then shall appear the signs of the truth: first, the sign of an outspreading in heaven, then the sign of the sound of the trumpet. And third, the resurrection of the dead -- yet not of all, but as it is said: "The Lord shall come and all His saints with Him." Then shall the world see the Lord coming upon the clouds of heaven.

The Apocalypse of Peter

[1]... many of them will be false prophets, and will teach divers ways and doctrines of perdition: but these will become sons of perdition. [3]. And then God will come unto my faithful ones who hunger and thirst and are afflicted and purify their souls in this life; and he will judge the sons of lawlessness. [4]. And furthermore the Lord said: Let us go into the mountain: Let us pray. [5]. And going with him, we, the twelve disciples, begged that he would show us one of our brethren, the righteous who are gone forth out of the world, in order that we might see of what manner of form they are, and having taken courage, might also encourage the men who hear us. [6]. And as we prayed, suddenly there appeared two men standing before the Lord towards the East, on whom we were not able to look; [7], for there came forth from their countenance a ray as of the sun, and their raiment was shining, such as eye of man never saw; for no mouth is able to express or heart to conceive the glory with which they were endued, and the beauty of their appearance. [8]. And as we looked upon them, we were astounded; for their bodies were whiter than any snow and ruddier than any rose; [9], and the red thereof was mingled with the white, and I am utterly unable to express their beauty; [10], for their hair was curly and bright and seemly both on their face and shoulders, as it were a wreath woven of spikenard and divers-coloured flowers, or like a rainbow in the sky, such was their seemliness. [11]. Seeing therefore their beauty we became astounded at them, since they appeared suddenly. [12]. And I approached the Lord and said: Who are these? [13]. He saith to me: These are your brethren the righteous, whose forms ye desired to see. [14]. And I said to him: And where are all the righteous ones and what is the aeon in which they are and have this glory? [15]. And the Lord showed me a very great country outside of this world, exceeding bright with light, and the air there lighted with the rays of the sun, and the earth itself blooming with unfading flowers and full of spices and plants, fair-flowering and incorruptible and bearing blessed fruit. [16]. And so great was the perfume that it was borne thence even unto us. [17]. And the dwellers in that place were clad in the raiment of shining angels and their raiment was like unto their country; and angels hovered about them there. [18]. And the glory of the dwellers there was equal, and with one voice they sang praises alternately to the Lord God, rejoicing in that place. [19]. The Lord saith to us: This is the place of your high-priests, the righteous men. [20]. And over against that place I saw another, squalid, and it was the place of punishment; and those who were punished there and the punishing angels had their raiment dark like the air of the place. [21]. And there were certain there hanging by the tongue: and these were the blasphemers of the way of righteousness; and under them lay fire, burning and punishing them. [22]. And there was a great lake, full of flaming mire, in which were certain men that pervert righteousness, and tormenting angels afflicted them. [23]. And there were also others, women, hanged by their hair over that mire that bubbled up: and these were they who adorned themselves for adultery; and the men who mingled with them in the defilement of adultery, were hanging by the feet and their heads in that mire. And I said: I did not believe that I should come into this place. [24]. And I saw the murderers and those who conspired with them, cast into a certain strait place, full of evil snakes, and smitten by those beasts, and thus turning to and fro in that punishment; and worms, as it were clouds of darkness, afflicted them. And the souls of the murdered stood and looked upon the punishment of those murderers and said: O God, thy judgment is just. [25]. And near that place I saw another strait place into which the gore and the filth of those who were being punished ran down and became there as it were a lake: and there sat women having the gore up to their necks, and over against them sat many children who were born to them out of due time, crying; and there came forth from them sparks of fire and smote the women in the eyes: and these were the accursed who conceived and caused abortion. [26]. And other men and women were burning up to the middle and were cast into a dark place and were beaten by evil spirits, and their inwards were eaten by restless worms: and these were they who persecuted the righteous and delivered them up. [27]. And near those there were again women and men gnawing their own lips, and being punished and receiving a red-hot iron in their eyes: and these were they who blasphemed and slandered the way of righteousness. [28]. And over against these again other men and women gnawing their tongues and having flaming fire in their mouths: and these were the false witnesses. [29]. And in a certain other place there were pebbles sharper than swords or any spit, red-hot, and women and men in tattered and filthy raiment rolled about on them in punishment: and these were the rich who trusted in their riches and had no pity for orphans and widows, and despised the commandment of God. [30]. And in another great lake, full of pitch and blood and mire bubbling up, there stood men and women up to their knees: and these were the usurers and those who take interest on interest. [31]. And other men and women were being hurled down from a great cliff and reached the bottom, and again were driven by those who were set over them to climb up upon the cliff, and thence were hurled down again, and had no rest from this punishment: and these were they who defiled their bodies acting as women; and the women who were with them were those who lay with one another as a man with a woman. [32]. And alongside of that cliff there was a place full of much fire, and there stood men who with their own hands had made for themselves carven images instead of God. And alongside of these were other men and women, having rods and striking each other and never ceasing from such punishment. [33]. And others again near them, women and men, burning and turning themselves and roasting: and these were they that leaving the way of God

The Epistle of Barnabas

Barn. 1 - [1] I Bid you greeting, sons and daughters, in the name of the Lord that loved us, in peace. [2] Seeing that the ordinances of God are great and rich unto you, I rejoice with an exceeding great and overflowing joy at your blessed and glorious spirits; so innate is the grace of the spiritual gift that ye have received. [3] Wherefore also I the more congratulate myself hoping to be saved, for that I truly see the Spirit poured out among you from the riches of the fount of the Lord. So greatly did the much-desired sight of you astonish me respecting you. [4] Being therefore persuaded of this, and being conscious with myself that having said much among you I know that the Lord journeyed with me on the way of righteousness, I am wholly constrained also myself to this, to love you more than my own soul (for great faith and love dwelleth in you through the hope of the life which is His)--considering this therefore, that, [5] if it shall be my care to communicate to you some portion of that which I received, it shall turn to my reward for having ministered to such spirits, I was eager to send you a trifle, that along with your faith ye might have your knowledge also perfect. [6] Well then, there are three ordinances of the Lord; *the hope of life, which is the beginning and end of our faith; and righteousness, which is the beginning and end of judgment; love shown in gladness and exultation, the testimony of works of righteousness. [7] For the Lord made known to us by His prophets things past and present, giving us likewise the firstfruits of the taste of things future. And seeing each of these things severally coming to pass, according as He spake, we ought to offer a richer and higher offering to the fear of Him. But I, not as though I were a teacher, but as one of yourselves, will show forth a few things, whereby ye shall be gladdened in the present circumstances.

Barn. 2 - [1] Seeing then that the days are evil, and that the Active One himself has the authority, we ought to give heed to ourselves and to seek out the ordinances of the Lord. [2] The aids of our faith then are fear and patience, and our allies are long-suffering and self-restraint. [3] While these abide in a pure spirit in matters relating to the Lord, wisdom, understanding, science, knowledge rejoice with them. [4] For He hath made manifest to us by all the prophets that He wanteth neither sacrifices nor whole burnt offerings nor oblations, saying at one time; [5] "What to Me is the multitude of your sacrifices, saith the Lord. I am full of whole burnt-offerings, and the fat of lambs and the blood of bulls and of goats desire not, not though ye should come to be seen of Me. or who required these things at your hands? Ye shall continue no more to tread My court. If ye bring fine flour, it is in vain; incense is an abomination to Me; your new moons and your Sabbaths I cannot away with." [6] These things therefore He annulled, that the new law of our Lord Jesus Christ, being free from the yoke of constraint, might have its oblation not made by human hands. [7] And He saith again unto them; "Did I command your fathers when they "went forth from the land of Egypt to bring Me whole burnt offerings and sacrifices?" [8] "Nay, this was My command unto them, Let none of you bear a grudge of evil against his neighbor in his heart, and love you not a false oath." [9] So we ought to perceive, unless we are without understanding, the mind of the goodness of our Father; for He speaketh to us, desiring us not to go astray like them but to seek how we may approach Him. [10] Thus then speaketh He to us; "The sacrifice unto God is a broken "heart, the smell of a sweet savor unto the Lord is a heart that glorifies its Maker." We ought therefore, brethren, to learn accurately concerning our salvation, lest the Evil One having effected an entrance of error in us should fling us away from our life.

Barn. 3 - [1] He speaketh again therefore to them concerning these things; "Wherefore fast ye for Me, saith the Lord, so that your voice is heard this day crying aloud? This is not the fast which have chosen, saith the Lord; not a man abasing his soul;" [2] "not though ye should bend your neck as a hoop, and put on sackcloth and make your bed of ashes, not even so shall ye call a fast that is acceptable." [3] But unto us He saith; "Behold, this is the fast which I have chosen, "saith the Lord; loosen every band of wickedness, untie the tightened cords of forcible contracts, send away the broken ones released and tear in pieces every unjust bond. Break thy bread to the hungry, and if thou seest one naked clothe him; bring the shelterless into thy house, and if thou seest a humble man, thou shalt not despise him, neither shall any one of thy household and of thine own seed." [4] "Then shall thy light break forth in the morning, and thy healing shall arise quickly, and righteousness shall go forth before thy face, and the glory of God shall environ thee. [5] "Then shalt thou cry out and God shall hear thee; while thou art still speaking, He shall say 'Lo, I am here'; if thou shalt take away from thee the yoke and the stretching forth of the finger and the word of murmuring, and shalt give thy bread to the hungry heartily, and shalt pity the abased soul." [6] To this end therefore, my brethren, He that is long-suffering, foreseeing that the people whom He had prepared in His well-beloved would believe in simplicity, manifested to us beforehand concerning all things, that we might not as novices shipwreck ourselves upon their law.

Barn. 4 - [1] It behooves us therefore to investigate deeply concerning the present, and to search out the things which have power to save us. Let us therefore flee altogether from all the works of lawlessness, lest the works of lawlessness overpower us; and let us loathe the error of the present time, that we may be loved for that which is to come. [2] Let us give no relaxation to our soul that it should have liberty to consort with sinners and wicked men, lest haply we be made like unto them. [3] The last offence is at hand, concerning which the scripture speaketh, as Enoch saith. "For to this end the Master hath cut the seasons and "the days short, that His beloved might hasten and come to His inheritance." [4] And the prophet also speaketh on this wise; "Ten reigns shall reign "upon the earth, and after them shall arise another king, who shall bring low three of the kings under one." [5] In like manner Daniel speaketh concerning the same; "And I saw the forth beast to be wicked and strong and more intractable than all the beasts of the earth, and how there arose from him ten horns, and from these a little horn and excrescence, and how that it abased under one three of the great horns." [6] Ye ought therefore to understand. Moreover I ask you this one thing besides, as being one of yourselves and loving you all in particular more than my own soul, to give heed to yourselves now, and not to liken yourselves to certain persons who pile up sin upon sin, saying that our covenant remains to them also. [7] Ours it is; but they lost it in this way for ever, when Moses had just received it. For the scripture saith; "And Moses was in the mountain fasting forty days and forty nights, and he received the covenant from the Lord, even tablets of stone written with the finger of the hand of the Lord." [8] But they lost it by turning unto idols. For thus saith the Lord; "Moses, Moses, come down quickly; for thy people whom thou broughtest out of the land of Egypt hath done unlawfully." And Moses understood, and threw the two tables from his hands; and their covenant was broken in pieces, that the covenant of the beloved Jesus might be sealed unto our hearts in the hope which springeth from faith in Him. [9] But though I would fain write many things, not as a teacher, but as becometh one who loveth you not to fall short of that which we possess, I was anxious to write to you, being your devoted slave. Wherefore let us take heed in these last days. For the whole time of our faith shall profit us nothing, unless we now, in the season of lawlessness and in the offenses that shall be, as becometh sons of God, offer resistance, that the Black One may not effect an entrance. [10] Let us flee from all vanity, let us entirely hate the works of the evil way. Do not entering in privily stand apart by yourselves, as if ye were already justified, but assemble yourselves together and consult concerning the common welfare. [11] For the scripture saith; "Woe unto them that are wise for themselves, and understanding in their own sight." Let us become spiritual, let us become a temple perfect unto God. As far as in us lies, let us exercise ourselves in the fear of God, [and] let us strive to keep His commandments, that we may rejoice in His ordinances. [12] The Lord judgeth the world without respect of persons; each man shall receive according to his deeds. If he be good, his righteousness shall go before him in the way; if he be evil, the recompense of his evil- doing is before him; lest perchance, [13] if we relax as men that are called, we should slumber over our sins, and the prince of evil receive power against us and thrust us out from the kingdom of the Lord. [14] Moreover understand this also, my brothers. When ye see that after so many signs and wonders wrought in Israel, even then they were abandoned, let us give heed, lest haply we be found, as the scripture saith, "many are called but few are chosen."

Barn. 5 - [1] For to this end the Lord endured to deliver His flesh unto corruption, that by the remission of sins we might be cleansed, which cleansing is through the blood of His sprinkling. [2] For the scripture concerning Him containeth some things relating to Israel, and some things relating to us. And it speaketh thus; "He was wounded for your transgressions, and He hath been bruised for our sins; by His stripes we were healed. As a sheep He was led to slaughter, as a lamb is dumb before his shearer." 3 We ought therefore to be very thankful unto the Lord, for that He both revealed unto us the past, and made us wise in the present, and as regards the future we are not without understanding. 4 Now the scripture saith; "Not unjustly is the net spread for the birds." He meaneth this that a man shall justly perish, who having the knowledge of the way of righteousness forceth himself into the way of darkness. 5 There is yet this also, my brethren; if the Lord endured to suffer for our souls, though He was Lord of the whole world, unto whom God said from the foundation of the world, "Let us make man after our image and likeness", how then did He endure to suffer at the hand of men? 6 Understand ye. The prophets, receiving grace from Him, prophesied concerning Him. But He Himself endured that He might destroy death and show forth the resurrection of the dead, for that He must needs be manifested in the flesh; 7 that at the same time He might redeem the promise made to the fathers, and by preparing the new people for Himself might show, while He was on earth, that having brought about the resurrection He will Himself exercise judgment. 8 Yea and further, He preached teaching Israel and performing so many wonders and miracles, and He loved him exceedingly. 9 And when He chose His own apostles who were to proclaim His Gospel, who that He might show that "He came not to call the righteous but sinners" were sinners above every sin, then He manifested Himself to be the Son of God. 10 For if He had not come in the flesh neither would men have looked upon Him and been saved, forasmuch as when they look upon the sun that shall cease to be, which is the work of His own hands, they cannot face its rays. 11 Therefore the Son of God came in the flesh to this end, that He might sum up the complete tale of their sins against those who persecuted and slew His prophets. 12 To this end therefore He endured. For God saith of the wounds of His flesh that they came from them; "When they shall smite their own shepherd, then shall the sheep of the flock be lost." 13 But He Himself desired so to suffer; for it was necessary for Him to suffer on a tree. For he that prophesied said concerning Him, "Spare My soul form the sword;" and, "Pierce My flesh with nails, for the congregations of evil-doers have risen up against Me." 14 And again He saith; "Behold I have given My back to stripes, and My cheeks to smitings, and My face did I set as a hard rock."

Barn. 6 - 1 When then He gave the commandment, what saith He? "Who is he that disputeth with Me? Let him oppose Me. Or who is he that goeth to law with Me? Let him draw nigh unto the servant of the Lord," 2 "Woe unto you, for ye all shall wax old as a garment, and the moth shall consume you." And again the prophet saith, seeing that as a hard stone He was ordained for crushing; "Behold I will put into the fountains of Zion a stone very precious, elect, a chief corner-stone, honorable." 3 Then again what saith He; "And whosoever shall set his hope on Him, shall live forever." Is our hope then set upon a stone? Far be it. But it is because the Lord hath set His flesh in strength. For He saith; "And He set Me as a hard rock." 4 And the prophet saith again; "The stone which the builders rejected, this became the head and the corner." And again He saith; "This is the great and wonderful day, which the Lord made." 5 I write to you the more simply, that ye may understand, I who am the offscouring of your love. 6 What then saith the prophet again? "The assembly of evildoers gathered around Me, they surrounded Me as bees surround a comb"; and; "For My garment they cast a lot." 7 Forasmuch then as He was about to be manifested in the flesh and

to suffer, His suffering was manifested beforehand. For the prophet saith concerning Israel; "Woe unto their soul, for they have counseled evil counsel against themselves saying, Let us bind the righteous one, for he is unprofitable for us." 8 What sayeth the other prophet Moses unto them? "Behold, these things saith the Lord God; enter into the good land which the Lord swear unto Abraham, Isaac, and Jacob, and inherit it, a land flowing with milk and honey." 9 But what saith knowledge? Understand ye. Set your hope on Him who is about to be manifested to you in the flesh, even Jesus. For man is earth suffering; for from the face of the earth came the creation of Adam. 10 What then saith He? "Into the good land, a land flowing with milk and honey." Blessed is our Lord, brethren, who established among us wisdom and understanding of His secret things. For the prophet speaketh a parable concerning the Lord. Who shall comprehend, save he that is wise and prudent and that loveth his Lord? 11 Forasmuch then as He renewed us in the remission of sins, He made us to be a new type, so that we should have the soul of children, as if He were recreating us. 12 For the scripture saith concerning us, how He saith to the Son; "Let us make man after our image and after our likeness, and let them rule over the beasts of the earth and the fowls of the heaven and the fishes of the sea." And the Lord said when He saw the fair creation of us men; "Increase and multiply and fill the earth." These words refer to the Son. 13 Again I will shew thee how the Lord speaketh concerning us. He made a second creation at the last; and the Lord saith; "Behold I make the last things as the first." In reference to this then the prophet preached; "Enter into a land flowing with milk and honey, and be lords over it." 14 Behold then we have been created anew, as He saith again in another prophet; "Behold, saith the Lord, I will take out from these", that is to say, from those whom the Spirit of the Lord foresaw, "their stony hearts, and will put into them hearts of flesh;" for He Himself was to be manifested in the flesh and to dwell in us. 15 For a holy temple unto the Lord, my brethren, is the abode of our heart. 16 For the Lord saith again; "For wherein shall I appear unto the Lord my God and be glorified? I will make confession unto Thee in the assembly of my brethren, and I will sing unto Thee in the midst of the assembly of the saints." We therefore are they whom He brought into the good land. 17 What then is the milk and the honey Because the child is first kept alive by honey, and then by milk. So in like manner we also, being kept alive by our faith in the promise and by the word, shall live and be lords of the earth. 18 Now we have already said above; "And let them increase and multiply and rule over the fishes." But who is he that is able [now] to rule over beasts and fishes and fowls of the heaven; for we ought to perceive that to rule implieth power, so that one should give orders and have dominion. 19 If then this cometh not to pass now, assuredly He spake to us for the hereafter, when we ourselves shall be made perfect so that we may become heirs of the covenant of the Lord.

Barn. 7 - 1 Understand therefore, children of gladness, that the good Lord manifested all things to us beforehand, that we might know to whom we ought in all things to render thanksgiving and praise. 2 If then the Son of God, being Lord and future Judge of quick and dead, suffered that His wound might give us life, let us believe that the Son of God could not suffer except for our sakes. 3 But moreover when crucified He had vinegar and gall given Him to drink. Hear how on this matter the priests of the temple have revealed. Seeing that there is a commandment in scripture, "Whatsoever shall not observe the fast shall surely die," the Lord commanded, because He was in His own person about to offer the vessel of His Spirit a sacrifice for our sins, that the type also which was given in Isaac who was offered upon the alter should be fulfilled.

4 What then saith He in the prophet? "And let them eat of the goat that is offered at the fast for all their sins." Attend carefully; "And let all the priests alone eat the entrails unwashed with vinegar." 5 Wherefore? Since ye are to give Me, who am to offer My flesh for the sins of My new people, gall with vinegar to drink, eat ye alone, while the people fasteth and waileth in sackcloth and ashes; that He might shew that He must suffer at their hands." 6 Attend ye to the commandments which He gave. "Take two goats, fair and alike, and offer them, and let the priest take the one for a whole burnt offering for sins." 7 But the other one--what must they do with it? "Accursed," saith He, "is the one." Give heed how the type of Jesus is revealed. 8 "And do ye all spit upon it and goad it, and place scarlet wool about its head, and so let it be cast into the wilderness." And when it is so done, he that taketh the goat into the wilderness leadeth it, and taketh off the wool, and putteth it upon the branch which is called Rachia, the same whereof we are wont to eat the shoots when we find them in the country. Of this briar alone is the fruit thus sweet. 9 What then meaneth this? Give heed. "The one at the alter, and the other accursed." And moreover the accursed one crowned. For they shall see Him in that day wearing the long scarlet robe about His flesh, and shall say, Is not this He, Whom once we crucified and set at nought and spat upon; verily this was He, Who then said that He was the Son of God. 10 For how is He like the goat? For this reason it says "the goats shall be fair and alike," that, when they shall see Him coming then, they may be astonished at the likeness of the goat. Therefore behold the type of Jesus that was to suffer. 11 But what meaneth it, that they place the wool in the midst of the thorns? It is a type of Jesus set forth for the Church, since whosoever should desire to take away the scarlet wool it behoved him to suffer many things owing to the terrible nature of the thorn, and through affliction to win the mastery over it. Thus, He saith, they that desire to see Me, and to attain unto My kingdom, must lay hold on Me through tribulation and affliction.

Barn. 8 - 1 But what think ye meaneth the type, where the commandment is given to Israel that those men, whose sins are full grown, offer an heifer and slaughter and burn it, and then that the children take up the ashes, and cast them into vessels, and twist the scarlet wool on a tree (see here again is the type of the cross and the scarlet wool, and the hyssop, and that this done the children should sprinkle the people one by one, that they may be purified from their sins? 2 Understand ye how in all plainness it is spoken unto you; the calf is Jesus, the men that offer it, being sinners, are they that offered Him for the slaughter. After this it is no more men (who offer; the glory is no more for sinners. 3 The children who sprinkle are they that preached unto us the forgiveness of sins and the purification of our heart, they to whom, being twelve in number for a testimony unto the tribes (for there are twelve tribes of Israel, He gave authority over the Gospel, that they should preach it. 4 But wherefore are the children that sprinkle three in number? For a testimony unto Abraham, Isaac and Jacob, because these are mighty before God. 5 Then there is the placing the wool on the tree. This means that the kingdom of Jesus is on the cross, and that they who set their hope on Him shall live for ever. 6 And why is there the wool and the hyssop at the same time? Because in His kingdom there shall be evil and foul days, in which we shall be saved; for he who suffers pain in the flesh is healed through the foulness of the hyssop. 7 Now to us indeed it is manifest that these things so befell for this reason, but to them they were dark, because they heard not the voice of the Lord.

Barn. 9 - 1 Furthermore He saith concerning the ears, how that it is our heart which He circumcised. The Lord saith in the prophet; "With the hearing of the ears they listened to Me." And again He

saith; They that are afar off shall hear with their ears, and shall perceive what I have done." And; "Be ye circumcised in your hearts," saith the Lord. 2 And again He saith; "Hear, O Israel, for thus saith the Lord thy God. Who is he that desireth to live forever, let him hear with his ears the voice of My servant." And again He saith; "Hear, O heaven, and give ear, O earth, for the Lord hath spoken these things for a testimony." And again He saith; Hear the words of the Lord, ye rulers of this people." And again He saith; "Hear, O my children, the voice of one crying in the wilderness." Therefore He circumcised our ears, that hearing the word we might believe. 3 But moreover the circumcision, in which they have confidence, is abolished; for He hath said that a circumcision not of the flesh should be practiced. But they transgressed, for an evil angel taught them cleverness. 4 He saith unto them; "Thus saith the Lord your God" (so I find the commandment; "sow not upon thorns, be ye circumcised in to your "Lord." And what saith He? "Be ye circumcised in the hardness of "your heart; and then ye will not harden your neck." Take this again; "Behold, sayith the Lord, all the Gentiles are uncircumcised "in their foreskin, but this people is uncircumcised in their "hearts." 5 But thou wilt say; In truth the people hath been circumcised for a seal. Nay, but so likewise is every Syrian and Arabian and all the priests of the idols. Do all those then too belong to their covenant? Moreover the Egyptians also are included among the circumcised. 6 Learn therefore, children of love, concerning all things abundantly, that Abraham, who first appointed circumcision, looked forward in the spirit unto Jesus, when he circumcised having received the ordinances of three letters. 7 For the scripture saith; "And Abraham circumcised of his household "eighteen males and three hundred." What then was the knowledge given unto him? Understand ye that He saith "the eighteen" first, and then after an interval "three hundred" In the eighteen 'I' stands for ten, 'H' for eight. Here thou hast JESUS (IHSOYS). And because the cross in the "T" was to have grace, He saith also "three hundred". So He revealeth Jesus in the two letters, and in the remaining one the cross. 8 He who placed within us the innate gift of His covenant knoweth; no man hath ever learnt from me a more genuine word; but I know that ye are worthy.

Barn. 10 - 1 But forasmuch as Moses said; "Ye shall not eat seine nor eagle nor "falcon nor crow nor any fish which hath no scale upon it", he received in his understanding three ordinances. 2 Yea and further He saith unto them in Deuteronomy; "And I will lay "as a covenant upon this people My ordinances." So then it is not a commandment of God that they should not bite with their teeth, but Moses spake it in spirit. 3 Accordingly he mentioned the swine with this intent. Thou shalt not cleave, saith he, to such men who are like unto swine; that is, when they are in luxury they forget the Lord, but when they are in want they recognize the Lord, just as the swine when it eateth knoweth not his lord, but when it is hungry it crieth out, and when it has received food again it is silent. 4 "Neither shalt thou eat eagle nor falcon nor kite nor crow." Thou shalt not, He saith, cleave unto, or be likened to, such men who now not how to provide food for themselves by toil and sweat, but in their lawlessness seize what belongeth to others, and as if they were walking in guilelessness watch and search about for some one to rob in their rapacity, just as these birds alone do not provide food for themselves, but sit idle and seek how they may eat the meat that belongeth to others, being pestilent in their evil-doings." 5 "And thou shalt not eat," saith He, "lamprey nor polypus nor cuttle fish" . Thou shalt not, He meaneth, become like unto such men, who are desperately wicked, and are already condemned to death, just as these fishes alone are accursed and swim in the depths, not swimming on the surface like the rest, but dwell on the ground beneath the deep sea. 6 "Moreover thou shalt not eat the hare." Why so? Thou shalt not be found a corrupter of boys, nor shalt thou become like such persons; for the hare gaineth one passage in the body every year; for according to the number of years it lives it has just so many orifices. 7 Again, "neither shalt thou eat the hyena;" thou shalt not, saith He, become an adulterer or a fornicator, neither shalt thou resemble such persons. Why so? Because this animal changeth its nature year by year, and becometh at one time male and at another female. 8 Moreover He hath hated the weasel also and with good reason. Thou shalt not, saith He, become such as those men of whom we hear as working iniquity with their mouth for uncleanness, neither shalt thou cleave unto impure women who work iniquity with their mouth. For this animal conceiveth with its mouth. 9 Concerning meats then Moses received three decrees to this effect and uttered them in a spiritual sense; but they accepted them according to the lust of the flesh, as though they referred to eating. 10 And David also receiveth knowledge of the same three decrees, and saith; "Blessed is the man who hath not gone in the council of the ungodly"--even as the fishes go in darkness into the depths; "and hath not stood in the path of sinners"--just as they who pretend to fear the Lord sin like swine; "and hath not sat on the seat of the destroyers"--as the birds that are seated for prey. Ye have now the complete lesson concerning eating. 11 Again Moses saith; "Ye shall everything that divideth the hoof and cheweth the cud." What meaneth he? He that receiveth the food knoweth Him that giveth him the food, and being refreshed appeareth to rejoice in him. Well said he, having regard to the commandment. What then meaneth he? Cleave unto those that fear the Lord, with those who meditate in their heart on the distinction of the word which they have received, with those who tell of the ordinances of the Lord and keep them, with those who know that meditation is a work of gladness and who chew the cud of the word of the Lord. But why that which divideth the hoof? Because the righteous man both walketh in this world, and at the same time looketh for the holy world to come. Ye see how wise a lawgiver Moses was. 12 But whence should they perceive or understand these things? Howbeit we having justly perceived the commandments tell them as the Lord willed. To this end He circumcised our ears and hearts, that we might understand these things.

Barn. 11 - 1 But let us enquire whether the Lord took care to signify before hand concerning the water and the cross. Now concerning the water it is written in reference to Israel, how that they would not receive the baptism which bringeth remission of sins, but would build for themselves. 2 For the prophet saith; "Be astonished, O heaven, and let the earth shudder the more at this, for this people hath done two evil things; they abandoned Me the fountain of life, and they digged for themselves a pit of death." 3 "Is My holy mountain of Sinai a desert rock? for ye shall be as the fledglings of a bird, which flutter aloft when deprived of their nest." 4 And again the prophet saith; "I will go before thee, and level mountains and crush gates of brass and break in pieces bolts of iron, and I will give thee treasures dark, concealed, unseen, that they may know that I am the Lord God." 5 And; "Thou shalt dwell in a lofty cave of a strong rock." And; "His water shall be sure; ye shall see the King in glory, and your soul shall meditate on the fear of the Lord." 6 And again He saith in another prophet; "And He that doeth these things shall be as the tree that is planted by the parting streams of waters, which shall yield his fruit at his proper season, and his leaf shall not fall off, and all things whatsoever he doeth shall prosper." 7 "Not so are the ungodly, not so, but are as the dust which the wind scattereth from the face of the earth. Therefore ungodly men shall not stand in judgment, neither sinners in the council of the righteous; for the

Lord knoweth the way of the righteous, and the way of the ungodly shall perish." 8 Ye perceive how He pointed out the water and the cross at the same time. For this is the meaning; Blessed are they that set their hope on the cross, and go down into the water; for He speaketh of the reward at "his proper season"; then, saith He, I will repay. But now what saith He? "His leaves shall not fall off"; He meaneth by this that every word, which shall come forth from you through your mouth in faith and love, shall be for the conversion and hope of many. 9 And again another prophet saith; "And the land of Jacob was praised above the whole earth." He meaneth this; He glorifieth the vessel of His Spirit. 10 Next what saith He? "And there was a river streaming from the right hand, and beautiful trees rose up from it; and whosoever shall eat of them shall live forever." 11 This He saith, because we go down into the water laden with sins and filth, and rise up from it bearing fruit in the heart, resting our fear and hope on Jesus in the spirit. "And whosoever shall eat of these shall live forever"; He meaneth this; whosoever, saith He, shall hear these things spoken and shall believe, shall live forever.

Barn. 12 - 1 In like manner again He defineth concerning the cross in another prophet, who saith; "And when shall these things be accomplished? saith the Lord. Whenever a tree shall be bended and stand upright, and whensoever blood shall drop from a tree." Again thou art taught concerning the cross, and Him that was to be crucified. 2 And He saith again in Moses, when war was waged against Israel by men of another nation, and that He might remind them when the war was waged against them that for their sins they were delivered unto death; the Spirit saith to the heart of Moses, that he should make a type of the cross and of Him that was to suffer, that unless, saith He, they shall set their hope on Him, war shall be waged against them for ever. Moses therefore pileth arms one upon another in the midst of the encounter, and standing on higher ground than any he stretched out his hands, and so Israel was again victorious. Then, whenever he lowered them, they were slain with the sword. 3 Wherefore was this? That they might learn that they cannot be saved, unless they should set their hope on Him. 4 And again in another prophet He saith; "The whole day long have I stretched out My hands to a disobedient people that did gainsay My righteous way." 5 Again Moses maketh a type of Jesus, how that He must suffer, and that He Himself whom they shall think to have destroyed shall make alive in an emblem when Israel was falling. For the Lord caused all manner of serpents to bite them, and they died (forasmuch as the transgression was wrought in Eve through the serpent), that He might convince them that by reason of their transgression they should be delivered over to the affliction of death. 6 Yea and further though Moses gave the commandment; "Ye shall not have a molten or a carved image for your God", yet he himself made one that he might show them a type of Jesus. So Moses maketh a brazen serpent, and setteth it up conspicuously, and summoneth the people by proclamation. 7 When therefore they were assembled together they entreated Moses that he should offer up intercession for them that they might be healed. And Moses said unto them; Whensoever, said he, one of you shall be bitten, let him come to the serpent which is placed on the tree, and let him believe and hope that the serpent being himself dead can make alive; and forthwith he shall be saved. And so they did. Here again thou hast in these things also the glory of Jesus, how that in Him and unto Him are all things. 8 What again saith Moses unto Jesus (Joshua) the son of Nun, when he giveth him this name, as being a prophet, that all the people might give ear to him alone, because the Father revealeth all things concerning His Son Jesus? 9 Moses therefore saith to Jesus the son of Nun, giving him this name, when he sent him as a spy on the land; "Take a book in thy hands, and write what the Lord saith, how the Son of God shall cut up by the roots all the house of Amalek in the last days." [10] Behold again it is Jesus, not a son of man, but the Son of God, and He was revealed in the flesh in a figure. Since then men will say that Christ is the son of David, David himself prophesieth being afraid and understanding the error of sinners; "The Lord said unto my Lord, Sit thou on My right hand until I set thine enemies for a footstool under Thy feet." [1] And again thus sayith Isaiah; "The Lord said unto my Christ the Lord, of whose right hand I laid hold, that the nations should give ear before Him, and I will break down the strength of kings. "See how David calleth Him Lord, and calleth Him not Son."

Barn. 13 - [1] Now let us see whether this people or the first people hath the inheritance, and whether the covenant had reference to us or to them. [2] Hear then what the scripture saith concerning the people; "And Isaac prayed concerning Rebecca his wife, for she was barren. And she conceived. Then Rebecca went out to enquire of the Lord. And the Lord said unto her; Two nations are in thy womb, and two peoples in thy belly, and one people shall vanquish another people, and the greater shall serve the less." [3] Ye ought to understand who Isaac is, and who Rebecca is, and in whose case He hath shown that the one people is greater than the other. [4] And in another prophecy Jacob speaketh more plainly to Joseph his son, saying; "Behold, the Lord hath not bereft me of thy face; bring me thy sons, that I may bless them." [5] And he brought Ephraim and Manasseh, desiring that Manasseh should be blessed, because he was the elder; for Joseph led him by the right hand of his father Jacob. But Jacob saw in the spirit a type of the people that should come afterwards. And what saith He? "And Jacob crossed his hands, and placed his right hand on the head of Ephraim, the second and younger, and blessed him. And Joseph said unto Jacob, Transfer thy right hand to the head of Manasseh, for he is my first born son. And Jacob said to Joseph, I know it, my son, I know it; but the greater shall serve the less. Yet this one also shall be blessed." [6] Mark in whose cases He ordained that this people should be first and heir of the covenant. [7] If then besides this He also recorded it through Abraham, we attain the completion of our knowledge. What then saith he to Abraham when he alone believed, and was ascribed for righteousness? "Behold I have made thee, Abraham, a father of nations that believe in God in uncircumcision."

Barn. 14 - [1] Yea verily, but as regards the covenant which He sware to the fathers to give it to the people let us see whether He hath actually given it. He hath given it, but they themselves were not found worthy to receive it by reason of their sins. [2] For the prophet saith; "And Moses was fasting in Mount Sinai forty days and forty nights, that he might receive the covenant of the Lord to give to the people. And [Moses] received from the Lord the two tables which were written by the finger of the hand of the Lord in the spirit." And Moses took them, and brought them down to give them to the people. [3] And the Lord said unto Moses; "Moses, Moses, come down quickly; for thy people, whom thou leddest forth from the land of Egypt, hath done wickedly. And Moses perceived that they had made for themselves again molten images, and he cast them out of his hands and the tables of the covenant of the Lord were broken in pieces." [4] Moses received them, but they themselves were not found worthy. But how did we receive them? Mark this. Moses received them being a servant, but the Lord himself gave them to us to be the people of His inheritance, having endured patiently for our sakes. [5] But He was made manifest, in order that at the same time they might be perfected in their sins, and we might receive the covenant through Him who inherited it, even the Lord Jesus, who was prepared beforehand hereunto, that appearing in person He might redeem out of darkness our hearts which had already been paid over unto death and delivered up to the iniquity of error, and thus establish the covenant in us through the word. [6] For it is written how the Father chargeth Him to deliver us from darkness, and to prepare a holy people for Himself. [7] Therefore saith the prophet; "I the Lord thy God called thee in righteousness, and I will lay hold of thy hand and will strengthen thee, and I have given thee to be a covenant of the race, a light to the Gentiles, to open the eyes of the blind, and to bring forth them that are bound from their fetters, and them that sit in darkness from their prison house." We perceive then whence we were ransomed. [8] Again the prophet saith; "Behold I have set Thee to be a light unto the Gentiles, that Thou shouldest be for salvation unto the ends of the earth; thus saith the Lord that ransomed thee, even God." [9] Again the prophet saith; "The Spirit of the Lord is upon Me, wherefore He anointed Me to preach good tidings to the humble; He hath sent Me to heal them that are broken-hearted, to preach release to the captives and recovery of sight to the blind, to proclaim the acceptable year of the Lord and the day of recompense, to comfort all that mourn."

Barn. 15 - [1] Moreover concerning the Sabbath likewise it is written in the Ten Words, in which He spake to Moses face to face on Mount Sinai; "And ye shall hallow the Sabbath of the Lord with pure hands and with a pure heart." [2] And in another place He saith; "If my sons observe the Sabbath then I will bestow My mercy upon them." [3] Of the Sabbath He speaketh in the beginning of the creation; "And God made the works of His hands in six days, and He ended on the seventh day, and rested on it, and He hallowed it." [4] Give heed, children, what this meaneth; "He ended in six days." He meaneth this, that in six thousand years the Lord shall bring all things to an end; for the day with Him signifyeth a thousand years; and this He himself beareth me witness, saying; "Behold, the day of the Lord shall be as a thousand years." Therefore, children, in six days, that is in six thousand years, everything shall come to an end. [5] "And He rested on the seventh day." this He meaneth; when His Son shall come, and shall abolish the time of the Lawless One, and shall judge the ungodly, and shall change the sun and the moon and the stars, then shall he truly rest on the seventh day. [6] Yea and furthermore He saith; "Thou shalt hallow it with pure hands and with a pure heart." If therefore a man is able now to hallow the day which God hallowed, though he be pure in heart, we have gone utterly astray. [7] But if after all then and not till then shall we truly rest and hallow it, when we shall ourselves be able to do so after being justified and receiving the promise, when iniquity is no more and all things have been made new by the Lord, we shall be able to hallow it then, because we ourselves shall have been hallowed first. [8] Finally He saith to them; "Your new moons and your Sabbaths I cannot away with." Ye see what is His meaning ; it is not your present Sabbaths that are acceptable [unto Me], but the Sabbath which I have made, in the which, when I have set all things at rest, I will make the beginning of the eighth day which is the beginning of another world. [9] Wherefore also we keep the eighth day for rejoicing, in the which also Jesus rose from the dead, and having been manifested ascended into the heavens.

Barn. 16 - [1] Moreover I will tell you likewise concerning the temple, how these wretched men being led astray set their hope on the building, and not on their God that made them, as being a house of God. [2] For like the Gentiles almost they consecrated Him in the temple. But what saith the Lord abolishing the temple? Learn ye. "Who hath measured the heaven with a span, or hath measured the earth with his hand? Have not I, saith the Lord? The heaven is My throne and the earth the footstool of My feet. What manner of house will ye build for Me? Or what shall be my resting place?" Ye perceive that their hope is vain. [3] Furthermore He saith again;

"Behold they that pulled down this temple themselves shall build it." [4] So it cometh to pass; for because they went to war it was pulled down by their enemies. Now also the very servants of their enemies shall build it up. [5] Again, it was revealed how the city and the temple and the people of Israel should be betrayed. For the scripture saith; "And it shall be in the last days, that the Lord shall deliver up the sheep of the pasture and the fold and the tower thereof to destruction." And it came to pass as the Lord spake. [6] But let us enquire whether there be any temple of God. There is; in the place where he himself undertakes to make and finish it. For it is written "And it shall come to pass, when the week is being accomplished, the temple of God shall be built gloriously in the name of the Lord." [7] I find then that there is a temple, How then shall it be built in the name of the Lord? Understand ye. Before we believed on God, the abode of our heart was corrupt and weak, a temple truly built by hands; for it was full of idolatry and was a house of demons, because we did whatsoever was contrary to God. [8] "But it shall be built in the name of the Lord." Give heed then that the temple of the Lord may be built gloriously. [9] How? Understand ye. By receiving the remission of our sins and hoping on the Name we became new, created afresh from the beginning. Wherefore God dwelleth truly in our habitation within us. How? The word of his faith, the calling of his promise, the wisdom of the ordinances, the commandments of the teaching, He Himself prophesying in us, He Himself dwelling in us, opening for us who had been in bondage unto death the door of the temple, which is the mouth, and giving us repentance leadeth us to the incorruptible temple. [10] For he that desireth to be saved looketh not to the man, but to Him that dwelleth and speaketh in him, being amazed at this that he has never at any time heard these words from the mouth of the speaker, nor himself ever desired to hear them. This is the spiritual temple built up to the Lord.

Barn. 17 - [1] So far as it was possible with all simplicity to declare it unto you, my soul hopeth that I have not omitted anything [of the matters pertaining unto salvation and so failed in my desire]. [2] For if I should write to you concerning things immediate or future, ye would not understand them, because they are put in parables. So much then for this.

Barn. 18 - [1] But let us pass on to another lesson and teaching. There are two ways of teaching and of power, the one of light and the other of darkness; and there is a great difference between the two ways. For on the one are stationed the light giving angels of God, on the other the angels of Satan. [2] And the one is the Lord from all eternity and unto all eternity, whereas the other is Lord of the season of iniquity that now is.

Barn. 19 - [1] This then is the way of light, if anyone desiring to travel on the way to his appointed place would be zealous in his works. The knowledge then which is given to us whereby we may walk therein is as follows. [2] Thou shalt love Him that made thee, thou shalt fear Him that created thee, thou shalt glorify Him that redeemed thee from death; thou shalt be simple in heart and rich in spirit; thou shalt not cleave to those who walk the way of death; thou shalt hate everything that is not pleasing to God; thou shalt hate all hypocrisy; thou shalt never forsake the commandments of the Lord. [3] Thou shalt not exalt thyself, but shalt be lowly minded in all things. Thou shalt not assume glory to thyself. Thou shalt not entertain a wicked design against thy neighbor; thou shalt not admit boldness into thy soul. [4] Thou shalt not commit fornication, "thou shalt not commit adultery", thou shalt not corrupt boys. The word of God shall not come forth from thee where any are unclean. Thou shalt not make a difference in a person to reprove him for a transgression. Thou shalt be meek, thou shalt be "quiet", thou shalt be "fearing the words" which thou hast heard. Thou shalt not bear a grudge against

361

thy brother. [5] Thou shalt not doubt whether a thing shall be or not be. "Thou shalt not take the name of the Lord in vain." Thou shalt love thy neighbor more than thine own soul. Thou shalt not murder a child by abortion, nor again shalt thou kill it when it is born. Thou shalt not withhold thy hand from thy son or daughter, but from their youth thou shalt teach them the fear of God. [6] Thou shalt not be found coveting thy neighbors goods; thou shalt not be found greedy of gain. Neither shalt thou cleave with thy soul to the lofty, but shalt walk with the humble and righteous. The accidents that befall thee thou shalt receive as good, knowing that nothing is done without God. Thou shalt not be double minded nor double tongued. [7] Thou shalt be subject unto thy masters as to a type of God in shame and fear. Thou shalt not command in bitterness thy bondservant or thine handmaid who set their hope on the same God, lest haply, they should cease to fear the God who is over both of you; for He came not to call with respect of persons, but to call those whom the Spirit hath prepared. [8] Thou shalt make thy neighbor partake in all things, and shalt not say "that anything is thine own." For if ye are fellow partakers in that which is imperishable, how much rather shall ye be in the things which are perishable. Thou shalt not be hasty with thine own tongue, for the mouth is the snare of death. So far as thou art able, thou shalt be pure for thy soul's sake. [9] "Be not thou found holding out thy hands to receive, and drawing them in to give." Thou shalt love as the apple of thine eye every one "that speaketh unto thee the word of the Lord. [10] "Thou shalt remember" the day of judgment night and day, and thou shalt seek out day by day the persons of the saints, either laboring by word and going to exhort them and meditating how thou mayest save souls by thy word, or thou shalt work with thy hands for a ransom for thy sins. [11] Thou shall not hesitate to give, neither shalt thou murmur when giving, but thou shalt know who is the good paymaster of thy reward. Thou shalt keep those things which thou hast received, neither adding to them nor taking away from them. Thou shalt utterly hate the Evil One. Thou shalt judge righteously. [12] Thou shalt not make a schism, but thou shalt pacify them that contend by bringing them together. Thou shalt confess thy sins. Thou shalt not betake thyself to prayer with an evil conscience. This is the way of light.

Barn. 20 - [1] But the way of the Black One is crooked and full of a curse. For it is a way of eternal death with punishment wherein are the things that destroy men's souls--idolatry, boldness, exhalation of power, hypocrisy, doubleness of heart, adultery, murder, plundering, pride, transgression, treachery, malice, stubbornness, witchcraft, magic, covetousness, absence of the fear of God; [2] persecutors of good men, hating the truth, loving lies, not perceiving the reward of righteousness, not "cleaving to the good" nor to the righteous judgment, paying no heed to the widow and the orphan, wakeful not for the fear of God but for that which is evil; men from whom gentleness and forbearance stand aloof and far off; loving vain things, pursuing a recompense, not pitying the poor man, not toiling for him that is oppressed with toil, ready to slander, not recognizing Him that made them murderers of children, corrupters of the creatures of God, turning away from him that is in want, oppressing him that is afflicted, advocates of the wealthy, unjust judges of the poor, sinful in all things.

Barn. 21 - ([21:1] It is good therefore to learn the ordinances of the Lord, as many as have been written above, and to walk in them. For he that doeth these things shall be glorified in the kingdom of God; whereas he that chooseth their opposites shall perish together with his works. For this cause is the resurrection, for this the recompense. ([21:2] I entreat those of you who are in a higher station, if ye will receive any counsel of good advice from me, keep amongst you those to whom ye may do good. Fail not. ([21:3] The day is at hand, in which everything shall be destroyed together with the Evil One. "The Lord is at hand and his reward." (21:4 Again and again I entreat you; be good lawgivers one to another; continue faithful councilors to yourselves; take away from you all hypocrisy. (21:5 And may God, who is Lord of the whole world, give you wisdom, judgment, learning, knowledge of His ordinances, patience. (21:6 And be ye taught of God, seeking diligently what the Lord requireth of you, and act that ye may be found in the day of judgment. (21:7 But if you have any remembrance of good, call me to mind when ye practice these things these things, that both my desire and my watchfulness may lead to some good result. I entreat you asking it as a favor. (21:8 So long as the good vessel (of the body) is with you, be lacking in none of these things, but search them out constantly, and fulfill every commandment; for they deserve it. (21:9 For this reason I was the more eager to write to you so far as I was able, that I might give you joy. Fare ye well, children of love and peace. The Lord of glory and of every grace be with your spirit.

3 Corinthians

There are various phrases and whole sentences, especially in the Armenian and the Milan MS. of the Latin, which are absent from the Coptic and the Laon MS. and are regarded, rightly, as interpolations. These will be distinguished by uppercase capitals.

1 Paul, a prisoner of Jesus Christ, unto the brethren which are in Corinth, greeting. 2 Being in the midst of many tribulations, I marvel not if the teachings of the evil one run abroad apace. 3 For my Lord Jesus Christ will hasten his coming, and will set at nought (no longer endure the insolence of) them that falsify his words. 4 For I delivered unto you in the beginning the things which I received of the HOLY apostles which were before me, who were at all times with Jesus Christ: 5 namely, that our Lord Jesus Christ was born of Mary WHICH IS of the seed of David ACCORDING TO THE FLESH, the Holy Ghost being sent forth from heaven from the Father unto her by the angel Gabriel, 6 that he (Jesus) might come down into this world and redeem all flesh by his flesh, and raise us up from the dead in the flesh, like as he hath shown to us in himself for an ensample. 7 And because man was formed by his Father, 8 therefore was he sought when he was lost, that he might be quickened by adoption. 9 For to this end did God Almighty who made heaven and earth first send the prophets unto the Jews, that they might be drawn away from their sins. 10 For he designed to save the house of Israel: therefore he conferred a portion of the spirit of Christ upon the prophets and sent them unto the Jews first (or unto the first Jews), and they proclaimed the true worship of God for a long space of time. 11 But the prince of iniquity, desiring to be God, laid hands on them and slew them (banished them from God, Laon MS.), and bound all flesh by evil lusts (AND THE END OF THE WORLD BY JUDGEMENT DREW NEAR). 12 But God Almighty, who is righteous, would not cast away his own creation, BUT HAD COMPASSION ON THEM FROM HEAVEN, 13 and sent his spirit into Mary IN GALILEE, [14 Milan MS. and Arm.: who believed with all her heart and received the Holy Ghost in her womb, that Jesus might come into the world,] 15 that by that flesh whereby that wicked one had brought in death (had triumphed), by the same he should be shown to be overcome. 16 For by his own body Jesus Christ saved all flesh [AND RESTORED IT UNTO LIFE], 17 that he might show forth the temple of righteousness in his body. 18 In whom (or whereby) we are saved (Milan, Paris: in whom if we believe we are set free). 19 They therefore (Paris MS.; Arm. has: Know therefore that. Laon has: They therefore who agree with them) are not children of righteousness but children of wrath who reject the wisdom (providence?) of God, saying that the heaven

and the earth and all that are in them are not the work of God. 20 They therefore are children of wrath, for cursed are they, following the teaching of the serpent, 21 whom do ye drive out from you and flee from their doctrine. [Arm., Milan, Paris: 22 For ye are not children of disobedience, but of the well-beloved church. 23 Therefore is the time of the resurrection proclaimed unto all.] 24 And as for that which they say, that there is no resurrection of the flesh, they indeed shall have no resurrection UNTO LIFE, BUT UNTO JUDGEMENT, 25 because they believe not in him that is risen from the dead, NOT BELIEVING NOR UNDERSTANDING, 26 for they know not, O Corinthians, the seeds of wheat or of other seeds (grain), how they are cast bare into the earth and are corrupted and rise again by the will of God with bodies, and clothed.[1] 27 And not only that [body] which is cast in riseth again, but manifold more blessing itself [i.e. fertile and prospering]. 28 And if we must not take an example from seeds ONLY, BUT FROM MORE NOBLE BODIES, 29 ye know how Jonas the son of Amathi, when he would not preach to them of Nineve, BUT FLED, was swallowed by the sea-monster; 30 and after three days and three nights God heard the prayer of Jonas out of the lowest hell, and no part of him was consumed, not even an hair nor an eyelash. 31 How much more, O YE OF LITTLE FAITH, shall he raise up you that have believed in Christ Jesus, like as he himself arose. 32 Likewise also a dead man was cast upon the bones of the prophet Helisaetis by the children of Israel, and he arose, both body and soul and bones and spirit (Laon: arose in his body); how much more shall ye which have been cast upon the body and bones and spirit of the Lord [Milan, Paris: how much more, O ye of little faith, shall ye which have been cast on him] arise again in that day having your flesh whole, EVEN AS HE AROSE? [33 Arm., Milan, Paris: Likewise also concerning the prophet Helias: he raised up the widow's son from death: how much more shall the Lord Jesus raise you up from death at the sound of the trumpet, in the twinkling of an eye? for he hath showed us an ensample in his own body.] 34 If, then, ye receive any other doctrine, God shall be witness against you; and let no man trouble me, 35 for I bear these bonds that I may win Christ, and I therefore bear his marks in my body that I may attain unto the resurrection of the dead. 86 And whoso receiveth (abideth in) the rule which he hath received by the blessed prophets and the holy gospel, shall receive a recompense from the Lord, AND WHEN HE RISETH FROM THE DEAD SHALL OBTAIN ETERNAL LIFE. 37 But whoso trans- gresseth these things, with him is the fire, and with them that walk in like manner (Milan, Paris: with them that go before in the same way, who are men without God), 38 which are a generation of vipers, 39 whom do ye reject in the power of the Lord, 40 and peace, GRACE, AND LOVE shall be with you.

Clement 1 - The First Epistle of Clement

1 Clem. 1 - THE Church of God which is at Rome, to the Church of God which is at Corinth, elect, sanctified by the will of God, through Jesus Christ our Lord: grace and peace from the Almighty God, by Jesus Christ be multiplied unto you. 2 Brethren, the sudden and unexpected dangers and calamities that have fallen upon us, have, we fear, made us the more slow in our consideration of those things which you inquired of us: 3 As also of that wicked and detestable sedition, so unbecoming the elect of God, which a few heady and self-willed men have fomented to such a degree of madness, that your venerable and renowned name, so worthy of all men to be beloved, is greatly blasphemed thereby. 4 For who that has ever been among you has not experimented the firmness of your faith, and its fruitfulness in all good works; and admired the temper

and moderation of your religion in Christ; and published abroad the magnificence of your hospitality, and thought you happy in your perfect and certain knowledge of the Gospel?

5 For ye did all things without respect of persons and walked according to the laws of God; being subject to those who had the rule over you, and giving the honour that was fitting to the aged among you. 6 Ye commanded the young men to think those things that were modest and grave. 7 The women ye exhorted to do all things with an unblameable and seemly, and pure conscience; loving their own husbands, as was fitting: and that keeping themselves within the bounds of a due obedience, they should order their houses gravely, with all discretion. 8. Ye were all of you humble minded, not boasting of any thing: desiring rather to be subject than to govern; to give than to receive; being 9 content with the portion God hath dispensed to you; And hearkening diligently to his word, ye 10 were enlarged in your bowels, having his 11 suffering always before your eyes. Thus a firm, and 12 blessed and profitable peace was given unto you; and an unsatiable desire of doing good; and a plentiful effusion of the Holy Ghost was upon all of you. And being full of 13 good designs, ye did with 14 great readiness of mind, and with a religious confidence stretch forth your hands to God Almighty; beseeching him to be merciful unto you, if in any thing ye had unwillingly sinned against him. Ye contended day and night for the whole brotherhood; that 15 with compassion and a good conscience, the number of his elect might be saved. Ye were sincere, and without offence towards each other; not mindful of injuries; all sedition and schism was an abomination unto you. Ye bewailed every one his neighbour's sins, esteeming their defects your own. Ye 16 were kind one to another without grudging; being ready to every good work. And being adorned with a conversation altogether virtuous and religious, ye did all things in the fear of God; whose commandments were written upon the tables of your heart.

1 Clem. 2 - ALL honour and enlargement was given unto you; and so was fulfilled that which is written, my beloved did eat and drink, he was enlarged and waxed fat, and he kicked. 2 From hence came emulation, and envy, and strife, and sedition; persecution and disorder, war and captivity. 3 So they who were of no renown, lifted up themselves against the honourable; those of no reputation, against those who were in respect; the foolish against the wise; the young men against the aged. 4 Therefore righteousness and peace are departed from you, because every one hath forsaken the fear of God; and is grown blind in his faith; nor walketh by the rule of God's commandments nor liveth as is fitting in Christ: 5 But every onefollows his own wicked lusts: having taken up an unjust and wicked envy, by which death first entered into the world.

1 Clem. 3 - FOR thus it is written, And in process of time it came to pass that Cain brought of the fruit of the ground an offering unto the Lord. And Abel, he also brought of the firstlings of his flock, and of the fat thereof: 2 And the Lord had respect unto Abel, and to his offering. But unto Cain and unto his offering he had not respect. And Cain was very sorrowful, and his countenance fell. 3 And the Lord said unto Cain, Why art thou sorrowful? And why is thy countenance fallen? If thou shalt offer aright, but not divide aright, hast thou not sinned? Hold thy peace: unto thee shall be his desire, and thou shalt rule over him. 4 And Cain said unto Abel his brother, Let us go down into the field. And it came to pass, as they were in the field, that Cain rose up against Abel his brother, and slew him. 5 Ye see, brethren, how envy and emulation wrought the death of a brother. For this our fatherJacob fled from the face of his brother Esau. 6 It was this that caused Joseph to be persecuted even unto death, and to come into bondage. Envy forced Moses to flee from the face of Pharaoh king of Egypt, when he heard his own

countrymen ask him, Who made thee a Judge, and a ruler over us? Wilt thou kill me as thou didst the Egyptian yesterday? 7 Through envy Aaron and Miriam were shut out of the camp, from the rest of the congregation seven days. 8 Emulation sent Dathan and Abiram quick into the grave because they raised up a sedition against Moses the servant of God. 9 For this David was not only hated of strangers, but was persecuted even by Saul the king of Israel. 10 But not to insist upon antient examples, let us come to those worthies that have been nearest to us; and take the brave examples of our own age. 11 Through zeal and envy, the most faithful and righteous pillars of the church have been persecuted even to the most grievous deaths. 12 Let us set before our eyes the holy Apostles; Peter by unjust envy underwent not one or two, but many sufferings; til at last being martyred, he went to the place of glory that was due unto him. 13 For the same cause did Paul in like manner receive the reward of his patience. Seven times he was in bonds; he was whipped, was stoned; he preached both in the East and in the West; leaving behind him the glorious report of his faith: 14 And so having taught the whole world righteousness, and for that end travelled even to the utmost bounds of the West; he at last suffered martyrdom by the command of the governors, 15 And departed out of the world, and went unto his holy place; being become a most eminent pattern of patience unto all ages. 16 To these Holy Apostles were joined a very great number of others, who having through envy undergone in like manner many pains and torments, have left a glorious example to us. 17 For this not only men but women have been persecuted: and having suffered very grievous and cruel punishments, have finished the course of their faith with firmness; and though weak in body, yet received a glorious reward. 18 This has alienated the minds even of women from their husbands; and changed what was once said by our father Adam; This is now bone of my bone, and flesh of my flesh. 19 In a word, envy and strife, have overturned whole cities, and rooted out great nations from off the earth.

1 Clem. 4 - 1 He exhorts them to live by the rules, and repent of their divisions, and they shall be forgiven. THESE things, beloved, we write unto you, not only for your instruction, but also for our own remembrance. 2 For we are all in the same 17 lists, and the same combat is prepared for us all. 3 Wherefore let us lay aside all vain and empty cares; and let us come up to the glorious and venerable rule of our holy calling. 4 Let us consider what is good, and acceptable and well-pleasing in the sight of him that made us. 5 Let us look steadfastly to the blood of Christ, and see how precious his blood is in the sight of God: which being shed for our salvation, has obtained the grace of repentance for all the world. 6 Let us search into all the ages that have gone before us; and let us learn that our Lord has in every one of them still given place for repentance to all such as would turn to him. 7 Noah preached repentance; and as many as hearkened to him were saved. Jonah denounced destruction against the Ninevites: 8 Howbeit they repenting of their sins, appeased God by their prayers: and were saved, though they were strangers to the covenant of God. 9 Hence we find how all the ministers of the grace of God have spoken by the Holy Spirit of repentance. And even the Lord of all has himself declared with an oath concerning it; 10 As I live, saith the Lord, I desire not the death of a sinner, but that he should repent. Adding farther this good sentence, saying: Turn from your iniquity, O house of Israel. 11 Say unto the children of my people, Though your sins should reach from earth to heaven; and though they shall be redder than scarlet, and blacker than sackcloth; yet if ye shall turn to me with all your heart, and shall call me father, I will hearken to you, as to a holy people. 12 And in another place he saith on this wise: Wash ye, make you clean; put away the evil of your doings from before mine eyes; cease to do evil, learn to do well;

seek judgment, relieve the oppressed, judge the fatherless, plead for the widow. 13 Come now and let us reason together, saith the Lord: though your sins be as scarlet, they shall be as white as snow; though they be red as crimson, they shall be as wool. 14 If ye be willing and obedient, ye shall eat the good of the land; but if ye refuse and rebel, ye shall be devoured with the sword; for the mouth of the Lord hath spoken it. 15 These things has God established by his Almighty will, desiring that all his beloved should come to repentance.

1 Clem. 5 - 1 He sets before them the examples of holy men, whose piety is recorded in the Scriptures. WHEREFORE let us obey his excellent and glorious will; and imploring his mercy and goodness, let us fall down upon our faces before him, and 11 cast ourselves upon his mercy; laying aside all vanity, and contention, and envy which leads unto death. 2 Let us look up to those who have the most perfectly ministered to his excellent glory. Let us take Enoch for our example; who being found righteous in obedience, was translated, and his death was not known. 3 Noah being proved to be faithful, did by his ministry preach regeneration to the world; and the Lord saved by him all the living creatures, that went with one accord into the ark. 4 Abraham, who was called God's friend, was in like manner found faithful; inasmuch as he obeyed the commands of God. 5 By obedience he went out of his own country, and from his own kindred, and from his father's house: that so forsaking a small country, and a weak affinity, and a little house, he might inherit the promises of God. 6 For thus God said unto him; get thee out of thy country, and from thy kindred, and from thy father's house, unto a land that I will show thee. 7 And I will make thee a great nation, and will bless thee, and make thy name great, and thou shalt be blessed. And I will bless them that bless thee, and curse them that curse thee; and in thee shall all families of the earth be blessed. 8 And again when he separated himself from Lot, God said unto him; Lift up now thine eyes, and look from the place where thou art northward and southward and eastward and westward for all the land which thou seest, to thee will I give it, and to thy seed for ever. 9 And I will make thy seed as the dust of the earth, so that if a man can number the dust of the earth, then shall thy seed also be numbered. 10 And again he saith: and God brought forth Abraham, and said unto him; Look now toward heaven, and tell the stars, if thou be able to number them: so shall thy seed be. 11 And Abraham believed God, and it was counted to him for righteousness. 12 Through faith and hospitality, he had a son given him in his old age; and through obedience he offered him up in sacrifice to God, upon one of the mountains which God showed unto him.

1 Clem. 6 - 1 And particularly such as have been eminent for their kindness and charity to their neighbours.

BY hospitality and godliness was Lot saved out of Sodom, when all the country round about was destroyed by fire and brimstone: 2 The Lord thereby making it manifest, that he will not forsake those that trust in him; but will bring the disobedient to punishment and correction. 3 For his wife who went out with him, being of a different mind, and not continuing in the same obedience, was for that reason set forth for an example, being turned into a pillar of salt unto this day. 4 That so all men may know, that those who are double minded, and distrustful of the power of God, are prepared for condemnation, and to be a sign to all succeeding ages. 5 By faith and hospitality was Rahab the harlot saved. For when the spies were sent by Joshua the son of Nun, to search out Jericho and the king of Jericho knew that they were come to spy out his country; he sent men to take them, so that they might be put to death. 6 Rahab therefore being hospitable, received them, and hid them under the stalks of flax, on the top of her house. 7 And when the messengers that were sent by the king came unto her, and asked her,

saying, There came men unto thee to spy out the land, bring them forth, for so hath the king commanded: She answered, The two men whom ye seek came unto me, but presently they departed, and are gone: Not discovering them unto them. 8 Then she said to the spies, I know that the Lord your God has given this city into your hands; for the fear of you is fallen upon all that dwell therein. When, therefore, ye shall have taken it ye shall save me and my father's house. 9 And they answered her, saying, It shall be as thou hast spoken to us. Therefore, when thou shalt know that we are near thou shalt gather all thy family together upon the housetop, and they shall be saved: but all that shall be found without thy house, shall be destroyed. 10 And they gave her moreover a sign: that she should hang out of her house a scarlet rope; 11 sheaving thereby, that by the blood of our Lord, there should be redemption to all that believe and hope in God. Ye see, beloved, how there was not only faith, but prophecy too in this woman.

1 Clem. 7 1 What rules are given for this purpose. LET us, therefore, humble ourselves, brethren, laying aside all pride, and boasting, and foolishness, and anger: And let us do as it is written. 2 For thus saith the Holy Spirit; Let not the wise man glory in his wisdom, nor the strong man in his strength, nor the rich man in his riches; but let him that glorieth, glory in the Lord, to seek him, and to do judgment and justice. 3 Above all, remembering the words of the Lord Jesus, which he spake concerning equity and long suffering, saying, 4 Be ye merciful and ye shall obtain mercy; forgive, and ye shall be forgiven: as ye do, so shall it be done unto you: as ye give, so shall it be given unto you: as ye judge, so shall ye be judged; as ye are kind to others so shall God be kind to you: with what measure ye mete, with the same shall it be measured to you again. 5 By this command, and by these rules, let us establish ourselves, that so we may always walk obediently to his holy words; being humble minded: 6 For so says the Holy Scripture; upon whom shall I look, even upon him that is poor and of a contrite spirit, and that trembles at my word. 7 It is, therefore, just and righteous, men and brethren, that we should become obedient unto God, rather than follow such as through pride and sedition, have made themselves the ring-leaders of a detestable emulation. 8 For it is not an ordinary harm that we shall do ourselves but rather a very great danger that we shall run, if we shall rashly give up ourselves to the wills of men who promote strife and seditions, to turn us aside from that which is fitting. 9 But let us be kind to one another, according to the compassion and sweetness of him that made us. 10 For it is written, The merciful shall inherit the earth; and they that are without evil shall be left upon it: but the transgressors shall perish from off the face of it. 11 And again he saith, I have seen the wicked in great power and spreading himself like the cedar of Libanus. I passed by, and lo! he was not; I sought his place, but it could not be found. 12 Keep innocently, and do the thing that is right, for there shall be a remnant to the peaceable man. 13 Let us, therefore, hold fast to those who religiously follow peace; and not to such as only pretend to desire. 14 For he saith in a certain place, This people honoureth me with their lips, but their heart is far from me. 15 And again, They bless with their mouths, but curse in their hearts. 16 And again he saith, They loved him with their mouths, and with their tongues they lied to him. For their heart was not r right with him, neither were they, faithful in his covenant. 17 Let all deceitful lips become dumb, and the tongue that speaketh proud things. Who have said, with our tongue will we prevail; our lips are our own, who is Lord over us. 18 For the oppression of the poor, for the sighing of the needy, now will I arise saith the Lord; I will set him in safety, I will deal confidently with him.

1 Clem. 8 - He advises them to be humble; and that from the examples of Jesus and of holy men in all ages. FOR Christ is theirs who are humble, and not who exalt themselves over his flock. The sceptre of the majesty of God, our Lord Jesus Christ, came not in the shew of pride and arrogance, though he could have done so; but with humility as the Holy Ghost had before spoken concerning him. 2 For thus he saith, Lord, who hath believed our report, and to whom is the arm of the Lord revealed? For he shall grow up before him as a tender plant, and as a root out of a dry ground. 3 He hath no form or comeliness, and when we shall see him, there is no beauty that we should desire him. 4 He is despised and rejected of men; a man of sorrows and acquainted with grief. 5 And we hid, as it were, our faces from him; he was despised, and we esteemed him not. 6 Surely he hath born our griefs, and carried our sorrows: yet we did esteem him stricken, smitten of God, and afflicted. 7 But he was wounded for our transgressions; he was bruised for our iniquities; the chastisement of our peace was upon him; and with his stripes we are healed. 8 All we like sheep have gone astray; we have turned every one to his own way, and the Lord hath laid on him the iniquity of us all. 9 He was oppressed, and he was afflicted, yet he opened not his mouth: he is brought as a lamb to the slaughter; and as a sheep before her shearers is dumb, so he openeth not his mouth. 10 He was taken from prison, and from judgment; and who shall declare his generation? For he was cut off out of the land of the living, for the transgressions of my people was he stricken. 11 And he made his grave with the wicked, and with the rich in his death; because he had done no violence, neither was any deceit in his mouth. 12 Yet it pleased the Lord to bruise him, he hath put him to grief; when thou shalt make his soul an offering for sin, he shall see his seed, he shall prolong his days; and the pleasure of the Lord shall prosper in his hand. 13 He shall see of the travail of his soul and shall be satisfied; by his knowledge shall my righteous servant justify many: for he shall bear their iniquities. 14 Therefore will I divide him a portion with the great, and he shall divide the spoil with the strong; because he hath poured out his soul into death; and he was numbered with the transgressors, and he bare the sin of many, and made intercession for the transgressors. 15 And again he himself saith, 1 I am a worm and no man, a reproach of men, and despised of the people. All they that see me laugh me to scorn; they shoot out their lips, they shake their heads, saying: He trusted in the Lord that he would deliver him, let him deliver him seeing he delighted in him. 16 Ye see, beloved, what the pattern is that has been given to us. For if the Lord thus humbled himself, what should we do who are brought by him under the yoke of his grace? 17 Let us be followers of those who went about in goat-skins and sheep-skins; preaching the coming of Christ. 18 Such were Elias, and Elisæus, and Ezekiel the prophets. And let us add to these such others as have received the like testimony. 19 Abraham has been greatly witnessed of; having been called the friend of God. And yet he steadfastly beholding the glory of God, says with all humility, I am dust and ashes. 20 Again of Job it is thus written, That he was just and without blame, true; one that served God, and abstained from all evil. Yet he accusing himself, says, No man is free from pollution, no not though he should live but one day. 21 Moses was called faithful in all God's House; and by his conduct the Lord punished Israel by stripes and plagues. 22 And even this man, though thus greatly honoured, spake not greatly of himself; but when the oracle of God was delivered to him out of the bush he said, Who am I, that thou dost send me? I am of a slender voice, and a slow tongue. 23 And again he saith, I am as the smoke of the pot. 24 And what shall we say of David, so highly testified of in the Holy Scriptures? To whom God said I have found a man after my own heart, David the son of Jesse, with my holy oil

365

have I anointed him. 25 But yet be himself saith unto God, Have mercy upon me, O God, according to thy loving kindness; according unto the multitude of thy tender mercies, blot out my transgressions. 26 Wash me thoroughly from mine iniquity, and cleanse me from my sin! For I acknowledge my transgressions, and my sin is ever before me. 27 Against Thee only have I sinned, and done this evil in thy sight, that thou mightest be justified when thou speakest, and be clear when thou judgest. 28 Behold I was shapen in iniquity, and in sin did my mother conceive me. 29 Behold, thou desireth truth in the inward parts; and in the hidden part thou shalt make me to know wisdom. 30 Purge me with hyssop and I shall be clean, wash me and I shall be whiter than snow. 31 Make me to hear joy and gladness, that the bones which thou hast broken may rejoice. 32 Hide thy face from my sins, and blot out all mine iniquities. 33 Create in me a clean heart O God; and renew a right spirit within me. 34 Cast me not away from thy presence, and take not thy holy spirit from me. 35 Restore unto me the joy of thy salvation, and uphold me with thy free spirit. 36 Then I will teach transgressors thy ways, and sinners shall be converted unto thee. 37 Deliver me from blood-guiltiness, O God, thou God of my salvation, and my tongue shall sing aloud of thy righteousness. 38 O Lord open thou my lips, and my mouth shall show forth thy praise. 39 For thou desirest not sacrifice, else would I give it; thou delightest not in burnt offerings. 40 The sacrifices of God are a broken spirit, a broken and a contrite heart, O God, thou wilt not despise.

1 Clem. 9 - He again persuades them to compose their divisions. THUS has the humility and godly fear of these great and excellent men, recorded in the Scriptures, through obedience, made not only us, but also the generations before us better; even as many as have received his holy oracles with fear and truth. 2 Having therefore so many, and such great and glorious 1 examples, let us return to that peace which was the mark that from the beginning was set before us; 3 Let us look up to the Father and Creator of the whole world; and let us hold fast to his glorious and exceeding gifts and benefits of peace. 4 Let us consider and behold with the eyes of our understanding his long-suffering will; and think how gentle and patient he is towards his whole creation. 5 The heavens moving by his appointment, are subject to him in peace. 6 Day and night accomplish the courses that he has allotted unto them, not disturbing one another. 7 The sun and moon, and all the several companies and constellations of the stars, run the 6courses that he has appointed to them in concord, without departing in the least from them. 8 The fruitful earth yields its food plentifully in due season both to man and beast, and to all animals that are upon it, according to his will; not disputing, nor altering any thing of what was ordered by him. 9 So also the unfathomable and unsearchable floods of the deep, are kept in by his command; 10 And the conflux of the vast sea, being brought together by his order into its several collections, passes not the bounds that he has set to it; 11 But as he appointed it, so it remains. For he said, Hitherto shalt thou come, and thy floods shall be broken within thee. 12 The ocean, unpassable to mankind, and the worlds that are beyond it, are governed by the same commands of their great master. 13 Spring and summer, autumn and winter, give place peaceably to each other. 14 The several quarters of the winds fulfil their work in their seasons, without offending one another. 15 The ever-flowing fountains, made both for pleasure and health, never fail to reach out their breasts to support the life of men. 16 Even the smallest creatures 14 live together in peace and concord with each other. 17 All these has the Great Creator and Lord of all, commanded to observe peace and concord; being good to all. 18 But especially to us who flee to his mercy through our Lord Jesus Christ; to whom be glory and majesty for ever and ever. Amen.

1 Clem. 10 - He exhorts them to obedience, from the consideration of the goodness of God, and of his presence in every place. TAKE heed, beloved, that his many blessings be not to us to condemnation; except we shall walk worthy of him, doing with one consent what is good and pleasing in his sight. [2] The spirit of the Lord is a candle, searching out the inward of the belly. [3] Let us therefore consider how near he is to us; and how that none of our thoughts, or reasonings which we frame with in ourselves, are hid from him. [4] It is therefore just that we should not forsake our rank, by doing contrary to his will. [5] Let us choose to offend a few foolish and inconsiderate men, lifted up and glorying in their own pride, rather than God. [6] Let us reverence our Lord Jesus Christ whose blood was given for us. [7] Let us honour those who are set over us; let us respect the aged that are amongst us; and let us instruct the younger men, in the discipline and fear of the Lord. [8] Our wives let us [3] direct to do that which is good. [9] Let them show forth a lovely habit of purity in all their conversation; with a sincere affection of meekness. [10] Let the government of their tongues be made manifest by their silence. [11] Let their charity be without respect of persons alike towards all such as religiously fear God. [12] Let your children be bred up in the instruction of Christ: [13] And especially let them learn how great a power humility has with God; how much a pure and holy charity avails with him; how excellent and great his fear is; and how it will save all such as turn to him with holiness in a pure mind. [14] For he is the searcher of the thoughts and counsels of the heart; whose breath is in us, and when he pleases he can take it from us.

1 Clem. 11 Of faith, and particularly what we are to believe as to the resurrection. BUT all these things [9] must be confirmed by the faith which is in Christ; for so he himself bespeaks us by the Holy Ghost. [2] Come ye children and hearken unto me, and I will teach you the fear of the Lord. What man is there that desireth life, and loveth to see good days? [3] Keep thy tongue from evil, and thy lips that they speak no guile. [4] Depart from evil and do good; seek peace and ensue it. [5] The eyes of the Lord are upon the righteous, and his ears are open unto their prayers. [6] But the face of the Lord is against them that do evil, to cut off the remembrance of them from the earth. [7] The righteous cried, and the Lord heard him, and delivered him out of all his troubles. [8] Many are the troubles of the wicked; but they that trust in the Lord, mercy shall encompass them about. [9] Our all-merciful and beneficent Father hath bowels of compassion towards them that fear him; and kindly and lovingly bestows his graces upon all such as come to him with a simple mind. [10] Wherefore let us not [1] waver, neither let us have any doubt in our hearts, of his excellent and glorious gifts. [11] Let that be far from us which is written, Miserable are the double-minded, and those who are doubtful in their hearts. [12] Who say these things have we heard, and our fathers have told us these things. But behold we are grown old, and none of them has happened unto us. [13] O ye fools! consider the trees: take the vine for an example. First it sheds its leaves; then it buds; after that it spreads its leaves; then it flowers; then come the sour grapes; and after them follows the ripe fruit. Ye see how in a little time the fruit of the tree comes to maturity. [14] Of a truth, yet a little while and his will shall suddenly be accomplished. [15] The Holy Scripture itself bearing witness, That He shall quickly come and not tarry, and that the Lord shall suddenly come to his temple, even the holy ones whom ye look for. [16] Let us consider, beloved, how the Lord does continually shew us, that there shall be a future resurrection; of which he has made our Lord Jesus Christ the first fruits, raising him from the dead. [17] Let us contemplate, beloved, the resurrection that is continually made before our eyes. [18] Day and night manifest a resurrection to us. The night lies down, and the day arises: main the day departs, and the night comes on. [19] Let us behold the fruits of the earth. Every one sees how the seed is sown. The sower goes forth, and casts it upon the earth; and the seed which when it was sown fell upon the earth dry and naked, in time dissolves. [20] And from the dissolution, the great power of the providence of the Lord raises it again; and of one seed many arise, and bring forth fruit.

1 Clem. 12 The Resurrection further proved. LET us consider that wonderful type of the resurrection which is seen in the Eastern countries; that is to say, in Arabia. [2] There is a certain bird called a Phœnix; of this there is never but one at a time: and that lives five hundred years. And when the time of its dissolution draws near, that it must die, it makes itself a nest of frankincense, and myrrh, and other spices into which when its time is fulfilled it enters and dies. [3] But its flesh putrifying, breeds a certain worm, which being nourished with the juice of the dead bird brings forth feathers; and when it is grown to a perfect state, it takes up the nest in which the bones of its parents lie, and carries it from Arabia into Egypt, to a city called Heliopolis: [4] And flying in open day in the sight of all men, lays it upon the altar of the sun, and so returns from whence it came. [5] The priests then search into the records of the time; and find that it returned precisely at the end of five hundred years. [6] And shall we then think it to be any very great and strange thing for the Lord of all to raise up those that religiously him in the assurance of good faith, when even by a bird he shews us the greatness of his power to fulfil his promise? [7] For he says in a certain place, Thou shalt raise me up, and I shall confess unto thee. [8] And again I laid me down and slept, and awaked, because thou art with me. [9] And again, Job says, Thou shalt raise up this flesh of mine, that has suffered all these things. [10] Having therefore this hope, let us hold fast to him who is faithful in all his promises, and righteous in all his judgments; who has commanded us not to lie: how much more will he not himself lie? [11] For nothing is impossible with God but to lie. [12] Let his faith then be stirred up again in us; and let us consider that all things are nigh unto him. [13] By the word of his power he made all things; and by the same word he is able (whenever he will), to destroy them. [14] Who shall say unto him, what dost thou? or who shall resist the power of his strength? [15] When, and as he pleased, he will do all things; and nothing shall pass away of all that has been determined by him. [16] All things are open before him; nor can anything be hid from his council. [17] The heavens declare the glory of God, and the firmament sheweth his handy work. Day unto day uttereth speech, and night unto night sheweth knowledge. There is no speech nor language where their voice is not heard.

1 Clem. 13 It is impossible to escape the vengeance of God, if we continue in sin. SEEING then all things are seen and heard by God; let us fear him, and let us lay aside our wicked works which proceed from ill desires; that through his mercy we may be delivered from the condemnation to come. For whither can any of us flee from his mighty hand? Or what world shall receive any of those who run away from him? For thus saith the Scripture in a certain place, Whither shall I flee from thy Spirit, or where shall I hide myself from thy presence? If I ascend up into heaven, thou art there; if I shall go to the utmost part of the earth, there is thy right hand: If I shall make my bed in the deep, thy Spirit is there. Whither then shall any one go; or whither shall he run from him that comprehends all things? Let us therefore come to him with holiness of heart, lifting up chaste and undefiled hands unto him; loving our gracious and merciful Father, who has made us to partake of his election. For so it is written, When the Most High divided the nations, when he separated the sons of Adam, he set the bounds of the nations, according to the number of his angels; his people [paragraph continues]Jacob became the portion of the Lord, and Israel the lot of his inheritance. And in another place he saith, Behold the Lord taketh unto himself a nation, out of the midst of the nations, as a man taketh the first-fruits of his flower; the Most Holy shall come out of that nation.

1 Clem. 14 How we must live that we may please God. WHEREFORE we being a part of the Holy One, let us do all those things that pertain unto holiness: [2] Fleeing all evil-speaking against one another; all filthy and impure embraces, together with all drunkenness, youthful lusts, abominable concupiscences, detestable adultery, and execrable pride. [3] For God, saith he, resisteth the proud, but giveth grace to the humble. [4] Let us therefore hold fast to those to whom God has given His grace. [5] And let us put on concord, being humble, temperate; free from all whispering and detraction; and justified by our actions, not our words. [6] For he saith, Doth he that speaketh and heareth many things, and that is of a ready tongue, suppose that he is righteous? Blessed is he that is born of a woman, that liveth but a few days: use not therefore much speech. Let our praise be of God, not of ourselves; for God hateth those that commend themselves. [8] Let the witness of our good actions be given to us of others, as it was given to the holy men that went before us. [9] Rashness, and arrogance, and confidence, belong to them who are accursed of God: but equity, and humility, and mildness, to such as are blessed by him. [10] Let us then lay hold of his blessing, and let us consider what are the ways by which we may attain unto it. [11] Let us Look back upon those things that have happened from the beginning. [12] For what was our father Abraham blessed? Was it not because that through faith he wrought righteousness and truth? [13] Isaac being fully persuaded of what he knew was to come, cheerfully yielded himself up for a sacrifice. Jacob with humility departed out of his own country, fleeing from his brother, and went unto Laban and served him; and so the sceptre of the twelve tribes of Israel was given unto him. [14] Now what the greatness of this Gift was, will plainly appear, if we shall take the pains distinctly to consider all the parts of it. [15] For from him came the priests and Levites, who all ministered at the altar of God. [16] From him came our Lord Jesus Christ according to the flesh. [17] From him came the kings, and princes, and rulers in Judah. [18] Nor were the rest of his tribes in any small glory: God having promised that thy seed (says he) shall be as the stars of heaven. [19] They were all therefore greatly glorified, not for their own sake, or for their own works, or for the righteousness that they themselves wrought, but through his will. [20] And we also being called by the same will in Christ Jesus, are not justified by ourselves, neither by our own wisdom, or knowledge, or piety, or the works which we have done [4] in the holiness of our hearts: [21] But by that faith by which God Almighty has justified all men from the beginning; to whom be glory for ever and ever. Amen.

1 Clem. 15 We are justified by faith; yet this must not lessen our care to live well, nor our pleasure in it. WHAT shall we do therefore, brethren? Shall we be slothful in well-doing, and lay aside our charity? God forbid that any such thing should be done by us. [2] But rather let us hasten with all earnestness and readiness of mind, to perfect every good work. For even the Creator and Lord of all things himself rejoices in his own works. [3] By his [5] Almighty power he fixed the heavens, and by his incomprehensible wisdom he adorned them. [4] He also divided the earth from the water, with which it is encompassed; and fixed it as a secure tower, upon the foundation of his own will. [5] He also by his appointment, commanded all the living creatures that are upon it, to exist. [6] So likewise the sea, and all the

creatures that are in it; having first created them, he enclosed them therein by his power. [7] And above all, he with his holy and pure hands, formed man, the most excellent, and, as to his understanding, truly the greatest of all other creatures, the character of his own image. [8] For so God says, Let us make man in our image, after our own likeness So God created man, male and female created he them. [9] And having thus finished all these things, he commended all that he had made, and blessed them, and said, increase and multiply. [10] We see how all righteous men have been adorned with good works: Wherefore even the Lord himself, having adorned himself with his works, rejoiced. [11] Having therefore such an example, let us without delay, fulfil his will; and with all our strength, work the work of righteousness.

1 Clem. 16 This enforced from the examples of the holy angels, and from the exceeding greatness of that reward which God has prepared for us. THE good workman with confidence receives the bread of his labour; but the sluggish and lazy cannot look him in the face that set him on work. [2] We must therefore be ready and forward in well doing; for from him are all things. [3] And thus he foretells us, [11] behold the Lord cometh, and his reward is with him, even before his face, to render to every one according to his work. [4] He warns us therefore beforehand, with all his heart to this end, that we should not be slothful and negligent in well doing. [5] Let our boasting, therefore, and our confidence be in God: let us submit ourselves to his will. Let us consider the whole multitude of his angels, how ready they stand to minister unto his will. [6] As saith the scripture, thousands of thousands stood before him and ten thousand times ten thousand ministered unto him. And they cried, saying, Holy, holy, holy is the Lord of Sabaoth: The whole earth is full of his glory. [7] Wherefore let us also, being conscientiously gathered together in concord with one another; as it were with one mouth, cry earnestly unto him, that he would make us partakers of his great and glorious promises. [8] For he saith, Eye hath not seen, nor ear heard, neither have entered into the heart of man, the things which God has prepared for them that wait for him.

1 Clem. 17 [1] We must attain unto this reward by faith and obedience, which we must carry on in an orderly pursuing of the duties of our several stations, without envy or contention. The necessity of different orders among men. We have none of us anything but what we received of God: whom therefore we ought in every condition thankfully to obey. HOW blessed and wonderful, beloved, are the gifts of God. [2] Life in immortality! brightness in righteousness! truth in full assurance! faith in confidence! temperance in holiness! [3] And all this has God subjected to our understandings: [4] What therefore shall those things be which he has prepared for them that wait for him? [5] The Creator and Father of spirits, the Most Holy; he only knows both the greatness and beauty of them. [6] Let us therefore strive with all earnestness, that we may be found in the number of those that wait for him, that so we may receive the reward which he has promised. [7] But how, beloved, shall we do this? We must fix our minds by faith towards God, and seek those things that are pleasing and acceptable unto him. [8] We must act conformably to his holy will; and follow the way of truth, casting off from us all unrighteousness and iniquity, together with all covetousness, strife, evil manners, deceit, whispering, detractions; all hatred of God, pride and boasting; vainglory and ambition; [9] For they that do these things are odious to God; and not only they that do them, but also all such as approve of those that do them. [10] For thus saith the Scripture, But unto the wicked, God said, What hast thou to do to declare my statute, or that thou shouldst take my covenant in the mouth? Seeing that thou hatest instruction, and castest my words behind thee. [11] When thou sawest a thief, then thou consentedst with him; and hast been partaker with adulterers. Thou givest thy mouth to evil, and thy tongue frameth deceit. Thou sittest and speakest against thy brother; thou slanderest thine own mother's son. 12 These things hast thou done and I kept silence; thou thoughtest that I was altogether such a one as thyself: but I will reprove thee, and set them in order before thine eyes. 13 Now consider this ye that forget God, lest I tear you in pieces, and there be none to deliver. 14 Whoso offereth praise, glorifieth me: and to him that disposeth his way aright, will I shew the salvation of God. 15 This is the way, beloved, in which we may find our Saviour, even Jesus Christ the high-priest of all our offerings, the defender and helper of our weakness. 16 By him we look up to the highest heavens; and behold, as in a glass, his spotless and most excellent visage. 17 By him are the eyes of our hearts opened; by him our foolish and darkened understanding rejoiceth to behold his wonderful light. 18 By him would God have us to taste the knowledge of immortality: who being the brightness of his glory, is by so much greater than the angels, as he has by inheritance obtained a more excellent name than they. 19 For so it is written, who maketh his angels spirits, and his ministers a flame of fire: 20 But to his son, thus saith the Lord, Thou art my Son, today have I begotten thee. 21 Ask of me, and I will give thee the heathen for thy inheritance, and the utmost parts of the earth for thy possession. 22 And again he saith unto him, Sit thou on my right hand until I make thine enemies my footstool. 23 But who are his enemies? even the wicked, and such who oppose their own wills to the will of God. 24 Let us therefore march on, men and brethren, with all earnestness in his holy laws. 25 Let us consider those who fight under our earthly governors: How orderly, how readily, and with what exact obedience they perform those things that are commanded them. 26 All are not generals, nor colonels, nor captains, nor inferior officers: 27 But every one in his respective rank does what is commanded him by the king, and those who have the authority over him. 28 They who are great, cannot subsist without those that are little; nor the little without the great. 29 But there must be a mixture in all things, and then there will be use and profit too. 30 Let us, for example, take our body: the head without the feet is nothing, neither the feet without the head. 31 And even the smallest members of our body are yet both necessary and useful to the whole body. 32 But all conspire together, and are subject to one common use, namely, the preservation of the whole body. 33 Let therefore our whole body be saved in Christ Jesus; and let every one be subject to his neighbour, according to the order in which he is placed by the gift of God. 34 Let not the strong man despise the weak; and let the weak see that he reverence the strong.35 Let the rich man distribute to the necessity of the poor: and let the poor bless God, that he has given one unto him, by whom his want may be supplied. 36 Let the wise man shew forth his wisdom, not in words, but in good works. 37 Let him that is humble, not bear witness to himself, but let him leave it to another to bear witness of him. 38 Let him that is pure in the flesh, not grow proud of it, knowing that it was from another that he received the gift of continence. 39 Let us consider therefore, brethren, whereof we are made; who, and what kind of men we came into the world, as it were out of a sepulchre, and from outer darkness. 40 He that made us, and formed us, brought us into his own world; having presented us with his benefits, even before we were born. 41 Wherefore, having received all these things from him, we ought in everything to give thanks unto him; to whom be glory for ever and ever. Amen.

1 Clem. 18 From whence he exhorts them to do everything orderly in the Church, as the only way to please God. FOOLISH and unwise men who have neither prudence nor learning may mock and deride

368

us; being willing to set up themselves in their own conceits; 2 But what can a mortal man do? Or what strength is there in him that is made out of the dust? 3 For it is written, there was no shape before mine eyes; only I heard a sound and a voice. 4 For what? Shall man be pure before the Lord? Shall he be blameless in his works? 5 Behold, he trusteth not in his servants; and his angels he chargeth with folly. 6 Yes, the heaven is not clean in his sight, how much less they that dwell in houses of clay; of which also we ourselves were made? 7 He smote them as a moth: and from morning even unto the evening they endure not. Because they were not able to help themselves, they perished; he breathed upon them and they died, because they had no wisdom. 8 Call now if there be any that will answer thee; and to which of the angels wilt thou look? 9 For wrath killeth the foolish man, and envy slayeth him that is in error. 10 I have seen the foolish taking root, but lo, their habitation was presently consumed. 11 Their children were far from safety, they 12 perished at the gates of those who were lesser than themselves; and there was no man to help them. For what was prepared for them, the righteous 14 did eat: and they shall not be delivered from evil. 13 Seeing then these things are manifest unto us, it will behoove us, to take care that looking into the depths of the divine knowledge, we do all things in order, whatsoever our Lord has commanded us to do. 14 And particularly, that we perform our offerings and service to God, at their appointed seasons: for these he has commanded to be done, not rashly and disorderly, but at certain determinate times and hours. 15 And therefore he has ordained by his supreme will and authority, both where, and by what persons, they are to be performed; that so all things being piously done unto all well-pleasing, they may be acceptable unto him. 16 They therefore who make their offerings at the appointed seasons, are happy and accepted: because that obeying the commandments of the Lord, they are free from sin. 17 And the same care must be had of the persons that minister unto him. 18 For the chief-priest has his proper services; and to the priests their proper place is appointed; and to the Levites appertain their proper ministries: and the layman is confined within the bounds of what is commanded to laymen. 19 Let every one of you therefore, brethren, bless God in his proper station, with a good conscience, and with all gravity, not exceeding the rule of his service that is appointed to him. 20 The daily sacrifices are not offered everywhere; nor the peace-offerings, nor the sacrifices appointed for sins and transgressions; but only at Jerusalem: nor in any place there, but only at the altar before the temple; that which is offered being first diligently examined by the high-priest and the other minister we before mentioned. 21 They therefore who do anything which is not agreeable to His will are punished with death. 22 Consider, brethren, that by how much the better knowledge God has vouchsafed unto us by so much the greater danger are we exposed to.

1 Clem. 19 The orders of Ministers in Christ's Church established by the Apostles according to Christ's command, after the example of Moses. Therefore they who have been duly placed in the ministry according to their order cannot without great sin be put out of it. THE Apostles have preached to us from the Lord Jesus Christ; Jesus Christ from God. 2 Christ therefore was sent by God, the Apostles by Christ; so both were orderly sent, according to the will of God. 3 For having received their command, and being thoroughly assured by the resurrection of our Lord Jesus Christ; and convinced by the word of God, with the fulness of the Holy Spirit, they went abroad, publishing, That the kingdom of God was at hand. 4 And thus preaching through countries and cities, they appointed the first fruits of their conversion to be bishops and ministers over such as should afterwards believe, having first proved them by the

Spirit. 5 Nor was this any new thing: seeing that long before it was written concerning bishops and deacons. For thus saith the Scripture, in a certain place: I will appoint their overseers in righteousness, and their ministers in faith. 7 And what wonder if they, to whom such a work was committed by God in Christ, established such officers as we before mentioned; when even that blessed and faithful servant in all his house, Moses, set down in the Holy Scriptures all things that were commanded him. 8 Whom also all the rest of the prophets followed, bearing witness with one consent to those things that were appointed by him. 9 For he, perceiving an emulation to arise among the tribes concerning the priesthood, and that there was a strife about it, which of them should be adorned with that glorious name; commanded their twelve captains to bring to him twelve rods; every tribe being written upon its rod, according to its name. 10 And he took them and bound them together, and sealed them with the seals of the twelve princes of the tribes; and laid them up in the tabernacle of witness, upon the table of God. 11 And when he had shut the door of the tabernacle he sealed up the keys of it, in like manner as he had done the rods; and said unto them, Men and brethren, whichsoever tribe shall have its rod blossom, that tribe has God chosen to perform the office of a priest, and to minister unto him in holy things. 12 And when the morning was come, he called together all Israel, six hundred thousand men; and shewed to the princes their seals; and opened the tabernacle of witness; and brought forth the rods. 13 And the rod of Aaron was found not only to have blossomed, but also to have fruit upon it. 14 What think you, beloved? Did not Moses before know what should happen? 15 Yes verily: but to the end there might be no division, nor tumult in Israel, he did in this manner, that the name of the true and only God might be glorified, to him be honour for ever and ever, Amen. 16 So likewise our Apostles knew by our Lord Jesus Christ, that there should contentions arise, upon account of the ministry. 17 And therefore having a perfect fore-knowledge of this, they appointed persons, as we have before said, and then gave direction, how, when they should die, other chosen and approved men should succeed in their ministry. 18 Wherefore we cannot think that those may justly be thrown out of their ministry, who were either appointed by them, or afterwards chosen by other eminent men, with the consent of the whole church; and who have with all lowliness and innocency ministered to the flock of Christ, in peace, and without self-interest, and were for a long time commended by all. 19 For it would be no small sin in us, should we cast off those from their [1] ministry who holily and without blame fulfil the duties of it. 20 Blessed are those priests, who having finished their course before these times have obtained a fruitful and perfect dissolution: for they have no fear, lest any one should turn them out of the place which is now appointed for them. 21 But we see how you have put out some, who lived reputably among you, from the ministry, which by their innocence they had adorned.

1 Clem. 20 He exhorts them to peace from examples out of the Holy Scriptures, particularly from St. Paul's exhortation to them. YE are contentious, brethren, and zealous for things that pertain not unto salvation. 2 Look into the Holy Scriptures, which are the true words of the Holy Ghost. Ye know that there is nothing unjust or counterfeit written in them. 3 There you shall not find that righteous men were ever cast off by such as were good themselves. 4 They were persecuted, but it was by the wicked and unjust. 5 They were cast into prison; but they were cast in by those that were unholy. 6 They were stoned; but it was by transgressors. 7 They were killed; but by accursed men, and such as had taken up an unjust envy against them. 8 And all these things they underwent gloriously. 9 For what shall we say, brethren? Was Daniel cast into the den of lions,

by men fearing God? Ananias, Azarius, and Misael, were they cast into the fiery furnace by men, professing the excellent and glorious worship of the Most High? God forbid. 10 What kind of persons then were they that did these things? They were men abominable, full of all wickedness; who were incensed to so great a degree, as to bring those into sufferings, who with a holy and unblameable purpose of mind worshipped God: not knowing that the Most High is the protector and defender of all such as with a pure conscience serve his holy name: to whom be glory for ever and ever, Amen. 11 But they who with a full persuasion have endured these things, and are made partakers of glory and honour: and are exalted and lifted up by God in their memorial throughout all ages, Amen. 12 Wherefore it will behoove us also, brethren, to follow such examples as these; for it is written, Hold fast to such as are holy; for they that do so shall be sanctified. And again in another place he saith, 13 With the pure thou shalt be pure, (and with the elect thou shalt be elect), but with the perverse man thou shalt be perverse. 14 Let us therefore join ourselves to the innocent and righteous; for such are the elect of God. 15 Wherefore are there strifes, and anger, and divisions, and schisms, and wars, among us? 16 Have we not all one God, and one Christ? Is not one spirit of grace poured out upon us all? Have we not one calling in Christ? 17 Why then do we rend and tear in pieces the members of Christ; and raise seditious against our own body? And are come to such a height of madness, as to forget that we were members one of another? 18 Remember the words of our Lord Jesus, how he said, Wo to that man, (by whom offences come) It were better for him that he had never been born, than that he should have offended one of my elect. It were better for him, that a millstone should be tied about his neck, and he should be cast into the sea, than that he should offend one of my little ones. 19 Your schism has perverted many, has discouraged many: it has caused diffidence in many, and grief in us all. And yet your sedition continues still. 20 Take the epistle of the blessed Paul the Apostle into your hands; What was it that he wrote to you at his first preaching the Gospel among you? 21 Verily he did by the spirit admonish you concerning himself, and Cephas, and Apollos, because that even then ye had begun to fall into parties and factions among yourselves. 22 Nevertheless your partiality then led you into a much less sin: forasmuch as ye placed your affections upon Apostles, men of [11] eminent reputation in the church; and upon another, who was greatly tried and approved of by them. 23 But consider, we pray you, who are they that have now led you astray; and lessened the reputation of that brotherly love that was so eminent among you? 24 It is a shame, my beloved, yea, a very great shame, and unworthy of your Christian profession, to hear that the most firm and ancient church of the Corinthians should, by one or two persons, be led into a sedition against its priests. 25 And this report is come not only to us, but to those also that differ from us. 26 Insomuch that the name of the Lord is blasphemed through your folly; and even ye yourselves are brought into danger by it. 27 Let us therefore with all haste put an end to this sedition; and let us fall down before the Lord, and beseech Him with tears that He would be favourably reconciled to us, and restore us again to a seemly and holy course of brotherly love. 28 For this is the gate of righteousness, opening unto life: as it is written, Open unto me the gates of righteousness; I will go in unto them and will praise the Lord. This is the gate of the Lord, the righteous shall enter into it. 29 Although therefore many gates are opened, yet this gate of righteousness is that gate in Christ at which blessed are they that enter in, and direct their way in holiness and righteousness, doing all things without disorder. 30 Let a man be faithful, let him be powerful in the utterance of knowledge: let him be wise in making an exact judgment of words; let him be pure in all his actions. [31] But still by how much the more he seems to be [1] above others by reason of these things, by so much the more will it behoove him to be humble-minded; and to seek what is profitable to all men, and not his own advantage.

1 Clem. 21 [1] The value which God puts upon love and unity: the effects of a true charity, which is the gift of God, and must be obtained by prayer. HE that has the love that is in Christ, let him keep the commandments of Christ. [2] For who is able to express the obligation of the love of God? What man is sufficient to declare, and is fitting, the excellency of its beauty? [3] The height to which charity leads is inexpressible.[4] Charity unites us to God; charity covers the multitude of sins: charity endures all things, is long-suffering in all things. [5] There is nothing base and sordid in charity; charity lifts not itself up above others; admits of no divisions; is not seditious; but does all things in peace and concord. [6] By charity were all the elect of God made perfect: Without it nothing is pleasing and acceptable in the sight of God. [7] Through charity did the Lord join us unto himself; whilst for the love that he bore towards us, our Lord Jesus Christ gave his own blood for us, by the will of God; his flesh for our flesh; his soul, for our souls. [8] Ye see, beloved, how great and wonderful a thing charity is: and how that no expressions are sufficient to declare its perfection. [9] But who is fit to be found in it? Even such only as God shall vouchsafe to make so. [10] Let us therefore pray to him, and beseech him, that we may be worthy of it; that so we may live in charity; being unblameable, without human propensities, without respect of persons. [11] All the ages of the world, from Adam, even unto this day, are passed away; but they who have been made perfect in love, have by the grace of God obtained a place among the righteous; and shall be made manifest in the judgment of the kingdom of Christ. [12] For it is written, Enter into thy chambers for a little space, till my anger and indignation shall pass away: And I will remember the good day, and will raise you up out of your graves. [13] Happy then shall we be, beloved, if we shall have fulfilled the commandments of God, in the unity of love; that so, through love, our sins may be forgiven us. [14] For so it is written, Blessed are they whose iniquities are forgiven, and whose sins are covered. Blessed is the man to whom the Lord imputeth no sin, and in whose mouth there is no guile. [15] Now this blessing is fulfilled in those who are chosen by God through Jesus Christ our Lord, to whom be glory for ever and ever. Amen.

1 Clem. 22 [1] He exhorts such as have been concerned in these divisions to repent, and return to their unity, confessing their sin to God, which he enforces from the example of Moses, and of many among the heathen, and of Judith and Esther among the Jews. LET us therefore, as many as have transgressed by any of the [2] suggestions of the adversary, beg God's forgiveness. And as for those who have been the heads of the sedition and faction among you, let them look to the common end of our hope. [3] For as many as are endued with fear and charity, would rather they themselves should fall into trials than their neighbours: And choose to be themselves condemned, rather than that the good and just charity delivered to us, should suffer. [4] For it is seemly for a man to confess wherein he has transgressed. [5] And not to harden his heart, as the hearts of those were hardened, who raised up sedition against Moses the servant of God; whose punishment was manifest unto all men; for they went down alive into the grave, death swallowed them up. [6] Pharaoh and his host, and all the rulers of Egypt, their chariots also and their horsemen, were for no other cause drowned, in the bottom of the Red Sea, and perished; but because they hardened their foolish hearts, after so many signs done in the land of Egypt, by Moses the servant of God. [7] Beloved, God is rot indigent of any

thing; nor does he demand any thing of us, but that we should confess our sins unto him. [8] For so says the [9] Holy David, [10] I will confess unto the Lord, and it shall please him better than a young bullock that hath horns and hoof. Let the poor see it and be glad. And again he saith, [11] Offer unto God the sacrifice of praise, and pay thy vows unto the Most Highest. And call upon me in the day of trouble, and I will deliver thee, and thou shalt glorify me. [12] The sacrifice of God is a broken spirit. Ye know, beloved, ye know full well the Holy Scriptures; and have thoroughly searched into the oracles of God: call them therefore to your remembrance. For when Moses went up into the mount, and tarried there forty days and forty nights in fasting and humiliation; God said unto him, Arise, Moses, and get thee down quickly from hence, for thy people whom thou broughtest out of the land of Egypt, have committed wickedness: they have soon transgressed the way that I commanded them, and have made to themselves graven images. And the Lord said unto him, I have spoken unto thee several times, saying I have seen this people, and behold it is a stiffnecked people: let me therefore destroy them, and put out their name from under heaven. And I will make unto thee a great and a wonderful nation, that shall be much larger than this. [13] But Moses said, Not so, Lord; Forgive now this people their sin; or if thou wilt not, blot me also out of the book of! the living. O admirable charity! O insuperable perfection! The servant speaks freely to his Lord; He beseeches him either to forgive the people, or to destroy him together with them. [14]Who is there among you that is generous? Who that is compassionate? Who that has any charity? Let him say, if this sedition, this contention, and these schisms, be upon my account, I am ready to depart; to go away whithersoever you please; and do whatsoever ye shall command me: Only let the flock of Christ be in peace, with the elders that are set over it. [15] He that shall do this, shall get to himself a very great honour in the Lord; and there is no place but what will be ready to receive him: For the earth is the Lord's and the fulness thereof. [16] These things they who have their conversation towards God not to be repented of, both have done and will always be ready! to do. [17] Nay and even the Gentiles themselves have given us! examples of this kind. [18] For we read, How many kings and princes, in times of pestilence, being warned by their oracles, have given up themselves unto death: that by their own blood, they might deliver their country from destruction. [19] Others have forsaken their cities, so that they might put an end to the seditions of them. [20] We know how many among ourselves, have given up themselves unto bonds, that thereby they might free others from them. [21] Others have sold themselves into bondage that they might feed [10] their brethren with the price of themselves. [22] And even many women, being strengthened by the grace of God, have done many glorious and manly things on such occasions. [23] The blessed Judith, when her city was besieged, desired the elders, that they would suffer her to go into the camp of their enemies: and she went out exposing herself to danger for the love she bore to her country and her people that were besieged; and the Lord delivered Holofernes into the hands of a woman. [24] Nor did Esther, being perfect in faith, expose herself to any less hazard, for the delivery of the twelve tribes of Israel, in danger of being destroyed. For, by fasting and humbling herself, she entreated the Great Maker of all things, the God of spirits; so that beholding the humility of her soul, he delivered the people, for whose sake she was in peril.

1 Clem. 23 The benefit of mutual advice and correction. He entreats them to follow that which is here given to them. WHEREFORE let us also pray for such as are fallen into sin. That being endued with humility and moderation, they may submit not unto us, but to the will of God. 2 For by this means they shall obtain a fruitful and perfect remembrance, with mercy, both in our prayers to God, and in our mention of them before his saints. 3 Let us receive correction, at which no man ought to repine. 4 Beloved, the reproof and the correction which we exercise towards one another, is good, and exceeding profitable: for it unites us the more closely to the will of God. 5 For so says the Holy Scripture, The Lord corrected me, but he did not deliver me over unto death. 6 For whom the Lord loveth he chasteneth, and scourgeth every son whom he receiveth. The righteous, saith he, shall instruct me in mercy and reprove me; but let not oil of sinners make fat my head. 7 And again he saith, Happy is the man whom God correcteth; therefore despise not thou the chastening of the Almighty. 8 For he maketh sore and bindeth up; he woundeth and his hands make whole. 9 He shall deliver thee in six troubles; yea in seven there shall no evil touch thee. In famine he shall redeem thee from death; and in war from the power of the sword. 10 Thou shalt be hid from the scourge of the tongue; neither shalt thou be afraid of destruction when it cometh. 11 Thou shalt laugh at the wicked and sinners; neither shalt thou be afraid of the beasts of the earth. The wild beast shall be at peace with thee. 12 Then shalt thou know that thy house shall be in peace; and the habitation of thy tabernacle shall not err. Thou shalt know also that thy seed shall be great and thy offspring as the grass of the earth. 13 Thou shalt come to thy grave as the ripe corn, that is taken in due time; like as a shock of corn cometh in, in its season. 14 Ye see, beloved, how there shall be a defence to those that are corrected of the Lord. For being a good instructor, he is willing to admonish us by his holy discipline. 15 Do ye therefore who laid the first foundation of this sedition, submit yourselves unto your priests; and be instructed unto repentance, bending the knees of your hearts. 16 Learn to be subject, laying aside all proud and arrogant boasting of your tongues. 17 For it is better for you to be found little, and approved, in the sheepfold of Christ, than to seem to yourselves better than others, and be cast out of his fold. 18 For thus speaks the excellent and all virtuous wisdom, Behold I will pour out the word of my spirit upon you, I will make known my speech unto you. 19 Because I called and ye would not hear, I stretched out my words and ye regarded not. 20 But ye have set at nought all my counsel, and would none of my reproof. I will also laugh at your calamity, and mock when your fear cometh. 21 When your fear cometh as desolation, and your destruction as a whirlwind, when distress and anguish cometh upon you. 22 Then shall ye call upon me, but I will not hear you: the wicked shall seek me, but they shall not find me. For that they hated knowledge, and did not seek the fear of the Lord. 23 They would not hearken unto my counsel: they despised all my reproof. Therefore shall they eat of the fruit of their own ways; and be filled with their own wickedness.

1 Clem. 24 1 Recommends there to God. Desires speedily to hear that this Epistle has had a good effect upon them. NOW God, the inspector of all things, the Father of Spirits, and the Lord of all flesh, who hath chosen our Lord Jesus Christ, and us by him, to be his peculiar people; 2 Grant to every soul of man that calleth upon his glorious and holy name, faith, fear, peace, long-suffering, patience, temperance, holiness and sobriety, unto all well-pleasing in his sight; through our High-Priest and Protector Jesus Christ, by whom be glory, and majesty, and power, and honour, unto him now and for ever more. Amen. 3 The messengers whom we have sent unto you, Claudius, Ephebus, and Valerios Bito, with Fortunatus, send back to us again with all speed in peace, and with joy, that they may the sooner acquaint us with your peace and concord, so much prayed for and desired by us; and that we may rejoice in your good order. 4 The Grace of our Lord Jesus Christ be with you, and with

all that are anywhere called by God through him: To whom be honour and glory, and might and majesty, and eternal dominion, by Christ Jesus, from everlasting to everlasting. Amen.

Clement 2 - The Second epistle of Clement

2 Clem. 1 That we ought to value our salvation; and to skew that we do, by a sincere obedience. BRETHREN, we ought so to think of Jesus Christ as of God: as of the judge of the living, and the dead; nor should we think any less of our salvation. 2 For if we think meanly of him, we shall hope only to receive some small things from him. 3 And if we do so; we shall sin; not considering from whence we have been called, and by whom, and to what place; and how much Jesus Christ vouchsafed to suffer for our sakes. 4 What recompense then shall we render unto him? Or what fruit that may be worthy of what he has given to us? 5 For indeed how great are those advantages which we owe to him in relation to our holiness? He has illuminated us: as a father, he has called us his children; he has saved us who were lost and undone. 6 What praise shall we give to him? Or what reward that may be answerable to those things which we have received? 7 We were defective in our understandings; worshipping stones and wood; gold, and silver, and brass, the works of men's hands; and our whole life was nothing else but death. 8 Wherefore being encompassed with darkness, and having such a mist before our eyes, we have looked up, and through his will have laid aside the cloud wherewith we were surrounded. 9 For he had compassion upon us, and being moved in his bowels towards us, he saved us; having beheld in us much error, and destruction; and seen that we had no hope of salvation, but only through him. 10 For he called us who were not; and was pleased from nothing to give us being.

2 Clem. 2 1 That God had before prophesied by Isaiah, that the Gentiles should be saved. That this ought to engage such especially to live well; without which they will still miscarry. REJOICE, thou barren, that bearest not, break forth and cry thou that travailest not; for she that is desolate hath many more children than she that hath an husband. 2 In that he said, Rejoice thou barren that bearest not, he spake of us: for our church was barren before that children were given unto it. 3 And again; when he said, Cry thou that travailest not; he implied thus much: That after the manner of women in travail, we should not cease to put up our prayers unto God 5 abundantly. 4 And for what follows, because she that is desolate hath more children than she that hath an husband: it was therefore added, because our people which seem to have been forsaken by God, now believing in him, are become more than they who seemed to have God. 5 And another Scripture saith, I came not to call the righteous but sinners (to repentance). The meaning of which is this: that those who were lost must be saved. 6 For that is, indeed, truly great and wonderful, not to confirm those things that are yet standing, but those which are falling. 7 Even so did it seem good to Christ to save what was lost; and when he came into the world, he saved many, and called us who were already lost. 8 Seeing then he has shewed so great mercy towards us; and chiefly for that, we who are alive, do now no longer sacrifice to dead Gods, nor pay any worship to them, but have by him been brought to the knowledge of the Father of truth. 9 Whereby shall we shew that we do indeed know him, but by not denying him by whom we have come to the knowledge of him? 10 For even he himself saith, Whosoever shall confess me before men, him will I confess before my Father. This therefore is our reward if we shall confess him by whom we have been saved. 11 But, wherein must we confess him? Namely, in doing those things which he saith, and not disobeying his commandments: by worshipping him not with our lips only, but with all our heart, and with all our mind. For he saith in Isaiah: This people honoureth me with their lips, but their heart is far from me. 12 Let us then not only call him Lord; for that will not save us. For he saith: Not every one that saith unto me Lord, Lord, shall be saved, but he that doeth righteousness. 13 Wherefore, brethren, let us confess him by our works; by loving one another; in not committing adultery, not speaking evil against each other, not envying one another; but by being temperate, merciful, good. 14 Let us also have a mutual sense of one another's sufferings; and not be covetous of money: but let us, by our good works, confess God, and not by those that are otherwise. 15 Also let us not fear men: but rather God. Wherefore, if we should do such wicked things, the Lord hath said: Though ye should be joined unto me, even in my very bosom, and not keep my commandments, I would cast you off, and say unto you: Depart from me; I know not whence you are, ye workers of iniquity.

2 Clem. 3 1 That whilst we secure the other world, we need not fear what can befall us in this. That if we follow the interests of this present world, we cannot escape the punishment of the other. Which ought to bring us to repentance and holiness, and that presently: because in this world is the only time for repentance. WHEREFORE, brethren, leaving willingly for conscience sake our sojourning in this world, let us do the will of him who has called us, and not fear to depart out of this world. 2 For the Lord saith, Ye shall be as sheep in the midst of wolves. Peter answered and said, What if the wolves shall tear in pieces the sheep? Jesus said unto Peter, Let not the sheep fear the wolves after death: And ye also fear not those that kill you, and after that have no more that they can do unto you; but fear him who after you are dead, has power to cast both soul and body into hell-fire. 3 For consider, brethren, that the sojourning of this flesh in the present world, is but little, and of a short continuance, but the promise of Christ is great and wonderful, even the rest of the kingdom that is to come, and of eternal life. 4 What then must we do that we may attain unto it? We must order our conversation holily and righteously, and look upon all the things of this world as none of ours, and not desire them. For, if we desire to possess them we fall from the way of righteousness. 5 For thus saith the Lord, No servant can serve two masters. If therefore we shall desire to serve God and Mammon it will be without profit to us. For what will it profit, if one gain the whole world, and lose his own soul? 6 Now this world and that to come are two enemies. This speaketh of adultery and corruption, of covetousness and deceit; but renounces these things. 7 We cannot, therefore, be the friends of both; but we must resolve by forsaking the one, to enjoy the other. And we think it is better to hate the present things, as little, short-lived, and corruptible, and to love those which are to come, which are truly good and incorruptible. 8 For, if we do the will of Christ, we shall find rest: but if not, nothing shall deliver us from eternal punishment if we shall disobey his commands. For even thus saith the Scripture in the prophet Ezekiel, If Noah, Job, and Daniel should rise up, they shall not deliver their children in captivity. 9 Wherefore, if such righteous men are not able by their righteousness to deliver their children; how can we hope to enter into the kingdom of God, except we keep our baptism holy and undefiled? Or who shall be our advocate, unless we shall be found to have done what is holy and just? 10 Let us, therefore, my brethren, contend with all earnestness, knowing that our combat is at hand; and that many go long voyages to encounter for a corruptible reward. 11 And yet all are not crowned, but they only that labour much, and strive gloriously. Let us, therefore, so contend, that we may all be crowned. Let us run in the straight road, the race that is incorruptible: and let us in great numbers pass unto

it, and strive that we may receive the crown. But and if we cannot all be crowned, let us come as near to it as we are able. 12 Moreover, we must consider, that he who contends in a corruptible combat, if he be found doing anything that is not fair, is taken away and scourged, and cast out of the lists. What think ye then that he shall suffer, who does anything that is not fitting in the combat of immortality? 13 Thus speaks the prophet concerning those who keep not their seal; Their worm shall not die, and their fire shall not be quenched; and they shall be for a spectacle unto all flesh. 14 Let us therefore repent, whilst we are yet upon the earth: for we are as clay in the hand of the artificer. For as the potter if he make a vessel, and it be turned amiss in his hands, or broken, again forms it anew; but if he have gone so far as to throw it into the furnace of fire, he can no more bring any remedy to it. 15 So we, whilst we are in this world, 1 should repent with our whole heart for whatsoever evil we have done in the flesh; while we have yet the time of repentance, that we may be saved by the Lord. 16 For after we shall have departed out of this world, we shall no longer be able to confess our sins or repent 2 in the other. 17 Wherefore, brethren, let us doing the will of the Father, and keeping our flesh pure, and observing the commandments of the Lord, lay hold on eternal life: for the Lord saith in the gospel, If ye have not kept that which was little, who will give you that which is great? For I say unto you, he that is faithful in that which is least, is faithful also in much. 18 This, therefore, is what he saith; keep your bodies pure, and your seal without spot, that ye may receive eternal life.

2 Clem. 4 1 We shall rise, and be judged in our bodies; therefore we must live well in them, that we ought, for our own interest, to live well; though few seem to mind what really is for their advantage, and not deceive ourselves: seeing God will certainly judge us, and render to all of us according to our works. AND let not any one among you say, that this very flesh is not judged, neither raised up. Consider, in what were you saved; in what did you look up, if not whilst you were in this flesh. 2 We must, therefore, keep our flesh as the temple of God. For in like manner as ye were called in the flesh ye shall also come to judgment in the flesh. Our one Lord Jesus Christ, who has saved us, being first a spirit, was made flesh, and so called us; even so we also shall in this flesh receive the reward. 3 Let us, therefore, love one another, that we may attain unto the kingdom of God. Whilst we have time to be healed, let us deliver up ourselves to God our physician, giving our reward unto him. 4. And what reward shall we give? Repentance out of a pure heart. For he knows all things before hand, and searches out our very hearts. 5 Let us, therefore, give praise unto him: not only with our mouths, but with all our souls; that he may receive us as children. For so the Lord hath said; They are my brethren, who do the will of my father. 6 Wherefore, my brethren, let us do the will of the Father, who hath called us, that we may live. Let us pursue virtue, and forsake wickedness, which leadeth us into sins; and let us flee all ungodliness, that evils overtake us not. 7 For, if we shall do our diligence to live well, peace shall follow us. And yet how hard is it to find a man that does this? For almost all are led by human fears, choosing rather the present enjoyments, than the future promise. 8 For they know not how great a torment the present enjoyments bring with them; nor what delights the future promise 9 And if they themselves only did this, it might the more easily be endured; but now they go on to infect innocent souls with their evil doctrines; not knowing that both themselves, and those that hear them, shall receive a double condemnation. 10 Let us, therefore, serve God with a pure heart, and we shall be righteous: but if we shall not serve him because we do not believe the promise of God, we shall be miserable. 11 For thus saith the prophet; Miserable are the double minded who doubt in their heart, and say, these things we have heard, even in the time of our fathers, but we have seen none of them, though we have expected them from day to day. 12 O ye fools! compare yourselves to a tree; take the vine for an example. First it sheds its leaves, then it buds, then come the sour grapes, then the ripe fruit; even so my people have borne its disorders and afflictions, but shall hereafter receive good things. 13 Wherefore my brethren, let us not doubt in our minds, but let us expect with hope, that we may receive our reward; for he is faithful, who has promised he will render to every one a reward according to his works. 14 If, therefore, we shall do what is just in the sight of God we shall enter into his kingdom, I and shall receive the promises; 2 Which neither eye has seen, nor ear heard, nor have entered into the heart of man. 15 Wherefore let us every hour expect the kingdom of God in love and righteousness; because we know not the day of God's appearing.

2 Clem. 5 A Fragment. Of the Lord's kingdom. 1 For the Lord himself, being asked by a certain person, When his kingdom should come? answered, When two shall be one, and that which is without as that which is within; and the male with the female, neither male nor female. 2 Now two are one, when we speak the truth to each other, and there is (without hypocrisy) one soul in two bodies: 3 And that which is without as that which is within: He means this: he calls the soul that which is within, and the body that which is without. As therefore thy body appears, so let thy soul be seen by its good works. 4 And the male with the female neither male nor female: He means this; he calls our anger the male, our concupiscence the female. 5 When therefore a man is come to such a pass that he is subject neither to the one nor the other of these (both of which, through the prevalence of custom, and an evil education, cloud and darken the reason,) 6 But rather, having dispelled the mist arising from them, and being full of shame, shall by repentance have united both his soul and spirit in the obedience of reason; then, as Paul says, there is in us neither male nor female

Seven Epistles of St. Ignatius of Antioch

The epistle of Ignatius to the Ephesians

Ignatius, who is also called Theopharus, to the Church which is at Ephesus, in Asia, deservedly most happy, being blessed in the greatness and fulness of God the Father, and predestinated before the beginning of time, that it should be always for an enduring and unchangeable glory, being united and elected through the true passion by the will of the Father, and Jesus Christ, our God: Abundant happiness through Jesus Christ, and His undefiled grace.

Ign. Eph. I. - Praise of the Ephesians.

I have become acquainted with your name, much-beloved in God, which ye have acquired by the habit of righteousness, according to the faith and love in Jesus Christ our Saviour. Being the followers of God, and stirring up yourselves by the blood of God, ye have perfectly accomplished the work which was beseeming to you. For, on hearing that I came bound from Syria for the common name and hope, trusting through your prayers to be permitted to fight with beasts at Rome, that so by martyrdom I may indeed become the disciple of Him "who gave Himself for us, an offering and sacrifice to God,"[ye hastened to see me]. I received, therefore, your whole multitude in the name of God, through Onesimus, a man of inexpressible love, and your bishop in the flesh, whom I pray you by Jesus Christ to love, and that you would all seek to be like him. And blessed be He who has granted unto you, being worthy, to obtain such an excellent bishop.

Ign. Eph. II. - Congratulations and Entreaties.

As to my fellow-servant Burrhus, your deacon in regard to God and blessed in all things, I beg that he may continue longer, both for your honour and that of your bishop. And Crocus also, worthy both of God and you, whom I have received as the manifestationof your love, hath in all things refreshedme, as the Father of our Lord Jesus Christ shall also refreshhim; together with Onesimus, and Burrhus, and Euplus, and Fronto, by means of whom, I have, as to love, beheld all of you. May I always have joy of you, if indeed I be worthy of it. It is therefore befitting that you should in every way glorify Jesus Christ, who hath glorified you, that by a unanimous obedience "ye may be perfectly joined together in the same mind, and in the same judgment, and may all speak the same thing concerning the same thing,"and that, being subject to the bishop and the presbytery, ye may in all respects be sanctified.

Ign. Eph. III. - Exhortations to Unity.

I do not issue orders to you, as if I were some great person. For though I am bound for the name [of Christ], I am not yet perfect in Jesus Christ. For now I begin to be a disciple, and I speak to you as fellow- disciples with me. For it was needful for me to have been stirred up by you in faith, exhortation, patience, and long-suffering. But inasmuch as love suffers me not to be silent in regard to you, I have therefore taken upon me first to exhort you that ye would all run together in accordance with the will of God. For even Jesus Christ, our inseparable life, is the[manifested] will of the Father; as also bishops, settled everywhere to the utmost bounds [of the earth], are so by the will of Jesus Christ.

Ign. Eph. IV. - The same continued.

Wherefore it is fitting that ye should run together in accordance with the will of your bishop, which thing also ye do. For your justly renowned presbytery, worthy of God, is fitted as exactly to the bishop as the strings are to the harp. Therefore in your concord and harmonious love, Jesus Christ is sung. And do ye, man by man, become a choir, that being harmonious in love, and taking up the song of God in unison, ye may with one voice sing to the Father through Jesus Christ, so that He may both hear you, and perceive by your works that ye are indeed the members of His son. It is profitable, therefore, that you should live in an unblameable unity, that thus ye may always enjoy communion with God.

Ign. Eph. V. - The praise of unity.

For if I in this brief space of time, have enjoyed such fellowship with your bishop--I mean not of a mere human, but of a spiritual nature--how much more do I reckon you happy who are so joined to him as the Church is to Jesus Christ, and as Jesus Christ is to the Father, that so all things may agree in unity! Let no man deceive himself: if any one be not within the altar, he is deprived of the bread of God. For if the prayer of one or two possesses such power, how much more that of the bishop and the whole Church! He, therefore, that does not assemble with the Church, has evenby this manifested his pride, and condemned himself. For it is written, "God resisteth the proud."Let us be careful, then, not to set ourselves in opposition to the bishop, in order that we may be subject to God.

Ign. Eph. VI. - Have respect to the bishop as to Christ himself.

Now the more any one sees the bishop keeping silence, the more ought he to revere him. For we ought to receive every one whom the Master of the house sends to be over His household, as we would do Him that sent him. It is manifest, therefore, that we should look upon the bishop even as we would upon the Lord Himself. And indeed Onesimus himself greatly commends your good order in God, that ye all live according to the truth, and that no sect has any dwelling-place among you. Nor, indeed, do ye hearken to any one rather than to Jesus Christ speaking in truth.

Ign. Eph. VII.-- Beware of false teachers.

For some are in the habit of carrying about the name [of Jesus Christ] in wicked guile, while yet they practise things unworthy of God, whom ye must flee as ye would wild beasts. For they are ravening dogs, who bite secretly, against whom ye must be on your guard, inasmuch as they are men who can scarcely be cured. There is one Physician who is possessed both of flesh and spirit; both made and not made; God existing in flesh; true life in death; both of Mary and of God; first possible and then impossible, even Jesus Christ our Lord.

Ign. Eph. VIII. - Renewed praise of the Ephesians.

Let not then any one deceive you, as indeed ye are not deceived, inasmuch as ye are wholly devoted to God. For since there is no strife raging among you which might distress you, ye are certainly living in accordance with God's will. I am far inferior to you, and require to be sanctified by your Church of Ephesus, so renowned throughout the world. They that are carnal cannot do those things which are spiritual, nor they that are spiritual the things which are carnal; even as faith cannot do the works of unbelief, nor the unbelief the works of faith. But even those things which ye do according to the flesh are spiritual; for ye do all things in Jesus Christ.

Ign. Eph. IX. - Ye have given no heed to false teachers.

Nevertheless, I have heard of some who have passed on from this to you, having false doctrine, whom ye did not suffer to sow among you, but stopped your ears, that ye might not receive those things which were sown by them, as being stonesof the temple of the Father, prepared for the building of God the Father, and drawn up on high by the instrument of Jesus Christ, which is the cross,making use of the Holy Spirit as a rope, while your faith was the means by which you ascended, and your love the way which led up to God. Ye, therefore, as well as all your fellow-travellers, are God- bearers, temple-bearers, Christ-bearers, bearers of holiness, adorned in all respects with the commandments of Jesus Christ, in whom also I exult that I have been thought worthy, by means of this Epistle, to converse and rejoice with you, because with respect to your Christian life ye love nothing but God only.

Ign. Eph. X. - Exhortations to prayer, humility, etc.

And pray ye without ceasing in behalf of other men. For there is in them hope of repentance that they may attain to God. See, then, that they be instructed by your works, if in no other way. Be ye meek in response to their wrath, humble in opposition to their boasting: to their blasphemies return your prayers; in contrast to their error, be ye stedfast in the faith; and for their cruelty, manifest your gentleness. While we take care not to imitate their conduct, let us be found their brethren in all true kindness; and let us seek to be followers of the Lord (who ever more unjustly treated, more destitute, more condemned?), that so no plant of the devil may be found in you, but ye may remain in all holiness and sobriety in Jesus Christ, both with respect to the flesh and spirit.

Ign. Eph. XI.- An exhortation to fear God, etc.

The last times are come upon us. Let us therefore be of a reverent spirit, and fear the long-suffering of God, that it tend not to our condemnation. For let us either stand in awe of the wrath to come, or show regard for the grace which is at present displayed--one of two things. Only [in one way or another] let us be found in Christ Jesus unto the true life. Apart from Him, let nothing attract you, for whom I bear about these bonds, these spiritual jewels, by which may I arise through your prayers, of which I entreat I may always be a partaker, that I may be found in the lot of the Christians of Ephesus, who have always been of the same mind with the apostles through the power of Jesus Christ.

Ign. Eph. XII. - Praise of the Ephesians.

I know both who I am, and to whom I write. I am a condemned man, ye have been the objects of mercy; I am subject to danger, ye are established in safety. Ye are the persons through whom those pass that are cut off for the sake of God. Ye are initiated into the mysteries of the Gospel with Paul, the holy, the martyred, the deservedly most happy, at whose feet may I be found, when I shall attain to God; who in all his Epistles makes mention of you in Christ Jesus.

Ign. Eph. XIII.-- Exhortation To Meet Together Frequently For The Worship Of God.

Take heed, then, often to come together to give thanks to God, and show for th His praise. For when ye assemble frequently in the same place, the powers of Satan are destroyed, and the destruction at which he aims is prevented by the unity of your faith. Nothing is more precious than peace, by which all war, both in heaven and earth, is brought to an end.

Ign. Eph. XIV. - Exhortations to faith and love.

None of these things is hid from you, if ye perfectly possess that faith and love towards Christ Jesus which are the beginning and the end of life. For the beginning is faith, and the end is love. Now these two. being inseparably connected together, are of God, while all other things which are requisite for a holy life follow after them. No man [truly] making a profession of faith sinneth; nor does he that possesses love hate any one. The tree is made manifest by its fruit; so those that profess themselves to be Christians shall be recognised by their conduct. For there is not now a demand for mere profession, but that a man be found continuing in the power of faith to the end.

Ign. Eph. XV. - Exhortation to confess christ by silence as well as speech.

It is better for a man to be silent and be [a Christian], than to talk and not to be one. It is good to teach, if he who speaks also acts. There is then one Teacher, who spake and it was done; while even those things which He did in silence are worthy of the Father. He who possesses the word of Jesus, is truly able to hear even His very silence, that he may be perfect, and may both act as he speaks, and be recognised by his silence. There is nothing which is hid from God, but our very secrets are near to Him. Let us therefore do all things as those who have Him dwelling in us, that we may be His temples, and He may be in us as our God, which indeed He is, and will manifest Himself before our faces. Wherefore we justly love Him.

Ign. Eph. XVI.--The fate of false teachers.

Do not err, my brethren. Those that corrupt families shall not inherit the kingdom of God. If, then, those who do this as respects the flesh have suffered death, how much more shall this be the case with any one who corrupts by wicked doctrine the faith of God, for which Jesus Christ was crucified! Such an one becoming defiled [in this way], shall go away into everlasting fire, and so shall every one that hearkens unto him.

Ign. Eph. XVII.--beware of false doctrines.

For this end did the Lord suffer the ointment to be poured upon His head, that He might breathe immortality into His Church. Be not ye anointed with the bad odour of the doctrine of the prince of this world; let him not lead you away captive from the life which is set before you. And why are we not all prudent, since we have received the knowledge of God, which is Jesus Christ? Why do we foolishly perish, not recognising the gift which the Lord has of a truth sent to us?

Ign. Eph. XVIII. - The glory of the cross.

Let my spirit be counted as nothing for the sake of the cross, which is a stumbling-block" to those that do not believe, but to us salvation and life eternal. "Where is the wise man? where the disputer?"Where is the boasting of those who are styled prudent? For our God, Jesus

Christ, was, according to the appointment of God, conceived in the womb by Mary, of the seed of David, but by the Holy Ghost. He was born and baptized, that by His passion He might purify the water.

Ign. Eph. XIX. - Three celebrated mysteries.

Now the virginity of Mary was hidden from the prince of this world, as was also her offspring, and the death of the Lord; three mysteries of renown, which were wrought in silence by God. How, then, was He manifested to the world? A star shone forth in heaven above all the other stars, the light of Which was inexpressible, while its novelty struck men with astonishment. And all the rest of the stars, with the sun and moon, formed a chorus to this star, and its light was exceedingly great above them all. And there was agitation felt as to whence this new spectacle came, so unlike to everything else [in the heavens]. Hence every kind of magic was destroyed, and every bond of wickedness disappeared; ignorance was removed, and the old kingdom abolished, God Himself being manifested in human form for the renewal of eternal life. And now that took a beginning which had been prepared by God. Henceforth all things were in a state of tumult, because He meditated the abolition of death.

Ign. Eph. XX. - Promise of another letter.

If Jesus Christ shall graciously permit me through your prayers, and if it be His will, I shall, in a second little work which I will write to you, make further manifest to you [the nature of] the dispensation of which I have begun [to treat], with respect to the new man, Jesus Christ, in His faith and in His love, in His suffering and in His resurrection. Especially [will I do this 14] if the Lord make known to me that ye come togetherman by man in common through grace, individually, in one faith, and in Jesus Christ, who was of the seed of David according to the flesh, being both the Son of man and the Son of God, so that ye obey the bishop and the presbytery with an undivided mind, breaking one and the same bread, which is the medicine of immortality, and the antidote to prevent us from dying, but [which causes] that we should live for ever in Jesus Christ.

Ign. Eph. XXI. - Exhortations to stedfastness and unity.
Stand fast, brethren, in the faith of Jesus Christ, and in His love, in His passion, and in His resurrection. Do ye all come together in common, and individually, through grace, in one faith of God the Father, and of Jesus Christ His only-begotten Son, and "the first-born of every creature," but of the seed of David according to the flesh, being under the guidance of the Comforter, in obedience to the bishop and the presbytery with an undivided mind, breaking one and the same bread, which is the medicine of immortality, and the antidote which prevents us from dying, but a cleansing remedy driving away evil, [which causes] that we should live in God through Jesus Christ.

Ign. Eph. XXII. - Conclusion.
My soul be for yours and theirs whom, for the honour of God, ye have sent to Smyrna; whence also I write to you, giving thanks unto the Lord, and loving Polycarp even as I do you. Remember me, as Jesus Christ also remembered you. Pray ye for the Church which is in Syria, whence I am led bound to Rome, being the last of the faithful who are there, even as I have been thought worthy to be chosento show forth the honour of God. Farewell in God the Father, and in Jesus Christ, our common hope. My soul be for yours and theirswhom, for the honour of God, ye have sent to Smyrna; whence also I write to you, giving thanks to the Lord, and loving Polycarp even as I do you. Remember me, as Jesus Christ also remembers you, who is blessed for evermore. Pray ye for the Church of Antioch which is in Syria, whence I am led bound to Rome, being the last of the faithful that are there, whoyet have been thought worthy to carry these chains to the honour of God. Fare ye well in God the Father, and the Lord Jesus Christ, our common hope, and in the Holy Ghost. Fare ye well. Amen. Grace [be with you].

The Epistle of Ignatius to the Magnesians.

Ignatius, who is also called Theophorus, to the [Church] blessed in the grace of God the Father, in Jesus Christ our Saviour, in whom I salute the Church which is at Magnesia, near the Moeander, and wish it abundance of happiness in God the father, and in Jesus Christ. Ignatius, who is also called Theophorus, to the [Church] blessed in the grace of God the Father, in Jesus Christ our Saviour, in whom I salute the Church which is at Magnesia, near the Moeander, and wish it abundance of happiness in God the Father, and in Jesus Christ, our Lord, in whom may you have abundance of happiness.

Ign. Mag. I. - Reason of writing the epistle.

Having been informed of your godly love, so well-ordered, I rejoiced greatly, and determined to commune with you in the faith of Jesus Christ. For as one who has been thought worthy of the most honourable of all names, in those bonds which I bear about, I commend the Churches, in which I pray for a union both of the flesh and spirit of Jesus Christ, the constant source of our life, and of faith and love, to which nothing is to be preferred, but especially of Jesus and the Father, in whom, if we endure all the assaults of the prince of this world, and escape them, we shall enjoy God.

Ign. Mag. II. - I rejoice in your messengers.

Since, then, I have had the privilege of seeing you, through Damas your most worthy bishop, and through your worthy presbyters Bassus and Apollonius, and through my fellow-servant the deacon Sotio, whose friendship may I ever enjoy, inasmuch as he is subject to the bishop as to the grace of God, and to the presbytery as to the law of Jesus Christ, [I now write to you].

Ign. Mag. III. - Honour your youthful bishop.

Now it becomes you also not to treat your bishop too familiarly on account of his youth, but to yield him all reverence, having respect to the power of God the Father, as I have known even holy presbyters do, not judging rashly, from the manifest youthful appearance [of their bishop], but as being themselves prudent in God, submitting to him, or rather not to him, but to the Father of Jesus Christ, the bishop of us all. It is therefore fitting that you should, after no hypocritical fashion, obey [your bishop], in honour of Him who has wired us [so to do], since he that does not so deceives not [by such conduct] the bishop that is visible, but seeks to mock Him that is invisible. And all such conduct has reference not to man, but to God, who knows all secrets.

Ign. Mag. IV. - Some wickedly act independently of the bishop.

It is fitting, then, not only to be called Christians, but to be so in reality: as some indeed give one the title of bishop, but do all things without him. Now such persons seem to me to be not possessed of a good conscience, seeing they are not stedfastly gathered together according to the commandment.

Ign. Mag. V. - Death is the fate of all such.

Seeing, then, all things have an end, these two things are simultaneously set before us--death and life; and every one shall go unto his own place. For as there are two kinds of coins, the one of God, the other of the world, and each of these has its special character stamped upon it, [so is it also here.] The unbelieving are of this world; but the believing have, in love, the character of God the Father by Jesus Christ, by whom, if we are not in readiness to die into His passion, His life is not in us.

Ign. Mag. VI. - Preserve harmony.

Since therefore I have, in the persons before mentioned, beheld the whole multitude of you in faith and love, I exhort you to study to do all things with a divine harmony, while your bishop presides in the place of God, and your presbyters in the place of the assembly of the apostles, along with your deacons, who are most dear to me, and are entrusted with the ministry of Jesus Christ, who was with the Father before the beginning of time, and in the end was revealed. Do ye all then, imitating the same divine conduct, pay respect to one another, and let no one look upon his neighbour after the flesh, but do ye continually love each other in Jesus Christ. Let nothing exist among you that may divide you; but be ye united with your bishop, and those that preside over you, as a type and evidence of your immortality.

Ign. Mag. VII. - Do nothing without the bishop and presbyters.

As therefore the Lord did nothing without the Father, being united to Him, neither by Himself nor by the apostles, so neither do ye anything without the bishop and presbyters. Neither endeavour that anything appear reasonable and proper to yourselves apart; but being come together into the same place, let there be one prayer, one supplication, one mind, one hope, in love and in joy undefiled. There is one Jesus Christ, than whom nothing is more excellent. Do ye therefore all run together as into one temple of God, as to one altar, as to one Jesus Christ, who came forth from one Father, and is with and has gone to one.

Ign. Mag. VIII - Caution against false doctrines.

Be not deceived with strange doctrines, nor with old fables, which are unprofitable. For if we still live according to the Jewish law, we acknowledge that we have not received grace. For the divinest prophets lived according to Christ Jesus. On this account also they were persecuted, being inspired by His grace to fully convince the unbelieving that there is one God, who has manifested Himself by Jesus Christ His Son, who is His eternal Word, not proceeding forth from silence, and who in all things pleased Him that sent Him.

Ign. Mag. IX. - Let us live with christ.

If, therefore, those who were brought up in the ancient order of thingshave come to the possession of a newhope, no longer observing the Sabbath, but living in the observanceof the Lord's Day, on which also our life has sprung up again by Him and by His death--whom some deny, by which mystery we have obtained faith,and therefore endure, that we may be found the disciples of Jesus Christ, our only Master--how shall we be able to live apart from Him, whose disciples the prophets themselves in the Spirit did wait for Him as their Teacher? And therefore He whom they rightly waited for, being come, raised them from the dead.

Ign. Mag. X. - Beware of judaizing.

Let us not, therefore, be insensible to His kindness. For were He to reward us according to our works, we should cease to be. Therefore, having become His disciples, let us learn to live according to the principles of Christianity.For whosoever is called by any other name besides this, is not of God. Lay aside, therefore, the evil, the old, the sour leaven, and be ye changed into the new leaven, which is Jesus Christ. Be ye salted in Him, lest any one among you should be corrupted, since by your savour ye shall be convicted. It is absurd to professChrist Jesus, and to Judaize. For Christianity did not embraceJudaism, but Judaism Christianity, that so every tongue which believeth might be gathered together to God.

Ign. Mag. XI. - Iwrite these things to warn you.

These things [I address to you], my beloved, not that I know any of you to be in such a state;but, as less than any of you, I desire to guard you beforehand, that ye fall not upon the hooks of vain doctrine, but thatye attain to full assurance in regard to the birth, and passion, and resurrection which took place in the time of the government of Pontius Pilate, being truly and certainly accomplished by Jesus Christ, who is our hope,from which may no one of you ever be turned aside.

Ign. Mag. XII. - Ye are superior to me.

May I enjoy you in all respects, if indeed I be worthy! For though I am bound, I am not worthy to be compared to any of you that are at liberty. I know that ye are not puffed up, for ye have Jesus Christ in yourselves. And all the more when I commend you, I know that ye cherish modestyof spirit; as it is written, "The righteous man is his own accuser."

Ign. Mag. XIII. - Be established in faith and unity.

Study, therefore, to be established in the doctrines of the Lord and the apostles, that so all things, whatsoever ye do, may prosper both in the flesh and spirit; in faith and love; in the Son, and in the Father, and in the Spirit; in the beginning and in the end; with your most admirable bishop, and the well-compacted spiritual crown of your presbytery, and the deacons who are according to God. Be ye subject to the bishop, and to one another, as Jesus Christ to the Father, according to the flesh, and the apostles to Christ, and to the Father, and to the Spirit; that so there may be a union beth fleshly and spiritual.

Ign. Mag. XIV. - Your prayers requested.

Knowing as I do that ye are full of God, I have but briefly exhorted you. Be mindful of me in your prayers, that I may attain to God; and of the Church which is in Syria, whence I am not worthy to derive my name: for I stand in need of your united prayer in God, and your love, that the Church which is in Syria may be "deemed worthy of being refreshedby your Church.

Ign. Mag. XV. - Salutations.

The Ephesians from Smyrna (whence I also write to you), who are here for the glory of God, as ye also are, who have in all things refreshed me, salute you, along with Polycarp, the bishop of the Smyrnaeans. The rest of the Churches, in honour of Jesus Christ, also salute you. Fare ye well in the harmony of God, ye who have obtained the inseparable Spirit, who is Jesus Christ.

The Epistle of Ignatius to the Trallians

Ignatius, who is also called Theophorus, to the holy Church which is at Tralles, in Asia, beloved of God, the Father of Jesus Christ, elect, and worthy of God, possessing peace through the flesh, and blood, and passion of Jesus Christ, who is our hope, through our rising again to Him, which also I salute in its fulness, and in the apostalical character,and wish abundance of happiness.

Ign. Tral. I.- Acknowledgment of their excellence.

I know that ye possess an unblameable and sincere mind in patience, and that not only in present practice, but according to inherent nature, as Polybius your bishop has shown me, who has come to Smyrna by the will of God and Jesus Christ, and so sympathized in the joy which I, who am bound in Christ Jesus, possess, that I beheld your whole multitude in him. Having therefore received through him the testimony of your good-will, according to God, I gloried to find you, as I knew ye were, the followers of God.

Ign. Tral. II. - Be subject to the bishop, etc.

For, since ye are subject to the bishop as to Jesus Christ, ye appear to me to live not after the manner of men, but according to Jesus Christ, who died for us, in order, by believing in His death, ye may escape from death. It is therefore necessary that, as ye indeed do, so without the bishop ye should do nothing, but should also our hope, in whom, if we live, we shall be found in Him. It behoves you also, in every way, to please the deacons, who are [ministers] of the mysteries of Christ Jesus; for they are not ministers of meat and drink, but servants of the Church of God. They are bound, therefore, to avoid all grounds of accusation [against them], as they would a burning fire. Let them, then, prove themselves to be such.

Ign. Tral. III. - Honour the deacons, etc.

In like manner, let all reverence the deacons as an appointment of Jesus Christ, and the bishop as Jesus Christ, who is the Son of the Father, and the presbyters as the sanhedrin of God, and assembly of the apostles. Apart from these, there is no Church. Concerning all this, I am persuaded that ye are of the same opinion. For I have received the manifestations of your love, and still have it with me, in your bishop, whose very appearance is highly instructive, and his meekness of itself a power; whom I imagine even the ungodly must reverence, seeing they are also pleased that I do not spare myself. But shall I, when permitted to write on this point, reach such a height of self-esteem, that though being a condemned man, I should issue commands to you as if I were an apostle?

Ign. Tral. IV. - I have need of humility.

I have great knowledge in God, but I restrain myself, lest, I should perish through boasting. For now it is needful for me to be the more fearful; and not give heed to those that puff me up. For they that speak to me [in the way of commendation] scourge me. For I do indeed desire to suffer, but I know not if I be worthy to do so. For this longing, though it is not manifest to many, all the more vehemently assails me. I therefore have need of meekness, by which the prince of this world is brought to nought.

Ign. Tral. V. - I will not teach you profound doctrines.

Am I not able to write to you of heavenly things? But I fear to do so, lest I should inflict injury on you who are but babes [in Christ]. Pardon me in this respect, lest, as not being able to receive [such doctrines], ye should be strangled by them. For even I, though I am bound [for Christ], yet am not on that account able to understand heavenly things, and the places of the angels, and their gatherings under their respective princes, things visible and invisible. Without reference to such abstruse subjects, I am still but a learner [in other respects]; for many things are wanting to us, that we come not short of God.

Ign. Tral. VI. - Abstain from the poison of heretics.

I therefore, yet not I, but the love of Jesus Christ, entreat you that ye use Christian nourishment only, and abstain from herbage of a different kind; I mean heresy. For those [that are given to this] mix up Jesus Christ with their own poison, speaking things which are unworthy of credit, like those who administer a deadly drug in sweet wine, which he who is ignorant of does greedily take, with a fatal pleasure leading to his own death.

Ign. Tral. VII. - The same continued.

Be on your guard, therefore, against such persons. And this will be the case with you if you are not puffed up, and continue in intimate union with Jesus Christ our God, and the bishop, and the enactments of the apostles. He that is within the altar is pure, but he that is without is not pure; that is, he who does anything apart from the bishop, and presbytery, and deacons, such a man is not pure in his conscience.

Ign. Tral. VIII. - Be on your guard against the snares of the devil.

Not that I Know there is anything of this kind among you; but I put you on your guard, inasmuch as I love you greatly, and foresee the snares of the devil. Wherefore, clothing yourselves with meekness, be ye renewed in faith, that is the flesh of the Lord, and in love, that is the blood of Jesus Christ. Let no one of you cherish any grudge against his neighbour. Give no occasion to the Gentiles, lest by means of a few foolish men the whole multitude [of those that believe] in God be evil spoken of. For, "Woe to him by whose vanity my name is blasphemed among any."

Ign. Tral. IX, - Reference to the history of Christ.

Stop your ears, therefore, when any one speaks to you at variance with Jesus Christ, who was descended from David, and was also of Mary; who was truly born, and did eat and drink. He was truly persecuted under Pontius Pilate; He was truly crucified, and [truly] died, in the sight of beings in heaven, and on earth, and under the earth. He was also truly raised from the dead, His Father quickening Him, even as after the same manner His Father will so raise up us who believe in Him by Christ Jesus, apart from whom we do not possess the true life.

Ign. Tral. X. - The reality of Christ's passion.

But if, as some that are without God, that is, the unbelieving, say, that He only seemed to suffer (they themselves only seeming to exist), then why am I in bonds? Why do I long to be exposed to s the wild beasts? Do I therefore die in vain? Am I not then guilty of falsehood against [the cross of] the Lord?

Ign. Tral. XI. - Avoid the deadly errors of the docetae.

Flee, therefore, those evil offshoots [of Satan], which produce death-bearing fruit, whereof if any one tastes, he instantly dies. For these men are not the planting of the Father. For if they were, they would appear as branches of the cross, and their fruit would be incorruptible. By it He calls you through His passion, as being His members. The head, therefore, cannot be born by itself, without its members; God, who is [the Saviour] Himself, having promised their union.

Ign. Tral. XII. - Continue in unity and love.

I salute you from Smyrna, together with the Churches of God which are with me, who have refreshed me in all things, both in the flesh and in the spirit. My bonds, which I carry about with me for the sake of Jesus Christ (praying that I may attain to God), exhort you. Continue in harmony among yourselves, and in prayer with one another; for it becomes every one of you, and especially the presbyters, to refresh the bishop, to the hon-our of the Father, of Jesus Christ, and of the apostles. I entreat you in love to hear me, that I may not, by having written, be a testimony against you. And do ye also pray for me, who have need of your love, along with the mercy of God, that I may be worthy of the lot for which I am destined, and that I may not be found reprobate.

Ign. Tral. XIII. - Conclusion.

The love of the Smymaeans and Ephesians salutes you. Remember in your prayers the Church which is in Syria, from which also I am not worthy to receive my appellation, being the last of them. Fare ye well in Jesus Christ, while ye continue subject to the bishop, as to the command [of God], and in like manner to the presbytery. And do ye, every man, love one another with an undivided heart. Let my spirit be sanctified by yours, not only now, but also when I shall attain to God. For I am as yet exposed to danger. But the Father is faithful in Jesus Christ to fulfil both mine and your petitions: in whom may ye be found unblameable.

The Epistle of Ignatius to the Romans

Ignatius, who is also called Theophorus, to the Church which has obtained mercy, through the majesty of the Mast High Father, and Jesus Christ, His only-begotten Son; the Church which is beloved and enlightened by the will of Him that willeth all things which are according to the love of Jesus Christ our God, which also presides in the place of the report of the Romans, worthy of God, worthy of honour, worthy of the highest happiness, worthy of praise, worthy of obtaining her every desire, worthy of being deemed holy, and which presides over love, is named from Christ, and from the Father, which I also salute in the name of Jesus Christ, the San of the Father: to those who are united, both according ta the flesh and spirit, to every one of His commandments; who are filled inseparably with the grace of God, and are purified from every strange taint, [I wish] abundance of happiness unblameably, in Jesus Christ our God.

Ign. Rom. I. - As a prisoner, i hope to see you.

THROUGH prayer to God I have obtained the privilege of seeing your most worthy faces, and have even been granted more than I requested; for I hope as a prisoner in Christ Jesus to salute you, if indeed it be the will of God that I be thought worthy of attaining unto the end. For the beginning has been well or dered, if I may obtain grace to cling to my lot without hindrance unto the end. For I am afraid of your love, lest it should do me an injury. For it is easy for you to accomplish what you please; but it is difficult for me to attain to God, if ye spare me.

Ign. Rom. II. - Do not save me from martyrdom.

For it is not my desire to act towards you as a man-pleaser, but as pleasing God, even as also ye please Him. For neither shall I ever have such [another] opportunity of attaining to God; nor will ye, if ye shall now be silent, ever be entitled to the honour of a better work. For if ye are silent concerning me, I shall become God's; but if you show your love to my flesh, I shall again have to run my race. Pray, then, do not seek to confer any greater favour upon me than that I be sacrificed to God while the altar is still prepared; that, being gathered together in love, ye may sing praise to the Father, through Christ Jesus, that God has deemed me, the bishop of Syria, worthy to be sent for from the east unto the west. It is good to set from the world unto God, that I may rise again to Him.

Ign. Rom. III. - Pray rather that i may attain' to martyrdom.

Ye have never envied any one; ye have taught others. Now I desire that those things may be confirmed [by your conduct], which in your instructions ye enjoin [on others]. Only request in my behalf both inward and outward strength, that I may not only speak, but [truly] will; and that I may not merely be called a Christian, but really be found to be one. For if I be truly found [a Christian], I may also be called one, and be then deemed faithful, when I shall no longer appear to the world. Nothing visible is eternal. "For the things which are seen are temporal, but the things which are not seen are eternal." For our God, Jesus Christ, Bow that He is with the Father, is all the more revealed [in His glory]. Christianity is not a thing of silence only, but also of [manifest] greatness.

Ign. Rom. IV.--Allow me to fall a prey to the wild beasts.

I write to the Churches, and impress on them all, that I shall willingly die for God, unless ye hinder me. I beseech of you not to show an unseasonable good-will towards me. Suffer me to become food for the wild beasts, through whose instrumentality it will be granted me to attain to God. I am the wheat of God, and let me be ground by the teeth of the wild beasts, that I may be found the pure bread of Christ. Rather entice the wild beasts, that they may become my tomb, and may leave nothing of my body; so that when I have fallen asleep [in death], I may be no trouble to any one. Then shall I truly be a disciple of Christ, when the world shall not see so much as my body. Entreat Christ for me, that by these instruments I may be found a sacrifice [to God]. I do not, as Peter and Paul, issue commandments unto you. They were apostles; I am but a condemned man: they were free, while I am, even until now, a servant. But when I suffer, I shall be the freedman of Jesus, and shall rise again emancipated in Him. And now, being a prisoner, I learn not to desire anything worldly or vain.

Ign. Rom. V. - I desire to die.

From Syria even unto Rome I fight with beasts, both by land and sea, both by night and day, being bound to ten leopards, I mean a band of soldiers, who, even when they receive benefits, show themselves all the worse. But I am the more instructed by their injuries [to act as a disciple of Christ]; "yet am I not thereby justified." May I enjoy the wild beasts that are prepared for me; and I pray they may be found eager to rush upon me, which also I will entice to devour me speedily, and not deal with me as with some, whom, out of fear, they have not touched. But if they be unwilling to assail me, I will compel them to do so. Pardon me [in this]: I know what is for my benefit. Now I begin to be a disciple. And let no one, of things visible or invisible, envy me that I should attain to Jesus Christ. Let fire and the cross; let the crowds of wild beasts; let tearings, breakings, and dislocations of bones; let cutting off of members; let shatterings of the whole body; and let all the dreadful torments of the devil come upon me: only let me attain to Jesus Christ.

Ign. Rom. VI. - By death i shall attain true life.

All the pleasures of the world, and all the kingdoms of this earth, shall profit me nothing. It is better for me to die in behalf of Jesus Christ, than to reign over all the ends of the earth. "For what shall a man be profited, if he gain the whole world, but lose his own soul?" Him I seek, who died for us: Him I desire, who rose again for our sake. This is the gain which is laid up for me. Pardon me, brethren: do not hinder me from living, do not wish to keep me in a state of death; and while I desire to belong to God, do not ye give me over to the world. Suffer me to obtain pure light: when I have gone thither, I shall indeed be a man of God. Permit me to be an imitator of the passion of my God. If any one has Him within himself, let him consider what I desire, and let him have sympathy with me, as knowing how I am straitened.

Ign. Rom. VII. - Reason of desiring to die.

The prince of this world would fain carry me away, and corrupt my disposition towards God. Let none of you, therefore, who are [in Rome] help him; rather be ye on my side, that is, on the side of God. Do not speak of Jesus Christ, and yet set your desires on the world. Let not envy find a dwelling-place among you; nor even should I, when present with you, exhort you to it, be ye persuaded to listen to me, but rather give credit to those things which I now write to you. For though I am alive while I write to you, yet I am eager to die. My love has been crucified, and there is no fire in me desiring to be fed; but there is within me a water that liveth and speaketh, saying to me inwardly, Come to the Father. I have no delight in corruptible food, nor in the pleasures of this life. I desire the bread of God, the heavenly bread, the bread of life, which is the flesh of Jesus Christ, the Son of God, who became afterwards of the seed of David and Abraham; and I desire the drink of God, namely His blood, which is incorruptible love and eternal life.

Ign. Rom. VIII. - Be ye favourable to me.

I no longer wish to live after the manner of men, and my desire shall be fulfilled if ye consent. Be ye willing, then, that ye also may have your desires fulfilled. I entreat you in this brief letter; do ye give credit to me. Jesus Christ will reveal these things to you, [so that ye shall know] that I speak truly. He is the mouth altogether free from falsehood, by which the Father has truly spoken. Pray ye for me, that I may attain [the object of my desire]. I have not written to you according to the flesh, but according to the will of God. If I shall suffer, ye have wished [well] to me; but if I am rejected, ye have hated me.

Ign. Rom. IX. - Pray for the church in syria.

Remember in your prayers the Church in Syria, which now has God for its shepherd, instead of me. Jesus Christ alone will oversee it, and your love [will also regard it]. But as for me, I am ashamed to be counted one of them; for indeed I am not worthy, as being the very last of them, and one born out of due time. But I have obtained mercy to be somebody, if I shall attain to God. My spirit salutes you, and the love of the Churches that have received me in the name of

Jesus Christ, and not as a mere passer-by. For even those Churches which were notnear to me in the way, I mean according to the flesh, have gone before me,city by city, [to meet me.]

Ign. Rom. X. - Conclusion.

Now I write these things to you from Smyrna by the Ephesians, who are deservedly most happy. There is also with me, along with many others, Crocus, one dearly beloved by me. As to those who have gone before me from Syria to Rome for the glory of God, I believe that you are acquainted with them; to whom, [then,] do ye make known that I am at hand. For they are all worthy, both of God and of you; and it is becoming that you should refresh them in all things. I have written these things unto you, on the day before the ninth of the Kalends of September (thatis, on the twenty-third day of August). Fare ye well to the end, in the patience of Jesus Christ. Amen.

The Epistle of Ignatius to the Philadelphians

Ignatius, who is also called Theophorus, to the Church of God the Father, and our Lord Jesus Christ, which is at Philadelphia, in Asia, which has obtained mercy, and is established in the harmony of God, and rejoiceth unceasinglyin the passion of our Lord, and is filled with all mercy through his resurrection; which I salute in the blood of Jesus Christ, who is our eternal and enduring joy, especially if [men] are in unity with the bishop, the presbyters, and the deacons, who have been appointed according to the mind of Jesus Christ, whom He has established in security, after His own will, and by His Holy Spirit.

Ign. Phil. I. - Praise of the bishop.

WHICH bishop, I know, obtained the ministry which pertains to the common [weal], not of himself, neither by men, nor through vainglory, but by the love of God the Father, and the Lord Jesus Christ; at whose meekness I am struck with admiration, and who by his silence is able to accomplish more than those who vainly talk. For he is in harmony with the commandments [of God], even as the harp is with its strings. Wherefore my soul declares his mind towards God a happy one, knowing it to be virtuous and perfect, and that his stability as well as freedom from all anger is after the example of the infinitemeekness of the living God.

Ign. Phil. II. - Maintain union with the bishop.

Wherefore, as children of light and truth, flee from division and wicked doctrines; but where the shepherd is, there do ye as sheep follow. For there are many wolves that appear worthy of credit, who, by means of a pernicious pleasure, carry captives those that are running towards God; but in your unity they shall have no place.

Ign. Phil. III. - Avoid schismatics.

Keep yourselves from those evil plants which Jesus Christ does not tend, because they are not the planting of the Father. Not that I have found any division among you, but exceeding purity. For as many as are of God and of Jesus Christ are also with the bishop. And as many as shall, in the exercise of repentance, return into the unity of the Church, these, too, shall belong to God, that they may live according to Jesus Christ. Do not err, my brethren. If any man follows him that makes a schism in the Church, he shall not inherit the kingdom of God. If any one walks according to a strangeopinion, he agrees not with the passion [of Christ.].

Ign. Phil. IV. - Have but one eucharist, etc.

Take ye heed, then, to have but one Eucharist. For there is one flesh of our Lord Jesus Christ, and one cup to [show forth] the unity of His blood; one altar; as there is one bishop, along with the presbytery and deacons, my fellow-servants: that so, whatsoever ye do, ye may do it according to [the will of] God.

Ign. Phil. V. - Pray for me.

My brethren, I am greatly enlarged in loving you; and rejoicing exceedingly [over you], I seek to secure your safety. Yet it is not I, but Jesus Christ, for whose sake being bound I fear the more, inasmuch as I am not yet perfect. But your prayer to God shall make me perfect, that I may attain to that portion which through mercy has been allotted me, while I flee to the Gospel as to the flesh of Jesus, and to the apostles as to the presbytery of the Church. And let us also love the prophets, because they too have proclaimed the Gospel, and placed their hope in Him,and waited for Him; in whom also believing, they were saved, through union to Jesus Christ, being holy men, worthy of love and admiration, having had witness borne to them by Jesus Christ, and being reckoned along with in the Gospel of the common hope.

Ign. Phil. VI. - Do not accept judaism.

But if any one preach the Jewish lawunto you, listen not to him. For it is better to hearken to Christian doctrine from a man who has been circumcised, than to Judaism from one uncircumcised. But if either of such persons do not speak concerning Jesus Christ, they are in my judgment but as monuments and sepulchres of the dead, upon which are written only the names of men. Flee therefore the wicked devices and snares of the prince of this world, lest at any time being conqueredby his artifices, ye grow weak in your love. But be ye all joined togetherwith an undivided heart. And I thank my God that I have a good conscience in respect to you, and that no one has it in his power to boast, either privately or publicly, that I have burdenedany one either in much or in little. And I wish for all among whom I have spoken, that they may not possess that for a testimony against them.

Ign. Phil. VII. - I have exhorted you to unity.

For though some would nave deceived me according to the flesh, yet the Spirit, as being from God, is not deceived. For it knows both whence it comes and whither it goes,and detects the secrets [of the heart]. For, when I was among you, I cried, I spoke with a loud voice: Give heed to the bishop, and to the presbytery and deacons. Now, some suspected me of having spoken thus, as knowing beforehand the division caused by some among you.But He is my witness, for whose sake I am in bonds, that I got no intelligence from any man.But the Spirit proclaimed these words: Do nothing without the bishop; keep your bodiesas the temples of God;love unity; avoid divisions; be the followers of Jesus Christ, even as He is of His Father.

Ign. Phil. VIII. - The same continued.

I therefore did what belonged to me, as a man devoted tounity. For where there is division and wrath, God doth not dwell. To all them that repent, the Lord grants forgiveness, if they turn in penitence to the unity of God, and to communion with the bishop. I trust [as to you] in the grace of Jesus Christ, who shall free you from every bond. And I exhort you to do nothing out of strife, but according to the doctrine of Christ. When I heard some saying, If I do not find it in the ancientScriptures, I will not believe the Gospel; on my saying to them, It is written, they answered me, That remains to be proved. But to me Jesus Christ is in the place of all that is ancient: His cross, and death, and resurrection, and the faithwhich is by Him, are undefiled monuments of antiquity; by which I desire, through your prayers, to be justified.

Ign. Phil. IX. - The old testament is good: the new testament is better.

The priestsindeed are good, but the High Priest is better; to whom the holy of holies has been committed, and who alone has been trusted with the secrets of God. He is the door of the Father, by which enter in Abraham, and Isaac, and Jacob, and the prophets, and the apostles, and the Church. All these have for their object the attaining to the unity of God. But the Gospel possesses something transcendent [above the former dispensation], viz., the appearance of our Lord Jesus Christ, His passion and resurrection. For the beloved prophets announced Him, but the Gospel is the perfection of immortality. All these things are good together, if ye believe in love.

Ign. Phil. X. - Congratulate the inhabitants of antioch on the close of the persecution.

Since, according to your prayers, and the compassion which ye feel in Christ Jesus, it is reported to me that the Church which is at Antioch in Syria possesses peace, it will become you, as a Church of God, to elect a deacon to act as the ambassador of God [for you] to [the brethren there], that he may rejoice along with them when they are met together, and glorify the name[of God], Blessed is he in Jesus Christ, who shall be deemed worthy of such a ministry; and ye too shall be glorified. And if ye are willing, it is not beyond your power to do this, for the sakeof God; as also the nearest Churches have sent, in some cases bishops, and in others presbyters and deacons.

Ign. Phil. XI. - Thanks and salutation.

Now, as to Philo the deacon, of Cilicia, a man of reputation, who still ministers to me in the word of God, along with Rheus Agathopus, an elect man, who has followed me from Syria, not regardinghis life,--these bear witness in your behalf; and I myself give thanks to God for you, that ye have received them, even as the Lord you. But may those that dishonoured them be forgiven through the grace of Jesus Christ! The love of the brethren at Troas salutes you; whence also I write to you by Burrhus, who was sent along with me by the Ephesians and Smyrnaeans, to show their respect.May the Lord Jesus Christ honour them, in whom they hope, in flesh, and soul, and faith, and love, and concord! Fare ye well in Christ Jesus, our common hope.

The Epistle of Ignatius to the Smyrnaeans

Ignatius, who is also called Theophorus, to the Church of God the Father, and of the beloved Jesus Christ, which has through mercy obtained every kind of gift, which is filled with faith and love, and is deficient in no gift, most worthy of God, and adorned with holiness: the Church which is at Smyrna, in Asia, wishes abundance of happiness, through the immaculate Spirit and word of God.

Ign. Smyr. I. - Thanks to god for your faith.

I glorify God, even Jesus Christ, who has given you such wisdom. For I have observed that ye are perfected in an immoveable faith, as if ye were nailed to the cross of our Lord Jesus Christ, both in the flesh and in the spirit, and are established in love through the blood of Christ, being fully persuaded with respect to our Lord, that He was truly of the seed of David according to the flesh,and the Son of God according to the will and powerof God; that He was truly born of a virgin, was baptized by John, in order that all righteousness might be fulfilledby Him; and was truly, under Pontius Pilate and Herod the tetrarch, nailed[to the cross] for us in His flesh. Of this fruitwe are by His divinely-blessed passion, that He might set up a standard s for all ages, through His resurrection, to all His holy and faithful[followers], whether among Jews or Gentiles, in the one body of His Church.

Ign. Smyr. II. - Christ's true passion.

Now, He suffered all these things for our sakes, that we might be saved. And He suffered truly, even as also He truly raised up Himself, not, as certain unbelievers maintain, that He only seemed to suffer, as they themselves only seem to be[Christians]. And as they believe, so shall it happen unto them, when they shall be divested of their bodies, and be mere evil spirits.

Ign. Smyr. III. - Christ was possessed of a body after his resurrection.

For I know that after His resurrection also He was still possessed of flesh, and I believe that He is so now. When, for instance, He came to those who were with Peter, He said to them, "Lay hold, handle Me, and see that I am not an incorporeal spirit."And immediately they touched Him, and believed, being convinced both by His flesh and spirit. For this cause also they despised death, and were found its conquerors. And after his resurrection He did eat and drink with them, as being possessed of flesh, although spiritually He was united to the Father.

Ign. Smyr. IV. - Beware of these heretics.

I give you these instructions, beloved, assured that ye also hold the same opinions[as I do]. But I guard you beforehand from those beasts in the shape of men, whom you must not only not receive, but, if it be possible, not even meet with; only you must pray to God for them, if by any means they may be brought to repentance, which, however, will be very difficult. Yet Jesus Christ, who is our true life, has the power of[effecting] this. But if these things were done by our Lord only in appearance, then am I also only in appearance bound. And why have I also surrendered myself to death, to fire, to the sword, to the wild beasts? But,[in fact,] he who is near to the sword is near to God; he that is among the wild beasts is in company with God; provided only he be so m the name of Jesus Christ. I undergo all these things that I may suffer together with Him,He who became a perfect man inwardly strengthening me.

Ign. Smyr. V. - Their dangerous errors.

Some ignorantlydeny Him, or rather have been denied by Him, being the advocates of death rather than of the truth. These persons neither have the prophets persuaded, nor the law of Moses, nor the Gospel even to this day, nor the sufferings we have individually endured. For they think also the same thing regarding us. For what does any one profit me, if he commends me, but blasphemes my Lord, not confessing that He was[truly] possessed of a body?But he who does not acknowledge this, has in fact altogether denied Him, being enveloped in death.I have not, however, thought good to write the names of such persons, inasmuch as they are unbelievers. Yea, far be it from me to make any mention of them, until they repent and return to[a true belief in] Christ's passion, which is our resurrection.

Ign. Smyr. VI - Unbelievers in the blood of Christ shall be condemned.

Let no man deceive himself. Both the things which are in heaven, and the glorious angels,and rulers, both visible and invisible, if they believe not in the blood of Christ, shall, in consequence, incur condemnation."He that is able to receive it, let him receive it."Let not[high] place puff any one up: for that which is worth all is a faith and love, to which nothing is to same thing regarding us. For what does it profit, if any one commends me, but blasphemes my be preferred. But consider those who are of a different opinion with respect to the grace of Christ which has come unto us, how opposed they are to the will of God. They have no regard for love; no care for the widow, or the orphan, or the oppressed; of the bond, or of the free; of the hungry, or of the thirsty.

Ign. Smyr. VII. - Let us stand aloof from such heretics.

They abstain from the Eucharist and from prayer,because they confess not the Eucharist to be the flesh of our Saviour Jesus Christ, which suffered for our sins, and which the Father, of His goodness, raised up again. Those, therefore, who speak against this gift of God, incur deathin the midst of their disputes. But it were better for them to treat it with respect,that they also might rise again. It is fitting, therefore, that ye should keep aloof from such persons, and not to speak ofthem either in private or in public, but to give heed to the prophets, and above all, to the Gospel, in which the passion[of Christ] has been revealed to us, and the resurrection has been fully proved.But avoid all divisions, as the beginning of evils. They are ashamed of the cross; they mock at the passion; they make a jest of the resurrection. They are the offspring of that spirit who is the author of all evil, who led Adam,by means of his wife, to transgress the commandment, who slew Abel by the hands of Cain, who fought against Job, who was the accuser of Joshuathe son of Josedech, who sought to "sift the faith"(10)of the apostles, who stirred up the multitude of the Jews against the Lord, who also now "worketh in the children of disobedience;(12)from whom the Lord Jesus Christ will deliver us, who prayed that the faith of the apostles might not fail,not because He was not able of Himself to preserve it, but because He rejoiced in the pre-eminence of the Father. It is fitting, therefore, that ye should keep aloof from such persons, and neither in private nor in public to talk withthem; but to give heed to the law, and the prophets, and to those who have preached to you the word of salvation. But flee from all abominable heresies, and those that cause schisms, as the beginning of evils.

Ign. Smyr. VIII. - Let nothing be done without the bishop.

See that ye all follow the bishop, even as Jesus Christ does the Father, and the presbytery as ye would the apostles; and reverence the deacons, as being the institutionof God. Let no man do anything connected with the Church without the bishop. Let that be deemed a properEucharist, which is[administered] either even as, wherever Jesus Christ is, there is the Catholic Church. It is not lawful without the bishop either to baptize or to celebrate a love-feast; but whatsoever he shall approve of, that is also pleasing to God, so that everything that is done may be secure and valid.

Ign. Smyr. IX. - Honour the bishop.

Moreover,it is in accordance with reason that we should return to soberness[of conduct], and, while yet we have opportunity, exercise repentance towards God. It is well to reverenceboth God and the bishop. He who honours the bishop has been honoured by God; he who does anything without the knowledge of the bishop, does[in reality] serve the devil. Let all things, then, abound to you through grace, for ye are worthy. Ye have refreshed me in all things, and Jesus Christ[shall refresh] you. Ye have loved me when absent as well as when present. May God recompense you, for whose sake, while ye endure all things, ye shall attain unto Him.

Ign. Smyr. X. - Acknowledgment of their kindness.

Ye have done well in receiving Philo and Rheus Agathopus as servantsof Christ our God, who have followed me for the sake of God, and who give thanks to the Lord in your behalf, because ye have in every way refreshed them. None of these things shall be lost to you. May my spirit be for you,and my bonds, which ye have not despised or been ashamed of; nor shall Jesus Christ, our perfect hope, be ashamed of you.

Ign. Smyr. XI. - Request to them to send a messenger to antioch.

Your prayer has reached to the Church which is at Antioch in Syria. Coming from that place bound with chains, most acceptable to God,I salute all; I who am not worthy to be styled from thence, inasmuch as I am the least of them. Nevertheless, according to the will of God, I have been thought worthy[of this honour], not that I have any sense [of having deserved it], but by the grace of God, which I wish may be perfectly given to me, that through your prayers I may attain to God. In order, therefore, that your work may be complete both on earth and in heaven, it is fitting that, for the honour of God, your Church should elect some worthy delegate; so that he, journeying into Syria, may congratulate them that they

are[now] at peace, and are restored totheir proper greatness, and that their proper constitutionhas been re-established among them. It seems then to me a becoming thing, that you should send some one of your number with an epistle, so that, in company with them, he may rejoiceover the tranquility which, according to the will of God, they have obtained, and because that, through your prayers, they have now reached the harbour. As persons who are perfect, ye should also aim atthose things which are perfect. For when ye are desirous to do well, God is also ready to assist you.

Ign. Smyr. XII. - Salutations.

The love of the brethren at Troas salutes you; whence also I write to you by Burrhus, whom ye sent with me, together with the Ephesians, your brethren, and who has in all things refreshed me. And I would that all may imitate him, as being a pattern of a ministerof God. Grace will reward him in all things. I salute your most worthybishop, and your very venerablepresbytery, and your deacons, my fellow-servants, and all of you individually, as well as generally, in the name of Jesus Christ, and in His flesh and blood, in His passion and resurrection, both corporeal and spiritual, in union with God and you. Grace, mercy, peace, and patience, be with you for evermore!

Ign. Smyr. XIII - Conclusion.

I salute the families of my bretheren, with their wives and children, and the virgins who are called widows.Be ye strong, I pray, in the power of the Holy Ghost. Philo, who is with me, greets you. I salute the house of Tavias, and pray that it may be confirmed in faith and love, both corporeal and spiritual. I salute Alce, my well-beloved,and the incomparable Daphnus, and Eutecnus, and all by name. Fare ye well in the grace of God.

The Epistle of Ignatius to Polycarp

Ignatius, who is also called Theophorus, to Polycarp, Bishop of the Church of the Smyrnæans, or rather, who has, as his own bishop, God the Father, and the Lord Jesus Christ:[wishes] abundance of happiness.

Ign. Poly. I. - Commendation and exhortation.

having obtained good proof that thy mind is fixed in God as upon an immoveable rock, I loudly glorify[His name] that I have been thought worthy[to behold] thy blameless face,which may I ever enjoy in God! I entreat thee, by the grace with which thou art clothed, to press forward in thy course, and to exhort all that they may be saved. Maintain thy position with all care, both in the flesh and spirit. Have a regard to preserve unity, than which nothing is better. Bear with all, even as the Lord does with thee. Supportall in love, as also thou doest. Give thyself to prayer without ceasing.Implore additional understanding to what thou already hast. Be watchful, possessing a sleepless spirit. Speak to every man separately, as God enables thee.Bear the infirmities of all, as being a perfect athlete[in the Christian life]: where the labour is great, the gain is all the more.

Ign. Poly. II. - Exhortations.

If thou lovest the good disciples, no thanks are due to thee on that account; but rather seek by meekness to subdue the more troublesome. Every kind of wound is not healed with the same plaster. Mitigate violent attacks[of disease] by gentle applications.Be in all things "wise as a serpent, and harmless as a dove."For this purpose thou art composed of both flesh and spirit, that thou mayest deal tenderlywith those[evils] that present themselves visibly before thee. And as respects those that are not seen,pray that[God] would reveal them unto thee, in order that thou mayest be wanting in nothing, but mayest abound in every gift. The times call for thee, as pilots do for the winds, and as on tossed with tempest seeks for the haven, so that both thou[and those under thy care] may attain to

God. Be sober as an athlete of God: the prize set before thee is immortality and eternal life, of which thou art also persuaded. In all things may my soul be for thing,and my bonds also, which thou hast loved.

Ign. Poly. III. - Exhortations.

Let not those who seem worthy of credit, but teach strange doctrines,fill thee with apprehension. Stand firm, as does an anvil which is beaten. It is the part of a nobleathlete to be wounded, and yet to conquer. And especially, we ought to bear all things for the sake of God, that He also may bear with us. Be ever becoming more zealous than what thou art. Weigh carefully the times. Look for Him who is above all time, eternal and invisible, yet who became visible for our sakes; impalpable and impassible, yet who became passible on our account; and who in every kind of way suffered for our sakes.

Ign. Poly. IV. - Exhortations.

Let not widows be neglected. Be thou, after the Lord, their protector s and friend. Let nothing be done without thy consent; neither do thou anything without the approval of God, which indeed thou dost not, inasmuch as thou art stedfast. Let your assembling together be of of frequentoccurrence: seek after all by name. Do not despise either male or female slaves, yet neither let them be puffed up with conceit, but rather let them submit themselvesthe more, for the glory of God, that they my obtain from God a better liberty. Let them not long to be set free [from slavery] at the public expense, that they be not found slaves to their own desires.

Ign. Poly. V. - The duties of husbands and wives.

Flee evil arts; but all the more discourse in public regarding them.Speak to my sisters, that they love the Lord, and be satisfied with their husbands both in the flesh and spirit. In like manner also, exhort my brethren, in the name of Jesus Christ, that they love their wives, even as the Lord the Church.If any one can continue in a state of purity,to the honour of Him who is Lord of the flesh,let him so remain without boasting. If he begins to boast, he is undone; and if he reckon himself greater than the bishop, he is ruined. But it becomes both men and women who marry, to form their union with the approval of the bishop, that their marriage may be according to God, and not after their own lust. Let all things be done to the honour of God.

Ign. Poly. VI. - The duties of the christian flock.

Give ye heed to the bishop, that God also may give heed to you. My soul be for theirsthat are submissive to the bishop, to the presbyters, and to the deacons, and may my portion be along with them in God! Labour together with one another; strive in company together; run together; suffer together; sleep together; and awake together, as the stewards, and associates,and servants of God. Please ye Him under whom ye fight, and from whom ye receive your wages. Let none of you be found a deserter. Let your baptism endure as your arms; your faith as your helmet; your love as your spear; your patience as a complete panoply. Let your works be the chargeassigned to you, that ye may receive a worthy recompense. Be long-suffering, therefore, with one another, in meekness, as God is towards you. May I have joy of you for ever!

Ign. Poly. VII. - Request that polycarp would send a messenger to antioch.

Seeing that the Church which is at Antioch in Syria is, as report has informed me, at peace, through your prayers, I also am the more encouraged, resting without anxiety in God,if indeed by means of suffering I may attain to God, so that, through your prayers, I may be found a disciple[of Christ].It is fitting, O Polycarp, most blessed in God, to assemble a very solemncouncil, and to elect one whom you greatly love, and know to be a man of activity, who may be designated the messenger of God;and to bestow on him this honour

that he may go into Syria, and glorify your ever active love to the praise of Christ. A Christian has not power over himself, but must always be ready for s the service of God. Now, this work is both God's and yours, when ye shall have completed it to His glory. For I trust that, through grace, ye are prepared for every good work pertaining to God. Knowing, therefore, your energetic love of the truth, I have exhorted you by this brief Epistle.

Ign. Poly. VIII. - Let other churches also send to antioch.

Inasmuch as I have not been able to write to all the Churches, because I must suddenly sail from Troas to Neapolis, as the will(7)[of the emperor] enjoins,[I beg that] thou, as being acquainted with the purposeof God, wilt write to the adjacent Churches, that they also may act in like manner, such as are able to do so sending messengers,and the others transmitting letters through those persons who are sent by thee, that thoumayest be glorified by a workwhich shall be remembered for ever, as indeed thou art worthy to be. I salute all by name, and in particutar the wife of Epitropus, with all her house and children. I salute Attalus, my beloved. I salute him who shall be deemed worthy to go[from you] into Syria. Grace shall be with him for ever, and with Polycarp that sends him. I pray for your happiness for ever in our God, Jesus Christ, by whom continue ye in the unity and under the protection of God,I salute Alce, my dearly beloved. Fare ye well in the Lord.

Epistle of Polycarp to the Philippians

Polycarp and the presbyters who are with him to the church of God that temporarily resides in Philippi. May mercy and peace be multiplied to you from God Almighty and Jesus Christ our savior.

Poly. 1

I greatly rejoice together with you in our Lord Jesus Christ. For you have received the replicas of true love and have, as was incumbent upon you, sent ahead those who were confined in chains fitting for the saints, crowns for those who have truly been chosen by God and our Lord. And I rejoice that the secure root of your faith, proclaimed from ancient times, even now continues to abide and bear fruit in our Lord Jesus Christ. He persevered to the point of death on behalf of our sins; and God raised him up after loosing the labor pains of Hades. Even without seeing him, you believe in him with an inexpressible and glorious joy? that many long to experience. For you know that you have been saved by a gracious gift—not from works? but by the will of God through Jesus Christ.

Poly. 2

Therefore, bind up your loose robes and serve as God's slaves in reverential fear and truth, abandoning futile reasoning and the error that deceives many, and believing in the one who raised our Lord Jesus Christ from the dead and gave him glory and a throne at his right hand. Everything in heaven and on earth is subject to him; everything that breathes will serve him; he is coming as a judge of the living and the dead; and God will hold those who disobey him accountable for his blood. But the one who raised him from the dead will raise us as well, if we do his will, walking in his commandments and loving the things he loved, abstaining from every kind of injustice, greed, love of money, slander, and false witness, not paying back evil for evil, or abuse for abuse or blow for blow, or curse for curse, but remembering what the Lord said when he taught: "Do not judge lest you be judged; forgive and it will be forgiven you; show mercy that you may be shown mercy; the amount you dispense will be the amount you receive in return." And, "blessed are the poor and those persecuted for the sake of righteousness, because the kingdom of God belongs to them."

Poly. 3

I am writing these things about righteousness, brothers, not on my own initiative but at your request. For neither I nor anyone like me is able to replicate the wisdom of the blessed and glorious Paul. When he was with you he accurately and reliably taught the word of truth to those who were there at the time. And when he was absent he wrote you letters. If you carefully peer into them, you will be able to be built up in the faith that was given you. This faith is the mother of us all, with hope following close after, and the love of God, Christ, and neighbor leading the way. For anyone centered in these has fulfilled the commandment of righteousness. For the one who has love is far removed from all sin.

Poly. 4

The love of money is the beginning of all difficulties. And so, since we know that we brought nothing into the world and can take nothing out of it, we should arm our selves with the weapons of righteousness and teach one another, first of all, to walk in the commandment of the Lord. Then we should teach our wives to walk in the faith given them and in love and purity; to be affectionate towards their own husbands in all truth; to love everyone equally, with all self-restraint; and to discipline their children in the reverential fear of God. We should teach the widows to be self-controlled with respect to faith in the Lord, to pray without ceasing for everyone, and to be distant from all libel, slander, false witness, love of money, and all evil, knowing that they are God's altar and that each offering is inspected for a blemish and that nothing escapes his notice, whether thoughts, ideas, or any of the things hidden in the heart.

Poly. 5

Since we know that God is not mocked, we should walk in a manner worthy of his commandment and glory. So too the deacons should be blameless before his righteousness as ministers of God and of Christ, not of humans. They should not be slanderous or insincere, but free from the love of money, self-restrained in every way, compassionate, attentive, and proceeding according to the truth of the Lord, who became a minister for everyone. If we are pleasing to him in the present age we will receive also the age that is coming, just as he promised that he would raise us from the dead and that, if we conducted ourselves worthily of him, we would also rule together with him—so long as we believe. So too let the young men be blameless in all things, concerned above all else for their purity, keeping themselves in check with respect to all evil. For it is good to be cut off from the passions of the world, since every passion wages war against the spirit, and neither the sexually immoral, nor the effeminate, nor male prostitutes will inherit the kingdom of God nor will those who engage in aberrant behavior. Therefore we must abstain from all these things, and be subject to the presbyters and deacons as to God and Christ. And the virgins must walk in a blameless and pure conscience.

Poly. 6

The presbyters also should be compassionate, merciful to all, turning back those who have gone astray, caring for all who are sick, not neglecting the widow, the orphan, or the poor, but always taking thought for what is good before both God and others, abstaining from all anger, prejudice, and unfair judgment, avoiding all love of money, not quick to believe a rumor against anyone, not severe in judgment, knowing that we are all in debt because of sin. And so if we ask the Lord to forgive us, we ourselves also ought to forgive; for we are before the eyes of the Lord and of God, and everyone must appear before the judgment seat of Christ, each rendering an account of himself. And so we should serve as his slaves, with reverential fear and all respect, just as he commanded, as did the apostles who proclaimed the gospel to us and the prophets who

383

preached, in advance, the coming of our Lord. We should be zealous for what is good, avoiding stumbling blocks, false brothers, and those who carry the name of the Lord in hypocrisy, leading the empty-minded astray.

Poly. 7

For anyone who does not confess that Jesus Christ has come in the flesh is an antichrist; and whoever does not confess the witness of the cross is from the devil; and whoever distorts the words of the Lord for his own passions, saying that there is neither resurrection nor judgment—this one is the firstborn of Satan. And so, let us leave behind the idle speculation of the multitudes and false teachings and turn to the word that was delivered to us from the beginning, being alert in prayer and persistent in fasting. Through our entreaties let us ask the God who sees all things not to bring us into temptation, just as the Lord said, "For the spirit is willing but the flesh is weak."

Poly. 8

Thus we should persevere, unremitting in our hope and in the down payment of our righteousness, which is Christ Jesus, who bore our sins in his own body on the tree, who did not commit sin nor was deceit found in his mouth; but he endured all things on our account, that we might live in him. Therefore we should be imitators of his endurance, and if we suffer for his name, we should give him the glory. For he set this example for us through what he did, and we have believed it.

Poly. 9

Therefore I urge all of you to obey the word of righteousness and to practice all endurance, which you also observed with your own eyes not only in the most fortunate Ignatius, Zosimus, and Rufus, but also in others who lived among you, and in Paul himself and the other apostles. You should be convinced that none of them acted in vain, but in faith and righteousness, and that they are in the place they deserved, with the Lord, with whom they also suffered. For they did not love the present age; they loved the one who died for us and who was raised by God for our sakes.

Poly. 10

And so, you should stand firm in these things and follow the example of the Lord, secure and unmoveable in your faith, loving the brotherhood, caring for one another, united in the truth, waiting on one another in the gentleness of the Lord, looking down on no one. When you are able to do good, do not put it off, since giving to charity frees a person from death. Let all of you be subject to one another, keeping your interactions with the outsiders above reproach, that by your good works you may receive praise and the Lord not be blasphemed because of you. For woe to the one through whom the name of the Lord is blasphemed. Teach all, therefore, to conduct themselves in a sober way, as you yourselves are doing.

Poly. 11

I am extremely sad for Valens, once a presbyter among you, that he should so misunderstand the office that was given him. Thus I urge you to abstain from love of money and to be pure and truthful. Abstain from every kind of evil. For if someone cannot control himself in such things, how can he preach self-control to another? Anyone who cannot avoid the love of money will be defiled by idolatry and will be judged as if among the outsiders who know nothing about the judgment of the Lord. Or do we not realize that "the saints will judge the world?" For so Paul teaches. But I have neither perceived nor heard that you have any such thing in your midst, among whom the most fortunate Paul labored and who are found in the beginning of his epistle. For he exulted in you among all his churches, which alone knew God at that time; for we had not yet come to know him. And so, my brothers, I am very sad for that man and his wife; may the Lord give them true repentance. And you yourselves should act in a sober way in this matter. Rather than judge such people as enemies, call them back as frail and wayward members, so as to heal your entire body. For when you do this, you build yourselves up.

Poly. 12

I am confident that you are well trained in the sacred Scriptures and that nothing is hidden from you; but to me this has not been granted. Only, as it is written in these Scriptures, "Be angry and do not sin, and do not let the sun go down on your anger." How fortunate is the one who remembers this; and I believe this to be the case among you. So may the God and Father of our Lord Jesus Christ, and the eternal priest himself, the Son of God, Jesus Christ, build you up in faith and truth and in all gentleness, without anger, and in patience, forbearance, tolerance, and purity; and may he grant to you the lot and portion to be among his saints—and to us as well with you, and to everyone under heaven who is about to believe in our Lord and God, Jesus Christ, and in his Father, who raised him from the dead. Pray for all the saints. Pray also for kings and magistrates and rulers, as well as for those who persecute and hate you and for the enemies of the cross, that your fruit may be manifest to all and you may be made perfect in him.

Poly. 13

Both you and Ignatius have written to me that if anyone is going to Syria he should take along your letter. I will do so if I have the opportunity—either I or someone I send as a representative on your behalf and mine. We have forwarded to you the letters of Ignatius that he sent to us, along with all the others we had with us, just as you directed us to do. These accompany this letter; you will be able to profit greatly from them, for they deal with faith and endurance and all edification that is suitable in our Lord. And let us know what you have learned more definitely about Ignatius himself and those who are with him.

Poly. 14

I am writing these things to you through Crescens, whom commended to you recently [Or: when I was with you] and now commend again. For he has conducted himself blamelessly among us; and I believe that he will do the same among you. And his sister will be commended to you when she comes to you. Farewell in the Lord Jesus Christ in grace, with all who are yours. Amen.

The Martyrdom of Polycarp

The church of God that temporarily resides in Smyrna to the church of God that temporarily resides in Philomelium, and to all congregations of temporary residents everywhere, who belong to the holy and universal church. May the mercy, peace, and love of God the Father and of our Lord Jesus Christ be multiplied.

Mart. Poly. 1

We are writing you, brothers, about those who were martyred, along with the blessed Polycarp, who put an end to the persecution by, as it were, setting a seal on it through his death as a martyr. For nearly everything leading up to his death occurred so that the Lord might show us from above a martyrdom in conformity with the gospel. For Polycarp waited to be betrayed, as also did the Lord, that we in turn might imitate him, thinking not only of ourselves, but also of our neighbors. For anyone with true and certain love wants not only himself but also all the brothers to be saved.

Mart. Poly. 2

Blessed and noble, therefore, are all the martyrdoms that have occurred according to the will of God. For we must be reverent and attribute the ultimate authority to God. For who would not be astounded by their nobility, endurance, and love of the Master? For

they endured even when their skin was ripped to shreds by whips, revealing the very anatomy of their flesh, down to the inner veins and arteries, while bystanders felt pity and wailed. But they displayed such nobility that none of them either grumbled or moaned, clearly showing us all that in that hour, while under torture, the martyrs of Christ had journeyed far away from the flesh, or rather, that the Lord was standing by, speaking to them. And clinging to the gracious gift of Christ, they despised the torments of the world, in one hour purchasing for themselves eternal life. And the fire of their inhuman torturers was cold to them, because they kept their eyes on the goal of escaping the fire that is eternal and never extinguished. And with the eyes of their hearts they looked above to the good things preserved for those who endure, which no ear has heard nor eye seen, which have never entered into the human heart, but which the Lord revealed to them, who were no long humans but already angels. In a similar way, those who were condemned to the wild beasts endured horrible torments, stretched out on sharp shells and punished with various other kinds of tortures, that, if possible, he might force them to make a denial through continuous torment.

Mart. Poly. 3

For the devil devised many torments against them. But thanks be to God: he had no power over any of them. For the most noble Germanicus strengthened their cowardice through his endurance, and he fought the wild beasts impressively. For when the proconsul wanted to persuade him, saying "Take pity on your age," he forcefully dragged the wild beast onto himself, wanting to leave their unjust and lawless life without delay. Because of this, the entire multitude, astounded by the great nobility of the godly and reverent race of the Christians, cried out, "Away with the atheists! Find Polycarp!"

Mart. Poly. 4

But there was a person named Quintus, a Phrygian who had recently come from Phrygia, who was overcome with cowardice once he saw the wild beasts. This is the one who compelled both himself and several others to turn themselves in. But the insistent pleas of the proconsul convinced him to take the oath and offer a sacrifice. Because of this, brothers, we do not praise those who hand themselves over, since this is not what the gospel teaches.

Mart. Poly. 5

Now when the most marvelous Polycarp first heard, he was not disturbed, but wanted to remain in the city. But most of the others were persuading him to leave. And so he left for a small country house not far from the city and stayed there with a few others, night and day doing nothing but pray for everyone and for the churches throughout the world, as was his custom. Three days before he was arrested, while praying, he had a vision and saw his pillow being consumed by fire. Then he turned to those with him and said, "I must be burned alive."

Mart. Poly. 6

While they continued searching for him, he moved to a different country house—just as those who were seeking him arrived at the other. Since they could not find him, they arrested two young slaves, one of whom made a confession under torture. For it was impossible for him to keep in hiding, since the ones who betrayed him were members of his household. And the chief of police, who was called by the same name—for his name was Herod— was eager to lead him into the stadium, that he might fulfill his special destiny as a partner with Christ, while those who betrayed him might suffer the punishment of Judas himself.

Mart. Poly. 7

And so, taking the young slave, on the Day of Preparation around the dinner hour, the mounted police and horsemen went out with their usual weapons, as if running down a thief. And when the hour was late, they converged and found Polycarp lying down in a small room upstairs. He could have fled elsewhere even from there, but he chose not to, saying, "God's will be done." And so, when he heard them come in, he came downstairs and talked with them; and those who were there were astonished at how old and composed he was, and they wondered why there was so much haste to arrest an old man like him. Straight away he ordered them to be given everything they wanted to eat and drink, then and there. And he asked them for an hour to pray without being disturbed. When they gave their permission, he stood and prayed, being so filled with God's grace that for two hours he could not be silent. Those who heard him were amazed, and many of them regretted coming out for such a godly old man.

Mart. Poly. 8

Then he finished his prayer, having remembered everyone he had ever met, both small and great, reputable and disreputable, as well as the entire universal church throughout the world; and when it came time for him to leave, they seated him on a donkey and led him into the city. It was a great Sabbath. The chief of police Herod, along with his father Nicetas, met him and transferred him to their carriage. Sitting on either side, they were trying to persuade him, saying, "Why is it so wrong to save yourself by saying 'Caesar is Lord,' making a sacrifice, and so on?" He did not answer them at first; but when they persisted, he said, "I am not about to do what you advise." Having failed to persuade him, they began speaking horrible words and hastily shoved him out, so that when he came down out of the carriage he scraped his shin. But he did not turn around, but quickly walked on in haste as if he had not been hurt. And he was led into the stadium, where there was such an uproar that no one could be heard.

Mart. Poly. 9

But as he entered the stadium a voice came to Polycarp from heaven: "Be strong, Polycarp, and be a man [Or: be courageous]." No one saw who had spoken, but those among our people who were there heard the voice. Finally, when he was brought forward, there was a great uproar among those who heard that Polycarp had been arrested. When he was brought forward the proconsul asked if he was Polycarp. When he said he was, the proconsul began trying to persuade him to make a denial, saying, "Have respect for your age," along with other related things they customarily say: "Swear by the Fortune of Caesar, repent, and say 'Away with the atheists.'" But Polycarp looked with a stern face at the entire crowd of lawless Gentiles in the stadium; and gesturing to them with his hand, he sighed, looked up to heaven, and said, "Away with the atheists." The proconsul became more insistent and said, "Take the oath and I will release you. Revile Christ." But Polycarp responded, "For eighty-six years I have served him, and he has done me no wrong. How can I blaspheme my king who has saved me?"

Mart. Poly. 10

When the proconsul persisted and said, "Swear by the Fortune of Caesar," Polycarp answered, "If you are so foolish as to think that I will swear by the Fortune of Caesar, as you say, and if you pretend not to know who I am, listen closely: I am a Christian. But if you wish to learn an account of Christianity, appoint a day and listen." The proconsul replied, "Persuade the people." Polycarp said, "I think you deserve an account, for we are taught to render all due honor to rulers and authorities appointed by God, in so far as it does us no harm. But as to those, I do not consider them worthy to hear a reasoned defense."

Mart. Poly. 11

The proconsul said, "I have wild beasts, and I will cast you to them if you do not repent." He replied, "Call them! For it is impossible for us to repent from better to worse; it is good, though, to change from what is wicked to what is right." Again the proconsul said to him, "If you despise the wild beasts, I will have you consumed by fire, if you do not repent." Polycarp replied, "You threaten with a fire that burns for an hour and after a short while is extinguished; for you do not know about the fire of the coming judgment and eternal torment, reserved for the ungodly. But why are you waiting? Bring on what you wish."

Mart. Poly. 12

While he was saying these and many other things, he was filled with courage and joy, and his face was full of grace, so that not only did he not collapse to the ground from being unnerved at what he heard, but on the contrary, the proconsul was amazed and sent his herald into the center of the stadium to proclaim three times, "Polycarp has confessed himself to be a Christian." When the herald said this, the entire multitude of both Gentiles and Jews who lived in Smyrna cried out with uncontrollable rage and a great voice, "This is the teacher of impiety, the father of the Christians, the destroyer of our own gods, the one who teaches many not to sacrifice or worship the gods." Saying these things, they began calling out to Philip, the Asiarch, asking him to release a lion on Polycarp. But he said that he could not do so, since he had already concluded the animal hunts. Then they decided to call out in unison for him to burn Polycarp alive. For the vision that had been revealed about the pillow had to be fulfilled; for he had seen it burning while he prayed. And when he turned he said prophetically to the faithful who were with him, "I must be burned alive."

Mart. Poly. 13

These things then happened with incredible speed, quicker than can be described. The crowds immediately gathered together wood and kindling from the workplaces and the baths, with the Jews proving especially eager to assist, as is their custom. When the pyre was prepared, Polycarp laid aside all his garments and loosened his belt. He was also trying to undo his sandals, even though he was not accustomed to do so, since each of the faithful was always eager to do it, to see who could touch his skin most quickly. For he was adorned with every good thing because of his exemplary way of life, even before he bore his testimony unto death. Immediately the instruments prepared for the pyre were placed around him. When they were about to nail him, he said, "Leave me as I am; for the one who enables me to endure the fire will also enable me to remain in the pyre without moving, even without the security of your nails."

Mart. Poly. 14

So they did not nail him, but they tied him. And when he placed his hands behind his back and was tied, he was like an exceptional ram taken from a great flock for a sacrifice, prepared as a whole burnt offering that is acceptable to God. Looking up into heaven he said, "Lord God Almighty, Father of your beloved and blessed child Jesus Christ, through whom we have received knowledge of you, the God of angels, of powers, and of all creation, and of every race of the upright who live before you, I bless you for making me worthy of this day and hour, that I may receive a share among the number of the martyrs in the cup of your Christ, unto the resurrection of eternal life in both soul and body in the immortality of the Holy Spirit. Among them may I be received before you today as a sacrifice that is rich and acceptable, just as you prepared and revealed in advance and now fulfilled—the true God who does not lie. For this reason and for all things I praise you, I bless you, I glorify you through the eternal and heavenly high priest Jesus Christ, your beloved child, through whom be glory to you, with him and the Holy Spirit, both now and for the ages to come. Amen."

Mart. Poly. 15

When he sent up the "Amen" and finished the prayer, the men in charge of the fire touched it off. And as a great flame blazoned forth we beheld a marvel—we to whom it was granted to see, who have also been preserved to report the events to the others. For the fire, taking on the appearance of a vaulted room, like a boat's sail filled with the wind, formed a wall around the martyr's body. And he was in the center, not like burning flesh but like baking bread or like gold and silver being refined in a furnace. And we perceived a particularly sweet aroma, like wafting incense or some other precious perfume.

Mart. Poly. 16

Finally, when the lawless ones saw that his body could not be consumed by the fire, they ordered an executioner to go up and stab him with a dagger. When he did so, a dove came forth, along with such a quantity of blood that it extinguished the fire, striking the entire crowd with amazement that there could be so much difference between the unbelievers and the elect. One of the latter was this most astounding Polycarp, who in our time was an apostolic and prophetic teacher and bishop of the universal church in Smyrna. For every word that came forth from his mouth was fulfilled and will be fulfilled.

Mart. Poly. 17

But the jealous and envious Evil One, the enemy of the race of the upright, having seen the greatness of Polycarp's death as a martyr and the irreproachable way of life that he had from the beginning—and that he had received the crown of immortality and was awarded with the incontestible prize—made certain that his poor body was not taken away by us, even though many were desiring to do so and to have a share in [Or: to commune with; or: to have fellowship with] his holy flesh. So he incited Nicetas, the father of Herod and brother of Alce, to petition the magistrate not to hand over his body, "Lest," he said, "they desert the one who was crucified and begin to worship this one." The Jews instigated and strongly urged these things, and kept watch when we were about to take him from the fire. For they did not realize that we are never able to abandon Christ, who suffered for the salvation of the entire world of those who are being saved, the one who was blameless for sinners; nor are we able to worship any other. For we worship this one who is the Son of God, but we love the martyrs as disciples and imitators of the Lord. And they are worthy, because of their unsurpassable affection for their own king and teacher. May we also become partners and fellow disciples with them!

Mart. Poly. 18

When the centurion saw the contentiousness caused by the Jews, he placed Polycarp's body in the center and burned it, as is their custom. And so, afterwards, we removed his bones, which were more valuable than expensive gems and more precious than gold, and put them in a suitable place. There, whenever we can gather together in joy and happiness, the Lord will allow us to commemorate the birthday of his martyrdom, both in memory of those who have already engaged in the struggle and as a training and preparation for those who are about to do so.

Mart. Poly. 19

Such are the matters pertaining to the blessed Polycarp, who along with those from Philadelphia was the twelfth martyr in Smyrna; but he alone is remembered by all, discussed even by the outsiders in every place. For he was not only an exceptional teacher but also a superb martyr. Everyone longs to imitate his martyrdom, since it occurred in conformity with the gospel of Christ. Through endurance he overcame the unjust ruler and thus received the crown

of immortality. And now he rejoices together with the apostles and all those who are upright, and he glorifies God the Father and blesses our Lord Jesus Christ, the savior of our souls, pilot of our bodies, and shepherd of the universal church throughout the world.

Mart. Poly. 20

You had asked for a lengthier explanation of what took place, but for the present we have mentioned only the principal points through our brother Marcion. When you have learned these things, send our letter to the brothers who are further afield, that they may also glorify the Lord who selects his chosen ones from among his own slaves. And now to the one who is able to lead us all by his grace and gift into his eternal kingdom, through his child, the unique one, Jesus Christ, be the glory, honor, power, and greatness forever. Greet all the saints. Those who are with us greet you, as does Evaristus, the one who is writing the letter, with his entire household.

Mart. Poly. 21

But the blessed Polycarp bore his witness unto death on the second day of the new month of Xanthikos, February 23, on a great Sabbath, at 2:00 in the afternoon. But he was arrested by Herod while Philip of Tralles was high priest, Statius Quadratus was proconsul, and Jesus Christ was ruling as king forever. To him be the glory, honor, greatness, and eternal throne, from one generation to the next. Amen.

Mart. Poly. 22

We bid you farewell, brothers, you who conduct yourselves in the word of Jesus Christ according to the gospel; with him be glory to God, both Father and Holy Spirit [Or: God, and the Father, and the Holy Spirit], for the salvation of his holy chosen ones, just as the blessed Polycarp bore witness unto death. May we be found to have followed in his footsteps in the kingdom of Jesus Christ! Gaius transcribed these things from the papers of Irenaeus, a disciple of Polycarp; he also lived in the same city as Irenaeus. And I, Socrates, have written these things in Corinth from the copies made by Gaius. May grace be with everyone. And I, Pionius, then sought out these things and produced a copy from the one mentioned above, in accordance with a revelation of the blessed Polycarp, who showed it to me, as I will explain in what follows. And I gathered these papers together when they were nearly worn out by age, so that the Lord Jesus Christ may gather me together with his chosen ones into his heavenly kingdom. To him be the glory with the Father and the Holy Spirit forever and ever. Amen.

Epistle of Mathetes to Diognetus

Mat. Diog. 1 - occasion of the epistle

Since I see thee, most excellent Diognetus, exceedingly desirous to learn the mode of worshipping God prevalent among the Christians, and inquiring very carefully and earnestly concerning them, what God they trust in, and what form of religion they observe, so as all to look down upon the world itself, and despise death, while they neither esteem those to be gods that are reckoned such by the Greeks, nor hold to the superstition of the Jews; and what is the affection which they cherish among themselves; and why, in fine, this new kind or practice [of piety] has only now entered into the world, and not long ago; I cordially welcome this thy desire, and I implore God, who enables us both to speak and to hear, to grant to me so to speak, that, above all, I may hear you have been edified, and to you so to hear, that I who speak may have no cause of regret for having done so.

Mat. Diog. 2 - the vanity of idols

Come, then, after you have freed yourself from all prejudices possessing your mind, and laid aside what you have been accustomed to, as something apt to deceive you, and being made, as if from the beginning, a new man, inasmuch as, according to your own confession, you are to be the hearer of a new [system of] doctrine; come and contemplate, not with your eyes only, but with your understanding, the substance and the form of those whom ye declare and deem to be gods. Is not one of them a stone similar to that on which we tread? Is not a second brass, in no way superior to those vessels which are constructed for our ordinary use? Is not a third wood, and that already rotten? Is not a fourth silver, which needs a man to watch it, lest it be stolen? Is not a fifth iron, consumed by rust? Is not a sixth earthenware, in no degree more valuable than that which is formed for the humblest purposes? Are not all these of corruptible matter? Are they not fabricated by means of iron and fire? Did not the sculptor fashion one of them, the brazier a second, the silversmith a third, and the potter a fourth? Was not every one of them, before they were formed by the arts of these [workmen] into the shape of these [gods], each in its own way subject to change? Would not those things which are now vessels, formed of the same materials, become like to such, if they met with the same artificers? Might not these, which are now worshipped by you, again be made by men vessels similar to others? Are they not all deaf? Are they not blind? Are they not without life? Are they not destitute of feeling? Are they not incapable of motion? Are they not all liable to rot? Are they not all corruptible? These things ye call gods; these ye serve; these ye worship; and ye become altogether like to them. For this reason ye hate the Christians, because they do not deem these to be gods. But do not ye yourselves, who now think and suppose [such to be gods], much more cast contempt upon them than they [the Christians do]? Do ye not much more mock and insult them, when ye worship those that are made of stone and earthenware, without appointing any persons to guard them; but those made of silver and gold ye shut up by night, and appoint watchers to look after them by day, lest they be stolen? And by those gifts which ye mean to present to them, do ye not, if they are possessed of sense, rather punish [than honour] them? But if, on the other hand, they are destitute of sense, ye convict them of this fact, while ye worship them with blood and the smoke of sacrifices. Let any one of you suffer such indignities! Let any one of you endure to have such things done to himself! But not a single human being will, unless compelled to it, endure such treatment, since he is endowed with sense and reason. A stone, however, readily bears it, seeing it is insensible. Certainly you do not show [by your conduct] that he [your God] is possessed of sense. And as to the fact that Christians are not accustomed to serve such gods, I might easily find many other things to say; but if even what has been said does not seem to any one sufficient, I deem it idle to say anything further.

Mat. Diog. 3 - superstitions of the jews

And next, I imagine that you are most desirous of hearing something on this point, that the Christians do not observe the same forms of divine worship as do the Jews. The Jews, then, if they abstain from the kind of service above described, and deem it proper to worship one God as being Lord of all, [are right]; but if they offer Him worship in the way which we have described, they greatly err. For while the Gentiles, by offering such things to those that are destitute of sense and hearing, furnish an example of madness; they, on the other hand by thinking to offer these things to God as if He needed them, might justly reckon it rather an act of folly than of divine worship. For He that made heaven and earth, and all that is therein, and gives to us all the things of which we stand in need, certainly requires none of those things which He Himself bestows on such as think of furnishing them to Him. But those who imagine that, by means of blood, and the smoke of sacrifices and burnt-offerings,

387

they offer sacrifices [acceptable] to Him, and that by such honours they show Him respect,--these, by supposing that they can give anything to Him who stands in need of nothing, appear to me in no respect to differ from those who studiously confer the same honour on things destitute of sense, and which therefore are unable to enjoy such honours.

Mat. Diog. 4 - the other observances of the jews

But as to their scrupulosity concerning meats, and their superstition as respects the Sabbaths, and their boasting about circumcision, and their fancies about fasting and the new moons, which are utterly ridiculous and unworthy of notice,--I do not think that you require to learn anything from me. For, to accept some of those things which have been formed by God for the use of men as properly formed, and to reject others as useless and redundant,--how can this be lawful? And to speak falsely of God, as if He forbade us to do what is good on the Sabbath-days,--how is not this impious? And to glory in the circumcision of the flesh as a proof of election, and as if, on account of it, they were specially beloved by God,--how is it not a subject of ridicule? And as to their observing months and days, as if waiting upon the stars and the moon, and their distributing, according to their own tendencies, the appointments of God, and the vicissitudes of the seasons, some for festivities, and others for mourning,--who would deem this a part of divine worship, and not much rather a manifestation of folly? I suppose, then, you are sufficiently convinced that the Christians properly abstain from the vanity and error common [to both Jews and Gentiles], and from the busy-body spirit and vain boasting of the Jews; but you must not hope to learn the mystery of their peculiar mode of worshipping God from any mortal.

Mat. Diog. 5 - the manners of the christians

For the Christians are distinguished from other men neither by country, nor language, nor the customs which they observe. For they neither inhabit cities of their own, nor employ a peculiar form of speech, nor lead a life which is marked out by any singularity. The course of conduct which they follow has not been devised by any speculation or deliberation of inquisitive men; nor do they, like some, proclaim themselves the advocates of any merely human doctrines. But, inhabiting Greek as well as barbarian cities, according as the lot of each of them has determined, and following the customs of the natives in respect to clothing, food, and the rest of their ordinary conduct, they display to us their wonderful and confessedly striking method of life. They dwell in their own countries, but simply as sojourners. As citizens, they share in all things with others, and yet endure all things as if foreigners. Every foreign land is to them as their native country, and every land of their birth as a land of strangers. They marry, as do all [others]; they beget children; but they do not destroy their offspring. They have a common table, but not a common bed. They are in the flesh, but they do not live after the flesh. They pass their days on earth, but they are citizens of heaven. They obey the prescribed laws, and at the same time surpass the laws by their lives. They love all men, and are persecuted by all. They are unknown and condemned; they are put to death, and restored to life. They are poor, yet make many rich; they are in lack of all things, and yet abound in all; they are dishonoured, and yet in their very dishonour are glorified. They are evil spoken of, and yet are justified; they are reviled, and bless; they are insulted, and repay the insult with honour; they do good, yet are punished as evil-doers. When punished, they rejoice as if quickened into life; they are assailed by the Jews as foreigners, and are persecuted by the Greeks; yet those who hate them are unable to assign any reason for their hatred.

Mat. Diog. 6 - the relation of christians to the world

To sum up all in one word--what the soul is in the body, that are Christians in the world. The soul is dispersed through all the members of the body, and Christians are scattered through all the cities of the world. The soul dwells in the body, yet is not of the body; and Christians dwell in the world, yet are not of the world. The invisible soul is guarded by the visible body, and Christians are known indeed to be in the world, but their godliness remains invisible. The flesh hates the soul, and wars against it, though itself suffering no injury, because it is prevented from enjoying pleasures; the world also hates the Christians, though in nowise injured, because they abjure pleasures. The soul loves the flesh that hates it, and [loves also] the members; Christians likewise love those that hate them. The soul is imprisoned in the body, yet preserves that very body; and Christians are confined in the world as in a prison, and yet they are the preservers of the world. The immortal soul dwells in a mortal tabernacle; and Christians dwell as sojourners in corruptible [bodies], looking for an incorruptible dwelling in the heavens. The soul, when but ill-provided with food and drink, becomes better; in like manner, the Christians, though subjected day by day to punishment, increase the more in number. God has assigned them this illustrious position, which it were unlawful for them to forsake.

Mat. Diog. 7 -the manifestation of christ

For, as I said, this was no mere earthly invention which was delivered to them, nor is it a mere human system of opinion, which they judge it right to preserve so carefully, nor has a dispensation of mere human mysteries been committed to them, but truly God Himself, who is almighty, the Creator of all things, and invisible, has sent from heaven, and placed among men, [Him who is] the truth, and the holy and incomprehensible Word, and has firmly established Him in their hearts. He did not, as one might have imagined, send to men any servant, or angel, or ruler, or any one of those who bear sway over earthly things, or one of those to whom the government of things in the heavens has been entrusted, but the very Creator and Fashioner of all things--by whom He made the heavens--by whom he enclosed the sea within its proper bounds--whose ordinances all the stars faithfully observe--from whom the sun has received the measure of his daily course to be observed--whom the moon obeys, being commanded to shine in the night, and whom the stars also obey, following the moon in her course; by whom all things have been arranged, and placed within their proper limits, and to whom all are subject--the heavens and the things that are therein, the earth and the things that are therein, the sea and the things that are therein--fire, air, and the abyss--the things which are in the heights, the things which are in the depths, and the things which lie between. This [messenger] He sent to them. Was it then, as one might conceive, for the purpose of exercising tyranny, or of inspiring fear and terror? By no means, but under the influence of clemency and meekness. As a king sends his son, who is also a king, so sent He Him; as God He sent Him; as to men He sent Him; as a Saviour He sent Him, and as seeking to persuade, not to compel us; for violence has no place in the character of God. As calling us He sent Him, not as vengefully pursuing us; as loving us He sent Him, not as judging us. For He will yet send Him to judge us, and who shall endure His appearing? ... Do you not see them exposed to wild beasts, that they may be persuaded to deny the Lord, and yet not overcome? Do you not see that the more of them are punished, the greater becomes the number of the rest? This does not seem to be the work of man: this is the power of God; these are the evidences of His manifestation.

Mat. Diog. 8 - the miserable state of men before the coming of the word

For, who of men at all understood before His coming what God is? Do you accept of the vain and silly doctrines of those who are deemed trustworthy philosophers? of whom some said that fire was God, calling that God to which they themselves were by and by to come; and some water; and others some other of the elements formed by God. But if any one of these theories be worthy of approbation, every one of the rest of created things might also be declared to be God. But such declarations are simply the startling and erroneous utterances of deceivers; and no man has either seen Him, or made Him known, but He has revealed Himself. And He has manifested Himself through faith, to which alone it is given to behold God. For God, the Lord and Fashioner of all things, who made all things, and assigned them their several positions, proved Himself not merely a friend of mankind, but also long-suffering [in His dealings with them.] Yea, He was always of such a character, and still is, and will ever be, kind and good, and free from wrath, and true, and the only one who is [absolutely] good; and He formed in His mind a great and unspeakable conception, which He communicated to His Son alone. As long, then, as He held and preserved His own wise counsel in concealment, He appeared to neglect us, and to have no care over us. But after He revealed and laid open, through His beloved Son, the things which had been prepared from the beginning, He conferred every blessing all at once upon us, so that we should both share in His benefits, and see and be active [in His service]. Who of us would ever have expected these things? He was aware, then, of all things in His own mind, along with His Son, according to the relation subsisting between them.

Mat. Diog. 9 -- why the son was sent so late

As long then as the former time endured, He permitted us to be borne along by unruly impulses, being drawn away by the desire of pleasure and various lusts. This was not that He at all delighted in our sins, but that He simply endured them; nor that He approved the time of working iniquity which then was, but that He sought to form a mind conscious of righteousness, so that being convinced in that time of our unworthiness of attaining life through our own works, it should now, through the kindness of God, be vouchsafed to us; and having made it manifest that in ourselves we were unable to enter into the kingdom of God, we might through the power of God be made able. But when our wickedness had reached its height, and it had been clearly shown that its reward, punishment and death, was impending over us; and when the time had come which God had before appointed for manifesting His own kindness and power, how the one love of God, through exceeding regard for men, did not regard us with hatred, nor thrust us away, nor remember our iniquity against us, but showed great long-suffering, and bore with us, He Himself took on Him the burden of our iniquities, He gave His own Son as a ransom for us, the holy One for transgressors, the blameless One for the wicked, the righteous One for the unrighteous, the incorruptible One for the corruptible, the immortal One for them that are mortal. For what other thing was capable of covering our sins than His righteousness? By what other one was it possible that we, the wicked and ungodly, could be justified, than by the only Son of God? O sweet exchange! O unsearchable operation! O benefits surpassing all expectation! that the wickedness of many should be hid in a single righteous One, and that the righteousness of One should justify many transgressors! Having therefore convinced us in the former time that our nature was unable to attain to life, and having now revealed the Saviour who is able to save even those things which it was [formerly] impossible to save, by both these facts He desired to lead us to trust in His kindness, to esteem Him our Nourisher, Father, Teacher, Counsellor, Healer, our

Wisdom, Light, Honour, Glory, Power, and Life, so that we should not be anxious[concerning clothing and food.

Mat. Diog. 10 - the blessings that will flow from faith

If you also desire [to possess] this faith, you likewise shall receive first of all the knowledge of the Father. For God has loved mankind, on whose account He made the world, to whom He rendered subject all the things that are in it, to whom He gave reason and understanding, to whom alone He imparted the privilege of looking upwards to Himself, whom He formed after His own image, to whom He sent His only-begotten Son, to whom He has promised a kingdom in heaven, and will give it to those who have loved Him. And when you have attained this knowledge, with what joy do you think you will be filled? Or, how will you love Him who has first so loved you? And if you love Him, you will be an imitator of His kindness. And do not wonder that a man may become an imitator of God. He can, if he is willing. For it is not by ruling over his neighbours, or by seeking to hold the supremacy over those that are weaker, or by being rich, and showing violence towards those that are inferior, that happiness is found; nor can any one by these things become an imitator of God. But these things do not at all constitute His majesty. On the contrary he who takes upon himself the burden of his neighbour; he who, in whatsoever respect he may be superior, is ready to benefit another who is deficient; he who, whatsoever things he has received from God, by distributing these to the needy, becomes a god to those who receive [his benefits]: he is an imitator of God. Then thou shalt see, while still on earth, that God in the heavens rules over [the universe]; then thou shall begin to speak the mysteries of God; then shalt thou both love and admire those that suffer punishment because they will not deny God; then shall thou condemn the deceit and error of the world when thou shall know what it is to live truly in heaven, when thou shalt despise that which is here esteemed to be death, when thou shalt fear what is truly death, which is reserved for those who shall be condemned to the eternal fire, which shall afflict those even to the end that are committed to it. Then shalt thou admire those who for righteousness' sake endure the fire that is but for a moment, and shalt count them happy when thou shalt know [the nature of] that fire.

Mat. Diog. 11 - these things are worthy to be known and believed

I do not speak of things strange to me, nor do I aim at anything inconsistent with right reason; but having been a disciple of the Apostles, I am become a teacher of the Gentiles. I minister the things delivered to me to those that are disciples worthy of the truth. For who that is rightly taught and begotten by the loving Word, would not seek to learn accurately the things which have been clearly shown by the Word to His disciples, to whom the Word being manifested has revealed them, speaking plainly [to them], not understood indeed by the unbelieving, but conversing with the disciples, who, being esteemed faithful by Him, acquired a knowledge of the mysteries of the Father? For which s reason He sent the Word, that He might be manifested to the world; and He, being despised by the people [of the Jews], was, when preached by the Apostles, believed on by the Gentiles. This is He who was from the beginning, who appeared as if new, and was found old, and yet who is ever born afresh in the hearts of the saints. This is He who, being from everlasting, is to-day called the Son; through whom the Church is enriched, and grace, widely spread, increases in the saints. furnishing understanding, revealing mysteries, announcing times, rejoicing over the faithful. giving to those that seek, by whom the limits of faith are not broken through, nor the boundaries set by the fathers passed over. Then the fear of the law is chanted, and the

grace of the prophets is known, and the faith of the gospels is established, and the tradition of the Apostles is preserved[, and the grace of the Church exults; which grace if you grieve not, you shall know those things which the Word teaches, by whom He wills, and when He pleases. For whatever things we are moved to utter by the will of the Word commanding us, we communicate to you with pains, and from a love of the things that have been revealed to us.

Mat. Diog. 12 - the importance of knowledge to true spiritual life

When you have read and carefully listened to these things, you shall know what God bestows on such as rightly love Him, being made [as ye are] a paradise of delight, presenting in yourselves a tree bearing all kinds of produce and flourishing well, being adorned with various fruits. For in this place the tree of knowledge and the tree of life have been planted; but it is not the tree of knowledge that destroys--it is disobedience that proves destructive. Nor truly are those words without significance which are written, how God from the beginning planted the tree of life in the midst of paradise, revealing through knowledge the way to life, and when those who were first formed did not use this [knowledge] properly, they were, through the fraud of the Serpent, stripped naked. For neither can life exist without knowledge, nor is knowledge secure without life. Wherefore both were planted close together. The Apostle, perceiving the force [of this conjunction], and blaming that knowledge which, without true doctrine, is admitted to influence life, declares, "Knowledge puffeth up, but love edifieth." For he who thinks he knows anything without true knowledge, and such as is witnessed to by life, knows nothing, but is deceived by the Serpent, as not loving life. But he who combines knowledge with fear, and seeks after life, plants in hope, looking for fruit. Let your heart be your wisdom; and let your life be true knowledge inwardly received. Bearing this tree and displaying its fruit, thou shalt always gather in those things which are desired by God, which the Serpent cannot reach, and to which deception does not approach; nor is Eve then corrupted, but is trusted as a virgin; and salvation is manifested, and the Apostles are filled with understanding, and the Passover of the Lord advances, and the choirs are gathered together, and are arranged in proper order, and the Word rejoices in teaching the saints,--by whom the Father is glorified: to whom be glory for ever. Amen.

The Shepherd of Hermas

The first part of the book of hermas called his vision.

Vision I [1] Against filthy and proud thoughts; also the neglect of Hermas in chastising his children. HE who had bred me up sold a certain young maid at Rome; whom when I saw many years after, I remembered her, and began to love her as a sister. It happened some time afterwards, that I saw her washing in the river. Tyber; and I reached out my hand unto her, and brought her out of the river, [2] And when I saw her I thought with myself, saying, How happy should I be if I had such a wife, both for beauty and manners. This I thought with myself; nor did I think any thing more. But not long after, as I was walking, and musing on these thoughts, I began to honour this creature of God, thinking with myself; how noble and beautiful she was. [3] And when I had walked a little, I fell asleep; and the spirit caught me away, and carried me through a certain place towards the right hand, through which no man could pass. It was a place among rocks, very steep, and unpassable for water. [4] When I was past this place, I came into a plain; and there falling down upon my knees, I began to pray unto the Lord, and to confess my sins. [5] And as I was praying, the heaven was opened, and I saw the woman which I had coveted, saluting me from heaven, and saying,

Hermas, hail! and I looking upon her, answered, Lady, what dost thou do here? She answered me, I am taken up hither to accuse thee of sin before the Lord. [6] Lady, said I, wilt thou convince me? No, said she: but hear the words which I am about to speak unto thee. God who dwelleth in heaven, and hath made all things out of nothing, and hath multiplied them for his holy church's sake, is angry with thee because thou hast sinned against me. [7] And I answering said unto her, Lady, if I have sinned against thee, tell me where, or in what place, or when did I ever speak an unseemly or dishonest word unto thee? [8] Have I not always esteemed thee as a lady? Have I not always reverenced thee as a sister? Why then dost thou imagine these wicked things against me? [9] Then she, smiling upon me, said: the desire of naughtiness has risen up in thy heart. Does it not seem to thee to be an ill thing for a righteous man to have an evil desire rise up in his heart. [10] It is indeed a sin, and that a very great sin, to such a one; for a righteous man thinketh that which is righteous. And whilst he does so, and walketh uprightly, he shall have the Lord in heaven favourable unto him in all his business. [11] But as for those who think wickedly in their hearts, they take to themselves death and captivity; and especially those who love this present world, and glory in their riches, and regard not the good things that are to come; their souls wander up and down and know not where to fix. [12] Now this is the case of such as are double-minded, who trust not in the Lord, and despise and neglect their own life. [13] But do thou pray unto the Lord, and he will heal thy sins, and the sins of thy whole house, and of all his saints. [14] As soon as she had spoken these words the heaven were shut, and I remained utterly swallowed up with sadness and fear: and said within myself, if this be laid against me for sin, how can I be saved. [15] Or how should I ever be able to entreat the Lord for my many and great sins? With what words shall I beseech him to be merciful unto me? [16] As I was thinking over these things, and meditating in myself upon them, behold a chair was set over against me of the whitest wool, as bright as snow. [17] And there came an old woman in a bright garment, having a book in her hand, and sat alone, and saluted me, saying, Hermas, hail! and I being full of sorrow and weeping, answered, Hail Lady! [18] And she said unto me, Why art thou sad, Hermas, who wert wont to be patient, and modest, and always cheerful? I answered, and said to her, Lady, a reproach has been laid to my charge by an excellent woman, who tells me that I have sinned against her. [19] She replied, Far be any such thing from the servant of God. But it may be the desire of her has risen up in thy heart? For indeed such a thought maketh the servants of God guilty of sin. [20] Nor ought such a detestable thought to be in the servant of God: nor should he who is approved by the Spirit desire that which is evil; but especially Hermas, who contains himself from all wicked lusts, and is full of all simplicity, and of great innocence. [21] Nevertheless the Lord is not so much angry with thee for thine own sake, as upon the account of thy house, which has committed wickedness against the Lord, and against their parents. [22] And for that out of thy fondness towards thy sons, thou hast not admonished thy house, but hast permitted them to live wickedly; for this cause the Lord is angry with thee: but he will heal all the evils that are done in thy house. For through their sins and iniquities, thou art wholly consumed in secular affairs. [23] But now the mercy of God hath taken compassion upon thee, and upon thine house, and hath greatly comforted thee. Only as for thee, do not wander, but be of an even mind, and comfort thy house. [24] As the workman bringing forth his work, offers it to whomsoever he pleaseth; so shalt thou by teaching every day what is just, cut off a great sin. Wherefore cease not to admonish thy sons, for the Lord knows that they will repent with all their heart, and they shall be written in the book of life. [25] And when she had said this,

she added unto me; Wilt thou hear me read? I answered her, Lady, I will. [26] Hear then, said she; and opening the book she read, gloriously, greatly. and wonderfully, such things as I could not keep in my memory. For they were terrible words, such as no man could bear. [27] How it be I committed her last words to my remembrance; for they were but few, and of great use to us:-- [28] Behold the mighty Lord, who by his invisible power, and with his excellent wisdom made the world, and by his glorious counsel beautified his creature, and with the word of his strength fixed the heaven, and founded the earth upon the waters; and by his powerful virtue established the Holy Church, which he hath blessed. [29] Behold he will remove the heavens, and the mountains, the hills, and the seas; and all things shall be made plain for his elect; that he may render unto them the promise which he has promised, with much honour and joy; if so be that they shall keep the commandments of God, which they have received with great faith. [30] And when she had made an end of reading, she rose out of the chair; and behold four young men came, and carried the chair to the east. [31] And she called me unto her, and touched my breast, and said unto me, Did my reading please thee? I answered, Lady, these last things please me; but what went before was severe and hard. [32] She said unto me, these last things are for the righteous, butthe foregoing for the revolters and heathen. [33] And as she was talking with me, two men appeared, and took her upon their shoulders, and went to the east where the chair was. [34] And she went cheerfully away; and as she was going, said unto me, Hermas, be of good cheer.

Vision II Again, of his neglect in correcting his talkative wife; and of his lewd sons. AS I was on the way to Cuma, about the same time that I went the year before, I began to call to mind the vision I formerly had. And again the spirit carried me away, and brought me into the same place, in which I had been the year before. [2] And when I was come into the place, I fell down upon my knees, and began to pray unto the Lord, and to glorify his name, that he had esteemed me worthy, and had manifested unto me my former sins. [3] And when I arose from prayer, behold I saw over against me the old woman whom I had seen the last year, walking and reading in a certain book. [4] And she said unto me, Canst thou tell these things to the elect of God? I answered and said unto her, Lady, I cannot retain so many things in my memory, but give me the book, and I will write them down. [5] Take it, says she, and see that thou restore it again to me. [6] As soon as I had received it, I went aside into a certain place of the field, and transcribe every letter, for I found no syllables. [7] And as soon as I had finished what was written in the book, the book was suddenly caught out of my hand, but by whom I saw not. [8] After fifteen days, when I had fasted, and entreated the Lord with all earnestness, the knowledge of the writing was revealed unto me. Now the writing was this:-- [9] Thy seed, O Hermas! hath sinned against the Lord, and have betrayed their parents, through their great wickedness. And they have been called the betrayers of their parents, and have gone on in their treachery. [10] And now have they added lewdness to their other sins, and the pollutions of their naughtiness: thus have they filled up the measure of their iniquities. But do thou upbraid thy sons with all these words; and thy wife, who shall be as thy sister; and let her learn to refrain her tongue, with which she calumniates. [11] And when she shall hear these things, she will refrain herself, and shall obtain mercy. [12] And they also shall be instructed, when thou shalt have reproached them with these words, which the Lord has commanded to be revealed unto them. [13] Then shall their sins be forgiven, which they have heretofore committed, and the sins of all the saints who have sinned even unto this day; if they shall repent with all their hearts, and remove all doubts out of their hearts. [14] For the Lord hath sworn by his glory concerning his elect, having determined this very time, that if any one shall even now sin, he shall not be saved. 15 For the repentance of the righteous has its end; the days of repentance are fulfilled to all the saints; but to the heathen, there is repentance even unto the last day. 16 Thou shalt therefore say to those who are over the church, that they order their ways in righteousness; so that they may fully receive the promise with much glory. 17 Stand fast therefore ye that work righteousness and continue to do it, that your departure may be with the holy angels. 18 Happy are ye, as many as shall endure the great trial that is at hand, and whosoever shall not deny his life. 19 For the Lord hath sworn by his Son, that whoso, denieth his Son and HIM, being afraid of his life, he will also deny him in the world that is to come. 20 But those who shall never deny him, he will of his exceeding great mercy be favourable unto them. 21 But thou, O Hermas! remember not the evils which thy sons have done, neither neglect thy sister, but take care that they amend of their former sins. 22 For they will be instructed by this doctrine, if thou shalt not be mindful of what they have done wickedly. 23 For the remembrance of evils worketh death, but the forgetting of them eternal life. 24 But thou, O Hermas! hast undergone a great many worldly troubles for the offences of thy house, because thou hast neglected them, as things that did not belong unto thee; and thou art wholly taken up with thy great business. 25 Nevertheless, for this cause shalt thou be saved, that thou hast not departed from the living God, and thy simplicity and singular continency shall preserve thee, if thou shalt continue in them. 26 Yes, they shall save all such as do such things, and walk in innocence and simplicity. 27 They who are of this kind shall prevail against all impiety, and continue until life eternal. 28 Happy are all they that do righteousness, they shall not be consumed for ever. 29 But thou wilt say, Behold there is a great trial coming. If it seem good to thee, deny him again. 30 The Lord is nigh to them that turn to him, as it is written in the book of Heldam and Modal, who prophesied to the people of Israel in the wilderness. 31 Moreover, brethren, it was revealed to me, as I was sleeping, by a very goodly young man, saying unto me, What thinkest thou of that old woman from whom thou receivedst the book; who is she? I answered, a Sybil. 32 Thou art mistaken said he, she is not. I replied, Who is she then, sir? He answered me, It is the church of God. 33 And I said unto him, Why then does she appear old? She is therefore, said he, an old woman, because she was the first of all the creation, and the world was made for her. 34 After this I saw a vision at home in my own house, and the old woman, whom I had seen before, came to me and asked me whether I had yet delivered her book to the elders of the church? And I answered, that I had not yet. 35 She replied, Thou hast well done, for I have certain words more to tell thee. But when I shall have finished all the words, they shall be clearly understood by the elect. 36 And thou shalt write two books, and send one to Clement and one to Grapte. For Clement shall send it to the foreign cities, because it is permitted to him so to do: but Grapte shall admonish the widows and orphans. 37 But thou shalt read in this city with the elders of the church.

Vision III Of the building of the church triumphant, and of the several sorts of reprobates. THE vision which I saw, brethren, was this. 2 When I had often fasted and prayed unto the Lord, that he would manifest unto me the revelation, which he had promised by the old woman to show unto me; the same night she appeared unto me, and said unto me, 3 Because thou dost thus afflict thyself, and art so desirous to know all things, come into the field, where thou wilt, and about the sixth hour, I will appear unto thee, and show thee what thou must see. 4 I asked her, saying; Lady, into what part of the field? She answered, wherever thou wilt, only choose a good and a private place. And before I began to speak and tell her the place, she

said unto me; I will come where thou wilt. 5 I was therefore, brethren in the field and I observed the hours, and came into the place where I had appointed her to come. 6 And I beheld a bench placed; it was a linen pillow, and over it spread a covering of fine linen. 7 When I saw these things ordered in this manner, and that there was nobody in the place, I began to be astonished, and my hair stood on end, and a, kind of horror seized me; for I was alone. 8 But being come to myself, and calling to mind the glory of God, and taking courage, I fell down upon my knees and began again to confess my sins as before. 9 And whilst I was doing this, the old woman came thither with the six young men whom I had seen before, and stood behind me as I was praying, and heard me praying and confessing my sins unto the Lord. 10 And touching me, she said; Leave off praying now only for thy sins; pray also for righteousness, that thou mayest receive a part of it in thy house. 11 And she lifted me up from the place, and took me by the hand, and brought me to the seat; and said to the young men, go, and build. 12 As soon as they were departed, and we were alone, she said unto me; sit here. I answered her; Lady, let those who are elder sit first. She replied, Sit down as I bid you. 13 And when I would have sat on the right side, she suffered me not, but made a sign to me with her hand, that I should sit on the left. 14 As I was therefore musing, and full of sorrow, that she would not suffer me to sit on the right side, she said unto me, Hermas, why art thou sad? 15 The place which is on the right hand is theirs who have already attained unto God, and have suffered for his name-sake. But there is yet a great deal remaining unto thee, before thou canst sit with them. 16 But continue as thou doest, in thy sincerity, and thou shalt sit with them; as all others shall, who do their works, and shall bear what they have borne. 17 I said to her; Lady, I would know what it is that they have suffered? Hear then, said she: wild beasts, scourgings, imprisonments, and crosses for his name-sake. 18 For this cause the right hand of holiness belongs to them, and to all others as many as shall suffer for the name of God; but the left belongs to the rest. 19 Howbeit the gifts and the promises belong to both, to them on the right, and to those on the left hand; only that sitting on the right hand they have some glory above the others. 20 But thou art desirous to sit on the right hand with them, and yet thy defects are many. But thou shalt be purged from thy defects, as also all who doubt not shall be cleansed from all the sins which they have committed unto this day. 21 And when she had said this she would have departed. 22 Wherefore, falling down before her feet, I began to entreat her, for the Lord's sake, that she would show me the vision which she had promised. 23 Then she again took me by the hand, and lifted me up, and made me sit upon the seat at the left side; and holding up a certain bright wand, said unto me, Seest thou that great thing? I replied, Lady, I see nothing. 24 She answered, Dost thou not see over against thee a great tower, which is built upon the water with bright square stones? 25 For the tower was built upon a square by these six young men that came with her. 26 But many thousand of other men brought stones; some drew them out of the deep, others carried them from the ground, and gave them to the six young men; and they took them and built. 27 As for those stones which were drawn out of the deep, they put them all into the building; for they were polished, and their squares exactly answered one another, and so one was joined in such wise to the other, that there was no space to be seen where they joined, insomuch that the whole tower appeared to be built as it were of one stone. 28 But as for the other stones that were taken off from the ground, some of them they rejected, others they fitted into the building. 29 As for those which were rejected, some they cut out, and cast them at a distance from the tower; but many others of them lay round about the tower, which they made no use of in the building. 30 For some of these were rough, others had clefts in them, others were white and round, not proper for the building of the tower. 31 But I saw the other stones cast afar off from the tower, and falling into the highway, and yet not continuing in the way, but were rolled from the way into a desert place. 32 Others I saw falling into the fire and burning; others fell near the water, yet could not roll themselves into it, though very desirous to fall into the water. 33 And when she had showed me these things she would have departed; but I said to her, Lady, what doth it profit me to see these things, and not understand what they mean? 34 She answered and said unto me; You are very cunning, in that you are desirous to know those things which relate to the tower. Yea, said I, lady, that I may declare them unto the brethren, and they may rejoice, and hearing these things may glorify God with great glory. 35 Then she said, Many indeed shall hear them, and when they shall have heard them, some shall rejoice, and others weep. And yet even these, if they shall repent, shall rejoice too. 36 Hear therefore what I shall say concerning the parable of the tower, and after this be no longer importunate with me about the revelation. 37 For these revelations have an end, seeing they are fulfilled. But thou dost not leave off to desire revelations, for thou art very urgent. 38 As for the tower which thou seest built, it is myself, namely, the church, which have appeared to thee both now and heretofore. Wherefore ask what thou wilt concerning the tower, and I will reveal it unto thee, that thou mayest rejoice with the saints. 39 I said unto her, Lady, because thou hast thought me once worthy to receive from thee the revelation of all these things, declare them unto me. 40 She answered me, Whatsoever is fit to be revealed unto thee shall be revealed: only yet thy heart be with the Lord, and doubt not, whatsoever thou shalt see. 41 I asked her, Lady, why is the tower built upon the water? She replied, I said before to thee that thou wert very wise to inquire diligently concerning the building, therefore thou shalt find the truth. 42 Hear therefore why the tower is built upon the water: because your life is and shall be saved by water. For it is founded by the word of the almighty and honourable name, and is supported by the invisible power and virtue of God. 43 And I answering, said unto her, These things are very admirable; but, lady, who are those six young men that build? 44 They are, said she, the angels of God, who were first appointed, and to whom the Lord has delivered all his creatures, to frame and build them up, and to rule over them. For by these the building of the tower shall be finished. 45 And who are the rest who bring them stones? 46 They also are the holy angels of the Lord; but the others are more excellent than these. Wherefore when the whole building of the tower shall be finished, they shall all feast together beside the tower, and shall glorify God, because the structure of the tower is finished. 47 I asked her, saying, I would know the condition of the stones, and what the meaning of them is? 48 She answering, said unto me, Art thou better than all others that this should be revealed unto thee? For others are both before thee and better than thou art, to whom these visions should be made manifest. 49 Nevertheless, that the name of God may be glorified, it has been shown and shall be revealed unto thee, for the sake of those who are doubtful, and think in their hearts whether these things are so or not. 50 Tell them that all these things are true, and that there is nothing in them that is not true but all are firm and truly established. 51 Hear now then concerning the stones that are in the building. 52 The square and white stones which agree exactly in their joints, are the apostles, and bishops, and doctors, and ministers, who through the mercy of God have come in, and governed, and taught and ministered holily and modestly to the elect of God, both they that have fallen asleep, and which yet remain; and have always agreed with them, and have had peace within themselves, and have heard

each other. 53 For which cause their joints exactly meet together in the building of the tower. 54 They which are drawn out of the deep and put into the building, and whose joints agree with the other stones which are already built, are those which are already fallen asleep, and have suffered for the sake of the Lord's name. 55 And what are the other stones, lady, that are brought from the earth? I would know what are they. 56 She answered, They which lie upon the ground and are not polished, are those which God has approved, because they have walked in I the law of the Lord, and directed their ways in his commandments. 57 They which are brought and put in the building of the tower, are the young in faith and the faithful. And these are admonished by the angels to do well because iniquity is not found in them. 58 But who are those whom they rejected, and laid beside the tower? 59 They are such as have sinned and are willing to repent; for which cause they are not cast far from the tower, because they will be useful for the building, if they shall repent. 60 They therefore that are yet to repent, if they repent they shall become strong in the faith; that is, if they repent now, whilst the tower is building. For if the building shall be finished there will then be no place for them to be put in, but they shall be rejected; for he only has this privilege who shall now be put into the tower. 61 But would you know who they are that were cut out, and cast afar off from the tower? Lady said I, I desire it. 62 They are the children of iniquity, who believed only in hypocrisy, and departed not from their evil ways; for this cause they shall not be saved, because they are not of any use in the building by reason of their sins. 63 Wherefore they are cut out, and cast afar off, because of the anger of the Lord, and because they have provoked him to anger against them. 64 As for the great number of other stones which thou hast seen placed about the tower, but now put into the building; those which are rugged, are they who have known the truth, but have not continued in it, nor been joined to the saints, and therefore are unprofitable. 65 Those that have clefts in them, are they that keep up discord in their hearts against each other, and live not in peace; that are friendly when present with their brethren, but as soon as they are departed from one another, their wickedness still continues in their hearts: these are the clefts which are seen in those stones. 66 Those that are maimed and short, are they who have believed indeed, but still are in great measure full of wickedness; for this cause they are maimed and not whole. 67 But what are the white and round stones, lady, and which are not proper for the building of the tower? 68 She answering said unto me: How long wilt thou continue foolish and without understanding, asking everything and discerning nothing? 69 They are such as have faith indeed, but have withal the riches of this present world. When therefore any troubles arise, for the sake of their riches and traffic, they deny the Lord. 70 I answering, said unto her, When therefore will they be profitable to the Lord? When their riches shall be cut away, says she, in which they take delight, then they will be profitable unto the Lord for his building. 71 For as a round stone, unless it be cut away and is cast somewhat of its bulk, cannot be made square, so they who are rich in this world; unless their riches be pared off; cannot be made profitable unto the Lord. 72 Learn this from thy own experience: when thou wert rich, thou wast unprofitable; but now thou art profitable, and fit for the life which thou hast undertaken; for thou also once was one of those stones. 73 As for the rest of the stones which thou sawest cast afar off from the tower, and running in the way, and tumbled out of the way into desert places; they are such as have believed indeed, but through their doubting have forsaken the true way, thinking that they could find a better. But they wander and are miserable, going into desolate ways. 74 Then for those stones which fell into the fire and were burnt, they are those who have for ever departed from the living God; nor doth it ever come into their hearts to repent, by reason of the affection which they bear to their lusts and wickedness which they commit. 75 And what are the rest which fell by the water, and could not roll into the water? 76 They are such as have heard the word, and were willing to be baptised in the name of the Lord; but considering the great holiness which the truth requires, have withdrawn themselves, an walked again after wicked lusts. 77 Thus she finished the explanation of the tower. 78 But I being still urgent, asked her, Is there repentance allowed to all those stones which are thus cast away, and were not suitable to the building of the tower; and shall they find place in this tower? 79 They may repent, said she, yet they cannot come into this tower; but, they shall be placed in a much lower rank, and then only after they shall have been afflicted and fulfilled the days of their sins. 80 And for this cause they shall be removed, because they have received the word of righteousness: and then they shall be translated from their afflictions, if they shall have a true sense in their hearts of what they have done amiss. 81 But if they shall not have this sense in their hearts, they shall not be saved by reason of the hardness of their hearts. 82 When therefore I had done asking her concerning all these things, she said unto me, Wilt thou see something else? And being desirous of seeing it, I became very cheerful of countenances. 83 She therefore looking back upon me, and smiling a little, said unto me, Seest thou seven women about the tower? Lady, said I, I see them. 84 This tower, replied she, is supported by them, according to the command of the Lord: hear therefore the effects of them. 85 The first of them, which holds fast with her hand, is called Faith; The next, which is girt up, and looks manly, is named Abstinence: she is the daughter of Faith. 86 Whosoever therefore shall follow her shall be happy in all his life, because he shall abstain from all evil works, believing that if he shall contain himself from all concupiscence, he shall be the heir of eternal life. And what, lady, said I, are the other five? 87 They are, replied she, the daughters of one another. The first of them is called Simplicity; the next Innocence; the third Modesty; then Discipline; and the last of all is Charity. When therefore thou shalt have fulfilled the works of their mother, thou shalt be able to do all things. 88 Lady, said I, I would know what particular virtue every one of these has. 89 Hear then, replied she; they have equal virtues, and their virtues are knit together, and follow one another as they were born. 90 From Faith proceeds Abstinence; from Abstinence, Simplicity; from Simplicity, Innocence; from Innocence, Modesty; from Modesty, Discipline and Charity. Therefore the works of these are holy, and chaste, and right. 91 Whoever therefore shall serve these, and hold fast to their works, he shall have his dwelling in the tower with the saints of God. 92 Then I asked her concerning the times, whether the end were now at hand? 93 But she cried out with a loud voice, saying, O foolish man! Dost thou not see the tower yet a building? When therefore the tower shall be finished, and built, it shall have an end; and indeed it shall soon be accomplished. 94 But do not ask me any more questions. What has been said may suffice thee and all the saints for the refreshment of your spirits. For these things have not been revealed to thee only, but that thou mayest make them manifest unto all. 95 For therefore, O Hermas, after three days thou must understand these words which I begin to speak unto thee, that thou mayest speak them in the ears of the saints; that when thou shall have heard and done them, they may be cleansed from their iniquities, and thou together with them. 96 Hear me therefore, O my sons! I have bred you up in much simplicity, and innocency, and modesty, for the love of God, which has dropped down upon you in righteousness, that you should be sanctified and justified from all sin and wickedness; but ye will not cease from your evil doings. 97 Now therefore hearken unto me, and have peace one with

another, and visit one another, and receive one another, and do not enjoy the creatures of God alone. 98 Give freely to them that are in need. For some by too free feeding contract an infirmity in their flesh, and do injury to their bodies; whilst the flesh of others, who have not food, withers away, because they want sufficient nourishment, and the bodies are consumed. 99 Wherefore this intemperance is hurtful to you, who have, and do not contribute to them that want. Prepare for the judgment that is about to come upon you. 100 Ye that are the more eminent, search out them that are hungry, whilst the tower is yet unfinished. For when the tower shall be finished, ye shall be willing to do good, and shall not find any place in it. 101 Beware, therefore, ye that glory in your riches, lest perhaps they groan who are in want, and their sighing come up unto God, and ye be shut out with your goods without the gate of the tower. 102 Behold I now warn you who are set over the church, and love the highest seats, be not ye like unto those that work mischief. 103 And they indeed carry about their poison in boxes, but ye contain your poison and infection in your hearts, and will not purge them, and mix your sense with a pure heart, that ye might find mercy with the Great King. 104 Take heed, my children, that your dissensions deprive you not of your lives. How will ye instruct the elect of God, when ye yourselves want correction? Wherefore admonish one another, and be at peace among yourselves, that I, standing before your Father, may give an account of you unto the Lord. 105 And when she had made an end of talking with me, the six young men that built, came and carried her to the tower; and four others took up the seat on which she sat, and they also went away again to the tower. I saw not the faces of these, for their backs were towards me. 106 As she was going away, I asked her, that she would reveal to me what concerned the three forms, in which she had appeared unto me. 107 But she answering said unto me, concerning these things thou must ask some other, that they may be revealed unto thee. 108 Now, brethren, in the first vision the last year, she appeared unto me exceedingly old, and sitting in a chair. 109 In another vision, she had indeed a youthful face, but her flesh and hair were old; but she talked with me standing, and was more cheerful than the first time. 110 In the third vision, she was in all respects much younger, and comely to the eye; only she had the hair of an aged person: yet she looked cheerful, and sat upon a seat. 111 I was therefore very sad concerning these things, until I might understand the vision. 112 Wherefore I saw the same old woman in a vision of the night saying unto me, All prayer needeth humiliation. Fast, therefore, and thou shalt learn from the Lord that which thou dost ask. I fasted therefore one day. 113 The same night a young man appeared to me and said, Why dost thou thus often desire Revelations in thy prayers? Take heed that by asking many things, thou hurt not the body. Let these Revelations suffice thee. 114 Canst thou see more notable Revelations than those which thou hast already received? 115 I answered and said unto him, Sir, I only ask this one thing upon the account of the three figures of the old woman that appeared to me, that the Revelation may be complete. 116 He answered me, You are not without understanding, but your doubts make you so; for as much as you have not your heart with the Lord. 117 I replied and said, But we shall learn these things more carefully from you. 118 Hear then, says he, concerning the figures about which you inquire. 119 To begin; in the first vision she appeared to thee in the shape of an old woman sitting in, a chair, because your old spirit was decayed, and without strength, by reason of your infirmities, and the doubtfulness of your heart. 120 For as they who are old have no hope of renewing themselves, nor expect any thing but their departure; so you being weakened through your worldly affairs gave yourself up to sloth, and cast not away your solicitude from yourself upon the Lord: and your sense was confused, and you grew old in your sadness. 121 But, sir, I would know why she sat upon a chair? 122 He answered, because every one that is weak sitteth upon a chair by reason of his infirmity, that his weakness may be upheld. Behold therefore the figure of the first vision. 123 In the second vision you saw her standing, and having a youthful face, and more cheerful than her former; but her flesh and her hair were ancient. Hear, said he, this parable also. 124 When any one grows old, he despairs of himself by reason of his infirmity and poverty, and expects nothing but the last day of his life. 125 But on a sudden an inheritance is left to him, and he hears of it, and rises: and being become cheerful, be puts on new strength. And now he no longer sits down, but stands, and is delivered from his former sorrow; and sits not, but acts manfully. 126 So you, having heard the Revelation which God revealed unto you, because God had compassion upon you, and renewed your spirit, both laid aside your infirmities, and strength came to you, and you grew strong in the faith; and God, seeing your strength, rejoiced. 127 For this cause he showed you the building of the tower, and will show other things unto you, if you shall have peace with all your heart among each other. 128 But in the third vision you saw her yet younger, fair and cheerful, and of a serene countenance. 129 For, as if some good news comes to him that is sad, he straightway forgets his sadness, and regards nothing else but the good news which he has heard; and for the rest he is comforted, and his spirit is renewed through the joy which he has received even so you have been refreshed in your spirit by seeing these good things. 130 And for that you saw her sitting upon a bench, it denotes a strong position; because a bench has four feet, and stands strongly. And even the world itself is upheld by the four elements. 131 They therefore that repent perfectly, shall be young; and they that turn from their sins with their whole heart, shall be established. 132 And now you have the Revelation fully, ask no more to have any thing farther revealed unto you. 133 But if any thing is to be revealed, it shall be made manifest unto you.

Vision IV Of the trial, and tribulation that is about to come upon men. I SAW a vision brethren, twenty days after the former vision; a representation of the tribulation that is at hand. I was walking in the field way. 2 Now from the public way to the place whither I went is about ten furlongs; it is a way very little frequented: 3 And as I was walking alone, I entreated the Lord that he would confirm the Revelations which he had shown unto me by his Holy Church. 4 And would grant repentance to all his servants who had been offended, that his great and honourable name might be glorified, and because he thought me worthy to whom he might show his wonders, and, that I might honour him, and give thanks unto him. 5 And behold somewhat like a voice answered me; Doubt not, Hermas. Wherefore I began to think, and say within myself, why should I doubt, seeing I am thus settled by the Lord, and have seen such glorious things? 6 I had gone but a little farther, brethren, when behold I saw a dust rise up to heaven. I began to say within myself, is there a drove of cattle coming, that rises such a dust? 7 It was about a furlong off from me. And behold I saw the dust rise more and more, insomuch that I began to suspect that there was somewhat extraordinary in it. 8 And the sun shone a little; and behold I saw a great beast, as it were a whale; and fiery locusts came out of his mouth. The height of the beast was about a hundred feet, and he had a head like a large earthen vessel. 9 I began to weep, and to pray unto the Lord that he would deliver me from it. Then I called to mind the word which I had heard; Doubt not, Hermas. 10 Wherefore, brethren, putting on a divine faith, and remembering who it was that had taught me great things, I delivered myself bodily unto the beast. 11 Now the beast came on in such a

394

manner, as if it could at once have devoured a city. 12 I came near unto it, and the beast extended its whole bulk upon the ground, and put forth nothing but its tongue, nor once moved itself till I had quite passed by it. 13 Now the beast had upon its head four colours; first black, then a red and bloody colour, then a golden, and then a white. 14 After that I had passed by it, and was gone forward about thirty feet, behold there met me a certain virgin, well adorned as if she had been just come out of her bride-chamber; all in white, having on white shoes, and a veil down her face, and covered with shining hair. 15 Now I knew by my former visions that it was the church, and thereupon grew the more cheerful. She saluted me, saying, Hail, O Man! I returned the salutation, saying, Lady, Hail! 16 She answering said unto me, Did nothing meet you, O man! I replied, Lady, there met me such a beast, as seemed able to devour a whole people; but by the power of God, and through his singular mercy, I escaped it. 17 Thou didst escape it well, said she, because thou didst cast thy whole care upon God, and opened thy heart unto him, believing that thou couldst be safe by no other than by his great and honourable name. 18 For this cause the Lord sent his angel, who is over the beast, whose name is Hegrin, and stopped his mouth, that he should not devour thee, Thou hast escaped a great trial through thy faith, and because thou didst not doubt for such a terrible beast. 19 Go, therefore, and relate to the elect of God the great things that he hath done for thee. And thou shalt say unto them, that this beast is the figure of the trial that is about to come. 20 If, therefore, ye shall have prepared yourselves, ye may escape it, if your hearts be pure and without spot; and if ye shall serve God all the rest of your days without complaint. 21 Cast all your care upon the Lord, and he will direct them. Believe in God, ye doubtful, because he can do all things; he can both turn away his wrath from you, and send you help and security. 22 Woe to the doubtful, to those who shall hear these words, and shall despise them: it had been better for them that they had not been born. 23 Then I asked her concerning the four colours which the beast had upon its head. But she answered me saying; Again thou art curious in that thou asketh concerning these things. But I said to her, Lady, chew me what they are? 24 Hear, said she; The black which thou sawest denotes the world in which you dwell. The fiery and bloody colour signifies that this age must be destroyed by fire and blood. 25 The golden part are ye, who have escaped out of it; for as gold is tried by the fire, and is made profitable, so are ye also in like manner tried who dwell among the men of this world. 26 They therefore, that shall endure to the end, and be proved by them, shall be purged. And as gold, by this trial, is cleansed and loses its dross, so shall ye also cast away all sorrow and trouble, and be made pure for the building of the tower. 27 But the white colour denotes the time of the world which is to come, in which the elect of God shall dwell: because the elect of God shall be pure and without spot until life eternal. 28 Wherefore do not thou cease to speak these thing in the ears of the saints. Here ye have the figure of the great tribulation that is about to come; which, if you please, shall be nothing to you. 29 When she had spoken thus much, she departed; but I saw not whither she went. But suddenly I heard a noise, and I turned back, being afraid, for I thought that the beast was coming toward me.

The second part of the book of hermas, called his commands..
WHEN I had prayed at home, and was sat down upon the bed, a certain man came in to me with a reverend look, in the habit of a Shepherd, clothed with a white cloak, having his bag upon his back, and his staff in his hand, and saluted me. 2 I returned his salutation, and immediately he sat down by me, and said unto me, I am sent by

that venerable messenger, that I should dwell with thee all the remaining days of thy life. 3 But I thought that he was come to try me, and said unto him, Who are you? For I know to whom I am committed. He said unto me, Do you not know me? I answered no. I am, said he, that shepherd to whose care you are delivered. 4 Whilst he was yet speaking, his shape was changed; and when I knew that it was he to whom I was committed, I was ashamed, and a sudden fear came upon me, and I was utterly overcome with sadness, because I had spoken so foolishly unto him. 5 But he said unto me, Be not ashamed, but receive strength in thy mind, through the commands which I am about to deliver unto thee. For, said he, I am sent to show unto thee all those things again, which thou hast seen before, but especially such of them as may be of most use unto thee. 6 And first of all write my Commands and Similitudes, the rest thou shall so write as I shall show unto thee. But I therefore bid thee first of all write my Commands and Similitudes, that by often reading of them thou mayest the more easily keep them in memory. 7 Whereupon I wrote his Commands and Similitudes, as he bade me. 8 Which things if when you have heard, ye shall observe to do them, and shall walk according to them, and exercise yourselves in them with a pure mind, ye shall receive from the Lord those things which he has promised unto you. 9 But if having heard them ye shall not repent, but shall still go on to add to your sins, ye shall be punished by him. 10 All these things that Shepherd, the angel of repentance, commanded me to write.

Command I Of believing in one God. FIRST of all believe that there is one God who created and brought all things out of nothing into existence. 2 He comprehends all things, and is only infinite, not to be comprehended by any. 3 Who can neither be defined by any words, nor conceived by the mind. 4 Therefore believe in him, and fear him; and fearing him abstain from all evil. 5 Keep these things, and cast all lust and iniquity far from thee, and put on righteousness, and thou shalt live to God, if thou shalt keep his commandment.

Command II That we must avoid detraction, and do our alms-deeds with simplicity. HE said unto me, Be innocent and without disguise; so shalt thou be like an infant who knows no malice which destroys the life of man. 2 Especially see that thou speak evil of none, nor willingly hear any one speak evil of others. 3 For if thou observest not this, thou also who hearest shall be partaker of the sin of him that speaketh evil, by believing the slander, and thou also shalt have sin, because thou believedst him that spoke evil of thy brother. 4 Detraction is a pernicious thing; an inconstant, evil spirit; that never continues in peace, but is always in discord. Wherefore refrain thyself from it, and keep peace ever more with thy brother. 5 Put on an holy constancy, in which there are no sins, but all is full of joy; and do good of thy labours. 6 Give without distinction to all that are in want, not doubting to whom thou givest. 7 But give to all, for God will have us give to all, of all his own gifts. They therefore that receive shall give an account to God, both wherefore they received and for what end. 8 And they that receive without real need, shall give an account for it; but he that gives shall be innocent. 9 For he has fulfilled his duty as he received it from God; not making any choice to whom he should give, and to whom not. And this service he did with simplicity and to the glory of God. 10 Keep therefore this command according as I have delivered it into thee: that thy repentance nay be found to be sincere, and that good may come to thy house; and have a pure heart.

Command III Of avoiding lying, and the repentance of Hermas for his dissimulation. MOREOVER he said unto me love truth; and let all the speech be true which proceeds out of thy mouth. 2 That the spirit which the Lord hath given to dwell in thy flesh may be found true towards all men; and the Lord be glorified, who hath given such

a spirit unto thee: because God is true in all his words, and in him there is no lie. 3 They therefore that lie, deny the Lord, and become robbers of the Lord, not rendering to God what they received from him. 4 For they received the spirit free from lying: If therefore they make that a liar, they defile what was committed to them by the Lord, and become deceivers. 5 When I heard this, I wept bitterly; and when he saw me weeping, he said unto me, Why weepest thou? And I said, Because, sir, I doubt whether I can be saved. 6 He asked me, Wherefore? I replied, Because, sir, I never spake a true word in my life; but always lived in dissimulation, and affirmed a lie for truth to all men; and no man contradicted me, but all gave credit to my words. How then can I live, seeing I have done in this manner? 7 And he said unto me, Thou thinkest well and truly; for thou oughtest, as the servant of God, to have walked in the truth, and not have joined an evil conscience with the spirit of truth, nor have grieved the holy and true Spirit of God. 8 And I replied unto him, Sir, I never before hearkened so diligently to these things. He answered, Now thou hearest them Take care from henceforth, that even those things which thou hast formerly spoken falsely for the sake of thy business, may, by thy present truth receive pardon. 9 For even those things may be forgiven, if for the time to come thou shalt speak the truth; and by so doing thou mayest attain unto life. 10 And whosoever shall hearken unto this command, and do it, and shall depart from all lying, he shall live unto God.

Command IV Of putting away one's wife for adultery. FURTHERMORE, said he, I command thee, that thou keep thyself chaste; and that thou suffer not any thought of any other marriage, or of fornication, to enter into thy heart; for such a thought produces great sin. 2 But be thou at all times mindful of the Lord, and thou shalt never sin. For if such an evil thought should arise in thy heart, then thou shall be guilty of a great sin; and they who do such things, follow the way of death. 3 Look therefore to thyself, and keep thyself from such a thought; for where chastity remains in the heart of a righteous man, there an evil thought ought never to arise. 4 And I said unto him, Sir, suffer me to speak a little to you. He bade me say on. And I answered, Sir, if a man that is faithful in the Lord shall have a wife, and shall catch her in adultery; doth a man sin that continues to live still with her? 5 And he said unto me, As long as he is ignorant of her sin, he commits no fault in living with her; but if a man shall know his wife to, have offended, and she shall not repent of her sin, but go on still in her fornication, and a man shall continue nevertheless to live with her, he shall become guilty of her sin, and partake with her in her adultery. 6 And I said unto him, What therefore is to be done, if the woman continues on in her sin? He answered, Let her husband put her away, and let him continue by himself; but if he shall put away his wife and marry another, he also doth commit adultery. 7 And I said, What, if the woman that is so put away, should repent, and be willing to return to her husband, shall she not be received by him? He said unto me, Yes; and if her husband shall not receive her, he will sin, and commit a great offence against himself; for he ought to receive the offender, if she repents: only not often. 8 For, to the servants of God, there is but one repentance; and for this cause a man that putteth away his wife ought not to take another, because she may repent. 9 This act is alike both in the man and in the woman. Now they commit adultery, not only who pollute their flesh, but who also make an image. If therefore a woman perseveres in any thing of this kind, and repents not, depart from her; and live not with her, otherwise thou also shalt be partaker of her sin. 10 But it is therefore commanded that both the man and the woman should remain unmarried, because such persons may repent. 11 Nor do I in this administer any occasion for the doing of these things; but rather that whoso has offended, should not offend any more. [12] But for their former sins, God who has the power of healing will give a remedy; for he has the power of all things. [13] I asked him again, and said, Seeing the Lord hath thought me worthy that thou shouldest dwell with me continually, speak a few words unto me, because I understand nothing, and my heart is hardened through my former conversation; and open my understanding because I am very dull, and apprehend nothing at all. [14] And he answering said unto me, I am the minister of repentance, and give understanding to all that repent. Does it not seem to thee to be a very wise thing to repent? Because he that does so gets great understanding. [15] For he is sensible that he hath sinned and done wickedly in the sight of the Lord, and he remembers within himself that he has offended, and repents and does no more wickedly, but does that which is good, and humbles his soul and afflicts it, because he has offended. You see therefore that repentance is great wisdom. [16] And I said unto him, For this cause, sir, I inquire diligently into all things, because I am a sinner, that I may know what I must do that I may live; because my sins are many. [17] And he said unto me, Thou shalt live if thou shalt keep these my commandments. And whosoever shall hear and do these commands shall live unto God. [18] And I said unto him, I have even now heard from certain teachers, that there is no other repentance beside that of baptism, when we go down into the water, and receive the forgiveness of our sins; and that after that, we must sin no more, but live in purity. [19] And he said unto me, Thou hast been rightly informed. Never- the-less seeing now thou inquirest diligently into all things, I will manifest this also unto thee; yet not so as to give any occasion of sinning, either to those who shall hereafter believe, or to those who have already believed in the Lord. [20] For neither they who have newly believed, or shall hereafter believe, have any repentance of sins, but forgiveness of them. [21] But as to those who have been called to the faith, and since that are fallen into any gross sin, the Lord hath appointed repentance, because God knoweth the thoughts of all men's hearts, and their infirmities, and the manifold wickedness of the devil, who is always contriving something against the servants of God, and maliciously lays snares for them. [22] Therefore our merciful Lord had compassion towards his creature, and appointed that repentance, and gave unto me the power of it. And therefore I say unto thee, if any one after that great and holy calling shall be tempted by the devil and sin, he has one repentance. But if he shall often sin and repent, it shall not profit such a one; for he shall hardly live unto God. [23] And I said, Sir, I am restored again to life since I have thus diligently hearkened to these commands. For I perceive that if I shall not hereafter add any more of my sins, I shall be saved. [24] And he said, Thou shalt be saved: and so shall all others, as many as shall observe these commandments. [25] And again I said unto him, Sir, seeing thou hearest me patiently, show me yet one thing more. Tell me, saith he, what it is. [26] And I said, If a husband or a wife die, and the party which survives marry again, does he sin in so doing? He that marries says he, sins not: howbeit, if he shall remain single, he shall thereby gain to himself great honour before the Lord. [27] Keep therefore thy chastity and modesty, and thou shalt live unto God. Observe from hence forth those things which I speak with thee, and command thee to observe, from the time that I have been delivered unto thee, and dwell in thy house. [28] So shall thy former sins be forgiven, if thou shalt keep these my commandments. And in like manner shall all others be forgiven, who shall observe these my commandments.

Command V Of the sadness of the heart, and of patience. Be patient, says he, and long- suffering; so shalt thou have dominion over all wicked works, and shall fulfil all righteousness. [2] For if thou shalt be patient, the Holy Spirit which dwelleth in thee shall be pure,

and not be darkened by any evil spirit; but being full of joy shall be enlarged, and feast in the body in which it dwells, and serve the Lord with joy, and in great peace. [3] But if any anger shall overtake thee, presently the Holy Spirit which is in thee will be straightened and seek to depart from thee. [4] For he is choked by the evil spirit, and has not the liberty of serving the Lord as he would; for he is grieved by anger. When, therefore, both these spirits dwell together, it is destructive to a man. [5] As if one should take a little wormwood, and put it into a vessel of honey, the whole honey would be spoiled; and a great quantity of honey is corrupted by a very little wormwood, and loses the sweetness of honey, and is no longer acceptable to its Lord because the whole honey is made bitter, and loses its use. [6] But if no wormwood be put into the honey, it is sweet and profitable to its Lord. Thus is forbearance sweeter than honey, and profitable to the Lord who dwelleth in it. [7] But anger is unprofitable. If therefore anger shall be mixed with forbearance, the soul is distressed, and its prayer is not profitable with God. [8] And I said unto him, Sir, I would know the sinfulness of anger, that I may keep myself from it. And he said unto me, Thou shall know it; and if thou shalt not keep thyself from it, thou shalt lose thy hope with all thy house. Wherefore depart from it. [9] For I the messenger of righteousness am with thee, and all that depart from it: as many as shall repent with all their hearts, shall live unto God; and I will be with them, and will keep them all. [10] For all such as have repented have been justified by the most holy messenger, who is a minister of salvation. [11] And now, says he, hear the wickedness of anger; how evil and hurtful is is, and how it overthrows the servants of God; for it cannot hurt those that are full of faith because the power of God is with them; but it overthrows the doubtful, and those that are destitute of faith. [12] For as often as it sees such men, it casts itself into their hearts; and so a man or woman is in bitterness for nothing: for the things of life, or for sustenance, or for a vain word, if any should chance to fall in; or by reason of any friend, or for a debt, or for any other superfluous things of the like nature. [13] For these things are foolish, and superfluous, and vain to the servants of God. But equanimity is strong, and forcible; and of great power, and sitteth in great enlargement; is cheerful, rejoicing in peace; and glorifying God at all times I with meekness. [14] And this long-suffering dwells with those that are full of faith. But anger is foolish, and light, and empty. Now bitterness is bred through folly; by bitterness, anger; by anger, fury; and this fury arising from so many evil principles, worketh a great and incurable sin. [15] For when all these things, are in the same man in which the Holy Spirit dwells, the vessel cannot contain them, but runs over: and because the Spirit being tender cannot tarry with the evil one; it departs and dwells with him that is meek. [16] When, therefore, it is departed from the man in whom it dwelt, that man becomes destitute of the Holy Spirit, and is afterwards filled with wicked spirits, and is blinded with evil thoughts. Thus doth it happen to all angry men. [17] Wherefore depart then from anger, and put on equanimity, and resist: wrath; so then shalt be found with modesty and chastity by God. Take good heed, therefore, that thou neglect not this commandment. [18]. For if thou shalt obey this command, then thou shalt also be able to observe the other commandments which I shall command thee. [19] Wherefore strengthen thyself now in these commands, that then mayest live unto God. And whosoever shall observe these commandments shall live unto God.

Command VI That every man has two angels and of the suggestions of both. I COMMANDED thee, said he, in my first commandments, that thou shouldst keep faith and fear, and repentance. Yes, sir, said I. [2] He continued. But now I will shew thee the virtues of these commands, that then mayest know their effects; how they are prescribed alike to the just and unjust. [3] Do thou therefore believe the righteous, but give no credit to the unrighteous. For righteousness keepeth the right way, but unrighteousness the wicked way. 4 Do thou therefore keep the right way, and leave that which is evil. For the evil way has not a good end, but hath many stumbling- blocks; it is rugged and full of thorns, and leads to destruction; and it is hurtful to all such as walk in it. 5 But they who go in the right way walk with evenness, and without offence; because it is not rough nor thorny. 6 Thou seest therefore how it is best to walk in this way. Thou shalt therefore go, says he, and all others, as many as believe in God with all their heart, shall go through it. 7 And now, says he, I understand first of all what belongs to faith. There are two angels with man; one of righteousness, the other of iniquity. 8 And I said unto him, Sir, how shall I know that there are two such angels with man? Hear, says he, and understand. 9 The angel of righteousness, is mild and modest, and gentle, and quiet. When, therefore, he gets into thy heart, immediately he talks with thee of righteousness, of modesty, of chastity, of bountifulness, of forgiveness, of charity, and piety. 10 When all these things come into thy heart, know then that the angel of righteousness is with thee. Wherefore hearken to this angel and to his works. 11 Learn also the works of the angel of iniquity. He is first of all bitter, and angry, and foolish; and his works are pernicious, and overthrow the servants of God. When therefore these things come into thine heart; thou shalt know by his works, that this is the angel of iniquity. 12 And I said unto him, Sir, how shall I understand these things? Hear, says he, and understand; When anger overtakes thee, or bitterness, know that he is in thee: 13 As also, when the desire of many things, and of the best meats, and of drunkenness; when the love of what belongs to others, pride, and much speaking, and ambition; and the like things, come upon thee. 14 When therefore these things arise in thine heart, know that the angel of iniquity is with thee. Seeing therefore thou knowest his works, depart from them all, and give no credit to him: because his works are evil, and become not the servants of God. 15 Here therefore thou hast the works of both these angels. Understand now and believe the angel of righteousness, because his instruction is good. 16 For let a man be never so happy; yet if the thoughts of the other angel arise in his heart, that man or woman must needs sin. 17 But let man or woman be never so wicked, if the works of the angel of righteousness come into their hearts, that man or woman must needs do some good. 18 Thou seest therefore how it is good to follow the angel of righteousness. If therefore thou shall follow him, and submit to his works, thou shalt live unto God. And as many as shall submit to his work shall live also unto God.

Command VII That we must fear God but not the Devil. FEAR God, says he, and keep his commandments. For if thou keepest his commandments thou shalt be powerful in every work, and all thy works shall be excellent. For by fearing God, thou shalt do everything well. 2 This is that fear with which thou must be affected that thou mayest be saved. But fear not the Devil: for if thou fearest the Lord, thou shalt have dominion over him; because there is no power in him. 3 Now if there be no power in him, then neither is he to be feared: for every one that has power, is to be feared. But he that has no power is despised by every one. 4 Fear the works of the Devil, because they are evil. For by fearing the Lord, thou wilt fear and do not the works of the Devil, but keep thyself from them. 5 There is therefore a twofold fear; if thou wilt not do evil, fear the Lord and thou shalt not do it. But if thou wilt do good, the fear of the Lord is strong, and great and glorious. 6 Wherefore, fear God and thou shalt live: and whosoever shall fear him, and keep his commandments, their life is with the Lord. But they who keep them not, neither is there life in them.

Command VIII That we must flee from evil, and do good works. I HAVE told thee, said he, that there are two kinds of creatures of the Lord, and that there is a two-fold abstinence. From some things therefore thou must abstain, and from others not. 2 I answered, Declare to me, sir, from what I must abstain, and from what not. Hearken, said he, Keep thyself from evil, and do it not; yet abstain not from good, but do it. For if thou shalt abstain from what is good, and not do it, thou shalt sin. Abstain therefore from all evil, and thou shalt know all righteousness. 3 I said, What evil things are they from which I must abstain? Hearken, said he; from adultery, from drunkenness, from riots, from excess of eating, from daintiness and dishonesty, from pride, from fraud, from lying, from detraction, from hypocrisy, from remembrance of injuries, and from all evil speaking. 4 For these are the works of iniquity, from which the servant of God must abstain. For he that cannot keep himself from these things, cannot live unto God. 5 But hear, said he, what follows of these kind of things: for indeed many more there are from which the servant of God must abstain. From theft, and cheating; from false witness, from covetousness, from boasting, and all other things of the like nature. 6 Do these things seem to thee to be evil or not? Indeed they are very evil to the servants of God, Wherefore the servant of God must abstain from all these works. 7 Keep thyself therefore from them, that thou mayest live unto God, and be written among those that abstain from them. And thus have I shown thee what things thou must avoid: now learn from what thou must not abstain. 8 Abstain not from any good works, but do them. Hear, said he, what the virtue of those good works is which thou must do, that thou mayest be saved. The first of all is faith; the fear of the Lord; charity; concord; equity; truth; patience; chastity. 9 There is nothing better than these things in the life of men; who shall keep and do these things in their life. Hear next what follow these. 10 To minister to the widows; not to despise the fatherless and poor; to redeem the servants of God from necessity; to be hospitable (for in hospitality there is sometimes great fruit); not to be contentious, but be quiet. 11 To be humble above all men; to reverence the aged; to labour to be righteous; to respect the brotherhood; to bear affronts; to be long-suffering; not to cast away those that have fallen from the faith, but to convert them, and make them be of good cheer: to admonish sinners; not to oppress those that are our debtors; and all other things of a like kind. 12 Do these things seem to thee to be good or not? And I said, What can be better than these words? Live then, said he, in these commandments, and do not depart from them. For if thou shalt keep all these commandments, thou shalt live unto God. And all they that shall keep these commandments shall live unto God.

Command IX That we must ask of God daily; and without doubting. AGAIN he said unto me; remove from thee all doubting; and question nothing at all when thou askest any thing of the Lord; saying within thyself, how shall I be able to ask any thing of the Lord and receive it, seeing I have so greatly sinned against him? 2 Do not think thus, but turn unto the Lord with all thy heart, and ask of him without doubting, and thou shalt know the mercy of the Lord; bow that he will not forsake thee, but will fulfil the request of thy soul. 3 For God is not as men, mindful of the injuries he has received; but he forgets injuries, and has compassion upon his creature. 4 Wherefore purify thy heart from all the vices of this present world; and observe the commands I have before delivered unto thee from God; and thon shall receive whatsoever good things thou shalt ask, and nothing shall be wanting unto thee of all thy petitions; if thou shalt ask of the Lord without doubting. 5 But they that are not such, shall obtain none of those things which they ask. For they that are full of faith, ask all things with confidence, and receive from the Lord, because they ask without doubting. But he that doubts, shall hardly live unto God, except he repent. 6 Wherefore purify thy heart from doubting, and put on faith, and trust in God, and thou shall receive all that thou shalt ask. But if thou shouldest chance to ask something, and not immediately receive it, yet do not therefore doubt, because thou hast not presently received the petition of thy soul. 7 For it may be thou shalt not presently receive it for thy trial, or else for some sin which thou knowest not. But do not thou leave off to ask, and then thou shalt receive. Else if thou shalt cease to ask, thou must complain of thyself, and not of God, that he has not given unto thee what thou didst desire. 8 Consider therefore this doubting how cruel and pernicious it is; and how it utterly roots out many from the faith, who were very faithful and firm. For this doubting is the daughter of the Devil, and deals very wickedly with the servants of God. 9 Despise it therefore, and thou shalt rule over it on every occasion. Put on a firm and powerful faith: for faith promises all things and perfects all things. But doubting will not believe that it shall obtain any thing by all that it can do. 10. Thou seest therefore, says he, how faith cometh from above from God; and hath great power. But doubting is an earthly spirit, and proceedeth from the Devil, and has no strength. 11 Do thou therefore keep the virtue of faith, and depart from doubting, in which is no virtue, and thou shalt live unto God. And all shall live unto God, as many as do these things.

Command X Of the sadness of the heart; and that we must take, heed not to grieve the spirit of God that is in us. PUT all sadness far from thee; for it is the sister of doubting and of anger. How, sir, said I is it the sister of these? For sadness, and anger, and doubting, seem to me to be very different from one another. 2 And he answered: Art thou without sense that thou dost not understand it? For sadness is the most mischievous of all spirits, and the worst to the servants of God: It destroys the spirits of all men, and torments the Holy Spirit, and it saves again. 3 Sir, said I, I am very foolish, and understand not these things. I cannot apprehend how it can torment, and yet save. Hear, said he, and understand. They who never sought out the truth, nor inquired concerning the majesty of God, but only believed, are involved in the affairs of the heathen. 4 And there is another lying prophet that destroys the minds of the servants of God; that is of those that are doubtful, not of those that fully trust in the Lord. Now those doubtful persons come to him, as to a divine spirit, and inquire of him what shall befall them. 5 And this lying prophet, having no power in him of the Divine Spirit, answers them according to their demands, and fills their souls with promises according as they desire. Howbeit that prophet is vain, and answers vain things to those who are themselves vain. 6 And whatsoever is asked of him by vain men, he answers them vainly; nevertheless he speaketh some things truly. For the Devil fills him with his spirit, that he may overthrow some of the righteous. 7 Whosoever therefore are strong in the faith of the Lord, and have put on the truth; they are not joined to such spirits, but depart from them. But they that are doubtful, and often repenting, like the heathens, consult them, and heap up to themselves great sin, serving idols. 8 As many therefore as are such, inquire of them upon every occasion; worship idols, and are foolish; and void of the truth. For every spirit that is given from God needs not to be asked: but having the power of divinity speaks all things of itself, because he comes from above; from the power of God. 10 But he, that being asked speaks according to men's desires and concerning many other affairs of this present world, understands not the tidings which relate unto God. For these spirits are darkened through such affairs, and corrupted, and broken. 11 As good vines if they are neglected, are oppressed with weeds and

398

thorns, and at last killed by them; so are the men who believe such spirits. 12 They fall into many actions and businesses, and are void of sense, and when they think of things pertaining unto God, they understand nothing at all; but at any time they chance to hear any thing concerning the Lord, their thoughts are upon their business. 13 But they that have the fear of the Lord, and search out the truth concerning God, having all their thoughts towards the Lord; apprehend whatsoever is said to them, and forthwith understand it, because they have the fear of the Lord in them. 14 For where the spirit of the Lord dwells, there is also much understanding added. Wherefore join thyself to the Lord, and thou shalt understand all things. 15 Learn now, O unwise man! how sadness troubleth the Holy Spirit, and how it saves. When a man that is doubtful is engaged in any affair, and does not accomplish it by reason of his doubting; this sadness enters into him, and grieves the Holy Spirit, and makes him sad. 16 Again anger, when it over. takes any man for any business he is greatly moved; and then again sadness entereth into the heart of him, who was moved with anger, and he is troubled for what he hath done, and repenteth, because he hath done amiss. 17 This sadness therefore seemeth to bring salvation, because he repenteth of his evil deed. But both the other things, namely, doubting and sadness, such as before was mentioned, vex the spirit: doubting, because his work did not succeed; and sadness, because he angered the Holy Spirit. 18 Remove therefore sadness from thyself, and afflict not the Holy Spirit which dwelleth in thee, lest he entreat God, and depart from thee. For the spirit of the Lord which is given to dwell in the flesh, endureth no such sadness. 19 Wherefore clothe thyself with cheerfulness, which has always favour with the Lord, and thou shalt rejoice in it. For every cheerful man does well; and relishes those things that are good, and despises sadness. 20 But the sad man does always wickedly. First, he doth wickedly, because he grieveth the Holy Spirit, which is given to man being of a cheerful nature. And again he does ill, because be prays with sadness unto the Lord, and maketh not first a thankful acknowledgment unto him of former mercies, and obtains not of God what he asks. 21 For the prayer of a sad man has not always efficacy to come up to the altar of God. And I said unto him, Sir, why has not the prayer of a sad man virtue to come up to the altar of God? Because, said he, that sadness remaineth in his heart. 22 When therefore a man's prayer shall be accompanied with sadness, it will not suffer his requests to ascend pure to the altar of God. For as wine when it is mingled with vinegar, has not the sweetness it had before; so sadness being mixed with the Holy Spirit, suffers not a man's prayer to be the same as it would be otherwise. 23 Wherefore cleanse thyself from sadness, which is evil, and thou shalt live unto God. And all others shall live unto God, as many as shall lay aside sadness, and put on cheerfulness.

Command XI That the spirits and prophets are to be tried by their works; and of a twofold, spirit. HE showed me certain men sitting upon benches, and one sitting in a chair: and he said unto me; Seest thou those who sit upon the benches? Sir, said I, I see them. He answered, They are the faithful; and he who sits in the chair is an earthly spirit. 2 For he cometh not into the assembly of the faithful, but avoids it. But he joins himself to the doubtful and empty; and prophesies to them in corners and hidden places; and pleases them by speaking according to all the desires of their hearts. 3 For he placing himself among empty vessels, is not broken, but the one fitteth the other. But when he cometh into the company of just men, who are full of the spirit of God, and they pray unto the Lord; that man is emptied, because that earthly spirit flies from him, and he is dumb, and cannot speak anything. 4 As if in a store-house you shall stop up wine or oil, and among those vessels place an empty jar; and when afterwards you come to open it, you shall find it empty as you stopped it up; so those empty prophets when they come among the spirits of the just, are found to be such as they came. 5 I said, How then shall a man be able to discern them? Consider what I am going to say concerning both kinds of men; and as I speak unto thee so shalt thou prove the prophet of God, and the false prophet. 6 And first try the man who hath the spirit of God, because the spirit which is from above is humble, and quiet, and departs from all wickedness; and from the vain desires of the present world; and makes himself more humble than all men; and answers to none when he is asked; nor to every one singly: for the Spirit of God doth not speak to a man when he will, but when God pleases. 7 When therefore a man who hath the Spirit of God hath come into the church of the righteous, who have the faith of God, and they pray unto the Lord; then the holy angel of God fills that man with the blessed Spirit, and he speaks in the congregation as he is moved of God. 8 Thus therefore is the spirit, of God known, because whosoever speaketh by the Spirit of God, speaketh as the Lord will. 9 Hear now concerning the earthly spirit, which is empty and foolish, and without virtue. And first of all the man who is supposed to have the Spirit, (whereas he hath it not in reality), exalteth himself, and desires to have the first seat, and is wicked, and full of words. 10 And spends his time in pleasure, and in all manner of voluptuousness, and receives the reward of his divination; which if he receives not, he does not divine. 11 Should the Spirit of God receive reward, and divine? It doth not become a prophet of God so to do. 12 Thus you seethe life of each of these kind of prophets. Wherefore prove that man by his life and works, who says that he hath the Holy Spirit. And believe the Spirit which comes from God, and has power as such. But believe not the earthly and empty spirit, which is from the devil, in whom there is no faith nor virtue. 13 Hear now the similitude which I am about to speak unto thee. Take a stone, and throw it up towards heaven; or take a spout of water, and mount it up thitherward; and see if thou canst reach unto heaven. 14 Sir; said I, how can this be done? For neither of those things which you have mentioned, are possible to be done. And he answered, Therefore as these things cannot be done, so is the earthy spirit without virtue, and without effect. 15 Understand yet farther the power which cometh from above, in this similitude. The grains of hail that drop down are exceedingly small; and yet when they fall upon the head of a man, how do they cause pain to it. 16 And again, consider, the droppings of a house; how the little drops falling upon the earth, work a hollow in the stones. 17 So in like manner the least things which come from above, and fall upon the earth, have great force. Wherefore join thyself to this spirit, which has the power; and depart from the other which is empty.

Command XII Of a two fold desire: that the commands of God, are not impossible: and that the devil is not to be feared by them that believe. AGAIN he said unto me; remove from thee all evil desires, and put on good and holy desires. For having put on a good desire, thou shalt hate that which is evil, and bridle it as thou wilt. But an evil desire is dreadful, and hard to be tamed. 2 It is very horrible and wild; and by its wildness consumes men. And especially if a servant of God shall chance to fall into it, except he be very wise, he is ruined by it. For it destroys those who have not the garment of a good desire and are engaged in the affairs of this present world; and delivers them unto death. 3 Sir, said I, what are the works of an evil desire, which bring men unto death? Shew them to me that I may depart from them. Hear, said he, by what works an evil desire bringeth the servants of God unto death. 4 First of all, it is an evil desire to covet another man's wife, or for a woman to covet another's husband; as also to desire the dainties of riches; and

multitude of superfluous meats; and drunkenness; and many delights. 5 For in much delicacy there is folly; and many pleasures are needless to the servants of God. Such lusting therefore is evil and pernicious, which brings to death the servants of God. For all such lusting is from the devil. 6 Whosoever therefore shall depart from all evil desires, shall live unto God; but they that are subject unto them shall die forever. For this evil lusting is deadly. Do thou therefore put on the desire of righteousness, and being armed with the fear of the Lord resist all wicked lusting. 7 For this fear dwelleth in good desires; and, when evil coveting shall see thee armed with the fear of the Lord, and resisting it; it will fly far from thee, and not appear before thee, but be afraid of thy armour. 8 And thou shall have the victory, and be crowned for it; and shall attain to that desire which is good; and shall give the victory which thou hast obtained unto God, and shall serve him in doing what thou thyself wouldest do. 9 For if thou shalt serve good desires, and be subject to them; then thou shalt be able to get the dominion over thy wicked lustings; and they will be subject to thee, as thou wilt. 10 And I said, Sir, I would know how to serve that desire which is good? Hearken, said he, Fear God, and put thy trust in him, and love truth, and righteousness, and do that which is good. 10 If thou shalt do these things, thou shall be an approved servant of God, and serve him; and all others who shall in like manner serve a good desire, shall live unto God. 12 And when he had fulfilled these twelve commands, he said unto me, Thou hast now these commands, walk in them; and exhort those that hear them, to repent, and that they keep their repentance pure all the remaining days of their life. 13 And fulfil diligently this ministry which I commit to thee, and thou shalt receive great advantage by it, and find favour with all such as shall repent and believe thy words. For I am with thee, and will force them to believe. 14 And I said unto him, Sir, these commands are great and excellent, and able to cheer the heart of that man that shall be able to keep them. But, Sir, I cannot tell, whether they can be observed by any man? 15 He answered, Thou shalt easily keep these commands, and they shall not be hard: howbeit, if thou shalt suffer it once to enter into thine heart that they cannot be kept by any one, thou shalt not fulfil them. 16 But now I say unto thee, if thou shalt not observe these commands, and shall neglect them, thou shalt not be saved, nor thy children, nor thy house: because thou hast judged that these commands cannot be kept by man. 17 These things he spake very angrily unto me, insomuch that he greatly affrighted me, for he changed his countenance so that a man could not bear his anger. 18 And when he saw me altogether troubled and confounded, he began to speak more moderately and cheerfully, saying, O foolish, and without understanding! 19 Unconstant, not knowing the majesty of God how great and wonderful he is; who created the world for man, and hath made every creature subject unto him; and given him all power, that he should be able to fulfil all these commands. 20 He is able, said he, to fulfil all these commands, who has the Lord in his heart; but they who have the Lord only in their mouths, their hearts are hardened, and they are far from the Lord: to such persons these commands are hard and difficult. 21 Therefore, ye that are empty and light in the faith, put the Lord your God in your hearts; and ye shall perceive how that nothing is more easy than these commands, nor more pleasant, nor more gentle and holy. 22 And turn yourselves to the Lord your God, and forsake the devil and his pleasures, because they are evil, and bitter, and impure. And fear not the devil, because he has no power over you. 23 For I am with you, the messenger of repentance, who have the dominion over him. The devil doth indeed affright men but his terror is vain. Wherefore fear him not, and he will flee from you. 24 And I said unto him; Sir, hear me speak a few words unto you. He answered, Say on: A man indeed desires to keep the commandments of God, and there is no one but what prays unto God, that he may be able to keep his commandments; 25 But the devil is hard, and by his power rules over the servants of God. And he said; He cannot rule over the servants of God, who trust in him with all their hearts. 26 The devil may strive, but he cannot overcome them. 27 For if ye resist him, he will flee away with confusion from you. But they that are not full in the faith, fear the devil, as if he had some great power. For the devil tries the servants of God and if he finds them empty, he destroys them. 28 For as man, when he fills up vessels with good wine, and among them puts a few vessels half full, and comes to try and taste of the vessels, doth not try those that are full, because he knows that they are good, but tastes those that are half full, lest they should grow sour; (for vessels half full soon grow sour, and lose the taste of wine:) so the devil comes to the servants of God to try them. 29 They that are full of faith resist him stoutly, and he departs from them, because he finds no place where to enter into them then he goes to those that are not full of faith, and because he has a place of entrance he goes into them, and does what he will with them, and they become his servants. 30 But I, the messenger of repentance, say unto you, fear not the devil, for I am sent unto you, that I may be with you, as many as shall repent with your whole heart, and that I may confirm you in the faith. 31 Believe therefore, ye who by reason of your transgressions have forgot God. and your own salvation; and adding to your sins have made your life very heavy. 32 That if ye shall turn to the Lord with your whole hearts, and shall serve him according to his will; he will heal you of your former sins, and ye shall have dominion over all the works of the devil. 33 Be not then afraid in the least of his threatenings, for they are without force, as the nerves of a dead man. But hearken unto me, and fear the Lord Almighty, who is able to save and to destroy you; and keep his commands, that ye may live unto God. 34 And I said unto him; Sir, I am now confirmed in all the commands of the Lord whilst you are with me, and I know that you will break all the powers of the devil. 35 And we also shall overcome him, if we shall be able, through the help of the Lord, to keep these commands which you have delivered. 36 Thou shalt keep them, said he, if thou shalt purify thy heart towards the Lord. And all they also shall keep them who shall cleanse their hearts from the vain desires of the present world, and shall live unto God.

The third part of thebook of hermas, called his similitudes.
Similitude I That seeing we have no abiding city in this world, we ought to look after that which is to come. AND he said onto me; Ye know that ye who are the servants of the Lord, live here as in a pilgrimage; for your city is far off from this city. 2 If, therefore, ye know your city in which ye are to dwell, why do ye here buy estates, and provide yourselves with delicacies, and stately buildings, and supurfluous houses? For he that provides himself these things in this city, does not think of returning into his own city. 3 O foolish, and doubtful, and wretched man; who understandest not that all these things belong to other men, and are under the power of another. For the Lord of this city saith unto thee; Either obey my laws, or depart out of my city. 4 What therefore shalt thou do who art subject to a law in thine own city? Canst thou for thy estate, or for any of those things which thou hast provided, deny thy law? But if thou shalt deny it, and wilt afterwards return into thy own city, thou shalt not be received, but shall be excluded thence. 5 See therefore, that like a man in another country, thou procure no more to thyself than what is necessary, and sufficient for thee; and be ready, that when the God or Lord of this city shall drive thee out of it thou mayest oppose his law, and go into thine own city; where thou mayest with

all cheerfulness live according to thine own law with no wrong. 6 Take heed therefore ye that serve God, and have him in your hearts: work ye the works of God, being mindful both of his commands and of his promises, which he has promised; and be assured that he will make them good unto you; if ye shall keep his commandments. 7 Instead therefore of the possessions that ye would otherwise purchase, redeem those that are in want from their necessities, as every one is able; justify the widows; judge the cause of the fatherless; and spend your riches and your wealth in such works as these. 8 For this end has God enriched you, that ye might fulfil these kind of services. It is much better to do this, than to buy lands or houses; because all such things shall perish with this present time. 9 But what ye shall do for the name of the Lord, ye shall find in your city, and shall have joy without sadness or fear. Wherefore covet not the riches of the heathen; for they are destructive to the servants of God. 10 But trade with your own riches which you possess, by which ye may attain unto everlasting joy. 11 And do not commit adultery, nor touch any other man's wife, nor desire her; but covet that which is thy own business, and thou shalt be saved.
Similitude II As the vine is supported by the elm, so is the rich man helped by the prayers of the poor. AS I was walking into the field, and considered the elm and the vine, and thought with myself of their fruits, an angel appeared unto me, and said unto me; What is it that thou thinkest upon thus long within thyself? 2 And I said unto him, Sir, I think of this vine and this elm because their fruits are fair. And he said unto me; These two trees are set for a pattern to the servants of God. 3 And I said unto him, Sir, I would know in what the pattern of these trees which thou mentionest, does consist. Hearken, saith he; seest thou this vine and this elm? Sir, said I, I see them. 4 This vine, saith he, is fruitful, but the elm is a tree without fruit. Nevertheless this vine unless it were set by this elm, and supported by it, would not bear much fruit; but lying along upon the ground, would bear but ill fruit, because it did not hang upon the elm; whereas, being supported upon the elm, it bears fruit both for itself and for that. 5 See, therefore, how the elm gives no less, but rather more fruit, than the vine. How, Sir, said I, does it bear more fruit than the vine? Because, said he, the vine being supported upon the elm gives both much and good fruit; whereas, if it lay along upon the ground, it would bear but little, and that very ill too. 6 This similitude, therefore, is set forth to the servants of God; and it represents the rich and poor man. I answered, Sir, make this manifest unto me. Hear, said he; the rich man has wealth: howbeit towards the Lord he is poor; for he is taken up about his riches, and prays but little to the Lord; and the prayers which he makes are lazy and without force. 7 When therefore, the rich man reaches out to the poor those things which he wants, the poor man prays unto the Lord for the rich; and God grants unto the rich man all good things, because the poor man is rich in prayer; and his requests have great power with the Lord. 8 Then the rich man ministers all thing to the poor, because he perceives that he is heard by the Lord; and he the more willingly and without doubting, affords him what he wants, and takes care that nothing be lacking to him. 9 And the poor man gives thanks unto the Lord for the rich; because they both do their work from the Lord. 10 With men, therefore, the elm is not thought to give any fruit; and they know not, neither understand that its company being added to the vine, the vine bears a double increase, both for itself and for the elm. 11 Even so the poor praying unto the Lord for the rich, are heard by him; and their riches are increased, because they minister to the poor of their wealth. They are, therefore, both made partakers of each other's good works. 12 Whosoever, therefore, shall do these things, he shall not be forsaken by the Lord, but shall be written in the book of

life. [13] Happy are they who are rich, and perceive themselves to be increased: for he that is sensible of this, will be able to minister somewhat to others.

Similitude III As the greet trees in the winter cannot be distinguished from the dry; so neither can the righteous from the wicked in this present world. AGAIN he showed me many trees whose leaves were shed, and which seemed to me to be withered, for they were all alike. And he said unto me, Seest thou these trees? I said, Sir, I see that they look like dry trees. [2] He answering, said unto me; These trees are like unto the men who live in the present world. I replied: Sir, why are they like unto dried trees? Because, said he, neither the righteous, nor unrighteous, are known from one another; but all are alike in this present world. [3] For this world is as the winter to the righteous men, because they are not known, but dwell among sinners. [4] As in the winter all the trees having lost their leaves, are like dry trees; nor can it be discerned which are dry and which are green: so in this present world neither the righteous, nor wicked are discerned from each other; but they are all alike.

Similitude IV As in the summer the living trees are distinguished from the dry by their fruit and green leaves; so in the world to come the righteous shall be distinguished from the unrighteous by their happiness. AGAIN he showed me many other trees, of which some had leaves, and others appeared dry and withered. And he said unto me, Seest thou these trees I answered, Sir, I see them; some are dry, and others full of leaves. [2] These trees, saith be, which are green, are the righteous, who shall possess the world to come. For the world to come, is the summer to the righteous; but to sinners it is the winter. [3] When, therefore, the mercy of the Lord shall shine forth, then they who serve God shall be made manifest, and plain unto all. For as in the summer the fruit of every tree is shown and made manifest. so also the works of the righteous shall be declared and made manifest, and they shall all be restored in that world merry and joyful. [4] For the other kind of men, namely the wicked, like the trees which thou rawest dry, shall, as such, be found dry and without fruit in that other world; and like dry wood shall be burnt; and it shall be made manifest that they have done evil all the time of their life; [5] And they shall be burnt because they have sinned and have not repented of their sins. And also all the other nations shall be burnt, because they have not acknowledged God their Creator. [6] Do then, therefore, bring forth good fruit, that in the summer thy fruit may be known; and keep thyself from much business, and thou shalt not offend. For they who are involved in much business, sin much; because they are taken up with their affairs, and serve not God. [7] And how can a man that does not serve God, ask anything of God, and receive it? But they who serve him, ask and receive what they desire. [8] But if a man has only one thing to follow, he may serve God, because his mind is not taken off from God, but he serves him with a pure mind. [9] If, therefore, thou shalt do this, thou mayest have fruit in the world to come; and as many as shall do in like manner, shall bring forth fruit.

Similitude V Of a true fast, and the rewards of it: also of the cleanliness of the body. AS I was fasting, and sitting down in a certain mountain, and giving thanks unto God for all the things that he had done unto me; behold, I saw the Shepherd, who was wont to converse with me, sitting by me, and saying unto me: What has brought thee hither thus early in the morning? I answered, Sir, to-day I keep a station. [2] He answered, What is a station; I replied, it is a fast. He said, What is that fast? I answered, I fast as I have been wont to do. Ye know not, said he, what it is to fast unto God; nor is this a fast which ye keep, profiting nothing with God. [3] Sir, said I, what makes you speak thus? He replied, I speak it, because it is not the true fast which you think that you keep; but I will show you what

that is which is a complete fast, and acceptable unto God. [4] Hearken, said he, The Lord does not desire such a needless fast; for by fasting in this manner, thou advancest nothing in righteousness. [5] But the true fast is this: Do nothing wickedly in thy life, but serve God with a pure mind; and keep his commandments, and walk according to his precepts, nor suffer any wicked desire to enter into the mind. [6] But trust in the Lord, that if thou dost these things, any fearest him, and abstaineth from every evil work, thou shall live unto God. [7] If thou shalt do this, thou shall perfect a great fast, and an acceptable one unto the Lord. [8] Hearken unto the similitude which I am about to propose unto thee, as to this matter. [9] A certain man having a farm, and many servants, planted a vineyard in a certain part of his estate for his posterity: [10] And taking a journey into a far country, chose one of his servants which he thought the most faithful and approved, and delivered the vineyard into his care; commanding him that he should stake up the vines. Which if he did, and fulfilled his command, he promised to give him his liberty. Nor did he command him to do any thing more; and so went into a far country. [11] And after that servant had taken that charge upon him, he did whatsoever his lord commanded him. And when he had staked the vineyard, and found it to be full of weeds, he began to think within himself, saying: [12] I have done what my lord commanded me, I will now dig this vineyard, and when it is digged, it will be more beautiful; and the weeds being pulled up, it will bring forth more fruit and not be choked by the weeds. [13] So setting about this work he digged it, and plucked up all the weeds that were in it; and so the vineyard became very beautiful and prosperous, not being choked with weeds. [14] After some time the lord of the vineyard comes and goes into the vineyard, and when he saw that it was handsomely staked and digged, and the weeds plucked up that were in it, and the vines flourishing, he rejoiced greatly at the care of his servant. [15] And calling his son whom he loved, and who was to be his heir, and his friends with whom he was wont to consult; he tells them what he had commanded his servant to do, and what his servant had done more; and they immediately congratulated that servant, that he had received so full a testimony from his lord. [16] Then he said to them, I indeed promised this servant his liberty, if he observed the command which I gave him; and he observed it, and besides has done a good work to my vineyard, which has exceedingly pleased me. [17] Wherefore, for this work which he hath done, I will make him my heir together with my son; because that when he saw what was good, he neglected it not, but did it. [18] This design of the lord both his son and his friends approved, namely, that his servant should be heir together with his son. [19] Not long after this the master of the family calling together, his friends, sent from his supper several kinds of food to that servant. [20] Which when he had received, he took so much of them as was sufficient for himself, and divided the rest among his fellow-servants. [21] Which when they had received, they rejoiced; and wished that he might find yet greater favour with his lord, for what he had done to them. [22] When his lord heard all these things, he was again filled with great joy: and calling again his friends and his son together, he related to them what his servant had done with the meats which he had sent unto him. [23] They therefore so much the more assented to the master of the household; and he ought to make that servant his heir together with his son. [24] I said unto him, sir, I know not these smilitudes, neither can I understand them, unless you expound them unto me. I will, says he, expound, all things unto thee whatsoever I have talked with thee, or shown unto thee. [25] Keep the commandments of the Lord and thou shalt be approved, and shall be written in the number of those that keep his commandments. But if besides those things which the Lord hath commanded, thou shalt add some good thing; thou shall purchase to thyself a greater dignity, and be in more favour with the Lord than thou shouldst otherwise have been. ²⁶ If therefore thou shalt keep the commandments of the Lord, and shalt add to them these stations, thou shall rejoice; but especially if thou shalt keep them according to my commands. ²⁷ I said unto him, sir, whatsoever thou shah command me, I will observe; for I know that thou wilt be with me. I will, said he, be with thee who hast taken up such a resolution; and I will be with all those who purpose in like manner. ²⁸ This fast, saith he, whilst thou dost also observe the commandments of the Lord, is exceeding good; therefore thus shalt thou keep it. ²⁹ First of all, take heed to thyself, and keep thyself from every wicked act, and from every filthy word, and from every hurtful desire; and purify thy mind from all the vanity of this present world. If thou shalt observe these things, this fast shall be right. ³⁰ Thus therefore do. Having performed what is before written, that day on which thou fastest thou shalt taste nothing at all but bread and water; and computing the quantity of food which thou art want to eat upon other days, thou shalt lay aside the expense which thou shouldest have made that day, and give it unto the widow, the fatherless, and the poor. ³¹ And thus thou shalt perfect the humiliation of thy soul; that he who receives of it may satisfy his soul, and his prayer come up to the Lord God for thee. ³² If therefore thou shalt thus accomplish thy fast, as I command thee, thy sacrifice shall be acceptable unto the Lord, and thy fast shall be written in his book. ³³ This station, thus performed, is good and pleasing and acceptable unto the Lord. These things if thou shalt observe with thy children and with all thy house, thou shalt be happy. ³⁴ And whosoever, when they hear these things, shall do them, they also shall be happy; and whatsoever they shall ask of the Lord they shall receive it. ³⁵ And I prayed him that he would expound unto me the similitude of the farm, and the Lord, and of the vineyard, and of the servant that had staked the vineyard; and of the weeds that were plucked out of the vineyard; and of his son and his friends which he took into counsel with him; for I understand that that was a similitude. ³⁶ He said unto me, Thou art very bold in asking; for thou oughtest not to ask any thing; because if it be fitting to show it unto thee, it shall be showed unto thee. ³⁷ I answered him; Sir, whatsoever thou shalt show me, without explaining it unto me, I shall in vain see it, if I do not understand what it is. And if thou shalt propose any similitudes, and not expound them, I shall in vain hear them. ³⁸ He answered me again, saying: Whosoever is the servant of God, and has the Lord in his heart, he desires understanding of him, and receives it; and he explains every similitude, and understands the words of the Lord which need an inquiry. ³⁹ But they that are lazy and slow to pray, doubt to seek from the Lord: although the Lord be of such an extraordinary goodness, that without ceasing he giveth all things to them that ask of him. ⁴⁰ Thou therefore who art strengthened by that venerable messenger, and hast received such a powerful gift of prayer; seeing thou art not slothful, why dost thou not now ask understanding of the Lord, and receive it? ⁴¹ I said unto him; seeing I have thee present, it is necessary that I should seek it of thee, and ask thee; for thou shewest all things unto me, and speakest to me when thou art present. ⁴² But if I should see or hear these things when thou wert not present, I would then ask the Lord that he would chew them unto me. ⁴³ And he replied, I said a little before that thou wert subtle and bold, in that thou asketh the meaning of these similitudes. ⁴⁴ But because thou still persistest, I will unfold to thee this parable which then desirest, that thou mayest make it known unto all men. ⁴⁵ Hear, therefore, said he, and understand. The farm before mentioned denotes the whole earth. The Lord of the farm is he, who created and finished all things; and gave virtue

unto them. ⁴⁶ His son is the Holy Spirit; the servant is the Son of God: the vineyard is the people whom he saves. The stakes are the messengers which are set oven them by the Lord, to support his people. The weeds that are plucked up out of the vineyard, are the sins which the servants of God had committed. ⁴⁷ The food which he sent him from his supper, are the commands which he gave to his people by his Son. The friends whom he called to counsel with him, are the holy angels whom he first created. The absence of the master of the household, is the time that remains unto his coming. ⁴⁸ I said unto him, Sir, all these things are very excellent, and wonderful, and good. But, continued I, could I or any other man besides, though never so wise, have understood these things? ⁴⁹ Wherefore now, sir, tell me, what I ask. He replied, ask me what thou wilt. Why, said I, is the Son of God in this parable, put in the place of a servant. ⁵⁰ Hearken, he said: the Son of God is not put in the condition of a servant, but in great power and authority. I said unto him, how, sir? I understand it not. ⁵¹ Because, said he, the Son set his messengers over those whom the Father delivered unto him, to keep every one of them; but he himself laboured very much, and suffered much, that he might blot out their offences. ⁵² For no vineyard can be digged without much labour and pains. Wherefore having blotted out the sins of his people, he showed to them the paths of life, giving them the law which he had received of the Father. ⁵³ You see, said he, that he is the Lord of his people, having received all power from his Father. But why the lord did take his son into counsel, about dividing the inheritance, and the good angels, hear now. ⁵⁴ That Holy Spirit, which was created first of all, he placed in the body in which God should dwell; namely, in a chosen body, as it seemed good to him. This body therefore into which the Holy Spirit was brought, served that Spirit, walking rightly and purely in modesty; nor ever defiled that Spirit. ⁵⁵ Seeing therefore the body at all times obeyed the Holy Spirit, and laboured rightly and chastely with him, nor faltered at anytime; that body being wearied conversed indeed servilely, but being mightily approved to God with the Holy Spirit, was accepted by him. ⁵⁶ For such a stout course pleased God, because he was not defiled in the earth, keeping the Holy Spirit. He called therefore to counsel his Son, and the good angels, that there might be some place of standing given to this body which had served the Holy Spirit without blame; lest it should seem to have lost the reward of its service. ⁵⁷ For every pure body shall receive its reward; that is found without spot, in which the Holy Spirit has been appointed to dwell. And thus you have now the exposition of this parable also. ⁵⁸ Sir, said I, I now understand your meaning, since I have heard this exposition. Hearken farther, said he: keep this thy body clean and pure, that the Spirit which shall dwell in it may bear witness unto it, and be judged to have been with thee. ⁵⁹ Also take heed that it be not instilled into thy mind that this body perishes, and thou abuse it to any lust. For if thou shalt defile thy body, thou shalt also at the same time defile the Holy Spirit; and if thou shalt defile the Holy Spirit, thou shall not live. ⁶⁰ And I said, What if through ignorance this should have been already committed, before a man heard these words; How can he attain into salvation, who has thus defiled his body? ⁶¹ He replied, As for men's former actions which through ignorance they have committed, God only can afford a remedy unto them; for all the power belongeth unto him. ⁶² But now guard thyself; and seeing God is almighty and merciful, he will grant a remedy to what thou hast formerly done amiss, if for the time, to come thou shalt not defile thy body and spirit: ⁶³ For they are companions together, and the one cannot be defiled but the other will be so too. Keep therefore both of them pure, and thou shalt live unto God.

Similitude VI Of two sorts of voluptuous men, and of their death and defection; and of the continuance of their pains. AS I was sitting at home, and praising God for all the things which I had seen; and was thinking concerning the commands, that they were exceedingly good, and great, and honest, and pleasant, and such as were able to bring a man to salvation; I said thus within myself, I shall be happy if I walk according to these commands; and whosoever shall walk in them shall live unto God. 2 Whilst I was speaking on this wise within myself, I saw him whom I had before been wont to see, sitting by me; and he spake thus unto me: 3 What doubtest thou concerning my commands which I have delivered unto thee? They are good, doubt not, but trust in the Lord, and thou shalt walk in them; for I will give thee strength to fulfil them. 4 These commands are profitable to those who shall repent of the sins which they have formerly committed; if for the time to come they shall not continue in them. 5 Whosoever therefore ye be that repent, cast away from you the naughtiness of the present world; and put on all virtue, and righteousness, and so shall ye be able to keep these commands; and not sin from henceforth any more. 6 For if ye shall keep yourselves from sin for the time to come, ye shall cut off a great deal of your former sins. Walk in my commands, and ye shall live unto God: These things have I spoken unto you. 7 And when he, had said this, he added; let us go into the field, and I will show thee shepherds of sheep. I replied, sir, let us go. 8 And we came into a certain field, and there he showed me a young shepherd, finely arrayed, with his garments of a purple colour. And he fed large flocks; and his sheep were full of pleasure, and in much delight and cheerfulness; and they skipping, ran here and there. 9 And the shepherd took very great satisfaction in his flock; and the countenance of that shepherd was cheerful, running up and down among his flock. 10 Then the angel said unto me, Seest then this shepherd? I answered, sir, I see him. He said unto me, this is the messenger of delight and pleasure. He therefore corrupts the minds of the servants of God, and turns them from the truth, delighting them with many pleasures, and they perish. 11 For they forget the commands of the living God, and live in luxury and in vain pleasures, and are corrupted by the evil angel, some of them even unto death; and others to a falling away. 12 I replied; I understand not what you mean, by saying unto death, and to a falling away. Hear, says he; all those sheep which thou sawest exceeding joyful, are such as have for ever departed from God, and given selves up to the lusts of this present time. 13 To these therefore there is no return, by repentance, unto life; because, to their other sins they have added this, that they have blasphemed the name of the lord: These kind of men are ordained unto death. 14 But those sheep which thou sawest not leaping, but feeding in one place; are such as have indeed given themselves up to pleasure and delights; but have not spoken anything wickedly against the Lord. 15 These therefore are only fallen off from the truth, and so have yet hope laid up for them in repentance. For such a falling off hath some hope still left of a renewal; but they that are dead, are utterly gone for ever. 16 Again we went a little farther forward, and he showed me a great shepherd, who had as it were a rustic figure; clad with a white goat's skin, having his bag upon his shoulder, and in his hand a stick full of knots, and very hard, and a whip in his other hand; and his countenance was stern and sour, enough to affright a man; such was his look. 17 He took from that young shepherd such sheep as lived in pleasures, but did not skip up and down; and drove them into a certain steep craggy place fall of thorns and briars, insomuch that they could not get themselves free from them: 18 But being entangled in them, fed upon thorns and briars, and were grievously tormented with his whipping. For he still drove them on, and afforded them not any place, or time, to stand still. 19 When

therefore I saw them so cruelly whipped and afflicted, I was grieved for them; because they were greatly tormented, nor had they any rest afforded them. 20 And I said unto the shepherd that was with me: Sir, who is this cruel and implacable shepherd, who is moved with no compassion towards these sheep? He answered, This shepherd is indeed one of the holy angels, but is appointed for the punishment of sinners. 21 To him therefore are delivered those who have erred from God, and served the lusts and pleasures of this world. For this cause he punishes them every one according to their deserts, with cruel and various kinds of pains. 22 Sir, said I, I would know what kind of pains they are which every one undergoes? Hearken, said he; The several pains and torments are those which men every day undergo in their present lives. For some suffer losses; others poverty; others divers sicknesses. Some are unsettled; others suffer injuries from those that are unworthy; others fall under many other trials and inconveniences. 23 For many with an unsettled design at many things, and it profiteth them not; and they say that they have not success in their undertakings. 24 They do not call to their mind what they have done amiss, and they complain of the Lord. When therefore they shall have undergone all kind of vexation and inconvenience; then they are delivered over to me for good instruction, and are confirmed in the Faith of the Lord, and serve the Lord all the rest of their days with a pure mind. 25 And when they begin to repent of their sins, then they call to mind their works which they have done amiss, and give honour to God, saying, that he is a just Judge, and they have deservedly suffered all things according to their deeds. 26 Then for what remains of their lives, they serve God with a pure mind; and have success in all their undertakings, and receive from the Lord whatever they desire. 27 And then they give thanks unto the Lord that they were delivered unto me; nor do they suffer any more cruelty. 28 I said unto him; Sir, I entreat you still to show me now one thing. What, said he, dost thou ask? I said unto him; Are they who depart from the fear of God, tormented for the same time that they enjoyed their false delight and pleasures? He answered me; they are tormented for the same time. 29 And I said unto him; They are then tormented but little; whereas they who enjoy their pleasures so as to forget God, ought to endure seven times as much punishment. 30 He answered me; Thou art foolish, neither understandest thou the efficacy of this punishment. I said unto him; Sir, if I understood it, I would not desire you to tell me. 31 Hearken, said he, and learn what the force of both is, both of the pleasure and of the punishment. An hour of pleasure is terminated within its own space: but one hour of punishment has the efficacy of thirty days. a Whosoever therefore enjoys his false pleasure for one day, and is one day, tormented; that one day of punishment is equivalent to a whole year's space. 32 Thus look how many days any one pursues his pleasures, so many years is he punished for it. You see therefore how that the time of worldly enjoyments is but short; but that of pain and torments, a great deal more. 33 I replied; Sir, forasmuch as I do not understand at all these times of pleasure and pain; I entreat you that you would explain yourself more clearly concerning them. He answered me, saying; Thy foolishness still sticks unto thee. 34. Shouldst thou not rather purify thy mind, and serve God? Take heed, lest when thy time is fulfilled, thou be found still unwise. Hear then, as thou desirest, that thou mayest the more easily understand. 35 He that gives himself up one day to his pleasures and delights, and does whatsoever his soul desires, is full of great folly, nor understands what he does, but the day following forgets what he did the day before. 36 For delight and worldly pleasure are not kept in memory, by reason of the folly that is rooted in them. But when pain and torment befal a man a day, he is in effect troubled the whole year after; because his punishment continues firm in his memory. 37 Wherefore he remembers it with sorrow the whole year; and then calls to mind his vain pleasure and delight, and perceives that for the sake of that he was punished. 38 Whosoever therefore have delivered themselves over to such pleasures, are thus punished; because that when they had life, they rendered themselves liable to death. 39 I said unto him; Sir, what pleasures are hurtful? He answered; That is pleasure to every man which he doth willingly. 40 For the angry man, gratifying his passion, perceives pleasure in it; and so the adulterer, and drunkard; the slanderer and liar; the covetous man and the defrauder; and whosoever commits anything like unto these, he followeth his evil disposition, because he receives a satisfaction in the doing of it. 41 All these pleasures and delights are hurtful to the servants of God. For these therefore they are tormented and suffer punishment. 42 There are also pleasures that bring salvation unto men. For many, when they do what is good, find pleasure in it, and are attracted by the delights of it. 43 Now this pleasure is profitable to the servants of God, and brings life to such men; but those hurtful pleasures, which were before mentioned, bring torments and punishment. 44 And whosoever shall continue in them, and shall not repent of what they have done, shall bring death upon themselves.

Similitude VII That they who repent, must bring forth, fruits worthy of repent once. AFTER a few days I saw the same person that before talked with me, in the same field, in which I had seen those shepherds, And he said unto me; What seekest thou? Sir, said I, I came to entreat you that You would command the shepherd, who is the minister of punishment, to depart out of my house, because he greatly afflicts me. 3 And he answered, It is necessary for thee to endure inconveniencies and vexations; for so that good angel hath commanded concerning thee, because he would try thee. 4 Sir, said I; What so great offence have I committed, that I should be delivered to this messenger? Hearken, said he: Thou art indeed guilty of many sins, yet not so many that thou shouldest be delivered to this messenger. 5 But thy house hath committed many sins and offences, and therefore that good messenger being grieved at their doings commanded that for some time thou shouldst suffer affliction; that they may both repent of what they have done, and may wash themselves from all the lusts of this present world. 6 When therefore they shall have repented, and be purified, then that messenger which is appointed over thy punishment, shall depart from thee. 7 I said unto him; Sir, if they have behaved themselves so as to anger that good angel, yet what have I done? He answered: They cannot otherwise be afflicted, unless thou, who art the head of the family, suffer. 8 For whatsoever thou shalt suffer, they must needs feel it but as long as thou shalt stand well established, they cannot experience any vexation. 9 I replied; But, sir, behold they also now repent with all their hearts. I know, says he, that they repent with all their hearts; but dost thou therefore think that their offences who repent, are immediately blotted out. 10 No, they are not presently; but he that repents must afflict his soul and show himself humble in all his affairs, and undergo many and divers vexations. 11 And when he shall have suffered all things that were appointed for him; then perhaps HE that made him, and formed all things besides, will be moved with compassion towards him, and afford him some remedy; and especially if HE shall perceive his heart who repents, to be free from every evil work. 12 But at present it is expedient for thee, and for thy house, to be grieved; and it is needful that thou shoudest endure much vexation, as the angel of the Lord who committed thee unto me, has commanded. 13 Rather give thanks unto the Lord, that knowing what was to come he thought thee worthy, to whom he should foretel that trouble was coming upon thee, who art able to bear it. 14 I said unto him; Sir, but

be thou also with me, and I shall easily undergo any trouble. I will, said he, be with thee; and I will entreat the messenger who is set over thy punishment, that he would moderate his afflictions towards thee. 15 And moreover thou shalt suffer adversity but for a little time; and then thou shalt again be restored to thy former state; only continue on in the humility of thy mind. 16 Obey the Lord with a pure heart; thou, and thy house, and thy children; and. walk in the commands which I have delivered unto thee; and then thy repentance may be firm and pure. 17 And if thou shalt keep these things with thy house, thy inconveniencies shall depart from thee. 18 And all vexation shall in like manner depart from those, whosoever shall walk according to these commands.

Similitude VIII That there are many kinds of elect, and of repenting sinners: and how all of theca shall receive a reward proportionable to the measure of their repentance and good works. AGAIN he showed me a willow which covered the fields and the mountains, under whose shadow came all such as were called by the name of the Lord. 2 And by that willow stood an. angel of the Lord very excellent and lofty, and did cut down bows from the willow with a great hook; and reached out to the people that were under the shadow of the willow, little rods, as it were about a foot long. 3 And when all of them had taken them, he laid aside his hook, and the tree continued entire, as I had before seen it; at which I wondered, and mused within myself. 4 Then that shepherd said unto me; Forbear to wonder that the tree continues whole, not-with-standing so many boughs have been cut off from it: but stay a little, for now it shall be shown thee, what that angel means, who gave those rods to the people. 5 So he again demanded the rods of them; and in the same order that every one had received them, was he called to him, and restored his rod; which when he had received, he examined them. 6 From some he received them dry and rotten, and as it were touched with the moth; those he commanded to be separated from the rest, and placed by themselves. Others gave in their rods dry indeed, but not touched with the moth: these also he ordered to be set by themselves. 7 Others gave in their rods half dry; these also were set apart, Others gave in their rods half dry and cleft; these too were set by themselves. Others brought in their rods half dry and half green, and these were in like manner placed by themselves. 8 Others delivered up their rods two parts green, and the third dry; and they too were set apart. Others brought their rods two parts dry, and the third green; and were also placed by themselves. 9 Others delivered up their rods less dry (for there was but a very little, to wit, their tops dry), but they had clefts, and these were set in like manner by themselves. In the rods of others there was but a little green, and the rest dry; and these were set aside by themselves. 10 Others came, and brought their rods green as they had received them, and the greatest part of the people brought their rods thus; and the messenger greatly rejoiced at these, and they also were put apart by themselves. 11 Others brought in their rods not only green, but full of branches; and these were set aside, being also received by the angel with great joy. Others brought their rods green with branches, and those also some fruit upon them. 12 They who had such rods, were very cheerful; and the angel himself took great joy at them; nor was the shepherd that stood with me, less pleased with them. 13 Then the angel of the Lord commanded crowns to be brought, and the crowns were brought made of palms; and the angel crowned those men in whose rods he found the young branches with fruit, and commanded them to go into the tower. 14 He also sent those into the tower, in whose hands he found branches without fruit, giving a seal unto them. For they had the same garment, that is, one white as snow; with which he bade them go into the tower And so he did to those who returned their rods green as they had received them; giving them a white garment, and so sent them away to go into the tower. [15] Having done this, he said to the shepherd that was with me, I go my way; but do thou send these within the walls, every one into the place in which he has deserved to dwell; examining first their rods, but examine them diligently that no one deceive thee; and if any one shall escape thee, I will try them upon the altar. Having said this to the shepherd, he departed. [16] After he was gone, the shepherd said unto me; Let us take the rods from them, and plant them; if perchance they may grow green again. I said unto him; Sir, how can those dry rods ever grow green again? [17] He answered me; That tree. is a willow, and always loves to live. If therefore these rods shall be planted, and receive a little moisture, many of them will recover themselves. [18] Wherefore I will try, and will pour water upon them, and if any of them can live, I will rejoice with them; but if not, at least by this means I shall be found not to have neglected my part. [19] Then he commanded me to call them; and they all came unto him, every one in the rank in which he stood, and gave him their rods; which having received he planted every one of them in their several orders. [20] And after he had planted them all, he poured much water upon them, insomuch that they were covered with water, and did not appear above it. Then when he had watered them, he said unto me; Let us depart, and after a little time we will return and visit them. [21] For he who created this tree, would have all those live that received rods from it. And I hope now that these rods are thus watered, many of them receiving in the moisture, will recover: [22] I said unto him, Sir, tell me what this tree denotes? For I am greatly astonished, that after so many branches have been cut off, it seems still to be whole: nor does there any thing the less of it appear to remain, which greatly amazes me. [23] He answered, Hearken. This great tree which covers the plains and the mountains, and all the earth, is the law of God, published throughout the whole world. [24] Now this law is the Son of God, who is preached to all the ends of the earth. The people that stand under its shadow, are those which have heard his preaching, and believed. [25] The great and venerable angel which you saw, was Michael who had the power over his people, and governs them. For he has planted the law in the hearts of those who have believed: and therefore he visits them to whom lie has given the law, to see if they have kept it. [26] And he examines every one's rod; and of those, many that are weakened: for those rods are the law of the Lord. Then he discerns all those who have not kept the law, knowing the place of every one of them. [27] I said unto him, Sir, why did he send away some to the tower, and left others here to you? He replied, those who have transgressed the law, which they received from him, are left in my power, that they may repent of their sins: but they who fulfilled this law and kept it, are under his power. [28] But who then, said I, are those, who went into the tower crowned? He replied, all such as having striven with the devil, have overcome him, are crowned: and they are those, who have suffered hard things, that they might keep the law. [29] But they who gave up their rods green, and with young branches, but without fruit, have indeed endured trouble for the same law, but have not suffered death; neither have they denied their holy law. [30] They who delivered up their rods green as they received them, are those who were modest and just, and have lived with a very pure mind, and kept the commandments of God. [31] The rest thou shalt know, when I shall have considered those rods which I have planted and watered. [32] After a few days we returned, and in the same place stood that glorious angel, and I stood by him. Then he said unto me; Gird thyself with a towel, and serve me. [33] And I girded myself with a clean towel, which was made of coarse cloth. And when he saw me girded, and ready to minister unto him, he said, Call those men

405

whose rods have been planted, every one in his order as he gave them. [34] And he brought me into the field, and I called them all, and they all stood ready in their several ranks. Then he said unto them; let every one pluck up his rod, and bring it unto me. And first they delivered theirs, whose rods had been dry and rotten. [35] And those whose rods still continued so, he commanded to stand apart. Then they came whose rods had been dry but not rotten. Some of these delivered. in their rods green; others dry and rotten, as if they had been touched by the moth. [36] Those who gave them up green, he commanded to stand apart: but those whose rods were dry and rotten, he caused to stand with the first sort. Then came they whose rods had been half dry, and cleft: many of these gave up their rods green, and uncleft. [37] Others delivered them up green with branches, like unto theirs who went crowned into the tower. Others delivered them up dry, but not rotten; and some gave them up as they were before, all dry, and cleft. [38] Every one of these he ordered to stand apart; some by themselves, others in their respective ranks. [32] Then came they whose rods had been green, but cleft. These delivered their rods altogether green, and stood in their own order. And the shepherd rejoiced at these, because they were all changed, and free from their clefts. [40] Then they gave in their rods, who had them half green and half dry. Of these some were found wholly green, others half dry: others green, with young shoots. And all these were sent away, every one to his proper rank. [41] Then they gave up their rods, who had them before two parts green, and the third dry. Many of those gave in their rods green; many half dry; the rest dry but not rotten. So these were sent away, each to his proper place. [42] Then came they who before had their rods two parts dry and the third green; many of these delivered up their rods half dry, others dry and rotten; others half dry and cleft: but few green. And all these were set every one in his own rank. [43] Then they reached in their rods, in which there was before but a little green, and the rest dry. Their rods were for the most part found green, having little boughs, with fruit upon them; and the rest altogether green. [44] And the shepherd upon sight of these rejoiced exceedingly, because he had found them thus; and they also went to their proper orders. [45] Now after he had examined all their rods, he said unto me, I told thee that this tree loved life thou seest how many have repented, and attained unto salvation. Sir, said I, I see it. [46] That thou mightest know saith he, that the goodness and mercy of the Lord is great, and to be had in honour; who gave his spirit to them that were found worthy of repentance. [47] I answered, Sir, why then did not all of them repent? He replied, Those whose minds the Lords foresaw would be pure, and that they would serve him with all their hearts, to them he gave repentance. [48] But for those whose deceit and wickedness he beheld, and perceived that they would not truly return unto him; to them he denied any return unto repentance, lest they should again blaspheme his law with wicked words. [49] I said unto him; Now, Sir, make known unto me, what is the place of every one of those, who have given up their rods, and what their portion; that when they may have not kept their seal entire, but have wasted the seal which they received, shall hear and believe these thins, and may acknowledge their evil deeds and repent; [50] And receiving again their seal from you, may give glory to God, that he was moved with compassion towards them, and sent you to renew their spirits. [51] Hearken, said he; they whose rods have been found and rotten, and as it were touched with the moth; are the deserters and the betrayers of the church; [52] Who with the rest of their crimes, have also blasphemed the Lord, and denied his name when he had called upon them. Therefore all these are dead unto God and thou seest that none of them have repented, although they have heard my commands which thou bast delivered unto them. From these men therefore life is far distant. 53 They also who have delivered up their rods dry, but not rotten, have not been far from them. For they have been counterfeits, and brought in evil doctrines, and have perverted the servants of God, especially those who had sinned; not suffering them to return unto repentance, but keeping them back by their false doctrines. 54 These therefore have hope; and thou seest that many of them have repented, since the time that thou hast laid my commands before them; and many more will yet repent. But they, that shall not repent; shall lose both repentance and life. 55 But they that have repented, their place is begun to be within the first walls, and some of them are even gone into the tower. Thou seest therefore, said he, that in the repentance of sinners there is life; but for those who repent not, death is prepared. 56 Hear now concerning those who gave in their rods half dry and full of clefts. Those whose rods were only half dry, are the doubtful; for they are neither living nor dead. 57 But they who delivered in their rods, not only half dry but also full of clefts, are both doubtful and evil speakers; who detract from those that are absent, and have never peace among themselves, and who envy one another. 58 Howbeit, to those also repentance is offered; for thou seest that some of these have repented. 59 Now all those of this kind who have quickly repented, shall have a place in the tower; and they who have been more slow in their repentance, shall dwell within the walls: but they that shall not repent, and shall continue on in their wicked doings, shall die the death. 60 As for those who had their rods green, but yet cleft; they are such as were always faithful and good, but they had some envy and strife among themselves concerning dignity and pre-eminence. 61 Now all such as are vain, and without understanding, contend with one another about these things. 62 Nevertheless, seeing they are otherwise good, if when they shall hear these commands they shall amend themselves, and shall at my persuasion suddenly repent; they shall at last dwell in the tower, like those who have truly and worthily repented. 63 But if any one shall again return to his dissension; he shall be shut out from the tower, and shall lose his life. For the life of those who keep the commandments of the Lord, consists in doing what they are commanded; not in principality, or in any other dignity. 64 For by forbearance and humility of mind, men shall attain unto life; but by seditions and contempt of the law, they shall purchase death unto themselves. 65 They who in their rods had half dry and half green, are those who are engaged in many affairs of the world, and are not joined to the saints. For which cause half of them liveth, and half is dead. 66 Wherefore many of these since the time that they have heard my commands, have repented, and begun to dwell in the tower. But some of them have wholly fallen away; to these there is no more place for repentance. 67 For by reason of their present interests, they have blasphemed and denied God: and for this wickedness they have lost life. And of these many are still in doubt, yet these may return; and if they shall quickly repent, they shall have a place in the tower; but if they shall be more slow, they shall dwell within the walls; but if they shall not repent, they shall die. 68 As for those who had two parts of their rods green, and the third dry; they have by manifold ways denied the Lord. Of these many have repented, and found a place in the tower: and many have altogether departed from God. These have utterly lost life. 69 And some being in a doubtful state, have raise up dissensions: these may yet return, if they shall suddenly repent and not continue in their lusts; but if they shall continue in their evil-doing they shall die. 70 They who gave in their rods two parts dry, and the other been, are those who have indeed been faithful, but withal rich and full of good things; and thereupon have desired to be famous among the heathen which are without, and have thereby fallen into great pride, and begun to

406

aim at high matters, and to forsake the truth. 71 Nor were they joined to the saints, but lived with the heathen; and this life seemed the more pleasant to them. Howbeit they have not departed from God, but continued in the faith; only they have not wrought the works of faith. 72 Many therefore of these have repented; and begun to dwell in the tower. Yet others still living among the heathen. people, and being lifted up with their vanities, have utterly fallen away from God, and followed the works and wickedness of the heathen. These kind of men therefore are reckoned among strangers to the Gospel. 73 Others of these began to be doubtful in their minds; despairing by reason of their wicked doings ever to attain unto salvation Others being thus made doubtful, did moreover stir up dissensions. 74 To these therefore, and to those who by reason of their doings are become doubtful, there is still hope of return; but they must repent quickly, that their place may be in the tower. But they that repent not, and continue still in their pleasures, are nigh unto death. 75 As for those who gave in their rods green, excepting their tops, which only were dry, and had clefts; these were always good, and faithful, and upright before God: nevertheless they sinned a little, by reason of their empty pleasures and trifling thoughts which they had within themselves. 76 Wherefore many of them when they heard my words, repented forthwith, and began to dwell in the tower. Nevertheless some grew doubtful, and others to their doubtful minds added dissensions. To these therefore there is still hope of return, because they were always good; but they shall not hardly be moved. 77 As for those, lastly, who gave in their rods dry, their tops only excepted, which alone were green; they are such as have believed indeed in God, but have lived in wickedness; yet without departing from God: having always willingly borne the name of the Lord, and readily received into their houses the servants of God. 78 Wherefore hearing these things they returned, and without delay repented, and lived in all righteousness. And some of them suffered death: others readily underwent many trials, being mindful of their evil doings. 79 If And when he had ended his explications of all the rods, he said unto me, Go, and say unto all men that they repent, and they shall live unto God; because the Lord being moved with great clemency hath sent me to preach repentance unto all: 80 Even unto those who by reason of their evil doings, deserve not to attain unto salvation. But the Lord will by patient, and keep the invitation that was made by his Son. 81 I said unto him, sir, I hope that all when they shall hear these things, will repent. For I trust that everyone acknowledging his crimes, and taking up the fear of the Lord, will return unto repentance. 82 He said unto me, Whosoever shall repent with all their hearts, and cleanse themselves from all the evils that I have before mentioned, and not add anything more to their sins, shall receive from the Lord cure of their former iniquities, if they do not make any doubt of these commands, and shall live unto God. 83 But they that shall continue to add to their transgressions, and still converse with the lusts of the present world, shall condemn themselves unto death. But do thou walk in these commands, and whosoever shall Walk in these, and exercise them rightly, shall live unto God. 84 And having showed me all these things, he said; I will show thee the rest in a few days.

Similitude IX The greatest mysteries of the militant and triumphant Church which is to be built. AFTER I had Written the Commands and similitudes of the Shepherd, the Angel of Repentance came unto me, and said to me, I will show thee all those things which the Spirit spake with thee under the figure of the church. For that Spirit is the Son of God. 2 And because thou wert weak in body, it was not declared unto thee by the angel, until thou wert strengthened by the Spirit, and increased in force, that thou mightest also see the angel: 3 For then indeed the building of the tower was very well and gloriously shown unto thee by the church; nevertheless thou sawest all things shown unto thee as it were by a virgin. ⁴ But now thou art enlightened by the angel, and yet by the same Spirit. But thou must consider all things diligently; for therefore am I sent into thy house by that venerable messenger, that when thou shalt have seen all things powerfully, thou mayest not be afraid as before. ⁵ And he led me to the height of a mountain in Arcadia, and we sat upon its top. And he showed me a great plain, and about it twelve mountains in different figures. ⁶ The first was black as soot. The second was smooth, without herbs. The third was full of thorns and thistles. The fourth had herbs half dried; of which the upper part was green, but that next the root was dry; and some of the herbs, when the sun grew hot, were dry. ⁷ The fifth mountain was very rugged; but yet had green herbs. The sixth mountain was full of clefts, some lesser, and some greater; and in these clefts grew grass, not flourishing, but which seemed to be withering. ⁸ The seventh mountain had delightful pasture, and was wholly fruitful; and all kinds of cattle, and of the birds of heaven; fed upon it; and the more they fed on it, the more and better did the grass grow. ⁹ The eighth mountain was full of fountains, and from those fountains were watered all kinds of the creatures of Cod. The ninth mountain had no water at all, but was wholly destitute of it; and nourished deadly serpents, very destructive to men. ¹⁰ The tenth mountain was full of tall trees, and altogether shady; and under the shade of them lay cattle resting and chewing the cud. ¹¹ The eleventh mountain was full of the thickest trees, and those trees seemed to be loaded with several sorts of fruits; that whosoever saw them could not choose but desire to eat of their fruit. ¹² The twelfth mountain was altogether white, and of a most pleasant aspect, and itself gave a most excellent beauty to itself. ¹³ In the middle of the plain he showed me a huge white rock, which rose out of the plain, and the rock was higher than those mountains, and was square; so that it seemed capable of supporting the whole world. ¹⁴ It looked to me to be old, yet it had in it a new gate, which seemed to have been newly hewn out of it. Now that gate was bright beyond the sun itself; insomuch, that I greatly wondered at its light. ¹⁵ About the gate stood twelve virgins; of which four that stood at the corners of the gate, seemed to me to be the chiefest, although the rest were also of worth: and they stood in the four parts of the gate. ¹⁶ It added also to the grace of those virgins, that they stood in pairs, clothed with linen garments, and decently girded, their right arms being at liberty, as if they were about to lift up some burthen; for so they were adorned, and were exceeding cheerful and ready. ¹⁷ When I saw this, I wondered with myself to see such great and noble things. And again I admired upon the account of those virgins, that they were so handsome and delicate; and stood with such firmness and constancy, as if they would carry the whole heaven. ¹⁸ And as I was thinking thus within myself, the shepherd said unto me; What thickest thou within thyself? Why art thou disquieted, and fillest thyself with care? ¹⁹ Do not seem to consider, as if thou wert wise, what thou doest not understand, but pray unto the Lord, that thou mayest have ability to understand it. What is to come thou canst not understand, but thou seest that which is before thee. ²⁰ Be not therefore disquieted at those things which thou canst not see; but get the understanding of those which thou seest. ²¹ Forbear to be curious; and I will show thee all things that I ought to declare unto thee: but first consider what yet remains. ²² And when he had said this unto me I looked up, and behold I saw six tall and venerable men coming; their countenances were all alike, and they called a certain multitude of men; and they who came at their call were also tall and stout. ²³ And those six commanded them to build a certain tower over that gate. And immediately there began to be a great noise of those men

407

running here and there about the gate, who were come together to build the tower. ²⁴ But those virgins which stood about the gate perceived that the building of the tower was to be hastened by them. And they stretched out their hands, as if they were to receive somewhat from them to do. ²⁵ Then those six men commanded, that they should lift up stones out of a certain deep place, and prepare them for the building of the tower. And there were lifted up ten white stones, square, and not cut round. ²⁶ Then those six men called the ten virgins to them, and commanded them to carry all the stones that were to be put into the building, and having carried them through the gate to deliver them to those that were about to build the tower. ²⁷ Immediately the virgins began all of them together to lift up those stones, that were before taken out of the deep. ²⁸ And they who also stood about the gate did carry stones in such a manner, that those stones which seemed to be the strongest were laid at the corners, and the rest were put into the sides; ²⁹ And thus they carried all the stones, and bringing them through the gate delivered them to the builders, as they had been commanded: who receiving them at their hands, built with them. ³⁰ But this building was made upon that great rock, and over the gate; and by these the whole tower was supported. But the building of the ten stones filled the whole gate, which began to be made for the foundation of that tower. ³¹ After those ten stones did five and twenty others rise up out of the deep; and these were placed in the building of the same tower; being lifted up by those virgins, as the others had been before. ³² After these did fire and thirty others rise up; and these were also in like manner fitted into the same work. Then forty other stones were brought up, and all these were added unto the building of that tower. ³³ So there began to be four ranks in the foundation of that tower; and the stones ceased to rise out of the deep; and they also which built rested a little. ³⁴ Again, those six men commanded the multitude, that they should bring stones out of those twelve mountains to the building of the same tower. ³⁵ So they cut out of all the mountains stones of divers colours, and brought them and gave them to the virgins; which when they had received they carried them, and delivered them into the building of the tower. ³⁶ In which when they were built they became white, and different from what they were before; for they were all alike, and did change their former colours. And some were reached up by the men themselves, which when they came into the building, continued such is they were put in. ³⁷ These neither became white, nor different from what they were before; because they were not carried by the virgins through the gate. Wherefore these stones were disagreeable in the building; which, when these six men perceived they commanded them to be removed, and put again in the place from which they were brought. ³⁸ And they said to those who brought these stones; Do not ye reach up to us any stones for this building, but lay them down by the tower, that these virgins may carry them and reach them to us. ³⁹ For unless they shall be carried by these virgins through this gate, they cannot change their colours: therefore do not labour in vain. ⁴⁰ So the building that day was done; howbeit the tower was not finished, for it was afterwards to be built; therefore now also there was some delay made of it. ⁴¹ And these six men commanded those that built to depart, and as it were to rest for some time; but they ordered those virgins that they should not depart from the tower; so now they seemed to me to be left for the guarding of it. ⁴² When all were departed, I said unto the shepherd; Sir, why is not the building of the tower finished? Because it cannot, said he, be finished until its Lord comes, and approves of the building; that if he shall find any stones in it that are not good they may be changed; for this tower is built according to his will. ⁴³ Sir, said I, I would know what the building of this tower signifies; as also I would be informed concerning this rock, and this gate; 44 And concerning the mountains, and the virgins, and the stones that did rise out of the deep, and were not cut, but put into the building just as they came forth; and why the ten stones were first laid in the foundation; then the twenty-five, then thirty- five; then forty? 45 Also concerning those stones that were put into the building, and again taken out, and carried back into their places? Fulfil, I pray, the desire of my soul as to all these things, and manifest all unto me. 46 And he said unto me; If thou shalt not be dull, thou shall know all, and shall see all the other things that are about to happen in this, tower: and shall understand diligently all these similitudes. 47 And after a few days we came into the same place where we had sat before; and he said unto me, Let us go unto the tower; for the Lord of it will come and examine it. 48 So we came thither, and found none but those virgins there. And he asked them whether the Lord of that tower was come thither? And they replied, that he would be there presently to examine the building. 49 After a very little while I saw a great multitude of men coming, and in the middle of them a man so tall, that he surpassed the tower in height. 50 About him were those six, who before commanded in the building, and all the rest of those who had built that tower, and many others of great dignity: and the virgins that kept the tower ran to meet him, and kissed him, and began to walk near unto him. 51 But he examined the building with so much care, that he handled every stone; and struck every one with a rod which he held in his hand: 52 Of which some being so struck turned black as soot; others were rough; some looked as if they had cracks in them; others seemed maimed; some neither black nor white; some looked sharp, and agreed not with the other stones, and others were full of spots. 53 These were the several kinds of those stones which were not found proper in the building; all which the Lord commanded to be taken out of the tower, and laid near it, and other stones to be brought and put in their places. 54 And they that built, asked him from which of the mountains he would have stones brought to put in the place of those that were laid aside. But he forbad them to bring any from the mountains, and commanded that they should take them out of a certain field that was near. 55 So they digged in the field, and found many bright square stones, and some also that were round. Howbeit, all that were found in that field were taken away, and carried through the gate by those virgins; and those of them that were square were fitted and put into the places of those that were pulled out. 56 But the round ones were not put into the building, because they were hard, and it would have required too much time to cut them but they were placed about the tower, as if they should hereafter be cut square, and put into the building; for they were very white. 57 When he who was chief in dignity, and lord of the whole tower saw this, he called to him the shepherd that was with me, and gave him the stones that were rejected and laid about the tower, and said unto him; cleanse these stones with all care, and fit them into the building of the tower, that they may agree with the rest; but those that will not suit with the rest, cast away afar off from the tower. 58 When he had thus commanded him, he departed, with all those that came with him to the tower but those virgins still stood about the tower to keep it. 59 And I said unto that shepherd; How can these stones, seeing they have been rejected, return into the building of this tower? He replied; I will cut off the greatest part from these stones, and will add them to the building, and they will agree with the rest. 60 And I said, Sir, how will they be able to fill the same place, when they shall be so much cut away? He answered; They that shall be found too little shall be put into the middle of the building, and the greater shall be placed without, and keep them in. 61 When he had said thus unto me, he added; Let us go, and after three days we will return, and I will put these stones, being cleansed,

408

into the tower. 62 For all these that are about the tower must be cleansed, lest the master of the house chance to come upon the sudden, and find those which are about the tower unclean; and be so exasperated that these stones should never be put into the building of this tower, and I shall be looked upon to have been unmindful of my master's commands. 63 When therefore we came after three days to the tower, he said unto me; Let us examine all these stones, and let us see which of them may go into the building. I answered, Sir, let us see. 64 And first of all we began to consider those which had been black; for they were found just such as they were when they were pulled out of the tower: wherefore he commanded them to be removed from the tower and put by themselves. 65 Then he examined those which had been rough; and commanded many of those to be cut round, and to be fitted by the virgins into the building of the tower; so they took them, and fitted them into the middle of the building and he commanded the rest to be laid by with the black ones, for they also were become black. 66 Next he considered those which were full of cracks, and many of those also he ordered to be pared away, and so to be added to the rest of the building, by the came virgins. 67 These were placed without because they were found entire; but the residue through the multitude of their cracks could not be reformed, and therefore were cast away from the building of the tower. 68 Then he considered those that had been maimed; many of these had cracks, and were become black; others had large clefts; these he commanded to be placed with those that were reected; 69 But the rest being cleansed and reformed, he commanded to be put into the building. These therefore those virgins took up, and fitted into the middle of the building, because they were but weak. 70 After these he examined those which were found half white and half black, and many of those which were now black; these also he ordered to be laid among those that were cast away. 71 The rest were found altogether white; those were taken up by the virgins, and fitted into the same tower: and they were put in the outside, because they were found entire; that so they might keep in those that were placed in the middle, for nothing was cut off from them. 72 Next he looked upon those which had been hard and sharp; but few of these were made use of, because they could not be cut, for they were found very hard: but the rest were formed, and fitted by the virgins into the middle of the building, because they were more weak. 73 Then he considered those which had spots; of these a few were found black, and they were carried to their fellows. The rest were white and entire; and they were fitted by the virgins into the building, and placed in the outside, by reason of their strength. 74 After this he came to consider those stones which were white and round: and he said unto me, What shall we do with these stones? I answered, Sir, I cannot tell. 75 He replied, Canst thou think of nothing then for these? I answered, Sir, I understand not this art; neither am I a stone-cutter, nor can I tell anything. 76 And he said, seest thou not that they are very round? Now to make them square, I must cut off a great deal from them; howbeit, it is necessary that some of these should go into the building of the tower. 77 I answered; If it be necessary, why do you perplex yourself, and not rather choose, if you have any choice among them, and fit them into the building. 78 Upon this he chose out the largest and brightest, and squared them; which, when he had done the virgins took them up, and fitted them into the building. 79 And the rest that remained were carried back into the same field from which they were taken; howbeit, they were not cast away; because, said he, there is yet a little wanting to this tower, which is to be built; and perhaps the Lord will have these stones fitted into this building, because they are exceeding white. 80 Then there were called twelve very stately women, clothed with a black garment, girded, and their shoulders free, and their hair loose. These seemed to me to be country women. [81] And the shepherd commanded them to take up those stones which were cast out of the building, and carry them back to the mountains out of which they were taken. [82] And they took them all up joyfully, and carried them back to their places from whence they had been taken. [83] When not one stone remained about the tower, he said unto me, Let us go about this tower, and see whether anything be wanting to it. [84] We began therefore to go round about it; and when he saw that it was handsomely built, he began to be very glad; for it was so beautifully framed, that any one that had seen it must have been in love with the building. [85] For it seemed to be all but one stone, nor did a joint any where appear; but it looked as if it had all been cut out of one rock. [86] And when I diligently considered what a tower it was, I was extremely pleased: and he said unto me, Bring hither some lime and little shells, that I may fill up the spaces of those stones that were taken out of the building, and put in again; for all things about the tower must be made even. [87] And I did as he commanded me, and brought them unto him and he said unto me, Be ready to help me, and this work will quickly be finished. [88] He therefore filled up the spaces of those stones, and commanded the place about the tower to be cleansed. [89] Then those virgins took besoms, and cleansed all the place around, and took away all the rubbish, and threw water on; which being done, the palace became delightful, and the tower beauteous. [90] Then he said unto me, All is now clean if the Lord should come to finish the tower, he will find nothing whereby to complain of us. [91] When he had said this he would have departed. But I laid hold on his bag, and began to entreat him for the Lord's sake, that he would explain to me all things that he had shown me. [92] He said unto me, I have at present a little business; but I will suddenly explain all things unto thee. Tarry here for me till I come. [93] I said unto him, Sir, what shall I do here alone? He answered, Thou art not alone, seeing all these virgins are with thee. [94] I said, Sir, deliver me then unto them. Then he called them and said unto them, I commend this man unto you until I shall come; [95] So I remained with those virgins: now they were cheerful and courteous unto me; especially the four, which seemed to be the chiefest among them. [96] Then those virgins said unto me, that shepherd will not return hither to-day. I said unto them, What then shall I do? They answered, Tarry for him till the evening, if perhaps he may come and speak with thee; but if not, yet thou shalt continue with us till he does come. [97] I said unto them, I will tarry for him till evening; but if he comes not by that time, I will go home, and return hither again the next morning. [98] They answered me, As thou art delivered unto us, thou mayest not depart from us. I said, Where shall I tarry? [99] They replied, Thou shalt sleep with us as a brother, not as a husband; for thou art our brother, and we are ready from henceforth to dwell with thee; for thou art very dear to as. [100] Howbeit I was ashamed to continue with them. But she that seemed to be the chiefest amongst them, embraced me, and began to kiss me. And the rest when they saw that I was kissed by her, began also to kiss me as a brother; and led me about the tower, and played with me. [101] Some of them also sung psalms, others made up the chorus with them. But I walked about the tower with them, rejoicing silently, and seeming to myself to be grown young again. [102] When the evening came on, I would forthwith have gone home, but they withheld me, and suffered me not to depart. Wherefore I continued with them that night near the same tower. [103] So they spread their linen garments upon the ground; and placed me in the middle, nor did they anything else, only they prayed. [104] I also prayed with them without ceasing, nor less than they. Who, when they saw me pray in that manner, rejoiced greatly:

409

and I continued there with their till the next day. [105] And when we had worshipped God, then the shepherd came and said unto them: You have done no injury to this man? They answered, Ask him. I said unto him, Sir, I have received a great deal of satisfaction in that I have remained with them. [106] And he said unto me, How didst thou sup? I answered, Sir, I feasted the whole night upon the words of the Lord. They received thee well then, said he? I said, Sir, very well. [107] He answered, Wilt thou now learn what thou didst desire? I replied, Sir, I will: and first I pray thee that thou shouldest show me all things in the order that I asked them. [108] He answered, I will do all as thou wouldst have me, nor will I hide any thing from thee. [109] First of all, Sir, said I, tell me, what this rock and this gate denote? Hearken, said he; this rock, and this gate, are the Son of God. I replied, Sir, how can that be; seeing the rock is old, but the gate new? [110] Hear, said he, O foolish man! and understand. The Son of God is indeed more ancient than any creature; insomuch that he was in council with his Father at the creation oft all things. [111] But the gate is therefore new, because he appeared in the last days in the fullness of time; that they who shall attain unto salvation, may by it enter into the kingdom of God. [112] You have seen, said he, those stones which were carried through the gate, how they were placed in the building of the tower; but that those which were not carried through the gate, were sent away into their own places? [113] I answered, sir, I saw it. Thus, said he, no man shall enter into the kingdom of God, but he who shall take upon him the name of the Son of God. [114] For if you would enter into any city, and that city should he encompassed with a wall, and had only one gate, could you enter into that city except by that gate? [115] I answered, Sir, how could I do otherwise? As therefore, said he, there would be no other way of entering into that city but by its gate, so neither can any one enter into the kingdom of God, but only by the name of his Son, who is most dear unto him. [116] And he said unto me, Didst thou see the multitude of those that built that tower? Sir, said I, I saw it. He answered, All those are the angels, venerable in their dignity, [117] With those is the Lord encompassed as with a wall: but the gate is the Son of God, who is the only way of coming unto God. For no man shall go to God, but by his Son. [118] Thou sawest also, said he, the six men, and in the middle of them that venerable great man, who walked about the tower, and rejected the stones out of the tower? [119] Sir, said I, I saw them. He answered, that tall man was the Son of God; and those six were his angels of most eminent dignity, which stand about him on the right hand and on the left. [120] Of these excellent angels none comes in unto God without him. He added, Whosoever there. fore shall not take upon him his name, he shall nor enter into the kingdom of God. [121] Then I said, What is this tower? This, said he, is the church. And what, Sir, are these virgins? He said unto me, These are the holy spirits, for no man can enter into the kingdom of God, except these clothe him with their garment, [122] For it will avail thee nothing to take up the name of the Son of God, unless thou shalt also receive their garment from them. For these virgins are the powers of the Son of God. So shall a man in vain bear his name, unless he shall be also endued with his powers. [123] And he said unto me, sawest thou those stones that were cast away? They bore indeed the name, but put not on their garment. I said, Sir, what is their garment? Their very names, said he, are their garment. [124] Therefore whosoever beareth the name of the Son of God, ought to bear their names also; for the Son of God also himself beareth their names. [125] As for those stones, continued he, which being delivered by their hands, thou sawest remain in the building, they were clothed with their power; for which cause thou seest the whole tower of the same colour with the rock, and made as it were of one stone. [126] So also those who have believed in God by his Son, have put on his spirit. Behold there shall be one spirit, and one body, and one colour of their garments; and all they shall attain this, who shall bear the names of these virgins. [127] And I said, Sir, why then were those stones cast away which were rejected, seeing they also were carried through the gate, and delivered by the hands of these virgins into the building of this tower? [128] Seeing, said he thou takest care to inquire diligently into all things, hear also concerning those stones which were rejected. All these received the name of the Son of God, and with that the power of these virgins. [129] Having therefore received these spirits, they were perfected, and brought into the number of the servants of God; and they began to be one body, and to have one garment, for they were endued with the same righteousness, which they alike exercised. [130] But after that they beheld those women which thou sawest clothed with a black garment, with their shoulders at liberty and their hair loose; they fixed their desires upon them, being tempted with their beauty; and were clothed with their power, and cast off the clothing of the virgins: [131] Therefore were they cast off from the house of God, and delivered to those women. But they that were not corrupted with their beauty, remained in the house of God. This, said he, is the signification of those stones which were rejected. [132] And I said, sir, what if any of these men shall repent, and cast away their desire of those women, and be converted, and return to these virgins, and put on again their virtue; shall they not enter into the house of God? [133] They shall enter, said he, if they shall lay aside all the works of those women, and shall resume the power of these virgins, and shall walk in their works. [134] And for this cause there is a stop in the building, that if they shall repent, they may be added to the building of this tower; but if they shall not repent, that others may be built in their places, and so they may be utterly cast away. [135] For all these things I gave thanks unto the Lord, that being moved with mercy towards all those upon whom his name is carried, he sent to us the angel of repentance to preside over us who have sinned against him; and that he has refreshed our spirits which were almost gone, and who had no hope of salvation, but are now refreshed to the renewal of life. [136] Then I said, Show me now sir, why this tower is not built upon the ground, but upon a rock, and upon the gate? He replied, Thou art foolish, and without understanding, therefore thou asketh this. [137] And I said, sir, I must needs ask all things of you because I understand nothing at all. For all your answers are great and excellent; and which a man can hardly understand. [138] Hear, said he: The name of the Son of God is great and without bounds, and the whole world is supported by it. If therefore, said I, every creature of God be sustained by his Son, why should he not support those also who have been invited by him, and who carry his name, and walk in his commandments? [139] Seest thou not, said he, that he doth support them, who with all their heart, bear his name? He therefore is their foundation, and gladly supports those who do not deny his name, but willingly bear it. [140] And I said: Sir, tell me the names of these virgins; and of those women that were clothed with the black garment. [141] Hear, said he, the names of those virgins which are the more powerful, and stand at the corners of the gate. These are their names: [142] The first is called Faith; the second Continence; the third Power; the fourth Patience; the rest which stand beneath these are, Simplicity, Innocence, Chastity, Cheerfulness, Truth, Understanding, Concord, Charity. [143] Whosoever therefore bear these names, and the name of the Son of God, shall enter into the kingdom of God. [144] Hear now, said he, the names of those women, which were clothed with the black garment. Of these, four are the principal: the first is Perfidiousness; the second, Incontinence; the third, Infidelity; the fourth, Pleasure. [145] And the rest which follow are called thus,

Sadness, Malice, Lust, Anger, Lying, Foolishness, Pride, and Hatred. The servant of God, which carries these spirits, shall see indeed the kingdom of God, but he shall not enter into it. [146] But, sir, what are those stones which were taken out of the deep and fitted into the building? The ten, said he, which were placed at the foundation, are the first age; the following five-and- twenty, are the second, of righteous men. [147] The next thirty-five, are the prophets and ministers of the Lord. And the forty, are the Apostles and doctors of the preaching of the Son of God. [148] And I said, sir, why did the virgins put even those stones into the building after they were carried through the gate? And he said, Because these first carried those spirits, and they departed not one from the other, neither the men from the spirits, nor the spirits from the men: [149] But the spirits were joined to those men even to the day of their death; who if they had not had these spirits with them, they could not have been useful to the building of this tower. [150] And I said, sir, show me this farther. He answered, What dost then ask? Why did these stones come out of the deep, and were placed into the building of this tower, seeing that they long ago carried those holy spirits? [151] It was necessary, said he, for them to ascend by water, that they might be at rest. For they could not otherwise enter into the kingdom of God, but by laying aside the mortality of their former life. [152] They therefore being dead, were nevertheless sealed with the seal of the Son of God, and so entered into the kingdom of God. [153] For before a man receives the name of the Son of God, he is ordained unto death; but when he receives that seal, he is freed from death, and assigned unto life. [154] Now that seal is the water of baptism, into which men go down under the obligation unto death, but come up appointed unto life. [155] Wherefore to those also was this seal preached, and they made use of it, that they might enter into the kingdom of God. [156] And I said, Why then, sir, did these forty stones also ascend with them out of the deep, having already received that seal? [157] He answered, Because these Apostles and teachers, who preached the name of the Son of God, dying after they had received his faith and power, preached to them who were dead before: and they gave this seal to them. [158] They went down therefore into the water with them, and again came up. But these went down whilst they were alive, and came up again alive: whereas those who were before dead, went down dead, but came up alive; [159] Through these therefore they received life, and knew the Son of God: for which cause they came up with them, and were fit to come into the building of the tower; and were not cut, but put in entire; because they died in righteousness, and in great purity; only this seal was wanting to them. [160] Thus you have the explication of these things. [161] I answered: Sir, tell me now what concerns those mountains; why are they so different, some of one form, and some of another? [162] Hear, said he; These twelve mountains which thou seest, are twelve nations, which make up the whole world. Wherefore the Son of God is preached to them, by those whom he sent unto them. [163] But why, said I, are they different, and every one of a figure? He replied, Hearken. Those twelve nations which possess the whole world, are twelve people. [164] And as thou hast beheld these mountains different, so are they. I will therefore open to thee the meaning and actions of every mountain. [165] But first, sir, said I, show me this; Seeing these mountains are so different, how have they agreed in the building of this tower; and been brought to one colour; and are no less bright than those that came out of the deep? [166] Because, replied he, all the nations which are under heaven, have heard and believed in the same one name of the Son of God by whom they are called. [167] Wherefore having received his seal, they have all been made partakers of the same understanding and knowledge; and their faith and charity have been the same; and they have carried the

410

spirits of these virgins together with his name. [168] And therefore the building of this tower appeared to be of the same colour, and did shine like the brightness of the sun. [169] But after that they had thus agreed in one mind, there began to be one body of them all; howbeit some of them polluted themselves, and were cast off from those of the righteous, and again returned to their former state, and became even worse than they were before. [170] How, air, said I, were they worse who knew the Lord? He answered: If he who knows not the Lord liveth wickedly, the punishment of his wickedness attends him; [171] But he who has known the Lord, ought to abstain altogether from all wickedness, and more and more to be the servant of righteousness. [172] And does not he then seem to thee to sin more who ought to follow goodness, if he shall prefer the part of sin; than he who offends without knowing the power of God? [173] Wherefore these are indeed ordained unto death; but they who have known the Lord, and have seen his wonderful works, if they shall live wickedly, they shall be doubly punished, and shall die for ever. [174] As therefore thou hast seen that after the stones were cast out of the tower, which had been rejected, they were delivered to wicked and cruel spirits; and thou beheldest the tower so cleansed, as if it had all been made of one stone: [175] So the church of God, when it shall be purified: (the wicked and counterfeits, the mischievous and doubtful, and all that have behaved themselves wickedly in it, and committed divers kinds of sin, being cast out) shall become one body, and there shall be one understanding, one opinion, one faith, and the same charity. [176] And then shall the Son of God rejoice among them, and shall receive his people with a pure will. [177] And I said; Sir, all these things are great and honourable; but now show unto me the effect and force of every mountain: that every soul which trusteth in the Lord, when it shall hear these things may honour his great, and wonderful, and holy name. [178] Hear, said he, the variety of these mountains, that is, of the twelve nations. [179] They who have believed of the first mountain, which is black, are those who have revolted from the faith, and spoken wicked things against the Lord; and betrayed the servants of God. [180] These are condemned to death; there is no repentance for them: and therefore they are black, because their kind is wicked. [181] Of the second mountain which was smooth, are the hypocrites, who have believed, and the teachers of naughtiness: and these are next to the foregoing, which have not in them the fruit of righteousness. [182] For as their mountain is barren and without fruit so also such kind of men have indeed the name of Christians, but are empty of faith; nor is there any fruit of the truth in them. [183] Nevertheless there is room left to them of repentance, if they shall speedily pursue it; but if they shall delay, they also shall be partakers of death with the foregoing kind. [184] I said, air, why is there room left to those for repentance, and not to the foregoing kind, seeing their sins are well nigh the same? [185] There is therefore, said he, to these a return unto life by repentance, because they have not blasphemed against their Lord, nor betrayed the servants of God: but by their desire of gain have deceived men, leading them according to the lusts of sinners; wherefore they shall suffer for this thing. [186] Howbeit there is still left them room for repentance, because they have not spoken any thing wickedly against the Lord. [187] They who are of the third mountain which had thorns and brambles, are those who believed, but were some of them rich; others taken up with many affairs: the brambles are their riches; the thorns, those affairs in which they were engaged. [188] Now they who are entangled in much business, and in diversity of affairs, join not themselves to the servants of God, but wander, being called away by those affairs with which they are choked. [189] And so they which are rich, with difficulty yield themselves to the conversation of the servants of God; fearing lest any thing should be asked of them.

411

These therefore shall hardly enter the kingdom of God. [190] For as men walk with difficulty bare-foot over thorns, even so these kind of men shall scarcely enter into the kingdom of God. [191] Nevertheless there is afforded to all these a return unto repentance, if they shall quickly return to it; because in their for-mer days they having neglected to work, in the time that is to come they may do some good. [192] If therefore having repented they shall do the works of righteousness, they shall live; but if they shall continue in their evil courses, they shall be delivered to those women who will take away their lives. [193] As for the fourth mountain, which had many herbs, the upper part of which is green, but the roots dry, and some of which being touched with the heat of the sun, are withered; [194] It denotes the doubtful, who have believed, and some others who carry the Lord on their tongues, but have him not in their hearts: therefore their grass is dry, and without root; because they live only in words, but their works are dead. [195] These therefore are neither dead nor living, and withal are doubtful. For the doubtful are neither green nor dry; that is neither dead nor alive. [196] For as the herbs dry away at the sight of the sun, so the doubtful, as soon as they hear of persecution, and fear inconveniencies, return to their idols, and again serve them, and are ashamed to bear the name of their Lord. [197] This kind of men then is neither dead nor alive; nevertheless these also may live, if they shall presently repent; but if not, they shall be delivered to those women, who shall take away their lives. [198] As concerning the fifth mountain that is craggy, and yet has green grass; they are of this kind who have believed, and are faithful indeed, but believe with difficulty, and are bold and self-conceited; and would be thought to know all things, but really know nothing. [199] Wherefore, by reason of this confidence, knowledge is departed from them; and a rash presumption is entered into them. [200] But they carry themselves high, and as prudent men; and though they are fools, yet would seem to be teachers. [201] Now by reason of this folly many of them whilst they magnify themselves, are become vain and empty. For boldness and vain confidence is a very evil spirit. [202] Wherefore many of these are cast away; but others acknowledging their error, have repented, and submitted themselves to those who are knowing. [203] And to all the rest of this kind, there is repentance allowed; forasmuch as they were not so much wicked as foolish, and void of understanding. [204] If these therefore shall repent, they shall live unto God; but if not, they shall dwell with those women, who shall exercise their wickedness upon them. [205] For what concerns the sixth mountain having greater and lesser clefts, they are such as have believed; but those in which were lesser clefts are they who have had controversies among themselves; and by reason of their quarrels languish in the faith: [206] Nevertheless many of these have repented, and so will the rest when they shall hear my commands; for their controversies are but small, and they will easily return unto repentance. [207] But those who have the greater clefts, will be as stiff stones, mindful of grudges and offences, and full of anger among themselves. These therefore are cast from the tower, and refused to be put into its building; for this kind of men shall hardly live. [208] Our God and Lord, who ruleth over all things, and has power over all his creatures, will not remember our offences, but is easily appeased by those who confess their sins: but man being languid, mortal, infirm, and full of sins, perseveres in his anger against man; as if it were in his power to save or destroy him. [209] But I, as the angel who am set over your repentance, admonish you, that whosoever among you has any such purpose he should lay it aside, and return unto repentance; and the Lord will heal your former sins, if you shall purge yourself from this evil spirit; but if you shall not do it, ye shall be delivered to him unto death. [210] As for the seventh mountain in which the grass was green and flourishing, and the whole mountain faithful; and all kind of cattle fed upon the grass of it, and the more the grass was eaten, so much the more it flourished; [211] They are such as believed, and were always good and upright; and without any differences among themselves, but still rejoiced in the servants of God, having put on the spirit of these virgins; and been always forward to show mercy to all men, readily giving to all men of their labours without upbraiding, and without deliberation. [212] Wherefore the Lord seeing their simplicity and innocence, has increased them in the works of their hands, and given them grace in all their works. [213] But I, who am the angel appointed over your repentance, exhort you, that as many as are of this kind would continue in the same purpose, that your seed may not be rooted out for ever. [214] For the Lord hath tried you, and written you into our number; and all your seed shall dwell with the Son of God; for ye are all of his spirit. [215] As concerning the eighth mountain in which were a great many springs, by which every kind of all the creatures of God was watered; they are such as have believed the Apostles which the Lord sent into all the world to preach; [216] And some of them being teachers have preached and taught purely and sincerely, and have not in the least yielded to any evil, desires, but have constantly walked in righteousness and truth. [217] These therefore have their conversations among the angels. [218] Again; as for what concerns the ninth mountain which is a desert, and full of serpents; they are such as have believed, but had many stains: [219] These are such ministers as discharge their ministry amiss; ravishing away the goods of the widows and fatherless; and serve themselves, not others, out of those things which they have received. [220] These, if they continue in this covetousness, have delivered themselves unto death, nor shall there be any hope of life for them. But if they shall be converted, and shall discharge their ministry sincerely, they may live. [221] As for those which were found rough, they are such as have denied the name of the Lord, and not returned again to the Lord, but have become savage and wild; not applying themelves to the servants of God; but being separated from them, have for a little carelessness lost their lives. [222] For as a vine that is forsaken in a hedge, and never dressed, perishes and is choked by the weeds, and in time becomes wild, and ceases to be useful to its lord; so this kind of men despairing of themselves, and being soured, have begun to be unprofitable to their Lord. [223] Howbeit, to these there is, after all, repentance allowed, if they shall not be found from their hearts to have denied Christ; but if any of these shall be found to have denied him from his heart, I cannot tell whether such a one can attain unto life. [224] I say therefore that if any one hath denied, he should in these days return unto repentance; for it cannot be that anyone who now denies the Lord, can afterwards attain unto salvation nevertheless repentance is promised unto them who have formerly denied. [225] But he who will repent must hasten on his repentance, before the building of this tower is finished; otherwise, he shall be delivered by those women unto death. [226] But they that are maimed, are the deceitful; and those who mix with one another, are the serpents that you saw mingled in that mountain. [227] For as the poison of serpents is deadly unto men, so the words of such persons infect and destroy men. They are therefore maimed in their faith, by reason of that kind of life which they lead. [228] Howbeit some of them, having repented, have been saved; and so shall others of the same kind be also saved, if they shall repent; but if not, they shall die by those women who power and force posses, [229] For what concerns the tenth mountain, in which were the trees covering the cattle, they are such as have believed; and some of them have been bishops, that is, governors of the churches. [230] Others, are such stones as have not feignedly, but with a cheerful mind entertained the servants of God. [231] Then, such as have been set over inferior

ministries, and have protected the poor and the widows; and have always kept a chaste conversation: therefore they also are protected by the Lord. [232] Whosoever shall do on this wise, are honoured with the Lord; and their place is among the angels, if they shall continue to obey the Lord even unto the end. [233] As to the eleventh mountain in which were trees loaded with several sorts of fruit; they are such as have believed, and suffered death, for the name of the Lord; and have endured with a heavy mind, and have given up their lives with all their hearts. [234] And I said, Why then, sir, have all these fruit indeed, but yet some fairer than others? [235] Hearken, said he: Whosoever have suffered for the name of the Lord are esteemed honourable by the Lord; and all their offences are blotted out, because they have suffered death for the name of the Son of God. [236] Hear now, why their fruits are different, and some of them excel others. They who were brought before magistrates, and being asked, denied not the Lord, but suffered with a ready mind; these are more honourable with the Lord. The fruits therefore that are the most fair are these. [237] But they who were fearful and doubtful, and have deliberated with themselves whether they should confess or deny Christ, and yet have suffered; their fruits are smaller, because that this thought came into their hearts. [238] For it is a wicked and evil thought for a servant to deliberate whether he should deny his master: Take heed therefore ye who have such thoughts, that this mind Pontinrie not in you, and ye die unto God. [239] But ye who suffer death for his name sake, ought to honour the Lord, that he has esteemed you worthy to bear his name; and that you should be delivered from all your sins. [240] And why therefore do you not rather esteem yourselves happy? Ye think verily that if any one among you suffer, he performs a great work! Yet the Lord giveth you life, and ye understand it not. For your offences did oppress you; and if you had not suffered for his name sake, ye would now be dead unto the Lord. [241] Wherefore I speak this unto you who deliberate whether ye should confess or deny him. Confess that ye have the Lord for your God, lest at any time denying him, ye be delivered up into bonds. [242] For if all nations punish their servants which deny their masters; what think you that the Lord will do unto you, who has the power of all things? [243] Remove therefore out of your hearts these doubts, that ye may live for ever unto God. [244] As for the twelfth mountain, which was white, they are such as have believed like sincere children, into whose thoughts there never came any malice, nor have they ever known what sin was, but have always continued in their integrity. [245] Wherefore this kind of men shall without all doubt inherit the kingdom of God; because they have never in any thing defiled the commandments of God, but have continued with sincerity in the same condition all the days of their lives. [246] Whosoever therefore, said he, shall continue as children without malice; shall be more honourable than all those of whom I have yet spoken: for all such children are honoured by the Lord, and esteemed the first of all. [247] Happy therefore are ye who shall remove all malice from you, and put on innocence; be. cause ye shall first see the Lord. [248] And after he had thus ended his explication of all the mountains, I said unto him, Sir, show me now also what concerns the stones that were brought out of the plain, and put into the tower in the room of those that were rejected. [249] As also concerning those round stones which were added into the building of the tower; and also of those who still continued round. [250] Hear now, says he, concerning those stones which were brought out of the plain into the building of the tower, and placed in the room of those that were rejected: they are the roots of that white mountain. [251] Wherefore because those who have believed of that mountain, were very innocent; the lord of this tower commanded that they which were of the roots of this mountain should be placed into the building. 252 For he knew that if they were put into, this building they would continue bright; nor would any of them any more be made black. 253 But if he had added after this manner, from the rest of the mountains, he would almost have needed again to visit the tower, and to cleanse it. 254 Now all these white stones are the young men who have believed, or shall believe; for they are all of the same kind. Happy is this kind, because it is innocent. 255 Hear now also concerning those round and bright stones; all these are of this white mountain. But they are therefore found round, because their riches have a little darkened them from the truth, and dazzled their eyes. 256 Howbeit they have never departed from the Lord, nor has any wicked word proceeded out of their mouths; but all righteousness, and virtue, and truth. 257 When therefore the Lord saw their minds, and that they might adorn the truth; he commanded that they should continue good, and that their riches should be pared away: 258 For he would not have them taken wholly away, to the end they might do some good with that which was left, and live unto God; because they also are of a good kind. 259 Therefore was there little cut off from them, and so they were put into the building of this tower. 260 As for the rest which continued still round, and were not found fit for the building of this tower, because they have not yet received the seal; they were carried back to their place, be. cause they were found very round. 261 But this present world must be cut away from them, and the vanities of their riches; and then they will be fit for the kingdom of God. For they must enter into the kingdom of God, because God has blessed this innocent kind. 262 Of this kind therefore none shall fall away: for though any of them being tempted by the devil should offend, he shall soon return to his Lord God. 263 I the angel of repentance esteem you happy, whosoever are innocent as little children, because your portion is good and honourable with the Lord. 264 And I say unto all you who have received this seal; keep simplicity, and remember not the offences which are committed against you, nor continue in malice, or in bitterness, through the memory of offences. 265 But become one spirit, and provide remedies for these evil rents, and remove them from you; that the lord of the sheep may rejoice at it; for he will rejoice, if he shall find all whole. 266 But if any of these sheep shall be found scattered away, Woe shall be to the shepherds; and if the shepherds themselves shall be scattered; what will they answer to the lord of the sheep-fold? Will they say that they were troubled by the sheep? But they shall not be believed. 267 For it is an incredible thing that the shepherd should suffer by his flock; and he shall be the more punished for his life. 268 Now I am the shepherd; and especially must give an account of you. 269 Wherefore take care of yourselves whilst the tower is, yet building. The Lord dwells in those that love peace, for peace is beloved; but he is far off from the contentious, and those who are full of malice. 270 Wherefore restore unto him the Spirit entire, as ye received it. For if thou shalt give unto a fuller a garment new and whole, thou wilt expect to receive it whole again; if therefore the fuller shall restore it unto thee torn, wouldst thou receive it? 271 Wouldst thou not presently be angry, and reproach him, saying: I gave my garment to thee whole, why halt thou rent it, and made it useless to me? Now it is of no use to me, by reason of the rent which thou hast made in it. Wouldst thou not say all this to a fuller, for the rent which he made in thy garment? 272 If therefore thou wouldst be concerned for thy garment, and complain that thou hadst not received it whole; what thinkest thou that the Lord will do, who gave his Spirit to thee entire, and thou hast rendered him altogether unprofitable, so that he can be of no use unto his Lord? For being corrupted by thee, he is no longer profitable to him. 273 Will not therefore the Lord do the same concerning his Spirit, by reason of thy deed? Undoubtedly, said I, he will do the

same to all those whom he shall find to continue in the remembrance of injuries. 274 Tread not then under foot he said, his mercy; but rather honour him, because he is so patient with respect to your offences, and not like one of you; but repent, for it will be profitable for you. 275 All these things which are above written, I the shepherd and angel of repentance, have shown and spoken to the servants of God. 276 If therefore ye shall believe and hearken to these words, and shall walk in them and correct your ways, ye shall live. But if ye shall, continue in malice, and in the remembrance of injuries, no such sinners shall live unto God. 277 All these things which were to be spoken by me, I have thus delivered unto you. Then the shepherd said unto me, Hast thou asked all things of me? I answered, sir, I have. 278 Why then, said he, hast thou not asked concerning the spaces of these stones that were put in the building, that I may explain that also unto thee? I answered, sir, I forgot it. Hear, then, said he, concerning these also. 279 They are those who have now heard these commands, and have repented with all their hearts; 280 And when the Lord saw that their repentance was good and pure, and that they could continue in it, he commanded their former sins to be blotted out. For these spaces were their sins, and they are therefore made even that they might not appear.

Similitude X Of Repentance and alms-deeds. AFTER I had written this book, the angel which had delivered me to that shepherd, came into the house where I was and sat upon the bed, and that shepherd stood at his right hand. 2 Then he called me and said unto me; I delivered thee and thy house to this shepherd, that thou mightest be protected by him. I said, Yes, Lord. 3 If therefore, said he, thou wilt be protected from all vexations and from all cruelty, and have success in every good word and work, and have all virtue and righteousness; walk in those commands which he has given thee, and thou shalt have dominion over all sin. 4 For if thou keepest those commands, all the lust and pleasure of this present world shall be subject to thee; and success shall follow thee in every good undertaking. 5 Take therefore his gravity and modesty towards thee, and say unto all, that he is in great honour and renown with God, and is a prince of great authority, and powerful in his office. 6 To him only is the power of repentance committed throughout the whole world. Does he not seem to thee to be of great authority? 7 But ye despise his goodness, and the modesty which he shows towards you. 8 I said unto him; Sir, ask him since the time that he came into my house whether I have done any thing disorderly, or have offended him in any thing? 9 I know, said he, that thou hast done nothing disorderly, neither wilt thou hereafter do any such thing, and therefore I speak these things with thee that then mayest persevere; for he has given me a good account concerning thee. 10 But thou shalt speak these things to others, that they who either have repented, or shall repent, may be like-minded with thee, and he may give me as good an account of them also; and that I may do the same unto the Lord. 11 I answered; Sir, I declare to all men the wonderful works of God; and I hope that all who love them, and have before sinned, when they shall hear these things, will repent, and recover life. 12 Continue therefore, said he, in this ministry, and fulfil it. And whosoever shall do according to the commands of this shepherd, he shall live; and shall have great honour both here and with the Lord. 13 But they that shall not keep his commands, flee from their life, and are adversaries to it. And they that follow not his commands, shall deliver themselves unto death; and shall be every one guilty of his own blood. 14 But I say unto thee, keep these commandments, and thou shalt find a cure for all thy sins. 15 Moreover, I have sent these virgins to dwell with thee; for I have seen that they are very kind to thee. Thou shalt therefore have them for thy helpers, that thou mayest the better keep the commands which he hath given thee; for these commands cannot be kept without these virgins. 16 And as I see how they are willing to be with thee, I will also command them that they shall not all depart from thy house. 17 Only do thou purify thy house; for they will readily dwell in a clean house. For they are clean and chaste, and industrious; and all of them have grace with the Lord. 18 If therefore thou shalt have thy house pure, they will abide with thee. But, if it shall be never so little polluted, they will immediately depart from thy house; for these virgins cannot endure any manner of pollution. 19 I said unto him; Sir, I hope that I shall so please them, that they shall always delight to dwell in my house. And as be to whom you have committed me, makes no complaint of me; so neither shall they complain. 20 Then he said to that shepherd: I see that the servant of God will live and keep these commandments, and place these virgins in a pure habitation. 21 When he had said this, he delivered me again to that shepherd, and called the virgins, and said unto them; Forasmuch as I see that ye will readily dwell in this man's house, I commend him and his family to you, that ye may not at all depart from his house. And they willingly heard these words. 22 Then he said unto me, Go on manfully in thy ministry; declare to all men the great things of God, and thou shalt find grace in this ministry. 23 And whosover shall walk in these commands, shall live, and be happy in his life. But he that shall neglect them, shall not live, and shall be unhappy in his life. 24 Say unto all that whosoever can do well, cease not to exercise themselves in good works, for it is profitable unto them. For I would that all men should be delivered from the inconveniences they lie under. 25 For he that wants, and suffers inconveniences in his daily life, is in great torment and necessity. Whosoever therefore delivers such a soul from necessity, gets great joy unto himself. 26 For he that is grieved with such inconveniencies is equally tormented, as if he were in chains. And many upon the account of such calamities, being not able to bear them, have chosen even to destroy themselves. 27 He therefore that knows the calamity of such a man, and does not free him from it, commits a great sin, and is guilty of his blood. 28 Wherefore exercise yourselves in good works, as many as have received ability from the Lord; lest whilst ye delay to do them, the building of the tower be finished; because for your sakes the building is stopped. 29 Except therefore ye shall make haste to do well, the tower shall be finished, and ye shall be shut out of it. 30 And after he had thus spoken with me, he rose up from the bed and departed, taking the shepherd and virgins with him. 31 Howbeit he said unto me, that he would send back the shepherd and virgins unto my house. Amen.

Odes of Solomon

Ode 1 1 The Lord is on my head like a crown, and I shall not be without Him. 2 They wove for me a crown of truth, and it caused thy branches to bud in me. 3 For it is not like a withered crown which buddeth not: but thou livest upon my head, and thou hast blossomed upon my head. 4 Thy fruits are full-grown and perfect, they are full of thy salvation.

Ode 2 No part of this Ode has ever been identified

Ode 3 The first words of this Ode have disappeared. 1 ... I put on. 2 And his members are with him. And on them do I stand, and He loves me: 3 For I should not have known love the Lord, if not loved me. 4 For who is able to distinguish love except the one that is loved? 5. I love the beloved and my soul loves Him: 6 And where His rest is, there also am I; 7 And I shall be no strangers for with the Lord Most High and Merciful there is no grudging. 8 I have been united to Him, for the Lover has found the Beloved, 9 And because I shall love Him that is the Son, I shall become a son;. 10 For he that

is joined to Him that is immortal, will also himself become immortal; 11 And he who has pleasure in the Living One, will become living. 12 This is the Spirit of the Lord, which doth not lie, which teacheth the sons of men to know His ways. 13 Be wise and understanding and vigilant. Hallelujah.

Ode 4 1 No man, O my God, changeth thy holy place; 2 And it is not (possible) that he should change it and put it in another place: because he hath no power over it: 3 For thy sanctuary thou hast designed before thou didst make (other) places: 4 That which is the elder shall not be altered by those that are younger than itself. 5 Thou has given thy heart, O Lord, to thy believers: never wilt thou fail, nor be without fruits: 6 For one hour of thy Faith is days and years. 7 For who is there put on thy grace, and be hurt? 8 For thy seal is known: and thy creatures know it: and thy (heavenly) hosts possess it: and the elect archangels are clad with it. 9 Thou hast given us thy fellowship: it was not that thou wast in need of us: but that we are in need of thee: 10 Distill thy dews upon us and open thy rich fountains that pour forth to us milk and honey: 11 For there is no repentance with thee that thou shouldest repent of anything that thou hast promised: 12 And the end was revealed before thee: for what thou gavest, thou gavest freely: 13 So that thou mayest not draw them back and take them again: 14 For all was revealed before thee as God, and ordered from the beginning before thee: and thou, O God, hast made all things. Hallelujah,

Ode 5 1 I will give thanks unto thee, O Lord, because I love thee; 2 O Most High, thou wilt not forsake me for thou art my hope: 3 Freely I have received thy grace, I shall live thereby: 4 My persecutors will come and not see me: 5 A cloud of darkness shall fall on their eyes; and an air of thick gloom shall darken them: 6 And they shall have no light to see: they may not take hold upon me. 7 Let their counsel become thick darkness, and what they have cunningly devised, let it return upon their own heads: 8 For they have devised a counsel and it did not succeed: 9 For my hope is upon the Lord and I will not fear, and because the Lord is my salvation, I will not fear: and He is a garland on my head and I shall not be moved; even if everything should be shaken, I stand firm; 11 And if all things visible should perish, I shall not die; because the Lord is with me I and I am with Him. Hallelujah.

Ode 6 1 As the hand moves over the harp, and the strings speak, 2 So speaks in my members the Spirit of the Lord, and I speak by His love. 3 For it destroys what is foreign and everything that is bitter: 4 For thus it was from the beginning and will be to the end, that nothing should be His adversary, and nothing should stand up against Him. 5 The Lord has multiplied the knowledge of Himself, and is zealous that these things should be known, which by His grace have been given to us. 6 And the praise of His name He gave us: our spirits praise His holy Spirit. 7 For there went forth a stream and became a river great and broad; 8 For it flooded and broke up everything and it brought (water) to the Temple; 9 And the restrainers of the children of men were not able to restrain it, nor the arts of those whose business it is to restrain waters; 10 For it spread over the face of the whole earth, and filled everything: and all the thirsty upon earth were given to drink of it; 11 And thirst was relieved and quenched: for from the Most High the draught was given. 12 Blessed then are the ministers of that draught who are entrusted with that water 13 They have assuaged the dry lips, and the will that had fainted they have raised up; 14 And souls that were near departing they have caught back from death: 15 And limbs that had fallen they straightened and set up: 16 They gave strength for their feebleness and light to their eyes: 17 For everyone knew them in the Lord, and they lived by the water of life forever. Hallelujah.

Ode 7 [1] As the impulse of anger against evil, so is the impulse of joy over what is lovely, and brings in of its fruits without restraint: [2] My joy is the Lord and my impulse is toward Him: this path of mine is excellent: [3] For I have a helper, the Lord. [4] He hath caused me to know Himself, without grudging, by His simplicity: His kindness has humbled His greatness. [5] He became like me, in order that I might receive Him: He was reckoned like myself in order that I might put Him on; [7] And I trembled not when I saw Him: because He was gracious to me: [8] Like my nature He became that I might learn Him and like my form, that I might not turn back from Him: [9] The Father of knowledge is the word of knowledge: [10] He who created wisdom is wiser than His works: [11] And He who created me when yet I was not knew what I should do when I came into being: [12] Wherefore He pitied me in His abundant grace: and granted me to ask from Him and to receive from His sacrifice: [13] Because He it is that is incorrupt, the fulness of the ages and the of them. [14] He hath given Him to be seen of them that are His, in order that they may recognize Him that made them: and that they might not suppose that they came of themselves: [15] For knowledge He hath appointed as its way, hath widened it and extended it; and brought to all perfection; [16] And set over it the traces of His light, and I walked therein from the beginning even to the end. [17] For by Him it was wrought, and He was resting in the Son, and for its salvation He will take hold of everything. [18] And the Most High shall be known in His Saints, to announce to those that have songs of the coming of the Lord: [19] That they may go forth to meet Him, and may sing to Him with joy and with the harp of many tones: [20] The seers shall come before Him and they shall be seen before Him, [21] And they shall praise the Lord for His love: because He is near and beholdeth. [22] And hatred shall be taken from the earth, and along with jealousy it shall be drowned: [23] For ignorance hath been destroyed, because the knowledge of the Lord hath arrived. [24] They who make songs shall sing the grace of the Lord Most High; [25] And they shall bring their songs, and their heart shall be like the day: and like the excellent beauty of the Lord their pleasant song; [26] And there shall neither be anything that breathes without knowledge nor any that is dumb: [27] For He hath given a mouth to His creation, to open the voice of the mouth towards Him, to praise Him: [28] Confess ye His power, and show forth His grace. Hallelujah.

Ode 8 [1] Open ye, open ye your hearts to the exultation of the Lord: [2] And let your love be multiplied from the heart and even to the lips, [3] To bring forth fruit to the Lord, living [fruit], holy [fruit], and to talk with watchfulness in His light. [4] Rise up, and stand erect, ye who sometime were brought low: [5] Tell forth ye who were in silence, that your mouth hath been opened. [6] Ye, therefore, that were despised be henceforth lifted up, because your righteousness hath been exalted. [7] For the right hand of the Lord is with you: and He is your helper: [8]. And peace was prepared for you, before ever your war was. [9]. Hear the word of truth, and receive the knowledge of the Most High. [10] Your flesh has not known what I am saying to you: neither have your hearts known what I am showing to you. [11] Keep. my secret, ye who are kept by it. [12] Keep my faith, ye who are kept by it. [13] And understand my knowledge, ye who know me in truth, [14] Love me with affection, ye who love! [15] For I do not turn away my face from them that are mine; [16] For I know them and before they came into being I took knowledge of them, and on their faces I set my seal: [17] I fashioned their members: my own breasts I prepared for them, that they might drink my holy milk and live thereby [18] I took pleasure in them and am not ashamed of them: [19] For my workmanship are they and the strength of my thoughts: [20] Who then shall rise up against my handiwork, or who is there that is not subject to them? [21] I willed and fashioned mind and

heart: and they are mine, and by my own right hand I set my elect ones: [22] And my righteousness goeth before them and they shall not be deprived of my name, for it is with them. [23] Ask, and abound and abide in the love of the Lord, [24] And yet beloved ones in the Beloved: those who are kept, in Him that liveth: [25] And they that are saved in Him that was saved; [26] And ye shall be found incorrupt in all ages to the name of your Father. Hallelujah.

Ode 9 [1] Open your ears and I will speak to you. Give me your souls that I may also give you my soul, [2] The word of the Lord and His good pleasures, the holy thought which He has devised concerning his Messiah. [3] For in the will of the Lord is your salvation, and His thought is everlasting life; and your end is immortality. [4] Be enriched in God the Father, and receive the thought of the Most High. [5] Be strong and be redeemed by His grace. [6] For I announce to you peace, to you His saints; [6] That none of those who hear may fall in war, and that those again who have known Him may not perish, and that those who receive may not be ashamed. [8] An everlasting crown forever is Truth. Blessed are they who set it on their heads: [9] A stone of great price is it; and there have been wars on account of the crown. [10] And righteousness hath taken it and hath given it to you. [11] Put on the crown in the true covenant of the Lord. [12] And all those who have conquered shall be written in His book. [13] For their book is victory which is yours. And she (Victory) sees you before her and wills that you shall be saved. Hallelujah.

Ode 10 [1] The Lord hath directed my mouth by His word: and He hath opened my heart by His light: and He hath caused to dwell in me His deathless life; [2] And gave me that I might speak the fruit peace: [3] To convert the souls of them who are willing to come to Him; and to lead captive a good captivity for freedom. [4] I was strengthened and made mighty and took the world captive; [5] And it became to me for the praise of the Most High, and of God my Father. [6] And the Gentiles were gathered together who were scattered abroad. [7] And I was unpolluted by my love for them, because they confessed me in high places: and the traces of the light were set upon their heart: [8] And they walked in my life and were saved and be came my people for ever and ever. Hallelujah.

Ode 11 [1] My heart was cloven and its flower appeared; and grace sprang up in it: and it brought forth fruit to the Lord, [2] For the Most High clave my heart by His Holy Spirit and searched my affection towards Him: and filled me with His love. [3] And His opening of me became my salvation; and I ran in His way in His peace even in the way of truth: [4] from the beginning and even to the end I acquired His knowledge: [5] And I was established upon the rock of truth, where He had set me up: [6] And speaking waters touched my lips from the fountain of the Lord plenteously: [7] And I drank and was inebriated with the living water that doth not die; [8] And my inebriation was not one without knowledge, but I forsook vanity and turned to the Most High my God, [9] And I was enriched by His bounty, and I forsook the folly which is diffused over the earth; and I stripped it off and cast it from me: [10] And the Lord renewed me in His raiment, and possessed me by His light, and from above He gave me rest in incorruption; [11] And I became like the land which blossoms and rejoices in its fruits: [12] And the Lord was like the sun shining on the face of the land; [13] He lightened my eyes and my face received the dew; the pleasant odour of the Lord; [14] And He carried me to His Paradise; where is the abundance of the pleasure, of the Lord; [15] And I worshipped the Lord on account of His glory; and I said, Blessed, O Lord, are they who are planted in thy land and those who have a place in thy Paradise; [16] And they grow by the fruits of the trees. And they have changed from darkness to light. [17] Behold! all thy servants are fair, who do good works, and turn away from wickedness to the pleasantness that is thine: [18] And they have turned back the bitterness of the trees from them, when they were planted in thy land; ¹⁹ And everything became like a relic of thyself, and memorial for ever of thy faithful works. ²⁰ For there is abundant room in thy Paradise, and nothing is useless therein; ²¹ But everything is filled with fruit; glory be to thee, O God, the delight of Paradise for ever. Hallelujah.

Ode 12 ¹ He hath filled me with words of truth; that I may speak the same; ² And like the flow of waters flows truth from my mouth, and my lips show forth His fruit. ³ And He has caused His knowledge to abound in me, because the mouth of the Lord is the true Word, and the door of His light; ⁴ And the Most High hath given it to His words, which are the interpreters of His own beauty, and the repeaters of His praise, and the confessors of His counsel and the heralds of His thought and the chasteners of His servants. ⁵ For the swiftness of the Word is inexpressible, and like its expression is its swiftness and force; ⁶ And its course knows no limit. Never doth it fail, but it stands sure, and it knows not descent nor the way of it. ⁷ For as its work is, so is its end: for it is light and the dawning of thought; ⁸ And by it the worlds talk one to the other; and in the Word there were those that were silent; ⁹ And from it came love and concord; and they spake one to the other whatever was theirs; and they were penetrated by the Word; ¹⁰ And they knew Him who made them, because they were in concord; for the mouth of the Most High spake to them; and His explanation ran by means of it: ¹¹ For the dwelling-place of the Word is man: and its truth is love. ¹² Blessed are they who by means thereof have understood everything, and have known the Lord in His truth. Hallelujah.

Ode 13 ¹ Behold! the Lord is our mirror: open the eyes and see them in Him: and learn the manner of your face: ² And tell forth praise to His spirit: and wipe off the filth from your face: and love His holiness, and clothe yourselves therewith: ³ And be without stain at all times before Him. Hallelujah.

Ode 14 ¹ As the eyes of a son to his father so are my eyes, O Lord at all times towards thee. ² For with thee are my consolations and my delight. ³ Turn not away thy mercies from me, O Lord: and take not thy kindness from me. ⁴ Stretch out to me, O Lord, at all times thy right hand: and be my guide even unto the end, according to thy good pleasure. ⁵ Let me be well-pleasing before thee, because of thy glory and because of thy name: ⁶ Let me be preserved from evil, and let thy meekness, O Lord, abide with me, and the fruits of thy love. ⁷ Teach me the Psalms of thy truth, that I may bring forth fruit in thee: ⁸ And open to me the harp of thy Holy Spirit, that with all its notes I may praise thee, O Lord. ⁹ And according to the multitude of thy tender mercies, so thou shalt give to me; and hasten to grant our petitions; and thou art able for all our needs. Hallelujah.

Ode 15 ¹ As the sun is the joy to them that seek for its daybreak, so is my joy the Lord; ² Because He is my Sun and His rays have lifted me up and His light hath dispelled all darkness from my face. In Him I have acquired eyes and have seen His holy day: ⁴ Ears have become mine and I have heard His truth. ⁵ The thought of knowledge hath been mine, and I have been delighted through Him. ⁶ The way of error I have left, and have walked towards Him and have received salvation from Him, without grudging. ⁷ And according to His bounty He hath given to me and according to His excellent beauty He hath made me. ⁸ I have put on incorruption through His name: and have put off corruption by His grace. ⁹ Death hath been destroyed before my face: and Sheol hath been abolished by my word: ¹⁰ And there hath gone up deathless life in the Lord's land, ¹¹ And it hath been made known to His faithful ones, and hath been given without stint to all those that trust in Him. Hallelujah.

Ode 16 ¹ As the work of the husband man is the ploughshare: and the work of the steersman is the guidance of the ship: ² So also my work is the Psalm of the Lord: my craft and praises: ³ Because His love hath nourished my heart, and even to my lips His fruits He poured out. ⁴ For my love is the Lord, and I therefore I will sing unto Him: ⁵ For I am made strong in His praise, and I have faith in Him. ⁶ I will open my mouth and His spirit will utter in me the glory of the Lord and His beauty; the work of His hands and the operation of His fingers: ⁷ The multitude of His mercies and the strength of His word. ⁸ For the word of the Lord searches out all things, both the invisible and that which reveals His thought; ⁹ For the eye sees His works and the ear hears His thought; ¹⁰ He spread out the earth and He settled the waters in the sea: ¹¹ He measured the heavens and fixed the stars: and He established the creation and set it up: ¹² And He rested from His works: ¹³ And created things run in their courses, and do their works: ¹⁴ And they know not how to stand and be idle; and His heavenly hosts are subject to His word. ¹⁵ The treasure-chamber of the light is the sun, and the treasury of the darkness is the night: ¹⁶ And He made the sun for the day that it may be bright, but night brings darkness over the face of the land; ¹⁷ And their alternations one to the other speak the beauty of God: ¹⁸ And there is nothing that is without the Lord; for He was before any thing came into being: ¹⁹ And the worlds were made by His word, and by the thought of His heart. Glory and honour to His name. Hallelujah.

Ode 17 ¹ I was crowned by my God: my crown is living: ² And I was justified in my Lord: my incorruptible salvation is He. ³ I was loosed from vanity, and I was not condemned: ⁴ The choking bonds were cut off by her hands: I received the face and the fashion of a new person: and I walked in it and was saved; ⁵ And the thought of truth led me on. And I walked after it and did not wander: ⁶ And all. that have seen me were amazed: and I was regarded by them as a strange person: ⁷ And He who knew and brought me up is the Most High in all His perfection. And He glorified me by His kindness, and raised my thoughts to the height of His truth. ⁸ And from thence He gave me the way of His precepts and I opened the doors that were closed,. ⁹ And brake in pieces the bars of iron: but my iron melted and dissolved before me; ¹⁰ Nothing appeared closed to me: because I was the door of everything. ¹¹ And I went over all my bond men to loose them; that I might not leave any man bound or binding: ¹² And I imparted my knowledge without grudging: and my prayer was in my love: ¹³ And I sowed my fruits in hearts, and transformed them into myself: and they received my blessing and lived; ¹⁴ And they were gathered to me and were saved; because they were to me as my own members and I was their head. Glory to thee our head the Lord Messiah. Hallelujah.

Ode 18 ¹ My heart was lifted up in the love of the Most High and was enlarged: that I might praise Him for His name's sake. ² My members were strengthened that they might not fall from His strength. ³ Sicknesses removed from my body, and it stood to the Lord by His will. For His kingdom is true. ⁴ O Lord, for the sake of them that are deficient do not remove thy word from me! ⁵ Neither for the sake of their works do thou restrain from me thy perfection! ⁶ Let not the luminary be conquered by the darkness; nor let truth flee away from falsehood. ⁷ Thou wilt appoint me to victory; our Salvation is thy right hand. And thou wilt receive men from all quarters. ⁸ And thou wilt preserve whosoever is held in evils: ⁹ Thou art my God. Falsehood and death are not in thy mouth: ¹⁰ For thy will is perfection; and vanity thou knowest not, ¹¹ Nor does it know thee. ¹² And error thou knowest not, ¹³ Neither does it know thee. ¹⁴ And ignorance appeared like a blind man; and like the foam of the sea, ¹⁵ And they supposed of that vain thing that it was something great; 16 And they too came in likeness of it and became vain; and those have understood who have known and meditated; 17 And they have not been corrupt in their imagination; for such were in the mind of the Lord; 18 And they mocked at them that were walking in error; 19 And they spake truth from the inspiration which the Most High breathed into them; Praise and great comeliness to His name. Hallelujah.

Ode 19 1 A cup of milk was offered to me: and I drank it in the sweetness of the delight of the Lord. 2 The Son is the cup and He who was milked is the Father: 3 And the Holy Spirit milked Him: because His breasts were full, and it was necessary for Him that His milk should be sufficiently released; 4 And the Holy Spirit opened His bosom and mingled the milk from the two breasts of the Father and gave the mixture to the world without their knowing: 5 And they who receive in its fulness are the ones on the right hand. 6 The Spirit opened the womb of the Virgin and she received conception and brought forth; and the Virgin became a Mother with many mercies; 7 And she travailed and brought forth a Son, without incurring pain; 8 And because she was not sufficiently prepared, and she had not sought a midwife (for He brought her to bear) she brought forth, as if she were a man, of her own will; 9 And she brought Him forth openly, and acquired Him with great dignity, 10 And loved Him in His swaddling clothes and guarded Him kindly, and showed Him in Majesty. Hallelujah.

Ode 20 1 I am a priest of the Lord, and to Him I do priestly service: and to Him I offer the sacrifice of His thought. 2 For His thought is not like the thought of the world nor the thought of the flesh, nor like them that serve carnally. 3 The sacrifice of the Lord is righteousness, and purity of heart and lips. 4 Present your reins before Him blamelessly: and let not thy heart do violence to heart, nor thy soul to soul. 5 Thou shalt not acquire a stranger by the price of thy silver neither shalt thou seek to devour thy neighbour, 6 Neither shalt thou deprive him of the covering of his nakedness. 7 But put on the grace of the Lord without stint; and come into His Paradise and make thee a garland from its tree,. 8 And put it on thy head and be glad; and recline on His rest, and glory shall go before thee, 9 And thou shalt receive of His kindness and of His grace; and thou shalt be flourishing in truth in the praise of His holiness. Praise and honour be to His name. Hallelujah.

Ode 21 1 My arms I lifted up to the Most High, even to the grace of the Lord: because He had cast off my bonds from me: and my Helper had lifted me up to His grace and to His salvation: 2 And I put off darkness and clothed myself with light, 3 And my soul acquired a body free from sorrow or affliction or pains 4 And increasingly helpful to me was the thought of the Lord, and His fellowship in incorruption: 5 And I was lifted up in His light; and I served before Him, 6 And I became near to Him, praising and confessing Him; 7 My heart ran over and was found in my mouth: and it arose upon my lips; and the exultation of the Lord increased on my face, and His praise likewise. Hallelujah.

Ode 22 1 He who brought me down from on high, also brought me up from the regions below; 2 And He who gathers together the things that are betwixt is He also who cast me down: 3 He who scattered my enemies had existed from ancient and my adversaries: 4 He who gave me authority over bonds that I might loose them; 5 He that overthrew by my hands the dragon with seven heads: and thou hast set me over his roots that I might destroy his seed. 6 Thou wast there and didst help me, and in every place thy name was a rampart to me. 7 Thy right hand destroyed his Wicked poison; and thy hand levelled the way for those who believe in thee. 8 And thou didst choose them from the graves and didst separate them from the dead. 9 Thou didst take dead bones and didst

cover them with bodies. 10 They were motionless, and thou didst give them energy for life. 11 Thy way was without corruption and thy face; thou didst bring thy world to corruption: that everything might be dissolved, and then renewed, 12 And that the foundation for everything might be thy rock: and on it thou didst build thy kingdom; and it became the dwelling place of the saints. Hallelujah.

Ode 23 1 Joy is of the saints! and who shall put it on, but they alone? 2 Grace is of the elect! and who shall receive it except those who trust in it from the beginning? 3 Love is of the elect? And who shall put it on except those who have possessed it from the beginning? 4 Walk ye in the knowledge of the Most High without grudging: to His exultation and to the perfection of His knowledge. 5 And His thought was like a letter; His will descended from on high, and it was sent like an arrow which is violently from the bow: 6 And many hands rushed to the letter to seize it and to take and read it: 7 And it escaped their fingers and they were affrighted at it and at the seal that was upon it. 8 Because it was not permitted to them to loose its seal: for the power that was over the seal was greater than they. 9 But those who saw it went after the letter that they might know where it would alight, and who should read it and who should hear it. 10 But a wheel received it and came over it: 11 And there was with it a sign of the Kingdom and of the Government: 12 And everything which tried to move the wheel it mowed and cut down: 13 And it gathered the multitude of adversaries, and bridged the rivers and crossed over and rooted up many forests and made a broad path. 14 The head went down to the feet for down to the feet ran the wheel, and that which was a sign upon it. 15 The letter was one of command, for there were included in it all districts; 16 And there was seen at its head, the head which was revealed even the Son of Truth from the Most High Father, 17 And He inherited and took possession of everything. And the thought of many was brought to nought. 18 And all the apostates hasted and fled away. And those who persecuted and were enraged became extinct, 19 And the letter was a great volume, which was wholly written by the finger of God: 20 And the name of the Father was on it and of the Son and of the Holy Spirit, to rule for ever and ever. Hallelujah.

Ode 24 1 The Dove fluttered over the Messiah, because He was her head; and she sang over Him and her voice was heard: 2 And the inhabitants were afraid and the sojourners were moved: 3 The birds dropped their wings and all creeping things died in their holes: and the abysses were opened which had been hidden; and they cried to the Lord like women in travail: 4 And no food was given to them, because it did not belong to them; 5 And they sealed up the abysses with the seal of the Lord. And they perished, in the thought those that had existed from ancient times; 6 For they were corrupt from the beginning; and the end of their corruption was life: 7 And every one of them that was imperfect perished: for it was not possible to give them a word that they might remain: 8 And the Lord destroyed the imaginations of all them that had not the truth with them. 9 For they who in their hearts were lifted up were deficient in wisdom and so they were rejected, because the truth was not with them. 10 For the Lord disclosed His way and spread abroad His grace: and those who understood it, know His holiness. Hallelujah.

Ode 25 1 I was rescued from my bonds and unto thee, my God, I fled: 2 For thou art the right hand of my Salvation and my helper. 3 Thou hast restrained those that rise up against me, 4 And I shall see him no more: because thy face was with me, which saved me by thy grace. 5 But I was despised and rejected in the eyes of many: and I was in their eyes like lead, 6 And strength was mine from thyself and help. 7 Thou didst set me a lamp at my right hand and at my left: and in me there shall be nothing that is not bright: 8 And I was clothed with the covering of thy Spirit, and thou didst remove from me my raiment of skin; 9 For thy right hand lifted me up and removed sickness from me: 10 And I became mighty in the truth, and holy by thy righteousness; and all my adversaries were afraid of me; 11 And I became admirable by the name of the Lord, and I was justified by His gentleness, and His rest is for ever and ever. Hallelujah.

Ode 26 1 I poured out praise to the Lord, for I am His: 2 And I will speak His holy song for my heart is with Him. 3 For His harp is in my hands, and the Odes of His rest shall not be silent. 4 I will cry unto him from my whole heart: I will praise and exalt Him with all my members. 5 For from the east and even to the west is His praise: 6 And from the south and even to the north is the confession of Him: 7 And from the top of the hills to their utmost bound is His perfection. 8 Who can write the Psalms of the Lord, or who read them? 9 Or who can train his soul for life that his soul may be saved, 10 Or who can rest on the Most High, so that with His mouth he may speak? 11 Who is able to interpret the wonders of the Lord? 12 For he who could interpret would be dissolved and would become that which is interpreted. 13 For it suffices to know and to rest: for in rest the singers stand, 14 Like a river which has an abundant fountain, and flows to the help of them that seek it. Hallelujah.

Ode 27 1 I stretched out my hands and sanctified my Lord: 2 For the extension of my hands is His sign: 3 And .my expansion is the upright tree [or cross].

Ode 28 1 As the wings of doves over their nestlings; and the mouth of their nestlings towards their mouths, 2 So also are the wings of the Spirit over my heart: 3 My heart is delighted and exults: like the babe who exults in the womb of his mother: 4 I believed; therefore I was at rest; for faithful is He in whom I have believed: 5 He has richly blessed me and my head is with Him: and the sword shall not divide me from Him, nor the scimitar; 6 For I am ready before destruction comes; and I have been set on His immortal pinions: 7 And He showed me His sign: forth and given me to drink, and from that life is the spirit within me and it cannot die, for it lives. 8 They who saw me marvelled at me, because I was persecuted, and they supposed that I was swallowed up: for I seemed to them as one of the lost; 9 And my oppression became my salvation; and I was their reprobation because there was no seal in me; 10 Because I did good to every man I was hated, 11 And they came round me like mad dogs, who ignorantly attack their masters, 12 For their thought is corrupt and their understanding perverted. 13 But I was carrying water in my right hand and their bitterness I endured by my sweetness: 14 And I did not perish, for I was not their brother nor was my birth like theirs. 15 And they sought for my death and did not find it: for I was older than the memorial of them; 16 And vainly did they make attack upon me and those who, without reward, came after me: 17 They sought to destroy the memorial of him who was before them. 18 For the thought of the Most High cannot be anticipated; and His heart is superior to all wisdom. Hallelujah.

Ode 29 1 The Lord is my hope: in Him I shall not be confounded. 2 For according to His praise He made me, and according to His goodness even so He gave unto me: 3 And according to His mercies He exalted me: and according to His excellent beauty He set me on high: 4 And brought me up out of the depths of Sheol: and from the mouth of death He drew me: 5 And thou didst lay my enemies low and He justified me by His grace. 6 For I believed in the Lord's Messiah: and it appeared to me that He is the Lord; 7 And He showed him His sign: and He led, me by His light, and gave me the rod of His power 8 That I might subdue the imaginations of the peoples; and the power of the men

418

of might to bring them low: 9 To make war by His word, and to take victory by His power. 10 And the Lord overthrew my enemy by His word: and he became like the stubble which the wind carries away; 11 And I gave praise to the Most High because He exalted me His servant and the son of His handmaid. Hallelujah.

Ode 30 1 Fill ye waters for yourselves from the living fountain, of the Lord, for it is opened to you: 2 And come all ye thirsty and take the draught; and rest by the fountain of the Lord. 3 For fair it is and pure and gives rest to the soul, Much ore pleasant are its waters than honey; 4 And the honeycomb of bees is not to be compared with it. 5 For it flows forth from the lips of the Lord and from the heart of the Lord is its name. 6 And it came infinitely and invisibly: and until it was set in the midst they did not know it: 7 Blessed are they who have drunk therefrom and have found rest thereby. Hallelujah.

Ode 31 1 The abysses were dissolved before the Lord: and darkness was destroyed by His appearance: 2 Error went astray and perished at His hand: and folly found no path to walk in, and was submerged by the truth of the Lord. 3 He opened His mouth and spake grace and joy: and He spake a new song of praise to His name: 4 And He lifted up His voice to the Most High and offered the sons that were with Him. 5 And His face was justified, for thus His holy Father had given to Him. 6 Come forth, ye that have been afflicted and receive joy, and possess your souls by His grace; and take to you immortal life. 7 And they made me a debtor when I rose up, me who had been a debtor: and they divided my spoil, though nothing was due to them. 8 But I endured and held my peace and was silent as if not moved by them. 9 But I stood unshaken like a firm rock which is beaten by the waves and endures. 10 An I bore their bitterness for humility's sake: 11 In order, that I might redeem my people, and inherit it and that I might not make void my promises to the fathers to whom I promised the salvation of their seed. Hallelujah.

Ode 32 1 To the blessed there is joy from their hearts, and light from Him that dwells in them: 2 And words from the Truth, who was self-originate: for He is strengthened by the holy power of the Most High: and He is unperturbed for ever and ever. Hallelujah.

Ode 33 1 Again Grace ran and forsook corruption, and came down in Him to bring it to nought; 2 And He destroyed perdition from before Him, and devastated all its order; 3 And He stood on a lofty summit and uttered His voice from one end of the earth to the other: 4 And drew to Him all those who obeyed Him; and there did not appear as it were an evil person. 5 But there stood a perfect virgin who was proclaiming and calling and saying, 6 O ye sons of men, return ye, and ye daughters of men, come ye: 7 And forsake the ways of that corruption and draw near unto me, and I will enter into you, and will bring you forth from perdition, 8 And make you wise in the ways of truth: that you be not destroyed nor perish: 9 Hear ye me and be redeemed. For the grace of God I am telling among you: and by my means you shall be redeemed and become blessed. 10 I am your judge; and they who have put me on shall not be injured: but they shall possess the new world that is incorrupt: 11 My chosen ones walk in me, and my ways I will make known to them that seek me, and I will make them trust in my name. Hallelujah.

Ode 34 1 No way is hard where there is a simple heart. 2 Nor is there any wound where the thoughts are upright: 3 Nor is there any storm in the depth of the illuminated thought: 4 Where one is surrounded on every side by beauty, there is nothing that is divided. 5 The likeness of what is below is that which is above; for everything is above: what is below is nothing but the imagination of those that are without knowledge. 6 Grace has been revealed for your salvation. Believe and live and be saved. Hallelujah.

Ode 35 1 The dew of the Lord in quietness He distilled upon me: 2 And the cloud of peace He caused to rise over my head, which guarded me continually; [3] It was to me for salvation: everything was shaken and they were affrighted; [4] And there came forth from them a smoke and a judgment; and I was keeping quiet in the order of the Lord: [5] More than shelter was He to me and more than foundation. [6] And I was carried like a child by mother: and He gave me milk, the dew of the Lord: [7] And I grew great by His bounty, and rested in His perfection, [8] And I spread out my hands in the lifting up of my soul: and I was made right with the Most High and I was redeemed with Him. Hallelujah.

Ode 36 [1] I rested in the Spirit of the Lord: and the Spirit raised me on high: [2] And made me stand on my feet in the height of the Lord, before His perfection and His glory, while I was praising Him by the composition of His songs. [3] The Spirit brought me forth before the face of the Lord: and, although a son of man, I was named the Illuminate, the Son of God: [4] While I praised amongst the praising ones, and great was I amongst the mighty ones. [5] For according to the greatness of the Most High, so He made me: and like His own newness He renewed me; and He anointed me from His own perfection: [6] And I became one of His Neighbours; and my mouth was opened; like a cloud of dew; [7] And my heart poured out as it were a gushing stream of righteousness, [8] And my access to Him was in peace; and I was established by the Spirit of His government. Hallelujah.

Ode 37 [1] I stretched out my hands to my Lord: and to the Most High I raised my voice: [2] And I spake with the lips of my heart; and He heard me when my voice reached Him: [3] His answer came to me and gave me the fruits of my labours; [4] And it gave me rest by the grace of the Lord. Hallelujah.

Ode 38 [1] I went up to the light of truth as if into a chariot: [2] And the Truth took me and led me: and carried me across pits and gulleys; and from the rocks and the waves it preserved me: [3] And it became to me a haven of Salvation: and set me on the arms of immortal life: [4] And it went with me and made me rest, and suffered me not to wander because it was the Truth. [5] And I ran no risk, because I walked with Him; [5] And I did not make an error [4] anything because I obeyed the Truth. [7] For Error flees away from it and meets it not: but the Truth proceeds in the right path, and [8] What ever I did not know, it made clear to me, all the poisons of error, and the plagues of death which they think to be sweetness: [9] And I saw the destroyer of destruction, when the bride who is corrupted is adorned: and the bridegroom who corrupts and is corrupted; [10] And I asked the Truth, 'Who are these?'; and He said to me, 'This is the deceiver and the error: [11] And they are alike in the beloved and in his bride: and they lead astray and corrupt the whole world: [12] And they invite many to the banquet, [13] And give them to drink of the wine of their intoxication, and remove their wisdom and knowledge, and so they make them without intelligence; [14] And then they leave them; and then these go about like madmen corrupting: seeing that they are with out heart, nor do they seek for it.' [15] And I was made wise so as not to fall into the hands of the deceiver; and I congratulated myself because the Truth went with me, [16] And I was established and lived and was redeemed, [17] And my foundations were laid on the hand of the Lord: because He established me. [18] For He set the root and watered it and fixed it and blessed it; and its fruits are for ever. [19] It struck deep and sprung up and spread out and was full and enlarged; [20] And the Lord alone was glorified in His planting and in His husbandry: by His care and by the blessing of His lips, [21] By the beautiful planting of His right hand: and by the discovery of His planting, and by the thought of His mind. Hallelujah.

Ode 39 [1] Great rivers are the power of the Lord: [2] And they carry headlong those who despise Him: and entangle their paths: [3] And

they sweep away their fords, and catch their bodies and destroy their lives. [4] For they are more swift than lightning and more rapid, and those who cross them in faith are not moved; [5] And those who walk on them without blemish shall not be afraid. [6] For the sign in them is the Lord; and the sign is the way of those who cross in the name of the Lord; [7] Put on, therefore the name of the Most High, and know Him and you shall cross without danger, for the rivers will be subject to you. [8] The Lord has bridged them by His word; and He walked and crossed them on foot: [9] And His footsteps stand firm on the water, and are not injured; they are as firm as a tree that is truly set up. [10] And the waves were lifted up on this side and on that, but the footsteps of our Lord Messiah stand firm and are not obliterated and are not defaced. [11] And a way has been appointed for those who cross after Him and for those who adhere to the course of faith in Him and worship His name. Hallelujah.

Ode 40 [1] As the honey distills from the comb of the bees, [2] And the milk flows from the woman that loves her children; [3] So also is my hope on Thee, my God. [4] As the fountain gushes out its water. [5] So my heart gushes out the praise of the Lord and my lips utter praise to Him, and my tongue His psalms, [6] And my face exults with His gladness and my spirit exults in His love and my soul shines in Him: [7] And reverence confides in Him; and redemption in Him stands assured: [8] And His inheritance is immortal life, and those who participate in it are incorrupt. Hallelujah.

Ode 41 [1] All the Lord's children will praise Him, and will collect the truth of His faith. [2] And His children shall be known to Him. Therefore we will sing in His love: [3] We live in the Lord by His grace: and life we receive in His Messiah: [4] For a great day has shined upon us: and marvellous is He who has given us of His glory. [5] Let us, therefore all of us unite together in the name of the Lord, and let us honour Him in His goodness, [6] And let our faces shine in His light: and let our hearts meditate in His love by night and by day. [7] Let us exult with the joy of the Lord. [8] All those will be astonished that see me, For from another race am I; [9] For the Father of truth remembered me: He who possessed me from the beginning: [10] For His bounty begat me, and the thought of His heart: [11] And His Word is with us in all our way; [12] The Saviour who makes alive and does not reject our souls; [13] The man who was humbled, and exalted by His own righteousness, [14] The Son of the Most High appeared in the perfection of His Father; [15] And light dawned from the Word that was beforetime in Him;. [16] The Messiah is truly one; and He was known before the foundation of the world, [17] That He might save souls forever by the truth of His name: a new song arises from those who love Him. Hallelujah.

Ode 42 [1] I stretched out my hands and approached my Lord: [2] For the stretching of my hands is His sign: [2] My expansion is the outspread tree which was set up on the way of the Righteous One. [4] And I became of no account to those who did not take hold of me and I shall be with those who love me. [5] All my persecutors are dead; and they sought after me who hoped in me, because I was alive: [6] And I rose up and am with them; and I will speak by their mouths. [7] For they have despised those who persecuted them; [8] And I lifted up over them the yoke of my love; [9] Like the arm of the bridegroom over the bride, [10] So was my yoke over those that know me: [11] And as the couch that is spread in the house of the bridegroom and bride, [12] So is my love over those that believe in me. [13] And I was not rejected though I was reckoned to be so. [14] I did not perish, though they devised it against me. [13] Sheol saw me and was made miserable: [16] Death cast me up and many along with me. [17] I had gall and bitterness, and I went down with him to the utmost of his depth: [18] And the feet and the head he let go, for they were not able to endure my face: [19] And I made a congregation of living men amongst his dead men, and I spake with them by living lips: 20 Because my word shall not be void: 21 And those who had died ran towards me: and they cried and said, Son of God, have pity on us, and do with us according to thy kindness. 22 And bring us out from the bonds of darkness: and open to us the door by which we shall come out to thee. 23 For we see that our death has not touched thee. 24 Let us also be redeemed with thee: for thou art our Redeemer. 25 And I heard their voice; and my name I sealed upon their heads: 26 For they are free men and they are mine. Hallelujah.

Apology of Aristides

[To the Emperor] Caesar Titus Hadrianus Antoninus Augustus Pius, from Marcianus Aristides, a philosopher of Athens.

Ap. Arist. 1. I, O king, by the grace of God came into this world; and having contemplated the heavens and the earth and the seas, and beheld the sun and the rest of the orderly creation, I was amazed at the arrangement of the world; and I comprehended that the world and all that is therein are moved by the impulse of another, and I understood that he that moveth them is God, who is hidden in them and concealed from them: and this is well known, that that which moveth is more powerful than that which is moved. And that I should investigate concerning this Mover of all, as to how He exists—for this is evident to me, for He is incomprehensible in His nature—and that I should dispute concerning the stedfastness of His government, so as to comprehend it fully, is not profitable for me; for no one is able perfectly to comprehend it. But I say concerning the Mover of the world, that He is God of all, who made all for the sake of man; and it is evident to me that this is expedient, that one should fear God, and not grieve man. Now I say that God is not begotten, not made; a constant nature, without beginning and without end; immortal, complete, and incomprehensible: and in saying that He is complete, I mean this; that there is no deficiency in Him, and He stands in need of nought, but everything stands in need of Him: and in saying that He is without beginning, I mean this; that everything which has a beginning has also an end; and that which has an end is dissoluble. He has no name; for everything that has a name is associated with the created; He has no likeness, nor composition of members; for he who possesses this is associated with things fashioned. He is not male, nor is He female: the heavens do not contain Him; but the heavens and all things visible and invisible are contained in Him. Adversary He has none; for there is none that is more powerful than He; anger and wrath He possesses not, for there is nothing that can stand against Him. Error and forgetfulness are not in His nature, for He is altogether wisdom and understanding, and in Him consists all that consists. He asks no sacrifice and no libation, nor any of the things that are visible; He asks not anything from anyone; but all ask from Him.

Ap. Arist. 2. Since then it has been spoken to you by us concerning God, as far as our mind was capable of discoursing concerning Him, let us now come to the race of men, in order that we may know which of them hold any part of that truth which we have spoken concerning Him, and which of them are in error therefrom. This is plain to you, O king, that there are four races of men in this world; Barbarians and Greeks, Jews and Christians. Now the Barbarians reckon the head of the race of their religion from Kronos and from Rhea and the rest of their gods: but the Greeks from Helenus, who is said to be from Zeus; and from Helenus was born Aeolus and Xythus, and the rest of the family from Inachus and Phoroneus, and last of all from Danaus the Egyptian and from Kadmus and from Dionysus. Moreover the Jews reckon the head of their race from Abraham, who begat Isaac, from whom was born Jacob, who begat twelve sons who removed from Syria and settled in Egypt, and there

were called the race of the Hebrews by their lawgiver: but at last they were named Jews. The Christians, then, reckon the beginning of their religion from Jesus Christ, who is named the Son of God most High; and it is said that God came down from heaven, and from a Hebrew virgin took and clad Himself with flesh, and in a daughter of man there dwelt the Son of God. This is taught from that Gospel which a little while ago was spoken among them as being preached; wherein if ye also will read, ye will comprehend the power that is upon it. This Jesus, then, was born of the tribe of the Hebrews; and He had twelve disciples, in order that a certain dispensation of His might be fulfilled. He was pierced by the Jews; and He died and was buried; and they say that after three days He rose and ascended to heaven; and then these twelve disciples went forth into the known parts of the world, and taught concerning His greatness with all humility and sobriety; and on this account those also who to-day believe in this preaching are called Christians, who are well known. There are then four races of mankind, as I said before, Barbarians and Greeks, Jews and Christians. To God then ministers wind, and to angels fire; but to demons water, and to men earth.

Ap. Arist. 3. Let us then begin with the Barbarians, and by degrees we will proceed to the rest of the peoples, in order that we may understand which of them hold the truth concerning God, and which of them error. The Barbarians then, inasmuch as they did not comprehend God, erred with the elements; and they began to serve created things instead of the Creator of them, and on this account they made likenesses and they enclosed them in temples; and lo! they worship them and guard them with great precaution, that their gods may not be stolen by robbers; and the Barbarians have not understood that whatsoever watches must be greater than that which is watched; and that whatsoever creates must be greater than that whatever is created: if so be then that their gods are too weak for their own salvation, how will they furnish salvation to mankind? The Barbarians then have erred with a great error in worshipping dead images which profit them not. And it comes to me to wonder also, O king, at their philosophers, how they too have erred and have named gods those likenesses which have been made in honour of the elements; and the wise men have not understood that these very elements are corruptible and dissoluble; for if a little part of the element be dissolved or corrupted, all of it is dissolved and corrupted. If then these elements are dissolved and corrupted, and compelled to be subject to another harder than themselves, and are not in their nature gods, how can they call gods those likenesses which are made in their honour? Great then is the error which their philosophers have brought upon their followers.

Ap. Arist. 4. Let us turn then, O king, to the elements themselves, in order that we may shew concerning them that they are not gods, but a creation, corruptible and changeable, which is in the likeness of man. But God is incorruptible and unchangeable and invisible, while seeing, turning and changing all things. Those therefore who think concerning earth that it is God have already erred, since it is digged and planted and delved; and since it receives the defilement of the excrement of men and of beasts and of cattle: and since sometimes it becomes what is useless; for if it be burned it becomes dead, for from baked clay there springs nothing: and again, if water be collected on it, it becomes corrupted along with its fruits: and lo! it is trodden on by men and beasts, and it receives the impurity of the blood of the slain; and it is digged and filled with the dead and becomes a repository for bodies: none of which things can that holy and venerable and blessed and incorruptible nature receive. And from this we have perceived that the earth is not God but a creature of God.

Ap. Arist. 5. And in like manner again have those erred who have thought concerning water that it is God. For water was created for the use of man and in many ways it is made subject to him. For it is changed, and receives defilement, and is corrupted, and loses its own nature when cooked with many things, and receives colours which are not its own; being moreover hardened by the cold and mixed and mingled with the excrement of men and beasts and with the blood of the slain: and it is compelled by workmen, by means of the compulsion of channels, to flow and be conducted against its own will, and to come into gardens and other places, so as to cleanse and carry out all the filth of men, and wash away all defilement, and supply man's need of itself. Wherefore it is impossible that water should be God, but it is a work of God and a part of the world. So too those have erred not a little who thought concerning fire that it is God: for it too was created for the need of men: and in many ways it is made subject to them, in the service of food and in the preparation of ornaments and the other things of which your majesty is aware: whilst in many ways it is extinguished and destroyed. And again those who have thought concerning the blast of winds that it is God, these also have erred: and this is evident to us, that these winds are subject to another, since sometimes their blast is increased and sometimes it is diminished and ceases, according to the commandment of Him who subjects them. Since for the sake of man they were created by God, in order that they might fulfil the needs of trees and fruits and seeds, and that they might transport ships upon the sea; those ships which bring to men their necessary things, from a place where they are found to a place where they are not found; and furnish the different parts of the world. Since then this wind is sometimes increased and sometimes diminished, there is one place in which it does good and another where it does harm, according to the nod of Him who rules it: and even men are able by means of well-known instruments to catch and coerce it that it may fulfil for them the necessities which they demand of it: and over itself it has no power at all; wherefore it is not possible that winds should be called gods, but a work of God.

Ap. Arist. 6. So too those have erred who have thought concerning the sun that he is God. For lo! we see him, that by the necessity of another he is moved and turned and runs his course; and he proceeds from degree to degree, rising and setting every day, in order that he may warm the shoots of plants and shrubs, and may bring forth in the air which is mingled with him every herb which is on the earth. And in calculation the sun has a part with the rest of the stars in his course, and although he is one in his nature, he is mixed with many parts, according to the advantage of the needs of men: and that not according to his own will, but according to the will of Him that ruleth him. Wherefore it is not possible that the sun should be God, but a work of God; and in like manner also the moon and stars.

Ap. Arist. 7. But those who have thought concerning men of old, that some of them are gods, these have greatly erred: as thou, even thou, O king, art aware, that man consists of the four elements and of soul and spirit, and therefore is he even called World, and apart from any one of these parts he does not exist. He has beginning and end, and he is born and also suffers corruption. But God, as I have said, has none of this in His nature, but He is unmade and incorruptible. On this account, then, it is impossible that we should represent him as God who is man by nature, one to whom sometimes, when he looketh for joy, grief happens; and for laughter, and weeping befals him; one that is passionate and jealous, envious and regretful, along with the rest of the other defects: and in many ways more corrupted than the elements or even than the beasts. And thence, O king, it is right for us to understand the error of the

Barbarians, that, whereas they have not investigated concerning the true God, they have fallen away from the truth and have gone after the desire of their own mind, in serving elements subject to dissolution, and dead images: and on account of their error they do not perceive who is the true God.

Ap. Arist. 8. Let us return now to the Greeks in order that we may know what opinion they have concerning the true God. The Greeks then because they are wiser than the Barbarians have erred even more than the Barbarians, in that they have introduced many gods that are made; and some of them they have represented as male and some of them as female; and in such a way that some of their gods were found to be adulterers and murderers, and jealous and envious, and angry and passionate, and murderers of fathers, and thieves and plunderers. And they say that some of them were lame and maimed; and some of them wizards, and some of them utterly mad; and some of them played on harps; and some of them wandered on mountains: and some of them died outright; and some were struck by lightning, and some were made subject to men, and some went off in flight, and some were stolen by men; and lo! some of them were wept and bewailed by men; and some, they say, went down to Hades; and some were sorely wounded, and some were changed into the likeness of beasts in order that they might commit adultery with the race of mortal women; and some of them have been reviled for sleeping with males: and some of them, they say, were in wedlock with their mothers and sisters and daughters; and they say of their gods that they committed adultery with the daughters of men, and from them was born a certain race which was also mortal. And of some of their goddesses they say that they contended about beauty and came for judgment before men. The Greeks, then, O king, have brought forward what is wicked, ridiculous and foolish concerning their gods and themselves; in that they called such like persons gods, who are no gods: and hence men have taken occasion to commit adultery and fornication, and to plunder and do everything that is wicked and hateful and abominable. For if those who are called their gods have done all those things that are written above, how much more shall men do them who believe in those who have done these things! and from the wickedness of this error, lo! there have happened to men frequent wars and mighty famines, and bitter captivity and deprivation of all things: and lo! they endure them, and all these things befal them from this cause alone: and when they endure them they do not perceive in their conscience that because of their error these things happen to them.

Ap. Arist. 9. Now let us come to the history of these their gods in order that we may prove accurately concerning all those things which we have said above. Before everything else the Greeks introduce as a god Kronos, which is interpreted Chiun; and the worshippers of this deity sacrifice to him their children: and some of them they burn while yet living. Concerning him they say that he took him Rhea to wife; and from her he begat many sons; from whom he begat also Dios, who is called Zeus; and at the last he went mad and, for fear of an oracle which was told him, began to eat his children. And from him Zeus was stolen away, and he did not perceive it: and at the last Zeus bound him and cut off his genitals and cast them in the sea: whence, as they say in the fable, was born Aphrodite, who is called Astera: and he cast Kronos bound into darkness. Great then is the error and scorn which the Greeks have introduced concerning the head of their gods, in that they have said all these things about him, O king. It is not possible that God should be bound or amputated; otherwise it is a great misfortune. And after Kronos they introduce another god, Zeus; and they say concerning this one, that he received the headship and became king of all the gods; and they say concerning him that he was changed into cattle and everything else, in order that he might commit adultery with mortal women, and might raise up to himself children from them. Since at one time they say he was changed into a bull on account of his passion for Europa and for Pasiphae; and again he was changed into the likeness of gold on account of his passion for Danae: and into a swan, through his passion for Lcda; and into a man through his passion for Antiope; and into lightning on account of his passion for the Moon: so that from these he begat many children: for they say that from Antiope he begat Zethus and Amphion; and from the Moon, Dionysus; from Alkmena, Herakles; and from Leto, Apollo and Artemis; and from Danae, Perseus; and from Leda, Castor and Polydeuces and Helene; and from Mnemosyne he begat nine daughters, those whom he called the Muses; and from Europa, Minos and Rhadamanthus and Sarpedon. But last of all he was changed into the likeness of an eagle on account of his passion for Ganymede the shepherd.Because of these stories, O king, much evil has befallen the race of men who are at this present day, since they imitate their gods, and commit adultery, and are defiled with their mothers and sisters, and in sleeping with males: and some of them have dared to kill even their fathers. For if he, who is said to be the head and king of their gods, has done these things, how much more shall his worshippers imitate him! And great is the madness which the Greeks have introduced into their history concerning him: for it is not possible that a god should commit adultery or fornication, or should approach to sleep with males, or that he should be a parricide; otherwise he is much worse than a destructive demon.

Ap. Arist. 10. And again they introduce another god, Hephaestus; and they say of him that he is lame and wearing a cap on his head, and holding in his hand tongs and hammer; and working in brass in order that therefrom he may find his needed sustenance. Is then this god so much in need? Whereas it is impossible for a god to be needy or lame: otherwise he is very weak.And again they introduce another god and call him Hermes; and they say that he is a thief, loving avarice and coveting gains, and a magician and maimed and an athlete and an interpreter of words: whereas it is impossible for a god to be a magician, or avaricious, or maimed, or coveting anything that is not his, or an athlete: and if it be found to be otherwise, he is of no use.And after him they introduce another god, Asclepius; and they say that he is a physician and prepares medicines and bandages in order that he may satisfy his need of sustenance. Is then this god in need? And he at last was struck by lightning by Zeus, on account of Tyndareus the Lacedemonian; and so he died. If then Asclepius was a god, and when struck by lightning was unable to help himself, how is it that he was able to help others? Whereas it is an impossible thing that the divine nature should be in need, or that it should be struck by lightning.And again they introduce another god and call him Ares, and they say that he is a warrior and jealous, and covets sheep and things which do not belong to him, and acquires possessions through his weapons; and of him they say that at last he committed adultery with Aphrodite and was bound by a tiny boy Eros, and by Hephaestus the husband of Aphrodite: whereas it is impossible that a god should be a warrior or a prisoner or an adulterer.And again they say of Dionysus that he too is a god, who celebrates festivals by night and teaches drunkenness, and carries off women that do not belong to him: and at the last they say that he went mad and left his female attendants and tied to the wilderness; and in this madness of his he ate serpents; and at the last he was killed by Titan. If then Dionysus was a god, and when slain was not able to help himself; how is it that he was able to help others?Herakles, too, they introduce, and they say of him that he is a god, a hater of things hateful, a tyrant and a warrior, and a slayer of the wicked: and of him they say that at the last he went mad and

422

slew his children and cast himself into the fire and died. If therefore Herakles be a god and in all these evils was unable to stand up for himself, how was it that others were asking help from him? Whereas it is impossible that a god should be mad or drunken or a slayer of his children, or destroyed by fire.

Ap. Arist. 11. And after him they introduce another god and call him Apollo: and they say of him that he is jealous and. changeable; and sometimes he holds a bow and a quiver, and sometimes a lyre and a plectrum; and he gives oracles to men, in order that he may receive a reward from them. Is then this god in need of reward? Whereas it is disgraceful that all these things should be found in a god.And after him they introduce Artemis a goddess, the sister of Apollo; and they say that she was a huntress; and she carried a bow and arrows, and went about on mountains leading dogs, either to hunt the deer or the wild boars. Whereas it is disgraceful that a maid should go about by herself on mountains and follow the chase of beasts. And therefore it is not possible that Artemis should be a goddess.Again they say of Aphrodite that she forsooth is a goddess; and sometimes forsooth she dwells with their gods, and sometimes she commits adultery with men; and sometimes she has Ares for her lover and sometimes Adonis, who is Tammuz: and sometimes forsooth Aphrodite is wailing and weeping for the death of Tammuz: and they say that she went down to Hades in order that she might ransom Adonis from Persephone, who was the daughter of Hades. If then Aphrodite be a goddess and was unable to help her lover in his death, how is she able to help others? And this is a thing impossible to be listened to, that the divine nature should come to weeping and wailing and adultery.

And again they say of Tammuz that he is a god; and he is forsooth a hunter and an adulterer; and they say that he was killed by a blow from a wild boar, and was not able to help himself, And if he was not able to help himself, how is he able to take care of the human race? And this is impossible, that a god should be an adulterer or a hunter or that he should have died by violence.And again they say of Rhea that she forsooth is the mother of their gods; and they say of her that she had at one time a lover Atys, and she was rejoicing in corruptible men; and at the last she established lamentations, and was bewailing her lover Atys. If then the mother of their gods was not able to help her lover and rescue him from death, how is it possible that she should help others? It is disgraceful then that a goddess should lament and weep, and that she should have joy over corruptible beings. Again they bring forward Kore; and they say that she was a goddess and that she was carried off by Pluto and was not able to help herself. If then she is a goddess and was not able to help herself, how is she able to help others? For a goddess who is carried off is extremely weak.All these things, then, O king, the Greeks have introduced forward about their gods, and have invented and said concerning them: whence all men have taken occasion to do all wicked and impure things: and thereby the whole earth has been corrupted.

Ap. Arist. 12. Now the Egyptians, because they arc more evil and ignorant than all peoples upon the earth, have erred more than all men. For the worship of the Barbarians and the Greeks did not suffice them, but they introduced also the nature of beasts, and said concerning it that they were gods: and also of the creeping things which are found on the dry land and in the waters, and of the plants and herbs they have said that some of them are gods, and they have become corrupt in all madness and impurity more than all peoples that are upon the earth. For of old time they worshipped Isis; and they say that she forsooth is a goddess, who had forsooth a husband Osiris, her brother; but when forsooth Osiris was killed by his brother Typhon, Isis fled with her son Horus to Byblos in Syria and was there for a certain time until that her son was grown: and he contended with his uncle Typhon and killed him, and thereupon Isis returned and went about with her son Horus, and was seeking for the body of Osiris her lord, and bitterly bewailing his death. If therefore Isis be a goddess, and was not able to help Osiris her brother and lord, how is it possible that she should help others? Whereas it is impossible that the divine nature should be afraid and flee, or weep and wail. Otherwise it is a great misfortune.But of Osiris they say that he is a god, a beneficent one; and he was killed by Typhon and could not help himself; and it is evident that this cannot be said of Deity.And again they say of Typhon, his brother, that he is a god, a fratricide, and slain by his brother's son and wife since he was unable to help himself. And how can one who does not help himself be a god?Now because the Egyptians are more ignorant than the rest of the peoples, these and the like gods did not suffice them, but they also put the name of gods on the beasts which are merely soulless. For some men among them worship the sheep, and others the calf; and some of them the pig, and others the shadfish; and some of them the crocodile, and the hawk, and the cormorant, and the kite, and the vulture, and the eagle, and the crow; some of them worship the cat, and others the fish Shibbuta; some of them the dog, and some of them the serpent, and some the asp, and others the lion, and others garlic, and onions, and thorns, and others the leopard, and the like.And the poor wretches do not perceive with regard to all these things that they are nought; while every day they look upon their gods, who are eaten and destroyed by men, yea even by their own fellows; and some of them being burned, and some of them dying and putrifying and becoming refuse; and they do not understand that they are destroyed in many ways.And accordingly the Egyptians have not understood that the like of these are not gods, since their salvation is not within their own power; and if they are too weak for their own salvation, then as regards the salvation of their worshippers pray whence will they have the power to help them?

Ap. Arist. 13. The Egyptians then have erred with a great error, above all peoples that are upon the face of the earth. But it is a matter of wonder, O king, concerning the Greeks, whereas they excel all the rest of the peoples in their manners and in their reason, how thus they have gone astray after dead idols and senseless images: while they see their gods sawn and polished by their makers, and curtailed and cut and burnt and shaped and transformed into every shape by them. And when they are grown old and fail by the length of time, and are melted and broken in pieces, how is it that they do not understand concerning them that they are not gods? And those who have not ability for their own preservation, how will they be able to take care of men? But even the poets and philosophers among them being in error have introduced concerning them that they are gods, things like these which are made for the honour of God Almighty; and being in error they seek to make them like to God as to whom no man has ever seen to whom He is like; nor is he able to see Him; and together with these things they introduce concerning Deity as if it were that deficiency were found with it; in that they say that He accepts sacrifice and asks for burnt-offering and libation and murders of men and temples. But God is not needy, and none of these things is sought for by Him: and it is clear that men are in error in those things that they imagine. But their poets and philosophers introduce and say, that the nature of all their gods is one; but they have not understood of God our Lord, that while He is one, He is yet in all. They, then, are in error; for if, while the body of man is many in its parts, no member is afraid of its fellow, but whilst it is a composite body, all is on an equality with all: so also God who is one in His nature has a single essence proper to Him,

423

and He is equal in His nature and His essence, nor is He afraid of Himself. If therefore the nature of the gods is one, it is not proper that a god should persecute a god, nor kill nor do him that which is evil.If then gods were persecuted and transfixed by gods, and some of them were carried off and some were struck by lightning; it is clear that the nature of their gods is not one, and hence it is clear, O king, that that is an error which they speculate about the nature of their gods, and that they reduce them to one nature. If then it is proper that we should admire a god who is visible and does not see, how much more is this worthy of admiration that a man should believe in a nature which is invisible and all-seeing! and if again it is right that a man should investigate the works of an artificer, how much more is it right that he should praise the Maker of the artificer! For behold! while the Greeks have established laws, they have not understood that by their laws they were condemning their gods; for if their laws are just, their gods are unjust, who have committed transgression in killing one another and practising sorcery, committing adultery, plundering, stealing and sleeping with males, along with the rest of their other doings. But if their gods excellently and as they describe have done all these things, then the laws of the Greeks are unjust; and they are not laid down according to the will of the gods; and in this the whole world has erred. For as for the histories of their gods, some of them are myths, some of them physical, and some hymns and songs: the hymns and songs, then, are empty words and sound; and as to the physical, if they were done as they say, then they are not gods, since they have done these things and suffered and endured these things: and these myths arc flimsy words, altogether devoid of force.

Ap. Arist. 14. Let us come now, O king, also to the history of the Jews and let us see what sort of opinion they have concerning God. The Jews then say that God is one, Creator of all and almighty: and that it is not proper for us that anything else should be worshipped, but this God only: and in this they appear to be much nearer to the truth than all the peoples, in that they worship God more exceedingly and not His works; and they imitate God by reason of the love which they have for man; for they have compassion on the poor and ransom the captive and bury the dead, and do things of a similar nature to these: things which are acceptable to God and are well-pleasing also to men, things which they have received from their fathers of old. Nevertheless they too have gone astray from accurate knowledge, and they suppose in their minds that they are serving God, but in the methods of their actions their service is to angels and not to God, in that they observe sabbaths and new moons and the passover and the great fast, and the fast, and circumcision, and cleanness of meats: which things not even thus have they perfectly observed.

Ap. Arist. 15. Now the Christians, O king, by going about and seeking have found the truth, and as we have comprehended from their writings they are nearer to the truth and to exact knowledge than the rest of the peoples. For they know and believe in God, the Maker of heaven and earth, in whom are all things and from whom are all things: He who has no other god as His fellow: from whom they have received those commandments which they have engraved on their minds, which they keep in the hope and expectation of the world to come; so that on this account they do not commit adultery nor fornication, they do not bear false witness, they do not deny a deposit, nor covet what is not theirs: they honour father and mother; they do good to those who are their neighbours, and when they are judges they judge uprightly; and they do not worship idols in the form of man; and whatever they do not wish that others should do to them, they do not practise towards any one, and they do not eat of the meats of idol sacrifices, for they are undefiled: and those who grieve them they comfort, and make them their friends; and they do good to their enemies: and their wives, O king, are pure as virgins, and their daughters modest: and their men abstain from all unlawful wedlock and from all impurity, in the hope of the recompense that is to come in another world: but as for their servants or handmaids, or their children if any of them have any, they persuade them to become Christians for the love that they have towards them; and when they have become so, they call them without distinction brethren: they do not worship strange gods: and they walk in all humility and kindness, and falsehood is not found among them, and they love one another: and from the widows they do not turn away their countenance: and they rescue the orphan from him who does him violence: and he who has gives to him who has not, without grudging; and when they see the stranger they bring him to their dwellings, and rejoice over him as over a true brother; for they do not call brothers those who are after the flesh, but those who are in the spirit and in God: but when one of their poor passes away from the world, and any of them sees him, then he provides for his burial according to his ability; and if they hear that any of their number is imprisoned or oppressed for the name of their Messiah, all of them provide for his needs, and if it is possible that he may be delivered, they deliver him. And if there is among them a man that is poor or needy, and they have not an abundance of necessaries, they fast two or three days that they may supply the needy with their necessary food. And they observe scrupulously the commandments of their Messiah: they live honestly and soberly, as the Lord their God commanded them: every morning and at all hours on account of the goodnesses of God toward them they praise and laud Him: and over their food and over their drink they render Him thanks. And if any righteous person of their number passes away from the world they rejoice and give thanks to God, and they follow his body, as if he were moving from one place to another: and when a child is born to any one of them, they praise God, and if again it chance to die in its infancy, they praise God mightily, as for one who has passed through the world without sins. And if again they see that one of their number has died in his iniquity or in his sins, over this one they weep bitterly and sigh, as over one who is about to go to punishment: such is the ordinance of the law of the Christians, O king, and such their conduct.

Ap. Arist. 16. As men who know God, they ask from Him petitions which are proper for Him to give and for them to receive: and thus they accomplish the course of their lives. And because they acknowledge the goodnesses of God towards them, lo! on account of them there flows forth the beauty that is in the world. And truly they are of the number of those that have found the truth by going about and seeking it, and as far as we have comprehended, we have understood that they only are near to the knowledge of the truth. But the good deeds which they do, they do not proclaim in the ears of the multitude, and they take care that no one shall perceive them, and hide their gift, as he who has found a treasure and hides it. And they labour to become righteous as those that expect to see their Messiah and receive from Him the promises made to them with great glory. But their sayings and their ordinances, O king, and the glory of their service, and the expectation of their recompense of reward, according to the doing of each one of them, which they expect in another world, thou art able to know from their writings. It sufficeth for us that we have briefly made known to your majesty concerning the conversation and the truth of the Christians. For truly great and wonderful is their teaching to him that is willing to examine and understand it. And truly this people is a new people, and there is something divine mingled with it. Take now their writings and read in them, and lo! ye will find that not of myself have

424

I brought these things forward nor as their advocate have I said them, but as I have read in their writings, these things I firmly believe, and those things also that are to come. And therefore I was constrained to set forth the truth to them that take pleasure therein and seek after the world to come. And I have no doubt that the world stands by reason of the intercession of Christians. But the rest of the peoples are deceived and deceivers, rolling themselves before the elements of the world, according as the sight of their understanding is unwilling to pass by them; and they grope as if in the dark, because they are unwilling to know the truth, and like drunken men they stagger and thrust one another and fall down.

Ap. Arist. 17. Thus far, O king, it is I that have spoken. For as to what remains, as was said above, there are found in their other writings words which are difficult to speak, or that one should repeat them; things which are not only said, but actually done. The Greeks, then, O king, because they practise foul things in sleeping with males, and with mother and sister and daughter, turn the ridicule of their foulness upon the Christians; but the Christians are honest and pious, and the truth is set before their eyes, and they are long-suffering; and therefore while they know their error and are buffeted by them, they endure and suffer them: and more exceedingly do they pity them as men who are destitute of knowledge: and in their behalf they offer up prayers that they may turn from their error. And when it chances that one of them turns, he is ashamed before the Christians of the deeds that are done by him: and he confesses to God, saying, In ignorance I did these things: and he cleanses his heart, and his sins are forgiven him, because he did them in ignorance in former time, when he was blaspheming and reviling the true knowledge of the Christians. And truly blessed is the race of the Christians, more than all men that are upon the face of the earth. Let the tongues of those now be silenced who talk vanity, and who oppress the Christians, and let them now speak the truth. For it is better that they should worship the true God rather than that they should worship a sound without intelligence; and truly divine is that which is spoken by the mouth of the Christians, and their teaching is the gateway of light. Let all those then approach thereunto who do not know God, and let them receive incorruptible words, those which are so always and from eternity: let them, therefore, anticipate the dread judgment which is to come by Jesus the Messiah upon the whole race of men.

Ethiopian Orthodox Canonical Texts

Introduction

This section presents a unique and profound collection of texts that are integral to the Ethiopian Orthodox Christian tradition. These writings, which are not included in the canonical scriptures of other Christian denominations, provide invaluable insights into the rich theological, liturgical, and cultural heritage of Ethiopian Christianity. They reflect the distinct spiritual journey and doctrinal development of a community that has preserved ancient Christian traditions through centuries of historical change.

Historical Context

The texts in this section span various periods, reflecting the long and continuous tradition of the Ethiopian Orthodox Church. They include works that date back to the early centuries of Christianity as well as medieval writings that have shaped the religious identity of the Ethiopian faithful. The Ethiopian Orthodox Tewahedo Church, one of the oldest Christian communities in the world, developed its unique canon in relative isolation from the broader Christian world. This canon includes books that were revered and transmitted within the Ethiopian community but did not gain widespread acceptance elsewhere.

Theological Significance

The "Ethiopian Orthodox Canonical Texts" offer profound insights into the spirituality, theology, and ecclesial life of the Ethiopian Orthodox Church. Among these, several texts stand out for their historical and theological importance:

- **1 Meqabyan, 2 Meqabyan, 3 Meqabyan:** These books, often referred to as the Ethiopian Maccabees, are distinct from the Maccabean texts found in other Christian traditions. They provide unique historical and moral narratives that reflect the spiritual ethos of Ethiopian Christianity.
- **Letter of Jeremiah:** This letter, also included in some versions of the Septuagint, offers a critical perspective on idolatry and emphasizes the importance of fidelity to God.
- **Ezra and Nehemiah:** These texts, known as I and II Ezra in the Ethiopian canon, detail the return from exile and the rebuilding of Jerusalem, providing a foundation for understanding the restoration themes in Ethiopian liturgy and theology.
- **Proverbs Messale and Tagsas:** These are collections of proverbs and wisdom literature that offer moral and ethical guidance, reflecting the practical theology of the Ethiopian Church.
- **Ecclesiastes and Song of Solomon:** These wisdom texts are cherished for their poetic and philosophical reflections on life, love, and divine wisdom.

Rationale for Inclusion

The inclusion of these writings in "Apocrypha Complete" enriches our understanding of the diverse expressions of Christian faith across different cultures and historical contexts. The Ethiopian Orthodox Canonical Texts illuminate the distinct theological perspectives and religious practices of the Ethiopian Orthodox Church. Their study provides a deeper appreciation of the spiritual and doctrinal contributions of Ethiopian Christianity to the broader Christian tradition.

By exploring these texts, you can gain a greater understanding of how the Ethiopian Orthodox Church has maintained its ancient traditions and developed its unique religious identity.

Embarking on the exploration of these texts within "Apocrypha Complete," you can appreciate the depth and breadth of Ethiopian Orthodox literature. Each document, whether historical, doctrinal, or liturgical, contributes uniquely to the tapestry of Christian history, offering insights that challenge and enrich our understanding of the faith.

Letter of Jeremiah

A copy of an epistle, which Jeremy sent unto them which were to be led captives into Babylon by the king of the Babylonians, to certify them, as it was commanded him of God.[1] Because of the sins which ye have committed before God, ye shall be led away captives into Babylon by Nabuchodonosor king of the Babylonians.[2] So when ye be come unto Babylon, ye shall remain there many years, and for a long season, namely, seven generations: and after that I will bring you away peaceably from thence.[3] Now shall ye see in Babylon gods of silver, and of gold, and of wood, borne upon shoulders, which cause the nations to fear.[4] Beware therefore that ye in no wise be like to strangers, neither be ye and of them, when ye see the multitude before them and behind them, worshipping them.[5] But say ye in your hearts, O Lord, we must worship thee.[6] For mine angel is with you, and I myself caring for your souls.[7] As for their tongue, it is polished by the workman, and they themselves are gilded and laid over with silver; yet are they but false, and cannot speak.[8] And taking gold, as it were for a virgin that loveth to go gay, they make crowns for the heads of their gods.[9] Sometimes also the priests convey from their gods gold and silver, and bestow it upon themselves.[10] Yea, they will give thereof to the common harlots, and deck them as men with garments, [being] gods of silver, and gods of gold, and wood.[11] Yet cannot these gods save themselves from rust and moth, though they be covered with purple raiment.[12] They wipe their faces because of the dust of the temple, when there is much upon them.[13] And he that cannot put to death one that offendeth him holdeth a sceptre, as though he were a judge of the country.[14] He hath also in his right hand a dagger and an ax: but cannot deliver himself from war and thieves.[15] Whereby they are known not to be gods: therefore fear them not.[16] For like as a vessel that a man useth is nothing worth when it is broken; even so it is with their gods: when they be set up in the temple, their eyes be full of dust through the feet of them that come in.[17] And as the doors are made sure on every side upon him that offendeth the king, as being committed to suffer death: even so the priests make fast their temples with doors, with locks, and bars, lest their gods be spoiled with robbers.[18] They light them candles, yea, more than for themselves, whereof they cannot see one.[19] They are as one of the beams of the temple, yet they say their hearts are gnawed upon by things creeping out of the earth; and when they eat them and their clothes, they feel it not.[20] Their faces are blacked through the smoke that cometh out of the temple.[21] Upon their bodies and heads sit bats, swallows, and birds, and the cats also.[22] By this ye may know that they are no gods: therefore fear them not.[23] Notwithstanding the gold that is about them to make them beautiful, except they wipe off the rust, they will not shine: for neither when they were molten did they feel it.[24] The things wherein there is no breath are bought for a most high price.[25] They are borne upon shoulders, having no feet whereby they declare unto men that they be nothing worth.[26] They also that serve them are ashamed: for if they fall to the ground at any time, they cannot rise up again of themselves: neither, if one set them upright, can they move of themselves: neither, if they be bowed down, can they make themselves straight: but they set gifts before them as unto dead men.[27] As for the things that are sacrificed unto them, their priests sell and abuse; in like manner their wives lay up part thereof in salt; but unto the poor and impotent they give nothing of it.[28] Menstruous women and women in childbed eat their sacrifices: by these things ye may know that they are no gods: fear them not.[29] For how can they be called gods? because women set meat before the gods of silver, gold, and wood.[30] And the priests sit in their temples, having their clothes rent, and their heads and beards shaven, and nothing upon their heads.[31] They roar and cry before their gods, as men do at the feast when one is dead.[32] The priests also take off their garments, and clothe their wives and children.[33] Whether it be evil that one doeth unto them, or good, they are not able to recompense it: they can neither set up a king, nor put him down.[34] In like manner, they can neither give riches nor money: though a man make a vow unto them, and keep it not, they will not require it.[35] They can save no man from death, neither deliver the weak from the mighty.[36] They cannot restore a blind man to his sight, nor help any man in his distress.[37] They can shew no mercy to the widow, nor do good to the fatherless.[38] Their gods of wood, and which are overlaid with gold and silver, are like the stones that be hewn out of the mountain: they that worship them shall be confounded.[39] How should a man then think and say that they are gods, when even the Chaldeans themselves dishonour them?[40] Who if they shall see one dumb that cannot speak, they bring him, and intreat Bel that he may speak, as though he were able to understand.[41] Yet they cannot understand this themselves, and leave them: for they have no knowledge.[42] The women also with cords about them, sitting in the ways, burn bran for perfume: but if any of them, drawn by some that passeth by, lie with him, she reproacheth her fellow, that she was not thought as worthy as herself, nor her cord broken.[43] Whatsoever is done among them is false: how may it then be thought or said that they are gods?[44] They are made of carpenters and goldsmiths: they can be nothing else than the workmen will have them to be.[45] And they themselves that made them can never continue long; how should then the things that are made of them be gods?[46] For they left lies and reproaches to them that come after.[47] For when there cometh any war or plague upon them, the priests consult with themselves, where they may be hidden with them.[48] How then cannot men perceive that they be no gods, which can neither save themselves from war, nor from plague?[49] For seeing they be but of wood, and overlaid with silver and gold, it shall be known hereafter that they are false:[50] And it shall manifestly appear to all nations and kings that they are no gods, but the works of men's hands, and that there is no work of God in them.[51] Who then may not know that they are no gods?[52] For neither can they set up a king in the land, nor give rain unto men.[53] Neither can they judge their own cause, nor redress a wrong, being unable: for they are as crows between heaven and earth.[54] Whereupon when fire falleth upon the house of gods of wood, or laid over with gold or silver, their priests will flee away, and escape; but they themselves shall be burned asunder like beams.[55] Moreover they cannot withstand any king or enemies: how can it then be thought or said that they be gods?[56] Neither are those gods of wood, and laid over with silver or gold, able to escape either from thieves or robbers.[57] Whose gold, and silver, and garments wherewith they are clothed, they that are strong take, and go away withal: neither are they able to help themselves.[58] Therefore it is better to be a king that sheweth his power, or else a profitable vessel in an house, which the owner shall have use of, than such false gods; or to be a door in an house, to keep such things therein, than such false gods. or a pillar of wood in a a palace, than such false gods.[59] For sun, moon, and stars, being bright and sent to do their offices, are obedient.[60] In like manner the lightning when it breaketh forth is easy to be seen; and after the same manner the wind bloweth in every country.[61] And when God commandeth the clouds to go over the whole world, they do as they are bidden.[62] And the fire sent from above to consume hills and woods doeth as it is commanded: but these are like unto them neither in shew nor power.[63] Wherefore it is neither to be supposed nor said that they are gods, seeing, they are able neither to judge causes, nor to do good unto men.[64] Knowing therefore that they are no gods, fear them not,[65] For they can neither curse nor bless kings:[66] Neither can they shew signs in the heavens among the heathen, nor shine as the sun, nor give light as the moon.[67] The beasts are better than they: for they can get under a cover and help themselves.[68] It is then by no means manifest unto us that they are gods: therefore fear them not.[69] For as a scarecrow in a garden of cucumbers keepeth nothing: so are their gods of wood, and laid over with silver and gold.[70] And likewise their gods of wood, and laid over with silver and gold, are like to a white thorn in an orchard, that every bird sitteth upon; as also to a dead body, that is east into the dark.[71] And ye shall know them to be no gods by the bright purple that rotteth upon then1: and they themselves afterward shall be eaten, and shall be a reproach in the country.[72] Better therefore is the just man that hath none idols: for he shall be far from reproach.

1 Meqabyan

This is what Meqabyan said about the kingdoms of Moab and Midian:

1 Meq. 1

426

[1] There was a man named Tseerutsaydan who loved sin. He would boast about his abundant horses and the strength of his troops under his command. [2] He had many priests serving the idols he worshipped, bowing and offering sacrifices to them day and night. [3] But in his heart's dullness, it seemed to him that these idols provided him with strength and power. [4] In his heart, he believed these idols granted him authority over all his dominions. [5] And at the time of formation, it seemed to him that they granted him all the desired authority as well. [6] He would offer sacrifices to them day and night. [7] He appointed priests to serve his idols. [8] While they ate from those defiled sacrifices, they would falsely assure him that the idols ate night and day. [9] They also made other people zealous like themselves, to offer sacrifices and eat. And again, they induced others to offer sacrifices and eat like them. [10] But he trusted in his idols, which neither profited nor benefited. [11] Due to his brief lifespan and the dullness of his heart, it seemed to him that they adored him, fed him, and crowned him. It seemed to him they adored him because Satan had deafened his reasoning, preventing him from knowing his Creator who brought him from non-existence to existence, and preventing him and his relatives from recognizing their Creator, leading them instead toward the eternal fire of Gehenna, judged alongside those they falsely called gods. [12] Since they are always worthless, he should regard them as dead. [13] As the authority of Satan, which misled them, resides in the idol's form, and as he guides their thoughts according to their desires, he will bring judgment upon the idols in which they believed and in which the children of Adam trusted, whose reasoning turned to ashes. [14] They will be astonished when they realize he fulfilled what they envisioned for them, leading them to sacrifice their sons and daughters, spilling the blood of their pure children. [15] They felt no sorrow, for Satan relished the sacrifices made to fulfill their wicked plans, dragging them down to Gehenna with him, where there are no exits, enduring eternal suffering. [16] But Tseerutsaydan was proud; he had fifty idols made in the form of males and twenty in the form of females. [17] He boasted about these useless idols and glorified them while offering sacrifices morning and evening. [18] He ordered people to offer sacrifices to the idols and eat from those defiled sacrifices, inciting them to commit more evils. [19] He constructed five temples for his sculpted idols made of iron, brass, and lead. [20] He adorned them with silver and gold and surrounded the temples with veiled curtains, setting up tents for them. [21] He appointed guardians for them and continuously offered sacrifices: ten fattened oxen, ten sterile cows, ten fattened sheep ewes, and ten barren goats, along with winged birds. [22] But he believed his idols consumed these offerings. He presented them with fifty measures of grapes and fifty dishes of wheat mixed with oil. [23] He instructed his priests: "Take and feed them. Let my gods eat what I have slaughtered for them and drink the wine I have presented. If it is not enough, I will add more." [24] He ordered everyone to eat and drink from those defiled sacrifices. [25] But in his wicked malice, he sent his troops throughout the kingdom to find anyone who did not sacrifice or bow, to separate and identify them, bring them forth, and punish them with fire and sword in his presence, to plunder their wealth and burn their homes to the ground, destroying all their possessions. [26] "For they are kind and great ones, for they have adored us with their mercy, and I will display punishment and tribulation for anyone who does not worship my gods and offer sacrifices to them. [27] I will show him punishment and tribulation, for they have adored the earth, heaven, the vast sea, moon, sun, stars, rain, winds, and all that lives in this world for our nourishment and satisfaction." [28] But those who worship them will be punished with severe tribulation and will not be treated kindly.

1 Meq. 2

[1] There was a man from the tribe of Benjamin named Meqabees; [2] he had three children who were handsome and strong warriors. They were beloved by everyone in the Midian and Moab region under Tseerutsaydan's rule. [3] As the king had commanded, when he found them: "Do not you bow to Tseerutsaydan's gods? Do not you offer sacrifices? [4] But if you refuse, we will take you to the king, and we will destroy all your wealth as the king has ordered." [5] These young, handsome men replied, saying, "As for the One we bow to, He is our Father and Creator, who made the earth, heaven, and all within it, the sea, the moon, the sun, the clouds, and the stars. He is the True Creator whom we worship and in whom we believe." [6] And these royal youths were four in number, and their servants, bearing shields and spears, numbered a hundred. [7] When they tried to capture these holy ones, they escaped from their grasp, as none could touch them. As these youths were mighty in strength, they took up shields and spears. [8] One of them could strangle and kill a panther, easily as if it were a chicken. [9] One could kill a lion with a single rock or by striking it once with a stick. [10] Another could kill a hundred men by striking at the right time with a sword. Their names and deeds were renowned throughout all Babylon and Moab. [11] They were mighty in strength, beloved for their character and beauty. [12] Moreover, their appearance was marvelous, but because they worshipped GOD and did not fear death, their moral beauty surpassed all. [13] When they terrified the troops, no one could capture them, but those who were warriors escaped to a high mountain. [14] Those troops returned to the city and locked the fortress gates, terrorizing the people by saying, "Unless you bring those warriors, the Meqabees, we will burn your city to the ground, report to the king, and destroy your land." [15] Then the people of the land, rich and poor, daughters and sons, children orphaned by their parents, and elderly women, all came out together, raising their voices toward the mountain, shouting to them, "Do not destroy us and our land because of you." [16] They all wept together, afraid because of GOD. [17] Turning their faces eastward and stretching out their hands, they all prayed to GOD together, "Lord, should we deny these men who have destroyed Your command and Your law? [18] Yet he believed in silver, gold, stone, and wood, made by human hands, but we do not wish to hear that sinful word from him who does not believe in Your law," they said. [19] "You are the Creator who saves and who destroys. Let him become like those who adored him, as for him, he is the one who spills human blood and eats human flesh. [20] But we do not wish to see that sinful face or hear his words," they said. [21] "However, if You command us, we will go to him, because we believe in You. We will go and offer our bodies to death, and when he says, 'Offer sacrifices to my gods,' we will not listen to that sinful word. [22] But we believe in You, Lord, who examines the kidneys and thoughts, our Fathers' Creator, Abraham, Isaac, and Jacob, who followed Your covenant and lived steadfastly in Your law. [23] You examine a person's reasoning and help both sinners and the righteous, and nothing is hidden from You, and those who seek refuge are known to You. [24] But we have no other Creator besides You. [25] So that we may offer our bodies for death because of Your glorified name, yet be Power and Strength and a Shelter for us in this work that we are ruled for You. [26] And when the children of Israel entered Egypt, You heard Jacob's plea, and now, glorified God, we beg You." [27] And when the two men, who were exceedingly handsome, were seen standing before them, when fiery swords that terrified like lightning struck and decapitated them, killing them, at that moment they arose as well as before. [28] Their appearance became even more handsome, and they shone brighter than the sun, becoming more beautiful than before.

1 Meq. 3

[1] Just as you have seen before you these servants of the Most High GOD, Abia, Seela, and Fentos, who died and rose again, you too shall rise after death, and your faces shall shine like the sun in the Kingdom of Heaven. [2] And they went with those men and received martyrdom there. [3] At that time, they prayed, praised, and bowed to GOD. Death did not frighten them, nor did the king's punishment scare them. [4] They approached those young men and became like sheep without malice, yet they did not frighten them. When they reached them, they seized, beat, bound, and whipped them, then delivered them to the king and stood them before him. [5] The king asked them, "Why do you stubborn ones not offer sacrifices and bow to my gods?" [6] Those brothers, cleansed from sin, honored, chosen, and radiant, shining like a precious jewel of immense value, Seela, Abia, and Fentos, answered him in unison. [7] They said to the king, who was a calamity, "As for us, we will neither bow nor offer sacrifices to defiled idols that lack knowledge and reasoning." [8] Again, they said to him, "We will not bow to idols made of silver, gold, stone, or wood by human hands, which have no reasoning, soul, or knowledge, and which do not benefit their worshippers nor harm their foes." [9] The king responded, "Why do you act like this, when they know who insults them and who mistreats them? Why do you insult the glorified gods?" [10] They replied, "As they are mere trifles to us, we will insult them and not glorify them." [11] The king responded, "I will punish you according to the evil of your deeds; I will mar your beauty with whipping, severe tribulation, and fire. [12] Now tell me, will you give sacrifices to my gods or not? Because if you do not, I will punish you with the sword and whipping." [13] They answered, "As for us, we will neither offer sacrifices nor bow to defiled idols." The king ordered that they be beaten with heavy sticks and then whipped with scourges, and afterward, they were mutilated until their inner organs were exposed. [14] After this, they were bound and imprisoned severely in a jail until he consulted on how to execute them more cruelly. [15] Without kindness, they were taken and placed under strict confinement in prison, fastened with iron shackles. [16] The king Tseerutsaydan said, "These youths who have erred have exhausted me. What can solidify their thinking? Their evil deeds match their strength. If I say they will convert, they make their reasoning more wicked. [17] I will inflict upon them punishment according to the measure of their wickedness; I will burn their flesh in fire until it turns to ash, and then I will scatter their ashes like dust on the mountains." [18] After saying this, he waited three days and then ordered that the honored men be brought to him. When the honored men approached, he commanded that a fire be kindled in the great pit oven and that it be fueled with malicious substances that would ignite the fire, boiling fat, soapberries, sea foam, resin, and sulfur. [19] When the fire blazed in the pit, the messengers went to the king and reported, "We have done as you commanded, now send the men to be cast in." [20] He ordered that they be taken and thrown into the fiery pit, and the youths did as the king commanded. When the honored men entered the fire, they gave up their souls to GOD. [21] When the ones who cast them saw this, angels received and took their souls to Paradise, where Isaac, Abraham, and Jacob reside, where the blessed are found.

1 Meq. 4

[1] And when the criminal saw that they were dead, he ordered their bodies to be burned to ashes and scattered in the wind, but the fire could not burn the hair of their corpses, and they were cast out of the pit. [2] They reignited the fire on them from morning until evening, but it did not consume them; they said, "Let us now cast their corpses into the sea." [3] They did as the king commanded,

casting them into the sea. Even though they added heavy stones, iron weights, and a millstone that turns by a donkey, the sea did not sink them. For the Spirit of Support from GOD was with them; they floated on the sea and did not sink. All the king's malice failed to destroy them. 4 "Since their death has wearied me more than their life, let me throw their bodies to the beasts to eat them. But what can I do?" he said. 5 The youths did as he commanded; neither vultures nor beasts touched the corpses. Birds and vultures shielded them with their wings from burning in the sun, and the five martyrs' bodies lay for fourteen days. 6 When they were seen, their bodies shone like the sun, and angels encircled their corpses as light encircles a tent. 7 He sought advice, not knowing what to do, and afterward he dug a grave and buried the five martyrs. 8 That night, as the king who had forgotten GOD's law lay in bed, he saw the five martyrs standing before him at night, brandishing swords and causing him fear. 9 It seemed to him that they entered his house at night to commit a crime. When he awoke from his sleep, he was scared and wished to flee from his bedroom to the hall. It appeared to him as if they were killing him, making it seem as though they committed a crime against him, and he was frightened, his knees trembling. 10 Because of this, he said, "My lords, what do you want? As for me, what should I do for you?" 11 They replied, "Aren't we the ones you burned in the fire and commanded to be thrown into the sea? As GOD has preserved our bodies because we believed in Him, you failed to destroy us. A person who believes in Him will not perish. Let glory and praise be due to GOD. We, who believed in Him, were not shamed by the tribulation." 12 "Since I did not know such a punishment would come upon me, what compensation should I give you for what I did to you?" 13 "Now separate from me the reward I should give you, lest you take my body to death and lower me to Sheol while I am alive." 14 "As I have wronged you, forgive my sin, for it was by the kindness of your Father GOD's law," he told them. 15 The honored martyrs replied, "Because you did evil to us, we will not repay you with evil, for GOD is the one who imposes hardship on a soul. He is the one who will punish you. But we appeared to you, showing you were well for a brief time because of your deaf reasoning. It seemed to you that you had killed us, but you actually prepared welfare for us." 16 "Your priests of idols and you will descend to Gehenna forever, where there are no exits." 17 "Woe to your idols, to which you have bowed, forsaking bowing to GOD who created you, who were despised as if you were spit out; and to you who worship them, not knowing GOD who created you, bringing you from nonexistence to existence. Aren't you like smoke today and will perish tomorrow?" 18 The king asked them, "What should I command so that I might do for you all that you wish?" 19 "It is to save your own soul lest you enter the fire of Gehenna. But it is not to save our own souls to teach you. Your idols are of silver and gold, of stone and wood, which have no reasoning, no soul, no knowledge. They neither kill nor save, benefit their friends nor harm their enemies, lower nor honor, enrich nor impoverish. They mislead you through the authority of demons, who do not wish for anyone to be saved, yet they cannot uproot nor plant." 20 "They especially do not wish for people like you to be saved from death, you dull-hearted ones, for whom it seems they have cared, when you are the ones who made them." 21 "As Satan's and demons' authority has resided in them, they will return to you as you love, to drown you in the sea of Gehenna." 22 "But you, abandon your errors and let this also be our reward for our death, that we might benefit our souls by worshiping our Creator, GOD ," they told him. 23 But he was alarmed and utterly astonished; as all five appeared before him drawing their swords, he was afraid, and because of this, he bowed to them. 24 "Now I know that after those

428

who are dust die, they will truly arise. As for me, only a little time remains before I die." 25 After this, they disappeared from the king's presence. From that day onward, Tseerutsaydan, who was extremely arrogant, ceased burning their corpses. 26 They had misled many for generations, reveling in their idols and delusional reasoning, leading many astray from worshipping GOD, the Creator, until they stopped following Him. They sacrificed their daughters and sons to demons, engaging in seductive and disturbing actions according to their corrupted reasoning, as taught by their father Satan, to carry out the seduction and disturbances that GOD detests. 27 They committed incest, defiling their mothers, aunts, and sisters, and indulged in all sorts of filthy acts, as Satan had solidified their perverted reasoning. They declared, "We will not return." 28 Tseerutsaydan, unaware of his Creator, was filled with pride, boasting about his idols. 29 If they say, "How will GOD grant the kingdom to those who do not know Him by law and worship?" they will surely turn back to Him in repentance. If they truly repent, He would love them and preserve their kingdom. But if they refuse, a fire will consume them in the fire of Gehenna forever. 30 A king should fear his Creator, GOD, as much as he enjoys his fame, and a judge should govern according to his Creator while delivering just judgments, as much as he enjoys his rule. 31 Elders, chiefs, ambassadors, and vassal kings should obey their Creator as much as they enjoy their wealth and power. 32 For He is the Lord of heaven and earth, who created all creation, because there is no other Creator in heaven or on earth who can impoverish and enrich. He is the one who honors and humiliates.

1 Meq. 5

1 "The one warrior out of sixty warriors was proud. GOD made his body, from his feet to his head, swell with just a spoonful of sulfur, and he died from the plague. 2 Again, Keeram, who built an iron bed, was proud because of his great power, and GOD concealed him in death. 3 And again, Nebuchadnezzar was proud, saying, 'There is no other king besides me, and I am the Creator who makes the sun rise in this world,' boasting of his great arrogance. 4 GOD removed him from people and sent him into the wilderness for seven years, where he lived among the birds of heaven and the beasts of the field until he recognized that GOD was the one who created him. 5 When he acknowledged Him in worship, GOD returned him to his kingdom. Who among those not from Earth was so boldly proud against GOD, the Creator? 6 And who is it that violated HIS LAW and HIS order, and the earth did not swallow him up? 7 And you, Tseerutsaydan, wish to be proud against your Creator, and again, you have provoked Him to destroy you like the others, to lower you to a grave because of your arrogance. 8 And again, after they entered Sheol, where there is grinding of teeth and mourning, which is the fulfillment of darkness, you should expect Him to lower you into the deep pit of Gehenna, where there are no exits forever. 9 As for you, you are a man who will die and be destroyed tomorrow like the arrogant kings before you, who left this living world. 10 As for us, we say, 'You are in ruins, but you are not GOD, for GOD is the one who created the earth and heaven and you.' 11 He humiliates the arrogant and honors those who are humbled. He gives strength to the weary. 12 He kills the healthy and raises up those from the earth, who were dead and buried in the grave. 13 And He frees slaves to life from the domination of sin. 14 Oh, King Tseerutsaydan, why do you boast about your defiled idols that bring no benefit? 15 But GOD created the earth and the heavens and the great seas. He created the moon and the sun and established the ages. 16 A man grazes in his field, and he continues plowing until dusk; the stars in the sky are established by His word. 17 He calls to everything in heaven; nothing happens without

GOD knowing it. ¹⁸ He commands the angels of heaven to serve Him and to praise His glorified name. Angels are sent to all people who inherit life. ¹⁹ Raphael, who was a servant, was sent to Tobit, and he saved Tobias from death in the land of Raguel. ²⁰ The holy Michael was sent to Gideon to make him notice by means that he would destroy the sons of Elope; and he was sent to the prophet Moses when he made Israel cross the Red Sea. ²¹ As only GOD has said, He led them; there was no different idol with them. ²² And He sent them forth to the crops of the earth. ²³ And He fed them with the grain of His planting. As He loved them completely, He nurtured them, feeding them honey solid as a rock. ²⁴ And that you might keep His people properly, and that you might execute GOD's Law, who created you, He crowned you, giving you authority over the four kingdoms. ²⁵ For He crowned you, making you loftier than all, and your Creator has completely crowned you so that you might love GOD. ²⁶ And it is right that you should love your Creator, GOD, as He loved you and entrusted you over all people. And you, perform GOD's Law so that your days may be extended in this world and that He may live with you in support. ²⁷ And perform GOD's Law so that He may stand for you as a Guardian against your enemies, and that He may seat you on your throne, and that He may shelter you under the wing of His support. ²⁸ If you do not know, GOD chose and crowned you over Israel just as He chose Saul from the children of Israel when he was looking after his father's donkeys, and He crowned him over his people Israel, and he sat with Israel on his throne. ²⁹ And He gave him great fortune, distinguishing him from his people. GOD crowned you over His people. Therefore, from now on, beware, maintain His people. ³⁰ For GOD has appointed you over them so that you may kill and save, keep them from evil deeds, those who do good deeds, and those who do evil deeds to good deeds," he told him. ³¹ "And as GOD has appointed you over everything that you may perform His Law, whether you whip or save, repay the evil deeds, those who do good deeds, and those who do good deeds and evil deeds. ³² For you are a servant of GOD who rules all in heaven, and you, perform GOD's Law so that He may perform your will for you in all your thoughts and in all that you ask while you entreat before Him. ³³ No one rules over Him, but He rules over all. ³⁴ No one appoints Him, but He appoints all. ³⁵ No one dismisses Him, but He dismisses all. ³⁶ No one reproaches Him, but He reproaches all. ³⁷ No one makes Him diligent, but He makes all diligent. As the rulership of heaven and earth belongs to Him, no one escapes from His authority; everything is exposed before Him, but nothing is hidden from His face. ³⁸ He sees all, but no one sees Him. He hears the prayer of the person who prays to Him, saying, 'Save me,' for He created man in His own image, and He accepts his supplication. ³⁹ As He is a King who lives forever, He feeds everyone from His unchanging nature.

1 Meq. 6

¹ As He truly crowns the kings who perform His Law, the kings wrote rightly because of Him. ² As they have performed GOD's Law, He will illuminate them with a light that is beyond examination, in the dwellings of Isaac, Abraham, Jacob, Solomon, David, and Hezekiah, in the garden where all the beautiful kings whose dwelling was in light reside. ³ The hall of heaven is utterly radiant, unlike the halls of the earth. Its floor, adorned with silver, gold, and jewels, is immaculate. ⁴ And its shining features are beyond human reasoning. The hall of heaven shines like jewels. ⁵ As GOD, who knows nature, knew, the hall of heaven He created is beyond human reasoning and shines in absolute light. Its floor, made of silver, gold, jewels, white silk, and blue silk, is immaculate. ⁶ It is extremely beautiful like this. ⁷ The righteous, who have stood firm in religion and virtue, are

the ones who will inherit it by the grace and forgiveness of GOD. ⁸ And there is a river of welfare flowing from it, shining like the sun. There is a tent of light within it, surrounded by the fragrance of grace. ⁹ A garden of beautiful and beloved fruits, with different appearances and tastes, surrounds the place. There is a place for oil and grapes there. It is extremely beautiful, and the fragrance of its fruits is sweet. ¹⁰ When a fleshly, blood-filled person enters it, his soul would have departed from his body due to the abundance of bliss found there because of its aromatic flavor. ¹¹ The beautiful kings who have executed GOD's Law will be joyful there. Their honor and place are recognized in the Kingdom of Heaven, which stands firm forever, where welfare is found. ¹² He demonstrated that their rule on earth was famous and honored, and their rule in heaven is famous and honored. They will be honored and exalted in heaven just as they were honored and bowed to in this world. If they do good deeds in this world, they will be joyful. ¹³ But the kings who were evil in their rule and their kingdoms that GOD gave them, who do not judge truly and justly, as they ignored the cries of the destitute and poor, did not judge truthfully and save the refugee and the wronged orphan. ¹⁴ They did not save the destitute and poor from the hands of the rich who robbed them, did not share their food and satisfy those who were hungry, did not share their drink and give drink to those who were thirsty, and did not listen to the cry of the poor. ¹⁵ He will take them to Gehenna, which is a dark ending. When that great day comes upon them, when GOD comes, and when His wrath is executed on them as David spoke in his praises, 'Lord, do not reprimand me in Your Judgment, and do not correct me in Your discipline,' their troubles and humiliations will increase according to their great fame. ¹⁶ When nobles and kings, who rule this world, exist in this world, there are people who do not keep your law. ¹⁷ But GOD, who rules all, is there in heaven. The souls and well-being of all people have been captured by His authority. He is the one who honors those who glorify Him, for He rules all and loves those who love Him. ¹⁸ As He is the Lord of the earth and heaven, He examines and knows what the kidneys carry and what the mind thinks. And for a person who prays to Him with a pure mind, He will give him the reward of his supplication. ¹⁹ He will destroy the arrogance of the powerful, who commit evil deeds against the orphan whose parents are dead, and against elderly women. ²⁰ It is not by your power that you have seized this kingdom; it is not by your ability that you have sat on this throne; He has tested you so that it might be possible for you to rule like Saul, who ruled his people at that time. He placed you on the throne of the kingdom, but it is not by your power that you have seized this kingdom. It happened when He tested you as He tested Saul, who disregarded the word of the prophet Samuel and the word of GOD and did not serve his army or the king of Amalek, but it is not by your ability that you have seized this kingdom. ²¹ And GOD told the prophet Samuel, 'Go, because they have grieved Me by destroying the LAW and worshiping idols, by bowing to the idol, by their mosques, and by all their detestable acts without benefit. Tell Saul, 'Go to the land of Amalek and destroy all their hosts and all their kings, from people to livestock.'' ²² Because they grieved GOD, for this reason, He sent Saul to destroy them. ²³ But he spared their king from death, and he spared many of their livestock, beauties, daughters, and handsome youths from death. As he scorned My command and did not listen to My command, because of this, GOD told the prophet Samuel, 'Go and divide his kingdom.' ²⁴ Because of his place, anoint the son of Jesse, David, to reign over Israel. ²⁵ But a demon will torment and throw him. ²⁶ As he refused when I gave him a kingdom to execute My Law, when he refused Me to execute My Law, I removed him from his kingdom that was due to him. But you, go and tell him, saying, 'Thus, will you disregard GOD who crowned you over His people Israel, who seated you on His Royal Throne?' ²⁷ But you, tell him, 'You did not know GOD who bestowed upon you so much honor and fame.' He told him. ²⁸ And the prophet Samuel went to King Saul and entered while he was sitting at the dining table, and when the king of Amalek, Agag, was sitting on his left. ²⁹ 'Why have you completely disregarded GOD who commanded you to destroy the livestock and people?' he told him. ³⁰ At that time, the king was afraid and rose from his throne, telling Samuel, 'Return with us,' and he grabbed his clothes, but Samuel refused to return. Samuel's clothes were torn. ³¹ And Samuel told Saul, 'GOD has divided your kingdom.' ³² And again, Saul told Samuel before the people, 'Honor me and atone for my sin before GOD that He might forgive me.' And as he was afraid of the word of GOD who created him, but as he was not afraid of the king who is dead, Samuel refused to return in his word. ³³ Because of this, he pierced the king of Amalek, Agag, before he swallowed what he chewed. ³⁴ And a demon seized Saul, who destroyed the LAW of GOD, and because He is the King of Kings who rules all, GOD struck on the head a king who sinned, so it would not disgrace him. ³⁵ For He is the Lord of all creation, who dismisses the authority of all nobles and kings who do not fear Him, but no one rules over Him. ³⁶ As He said, 'The lineage of David shall go while it is famous and honored, but the lineage of Saul shall go while it is humiliated.' He destroyed the kingdom from his child and from Saul. ³⁷ Because it grieved Him, and because He destroyed the wicked who grieved Him by their evil deeds, GOD avenged and destroyed the children of Saul's family. For a person who does not avenge the enemy of GOD, when it is possible for him to avenge and destroy, and he has the authority, a person who does not avenge and destroy the sinner and does not avenge and destroy one who does not keep GOD's LAW, as he is an enemy of GOD, He destroyed the children of Saul's family.

1 Meq. 7

¹ Whether you are a king or a ruler, what significant thing are you? ² Isn't it GOD who created you, bringing you from nonexistence to existence, so that you might execute His Law, live firmly by His command, and fear His judgment? Just as you are angry with your servants and rule over them, so also GOD is angry with you and rules over you. ³ Just as you mercilessly beat those who commit sins, so also GOD will strike you and lower you to Gehenna, where there are no exits forever. ⁴ Just as you whip someone who has not been governed by you and has not brought a tribute to you, what is it that you do not bring a tribute to GOD? ⁵ As He is the one who created you so that they might fear you, and crowned you over all creation so that you might truly keep His people, why is it that you do not fear your Creator, GOD? ⁶ Judge truly and justly as GOD appointed you, and do not look at faces and show favor to either small or great. Whom will you fear except Him? Keep His worship and the nine commands. ⁷ As Moses commanded the children of Israel, saying, 'I have set before you water and fire; choose what you love' - do not go to the right or the left. ⁸ Listen to His word that I tell you, so that you may listen to His word and execute His command, lest you say, 'It is beyond the sea, or beyond the depth, or beyond the river, who will bring it to me so that I may see it and hear His word and execute His command?' ⁹ Lest you say, 'Who will ascend to heaven again and bring down that word of GOD to me so that I may hear and execute it?' - The word of GOD is what has approached; behold, teach it with your mouth and give charity with your hand. ¹⁰ And you did not listen to your Creator, GOD, unless you listened to His book, and you did not love Him or keep His command unless you kept His LAW. ¹¹ And you must enter Gehenna forever unless you loved His command and unless

you executed GOD's Law, who honored and made you famous apart from all your people so that you might truly keep them. You must enter Gehenna forever. ¹² He made you above all, and He crowned you over all His people so that you might rule His people truly and justly while thinking of the name of your Creator who created you and gave you a kingdom. ¹³ There are those whom you whip among those who wronged you, and there are those whom you forgive while thinking of GOD's deeds, and there are those for whom you judge truly and justly, straightening your reasoning. ¹⁴ And do not favor by looking at faces when they argue before you. Since the physique of the earth is your possession, do not accept a bribe so that you may forgive the sinful person and wrong the innocent person. ¹⁵ If you execute His Law, GOD will multiply your days in this world for you, but if you grieve Him, He will reduce your days. ¹⁶ Consider that you will rise after you die, and that you will be examined standing before Him for all the deeds you have done, whether they are good or evil. ¹⁷ If you do good deeds, you will live in a garden in the Kingdom of Heaven, in houses where kind kings reside, where there is light. GOD will not disgrace your royal authority, but if you do evil deeds, you will live in Sheol Gehenna, where evil kings reside. ¹⁸ But when you observe your famous fearfulness, your awards from warriors, your hanging shields and spears, and when you observe your horses and your troops under your command, those who beat drums, and people who play the harp before you... ¹⁹ And when you observe all this, you elevate your reasoning, stiffen the collar of your reasoning, and do not think of GOD who gave you all this honor. However, when He tells you, 'Give up all this,' you are not the one who gives it up. ²⁰ For you have completely neglected the appointment He appointed for you, and He will give your rule to another. ²¹ As death will suddenly come upon you, and judgment will be executed at the time of resurrection, and as all human deeds will be examined, He will fully investigate and judge you. ²² No one will honor the kings of this world, for because He is the true Judge, at the time of judgment, the poor and the rich will stand together. The crowns of the nobles of this world in which they boasted will fall. ²³ Judgment is prepared, and a soul will tremble. At that time, the deeds of sinners and the righteous will be examined. ²⁴ And no one will be hidden. When a daughter comes for delivery, and when the fetus in her belly comes for birth, just as she cannot prevent her womb, the earth also cannot prevent its inhabitants upon it; it will return them. ²⁵ And just as clouds cannot prevent rain unless they carry and pour it to the place GOD commanded them - for the word of GOD has created all, bringing from nonexistence to existence - and the word of GOD has again introduced all to the grave; likewise, after the time of resurrection has arrived, it is not possible that the dead will not rise. ²⁶ As Moses said, 'It is by the words that proceed from the mouth of GOD, and not only by bread, that a person is saved'; and the word of GOD will again raise all people from the graves. ²⁷ Behold, it is known that the dead will rise by the word of GOD. ²⁸ And again, GOD said this in the Law of Moses because of the nobles and kings who execute His Law. As the day has arrived when they are appointed for destruction, I will avenge and destroy them on the day when judgment is judged and at the time when their feet stumble, He said. ²⁹ And again, GOD told those who know His judgment, 'Know well that I am your Creator, GOD, and I kill and I save. I chastise in tribulation and I forgive. I lower to Sheol and again I send to the garden, and no one will escape from My authority,' He told them. ³⁰ GOD said this because of the nobles and kings who did not keep His LAW. As earthly kingdoms are passing and they pass from morning until evening, keep My ordinance and My LAW so that you may enter the Kingdom of Heaven, which stands firm forever, He said. [31] For GOD's calling of the righteous is for glory, and sinners for tribulation. He will make the sinner miserable but will honor the righteous. [32] He will dismiss the one who did not execute His Law, but He will appoint the one who executed His Law.

1 Meq. 8

[1] Listen, I will tell you how the dead will rise: They will plant a plant, it will be fertile, and grapes will sprout vines. As the Lord brings forth fruit to consume, they will extract wine from it. [2] Understand that the plant you planted was small, but today it has grown, bearing fruit, tips, and leaves. [3] The Lord gave its roots water to drink from the Earth and Water - from both sources. [4] But He nourished its wood with fire and wind. The roots provide water for the leaves, and the Earth gives solidity to the wood. [5] But the soul that the Lord created within them allows them to bear fruit, and similarly, the dead will rise. [6] When the soul was separated from the body, as they each returned to their own elements, He said: "Gather souls from the four elements - from Earth and Water, wind and fire." [7] But the nature of the Earth lived, solidified within its form and became Earth; and the nature of Water lived, solidified within its form and became Water. [8] And the nature of the wind lived, solidified within its form and became wind; and the nature of fire lived, solidified within its form and became a fierce fire. [9] But a soul that the Lord separated from the body will return to its Creator until He raises it, united with the body at the time of His choosing, placing it in a Garden in the place He loves. [10] He places righteous souls in a House of Light in a Garden, but to send away the souls of sinners, He also places them in a house of darkness in Sheol until the time He loves. [11] The Lord told the prophet Ezekiel: "Call souls from the four corners, that they might be gathered and become one body." [12] When He spoke in one word, saying thus, the souls were gathered from the four corners. [13] And the nature of Water brought greenery, and again the nature of fire brought fire. [14] And again, the nature of Earth brought forth the earth, and the nature of wind brought wind. [15] And the Lord brought a soul from the Garden place where He placed it. They were gathered by one word, and a resurrection was made. [16] And again, I will show you the example that is beside you: the day ends, you sleep; the night passes, and you rise from your bed. But when you slept, it was an example of your death. [17] And when you awoke, it was an example of your rising. But the night, when all people sleep, their bodies obscured by darkness, is an example of this world. [18] But the morning light, when darkness is banished and light fills the world, and when people arise and move towards the fields, is an example of the resurrection of the dead. [19] And this Kingdom of Heaven, where man is renewed, is like this: the resurrection of the dead is like this; as this world passes, it is an example of the night. [20] As David said, "He placed His example in the Sun" - as the sun shines when it rises, it is an example of the Kingdom of Heaven. [21] And as the sun shines in this world today, when Christ comes, He will shine like the sun in the new Kingdom of Heaven, as He has said, "I am a sun that does not set and a torch that is not extinguished" - He, the Lord, is her light. [22] And He will quickly raise the dead again. I will bring you another example from the food that you sow and by which you are saved: whether it is a grain of wheat, barley, lentil, or any seed sown upon the Earth, none will grow unless it has been demolished and rotted. [23] And as you see the flesh of a person, when it has been demolished and rotted, the Earth consumes its flesh with the skin. [24] And when the Earth has consumed its flesh, it grows, encircling a seed sevenfold. The Lord sends a cloud that captures rain as He loves, and roots grow in the Earth and sprout leaves. [25] And if it were demolished and rotted, it cannot grow. But after it has grown, it produces many buds. [26] And by the Lord's decree, fruit is given to those buds that grew, and He wraps its flesh in straw. [27] Look at how much the seed kernel you sowed has multiplied, yet the silver and the leaf, the ear, and the straw are not counted for you. [28] Do not be ignorant and see your seed multiply, and likewise, think that the dead will receive the resurrection, that they will rise, and their hardships will be like their deeds. [29] Listen, if you sow wheat, it will not grow as barley, nor as wheat if you sow barley. And let me tell you again, it will not grow: if you sow wheat, will you harvest barley? If you sow watercress, will you harvest linseed? [30] What about different kinds of plants: if you plant figs, will they really grow as nuts for you? Or if you plant almonds, will they grow as grapes for you? [31] If you plant sweet fruit, will it grow as bitter for you? Or if you plant bitter fruit, is it possible for it to become sweet for you? [32] Similarly, if a sinner dies, is it possible for them to rise as righteous in the time of Resurrection? Or if a righteous person dies, is it possible for them to rise as a sinner in the time of Resurrection? Everyone will receive their due according to their deeds, yet they will receive their reward according to their sins and their hands' work, yet none will be convicted by another's sin. [33] A highland tree is planted, and it sends forth long branches; it will completely dry up unless Heaven sends rain and its leaves become verdant. [34] And the cedar will be uprooted from its roots unless summer rain falls upon it. [35] Similarly, the dead will not rise unless the dew of salvation falls upon them, commanded by the Lord.

1 Meq. 9

[1] Unless the highland mountains and the Gielabuhie regions receive a forgiving rain commanded by the Lord, they will not grow grass for the beasts and animals. [2] And the Elam mountains and Gilead mountains will not produce green leaves for sheep and goats, nor for the oribi and animals in the wilderness, nor for the ibexes and hartebeests. [3] Similarly, forgiveness and dew commanded by the Lord will not fall upon doubters and criminals who have made error and crime their trade. The dead will not rise, and those like Deemas and Qophros, who worship idols and engage in dubious activities, will not be revived. [4] And those who practice root digging and sorcery, causing conflicts among people, will not be revived. [5] And those who have strayed from the LAW, including the people of Miedon and Atiena who believe in their idols, and those who entertain these beliefs with music and dances, will not rise unless the forgiving dew ordained by the Lord falls upon them. [6] These individuals will face judgment on the day when the dead rise and the Final Judgment occurs, even those who preserved themselves through their deeds will err due to their idolatry. [7] O wasteful and foolish heart, do you think the dead will not rise? [8] When the chief angel, Hola Meeka'iel, blows the trumpet, then the dead will arise. You will not remain in the grave without rising. Do not believe otherwise. [9] Hills and mountains will be flattened and become clear paths. [10] And a Resurrection will be conducted for all those with flesh.

1 Meq. 10

[1] But if it were not so, the ancient ones could have been buried in the graves of their fathers, starting from Adam to Seth, Abel, Shem, Noah, Isaac, Abraham, Joseph, Jacob, Aaron, and Moses. But why did they not desire to be buried elsewhere? [2] Is it not that they should rise together with their relatives at the time of Resurrection? Or is it lest their bones be mixed with those of evildoers and idol worshipers? Why did they not desire to be buried elsewhere? [3] But you, do not mislead your reasoning by asking, 'How will the dead arise after they have died, those buried in a grave by tens of thousands whose bodies were destroyed and rotted?' [4] When you look at a grave, you utter this out of your foolish thinking, saying, 'Not even a handful of earth will be found. How will the dead

arise?' 5 Would you claim that the seed you planted will not grow? Indeed, even the seed you sowed will grow. 6 Similarly, the souls the Lord planted will quickly rise, as He created man in His truth, bringing them from nonexistence to existence. He will revive them swiftly with His salvational word; He will not delay their awakening. 7 And as He has returned them from living to the grave in death, is it not possible for Him to return them from death to life? 8 Salvation and resurrection are possible for the Lord.

1 Meq. 11

1 Armon was destroyed, and its fortress was demolished, as the Lord brought hardships upon them due to their evil and the deeds they performed with their hands. The people who worship idols in Edom and Zabulon will be humbled at that time, as the Lord approaches. He will convict those who committed wicked acts from their youth and did not cease even in their old age because of their idols and evil deeds. Sidon and Tyre will mourn. 2 Because they committed sins, seduced others into fornication, and worshiped idols, the Lord will seek vengeance and destroy them for not living according to the command of their Creator, the Lord. The children of Judah will be in despair. 3 They established themselves in killing prophets and in righteousness, but since they did not live according to the Nine Laws and true Worship, their sins will be revealed when the dead rise. 4 At that time, the Lord will examine them with His inherent wisdom, seek vengeance, and destroy them for all the sins they committed from their youth to their old age. 5 They will enter the grave and become dust, just like their ancestors who lived in sin, and at the time of Resurrection, He will seek vengeance and destroy those who disregarded the Lord's LAW. 6 They will be judged for claiming, 'Their way of life, their thoughts, have become like the laws of Sodom.' 7 Their kin are like those of Gomorrah, their laws lead to destruction, and their deeds are evil. 8 Their laws are as deadly as snake poison, as viper venom that kills from close by.

1 Meq. 12

1 O child of Jerusalem, your sins are like those of Sodom and Gomorrah. O child of Jerusalem, your suffering has been spoken by a prophet . 2 Your tribulation is like the tribulation of Sodom and Gomorrah, your laws and reasoning entrenched in adultery and arrogance. 3 Apart from adultery and arrogance, no rain of pardon or humility has fallen from your reasonings. Your law of reasoning has become barren, aside from shedding human blood, robbing, and forgetting your Creator, the Lord. 4 You did not recognize your Creator, aside from your evil deeds and idols. You are content with your deeds, lusting after men and animals. 5 Because your eyes of understanding have been blinded, preventing you from seeing the secrets, and your ears have been deafened, preventing you from hearing or following the Lord's loving commands, you did not know the Lord in your actions, and your reasoning has become like the laws of Sodom. Your kindred are like the grapevines of Gomorrah that produce bitter fruit. 6 If you inspect your deeds, they are poisonous and lethal, for they are rooted in a curse from the day they were committed, and their foundation is set in an era of destruction. 7 As your way of living, your reasoning, is entrenched in sinful deeds, as your bodies are committed to the burning works of Satan to commit sin, your way of living, your reasoning, does not produce any righteous deeds at any time. 8 And when he was shamed and baptized (by one led astray), it was for punishment and destruction. He will solidify the judgments on those who drank and followed these teachings and will make those who destroy the truth - repulsive individuals who turned away from the Lord. 9 Because they have lived according to their evil deeds, he will make them dwellings of the Devil, and eating sacrifices offered to idols has begun in the House of Israel. She proceeds to the mountains and

432

trees, 10 And she worships the idols that the people in her region worship. Her daughters and sons are for demons who do not know the distinction between good and evil. 11 They spill innocent blood; they gush and pour wine from Sodom for the idols forever. 12 And she glorifies and worships Dagon, which the Philistines worship. She sacrifices to him from her flocks and her fattened cows so that she may find favor in the idle teachings of demons, who taught her to make sacrifices for them, and in their gushing and pouring of wine, that she might act according to their wishes. 13 She sacrifices to him so that she may find favor in the idle teachings of demons, which they taught her so that she would not know her Creator, the Lord, who feeds her at all times and who cared for and raised her from her infancy to her prime, and then again until the day she dies. 14 And again, I, the Lord, will seek vengeance and judge him in the time of Resurrection, and as she did not return to my LAW and did not live according to my Command, her time when she lives in Hell will be eternal. 15 If they were true gods, let her idols rise with her and descend into Hell to save her when I, the Lord, am angry and destroy her, and when I distance all the priests of the idols who conspired with her. 16 As she has committed sin and insulted the Holy Items and my Dwelling, the Temple, I, the Lord, made her desolate by all this. 17 When they told her, 'Look, this is the people of the Lord, and she is the worshipper of the Lord, the God of Israel, and the renowned kingdom of Jerusalem, which was set apart from those who were set apart, she is the dwelling place of the Most High Lord's Name' - I, the Lord, made her desolate as she brought sorrow to my Name that was called upon her. 18 She boasts in me that she was my servant and that I was her Lord. She flirts with me like a criminal, yet she is not one who fears me and follows my commands as I am her Lord. 19 They became an obstacle to her, misleading her so that they might distance her from me, yet she is governed by other idols that neither feed nor clothe her. 20 She offers sacrifices to them, eats the sacrifices, spills blood for them, gushes and drinks from the wine for them. She burns incense for them and makes the fragrance of incense pleasing for them. Her idols command her, and she is commanded by them. 21 Again, she sacrifices her daughters and sons for them, and as she offers praises to them because of their love, she finds pleasure in what she says with her tongue and in her actions. 22 Woe to her on the day of Final Judgment, and woe to her idols that she loves and unites with. She will descend with them to Hell, below Sheol, where the worm does not sleep, and the fire is not extinguished. 23 Woe to you, wretched child of Jerusalem, for you have abandoned me, your Creator, and have worshipped different idols. 24 And I, the Lord, will bring hardships upon you according to your deeds. As you have saddened me and ignored my Word and have not done righteous works, I, the Lord, will judge you according to your pretensions. 25 Because you have saddened my Word and have not lived according to my LAW, which you swore with me that you might keep my LAW and that I, the Lord, might live with you in support and save you from all who fight against you, and also that you might keep my Order that I, the Lord, commanded you. I, the Lord, will ignore you and will not quickly save you from tribulation. 26 You did not keep all this, and I, the Lord, ignored you. As I created you and as you did not keep my Command nor my Word, I, the Lord, will judge you in the time of Judgment. I honored you that you might be my kin. 27 As Sodom and Gomorrah were separated from me, so you were separated from me. 28 And I judged and destroyed them. Just as Sodom and Gomorrah were separated from me, so you separated from me. And now, just as I was angry and destroyed them, I, the Lord, am angry and have destroyed you. As you are from the kindred of Sodom and Gomorrah, whom I, the Lord, destroyed, I have destroyed you. As those whom I created have saddened me by going to a young woman and lusting unlawfully, with animals and men as if going to daughters, I have obliterated their names from this world so that they may not live in their righteousness. ²⁹ There is no fear of the Lord in their faces, from a child to an elder. They aid each other in all their wicked deeds, yet He does not grow angry with each one so that they might stop working her. As their deeds are evil, they are full of sin and iniquity. ³⁰ All wicked deeds - theft, arrogance, and greed - are conceived in their minds. ³¹ And because of this, the Lord ignored them and destroyed their lands. They are there so that He might burn them with fire until their very roots perish. They are utterly destroyed forever, yet He did not allow even one of them to remain. ³² As they were entrenched in sin, they will wait in destruction forever until the Day of the Advent when Final Judgment is done, for they have saddened me with their wicked deeds, and I, the Lord, will not pardon nor forgive them. ³³ And I, the Lord, ignored them. For you will find no excuse when I, the Lord, become angry and take you because all your deeds were theft and sin, adultery and greed, lying and all wrongdoings, and obstacles that I, the Lord, do not love. And you, child of Jerusalem, who were wretched, on the day of Judgment, you will be captured in Judgment like them. ³⁴ I made you for honor, but you have degraded yourself. I called you my treasure, but you have become another's. ³⁵ I betrothed you for honor, but you have become for the Devil. And I, the Lord, will seek vengeance and destroy you according to your evil deeds. ³⁶ Because you did not listen to all my Words, and because you did not keep the Command I commanded you when I loved you, I, the Lord, will multiply and exact firm vengeance upon you, for I am the Lord who created you. And I, the Lord, will judge all sinners like you, and on the day when Judgment is done, I, the Lord, will bring hardships upon them according to their wicked deeds. ³⁷ As you did not keep my Word, and as you have ignored my Judgment, I, the Lord, will judge you along with them. ³⁸ Woe to you, Sodom and Gomorrah, who have no fear of the Lord in your thinking. ³⁹ Likewise, woe to your sister, child of Jerusalem, upon whom judgment will be passed together with you in the Fire of Hell, for you both will descend together to Hell that was prepared for you, where there are no exits forever. And woe to all sinners who committed your sins. ⁴⁰ As you did not keep my Command nor my Word, both you and she who did not keep my Command nor my Word will descend to Sheol together on the day when Judgment is judged. ⁴¹ But kind persons who kept my Command and my Word will inherit the wealth that sinner persons accumulated, and as the Lord commanded, kind persons will share the spoils that evil persons seized, and kind persons will be completely at peace. ⁴² But wrongdoers and sinful persons will weep, and they will be sad because of all their sins , having strayed from my Command. ⁴³ He who keeps my Word and lives according to my Command is the one who will find my blessing and be honored alongside me. ⁴⁴ Every person who keeps my Word and lives according to my Command will enjoy the bounty from the Earth and will live, entering the Garden where righteous kings with upright reasoning enter.

1 Meq. 13

¹ As they will be miserable and perish by my wrath when I seize them, woe to Tyre and Sidon and all the regions of Judah who make themselves arrogant today. ² The conquering Lord has spoken thus. He has said: The child of the Devil, who is completely arrogant, will emerge from them - the False Messiah who is the true enemy, who tightens his collar of reasoning, who boasts and does not recognize his Creator. And He said: Woe to them. And the Lord who rules all has said: I created him for the pattern of my anger, that I might reveal my power in him. ³ And this Capernaum, Samaria, Galilee,

433

Damascus, Syria, Achaia, Cyprus, and all the regions of Jordan are families who have stiffened their necks, who live entrenched in their sins, and whom the shadow of death and darkness have covered, for the Devil has shrouded their reasoning in sin, and they are commanded by that arrogant Devil. They did not return to fearing the Lord. ⁴ At that time, woe to those who are led by demons and who offer sacrifices in their names. As they have denied the Lord who created them, they are like mindless animals. For the False Messiah, who has forgotten the Lord's LAW and is the child of the Devil, will establish his image in all places (for he has said, 'I am a god'), and he will be content in his reasoning, his actions, and in all his sins, treachery, and wickedness - in theft and all the adulteries committed by a person. ⁵ Because it is considered by the Lord that he acts in this way, the time is recognized for their sinfulness. ⁶ The sun will darken, the moon will turn to blood, and the stars will be shaken from the heavens. All deeds will pass by the miracles that the Lord will perform in the Era of Fulfillment, so He might pass the earth and all who live in the sin of those dwelling within it. ⁷ As the Lord was proud of the creation He created, and as He swiftly accomplished all He loved in one moment, the lord of death will destroy the insignificant enemy, the Devil. ⁸ For the Lord who rules all has said: I will judge and destroy, but after the Coming, the Devil will have no authority. ⁹ And on the day when he is seized by my anger, he will descend to Hell, for which he applied and where severe punishment exists. As he will take all who are with him to punishment, destruction, and treachery, because I, the Lord, was the one who expelled from Hell and who leads into Hell, he will descend into Hell. ¹⁰ As He grants strength and power to the weak and likewise gives weakness to the strong and firm, let not the strong boast in their strength. ¹¹ As He is the Ruler and as He judges and rescues the oppressed from the hands of those oppressing them, He will avenge the grievances of the widows and the orphaned children upon him. ¹² Woe to you who boast and stiffen your neck in reasoning, for it seems to you that I, the Lord, will not govern nor judge and destroy you. For in his boasting and arrogance, he has said, 'I will extend my throne into the stars of heaven, and I will be like the Most High Lord.' ¹³ And as He has said, 'How did the Devil fall from heaven, he who shone like the morning star, who was created before all others?' Woe to you. ¹⁴ And you dared and spoke this in your arrogance, and you did not consider the Lord who created you with His authority. Why did you exalt yourself so that you would descend to Hell with your reasoning firmness? ¹⁵ You have been separated from all angels like you, for they praise their Creator with humble reasoning because they know that He is the one who created them from fire and wind, and because they do not stray from His Command, and because they keep their reasoning from treachery so as not to completely stray from His Command. ¹⁶ But you committed grave treachery in your reasoning arrogance. You have become a wretched man, separate from your companions, for you have cherished all sin and iniquity - theft and treachery, through which people who have forgotten the Lord's LAW and sinners like you are entrenched, those who are from your family and commit crimes like you, those who live according to your command and your will, through which you teach sin. ¹⁷ Woe to you, for the demons you led astray in your malice, you will descend to Hell together. ¹⁸ O you children of the Lord who were misled by that misleading criminal, the Devil, woe to you. As you have gone astray like him by the teachings he gave you and that his followers taught you, you will descend to Hell together, where there are no exits forever. ¹⁹ And previously, when the Lord's servant Moses was there, you saddened the Lord at the Waters of Meribah and at Kadesh, by Amalek and at Mount Sinai. ²⁰ Moreover, when you sent scouts to Canaan, and they told you, 'The journey is long, and the ramparts and fortresses that reach up to the heavens are strong, and mighty warriors dwell there,' you became upset, wanting to return to Egypt, where you performed laborious tasks, and you saddened the Lord's word. 21 You did not remember the Lord who lifted you out of adversity, who performed great miracles in Egypt, and who led you with the authority of His Angel. He covered you with a cloud by day so the sun would not burn you, and He shone a pillar of fire for you by night so that your feet would not stumble in the darkness. 22 And when the army and Pharaoh scared you, you cried out to Moses, and Moses cried out to the Lord, and He stayed with His Angel and protected you so that you would not encounter Pharaoh. 23 But He led them into the Red Sea in distress. The Lord led only Israel, for He said: There was no other god with them, but He buried their enemies in the sea at once, and He did not save any who fled from them. 24 And He led Israel across the sea on foot. There were no difficulties arising from the Egyptians. He delivered them to Mount Sinai, and there He fed them manna for forty years. 25 As the children of Israel always saddened the Lord, despite all the good things He did for them, they neglected to worship the Lord. 26 They harbored evil in their reasoning from their youth to their old age, for the Lord's word spoke thus in the Torah, where the birth of the fathers was recorded. As He said, 'The reasoning of the children of Adam is ashes, and all their deeds are geared toward theft, and they rush toward evil. There is none among them who loves righteous deeds, apart from accumulating wealth through violence, swearing falsely, harming their neighbors, and engaging in theft and robbery.' They harbored evil in their reasoning. 27 And all proceed toward wicked deeds in the time they live. The children of Israel, who completely disregarded the Lord's LAW, saddened the Lord from ancient times until the era of fulfillment.

1 Meq. 14

1 And when the Lord destroyed the descendants of Cain - the kindreds who came before - with the waters of destruction because of their sins, He baptized the Earth with the waters of destruction and cleansed her from all the sins of Cain's children. 2 As He said, "I was saddened because I created man." He destroyed all wrongdoers, sparing only eight persons. After this, He multiplied them, and they filled the Earth, sharing the inheritance of their father Adam. 3 But Noah made an oath with the Lord. They swore to the Lord not to let the Earth be destroyed again by the waters of destruction, nor let Noah's children consume what is dead or has died naturally, nor to worship other idols apart from the Lord who created them. He would be a loving Father to them, not destroy them all at once for their meaningless sins, not withhold early and latter rains, and would provide food for livestock and people at all times, including grass, grain, fruit, and plants, so that they might perform good deeds pleasing to the Lord. 4 After He gave them this command, the children of Israel saddened the Lord with their sins. They did not adhere to His law like their forefathers Isaac, Abraham, and Jacob, who did not ignore the Lord's laws. 5 From the least to the greatest, those children of Israel who did not keep the Lord's law were corrupt in their actions. 6 Whether they were priests, leaders, or scribes, everyone ignored the Lord's law. 7 They did not abide by the Lord's order or His law that Moses commanded them in Deuteronomy, saying, "Love your Creator, the Lord, with all your body and all your reasoning." 8 They did not adhere to the Lord's order or His law that Moses commanded them in the scripture where the law was written, saying, "Love your neighbor as yourself. Do not worship different idols. Do not pursue a young woman. Do not kill a soul. Do not steal. 9 Do not bear false witness. Whether it is his donkey or his ox, do not covet your neighbor's possessions or anything that your brother has acquired." 10 However, after he commanded them all this, the children of Israel, who were evil, returned to treachery, sin, robbery, immorality, to lying, stealing, and worshipping idols. 11 The children of Israel saddened the Lord at Horeb by making a golden calf that grazed on grass. They bowed down, saying, "Look, these are our gods who led us out of Egypt." 12 They were content with their handiwork. If they ate and drank and sat down, they rose to dance. 13 As the Lord told Moses, "Your relatives whom you led out of the land of Egypt, where they were enslaved, have deviated from the law and committed wrongdoing. They made an image of a calf and bowed down to the idol." Because of this, Moses became angry and came down from Mount Sinai. 14 While Moses was angry with his relatives, he descended with his confidant Joshua. When Joshua heard the noise, he said, "Look, I hear the sound of warriors in the camp of Israel." 15 But Moses told Joshua, "It is the sound of Israel playing after drinking undiluted wine. It is not the sound of victory nor defeat." Then he descended, shattered the idol, and ground it into dust, mixing it into the water that the children of Israel drank near the mountain. 16 After this, he commanded the priests to kill each other because of the sin they committed before the Lord. 17 They understood that defying the Lord was worse than killing themselves or their fathers, and they did as he commanded them. 18 Moses told them, "Because you saddened the Lord who fed you, cherished you, led you out of the house of bondage, and bequeathed you the inheritance that He swore to your forefathers to give to them and their children after them, because of this, you made the Lord angry." 19 For they pursued sin and evil, and they did not stop saddening the Lord there. 20 They were not like their forefathers Isaac, Abraham, and Jacob, who pleased the Lord with their good deeds, so that He might give them what is on Earth and what He prepared for those who love Him in Heaven, from their youth to their old age. They were not like Abraham, Isaac, and Jacob, who pleased the Lord with their actions so that He might grant them an Earthly inheritance where righteousness abides in this world and a delightful garden prepared for the righteous in the afterlife, which He prepared for Abraham, Isaac, and Jacob, who pleased the Lord while they were alive and loved Him, beyond what eye has seen, ear has heard, or mind has conceived. 21 And their children, who denied the Lord and were evil, living according to their misguided thoughts, did not listen to the Lord's command, He who fed them, cherished them, and protected them from their infancy. 22 They did not think of the Lord who led them out of the land of Egypt, saved them from hard labor, and from a harsh rule. 23 But they completely saddened Him, and He raised up nations in their region against them, who rose up against them in hostility and also levied taxes on them, just as they had desired.

1 Meq. 15

1 And at that time, the people of Midian rose against them in enmity, and they mobilized their armies against Israel to fight them. Their king was named 'Akrandis; he quickly gathered numerous armies from Keeliqyas, Syria, and Damascus. 2 Camping beyond the Jordan, he sent messengers saying, "So that I may seize your wealth, pay tribute to Israel for me." He told them, "But if you do not pay the tribute, I have come to punish you and will seize your livestock, take your mares, and capture your children." 3 "I will seize and take you to a land unknown to you, where I will make you water carriers and wood gatherers," he told them. 4 "Do not boast, saying, 'We are the descendants of the Lord, and nothing can happen to us.' Is it not the Lord who sent me to destroy you and plunder your wealth? Am I not the one whom the Lord sent to gather all your kin?" 5 "Have the other gods really saved the other tribes that I destroyed? I seized

their horses and mares, I killed them and captured their children. [6] If you do not deliver the tribute I have commanded you, I will destroy you just like them," he said. And he crossed the Jordan to plunder their livestock, their wealth, and to capture their wives. [7] After this, the children of Israel wept bitterly before the Lord, and they cried out loudly, but they lacked anyone to help them. [8] Because the Lord empowered the three brothers, whose names were Judah, Mebikyas, and Maccabees, who were handsome and were warriors in their strength. [9] The children of Israel wept bitterly there. When they heard the news, it saddened them deeply, echoing the cries from all the children of Israel, the child orphaned by his parents, the widows, their officials, and their priests, all the families of Israel, both daughters and sons, and all the children. They wept, sprinkling ashes on their heads, and their nobles wore sackcloth. [10] But those brothers, who were attractive and comely, agreed to save them. They consulted, saying, "Let us go and offer our bodies to death for these people." [11] Encouraging each other, "Take heart, take heart," they went, girding their swords around their waists and holding their spears in their hands, prepared to confront the warrior. [12] They reached their camp. Mebikyas attacked the king (the warrior) while he was seated at the dinner table. He cut off his neck with a single blow while he was eating, and Maccabees and Judah struck down his soldiers to the left and right with the sword, killing them. [13] When their king was defeated, they plunged their spears into the hearts of their companions, and they all fled, their bows were broken, and they were defeated. [14] But those brothers, who were attractive and comely, were saved from death. No evil befell them because, as the Lord returned punishment to their enemies, they slaughtered one another and were decimated. [15] They were defeated and died, and as they crossed the Jordan, they discarded all their wealth. All their wealth remained, and when the children of Israel saw that their enemies had fled, they went to their camp and took for themselves both what was plundered and the wealth. [16] The Lord saved Israel in this manner through the brothers and by Mebikyas's hand. [17] Israel rested for a few days while they made the Lord pleased. [18] But after that, they returned to their sins. The children of Israel neglected worshipping the Lord as they should. [19] And He will again afflict them with tribes unknown to them who will harvest their fields, destroy their vineyards, plunder their flocks, slaughter and feed on their livestock in front of them... [20] and who will capture their wives, their daughters, and their sons. Because they always saddened the Lord; as they are families who ignored the law, they will have their children dashed against the rocks in front of them; they will not save them.

1 Meq. 16

[1] Those who do this are the people of Tyre and Sidon and those who live beyond the Jordan River and along the seashore - the people of Keran and Gilead, the Jebusites, the Canaanites, Edom, and the Gergesites, and the Amalekites. [2] All these people do the same, living firmly in each of their tribes, countries, regions, and according to all their deeds and languages, and all live firmly as the Lord created them. [3] And there are people among them who know the Lord and whose deeds were beautiful. [4] And there are people among them whose deeds were evil and who do not know the Lord who created them, and as they committed sins, He handed them over to the king of Syria, Shalmaneser. [5] As he plundered and took the wealth of Damascus and as he shared the spoils of Samaria before the king of Egypt, He handed them over to the hand of Shalmaneser. [6] The region of Gilead and also the people in Persia and Media, Cappadocia, and Sicyonia, who live in the western mountains, in the fortress of Gilead, and Phasga, which is part of the land of Judah... [7] and these people who live in that region are families who

do not know the Lord nor keep His Command, and whose necks of reasoning were stiff. [8] And He will repay them for their evil deeds and the works of their hands. [9] For the families of Gilead and the region of Caesarea and the Amalekites have joined together to destroy the Lord's land filled with truth and within which the worship of the Lord, the Most Glorious and Conquering, is praised, He Who is served fearfully and tremblingly by countless angels in the chariots of Cherubiel, standing before Him. And He will repay them for their evil deeds and the works of their hands.

1 Meq. 17

[1] The people of Amalek and Edom do not worship the Lord by whose authority the dominion of Earth and Heaven was seized, as they are offenders who do not live by the deeds of truth. They have no fear of demolishing His dwelling, the Temple. [2] They have no fear of the Lord before them, except for shedding blood, adultery, consuming what was struck down, and sacrificing to idols, and all that is like consuming what died naturally. These are despised sinners. [3] They have neither decency nor religion, as they are those who hated righteous deeds, and as they do not know the Lord, and as they do not know the deeds of love, other than robbing a person's wealth and from sin, and other than disturbing a person and all detested deeds, apart from games and songs as their father, the Devil, taught them. They have neither decency nor religion. [4] As he has ruled them with his host of demons, he teaches them all evil deeds for each of their own benefits - all robbery and sin, theft and falsehood, robbing money and consuming what was struck down and what died naturally, and the deeds of adultery. [5] And he teaches them all that is like this - and going towards a young woman - and shedding blood - eating what was sacrificed to idols and what died naturally - and killing a person's soul violently - and envy and winking and greed and all evil deeds that the Lord does not love. The Devil, their enemy, teaches them these teachings to distance them from the Lord's LAW, who rules the whole world. [6] But the Lord's deeds are innocence and humility - not annoying a brother and loving a companion - being harmonious and loving towards all people. [7] Do not be hypocrites for the sake of favoring someone's face, and do not be wrongdoers nor complete robbers, nor people who go towards a young woman, nor people who commit iniquity and evil deeds towards their companion, nor who coax to wrong their companion violently. [8] They wink and shake their heads and incite evil. They discourage to mislead so that they might lower them forever in the Definite Judgment of Eternity.

1 Meq. 18

[1] Consider that you will go into death towards the Lord in whose hand all things lie, and you will stand before Him so that He may judge you for all the sins you have committed. [2] As those who are proud and evil, and the children of powerful ones, are no stronger than them - were likewise previously - because they relied on their stature, power, and solid authority, they did not place the Lord before them, and they did not realize that He was their Creator who brought them from nonexistence to existence. [3] And when their fathers, resembling "Angels," were praised on Mount Holy with the Angels, when their agreement misled them, they descended into this world where the Definite Judgment will be carried out forever. [4] As the Lord created human flesh for them in antiquity, to lead them astray because of their arrogant reasoning and to test them whether they would keep His laws and commands, they married women from Cain's descendants. [5] But they did not keep His laws. He cast them into the fire of Hell along with their father, the Devil, for the Lord was angry with the descendants of Seth who acted wickedly like the people, and the lifespan of people was reduced because of their sins. [6] And they led Adam's children into sin with them. He cast

them into Sheol, where they will receive their judgment. [7] Since the lifespan of people was reduced because the descendants of Seth erred with Cain's descendants, when people's lifespan was nine hundred years in antiquity, they were reduced to living only one hundred twenty years. [8] And as they are flesh and blood, the Lord said, "My spirit shall not abide in man forever." [9] Because our lifespan was reduced, because of our sins and iniquities, our lifespan was reduced from that of our forefathers. And when they are young again, they are dying. [10] But our forefathers' lifespan was extended because they kept the Lord's laws and did not sadden the Lord. [11] But our forefathers' lifespan was extended because they were strict with their daughters and sons, teaching them, and because they were strict with their sons not to violate the Lord's laws that they taught them. Because they did not violate the Lord's laws with their daughters and sons, indeed, their lifespan was truly extended.

1 Meq. 19

[1] When the descendants of Cain multiplied, they created drums, harps, lyres, and violins; they made songs and all sorts of games. [2] Children who were attractive and comely were born to Cain from the wife of the righteous man Abel, whom he killed because of her, for she was attractive. And after he killed his brother, he took that woman, who was his possession. [3] Separating from his father, he took them and went to the region of Nod, which is towards the West, and those attractive children were as beautiful as their mother. [4] And because the descendants of Seth descended towards Cain's descendants, and after they saw them, they did not wait even an hour, and they took the daughters whom they chose for themselves as wives. [5] As they have led us into error along with them because of their mistake, because the Lord was angry with us and with them. [6] And the Devil, having deceived them by saying, "You will become like gods, like your Creator, the Lord," led our mother Eve and our father Adam into his deception. [7] But it seemed true to them in their folly; they abandoned the Lord's law, He who created them from nonexistence to existence, that they might bow down and praise His glorious name. [8] But their Creator humbled those Adam and Eve who aspired to divinity, and He humbled the one who was arrogant. [9] As David said, "Adam fell through the Devil's pride," He disgraced them, for our father Adam was judged for the Devil's pride by His true judgment. [10] And the descendants of Seth, who erred with the descendants of Cain, led us into their sin. Because of this, our lifespan that the Lord gave us was less than that of our ancestors. [11] But they had performed good deeds because they had anchored their thoughts in the Lord. They were like the righteous Abel, innocent ones like Abel. But those people who live according to the deeds of Abel love the Lord. [12] But the Lord disregards the wicked, and their Definite Judgment is prepared for them in their bodies, and it is written in the records of their thoughts. And when Judgment is passed, it will be read before men and angels and all creations. [13] At that time, they will be ashamed. The wrongdoers and those who refused to do the Lord's deeds will be ashamed. [14] And a terrifying word will be given to them, saying, "Place them in Hell, where there is no exit forever."

1 Meq. 20

[1] My brothers, consider this: do not forget what has been told to you before - that JAH preserves the true work of those who do good deeds. [2] He multiplies their descendants in this world - and their names will be invoked for blessings forever; their children will not suffer for food in this world. [3] He will fight for them because they belong to Him - and He will not deliver them into the hands of their enemies - He will rescue them from the hands of those who despise

them. [4] And for those who love His name - He will be their helper in times of trouble; He will protect them and forgive all their sins.

1 Meq. 21

[1] David trusted in JAH - for He had faith in him - and He was his refuge from King Saul. [2] As he had faith in Him and kept His laws during the uprisings of his son Absalom, the Philistines, the Edomites, the Amalekites, and when one of the four giants arose - JAH delivered David from all these troubles brought upon him by his adversaries. [3] Success is by JAH's decree - they were overcome by their enemies - yet JAH did not save the wicked kings who did not believe in Him. [4] Hezekiah trusted in JAH - He saved him from the hands of the arrogant Sennacherib. [5] But his son Manasseh was defeated by his enemies because he did not place his trust in JAH - as he did not trust in JAH and did not revere JAH who greatly honored and exalted him - they bound him and took him to their land - but those enemies who defeated Manasseh were not like him. [6] At that time He deprived him of the kingdom He had given him - because he did not perform righteous acts before his Creator JAH - so that his reign might be extended and that He might fight his enemies for him and that he might have power and stability from behind and before. [7] It is better to trust in JAH than in many armies - than in horses, bows, and shields. [8] Trusting in JAH is superior - a person who trusts in Him will stand firm, be honored, and exalted. [9] JAH does not show favoritism - but those who did not believe in JAH and trusted in their abundance of wealth became those who were removed from the grace and honor that He gave them. [10] He will protect those who trust in Him - but He will let those who deny Him be plundered by their enemies - as they did not direct their minds to follow JAH or keep His laws - He will not quickly assist them in their times of trouble or when their enemies confront them. [11] But for a person disciplined in worshipping JAH and keeping His laws - He will be a refuge in their time of trouble. [12] By destroying their enemies, plundering their livestock, capturing the people of their enemies, sending down abundant rains, causing sprouts to grow, bringing in heaps of grain, providing the first and latter rains, making the grass green, giving rain at the appropriate times so their subjects under their authority may prosper - He will make them prosper. [13] He will make them prosper - so they may consume the wealth of others, be satisfied from the plunder taken from their enemies, plunder animals, sheep, and cattle, eat from the tables of others, and take their enemies' children captive. [14] JAH will do all this for the person He loves - but He will allow the enemies to plunder those who hate Him. [15] He will bind their feet and hands and deliver them into the hands of their enemies - He will make them a mockery to their foes - as they have become murderers who broke JAH's laws - He will not allow them to prosper in their descendants' homes. [16] They will not stand in the time of judgment - and to inflict the deserved punishment on those who do evil - He will also give to those who commit wicked acts the due recompense for their sins. [17] But it has been decreed by JAH to give to those who perform righteous deeds their reward - to keep them under His protection. [18] For He is empowered over all the nations He created to do good deeds and to provide them with eternal well-being so that they may praise JAH who created them - and He ordered that He may keep His law - aside from mankind, none of the creations He made has strayed from His command. [19] As JAH commanded all living beings, each in their works - they all know and are maintained under His law. [20] But man has become bold against JAH, who crowned everything in each of their domains - over animals, beasts, and birds of the sky. [21] Whether in the sea or on land - JAH gave all creatures He created to Adam, their father - JAH gave them so that he might do as he pleases with

them, so that they might eat them like crops grown from the earth, and that they might rule and govern over them, whether beasts or animals, they might be subject to man - and He appointed them over everything He created so that those who reign might be under the command of JAH who granted them honor, and that they might honor Him. 22 But if they deviate from His laws, He will strip them of the dominion He granted them - as He is the ruler of heaven and earth - He will grant it to those who fulfill His covenant. 23 He appoints those He loves to appoint, and dismisses those He wishes to dismiss - He kills, He saves, He disciplines in times of trouble, He forgives. 24 There is no creator like Him - as He is the sovereign over all the nations He created - there is none other apart from Him, the Creator, in heaven above or on earth below - there is none who can challenge Him. 25 He appoints, He dismisses, He kills, He saves, He disciplines in times of trouble, He forgives, He impoverishes, He exalts. 26 He listens to those who pray to Him earnestly - He accepts the pleas of those who fulfill His covenant with a pure mind; He listens to their prayers - He fulfills their requests in everything they have asked Him for. 27 And He makes both the great and the small subject to them - all this is their inheritance on the hills and mountains, at the roots of trees, in caves, wells of the earth, and all their kin, on both dry land and sea. 28 And for those who fulfill the covenant of their Creator, all this is their inheritance - and He will not deprive them of their abundance - He will give them their due reward of praise. 29 And He will grant them the honor He has prepared in heaven for their forefathers Isaac, Abraham, and Jacob - He will give them what He has prepared for Hezekiah, David, and Samuel who did not stray from His laws and His command. 30 That they may prosper in His sovereignty - He will give those who have served Him from antiquity the honor He prepared for their forefathers Isaac, Abraham, and Jacob - for whom He swore to give them an inheritance.

1 Meq. 22

1 Please reflect on the names of those who perform righteous deeds and do not forget their actions. 2 Ensure that your name is mentioned among theirs, so that you may rejoice with them in the Kingdom of Heaven, the Place of Light prepared for the noble and kings who abided by JAH's covenant and were kind-hearted. 3 Also, be aware and convinced of the names of wicked nobles and kings - they will be condemned and scorned among men after their death. 4 Because they did not align their actions with their knowledge and understanding, be convinced that unless they lived according to JAH's covenant, they will face greater judgment in the Kingdom of Heaven than criminals and those who neglected JAH's laws. 5 Be kind, innocent, and honest, but do not follow the path of those who have forgotten JAH's laws, upon whom JAH has poured out His wrath because of their wicked deeds. 6 Judge truthfully and rescue the orphan whose parents have died, and the widow from the hands of sinners who rob them. 7 Act as a fatherly guardian to the orphan whose parents have died, protect him from the wealthy who exploit him, stand by him, and be moved when you see the tears of the orphan, lest you find yourself in the fiery sea where sinners who have not repented are punished. 8 And direct your steps towards the path of Love and Unity, for JAH's eyes observe His friends, and His ears hear their plea - seek Love and follow her. 9 But JAH's wrathful countenance is turned towards those who do evil deeds, to obliterate their name from this world, and He will not spare anyone who lurks near cliffs or mountains. 10 As I am JAH, who is zealous for my divinity, I am a Creator who avenges and destroys those who despise me and do not adhere to my words - I will not turn my merciful face back to them until I have destroyed those who do not abide by my word. 11 And I shall honor those who honor me and keep my commands.

1 Meq. 23

1 Do not follow in the way of Cain, who killed his brother in innocence, mistakenly believing his brother bore love for him. 2 And he murdered his brother out of envy for a woman - those who create envy, iniquity, and betrayal against their companions are like him. 3 But because Abel was as innocent as a lamb, and his blood was as pure as the blood of a clean sheep sacrificed to JAH with a pure heart, they followed Cain's path, which is not Abel's path. 4 Because all who live in innocence are beloved by JAH, like the kind man Abel - they have been as innocent as Abel, but those who conduct themselves according to Abel's righteousness truly love JAH. 5 However, JAH disregards the wicked ones - and their definitive judgment will apply to them; it is inscribed in the records of their thoughts, and at the time of judgment, it will be read before men, angels, and all creation. 6 At that time, they will be shamed - wrongdoers and those who refused to live according to JAH's covenant will face humiliation. 7 A terrifying decree will be pronounced against them, stating - Place them in Hell, from which there is no escape, forever.

1 Meq. 24

1 When Gideon trusted in JAH, he defeated the uncircumcised peoples' armies, which were vast, with just a few tens of thousands, outnumbering them like locusts. 2 There is no Creator apart from me - oh nobles and kings, do not put your faith in various idols. 3 I am your Creator, JAH, who brought you from your mothers' wombs, raised you, fed you, and clothed you. Why do you make excuses? Why do you worship other gods apart from me? 4 I have done all this for you – what have you offered me? You should live according to my laws, commands, and decrees, so I may ensure your well-being. But what more can I ask from you? 5 JAH, the ruler of all, thus declares: Rescue yourselves from idol worship, sorcery, and the spread of negativity. 6 For JAH's punishment will come upon those who engage in these acts, and upon those who listen to and follow them, who are their friends and live by their commands - free yourselves from the worship of idols. 7 As people, unknown and unkind to you, will rise against you - unless you, who revered and followed JAH's ways, they will consume what you have labored for, just as the prophets, Enoch, and Asaph had spoken. Unless you follow JAH's ways, others will consume what you have toiled for. 8 Wicked people will come in disguise, they adhere to no law other than indulging in eating, drinking, and adorning themselves with silver and gold, living in sin and all the deeds JAH detests. 9 They are set for feasting and drinking - from morning until evening, they engage in malicious deeds; their paths are filled with misery and tribulation, yet they know not the path of Love. 10 They are ignorant of the deeds of Love and Unity, lacking the fear of JAH in their demeanor; they are corrupt, godless, and without moral virtue; they are greedy, indulging alone, drunken, boundless in sin, engaging in seduction, bloodshed, theft, treachery, and ruthless robbery. 11 They are fault-finders lacking love and law; they do not fear JAH, their Creator, and show no reverence. 12 They feel no shame before the one they face; they do not respect the elderly or the grey-haired. When they hear, 'There is wealth in this world,' they consider it solely theirs before even seeing it, for they lack the fear of JAH. 13 The nobles exploit the trust placed in them; they are cynics with no truth in their speech, inconsistent from morning to evening. 14 They ignore the cries of the afflicted and the poor; their rulers hasten towards evil, troubling the innocent who have sheltered refugees from the greed of the wealthy. 15 Let them protect the wronged and the refugee, but let not the rulers deny them justice

for any reason. [16] They are the ones who levy heavy taxes, plunder wealth unjustly, and are known as criminals. Their deeds are malevolent; they are unkind even when consuming the calf with its mother and a bird with its egg. They claim everything they see and hear as their own. [17] They gather wealth selfishly, indifferent to the sick and the poor, and violently strip away from those who have nothing, amassing riches only for their own enjoyment. [18] For they will vanish swiftly like a scarab emerging from its hole, leaving no trace and never returning home, because they did not perform righteous deeds in their lifetime - woe to them when JAH becomes angry and acts against them. [19] When JAH abandons them, they will perish together under one punishment; He has been patient as if awaiting their repentance, not destroying them hastily - yet, they will meet their end when their time comes. [20] But if they do not repent, He will destroy them quickly, as He did with those before them who did not observe His laws appropriately. [21] They are those who consume human flesh and drink human blood, dressing in violence and sin. There is no fear of JAH in their eyes; they wake from their beds restless to commit sin. [22] Their activities revolve around eating and drinking, heading towards destruction and sin, aiming to ruin many lives in this world.

1 Meq. 25

[1] As their actions are crooked, and all those who are entrenched in Satan's misleading works, JAH, the ruler of all, has declared, "Woe to your body when I am angry and seize it. [2] But because they do not recognize JAH's works, for they have turned them away and have neglected my laws. [3] And later, in the era of fulfillment, I will bring suffering upon them equivalent to their wickedness; just as their sins are recorded before me, I will avenge and destroy them on the day of Judgment. [4] As I, JAH, fill everything from horizon to horizon, and all creation is under my dominion, no one can escape my authority in heaven, on earth, or in the depths or the sea. [5] I command the snake that crawls beneath the earth, the fish within the sea, the birds in the sky, and the desert donkey in the wilderness, for they are all my property from one horizon to the other. [6] As I am the one who performs marvelous deeds and performs miracles before me, no one can escape my authority on earth or in heaven. No one can ask me, 'Where are you going? What are you doing?' [7] I issue commands to the chief angels and hosts. All nations whose names are called belong to me, as do the beasts in the wilderness, all birds in the sky, and livestock; they are my possessions. [8] This comes from the Azieb wind and settles into the drought of Mesie. Later, in the era of fulfillment, the Eritrean sea will vanish, heard from afar, because of JAH, who will approach it, feared and renowned. [9] For He rules over the dead and those present, and it will vanish, being heard along with Saba, Noba, Hindekie, Ethiopia's boundaries, and all those regions. [10] And He observes all from a lofty authority and purity, for His authority surpasses all other powers, and He maintains congregations under His dominion. [11] For His authority stands above all others, His kingdom surpasses all kingdoms, and His power governs the entire world because He is capable of everything, and nothing can withstand Him. [12] He controls all the clouds in the sky, causes grass to grow for the livestock on the earth, and produces fruit on the trees. [13] He feeds everyone according to their kind, as He loves, sustains all He has created with each type of fruit and food, feeds ants and locusts beneath the earth, livestock on the ground, and beasts, and to a person who prays to Him, He grants their prayers and does not ignore the pleas of an orphan or widows. [14] As the rebellion of evil people is like a swirling wind and the counsel of wrongdoers like misty urine, He would rather accept the pleas of those who beg Him at all times and those who are pure. [15] And as their bodies are like a flying bird and their attractive features, which are of silver and gold, are perishable in this world, scrutiny will benefit those who have forgotten JAH's law but not their gold, and moths will consume their garments. [16] And weevils will entirely devour the richness of the wheat and barley, and everything will pass like the day that went by yesterday, like a word that leaves a mouth and does not return. The money of sinful people is also like this, and their 'beautiful lifestyle' is like a passing shadow; sinful people's wealth before JAH is like clothing of lies. [17] However, if righteous people are honored, JAH will not ignore them because they have been honored while they were kind to the poor and have heard the justice of the suffering and the orphan. JAH will not disregard them because they, without neglecting their own children, honor Him while clothing the naked with the garments JAH provided them to give to the suffering refugee. [18] They do not favor the judgment of loyal people, and they do not allow a hired worker's wages to stay with them. As JAH's affairs are true and honored like a sword with two edges, they will not commit iniquity in their seasons or in their balance measurements.

1 Meq. 26

[1] But the poor will reconsider their situation in their beds - if the rich do not accept them, they will be like dry wood lacking greenery, and a root will not be fertile if it lies where there is no moisture, nor will a leaf be fertile if it has no root. [2] Just as a leaf serves a flower by being an ornament to the fruit, unless the leaf is fertile, it will not bear fruit. Likewise, the fulfillment of a man is his religion; without religion, a person has no virtue. [3] If he firmly practices his religion, he performs virtuous deeds, and JAH is pleased with a person who works in truth and righteousness. [4] And for the person who prays to Him, He will grant his plea and reward his sincerity; He will not mistreat the truthful person because of the true work he has performed. [5] As JAH is truthful and loves things of truth, He will not justify the sinner without repentance because of the evil work he has done. Since all souls are held within His power because He is the one who rules both Earth and Heaven, He will not favor the rich over the poor at the time of judgment; He will not absolve them without repentance.

1 Meq. 27

[1] He created, having brought the entire world from non-existence into existence, and He fully prepared the hills and mountains, and established the Earth upon the waters. Lest the sea be agitated, He outlined it with sand. For in His first word, JAH said, "Let there be light." [2] Light was created when this world was enveloped in darkness. JAH created all creations, prepared this world, and established it with what is right and with just measures. He said, "Let the evening be dark." [3] And again, JAH said, "Let there be light," and it dawned, and there was light. He lifted the upper waters towards the heavens. [4] He stretched it out like a tent, established it with wind, and placed the lower waters within a basin. [5] He locked the sea with sand and solidified them with His authority, lest they be submerged in water. He placed animals and beasts within it, and He placed within it Leviathan and Behemoth, who are great beasts, and He placed within it countless animals, both visible and invisible. [6] On the third day, JAH created plants on Earth, all the roots, trees, and fruits that produce according to their kinds, and a tree of welfare, beautiful to look upon. [7] And He created a tree of welfare that was both beautiful to behold and sweet to eat, and He created grass and all plants whose seeds come from within them to be food for birds, livestock, and beasts. [8] It turned to dusk and then dawned, and on the fourth day, He said, "Let there be lights in the heaven named cosmos." JAH, having created the moon, the sun, and the stars, placed them in the heaven named cosmos so that they might illuminate this world and provide light for day and

night. ⁹ And after this, the moon, the sun, and the stars alternated between night and day. ¹⁰ And on the fifth day, JAH created all the animals and beasts that live in the water and all the birds that fly in the sky, everything that is visible and invisible. ¹¹ And on the sixth day, He created livestock, beasts, and others, and having created and prepared all, He created Adam in His image and likeness. ¹² He gave him all the animals and beasts He created to reign over them, and again, all animals, beasts, and all fishes, Leviathan and Behemoth that are in the sea. ¹³ And He gave him all the cattle that live in this world and sheep, the animals unseen and those seen. ¹⁴ And He placed Adam, whom He created in His image and likeness, in the Garden, that he might eat and might cultivate plants and praise JAH there. ¹⁵ And lest he break His commandment, He said, "The moment you eat from the fig tree, you will surely die." ¹⁶ And He commanded him not to eat from the fig tree that brings death, that opens the eyes to good and evil, that brings death. ¹⁷ Our mother Eve was deceived by a misleading snake, and she ate from that fig tree and gave some to our father Adam. ¹⁸ And Adam, having eaten from that fig tree, brought death upon his children and upon himself. ¹⁹ Since he broke His command and ate from the fig tree that JAH commanded saying, "Do not eat from it," JAH was angered with our father Adam and expelled and sent him away from the Garden, and He gave him the earth that grows thistles and thorns, which He cursed because he broke His command at that time, so that he might eat his food by toiling and laboring over the land. ²⁰ And when JAH sent him forth to this land, Adam returned to complete sorrow, and having toiled and labored to cultivate the Earth, he began to eat in weariness and in struggles.

1 Meq. 28

¹ And after his children lived and multiplied, there were among them those who praised and honored JAH and did not break His command. ² There were prophets who spoke of what had happened and what would happen in the future, and among his children, there were sinners who spoke lies and wronged others. Adam's firstborn, Cain, became evil and killed his brother Abel. ³ JAH pronounced judgment on Cain because he killed his brother Abel, and JAH was vexed with the Earth because it drank his blood. ⁴ And JAH said to Cain, "Where is your brother Abel?" and Cain, in his heart's arrogance, said, "Am I my brother Abel's keeper?" ⁵ Abel became a pure man, but Cain became a sinful man by killing a good man, his brother Abel. ⁶ Then a kind child, Seth, was born; Adam had sixty children; there were kind people and evil people among them. ⁷ And there are kind people among them, and there are those who were prophets and those who were traitors and sinners. ⁸ There are blessed people who were kind people, who followed their father Adam's teachings and all he instructed to his child Seth, from Adam up to Noah, who was a kind man who kept JAH's laws. ⁹ And he established JAH's law for his children, telling them, "Guard," lest they break JAH's law, so that they might inform their children just as their father Noah instructed them, and that they might keep JAH's law. ¹⁰ And they lived while they taught their children, generations born after them. ¹¹ But Satan was alive when he spoke to their fathers, having settled in idols that led to the grave and that had vows upon them, and having overcome the people who told him it was right, and when they did everything that Satan, the teacher of sin, commanded them. ¹² And they lived while they worshipped the idols according to their customs until a kind man, Abraham, who fulfilled JAH's covenant, came along. ¹³ For he lived upright in the law beforehand, separate from his cousins, and JAH swore an oath with him, having made a covenant with wind and fire. ¹⁴ JAH swore to him that He would give him a land as an inheritance and that He would give his descendants until eternity. ¹⁵ And He swore to Isaac

just as he had to Abraham, that He might give Isaac the inheritance of his father Abraham, and He swore to Jacob that He might give him the inheritance of his father Isaac, just as He swore to Isaac. ¹⁶ And He separated their descendants, who were born after them from Jacob, into the twelve tribes of Israel, and made them priests and kings, blessing them saying, "Multiply and be very numerous." ¹⁷ And He gave them their father's inheritance, but even though He fed them and loved them, they continued to sadden JAH in everything. ¹⁸ And when He destroys them, at that time they will seek Him in worship, and they will turn back from sin and turn to JAH, for He loves them, and JAH will forgive them. ¹⁹ For being kind to all He created, He will forgive them, and it is because of their fathers' deeds that He loves them, not because of their own deeds. ²⁰ And He will extend His right hand abundantly to satisfy the hungry, and He will open His eyes to pardon and multiply grain for food. ²¹ He gives food to the young crows and to beasts that beg Him. When they cry to Him, He will save the children of Israel from the hands of their enemies who have delayed them. ²² And they will return to sin again to sadden Him, and He will stir up their enemy nations in their region against them. They will destroy them, kill them, and capture them. ²³ And again, they will cry out to JAH in mourning and sorrow, and then He will send help and save them through the hands of prophets. ²⁴ And there were times when He saved them through the hands of princes, and when they saddened JAH, their enemies imposed taxes on them and captured them. ²⁵ David arose and saved them from the hands of the Philistines; and again, they saddened JAH, and JAH stirred up peoples who troubled them. ²⁶ And there were times when He saved them through the hands of Jephthah, and again, they forgot JAH who saved them in their time of trouble. As JAH brought hardship upon them, He will stir up against them evil enemies who will impose suffering on them and completely capture them. ²⁷ And when they were distressed by suffering, they were overwhelmed and again cried out to Him, and He saved them through the hands of Gideon; and again, they saddened JAH with the works of their hands. ²⁸ And again, He stirred up against them peoples who imposed suffering on them, and they returned, wept, and cried out to JAH. ²⁹ And again, He saved them from the peoples through the hands of Samson; and they rested a little from the suffering. Then they rose up to sadden JAH with their former sins. ³⁰ And again, He stirred up against them other peoples who troubled them, and again they cried and wept to JAH for Him to send help for them, and He saved them from the peoples through the hands of Barak and Deborah. ³¹ Again, they lived for a short season while they worshipped JAH, and again, they forgot JAH in their former sins and saddened Him. ³² And He stirred up against them other peoples who troubled them, and again He saved them through the hands of Judith; and after sitting for a short season, they rose up to sadden JAH with their sins as before. ³³ And He stirred up against them peoples who ruled over them, and they cried and wept to JAH; for He had struck on his head Abimelech, who was a warrior who came to fight the land of Judah. ³⁴ And He saved them through the children of the area and by the hand of Mattathias; and when that warrior died, his army fled and was scattered, and the children of Israel pursued and fought them up to the Jabbok River, and they did not spare even one person from them. ³⁵ After this, they waited for a little while and then rose up to sadden JAH; and He stirred up against them peoples who ruled over them, and again they cried out completely to JAH; and JAH ignored their crying and their mourning, for they had saddened JAH every time and had broken His law. ³⁶ And they were captured and taken along with their priests to the land of the Babylonians. ³⁷ And then the children of Israel who were traitors did not stop saddening JAH while they committed sins and worshipped idols. 38 JAH became angry and decided to destroy them once for their sins; Haman had put ten thousand pieces of gold into the king's treasury, and on the day it was known, he incited anger in King Ahasuerus, saying that he should not allow the children to survive in the Persian empire, from India to Ethiopia, when he told him that he should destroy them. 39 He did so; and he wrote a letter in which a decree was written by the king's authority, and he gave him a seal in his hand to deliver it to the Persian empire. 40 He gave him a seal so that he might destroy them on the day he chose to destroy them, as the king commanded, but he ordered that he should bring their money, the gold and silver, to the king's treasury. 41 And when the children of Israel heard about this, they cried and wept to JAH, and they informed Mordecai, and Mordecai informed Esther. 42 And Esther said, "Fast, pray, and let all the kindreds of the children of Israel cry out to JAH wherever you are." 43 And Mordecai wore sackcloth and sprinkled dust on himself, and the children of Israel fasted, prayed, and repented in the land where they were. 44 And Esther was deeply saddened, and being a queen, she wore sackcloth, sprinkled dust, shaved her head, and did not anoint herself with perfume as the Persian queens did, and in her deep thought, she cried and wept to her father's Creator, JAH. 45 And because of this, He made her favored by King Ahasuerus of Persia, and she prepared a fine meal for her father's Creator. 46 And Haman and the king came to the meal that Esther had prepared, and as he liked to do to Mordecai, JAH inflicted the hardship on Haman, and they hanged him on a high wood. 47 The king's decree was commanded so that they would leave the Israelites alone as they were in all their agreements, and that they should not tax them, rob them, wrong them, or take their money from them. 48 As JAH will pardon Israel for doing this when they cried out in repentance, they will be loved and honored in the Persian country where they lived, but a royal decree was commanded so that they should not destroy their land or plunder their livestock. 49 And at the time they saddened Him, He will stir up against them peoples who will trouble them; at that time, they will cry and wean completely so that He might send them help and save them from the hands of peoples who impose suffering on them.

1 Meq. 29

1 And when the Egyptians also made the children of Israel work by making them make bricks under difficult conditions, and when they oppressed them by making them work with all their might, kicking mud without straw and heating bricks... 2 And when they set taskmasters over them to rush the workers, they cried out to JAH to save them from making all the Egyptian bricks. 3 At that time, He sent them Aaron and Moses to help them, for JAH had sent them to bring His kindred out from under Pharaoh's rule, and He saved them from the brickmaking work because in his arrogance, Pharaoh refused to let Israel go to worship and offer sacrifices to JAH in the wilderness. JAH sent them so that they might bring His kindred Israel out from under the rule of the Egyptian king Pharaoh, and they saved them. 4 For JAH neglects the arrogant ones, and He drowned Pharaoh in the Red Sea along with his army because of his arrogance. 5 And just like him, He will destroy those who did not perform noble deeds in all the kingdoms that He appointed and crowned them, so that those who disregard JAH's word when they are nobles and kings may fulfill His covenant with Him, and that they may pay those who work in noble things their wages, and that they may honor His glorious name. 6 JAH, the ruler of all, said, "But if they will straighten out My kingdom, I will straighten out their kingdom for them. 7 Perform noble deeds for Me, and I will perform noble deeds for you. Keep My laws, and I will preserve your

440

lives. Live by My laws, and I will establish honesty within you, as within your minds. 8 Love Me, and I will care for your well-being. Draw near to Me, and I will heal you." 9 JAH, the ruler of all, said, "Believe in Me, and I will save you from tribulation. 10 Do not live in discord; as JAH, the ruler of all, loves righteous deeds, He said, "You - come closer to Me, and I will come closer to you. You sinners and traitors, wash your hands of sin and distance your thoughts from evil. 11 And I will remove My anger from you and return to you in mercy and forgiveness. 12 I will remove from you criminals and enemies who commit wickedness, just as I saved My servant David from his enemies who confronted him, from their great malice, from the hand of Goliath, who was a warrior, and also from the hand of Saul, who sought to kill him, and from the hand of his son Absalom, who desired to take his kingdom. 13 I will save those who keep My laws and fulfill My covenant like him. I will grant them honor, and they will be peaceful in the present world and in the world to come. I will crown them over all so that they may be at peace. 14 They will be united with kings who served JAH and were honored in their righteous way of life, like the prophet Samuel, who served Him in his righteous way of life from his childhood, whom JAH, being the Law, chose. 15 He told him to inform Eli, who was an elder servant, and when he served in JAH's house, the Temple, Samuel's deeds were also merciful and beloved. 16 And when he grew while serving in JAH's house, the Temple, He appointed him and anointed him so that he could appoint his people and that kings might be anointed according to JAH's covenant. Because JAH loved him and chose the tribe from the children of Israel, when he fulfilled JAH's covenant who created him, He gave him the anointing of the kingdom in his hand. 17 And when Saul was in his kingdom, JAH told His prophet Samuel, "Go, because I have loved Jesse's son David, who was born from the tribe of Judah, and anoint him."

1 Meq. 30

1 I have detested Saul's lineage because he saddened me by violating my word. 2 And I have ignored him because he did not keep my law, and I will not grant kingship to his lineage again. 3 And those who did not keep my law, my word, and my commands like him, I will destroy their kingdom and their children's inheritance forever. 4 And as they did not make me renowned when I made them renowned, I will destroy them, and I will not lift them up again—even though I honored them—as they did not honor me, I will not make them renowned again. 5 Because they did not do good for me when I did good for them, and because they did not forgive me when I forgave them. 6 And as they did not make me a ruler when I made them rulers over all, as they did not honor me when I honored them above all, I will not make them renowned nor honor them again, because they did not keep my law. 7 And I withheld the gift I gave them, and I will not return the wealth I withheld from them according to the extent of my anger and oath. JAH, who rules all, has said this. He said, "I will honor those who honored me and love those who loved me." 8 I will separate those who did not honor me nor keep my law from the gift I gave them. 9 JAH, who rules all, said, "I love those who loved me and make renowned those who made me renowned." 10 As I, JAH, who rules all, there is none who can escape my authority on earth or in heaven, for I am JAH who kills and saves, saddens and forgives. 11 As renown and honor are my possessions, I will honor those whom I loved, for I am the one who judges and avenges, destroys, and makes miserable those whom I hated. 12 For I am the one who forgives those who love me and call upon my name at all times, for I am the one who provides food for the wealthy and the poor. 13 And I provide for birds and animals, fish in the sea, beasts, and flowers, yet I am not only the provider for humans. 14 I provide for crocodiles and whales, gophers and

hippos, and badgers... [15] And all that lives in the water, all that flies in the wind, yet I am not only the provider for humans— all these are my possessions. [16] I am the one who provides for all who seek me by all that is due and loved.

1 Meq. 31

[1] Kings do not reign without my agreement, and sufferers are by my command - yet they are not poor without my command - and the powerful are by my agreement, yet they are not strong without my agreement. [2] I granted David belovedness and Solomon wisdom, and I extended Hezekiah's years. [3] I reduced Goliath's time and granted Samson power, and then again I diminished his power. [4] And I saved my servant David from the warrior Goliath's hand. [5] And again, I saved him from King Saul's hand and from the second warrior who challenged him - because he kept my command - and I saved him from the people who challenged and fought him. [6] And I loved him - and I love all the nobles and kings who keep my law - as they have pleased me - I will grant them victory and power over their enemies. [7] And so that they may inherit their fathers' land - I will grant them the cleansed and shining land of inheritance that I swore to their fathers.

1 Meq. 32

[1] JAH, who rules all, said - You nobles and also you kings - listen to me in my word - and keep my command - lest you sadden me and worship like the children of Israel who saddened me and worshipped other idols - those whom I kept and saved when I, JAH, am their Creator - JAH, who rules all, said - Listen to me in my word; and all whom I raised and loved and fed since they were born from their mother and father. [2] And whom I sent forth toward Earth's harvests - and whom I fed the richness found from Earth as due - and whom I gave the grapevine and the olive-tree fruit that they did not plant and the clear water well that they did not dig. [3] Listen to me in my word lest you sadden me like the children of Israel who saddened me worshipping other idols when I, JAH, am their Creator - He told them - Who fed them sheep's milk and honeycomb with the husked wheat - and Who clothed them with ornamental clothes - and Who gave them all their desires. [4] And without it, I deprived them of all they prayed to me for.

1 Meq. 33

[1] As David spoke saying - "The children of Israel were fed manna that Angels lowered" - and again listen to me in my word lest you sadden me like the children of Israel saddened me worshipping idols when I, JAH, am their Creator, who fed them sweet manna in the wilderness - He said - I did all this for them so they might worship me correctly and truthfully. [2] JAH, who rules all, said - But they did not worship me - and I neglected them - they saddened me and were firmly rooted in the law of idols that were not my law. [3] And I will bring hardships upon them corresponding to their sins - as they have neglected my worship and did not adhere to my counsel and my order - I neglected them in the measure of sin they committed with their hands - and I will cast them into Gehenna in the definitive judgment that is carried out in Heaven. [4] Because they did not keep my law - and because I was vexed with them - I will reduce their era in this world. [5] If you are a king - are you not a man who will die and be destroyed and tomorrow become worms and dust? [6] But today you boast and are proud as if you will never die. [7] JAH, who rules all, said - But you, who are well today, are a man who will die tomorrow. [8] But if you keep my command and my word - I will bequeath you a honored country with honored kings who followed my decree - whose dwellings were light and whose crowns were beautiful - and whose thrones were of silver and gold and whom people who sit upon them adorned - He said. [9] And they will be peaceful within his country, which is a place set aside for those who

conducted good deeds. [10] But for those who commit sin - as they did not keep my law - said JAH, who rules all... [11] It is not right for them to enter that country where honored kings will enter.

1 Meq. 34

[1] The kingdom of Media will perish - but the kingdom of Rome will entirely rise upon the kingdom of Macedonia - and the kingdom of Nineveh will rise upon the kingdom of Persia. [2] And the kingdom of Ethiopia will rise upon the kingdom of Alexandria - as peoples will arise - the kingdom of Moab will rise upon the kingdom of Amalek. [3] And brother will rise against brother - and JAH will avenge and destroy as He has said that it shall perish. [4] Kingdom will rise against kingdom - and people against people and country against country - He said. [5] And there will be arguments and there will be battles - famine - plague - earthquake - drought - as Love has perished from this world - JAH's punishment descended upon it. [6] For the day has suddenly arrived when JAH will come - Who terrifies like lightning that is seen from the East to the West. [7] On the day when HE, JAH, judges Judgment - at that time everyone will receive their hardship according to their weakness and the firmness of their sin - for He has said I will avenge them on the day when HE, JAH, judges Judgment and on the day when their feet are hindered - for the day when they are counted for destruction has arrived. [8] At that time JAH will destroy in Gehenna forever those who do not live by his law - who commit sin. [9] And those who live in the western islands and in Nuba and Hindake - in Sheba and Ethiopia and the people of Egypt - all people who live in them... [10] At that time will know I that I am JAH who rules the Earth and Heaven - and who gives love and honor - and who saves and kills. [11] I am who sends forth the sun - who sends it toward its setting - who brings the evil and the good. [12] I am who brings peoples whom you do not know - who slaughter and eat the wealth for which you have toiled - your sheep and your herds of cattle. [13] And they will capture your children while they smash them before you - and you cannot save them. Because JAH's Spirit of Support did not dwell in you - as you did not fear JAH's command that you heard - He will destroy your extravagances and your assignments. [14] But a person in whom JAH's Spirit of Support has dwelt will know everything - as Nebuchadnezzar said to Daniel, saying, "I see JAH's Spirit of Support that has dwelt in you." [15] And a person in whom JAH's Spirit of Support has dwelt will know everything - and what was hidden will be revealed to him - and he will know all that was revealed and that was hidden - yet there is nothing hidden from a person in whom JAH's Spirit of Support has dwelt. [16] But as we are people who will die tomorrow - our sins that we have concealed and committed will be revealed. [17] And as they test silver and gold in fire - like there are sinners - later on the Day of Advent, they will be tested - because they did not keep JAH's command. [18] At that time all the works of all people and all the children of Israel will be examined.

1 Meq. 35

[1] As JAH is vexed with you because you did not judge a true judgment for the child whose parents died on him - woe to you, nobles of Israel. [2] Woe to you, people who go to the drinking house morning and evening and get drunk - who are biased in judgment - and who do not hear the widow's justice or the orphan's - who live in sin and seduction. [3] JAH said to the nobles of Israel thus: - Unless you lived by my command and kept my law and loved what I love - woe to you - He told them. [4] And I will bring destruction, punishment, and tribulation upon you - and you will perish like what weevils and moths ate - and your tracks and your region will not be found - He told them. [5] And your country will become a wilderness - and all people who formerly saw her will clap their hands - they

will marvel at her while saying, "Wasn't this country filled with her abundance and all who loved her? JAH made her so because of the sin of the people who lived in her." 6 They will say, "Because she made her heart proud - and because she elevated herself - and because she stiffened her neck of reasoning until JAH made her miserable on Earth - and because she became a desert due to the arrogance of the people who lived in her - and because thorns and thistles grew on her - woe to her." 7 And she will grow weeds and nettles - and she will become a wilderness and a desert - and beasts will live within her. 8 For JAH's judgment has settled on her - and for she will receive JAH's judgment cup because of her arrogant reasoning by the sin of the people who live in her - and she has become terrifying for people who approach her.

1 Meq. 36

1 Macedonian people - do not boast - as JAH is there Who will destroy you - Amalekites - do not stiffen your neck of reasoning. 2 For you will be exalted up to Heaven and you will descend to Gehenna. 3 When Israel formerly entered into the land of Egypt in Moab and the kingdom of Midian He said - Do not boast - for it is not right to pretend before JAH that you might delude Him . 4 You, Ishmael's descendants - slave child - why do you stiffen your neck of reasoning with what was not your wealth? Do you not think that JAH will judge upon you when He rises to be judged on Earth - on the day when it is judged upon you? 5 JAH, who rules all, said - At that time you will receive your hardship according to the work of your hands - why then do you elevate your reasoning? Why then do you stiffen your neck of reasoning? 6 And I will deal with you as you dealt with people who were not your relatives - because you do what you love so that you may commit sin - and I will neglect you in the place where they sent you. 7 JAH, who rules all, said - And I will do this to you - He said - But if you performed good deeds and if you love what I love - I also will listen to you in all that you prayed for. 8 And if you fulfill my agreement for me - I will fulfill your agreement for you - and I will dispute your enemies for you - and I will bless your children and your descendants for you. 9 And I will increase your flocks of sheep and cattle for you - and if you lived by my command and also if you did what I love - JAH, who rules all, said - I will bless for you everything you possess in your hand. 10 But if you do not follow my agreement - if you do not live by my law and my command - all this tribulation that was previously told will find you - because you did not endure tribulation by my command - and because you did not live by my law - and you cannot escape from my anger that will come upon you every time. 11 And as you did not love what I love - when I am Who created you bringing you from non-existence to existence... 12 All this was your wealth - that you might kill and heal to do all that you loved - that you might build and destroy - that you might honor and insult - that you might elevate and degrade - and as you have neglected my worship and my praise when I am Who gave you dominion and also honor among people who are beneath your authority - you cannot escape from my anger that will come upon you. 13 And if you did JAH's agreement and if you lived formed up in His command - He will love you so that you may be at peace with Him in His sovereignty - and that you may share with people who inherited an honored country. 14 For He has said - If they endure me - I will bequeath them being loved and honored - for I will make them peaceful in the temple where prayer is prayed - for JAH, who rules all, has said - And they will be loved and chosen like unto a sacrifice. 15 Do not neglect to do work by which welfare is done and a good thing so that you may cross from death to life. 16 But people who perform good deeds - JAH will keep them in all His good work - so that they may be His servants like Job whom JAH preserved

442

from all tribulation. 17 JAH will preserve them in all good work - so that they may be His servants for Him like Abraham whom He saved when he killed the kings - and like Moses whom He saved from the hands of the Canaanites and Pharaoh's hand - in whom Abraham lived - and who were also disturbing his body evening and morning night and day so that they might make him worship idols. 18 But when they took him toward the idols that were their wealth - he would endure the tribulation while he refused. 19 For Abraham, who believed Him from his childhood, was for JAH His trusted friend - and while he refused he would worship JAH Who created him. 20 As he entirely loved JAH - he did not stop worshipping JAH until he died - and he did not depart from His law until he died - and he taught his children that they might keep JAH's law. 21 And like their father Abraham kept His law - they did not depart from JAH's law - as He told the angels saying - I have a friend in this world called Abraham - Abraham's children Jacob and Isaac - who are His servants because whom JAH spoke - did not depart from JAH's law. 22 JAH Who was praised with them and Who rules all said - Abraham is my friend - Isaac is my confidant - and Jacob is my friend whom my reasoning loved. 23 But when He entirely loved the children of Israel - they lived continually saddening Him - and He lived enduring them and feeding them manna in the wilderness. 24 Their clothes did not wear out - for they were fed manna which is the bread of knowledge - and their feet did not swell. 25 But their reasonings would distance from JAH every time - as they were who commit sin from antiquity - they had no hope to be saved. 26 They became like a crooked bow - yet they did not become like their fathers Isaac, Abraham, and Jacob who served JAH in their beautiful way of life - they would sadden Him every time by their idols on the mountains and the hills - they would eat on the mountain and at the caves and the roots of trees. 27 They would slaughter a bull - they would offer a sacrifice - and they would be joyful in their handiwork - they would eat the remainder of the sacrifice - they would drink from their offering - and they would play with demons while they sang. 28 And demons would admire all their games and their songs for them - and they would indulge their drunkenness and adultery without limit - and they would commit the theft and greed that JAH does not love. 29 For the idols of Canaan - and for the idols of Midian and for Baal - and for Aphrodite and Dagon and Seraphim and Artemis who are idols of Greece... 30 And for all the idols of the peoples in their area - they would offer sacrifices; and all Israel would worship idols just as peoples worship idols according to what they see and hear - they would make their games and their songs and their boasting as peoples do. 31 All the tribes of Israel do likewise - who say 'We will worship JAH' - without keeping His command and His law that Moses told them in the Torah so that they might keep JAH's law and stay away from worshipping idols. 32 Lest they worship separate idols - apart from their creator who fed them the honey found in the comb who fed them the cultivated grain and sent them forth to the crops of the earth - and who fed them the manna... 33 Moses commanded them saying 'Do not worship' - for He is their creator - and for He feeds those who loved Him - and He will not deprive those who loved Him and desired Him. 34 But they did not stop saddening JAH - and they would sadden JAH when He made them at peace. 35 And when He saddened them - they would cry out to Him - and He would save them from the tribulation that befell them - and they would again be completely at peace and would live many years. 36 And at that time they would totally return their heart to sin so that they might sadden JAH as before - and He would stir up peoples in their area to destroy them - and they would be distressed and taxed by them. 37 And again they would completely return and cry out to their Creator JAH. ³⁸ And He would forgive them - it is because of their forefathers - Noah, Isaac, Abraham, and Jacob - who served JAH in their beautiful way of life from antiquity - for whom He established His oath - but it is not because of their own deeds that He forgave them. ³⁹ And He loved those who kept His law loving that they might multiply their children like the stars of the heavens and the sand of the sea. ⁴⁰ But when the dead rise and they become like the sand of the sea - they are sinful souls that will be separated from the children of Israel and will enter into Gehenna. ⁴¹ As JAH told Abraham - Look up to the heavens at night and count the stars if you can count them - likewise as He told him - Your children and the righteous ones will shine in the heavens like the stars - they are like stars that shine in the heavens - but what they have are kind souls born of Israel. ⁴² And again as He told him - Stand by the edge of the river and the sea - and look at what is amidst the sand - count if you can count - and your sinful children will likewise - who will descend to Gehenna when the dead rise - they are sinful souls. ⁴³ And Abraham believed in JAH - because of this it was counted to him as righteousness - he found his reward in this world - and after his wife Sarah aged, she bore a child named Isaac. ⁴⁴ For he believed that those who performed good deeds will rise and go to the Kingdom of Heaven that remains forever - and he will find a Kingdom in Heaven. ⁴⁵ But because he believed that those who committed sin will go to Gehenna that remains forever when the dead rise - but that righteous ones who performed good deeds will reign with Him forever. ⁴⁶ But because he believed that judgment will forever be true without falsehood upon those who committed sin - he will find the Kingdom of Life in Heaven.

2 Meqabyan

2 Meq. 1

¹ This is a book that speaks of the Maccabees who found Israel in Mesopotamia, part of Syria, and killed them in their region from the Yabbock to the Jerusalem square - and destroyed the land. ² Because the people of Syria and Edomites and the Amalekites were united with the Moabite Maccabees who destroyed the country of Jerusalem - as they camped from Samaria to the Jerusalem square and all its region - they killed in war, not sparing those who fled except for a few. ³ And when the children of Israel transgressed, He raised the Moabite Maccabees against them - and he killed them by the sword. ⁴ Because of this, the enemies of GOD boasted about His honored country - and they swore in their crime. ⁵ And the people of Eloph and Edom camped - as He sent them because they pretended to follow GOD's Word - they began to revenge and destroy GOD's country. ⁶ And the country of Maccabees is Riemath, part of Moab - and he arose from his country in power and also swore with those with him. ⁷ And they camped in the Gilead region, part of Mesopotamia up to Syria, that they might destroy GOD's country - and there he requested the Amalekites and Elophites. He gave them much silver and gold and chariots and horses that they might join him in crime. ⁸ They came together and crushed the fortress - people living there shed blood like water. ⁹ And they made Jerusalem like a booth for vineyard keepers - and he made a voice heard within her - he did all the sinful work that GOD hates - and they also defiled GOD's country that was filled with praise and honor. ¹⁰ They made the flesh of your friends and the corpses of your slaves food for wild beasts and birds of heaven. ¹¹ And they robbed children whose parents had died on them and widows - for without fearing GOD they did as Satan taught them - and until GOD, Who examines kidneys and reasonings, was vexed - they ripped out fetuses from pregnant daughters' bellies. ¹² They returned to their country while they were happy because they did evil work upon GOD's kindreds - and they took the plunder they captured from the honored country. ¹³ When they returned and entered their houses, they made festivities, songs, and clapping.

2 Meq. 2

¹ The prophet, whom they call Re'ay, told him thus: "Today be merry a little on the time when festivities were made - GOD, Whom Israel glorified, has that He might avenge and destroy you in the punishment you didn't doubt. ² Will you say, 'My horses are swift, because I will escape by running'? ³ As for me, I tell you - People who will follow you are swifter than vultures - you won't escape from GOD's Judgment and destruction that shall come upon you. ⁴ Will you say, 'I wear iron clothes, and spear throwing and bow stinging can't harm me'?; GOD Who honors Israel said - It isn't by spear throwing that I will avenge and destroy you," He told him. "I shall bring upon you heart sickness and itch and rheumatism sickness that are worse and stronger than spear throwing and bow stinging - yet it isn't by this that I shall avenge and destroy you. ⁵ You have aroused My anger - I shall bring heart sickness upon you - and you will lack one who helps you - and you won't escape from My Authority until I destroy your name invocation from this world. ⁶ As you have stiffened your neck of reasoning - and as you have elevated yourself upon My country - when I quickly did this thing like a blink of an eye - you will know I, that I was your Creator - as you are before Me like grass before the wind that fire eats - and as you are like the dust that winds spill and scatter from Earth - you are like them before Me. ⁷ For you have aroused My anger - and because you didn't know your Creator - and I shall neglect all your kindred - and neither will I preserve him who neared your fortress. ⁸ And now return from all your sins that you worked - if you return from your sin and fully appease in mourning and sadness before GOD - and if you beg toward Him in clean reasoning - GOD will forgive you all your sins that you worked before Him," he told him. ⁹ At that time, Maccabees wore dust and mourned before GOD because of his sin - for GOD was vexed upon him. ¹⁰ For His eyes are revealed - for He doesn't withhold - and for His ears are opened - for He doesn't neglect - and for He doesn't make the word He spoke false - and for He quickly does it at one time - for GOD knew lest He preserves the punishment He spoke by the prophet's word. ¹¹ He cast his clothes and wore sackcloth and sprinkled dust on his head and cried and wept before his Creator GOD because of his sin that he worked.

2 Meq. 3

¹ And the prophet came from Riemath and told him - for Riemath, that is part of Moab, is near Syria. ² He dug a pit and entered up to his neck and wept firm tears - and he entered repentance because of his sin that he worked before GOD. ³ And GOD told the prophet thus: "Return from the land of Judah, Riemath to the Moabite official Maccabees," He told him. Tell him, "GOD told you thus" - Tell him, "He told you, 'I, GOD Who am your Creator, sent you by My Accord that you might destroy My country - lest you say, 'I destroyed the honored country Jerusalem by my firmness and my army's abundance' - yet it wasn't you who did this thing. ⁴ For she has saddened Me by all her greed and her betrayal and her lustfulness. ⁵ And I neglected and cast her by your hand - and now GOD has forgiven you your sin because of your children whom you fathered - it isn't because you who stiffened your neck of reasoning and say 'I encircled the country Jerusalem by my firmness of authority.' ⁶ As people who doubt aren't disciplined to enter repentance - don't be a doubter - and now enter repentance being disciplined in your complete reasoning." ⁷ However, people are admired who enter repentance in their complete reasonings and who don't again return toward desire and sin by all that entered toward

repentance because they sinned. 8 People are admired who return toward their Creator GOD being disciplined in mourning and sadness - in bowing and many pleas. People are admired who are disciplined and enter repentance - for He has told them, "You are My treasures who entered repentance after you misled people who entered repentance. 9 He told arrogant Maccabees on the time he returned toward Him in repentance after he misled - "I forgive you your sin because of your fear and your alarm; for I am GOD, your Creator, Who brings hardship upon children by a father's sin up to seven generations if the child works the sin that the father worked - and Who does Charity up to ten thousand generations for people who love Me and keep My LAW. 10 And now I will affirm My Oath with you because of these your children whom you fathered - and GOD Who rules all and Who honored Israel said - 'I will accept the repentance you made because of your sin that you worked. 11 At that time, he proceeded from the pit and bowed to the prophet - he swore saying, "As I have saddened GOD - make me as you loved - but let GOD do to me thus so lest I separate from you - as we have no LAW - I didn't live firmed up in His Command as my fathers did - you know that our fathers taught us and that we worship idols. 12 For I am a sinner who lived firmed up in my sin - who stiffened up in my collar of reasoning and my reasoning's arrogance whereby I saddened GOD's Command - but up to now I hadn't heard GOD's servants the prophets' Word - and I didn't live firmed up in His LAW and His Command that He commanded me." 13 He told him saying, "As there is none from your kindred preceding you who trusted his sin - I knew that the prophet received repentance today." 14 "But now quit your worshiping of idols and return toward knowing GOD that you might have true repentance," he told him. He fell and bowed at the prophet's feet - and the prophet lifted him up and commanded him all the goodly Work that is due to him. 15 And he returned toward his house doing also as GOD commanded him. 16 And that Maccabees returned his body toward worshiping GOD - and he destroyed from his house the idols and also the sorcery - people who worship idols and pessimists and magicians. 17 And morning and evening like his fathers did - he would examine the children he captured and brought from Jerusalem in all GOD's Commands and His Order and His LAW. 18 And from the children he captured - he appointed knowledgeable ones upon his house. 19 And again from the infants he appointed knowledgeable children who keep leveled children who were small - who enter toward the bedding that they might teach them GOD's LAW that the children of Israel do - he would hear from captured Israelite children the Order and the LAW and the Nine Laws - that Moabite people's order and their mosques that they make were vain. 20 He destroyed their mosques - their idols and their sorcery - and the sacrifice and the grapes sacrificed for the idols morning and evening from the goat kids and fattened sheep flocks. 21 And he destroyed his idols whom he worshiped and begged and believed in all his Work while he sacrificed sacrifice afternoon and at noon - and for all priests told him - and his idols for whom he did their accord. 22 As it would seem to him that they save him in all that they told - he wouldn't scorn all the thing they told him. 23 But that Maccabees quit their Work. 24 After he heard the Ra'ay thing - whom they call a prophet - he accomplished his Work in repentance - as Israelite children would sadden Him at one time - and on the time He chastised them in the tribulation - as they know and also cry toward GOD - all His kindreds worked goodly Work more than Israelite children in that season. 25 On the time He heard that they were seized and abused by peoples' hands who firmed up tribulation upon them and that they cried toward Him - He thought of their fathers' oath and at that time He would forgive them because of their fathers Isaac - Abraham - and Jacob. 26 And on the time He saved them - they would forget GOD Who saved them from tribulation - and they would return toward worshiping the idols. 27 And at that time He would arouse upon them peoples who firmed up tribulation upon them - and on the time they firmed up tribulation upon them and saddened them - they would cry toward GOD - as He loves them because they were His Authority's Creation - at that time He would be nice and forgive them. 28 And on the time He kept them - they again returned toward sin that they might sadden Him by their hands' Work that was firm and by worshiping idols in their councils. 29 But He would arouse upon them Moab and Eloph - Syria - Midian and Egyptian people; and on the time their enemies defeated them - they would cry and weep - on the time they firmed up upon them and taxed them and ruled them - GOD would arouse princes for them that He might save them on the time He loved.

2 Meq. 4

1 And in Joshua's time was a day when He saved them. 2 And in Gideon's time was a day when He saved them. 3 And in Samson's time and in Deborah's and Barak's and Judith's time was a day when He saved them - lodging whether upon male or upon daughter - He would arouse princes for them that they might save them from their enemies' hands who firmed up tribulation upon them. 4 And as GOD loved - He would save them from people who firmed up tribulation upon them. 5 And they would be totally Merry in all the Work that He accomplished for them - they would be Merry in their land's seed and in multiplying all their flocks in the wilderness and their livestock. 6 And He would bless their plants and their livestock for them - for He saw them up in the Eye of Mercy - and for He wouldn't diminish their livestock upon them - for they are kind people's children and He would totally love them. 7 But on the time they were evil in their Work - He would cast them into their enemies' hands. 8 And on the time He destroyed them - they would seek Him in worship - and they would return from sin and march toward GOD in repentance. 9 And on the time they returned in their complete reasoning - He would atone their sin for them - He wouldn't think of their former sin upon them - for He knows them that they were flesh and blood - for they have this world's misleading thoughts upon them - and for they have demons in them. 10 But on the time that Maccabees heard this Order that GOD worked in His worshiping place the Temple - he was slain in repentance. 11 After he saw and heard this - he didn't scorn working goodly Work; he didn't scorn working all the goodly Work that Israelite children work on the time GOD forgave them - and after they trespassed from His LAW - they weep and would cry on the time GOD whipped them - and again He would forgive them - and they would keep His LAW. 12 And Maccabees likewise would straighten up his Work - and he would keep His LAW - and he would live firmed up in Israel's Creator GOD's Command. 13 At that time after he heard all the Work whereby Israelite children boast - He would boast like them in keeping GOD's LAW. 14 He would urge his kindred and children that they might live firmed up in GOD's Command and all His LAW. 15 And he would forbid the food that Israel forbids - and he would hear and keep the Law that Israel keeps - and when his kindred are another Moabite man - he would forbid the food that Israel forbids. 16 And he would send forth tithes - he would give all that were firstborn and that he owned from his cows and his sheep and his donkeys - and turning his face toward Jerusalem he would sacrifice the sacrifice that Israel sacrifices. 17 He would sacrifice sin and vow sacrifices - a sacrifice whereby welfare is done and an accord sacrifice - and the continual sacrifice. 18 And he would give his first crops - and he would press and pour the grapes that Israel

pours - and he would give this for his priest whom he appointed - and likewise he would do all that Israel does - and he would sweeten his incense. ¹⁹ He built a candlestick and a basin and a seat and a tent and the four links of rings - and diluted oil for the Holy of Holies lamps - and the curtain that Israel made in the Holy of Holies on the time they served GOD. ²⁰ And as they worked goodly Work on the time they lived firmed up in His Order and His LAW and on the time GOD didn't neglect and cast them into their enemies' hands - Maccabees also would work goodly Work like them. ²¹ He would beg toward Israel's Creator GOD every time that He might be his Teacher and lest He separate him from Israelite children whom He chose and who did His Accord. ²² And again he would beg Him that He might give him children in Zion and a house in Jerusalem - that He might give them Heavenly Seed of Virtue in Zion and a Heavenly House of Soul in Jerusalem - and that He might save him from the destruction spoken by the prophet's tongue - that He might accept his repentance in all the mourning he wept before GOD being sad and entering repentance... ²³ and lest He destroy children in this world upon him - and that He might keep him in his proceeding and entering. ²⁴ Kindreds from Moabite people under Maccabees' Authority were Merry that they might believe - for their chief lived firmed up in straight Work - and they would check up his judgment and fulfill his accord - and they would scorn their country's language and their country's justice - they would understand that Maccabees' Work surpassed and was straight. ²⁵ And they would come and hear Maccabees' charity and True judgments. ²⁶ He had much money - he had daughter slaves and male slaves and camels and donkeys - and he had five hundred horses that wear breastplates - he would totally defeat the Amalekites and Elophites and Syrian people - but formerly when he worshipped idols he lived when they defeated him. ²⁷ He prevailed - yet but from his worshiping GOD onward - when he went toward battle there are none who defeated him. ²⁸ But they would come in their idols' Power that they might fight him - and they would call their idols' names and curse him - however there were none who defeat him - for he has made his faith upon his Creator GOD. ²⁹ And when he did thus and when he defeated his enemies - he lived when he ruled peoples in his Authority. ³⁰ He would avenge and destroy wronged people's enemy for them - he would judge Truth for a child whose mother and father died upon him. ³¹ And he would receive widows in their trouble time - and he would give from his food and satisfy those who hungered - and he would clothe the naked from his clothes. ³² And he would be Merry in his hands' Work - and he would give from the money he had without begrudging - and he would give tithes for the Temple - Maccabees died having lived in Merriness when he did this.

2 Meq. 5

¹ And he died leaving his children who were small - and they grew up as their father taught them - they kept their house's Order - and they would keep all their kindred - and they wouldn't make poor ones cry - nor widows nor a child whose mother and father died upon him. ² They would fear GOD - and they would give their money alms for poor ones - and they would keep all the trust their father told them - and they would calm the child whose mother and father died upon them and widows in their trouble time - and they would be their mother and father - they would make them cast from people's hands who wronged them - and calm them from all the disturbance and sadness that found them. ³ They lived five years while they did thus. ⁴ After this, the Chaldeans' king Tserutsaydan came - he destroyed all their country - and he captured Maccabees' children and destroyed all their villages. ⁵ And he plundered all their money - they lived firmed up in all evil Work and sin - in adultery - insult and greed and not thinking of their Creator - yet people who

don't live firmed up in GOD's LAW and His Command and who worship idols seized them also and took them to their country. ⁶ They eat what a beast bit and the blood and the carcass - and what a scavenger beat and cast - all that GOD doesn't love - yet they have no order from all the true Commands written in the Torah. ⁷ They don't know GOD their Creator - Who sent them forth from their mothers' wombs and fed them by what is due - was their Medicine. ⁸ They marry from their aunt and their father's wife - their stepmother - and they go toward robbery and evil and sin and adultery - yet they have no order in Judgment time - and they work all evil Work and they marry their aunts and their sisters and they have no LAW. ⁹ And all their roads are dark and slippery - and their Work are sin and adultery. ¹⁰ But those Maccabees' children would keep in all their Order - they wouldn't eat what a scavenger beat nor what died and lodged - they wouldn't work all the Work that the Chaldeans' children work - for their many Works are evil that weren't written in this book - that sinners work - and doubters and criminals - betrayers totally filled with robbery and sin and pagans' children. ¹¹ All the Work their Creator GOD loves aren't there with them. ¹² And again they would worship an idol called Baal Peor - they would trust it like their Creator GOD when it was deaf and dumb. For it is the idol that a person's hand worked - for it is the person's hand Work that a smith worked who works silver and gold - that has no breath nor knowledge - and it had nothing that it sees up nor hears. ¹³ It doesn't eat nor drink. ¹⁴ It doesn't kill nor save. ¹⁵ It doesn't plant nor uproot. ¹⁶ It doesn't harm its enemy nor benefit its friend. ¹⁷ It doesn't impoverish nor honor. ¹⁸ It will be a hindrance to mislead the Chaldeans' people who were lazy - yet it doesn't chastise nor forgive.

2 Meq. 6

¹ GOD's enemy Tserutsaydan, who was arrogant, appointed those who veil and falsehood priests for his idols. ² He would sacrifice sacrifice for them and pour the grapes for them. ³ And it would seem to him that they eat and drink. ⁴ And while it dawned, he would give them cows and donkeys and heifers - and he would sacrifice sacrifice morning and evening - and he would eat from that defiled sacrifice. ⁵ And again he would disturb and obligate other people that they might sacrifice for his idols - yet it wasn't only they who did it. ⁶ On the time they saw Maccabees' children that they were handsome and that they worship their Creator GOD - the idols' priests loved that they might mislead them to sacrifice sacrifice and to eat from that hated sacrifice - but these honored Maccabees' children refused them. ⁷ As they keep their father's command - and as they have firmed up in working goodly Work - and as they totally fear GOD - it failed them to agree... ⁸ on the time they bound them and insulted them and robbed them. ⁹ They told the king Tserutsaydan that they refused to sacrifice and bowing for his idols. ¹⁰ And because of this the king was vexed - he was sad and commanded that they might bring them - and they brought and stood them before him - and the king told them for his idols - "Sacrifice a sacrifice for my idols." ¹¹ And they spoke and told him - "And we won't answer you in this thing - and we won't sacrifice sacrifice for your defiled idols." ¹² He frightened them by Works that abounded - yet he couldn't able for them - for they have disciplined their reasonings believing in GOD. ¹³ He flamed a fire and cast them into the fire - and they gave their bodies for GOD. ¹⁴ After they died, they arose and were seen for him at night drawing their swords when he had reclined on his lordship throne - and he totally feared. ¹⁵ "My lords - tell me alright - what should I do for you? Don't take my body into death - that I might do all you commanded me." ¹⁶ They told him all that is due to him while they said - "Think that GOD was your Creator - and GOD is there Who shall dismiss

from this your kingdom where you are arrogant - and Who shall lower you toward Hell of Fire with your father the Devil - as we worshipped our Creator GOD without an iniquity living that we wronged you - and as you burned us in fire - you will finish all your hardship by that also. [17] For He is Who Created all - Earth and Heaven and sea and all that are within her. [18] And for He is Who Created the moon and Sun and stars - and for He Who Created all the Creation is GOD. [19] For there is no other creator without Him on Earth nor Heaven - for He is Who able to all - and for there is nothing that fails Him. As He is Who kills and Who saves - Who whips in tribulation and Who forgives - when we bowed for Him in fearing GOD - as you burned us in fire - you will finish your hardship by that," they told him. [20] "As He is Who rules Earth and Heaven - there is none who escape from His Authority. [21] There is none from the Creation He Created who departed from His Command - apart from you who are a criminal - and criminals like you whose reasonings your father Satan hid - and you and those your priests and your idols will descend together toward Hell where are no exits until Eternity. [22] Your teacher is Satan who taught you this evil Work that you might do evil upon Us - yet as it isn't only you who do this - you will descend toward Hell together. [23] For you make yourself like your Creator GOD - yet you didn't know GOD Who Created you. [24] And you are arrogant in your idols and your hand Work until GOD makes you wretched - He shall convict you upon all your sin and iniquity that you worked in this world.

2 Meq. 7

[1] Woe to you who don't know GOD Who Created you - for your idols who are like you - and for you - and for you have that you might regret a regret that won't profit on the time you were sad being seized in Hell's difficulty - and woe to you - for you who don't keep His Word and His LAW. [2] You will have no exit from it until Eternity - your priests and you who sacrifice for them like your Creator GOD - for your idols who have no breath nor soul - who won't avenge and destroy him who did evil upon them - nor do goodly thing for him who did a goodly thing for them. [3] Woe to you who sacrifice for them - for they are a person's hands Work where Satan lives - lodging there to mislead lazy ones' reasoning like you - that he might lower you toward Hell of Fire - and the priests who serve demons commanded for you and your idols. [4] As you don't know that there is nothing that will profit you - you wrong and err. [5] As for the animals that GOD Created to be food for you - and dogs and beasts - they are better than you - for besides one death there are no more condemnation upon them. [6] But as you will die and receive hardship in Hell's Fire where are no exits until Eternity - animals are better." [7] Having spoken this - they went and were hidden from him. [8] But that Tserutsaydan lodged when he trembled - seized by a firm fright - and fright didn't quit him until it dawned.

2 Meq. 8

[1] And he lived firmed up in reasoning's malice and arrogance. [2] And as iron has been called firm - like Daniel saw it upon his kingdom - he turned into people's countries in his area. [3] He lived firmed up in evil and all his laziness and in disturbing people. [4] And he totally destroyed what We spoke formerly - and he ate a person's money. [5] For he is diligent for evil like his father the Devil who stiffened up his collar of reasoning - and he destroyed what remained with his army. [6] He says, "My era has become like the Sun's era" - yet he doesn't know GOD that He was his Creator. [7] And in his reasoning, he thinks that the Sun is found from him. [8] He arises in Power - he camps in the Tribe of Zebulun's lot and begins a formation in Macedonia - and he receives his food from Samaria - and they give him presents from Samaria. [9] He camps in the nomads' region - and he reaches up to Sidon - and he imposes a tax on Achaia

- and he elevates his collar of reasoning up to the flowing sea - and he returns and sends messengers up to the Indian sea. [10] And likewise, he elevates his collar of reasoning up to Heaven. [11] He lives firmed up in being arrogant and in evil - yet he doesn't have humbling himself. [12] And his path is toward darkness and slipperiness - and toward crime and being arrogant - and toward shedding blood and tribulation. [13] And all his Work is what GOD hates - he does like robbery and evil and sin teacher the Devil taught him - he makes a child cry whose mother and father died upon him - and he isn't nice to a poor one. [14] And he defeated and destroyed people's kings by his authority. [15] And he ruled enemies' chiefs - and he ruled many people - and he taxed them as he loved. [16] Even if he destroyed - he didn't quit - there is no person whom he didn't snatch from the Tigris sea to the Jer icho sea. [17] He would bow to idols - he would eat what died and lodged - the blood - what a sword bloated and cut - and what was sacrificed for idols - all his Work is without justice - yet he has no justice - as he has been who alarms people beneath his authority - he would tax them tax as he loved. [18] As he does all that he loves before him - there is no fearing GOD before him - and he lives in malice before GOD Who Created him. [19] He didn't do it like his Creator - and like he did evil upon his companion on the time he was vexed and seized him - GOD shall also pay him his hardship. [20] As GOD has said - "I shall avenge and destroy sinful people who don't live by My Command - that I might destroy their name invocation from this world - as He destroyed people who were preceding him - He shall avenge and destroy him on the time when He destroys. [21] And as evil people did evil things - they shall receive their hardship. [22] But being commanded from GOD - goodly Work shall follow people who work goodly Work. [23] For as Joshua destroyed the five Canaanite kings in a cave in one day - and as he made the Sun stand in Gibeon by his prayer that he might destroy their armies - Sun has stood amidst Heaven until he destroyed the kings of Ai and Canaan and Perizzites and Hivites and Jebusites' armies - and as he killed around twenty thousand people at one time - and as he killed them - and as he bound them making foot from neck - and as he killed them in a cave by spear - and as he fitted a stone upon them... [24] Tribulation like this shall find all people who sadden GOD in their evil Work.

2 Meq. 9

[1] "O you weak man who isn't GOD - why are you proud? You who are seen today being a man are Earth's ashes tomorrow - and you will totally be worms in your grave. [2] For your teacher is the Devil who returns all people's sin hardship toward himself because he misled Our father Adam - and Hell will find you again - and it will find people who work your sin. [3] For in stiffening up his collar of reasoning and making himself proud - like he refused to bow to Adam whom the Creator Created... [4] you also have refused to bow to your Creator GOD like your teacher the Devil did. [5] Like your preceding fathers - who don't know their Creator GOD in worship - will go toward Hell - you also will go toward Hell. [6] Like He avenged and destroyed them because of their evil Work that they worked in this world - and like they descended toward Hell... [7] you also will descend toward Hell like them. [8] As you have aroused His anger - and as you have neglected to worship GOD Who gave you Authority over the five kingdoms - does it seem to you that you will escape from GOD's Authority? [9] You don't do this that you do His Accord - thus He examined you - but if you work goodly Work in this world - GOD will accomplish all your Work for you - and He will bless all the Work you seized in your hand for you - and He will subject your Ancestors of enemies and your day enemies for you. [10] You will be Merry in your enterings and your leavings and in your child birthed from your loins - and in your flocks and your

fatnesses - and in all Work where you placed your hand - and in all that you thought in your heart - as Authority has been given you from alongside GOD that you might do this and might work and plant and demolish - all will be commanded for you. ¹¹ However, if you won't hear GOD's Word nor live firmed up in His LAW - like criminals who were preceding you - and who don't worship GOD as is due - and who didn't believe firmed up in HIS straight LAW - there is nothing by which you will escape from GOD's Authority - for GOD's Judgment is Truth. ¹² All are totally revealed before Him - yet there is nothing hidden from before Him. ¹³ He is Who seizes the kings' Authority and Who overturns powerful ones' thrones. ¹⁴ He is Who Elevates those who were downbased and Who lifts up those who fell. ¹⁵ He is Who looses those who were bound and Who arouses those who died - as pardon dew is found from alongside Him - on the time He loved He shall arouse people whose flesh were demolished and rotten and were like unto dust. ¹⁶ And having aroused and judged people who worked evil Work - He will take them toward Hell - for they have saddened Him. ¹⁷ For they are who demolished GOD's Order and His LAW - and He will destroy their child from this world. ¹⁸ As kind people's Work are more difficult than sinful people's Work - sinful people don't love that they might live in kind people's counsel. ¹⁹ Like Heavens were distanced from Earth - likewise kind people's Work were distanced from evil people's Work. ²⁰ But sinful people's Work are robbery and sin - adultery and iniquity - greed and betrayal Work - it is being drunk in iniquity and robbing a person's money. ²¹ It is quickly going toward shedding a person's blood - and it is going toward destruction that doesn't benefit - and it is making a child weep whose mother and father died upon him - it is eating blood and what died and lodged - and it is eating camel and pig flesh - and it is going toward a young woman in her blood before she is cleansed - and toward a young woman in childbirth. ²² All this is sinful people's Work - it is Satan's trap that was a wide and prepared path - and that takes toward Hell that lives firmed up forever - and toward Sheol. ²³ But righteous people's path that was totally narrow is what takes toward welfare - and innocence and humbleness - and Unity and Love - and prayer and fast - and flesh purity - toward keeping from what doesn't benefit - from eating what a sword bloated and cut and what died and lodged - and from going toward a young man's wife and from adultery. ²⁴ They keep from what wasn't commanded by LAW - from eating disgusting food and from all hated Work - and from all the Work that GOD doesn't love - for sinful people do all this. ²⁵ As for kind people - they distance from all the Work that GOD doesn't love. ²⁶ He loves them and shall keep them from all their tribulation like Trust money. ²⁷ For they keep His Order and His LAW and all that He loves - but Satan rules sinful people.

2 Meq. 10

¹ Fear GOD Who Created you and kept you until today - yet you, the nobles and the kings, don't go on Satan's path. ² Live in the LAW and Command of GOD Who rules all - yet don't go on Satan's path. ³ As on the time Israelite children came toward Amalek that they might inherit the Hittites' and Canaanites' and Perizzites' country - Sihon's son Balak and Balaam... ⁴ whom you cursed are cursed - and he whom you blessed is blessed - don't go on Satan's road - for he has said, "And I will give you much silver and gold that honor you - that you might curse for me and - and having cursed - that you might destroy for me." ⁵ And because Balaam has come making his sorcery reward a morale - and because Sihon's son Balak has shown him the place where Israelite children camped. ⁶ For he has done his pessimism - and for he has sacrificed his sacrifice - and for he has slaughtered from his fattened cows and sheep - and for

447

he has loved that he might curse and destroy Israelite children. ⁷ He returned a curse toward a bless - yet but as GOD didn't love that he might curse them by His Word - don't go on Satan's road. ⁸ "As you are the kindred that GOD chose - as you are GOD's Lodging that shall come from Heaven - let people be cursed who curse you - and let people who bless you be blessed," he said. ⁹ On the time he blessed them before him - after this, Sihon's son Balak was sad - and he totally vexed and commanded that he might curse them. ¹⁰ Because the kindred that GOD blessed have come toward this country - and Balaam told him, "I won't curse Israel whom GOD blessed." ¹¹ And Sihon's son Balak told Balaam, "As for me - I had loved that you might curse for me - you blessed them before me - yet but you didn't curse them - if you had cursed for me and told me 'Give me' - as for me - I would have given you a house full of silver and gold - but you totally blessed them - and you didn't do a goodly thing for me - and I won't do a goodly thing for you." ¹² Balaam said, "What GOD told me Speak with my tongue - I will speak it - yet as for me - I can't dare to ignore GOD's thing. ¹³ Lest I curse a blessed kindred - as GOD shall vex upon me if I love money - as for me - I don't love money more than my soul. ¹⁴ As GOD has told their father Jacob - 'Let people who bless you be blessed and let people who curse you be cursed - lest I curse blessed Jacob - as for me - I don't love money more than my soul," he said - and as GOD has told him - "He who blesses you is blessed... ¹⁵ and a person who unjustly curses you is cursed - accomplish your path and your Work that GOD might love you. ¹⁶ And don't be like unto former people who saddened GOD in their sin and whom He neglected - and there are them whom He destroyed in the Flood. ¹⁷ And there are them whom He destroyed by their haters' hands - there are them whom He destroyed by their enemies' hands - bringing enemies who were evil people who firmed up tribulation upon them - and they captured their lords with their priests and their prophets. ¹⁸ And they delivered them to a foreign country they don't know - they totally captured them - and they plundered their livestock upon them and destroyed their country. ¹⁹ For they have demolished the honored country Jerusalem's fences and ramparts - and they made Jerusalem like a field. ²⁰ And the priests were captured - and the LAW was demolished - and warriors fought in war and fell. ²¹ And widows were captured - as they have been captured - they wept for themselves - yet they didn't weep for their husbands who died. ²² And the children wept - and elders were ashamed - and they weren't nice to neither a grey-haired person nor an elder. ²³ They destroyed all they found in the country - yet they weren't nice to beauties nor to those in LAW - as GOD was vexed upon His kindreds on the time He loved that He might beforehand destroy His Lodging the Temple - they captured and took them to a country they don't know and to people. ²⁴ As they sadden their Creator every time - because of this on the time GOD neglected Israelite children - GOD made Jerusalem to be ploughed like a field. ²⁵ For He is nice to them because of their fathers - but He didn't destroy them at one time - as He loves their fathers Isaac and Abraham and Jacob who reigned truly and lived firmed up in straight LAW before their Creator - it is because of their fathers' kindness - yet it isn't because of their own kindness that he forgives them. ²⁶ And He appointed them upon honors that were twofold - and they found two Kingdoms - on Earth and in Heaven. ²⁷ And you, the kings and the nobles who live in this passing world - like unto your fathers who lived firmed up in Work that is due and who were preceding you likewise inherited the Kingdom of Heaven - and like unto them names were beautiful for a child's children - think of them. ²⁸ And you - straighten up your Work - that He might straighten up your

Kingdom for you - and that your name might be called in goodly invocation like unto the kind kings who were preceding you who served GOD in their beautiful lifestyle.

2 Meq. 11

[1] Remember the servant of GOD, Moses, who was not angry as he led this people in his humility and prayers, and not a single person was destroyed. He prayed to GOD in his innocence for his sister and brother who spoke against him, wishing that GOD might destroy them while he said, "As they have wronged You, Lord, forgive and do not abandon Your people" - and he atoned for their sins, but GOD remembered his servant Moses who was not angry. [2] "For I have wronged You, and forgive me, Your servant who am a sinner, for You are Merciful, and You are a Forgiver, and forgive their sins." [3] And Moses likewise atoned for the sins of his sister and brother who spoke against him. [4] Because he was called innocent. [5] And GOD loved him more than all the priests' children who were his brethren - for He appointed the priests - and GOD made him like Himself alongside them. [6] But He also sank beneath the Earth the children of Korah who challenged - He lowered them toward Sheol with their livestock and their tents when they said "We are here - we are here in flesh and soul" - as his Creator GOD loved him - and as he did not depart from His Command - all the words he spoke would be done for him like unto GOD's Word. [7] And unless you demolished GOD's Command likewise - GOD will do your will for you and will love your thing for you - and He will preserve your Kingdom for you. [8] And Dathan and the children of Korah who departed from Moses' command grumbled against him because he told them, "Straighten up your reasonings to be ruled by GOD." [9] They grumbled saying, "How are we not Levite children who perform priesthood Work in the special Tent?" [10] They went and offered incense seizing their censers that they might offer up - but GOD did not accept their plea - and they were burnt by the fire in their censers - and they melted like unto the wax that fire melts - and not even one person remained from them - as He has said - Their censers were honored by their bodies being burnt - apart from those censers that entered toward GOD's Dwelling for GOD's Command - neither their clothes nor their bones remained. [11] Because of this GOD told Aaron and Moses - Gather their censers toward the Tent - make it an instrument for My Dwelling wherefor I prepared all beginning from outside up to within. [12] And he prepared the sacred Tent instruments - he prepared the rings and the joiners - the sea of Cherubim image. [13] He made the cups - the curtains - the Tent area grounds for the mobilization - the altar and the jugs whereby they sacrifice in the special Tent. [14] They offered the sacrifice that they sacrifice by their agreement - the sacrifice whereby welfare is made - the sacrifice whereby He atones for sin - and the vow sacrifice and the morning and the evening sacrifice. [15] All that He commanded for Moses - he commanded them in the special Tent - that they might perform Work in it. [16] They did not scorn being ruled by their Creator GOD - that His Name might be praised by them in the LAW Dwelling Tent of their Creator GOD Who gave them a promise that He might give them to inherit their fathers' inheritance that produces honey and milk that He swore to Abraham. [17] They did not scorn being ruled by their Creator GOD - Who swore to Isaac and established His Worship for Jacob... [18] and Who established for Aaron and Moses the Tent where His Worship is kept... [19] and Who established His Worship for both Elijah and Samuel in the Temple and Tent that Solomon built up until it became GOD's Dwelling in Jerusalem - and up until GOD's Name Dwelling became GOD's Dwelling that honored Israel. [20] For it is a supplication - and for it is a sin atonement where it is overturned for those who live in innocence

and for the priests. [21] And for it is a place for those who do His Accord where He will hear their pleas... [22] and GOD's LAW Construction that honored Israel. [23] For it is where sacrifices are offered and where Incense is burned up that GOD Who honored Israel may be in a goodly Fragrance. [24] And He would speak being upon the joiner where He forgives in the special Tent - GOD's Light would be revealed for the children of Jacob whom He chose and for friends who live firmed up in His LAW and His Command. [25] But those who ignored GOD's LAW will be like unto the children of Korah whom the Earth sank - and likewise sinful people have that they might enter toward Hell that has no exits until Eternity.

2 Meq. 12

[1] You who did not keep the LAW He commanded you in the Tent - woe to you, Israelite nobles who also did not do His Accord - but you did your own will - and this is being arrogant and pride - greed and adultery - drinking and being drunk - and swearing falsely. [2] Because of this, I am angry - like chaff burnt before a fire - and like fire burns the mountain - and like a whirlwind scatters the crushed chaff from the Earth and scatters it toward Heaven - lest its trace be found in its place - I will destroy you like that. [3] GOD Who honored Israel said - I will likewise destroy all people who commit sin - and think of GOD Who rules all and for Whom nothing is impossible. [4] He loves those who love Him - and for those who live firmed up in His Command - He will atone for their iniquity and their sin for them - do not be dull and stingy of heart by not believing. [5] And make your reasonings straight to be ruled by GOD - and believe in Him that you might firm up your bodies - and I will save you from your enemy's hand in your day of tribulation. [6] And in your time of plea, I tell you - Look - I am there with you in Support - I will save you from your enemy's hand - as you have believed in Me - and as you have done My Command - and as you did not depart from My LAW - and as you have loved what I love - GOD Who rules all said - I will not neglect you on your day of tribulation. [7] He loves those who love Him - for He is a Forgiver - and He is kind - and He keeps those who keep His LAW - like a trust money. [8] He returns His anger many times - because He knew them that they are flesh and blood - as He is a Forgiver - He didn't destroy all in His chastisement - and when their souls were separated from their flesh - they will return to their Earthliness. [9] As He created them bringing from non-living to living - they won't know the place where they lived until GOD loves that He might bring them from non-living to living - again He separated their souls from their flesh - and Earth nature returned to its Earthliness. [10] And again His Accord shall bring them from non-living to living." [11] But King Tseerutsaydan who denied GOD multiplied being arrogant before GOD - he made himself lofty until the day that he loved when he left Him. [12] "And my era has become like unto the era of Heaven - and I am the one who sends forth the Sun - and I won't die until Eternity," he said. [13] And before he finished speaking this thing, the Angel of Death, whose name is called Thilimyakos, alit and struck his heart - he died at that moment - as he did not praise his Creator - he was separated from his beautiful lifestyle and perished arising from his abundance of arrogance and his evil deeds. [14] But when the king of the Chaldeans' army had camped in the city and the country squares loving to fight him - when he died - they proceeded and destroyed his country - they plundered all his livestock - and they did not preserve an elder who approached and saw the ramparts. [15] They plundered all his money - and they took even his little money - and they burned his country in fire and returned to their country.

2 Meq. 13

¹ But these five Maccabee children who believed gave their bodies for death refusing to eat the sacrifice offered to idols. ² For they knew that pretending with GOD surpasses pretending with people - and GOD's anger surpasses the king's anger. ³ Having known that this world will totally pass and that the Righteous Life will not live forever - they gave their bodies to fire that they might be saved from fire in Heaven. ⁴ And as they knew that being made Joyful in Heaven for one day is better than living many ages in this world - and that finding Your Pardon for one hour, Lord, is better than many ages - they gave their bodies to fire. ⁵ What is our era? Like a shadow - like passing wax melted and perishes on the edge of a fire - isn't it like that? ⁶ But You, Lord, live forever - and Your Era is not completed - and Your Name invocation is for children's children. ⁷ And the Maccabee children thought all this - refusing to eat a disgusting sacrifice they chose believing in GOD. ⁸ Knowing that they will rise with those who are dead - and because of GOD - knowing that Judgment will be judged after the Resurrection of the Council - because of this, they gave their bodies for martyrdom. ⁹ You people who do not know or believe that the dead rise - knowing that the Life they find later will surpass this passing Earthly Life - arising from these five Maccabee children who gave their bodies together for death and whose appearance was handsome - after this, they knew Resurrection. ¹⁰ Because they believed in Him knowing that all shall pass - and because they did not bow to idols - because they did not eat a disgusting sacrifice that does not give Support - they gave their bodies for death that they might find favor from GOD. ¹¹ For because knowing that He will make them Joyful in flesh and soul in a later era - they did not taste this world's flavor and considered death's tribulation not a serious thing for those who have children and a wife - and knowing that Resurrection will be made in flesh and soul on the Day of Coming - they gave their bodies for death. ¹² And knowing that those who kept GOD's LAW - with the nobles and the kings who believed GOD's Word and were kind... ¹³ shall live reigning for children's children many eras in the Kingdom of Heaven where there is no sadness and tribulation nor death - and knowing in their reasonings what will be done later - like wax melts amidst fire - because of this, they gave their bodies for death. ¹⁴ Believing that their faces will shine seven hands more than the Sun - and that they will be Joyful in His Love when all arise in flesh and soul - they gave their bodies for death.

2 Meq. 14

¹ But the Samaritans and 'Ayhuds thing - the Sadducees who do not believe in the resurrection of the dead - and the Pharisees thing completely sadden me - and it helps my reasoning - "We will die tomorrow," 'Ayhuds say - "Let us eat and drink - we will die tomorrow - there are no Righteous Life we will see in the grave." ² But the Samaritans say - "As our flesh will be dust - it will not rise. ³ Because it was invisible like the wind and like the voice of thunder - look - it is here - and because it was what they do not call invisible - as the soul will not rise if the flesh dies - when the Resurrection is done, we will believe our souls rising. ⁴ But as beasts will eat it and as worms will eat it in the grave - our flesh is seen alongside all - it will become dust and ashes. ⁵ And those beasts who ate it will become dust - for they have been like grass - and for they have become dust like those who were not created - and for their trace will not be found - but our flesh will not rise." ⁶ And the Pharisees say - "We believe as for those who are dead rising - however, He will bring and Unite souls with another flesh that is in Heaven - that is not on Earth - where will demolished and rotten flesh be found?" ⁷ But the Sadducees say - "After our soul departed from our flesh - we will not rise with those who are dead - and flesh and soul have no rising after they die - and after we die, we will not

449

rise." ⁸ And because they completely err - and as they speak insult on the LORDSHIP of GOD - their thing saddens me. ⁹ As they did not believe GOD Who honored them - they have no hope to be saved - however, they have no hope to die and rise and be saved. ¹⁰ At that time, they will see the tribulation that will come upon them and will have no ending - and where there is no calm nor welfare - and it has the sadness that has no rest nor calm in their reasoning. ¹¹ And a fire that does not perish and worms that do not sleep will come upon them. ¹² And in the place where their flesh is, there will be fire - sulfur - whirlwind - frost - hail - sleet - all this will rain over them. ¹³ For those who do not believe in the resurrection of the dead - there is the fire of Hell upon them.

2 Meq. 15

¹ Those who have earned rewards through their good deeds will be joyful, while those who disbelieved, claiming "the dead will not rise," will be saddened upon witnessing the resurrection and realizing that their evil deeds brought no benefit. ² Their deeds will condemn them, and they will recognize their own condemnation without anyone disputing it. ³ On the day of judgment and mourning, when JAH comes and the final judgment is made, those who ignored JAH's laws will stand where they are. ⁴ It will be a day of total darkness, mist, visible lightning, and audible thunder... ⁵ A day marked by earthquakes, terror, heatwaves, and frost... ⁶ A day when the wicked who committed evil will face their due suffering, the righteous will receive their rewards as per their deeds, and those who forgot JAH's laws will face punishment as sinners do, standing in their respective places. ⁷ For on that day, no master will be more honored than his servant, no mistress more than her maid... ⁸ No king more honored than a pauper, no elder more than an infant, no father more than his child, no mother more than her offspring... ⁹ No rich person will be more honored than a poor one, no arrogant more than the humbled, no great more than the small - this is the day of judgment, the day sentences and suffering are dispensed, and the day all receive their due according to their sins. ¹⁰ And it is also the day when those who have performed good deeds receive their rewards, and those who have sinned face their suffering. ¹¹ As it is the day when those who have found their rewards are made joyful, those who ignored JAH's laws will remain standing in their places. Those who lied, who trivialized the notion saying, "The dead do not rise," will witness the resurrection. ¹² Then, sinners of this world, who failed to do good deeds, will lament over their sins as grief engulfs them relentlessly. ¹³ Conversely, the righteous, those who performed good deeds, their bliss is eternal, for they acted righteously while in this world. ¹⁴ They knew they would rise after death and did not stray from their Creator's laws. ¹⁵ Because they adhered to His commandments, they will inherit dual blessings: their offspring will multiply in this world, and they themselves will be honored. ¹⁶ They will inherit the Kingdom of Heaven, the place of bliss promised to their ancestors, at the resurrection and when the rich become poor. ¹⁷ Those who sinned, disbelieving in resurrection, neglecting JAH's laws, and overlooking the Day of Resurrection, will weep. ¹⁸ They will witness the endless torment that awaits them, a place devoid of peace or comfort, marked by endless grief and unrest. ¹⁹ A fire that never dies and worms that never rest will be their fate. ²⁰ Their flesh will be tormented by fire, sulfur, whirlwinds, frost, hail, and sleet – all these will descend upon them. ²¹ For those who disbelieve in the resurrection, the fire of Gehenna awaits.

2 Meq. 16

¹ Please consider what is on your flesh - and your feet and your hands' nails - and your head's hair - for they grow quickly the moment you cut them - know the Resurrection by this - that you

have reasoning - and that you have religion and knowledge. [2] Your feet and your hands' nails and your head's hair - you ask, "Where do these come from?" - isn't it GOD Who prepared them to grow - that you might know the resurrection that will be done on your flesh that is not on another flesh - that you might know that you will rise after you die? [3] Because you misled people while you said, "There is no Resurrection of the dead ones" - when the dead ones rise, you will receive your hardship as you have sinned. [4] And as even what you planted now will not remain refusing that it might grow - whether it be wheat or barley - you will see it when the day arrives when you receive your hardship. [5] And again - the plant you planted will not say, "I will not grow" - and be it a fig wood or a grape vine - its fruit and its leaf will not be changed. [6] If you plant grapes, they will not change to be figs - and if you plant figs, they will not change to be grapes - and if you sow wheat, it will not change to be barley. [7] All - in each of the seeds - in each of their kinds - each of the fruits - each of the woods - each of the leaves - each of the roots - produce fruit having received Blessing Dew from GOD - yet if you sow barley also it will not change to be wheat. [8] And all likewise - that a grave might produce flesh and soul - it shall produce people just as GOD sowed upon it - the flesh and soul that GOD sowed shall arise being United - yet people who did goodly Work will not be changed into people who did evil Work - and people who did evil Work also will not be changed into people who did goodly Work. [9] Upon the moment the hour arrived when a drum is beaten - the dead shall arise by the Blessing Dew from GOD - people who did goodly Work shall arise in a Life Resurrection - and their reward is the Garden where there are Righteous Life that GOD prepared for kind people - where there is no tribulation nor disease - and that is the dwelling of clean ones where they will not again die after this. [10] But people who did evil Work shall arise in a Definite Judgment arising - and with Satan who misled them... [11] and with his armies - demons who do not love that even one person might be saved from all Adam's children... [12] they shall descend toward Hell that was darkness edge - where there is teeth grinding and mourning - where there is no charity nor pardon - and where there are no exits until Eternity - that is beneath Sheol forever. For they did not do goodly Work in their Life in this world when they were in their flesh. [13] Because of this, it shall be judged upon them when flesh and soul arise being United. [14] Woe to sinful people's souls who take them toward destruction - who have no welfare nor rest - nor escaping from the tribulation that found them - nor proceeding from Hell until Eternity. [15] As they have lived firmed up in Cain's Work - and as they have perished by Balaam's iniquity price - and as they have lacked what they will do - woe to sinful people - for they pretext to receive interest and gifts that in regression they might take a stranger's money that was not their own. [16] They shall receive their hardship in Hell by their sin that they worked.

2 Meq. 17

[1] A wheat kernel will not grow nor bear fruit unless it is demolished. But if a wheat kernel is demolished, it will send roots toward the Earth - it will send forth leaves - there will be buds - it will bear fruit. [2] You know that the one wheat kernel will become many kernels. [3] And all likewise - this kernel grows rising up from Water and wind and Earth's dew - for wheat cannot bear fruit without the Sun - but the Sun exists because of fire's stead. [4] And the wind exists because of a soul's stead - and wheat cannot bear fruit without wind - and the Water gives Earth to drink and scatters her. [5] And after the Earth that is ashes drank Water, it produces roots - and it tips are lofty upward - it bears fruit around what GOD blessed her. [6] But a wheat kernel is Adam's example - in whom lodged a resonating soul that GOD created - and likewise a grape vine drinks Water and sends forth roots - and the thin root types drink Water. [7] For Blessing Dew from GOD gives drink to vine tips that were long - and it sends the Water upward toward the leaf tips - it buds up from the Sun's heat - and by GOD's Accord, it bears fruit. [8] It shall be a goodly fragrance that makes reasoning Joyful - and upon eating it, it shall satiate like unto Water that does not make thirsty and grain that does not make hungry - and upon immersing it, it will be the blood of the cluster. [9] And like it was told in the Psalm saying - "Grapes make a person's reasoning Joyful" - upon drinking it, it makes a person's heart Joyful - and upon a person who came loose opened his mouth and drank it - he is drunk - he drinks and fills in his lungs - and the blood flows toward his heart. [10] As grapes' drunkenness totally misleads - and as it deprives him of his mind - it makes the pit and the cliff like unto a wide meadow - and he does not know obstacles and thorns upon his feet and hands. [11] GOD did this upon its fruit and grape vine that His Name might be praised by people who believe in the dead's resurrection and who do His Accord. [12] In the Kingdom of Heaven, He shall make joyful those who believe in the dead's resurrection.

2 Meq. 18

[1] You people who do not believe in the dead's resurrection - what error do you err in! And upon the time they took you toward the place you do not know - you will regret a useless regret - and because you did not believe in the resurrection that the dead shall have United in soul and flesh - and upon the time people cast you toward Hell... [2] if you work whether good or evil - you will receive your reward according to your Work - for you have misled your companions' reasoning while you said, "We know that the dead - who were dust and ashes - will not rise." [3] As their death has no exit - and as they have no Power for their punishment that shall come upon them - and as they were not firm in their tribulation - because they misled their companions - for they have that they might stand in GOD's Square. [4] Upon the time He is angry at them in His wrath they will totally fear - because they did not know that they were created bringing from non-living to living - as they speak GOD's LAW without knowing - it shall be judged upon them all because they did evil. [5] They do not know Hell where they will go - for because they were angry and because they were crooked in their Work - they teach to their companions like unto their reasoning's thirst measure - and for they are evil ones who teach a crooked thing while they said, "There is no Resurrection of dead ones." [6] At that time, they shall know that the dead shall rise - and they shall know that it shall be judged upon them because they did not believe in the dead's resurrection that is for all Adam's children. [7] For all of us are Adam's children - and for we have died because of Adam - and for the judgment of death has found us all from GOD because of our father Adam's error. [8] We will again rise there with our father Adam that we might receive our hardship by our Work that we worked - for the world has been doomed to death by our father Adam's ignorance. [9] By Adam breaking GOD's Command - because of this, we received hardship - our flesh in the grave melted like wax - and our bodies perished. [10] And the Earth drank our marrow - we perished and our comeliness perished in the grave - and our flesh was buried in the grave - and our beautiful words were buried in the Earth. [11] And worms proceeded from our shining eyes - and our features perished in the grave and became dust. [12] Where are the youth's features' comeliness - who were attractive - whose stance was handsome and whose word thing succeeded? Where are the warriors' firmness? [13] Where are the kings' armies - or where are the nobles' lordship? Where are adorning in horses and adorning in silver and gold and adorning in shining weapons? Didn't it

perish? [14] Where are the sweet grape drinks - and what about the food's flavor?

2 Meq. 19

[1] O Earth who gathered the nobles and the kings and rich ones and elders and daughters who were attractive and beauties who were attractive - woe arising from you. [2] O Earth who gathered people who were warriors - those who had comeliness - and those who were fine of leg - and those who had reasoning and knowledge - and those whose words had words that were beautiful like unto a humming harp and like unto a lyre and a violin beat... [3] and those who had a tune that made Joyful like unto grape drink makes Joyful - and those whose eyes shine like unto a morning star... [4] and those who sketch what was firm like unto their right hands lift up what is given and withheld and like unto they were - and those whose feet were beautiful to look at - and those who run like rushing wheels - woe arising from you. [5] O death who separated attractive people's souls from their flesh - woe arising from you - for you have been sent by GOD's Accord. [6] As you have gathered many people whom GOD produced from you and returned toward you - you Earth - woe arising from you - we were found from you - we returned toward you by GOD's Accord - we were Joyful over you by GOD's Accord. [7] You became a carpet for our corpses - we walked over you - and we were buried within you - we ate your fruit - and you ate our flesh. [8] And we drank the Water found from your springs - and you drank our blood springs - we ate the fruit found from your Earthliness - and you ate our body's flesh. [9] Like GOD commanded you to be our food - we ate grain from your Earthliness that had beautiful dew - and you received our flesh's comeliness and made it dust for your food like GOD commanded you. [10] O death who gathered the nobles and the kings who were powerful - woe arising from you - you did not fear arising from their fame and their frightening - like unto GOD Who created them commanded you - o death - woe arising from you - and you did not scorn the sufferer. [11] And you were not kind to people whose features are beautiful - and you did not spare powerful ones and warriors - you did not spare poor nor rich ones - neither kind nor evil ones - neither children nor elders - neither daughters nor males. [12] You did not spare people who think a good thing and who did not depart from the LAW - and you did not spare those who were like animals in their Work - who think an evil thing - who were totally beautiful in their features' comeliness - in their things' flavor and in their words - o death - woe arising from you. [13] You did not spare people whose words were angry and whose mouths were full of curses - you gathered people who live in darkness and in light and their souls in your places - o death - woe arising from you. [14] And Earth gathered the people's flesh who live whether in a cave or on Earth - until a drum is beaten and the dead arise. [15] As the dead shall arise quickly like unto an eye wink by GOD's Command and upon a drum being beaten - people who did evil Work shall receive their hardship in the abundance measure of their sin that they worked it - and people who did goodly Work shall be Joyful.

2 Meq. 20

[1] And believe I that all Our Work that We worked in this world will not remain nor be hidden when We stand before Him fearing and trembling. [2] And upon the time We didn't bring provisions for Our path - and upon the time We won't have clothes for Our bodies... [3] upon the time We won't have a staff for Our hands nor shoes for Our feet... [4] and upon the time We won't know the paths where demons take Us - whether it be slippery or smooth - or be it dark - and whether it be thorns or nettles - or whether it be a Water's depth or a pit's depth - believe I that Our Work that We worked in this world will not remain nor be hidden. [5] We won't know the

demons who take Us - and We won't hear their thing. [6] As they are black ones - and as they lead Us toward darkness - We don't see their faces. [7] And like unto the prophet spoke saying - "When My soul was separated from My flesh - Lord My Lord - You know My path - and they hid a trap on that path where I went - and I saw returning toward the right - I lacked someone who knows Me - and I have nothing there by which I will escape" - as they take Us toward darkness - We won't see their faces. [8] As he knows that demons ridicule upon him - and as they will lead him toward the path he doesn't know - he speaks this because of that - and if he returns leftward and rightward - there is no one who knows him. [9] He is alone among demons - and yet there is none who knows him. [10] Angels of Light who are subtle are those who are sent toward kind people that they might receive righteous ones' souls - and might take toward a Light place - toward the Garden - where welfare is found. [11] Demons and Angels of darkness are those who are sent that they might receive them and might take them toward Hell that was prepared for them that they might receive their hardship by their sin that they worked. [12] Woe to sinful people's souls who take them toward destruction - who have no welfare nor rest - nor escaping from the tribulation that found them - nor proceeding from Hell until Eternity. [13] As they have lived firmed up in Cain's Work - and as they have perished by Balaam's iniquity price - and as they have lacked what they will do - woe to sinful people - for they pretexts to receive interest and gifts that in regression they might take a stranger's money that was not their own. [14] They shall receive their hardship in Hell by their sin that they worked.

2 Meq. 21

[1] Where are people who gather a stranger's money that was not their own hands' Work nor their own money? [2] For they took a person's money for free - and for they shall be gathered without knowing the day of their death that shall arrive upon them - however, they leave their money for a stranger. [3] For like their fathers - they are sinners' lineages who worry and seize sinners like them whether it be by theft or by robbery - and their children will not be Joyful by their fathers' money. [4] As they have gathered for them in wrongdoing - and as it seems to them that they will not die - like unto people who wrong their companions will not boast - sinners' destruction is likewise in one moment. [5] You lazy ones - think that you will perish and that your money will perish with you - and if your silver and your gold abound, it shall become rust ed. [6] And if you birth many children, they shall be for many graves - and if you build many houses, they shall be demolished. [7] For you did not fulfill your Creator GOD's Accord - and if you multiply livestock, they shall be for your enemies' capture - and all the money you seized in your hands will not be found - for it has not been blessed. [8] Whether it be in a house or in a forest - and be it in a wilderness or a pasture place - and be it in a grape threshing floor or in a grain threshing floor - it will not be found. [9] Because you did not keep GOD's Command - as GOD will not save you with all your household from the tribulation - there shall be sadness upon you arising from all your enemies - yet you will not be Joyful in your children born from your nature. [10] But from His abundance - He will not trouble those who kept His Order and His LAW - He gives to all who begged Him - yet He blesses their children born from their nature and also their land's fruit for them. [11] And He makes them rulers over all people in their area that they might rule lest they be those who are ruled - and He gives them all His abundance in their pasture place. [12] He blesses for them all they seized in their hand - all their field's fruit - and all their livestock's places - and He makes them Joyful in their children born from their nature. [13] And He does not diminish their livestock upon them - He saves them from all their tribulation and from weariness

and illness and destruction - and from their enemy they do not know and from him they know. 14 And He will dispute for them in the time of judgment - and He shall save them from an evil thing and from tribulation and from all who dispute them - in the first era if a priest lived who performs the Tent Work - who keeps the LAW and keeps the Tent Order and lives firmed up in GOD's Accord - by the first Order and all the LAW as they would give him the tithe and what was birthed first beginning from man up to livestock - He would save them from all the tribulation. 15 Like Moses commanded Nun's child Joshua - there was a sanctuary country in all their country - by not knowing and by knowing up to when they judged judgment on whom they convicted and for whom they acquitted... 16 if a person lived who killed a soul - he would be measured there that he might be saved. 17 He told them - "Examine in your reasonings that he had a quarrel with him formerly - and be it by axe or be it by a stone or be it by wood - as it has fallen from his hand by not knowing - if he says "That person upon whom it fell died on me" - examine and save him - if he did it unknowingly make him be saved. 18 But if he does it knowingly - he will receive his hardship according to his sin - and there is none who will pardon him; but if he killed him unknowingly - as he has done it unknowingly - examine and save him lest he dies. 19 He worked for them that they might distance from all the sin - yet Moses would work like this for the children of Israel lest they depart from GOD's LAW. 20 He commanded them that Adam's children - who live firmed up in GOD's Command from worshipping idols and eating what is dead and lodged and what a sword bloated and cut - and who distance from all evil work like he worked for them - that they might work it and might totally distance from all that is not due. 21 He commanded them lest they depart from the Command He worked for them in the Tent example in Heaven - that they might save their bodies and might find their dwelling with their fathers. 22 As they have been birthed from Seth and Adam who did GOD's Accord - people who believed in GOD's Word and lived firmed up in His Command will be called kind people's children. 23 As We are Adam's children - as He has created Us in His Example and His Appearance that We might do all goodly Work that makes GOD Joyful - He will not scorn it. 24 As He totally will not separate His friends - if We do goodly Work - We shall inherit the Kingdom of Heaven where there is welfare with people who do goodly Work. 25 He totally loves those who beg Him cleanly - and He hears them in their prayer - and He accepts the repentance of those who are disciplined and enter repentance - He gives firmness and Power for those who keep His Order and His LAW and His Command. 26 Those who did His Accord shall be Joyful with Him in His Kingdom forever - and whether they be people who preceded or who arose later - they will present praise for Him beginning from today until Eternity.

3 Meqabyan

3 Meq. 1

1 Christ shall bring joy to the people of Egypt - because He will come to them in a future era to avenge and destroy the Devil - who wronged those who were kind and innocent - and who misled people - and who hated His Creator's Work. 2 He will avenge and destroy him - He will return his dominion to misery and being debased - for he was arrogant in his reasoning. 3 He will return his dominion to being debased - for he has said, "I will enter into the midst of the sea, and I will proceed to Heaven, and I will look up at the depths, and I will capture and seize the children of Adam like birds' chicks - who is higher than me? 4 Because I became the reason that I might distance them from the straight LAW of GOD - as I

will strengthen upon people who live in this world unless they did GOD's Accord - there is none who will depose me from my authority," he said. 5 "For I will be the reason to return them to a path that was smooth to go to Hell with me. 6 People who loved Him and kept His LAW hate me because of this thing - but people who departed from their Lord's LAW and who erred will come towards me and love me and keep my oath - as I will make their reasoning evil and change their thoughts lest they return to their Creator GOD - they will do my command just as I commanded them. 7 And when I showed them the wealth of this world, I will mislead their reasoning from the straight LAW - and when I showed them beautiful and attractive daughters, I will distance them with these from the straight LAW. 8 And when I showed them shining Indian jewels, silver, and gold, I will distance them with this also from the straight LAW so they might return to my Work. 9 And when I showed them fine garments, red silk, and white silk - and linens and white silk - I will distance them with this also from the straight LAW - and I will turn them towards my thoughts - when I multiplied money and livestock like the sand and showed them - by this also I will turn them towards my Work. 10 And when I showed them jealousy, pride, anger, and quarrels - by all this I will turn them towards my Work. 11 And when I showed them omens, I will lodge in their reasoning - and I will lodge a sign for each of the races in their reasoning - and I showed them words and misled them. 12 And for people in whom I lodged my lodging, I will show them signs - whether it be in the movement of stars, or in the progression of clouds, or in the flickering of fire, or in the cries of animals and birds - as they are my lodgings - I will lodge signs in their reasoning by all this. 13 They will speak and give signs to their companions - and just as those doubters told them - I will precede and be a sign for them. 14 I will make their words signs for them - that people who examined them might be misled - and that they might give a reward to sorcerers - and that they might tell their companions saying, 'There are no sages like so-and-so and so-and-so for whom it is done just as they spoke - and who know prophecy - and who distinguish good and evil - and for whom everything is as they spoke - and for whom it is done just as they worded.' 15 I will be pleased when they speak this - that people who perish and err by me might totally abound and that the children of Adam might perish - for GOD has debased me from my rank because of their father Adam - on my saying 'I will not bow to Adam who is debased from me.' 16 And I will lead to destruction all his children who live firm in my command - I have a Oath from GOD Who Irritated me - that all people whom I misled might descend to Hell with me. 17 And when He multiplied His anger upon me - and when He commanded that they might bind and cast me into Hell - when my Creator commanded saying thus - I interceded with my Lord - I interceded before Him saying, 'As You have vexed upon me - and as You have admonished me by Your chastisement - and as You have chastised me by Your wrath - Lord my Lord - adjourn me that I might speak one thing before You.' 18 And my Lord answered to me saying, Speak - I will hear you - at that time I began my plea towards Him saying, 'After I was debased from my rank - let the people whom I misled be like me in Hell where I will receive tribulation. 19 And make them for Your Lordship who refused me - who didn't err by me - who didn't keep my command - that they might do Your Command and might fulfill Your Accord and might keep Your Word - when they didn't err by me as I misled them having refused as I taught them - and when You loved me - let them take the crown You gave to me. 20 Give them the crown of the authorities called Satans who were sent with me - seat them on my throne on Your Right that was a wilderness from me and my hosts. 21 And let them praise You as You loved -

and let them be like my hosts and like me - because You hated me and loved those who were Created from ashes and Earth - as my authority has perished - and as their authority has been exalted - let them praise You as You loved.' 22 My Lord answered to me saying, As you have misled them while they looked up and while they heard - if you misled them without them loving My Order - let them be for you like your accord and like your word. 23 If they abandoned the Books Word and My Command and came towards you - and if you misled them while their destruction also saddened Me - let them receive tribulation in Hell like you - He told me. 24 You will receive tribulation in Hell until Eternity - yet you will have no exits from Hell until Eternity - for those whom you misled nor for you.

3 Meq. 2

1 But I will bequeath your throne and lordship to those whom it failed you to mislead - like My servant Job ~ GOD Who rules all said - I will give the Kingdom of Heaven to people whom it failed you to mislead. 2 And I provoke upon the children of Adam in all - if it were possible for me to mislead them - I won't leave them so that they might stand firm in goodly Work - for I provoke upon all the children of Adam - and I sweeten this world's Righteousness for them. 3 Be it by loving drink and food and clothes - or by loving things - or by withholding and giving... 4 or be it by loving to hear and see - or be it by loving to touch and go - or be it by multiplying pride and things - or be it by loving dreams and sleep... 5 or be it by multiplying drunkenness and drink - or be it by multiplying insults and anger - be it by speaking idly and pointless things... 6 or be it by quarrels and by gossiping about their companion - or be it by looking upon this world's daughters who are attractive - be it by smelling perfumes that mislead them... 7 I hate them by all this lest they be able to be saved - I distance them from GOD's LAW that they might enter with me into the destruction whereby I was debased from my rank." 8 And the prophet told him, "You who destroy people - perish - for the time you departed from GOD's LAW and committed crime in your firm reasoning and your arrogance - and by saddening your Creator and not worshipping your Creator in your firm reasoning - will you thus be arrogant upon GOD's Creation? 9 When your Creator was vexed upon you - He debased you from your rank because of your evil Work - why do you lead Adam into sin - him whom his Creator Created from Earth - whom He made like unto Him loved - and whom He placed to praise Him?" he told him. 10 "When you - who are cunning and were Created from wind and fire - were arrogant in saying 'I am the Creator'... 11 when you boasted - as GOD has seen your evil Work and you have denied GOD with your hosts - He Created Adam who will praise because of your place - that he might praise His Name without diminishing. 12 As you have made yourself prouder than all Angel hosts who are like you - because of your arrogance GOD Created Adam with his children that they might praise GOD's Name because of the praise that you praised with your hosts whom He scorned. 13 And because of this thing GOD destroyed you separating from all Angel chiefs like you - and your hosts Irritated in one counsel with you - and you - you proceeded and erred from GOD's praise because of your useless reasoning arrogance and because of your reasoning firmness - and you were arrogant upon your Creator - that aren't upon another. 14 Because of this thing He Created Adam from Earth that He might be praised by debased people - and He gave him a Command and Law saying Do not eat lest you eat from the fig fruit. 15 And He appointed him upon all the Creation He Created - He notified him saying - Do not eat from one fig fruit that brings death - lest you bring death upon yourself - yet eat fruit from all the woods amidst the Garden. 16 And when you heard this Word - you lodged treachery in him arising from the thing

you spoke in your tongue to Eve who was found from Adam's side bone. 17 You misled Adam who was clean - in firm treachery that you might make him a Lawbreaker like you. 18 When you misled Eve - who was Created being like an innocent dove and who doesn't know your malice - you made her betray by your thing that succeeded and your crooked word - and after you misled that Eve who was Created beforehand - she also went and misled GOD's Creation Adam who was Created from Earth beforehand. 19 And you made him betray a disturbance that isn't by your arrogance - and you made him deny so that he might deny his Creator's Word - and you destroyed Adam in your arrogance. 20 And in your malice you distanced him from his Creator's Love - and by your reason you sent him away from the Garden where Righteousness is - and by your hindrance you made him abandon the Garden's food. 21 From the Beginning you quarreled with the innocent Creation Adam that you might lower him towards Sheol where you will receive hardship - and that you might send him away from the Love that brought him and Created him from not living to true living - and by your false thing you made him thirst for a drink from the Garden. 22 And when he is Earthly - He made him a cunning Angel who completely praises his Creator in his flesh and his soul and his reasoning. 23 And He Created many thoughts for him - like unto harps praised in each of their styles.

3 Meq. 3

1 But He Created one thought for you - that you might completely praise while you were sent to where your Creator sent you. 2 But for Adam were given five thoughts that were evil and five thoughts that were goodly - ten thoughts. 3 And again he has many thoughts like unto sea waves - and like unto a whirlwind that scatters dust lifted up from Earth - and like unto the sea waves that shake - and arising from him unnumbered thoughts abundance in his heart like unto unnumbered raindrops - Adam's thoughts are like that. 4 But your thought is one - as you aren't fleshly - you have no other thought. 5 But you lodged in a snake's reasoning - in evil treachery you destroyed Adam who was one limb - and Eve heard the snake's thing - and having heard - she did as she commanded her. 6 After she ate a fig fruit - she came and misled GOD's first Creation Adam - and she brought death upon him and upon her children because she infringed her Creator's Command. 7 They proceeded from the Garden by GOD by His true Judgment - He calmed them in the land where they were sent by their children born from their nature and by their crops found from Earth - yet He didn't distance them from the Garden's quarreling. 8 And when you expelled them directly from the Garden - that they might plant plants and children to be calmed and to renew their reasoning in the Earth's fruit that Earth prepared from her Earthliness - and that they might be calmed by Earth's fruit and the Garden's fruit that GOD gave them... 9 GOD gave them woods more verdant than the Garden's woods - and Eve and Adam - whom you sent away from the Garden upon their eating it - were totally calmed from sadness. 10 As GOD knows to calm His Creation - their reasonings are calmed because of their children and because of the crops found from Earth. 11 As they have been sent towards this world that grows nettles and thorns - they firm up their reasonings in Water and grain.

3 Meq. 4

1 The Lord has that He might ransom Adam - and He shall shame you - He will save a sheep from a wolf's mouth (Adam from the Devil). 2 However you will go towards Hell seizing with you the people whom you ruled. 3 People who kept their Creator GOD's LAW shall be Merry with their Creator GOD Who hid them from evil Work that He might make them His fortune - and that they might praise Him with honored Angels who didn't infringe their

Creator GOD's LAW like you. 4 But GOD - Who chose and gave you more than all Angels like you that you might praise Him with His servant Angels - withheld from you a lofty throne in your arrogance. 5 But you became famous and were called one who loves godhood - and your hosts were called demons. 6 But people who loved GOD shall be His relatives like unto honored Angels - and the Seraphiel and Cherubiel who praise Him stretch forth their wings and praise without slackness. 7 But in your arrogance and your laziness you destroyed your praise that you might praise Him every time with your host and your relatives Created in your likeness. 8 Lest the praise of GOD - Who Created you making a tenth tribe - be diminished when you forgot the praise of GOD Who Created you - it having seemed to you that it isn't possible for Him to Create a Creation like you - and lest the praise of GOD - Who Created you - be diminished when you were separated from your brethren Unity - He Created Adam because of your place. 9 But in your reasoning arrogance you neglected the praise of GOD Who Created you - and He was vexed upon you - He ridiculed you - and He bound and banished you into Hell with your hosts also. 10 He brought Soil from Earth with His glorified Hands - and adding fire and Water and wind - He Created Adam in His Image and His Likeness. 11 He appointed him upon all the Creation He Created in His Authority - that His praise might be filled by the praise you would praise Him - Adam's praise became one with Angels' praise - and their praises were equal. 12 But in your collar of reasoning firmness and your arrogance you were debased from your rank - and having departed from GOD's Lordship - Who Created you - you destroyed yourself. 13 Know that His praise wasn't diminished - for GOD has Created Adam who praised Him in his reasoning counsel lest GOD's Godliness praise be diminished. 14 For He knows all before it is done - and He knew you before He Created you that you will demolish His Command - as there is a counsel hidden alongside Him before He Created the world - when you denied Him - He Created His servant Adam in His Image and His Likeness. 15 Like Solomon spoke saying - 'Before hills were Created and before the world began being Created - and before winds that are Earth's foundations were Created... 16 and before He established hills and mountains' foundations - and before this world's Work established - and before the moon and the Sun's light shone - before eras and stars' caretaking were known... 17 and before daylight and night alternated - and before the sea was delineated by sand - before all the Created Creations were Created... 18 and before all seen today were seen - before all the names called today were called - He Created I, Solomon' - Angels like you and you and His servant Adam were in GOD's Reasoning. 19 He Created Adam that His glorified Name might be praised when you mutinied - and that He might be praised by His debased servant Adam who was Created from Earth when you were arrogant. 20 For being in Heaven GOD hears the poor ones' plea - and He loves the debased people's praise. 21 He loves to save having lodged in people who fear Him - yet as He doesn't love horse Power - and as He doesn't step meaning for the lap of a concubine - GOD shall ignore arrogant ones' things. 22 And they shall weep while they cried because of their sin that they worked. 23 It failed you to plead in repentance. 24 But Adam who was Created from Earth returned in repentance while he totally wept before GOD because of his sin. 25 But in your collar of reasoning firmness and your heart's arrogance you didn't know Love's Work and you didn't know repentance - it failed you to plead before your Creator GOD in repentance and mourning and sadness. 26 But that Adam who is ashes and Earth returned towards repentance in mourning and sadness - and he returned towards humbleness and Love's Work. 27 But you didn't humble your reasoning and yourself

for GOD Who Created you. 28 As for Adam - he humbled himself and pleaded upon the iniquity he wronged - he wasn't proud. 29 As you have totally produced crime - it was found from you - yet it isn't him who produced that error - in your arrogance you took him with you towards your destruction. 30 Before he Created you both - as He has known you that you were sinners - and as He has known your Works - He knows that this that was done was in your heart's arrogance. 31 But He returned that Adam - who was without arrogance or malice - in repentance mourning and sadness. 32 For a person who wrongs and doesn't plead in repentance has multiplied his iniquity more than his earlier iniquity - but in your heart's arrogance it failed you to plead in repentance - but a person who pleads and weeps entering repentance before His Creator GOD... 33 he entered repentance for true - and he found Work whereby he will be saved that he might fear his Lord's Heart - and he pleaded before his Creator - for he has pleaded before Him in bowing and much repentance - and arising from the earlier tribulation the Lord shall lighten his sin for him lest He vex upon His servant - and He will forgive him his former sin. 34 If he didn't return towards his former sin and if he did this - this is perfect repentance - Adam didn't forget to think of his Creator nor to implore his Creator GOD in repentance. 35 And you - plead in repentance towards your Creator GOD - and don't wrong them because they were flesh and blood - for GOD Who Created them knows their weakness - and don't wrong the people He Created by His Authority. 36 And after their soul were separated from their flesh - their flesh shall be dust until the day that GOD loves.

3 Meq. 5

1 Know GOD Who Created you - as GOD has Created you in His Image and His Likeness when you are Earth - don't forget GOD Who established you up and saved you and Whom 'Israel' glorified - He placed you in a Garden that you might be Merry and might dig Earth. 2 When you demolished His Command - He sent you away from the Garden towards this world that He cursed because of you - that grows nettles and thorns. 3 For you are Earth - and for she is Earth - for you are dust - and for she is dust - for you are Soil - and for she is Soil - for you are fed the grain found from her - and for you will return towards her - for you will be Soil until He loves that He might raise you - and for He shall examine you the sin you worked and all the iniquity. 4 Know what you will answer Him at that time - think of the good and evil you worked in this world - examine whether the evil would abound or whether the good would abound - try. 5 If you work a goodly thing - it is a goodly thing for you that you might be Merry on the day when people who dead will arise. 6 But if you work evil Work - woe for you - for you will receive your hardship like your hands' Work and like your reasoning's evil - for if you work an evil thing upon your companion and if you didn't fear GOD - you will receive your hardship. 7 And if you betray your companion and if you call GOD's Name and swear in a lie - as you will receive your hardship like your Work - woe for you. 8 And you tell your false thing to your companion simulating Truth - but you know that you spoke a lie. 9 And you persuade the people with you your false thing simulating Truth - and you multiply false things that weren't Truth - and you will receive your hardship like your sin - you deny your companion while you tell your companion 'I will give you' what you won't give him. 10 And on the time you said 'I will give' in your pure reasoning - demons make application for you like dogs - and they make you forget all - and if you withhold or if you love that you might give - they don't know the person for whom they gather - yet as He has said - They shall fatten - this world's money tempts you that you might fatten the money that won't benefit you and that you won't eat. 11 And again - as He has said - 'Adam's liar children

make a balance false - as for them - they go from robbery to robbery - this world's money tempts you. ¹² O people - don't make hope in distorting scales and balances - and in stealing a person's money - and in making a person's money one in downgression - and in infringing your companions' money - and in stealing his field - in all the lies you do for your own profit that aren't for your companions. ¹³ If you do this you will receive your hardship like your Work. ¹⁴ O people - be fed by your hands' Work that were straight - yet don't desire robbery - don't love that you might totally rob and eat a person's money without justice by what isn't due. ¹⁵ And if you eat it - it won't satisfy you - on the time you die you will leave it for another - yet even if you fatten - it won't benefit you. ¹⁶ And if your money abounds - don't distort your reasonings - as sinner people's money are like the smoke that proceeds from a griddle and the wind takes it - better than sinner people's money are the little money they accumulated in Truth.

3 Meq. 6

¹ Think of the day when you will die - on the time your souls were separated from your flesh - and on the time you leave your money for another - and on the time you go on the path you don't know - think of the tribulation that shall come upon you. ² And the demons that will receive you are evil - and their features are ugly - and they are frightening in their splendor - and they won't hear your words - and you won't hear their words. ³ And because you didn't do your Creator GOD's Accord - they won't hear you in your plea on the time you begged them - because of this thing they will totally frighten you. ⁴ But people who fulfilled GOD's Accord have no fear - for demons fear them. But demons shall ridicule sinner people's souls upon them. ⁵ But kind people's souls shall be Merry upon Angels in Righteousness - for they shall totally make them Merry because they scorned this world - but angels who are evil shall receive sinner people's souls. ⁶ Pardon Angels shall receive kind people and righteous ones' souls - for they are sent from GOD that they might calm righteous ones ' souls - as Angels that were evil are sent from the Devil that they might ridicule upon sinner people's souls - demons shall receive sinner people's souls. ⁷ Sinner people - woe for you - weep for yourselves before the day when you die arrives upon you - on the time you reach towards GOD... ⁸ enter repentance in your era that is there before your era passes - that you might live in Merriness and Righteousness without tribulation nor disease - yet as after you die your era won't return that passed - weep. ⁹ Lest it be upon you towards a vain accord that distances from GOD - in your firm criticism make loving to be lavished and food and Righteousness not be found in you - as a body that is sated without measure won't think of GOD's Name - the Devil's wealth shall lodge upon it - yet as the Holy Spirit won't lodge in it - make loving the Righteousness not be found in you. ¹⁰ Like Moses spoke - Moses having said - "Jacob ate and was sated and fattened and tall and wide - and GOD Who Created him was separated from him. ¹¹ And his lifestyle distanced from GOD" - as a body that is sated without measure nor moderation won't think of GOD's Name - make loving Righteousness not be found alongside you - as belly satiety without measure is being like a boar and like a wandering horse - make drinking and eating without measure and adultery not be found in you. ¹² But a person who eats in measure shall live firmed up in GOD's Support - and he shall live firmed up like the horizon and like a tower that has a stone fence; a person who forgot GOD's LAW shall flee without one living who chases him. ¹³ A kind person shall live in being respected like a lion. ¹⁴ But people who don't love GOD won't keep His LAW - and their reasonings aren't straight. ¹⁵ And GOD shall bring sadness and alarm upon them when they are in this world - and being seized in trembling and fright

- and being seized in the tribulations without number by their money being snatched - being bound by their hands in chains from their masters' hands... ¹⁶ lest they be who rested from the tribulation - and lest their lifestyle be in Righteousness - lest they rest when they are in alarming tribulations that are upon each of their own selves - He shall bring sadness and alarm upon them.

3 Meq. 7

¹ But like David spoke saying - "I believed in GOD - I won't fear having said, 'What would a person make me?'" - there is no fright and alarm upon people who believed in GOD. ² And again like he spoke saying - "If warriors surround me - I believed in Him - I begged GOD one thing - I seek that" - people who believed in Him have no fright upon them - a person who believed in Him shall live in Life forever - and he won't fear arising from an evil thing. ³ Who is a person who shamed believing in GOD? how about who ignored Him for a desire? ⁴ As He has said - I love him who loved Me - and I shall honor him who glorified Me - I shall keep him who returned towards Me in repentance - who is a person who shamed believing in Him? ⁵ Judge Truth and save the widow's body - save them that GOD might save you from all that oppose you in an evil thing - keep them - as kind people's children are honored - they are given making a profit - and yet He shall save your children after you - for they won't be troubled for grain.

3 Meq. 8

¹ Job believed in GOD - as he didn't neglect to praise his Creator GOD - GOD saved him from all the tribulation that the enemy of Adam's children, the Devil, brought upon him - he said, "GOD gave - GOD withheld - it happened as GOD loved upon me - and let GOD's Name be praised by all upon Earth and in Heaven" - yet as he didn't sadden his reasoning - GOD saved him. ² And on the time GOD saw that Job's heart was cleansed from sin - He received him in much honor. ³ And He gave him money that abounded more than his money that preceded - for he has totally endured his tribulation - and He cured him from his wounds because of him enduring all the tribulation that arrived upon him. ⁴ And if you like him endure the tribulation arising from demons sent towards you - you will be admired. ⁵ Endure the tribulation - that GOD might be for you a fortress Refuge from people who hate you - and that He might be a fortress Refuge for your children's children and for your children after you - don't sadden your reasonings arising from the tribulation that came upon you - believe in Him - and He shall be a fortress Refuge for you. ⁶ Beg Him - He will hear you - make hope - and He will forgive you - beg Him - and He will be a Father for you; ⁷ Think of Mordecai and Esther - Judith and Gideon and Deborah and Barak and Jephthah and Samson... ⁸ and other people like them who were disciplined for believing in GOD and whose enemies didn't defeat them. ⁹ For GOD is True - and for He doesn't favor having seen a face - but people received hardship who love that they might work sin upon themselves - all people who fear Him and keep His LAW shall keep bodies - and He shall give them being loved and honor. ¹⁰ He shall make them Merry in their proceeding and their entering - in their Life and their death - and in their rising and sitting - For He saves - and He secludes. ¹¹ For He saddens - and He pardons. ¹² For He makes poor - and He honors - He makes wretched - and as He honors - He makes them Merry.

3 Meq. 9

¹ And whether it be what is in Heaven - or whether it be what is upon Earth - be it either subtle or stout - everything and all His money live being firmed up in His Order. ² There is nothing that departed from GOD's LAW and His Order - Who Created all the world - be it a vulture's track that flies in Heaven - He commands towards its destination where He loved. ³ And He commands an

Earth snake's path that lives in a cave towards where He loved - and a boat's path that goes upon the sea - apart from only GOD there is none who knows its path. 4 And apart from only GOD - there is none who knows the path where a soul goes on the time it was separated from its flesh - be it a righteous or a sinner soul. 5 Who knows where it will turn - that it would turn into wilderness or on a mountain? or that it would fly like a bird - that it would be like Heaven's dew that alights on a mountain... 6 or that it would be like deep wind - or that it would be like lightning that straightens up its path... 7 or that it would be like stars that shine amidst the deep - or that it would be like sand on a sea shore that are piled amidst the deep... 8 or that it would be like a horizon stone that firmed up on the sea's deep edge - or like a tree that gives its beautiful fruit that grew by a Water spout... 9 or that it would be that I likened unto the reed that the heat of the Sun burnt - and that wind lift and took towards another place where it didn't grow - and whose trace isn't found... 10 or that it would be like unto misty urine whose trace isn't found - who knows GOD's Work? who are His counselors? how about with whom did He counsel? 11 As GOD's Thoughts are hidden from people - who will examine and know His Work? 12 As He has Created Earth upon Water - and as He has firmed her up without stakes - there is none who examines and knows GOD's Counsel or His Wisdom - and He Created Heaven in His perfect Wisdom and firmed it up in winds - and He stretched forth a lofty cosmos like a tent. 13 He commanded clouds that they might rain rain upon Earth - and He grows grass - and He grows fruits without number to be food for people - that we might believe in GOD and be Merry in Unity. 14 GOD is Who gives Adam's children the Merriness and all the fatness and all the satiety - GOD is Who gives that they might satisfy and praise GOD Who gave them fruit from Earth... 15 and Who dressed them in beautiful robes - Who gave them all the loved plenty - the Merriness and the Righteousness that are given for people who fulfill GOD's Accord. 16 He gives being loved and honor in the house He prepared and in the Kingdom of Heaven for their fathers who keep GOD's LAW. 17 He gives being loved and honor in the place He prepared and in the Kingdom of Heaven for their fathers who lived firmed up in His Worship and His LAW - and who didn't depart from His LAW - whom He famed and raised that they might keep His Order and His LAW - and I have seen what GOD does for His friends in this world by weakening their enemies and by keeping their bodies. 18 I have seen that He gives them all they begged Him and that He fulfills their accord for them - don't depart from GOD - and fulfill GOD's Accord. 19 Don't depart from His Command and His LAW - lest He vex upon you and lest He destroy you at one time - and lest He vex and whip you in the tribulation from where you lived formerly - lest you depart from your fathers' Order where you were formerly - and lest your lodging be in Hell where are no exits until Eternity. 20 Keep your Creator GOD's LAW when your soul is separated from your flesh that He might do goodly Work for you on the time you stood before GOD. 21 For Earth and Heaven's Kingdoms are for Him - and for Kingdom and capability are for Him - and for being nice and pardoning are only for Him. 22 As He makes rich and He makes poor - as He makes wretched and as He honors - keep GOD's LAW. 23 And David spoke because of Him while he said - "Man seems vain - and his era passes like a shadow." 24 He spoke because of Him saying - "But Lord - You live forever - and Your Name Invocation is for a child's children." 25 And again he said - "Your Kingdom is all the world's Kingdom - and Your Rulership is for a child's children" - You returned a kingdom for David bringing from Saul. 26 But there is none who will appoint You - there is none who can dismiss - You see all - yet there is none who can see You. 27 And Your kingdom won't perish forever for a child's children - there is none who will rule Him - but He rules all - He sees all - but there is none who sees Him. 28 As He has Created man in His Image and in His likeness that they might praise Him and might know His Worship in straight reasoning without doubt - He examines and knows what kidneys smoked up and what a reasoning transported. 29 Yet they bow to stone - for wood - and for silver and gold that a person's hand worked. 30 And they sacrifice sacrifice for them up until their sacrifice smoke proceeds towards Heaven - that their sin might live firmed up before GOD - but yet they refused to worship GOD Who Created them - He shall accuse them because of all their sin that they worked in worshiping their idols. 31 They learned bowing to idols and all stained Work that isn't due - naysaying by stars - sorcery - worshiping idols - evil accord - and all the Work that GOD doesn't love - yet they didn't keep GOD's Command that they learned. 32 As they didn't love to worship GOD that they might save their bodies from sin and iniquity by His servants the Angels and by money that they praise before GOD - they work all this in lacking goodly Work. 33 And on the time they all arose together from the graves where they were buried and where their bodies perished - their souls shall stand empty before GOD - and their souls lived in the Kingdom of Heaven prepared for kind people. 34 But sinner people's souls shall live in Hell - and on the time graves were opened - people who dead shall arise - and souls shall return towards the flesh that they were separated formerly. 35 Like they were birthed in their nakedness from their mother's belly - they shall stand in their nakedness before GOD - and their sins that they worked Beginning from their infancy until that time shall be revealed. 36 They shall receive their sin's hardship upon their bodies - and whether their little or much sin - they shall receive their hardship like their sin.

3 Meq. 10

1 For the blood of the soul found from GOD shall lodge in them like it lodged in them formerly - and if you didn't believe people who dead arising - hear that Creations shall arise in the rainy season without being birthed from their mother nor father. 2 And He commanded them formerly by His Word that they died. 3 And their flesh being demolished and rotten and again renewed - they shall arise like He loved. 4 And again on the time rain alighted and on the time it sated Earth - they shall live having arisen like they were Created formerly. 5 As those who are everliving in a bloody soul and who live in this world and those whom Water produced have been Created - He having said Make them be Created - and as GOD's Authority lodges on the Water - she gives them a bloody soul by His Authority and by His Word. 6 As they are Created by His Authority and by His Word without a father nor mother - you blind of reasoning who say "People who dead won't arise" - if you have knowledge or Wisdom - how will you say people who dead won't arise by their Creator GOD's Word? 7 As people who dead - who were ashes and dust in a grave - shall arise by GOD's Word - as for you - enter repentance and return to your religion. 8 Like His Word spoke formerly - they shall arise by the Pardon Dew found from GOD - and that Word shall turn all the world and arouse the people who dead like He loved. 9 And know that you will arise and stand before Him - and make it not seem to you in your reasoning dullness that you will remain in a grave. 10 It isn't thus - you will arise and receive your hardship like the Work's measure that you worked - whether it be goodly or evil - yet make it not seem to you that you will remain - for this Day is the day when they will receive hardship. 11 And in Resurrection time you will receive your hardship by all your sin that you worked - you will finish your sin's hardship that was written Beginning from your infancy until that time - and

you have no reason that you will pretext upon your sin like this world's Work that you might deny your sin. [12] Like you make your false word truth before you - and like you make the lie's thing that you spoke truth - you have no reason that you will pretext like this world's Work. [13] Because it was that she knows upon you all your evil Work you worked - and because it was that she will reveal upon you before her Creator GOD - as GOD's Word shall lodge upon you and speak upon you - you have no reason upon what you pretext. [14] You will shame there because of your sin that you worked - it is that you might be thanked with people who are thanked upon their beautiful Work - yet lest you shame before man and Angels on the day when Judgment is judged - quickly enter repentance in this world before you arrive towards there. [15] People who praise GOD with Angels shall receive their reward from their Creator without shaming - and they shall be Merry in the Kingdom of Heaven - however unless you worked goodly Work when you are in your flesh in Life - you have no fortune with righteous ones. [16] As you weren't prepared when you have knowledge and when you have this world where you enter repentance - there shall be a useless regret upon you - and for you didn't give a morsel for the hungry when you have money. [17] And for you didn't clothe the naked when you have clothes - and for you didn't save the wronged when you have Authority. [18] For you didn't teach the sinner person when you have knowledge - that he might return and enter repentance - and that GOD might forgive him his sin that he formerly worked in ignorance - and for you didn't fight with demons who quarrel with you when you have Power that you able to prevail. [19] And for you didn't fast nor pray when you have firmness that you might weaken your infancy Power that is upon flesh - and that you might subject yourself for Rightness that isn't favoring upon flesh... [20] that isn't favoring Righteousness when it is in this world in beautiful drink and sweet food - and that isn't adorning in thin clothes and silver and gold... [21] and as you didn't fast nor pray when you have firmness that you might subject yourself for Rightness that isn't adorning in honored Indian jewels called emerald and phazyon - there shall be a useless regret upon you - this isn't a person's ornament that is due. [22] As for a person's ornament - it is purity - Wisdom - knowledge - loving one another by what is due without envying nor jealousy nor doubting nor quarrels - while you loved your companion like yourself... [23] and without you doing an evil thing upon a person who did an evil thing upon you - it is loving one another by what is due - that you might enter towards the Kingdom of Heaven that is given for a person who endured the tribulation - that He might give you the honored Kingdom of Heaven and your reward upon making hope in the Kingdom of Heaven in Resurrection time with honored people in knowledge and Wisdom. [24] And don't say "After we die we won't arise" - for the Devil cuts off hope of people who speak and think this lest they be saved in Resurrection time - they will know that they have hardship upon them on the time Advent arrived upon them - in Resurrection time people will be totally sad who worked sin in not knowing that He might think of their sin upon them - for they didn't believe in Him that they will arise on that Day. [25] Because of this thing they shall be reproached like their Work's evil measure that they worked in this world - and they shall see the Resurrection that they denied whereby they will arise together in flesh. [26] They shall weep at that time because they didn't work goodly Work - it would have been better for them if they wept in this world if it is possible for them lest they be who weep in Hell. [27] If we didn't weep in this world by our accord - demons will make us weep without our accord in Hell - if we didn't enter repentance in this world - we prepare worthless and useless cries and mourning in Hell. [28] Prepare goodly Work -

that you might cross from death to Life - and that you might go from this passing world to the Kingdom of Heaven - and that you might see the Kingdom of Heaven's Light that surpasses light in this world. [29] Refuse Righteousness that is in this world - that you might be Merry without measure in the Kingdom of Heaven in Righteousness that isn't fulfilled Beginning from today until Eternity with people who believe people who dead arising.

Ezra (I Ezra)

1Ezra. 1

[1] Now in the first year of Cyrus king of Persia, that the word of the LORD by the mouth of Jeremiah might be fulfilled, the LORD stirred up the spirit of Cyrus king of Persia, that he made a proclamation throughout all his kingdom, and put it also in writing, saying, [2] Thus saith Cyrus king of Persia, The LORD God of heaven hath given me all the kingdoms of the earth; and he hath charged me to build him an house at Jerusalem, which is in Judah. [3] Who is there among you of all his people? his God be with him, and let him go up to Jerusalem, which is in Judah, and build the house of the LORD God of Israel, (he is the God,) which is in Jerusalem. [4] And whosoever remaineth in any place where he sojourneth, let the men of his place help him with silver, and with gold, and with goods, and with beasts, beside the freewill offering for the house of God that is in Jerusalem. [5] Then rose up the chief of the fathers of Judah and Benjamin, and the priests, and the Levites, with all them whose spirit God had raised, to go up to build the house of the LORD which is in Jerusalem. [6] And all they that were about them strengthened their hands with vessels of silver, with gold, with goods, and with beasts, and with precious things, beside all that was willingly offered. [7] Also Cyrus the king brought forth the vessels of the house of the LORD, which Nebuchadnezzar had brought forth out of Jerusalem, and had put them in the house of his gods; [8] Even those did Cyrus king of Persia bring forth by the hand of Mithredath the treasurer, and numbered them unto Sheshbazzar, the prince of Judah. [9] And this is the number of them: thirty chargers of gold, a thousand chargers of silver, nine and twenty knives, [10] Thirty basons of gold, silver basons of a second sort four hundred and ten, and other vessels a thousand. [11] All the vessels of gold and of silver were five thousand and four hundred. All these did Sheshbazzar bring up with them of the captivity that were brought up from Babylon unto Jerusalem.

1Ezra. 2

[1] Now these are the children of the province that went up out of the captivity, of those which had been carried away, whom Nebuchadnezzar the king of Babylon had carried away unto Babylon, and came again unto Jerusalem and Judah, every one unto his city; [2] Which came with Zerubbabel: Jeshua, Nehemiah, Seraiah, Reelaiah, Mordecai, Bilshan, Mispar, Bigvai, Rehum, Baanah. The number of the men of the people of Israel: [3] The children of Parosh, two thousand an hundred seventy and two. [4] The children of Shephatiah, three hundred seventy and two. [5] The children of Arah, seven hundred seventy and five. [6] The children of Pahath-moab, of the children of Jeshua and Joab, two thousand eight hundred and twelve. [7] The children of Elam, a thousand two hundred fifty and four. [8] The children of Zattu, nine hundred forty and five. [9] The children of Zaccai, seven hundred and threescore. [10] The children of Bani, six hundred forty and two. [11] The children of Bebai, six hundred twenty and three. [12] The children of Azgad, a thousand two hundred twenty and two. [13] The children of Adonikam, six hundred sixty and six. [14] The children of Bigvai, two thousand fifty and six. [15] The children of Adin, four hundred fifty and four. [16] The children of Ater of Hezekiah, ninety and eight. [17] The children of Bezai, three hundred twenty and three. [18] The children of Jorah, an

hundred and twelve.[19] The children of Hashum, two hundred twenty and three.[20] The children of Gibbar, ninety and five.[21] The children of Bethlehem, an hundred twenty and three.[22] The men of Netophah, fifty and six.[23] The men of Anathoth, an hundred twenty and eight.[24] The children of Azmaveth, forty and two.[25] The children of Kirjath-arim, Chephirah, and Beeroth, seven hundred and forty and three.[26] The children of Ramah and Geba, six hundred twenty and one.[27] The men of Michmas, an hundred twenty and two.[28] The men of Bethel and Ai, two hundred twenty and three.[29] The children of Nebo, fifty and two.[30] The children of Magbish, an hundred fifty and six.[31] The children of the other Elam, a thousand two hundred fifty and four.[32] The children of Harim, three hundred and twenty.[33] The children of Lod, Hadid, and Ono, seven hundred twenty and five.[34] The children of Jericho, three hundred forty and five.[35] The children of Senaah, three thousand and six hundred and thirty.[36] The priests: the children of Jedaiah, of the house of Jeshua, nine hundred seventy and three.[37] The children of Immer, a thousand fifty and two.[38] The children of Pashur, a thousand two hundred forty and seven.[39] The children of Harim, a thousand and seventeen.[40] The Levites: the children of Jeshua and Kadmiel, of the children of Hodaviah, seventy and four.[41] The singers: the children of Asaph, an hundred twenty and eight.[42] The children of the porters: the children of Shallum, the children of Ater, the children of Talmon, the children of Akkub, the children of Hatita, the children of Shobai, in all an hundred thirty and nine.[43] The Nethinims: the children of Ziha, the children of Hasupha, the children of Tabbaoth,[44] The children of Keros, the children of Siaha, the children of Padon,[45] The children of Lebanah, the children of Hagabah, the children of Akkub,[46] The children of Hagab, the children of Shalmai, the children of Hanan,[47] The children of Giddel, the children of Gahar, the children of Reaiah,[48] The children of Rezin, the children of Nekoda, the children of Gazzam,[49] The children of Uzza, the children of Paseah, the children of Besai,[50] The children of Asnah, the children of Mehunim, the children of Nephusim,[51] The children of Bakbuk, the children of Hakupha, the children of Harhur,[52] The children of Bazluth, the children of Mehida, the children of Harsha,[53] The children of Barkos, the children of Sisera, the children of Thamah,[54] The children of Neziah, the children of Hatipha.[55] The children of Solomon's servants: the children of Sotai, the children of Sophereth, the children of Peruda,[56] The children of Jaalah, the children of Darkon, the children of Giddel,[57] The children of Shephatiah, the children of Hattil, the children of Pochereth of Zebaim, the children of Ami.[58] All the Nethinims, and the children of Solomon's servants, were three hundred ninety and two.[59] And these were they which went up from Tel-melah, Tel-harsa, Cherub, Addan, and Immer: but they could not shew their father's house, and their seed, whether they were of Israel:[60] The children of Delaiah, the children of Tobiah, the children of Nekoda, six hundred fifty and two.[61] And of the children of the priests: the children of Habaiah, the children of Koz, the children of Barzillai; which took a wife of the daughters of Barzillai the Gileadite, and was called after their name:[62] These sought their register among those that were reckoned by genealogy, but they were not found: therefore were they, as polluted, put from the priesthood.[63] And the Tirshatha said unto them, that they should not eat of the most holy things, till there stood up a priest with Urim and with Thummim.[64] The whole congregation together was forty and two thousand three hundred and threescore,[65] Beside their servants and their maids, of whom there were seven thousand three hundred thirty and seven: and there were among them two hundred singing men and singing women.[66] Their horses were seven hundred thirty and six; their

mules, two hundred forty and five;[67] Their camels, four hundred thirty and five; their asses, six thousand seven hundred and twenty.[68] And some of the chief of the fathers, when they came to the house of the LORD which is at Jerusalem, offered freely for the house of God to set it up in his place:[69] They gave after their ability unto the treasure of the work threescore and one thousand drams of gold, and five thousand pound of silver, and one hundred priests' garments.[70] So the priests, and the Levites, and some of the people, and the singers, and the porters, and the Nethinims, dwelt in their cities, and all Israel in their cities.

1Ezra. 3

[1] And when the seventh month was come, and the children of Israel were in the cities, the people gathered themselves together as one man to Jerusalem.[2] Then stood up Jeshua the son of Jozadak, and his brethren the priests, and Zerubbabel the son of Shealtiel, and his brethren, and builded the altar of the God of Israel, to offer burnt offerings thereon, as it is written in the law of Moses the man of God.[3] And they set the altar upon his bases; for fear was upon them because of the people of those countries: and they offered burnt offerings thereon unto the LORD, even burnt offerings morning and evening.[4] They kept also the feast of tabernacles, as it is written, and offered the daily burnt offerings by number, according to the custom, as the duty of every day required;[5] And afterward offered the continual burnt offering, both of the new moons, and of all the set feasts of the LORD that were consecrated, and of every one that willingly offered a freewill offering unto the LORD.[6] From the first day of the seventh month began they to offer burnt offerings unto the LORD. But the foundation of the temple of the LORD was not yet laid.[7] They gave money also unto the masons, and to the carpenters; and meat, and drink, and oil, unto them of Zidon, and to them of Tyre, to bring cedar trees from Lebanon to the sea of Joppa, according to the grant that they had of Cyrus king of Persia.[8] Now in the second year of their coming unto the house of God at Jerusalem, in the second month, began Zerubbabel the son of Shealtiel, and Jeshua the son of Jozadak, and the remnant of their brethren the priests and the Levites, and all they that were come out of the captivity unto Jerusalem; and appointed the Levites, from twenty years old and upward, to set forward the work of the house of the LORD.[9] Then stood Jeshua with his sons and his brethren, Kadmiel and his sons, the sons of Judah, together, to set forward the workmen in the house of God: the sons of Henadad, with their sons and their brethren the Levites.[10] And when the builders laid the foundation of the temple of the LORD, they set the priests in their apparel with trumpets, and the Levites the sons of Asaph with cymbals, to praise the LORD, after the ordinance of David king of Israel.[11] And they sang together by course in praising and giving thanks unto the LORD; because he is good, for his mercy endureth for ever toward Israel. And all the people shouted with a great shout, when they praised the LORD, because the foundation of the house of the LORD was laid.[12] But many of the priests and Levites and chief of the fathers, who were ancient men, that had seen the first house, when the foundation of this house was laid before their eyes, wept with a loud voice; and many shouted aloud for joy:[13] So that the people could not discern the noise of the shout of joy from the noise of the weeping of the people: for the people shouted with a loud shout, and the noise was heard afar off.

1Ezra. 4

[1] Now when the adversaries of Judah and Benjamin heard that the children of the captivity builded the temple unto the LORD God of Israel;[2] Then they came to Zerubbabel, and to the chief of the fathers, and said unto them, Let us build with you: for we seek your God, as ye do; and we do sacrifice unto him since the days of Esar-

haddon king of Assur, which brought us up hither.[3] But Zerubbabel, and Jeshua, and the rest of the chief of the fathers of Israel, said unto them, Ye have nothing to do with us to build an house unto our God; but we ourselves together will build unto the LORD God of Israel, as king Cyrus the king of Persia hath commanded us.[4] Then the people of the land weakened the hands of the people of Judah, and troubled them in building,[5] And hired counsellers against them, to frustrate their purpose, all the days of Cyrus king of Persia, even until the reign of Darius king of Persia.[6] And in the reign of Ahasuerus, in the beginning of his reign, wrote they unto him an accusation against the inhabitants of Judah and Jerusalem.[7] And in the days of Artaxerxes wrote Bishlam, Mithredath, Tabeel, and the rest of their companions, unto Artaxerxes king of Persia; and the writing of the letter was written in the Syrian tongue, and interpreted in the Syrian tongue.[8] Rehum the chancellor and Shimshai the scribe wrote a letter against Jerusalem to Artaxerxes the king in this sort:[9] Then wrote Rehum the chancellor, and Shimshai the scribe, and the rest of their companions; the Dinaites, the Apharsathchites, the Tarpelites, the Apharsites, the Archevites, the Babylonians, the Susanchites, the Dehavites, and the Elamites,[10] And the rest of the nations whom the great and noble Asnappar brought over, and set in the cities of Samaria, and the rest that are on this side the river, and at such a time.[11] This is the copy of the letter that they sent unto him, even unto Artaxerxes the king; Thy servants the men on this side the river, and at such a time.[12] Be it known unto the king, that the Jews which came up from thee to us are come unto Jerusalem, building the rebellious and the bad city, and have set up the walls thereof, and joined the foundations.[13] Be it known now unto the king, that, if this city be builded, and the walls set up again, then will they not pay toll, tribute, and custom, and so thou shalt endamage the revenue of the kings.[14] Now because we have maintenance from the king's palace, and it was not meet for us to see the king's dishonour, therefore have we sent and certified the king;[15] That search may be made in the book of the records of thy fathers: so shalt thou find in the book of the records, and know that this city is a rebellious city, and hurtful unto kings and provinces, and that they have moved sedition within the same of old time: for which cause was this city destroyed.[16] We certify the king that, if this city be builded again, and the walls thereof set up, by this means thou shalt have no portion on this side the river.[17] Then sent the king an answer unto Rehum the chancellor, and to Shimshai the scribe, and to the rest of their companions that dwell in Samaria, and unto the rest beyond the river, Peace, and at such a time.[18] The letter which ye sent unto us hath been plainly read before me.[19] And I commanded, and search hath been made, and it is found that this city of old time hath made insurrection against kings, and that rebellion and sedition have been made therein.[20] There have been mighty kings also over Jerusalem, which have ruled over all countries beyond the river; and toll, tribute, and custom, was paid unto them.[21] Give ye now commandment to cause these men to cease, and that this city be not builded, until another commandment shall be given from me.[22] Take heed now that ye fail not to do this: why should damage grow to the hurt of the kings?[23] Now when the copy of king Artaxerxes' letter was read before Rehum, and Shimshai the scribe, and their companions, they went up in haste to Jerusalem unto the Jews, and made them to cease by force and power.[24] Then ceased the work of the house of God which is at Jerusalem. So it ceased unto the second year of the reign of Darius king of Persia.

1Ezra. 5

[1] Then the prophets, Haggai the prophet, and Zechariah the son of Iddo, prophesied unto the Jews that were in Judah and Jerusalem in the name of the God of Israel, even unto them.[2] Then rose up Zerubbabel the son of Shealtiel, and Jeshua the son of Jozadak, and began to build the house of God which is at Jerusalem: and with them were the prophets of God helping them.[3] At the same time came to them Tatnai, governor on this side the river, and Shethar-boznai, and their companions, and said thus unto them, Who hath commanded you to build this house, and to make up this wall?[4] Then said we unto them after this manner, What are the names of the men that make this building?[5] But the eye of their God was upon the elders of the Jews, that they could not cause them to cease, till the matter came to Darius: and then they returned answer by letter concerning this matter.[6] The copy of the letter that Tatnai, governor on this side the river, and Shethar-boznai, and his companions the Apharsachites, which were on this side the river, sent unto Darius the king:[7] They sent a letter unto him, wherein was written thus; Unto Darius the king, all peace.[8] Be it known unto the king, that we went into the province of Judea, to the house of the great God, which is builded with great stones, and timber is laid in the walls, and this work goeth fast on, and prospereth in their hands.[9] Then asked we those elders, and said unto them thus, Who commanded you to build this house, and to make up these walls?[10] We asked their names also, to certify thee, that we might write the names of the men that were the chief of them.[11] And thus they returned us answer, saying, We are the servants of the God of heaven and earth, and build the house that was builded these many years ago, which a great king of Israel builded and set up.[12] But after that our fathers had provoked the God of heaven unto wrath, he gave them into the hand of Nebuchadnezzar the king of Babylon, the Chaldean, who destroyed this house, and carried the people away into Babylon.[13] But in the first year of Cyrus the king of Babylon the same king Cyrus made a decree to build this house of God.[14] And the vessels also of gold and silver of the house of God, which Nebuchadnezzar took out of the temple that was in Jerusalem, and brought them into the temple of Babylon, those did Cyrus the king take out of the temple of Babylon, and they were delivered unto one, whose name was Sheshbazzar, whom he had made governor;[15] And said unto him, Take these vessels, go, carry them into the temple that is in Jerusalem, and let the house of God be builded in his place.[16] Then came the same Sheshbazzar, and laid the foundation of the house of God which is in Jerusalem: and since that time even until now hath it been in building, and yet it is not finished.[17] Now therefore, if it seem good to the king, let there be search made in the king's treasure house, which is there at Babylon, whether it be so, that a decree was made of Cyrus the king to build this house of God at Jerusalem, and let the king send his pleasure to us concerning this matter.

1Ezra. 6

[1] Then Darius the king made a decree, and search was made in the house of the rolls, where the treasures were laid up in Babylon.[2] And there was found at Achmetha, in the palace that is in the province of the Medes, a roll, and therein was a record thus written:[3] In the first year of Cyrus the king the same Cyrus the king made a decree concerning the house of God at Jerusalem, Let the house be builded, the place where they offered sacrifices, and let the foundations thereof be strongly laid; the height thereof threescore cubits, and the breadth thereof threescore cubits;[4] With three rows of great stones, and a row of new timber: and let the expences be given out of the king's house:[5] And also let the golden and silver vessels of the house of God, which Nebuchadnezzar took forth out of the temple which is at Jerusalem, and brought unto Babylon, be restored, and brought again unto the temple which is at Jerusalem, every one to his place, and place them in the house of God.[6] Now therefore, Tatnai,

governor beyond the river, Shethar-boznai, and your companions the Apharsachites, which are beyond the river, be ye far from thence:[7] Let the work of this house of God alone; let the governor of the Jews and the elders of the Jews build this house of God in his place.[8] Moreover I made a decree what ye shall do to the elders of these Jews for the building of this house of God: that of the king's goods, even of the tribute beyond the river, forthwith expences be given unto these men, that they be not hindered.[9] And that which they have need of, both young bullocks, and rams, and lambs, for the burnt offerings of the God of heaven, wheat, salt, wine, and oil, according to the appointment of the priests which are at Jerusalem, let it be given them day by day without fail:[10] That they may offer sacrifices of sweet savours unto the God of heaven, and pray for the life of the king, and of his sons.[11] Also I have made a decree, that whosoever shall alter this word, let timber be pulled down from his house, and being set up, let him be hanged thereon; and let his house be made a dunghill for this.[12] And the God that hath caused his name to dwell there destroy all kings and people, that shall put to their hand to alter and to destroy this house of God which is at Jerusalem. I Darius have made a decree; let it be done with speed.[13] Then Tatnai, governor on this side the river, Shethar-boznai, and their companions, according to that which Darius the king had sent, so they did speedily.[14] And the elders of the Jews builded, and they prospered through the prophesying of Haggai the prophet and Zechariah the son of Iddo. And they builded, and finished it, according to the commandment of the God of Israel, and according to the commandment of Cyrus, and Darius, and Artaxerxes king of Persia.[15] And this house was finished on the third day of the month Adar, which was in the sixth year of the reign of Darius the king.[16] And the children of Israel, the priests, and the Levites, and the rest of the children of the captivity, kept the dedication of this house of God with joy,[17] And offered at the dedication of this house of God an hundred bullocks, two hundred rams, four hundred lambs; and for a sin offering for all Israel, twelve he goats, according to the number of the tribes of Israel.[18] And they set the priests in their divisions, and the Levites in their courses, for the service of God, which is at Jerusalem; as it is written in the book of Moses.[19] And the children of the captivity kept the passover upon the fourteenth day of the first month.[20] For the priests and the Levites were purified together, all of them were pure, and killed the passover for all the children of the captivity, and for their brethren the priests, and for themselves.[21] And the children of Israel, which were come again out of captivity, and all such as had separated themselves unto them from the filthiness of the heathen of the land, to seek the LORD God of Israel, did eat,[22] And kept the feast of unleavened bread seven days with joy: for the LORD had made them joyful, and turned the heart of the king of Assyria unto them, to strengthen their hands in the work of the house of God, the God of Israel.

1Ezra. 7

[1] Now after these things, in the reign of Artaxerxes king of Persia, Ezra the son of Seraiah, the son of Azariah, the son of Hilkiah,[2] The son of Shallum, the son of Zadok, the son of Ahitub,[3] The son of Amariah, the son of Azariah, the son of Meraioth,[4] The son of Zerahiah, the son of Uzzi, the son of Bukki,[5] The son of Abishua, the son of Phinehas, the son of Eleazar, the son of Aaron the chief priest:[6] This Ezra went up from Babylon; and he was a ready scribe in the law of Moses, which the LORD God of Israel had given: and the king granted him all his request, according to the hand of the LORD his God upon him.[7] And there went up some of the children of Israel, and of the priests, and the Levites, and the singers, and the porters, and the Nethinims, unto Jerusalem, in the seventh year of Artaxerxes the king.[8] And he came to Jerusalem in the fifth month, which was in the seventh year of the king.[9] For upon the first day of the first month began he to go up from Babylon, and on the first day of the fifth month came he to Jerusalem, according to the good hand of his God upon him.[10] For Ezra had prepared his heart to seek the law of the LORD, and to do it, and to teach in Israel statutes and judgments.[11] Now this is the copy of the letter that the king Artaxerxes gave unto Ezra the priest, the scribe, even a scribe of the words of the commandments of the LORD, and of his statutes to Israel.[12] Artaxerxes, king of kings, unto Ezra the priest, a scribe of the law of the God of heaven, perfect peace, and at such a time.[13] I make a decree, that all they of the people of Israel, and of his priests and Levites, in my realm, which are minded of their own freewill to go up to Jerusalem, go with thee.[14] Forasmuch as thou art sent of the king, and of his seven counsellers, to inquire concerning Judah and Jerusalem, according to the law of thy God which is in thine hand;[15] And to carry the silver and gold, which the king and his counsellers have freely offered unto the God of Israel, whose habitation is in Jerusalem,[16] And all the silver and gold that thou canst find in all the province of Babylon, with the freewill offering of the people, and of the priests, offering willingly for the house of their God which is in Jerusalem:[17] That thou mayest buy speedily with this money bullocks, rams, lambs, with their meat offerings and their drink offerings, and offer them upon the altar of the house of your God which is in Jerusalem.[18] And whatsoever shall seem good to thee, and to thy brethren, to do with the rest of the silver and the gold, that do after the will of your God.[19] The vessels also that are given thee for the service of the house of thy God, those deliver thou before the God of Jerusalem.[20] And whatsoever more shall be needful for the house of thy God, which thou shalt have occasion to bestow, bestow it out of the king's treasure house.[21] And I, even I Artaxerxes the king, do make a decree to all the treasurers which are beyond the river, that whatsoever Ezra the priest, the scribe of the law of the God of heaven, shall require of you, it be done speedily,[22] Unto an hundred talents of silver, and to an hundred measures of wheat, and to an hundred baths of wine, and to an hundred baths of oil, and salt without prescribing how much.[23] Whatsoever is commanded by the God of heaven, let it be diligently done for the house of the God of heaven: for why should there be wrath against the realm of the king and his sons?[24] Also we certify you, that touching any of the priests and Levites, singers, porters, Nethinims, or ministers of this house of God, it shall not be lawful to impose toll, tribute, or custom, upon them.[25] And thou, Ezra, after the wisdom of thy God, that is in thine hand, set magistrates and judges, which may judge all the people that are beyond the river, all such as know the laws of thy God; and teach ye them that know them not.[26] And whosoever will not do the law of thy God, and the law of the king, let judgment be executed speedily upon him, whether it be unto death, or to banishment, or to confiscation of goods, or to imprisonment.[27] Blessed be the LORD God of our fathers, which hath put such a thing as this in the king's heart, to beautify the house of the LORD which is in Jerusalem:[28] And hath extended mercy unto me before the king, and his counsellers, and before all the king's mighty princes. And I was strengthened as the hand of the LORD my God was upon me, and I gathered together out of Israel chief men to go up with me.

1Ezra. 8

[1] These are now the chief of their fathers, and this is the genealogy of them that went up with me from Babylon, in the reign of Artaxerxes the king.[2] Of the sons of Phinehas; Gershom: of the sons of Ithamar; Daniel: of the sons of David; Hattush.[3] Of the sons of Shechaniah, of the sons of Pharosh; Zechariah: and with him were

reckoned by genealogy of the males an hundred and fifty.[4] Of the sons of Pahath-moab; Elihoenai the son of Zerahiah, and with him two hundred males.[5] Of the sons of Shechaniah; the son of Jahaziel, and with him three hundred males.[6] Of the sons also of Adin; Ebed the son of Jonathan, and with him fifty males.[7] And of the sons of Elam; Jeshaiah the son of Athaliah, and with him seventy males.[8] And of the sons of Shephatiah; Zebadiah the son of Michael, and with him fourscore males.[9] Of the sons of Joab; Obadiah the son of Jehiel, and with him two hundred and eighteen males.[10] And of the sons of Shelomith; the son of Josiphiah, and with him an hundred and threescore males.[11] And of the sons of Bebai; Zechariah the son of Bebai, and with him twenty and eight males.[12] And of the sons of Azgad; Johanan the son of Hakkatan, and with him an hundred and ten males.[13] And of the last sons of Adonikam, whose names are these, Eliphelet, Jeiel, and Shemaiah, and with them threescore males.[14] Of the sons also of Bigvai; Uthai, and Zabbud, and with them seventy males.[15] And I gathered them together to the river that runneth to Ahava; and there abode we in tents three days: and I viewed the people, and the priests, and found there none of the sons of Levi.[16] Then sent I for Eliezer, for Ariel, for Shemaiah, and for Elnathan, and for Jarib, and for Elnathan, and for Nathan, and for Zechariah, and for Meshullam, chief men; also for Joiarib, and for Elnathan, men of understanding.[17] And I sent them with commandment unto Iddo the chief at the place Casiphia, and I told them what they should say unto Iddo, and to his brethren the Nethinims, at the place Casiphia, that they should bring unto us ministers for the house of our God.[18] And by the good hand of our God upon us they brought us a man of understanding, of the sons of Mahli, the son of Levi, the son of Israel; and Sherebiah, with his sons and his brethren, eighteen;[19] And Hashabiah, and with him Jeshaiah of the sons of Merari, his brethren and their sons, twenty;[20] Also of the Nethinims, whom David and the princes had appointed for the service of the Levites, two hundred and twenty Nethinims: all of them were expressed by name.[21] Then I proclaimed a fast there, at the river of Ahava, that we might afflict ourselves before our God, to seek of him a right way for us, and for our little ones, and for all our substance.[22] For I was ashamed to require of the king a band of soldiers and horsemen to help us against the enemy in the way: because we had spoken unto the king, saying, The hand of our God is upon all them for good that seek him; but his power and his wrath is against all them that forsake him.[23] So we fasted and besought our God for this: and he was intreated of us.[24] Then I separated twelve of the chief of the priests, Sherebiah, Hashabiah, and ten of their brethren with them,[25] And weighed unto them the silver, and the gold, and the vessels, even the offering of the house of our God, which the king, and his counsellers, and his lords, and all Israel there present, had offered:[26] I even weighed unto their hand six hundred and fifty talents of silver, and silver vessels an hundred talents, and of gold an hundred talents;[27] Also twenty basons of gold, of a thousand drams; and two vessels of fine copper, precious as gold.[28] And I said unto them, Ye are holy unto the LORD; the vessels are holy also; and the silver and the gold are a freewill offering unto the LORD God of your fathers.[29] Watch ye, and keep them, until ye weigh them before the chief of the priests and the Levites, and chief of the fathers of Israel, at Jerusalem, in the chambers of the house of the LORD.[30] So took the priests and the Levites the weight of the silver, and the gold, and the vessels, to bring them to Jerusalem unto the house of our God.[31] Then we departed from the river of Ahava on the twelfth day of the first month, to go unto Jerusalem: and the hand of our God was upon us, and he delivered us from the hand of the enemy, and of such as lay in wait by the way.[32] And we came to Jerusalem,

and abode there three days.[33] Now on the fourth day was the silver and the gold and the vessels weighed in the house of our God by the hand of Meremoth the son of Uriah the priest; and with him was Eleazar the son of Phinehas; and with them was Jozabad the son of Jeshua, and Noadiah the son of Binnui, Levites;[34] By number and by weight of every one: and all the weight was written at that time.[35] Also the children of those that had been carried away, which were come out of the captivity, offered burnt offerings unto the God of Israel, twelve bullocks for all Israel, ninety and six rams, seventy and seven lambs, twelve he goats for a sin offering: all this was a burnt offering unto the LORD.[36] And they delivered the king's commissions unto the king's lieutenants, and to the governors on this side the river: and they furthered the people, and the house of God.

1Ezra. 9

[1] Now when these things were done, the princes came to me, saying, The people of Israel, and the priests, and the Levites, have not separated themselves from the people of the lands, doing according to their abominations, even of the Canaanites, the Hittites, the Perizzites, the Jebusites, the Ammonites, the Moabites, the Egyptians, and the Amorites.[2] For they have taken of their daughters for themselves, and for their sons: so that the holy seed have mingled themselves with the people of those lands: yea, the hand of the princes and rulers hath been chief in this trespass.[3] And when I heard this thing, I rent my garment and my mantle, and plucked off the hair of my head and of my beard, and sat down astonied.[4] Then were assembled unto me every one that trembled at the words of the God of Israel, because of the transgression of those that had been carried away; and I sat astonied until the evening sacrifice.[5] And at the evening sacrifice I arose up from my heaviness; and having rent my garment and my mantle, I fell upon my knees, and spread out my hands unto the LORD my God.[6] And said, O my God, I am ashamed and blush to lift up my face to thee, my God: for our iniquities are increased over our head, and our trespass is grown up unto the heavens.[7] Since the days of our fathers have we been in a great trespass unto this day; and for our iniquities have we, our kings, and our priests, been delivered into the hand of the kings of the lands, to the sword, to captivity, and to a spoil, and to confusion of face, as it is this day.[8] And now for a little space grace hath been shewed from the LORD our God, to leave us a remnant to escape, and to give us a nail in his holy place, that our God may lighten our eyes, and give us a little reviving in our bondage.[9] For we were bondmen; yet our God hath not forsaken us in our bondage, but hath extended mercy unto us in the sight of the kings of Persia, to give us a reviving, to set up the house of our God, and to repair the desolations thereof, and to give us a wall in Judah and in Jerusalem.[10] And now, O our God, what shall we say after this? for we have forsaken thy commandments,[11] Which thou hast commanded by thy servants the prophets, saying, The land, unto which ye go to possess it, is an unclean land with the filthiness of the people of the lands, with their abominations, which have filled it from one end to another with their uncleanness.[12] Now therefore give not your daughters unto their sons, neither take their daughters unto your sons, nor seek their peace or their wealth for ever: that ye may be strong, and eat the good of the land, and leave it for an inheritance to your children for ever.[13] And after all that is come upon us for our evil deeds, and for our great trespass, seeing that thou our God hast punished us less than our iniquities deserve, and hast given us such deliverance as this;[14] Should we again break thy commandments, and join in affinity with the people of these abominations? wouldest not thou be angry with us till thou hadst consumed us, so that there should be no remnant nor escaping?[15] O

LORD God of Israel, thou art righteous: for we remain yet escaped, as it is this day: behold, we are before thee in our trespasses: for we cannot stand before thee because of this.

1Ezra. 10

[1] Now when Ezra had prayed, and when he had confessed, weeping and casting himself down before the house of God, there assembled unto him out of Israel a very great congregation of men and women and children: for the people wept very sore. [2] And Shechaniah the son of Jehiel, one of the sons of Elam, answered and said unto Ezra, We have trespassed against our God, and have taken strange wives of the people of the land: yet now there is hope in Israel concerning this thing. [3] Now therefore let us make a covenant with our God to put away all the wives, and such as are born of them, according to the counsel of my lord, and of those that tremble at the commandment of our God; and let it be done according to the law. [4] Arise; for this matter belongeth unto thee: we also will be with thee: be of good courage, and do it. [5] Then arose Ezra, and made the chief priests, the Levites, and all Israel, to swear that they should do according to this word. And they sware. [6] Then Ezra rose up from before the house of God, and went into the chamber of Johanan the son of Eliashib: and when he came thither, he did eat no bread, nor drink water: for he mourned because of the transgression of them that had been carried away. [7] And they made proclamation throughout Judah and Jerusalem unto all the children of the captivity, that they should gather themselves together unto Jerusalem; [8] And that whosoever would not come within three days, according to the counsel of the princes and the elders, all his substance should be forfeited, and himself separated from the congregation of those that had been carried away. [9] Then all the men of Judah and Benjamin gathered themselves together unto Jerusalem within three days. It was the ninth month, on the twentieth day of the month; and all the people sat in the street of the house of God, trembling because of this matter, and for the great rain. [10] And Ezra the priest stood up, and said unto them, Ye have transgressed, and have taken strange wives, to increase the trespass of Israel. [11] Now therefore make confession unto the LORD God of your fathers, and do his pleasure: and separate yourselves from the people of the land, and from the strange wives. [12] Then all the congregation answered and said with a loud voice, As thou hast said, so must we do. [13] But the people are many, and it is a time of much rain, and we are not able to stand without, neither is this a work of one day or two: for we are many that have transgressed in this thing. [14] Let now our rulers of all the congregation stand, and let all them which have taken strange wives in our cities come at appointed times, and with them the elders of every city, and the judges thereof, until the fierce wrath of our God for this matter be turned from us. [15] Only Jonathan the son of Asahel and Jahaziah the son of Tikvah were employed about this matter: and Meshullam and Shabbethai the Levite helped them. [16] And the children of the captivity did so. And Ezra the priest, with certain chief of the fathers, after the house of their fathers, and all of them by their names, were separated, and sat down in the first day of the tenth month to examine the matter. [17] And they made an end with all the men that had taken strange wives by the first day of the first month. [18] And among the sons of the priests there were found that had taken strange wives: namely, of the sons of Jeshua the son of Jozadak, and his brethren; Maaseiah, and Eliezer, and Jarib, and Gedaliah. [19] And they gave their hands that they would put away their wives; and being guilty, they offered a ram of the flock for their trespass. [20] And of the sons of Immer; Hanani, and Zebadiah. [21] And of the sons of Harim; Maaseiah, and Elijah, and Shemaiah, and Jehiel, and Uzziah. [22] And of the sons of Pashur; Elioenai, Maaseiah, Ishmael, Nethaneel, Jozabad, and Elasah. [23] Also of the Levites; Jozabad, and Shimei, and Kelaiah, (the same is Kelita,) Pethahiah, Judah, and Eliezer. [24] Of the singers also; Eliashib: and of the porters; Shallum, and Telem, and Uri. [25] Moreover of Israel: of the sons of Parosh; Ramiah, and Jeziah, and Malchiah, and Miamin, and Eleazar, and Malchijah, and Benaiah. [26] And of the sons of Elam; Mattaniah, Zechariah, and Jehiel, and Abdi, and Jeremoth, and Eliah. [27] And of the sons of Zattu; Elioenai, Eliashib, Mattaniah, and Jeremoth, and Zabad, and Aziza. [28] Of the sons also of Bebai; Jehohanan, Hananiah, Zabbai, and Athlai. [29] And of the sons of Bani; Meshullam, Malluch, and Adaiah, Jashub, and Sheal, and Ramoth. [30] And of the sons of Pahath-moab; Adna, and Chelal, Benaiah, Maaseiah, Mattaniah, Bezaleel, and Binnui, and Manasseh. [31] And of the sons of Harim; Eliezer, Ishijah, Malchiah, Shemaiah, Shimeon, [32] Benjamin, Malluch, and Shemariah. [33] Of the sons of Hashum; Mattenai, Mattathah, Zabad, Eliphelet, Jeremai, Manasseh, and Shimei. [34] Of the sons of Bani; Maadai, Amram, and Uel, [35] Benaiah, Bedeiah, Chelluh, [36] Vaniah, Meremoth, Eliashib, [37] Mattaniah, Mattenai, and Jaasau, [38] And Bani, and Binnui, Shimei, [39] And Shelemiah, and Nathan, and Adaiah, [40] Machnadebai, Shashai, Sharai, [41] Azareel, and Shelemiah, Shemariah, [42] Shallum, Amariah, and Joseph. [43] Of the sons of Nebo; Jeiel, Mattithiah, Zabad, Zebina, Jadau, and Joel, Benaiah. [44] All these had taken strange wives: and some of them had wives by whom they had children.

Nehemiah (II Ezra)

Neh.1

[1] The words of Nehemiah the son of Hachaliah. And it came to pass in the month Chisleu, in the twentieth year, as I was in Shushan the palace, [2] That Hanani, one of my brethren, came, he and certain men of Judah; and I asked them concerning the Jews that had escaped, which were left of the captivity, and concerning Jerusalem. [3] And they said unto me, The remnant that are left of the captivity there in the province are in great affliction and reproach: the wall of Jerusalem also is broken down, and the gates thereof are burned with fire. [4] And it came to pass, when I heard these words, that I sat down and wept, and mourned certain days, and fasted, and prayed before the God of heaven, [5] And said, I beseech thee, O LORD God of heaven, the great and terrible God, that keepeth covenant and mercy for them that love him and observe his commandments: [6] Let thine ear now be attentive, and thine eyes open, that thou mayest hear the prayer of thy servant, which I pray before thee now, day and night, for the children of Israel thy servants, and confess the sins of the children of Israel, which we have sinned against thee: both I and my father's house have sinned. [7] We have dealt very corruptly against thee, and have not kept the commandments, nor the statutes, nor the judgments, which thou commandedst thy servant Moses. [8] Remember, I beseech thee, the word that thou commandedst thy servant Moses, saying, If ye transgress, I will scatter you abroad among the nations: [9] But if ye turn unto me, and keep my commandments, and do them; though there were of you cast out unto the uttermost part of the heaven, yet will I gather them from thence, and will bring them unto the place that I have chosen to set my name there. [10] Now these are thy servants and thy people, whom thou hast redeemed by thy great power, and by thy strong hand. [11] O Lord, I beseech thee, let now thine ear be attentive to the prayer of thy servant, and to the prayer of thy servants, who desire to fear thy name: and prosper, I pray thee, thy servant this day, and grant him mercy in the sight of this man. For I was the king's cupbearer.

Neh.2

[1] And it came to pass in the month Nisan, in the twentieth year of Artaxerxes the king, that wine was before him: and I took up the wine, and gave it unto the king. Now I had not been beforetime sad in his presence.[2] Wherefore the king said unto me, Why is thy countenance sad, seeing thou art not sick? this is nothing else but sorrow of heart. Then I was very sore afraid,[3] And said unto the king, Let the king live for ever: why should not my countenance be sad, when the city, the place of my fathers' sepulchres, lieth waste, and the gates thereof are consumed with fire?[4] Then the king said unto me, For what dost thou make request? So I prayed to the God of heaven.[5] And I said unto the king, If it please the king, and if thy servant have found favour in thy sight, that thou wouldest send me unto Judah, unto the city of my fathers' sepulchres, that I may build it.[6] And the king said unto me, (the queen also sitting by him,) For how long shall thy journey be? and when wilt thou return? So it pleased the king to send me; and I set him a time.[7] Moreover I said unto the king, If it please the king, let letters be given me to the governors beyond the river, that they may convey me over till I come into Judah;[8] And a letter unto Asaph the keeper of the king's forest, that he may give me timber to make beams for the gates of the palace which appertained to the house, and for the wall of the city, and for the house that I shall enter into. And the king granted me, according to the good hand of my God upon me.[9] Then I came to the governors beyond the river, and gave them the king's letters. Now the king had sent captains of the army and horsemen with me.[10] When Sanballat the Horonite, and Tobiah the servant, the Ammonite, heard of it, it grieved them exceedingly that there was come a man to seek the welfare of the children of Israel.[11] So I came to Jerusalem, and was there three days.[12] And I arose in the night, I and some few men with me; neither told I any man what my God had put in my heart to do at Jerusalem: neither was there any beast with me, save the beast that I rode upon.[13] And I went out by night by the gate of the valley, even before the dragon well, and to the dung port, and viewed the walls of Jerusalem, which were broken down, and the gates thereof were consumed with fire.[14] Then I went on to the gate of the fountain, and to the king's pool: but there was no place for the beast that was under me to pass.[15] Then went I up in the night by the brook, and viewed the wall, and turned back, and entered by the gate of the valley, and so returned.[16] And the rulers knew not whither I went, or what I did; neither had I as yet told it to the Jews, nor to the priests, nor to the nobles, nor to the rulers, nor to the rest that did the work.[17] Then said I unto them, Ye see the distress that we are in, how Jerusalem lieth waste, and the gates thereof are burned with fire: come, and let us build up the wall of Jerusalem, that we be no more a reproach.[18] Then I told them of the hand of my God which was good upon me; as also the king's words that he had spoken unto me. And they said, Let us rise up and build. So they strengthened their hands for this good work.[19] But when Sanballat the Horonite, and Tobiah the servant, the Ammonite, and Geshem the Arabian, heard it, they laughed us to scorn, and despised us, and said, What is this thing that ye do? will ye rebel against the king?[20] Then answered I them, and said unto them, The God of heaven, he will prosper us; therefore we his servants will arise and build: but ye have no portion, nor right, nor memorial, in Jerusalem.

Neh.3

[1] Then Eliashib the high priest rose up with his brethren the priests, and they builded the sheep gate; they sanctified it, and set up the doors of it; even unto the tower of Meah they sanctified it, unto the tower of Hananeel.[2] And next unto him builded the men of Jericho. And next to them builded Zaccur the son of Imri.[3] But the fish gate did the sons of Hassenaah build, who also laid the beams thereof, and set up the doors thereof, the locks thereof, and the bars thereof.[4] And next unto them repaired Meremoth the son of Urijah, the son of Koz. And next unto them repaired Meshullam the son of Berechiah, the son of Meshezabeel. And next unto them repaired Zadok the son of Baana.[5] And next unto them the Tekoites repaired; but their nobles put not their necks to the work of their Lord.[6] Moreover the old gate repaired Jehoiada the son of Paseah, and Meshullam the son of Besodeiah; they laid the beams thereof, and set up the doors thereof, and the locks thereof, and the bars thereof.[7] And next unto them repaired Melatiah the Gibeonite, and Jadon the Meronothite, the men of Gibeon, and of Mizpah, unto the throne of the governor on this side the river.[8] Next unto him repaired Uzziel the son of Harhaiah, of the goldsmiths. Next unto him also repaired Hananiah the son of one of the apothecaries, and they fortified Jerusalem unto the broad wall.[9] And next unto them repaired Rephaiah the son of Hur, the ruler of the half part of Jerusalem.[10] And next unto them repaired Jedaiah the son of Harumaph, even over against his house. And next unto him repaired Hattush the son of Hashabniah.[11] Malchijah the son of Harim, and Hashub the son of Pahath-moab, repaired the other piece, and the tower of the furnaces.[12] And next unto him repaired Shallum the son of Halohesh, the ruler of the half part of Jerusalem, he and his daughters.[13] The valley gate repaired Hanun, and the inhabitants of Zanoah; they built it, and set up the doors thereof, the locks thereof, and the bars thereof, and a thousand cubits on the wall unto the dung gate.[14] But the dung gate repaired Malchiah the son of Rechab, the ruler of part of Beth-haccerem; he built it, and set up the doors thereof, the locks thereof, and the bars thereof.[15] But the gate of the fountain repaired Shallun the son of Col-hozeh, the ruler of part of Mizpah; he built it, and covered it, and set up the doors thereof, the locks thereof, and the bars thereof, and the wall of the pool of Siloah by the king's garden, and unto the stairs that go down from the city of David.[16] After him repaired Nehemiah the son of Azbuk, the ruler of the half part of Beth-zur, unto the place over against the sepulchres of David, and to the pool that was made, and unto the house of the mighty.[17] After him repaired the Levites, Rehum the son of Bani. Next unto him repaired Hashabiah, the ruler of the half part of Keilah, in his part.[18] After him repaired their brethren, Bavai the son of Henadad, the ruler of the half part of Keilah.[19] And next to him repaired Ezer the son of Jeshua, the ruler of Mizpah, another piece over against the going up to the armoury at the turning of the wall.[20] After him Baruch the son of Zabbai earnestly repaired the other piece, from the turning of the wall unto the door of the house of Eliashib the high priest.[21] After him repaired Meremoth the son of Urijah the son of Koz another piece, from the door of the house of Eliashib even to the end of the house of Eliashib.[22] And after him repaired the priests, the men of the plain.[23] After him repaired Benjamin and Hashub over against their house. After him repaired Azariah the son of Maaseiah the son of Ananiah by his house.[24] After him repaired Binnui the son of Henadad another piece, from the house of Azariah unto the turning of the wall, even unto the corner.[25] Palal the son of Uzai, over against the turning of the wall, and the tower which lieth out from the king's high house, that was by the court of the prison. After him Pedaiah the son of Parosh.[26] Moreover the Nethinims dwelt in Ophel, unto the place over against the water gate toward the east, and the tower that lieth out.[27] After them the Tekoites repaired another piece, over against the great tower that lieth out, even unto the wall of Ophel.[28] From above the horse gate repaired the priests, every one over against his house.[29] After them repaired Zadok the son of Immer over against his house. After him repaired also Shemaiah the son of Shechaniah, the keeper of the east gate.[30] After him repaired Hananiah the son

of Shelemiah, and Hanun the sixth son of Zalaph, another piece. After him repaired Meshullam the son of Berechiah over against his chamber.[31] After him repaired Malchiah the goldsmith's son unto the place of the Nethinims, and of the merchants, over against the gate Miphkad, and to the going up of the corner.[32] And between the going up of the corner unto the sheep gate repaired the goldsmiths and the merchants.

Neh.4

[1] But it came to pass, that when Sanballat heard that we builded the wall, he was wroth, and took great indignation, and mocked the Jews.[2] And he spake before his brethren and the army of Samaria, and said, What do these feeble Jews? will they fortify themselves? will they sacrifice? will they make an end in a day? will they revive the stones out of the heaps of the rubbish which are burned?[3] Now Tobiah the Ammonite was by him, and he said, Even that which they build, if a fox go up, he shall even break down their stone wall.[4] Hear, O our God; for we are despised: and turn their reproach upon their own head, and give them for a prey in the land of captivity:[5] And cover not their iniquity, and let not their sin be blotted out from before thee: for they have provoked thee to anger before the builders.[6] So built we the wall; and all the wall was joined together unto the half thereof: for the people had a mind to work.[7] But it came to pass, that when Sanballat, and Tobiah, and the Arabians, and the Ammonites, and the Ashdodites, heard that the walls of Jerusalem were made up, and that the breaches began to be stopped, then they were very wroth,[8] And conspired all of them together to come and to fight against Jerusalem, and to hinder it.[9] Nevertheless we made our prayer unto our God, and set a watch against them day and night, because of them.[10] And Judah said, The strength of the bearers of burdens is decayed, and there is much rubbish; so that we are not able to build the wall.[11] And our adversaries said, They shall not know, neither see, till we come in the midst among them, and slay them, and cause the work to cease.[12] And it came to pass, that when the Jews which dwelt by them came, they said unto us ten times, From all places whence ye shall return unto us they will be upon you.[13] Therefore set I in the lower places behind the wall, and on the higher places, I even set the people after their families with their swords, their spears, and their bows.[14] And I looked, and rose up, and said unto the nobles, and to the rulers, and to the rest of the people, Be not ye afraid of them: remember the Lord, which is great and terrible, and fight for your brethren, your sons, and your daughters, your wives, and your houses.[15] And it came to pass, when our enemies heard that it was known unto us, and God had brought their counsel to nought, that we returned all of us to the wall, every one unto his work.[16] And it came to pass from that time forth, that the half of my servants wrought in the work, and the other half of them held both the spears, the shields, and the bows, and the habergeons; and the rulers were behind all the house of Judah.[17] They which builded on the wall, and they that bare burdens, with those that laded, every one with one of his hands wrought in the work, and with the other hand held a weapon.[18] For the builders, every one had his sword girded by his side, and so builded. And he that sounded the trumpet was by me.[19] And I said unto the nobles, and to the rulers, and to the rest of the people, The work is great and large, and we are separated upon the wall, one far from another.[20] In what place therefore ye hear the sound of the trumpet, resort ye thither unto us: our God shall fight for us.[21] So we laboured in the work: and half of them held the spears from the rising of the morning till the stars appeared.[22] Likewise at the same time said I unto the people, Let every one with his servant lodge within Jerusalem, that in the night they may be a guard to us, and labour on the day.[23] So neither I, nor

my brethren, nor my servants, nor the men of the guard which followed me, none of us put off our clothes, saving that every one put them off for washing.

Neh.5

[1] And there was a great cry of the people and of their wives against their brethren the Jews.[2] For there were that said, We, our sons, and our daughters, are many: therefore we take up corn for them, that we may eat, and live.[3] Some also there were that said, We have mortgaged our lands, vineyards, and houses, that we might buy corn, because of the dearth.[4] There were also that said, We have borrowed money for the king's tribute, and that upon our lands and vineyards.[5] Yet now our flesh is as the flesh of our brethren, our children as their children: and, lo, we bring into bondage our sons and our daughters to be servants, and some of our daughters are brought unto bondage already: neither is it in our power to redeem them; for other men have our lands and vineyards.[6] And I was very angry when I heard their cry and these words.[7] Then I consulted with myself, and I rebuked the nobles, and the rulers, and said unto them, Ye exact usury, every one of his brother. And I set a great assembly against them.[8] And I said unto them, We after our ability have redeemed our brethren the Jews, which were sold unto the heathen; and will ye even sell your brethren? or shall they be sold unto us? Then held they their peace, and found nothing to answer.[9] Also I said, It is not good that ye do: ought ye not to walk in the fear of our God because of the reproach of the heathen our enemies?[10] I likewise, and my brethren, and my servants, might exact of them money and corn: I pray you, let us leave off this usury.[11] Restore, I pray you, to them, even this day, their lands, their vineyards, their oliveyards, and their houses, also the the hundredth part of the money, and of the corn, the wine, and the oil, that ye exact of them.[12] Then said they, We will restore them, and will require nothing of them; so will we do as thou sayest. Then I called the priests, and took an oath of them, that they should do according to this promise.[13] Also I shook my lap, and said, So God shake out every man from his house, and from his labour, that performeth not this promise, even thus be he shaken out, and emptied. And all the congregation said, Amen, and praised the LORD. And the people did according to this promise.[14] Moreover from the time that I was appointed to be their governor in the land of Judah, from the twentieth year even unto the two and thirtieth year of Artaxerxes the king, that is, twelve years, I and my brethren have not eaten the bread of the governor.[15] But the former governors that had been before me were chargeable unto the people, and had taken of them bread and wine, beside forty shekels of silver; yea, even their servants bare rule over the people: but so did not I, because of the fear of God.[16] Yea, also I continued in the work of this wall, neither bought we any land: and all my servants were gathered thither unto the work.[17] Moreover there were at my table an hundred and fifty of the Jews and rulers, beside those that came unto us from among the heathen that are about us.[18] Now that which was prepared for me daily was one ox and six choice sheep; also fowls were prepared for me, and once in ten days store of all sorts of wine: yet for all this required not I the bread of the governor, because the bondage was heavy upon this people.[19] Think upon me, my God, for good, according to all that I have done for this people.

Neh.6

[1] Now it came to pass, when Sanballat, and Tobiah, and Geshem the Arabian, and the rest of our enemies, heard that I had builded the wall, and that there was no breach left therein; (though at that time I had not set up the doors upon the gates;)[2] That Sanballat and Geshem sent unto me, saying, Come, let us meet together in some one of the villages in the plain of Ono. But they thought to do me

mischief.[3] And I sent messengers unto them, saying, I am doing a great work, so that I cannot come down: why should the work cease, whilst I leave it, and come down to you?[4] Yet they sent unto me four times after this sort; and I answered them after the same manner.[5] Then sent Sanballat his servant unto me in like manner the fifth time with an open letter in his hand;[6] Wherein was written, It is reported among the heathen, and Gashmu saith it, that thou and the Jews think to rebel: for which cause thou buildest the wall, that thou mayest be their king, according to these words.[7] And thou hast also appointed prophets to preach of thee at Jerusalem, saying, There is a king in Judah: and now shall it be reported to the king according to these words. Come now therefore, and let us take counsel together.[8] Then I sent unto him, saying, There are no such things done as thou sayest, but thou feignest them out of thine own heart.[9] For they all made us afraid, saying, Their hands shall be weakened from the work, that it be not done. Now therefore, O God, strengthen my hands.[10] Afterward I came unto the house of Shemaiah the son of Delaiah the son of Mehetabeel, who was shut up; and he said, Let us meet together in the house of God, within the temple, and let us shut the doors of the temple: for they will come to slay thee; yea, in the night will they come to slay thee.[11] And I said, Should such a man as I flee? and who is there, that, being as I am, would go into the temple to save his life? I will not go in.[12] And, lo, I perceived that God had not sent him; but that he pronounced this prophecy against me: for Tobiah and Sanballat had hired him.[13] Therefore was he hired, that I should be afraid, and do so, and sin, and that they might have matter for an evil report, that they might reproach me.[14] My God, think thou upon Tobiah and Sanballat according to these their works, and on the prophetess Noadiah, and the rest of the prophets, that would have put me in fear.[15] So the wall was finished in the twenty and fifth day of the month Elul, in fifty and two days.[16] And it came to pass, that when all our enemies heard thereof, and all the heathen that were about us saw these things, they were much cast down in their own eyes: for they perceived that this work was wrought of our God.[17] Moreover in those days the nobles of Judah sent many letters unto Tobiah, and the letters of Tobiah came unto them.[18] For there were many in Judah sworn unto him, because he was the son in law of Shechaniah the son of Arah; and his son Johanan had taken the daughter of Meshullam the son of Berechiah.[19] Also they reported his good deeds before me, and uttered my words to him. And Tobiah sent letters to put me in fear.

Neh.7

[1] Now it came to pass, when the wall was built, and I had set up the doors, and the porters and the singers and the Levites were appointed,[2] That I gave my brother Hanani, and Hananiah the ruler of the palace, charge over Jerusalem: for he was a faithful man, and feared God above many.[3] And I said unto them, Let not the gates of Jerusalem be opened until the sun be hot; and while they stand by, let them shut the doors, and bar them: and appoint watches of the inhabitants of Jerusalem, every one in his watch, and every one to be over against his house.[4] Now the city was large and great: but the people were few therein, and the houses were not builded.[5] And my God put into mine heart to gather together the nobles, and the rulers, and the people, that they might be reckoned by genealogy. And I found a register of the genealogy of them which came up at the first, and found written therein,[6] These are the children of the province, that went up out of the captivity, of those that had been carried away, whom Nebuchadnezzar the king of Babylon had carried away, and came again to Jerusalem and to Judah, every one unto his city;[7] Who came with Zerubbabel, Jeshua, Nehemiah, Azariah, Raamiah, Nahamani, Mordecai, Bilshan, Mispereth, Bigvai,

Nehum, Baanah. The number, I say, of the men of the people of Israel was this;[8] The children of Parosh, two thousand an hundred seventy and two.[9] The children of Shephatiah, three hundred seventy and two.[10] The children of Arah, six hundred fifty and two.[11] The children of Pahath-moab, of the children of Jeshua and Joab, two thousand and eight hundred and eighteen.[12] The children of Elam, a thousand two hundred fifty and four.[13] The children of Zattu, eight hundred forty and five.[14] The children of Zaccai, seven hundred and threescore.[15] The children of Binnui, six hundred forty and eight.[16] The children of Bebai, six hundred twenty and eight.[17] The children of Azgad, two thousand three hundred twenty and two.[18] The children of Adonikam, six hundred threescore and seven.[19] The children of Bigvai, two thousand threescore and seven.[20] The children of Adin, six hundred fifty and five.[21] The children of Ater of Hezekiah, ninety and eight.[22] The children of Hashum, three hundred twenty and eight.[23] The children of Bezai, three hundred twenty and four.[24] The children of Hariph, an hundred and twelve.[25] The children of Gibeon, ninety and five.[26] The men of Bethlehem and Netophah, an hundred fourscore and eight.[27] The men of Anathoth, an hundred twenty and eight.[28] The men of Beth-azmaveth, forty and two.[29] The men of Kirjath-jearim, Chephirah, and Beeroth, seven hundred forty and three.[30] The men of Ramah and Geba, six hundred twenty and one.[31] The men of Michmas, an hundred and twenty and two.[32] The men of Bethel and Ai, an hundred twenty and three.[33] The men of the other Nebo, fifty and two.[34] The children of the other Elam, a thousand two hundred fifty and four.[35] The children of Harim, three hundred and twenty.[36] The children of Jericho, three hundred forty and five.[37] The children of Lod, Hadid, and Ono, seven hundred twenty and one.[38] The children of Senaah, three thousand nine hundred and thirty.[39] The priests: the children of Jedaiah, of the house of Jeshua, nine hundred seventy and three.[40] The children of Immer, a thousand fifty and two.[41] The children of Pashur, a thousand two hundred forty and seven.[42] The children of Harim, a thousand and seventeen.[43] The Levites: the children of Jeshua, of Kadmiel, and of the children of Hodevah, seventy and four.[44] The singers: the children of Asaph, an hundred forty and eight.[45] The porters: the children of Shallum, the children of Ater, the children of Talmon, the children of Akkub, the children of Hatita, the children of Shobai, an hundred thirty and eight.[46] The Nethinims: the children of Ziha, the children of Hashupha, the children of Tabbaoth,[47] The children of Keros, the children of Sia, the children of Padon,[48] The children of Lebana, the children of Hagaba, the children of Shalmai,[49] The children of Hanan, the children of Giddel, the children of Gahar,[50] The children of Reaiah, the children of Rezin, the children of Nekoda,[51] The children of Gazzam, the children of Uzza, the children of Phaseah,[52] The children of Besai, the children of Meunim, the children of Nephishesim,[53] The children of Bakbuk, the children of Hakupha, the children of Harhur,[54] The children of Bazlith, the children of Mehida, the children of Harsha,[55] The children of Barkos, the children of Sisera, the children of Tamah,[56] The children of Neziah, the children of Hatipha.[57] The children of Solomon's servants: the children of Sotai, the children of Sophereth, the children of Perida,[58] The children of Jaala, the children of Darkon, the children of Giddel,[59] The children of Shephatiah, the children of Hattil, the children of Pochereth of Zebaim, the children of Amon.[60] All the Nethinims, and the children of Solomon's servants, were three hundred ninety and two.[61] And these were they which went up also from Telmelah, Telharesha, Cherub, Addon, and Immer: but they could not shew their father's house, nor their seed, whether they were of Israel.[62] The children of Delaiah, the children of Tobiah, the children of Nekoda, six hundred forty and two.[63] And of the priests: the children of Habaiah, the children of Koz, the children of Barzillai, which took one of the daughters of Barzillai the Gileadite to wife, and was called after their name.[64] These sought their register among those that were reckoned by genealogy, but it was not found: therefore were they, as polluted, put from the priesthood.[65] And the Tirshatha said unto them, that they should not eat of the most holy things, till there stood up a priest with Urim and Thummim.[66] The whole congregation together was forty and two thousand three hundred and threescore,[67] Beside their manservants and their maidservants, of whom there were seven thousand three hundred thirty and seven: and they had two hundred forty and five singing men and singing women.[68] Their horses, seven hundred thirty and six: their mules, two hundred forty and five:[69] Their camels, four hundred thirty and five: six thousand seven hundred and twenty asses.[70] And some of the chief of the fathers gave unto the work. The Tirshatha gave to the treasure a thousand drams of gold, fifty basons, five hundred and thirty priests' garments.[71] And some of the chief of the fathers gave to the treasure of the work twenty thousand drams of gold, and two thousand and two hundred pound of silver.[72] And that which the rest of the people gave was twenty thousand drams of gold, and two thousand pound of silver, and threescore and seven priests' garments.[73] So the priests, and the Levites, and the porters, and the singers, and some of the people, and the Nethinims, and all Israel, dwelt in their cities; and when the seventh month came, the children of Israel were in their cities.

Neh.8

[1] And all the people gathered themselves together as one man into the street that was before the water gate; and they spake unto Ezra the scribe to bring the book of the law of Moses, which the LORD had commanded to Israel.[2] And Ezra the priest brought the law before the congregation both of men and women, and all that could hear with understanding, upon the first day of the seventh month.[3] And he read therein before the street that was before the water gate from the morning until midday, before the men and the women, and those that could understand; and the ears of all the people were attentive unto the book of the law.[4] And Ezra the scribe stood upon a pulpit of wood, which they had made for the purpose; and beside him stood Mattithiah, and Shema, and Anaiah, and Urijah, and Hilkiah, and Maaseiah, on his right hand; and on his left hand, Pedaiah, and Mishael, and Malchiah, and Hashum, and Hashbadana, Zechariah, and Meshullam.[5] And Ezra opened the book in the sight of all the people; (for he was above all the people;) and when he opened it, all the people stood up:[6] And Ezra blessed the LORD, the great God. And all the people answered, Amen, Amen, with lifting up their hands: and they bowed their heads, and worshipped the LORD with their faces to the ground.[7] Also Jeshua, and Bani, and Sherebiah, Jamin, Akkub, Shabbethai, Hodijah, Maaseiah, Kelita, Azariah, Jozabad, Hanan, Pelaiah, and the Levites, caused the people to understand the law: and the people stood in their place.[8] So they read in the book in the law of God distinctly, and gave the sense, and caused them to understand the reading.[9] And Nehemiah, which is the Tirshatha, and Ezra the priest the scribe, and the Levites that taught the people, said unto all the people, This day is holy unto the LORD your God; mourn not, nor weep. For all the people wept, when they heard the words of the law.[10] Then he said unto them, Go your way, eat the fat, and drink the sweet, and send portions unto them for whom nothing is prepared: for this day is holy unto our Lord: neither be ye sorry; for the joy of the LORD is your strength.[11] So the Levites stilled all the people, saying, Hold your peace, for the day is holy; neither be ye grieved.[12] And all the people went their way to eat, and to drink, and

to send portions, and to make great mirth, because they had understood the words that were declared unto them.[13] And on the second day were gathered together the chief of the fathers of all the people, the priests, and the Levites, unto Ezra the scribe, even to understand the words of the law.[14] And they found written in the law which the LORD had commanded by Moses, that the children of Israel should dwell in booths in the feast of the seventh month:[15] And that they should publish and proclaim in all their cities, and in Jerusalem, saying, Go forth unto the mount, and fetch olive branches, and pine branches, and myrtle branches, and palm branches, and branches of thick trees, to make booths, as it is written.[16] So the people went forth, and brought them, and made themselves booths, every one upon the roof of his house, and in their courts, and in the courts of the house of God, and in the street of the water gate, and in the street of the gate of Ephraim.[17] And all the congregation of them that were come again out of the captivity made booths, and sat under the booths: for since the days of Jeshua the son of Nun unto that day had not the children of Israel done so. And there was very great gladness.[18] Also day by day, from the first day unto the last day, he read in the book of the law of God. And they kept the feast seven days; and on the eighth day was a solemn assembly, according unto the manner.

Neh.9

[1] Now in the twenty and fourth day of this month the children of Israel were assembled with fasting, and with sackclothes, and earth upon them.[2] And the seed of Israel separated themselves from all strangers, and stood and confessed their sins, and the iniquities of their fathers.[3] And they stood up in their place, and read in the book of the law of the LORD their God one fourth part of the day; and another fourth part they confessed, and worshipped the LORD their God.[4] Then stood up upon the stairs, of the Levites, Jeshua, and Bani, Kadmiel, Shebaniah, Bunni, Sherebiah, Bani, and Chenani, and cried with a loud voice unto the LORD their God.[5] Then the Levites, Jeshua, and Kadmiel, Bani, Hashabniah, Sherebiah, Hodijah, Shebaniah, and Pethahiah, said, Stand up and bless the LORD your God for ever and ever: and blessed be thy glorious name, which is exalted above all blessing and praise.[6] Thou, even thou, art LORD alone; thou hast made heaven, the heaven of heavens, with all their host, the earth, and all things that are therein, the seas, and all that is therein, and thou preservest them all; and the host of heaven worshippeth thee.[7] Thou art the LORD the God, who didst choose Abram, and broughtest him forth out of Ur of the Chaldees, and gavest him the name of Abraham;[8] And foundest his heart faithful before thee, and madest a covenant with him to give the land of the Canaanites, the Hittites, the Amorites, and the Perizzites, and the Jebusites, and the Girgashites, to give it, I say, to his seed, and hast performed thy words; for thou art righteous:[9] And didst see the affliction of our fathers in Egypt, and heardest their cry by the Red sea;[10] And shewedst signs and wonders upon Pharoah, and on all his servants, and on all the people of his land: for thou knewest that they dealt proudly against them. So didst thou get thee a name, as it is this day.[11] And thou didst divide the sea before them, so that they went through the midst of the sea on the dry land; and their persecutors thou threwest into the deeps, as a stone into the mighty waters.[12] Moreover thou leddest them in the day by a cloudy pillar; and in the night by a pillar of fire, to give them light in the way wherein they should go.[13] Thou camest down also upon mount Sinai, and spakest with them from heaven, and gavest them right judgments, and true laws, good statutes and commandments:[14] And madest known unto them thy holy sabbath, and commandedst them precepts, statutes, and laws, by the hand of Moses thy servant:[15] And gavest them bread from heaven for their hunger, and broughtest

forth water for them out of the rock for their thirst, and promisedst them that they should go in to possess the land which thou hadst sworn to give them.¹⁶ But they and our fathers dealt proudly, and hardened their necks, and hearkened not to thy commandments,¹⁷ And refused to obey, neither were mindful of thy wonders that thou didst among them; but hardened their necks, and in their rebellion appointed a captain to return to their bondage: but thou art a God ready to pardon, gracious and merciful, slow to anger, and of great kindness, and forsookest them not.¹⁸ Yea, when they had made them a molten calf, and said, This is thy God that brought thee up out of Egypt, and had wrought great provocations;¹⁹ Yet thou in thy manifold mercies forsookest them not in the wilderness: the pillar of the cloud departed not from them by day, to lead them in the way; neither the pillar of fire by night, to shew them light, and the way wherein they should go.²⁰ Thou gavest also thy good spirit to instruct them, and withheldest not thy manna from their mouth, and gavest them water for their thirst.²¹ Yea, forty years didst thou sustain them in the wilderness, so that they lacked nothing; their clothes waxed not old, and their feet swelled not.²² Moreover thou gavest them kingdoms and nations, and didst divide them into corners: so they possessed the land of Sihon, and the land of the king of Heshbon, and the land of Og king of Bashan.²³ Their children also multipliedst thou as the stars of heaven, and broughtest them into the land, concerning which thou hadst promised to their fathers, that they should go in to possess it.²⁴ So the children went in and possessed the land, and thou subduedst before them the inhabitants of the land, the Canaanites, and gavest them into their hands, with their kings, and the people of the land, that they might do with them as they would.²⁵ And they took strong cities, and a fat land, and possessed houses full of all goods, wells digged, vineyards, and oliveyards, and fruit trees in abundance: so they did eat, and were filled, and became fat, and delighted themselves in thy great goodness.²⁶ Nevertheless they were disobedient, and rebelled against thee, and cast thy law behind their backs, and slew thy prophets which testified against them to turn them to thee, and they wrought great provocations.²⁷ Therefore thou deliveredst them into the hand of their enemies, who vexed them: and in the time of their trouble, when they cried unto thee, thou heardest them from heaven; and according to thy manifold mercies thou gavest them saviours, who saved them out of the hand of their enemies.²⁸ But after they had rest, they did evil again before thee: therefore leftest thou them in the hand of their enemies, so that they had the dominion over them: yet when they returned, and cried unto thee, thou heardest them from heaven; and many times didst thou deliver them according to thy mercies;²⁹ And testifiedst against them, that thou mightest bring them again unto thy law: yet they dealt proudly, and hearkened not unto thy commandments, but sinned against thy judgments, (which if a man do, he shall live in them;) and withdrew the shoulder, and hardened their neck, and would not hear.³⁰ Yet many years didst thou forbear them, and testifiedst against them by thy spirit in thy prophets: yet would they not give ear: therefore gavest thou them into the hand of the people of the lands.³¹ Nevertheless for thy great mercies' sake thou didst not utterly consume them, nor forsake them; for thou art a gracious and merciful God.³² Now therefore, our God, the great, the mighty, and the terrible God, who keepest covenant and mercy, let not all the trouble seem little before thee, that hath come upon us, on our kings, on our princes, and on our priests, and on our prophets, and on our fathers, and on all thy people, since the time of the kings of Assyria unto this day.³³ Howbeit thou art just in all that is brought upon us; for thou hast done right, but we have done wickedly:³⁴ Neither have our kings, our princes, our priests, nor our

fathers, kept thy law, nor hearkened unto thy commandments and thy testimonies, wherewith thou didst testify against them.³⁵ For they have not served thee in their kingdom, and in thy great goodness that thou gavest them, and in the large and fat land which thou gavest before them, neither turned they from their wicked works.³⁶ Behold, we are servants this day, and for the land that thou gavest unto our fathers to eat the fruit thereof and the good thereof, behold, we are servants in it:³⁷ And it yieldeth much increase unto the kings whom thou hast set over us because of our sins: also they have dominion over our bodies, and over our cattle, at their pleasure, and we are in great distress.³⁸ And because of all this we make a sure covenant, and write it; and our princes, Levites, and priests, seal unto it.

Neh.10

¹ Now those that sealed were, Nehemiah, the Tirshatha, the son of Hachaliah, and Zidkijah,² Seraiah, Azariah, Jeremiah,³ Pashur, Amariah, Malchijah,⁴ Hattush, Shebaniah, Malluch,⁵ Harim, Meremoth, Obadiah,⁶ Daniel, Ginnethon, Baruch,⁷ Meshullam, Abijah, Mijamin,⁸ Maaziah, Bilgai, Shemaiah: these were the priests.⁹ And the Levites: both Jeshua the son of Azaniah, Binnui of the sons of Henadad, Kadmiel;¹⁰ And their brethren, Shebaniah, Hodijah, Kelita, Pelaiah, Hanan,¹¹ Micha, Rehob, Hashabiah,¹² Zaccur, Sherebiah, Shebaniah,¹³ Hodijah, Bani, Beninu.¹⁴ The chief of the people; Parosh, Pahath-moab, Elam, Zatthu, Bani,¹⁵ Bunni, Azgad, Bebai,¹⁶ Adonijah, Bigvai, Adin,¹⁷ Ater, Hizkijah, Azzur,¹⁸ Hodijah, Hashum, Bezai,¹⁹ Hariph, Anathoth, Nebai,²⁰ Magpiash, Meshullam, Hezir,²¹ Meshezabeel, Zadok, Jaddua,²² Pelatiah, Hanan, Anaiah,²³ Hoshea, Hananiah, Hashub,²⁴ Hallohesh, Pileha, Shobek,²⁵ Rehum, Hashabnah, Maaseiah,²⁶ And Ahijah, Hanan, Anan,²⁷ Malluch, Harim, Baanah.²⁸ And the rest of the people, the priests, the Levites, the porters, the singers, the Nethinims, and all they that had separated themselves from the people of the lands unto the law of God, their wives, their sons, and their daughters, every one having knowledge, and having understanding;²⁹ They clave to their brethren, their nobles, and entered into a curse, and into an oath, to walk in God's law, which was given by Moses the servant of God, and to observe and do all the commandments of the LORD our Lord, and his judgments and his statutes;³⁰ And that we would not give our daughters unto the people of the land, nor take their daughters for our sons:³¹ And if the people of the land bring ware or any victuals on the sabbath day to sell, that we would not buy it of them on the sabbath, or on the holy day: and that we would leave the seventh year, and the exaction of every debt.³² Also we made ordinances for us, to charge ourselves yearly with the third part of a shekel for the service of the house of our God;³³ For the shewbread, and for the continual meat offering, and for the continual burnt offering, of the sabbaths, of the new moons, for the set feasts, and for the holy things, and for the sin offerings to make an atonement for Israel, and for all the work of the house of our God.³⁴ And we cast the lots among the priests, the Levites, and the people, for the wood offering, to bring it into the house of our God, after the houses of our fathers, at times appointed year by year, to burn upon the altar of the LORD our God, as it is written in the law:³⁵ And to bring the firstfruits of our ground, and the firstfruits of all fruit of all trees, year by year, unto the house of the LORD:³⁶ Also the firstborn of our sons, and of our cattle, as it is written in the law, and the firstlings of our herds and of our flocks, to bring to the house of our God, unto the priests that minister in the house of our God:³⁷ And that we should bring the firstfruits of our dough, and our offerings, and the fruit of all manner of trees, of wine and of oil, unto the priests, to the chambers of the house of our God; and the tithes of our

ground unto the Levites, that the same Levites might have the tithes in all the cities of our tillage.[38] And the priest the son of Aaron shall be with the Levites, when the Levites take tithes: and the Levites shall bring up the tithe of the tithes unto the house of our God, to the chambers, into the treasure house.[39] For the children of Israel and the children of Levi shall bring the offering of the corn, of the new wine, and the oil, unto the chambers, where are the vessels of the sanctuary, and the priests that minister, and the porters, and the singers: and we will not forsake the house of our God.

Neh.11

[1] And the rulers of the people dwelt at Jerusalem: the rest of the people also cast lots, to bring one of ten to dwell in Jerusalem the holy city, and nine parts to dwell in other cities.[2] And the people blessed all the men, that willingly offered themselves to dwell at Jerusalem.[3] Now these are the chief of the province that dwelt in Jerusalem: but in the cities of Judah dwelt every one in his possession in their cities, to wit, Israel, the priests, and the Levites, and the Nethinims, and the children of Solomon's servants.[4] And at Jerusalem dwelt certain of the children of Judah, and of the children of Benjamin. Of the children of Judah; Athaiah the son of Uzziah, the son of Zechariah, the son of Amariah, the son of Shephatiah, the son of Mahalaleel, of the children of Perez;[5] And Maaseiah the son of Baruch, the son of Col-hozeh, the son of Hazaiah, the son of Adaiah, the son of Joiarib, the son of Zechariah, the son of Shiloni.[6] All the sons of Perez that dwelt at Jerusalem were four hundred threescore and eight valiant men.[7] And these are the sons of Benjamin; Sallu the son of Meshullam, the son of Joed, the son of Pedaiah, the son of Kolaiah, the son of Maaseiah, the son of Ithiel, the son of Jesaiah.[8] And after him Gabbai, Sallai, nine hundred twenty and eight.[9] And Joel the son of Zichri was their overseer: and Judah the son of Senuah was second over the city.[10] Of the priests: Jedaiah the son of Joiarib, Jachin.[11] Seraiah the son of Hilkiah, the son of Meshullam, the son of Zadok, the son of Meraioth, the son of Ahitub, was the ruler of the house of God.[12] And their brethren that did the work of the house were eight hundred twenty and two: and Adaiah the son of Jeroham, the son of Pelaliah, the son of Amzi, the son of Zechariah, the son of Pashur, the son of Malchiah,[13] And his brethren, chief of the fathers, two hundred forty and two: and Amashai the son of Azareel, the son of Ahasai, the son of Meshillemoth, the son of Immer,[14] And their brethren, mighty men of valour, an hundred twenty and eight: and their overseer was Zabdiel, the son of one of the great men.[15] Also of the Levites: Shemaiah the son of Hashub, the son of Azrikam, the son of Hashabiah, the son of Bunni;[16] And Shabbethai and Jozabad, of the chief of the Levites, had the oversight of the outward business of the house of God.[17] And Mattaniah the son of Micha, the son of Zabdi, the son of Asaph, was the principal to begin the thanksgiving in prayer: and Bakbukiah the second among his brethren, and Abda the son of Shammua, the son of Galal, the son of Jeduthun.[18] All the Levites in the holy city were two hundred fourscore and four.[19] Moreover the porters, Akkub, Talmon, and their brethren that kept the gates, were an hundred seventy and two.[20] And the residue of Israel, of the priests, and the Levites, were in all the cities of Judah, every one in his inheritance.[21] But the Nethinims dwelt in Ophel: and Ziha and Gispa were over the Nethinims.[22] The overseer also of the Levites at Jerusalem was Uzzi the son of Bani, the son of Hashabiah, the son of Mattaniah, the son of Micha. Of the sons of Asaph, the singers were over the business of the house of God.[23] For it was the king's commandment concerning them, that a certain portion should be for the singers, due for every day.[24] And Pethahiah the son of Meshezabeel, of the children of Zerah the son of Judah, was at the king's hand in all

matters concerning the people.[25] And for the villages, with their fields, some of the children of Judah dwelt at Kirjath-arba, and in the villages thereof, and at Dibon, and in the villages thereof, and at Jekabzeel, and in the villages thereof,[26] And at Jeshua, and at Moladah, and at Beth-phelet,[27] And at Hazar-shual, and at Beer-sheba, and in the villages thereof,[28] And at Ziklag, and at Mekonah, and in the villages thereof,[29] And at En-rimmon, and at Zareah, and at Jarmuth,[30] Zanoah, Adullam, and in their villages, at Lachish, and the fields thereof, at Azekah, and in the villages thereof. And they dwelt from Beer-sheba unto the valley of Hinnom.[31] The children also of Benjamin from Geba dwelt at Michmash, and Aija, and Bethel, and in their villages,[32] And at Anathoth, Nob, Ananiah,[33] Hazor, Ramah, Gittaim,[34] Hadid, Zeboim, Neballat,[35] Lod, and Ono, the valley of craftsmen.[36] And of the Levites were divisions in Judah, and in Benjamin.

Neh.12

[1] Now these are the priests and the Levites that went up with Zerubbabel the son of Shealtiel, and Jeshua: Seraiah, Jeremiah, Ezra,[2] Amariah, Malluch, Hattush,[3] Shechaniah, Rehum, Meremoth,[4] Iddo, Ginnetho, Abijah,[5] Miamin, Maadiah, Bilgah,[6] Shemaiah, and Joiarib, Jediah,[7] Sallu, Amok, Hilkiah, Jedaiah. These were the chief of the priests and of their brethren in the days of Jeshua.[8] Moreover the Levites: Jeshua, Binnui, Kadmiel, Sherebiah, Judah, and Mattaniah, which was over the thanksgiving, he and his brethren.[9] Also Bakbukiah and Unni, their brethren, were over against them in the watches.[10] And Jeshua begat Joiakim, Joiakim also begat Eliashib, and Eliashib begat Joiada,[11] And Joiada begat Jonathan, and Jonathan begat Jaddua.[12] And in the days of Joiakim were priests, the chief of the fathers: of Seraiah, Meraiah; of Jeremiah, Hananiah;[13] Of Ezra, Meshullam; of Amariah, Jehohanan;[14] Of Melicu, Jonathan; of Shebaniah, Joseph;[15] Of Harim, Adna; of Meraioth, Helkai;[16] Of Iddo, Zechariah; of Ginnethon, Meshullam;[17] Of Abijah, Zichri; of Miniamin, of Moadiah, Piltai;[18] Of Bilgah, Shammua; of Shemaiah, Jehonathan;[19] And of Joiarib, Mattenai; of Jedaiah, Uzzi;[20] Of Sallai, Kallai; of Amok, Eber;[21] Of Hilkiah, Hashabiah; of Jedaiah, Nethaneel.[22] The Levites in the days of Eliashib, Joiada, and Johanan, and Jaddua, were recorded chief of the fathers: also the priests, to the reign of Darius the Persian.[23] The sons of Levi, the chief of the fathers, were written in the book of the chronicles, even until the days of Johanan the son of Eliashib.[24] And the chief of the Levites: Hashabiah, Sherebiah, and Jeshua the son of Kadmiel, with their brethren over against them, to praise and to give thanks, according to the commandment of David the man of God, ward over against ward.[25] Mattaniah, and Bakbukiah, Obadiah, Meshullam, Talmon, Akkub, were porters keeping the ward at the thresholds of the gates.[26] These were in the days of Joiakim the son of Jeshua, the son of Jozadak, and in the days of Nehemiah the governor, and of Ezra the priest, the scribe.[27] And at the dedication of the wall of Jerusalem they sought the Levites out of all their places, to bring them to Jerusalem, to keep the dedication with gladness, both with thanksgivings, and with singing, with cymbals, psalteries, and with harps.[28] And the sons of the singers gathered themselves together, both out of the plain country round about Jerusalem, and from the villages of Netophathi;[29] Also from the house of Gilgal, and out of the fields of Geba and Azmaveth: for the singers had builded them villages round about Jerusalem.[30] And the priests and the Levites purified themselves, and purified the people, and the gates, and the wall.[31] Then I brought up the princes of Judah upon the wall, and appointed two great companies of them that gave thanks, whereof one went on the right hand upon the wall toward the dung gate:[32] And after them went Hoshaiah, and half of

the princes of Judah,[33] And Azariah, Ezra, and Meshullam,[34] Judah, and Benjamin, and Shemaiah, and Jeremiah,[35] And certain of the priests' sons with trumpets; namely, Zechariah the son of Jonathan, the son of Shemaiah, the son of Mattaniah, the son of Michaiah, the son of Zaccur, the son of Asaph:[36] And his brethren, Shemaiah, and Azarael, Milalai, Gilalai, Maai, Nethaneel, and Judah, Hanani, with the musical instruments of David the man of God, and Ezra the scribe before them.[37] And at the fountain gate, which was over against them, they went up by the stairs of the city of David, at the going up of the wall, above the house of David, even unto the water gate eastward.[38] And the other company of them that gave thanks went over against them, and I after them, and the half of the people upon the wall, from beyond the tower of the furnaces even unto the broad wall;[39] And from above the gate of Ephraim, and above the old gate, and above the fish gate, and the tower of Hananeel, and the tower of Meah, even unto the sheep gate: and they stood still in the prison gate.[40] So stood the two companies of them that gave thanks in the house of God, and I, and the half of the rulers with me:[41] And the priests; Eliakim, Maaseiah, Miniamin, Michaiah, Elioenai, Zechariah, and Hananiah, with trumpets;[42] And Maaseiah, and Shemaiah, and Eleazar, and Uzzi, and Jehohanan, and Malchijah, and Elam, and Ezer. And the singers sang loud, with Jezrahiah their overseer.[43] Also that day they offered great sacrifices, and rejoiced: for God had made them rejoice with great joy: the wives also and the children rejoiced: so that the joy of Jerusalem was heard even afar off.[44] And at that time were some appointed over the chambers for the treasures, for the offerings, for the firstfruits, and for the tithes, to gather into them out of the fields of the cities the portions of the law for the priests and Levites: for Judah rejoiced for the priests and for the Levites that waited.[45] And both the singers and the porters kept the ward of their God, and the ward of the purification, according to the commandment of David, and of Solomon his son.[46] For in the days of David and Asaph of old there were chief of the singers, and songs of praise and thanksgiving unto God.[47] And all Israel in the days of Zerubbabel, and in the days of Nehemiah, gave the portions of the singers and the porters, every day his portion: and they sanctified holy things unto the Levites; and the Levites sanctified them unto the children of Aaron.

Neh.13

[1] On that day they read in the book of Moses in the audience of the people; and therein was found written, that the Ammonite and the Moabite should not come into the congregation of God for ever;[2] Because they met not the children of Israel with bread and with water, but hired Balaam against them, that he should curse them: howbeit our God turned the curse into a blessing.[3] Now it came to pass, when they had heard the law, that they separated from Israel all the mixed multitude.[4] And before this, Eliashib the priest, having the oversight of the chamber of the house of our God, was allied unto Tobiah:[5] And he had prepared for him a great chamber, where aforetime they laid the meat offerings, the frankincense, and the vessels, and the tithes of the corn, the new wine, and the oil, which was commanded to be given to the Levites, and the singers, and the porters; and the offerings of the priests.[6] But in all this time was not I at Jerusalem: for in the two and thirtieth year of Artaxerxes king of Babylon came I unto the king, and after certain days obtained I leave of the king:[7] And I came to Jerusalem, and understood of the evil that Eliashib did for Tobiah, in preparing him a chamber in the courts of the house of God.[8] And it grieved me sore: therefore I cast forth all the household stuff of Tobiah out of the chamber.[9] Then I commanded, and they cleansed the chambers: and thither brought I again the vessels of the house of God, with the meat offering and the frankincense.[10] And I perceived that the portions of the Levites

had not been given them: for the Levites and the singers, that did the work, were fled every one to his field.[11] Then contended I with the rulers, and said, Why is the house of God forsaken? And I gathered them together, and set them in their place.[12] Then brought all Judah the tithe of the corn and the new wine and the oil unto the treasuries.[13] And I made treasurers over the treasuries, Shelemiah the priest, and Zadok the scribe, and of the Levites, Pedaiah: and next to them was Hanan the son of Zaccur, the son of Mattaniah: for they were counted faithful, and their office was to distribute unto their brethren.[14] Remember me, O my God, concerning this, and wipe not out my good deeds that I have done for the house of my God, and for the offices thereof.[15] In those days saw I in Judah some treading wine presses on the sabbath, and bringing in sheaves, and lading asses; as also wine, grapes, and figs, and all manner of burdens, which they brought into Jerusalem on the sabbath day: and I testified against them in the day wherein they sold victuals.[16] There dwelt men of Tyre also therein, which brought fish, and all manner of ware, and sold on the sabbath unto the children of Judah, and in Jerusalem.[17] Then I contended with the nobles of Judah, and said unto them, What evil thing is this that ye do, and profane the sabbath day?[18] Did not your fathers thus, and did not our God bring all this evil upon us, and upon this city? yet ye bring more wrath upon Israel by profaning the sabbath.[19] And it came to pass, that when the gates of Jerusalem began to be dark before the sabbath, I commanded that the gates should be shut, and charged that they should not be opened till after the sabbath: and some of my servants set I at the gates, that there should no burden be brought in on the sabbath day.[20] So the merchants and sellers of all kind of ware lodged without Jerusalem once or twice.[21] Then I testified against them, and said unto them, Why lodge ye about the wall? if ye do so again, I will lay hands on you. From that time forth came they no more on the sabbath.[22] And I commanded the Levites that they should cleanse themselves, and that they should come and keep the gates, to sanctify the sabbath day. Remember me, O my God, concerning this also, and spare me according to the greatness of thy mercy.[23] In those days also saw I Jews that had married wives of Ashdod, of Ammon, and of Moab:[24] And their children spake half in the speech of Ashdod, and could not speak in the Jews' language, but according to the language of each people.[25] And I contended with them, and cursed them, and smote certain of them, and plucked off their hair, and made them swear by God, saying, Ye shall not give your daughters unto their sons, nor take their daughters unto your sons, or for yourselves.[26] Did not Solomon king of Israel sin by these things? yet among many nations was there no king like him, who was beloved of his God, and God made him king over all Israel: nevertheless even him did outlandish women cause to sin.[27] Shall we then hearken unto you to do all this great evil, to transgress against our God in marrying strange wives?[28] And one of the sons of Joiada, the son of Eliashib the high priest, was son in law to Sanballat the Horonite: therefore I chased him from me.[29] Remember them, O my God, because they have defiled the priesthood, and the covenant of the priesthood, and of the Levites.[30] Thus cleansed I them from all strangers, and appointed the wards of the priests and the Levites, every one in his business;[31] And for the wood offering, at times appointed, and for the firstfruits. Remember me, O my God, for good.

Esther

Esth.1

[1] Now it came to pass in the days of Ahasuerus, (this is Ahasuerus which reigned, from India even unto Ethiopia, over an hundred and seven and twenty provinces:)[2] That in those days, when the king

Ahasuerus sat on the throne of his kingdom, which was in Shushan the palace,³ In the third year of his reign, he made a feast unto all his princes and his servants; the power of Persia and Media, the nobles and princes of the provinces, being before him:⁴ When he shewed the riches of his glorious kingdom and the honour of his excellent majesty many days, even an hundred and fourscore days.⁵ And when these days were expired, the king made a feast unto all the people that were present in Shushan the palace, both unto great and small, seven days, in the court of the garden of the king's palace;⁶ Where were white, green, and blue, hangings, fastened with cords of fine linen and purple to silver rings and pillars of marble: the beds were of gold and silver, upon a pavement of red, and blue, and white, and black, marble.⁷ And they gave them drink in vessels of gold, (the vessels being diverse one from another,) and royal wine in abundance, according to the state of the king.⁸ And the drinking was according to the law; none did compel: for so the king had appointed to all the officers of his house, that they should do according to every man's pleasure.⁹ Also Vashti the queen made a feast for the women in the royal house which belonged to king Ahasuerus.¹⁰ On the seventh day, when the heart of the king was merry with wine, he commanded Mehuman, Biztha, Harbona, Bigtha, and Abagtha, Zethar, and Carcas, the seven chamberlains that served in the presence of Ahasuerus the king,¹¹ To bring Vashti the queen before the king with the crown royal, to shew the people and the princes her beauty: for she was fair to look on.¹² But the queen Vashti refused to come at the king's commandment by his chamberlains: therefore was the king very wroth, and his anger burned in him.¹³ Then the king said to the wise men, which knew the times, (for so was the king's manner toward all that knew law and judgment:¹⁴ And the next unto him was Carshena, Shethar, Admatha, Tarshish, Meres, Marsena, and Memucan, the seven princes of Persia and Media, which saw the king's face, and which sat the first in the kingdom;)¹⁵ What shall we do unto the queen Vashti according to law, because she hath not performed the commandment of the king Ahasuerus by the chamberlains?¹⁶ And Memucan answered before the king and the princes, Vashti the queen hath not done wrong to the king only, but also to all the princes, and to all the people that are in all the provinces of the king Ahasuerus.¹⁷ For this deed of the queen shall come abroad unto all women, so that they shall despise their husbands in their eyes, when it shall be reported, The king Ahasuerus commanded Vashti the queen to be brought in before him, but she came not.¹⁸ Likewise shall the ladies of Persia and Media say this day unto all the king's princes, which have heard of the deed of the queen. Thus shall there arise too much contempt and wrath.¹⁹ If it please the king, let there go a royal commandment from him, and let it be written among the laws of the Persians and the Medes, that it be not altered, That Vashti come no more before king Ahasuerus; and let the king give her royal estate unto another that is better than she.²⁰ And when the king's decree which he shall make shall be published throughout all his empire, (for it is great,) all the wives shall give to their husbands honour, both to great and small.²¹ And the saying pleased the king and the princes; and the king did according to the word of Memucan:²² For he sent letters into all the king's provinces, into every province according to the writing thereof, and to every people after their language, that every man should bear rule in his own house, and that it should be published according to the language of every people.

Esth.2

¹ After these things, when the wrath of king Ahasuerus was appeased, he remembered Vashti, and what she had done, and what was decreed against her.² Then said the king's servants that ministered unto him, Let there be fair young virgins sought for the king:³ And let the king appoint officers in all the provinces of his kingdom, that they may gather together all the fair young virgins unto Shushan the palace, to the house of the women unto the custody of Hege the king's chamberlain, keeper of the women; and let their things for purification be given them:⁴ And let the maiden which pleaseth the king be queen instead of Vashti. And the thing pleased the king; and he did so.⁵ Now in Shushan the palace there was a certain Jew, whose name was Mordecai, the son of Jair, the son of Shimei, the son of Kish, a Benjamite;⁶ Who had been carried away from Jerusalem with the captivity which had been carried away with Jeconiah king of Judah, whom Nebuchadnezzar the king of Babylon had carried away.⁷ And he brought up Hadassah, that is, Esther, his uncle's daughter: for she had neither father nor mother, and the maid was fair and beautiful; whom Mordecai, when her father and mother were dead, took for his own daughter.⁸ So it came to pass, when the king's commandment and his decree was heard, and when many maidens were gathered together unto Shushan the palace, to the custody of Hegai, that Esther was brought also unto the king's house, to the custody of Hegai, keeper of the women.⁹ And the maiden pleased him, and she obtained kindness of him; and he speedily gave her her things for purification, with such things as belonged to her, and seven maidens, which were meet to be given her, out of the king's house: and he preferred her and her maids unto the best place of the house of the women.¹⁰ Esther had not shewed her people nor her kindred: for Mordecai had charged her that she should not shew it.¹¹ And Mordecai walked every day before the court of the women's house, to know how Esther did, and what should become of her.¹² Now when every maid's turn was come to go in to king Ahasuerus, after that she had been twelve months, according to the manner of the women, (for so were the days of their purifications accomplished, to wit, six months with oil of myrrh, and six months with sweet odours, and with other things for the purifying of the women;)¹³ Then thus came every maiden unto the king; whatsoever she desired was given her to go with her out of the house of the women unto the king's house.¹⁴ In the evening she went, and on the morrow she returned into the second house of the women, to the custody of Shaashgaz, the king's chamberlain, which kept the concubines: she came in unto the king no more, except the king delighted in her, and that she were called by name.¹⁵ Now when the turn of Esther, the daughter of Abihail the uncle of Mordecai, who had taken her for his daughter, was come to go in unto the king, she required nothing but what Hegai the king's chamberlain, the keeper of the women, appointed. And Esther obtained favour in the sight of all them that looked upon her.¹⁶ So Esther was taken unto king Ahasuerus into his house royal in the tenth month, which is the month Tebeth, in the seventh year of his reign.¹⁷ And the king loved Esther above all the women, and she obtained grace and favour in his sight more than all the virgins; so that he set the royal crown upon her head, and made her queen instead of Vashti.¹⁸ Then the king made a great feast unto all his princes and his servants, even Esther's feast; and he made a release to the provinces, and gave gifts, according to the state of the king.¹⁹ And when the virgins were gathered together the second time, then Mordecai sat in the king's gate.²⁰ Esther had not yet shewed her kindred nor her people; as Mordecai had charged her: for Esther did the commandment of Mordecai, like as when she was brought up with him.²¹ In those days, while Mordecai sat in the king's gate, two of the king's chamberlains, Bigthan and Teresh, of those which kept the door, were wroth, and sought to lay hand on the king Ahasuerus.²² And the thing was known to Mordecai, who told it unto Esther the queen; and Esther certified the king thereof

in Mordecai's name.[23] And when inquisition was made of the matter, it was found out; therefore they were both hanged on a tree: and it was written in the book of the chronicles before the king.

Esth.3

[1] After these things did king Ahasuerus promote Haman the son of Hammedatha the Agagite, and advanced him, and set his seat above all the princes that were with him.[2] And all the king's servants, that were in the king's gate, bowed, and reverenced Haman: for the king had so commanded concerning him. But Mordecai bowed not, nor did him reverence.[3] Then the king's servants, which were in the king's gate, said unto Mordecai, Why transgressest thou the king's commandment?[4] Now it came to pass, when they spake daily unto him, and he hearkened not unto them, that they told Haman, to see whether Mordecai's matters would stand: for he had told them that he was a Jew.[5] And when Haman saw that Mordecai bowed not, nor did him reverence, then was Haman full of wrath.[6] And he thought scorn to lay hands on Mordecai alone; for they had shewed him the people of Mordecai: wherefore Haman sought to destroy all the Jews that were throughout the whole kingdom of Ahasuerus, even the people of Mordecai.[7] In the first month, that is, the month Nisan, in the twelfth year of king Ahasuerus, they cast Pur, that is, the lot, before Haman from day to day, and from month to month, to the twelfth month, that is, the month Adar.[8] And Haman said unto king Ahasuerus, There is a certain people scattered abroad and dispersed among the people in all the provinces of thy kingdom; and their laws are diverse from all people; neither keep they the king's laws: therefore it is not for the king's profit to suffer them.[9] If it please the king, let it be written that they may be destroyed: and I will pay ten thousand talents of silver to the hands of those that have the charge of the business, to bring it into the king's treasuries.[10] And the king took his ring from his hand, and gave it unto Haman the son of Hammedatha the Agagite, the Jews' enemy.[11] And the king said unto Haman, The silver is given to thee, the people also, to do with them as it seemeth good to thee.[12] Then were the king's scribes called on the thirteenth day of the first month, and there was written according to all that Haman had commanded unto the king's lieutenants, and to the governors that were over every province, and to the rulers of every people of every province according to the writing thereof, and to every people after their language; in the name of king Ahasuerus was it written, and sealed with the king's ring.[13] And the letters were sent by posts into all the king's provinces, to destroy, to kill, and to cause to perish, all Jews, both young and old, little children and women, in one day, even upon the thirteenth day of the twelfth month, which is the month Adar, and to take the spoil of them for a prey.[14] The copy of the writing for a commandment to be given in every province was published unto all people, that they should be ready against that day.[15] The posts went out, being hastened by the king's commandment, and the decree was given in Shushan the palace. And the king and Haman sat down to drink; but the city Shushan was perplexed.

Esth.4

[1] When Mordecai perceived all that was done, Mordecai rent his clothes, and put on sackcloth with ashes, and went out into the midst of the city, and cried with a loud and a bitter cry;[2] And came even before the king's gate: for none might enter into the king's gate clothed with sackcloth.[3] And in every province, whithersoever the king's commandment and his decree came, there was great mourning among the Jews, and fasting, and weeping, and wailing; and many lay in sackcloth and ashes.[4] So Esther's maids and her chamberlains came and told it her. Then was the queen exceedingly grieved; and she sent raiment to clothe Mordecai, and to take away his sackcloth from him: but he received it not.[5] Then called Esther

for Hatach, one of the king's chamberlains, whom he had appointed to attend upon her, and gave him a commandment to Mordecai, to know what it was, and why it was.[6] So Hatach went forth to Mordecai unto the street of the city, which was before the king's gate.[7] And Mordecai told him of all that had happened unto him, and of the sum of the money that Haman had promised to pay to the king's treasuries for the Jews, to destroy them.[8] Also he gave him the copy of the writing of the decree that was given at Shushan to destroy them, to shew it unto Esther, and to declare it unto her, and to charge her that she should go in unto the king, to make supplication unto him, and to make request before him for her people.[9] And Hatach came and told Esther the words of Mordecai.[10] Again Esther spake unto Hatach, and gave him commandment unto Mordecai;[11] All the king's servants, and the people of the king's provinces, do know, that whosoever, whether man or woman, shall come unto the king into the inner court, who is not called, there is one law of his to put him to death, except such to whom the king shall hold out the golden sceptre, that he may live: but I have not been called to come in unto the king these thirty days.[12] And they told to Mordecai Esther's words.[13] Then Mordecai commanded to answer Esther, Think not with thyself that thou shalt escape in the king's house, more than all the Jews.[14] For if thou altogether holdest thy peace at this time, then shall there enlargement and deliverance arise to the Jews from another place; but thou and thy father's house shall be destroyed: and who knoweth whether thou art come to the kingdom for such a time as this?[15] Then Esther bade them return Mordecai this answer,[16] Go, gather together all the Jews that are present in Shushan, and fast ye for me, and neither eat nor drink three days, night or day: I also and my maidens will fast likewise; and so will I go in unto the king, which is not according to the law: and if I perish, I perish.[17] So Mordecai went his way, and did according to all that Esther had commanded him.

Esth.5

[1] Now it came to pass on the third day, that Esther put on her royal apparel, and stood in the inner court of the king's house, over against the king's house: and the king sat upon his royal throne in the royal house, over against the gate of the house.[2] And it was so, when the king saw Esther the queen standing in the court, that she obtained favour in his sight: and the king held out to Esther the golden sceptre that was in his hand. So Esther drew near, and touched the top of the sceptre.[3] Then said the king unto her, What wilt thou, queen Esther? and what is thy request? it shall be even given thee to the half of the kingdom.[4] And Esther answered, If it seem good unto the king, let the king and Haman come this day unto the banquet that I have prepared for him.[5] Then the king said, Cause Haman to make haste, that he may do as Esther hath said. So the king and Haman came to the banquet that Esther had prepared.[6] And the king said unto Esther at the banquet of wine, What is thy petition? and it shall be granted thee: and what is thy request? even to the half of the kingdom it shall be performed.[7] Then answered Esther, and said, My petition and my request is;[8] If I have found favour in the sight of the king, and if it please the king to grant my petition, and to perform my request, let the king and Haman come to the banquet that I shall prepare for them, and I will do tomorrow as the king hath said.[9] Then went Haman forth that day joyful and with a glad heart: but when Haman saw Mordecai in the king's gate, that he stood not up, nor moved for him, he was full of indignation against Mordecai.[10] Nevertheless Haman refrained himself: and when he came home, he sent and called for his friends, and Zeresh his wife.[11] And Haman told them of the glory of his riches, and the multitude of his children, and all the things wherein the king had

promoted him, and how he had advanced him above the princes and servants of the king.[12] Haman said moreover, Yea, Esther the queen did let no man come in with the king unto the banquet that she had prepared but myself; and to morrow am I invited unto her also with the king.[13] Yet all this availeth me nothing, so long as I see Mordecai the Jew sitting at the king's gate.[14] Then said Zeresh his wife and all his friends unto him, Let a gallows be made of fifty cubits high, and tomorrow speak thou unto the king that Mordecai may be hanged thereon: then go thou in merrily with the king unto the banquet. And the thing pleased Haman; and he caused the gallows to be made.

Esth.6

[1] On that night could not the king sleep, and he commanded to bring the book of records of the chronicles; and they were read before the king.[2] And it was found written, that Mordecai had told of Bigthana and Teresh, two of the king's chamberlains, the keepers of the door, who sought to lay hand on the king Ahasuerus.[3] And the king said, What honour and dignity hath been done to Mordecai for this? Then said the king's servants that ministered unto him, There is nothing done for him.[4] And the king said, Who is in the court? Now Haman was come into the outward court of the king's house, to speak unto the king to hang Mordecai on the gallows that he had prepared for him.[5] And the king's servants said unto him, Behold, Haman standeth in the court. And the king said, Let him come in.[6] So Haman came in. And the king said unto him, What shall be done unto the man whom the king delighteth to honour? Now Haman thought in his heart, To whom would the king delight to do honour more than to myself?[7] And Haman answered the king, For the man whom the king delighteth to honour,[8] Let the royal apparel be brought which the king useth to wear, and the horse that the king rideth upon, and the crown royal which is set upon his head:[9] And let this apparel and horse be delivered to the hand of one of the king's most noble princes, that they may array the man withal whom the king delighteth to honour, and bring him on horseback through the street of the city, and proclaim before him, Thus shall it be done to the man whom the king delighteth to honour.[10] Then the king said to Haman, Make haste, and take the apparel and the horse, as thou hast said, and do even so to Mordecai the Jew, that sitteth at the king's gate: let nothing fail of all that thou has spoken.[11] Then took Haman the apparel and the horse, and arrayed Mordecai, and brought him on horseback through the street of the city, and proclaimed before him, Thus shall it be done unto the man whom the king delighteth to honour.[12] And Mordecai came again to the king's gate. But Haman hasted to his house mourning, and having his head covered.[13] And Haman told Zeresh his wife and all his friends every thing that had befallen him. Then said his wise men and Zeresh his wife unto him, If Mordecai be of the seed of the Jews, before whom thou hast begun to fall, thou shalt not prevail against him, but shalt surely fall before him.[14] And while they were yet talking with him, came the king's chamberlains, and hasted to bring Haman unto the banquet that Esther had prepared.

Esth.7

[1] So the king and Haman came to banquet with Esther the queen.[2] And the king said again unto Esther on the second day at the banquet of wine, What is thy petition, queen Esther? and it shall be granted thee: and what is thy request? and it shall be performed, even to the half of the kingdom.[3] Then Esther the queen answered and said, If I have found favour in thy sight, O king, and if it please the king, let my life be given me at my petition, and my people at my request:[4] For we are sold, I and my people, to be destroyed, to be slain, and to perish. But if we had been sold for bondmen and bondwomen, I had held my tongue, although the enemy could not countervail the king's damage.[5] Then the king Ahasuerus answered and said unto Esther the queen, Who is he, and where is he, that durst presume in his heart to do so?[6] And Esther said, The adversary and enemy is this wicked Haman. Then Haman was afraid before the king and the queen.[7] And the king arising from the banquet of wine in his wrath went into the palace garden: and Haman stood up to make request for his life to Esther the queen; for he saw that there was evil determined against him by the king.[8] Then the king returned out of the palace garden into the place of the banquet of wine; and Haman was fallen upon the bed whereon Esther was. Then said the king, Will he force the queen also before me in the house? As the word went out of the king's mouth, they covered Haman's face.[9] And Harbonah, one of the chamberlains, said before the king, Behold also, the gallows fifty cubits high, which Haman had made for Mordecai, who had spoken good for the king, standeth in the house of Haman. Then the king said, Hang him thereon.[10] So they hanged Haman on the gallows that he had prepared for Mordecai. Then was the king's wrath pacified.

Esth.8

[1] On that day did the king Ahasuerus give the house of Haman the Jews' enemy unto Esther the queen. And Mordecai came before the king; for Esther had told what he was unto her.[2] And the king took off his ring, which he had taken from Haman, and gave it unto Mordecai. And Esther set Mordecai over the house of Haman.[3] And Esther spake yet again before the king, and fell down at his feet, and besought him with tears to put away the mischief of Haman the Agagite, and his device that he had devised against the Jews.[4] Then the king held out the golden sceptre toward Esther. So Esther arose, and stood before the king,[5] And said, If it please the king, and if I have found favour in his sight, and the thing seem right before the king, and I be pleasing in his eyes, let it be written to reverse the letters devised by Haman the son of Hammedatha the Agagite, which he wrote to destroy the Jews which are in all the king's provinces:[6] For how can I endure to see the evil that shall come unto my people? or how can I endure to see the destruction of my kindred?[7] Then the king Ahasuerus said unto Esther the queen and to Mordecai the Jew, Behold, I have given Esther the house of Haman, and him they have hanged upon the gallows, because he laid his hand upon the Jews.[8] Write ye also for the Jews, as it liketh you, in the king's name, and seal it with the king's ring: for the writing which is written in the king's name, and sealed with the king's ring, may no man reverse.[9] Then were the king's scribes called at that time in the third month, that is, the month Sivan, on the three and twentieth day thereof; and it was written according to all that Mordecai commanded unto the Jews, and to the lieutenants, and the deputies and rulers of the provinces which are from India unto Ethiopia, an hundred twenty and seven provinces, unto every province according to the writing thereof, and unto every people after their language, and to the Jews according to their writing, and according to their language.[10] And he wrote in the king Ahasuerus' name, and sealed it with the king's ring, and sent letters by posts on horseback, and riders on mules, camels, and young dromedaries:[11] Wherein the king granted the Jews which were in every city to gather themselves together, and to stand for their life, to destroy, to slay, and to cause to perish, all the power of the people and province that would assault them, both little ones and women, and to take the spoil of them for a prey,[12] Upon one day in all the provinces of king Ahasuerus, namely, upon the thirteenth day of the twelfth month, which is the month Adar.[13] The copy of the writing for a commandment to be given in every province was published unto all people, and that the Jews should be ready against that day to avenge themselves on their enemies.[14] So the posts that rode

upon mules and camels went out, being hastened and pressed on by the king's commandment. And the decree was given at Shushan the palace.¹⁵ And Mordecai went out from the presence of the king in royal apparel of blue and white, and with a great crown of gold, and with a garment of fine linen and purple: and the city of Shushan rejoiced and was glad.¹⁶ The Jews had light, and gladness, and joy, and honour.¹⁷ And in every province, and in every city, whithersoever the king's commandment and his decree came, the Jews had joy and gladness, a feast and a good day. And many of the people of the land became Jews; for the fear of the Jews fell upon them.

Esth.9

¹ Now in the twelfth month, that is, the month Adar, on the thirteenth day of the same, when the king's commandment and his decree drew near to be put in execution, in the day that the enemies of the Jews hoped to have power over them, (though it was turned to the contrary, that the Jews had rule over them that hated them;)² The Jews gathered themselves together in their cities throughout all the provinces of the king Ahasuerus, to lay hand on such as sought their hurt: and no man could withstand them; for the fear of them fell upon all people.³ And all the rulers of the provinces, and the lieutenants, and the deputies, and officers of the king, helped the Jews; because the fear of Mordecai fell upon them.⁴ For Mordecai was great in the king's house, and his fame went out throughout all the provinces: for this man Mordecai waxed greater and greater.⁵ Thus the Jews smote all their enemies with the stroke of the sword, and slaughter, and destruction, and did what they would unto those that hated them.⁶ And in Shushan the palace the Jews slew and destroyed five hundred men.⁷ And Parshandatha, and Dalphon, and Aspatha,⁸ And Poratha, and Adalia, and Aridatha,⁹ And Parmashta, and Arisai, and Aridai, and Vajezatha,¹⁰ The ten sons of Haman the son of Hammedatha, the enemy of the Jews, slew they; but on the spoil laid they not their hand.¹¹ On that day the number of those that were slain in Shushan the palace was brought before the king.¹² And the king said unto Esther the queen, The Jews have slain and destroyed five hundred men in Shushan the palace, and the ten sons of Haman; what have they done in the rest of the king's provinces? now what is thy petition? and it shall be granted thee: or what is thy request further? and it shall be done.¹³ Then said Esther, If it please the king, let it be granted to the Jews which are in Shushan to do tomorrow also according unto this day's decree, and let Haman's ten sons be hanged upon the gallows.¹⁴ And the king commanded it so to be done: and the decree was given at Shushan; and they hanged Haman's ten sons.¹⁵ For the Jews that were in Shushan gathered themselves together on the fourteenth day also of the month Adar, and slew three hundred men at Shushan; but on the prey they laid not their hand.¹⁶ But the other Jews that were in the king's provinces gathered themselves together, and stood for their lives, and had rest from their enemies, and slew of their foes seventy and five thousand, but they laid not their hands on the prey,¹⁷ On the thirteenth day of the month Adar; and on the fourteenth day of the same rested they, and made it a day of feasting and gladness.¹⁸ But the Jews that were at Shushan assembled together on the thirteenth day thereof; and on the fourteenth thereof; and on the fifteenth day of the same they rested, and made it a day of feasting and gladness.¹⁹ Therefore the Jews of the villages, that dwelt in the unwalled towns, made the fourteenth day of the month Adar a day of gladness and feasting, and a good day, and of sending portions one to another.²⁰ And Mordecai wrote these things, and sent letters unto all the Jews that were in all the provinces of the king Ahasuerus, both nigh and far,²¹ To stablish this among them, that they should keep the

fourteenth day of the month Adar, and the fifteenth day of the same, yearly,²² As the days wherein the Jews rested from their enemies, and the month which was turned unto them from sorrow to joy, and from mourning into a good day: that they should make them days of feasting and joy, and of sending portions one to another, and gifts to the poor.²³ And the Jews undertook to do as they had begun, and as Mordecai had written unto them;²⁴ Because Haman the son of Hammedatha, the Agagite, the enemy of all the Jews, had devised against the Jews to destroy them, and had cast Pur, that is, the lot, to consume them, and to destroy them;²⁵ But when Esther came before the king, he commanded by letters that his wicked device, which he devised against the Jews, should return upon his own head, and that he and his sons should be hanged on the gallows.²⁶ Wherefore they called these days Purim after the name of Pur. Therefore for all the words of this letter, and of that which they had seen concerning this matter, and which had come unto them,²⁷ The Jews ordained, and took upon them, and upon their seed, and upon all such as joined themselves unto them, so as it should not fail, that they would keep these two days according to their writing, and according to their appointed time every year;²⁸ And that these days should be remembered and kept throughout every generation, every family, every province, and every city; and that these days of Purim should not fail from among the Jews, nor the memorial of them perish from their seed.²⁹ Then Esther the queen, the daughter of Abihail, and Mordecai the Jew, wrote with all authority, to confirm this second letter of Purim.³⁰ And he sent the letters unto all the Jews, to the hundred twenty and seven provinces of the kingdom of Ahasuerus, with words of peace and truth,³¹ To confirm these days of Purim in their times appointed, according as Mordecai the Jew and Esther the queen had enjoined them, and as they had decreed for themselves and for their seed, the matters of the fastings and their cry.³² And the decree of Esther confirmed these matters of Purim; and it was written in the book.

Esth.10

¹ And the king Ahasuerus laid a tribute upon the land, and upon the isles of the sea.² And all the acts of his power and of his might, and the declaration of the greatness of Mordecai, whereunto the king advanced him, are they not written in the book of the chronicles of the kings of Media and Persia?³ For Mordecai the Jew was next unto king Ahasuerus, and great among the Jews, and accepted of the multitude of his brethren, seeking the wealth of his people, and speaking peace to all his seed.

Proverbs Messale and Tagsas

Prov.1

¹ The proverbs of Solomon the son of David, king of Israel;² To know wisdom and instruction; to perceive the words of understanding;³ To receive the instruction of wisdom, justice, and judgment, and equity;⁴ To give subtilty to the simple, to the young man knowledge and discretion.⁵ A wise man will hear, and will increase learning; and a man of understanding shall attain unto wise counsels:⁶ To understand a proverb, and the interpretation; the words of the wise, and their dark sayings.⁷ The fear of the LORD is the beginning of knowledge: but fools despise wisdom and instruction.⁸ My son, hear the instruction of thy father, and forsake not the law of thy mother:⁹ For they shall be an ornament of grace unto thy head, and chains about thy neck.¹⁰ My son, if sinners entice thee, consent thou not.¹¹ If they say, Come with us, let us lay wait for blood, let us lurk privily for the innocent without cause:¹² Let us swallow them up alive as the grave; and whole, as those that go down into the pit:¹³ We shall find all precious substance, we shall fill our

houses with spoil:[14] Cast in thy lot among us; let us all have one purse:[15] My son, walk not thou in the way with them; refrain thy foot from their path:[16] For their feet run to evil, and make haste to shed blood.[17] Surely in vain the net is spread in the sight of any bird.[18] And they lay wait for their own blood; they lurk privily for their own lives.[19] So are the ways of every one that is greedy of gain; which taketh away the life of the owners thereof.[20] Wisdom crieth without; she uttereth her voice in the streets:[21] She crieth in the chief place of concourse, in the openings of the gates: in the city she uttereth her words, saying,[22] How long, ye simple ones, will ye love simplicity? and the scorners delight in their scorning, and fools hate knowledge?[23] Turn you at my reproof: behold, I will pour out my spirit unto you, I will make known my words unto you.[24] Because I have called, and ye refused; I have stretched out my hand, and no man regarded;[25] But ye have set at nought all my counsel, and would none of my reproof:[26] I also will laugh at your calamity; I will mock when your fear cometh;[27] When your fear cometh as desolation, and your destruction cometh as a whirlwind; when distress and anguish cometh upon you.[28] Then shall they call upon me, but I will not answer; they shall seek me early, but they shall not find me:[29] For that they hated knowledge, and did not choose the fear of the LORD:[30] They would none of my counsel: they despised all my reproof.[31] Therefore shall they eat of the fruit of their own way, and be filled with their own devices.[32] For the turning away of the simple shall slay them, and the prosperity of fools shall destroy them.[33] But whoso hearkeneth unto me shall dwell safely, and shall be quiet from fear of evil.

Prov.2

[1] My son, if thou wilt receive my words, and hide my commandments with thee;[2] So that thou incline thine ear unto wisdom, and apply thine heart to understanding;[3] Yea, if thou criest after knowledge, and liftest up thy voice for understanding;[4] If thou seekest her as silver, and searchest for her as for hid treasures;[5] Then shalt thou understand the fear of the LORD, and find the knowledge of God.[6] For the LORD giveth wisdom: out of his mouth cometh knowledge and understanding.[7] He layeth up sound wisdom for the righteous: he is a buckler to them that walk uprightly.[8] He keepeth the paths of judgment, and preserveth the way of his saints.[9] Then shalt thou understand righteousness, and judgment, and equity; yea, every good path.[10] When wisdom entereth into thine heart, and knowledge is pleasant unto thy soul;[11] Discretion shall preserve thee, understanding shall keep thee:[12] To deliver thee from the way of the evil man, from the man that speaketh froward things;[13] Who leave the paths of uprightness, to walk in the ways of darkness;[14] Who rejoice to do evil, and delight in the frowardness of the wicked;[15] Whose ways are crooked, and they froward in their paths:[16] To deliver thee from the strange woman, even from the stranger which flattereth with her words;[17] Which forsaketh the guide of her youth, and forgetteth the covenant of her God.[18] For her house inclineth unto death, and her paths unto the dead.[19] None that go unto her return again, neither take they hold of the paths of life.[20] That thou mayest walk in the way of good men, and keep the paths of the righteous.[21] For the upright shall dwell in the land, and the perfect shall remain in it.[22] But the wicked shall be cut off from the earth, and the transgressors shall be rooted out of it.

Prov.3

[1] My son, forget not my law; but let thine heart keep my commandments:[2] For length of days, and long life, and peace, shall they add to thee.[3] Let not mercy and truth forsake thee: bind them about thy neck; write them upon the table of thine heart:[4] So shalt thou find favour and good understanding in the sight of God and

man.[5] Trust in the LORD with all thine heart; and lean not unto thine own understanding.[6] In all thy ways acknowledge him, and he shall direct thy paths.[7] Be not wise in thine own eyes: fear the LORD, and depart from evil.[8] It shall be health to thy navel, and marrow to thy bones.[9] Honour the LORD with thy substance, and with the firstfruits of all thine increase:[10] So shall thy barns be filled with plenty, and thy presses shall burst out with new wine.[11] My son, despise not the chastening of the LORD; neither be weary of his correction:[12] For whom the LORD loveth he correcteth; even as a father the son in whom he delighteth.[13] Happy is the man that findeth wisdom, and the man that getteth understanding.[14] For the merchandise of it is better than the merchandise of silver, and the gain thereof than fine gold.[15] She is more precious than rubies: and all the things thou canst desire are not to be compared unto her.[16] Length of days is in her right hand; and in her left hand riches and honour.[17] Her ways are ways of pleasantness, and all her paths are peace.[18] She is a tree of life to them that lay hold upon her: and happy is every one that retaineth her.[19] The LORD by wisdom hath founded the earth; by understanding hath he established the heavens.[20] By his knowledge the depths are broken up, and the clouds drop down the dew.[21] My son, let not them depart from thine eyes: keep sound wisdom and discretion:[22] So shall they be life unto thy soul, and grace to thy neck.[23] Then shalt thou walk in thy way safely, and thy foot shall not stumble.[24] When thou liest down, thou shalt not be afraid: yea, thou shalt lie down, and thy sleep shall be sweet.[25] Be not afraid of sudden fear, neither of the desolation of the wicked, when it cometh.[26] For the LORD shall be thy confidence, and shall keep thy foot from being taken.[27] Withhold not good from them to whom it is due, when it is in the power of thine hand to do it.[28] Say not unto thy neighbour, Go, and come again, and to morrow I will give; when thou hast it by thee.[29] Devise not evil against thy neighbour, seeing he dwelleth securely by thee.[30] Strive not with a man without cause, if he have done thee no harm.[31] Envy thou not the oppressor, and choose none of his ways.[32] For the froward is abomination to the LORD: but his secret is with the righteous.[33] The curse of the LORD is in the house of the wicked: but he blesseth the habitation of the just.[34] Surely he scorneth the scorners: but he giveth grace unto the lowly.[35] The wise shall inherit glory: but shame shall be the promotion of fools.

Prov.4

[1] Hear, ye children, the instruction of a father, and attend to know understanding.[2] For I give you good doctrine, forsake ye not my law.[3] For I was my father's son, tender and only beloved in the sight of my mother.[4] He taught me also, and said unto me, Let thine heart retain my words: keep my commandments, and live.[5] Get wisdom, get understanding: forget it not; neither decline from the words of my mouth.[6] Forsake her not, and she shall preserve thee: love her, and she shall keep thee.[7] Wisdom is the principal thing; therefore get wisdom: and with all thy getting get understanding.[8] Exalt her, and she shall promote thee: she shall bring thee to honour, when thou dost embrace her.[9] She shall give to thine head an ornament of grace: a crown of glory shall she deliver to thee.[10] Hear, O my son, and receive my sayings; and the years of thy life shall be many.[11] I have taught thee in the way of wisdom; I have led thee in right paths.[12] When thou goest, thy steps shall not be straitened; and when thou runnest, thou shalt not stumble.[13] Take fast hold of instruction; let her not go: keep her; for she is thy life.[14] Enter not into the path of the wicked, and go not in the way of evil men.[15] Avoid it, pass not by it, turn from it, and pass away.[16] For they sleep not, except they have done mischief; and their sleep is taken away, unless they cause some to fall.[17] For they eat the bread of wickedness, and drink the wine of violence.[18] But the path of the just is as the shining light,

that shineth more and more unto the perfect day.[19] The way of the wicked is as darkness: they know not at what they stumble.[20] My son, attend to my words; incline thine ear unto my sayings.[21] Let them not depart from thine eyes; keep them in the midst of thine heart.[22] For they are life unto those that find them, and health to all their flesh.[23] Keep thy heart with all diligence; for out of it are the issues of life.[24] Put away from thee a froward mouth, and perverse lips put far from thee.[25] Let thine eyes look right on, and let thine eyelids look straight before thee.[26] Ponder the path of thy feet, and let all thy ways be established.[27] Turn not to the right hand nor to the left: remove thy foot from evil.

Prov.5

[1] My son, attend unto my wisdom, and bow thine ear to my understanding:[2] That thou mayest regard discretion, and that thy lips may keep knowledge.[3] For the lips of a strange woman drop as an honeycomb, and her mouth is smoother than oil:[4] But her end is bitter as wormwood, sharp as a twoedged sword.[5] Her feet go down to death; her steps take hold on hell.[6] Lest thou shouldest ponder the path of life, her ways are moveable, that thou canst not know them.[7] Hear me now therefore, O ye children, and depart not from the words of my mouth.[8] Remove thy way far from her, and come not nigh the door of her house:[9] Lest thou give thine honour unto others, and thy years unto the cruel:[10] Lest strangers be filled with thy wealth; and thy labours be in the house of a stranger;[11] And thou mourn at the last, when thy flesh and thy body are consumed,[12] And say, How have I hated instruction, and my heart despised reproof;[13] And have not obeyed the voice of my teachers, nor inclined mine ear to them that instructed me![14] I was almost in all evil in the midst of the congregation and assembly.[15] Drink waters out of thine own cistern, and running waters out of thine own well.[16] Let thy fountains be dispersed abroad, and rivers of waters in the streets.[17] Let them be only thine own, and not strangers' with thee.[18] Let thy fountain be blessed: and rejoice with the wife of thy youth.[19] Let her be as the loving hind and pleasant roe; let her breasts satisfy thee at all times; and be thou ravished always with her love.[20] And why wilt thou, my son, be ravished with a strange woman, and embrace the bosom of a stranger?[21] For the ways of man are before the eyes of the LORD, and he pondereth all his goings.[22] His own iniquities shall take the wicked himself, and he shall be holden with the cords of his sins.[23] He shall die without instruction; and in the greatness of his folly he shall go astray.

Prov.6

[1] My son, if thou be surety for thy friend, if thou hast stricken thy hand with a stranger,[2] Thou art snared with the words of thy mouth, thou art taken with the words of thy mouth.[3] Do this now, my son, deliver thyself, when thou art come into the hand of thy friend; go, humble thyself, and make sure thy friend.[4] Give not sleep to thine eyes, nor slumber to thine eyelids.[5] Deliver thyself as a roe from the hand of the hunter, and as a bird from the hand of the fowler.[6] Go to the ant, thou sluggard; consider her ways, and be wise:[7] Which having no guide, overseer, or ruler,[8] Provideth her meat in the summer, and gathereth her food in the harvest.[9] How long wilt thou sleep, O sluggard? when wilt thou arise out of thy sleep?[10] Yet a little sleep, a little slumber, a little folding of the hands to sleep:[11] So shall thy poverty come as one that travelleth, and thy want as an armed man.[12] A naughty person, a wicked man, walketh with a froward mouth.[13] He winketh with his eyes, he speaketh with his feet, he teacheth with his fingers;[14] Frowardness is in his heart, he deviseth mischief continually; he soweth discord.[15] Therefore shall his calamity come suddenly; suddenly shall he be broken without remedy.[16] These six things doth the LORD hate: yea, seven are an abomination unto him:[17] A proud look, a lying tongue, and hands

that shed innocent blood,[18] An heart that deviseth wicked imaginations, feet that be swift in running to mischief,[19] A false witness that speaketh lies, and he that soweth discord among brethren.[20] My son, keep thy father's commandment, and forsake not the law of thy mother:[21] Bind them continually upon thine heart, and tie them about thy neck.[22] When thou goest, it shall lead thee; when thou sleepest, it shall keep thee; and when thou awakest, it shall talk with thee.[23] For the commandment is a lamp; and the law is light; and reproofs of instruction are the way of life:[24] To keep thee from the evil woman, from the flattery of the tongue of a strange woman.[25] Lust not after her beauty in thine heart; neither let her take thee with her eyelids.[26] For by means of a whorish woman a man is brought to a piece of bread: and the adulteress will hunt for the precious life.[27] Can a man take fire in his bosom, and his clothes not be burned?[28] Can one go upon hot coals, and his feet not be burned?[29] So he that goeth in to his neighbour's wife; whosoever toucheth her shall not be innocent.[30] Men do not despise a thief, if he steal to satisfy his soul when he is hungry;[31] But if he be found, he shall restore sevenfold; he shall give all the substance of his house.[32] But whoso committeth adultery with a woman lacketh understanding: he that doeth it destroyeth his own soul.[33] A wound and dishonour shall he get; and his reproach shall not be wiped away.[34] For jealousy is the rage of a man: therefore he will not spare in the day of vengeance.[35] He will not regard any ransom; neither will he rest content, though thou givest many gifts.

Prov.7

[1] My son, keep my words, and lay up my commandments with thee.[2] Keep my commandments, and live; and my law as the apple of thine eye.[3] Bind them upon thy fingers, write them upon the table of thine heart.[4] Say unto wisdom, Thou art my sister; and call understanding thy kinswoman:[5] That they may keep thee from the strange woman, from the stranger which flattereth with her words.[6] For at the window of my house I looked through my casement,[7] And beheld among the simple ones, I discerned among the youths, a young man void of understanding,[8] Passing through the street near her corner; and he went the way to her house,[9] In the twilight, in the evening, in the black and dark night:[10] And, behold, there met him a woman with the attire of an harlot, and subtil of heart.[11] (She is loud and stubborn; her feet abide not in her house:[12] Now is she without, now in the streets, and lieth in wait at every corner.)[13] So she caught him, and kissed him, and with an impudent face said unto him,[14] I have peace offerings with me; this day have I payed my vows.[15] Therefore came I forth to meet thee, diligently to seek thy face, and I have found thee.[16] I have decked my bed with coverings of tapestry, with carved works, with fine linen of Egypt.[17] I have perfumed my bed with myrrh, aloes, and cinnamon.[18] Come, let us take our fill of love until the morning: let us solace ourselves with loves.[19] For the goodman is not at home, he is gone a long journey:[20] He hath taken a bag of money with him, and will come home at the day appointed.[21] With her much fair speech she caused him to yield, with the flattering of her lips she forced him.[22] He goeth after her straightway, as an ox goeth to the slaughter, or as a fool to the correction of the stocks;[23] Till a dart strike through his liver; as a bird hasteth to the snare, and knoweth not that it is for his life.[24] Hearken unto me now therefore, O ye children, and attend to the words of my mouth.[25] Let not thine heart decline to her ways, go not astray in her paths.[26] For she hath cast down many wounded: yea, many strong men have been slain by her.[27] Her house is the way to hell, going down to the chambers of death.

Prov.8

¹ Doth not wisdom cry? and understanding put forth her voice?² She standeth in the top of high places, by the way in the places of the paths.³ She crieth at the gates, at the entry of the city, at the coming in at the doors.⁴ Unto you, O men, I call; and my voice is to the sons of man.⁵ O ye simple, understand wisdom: and, ye fools, be ye of an understanding heart.⁶ Hear; for I will speak of excellent things; and the opening of my lips shall be right things.⁷ For my mouth shall speak truth; and wickedness is an abomination to my lips.⁸ All the words of my mouth are in righteousness; there is nothing froward or perverse in them.⁹ They are all plain to him that understandeth, and right to them that find knowledge.¹⁰ Receive my instruction, and not silver; and knowledge rather than choice gold.¹¹ For wisdom is better than rubies; and all the things that may be desired are not to be compared to it.¹² I wisdom dwell with prudence, and find out knowledge of witty inventions.¹³ The fear of the LORD is to hate evil: pride, and arrogancy, and the evil way, and the froward mouth, do I hate.¹⁴ Counsel is mine, and sound wisdom: I am understanding; I have strength.¹⁵ By me kings reign, and princes decree justice.¹⁶ By me princes rule, and nobles, even all the judges of the earth.¹⁷ I love them that love me; and those that seek me early shall find me.¹⁸ Riches and honour are with me; yea, durable riches and righteousness.¹⁹ My fruit is better than gold, yea, than fine gold; and my revenue than choice silver.²⁰ I lead in the way of righteousness, in the midst of the paths of judgment:²¹ That I may cause those that love me to inherit substance; and I will fill their treasures.²² The LORD possessed me in the beginning of his way, before his works of old.²³ I was set up from everlasting, from the beginning, or ever the earth was.²⁴ When there were no depths, I was brought forth; when there were no fountains abounding with water.²⁵ Before the mountains were settled, before the hills was I brought forth:²⁶ While as yet he had not made the earth, nor the fields, nor the highest part of the dust of the world.²⁷ When he prepared the heavens, I was there: when he set a compass upon the face of the depth:²⁸ When he established the clouds above: when he strengthened the fountains of the deep:²⁹ When he gave to the sea his decree, that the waters should not pass his commandment: when he appointed the foundations of the earth:³⁰ Then I was by him, as one brought up with him: and I was daily his delight, rejoicing always before him;³¹ Rejoicing in the habitable part of his earth; and my delights were with the sons of men.³² Now therefore hearken unto me, O ye children: for blessed are they that keep my ways.³³ Hear instruction, and be wise, and refuse it not.³⁴ Blessed is the man that heareth me, watching daily at my gates, waiting at the posts of my doors.³⁵ For whoso findeth me findeth life, and shall obtain favour of the LORD.³⁶ But he that sinneth against me wrongeth his own soul: all they that hate me love death.

Prov.9

¹ Wisdom hath builded her house, she hath hewn out her seven pillars:² She hath killed her beasts; she hath mingled her wine; she hath also furnished her table.³ She hath sent forth her maidens: she crieth upon the highest places of the city,⁴ Whoso is simple, let him turn in hither: as for him that wanteth understanding, she saith to him,⁵ Come, eat of my bread, and drink of the wine which I have mingled.⁶ Forsake the foolish, and live; and go in the way of understanding.⁷ He that reproveth a scorner getteth to himself shame: and he that rebuketh a wicked man getteth himself a blot.⁸ Reprove not a scorner, lest he hate thee: rebuke a wise man, and he will love thee.⁹ Give instruction to a wise man, and he will be yet wiser: teach a just man, and he will increase in learning.¹⁰ The fear of the LORD is the beginning of wisdom: and the knowledge of the holy is understanding.¹¹ For by me thy days shall be multiplied, and the years of thy life shall be increased.¹² If thou be

wise, thou shalt be wise for thyself: but if thou scornest, thou alone shalt bear it.¹³ A foolish woman is clamourous: she is simple, and knoweth nothing.¹⁴ For she sitteth at the door of her house, on a seat in the high places of the city,¹⁵ To call passengers who go right on their ways:¹⁶ Whoso is simple, let him turn in hither: and as for him that wanteth understanding, she saith to him,¹⁷ Stolen waters are sweet, and bread eaten in secret is pleasant.¹⁸ But he knoweth not that the dead are there; and that her guests are in the depths of hell.

Prov.10

¹ The proverbs of Solomon. A wise son maketh a glad father: but a foolish son is the heaviness of his mother.² Treasures of wickedness profit nothing: but righteousness delivereth from death.³ The LORD will not suffer the soul of the righteous to famish: but he casteth away the substance of the wicked.⁴ He becometh poor that dealeth with a slack hand: but the hand of the diligent maketh rich.⁵ He that gathereth in summer is a wise son: but he that sleepeth in harvest is a son that causeth shame.⁶ Blessings are upon the head of the just: but violence covereth the mouth of the wicked.⁷ The memory of the just is blessed: but the name of the wicked shall rot.⁸ The wise in heart will receive commandments: but a prating fool shall fall.⁹ He that walketh uprightly walketh surely: but he that perverteth his ways shall be known.¹⁰ He that winketh with the eye causeth sorrow: but a prating fool shall fall.¹¹ The mouth of a righteous man is a well of life: but violence covereth the mouth of the wicked.¹² Hatred stirreth up strifes: but love covereth all sins.¹³ In the lips of him that hath understanding wisdom is found: but a rod is for the back of him that is void of understanding.¹⁴ Wise men lay up knowledge: but the mouth of the foolish is near destruction.¹⁵ The rich man's wealth is his strong city: the destruction of the poor is their poverty.¹⁶ The labour of the righteous tendeth to life: the fruit of the wicked to sin.¹⁷ He is in the way of life that keepeth instruction: but he that refuseth reproof erreth.¹⁸ He that hideth hatred with lying lips, and he that uttereth a slander, is a fool.¹⁹ In the multitude of words there wanteth not sin: but he that refraineth his lips is wise.²⁰ The tongue of the just is as choice silver: the heart of the wicked is little worth.²¹ The lips of the righteous feed many: but fools die for want of wisdom.²² The blessing of the LORD, it maketh rich, and he addeth no sorrow with it.²³ It is as sport to a fool to do mischief: but a man of understanding hath wisdom.²⁴ The fear of the wicked, it shall come upon him: but the desire of the righteous shall be granted.²⁵ As the whirlwind passeth, so is the wicked no more: but the righteous is an everlasting foundation.²⁶ As vinegar to the teeth, and as smoke to the eyes, so is the sluggard to them that send him.²⁷ The fear of the LORD prolongeth days: but the years of the wicked shall be shortened.²⁸ The hope of the righteous shall be gladness: but the expectation of the wicked shall perish.²⁹ The way of the LORD is strength to the upright: but destruction shall be to the workers of iniquity.³⁰ The righteous shall never be removed: but the wicked shall not inhabit the earth.³¹ The mouth of the just bringeth forth wisdom: but the froward tongue shall be cut out.³² The lips of the righteous know what is acceptable: but the mouth of the wicked speaketh frowardness.

Prov.11

¹ A false balance is abomination to the LORD: but a just weight is his delight.² When pride cometh, then cometh shame: but with the lowly is wisdom.³ The integrity of the upright shall guide them: but the perverseness of transgressors shall destroy them.⁴ Riches profit not in the day of wrath: but righteousness delivereth from death.⁵ The righteousness of the perfect shall direct his way: but the wicked shall fall by his own wickedness.⁶ The righteousness of the

upright shall deliver them: but transgressors shall be taken in their own naughtiness.[7] When a wicked man dieth, his expectation shall perish: and the hope of unjust men perisheth.[8] The righteous is delivered out of trouble, and the wicked cometh in his stead.[9] An hypocrite with his mouth destroyeth his neighbour: but through knowledge shall the just be delivered.[10] When it goeth well with the righteous, the city rejoiceth: and when the wicked perish, there is shouting.[11] By the blessing of the upright the city is exalted: but it is overthrown by the mouth of the wicked.[12] He that is void of wisdom despiseth his neighbour: but a man of understanding holdeth his peace.[13] A talebearer revealeth secrets: but he that is of a faithful spirit concealeth the matter.[14] Where no counsel is, the people fall: but in the multitude of counsellers there is safety.[15] He that is surety for a stranger shall smart for it: and he that hateth suretiship is sure.[16] A gracious woman retaineth honour: and strong men retain riches.[17] The merciful man doeth good to his own soul: but he that is cruel troubleth his own flesh.[18] The wicked worketh a deceitful work: but to him that soweth righteousness shall be a sure reward.[19] As righteousness tendeth to life: so he that pursueth evil pursueth it to his own death.[20] They that are of a froward heart are abomination to the LORD: but such as are upright in their way are his delight.[21] Though hand join in hand, the wicked shall not be unpunished: but the seed of the righteous shall be delivered.[22] As a jewel of gold in a swine's snout, so is a fair woman which is without discretion.[23] The desire of the righteous is only good: but the expectation of the wicked is wrath.[24] There is that scattereth, and yet increaseth; and there is that withholdeth more than is meet, but it tendeth to poverty.[25] The liberal soul shall be made fat: and he that watereth shall be watered also himself.[26] He that withholdeth corn, the people shall curse him: but blessing shall be upon the head of him that selleth it.[27] He that diligently seeketh good procureth favour: but he that seeketh mischief, it shall come unto him.[28] He that trusteth in his riches shall fall: but the righteous shall flourish as a branch.[29] He that troubleth his own house shall inherit the wind: and the fool shall be servant to the wise of heart.[30] The fruit of the righteous is a tree of life; and he that winneth souls is wise.[31] Behold, the righteous shall be recompensed in the earth: much more the wicked and the sinner.

Prov.12

[1] Whoso loveth instruction loveth knowledge: but he that hateth reproof is brutish.[2] A good man obtaineth favour of the LORD: but a man of wicked devices will he condemn.[3] A man shall not be established by wickedness: but the root of the righteous shall not be moved.[4] A virtuous woman is a crown to her husband: but she that maketh ashamed is as rottenness in his bones.[5] The thoughts of the righteous are right: but the counsels of the wicked are deceit.[6] The words of the wicked are to lie in wait for blood: but the mouth of the upright shall deliver them.[7] The wicked are overthrown, and are not: but the house of the righteous shall stand.[8] A man shall be commended according to his wisdom: but he that is of a perverse heart shall be despised.[9] He that is despised, and hath a servant, is better than he that honoureth himself, and lacketh bread.[10] A righteous man regardeth the life of his beast: but the tender mercies of the wicked are cruel.[11] He that tilleth his land shall be satisfied with bread: but he that followeth vain persons is void of understanding.[12] The wicked desireth the net of evil men: but the root of the righteous yieldeth fruit.[13] The wicked is snared by the transgression of his lips: but the just shall come out of trouble.[14] A man shall be satisfied with good by the fruit of his mouth: and the recompence of a man's hands shall be rendered unto him.[15] The way of a fool is right in his own eyes: but he that hearkeneth unto counsel is wise.[16] A fool's wrath is presently known: but a prudent man

covereth shame.[17] He that speaketh truth sheweth forth righteousness: but a false witness deceit.[18] There is that speaketh like the piercings of a sword: but the tongue of the wise is health.[19] The lip of truth shall be established for ever: but a lying tongue is but for a moment.[20] Deceit is in the heart of them that imagine evil: but to the counsellers of peace is joy.[21] There shall no evil happen to the just: but the wicked shall be filled with mischief.[22] Lying lips are abomination to the LORD: but they that deal truly are his delight.[23] A prudent man concealeth knowledge: but the heart of fools proclaimeth foolishness.[24] The hand of the diligent shall bear rule: but the slothful shall be under tribute.[25] Heaviness in the heart of man maketh it stoop: but a good word maketh it glad.[26] The righteous is more excellent than his neighbour: but the way of the wicked seduceth them.[27] The slothful man roasteth not that which he took in hunting: but the substance of a diligent man is precious.[28] In the way of righteousness is life; and in the pathway thereof there is no death.

Prov.13

[1] A wise son heareth his father's instruction: but a scorner heareth not rebuke.[2] A man shall eat good by the fruit of his mouth: but the soul of the transgressors shall eat violence.[3] He that keepeth his mouth keepeth his life: but he that openeth wide his lips shall have destruction.[4] The soul of the sluggard desireth, and hath nothing: but the soul of the diligent shall be made fat.[5] A righteous man hateth lying: but a wicked man is loathsome, and cometh to shame.[6] Righteousness keepeth him that is upright in the way: but wickedness overthroweth the sinner.[7] There is that maketh himself rich, yet hath nothing: there is that maketh himself poor, yet hath great riches.[8] The ransom of a man's life are his riches: but the poor heareth not rebuke.[9] The light of the righteous rejoiceth: but the lamp of the wicked shall be put out.[10] Only by pride cometh contention: but with the well advised is wisdom.[11] Wealth gotten by vanity shall be diminished: but he that gathereth by labour shall increase.[12] Hope deferred maketh the heart sick: but when the desire cometh, it is a tree of life.[13] Whoso despiseth the word shall be destroyed: but he that feareth the commandment shall be rewarded.[14] The law of the wise is a fountain of life, to depart from the snares of death.[15] Good understanding giveth favour: but the way of transgressors is hard.[16] Every prudent man dealeth with knowledge: but a fool layeth open his folly.[17] A wicked messenger falleth into mischief: but a faithful ambassador is health.[18] Poverty and shame shall be to him that refuseth instruction: but he that regardeth reproof shall be honoured.[19] The desire accomplished is sweet to the soul: but it is abomination to fools to depart from evil.[20] He that walketh with wise men shall be wise: but a companion of fools shall be destroyed.[21] Evil pursueth sinners: but to the righteous good shall be repayed.[22] A good man leaveth an inheritance to his children's children: and the wealth of the sinner is laid up for the just.[23] Much food is in the tillage of the poor: but there is that is destroyed for want of judgment.[24] He that spareth his rod hateth his son: but he that loveth him chasteneth him betimes.[25] The righteous eateth to the satisfying of his soul: but the belly of the wicked shall want.

Prov.14

[1] Every wise woman buildeth her house: but the foolish plucketh it down with her hands.[2] He that walketh in his uprightness feareth the LORD: but he that is perverse in his ways despiseth him.[3] In the mouth of the foolish is a rod of pride: but the lips of the wise shall preserve them.[4] Where no oxen are, the crib is clean: but much increase is by the strength of the ox.[5] A faithful witness will not lie: but a false witness will utter lies.[6] A scorner seeketh wisdom, and findeth it not: but knowledge is easy unto him that

understandeth.⁷ Go from the presence of a foolish man, when thou perceivest not in him the lips of knowledge.⁸ The wisdom of the prudent is to understand his way: but the folly of fools is deceit.⁹ Fools make a mock at sin: but among the righteous there is favour.¹⁰ The heart knoweth his own bitterness; and a stranger doth not intermeddle with his joy.¹¹ The house of the wicked shall be overthrown: but the tabernacle of the upright shall flourish.¹² There is a way which seemeth right unto a man, but the end thereof are the ways of death.¹³ Even in laughter the heart is sorrowful; and the end of that mirth is heaviness.¹⁴ The backslider in heart shall be filled with his own ways: and a good man shall be satisfied from himself.¹⁵ The simple believeth every word: but the prudent man looketh well to his going.¹⁶ A wise man feareth, and departeth from evil: but the fool rageth, and is confident.¹⁷ He that is soon angry dealeth foolishly: and a man of wicked devices is hated.¹⁸ The simple inherit folly: but the prudent are crowned with knowledge.¹⁹ The evil bow before the good; and the wicked at the gates of the righteous.²⁰ The poor is hated even of his own neighbour: but the rich hath many friends.²¹ He that despiseth his neighbour sinneth: but he that hath mercy on the poor, happy is he.²² Do they not err that devise evil? but mercy and truth shall be to them that devise good.²³ In all labour there is profit: but the talk of the lips tendeth only to penury.²⁴ The crown of the wise is their riches: but the foolishness of fools is folly.²⁵ A true witness delivereth souls: but a deceitful witness speaketh lies.²⁶ In the fear of the LORD is strong confidence: and his children shall have a place of refuge.²⁷ The fear of the LORD is a fountain of life, to depart from the snares of death.²⁸ In the multitude of people is the king's honour: but in the want of people is the destruction of the prince.²⁹ He that is slow to wrath is of great understanding: but he that is hasty of spirit exalteth folly.³⁰ A sound heart is the life of the flesh: but envy the rottenness of the bones.³¹ He that oppresseth the poor reproacheth his Maker: but he that honoureth him hath mercy on the poor.³² The wicked is driven away in his wickedness: but the righteous hath hope in his death.³³ Wisdom resteth in the heart of him that hath understanding: but that which is in the midst of fools is made known.³⁴ Righteousness exalteth a nation: but sin is a reproach to any people.³⁵ The king's favour is toward a wise servant: but his wrath is against him that causeth shame.

Prov.15

¹ A soft answer turneth away wrath: but grievous words stir up anger.² The tongue of the wise useth knowledge aright: but the mouth of fools poureth out foolishness.³ The eyes of the LORD are in every place, beholding the evil and the good.⁴ A wholesome tongue is a tree of life: but perverseness therein is a breach in the spirit.⁵ A fool despiseth his father's instruction: but he that regardeth reproof is prudent.⁶ In the house of the righteous is much treasure: but in the revenues of the wicked is trouble.⁷ The lips of the wise disperse knowledge: but the heart of the foolish doeth not so.⁸ The sacrifice of the wicked is an abomination to the LORD: but the prayer of the upright is his delight.⁹ The way of the wicked is an abomination unto the LORD: but he loveth him that followeth after righteousness.¹⁰ Correction is grievous unto him that forsaketh the way: and he that hateth reproof shall die.¹¹ Hell and destruction are before the LORD: how much more then the hearts of the children of men?¹² A scorner loveth not one that reproveth him: neither will he go unto the wise.¹³ A merry heart maketh a cheerful countenance: but by sorrow of the heart the spirit is broken.¹⁴ The heart of him that hath understanding seeketh knowledge: but the mouth of fools feedeth on foolishness.¹⁵ All the days of the afflicted are evil: but he that is of a merry heart hath a continual feast.¹⁶ Better is little with the fear of the LORD than great treasure and trouble

therewith.¹⁷ Better is a dinner of herbs where love is, than a stalled ox and hatred therewith.¹⁸ A wrathful man stirreth up strife: but he that is slow to anger appeaseth strife.¹⁹ The way of the slothful man is as an hedge of thorns: but the way of the righteous is made plain.²⁰ A wise son maketh a glad father: but a foolish man despiseth his mother.²¹ Folly is joy to him that is destitute of wisdom: but a man of understanding walketh uprightly.²² Without counsel purposes are disappointed: but in the multitude of counsellers they are established.²³ A man hath joy by the answer of his mouth: and a word spoken in due season, how good is it!²⁴ The way of life is above to the wise, that he may depart from hell beneath.²⁵ The LORD will destroy the house of the proud: but he will establish the border of the widow.²⁶ The thoughts of the wicked are an abomination to the LORD: but the words of the pure are pleasant words.²⁷ He that is greedy of gain troubleth his own house; but he that hateth gifts shall live.²⁸ The heart of the righteous studieth to answer: but the mouth of the wicked poureth out evil things.²⁹ The LORD is far from the wicked: but he heareth the prayer of the righteous.³⁰ The light of the eyes rejoiceth the heart: and a good report maketh the bones fat.³¹ The ear that heareth the reproof of life abideth among the wise.³² He that refuseth instruction despiseth his own soul: but he that heareth reproof getteth understanding.³³ The fear of the LORD is the instruction of wisdom; and before honour is humility.

Prov.16

¹ The preparations of the heart in man, and the answer of the tongue, is from the LORD.² All the ways of a man are clean in his own eyes; but the LORD weigheth the spirits.³ Commit thy works unto the LORD, and thy thoughts shall be established.⁴ The LORD hath made all things for himself: yea, even the wicked for the day of evil.⁵ Every one that is proud in heart is an abomination to the LORD: though hand join in hand, he shall not be unpunished.⁶ By mercy and truth iniquity is purged: and by the fear of the LORD men depart from evil.⁷ When a man's ways please the LORD, he maketh even his enemies to be at peace with him.⁸ Better is a little with righteousness than great revenues without right.⁹ A man's heart deviseth his way: but the LORD directeth his steps.¹⁰ A divine sentence is in the lips of the king: his mouth transgresseth not in judgment.¹¹ A just weight and balance are the LORD's: all the weights of the bag are his work.¹² It is an abomination to kings to commit wickedness: for the throne is established by righteousness.¹³ Righteous lips are the delight of kings; and they love him that speaketh right.¹⁴ The wrath of a king is as messengers of death: but a wise man will pacify it.¹⁵ In the light of the king's countenance is life; and his favour is as a cloud of the latter rain.¹⁶ How much better is it to get wisdom than gold! and to get understanding rather to be chosen than silver!¹⁷ The highway of the upright is to depart from evil: he that keepeth his way preserveth his soul.¹⁸ Pride goeth before destruction, and an haughty spirit before a fall.¹⁹ Better it is to be of an humble spirit with the lowly, than to divide the spoil with the proud.²⁰ He that handleth a matter wisely shall find good: and whoso trusteth in the LORD, happy is he.²¹ The wise in heart shall be called prudent: and the sweetness of the lips increaseth learning.²² Understanding is a wellspring of life unto him that hath it: but the instruction of fools is folly.²³ The heart of the wise teacheth his mouth, and addeth learning to his lips.²⁴ Pleasant words are as an honeycomb, sweet to the soul, and health to the bones.²⁵ There is a way that seemeth right unto a man, but the end thereof are the ways of death.²⁶ He that laboureth laboureth for himself; for his mouth craveth it of him.²⁷ An ungodly man diggeth up evil: and in his lips there is as a burning fire.²⁸ A froward man soweth strife: and a whisperer separateth chief friends.²⁹ A violent man enticeth his neighbour, and leadeth him into the way that is not

good.³⁰ He shutteth his eyes to devise froward things: moving his lips he bringeth evil to pass.³¹ The hoary head is a crown of glory, if it be found in the way of righteousness.³² He that is slow to anger is better than the mighty; and he that ruleth his spirit than he that taketh a city.³³ The lot is cast into the lap; but the whole disposing thereof is of the LORD.

Prov.17

¹ Better is a dry morsel, and quietness therewith, than an house full of sacrifices with strife.² A wise servant shall have rule over a son that causeth shame, and shall have part of the inheritance among the brethren.³ The fining pot is for silver, and the furnace for gold: but the LORD trieth the hearts.⁴ A wicked doer giveth heed to false lips; and a liar giveth ear to a naughty tongue.⁵ Whoso mocketh the poor reproacheth his Maker: and he that is glad at calamities shall not be unpunished.⁶ Children's children are the crown of old men; and the glory of children are their fathers.⁷ Excellent speech becometh not a fool: much less do lying lips a prince.⁸ A gift is as a precious stone in the eyes of him that hath it: whithersoever it turneth, it prospereth.⁹ He that covereth a transgression seeketh love; but he that repeateth a matter separateth very friends.¹⁰ A reproof entereth more into a wise man than an hundred stripes into a fool.¹¹ An evil man seeketh only rebellion: therefore a cruel messenger shall be sent against him.¹² Let a bear robbed of her whelps meet a man, rather than a fool in his folly.¹³ Whoso rewardeth evil for good, evil shall not depart from his house.¹⁴ The beginning of strife is as when one letteth out water: therefore leave off contention, before it be meddled with.¹⁵ He that justifieth the wicked, and he that condemneth the just, even they both are abomination to the LORD.¹⁶ Wherefore is there a price in the hand of a fool to get wisdom, seeing he hath no heart to it?¹⁷ A friend loveth at all times, and a brother is born for adversity.¹⁸ A man void of understanding striketh hands, and becometh surety in the presence of his friend.¹⁹ He loveth transgression that loveth strife: and he that exalteth his gate seeketh destruction.²⁰ He that hath a froward heart findeth no good: and he that hath a perverse tongue falleth into mischief.²¹ He that begetteth a fool doeth it to his sorrow: and the father of a fool hath no joy.²² A merry heart doeth good like a medicine: but a broken spirit drieth the bones.²³ A wicked man taketh a gift out of the bosom to pervert the ways of judgment.²⁴ Wisdom is before him that hath understanding; but the eyes of a fool are in the ends of the earth.²⁵ A foolish son is a grief to his father, and bitterness to her that bare him.²⁶ Also to punish the just is not good, nor to strike princes for equity.²⁷ He that hath knowledge spareth his words: and a man of understanding is of an excellent spirit.²⁸ Even a fool, when he holdeth his peace, is counted wise: and he that shutteth his lips is esteemed a man of understanding.

Prov.18

¹ Through desire a man, having separated himself, seeketh and intermeddleth with all wisdom.² A fool hath no delight in understanding, but that his heart may discover itself.³ When the wicked cometh, then cometh also contempt, and with ignominy reproach.⁴ The words of a man's mouth are as deep waters, and the wellspring of wisdom as a flowing brook.⁵ It is not good to accept the person of the wicked, to overthrow the righteous in judgment.⁶ A fool's lips enter into contention, and his mouth calleth for strokes.⁷ A fool's mouth is his destruction, and his lips are the snare of his soul.⁸ The words of a talebearer are as wounds, and they go down into the innermost parts of the belly.⁹ He also that is slothful in his work is brother to him that is a great waster.¹⁰ The name of the LORD is a strong tower: the righteous runneth into it, and is safe.¹¹ The rich man's wealth is his strong city, and as an high

wall in his own conceit.¹² Before destruction the heart of man is haughty, and before honour is humility.¹³ He that answereth a matter before he heareth it, it is folly and shame unto him.¹⁴ The spirit of a man will sustain his infirmity; but a wounded spirit who can bear?¹⁵ The heart of the prudent getteth knowledge; and the ear of the wise seeketh knowledge.¹⁶ A man's gift maketh room for him, and bringeth him before great men.¹⁷ He that is first in his own cause seemeth just; but his neighbour cometh and searcheth him.¹⁸ The lot causeth contentions to cease, and parteth between the mighty.¹⁹ A brother offended is harder to be won than a strong city: and their contentions are like the bars of a castle.²⁰ A man's belly shall be satisfied with the fruit of his mouth; and with the increase of his lips shall he be filled.²¹ Death and life are in the power of the tongue: and they that love it shall eat the fruit thereof.²² Whoso findeth a wife findeth a good thing, and obtaineth favour of the LORD.²³ The poor useth intreaties; but the rich answereth roughly.²⁴ A man that hath friends must shew himself friendly: and there is a friend that sticketh closer than a brother.

Prov.19

¹ Better is the poor that walketh in his integrity, than he that is perverse in his lips, and is a fool.² Also, that the soul be without knowledge, it is not good; and he that hasteth with his feet sinneth.³ The foolishness of man perverteth his way: and his heart fretteth against the LORD.⁴ Wealth maketh many friends; but the poor is separated from his neighbour.⁵ A false witness shall not be unpunished, and he that speaketh lies shall not escape.⁶ Many will intreat the favour of the prince: and every man is a friend to him that giveth gifts.⁷ All the brethren of the poor do hate him: how much more do his friends go far from him? he pursueth them with words, yet they are wanting to him.⁸ He that getteth wisdom loveth his own soul: he that keepeth understanding shall find good.⁹ A false witness shall not be unpunished, and he that speaketh lies shall perish.¹⁰ Delight is not seemly for a fool; much less for a servant to have rule over princes.¹¹ The discretion of a man deferreth his anger; and it is his glory to pass over a transgression.¹² The king's wrath is as the roaring of a lion; but his favour is as dew upon the grass.¹³ A foolish son is the calamity of his father: and the contentions of a wife are a continual dropping.¹⁴ House and riches are the inheritance of fathers and a prudent wife is from the LORD.¹⁵ Slothfulness casteth into a deep sleep; and an idle soul shall suffer hunger.¹⁶ He that keepeth the commandment keepeth his own soul; but he that despiseth his ways shall die.¹⁷ He that hath pity upon the poor lendeth unto the LORD; and that which he hath given will he pay him again.¹⁸ Chasten thy son while there is hope, and let not thy soul spare for his crying.¹⁹ A man of great wrath shall suffer punishment: for if thou deliver him, yet thou must do it again.²⁰ Hear counsel, and receive instruction, that thou mayest be wise in thy latter end.²¹ There are many devices in a man's heart; nevertheless the counsel of the LORD, that shall stand.²² The desire of a man is his kindness: and a poor man is better than a liar.²³ The fear of the LORD tendeth to life: and he that hath it shall abide satisfied; he shall not be visited with evil.²⁴ A slothful man hideth his hand in his bosom, and will not so much as bring it to his mouth again.²⁵ Smite a scorner, and the simple will beware: and reprove one that hath understanding, and he will understand knowledge.²⁶ He that wasteth his father, and chaseth away his mother, is a son that causeth shame, and bringeth reproach.²⁷ Cease, my son, to hear the instruction that causeth to err from the words of knowledge.²⁸ An ungodly witness scorneth judgment: and the mouth of the wicked devoureth iniquity.²⁹ Judgments are prepared for scorners, and stripes for the back of fools.

Prov.20

¹ Wine is a mocker, strong drink is raging: and whosoever is deceived thereby is not wise.² The fear of a king is as the roaring of a lion: whoso provoketh him to anger sinneth against his own soul.³ It is an honour for a man to cease from strife: but every fool will be meddling.⁴ The sluggard will not plow by reason of the cold; therefore shall he beg in harvest, and have nothing.⁵ Counsel in the heart of man is like deep water; but a man of understanding will draw it out.⁶ Most men will proclaim every one his own goodness: but a faithful man who can find?⁷ The just man walketh in his integrity: his children are blessed after him.⁸ A king that sitteth in the throne of judgment scattereth away all evil with his eyes.⁹ Who can say, I have made my heart clean, I am pure from my sin?¹⁰ Divers weights, and divers measures, both of them are alike abomination to the LORD.¹¹ Even a child is known by his doings, whether his work be pure, and whether it be right.¹² The hearing ear, and the seeing eye, the LORD hath made even both of them.¹³ Love not sleep, lest thou come to poverty; open thine eyes, and thou shalt be satisfied with bread.¹⁴ It is naught, it is naught, saith the buyer: but when he is gone his way, then he boasteth.¹⁵ There is gold, and a multitude of rubies: but the lips of knowledge are a precious jewel.¹⁶ Take his garment that is surety for a stranger: and take a pledge of him for a strange woman.¹⁷ Bread of deceit is sweet to a man; but afterwards his mouth shall be filled with gravel.¹⁸ Every purpose is established by counsel: and with good advice make war.¹⁹ He that goeth about as a talebearer revealeth secrets: therefore meddle not with him that flattereth with his lips.²⁰ Whoso curseth his father or his mother, his lamp shall be put out in obscure darkness.²¹ An inheritance may be gotten hastily at the beginning; but the end thereof shall not be blessed.²² Say not thou, I will recompense evil; but wait on the LORD, and he shall save thee.²³ Divers weights are an abomination unto the LORD; and a false balance is not good.²⁴ Man's goings are of the LORD; how can a man then understand his own way?²⁵ It is a snare to the man who devoureth that which is holy, and after vows to make inquiry.²⁶ A wise king scattereth the wicked, and bringeth the wheel over them.²⁷ The spirit of man is the candle of the LORD, searching all the inward parts of the belly.²⁸ Mercy and truth preserve the king: and his throne is upholden by mercy.²⁹ The glory of young men is their strength: and the beauty of old men is the gray head.³⁰ The blueness of a wound cleanseth away evil: so do stripes the inward parts of the belly.

Prov.21

¹ The king's heart is in the hand of the LORD, as the rivers of water: he turneth it whithersoever he will.² Every way of a man is right in his own eyes: but the LORD pondereth the hearts.³ To do justice and judgment is more acceptable to the LORD than sacrifice.⁴ An high look, and a proud heart, and the plowing of the wicked, is sin.⁵ The thoughts of the diligent tend only to plenteousness; but of every one that is hasty only to want.⁶ The getting of treasures by a lying tongue is a vanity tossed to and fro of them that seek death.⁷ The robbery of the wicked shall destroy them; because they refuse to do judgment.⁸ The way of man is froward and strange: but as for the pure, his work is right.⁹ It is better to dwell in a corner of the housetop, than with a brawling woman in a wide house.¹⁰ The soul of the wicked desireth evil: his neighbour findeth no favour in his eyes.¹¹ When the scorner is punished, the simple is made wise: and when the wise is instructed, he receiveth knowledge.¹² The righteous man wisely considereth the house of the wicked: but God overthroweth the wicked for their wickedness.¹³ Whoso stoppeth his ears at the cry of the poor, he also shall cry himself, but shall not be heard.¹⁴ A gift in secret pacifieth anger: and a reward in the bosom strong wrath.¹⁵ It is joy to the just to do judgment: but destruction shall be to the workers of iniquity.¹⁶ The man that

wandereth out of the way of understanding shall remain in the congregation of the dead.¹⁷ He that loveth pleasure shall be a poor man: he that loveth wine and oil shall not be rich.¹⁸ The wicked shall be a ransom for the righteous, and the transgressor for the upright.¹⁹ It is better to dwell in the wilderness, than with a contentious and an angry woman.²⁰ There is treasure to be desired and oil in the dwelling of the wise; but a foolish man spendeth it up.²¹ He that followeth after righteousness and mercy findeth life, righteousness, and honour.²² A wise man scaleth the city of the mighty, and casteth down the strength of the confidence thereof.²³ Whoso keepeth his mouth and his tongue keepeth his soul from troubles.²⁴ Proud and haughty scorner is his name, who dealeth in proud wrath.²⁵ The desire of the slothful killeth him; for his hands refuse to labour.²⁶ He coveteth greedily all the day long: but the righteous giveth and spareth not.²⁷ The sacrifice of the wicked is abomination: how much more, when he bringeth it with a wicked mind?²⁸ A false witness shall perish: but the man that heareth speaketh constantly.²⁹ A wicked man hardeneth his face: but as for the upright, he directeth his way.³⁰ There is no wisdom nor understanding nor counsel against the LORD.³¹ The horse is prepared against the day of battle: but safety is of the LORD.

Prov.22

¹ A good name is rather to be chosen than great riches, and loving favour rather than silver and gold.² The rich and poor meet together: the LORD is the maker of them all.³ A prudent man foreseeth the evil, and hideth himself: but the simple pass on, and are punished.⁴ By humility and the fear of the LORD are riches, and honour, and life.⁵ Thorns and snares are in the way of the froward: he that doth keep his soul shall be far from them.⁶ Train up a child in the way he should go: and when he is old, he will not depart from it.⁷ The rich ruleth over the poor, and the borrower is servant to the lender.⁸ He that soweth iniquity shall reap vanity: and the rod of his anger shall fail.⁹ He that hath a bountiful eye shall be blessed; for he giveth of his bread to the poor.¹⁰ Cast out the scorner, and contention shall go out; yea, strife and reproach shall cease.¹¹ He that loveth pureness of heart, for the grace of his lips the king shall be his friend.¹² The eyes of the LORD preserve knowledge, and he overthroweth the words of the transgressor.¹³ The slothful man saith, There is a lion without, I shall be slain in the streets.¹⁴ The mouth of strange women is a deep pit: he that is abhorred of the LORD shall fall therein.¹⁵ Foolishness is bound in the heart of a child; but the rod of correction shall drive it far from him.¹⁶ He that oppresseth the poor to increase his riches, and he that giveth to the rich, shall surely come to want.¹⁷ Bow down thine ear, and hear the words of the wise, and apply thine heart unto my knowledge.¹⁸ For it is a pleasant thing if thou keep them within thee; they shall withal be fitted in thy lips.¹⁹ That thy trust may be in the LORD, I have made known to thee this day, even to thee.²⁰ Have not I written to thee excellent things in counsels and knowledge,²¹ That I might make thee know the certainty of the words of truth; that thou mightest answer the words of truth to them that send unto thee?²² Rob not the poor, because he is poor: neither oppress the afflicted in the gate:²³ For the LORD will plead their cause, and spoil the soul of those that spoiled them.²⁴ Make no friendship with an angry man; and with a furious man thou shalt not go:²⁵ Lest thou learn his ways, and get a snare to thy soul.²⁶ Be not thou one of them that strike hands, or of them that are sureties for debts.²⁷ If thou hast nothing to pay, why should he take away thy bed from under thee?²⁸ Remove not the ancient landmark, which thy fathers have set.²⁹ Seest thou a man diligent in his business? he shall stand before kings; he shall not stand before mean men.

Prov.23

¹ When thou sittest to eat with a ruler, consider diligently what is before thee:² And put a knife to thy throat, if thou be a man given to appetite.³ Be not desirous of his dainties: for they are deceitful meat.⁴ Labour not to be rich: cease from thine own wisdom.⁵ Wilt thou set thine eyes upon that which is not? for riches certainly make themselves wings; they fly away as an eagle toward heaven.⁶ Eat thou not the bread of him that hath an evil eye, neither desire thou his dainty meats:⁷ For as he thinketh in his heart, so is he: Eat and drink, saith he to thee; but his heart is not with thee.⁸ The morsel which thou hast eaten shalt thou vomit up, and lose thy sweet words.⁹ Speak not in the ears of a fool: for he will despise the wisdom of thy words.¹⁰ Remove not the old landmark; and enter not into the fields of the fatherless:¹¹ For their redeemer is mighty; he shall plead their cause with thee.¹² Apply thine heart unto instruction, and thine ears to the words of knowledge.¹³ Withhold not correction from the child: for if thou beatest him with the rod, he shall not die.¹⁴ Thou shalt beat him with the rod, and shalt deliver his soul from hell.¹⁵ My son, if thine heart be wise, my heart shall rejoice, even mine.¹⁶ Yea, my reins shall rejoice, when thy lips speak right things.¹⁷ Let not thine heart envy sinners: but be thou in the fear of the LORD all the day long.¹⁸ For surely there is an end; and thine expectation shall not be cut off.¹⁹ Hear thou, my son, and be wise, and guide thine heart in the way.²⁰ Be not among winebibbers; among riotous eaters of flesh:²¹ For the drunkard and the glutton shall come to poverty: and drowsiness shall clothe a man with rags.²² Hearken unto thy father that begat thee, and despise not thy mother when she is old.²³ Buy the truth, and sell it not; also wisdom, and instruction, and understanding.²⁴ The father of the righteous shall greatly rejoice: and he that begetteth a wise child shall have joy of him.²⁵ Thy father and thy mother shall be glad, and she that bare thee shall rejoice.²⁶ My son, give me thine heart, and let thine eyes observe my ways.²⁷ For a whore is a deep ditch; and a strange woman is a narrow pit.²⁸ She also lieth in wait as for a prey, and increaseth the transgressors among men.²⁹ Who hath woe? who hath sorrow? who hath contentions? who hath babbling? who hath wounds without cause? who hath redness of eyes?³⁰ They that tarry long at the wine; they that go to seek mixed wine.³¹ Look not thou upon the wine when it is red, when it giveth his colour in the cup, when it moveth itself aright.³² At the last it biteth like a serpent, and stingeth like an adder.³³ Thine eyes shall behold strange women, and thine heart shall utter perverse things.³⁴ Yea, thou shalt be as he that lieth down in the midst of the sea, or as he that lieth upon the top of a mast.³⁵ They have stricken me, shalt thou say, and I was not sick; they have beaten me, and I felt it not: when shall I awake? I will seek it yet again.

Prov.24

¹ Be not thou envious against evil men, neither desire to be with them.² For their heart studieth destruction, and their lips talk of mischief.³ Through wisdom is an house builded; and by understanding it is established:⁴ And by knowledge shall the chambers be filled with all precious and pleasant riches.⁵ A wise man is strong; yea, a man of knowledge increaseth strength.⁶ For by wise counsel thou shalt make thy war: and in multitude of counsellers there is safety.⁷ Wisdom is too high for a fool: he openeth not his mouth in the gate.⁸ He that deviseth to do evil shall be called a mischievous person.⁹ The thought of foolishness is sin: and the scorner is an abomination to men.¹⁰ If thou faint in the day of adversity, thy strength is small.¹¹ If thou forbear to deliver them that are drawn unto death, and those that are ready to be slain;¹² If thou sayest, Behold, we knew it not; doth not he that pondereth the heart consider it? and he that keepeth thy soul, doth not he know it? and shall not he render to every man according to his works?¹³ My son,

eat thou honey, because it is good; and the honeycomb, which is sweet to thy taste:¹⁴ So shall the knowledge of wisdom be unto thy soul: when thou hast found it, then there shall be a reward, and thy expectation shall not be cut off.¹⁵ Lay not wait, O wicked man, against the dwelling of the righteous; spoil not his resting place:¹⁶ For a just man falleth seven times, and riseth up again: but the wicked shall fall into mischief.¹⁷ Rejoice not when thine enemy falleth, and let not thine heart be glad when he stumbleth:¹⁸ Lest the LORD see it, and it displease him, and he turn away his wrath from him.¹⁹ Fret not thyself because of evil men, neither be thou envious at the wicked;²⁰ For there shall be no reward to the evil man; the candle of the wicked shall be put out.²¹ My son, fear thou the LORD and the king: and meddle not with them that are given to change:²² For their calamity shall rise suddenly; and who knoweth the ruin of them both?²³ These things also belong to the wise. It is not good to have respect of persons in judgment.²⁴ He that saith unto the wicked, Thou are righteous; him shall the people curse, nations shall abhor him:²⁵ But to them that rebuke him shall be delight, and a good blessing shall come upon them.²⁶ Every man shall kiss his lips that giveth a right answer.²⁷ Prepare thy work without, and make it fit for thyself in the field; and afterwards build thine house.²⁸ Be not a witness against thy neighbour without cause; and deceive not with thy lips.²⁹ Say not, I will do so to him as he hath done to me: I will render to the man according to his work.³⁰ I went by the field of the slothful, and by the vineyard of the man void of understanding;³¹ And, lo, it was all grown over with thorns, and nettles had covered the face thereof, and the stone wall thereof was broken down.³² Then I saw, and considered it well: I looked upon it, and received instruction.³³ Yet a little sleep, a little slumber, a little folding of the hands to sleep:³⁴ So shall thy poverty come as one that travelleth; and thy want as an armed man.

Prov.25

¹ These are also proverbs of Solomon, which the men of Hezekiah king of Judah copied out.² It is the glory of God to conceal a thing: but the honour of kings is to search out a matter.³ The heaven for height, and the earth for depth, and the heart of kings is unsearchable.⁴ Take away the dross from the silver, and there shall come forth a vessel for the finer.⁵ Take away the wicked from before the king, and his throne shall be established in righteousness.⁶ Put not forth thyself in the presence of the king, and stand not in the place of great men:⁷ For better it is that it be said unto thee, Come up hither; than that thou shouldest be put lower in the presence of the prince whom thine eyes have seen.⁸ Go not forth hastily to strive, lest thou know not what to do in the end thereof, when thy neighbour hath put thee to shame.⁹ Debate thy cause with thy neighbour himself; and discover not a secret to another:¹⁰ Lest he that heareth it put thee to shame, and thine infamy turn not away.¹¹ A word fitly spoken is like apples of gold in pictures of silver.¹² As an earring of gold, and an ornament of fine gold, so is a wise reprover upon an obedient ear.¹³ As the cold of snow in the time of harvest, so is a faithful messenger to them that send him: for he refresheth the soul of his masters.¹⁴ Whoso boasteth himself of a false gift is like clouds and wind without rain.¹⁵ By long forbearing is a prince persuaded, and a soft tongue breaketh the bone.¹⁶ Hast thou found honey? eat so much as is sufficient for thee, lest thou be filled therewith, and vomit it.¹⁷ Withdraw thy foot from thy neighbour's house; lest he be weary of thee, and so hate thee.¹⁸ A man that beareth false witness against his neighbour is a maul, and a sword, and a sharp arrow.¹⁹ Confidence in an unfaithful man in time of trouble is like a broken tooth, and a foot out of joint.²⁰ As he that taketh away a garment in cold weather, and as vinegar upon nitre, so is he that singeth songs to an heavy heart.²¹ If thine enemy

be hungry, give him bread to eat; and if he be thirsty, give him water to drink:²² For thou shalt heap coals of fire upon his head, and the LORD shall reward thee.²³ The north wind driveth away rain: so doth an angry countenance a backbiting tongue.²⁴ It is better to dwell in the corner of the housetop, than with a brawling woman and in a wide house.²⁵ As cold waters to a thirsty soul, so is good news from a far country.²⁶ A righteous man falling down before the wicked is as a troubled fountain, and a corrupt spring.²⁷ It is not good to eat much honey: so for men to search their own glory is not glory.²⁸ He that hath no rule over his own spirit is like a city that is broken down, and without walls.

Prov.26

¹ As snow in summer, and as rain in harvest, so honour is not seemly for a fool.² As the bird by wandering, as the swallow by flying, so the curse causeless shall not come.³ A whip for the horse, a bridle for the ass, and a rod for the fool's back.⁴ Answer not a fool according to his folly, lest thou also be like unto him.⁵ Answer a fool according to his folly, lest he be wise in his own conceit.⁶ He that sendeth a message by the hand of a fool cutteth off the feet, and drinketh damage.⁷ The legs of the lame are not equal: so is a parable in the mouth of fools.⁸ As he that bindeth a stone in a sling, so is he that giveth honour to a fool.⁹ As a thorn goeth up into the hand of a drunkard, so is a parable in the mouth of fools.¹⁰ The great God that formed all things both rewardeth the fool, and rewardeth transgressors.¹¹ As a dog returneth to his vomit, so a fool returneth to his folly.¹² Seest thou a man wise in his own conceit? there is more hope of a fool than of him.¹³ The slothful man saith, There is a lion in the way; a lion is in the streets.¹⁴ As the door turneth upon his hinges, so doth the slothful upon his bed.¹⁵ The slothful hideth his hand in his bosom; it grieveth him to bring it again to his mouth.¹⁶ The sluggard is wiser in his own conceit than seven men that can render a reason.¹⁷ He that passeth by, and meddleth with strife belonging not to him, is like one that taketh a dog by the ears.¹⁸ As a mad man who casteth firebrands, arrows, and death,¹⁹ So is the man that deceiveth his neighbour, and saith, Am not I in sport?²⁰ Where no wood is, there the fire goeth out: so where there is no talebearer, the strife ceaseth.²¹ As coals are to burning coals, and wood to fire; so is a contentious man to kindle strife.²² The words of a talebearer are as wounds, and they go down into the innermost parts of the belly.²³ Burning lips and a wicked heart are like a potsherd covered with silver dross.²⁴ He that hateth dissembleth with his lips, and layeth up deceit within him;²⁵ When he speaketh fair, believe him not: for there are seven abominations in his heart.²⁶ Whose hatred is covered by deceit, his wickedness shall be shewed before the whole congregation.²⁷ Whoso diggeth a pit shall fall therein: and he that rolleth a stone, it will return upon him.²⁸ A lying tongue hateth those that are afflicted by it; and a flattering mouth worketh ruin.

Prov.27

¹ Boast not thyself of to morrow; for thou knowest not what a day may bring forth.² Let another man praise thee, and not thine own mouth; a stranger, and not thine own lips.³ A stone is heavy, and the sand weighty; but a fool's wrath is heavier than them both.⁴ Wrath is cruel, and anger is outrageous; but who is able to stand before envy?⁵ Open rebuke is better than secret love.⁶ Faithful are the wounds of a friend; but the kisses of an enemy are deceitful.⁷ The full soul loatheth an honeycomb; but to the hungry soul every bitter thing is sweet.⁸ As a bird that wandereth from her nest, so is a man that wandereth from his place.⁹ Ointment and perfume rejoice the heart: so doth the sweetness of a man's friend by hearty counsel.¹⁰ Thine own friend, and thy father's friend, forsake not; neither go into thy brother's house in the day of thy calamity: for

better is a neighbour that is near than a brother far off.¹¹ My son, be wise, and make my heart glad, that I may answer him that reproacheth me.¹² A prudent man foreseeth the evil, and hideth himself; but the simple pass on, and are punished.¹³ Take his garment that is surety for a stranger, and take a pledge of him for a strange woman.¹⁴ He that blesseth his friend with a loud voice, rising early in the morning, it shall be counted a curse to him.¹⁵ A continual dropping in a very rainy day and a contentious woman are alike.¹⁶ Whosoever hideth her hideth the wind, and the ointment of his right hand, which bewrayeth itself.¹⁷ Iron sharpeneth iron; so a man sharpeneth the countenance of his friend.¹⁸ Whoso keepeth the fig tree shall eat the fruit thereof: so he that waiteth on his master shall be honoured.¹⁹ As in water face answereth to face, so the heart of man to man.²⁰ Hell and destruction are never full; so the eyes of man are never satisfied.²¹ As the fining pot for silver, and the furnace for gold; so is a man to his praise.²² Though thou shouldest bray a fool in a mortar among wheat with a pestle, yet will not his foolishness depart from him.²³ Be thou diligent to know the state of thy flocks, and look well to thy herds.²⁴ For riches are not for ever: and doth the crown endure to every generation?²⁵ The hay appeareth, and the tender grass sheweth itself, and herbs of the mountains are gathered.²⁶ The lambs are for thy clothing, and the goats are the price of the field.²⁷ And thou shalt have goats' milk enough for thy food, for the food of thy household, and for the maintenance for thy maidens.

Prov.28

¹ The wicked flee when no man pursueth: but the righteous are bold as a lion.² For the transgression of a land many are the princes thereof: but by a man of understanding and knowledge the state thereof shall be prolonged.³ A poor man that oppresseth the poor is like a sweeping rain which leaveth no food.⁴ They that forsake the law praise the wicked: but such as keep the law contend with them.⁵ Evil men understand not judgment: but they that seek the LORD understand all things.⁶ Better is the poor that walketh in his uprightness, than he that is perverse in his ways, though he be rich.⁷ Whoso keepeth the law is a wise son: but he that is a companion of riotous men shameth his father.⁸ He that by usury and unjust gain increaseth his substance, he shall gather it for him that will pity the poor.⁹ He that turneth away his ear from hearing the law, even his prayer shall be abomination.¹⁰ Whoso causeth the righteous to go astray in an evil way, he shall fall himself into his own pit: but the upright shall have good things in possession.¹¹ The rich man is wise in his own conceit; but the poor that hath understanding searcheth him out.¹² When righteous men do rejoice, there is great glory: but when the wicked rise, a man is hidden.¹³ He that covereth his sins shall not prosper: but whoso confesseth and forsaketh them shall have mercy.¹⁴ Happy is the man that feareth alway: but he that hardeneth his heart shall fall into mischief.¹⁵ As a roaring lion, and a ranging bear; so is a wicked ruler over the poor people.¹⁶ The prince that wanteth understanding is also a great oppressor: but he that hateth covetousness shall prolong his days.¹⁷ A man that doeth violence to the blood of any person shall flee to the pit; let no man stay him.¹⁸ Whoso walketh uprightly shall be saved: but he that is perverse in his ways shall fall at once.¹⁹ He that tilleth his land shall have plenty of bread: but he that followeth after vain persons shall have poverty enough.²⁰ A faithful man shall abound with blessings: but he that maketh haste to be rich shall not be innocent.²¹ To have respect of persons is not good: for for a piece of bread that man will transgress.²² He that hasteth to be rich hath an evil eye, and considereth not that poverty shall come upon him.²³ He that rebuketh a man afterwards shall find more favour than he that flattereth with the tongue.²⁴ Whoso robbeth his father

or his mother, and saith, It is no transgression; the same is the companion of a destroyer.[25] He that is of a proud heart stirreth up strife: but he that putteth his trust in the LORD shall be made fat.[26] He that trusteth in his own heart is a fool: but whoso walketh wisely, he shall be delivered.[27] He that giveth unto the poor shall not lack: but he that hideth his eyes shall have many a curse.[28] When the wicked rise, men hide themselves: but when they perish, the righteous increase.

Prov.29

[1] He, that being often reproved hardeneth his neck, shall suddenly be destroyed, and that without remedy.[2] When the righteous are in authority, the people rejoice: but when the wicked beareth rule, the people mourn.[3] Whoso loveth wisdom rejoiceth his father: but he that keepeth company with harlots spendeth his substance.[4] The king by judgment establisheth the land: but he that receiveth gifts overthroweth it.[5] A man that flattereth his neighbour spreadeth a net for his feet.[6] In the transgression of an evil man there is a snare: but the righteous doth sing and rejoice.[7] The righteous considereth the cause of the poor: but the wicked regardeth not to know it.[8] Scornful men bring a city into a snare: but wise men turn away wrath.[9] If a wise man contendeth with a foolish man, whether he rage or laugh, there is no rest.[10] The bloodthirsty hate the upright: but the just seek his soul.[11] A fool uttereth all his mind: but a wise man keepeth it in till afterwards.[12] If a ruler hearken to lies, all his servants are wicked.[13] The poor and the deceitful man meet together: the LORD lighteneth both their eyes.[14] The king that faithfully judgeth the poor, his throne shall be established for ever.[15] The rod and reproof give wisdom: but a child left to himself bringeth his mother to shame.[16] When the wicked are multiplied, transgression increaseth: but the righteous shall see their fall.[17] Correct thy son, and he shall give thee rest; yea, he shall give delight unto thy soul.[18] Where there is no vision, the people perish: but he that keepeth the law, happy is he.[19] A servant will not be corrected by words: for though he understand he will not answer.[20] Seest thou a man that is hasty in his words? there is more hope of a fool than of him.[21] He that delicately bringeth up his servant from a child shall have him become his son at the length.[22] An angry man stirreth up strife, and a furious man aboundeth in transgression.[23] A man's pride shall bring him low: but honour shall uphold the humble in spirit.[24] Whoso is partner with a thief hateth his own soul: he heareth cursing, and bewrayeth it not.[25] The fear of man bringeth a snare: but whoso putteth his trust in the LORD shall be safe.[26] Many seek the ruler's favour; but every man's judgment cometh from the LORD.[27] An unjust man is an abomination to the just: and he that is upright in the way is abomination to the wicked.

Prov.30

[1] The words of Agur the son of Jakeh, even the prophecy: the man spake unto Ithiel, even unto Ithiel and Ucal,[2] Surely I am more brutish than any man, and have not the understanding of a man.[3] I neither learned wisdom, nor have the knowledge of the holy.[4] Who hath ascended up into heaven, or descended? who hath gathered the wind in his fists? who hath bound the waters in a garment? who hath established all the ends of the earth? what is his name, and what is his son's name, if thou canst tell?[5] Every word of God is pure: he is a shield unto them that put their trust in him.[6] Add thou not unto his words, lest he reprove thee, and thou be found a liar.[7] Two things have I required of thee; deny me them not before I die:[8] Remove far from me vanity and lies: give me neither poverty nor riches; feed me with food convenient for me:[9] Lest I be full, and deny thee, and say, Who is the LORD? or lest I be poor, and steal, and take the name of my God in vain.[10] Accuse not a servant unto his master, lest he

curse thee, and thou be found guilty.[11] There is a generation that curseth their father, and doth not bless their mother.[12] There is a generation that are pure in their own eyes, and yet is not washed from their filthiness.[13] There is a generation, O how lofty are their eyes! and their eyelids are lifted up.[14] There is a generation, whose teeth are as swords, and their jaw teeth as knives, to devour the poor from off the earth, and the needy from among men.[15] The horseleach hath two daughters, crying, Give, give. There are three things that are never satisfied, yea, four things say not, It is enough:[16] The grave; and the barren womb; the earth that is not filled with water; and the fire that saith not, It is enough.[17] The eye that mocketh at his father, and despiseth to obey his mother, the ravens of the valley shall pick it out, and the young eagles shall eat it.[18] There be three things which are too wonderful for me, yea, four which I know not:[19] The way of an eagle in the air; the way of a serpent upon a rock; the way of a ship in the midst of the sea; and the way of a man with a maid.[20] Such is the way of an adulterous woman; she eateth, and wipeth her mouth, and saith, I have done no wickedness.[21] For three things the earth is disquieted, and for four which it cannot bear:[22] For a servant when he reigneth; and a fool when he is filled with meat;[23] For an odious woman when she is married; and an handmaid that is heir to her mistress.[24] There be four things which are little upon the earth, but they are exceeding wise:[25] The ants are a people not strong, yet they prepare their meat in the summer;[26] The conies are but a feeble folk, yet make they their houses in the rocks;[27] The locusts have no king, yet go they forth all of them by bands;[28] The spider taketh hold with her hands, and is in kings' palaces.[29] There be three things which go well, yea, four are comely in going:[30] A lion which is strongest among beasts, and turneth not away for any;[31] A greyhound; an he goat also; and a king, against whom there is no rising up.[32] If thou hast done foolishly in lifting up thyself, or if thou hast thought evil, lay thine hand upon thy mouth.[33] Surely the churning of milk bringeth forth butter, and the wringing of the nose bringeth forth blood: so the forcing of wrath bringeth forth strife.

Prov.31

[1] The words of king Lemuel, the prophecy that his mother taught him.[2] What, my son? and what, the son of my womb? and what, the son of my vows?[3] Give not thy strength unto women, nor thy ways to that which destroyeth kings.[4] It is not for kings, O Lemuel, it is not for kings to drink wine; nor for princes strong drink:[5] Lest they drink, and forget the law, and pervert the judgment of any of the afflicted.[6] Give strong drink unto him that is ready to perish, and wine unto those that be of heavy hearts.[7] Let him drink, and forget his poverty, and remember his misery no more.[8] Open thy mouth for the dumb in the cause of all such as are appointed to destruction.[9] Open thy mouth, judge righteously, and plead the cause of the poor and needy.[10] Who can find a virtuous woman? for her price is far above rubies.[11] The heart of her husband doth safely trust in her, so that he shall have no need of spoil.[12] She will do him good and not evil all the days of her life.[13] She seeketh wool, and flax, and worketh willingly with her hands.[14] She is like the merchants' ships; she bringeth her food from afar.[15] She riseth also while it is yet night, and giveth meat to her household, and a portion to her maidens.[16] She considereth a field, and buyeth it: with the fruit of her hands she planteth a vineyard.[17] She girdeth her loins with strength, and strengtheneth her arms.[18] She perceiveth that her merchandise is good: her candle goeth not out by night.[19] She layeth her hands to the spindle, and her hands hold the distaff.[20] She stretcheth out her hand to the poor; yea, she reacheth forth her hands to the needy.[21] She is not afraid of the snow for her household: for all her household are clothed with scarlet.[22] She

maketh herself coverings of tapestry; her clothing is silk and purple.²³ Her husband is known in the gates, when he sitteth among the elders of the land.²⁴ She maketh fine linen, and selleth it; and delivereth girdles unto the merchant.²⁵ Strength and honour are her clothing; and she shall rejoice in time to come.²⁶ She openeth her mouth with wisdom; and in her tongue is the law of kindness.²⁷ She looketh well to the ways of her household, and eateth not the bread of idleness.²⁸ Her children arise up, and call her blessed; her husband also, and he praiseth her.²⁹ Many daughters have done virtuously, but thou excellest them all.³⁰ Favour is deceitful, and beauty is vain: but a woman that feareth the LORD, she shall be praised.³¹ Give her of the fruit of her hands; and let her own works praise her in the gates.

Ecclesiastes

Ecc.1

[1] The words of the Preacher, the son of David, king in Jerusalem.[2] Vanity of vanities, saith the Preacher, vanity of vanities; all is vanity.[3] What profit hath a man of all his labour which he taketh under the sun?[4] One generation passeth away, and another generation cometh: but the earth abideth for ever.[5] The sun also ariseth, and the sun goeth down, and hasteth to his place where he arose.[6] The wind goeth toward the south, and turneth about unto the north; it whirleth about continually, and the wind returneth again according to his circuits.[7] All the rivers run into the sea; yet the sea is not full; unto the place from whence the rivers come, thither they return again.[8] All things are full of labour; man cannot utter it: the eye is not satisfied with seeing, nor the ear filled with hearing.[9] The thing that hath been, it is that which shall be; and that which is done is that which shall be done: and there is no new thing under the sun.[10] Is there any thing whereof it may be said, See, this is new? it hath been already of old time, which was before us.[11] There is no remembrance of former things; neither shall there be any remembrance of things that are to come with those that shall come after.[12] I the Preacher was king over Israel in Jerusalem.[13] And I gave my heart to seek and search out by wisdom concerning all things that are done under heaven: this sore travail hath God given to the sons of man to be exercised therewith.[14] I have seen all the works that are done under the sun; and, behold, all is vanity and vexation of spirit.[15] That which is crooked cannot be made straight: and that which is wanting cannot be numbered.[16] I communed with mine own heart, saying, Lo, I am come to great estate, and have gotten more wisdom than all they that have been before me in Jerusalem: yea, my heart had great experience of wisdom and knowledge.[17] And I gave my heart to know wisdom, and to know madness and folly: I perceived that this also is vexation of spirit.[18] For in much wisdom is much grief: and he that increaseth knowledge increaseth sorrow.

Ecc.2

[1] I said in mine heart, Go to now, I will prove thee with mirth, therefore enjoy pleasure: and, behold, this also is vanity.[2] I said of laughter, It is mad: and of mirth, What doeth it?[3] I sought in mine heart to give myself unto wine, yet acquainting mine heart with wisdom; and to lay hold on folly, till I might see what was that good for the sons of men, which they should do under the heaven all the days of their life.[4] I made me great works; I builded me houses; I planted me vineyards:[5] I made me gardens and orchards, and I planted trees in them of all kind of fruits:[6] I made me pools of water, to water therewith the wood that bringeth forth trees:[7] I got me servants and maidens, and had servants born in my house; also I had great possessions of great and small cattle above all that were in Jerusalem before me:[8] I gathered me also silver and gold, and the peculiar treasure of kings and of the provinces: I gat me men singers and women singers, and the delights of the sons of men, as musical instruments, and that of all sorts.[9] So I was great, and increased more than all that were before me in Jerusalem: also my wisdom remained with me.[10] And whatsoever mine eyes desired I kept not from them, I withheld not my heart from any joy; for my heart rejoiced in all my labour: and this was my portion of all my labour.[11] Then I looked on all the works that my hands had wrought, and on the labour that I had laboured to do: and, behold, all was vanity and vexation of spirit, and there was no profit under the sun.[12] And I turned myself to behold wisdom, and madness, and folly: for what can the man do that cometh after the king? even that which hath been already done.[13] Then I saw that wisdom excelleth folly, as far as light excelleth darkness.[14] The wise man's eyes are in his head; but the fool walketh in darkness: and I myself perceived also that one event happeneth to them all.[15] Then said I in my heart, As it happeneth to the fool, so it happeneth even to me; and why was I then more wise? Then I said in my heart, that this also is vanity.[16] For there is no remembrance of the wise more than of the fool for ever; seeing that which now is in the days to come shall all be forgotten. And how dieth the wise man? as the fool.[17] Therefore I hated life; because the work that is wrought under the sun is grievous unto me: for all is vanity and vexation of spirit.[18] Yea, I hated all my labour which I had taken under the sun: because I should leave it unto the man that shall be after me.[19] And who knoweth whether he shall be a wise man or a fool? yet shall he have rule over all my labour wherein I have laboured, and wherein I have shewed myself wise under the sun. This is also vanity.[20] Therefore I went about to cause my heart to despair of all the labour which I took under the sun.[21] For there is a man whose labour is in wisdom, and in knowledge, and in equity; yet to a man that hath not laboured therein shall he leave it for his portion. This also is vanity and a great evil.[22] For what hath man of all his labour, and of the vexation of his heart, wherein he hath laboured under the sun?[23] For all his days are sorrows, and his travail grief; yea, his heart taketh not rest in the night. This is also vanity.[24] There is nothing better for a man, than that he should eat and drink, and that he should make his soul enjoy good in his labour. This also I saw, that it was from the hand of God.[25] For who can eat, or who else can hasten hereunto, more than I?[26] For God giveth to a man that is good in his sight wisdom, and knowledge, and joy: but to the sinner he giveth travail, to gather and to heap up, that he may give to him that is good before God. This also is vanity and vexation of spirit.

Ecc.3

[1] To every thing there is a season, and a time to every purpose under the heaven:[2] A time to be born, and a time to die; a time to plant, and a time to pluck up that which is planted;[3] A time to kill, and a time to heal; a time to break down, and a time to build up;[4] A time to weep, and a time to laugh; a time to mourn, and a time to dance;[5] A time to cast away stones, and a time to gather stones together; a time to embrace, and a time to refrain from embracing;[6] A time to get, and a time to lose; a time to keep, and a time to cast away;[7] A time to rend, and a time to sew; a time to keep silence, and a time to speak;[8] A time to love, and a time to hate; a time of war, and a time of peace.[9] What profit hath he that worketh in that wherein he laboureth?[10] I have seen the travail, which God hath given to the sons of men to be exercised in it.[11] He hath made every thing beautiful in his time: also he hath set the world in their heart, so that no man can find out the work that God maketh from the beginning to the end.[12] I know that there is no good in them, but for a man to rejoice, and to do good in his life.[13] And also that every man should eat and drink, and enjoy the good of all his labour, it is the gift of God.[14] I know that, whatsoever God doeth, it shall be for

ever: nothing can be put to it, nor any thing taken from it: and God doeth it, that men should fear before him.[15] That which hath been is now; and that which is to be hath already been; and God requireth that which is past.[16] And moreover I saw under the sun the place of judgment, that wickedness was there; and the place of righteousness, that iniquity was there.[17] I said in mine heart, God shall judge the righteous and the wicked: for there is a time there for every purpose and for every work.[18] I said in mine heart concerning the estate of the sons of men, that God might manifest them, and that they might see that they themselves are beasts.[19] For that which befalleth the sons of men befalleth beasts; even one thing befalleth them: as the one dieth, so dieth the other; yea, they have all one breath; so that a man hath no preeminence above a beast: for all is vanity.[20] All go unto one place; all are of the dust, and all turn to dust again.[21] Who knoweth the spirit of man that goeth upward, and the spirit of the beast that goeth downward to the earth?[22] Wherefore I perceive that there is nothing better, than that a man should rejoice in his own works; for that is his portion: for who shall bring him to see what shall be after him?

Ecc.4

[1] So I returned, and considered all the oppressions that are done under the sun: and behold the tears of such as were oppressed, and they had no comforter; and on the side of their oppressors there was power; but they had no comforter.[2] Wherefore I praised the dead which are already dead more than the living which are yet alive.[3] Yea, better is he than both they, which hath not yet been, who hath not seen the evil work that is done under the sun.[4] Again, I considered all travail, and every right work, that for this a man is envied of his neighbour. This is also vanity and vexation of spirit.[5] The fool foldeth his hands together, and eateth his own flesh.[6] Better is an handful with quietness, than both the hands full with travail and vexation of spirit.[7] Then I returned, and I saw vanity under the sun.[8] There is one alone, and there is not a second; yea, he hath neither child nor brother: yet is there no end of all his labour; neither is his eye satisfied with riches; neither saith he, For whom do I labour, and bereave my soul of good? This is also vanity, yea, it is a sore travail.[9] Two are better than one; because they have a good reward for their labour.[10] For if they fall, the one will lift up his fellow: but woe to him that is alone when he falleth; for he hath not another to help him up.[11] Again, if two lie together, then they have heat: but how can one be warm alone?[12] And if one prevail against him, two shall withstand him; and a threefold cord is not quickly broken.[13] Better is a poor and a wise child than an old and foolish king, who will no more be admonished.[14] For out of prison he cometh to reign; whereas also he that is born in his kingdom becometh poor.[15] I considered all the living which walk under the sun, with the second child that shall stand up in his stead.[16] There is no end of all the people, even of all that have been before them: they also that come after shall not rejoice in him. Surely this also is vanity and vexation of spirit.

Ecc.5

[1] Keep thy foot when thou goest to the house of God, and be more ready to hear, than to give the sacrifice of fools: for they consider not that they do evil.[2] Be not rash with thy mouth, and let not thine heart be hasty to utter any thing before God: for God is in heaven, and thou upon earth: therefore let thy words be few.[3] For a dream cometh through the multitude of business; and a fool's voice is known by multitude of words.[4] When thou vowest a vow unto God, defer not to pay it; for he hath no pleasure in fools: pay that which thou hast vowed.[5] Better is it that thou shouldest not vow, than that thou shouldest vow and not pay.[6] Suffer not thy mouth to cause thy flesh to sin; neither say thou before the angel, that it was an error:

wherefore should God be angry at thy voice, and destroy the work of thine hands?[7] For in the multitude of dreams and many words there are also divers vanities: but fear thou God.[8] If thou seest the oppression of the poor, and violent perverting of judgment and justice in a province, marvel not at the matter: for he that is higher than the highest regardeth; and there be higher than they.[9] Moreover the profit of the earth is for all: the king himself is served by the field.[10] He that loveth silver shall not be satisfied with silver; nor he that loveth abundance with increase: this is also vanity.[11] When goods increase, they are increased that eat them: and what good is there to the owners thereof, saving the beholding of them with their eyes?[12] The sleep of a labouring man is sweet, whether he eat little or much: but the abundance of the rich will not suffer him to sleep.[13] There is a sore evil which I have seen under the sun, namely, riches kept for the owners thereof to their hurt.[14] But those riches perish by evil travail: and he begetteth a son, and there is nothing in his hand.[15] As he came forth of his mother's womb, naked shall he return to go as he came, and shall take nothing of his labour, which he may carry away in his hand.[16] And this also is a sore evil, that in all points as he came, so shall he go: and what profit hath he that hath laboured for the wind?[17] All his days also he eateth in darkness, and he hath much sorrow and wrath with his sickness.[18] Behold that which I have seen: it is good and comely for one to eat and to drink, and to enjoy the good of all his labour that he taketh under the sun all the days of his life, which God giveth him: for it is his portion.[19] Every man also to whom God hath given riches and wealth, and hath given him power to eat thereof, and to take his portion, and to rejoice in his labour; this is the gift of God.[20] For he shall not much remember the days of his life; because God answereth him in the joy of his heart.

Ecc.6

[1] There is an evil which I have seen under the sun, and it is common among men:[2] A man to whom God hath given riches, wealth, and honour, so that he wanteth nothing for his soul of all that he desireth, yet God giveth him not power to eat thereof, but a stranger eateth it: this is vanity, and it is an evil disease.[3] If a man beget an hundred children, and live many years, so that the days of his years be many, and his soul be not filled with good, and also that he have no burial; I say, that an untimely birth is better than he.[4] For he cometh in with vanity, and departeth in darkness, and his name shall be covered with darkness.[5] Moreover he hath not seen the sun, nor known any thing: this hath more rest than the other.[6] Yea, though he live a thousand years twice told, yet hath he seen no good: do not all go to one place?[7] All the labour of man is for his mouth, and yet the appetite is not filled.[8] For what hath the wise more than the fool? what hath the poor, that knoweth to walk before the living?[9] Better is the sight of the eyes than the wandering of the desire: this is also vanity and vexation of spirit.[10] That which hath been is named already, and it is known that it is man: neither may he contend with him that is mightier than he.[11] Seeing there be many things that increase vanity, what is man the better?[12] For who knoweth what is good for man in this life, all the days of his vain life which he spendeth as a shadow? for who can tell a man what shall be after him under the sun?

Ecc.7

[1] A good name is better than precious ointment; and the day of death than the day of one's birth.[2] It is better to go to the house of mourning, than to go to the house of feasting: for that is the end of all men; and the living will lay it to his heart.[3] Sorrow is better than laughter: for by the sadness of the countenance the heart is made better.[4] The heart of the wise is in the house of mourning; but the heart of fools is in the house of mirth.[5] It is better to hear the rebuke

of the wise, than for a man to hear the song of fools.[6] For as the crackling of thorns under a pot, so is the laughter of the fool: this also is vanity.[7] Surely oppression maketh a wise man mad; and a gift destroyeth the heart.[8] Better is the end of a thing than the beginning thereof: and the patient in spirit is better than the proud in spirit.[9] Be not hasty in thy spirit to be angry: for anger resteth in the bosom of fools.[10] Say not thou, What is the cause that the former days were better than these? for thou dost not inquire wisely concerning this.[11] Wisdom is good with an inheritance: and by it there is profit to them that see the sun.[12] For wisdom is a defence, and money is a defence: but the excellency of knowledge is, that wisdom giveth life to them that have it.[13] Consider the work of God: for who can make that straight, which he hath made crooked?[14] In the day of prosperity be joyful, but in the day of adversity consider: God also hath set the one over against the other, to the end that man should find nothing after him.[15] All things have I seen in the days of my vanity: there is a just man that perisheth in his righteousness, and there is a wicked man that prolongeth his life in his wickedness.[16] Be not righteous over much; neither make thyself over wise: why shouldest thou destroy thyself?[17] Be not over much wicked, neither be thou foolish: why shouldest thou die before thy time?[18] It is good that thou shouldest take hold of this; yea, also from this withdraw not thine hand: for he that feareth God shall come forth of them all.[19] Wisdom strengtheneth the wise more than ten mighty men which are in the city.[20] For there is not a just man upon earth, that doeth good, and sinneth not.[21] Also take no heed unto all words that are spoken; lest thou hear thy servant curse thee:[22] For oftentimes also thine own heart knoweth that thou thyself likewise hast cursed others.[23] All this have I proved by wisdom: I said, I will be wise; but it was far from me.[24] That which is far off, and exceeding deep, who can find it out?[25] I applied mine heart to know, and to search, and to seek out wisdom, and the reason of things, and to know the wickedness of folly, even of foolishness and madness:[26] And I find more bitter than death the woman, whose heart is snares and nets, and her hands as bands: whoso pleaseth God shall escape from her; but the sinner shall be taken by her.[27] Behold, this have I found, saith the preacher, counting one by one, to find out the account:[28] Which yet my soul seeketh, but I find not: one man among a thousand have I found; but a woman among all those have I not found.[29] Lo, this only have I found, that God hath made man upright; but they have sought out many inventions.

Ecc.8

[1] Who is as the wise man? and who knoweth the interpretation of a thing? a man's wisdom maketh his face to shine, and the boldness of his face shall be changed.[2] I counsel thee to keep the king's commandment, and that in regard of the oath of God.[3] Be not hasty to go out of his sight: stand not in an evil thing; for he doeth whatsoever pleaseth him.[4] Where the word of a king is, there is power: and who may say unto him, What doest thou?[5] Whoso keepeth the commandment shall feel no evil thing: and a wise man's heart discerneth both time and judgment.[6] Because to every purpose there is time and judgment, therefore the misery of man is great upon him.[7] For he knoweth not that which shall be: for who can tell him when it shall be?[8] There is no man that hath power over the spirit to retain the spirit; neither hath he power in the day of death: and there is no discharge in that war; neither shall wickedness deliver those that are given to it.[9] All this have I seen, and applied my heart unto every work that is done under the sun: there is a time wherein one man ruleth over another to his own hurt.[10] And so I saw the wicked buried, who had come and gone from the place of the holy, and they were forgotten in the city where they had so done: this is also vanity.[11] Because sentence against an evil work is not executed

speedily, therefore the heart of the sons of men is fully set in them to do evil.[12] Though a sinner do evil an hundred times, and his days be prolonged, yet surely I know that it shall be well with them that fear God, which fear before him:[13] But it shall not be well with the wicked, neither shall he prolong his days, which are as a shadow; because he feareth not before God.[14] There is a vanity which is done upon the earth; that there be just men, unto whom it happeneth according to the work of the wicked; again, there be wicked men, to whom it happeneth according to the work of the righteous: I said that this also is vanity.[15] Then I commended mirth, because a man hath no better thing under the sun, than to eat, and to drink, and to be merry: for that shall abide with him of his labour the days of his life, which God giveth him under the sun.[16] When I applied mine heart to know wisdom, and to see the business that is done upon the earth: (for also there is that neither day nor night seeth sleep with his eyes:)[17] Then I beheld all the work of God, that a man cannot find out the work that is done under the sun: because though a man labour to seek it out, yet he shall not find it; yea further; though a wise man think to know it, yet shall he not be able to find it.

Ecc.9

[1] For all this I considered in my heart even to declare all this, that the righteous, and the wise, and their works, are in the hand of God: no man knoweth either love or hatred by all that is before them.[2] All things come alike to all: there is one event to the righteous, and to the wicked; to the good and to the clean, and to the unclean; to him that sacrificeth, and to him that sacrificeth not: as is the good, so is the sinner; and he that sweareth, as he that feareth an oath.[3] This is an evil among all things that are done under the sun, that there is one event unto all: yea, also the heart of the sons of men is full of evil, and madness is in their heart while they live, and after that they go to the dead.[4] For to him that is joined to all the living there is hope: for a living dog is better than a dead lion.[5] For the living know that they shall die: but the dead know not any thing, neither have they any more a reward; for the memory of them is forgotten.[6] Also their love, and their hatred, and their envy, is now perished; neither have they any more a portion for ever in any thing that is done under the sun.[7] Go thy way, eat thy bread with joy, and drink thy wine with a merry heart; for God now accepteth thy works.[8] Let thy garments be always white; and let thy head lack no ointment.[9] Live joyfully with the wife whom thou lovest all the days of the life of thy vanity, which he hath given thee under the sun, all the days of thy vanity: for that is thy portion in this life, and in thy labour which thou takest under the sun.[10] Whatsoever thy hand findeth to do, do it with thy might; for there is no work, nor device, nor knowledge, nor wisdom, in the grave, whither thou goest.[11] I returned, and saw under the sun, that the race is not to the swift, nor the battle to the strong, neither yet bread to the wise, nor yet riches to men of understanding, nor yet favour to men of skill; but time and chance happeneth to them all.[12] For man also knoweth not his time: as the fishes that are taken in an evil net, and as the birds that are caught in the snare; so are the sons of men snared in an evil time, when it falleth suddenly upon them.[13] This wisdom have I seen also under the sun, and it seemed great unto me:[14] There was a little city, and few men within it; and there came a great king against it, and besieged it, and built great bulwarks against it:[15] Now there was found in it a poor wise man, and he by his wisdom delivered the city; yet no man remembered that same poor man.[16] Then said I, Wisdom is better than strength: nevertheless the poor man's wisdom is despised, and his words are not heard.[17] The words of wise men are heard in quiet more than the cry of him that ruleth among fools.[18] Wisdom is better than weapons of war: but one sinner destroyeth much good.

Ecc.10

[1] Dead flies cause the ointment of the apothecary to send forth a stinking savour: so doth a little folly him that is in reputation for wisdom and honour.[2] A wise man's heart is at his right hand; but a fool's heart at his left.[3] Yea also, when he that is a fool walketh by the way, his wisdom faileth him, and he saith to every one that he is a fool.[4] If the spirit of the ruler rise up against thee, leave not thy place; for yielding pacifieth great offences.[5] There is an evil which I have seen under the sun, as an error which proceedeth from the ruler:[6] Folly is set in great dignity, and the rich sit in low place.[7] I have seen servants upon horses, and princes walking as servants upon the earth.[8] He that diggeth a pit shall fall into it; and whoso breaketh an hedge, a serpent shall bite him.[9] Whoso removeth stones shall be hurt therewith; and he that cleaveth wood shall be endangered thereby.[10] If the iron be blunt, and he do not whet the edge, then must he put to more strength: but wisdom is profitable to direct.[11] Surely the serpent will bite without enchantment; and a babbler is no better.[12] The words of a wise man's mouth are gracious; but the lips of a fool will swallow up himself.[13] The beginning of the words of his mouth is foolishness: and the end of his talk is mischievous madness.[14] A fool also is full of words: a man cannot tell what shall be; and what shall be after him, who can tell him?[15] The labour of the foolish wearieth every one of them, because he knoweth not how to go to the city.[16] Woe to thee, O land, when thy king is a child, and thy princes eat in the morning![17] Blessed art thou, O land, when thy king is the son of nobles, and thy princes eat in due season, for strength, and not for drunkenness![18] By much slothfulness the building decayeth; and through idleness of the hands the house droppeth through.[19] A feast is made for laughter, and wine maketh merry: but money answereth all things.[20] Curse not the king, no not in thy thought; and curse not the rich in thy bedchamber: for a bird of the air shall carry the voice, and that which hath wings shall tell the matter.

Ecc.11

[1] Cast thy bread upon the waters: for thou shalt find it after many days.[2] Give a portion to seven, and also to eight; for thou knowest not what evil shall be upon the earth.[3] If the clouds be full of rain, they empty themselves upon the earth: and if the tree fall toward the south, or toward the north, in the place where the tree falleth, there it shall be.[4] He that observeth the wind shall not sow; and he that regardeth the clouds shall not reap.[5] As thou knowest not what is the way of the spirit, nor how the bones do grow in the womb of her that is with child: even so thou knowest not the works of God who maketh all.[6] In the morning sow thy seed, and in the evening withhold not thine hand: for thou knowest not whether shall prosper, either this or that, or whether they both shall be alike good.[7] Truly the light is sweet, and a pleasant thing it is for the eyes to behold the sun:[8] But if a man live many years, and rejoice in them all; yet let him remember the days of darkness; for they shall be many. All that cometh is vanity.[9] Rejoice, O young man, in thy youth; and let thy heart cheer thee in the days of thy youth, and walk in the ways of thine heart, and in the sight of thine eyes: but know thou, that for all these things God will bring thee into judgment.[10] Therefore remove sorrow from thy heart, and put away evil from thy flesh: for childhood and youth are vanity.

Ecc.12

[1] Remember now thy Creator in the days of thy youth, while the evil days come not, nor the years draw nigh, when thou shalt say, I have no pleasure in them;[2] While the sun, or the light, or the moon, or the stars, be not darkened, nor the clouds return after the rain:[3] In the day when the keepers of the house shall tremble, and the strong men shall bow themselves, and the grinders cease because they are few, and those that look out of the windows be darkened,[4] And the doors shall be shut in the streets, when the sound of the grinding is low, and he shall rise up at the voice of the bird, and all the daughters of musick shall be brought low;[5] Also when they shall be afraid of that which is high, and fears shall be in the way, and the almond tree shall flourish, and the grasshopper shall be a burden, and desire shall fail: because man goeth to his long home, and the mourners go about the streets:[6] Or ever the silver cord be loosed, or the golden bowl be broken, or the pitcher be broken at the fountain, or the wheel broken at the cistern.[7] Then shall the dust return to the earth as it was: and the spirit shall return unto God who gave it.[8] Vanity of vanities, saith the preacher; all is vanity.[9] And moreover, because the preacher was wise, he still taught the people knowledge; yea, he gave good heed, and sought out, and set in order many proverbs.[10] The preacher sought to find out acceptable words: and that which was written was upright, even words of truth.[11] The words of the wise are as goads, and as nails fastened by the masters of assemblies, which are given from one shepherd.[12] And further, by these, my son, be admonished: of making many books there is no end; and much study is a weariness of the flesh.[13] Let us hear the conclusion of the whole matter: Fear God, and keep his commandments: for this is the whole duty of man.[14] For God shall bring every work into judgment, with every secret thing, whether it be good, or whether it be evil.

Song of Solomon

Cant.1

[1] The song of songs, which is Solomon's.[2] Let him kiss me with the kisses of his mouth: for thy love is better than wine.[3] Because of the savour of thy good ointments thy name is as ointment poured forth, therefore do the virgins love thee.[4] Draw me, we will run after thee: the king hath brought me into his chambers: we will be glad and rejoice in thee, we will remember thy love more than wine: the upright love thee.[5] I am black, but comely, O ye daughters of Jerusalem, as the tents of Kedar, as the curtains of Solomon.[6] Look not upon me, because I am black, because the sun hath looked upon me: my mother's children were angry with me; they made me the keeper of the vineyards; but mine own vineyard have I not kept.[7] Tell me, O thou whom my soul loveth, where thou feedest, where thou makest thy flock to rest at noon: for why should I be as one that turneth aside by the flocks of thy companions?[8] If thou know not, O thou fairest among women, go thy way forth by the footsteps of the flock, and feed thy kids beside the shepherds' tents.[9] I have compared thee, O my love, to a company of horses in Pharaoh's chariots.[10] Thy cheeks are comely with rows of jewels, thy neck with chains of gold.[11] We will make thee borders of gold with studs of silver.[12] While the king sitteth at his table, my spikenard sendeth forth the smell thereof.[13] A bundle of myrrh is my wellbeloved unto me; he shall lie all night betwixt my breasts.[14] My beloved is unto me as a cluster of camphire in the vineyards of En-gedi.[15] Behold, thou art fair, my love; behold, thou art fair; thou hast doves' eyes.[16] Behold, thou art fair, my beloved, yea, pleasant: also our bed is green.[17] The beams of our house are cedar, and our rafters of fir.

Cant.2

[1] I am the rose of Sharon, and the lily of the valleys.[2] As the lily among thorns, so is my love among the daughters.[3] As the apple tree among the trees of the wood, so is my beloved among the sons. I sat down under his shadow with great delight, and his fruit was sweet to my taste.[4] He brought me to the banqueting house, and his banner over me was love.[5] Stay me with flagons, comfort me with apples: for I am sick of love.[6] His left hand is under my head, and his right hand doth embrace me.[7] I charge you, O ye daughters of

Jerusalem, by the roes, and by the hinds of the field, that ye stir not up, nor awake my love, till he please.[8] The voice of my beloved! behold, he cometh leaping upon the mountains, skipping upon the hills.[9] My beloved is like a roe or a young hart: behold, he standeth behind our wall, he looketh forth at the windows, shewing himself through the lattice.[10] My beloved spake, and said unto me, Rise up, my love, my fair one, and come away.[11] For, lo, the winter is past, the rain is over and gone;[12] The flowers appear on the earth; the time of the singing of birds is come, and the voice of the turtle is heard in our land;[13] The fig tree putteth forth her green figs, and the vines with the tender grape give a good smell. Arise, my love, my fair one, and come away.[14] O my dove, that art in the clefts of the rock, in the secret places of the stairs, let me see thy countenance, let me hear thy voice; for sweet is thy voice, and thy countenance is comely.[15] Take us the foxes, the little foxes, that spoil the vines: for our vines have tender grapes.[16] My beloved is mine, and I am his: he feedeth among the lilies.[17] Until the day break, and the shadows flee away, turn, my beloved, and be thou like a roe or a young hart upon the mountains of Bether.

Cant.3

[1] By night on my bed I sought him whom my soul loveth: I sought him, but I found him not.[2] I will rise now, and go about the city in the streets, and in the broad ways I will seek him whom my soul loveth: I sought him, but I found him not.[3] The watchmen that go about the city found me: to whom I said, Saw ye him whom my soul loveth?[4] It was but a little that I passed from them, but I found him whom my soul loveth: I held him, and would not let him go, until I had brought him into my mother's house, and into the chamber of her that conceived me.[5] I charge you, O ye daughters of Jerusalem, by the roes, and by the hinds of the field, that ye stir not up, nor awake my love, till he please.[6] Who is this that cometh out of the wilderness like pillars of smoke, perfumed with myrrh and frankincense, with all powders of the merchant?[7] Behold his bed, which is Solomon's; threescore valiant men are about it, of the valiant of Israel.[8] They all hold swords, being expert in war: every man hath his sword upon his thigh because of fear in the night.[9] King Solomon made himself a chariot of the wood of Lebanon.[10] He made the pillars thereof of silver, the bottom thereof of gold, the covering of it of purple, the midst thereof being paved with love, for the daughters of Jerusalem.[11] Go forth, O ye daughters of Zion, and behold king Solomon with the crown wherewith his mother crowned him in the day of his espousals, and in the day of the gladness of his heart.

Cant.4

[1] Behold, thou art fair, my love; behold, thou art fair; thou hast doves' eyes within thy locks: thy hair is as a flock of goats, that appear from mount Gilead.[2] Thy teeth are like a flock of sheep that are even shorn, which came up from the washing; whereof every one bear twins, and none is barren among them.[3] Thy lips are like a thread of scarlet, and thy speech is comely: thy temples are like a piece of a pomegranate within thy locks.[4] Thy neck is like the tower of David builded for an armoury, whereon there hang a thousand bucklers, all shields of mighty men.[5] Thy two breasts are like two young roes that are twins, which feed among the lilies.[6] Until the day break, and the shadows flee away, I will get me to the mountain of myrrh, and to the hill of frankincense.[7] Thou art all fair, my love; there is no spot in thee.[8] Come with me from Lebanon, my spouse, with me from Lebanon: look from the top of Amana, from the top of Shenir and Hermon, from the lions' dens, from the mountains of the leopards.[9] Thou hast ravished my heart, my sister, my spouse; thou hast ravished my heart with one of thine eyes, with one chain of thy neck.[10] How fair is thy love, my sister, my spouse! how much

better is thy love than wine! and the smell of thine ointments than all spices![11] Thy lips, O my spouse, drop as the honeycomb: honey and milk are under thy tongue; and the smell of thy garments is like the smell of Lebanon.[12] A garden inclosed is my sister, my spouse; a spring shut up, a fountain sealed.[13] Thy plants are an orchard of pomegranates, with pleasant fruits; camphire, with spikenard,[14] Spikenard and saffron; calamus and cinnamon, with all trees of frankincense; myrrh and aloes, with all the chief spices:[15] A fountain of gardens, a well of living waters, and streams from Lebanon.[16] Awake, O north wind; and come, thou south; blow upon my garden, that the spices thereof may flow out. Let my beloved come into his garden, and eat his pleasant fruits.

Cant.5

[1] I am come into my garden, my sister, my spouse: I have gathered my myrrh with my spice; I have eaten my honeycomb with my honey; I have drunk my wine with my milk: eat, O friends; drink, yea, drink abundantly, O beloved.[2] I sleep, but my heart waketh: it is the voice of my beloved that knocketh, saying, Open to me, my sister, my love, my dove, my undefiled: for my head is filled with dew, and my locks with the drops of the night.[3] I have put off my coat; how shall I put it on? I have washed my feet; how shall I defile them?[4] My beloved put in his hand by the hole of the door, and my bowels were moved for him.[5] I rose up to open to my beloved; and my hands dropped with myrrh, and my fingers with sweet smelling myrrh, upon the handles of the lock.[6] I opened to my beloved; but my beloved had withdrawn himself, and was gone: my soul failed when he spake: I sought him, but I could not find him; I called him, but he gave me no answer.[7] The watchmen that went about the city found me, they smote me, they wounded me; the keepers of the walls took away my veil from me.[8] I charge you, O daughters of Jerusalem, if ye find my beloved, that ye tell him, that I am sick of love.[9] What is thy beloved more than another beloved, O thou fairest among women? what is thy beloved more than another beloved, that thou dost so charge us?[10] My beloved is white and ruddy, the chiefest among ten thousand.[11] His head is as the most fine gold, his locks are bushy, and black as a raven.[12] His eyes are as the eyes of doves by the rivers of waters, washed with milk, and fitly set.[13] His cheeks are as a bed of spices, as sweet flowers: his lips like lilies, dropping sweet smelling myrrh.[14] His hands are as gold rings set with the beryl: his belly is as bright ivory overlaid with sapphires.[15] His legs are as pillars of marble, set upon sockets of fine gold: his countenance is as Lebanon, excellent as the cedars.[16] His mouth is most sweet: yea, he is altogether lovely. This is my beloved, and this is my friend, O daughters of Jerusalem.

Cant.6

[1] Whither is thy beloved gone, O thou fairest among women? whither is thy beloved turned aside? that we may seek him with thee.[2] My beloved is gone down into his garden, to the beds of spices, to feed in the gardens, and to gather lilies.[3] I am my beloved's, and my beloved is mine: he feedeth among the lilies.[4] Thou art beautiful, O my love, as Tirzah, comely as Jerusalem, terrible as an army with banners.[5] Turn away thine eyes from me, for they have overcome me: thy hair is as a flock of goats that appear from Gilead.[6] Thy teeth are as a flock of sheep which go up from the washing, whereof every one beareth twins, and there is not one barren among them.[7] As a piece of a pomegranate are thy temples within thy locks.[8] There are threescore queens, and fourscore concubines, and virgins without number.[9] My dove, my undefiled is but one; she is the only one of her mother, she is the choice one of her that bare her. The daughters saw her, and blessed her; yea, the queens and the concubines, and they praised her.[10] Who is she that looketh forth as the morning, fair as the moon, clear as the sun, and

terrible as an army with banners?[11] I went down into the garden of nuts to see the fruits of the valley, and to see whether the vine flourished, and the pomegranates budded.[12] Or ever I was aware, my soul made me like the chariots of Amminadib.[13] Return, return, O Shulamite; return, return, that we may look upon thee. What will ye see in the Shulamite? As it were the company of two armies.

Cant.7

[1] How beautiful are thy feet with shoes, O prince's daughter! the joints of thy thighs are like jewels, the work of the hands of a cunning workman.[2] Thy navel is like a round goblet, which wanteth not liquor: thy belly is like an heap of wheat set about with lilies.[3] Thy two breasts are like two young roes that are twins.[4] Thy neck is as a tower of ivory; thine eyes like the fishpools in Heshbon, by the gate of Bath-rabbim: thy nose is as the tower of Lebanon which looketh toward Damascus.[5] Thine head upon thee is like Carmel, and the hair of thine head like purple; the king is held in the galleries.[6] How fair and how pleasant art thou, O love, for delights![7] This thy stature is like to a palm tree, and thy breasts to clusters of grapes.[8] I said, I will go up to the palm tree, I will take hold of the boughs thereof: now also thy breasts shall be as clusters of the vine, and the smell of thy nose like apples;[9] And the roof of thy mouth like the best wine for my beloved, that goeth down sweetly, causing the lips of those that are asleep to speak.[10] I am my beloved's, and his desire is toward me.[11] Come, my beloved, let us go forth into the field; let us lodge in the villages.[12] Let us get up early to the vineyards; let us see if the vine flourish, whether the tender grape appear, and the pomegranates bud forth: there will I give thee my loves.[13] The mandrakes give a smell, and at our gates are all manner of pleasant fruits, new and old, which I have laid up for thee, O my beloved.

Cant.8

[1] O that thou wert as my brother, that sucked the breasts of my mother! when I should find thee without, I would kiss thee; yea, I should not be despised.[2] I would lead thee, and bring thee into my mother's house, who would instruct me: I would cause thee to drink of spiced wine of the juice of my pomegranate.[3] His left hand should be under my head, and his right hand should embrace me.[4] I charge you, O daughters of Jerusalem, that ye stir not up, nor awake my love, until he please.[5] Who is this that cometh up from the wilderness, leaning upon her beloved? I raised thee up under the apple tree: there thy mother brought thee forth: there she brought thee forth that bare thee.[6] Set me as a seal upon thine heart, as a seal upon thine arm: for love is strong as death; jealousy is cruel as the grave: the coals thereof are coals of fire, which hath a most vehement flame.[7] Many waters cannot quench love, neither can the floods drown it: if a man would give all the substance of his house for love, it would utterly be contemned.[8] We have a little sister, and she hath no breasts: what shall we do for our sister in the day when she shall be spoken for?[9] If she be a wall, we will build upon her a palace of silver: and if she be a door, we will inclose her with boards of cedar.[10] I am a wall, and my breasts like towers: then was I in his eyes as one that found favour.[11] Solomon had a vineyard at Baal-hamon; he let out the vineyard unto keepers; every one for the fruit thereof was to bring a thousand pieces of silver.[12] My vineyard, which is mine, is before me: thou, O Solomon, must have a thousand, and those that keep the fruit thereof two hundred.[13] Thou that dwellest in the gardens, the companions hearken to thy voice: cause me to hear it.[14] Make haste, my beloved, and be thou like to a roe or to a young hart upon the mountains of spices.

Made in United States
Troutdale, OR
06/08/2025